THE FACTS ON FILE
COMPANION TO THE

AMERICAN
NOVEL

VOLUME III
P–Z

EDITED BY ABBY H. P. WERLOCK
ASSISTANT EDITOR: JAMES P. WERLOCK

Facts On File
An imprint of Infobase Publishing

To my father,
Thomas Kennedy Potter, Jr. (1917–2003)

The Facts On File Companion to the American Novel

Copyright © 2006 by Abby H. P. Werlock

Facts On File, Inc.
An imprint of Infobase Publishing
132 West 31st Street
New York NY 10001

Library of Congress Cataloging-in-Publication Data
The Facts On File companion to the American novel / [edited by] Abby H. P. Werlock.
   p. cm.
Includes bibliographical references and index.
ISBN 0-8160-4528-3 (set: hardcover: alk. paper)
1. American fiction—Encyclopedias. 2. American fiction—Bio-bibliography. 3. American fiction—Stories, plots, etc. I. Title: Companion to the American novel. II. Werlock, Abby H. P.
III. Facts on File, Inc. IV. Title.

PS371.F33 2005
813′.003—dc22   2005012437

Facts On File books are available at special discounts when purchased in bulk quantities for businesses, associations, institutions, or sales promotions. Please call our Special Sales Department in New York at (212) 967-8800 or (800) 322-8755.

You can find Facts On File on the World Wide Web at http://www.factsonfile.com

Text design adapted by James Scotto-Lavino
Cover design by Cathy Rincon

Printed in the United States of America

VB Hermitage 10 9 8 7 6 5 4 3 2 1

This book is printed on acid-free paper.

CONTENTS

P

PACO'S STORY LARRY HEINEMANN (1986)

Paco's Story is Larry HEINEMANN's second Vietnam War novel, after *Close Quarters,* which was published in 1977. Both novels draw from Heinemann's 1967–68 tour of duty in Vietnam as a combat infantryman with the 25th Division. *Paco's Story* is one of the most significant fictional works on American experiences of the Vietnam War and its aftermath, and the novel has garnered Heinemann lasting recognition and a number of awards, including the 1987 National Book Award.

The opening introduces the reader to the novel's protagonist while he is still in Vietnam: A massive bombardment, probably "friendly fire," has devastated Alpha Company, and Paco is the only survivor. The reader follows Paco through treatments and hospitals, and then travels with him stateside to a quiet town, where he takes up a job as dishwasher at a diner named The Texas Lunch. In the end, Paco realizes that despite his dedication to the job and his modest attempts at making a life for himself, he will never be accepted as an equal within the community and resolves to leave town for good.

Interestingly, Paco never fully tells his own story. When found among the corpses, he is unable to answer questions about who he is and what has happened. Later, he tells his tale only in the most abbreviated form: "I was wounded in the war" (103). The details of Paco's Vietnam experiences and their lasting mark on his appearance and behavior are provided instead through the observations of him by others,

including the medic who finds him among the bodies and, unlike Paco, will "tell the story [of finding Paco]. . . . over and over again" (20); the bus driver who drops him off at a Texaco station outside the small town; the mechanic at the station who gives him a ride into town; and—most important—the disembodied voice belonging to an American soldier killed in the bombardment that narrates the past and present experiences of Paco throughout the book. Marilyn Durham has addressed the nature and effects of this peculiar narrative voice in the novel, writing that the voice possesses "a special authority," as it belongs to someone who had been there with Paco during the bombardment, and simultaneously conveys a sense of immediacy and invites our sympathy and identification with both the masses of dead and the sole survivor (100). Other critical commentary on *Paco's Story* ranges from attention to the structuring of the narrative to analysis of larger gender and class conflicts represented in the novel.

Nancy Anisfield provides a long catalog of novels on the Vietnam War that include a "final gut-wrenching climactic event" serving simultaneously to thrill and convince the reader of the permanent damage to the protagonist's psyche (*America Rediscovered* 1990, 276). *Paco's Story,* she argues, is quite different in that the physical and emotional devastation comes at the novel's opening—with the many torn, burned corpses and the details of Paco's long suffering among them— whereas the climax at the narrative's end involves a far more passive and interior event: Paco reads entries in the diary of Cathy, the niece of his landlord, and learns that he will never be viewed as a member of the community. In this analysis, however, Anisfield overlooks two surprising juxtapositions in the novel's closing chapters. The second-to-last chapter pairs Paco's thoughts about Cathy—whom he hears making love with her boyfriend in the adjacent apartment—with memories of the gang rape and execution of a young Vietnamese woman that he witnessed firsthand, and the final chapter pairs Paco's quiet break-in into Cathy's apartment with detailed descriptions of his nightly forays into the Vietnamese jungle to set booby traps to kill the enemy. The thrilling and devastating experiences that characterize the final chapters of much of the fiction on the Vietnam war, as identified by Anisfield, are thus also present in the closing chapters of Heinemann's novel. Indeed, at least one critic, Grant F. Scott, characterizes the rape of the Vietnamese woman as the "climactic moment" of the work (Scott, 69).

Like Scott, Susan Jeffords focuses on the larger gender conflicts underlying the actions in the novel and convincingly demonstrates a number of parallels between Paco and the raped and executed Vietnamese woman. Jeffords goes on to find multiple meanings in the scars covering Paco's body. For one, they serve as a metaphor for the war itself in their unreadability and purposelessness (209). Louis K. Greiff provides a gendered reading of a different sort, analyzing the functions of various names within *Paco's Story* while developing the argument that the book expresses a need "to establish the brotherhood of all American men of that generation who need reconciliation after a second Civil War" (Greiff, 382).

A second source of conflict—one based on class difference—is the focus of Milton J. Bates's discussion of the novel. In a book-length study, Bates argues that the military involvement in Vietnam intensified specific cultural conflicts already raging in American society during the 1960s and that these conflicts (including ones structured around race, class, gender, and generation) shape both the form and content of Vietnam fiction. In his chapter "The Class War," Bates describes various class divisions in 1960s America, including the disproportionately high numbers of working-class

youths sent overseas to fight the war, and then discusses how *Paco's Story*, alongside Norman Mailer's *Armies of the Night* and Oliver Stone's "Platoon," transforms such class conflicts into compelling tales. This range of critical approaches attests to the novel's richness and enduring interest.

SOURCES

Anisfield, Nancy. "After the Apocalypse: Narrative Movement in Larry Heinemann's *Paco's Story*." In *America Rediscovered: Critical Essays on Literature and Film of the Vietnam War*, edited by Owen W. Gilman, Jr., and Lorrie Smith, 275–281. New York: Garland, 1990.

Bates, Milton J. *The Wars We Took to Vietnam: Cultural Conflict and Storytelling*. Berkeley, Calif.: University of California Press, 1996.

Durham, Marilyn. "Narrative Strategies in Recent Vietnam War Fiction." In *America Rediscovered: Critical Essays on Literature and Film of the Vietnam War*, edited by Owen W. Gilman, Jr., and Lorrie Smith, 100–108. New York: Garland, 1990.

Greiff, Louis K. "In the Name of the Brother: Larry Heinemann's *Paco's Story* and Male America," *Critique* 41, no. 4 (Summer 2000): 381–389.

Heinemann, Larry. *Paco's Story*. New York: Farrar, Straus & Giroux, 1986.

Jeffords, Susan. "Tattoos, Scars, Diaries, and Writing Masculinity." In *The Vietnam War and American Culture*, edited by John Carlos Rowe and Rick Berg, 208–228. New York: Columbia University Press, 1991.

Scott, Grant F. "*Paco's Story* and the Ethics of Violence," *Critique* 36, no. 1 (Fall 1994): 69–80.

James Kelley

PAINTED BIRD, THE Jerzy Kosinski (1965)

Set for the most part in the eastern European countryside during World War II, *The Painted Bird* chronicles the largely nightmarish experiences of a young, dark-complexioned boy. His parents have sent him out of the city in which they have lived so that he might escape the Nazi persecution. Because the boy is never identified as Jewish and could very well be a gypsy, because he is never named, and because even the setting is never specifically identified, his seemingly singular, darkly fantastical passage to adulthood becomes, on many levels, emblematic of a whole generation's maturation under extraordinarily harsh conditions.

The title of the novel refers to an ordinary bird captured by one of the characters. He paints its feathers in bright colors and then rereleases it to join its flock. But the bird now looks so different that the others in the flock do not recognize it as one of their kind. At first they simply ignore it, then they try to drive it off, and finally they attack it savagely. The bird's predicament becomes symbolic of the main character's mounting desperation to be accepted and the perverse escalation in the peasants' rejection of him.

For the most part, the peasants among whom the boy lives are the antithesis of the kindly country folk that populate the bucolic pasturelands of genteel American fiction. These are more the hard-natured and often sadistic, the perpetually ruttish and often depraved, the superstitious and often madly deluded inbred brutes and freaks of Erskine CALDWELL's backcountry. First, he lives with an eccentric old woman who is regarded as a witch. He subsequently becomes attached to a bovine young woman named Ludmilla who becomes the victim of a vicious sexual assault—ironically, because she is perceived as dangerously promiscuous. Then he becomes infatuated with an elfin farm girl named Ewka, whose father and brothers subject her to grotesque sexual abuse. Later, he is dangled from a meat hook above a farmer's vicious dogs. And, at one point, he is hurled by a whole church congregation into the communal dung pit for a mishap that they regard as sacrilegious. This outrage leaves him mute.

A turning point of sorts occurs when he has a hand in an S.S. officer's falling into a dark cavity full of hungry rats. Eventually, he is befriended by soldiers of the liberating Soviet army, and he becomes particularly close to a renowned sniper who, in a sense, formalizes the lessons that the boy has learned about survival. After the war, he is placed in a loosely controlled orphanage in a city and essentially becomes a street kid. He and his friends not only become adept at negotiating the bombed out streets but engage in acts of revenge that are so disproportionate to the specific offenses against them that they amount to terrorism. The boy is saved from a criminal life only by his being reunited with his parents and by an accident that restores his speech and, more broadly, allows him a less sociopathic mode of self-expression and self-appraisal.

The Painted Bird has often been described as a picaresque with many mythic elements. Indeed, it seemed an extraordinary literary achievement for an author who had defected from Poland only a decade earlier. Its immediacy was partly explained by its being to some degree autobiographical. Moreover, it stood out from other novels about the Holocaust because it seemed to bridge the genres of novel and memoir, because it presented a child's perspective on the horrors, and because it dealt with circumstances outside the ghettos and the concentration camps.

In interviews, KOSINSKI quickly became a master at sketching just enough of his personal history to invite curiosity and then leaving much of the detail ambiguous. Eventually this predilection would come to seem, to some, more a deliberate misrepresentation than an eccentric artifice. When, late in his career, Kosinski was publicly accused of having hired out much of the writing of his novels, the effect was very damaging, for all the old insinuations about his distortions of the facts of his life resurfaced. For instance, although Kosinski had been sent into the countryside to escape the Nazis, his experiences were apparently much less grotesque and damaging than those endured by the boy in The Painted Bird. In the midst of all of this controversy over authorship and literary credibility, several right-wing Polish and Ukrainian groups even made scurrilous attacks against him, framed in anti-Semitic code words, for defaming the behavior and ignoring the sufferings of the peasantry of those countries during the war.

SOURCES

Carpenter, John. "Jerzy Kosinski and The Painted Bird," Cross Currents: A Yearbook of Central European Culture 11 (1992): 139–152.

Corngold, Stanley. "Jerzy Kosinski's The Painted Bird: Language Lost and Regained," Mosaic 6, no. 4 (1973): 153–167.

Granofsky, Ronald. "Circle and Line: Modern and Postmodern Constructs of the Self in Jerzy Kosinski's The Painted Bird," Essays in Literature 18 (Fall 1991): 254–268.

Harpham, Geoffrey Galt. "Survival in and of The Painted Bird: The Career of Jerzy Kozinski," Georgia Review 35 (Spring 1981): 142–157.

Jarniewicz, Jerzy. "The Terror of Normality in Jerzy Kosinski's The Painted Bird," Polish Review 49, no. 1 (2004): 641–652.

Lale, Meta, and John S. Williams. "The Narrator of *The Painted Bird*: A Case Study," *Renascence* 24 (1972): 198–206.

McGinnis, Wayne D. "Transcendence and Primitive Sympathy in Kosinski's *The Painted Bird*," *Studies in the Humanities* 8, no. 1 (1980): 22–27.

Meszaros, Patricia K. "Hero with a Thousand Faces, Child with No Name: Kosinski's *The Painted Bird*," *College Literature* 6 (1979): 232–244.

Piwinski, David J. "Kosinski's *The Painted Bird*," *Explicator* 40, no. 1 (Fall 1981): 62–63.

Richter, David H. "The Three Denouements of Jerzy Kosinski's *The Painted Bird*," *Contemporary Literature* 15 (1974): 370–385.

Sloan, James Park. "Kosinski's War." In *Critical Essays on Jerzy Kosinski,* edited by Barbara Tepa Lupack, 236–246. New York: G. K. Hall, 1998.

Spendal, R. J. "The Structure of *The Painted Bird*," *Journal of Narrative Technique* 6 (1976): 132–136.

Weales, Gerald. "Jerzy Kosinski: *The Painted Bird* and Other Disguises." In *Critical Essays on Jerzy Kosinski,* edited by Barbara Tepa Lupack, 142–152. New York: G. K. Hall, 1998.

Martin Kich

PALAHNIUK, CHUCK (1962–)

Chuck Palahniuk's experience is that of a man who liberated himself by writing. After graduating from the University of Oregon with a degree in journalism, he began a short-lived career as a news reporter in Portland. Discouraged, he quit and became a diesel mechanic at a Freightliner plant. He hated his job. At night, he went out drinking and occasionally got into bar brawls. He broke into open houses with his friends, raiding medicine cabinets for prescription drugs. He lived in the most extreme state of misery and deprivation until a self-help seminar prompted him to write.

Palahniuk would frantically jot down words and phrases on notes and scraps of paper at work and at the gym. Later, he synthesized them while listening to the music of Nine Inch Nails. He attended writing workshops led by his mentor Tom Spanbauer, from whom he learned the techniques of minimalism. His initial attempts at publication failed: His second novel, *Invisible Monsters,* was rejected by publishers for its allegedly "unpleasant" subject matter. His first published novel, the revolutionary *FIGHT CLUB* (1996), was written as an affront to those who refused to publish *Invisible Monsters* and as a diatribe against a culture that denied him and others recognition. It was received with critical acclaim. *Fight Club* won the Oregon Book Award and the Pacific Northwestern Booksellers' Award. In the past five years, he has published four novels: *Survivor* (1999), a revised version of *Invisible Monsters* (1999), *Choke* (2001), and *Lullaby* (2002), as well as numerous articles. His work has attracted the attention of musicians such as Trent Reznor and Marilyn Manson, as well as the filmmaking industry.

The first cinematic interpretation of his work, David Fincher's *Fight Club* (1999), ensured Palahniuk a lasting cult following. Part of his work's appeal for an ever-widening young readership lies in its orientation around the question of freedom. Palahniuk's antiheroes revolt against mainstream culture. In *Fight Club,* violence appears as a means through which members of a consumer culture are able to free themselves from their mechanical and meaningless lives. An underground boxing network, the fight club seems to break with the capitalist world and yet reveals itself as its reverse image. In the extraordinary *Invisible Monsters,* a fashion model is grotesquely disfigured by a shotgun blast. She moves from absolute visibility to absolute invisibility. Now an outsider, she becomes the enemy of the culture that refuses to acknowledge her. Her external position allows her to transform herself entirely. She teams up with Brandy Alexander, a pre-operation transsexual, who teaches her that the past is essentially linguistic. For the one who exists beyond all fields of visibility, she learns, anything is possible. Sexual compulsiveness affords Victor Mancini, the narrator of the wonderfully strange and fascinating *Choke,* a kind of transcendence from the colonial amusement-park world that he inhabits—a world that is frozen in an immemorial past.

Through their rebellion, Chuck Palahniuk's protagonists seek to provoke God's indifference. They prefer the chaos of a broken world to a culture that deprives them of freedom.

NOVELS

Choke. New York: Doubleday, 2001.
Diary. New York: Doubleday, 2003.

Fight Club. New York: W. W. Norton, 1996.
Invisible Monsters. New York: W. W. Norton, 1999.
Lullaby. New York: Doubleday, 2002.
Survivor. New York: W. W. Norton, 1999.

SOURCES

Gaughan, Thomas. Review of *Fight Club, Booklist* (July 1996): 1,804.
Kaufmann, Stanley. Review of *Fight Club, New Republic,* November 8, 1999, p. 64.
Maslin, Janet. "An Immature Con Man with a Mom Problem," *New York Times,* 24 May 2001.
Needham, George. Review of *Invisible Monsters, Booklist* (September 15, 1999): 233.
Ott, Bill. Review of *Fugitives and Refugees: A Walk in Portland, Oregon, Booklist* (July 2003): 1,858.
Patterson, Troy. "Hard to Swallow: In *Choke,* the Latest from the Author of *Fight Club.* Chuck Palahniuk's Hip Nihilism Comes to Naught," *Entertainment Weekly,* 25 May 2001, p. 72.
Unsigned. "Chuck Palahniuk: Road Trips and Romance," *PW* Interview, *Publishers Weekly* 249, no. 35 (September 2, 2002): 49.

OTHER

Donadoni, Serena. "Going for Broke." *Orlando Weekly* (October 15, 1999). Available online. URL: http://www.orlandoweekly.com/film/story.asp?id=1512. Accessed January 11, 2006.
Jeffries, Stuart. "Bruise Control." *Guardian Unlimited,* (May 12, 2000). Available online. URL: http://books.guardian.co.uk/departments/generalfiction/story/0,6000,219740,00.html. Accessed January 11, 2006.
Tomlinson, Sarah. "Is It Fistfighting, or Just Multitasking?" *Salon.com.* (October 13, 1999). Available online. URL: http://www.salon.com/ent/movies/int/1999/10/13/palahniuk. Accessed January 11, 2006.

Joseph Suglia

PALE FIRE VLADIMIR NABOKOV (1962) *Pale Fire,* Vladimir NABOKOV's 14th novel (his fifth in English), is unlike almost any other novel written before or since. A reader, not knowing this was a novel, might at first mistake it for an annotated volume of poetry: *Pale Fire* presents itself as a previously unpublished, 999-line poem by the murdered poet John Shade, along with commentary by his sometime colleague, Charles Kinbote. There is also a scholarly introduction and a self-referential index to the "study." However, Shade and his family, Kinbote and his homeland of Zembla, and "Pale Fire" (the poem) are all really the creations of Nabokov.

The foreword tells how the poem came into Kinbote's hands in the first place. Shade was murdered in his home, having lived in the same neighborhood as Kinbote. Throughout the foreword, Kinbote as narrator assures us that Shade and his wife, Sybil, liked and trusted him, though, he concedes, others had a difficult time understanding their relationship. What becomes clear in Kinbote's commentary on "Pale Fire," however, is that John and Sybil Shade could barely stand Charles Kinbote, but Kinbote is blissfully unaware of this.

Immediately following the foreword is the poem itself. "Pale Fire" is in iambic pentameter, separated into four cantos. Interestingly, the final line of the poem—"Trundling an empty barrow up the lane"—rhymes with the first—"I was the shadow of the waxwing slain"—suggesting a circular nature to the poem. The content of the poem is primarily autobiographical, dealing with the difficult life and premature death of John and Sybil Shade's daughter, Hazel. Hazel is never named directly in "Pale Fire" itself; instead the reference to her is "clarified" by Kinbote in the commentary section.

It is in this commentary section, as throughout Nabokov's LOLITA (1955), that the success of the novel depends on the unreliability of the narrator. While two narratives emerge in the commentary section—one telling the story of Hazel Shade and one regarding the political situation in Zembla—neither can be counted on as true because, as becomes more and more clear as the reader makes his or her way through *Pale Fire,* the narrator is either insane or not who he originally presents himself as. So, as a result, we can never be sure whether the tragic story of Hazel that Kinbote relates in the commentary was really intended by John Shade to tell this story.

Once the reader reaches the commentary section, it becomes immediately apparent that Kinbote is no traditional critic. From the beginning, he inserts personal recollections of his relationship with the Shades, as well as reminiscences of his life in his native land of

Zembla. For instance, while commenting on the first four lines of "Pale Fire," Kinbote inserts a thought beginning, "When, in the last year of Shade's life I had the fortune of being [Shade's] neighbor . . ." (45). Clearly, despite the continuing importance of New Criticism in literary circles in 1962, Kinbote is not a critic afraid to insert his own point of view. According to critic William Monroe, Nabokov is characterizing "the reductionist tendency of theory in the character of Charles Kinbote" (Monroe, 157).

Similarly, on the second page of the commentary, the first of several mentions is made of King Charles II the Beloved of Zembla, who, we are told, was born in 1915 and reigned as the last king of Zembla from 1936 to 1958. While, on the one hand, it might be considered natural for a critic comfortable writing in the first person to insert aspects of his or her own ethnic or national background into his or her work, the obsession of Kinbote with the fate of Charles II continues throughout the commentary section, with more and more details of how Charles's reign was brought to an end, shoving to the margins any serious explication of Shade's poem.

Eventually, Kinbote drops all pretenses, presenting himself as the exiled king in the flesh and bemoaning the fact that the bullet intended for his own assassination struck his "friend" Shade. Thus the commentary section concludes, with the index referring the reader not just to themes raised in the poem but also in the commentary section and having nothing to do with Hazel Shade's premature death or the Shade family in general. The index contains several spurious entries, including a reference to "word golf," with "see also" notes for "lass," "mass," and "male," all of which point back to the initial entry.

Critics remain perplexed as to the "solution" to *Pale Fire.* "As early as 1966–67, a number of critics began to raise with some insistance [*sic*] the question of who invented whom in *Pale Fire,*" writes Maurice Couturier. Is Kinbote crazy, or is he really the exiled king? Or is Shade the real narrator hiding behind his psychotic creation, Charles Kinbote? Nabokov biographer Brian Boyd writes that Kinbote "is actually Vseslav Botkin, a Russian émigré, whose paranoia is edging him towards suicide" (Boyd, "Shade"). As with Humbert, we are left

with no definitive answers, despite the fictional front and back matter offered by Nabokov.

SOURCES

Boyd, Brian. *Vladimir Nabokov: The American Years.* Princeton, N.J.: Princeton University Press, 1991.

Connolly, Julian W., ed. *Nabokov and His Fiction: New Perspectives.* New York: Cambridge University Press, 1999.

Monroe, William. *Power to Hurt: The Virtues of Alienation.* Urbana-Champaign: University of Illinois Press, 1998.

Nabokov, Vladimir. *Pale Fire.* New York: Putman, 1962.

Rampton, David. *Vladimir Nabokov.* New York: St. Martin's Press, 1993.

OTHER

Boyd, Brian. "Shade and Shape in *Pale Fire,*" *Nabokov Studies* 4 (1997): 173–224. Available online. URL: http://www.libraries.psu.edu/nabokov/boydpf1.htm. Accessed September 24, 2005.

Couturier, Maurice. " 'Which Is to Be Master' in *Pale Fire,*" *Zembla.* (January 29, 2005). Available online. URL: http://www.libraries.psu.edu/nabokov/coutpf.htm. Accessed September 24, 2005.

Andrew Mathis

PARADISE Toni Morrison **(1998)** Her first novel since being awarded the Nobel Prize in 1993, *Paradise* continues Morrison's long-standing project of memorializing (or remembering) details of African-American history that have been ignored by mainstream accounts of what it is to be American. This time, though, Morrison is also carefully interrogating that project. Not only does *Paradise* seek to fill in gaps in the American "grand narrative" of history, but it scrutinizes the process of re-creating "grand narratives" in its depiction of the town of Ruby. In this way, the novel continues the meditation on reading and readership that characterizes *Beloved* and *Jazz*; at issue as we read is how we can accurately and ethically "pass on" or "re-make" the story.

Inspired by an advertisement for an African-American town that Morrison came across in a late 19th-century newspaper that read, "Come prepared or not at all," *Paradise* takes root in a specific and largely unrecorded historical situation, the westward migration of former slaves into Oklahoma territory following the Civil War.

Ruby is an all-black town that has managed to survive as such into the 1970s, when the novel is largely set; however, the larger world "Out There" (and myriad unspeakable problems within) seems to be threatening the hegemony of the town's ruling families. These angry, inflexible men find exquisitely blamable victims in a group of wayward women residing in a house, known as "the Convent," at the edge of town. The violence of the eventual clash of the two groups and the town's irrational and uncompromising drive to maintain its "integrity" in the face of a world spinning out of control (i.e., the 1960s) are summed up and foreshadowed in the first line of the novel: "They shot the white girl first" (1).

Racial categorizations are both crucial and ignored in *Paradise,* since we begin with the murder of a "white girl" but are not told which of the convent women is actually white. This narrative strategy (which Morrison earlier experimented with in her short story "Recitatif") contrasts with the skin-conscious ideology of Ruby, which built itself up and maintained itself away from the larger white society and from the lighter-skinned blacks who once rejected Ruby's forefathers for the darkness of their skin. The town has created its own semireligious mythology, which begins in that moment of rejection—"The Disallowing"—and which centers itself on certain individuals and objects, such as the original leader of the ex-slaves, Zechariah Morgan, and the community oven. The irony of this creation myth is that in the violence with which it is enforced as the official history of the people, the men of Ruby have created an exclusive community just as brutally intolerant as the white and "light" ones that originally "disallowed" their grandfathers.

This strict patriarchy is contrasted with the loose atmosphere of "the Convent," which is actually an embezzler's lurid mansion turned Catholic "asylum" for Native American girls and mostly abandoned by the 1970s, although the harried women who come across it do seek "asylum" with Consolata, the last remaining occupant. At a glance, the Convent is a female-centered utopia, but actually the women there are as lost and damaged and in some cases as morally bankrupt as the men of Ruby. It is not until Consolata shakes off her alcoholic haze and forces the women to

come to terms with themselves and each other that the Convent begins to represent a real "haven" or utopia. It is at this point, however, that the men of Ruby gun down the women in cold blood.

In the final section of *Paradise,* each of the murdered women reappears as a ghost and a warrior. Their resurrection corresponds to Connie's ability to "step in" or, as she prefers to call it, "see in" to a dying person and bring him or her back to life. This "insight" is, as Philip Page describes it, an act "of extreme self-projection, of ultimate empathy, of total transfer of the self to the other" (641). It is also a model for reading. When the Convent women reappear, our "insight" into them helps give them new life. *Paradise,* then, explores racism, exclusion, notions of purity, the need for home, and the possibilities and dangers of rewriting history, but it places most of its hope for ethical action, for understanding, and even for rebirth in the act of reading.

SOURCES

Krumholz, Linda J. "Reading and Insight in Toni Morrison's *Paradise," African American Review* 36, no. 1 (2002): 21–34.

Matus, Jill. *Toni Morrison.* New York: St. Martin's Press, 1998.

Morrison, Toni. *Paradise.* New York: Knopf, 1998.

———. "Recitatif." In *Confirmation,* edited by Amiri and Amina Baraka, 243–261. New York: Morrow, 1983.

Page, Philip. "Furrowing All the Brows: Interpretation and the Transcendent in Toni Morrison's *Paradise," African American Review* 35, no. 4 (2001): 637–648.

Peterson, Nancy J. *Against Amnesia: Contemporary Woman Writers and the Crisis of Historical Memory.* Philadelphia: University of Pennsylvania Press, 2001.

Monika Hogan

PARETSKY, SARA (1947–) One of the most prominent detective fiction writers to emerge in the late 20th century, Sara Paretsky is the creator of the much admired sleuth V. I. (Victoria Iphigenia) Warshawski. Paretsky (and Warshawski) redefined the traditional private-eye novel as honed by Raymond CHANDLER and Dashiell HAMMETT. Unlike the male-created Philip Marlowe or Sam Spade, the street-smart loner-orphan Warshawski has an extensive community

of friends and supporters, and even shows her emotions on occasion. Moreover, as critic Jane S. Bakerman notes, Warshawski regularly "measures both her professional and personal humanity against her surviving relatives, the memories of her parents, and her constructed family of friends and lovers" (Bakerman, 135). In Paretsky's carefully plotted novels, her realistic and complicated characters travel the mean streets of Chicago.

Sara Paretsky was born on June 8, 1947, in Ames, Iowa, to David Paretsky, a scientist, and Mary Edwards, a librarian. She was educated at the University of Kansas, earning a bachelor's degree (1967), and at the University of Chicago (M.A. and Ph.d., 1977). In Paretsky's first novel, *Indemnity Only* (1982), the half-Polish, half-Italian Warshawski searches for a missing University of Chicago woman; she uncovers a corpse, a corrupt union, and an insurance scam. *Deadlock* (1984) is about corruption and crime in the insurance and shipping business, and *Killing Orders* (1985) reveals a criminal connection between the Catholic Church and a long-ago promise between Warshawski and her mother. Paretsky's pattern is to present a simple mystery that unfolds to reveal corruption in supposedly respectable institutions. For instance, *Bitter Medicine* (1987) exposes medical malfeasance in a large hospital, *Blood Shot* (1988) deals with a cover-up of environmental hazards in the chemical industry, and *Burn Marks* (1990) exposes the collusion of police and corporate executives that has ramifications for the homeless. Social concern are evident too in *Guardian Angel* (1992), involving the persecution of an old woman; *Tunnel Vision* (1994) focuses on social services and a homeless family; and *Hard Time* (1999) refers to Warshawski's own jail time, which grew from her confrontation with a media executive while she was investigating the murder of a homeless immigrant woman.

One of the founders of Sisters in Crime, Paretsky served as the organization's first president in 1986. In 1991 *Indemnity Only* was adapted for a feature-length film retitled *V. I. Warshawski* and starring Kathleen Turner as the private eye. In 1987 *Ms. Magazine* named Paretsky one of the Women of the Year; among Paretsky's numerous honors and awards is the Crime Writers Association Silver Dagger in 1988 for her novel *Blood Shot*.

NOVELS

Bitter Medicine. New York: Morrow, 1987.
Blacklist. New York: G. P. Putnam's Sons, 2003.
Blood Shot. New York: Delacorte, 1988. Published in England as *Toxic Shock.* London: Gollancz, 1988.
Burn Marks. New York: Delacorte, 1990.
Deadlock. New York: Dial, 1984.
Fire Sale. New York: G. P. Putnam's Sons, 2005.
Ghost Country. New York: Delacorte, 1998.
Guardian Angel. New York: Delacorte, 1992.
Hard Time. New York: Delacorte Press, 1999.
Indemnity Only. New York: Dial, 1982.
Killing Orders. New York: Morrow, 1985.
Total Recall. New York: Delacorte, 2001.
Tunnel Vision. New York: Delacorte, 1994.
V. I. Times Two: Photo Finish and Publicity Stunts. Chicago, Ill.: Women and Children First, 2002.

SOURCES

Bakerman, Jane, ed. *And Then There Were Nine: More Women of Mystery.* Bowling Green, Ohio: Bowling Green University Popular Press, 1985.
St. James Guide to Crime and Mystery Writers. 4th ed. Detroit, Mich.: St. James Press, 1996.

OTHER

First Person: Book Page. Available online. URL: http://www.bookpage.com/9806bp/sara_paretsky.html. Accessed September 24, 2005.
Sara Paretsky. Available online. URL: http://www.saraparetsky.com. Accessed September 24, 2005.
Valencia West "Sara Paretsky." Available online. URL: http://valencia.cc.fl.us/lrcwest/Author_Pathfinders/paretsky.hmtl. Accessed September 24, 2005.

PARIS TROUT Peter Dexter (1988) Published in 1988, *Paris Trout* is the third and most celebrated of journalist Peter Dexter's five novels. Described as a "masterpiece" by one reviewer, it won the National Book Award and was nominated for the National Book Critics Circle Award. Surprisingly, given its warm critical reception and best-seller status, scholars have for the most part ignored the novel, which was made into a movie in 1991.

Set in the small town of Cotton Point, Georgia, in the 1950s, events develop around the title character, a psychotic 59-year-old white merchant who acts as a loan shark to local African Americans. The chronologically ordered third-person narrative begins with Trout's murder of a poor and innocent young black girl and proceeds through his arrest, trial, conviction, sentencing, appeal, escape, and return.

Chapters move back and forth among the main characters, who include Trout, his wife Hanna, his lawyer Seagraves, and another attorney, Bonner, who represents Hanna in her divorce case. Critics have praised the characterization in the book; for instance, one said that the characters are "stroked boldly" with "voices that ring true," and another that they are portrayed with "marvelous sharpness." Some commentators have likened Dexter to William FAULKNER and Flannery O'CONNOR and have called *Paris Trout* "a southern novel" that ranks with "the best fiction of the South." Dexter, however, has insisted that the novel "could have happened anywhere," since it examines and condemns phenomena that are not unique to a particular region: violent and exploitative racism, classism, and sexism.

Read with an eye on race, class, and gender, *Paris Trout* reveals crimes of commission and omission. The very name of Cotton Point evokes a color and class line that is disturbingly at play in the novel. This is clearly seen when Trout justifies killing the girl on a race- and class-based "natural order of things" (77). Initially, the town's white community tacitly supports this rationale, as it looks the other way.

Race- and class-driven homicide is not Trout's only offense. He abuses his younger wife emotionally, psychologically, physically, and sexually after first stealing her life savings and putting her to work in his store. Here, too, the community accommodates. When she reports her abuse, Hanna is dismissed by the town's distinguished doctor and told that this kind of thing "is common enough even in the best households" (121). With Trout as blight, the race, class, and gender reading resolves through his death by suicide. Though Seagraves notes that it is not "easy to put him behind you," at the end the local newspaper, known as "The Conscience of the South," indicts Trout, who is buried in an isolated and "poisoned" site where the "Monument to the Unknown Confederate Dead . . . cast a shadow across his grave" (303).

While the novel should be read socio-culturally, an equally important if not more interesting approach

calls for a psychological or psychoanalytic reading, in particular of Trout and his disintegration. Although one critic objected that Dexter erred in making Trout "an out-and-out psychotic," the reader is challenged to ascertain the origins and dimensions of Trout's madness, and here the text is richly suggestive.

Trout is brutal, remorseless, possessive, and obsessive, and his mother seems to be at the core of his pathology. Trout wed late in life, after his mother was muted by a stroke, and the town speculation was that he had married "to replace his mother." This is implied in an early family photo in which young Paris sits in front of his mother, who touches him in "some secret connection," as his father stands to the side (119).

While on trial, Trout sketches scenes of animals shooting and killing each other, and also a family tree, at the top of which is his mother's name and a spider with a face. On a recess, Trout walks to the nursing home and stares silently at his naked mother as she is being bathed. Then, back in court, he states that "we were all somebody's baby once," and later that "we are all somebody's baby" (179).

Hanna is at first outspoken but after two years of marriage is silenced by Trout's threats and attacks, which include a degrading rape. Initially drawn to his "dark side," she acknowledges that Trout "had stolen her direction" and "isolated her." When she realizes that Trout fears he is losing control of her, Hanna drives him from the house, where there are "spider webs in the corners" (50), by playing off his paranoia.

Out of the house, Trout ironically moves into the honeymoon suite of the local hotel as his deterioration accelerates and his rage intensifies. After killing Bonner and Seagraves, Trout shoots his mother in the head, wets himself with urine, and kills himself with a gun in his mouth. Staying with an established motif, the narrator tells us that "at the corner of the ceiling, bits of . . . [Trout] hung in a spider web" (297).

Unlike the socio-cultural approach, a psychological or psychoanalytic reading does not resolve the many issues of the novel, and the reader is left to ponder Trout's psychosis and the place of his mother in it. Did he love her, and was he trying to release them both from frustration over the stroke? Did he hate her, and had she sexually abused him as a child? Hanna is the only main character who is alive at the end, and she provides no clues.

SOURCES

Axthelm, Pete. Review of *Paris Trout* by Pete Dexter, *Newsweek,* 26 September 1988, p. 75.

Dexter, Pete. *Paris Trout.* New York: Penguin Books, 1989.

Predmore, Richard. "Ownership in Dexter's *Paris Trout,*" *The Southern Quarterly* 33, nos. 2–3 (1995): 147–150.

Towers, Robert. Review of *Paris Trout* by Pete Dexter, *New York Review of Books,* 16 February 1989, pp. 18–20.

Wright, Elizabeth. *Psychoanalytic Criticism: Theory in Practice.* New York: Methuen, 1984.

Geoffrey C. Middlebrook

PASSING Nella Larsen (1929) Following her achievement with her first two novels, *Quicksand* (1928) and *Passing,* Nella Larsen was awarded a Guggenheim Fellowship in 1930, becoming the first female African-American writer to receive this prize and establishing herself as the most promising writer of the Harlem Renaissance.

Passing depicts the reencounter of two African-American girlhood friends, Irene Redfield and Clare Kendry, who have not seen each other for 12 years. The entanglement of the two women's lives is unraveled by a third-person narrator, mostly through the eyes of Irene Redfield. The novel opens in the Redfields' New York home, where Irene receives a letter from Clare, to which she is disinclined to reply due to the recollection of their chance meeting in Chicago. Two years before the arrival of the letter, the two women had met on a hot day on the rooftop of the luxurious Drayton Hotel in Chicago, their native city, where they were both visiting, and reminisced about the past and related their present lives to each other.

After the death of her father in a parlor fight, Clare was brought up by her father's aunts, who suppressed her African-American past. Daring, willful, selfish, and pretty, Clare secures her happiness as the wife of a wealthy businessman, John Bellew, and mother of a 10-year-old girl, Margery, as long as she can conceal her racial identity from her bigoted husband, who deeply dislikes African Americans. Unlike Clare, Irene takes advantage of her fair skin only sometimes, for the sake of entering hotels or restaurants, and adheres to stability, permanence, and her African-American identity. Happy and secure in her marriage with an African-American physician, Brian Redfield, and two sons, Brian Jr. and Theodore, Irene is also an active member of Harlem's uplift affairs.

Unable to resist Clare's insistent invitation, Irene visits her on the next day at her Chicago hotel, where she finds a common acquaintance, Gertrude Martin, whose husband, unlike Clare's, is aware of her racial identity. Irene's feeling of uneasiness in the company of the two passing women turns into perturbation when John Bellew makes racist comments, unaware that he is in the presence of three African-American women. Irene's loyalty to her own race prevents her from betraying Clare but not from severing her ties with her.

Two years later, still vividly feeling the bitterness of this experience, Irene leaves Clare's letter unanswered. Nevertheless, unpredictable Clare appears uninvited at the Redfields' residence and, whenever her husband leaves town on business, maintains a regular presence at the Redfields' parties and follows them to their Harlem outings on the pretext that she feels nostalgic for the African-American community. The opposition between the characters of conservative Irene and adventurous Clare contrasts with the affinity between those of Clare and Brian, as Irene's conformity to the stability of her life in Harlem remains unchanged despite Brian's desire to immigrate to Brazil. Irene's anxiety over Clare's recklessness in risking the safety of her meticulously constructed identity and marriage and the future of her daughter to her indulgence in amusement in Harlem, and her jealousy for the attraction between her husband and Clare bring her to the brink of wishing Clare dead.

On a cold December day in New York, with her African-American friend Felise Freeland, Irene runs into John Bellew, who notices the racial link between the two women. This meeting prompts John Bellew to seek the truth about his wife's identity, which he pursues at an African-American soirée in the sixth-floor apartment of the Freelands, where Clare is enjoying the evening in the company of the Redfields. Frightened by the raging Bellew's bolt into the apartment, Irene rushes to the side of Clare, who is calmly standing by the open window. At the novel's end, Clare tumbles to her death from the sixth-floor window. The unreliable narrator of the novel leaves it to the reader to decide whether, having lost everything, Claire has committed suicide or whether she is pushed down by her jealous friend Irene.

Considered one of the finest novels dealing with the themes of "racial passing" and the "tragic mulatto" of late 19th- and early 20th-century fiction, *Passing* also indicates the division within African-American society by social class. Without the middle-class veneer that Clare has acquired through her marriage to John Bellew, she would not be accepted to Harlem's bourgeoisie, which is represented by the Redfields, who consider themselves socially above their servants.

The novel explores the sexual aspect of passing. A dormant homoerotic desire exists beneath the ostensible irritation Irene feels toward Clare and the friendly affection Clare displays for Irene. Although Clare's racial passing and daring attitude to life seem to create Irene's repulsion toward her friend, Irene is subconsciously attracted to Clare's risk-taking tendency that she herself lacks. Clare's outward longing for the African-American community veils an inward lesbian yearning for her friend.

The similarity between the two women's personal sacrifices to preserve their marriages underlines women's plight in the 1920s, including the novel's journey into social as well as psychological realism. For both Clare and Irene, economic survival means dependence on a husband. Irene perceives that Clare's passing is a price paid for safety and security, which she highly values and also maintains through marriage. This aspect of the novel surpasses the issues of the limits of African-American women and addresses the question of limitations to the freedom of all women.

SOURCES

Davis, Thadious. *Nella Larsen, Novelist of the Harlem Renaissance: A Woman's Life Unveiled.* Baton Rouge: Louisiana University Press, 1996.

Goldsmith, Meredith. "Shopping to Pass, Passing to Shop: Bodily Self-Fashioning in the Fiction of Nella Larsen." In *Recovering the Black Female Body: Self-Representations by African American Women,* edited by Michael Bennett and Vanessa D. Dickerson, 97–120. New Brunswick, N.J.: Rutgers University Press, 2001.

Larsen, Nella. *Quicksand and Passing,* edited by Deborah E. McDowell. New Brunswick, N.J.: Rutgers University Press, 1986.

Larson, Charles R. *Invisible Darkness: Jean Toomer & Nella Larsen.* Iowa City: University of Iowa Press, 1993.

McLendon, Jacquelyn Y. *The Politics of Color in the Fiction of Jessie Fauset and Nella Larsen.* Charlottesville: University Press of Virginia, 1995.

Miller, Erica M. *The Other Reconstruction: Where Violence and Womanhood Meet in the Writings of Wells-Barnett, Grimké, and Larsen.* New York: Garland, 2000.

Sullivan, Neil. "Nella Larsen's Passing and the Fading Subject," *African American Review* 32, no. 3 (Fall 1998): 373–387.

Wall, Cheryl A. *Women of the Harlem Renaissance.* Bloomington: Indiana University Press, 1995.

Ferdâ Asya

PASTURES OF HEAVEN, THE JOHN STEINBECK (1932)

STEINBECK's biographer Jackson J. Benson notes that during the first two decades of the century, American and European authors were being influenced by a great deal of experimental fiction. Citing such works as Dos Passos's *Manhattan Transfer* (1925) and Joyce's *Ulysses* (1922) and *The Dubliners* (1916) as representative of the experimentation that was taking place, Benson suggests that during the 1920s and 1930s, Steinbeck was intrigued by innovation and that the construction of *The Pastures of Heaven,* his second novel, may have been influenced by these newly rebellious structures in fiction as well as by Sherwood Anderson's *Winesburg, Ohio,* published in 1919 and considered the first attempt in America at what was later labeled the short story cycle (Benson, 201).

As far as inspiration for the volume, most critics agree that the central idea for *Pastures* was supplied by Steinbeck's friend and fellow writer, Beth Ingels, who had been raised in Corral de Tierra, a little valley in the hills west of Salinas. Originally, Ingels envisioned a book about the strange people whose fates influenced the emotional development of a young girl and the interaction of people in a small confined valley (Benson, 208). However, when she repeated her ideas within the intellectual circle of friends fostered by John and Carol Steinbeck, it was inevitable that the more famous author would pick up on a potential story line and shape it to fit his own ends.

Yet the concept was hardly Ingels's exclusive property, and the resulting novel certainly includes many traits that indicate Steinbeck's personal thematic emphases rather than those of Ingels. In fact, already in 1930, Steinbeck wrote his friend Ted Miller about his desire to fashion together a series of short stories in *Decameron* fashion (Benson, 209). Thus, by combining his interest in experimental form and in Jungian actions motivated by the unconscious, along with the biblical myth of fallen Eden and separated generations, the essential qualities that comprise *The Pastures of Heaven* were generated.

According to Benson, another letter to Miller in May 1931 specifies Steinbeck's intention to interrelate the stories with each other and to draw a parallel to a Miltonian Lucifer (Benson, 211). Jay Parini in his 1994 biography suggests a further tie to Milton's *Paradise Lost*: "the fact that evil becomes a necessary agent of righteousness" (Parini, 130). He also calls attention to the influence of Steinbeck's reading of John Elof Boodin (*Cosmic Evolution*) and William Emerson Ritter (*The Natural History of Our Conduct*), both of whom theorized that evil was not entirely negative and that at times it even suggested or motivated creative possibilities. Both biographers also agree that initially the plan called for five to six stories that would then be combined with Steinbeck's in-progress novella, *Dissonant Symphony*. Eventually, however, *Pastures* was engendered as a separate work and gained a life of its own.

Pastures, like Steinbeck's earlier *To a God Unkown,* can be said to emphasize a mechanistic world in which there is no ultimate cause or design (Benson, 245). In fact, Benson suggests that *Pastures* provides one of the first indications that Steinbeck was attracted to "is-thinking" or non-teleological philosophy, a philosophical stance that grew even more significant during his association and long friendship with Ed Ricketts in the later 1930s. "Is thinking," the belief that one should not ask why or look for causes, was motivated by Steinbeck's desire to be totally objective, to merely see what things were and how they worked, not to "show exactly why people act as they do, but to show the psychological steps that precede and clear the way for an act" (Benson, 202). Another significant influence for the author at the time of the composition of *The Pastures of Heaven* were the writings of Carl Jung. In Jung's terminology, the shadow world of the residents of La Pastura may be far more responsible for their situations than the family they choose to blame.

Although *The Pastures of Heaven* sold poorly in its first printing, it was initially well received by critics, who noted its author's "development in creating greater social and psychological realism in his characters" (Lisca, 47). Recent assessments have tended to stress the book's reliance on biblical mythology and its portrait of a type of "fallen" Eden. John Timmerman, for example, states that "the Eden of *Pastures* measures what the inhabitants could be but more decisively what they are, mortals discovering the fallenness of human nature, not sons of God" (Timmerman, 56). Timmerman goes on to draw three distinct parallels to the biblical Eden myth in the story cycle, pointing out that *Pastures* displays not only disorientation from God that leads to enmity with neighbors but also an initiation into human knowledge of evil as a personal experience and an exile from the rich beneficence of Eden to a lifetime of toil and troubles (Timmerman, 56).

Similarly, Louis Owens recalls the words of Satan in Paradise Lost in his analysis, citing the lines "the mind itself is its own place and in itself / Can make a Heav'n of Hell, a Hell of Heav'n" (Owens, 75). But while giving credit to biblical allusion and acknowledging earlier critics in the process, Owens shifts his personal assessment to private human illusions, stressing their connection to the greater illusion of an American Eden that can somehow be regained (Owens, 88). Owens implies that Steinbeck's intent is to draw the reader into a deceptive trap of blaming the Munroes for the decay in *Pastures* rather than acknowledging that every dilemma faced there is attributable to human nature rather than to an individual scapegoat.

Perhaps the closest reading of the interconnectedness of the stories is provided in Fontenrose's *Steinbeck's Unhappy Valley*. In this insightful study, Fontenrose outlines the complexity of this outwardly simple book and explains how Steinbeck manipulates the effect of time and the importance of the locale (houses, gardens, and farms) in order to create generous parallel and antithetical elements that exist between each story and its precursors as well as its followers. Further chapters describe how the Battle farm impacts each of the sections or episodes and how religious and mythological referents also are incorporated, many times in a reversal of their original meaning.

Finally, in a more recent and as yet unpublished analysis of *Pastures,* Kevin Hearle places *Pastures* as a novel of social protest in which Steinbeck carefully dissects and dismantles the stereotypical American dreams of a pastoral idyllic setting where "all is well." Even after 70 years, the fields of Steinbeck's second novel can still be tilled effectively and produce new food for thought.

SOURCES

Astro, Richard, and Tetsumaro Hayashi, eds. *Steinbeck: The Man and His Work.* Corvallis: Oregon State University Press, 1971.

Benson, Jackson L. *The True Adventures of John Steinbeck, Writer: A Biography.* New York: Viking, 1984.

French, Warren. *John Steinbeck's Fiction Revisited.* New York: Twayne, 1994.

Hayashi, Tetsumaro, ed. *John Steinbeck: The Years of Greatness, 1936–1939.* Tuscaloosa: University of Alabama Press, 1993.

———. *A New Study Guide to Steinbeck's Major Works, with Critical Explications.* Metuchen, N.J.: Scarecrow Press, 1993.

Lisca, Peter. *John Steinbeck: Nature and Myth.* New York: Thomas Y. Crowell Company, 1978.

Owens, Louis. *John Steinbeck's Re-vision of America.* Athens: University of Georgia Press, 1985.

Parini, Jay. *John Steinbeck: A Biography.* New York: Holt, 1995.

Simmonds, Roy S. *John Steinbeck: The War Years, 1939–1945.* Lewisburg, Pa.: Bucknell University Press, 1996.

Timmerman, John. *John Steinbeck's Fiction: The Aesthetics of the Road Taken.* Norman: University of Oklahoma Press, 1986.

Michael J. Meyer

PATCHETT, ANN (1963–)

Ann Patchett is the author of four novels, the third of which, *Bel Canto* (2001), won the PEN/Faulkner Award and England's Orange Prize, and was a finalist for the National Book Critics Circle Award. She has been praised especially for her realistic and widely divergent characters. In the opinion of writer and reviewer Laurie Parker, Patchett's books seem almost like "oral histories recorded by a kind and forgiving transcriber," as Patchett creates "characters of such varied races and backgrounds, making each one's voice and life so utterly believable" (Miller).

Ann Patchett was born on December 2, 1963, in Los Angeles, California, to Frank Patchett, a police captain, and Jeanne Ray Wilkinson Patchett, a nurse. Patchett was educated at Sarah Lawrence College, where she earned her bachelor's degree in 1984, and the University of Iowa, where she earned her master of fine arts degree in 1987. Her first novel, *The Patron Saint of Liars* (1992), opens as Martha Rose, 23 years old and pregnant, flees her husband, Thomas, in California and heads east to Kentucky and St. Elizabeth's, a home for unwed mothers. Once at St. Elizabeth's, however, she not only realizes she cannot give up the baby but meets a man named Son who wants to marry her and adopt the child, Cecilia. The reappearance of Thomas, however, changes the lives of both Rose and Cecilia. *Taft* (1994) tells a tale about fathers: Black ex-jazz musician John Nickel is devastated when his only son is taken from him. Continuing to run his Memphis bar, Muddy's, he becomes involved in the lives of Fay, a white waitress who works for him, and her brother Carl. Nickel becomes obsessed with reconstructing the life of their father, Taft, and discovering truths about unconventional love and family.

In *The Magician's Assistant* (1997), Patchett creates an intriguing relationship among Sabine, architect and assistant to the magician Parsifal, a gay man in love with Phan, a quiet Vietnamese who designs computer software. When Phan dies of AIDS, Parsifal discovers that he, too, is afflicted with the disease, and marries Sabine—who has always been in love with him—to ensure that she will inherit his assets. After Parsifal's death, and a surprising disclosure, Sabine embarks on a love affair of her own. *Bel Canto* (2001), as Ann Patchett has discussed with several interviewers, is based on the 1996 takeover of the Japanese embassy in Lima, Peru, by Tupac Amaru terrorists. Although in reality, all women and children were released, Patchett's novel creates famous American opera singer Roxane Coss, the only woman who remains a hostage with the 57 men. She sings arias twice a day during the long ordeal that ultimately celebrate the triumph of human goodness in the face of evil.

Patchett wrote the screenplay for *The Patron Saint of Liars* that aired as a television film for CBS in 1998. She lives and writes in Nashville, Tennessee.

NOVELS

Bel Canto. New York: HarperCollins, 2001.
The Magician's Assistant. New York: Harcourt Brace, 1997.
The Patron Saint of Liars. Boston: Houghton Mifflin, 1992.
Taft. Boston: Houghton Mifflin, 1994.

SOURCES

Maslin, Janet. "Uninvited Guests Wearing You Down? Listen to Opera." *New York Times,* 31 May 2001, p. E–7.
Review of *Bel Canto. Publisher's Weekly* (April, 16, 2001): 42.

OTHER

Ann Patchett. Available online. URL: http://www.annpatch-ett.com. Accessed September 24, 2005.
Bookreporter. "On the Road with Ann Patchett, Week 1." Available online. URL: http://www.bookreporter.com.lectures/road/patchett-1asp. Accessed September 24, 2005.
Clark, Alex. "Danger Arias," *Guardian Unlimited* (July 14, 2001). Available online. URL: http://books.guardian.co.uk.reviews/generalfiction/0,6121,521254,00.html. Accessed September 24, 2005.
"A Conversation with Ann Patchett, Author of *Bel Canto.*" BookBrowse.com. Available online. URL: http://www.bookbrowse.com/author_interviews/full/index.cfm?author_number=645. Accessed September 24, 2005.
Miller, Laura. "*Bel Canto* by Ann Patchett," *Salon.com.* Available online. URL: http://dir.salon.com/books/review/2001/06/22/patchett/index.html?sid=1036831. Accessed September 24, 2005.
Parker, Laurie. Review of *The Magician's Assistant.* Bookpage.com. Available online. URL: http://www.bookpage.com/9710bp/fiction/themagiciansassistant.html. Accessed on September 24, 2005.
Patchett, Ann. "Ann Patchett: Turning a News Story into a Novel." *Bookpage.com* Available online. URL: http://www.bookpage.com/0106bp/ann_patchett.html. Accessed September 24, 2005.
Valby, Karen. Review of *Bel Canto, Entertainment Weekly* (June 8, 2001). Available online by subscription. URL: http://www.ew.com/ew/article/review/book/0,6115,256647_5_0_,00html. Accessed September 24, 2005.
Welch, Dave. "Ann Patchett Hits All the Right Notes." *Powells.com.* Available online. URL: http://www.powells.com.authors/patchett.html. Accessed September 24, 2005.

PEACOCK, NANCY (1954–)

Nancy Peacock is the author of *Life without Water* (1996), which has been praised for its realistic rendering of the hippie era of the 1960s, and *Home Across the Road* (1999), lauded for its poetically rendered stories of both a black family and a white family from 1855 until 1971.

Nancy Peacock was born on June 19, 1954, in Wilmington, Delaware, to Alton Edward Peacock, a chemist, and Margaret Weston Peacock, a social worker. Her parents divorced and Peacock lived with her mother in Alabama and in North Carolina. She worked as a dairy-farm milker and stable mucker before *Life Without Water,* set in Chatham County, North Carolina, during the turbulent 1960s, was published.

Cedar, born in 1969, grows in experience, as does her young mother Sara, who dropped out of college to be with Sol, Cedar's father and a marijuana-smoking hippie artist. Sara leaves Sol, taking Cedar to a commune on the West Coast, where Sara becomes pregnant by Daniel; he abandons her for another woman before the new baby is born. Despite her disillusionment with the free-love philosophy, Sara is admirable in the love she gives and shares with Cedar, who narrates the novel.

Home across the Road begins during slavery. As reviewer Judith Kicinski points out, the novel, centering on the slave Cally Redd, and her great-granddaughter China Redd, born free in 1912, has "the scope, but not the length, of an epic" (Skicinski, 107). Cally, a slave at the Roseberry plantation owned by the Redds, is part of the black Redd family, who eventually move to a house across the road. The five generations of the two families—along with several intricately employed symbols, including a heirloom pair of earrings—show the intertwining histories of the two families and two races in 100 years of race relations in the South. For the "black Redds," the earrings are not only a reminder of the repeated rapes and abuse they suffered at the hands of the "white Redds," but also, as critic Gene Hyde notes, a "powerful symbol for their tenacious independence" as they emerge from the legacy of slavery.

Nancy Peacock lives and works in Pittsboro, near Chapel Hill, North Carolina. She is reportedly writing a memoir.

NOVELS

Home across the Road. Atlanta, Ga.: Longstreet, 1999.
Life without Water. Atlanta, Ga.: Longstreet, 1996.

SOURCES

Chamberlain, Marlene. Review of *Home across the Road, Booklist* (November 15, 1999): 606.
Prose, Francine. "Up in Smoke," *New York Times Book Review,* November 24, 1996, p. 23.
Skicinski, Judith. Review of *Home Across the Road, Library Journal* 124, no. 17 (October 15, 1999): 107.
Unsigned review of *Home Across the Road, Publishers Weekly* 246, no. 43 (October 25, 1999): 52.
Unsigned review of *Life Without Water, Publishers Weekly* 243, no. 37 (September 9, 1996): 65.

OTHER

Barnhill, Anne C. "Lessons from a Flower Child." *The News & Record* (Piedmont Triad, N.C.) (November 24, 1996). HighBeam Research. Available online. URL: http://www.highbeam.com/library/doc3.asp?DOCID=1G1:74773774. Accessed September 24, 2005.
Hyde, Gene. "Three Novels By North Carolinians Living with the Legacy Of Slavery." *The News & Record* (Piedmont Triad, N.C.) (October 31, 1999). HighBeam Research. Available online. URL: http://www.highbeam.com/library/doc3.asp?DOCID=1G1:74539865. Accessed September 24, 2005.

PEARL, THE JOHN STEINBECK (1947) When STEINBECK and his close friend Edward F. Ricketts made a scientific expedition in the Gulf of California in 1940, they learned of a folktale that Steinbeck reported in the "Narrative" section of *The Log from the Sea of Cortez* (1941). It was a story of a native Mexican boy who accidentally found an enormous pearl. He knew its value was so great that he might get "drunk as long as he wished and marry any one of a number of girls" (103). But every pearl broker offered him so little that he refused to sell it, and instead hid it under a stone. Then he was waylaid, attacked, and tortured. Finally he got angry, cursed the pearl, and threw it into the sea to make himself a free man again, and "laughed a great deal about it" (103). Steinbeck considered the Indian boy "too heroic, too wise," and the legend "far too reasonable to be true," but he thought it "probably true" (103).

Nonetheless, Steinbeck nursed the story in his mind for four years before he started writing the novella *The Pearl,* expanding the original one-page narrative in *The Log* to a complex novella of more than 100 pages. He finished the first draft by early February 1945, and the story first appeared in the *Woman's Home Companion* (December 1945) under the title *The Pearl of the World.* Its publication in book form as *The Pearl* was delayed until December 1947, when the first edition appeared from the Viking Press.

In the early stages of the expansion of the story, Steinbeck had thoughts of making it into a screenplay. In the hopes of universalizing the young Indian boy, he converted him to a young married man, Kino, who has a wife, Juana, and an infant son, Coyotito. With these social responsibilities, he has far more obligations than the single native resident of the folktale. Although some of the details of the original story were retained (e.g., the pearl buyers' conspiracy, the physical attack on the pearl's owner), Steinbeck added still others, creating a scenario where the pearl becomes a necessity to its young discoverer and is equated with his very soul.

The novella begins with a description of Kino and his family in the early morning, living a simple and peaceful life. The opening scenes are developed effectively with symbolic imagery of light and darkness and musical sounds that fluctuate between the comforting soft "Song of the Family" and the threatening "Song of Evil" that is heard when a scorpion appears and stings Kino's baby son, Coyotito, on the shoulder. As the peacefulness of the small family suddenly turns into a panic, Kino's wife, Juana, sucks the poison from the wound but desperately wants to see the doctor in the town to make sure her child is safe. Unfortunately, the doctor refuses to see the baby because Kino has no money, his "fortune consisting of only several valueless seed pearls." Steinbeck makes sure to carefully associate the doctor as a descendent of the early Spanish invaders or "conquistadors," and to establish the fact that Kino's race has been exploited by such men in the past.

After the doctor's refusal, the family sets out to sea in search of food and the ever-elusive pearl sought by all divers. As he continues to dive, Kino sees a pale glimmer and to his amazement discovers a pearl that is as large as a seagull's egg. The find seems to be an answer to his prayers, since it will no doubt convince the doctor to pay a visit and assure Kino and Juana of their son's future health. As he gazes at the silver surface of the pearl in his small thatched hut on land, Kino is transformed by the potential he sees for a life change. Ignoring his present condition of happiness, he begins to envision what he can attain when he becomes rich. At first, he dreams of fine new clothes and a new harpoon, but the vision soon expands to include education for Coyotito and respectability accorded by a church wedding with his common-law wife. Steinbeck even inserts a passing reference to a rifle as a symbol of Kino's newfound power. Though he had previously lacked strength due to his poverty and lower social class, he can now forcefully assert his equality to others as a result of the potential wealth that accompanies the pearl. Angered at his former rejection by the doctor, he now sees the pearl as his salvation, a lever to force the physician to offer his medical advice, thus overcoming the stigma of Kino's native and peasant status.

As news of Kino's "pearl" spreads, the doctor surprisingly agrees to make a house call, changing his mind about treating Coyotito now that Kino possesses wealth beyond belief. Though Kino at first welcomes the doctor's visit, shortly after he administers medicine to Coyotito, the child begins to sicken, allowing the doctor a chance to "save" him. Kino's fears escalate as he considers the possibility that the physician has caused this relapse, rather than bringing the family healing and relief from worry and concern.

Not surprisingly, Kino hides the pearl, burying it in the ground and fearing that others, both friends and enemies, have a greed that surpasses even the doctor's. Despite his skills, the motives of the doctor remain suspect, and Steinbeck seems to suggest that his keen eye observes Kino's unintentional revelation of the treasure's hiding place. Later in the night, an intruder enters Kino's house and attempts to steal the pearl. Though Kino wounds the thief, he is also hurt in the struggle, prompting Juana to proclaim the pearl a thing of evil, a danger that is destined to destroy the family.

Reluctant to part with this windfall of good luck, Kino refuses to listen to his wife's warning and, for the moment at least, convinces her that the treasure will ultimately be beneficial. The following morning, he sets out to offer the pearl to the buyers in La Paz.

Unfortunately, however, he is unable to sell the pearl for the price he has expected and finds that they denigrate his find as "monstrous" and "ugly" because of its size. Nonetheless, he refuses to part with it for the offers made by the consortium of buyers, nor does he believe their claims of its worthlessness. All too soon, he comes to a realization that he and his people have always been cheated by the pearl buyers, who have set prices for pearls far below their real worth, depending upon native ignorance and naiveté to manipulate and dupe the local divers. Impetuously, Kino declares that he will sell his pearl in the capital, an act that defies the established social structure and suggests his unwillingness to be the pawn of those who have power. Although his actions are seemingly justified and correct, they are seen by his friends and relatives as a betrayal of his people's way of life and traditions, and as a defiance that will inevitably cause tragedy for the family as well as for the Indian society they belong to. He has stepped outside the well-known boundaries established for his people.

Before he sets out on his journey to escape the dishonesty and trickery of the buyers, he returns home a second time. Though he is forced to endure another physical attack, this time he kills the potential thief, only to discover later that his canoe has been ruthlessly destroyed and his house has been burnt down. Thus destitute and homeless, the three leave the village and become fugitives. Since the pearl is taken with them as a potential solution to their plight, it is not surprising that three "dark trackers" follow the family. For a while, they elude these men, but eventually a confrontation takes place in the barren mountains that separate Kino and his family from escape and redemption. In the ensuing struggle, Kino manages to kill the trackers, but a stray shot from a rifle hits Coyotito in the head, causing his death. Then, at last, Kino and Juana return to La Paz and walk straight to the beach. This time the gender differences seem to have disappeared as the couple walks hand in hand rather than separately. Kino offers Juana the opportunity to throw the great but cursed pearl back into the sea, but Steinbeck ultimately chooses to let his protagonist demonstrate the knowledge he has gained from his misfortunes, and it is Kino who tosses the treasure back into the murky depths from whence it came.

The story is a morality play as well as a parable. Steinbeck notes in his introductory remarks, "as with all retold tales that are in people's hearts, there are only good and bad things and black and white things and good and evil things and no in-between anywhere" (2). Yet this introductory statement may also be seen as a facetious comment, for there are many interpretations and lenses through which a reader can view the story's meaning.

Thus, everything in the story seems to possess a dual quality, the quality of which has been embodied, for instance, in the history of Mexico as a country of native Mexicans and the descendants of the conquistadors. For example, when a scorpion moves delicately down the rope to Coyotito at the outset of the novella, Kino hears in his mind "the Song of Evil" on top of "the Song of the Family," whereas Juana "repeated an ancient magic to guard against such evil, and on top of that she muttered a Hail Mary between clenched teeth" (10). Similarly, the great pearl is only beautiful when it is possessed in the hand of a person of pure heart. Its negative qualities are evident in the last scene of the story, when Kino looks into the surface of the pearl and finds that "it was gray and ulcerous. And the pearl was ugly like a malignant growth." The evil faces of the trackers Kino kills appear to "peer from it into his eyes," and Kino sees his son's body "with the top of his head shot away" (121) in its reflection. Once the pearl settles into the water at the end of the tale, however, "The lights on its surface were green and lovely" (122). Additionally, in order to overlap the dual quality of the landscape and environment, Steinbeck incorporates an atmosphere of hazy mirage into this story [whose locale is La Paz, though the author actually came across the story around Pulmo and in Estero de la Luna on the eastern coast of the Gulf (*Sea of Cortez,* "Log," 254)]. The use of such dubious imagery is designed to show how the local people "trust things of the spirit and things of the imagination, but they do not trust their eyes" (21).

The Pearl is "a brutal story but with flashes of beauty" (Steinbeck and Wallsten, 279), in which ruthless, deadly fights for survival take place in the dark. In the middle of chapter 3 in *The Pearl,* the people in the house can hear the swish of a tightly woven school of small fishes and the bouncing splash of the bigger fishes from the estuary as the slaughter goes on (47). The passage, based on a phenomenon Steinbeck witnessed not in La Paz but near Guaymas on the other side of the Gulf (*Sea of Cortez,* "Log," 240), symbolically falls between the doctor's two visits to Kino's house at night. One can readily suspect his medical treatment for the baby to be dishonest. One may even suspect that he is deeply involved in the whole criminal plot of robbing Kino of the great pearl.

Furthermore, the estuary, like a tide pool, represents a microcosm, just as a town represents a human habitat. To Steinbeck, a town epitomizes the universe, as does a human community like Tortilla Flat or Cannery Row in Monterey, California. The microcosm functions as part of a greater ecosystem. It is a motif Steinbeck persistently uses in his entire canon. The thesis of this interrelationship between the parts and the whole is considered to be developed from his "phalanx theory," which is first introduced in his June 21, 1933, letter to Carlton Sheffield and also in a letter to George Albee (ca. July 1933), both included in *Steinbeck: A Life in Letters* (74–77, 79–82).

Another significant landscape description in the story is that of the mountainous area where Kino's family arrives and finds an oasis and life-giving water during their desperate flight (107–108) from the dark trackers (just as Pepé Torres does in Steinbeck's short story "Flight"). In fact, the family surely would have died had they not found the little pools. Undoubtedly, the description of the pools is based on the camping place where Steinbeck and Ricketts stayed overnight on March 25, 1940, which is located close to Loreto (*Sea of Cortez,* "Log," 161–162). By incorporating facts into fiction, Steinbeck chooses to ignore the fact that it would have been almost impossible for the Kino family to walk to Loreto, which is located 220 miles away from La Paz.

Again, to Steinbeck, the little pools are, like the Great Tide Pool in *Cannery Row,* not only "places of life" but "places of killing because of the water" (108). Robert S. Hughes's poignant argument that "the two most important strands of Steinbeck's thinking in *Cannery Row* [are] the moral and the ecological" (119) is true of *The Pearl* as well. *The Pearl* is a symbolic parable with moral lessons, and also a realistic, humanistic novella with ecological and sociological insights. As Jackson J. Benson calls *Cannery Row* "an ecological parable" (25), *The Pearl* also fits this literary description. The surface stories of the two are quite different from each other, and yet on deeper levels they reveal similar thematic features.

In the final impressive scene of the novella, the only thing Kino holds in his hand is a rifle that he has taken from the dark trackers. At the outset of the story, Kino and Juana had a brush house, a canoe, and, most of all, their beloved son, Coyotito. As the story ends, they have lost everything. Many readers might question the ending: How will they be able to live when all they possess is a rifle, and nothing to live by and on? Surely Kino will always be in danger of being shot by another "dark thing." Nothing meaningful and productive can be achieved by violence. As Roy S. Simmonds contends, "The logical ending to the story is future tragedy and death" (182).

Fortunately, given the dualistic nature of life, another option exists: the possibility that Kino and Juana have walked through trial and temptation and have come out, not unscathed, but as survivors who are filled with an understanding of life's complexity, a vision which would have been impossible without undergoing the troubling discoveries about their own human natures that come with ownership of the pearl. Seen through Western eyes, the novel seems to condemn patriarchal class structure and the oppression of the poor, while from an Eastern perspective, it is Kino's own discontent and refusal to accept a lowly place in society (he is constantly striving for materialistic gain) that eventually causes his downfall. The complexity of the novella, its layers of meanings, cyclical pattern, and disturbing ambiguous ending, suggests that Steinbeck had truly discovered how to write without offering merely didactic or reductive moral messages. He had discovered the ambiguities that plague all human beings as they struggle between choices of good and evil.

SOURCES

Benson, Jackson J. *The True Adventures of John Steinbeck, Writer.* New York: Viking, 1984.

———, ed. *The Short Novels of John Steinbeck: Critical Essays with a Checklist to Steinbeck Criticism.* Durham, N.C.: Duke University Press, 1990.

Hughes, R. S. *John Steinbeck: A Study of the Short Fiction.* Boston: Twayne, 1989.

Simmonds, Roy S. *John Steinbeck: The War Years, 1939–1945.* Lewisburg, Pa.: Bucknell University Press, 1996.

Steinbeck, John. *The Pearl.* 1947.

———. *The Sea of Cortez.* 1941.

———. *Steinback: A Life in Letters.* Edited by Elaine Steinbeck and Robert Wallsten. New York: Viking, 1974.

Michael J. Meyer

PEMBROKE Mary E. Wilkins Freeman (1894)

Much of the fiction of Mary Wilkins FREEMAN invites feminist readings because her works deal with the struggles of women in patriarchal societies. However, Freeman's 1894 *Pembroke* resists a purely feminist reading primarily because of the negative portrayal of Deborah Thayer. Among the several rural New England households described in the novel, the father is generally the overbearing parent who stubbornly sticks to his "way" (11), thereby complicating the relationships of his children. The brothers-in-law Cephas Barnard and Silas Berry impose their own unreasonable will on their children, especially when it comes to their love interests. What prevents *Pembroke* from lumping all fathers into one type is that the character who seems to have the most profoundly negative impact on the next generation is actually the female character, Deborah Thayer, whose husband Caleb does whatever she says.

Although some critics attribute Rebecca Thayer's descent into "fallen woman" status on the spinelessness of her father Caleb, most readers wonder how anyone could stand up to a domineering woman like Mrs. Thayer. She even admits that her son Barney, whose rash actions dominate the text, inherited her stubborn streak. The novel presents more and more evidence that the heart of Barney's problem is not so much genetic as it is a matter of example. His mother had been a model of stubborn and unreasonable pride all his life, so it seems natural for him to refuse to marry Charlotte simply to spite her father. A consistent theme throughout the novel is often uttered by its characters with the expression, "You're putting your own eyes out" (122). Indeed, numerous inhabitants of *Pembroke* practice self-destructive behavior, thinking they are getting back at someone else. Despite Deborah Thayer's hopes that her oldest son, Barney, will finally marry Charlotte Barnard, she uses this conflict as an excuse to prevent her daughter Rebecca from marrying William Berry simply because he is Charlotte's cousin. Her ridiculous refusal to bend on this matter forces Rebecca to meet William secretly, and the end result is an unplanned pregnancy. When Deborah realizes that her daughter is expecting, she orders her out of the house, and Rebecca walks out into a blizzard without anything warm to wear. Mrs. Thayer then consciously keeps her husband from looking for their daughter by ordering him to keep on shucking corn, and he "obeyed" (195). She finally decides to send their son Barney to make William marry her.

Although Freeman's description of this conflict seems to absolve William of any error in judgment, it is a realistic representation of a society that places all the blame on the woman who "gets herself in trouble." The author's reticence on the subject of the baby that dies makes readers wonder about the exact cause of death. Tracing Rebecca's circumstances reveal that her mother was most to blame for everything bad that happened. If the baby died from the physical and psychological distress of the mother, Deborah Thayer is culpable. While the characters in the novel and many critics view most of the village of Pembroke's problems on Barney's stubborn action, the destructive will can perhaps better be traced to Deborah Thayer.

Toward the end of the novel, Deborah is absolved of the blame of her son Ephraim's death when she learns that Ephraim had been secretly sledding in the middle of the cold night. Since Ephraim has always been in poor health, such activity probably did cause his sudden death. However, if Deborah had not been so strict with Ephraim, he would not have been tempted to sneak out. Freeman's inclusion of the controlling Mrs. Thayer limits the gender bias of the novel. It is also unique that Freeman's male characters in this novel are the ones who most often "sob" (291) their dialogue, while the female characters seem stronger in many ways. Despite their earlier jilting, Charlotte Barnard and Sylvia Crane develop from unbearable patience into memorable forces by the end. *Pembroke* reveals the selfish motives behind the petty behavior of all its characters and explores the strengths and weaknesses of both genders.

In a comprehensive study of American realism and regionalism, Eric Sundquist aptly notes that "Freeman surpasses Jewett in her ability to combine contemporary social problems with a stylistically detailed apprehension of regional character" (Sundquist, 509). Mary E. Wilkins Freeman's writing style in *Pembroke* is straightforward and a pleasure to read, but the novel bears some striking similarities to *The Scarlet Letter*. Heather Kirk Thomas notes the way Charlotte Barnard becomes "analogous to Hawthorne's Hester Prynne" (Thomas, 32) when she sews for the village. Rebecca's embarrassment over having gotten pregnant before marriage is also described in a similar way to Hester Prynne's shame when seeing any stranger in town, for it seemed "her old disgrace had assumed in this new mind a hideous freshness" (308). Still, Freeman's overall depiction of women is original. Although the characters are extreme, they never seem exaggerated. Many examples are humorous in their irony, such as when Hannah Berry treats her sisters and niece abominably but defies anyone else to treat them badly. Like many of us with priorities out of whack, "Hannah Berry had a species of loyalty in her nature, inasmuch as she would tolerate ill-treatment of her kin from nobody but her own self" (273).

It is true that Mary Wilkins Freeman "devoted [herself] to telling the stories of female loneliness, isolation, and frustration" (Showalter, 70), in addition to describing the local color of settings, much as Jewett and Chopin did. Indeed, Sylvia Crane as the "old maid" is quite touching in *Pembroke*, but this novel actually presents the effect of lost love as being equally painful for its male characters. Both Richard Alger and Barney Thayer learn what they were missing because of their pride, and Freeman's narrative questions whether what is considered "proper" between men and women is something about which we should even worry.

SOURCES

Freeman, Mary E. Wilkins. *Pembroke.* 1894. Reprinted, Boston: Northeastern University Press, 2002.

Menke, Pamela Glenn. "The Catalyst of Color and Women's Regional Writing: *At Fault, Pembroke,* and *The Awakening,*" *Southern Quarterly: A Journal of the Arts in the South* 37, no. 3–4 (Spring–Summer 1999): 9–20.

Showalter, Elaine. *Sister's Choice: Tradition and Change in American Women's Writing.* Oxford: Clarendon Press, 1991.

Sundquist, Eric J. "Realism and Regionalism." In *Columbia Literary History of the United States,* edited by Emory Elliott, 501–524. New York: Columbia University Press, 1988.

Thomas, Heather Kirk. " 'It's Your Father's Way': The Father-Daughter Narrative and Female Development in Mary Wilkins Freeman's *Pembroke,*" *Studies in the Novel* 29, no. 1 (Spring 1997): 26–39.

Rachel G. Wall

PENHALLY Caroline Gordon (1931)

Released in 1931, *Penhally*—Caroline GORDON's first published novel—tells the story of four generations of the Llewellyn family and their lives on the great plantation of Penhally. Gordon divides the text into three sections and tells the story of the current generation in each section. Because Lucy and John's son—Frank—kills himself, Gordon gives us the story of his two sons—Nick and Chance—in the last section, thus encompassing the lives of the four generations. Within the text, one of the obvious concerns is that of land and the entailment of land to the firstborn male. Through her use of local color, Gordon develops the plot around Penhally, so much so that Penhally becomes the main protagonist. In fact, it could be easily argued that Gordon's primary focus is on land and how it affects familial relations: Gordon opens the novel with a land-related disturbance (between Nicholas and Ralph) and closes it with the murder of Nick by his brother Chance over Nick's decision to sell Penhally.

Although much of the novel evolves around land and the inherent evils of entailment, Gordon develops strong female characters that are often overlooked because they are hidden within the development of the novel—readers must look beyond the stereotypes. In contrast to the male characters, the female characters make well-thought-out choices that affect their lives and the lives of those around them. In fact, female characters from Cousin Jess to Alice Blair give strength and support to the tragic stories of the Llewellyns.

Whereas the male characters focus on land and inheritance and make grave mistakes in their decisions, female characters portray the ability to make reasonable choices even when faced with negative situations. And Gordon often portrays them in a humorous light. For instance, Gordon gives us this depiction of Cousin Jess: "Cousin Jess would come right along and take the bell out of his hand. She had an energy that contrasted oddly with her tired voice. She seemed always on the point of doing something for you, better, of course, than you could do it yourself" (55). This glimpse of Cousin Jess tells us that she has the ability to get things done, even if others have to listen to her bragging about her abilities.

For Nancylee Jonza, Alice is the most reliable and stable female character in Gordon's text. Alice knows that she must marry a man who is able to take care of his family, and we see this when she is contemplating her possible future with John: "On the face of it, John was the better match of the two. But the old gentleman was likely to make half a dozen more wills before he died. . . . John would never be able to fend for himself if he were cut off" (72). And even though this scene shows Alice's dependence on marriage, Gordon depicts Alice as strong and wise enough to be aware of her limited choices. Although limited, Alice is a character capable of making her own choices, choices that have the ability to change her life.

Another important female character in the novel is Lucy. Although our glimpses of Lucy are contrasting (in one scene she is pouring out buttermilk in front of a woman and her two children, thereby denying them the opportunity to utilize the buttermilk), Gordon gives us at least one scene where she stands up to her uncle, Nicholas. In this scene, Nicholas is contemplating how his power and influence intimidates most of his family as he addresses Lucy:

> Leaning back in his chair he waited, pleasantly alert, for her answer. He always enjoyed introducing his brother's name into conversation like that. It made people jump. They hardly ever knew how to take it, their assumption being usually that he chose to forget that he had ever

had a brother, while the attitude that he really took was that the brother, whose existence he perfectly recognized, was no more to him than a casual acquaintance.

But Lucy did not jump. (64)

And so we see Lucy as a woman who is not so easily intimidated. She calmly answers her uncle, and she refuses to bow to him. In addition, Gordon foreshadows the Llewellyn's ruin, for Nicholas's own disagreeable temperament will jeopardize the family's inheritance. In contrast to Lucy's iron will, Nicholas makes emotional decisions that are purely "in the moment." His inattention to others' feelings and his preoccupation with land and primogeniture serve to lay the groundwork for the family's eventual demise.

For Caroline Gordon, the South played an intrinsic part in her life and her novels. In *Penhally*, she uses the land and the estate to frame a novel that focuses on the eventual downfall of the Llewellyn family—a family grounded in the old traditions of the South. However, Gordon—through careful characterization and plot development—creates a text that is both entertaining and critical of a bygone era. Although much of the focus of *Penhally* is on male characters, Gordon writes about women who utilize their surroundings as best they can. These women—Cousin Jess, Alice, and Lucy—all portray able women who, through their comments, actions, and lives, add to the flavor of Gordon's novel.

SOURCES

Fraistat, Rose Ann C. *Caroline Gordon as Novelist and Woman of Letters*. Baton Rouge: Louisiana State University Press, 1984.

Gordon, Caroline. *Penhally*. Nashville, Tenn.: J. S. Sanders & Company, 1931.

Jonza, Nancylee Novell. *The Underground Stream: The Life and Art of Caroline Gordon*. Athens: University of Georgia Press, 1995.

Christopher Lee Massey

PEOPLE OF DARKNESS Tony Hillerman (1980)

It is not an overstatement to assert that the publication of Tony Hillerman's Navajo novels has been as significant to the history of the mystery-detective genre as Sir Arthur Conan Doyle's creation of Sherlock Holmes and Dashiell Hammett's and Raymond Chandler's popularization of the hard-boiled style through the novels and stories featuring Sam Spade and Philip Marlowe, respectively. Before Hillerman's series, the multicultural contributions to the genre were anomalies, curiosities ranging from Earl Derr Biggers's immensely popular series featuring Charlie Chan, a generally benign caricature of the "Oriental" sensibility, to Arthur W. Upfield's long-running Australian series featuring the half-Aborigine police detective Napoleon Bonaparte.

The commercial and critical success of Hillerman's series has made multiculturalism much more the norm than the exception in the genre. Not only are there now more than a dozen established series featuring Native American detectives, but there are even more series featuring African-American and Hispanic detectives, as well as series featuring detectives of European ancestry that emphasize ethnic heritage in a pointed and extended manner that was uncommon before Hillerman's series. Indeed, the much broadened popularity of the genre in all regions of the world and, even more, the increased demand for English translations of foreign contributions to the genre can be attributed to Hillerman's influence. And this new diversity in the genre has had the ancillary effect of greatly expanding the list of the occupations in which amateur detectives are employed, so that there are now established series featuring everything from meter readers to exotic dancers.

Hillerman's "Navajo" series now includes 19 novels. It has evolved in an unusual way. In three of his first four novels, the detective is Joe Leaphorn, a middle-aged Navajo tribal policeman (the second novel, *The Fly on the Wall* [1971], features an investigative reporter named John Cotton). Then in the fifth novel in the series, *People of Darkness* (1980), Hillerman introduces another detective, a younger tribal policeman named Jim Chee. Ironically, the younger Chee is more traditional in his attitudes than Leaphorn, whose greater experience as an investigator has its corollary in a more cosmopolitan and cynical sensibility. Chee is also the protagonist in the sixth and seventh novels in the series. There were pragmatic as well as creative reasons for the shift to Chee. Hillerman had sold the television rights to the Leaphorn character, and it would take him several years to regain the complete rights to the character. When Hillerman finally teamed Leaphorn and Chee in *Skinwalkers* (1986) and in *A Thief of Time* (1988), he achieved a sort of breakthrough commercially and critically. Although each of his earlier novels had had better sales, he became a fixture on the best-seller lists with these two novels, and critics responded enthusiastically to the greater dramatic, thematic, and tonal complexity generated by the pairing of the two very distinctive detectives. Although there may be other instances in which a novelist has developed two detectives separately before bringing them together, the only other example that comes immediately to my mind is James Crumley's delayed teaming of his investigators Milo Milodragovitch and C. W. Sughrue.

Interestingly, it is generally acknowledged that Hillerman's first few novels were very unevenly written. But by the time he wrote *People of Darkness,* his style had begun to complement his more intuitively exquisite conception of his narratives. The novel opens in Albuquerque, with a pickup truck exploding outside the offices of a bacteriologist at the University of New Mexico Hospital. Having accumulated 30 days of leave time, Jimmy Chee is hired by Rosemary Vines, the second wife of a well-to-do rancher, B. J. Vines, to recover a stolen box of keepsakes belonging to her husband. Mrs. Vines claims that the thieves are the "people of darkness," who are somehow connected to a Navajo named Dillon Charley. Her husband had given Dillon Charley something from the box of keepsakes before it was stolen, but Dillon Charley is now buried near the first Mrs. Vines. It turns out that the exploding pickup truck belonged to Dillon Charley's son, Emerson, who is now a cancer patient at the hospital. B. J. Vines tries to persuade Chee to drop his investigation of the missing box, claiming that his wife herself is responsible for its theft. Remaining on the case, Chee begins to focus on Cotton Wolf as a suspect in the explosion of the pickup truck. In the course of his investigation, Chee meets a teacher named Mary Landon, with whom he gradually develops a long-term

relationship. Meanwhile, Emerson Charley dies, ostensibly from his cancer, but his corpse disappears from the morgue. His son, Tomas Charley, reveals to Chee the whereabouts of Vines' missing box, but when Chee goes there with Mary, they find Tomas dead and are stalked by Cotton Wolf. It turns out that the whole case hinges on revelations about an explosion on an oil rig some 40 years earlier, when Dillon Charley had been the foreman of the rig's drilling crew.

SOURCES

Bakerman, Jane S. "Joe Leaphorn and the Navaho Way: Tony Hillerman's Indian Detective Fiction," *Clues: A Journal of Detection* 2 (Spring–Summer 1981): 9–16.

———. "Tony Hillerman's Joe Leaphorn and Jim Chee." In *Cops and Constables: American and British Fictional Policemen,* edited by Earl Bargainnier and George N. Dove, 98–112. Bowling Green, Ohio: Bowling Green State University Popular Press, 1986.

Browne, Ray B. "The Ethnic Detective: Arthur W. Upfield, Tony Hillerman, and Beyond." In *Mystery and Suspense Writers: The Literature of Crime, Detection, and Espionage,* I–II, edited by Robin W. Winks and Maureen Corrigan, 1,029–1,046. New York: Scribner, 1998.

Engel, Leonard. "Landscape and Place in Tony Hillerman's Mysteries," *Western American Literature* 28 (August 1993): 111–122.

Erisman, Fred. "Hillerman's Uses of the Southwest," *Roundup Quarterly* 1, no. 4 (Summer 1989): 9–18.

———. *Tony Hillerman.* Western Writers Series, No. 87. Boise, Idaho: Boise State University, 1989.

Grape, Jan. "Tony Hillerman," *Mystery Scene* 58 (1997): 42–45.

Hillerman, Tony. "Making Mysteries with Navajo Materials." In *Literature and Anthropology. Studies in Comparative Literature,* no. 20, edited by Philip Dennis and Wendell Aycock, 5–13. Lubbock: Texas Tech University Press, 1989.

O'Sullivan, Maurice J. "Tony Hillerman and the Navajo Way." In *Crime Fiction and Film in the Southwest: Bad Boys and Bad Girls in the Badlands,* edited by Steve Glassman and Maurice J. O'Sullivan, 163–176. Bowling Green, Ohio: Bowling Green State University Popular Press, 2001.

Parfit, Michael. "Weaving Mysteries That Tell of Life among the Navajos," *Smithsonian* 21 (December 1990): 92–105.

Roush, Jan. "The Developing Art of Tony Hillerman," *Western American Literature* 28 (August 1993): 99–110.

———. "Tony Hillerman." In *Updating the Literary West,* edited by Max Westbrook, 468–474. Fort Worth: Western

Literature Association/Texas Christian University Press, 1997.

Schneider, Jack W. "Crime and Navajo Punishment: Tony Hillerman's Novels of Detection," *Southwest Review* 67 (Spring 1982): 151–160.

Sobol, John. *Tony Hillerman: A Public Life.* Toronto: ECW, 1994.

Martin Kich

PERCY, WALKER (1916–1990)

In addition to essays on contemporary language and literature, Walker Percy wrote six novels during his lifetime, all populated by characters who are consumed by a need to understand their identities and to relate to other human beings. His ability to combine intellectual and existential issues with realistically drawn, witty characters, who understand what they see, distinguished Percy from the beginning of his career. His first novel, *The MOVIEGOER* (1961), won the National Book Award because it clearly portrayed one individual's attempt to find meaning in his shallow life. His second novel, *The LAST GENTLEMAN* (1966), was a runner-up for the same award; *LOVE IN THE RUINS* (1971) cemented Percy's reputation as a writer who could combine the ideas of Soren Kierkegaard, European existentialism, and Helen Keller with the role of language and his own brand of Roman Catholicism, in readable, intriguing, yet comic, fiction.

Walker Percy was born on May 28, 1916, in Birmingham, Alabama, to Leroy Pratt Percy and Martha Phinizy Percy. After his father committed suicide in 1929, and his mother was killed in an automobile accident two years later, Percy was adopted by his father's cousin, William Alexander Percy. Percy, a cultivated and wealthy intellectual known for his friendships with historians, novelists, poets, and psychologists—and later for his autobiography, *Lanterns on the Levee: Recollections of a Planter's Son* (1941)—provided a stimulating atmosphere for Percy and his two brothers at their new home in Greenville, Mississippi. Percy was educated at the University of North Carolina, earning his bachelor's degree in 1937 and his medical degree from Columbia University in 1941. Because of medical problems resulting from recurring tuberculosis, Percy decided to leave the medical profession for the world of letters. In 1946, he married Mary Bernice Townsend, with whom he lived, mostly in Covington, Louisiana, until his death in 1990.

In *The Moviegoer,* Binx Bolling coins the term "Everydayness" to describe his hollow existence, because Binx recognizes that he needs to overcome the despair and find meaningful human contact. His future seems brighter at the novel's end. In *The Last Gentleman* Percy focuses on Will Barrett, an engineer. His rambling odyssey from New York City to the South and then to the New Mexico desert causes a malaise so strong that he nearly commits suicide. (This separation of body and soul is one of Percy's recurring concepts.) Will reappears 20 years later (as a lawyer rather than an engineer) in Percy's fifth novel, *The Second Coming* (1980). There he demands proof of God's existence and finds love with Allie, a sanatorium escapee who helps him overcome his angst and suggests that together they can survive and grow.

Percy's third novel, *Love in the Ruins,* features Dr. Tom More, who is descended from the Elizabethan Sir Thomas More. He attempts with the help of his invention, the "Lapsometer," to cure people of their despair; ironically, however, instead of offering solutions, the Lapsometer merely makes people behave in extreme ways, providing grist for the mill of Percy's redoubtable humor. To wit, Tom waits for the apocalypse in the shell of an old Howard Johnson motel, pinned down by a sniper but comfortable as long as his Early Times bourbon does not run out. Tom More reappears in Percy's last novel, *The Thanatos Syndrome* (1987), in which he fights the scientists who are contaminating the public water supplies with a mind-altering drug that results in loss of individuality and free will. *LANCELOT* (1977), Percy's fourth novel, is perhaps the most powerful in its angry indictment of American cultural values. Lance, the insane protagonist who is angry over his wife's infidelity, commits multiple murders, for which he is imprisoned as the novel opens. However, even Lance's bitterness is ameliorated by Percy's use of dark humor.

Walker Percy died on May 10, 1990, of cancer, in Louisiana. Appreciation of Walker Percy's novels continues to rise, helped by hundreds of doctoral dissertations and articles, and scores of scholarly books on both his fiction and his nonfiction articles on language, religion, and philosophy.

NOVELS

Lancelot. New York: Farrar, Straus, 1977.

The Last Gentleman. New York: Farrar, Straus, 1966.

Love in the Ruins: The Adventures of a Bad Catholic at a Time Near the End of the World. New York: Farrar, Straus, 1971.

The Moviegoer. New York: Knopf, 1961.

The Second Coming. New York: Farrar, Straus, 1980.

The Thanatos Syndrome. New York: Farrar, Straus, 1987.

SOURCES

Allen, William Rodney. *Walker Percy: A Southern Wayfarer.* Jackson: University Press of Mississippi, 1986.

Bloom, Harold, ed. *Modern Critical Views: Walker Percy.* New York: Chelsea House, 1986.

Brinkmeyer, Robert H., Jr. *Three Catholic Writers of the South.* Jackson: University Press of Mississippi, 1985.

Ciuba, Gary M. *Walker Percy: Books of Revelation.* Athens: University of Georgia Press, 1991.

Coles, Robert. *Walker Percy: An American Search.* Boston: Little, Brown, 1978.

Crowley, J. Donald, and Sue Mitchell Crowley, eds. *Walker Percy: Critical Essays.* Boston: G. K. Hall, 1989.

Desmond, John F. *At the Crossroads: Ethical and Religious Themes in the Writings of Walker Percy.* Troy, N.Y.: Whitson Publishing Company, 1997.

Gretlund, Jan Nordby, and Karl Heinz, eds. *Walker Percy: Novelist and Philosopher.* Jackson: University Press of Mississippi, 1991.

Hardy, John Edward. *The Fiction of Walker Percy.* Urbana: University of Illinois Press, 1987.

Hobson, Linda Whitney. *Walker Percy: A Comprehensive Descriptive Bibliography.* Columbia, S.C.: Faust, 1988.

———. *Understanding Walker Percy.* Columbia: University of South Carolina Press, 1988.

Kramer, Victor, ed. *Andrew Lytle, Walker Percy, Peter Taylor: A Reference Guide.* Boston: G. K. Hall, 1983.

Lawson, Lewis A., ed. *Following Percy: Essays on Walker Percy's Work.* Albany, N.Y.: Whitston Publishing Co., 1987.

———. *Still Following Percy.* Jackson: University Press of Mississippi, 1996.

Lawson, Lewis A., and Victor A. Kramer, eds. *Conversations with Walker Percy.* Jackson: University Press of Mississippi, 1985.

———, eds. *More Conversations with Walker Percy.* Jackson: University Press of Mississippi, 1993.

Lawson, Lewis A., and Elzbieta Oleksy. *Walker Percy's Feminine Characters.* Albany, N.Y.: Whitston Publishing Co., 1995.

Poteat, Patricia Lewis. *Percy and the Old Modern Age.* Baton Rouge: Louisiana State University Press, 1985.

Quinlan, Kieran. *Walker Percy: The Last Catholic Novelist.* Baton Rouge: Louisiana State University Press, 1996.

Samway, Patrick H. *Walker Percy: A Life.* New York: Farrar, Straus, 1997.

Taylor, L. Jerome. *In Search of Self: Life, Death, and Walker Percy.* Cambridge, Mass.: Cowley, 1986.

Tharpe, Jac, ed. *Walker Percy: Art and Ethics.* Jackson: University Press of Mississippi, 1980.

———. *Walker Percy.* Boston: Twayne, 1983.

Tolson, Jay. *Pilgrim in the Ruins: A Life of Walker Percy.* Chapel Hill: University of North Carolina, 1994.

Wyatt-Brown, Bertram. *The House of Percy: Honor, Melancholy, and Imagination in a Southern Family.* New York: Oxford University Press, 1994.

OTHER

"Walker Percy: An Introduction." Available online. URL: http://metalab.unc.edu/wpercy/who.html. Accessed September 26, 2005.

PETRY, ANN (1908–1997)

PETRY, ANN (1908–1997)   Ann Petry, novelist and short story writer, occupies a secure place in American literature. Her subject matter includes not only racial oppression and poverty on the streets of Harlem but also the smug hypocrisy of small-town white America immediately after World War II, miscegenation, and the precarious nature of the American dream. Her most famous novel, *The STREET* (1946) sold more than a million copies, earning for Petry both popular and critical esteem. Two additional novels followed: *Country Place* (1947) and *The Narrows* (1953), as well as the short fiction collection *Miss Muriel and Other Stories* and several young adult novels. These include portraits of slave women and Harriet Tubman, a hero of the Underground Railroad.

Petry was born on October 12, 1908, in Old Saybrook, Connecticut, to Bertha James Lane, a chiropodist and hairdresser, and Peter Clark Lane, Jr., a pharmacist. Educated at the Connecticut College of Pharmacy, from which she graduated in 1921, Petry worked at the family drugstore until her marriage in 1938 to George Petry. They moved to New York, where Petry worked as a journalist and took creative writing classes at Columbia

University. From the experience of living in Harlem arose Petry's stylistically forceful novel, *The Street,* largely about Lutie Johnson's struggle to overcome poverty and racism. Three years later, Petry published *Country Place,* whose characters are white New England inhabitants of Lennox, Connecticut. The residents are unhappy and often unprincipled. The novel did not enjoy the success of *The Street;* at its end, the returning World War II character, Johnnie Roane, leaves Lennox in disgust at the racism and venality just below the surface of the American Dream he fought to defend. With *The Narrows,* Petry turned her attention to interracial relationships. Again set in a small New England town, the novel traces the love affair between Link Williams, an African-American graduate of Dartmouth College, and Camilo Treadway Sheffield, a white married woman and heiress to an enormous fortune. The relationship is doomed. Both this novel and *Country Place* deserve more attention than they have received to date.

Ann Petry's novels have been compared thematically with those of Richard WRIGHT, Gloria NAYLOR, Toni MORRISON, and Alice WALKER. She was also a naturalist in the tradition of Stephen CRANE, Chester HIMES, and Theodore DREISER. After Petry's death in 1997, her papers were moved to the Boston University Mugar Memorial Library.

NOVELS

Country Place. Boston: Houghton Mifflin, 1947.
The Narrows. Boston: Houghton Mifflin, 1953.
The Street. Boston: Houghton Mifflin, 1946.

SOURCES

Bell, Bernard W. *The Afro-American Novel and Its Tradition.* Amherst: University of Massachusetts Press, 1987.
Bone, Robert A. *The Negro Novel in America.* Rev. ed. New Haven, Conn.: Yale University Press, 1965, pp. 157, 180–185.
Christian, Barbara. *Black Women Novelists: The Development of a Tradition.* Westport, Conn.: Greenwood Press, 1980.
Conjuring: Black Women, Fiction, and Literary Tradition. Edited by Marjorie Pryse and Hortense J. Spillers. Bloomington: Indiana University Press, 1985.
Davis, Arthur Press. *From the Dark Tower: Afro-American Writers from 1900 to 1960.* Washington, D.C.: Howard University Press, 1974.
Gayle, Addison, Jr. *The Way of the New World: The Black Novel in America.* Garden City, N.Y.: Anchor/Doubleday, 1975.
Holladay, Hilary. *Ann Petry.* New York: Twayne, 1996.
Interviews with Black Writers. Edited by John O'Brien. New York: Liveright, 1973. Photograph, p. 153.
Littlejohn, David. *Black on White.* New York: Grossman, 1966.
Noble, Jeanne. *Beautiful, Also, Are the Souls of My Black Sisters.* Englewood Cliffs, N.J.: Prentice-Hall, 1978.
Washington, Mary Helen. *Invented Lives: Narratives of Black Women, 1860–1960.* New York: Doubleday, 1987.

PET SEMATARY STEPHEN KING (1983)

In 1980, during an interview with Abe Peck of *Rolling Stone,* Stephen KING said of *Pet Sematary:* "It's done, but it's put away. I have no plans to publish it in the near future. It's too horrible. It's worse than *The Shining* or any of the other things. It's terrifying" (Underwood, 100). The idea for *Pet Sematary* came from a sequence of events from King's own life and began as any of his novels do, with a "what if" question. He planned to expand his idea into a modern retelling of W. W. Jacob's "The Monkey's Paw." During the writing, however, King said, "the book ceased being a novel to me, and became instead a gloomy exercise, like an endless marathon run. It never left my mind; it never ceased to trouble me" (Winter, 131). *Pet Sematary* was written between January and May 1979, and it was published against King's wishes in 1982 to satisfy his ending contract with Doubleday. King wrote the screenplay for the movie in 1989, but he says he will never reread the novel. In spite of King's feelings, *Pet Sematary* is one of his best-known novels. The characters' realism in the beginning is due largely to the autobiographical elements from King's own life. His use of narration, point of view, and flashback pulls readers into the story immediately and keeps them captivated far beyond its conclusion.

Pet Sematary is divided into three parts. At the opening of part 1, entitled "The Pet Sematary," the Creed family arrives at their new home in Ludlow, Maine. Louis, the patriarch, has accepted a job as the resident physician at the University of Maine. The family quickly bonds with the Crandalls, an elderly couple who live across the road. Jed Crandall becomes a father figure for Louis, and the two men spend many evenings together. One afternoon, Jed takes the whole Creed family up a path behind the Creeds' house to see the Pet Sematary, a burial ground set up by children many decades before. Several days later, Louis deals with a tragedy at the university: An automobile-pedestrian accident kills a student, Victor Pascow. Pascow's is the first of many untimely deaths Louis deals with in the novel. As Thanksgiving comes, Rachel takes the children, five-year-old Ellie and two-year-old Gage, back to Chicago. While they are away, Church, Ellie's beloved cat, is hit and killed by a truck passing in front of the Creed home. Jed offers to help Louis bury Church and guides him up to the Pet Sematary, and then to the Micmac ancient burial ground beyond. Jed explains, "The Micmacs believed this hill was a magic place" (117). He also indicates that the Micmacs stopped using the burial ground because they believed it had been possessed by a Wendigo, an evil, cannibalistic spirit. Louis buries Church, and the next day, Church returns alive but different. Part two, "The Micmac Burial Ground," centers wholly on a second, far more dreadful tragedy that has befallen the Creed household. Another truck passing on the road in front of the house kills not a pet but a child. The family falls apart, and Louis feels the pull of the Micmac burial ground, believing that using it will restore his family to its prior, happier state. Jed warns Louis to stay away from the burial ground, saying, "Sometimes dead is better." Louis, in his grief, goes against Jed's warnings and uses the burial ground again to resurrect the child. Part three, "Oz the Gweat and Tewwible," is brief and acute. The deceased child returns to the Creed home, but as a soulless physical shell infected by the evil of the Wendigo. Louis must deal with the consequences of his choices as the remnants of his family are destroyed.

Typically, King introduces sections of his novels with pertinent song lyrics. In *Pet Sematary,* he deviates from this pattern to quote the story of Lazarus rising from the dead from the gospel of John. While the context of *Pet Sematary* is not overtly biblical, the story of Lazarus parallels the story line of human resurrection and its implications. The title page of "The Pet Sematary" shows the disciples telling Jesus that Lazarus is sleeping. Jesus corrects them and explains that Lazarus is, in fact, dead. "The Micmac Burial Ground" shows Lazarus dead for four days. Jesus promises Martha that her brother "shall rise again" (201). "Oz the Gweat and Tewwible" begins with Lazarus rising from the dead. Jesus orders Martha to "loose him" from his burial clothing and "let him go" (341). King's quotation of the Lazarus story opposes Louis Creed's self-proclaimed role of God. When faced with the very human powerlessness of death, Creed falls into a cataclysmic state of denial. He believes that he has found the power to restore life, as Christ restored Lazarus. His tunnel vision evokes both pity and anger in the rational reader as he works his family into complete destruction in a vain attempt to restore it.

Pet Sematary came to be as a result of several real-life events: the death of Naomi King's cat, "Smucky" (whose name appears on a headstone in the fictional pet sematary); the road in front of their rented Orrington, Maine, home where trucks regularly sped by; and an occasion where Owen, his youngest son, began running toward the road and King pulled him back to safety. The pet sematary was also real; it existed in the woods behind the Orrington house (Winter, 129). While King believes in the fantastic and fictional to create horror, he also believes firmly that the most effective way truly to frighten people is to show them events, people, and situations they see in everyday life. "The more frightened people become about the real world the easier they are to scare" (Nelson, 2).

King's exquisite command of narration, point of view, and flashback allows him to weave them together seamlessly. His realistic narration hooks the reader, and the scene is set by the family making a risky move across the country. By the end of page 3, readers are already rooting for this family man, his wife, and their two adorable children. While in third person, it is Louis who narrates parts 1, 2, and the early portion of 3. Readers view the world through his eyes. In the latter portion of part 3, King switches the point of view to a more omniscient approach, which again helps to engage the reader by showing a broader scope of the ultimate effects of Louis's actions. By far the most effective element in the novel is the use of a flashback during the novel's most horrific event. Rather than narrate the death of Louis's child directly, King allows him to remember it in graphic, nightmarish detail. Louis describes the moments prior to, during, and immediately following the accident with the guilt-ridden thoughts of a parent who believes he could have stopped this tragedy.

Pet Sematary is truly one of King's finest works; it is made all the more special because of the knowledge that it nearly was not published. It is far more than his original intention, a modern "The Monkey's Paw." Pet Sematary touches on religion, morality, and the worst fear for many, the death of a loved one.

SOURCES

King, Stephen. *Pet Sematary.* Garden City, N.Y.: Doubleday & Company, 1983.

Nelson, Harold. *Twentieth-Century Young Adult Writers.* 1st edition. Edited by Laura Standley Berger. Detroit, Mich.: St. James Press, 1994.

Underwood, Tim, and Chuck Miller, eds. *Bare Bones: Conversations on Terror with Stephen King.* New York: Warner Books, Inc., 1988.

Winter, Douglas E. *Stephen King: The Art of Darkness.* New York: New American Library, 1986.

Kelly Flanagan

PHANTOM TOLLBOOTH, THE NORTON JUSTER (1961)

Two generations of children have now experienced the wondrously wacky world that young Milo found when he drove his tiny electric car through the little purple tollbooth that had mysteriously appeared in his bedroom. What elevates *The Phantom Tollbooth*—best categorized as an allegorical fantasy—to its place in the canon of children's literature is the fact that Juster kept his eye on the prize the whole time—he educated children without them realizing it. The result is that children continue to form a deep attachment to this book, this allegory on the development of the mind. Milo's journey becomes their journey. When Milo returns from his adventure, he is better able to appreciate his life and the world around him. So too is the young reader.

Using puns, humor, and clever wordplay, Juster creates a world where literary terminology and mathematics are literally embodied by the characters. Poor Milo is always bored. In fact, "Wherever he was he wished he were somewhere else, and when he got there he wondered why he'd bothered" (9). He drives through the tollbooth for lack of anything better to do and finds himself in the Land of Expectations, the place you must always go before you get to where you're going (19). Soon after, he meets the watchdog Tock, whose job it is to make sure no one wastes time. Tock becomes Milo's faithful companion and together they arrive at the city of Dictionopolis, where all the world's words grow on trees and are sold at the marketplace. There they meet the Humbug and learn of the dispute between King Azaz of Dictionopolis and his brother, the Mathemagician of Digitopolis (where numbers are dug up in deep mines), over the superiority of letters or numbers. This argument led to the imprisonment of the princesses Rhyme and Reason, which, in turn, has aversely affected the entire Kingdom of Wisdom. Milo agrees to try to rescue the princesses, unite the two cities, and restore order to the kingdom.

At each turn, Milo is confronted by someone who at first frightens and then delights him as he learns more about the world. He narrowly escapes the Island of Conclusions, which you can only get to by jumping (and only leave by swimming through the Sea of Knowledge). In the city of Ignorance he meets the Terrible Trivium, from whom he learns the dangers of giving oneself over to petty tasks and forces of habit. In the land of Reality—which has become virtually invisible because people stopped noticing the things around them—he recognizes the dangers in just floating through the world without noticing the wonders around you. He finally realizes he can overcome the limitations he has placed on himself when he Princess Reason tells him, "What you can do is often simply a matter of what you *will* do" (247). By grasping the usefulness of both math and language, he becomes the hero of his own story.

Although widely used in classrooms to teach mathematical concepts or literary terminology, *The Phantom Tollbooth* actually serves as a commentary on the way the modern educational system may do children a disservice. Juster believes that throwing so much varied information at a child without linking it together allows the child to dismiss it as unimportant and not relevant to his life. Through the book, he shows the reader the power of information and education, for it is through the clear communication of ideas that Milo is ultimately successful.

SOURCES

Juster, Norman. *The Phantom Tollbooth*. New York: Random House, 1961.

Sadler, Glenn Edward, ed. *Teaching Children's Literature: Issues, Pedagogy, Resources*. New York: Modern Language Association of America, 1992.

Swinfen, Ann. *In Defence of Fantasy: A Study of the Genre in English and American Literature since 1945*. London: Routledge, 1984.

OTHER

Miller, Laura. "The Road to Dictionopolis: An interview with Norton Juster." Salon.com. Available online. URL: http://www.salon.com/books/inf/2001/03/12/juster. Accessed September 25, 2005.

Wendy Maas

PHELPS, ELIZABETH STUART (ELIZABETH WOOSTER STUART PHELPS WARD) (1815–1852)

Not to be confused with her daughter, Elizabeth Stuart Phelps Ward, a novelist and short story writer, this Elizabeth Phelps wrote short stories for magazines and novels, the most popular of which, *The Sunny Side; or, the Country Minister's Wife*, sold 100,000 copies the year it appeared. Phelps, moreover, penned the "Kitty Brown" books (1851–53), one of the earliest series of novels for girls. Her story "The Angel over the Right Shoulder" (1852), a work originally published as a Christmas book, is now routinely used in feminist history and literature courses.

Born on August 13, 1815, to Abigail Clark Stuart and Moses Stuart in Andover, Massachusetts, Phelps was reared in a religious and literary millieu. Her father, a Congregationalist minister, taught at Andover Theological Seminary. Phelps, who was educated at Abbot Academy and Mount Vernon School, began publishing stories in the Reverend Jacob Abbot's magazine under the name H. Trusta, an anagram of her own surname, a pseudonym she continued to use both on her adult novels and her children's books. Although she was in poor health with an illness characterized as a "cerebral disease," Elizabeth married Austin Phelps, who became a theology professor at the Andover Seminary, in 1842. Her daughter, Mary Gray Phelps, who legally had her name changed to her mother's (Elizabeth Stuart Phelps), was born in 1844.

Despite her blinding headaches, temporary paralysis, and partial blindness, Phelps continued to write. Her own favorite novel, published in the last year of her life, was *A Peep At "Number Five"; or, A Chapter in the Life of a City Pastor* (1852). Apparently autobiographical, it served as a companion piece to *The Sunny Side*. Phelps died in 1852 at age 37, fewer than three months after giving birth to her third child. She left a legacy of domestic, realistic novels that have been widely translated. Her papers are housed at the Andover Historical Society.

NOVELS

A Peep at "Number Five"; or, A Chapter in the Life of a City Pastor, as H. Trusta. Boston: Phillips, Sampson, 1852.

The Sunny Side; or, the Country Minister's Wife, as H. Trusta. Philadelphia and New York: American Sunday-School Union, 1851.

SOURCES

Fetterly, Judith, ed. "Elizabeth Stuart Phelps (1815–52)." In *Provisions: A Reader from 19th-Century Women*, 203–209. Bloomington: Indiana University Press, 1985.

Kessler, Carol Farley. *Elizabeth Stuart Phelps*. Boston: Twayne, 1982.

PHILADELPHIA FIRE JOHN EDGAR WIDEMAN (1990)

On May 13, 1985, Philadelphia police fired tear gas, water cannons, and automatic weapons, and dropped a satchel bomb upon a row of tenements on the 6200 block of Osage Avenue. Their target was a single row house, the home and headquarters of the MOVE Organization, an Afrocentric back-to-nature religious movement. After the smoke cleared from the bomb's resultant fire, 60 other homes had been destroyed, leaving more than 250 people homeless. Eleven MOVE members had been killed. Five were children.

Five years later, John Edgar WIDEMAN published *Philadelphia Fire*, his record-setting second PEN/Faulkner Award-winning novel (his first was the 1984 *Sent for You Yesterday*). In this novel, which *Time* found "reminiscent of Ralph ELLISON's *INVISIBLE MAN*," Wideman, a Pennsylvania native, explores the ruins of the Osage Avenue atrocity. What he seeks to understand is not the assault's cause so much as its aftermath. Working their way through the rubble are two writers, the novel's main protagonists, the imaginary Cudjoe and the very real Wideman, both of whose thoughts, temptations, and torments we gain access to in this haunting, memoir-tinged historical novel. While Wideman's subject here is harrowing, there remains more than a glimmer of hope in the two men's journeys through their pasts to discover themselves and the voices with which they can express their outrage and pain. And it is Wideman's voice suffused throughout this novel—his spirited and exuberant prose style, and his unflinching examination of our national and personal crises of conscience—that finally liberates us from the despair and self-destruction that court the two writers as they investigate this often overlooked American heartbreak.

Divided into three sections, the novel first focuses on Cudjoe and his quest through the city of Philadelphia to find a rumored child survivor of the bombing, Simba, and with him a story that Cudjoe hopes to write that will help save them both. Simba's vaporous escape from the flames parallels Cudjoe's own flight from his past and reminds him of his failures as a black schoolteacher in the late 1960s to "save" his young black students by teaching them to protest creatively through literature. (Whether ironic or not, Cudjoe shares his name with the famous leader of the Maroons in Jamaica, a group of runaway slaves who resisted British rule and fought bravely for their independence almost 300 years ago; the Maroon leader too was very much divided between peaceful reconciliation and sustained resistance.) As a writer struggling to piece together Simba's story and his own, Cudjoe must confront the ghosts from his own life as well as the ghosts of the city, not all of whom, we learn, are dead.

The city of Philadelphia, then, is itself a character in this drama, a force even, and a site of disaster and despair. It is a city of lost children in a book about lost children. Simba is still missing. Cudjoe is the prodigal son returning home from his self-exile abroad only to remember the students he left behind. And an underground kid cult splashes the city walls with cryptic graffiti manifestoes intimating a conspiracy to overthrow the adults who have forsaken them: adults like Wilson Goode, who was mayor at the time of the bombing, and the community's adults, who,

too, swiftly forgot about it. Also lost is Wideman's own son, who was incarcerated for manslaughter and with whom the author seeks sadly in the novel's second section to maintain telephone communication despite the decaying connection between them. This novel is not only about the struggle to speak up and out then, but also the struggle to speak at all. These are struggles fraught with fits, false starts, and ambivalence, and the novel evokes these uncertainties in its very form—in digressions, abrupt shifts in point of view, and a fragmented and snaking narrative. And yet, in its sweeping lyricism, the novel also captures moments of exhilaration and affirmation; for instance, we are reminded in Wideman's rhythmic description of a street basketball game, in his head-fake and jump-shot prose, that we must find hope and beauty in the everyday, the ordinary events made luminous through language and reverence.

It should here be noted that while this novel dazzles us aesthetically—riffing on postmodernist self-reflexivity and intertextuality and employing quite brilliantly at times a quasi-expressionistic jazz-inflected lyricism—it also owes much to the subtle moral shadings of Shakespeare (whose *The Tempest* Wideman explicitly references) and the revitalized realism and naturalism one finds in the works of Wideman's fine contemporaries Russell BANKS and Robert STONE. Moreover, as with other recent historical novels such as Cormac MCCARTHY's *BLOOD MERIDIAN* and Don DELILLO's *LIBRA*, *Philadelphia Fire* reimagines a historical event not only to better understand its effects on a community but also to probe philosophically the very nature of received and perceived historical "truth." The bombing, then, is not precisely the novel's centerpiece. Rather, the focus seems to be on the protagonist Cudjoe's quest through the wreckage of the past: the community's as well as his own personal past. In his journeys, he seeks not only to discover the truth about the atrocity and save a young boy's life in the process; he struggles also to discover and save himself, even if only through the fictions he tells himself, the histories he invents to order his world.

And Cudjoe's quest is also Wideman's. Both are writers and witnesses, each testifying in the novel to the possibilities and limitations of fictional testimonies to counteract the nightmares of histories personal, political, and national. Both struggle to express through writing their frustration, sorrow, and pain, yet neither finds true closure come the novel's end. Cudjoe attends a memorial service for the victims of the bombing. He stands holding a candle, frozen, wishing he could run, and outraged by the poor turnout, he begins populating the empty square with ghosts. Like Wideman, he can neither escape nor reverse the past; his fictions will not change history. The bomb has been dropped. It has destroyed and altered lives. The two writers cannot invent ways around these realities. Not merely the novel's backdrop, the bombing is intertwined with the writers' lives and the lives and histories of a city and its citizens. Whether those citizens are fictional like Cudjoe or actual like Wideman himself, many of them struggle to find meaning in and hope beyond the trauma caused in one day.

Theirs is not an uncommon struggle either; two decades later another American city will tremble, and its citizens, shaken by terror and disbelief, will look to the skies for meaning. Some of Wideman's characters, members of the Philadelphia community, react to the tragedy with anger, others with mourning, and too many with silence. Their responses remind us of September 11, 2001, and the myriad reactions of citizens across the nation and the actions they took (or did not) to restore order to their lives. For weeks after the terrorist attack, the nation saw most clearly what our democracy operating at its best and worst looks like: on one hand, individuals speaking up and people working together to ensure safety and bring hope and succor, and on the other, blind patriotism and a renewed racist hysteria. This novel examines such a traumatic event not by speculating on its causes and offering "clarifying" conspiracies; instead Wideman dramatizes the event's aftermath so as to capture the moral and spiritual crises we face when looking for someone to blame rather than a reason to reflect and imagine, for a moment at least, a better world. He focuses on the aftermath also to humanize more fully the many victims and survivors: some silent, others forgotten, yet many outspoken about the need to bear witness and remember history. And here we discover this novel's lesson: Never forget.

Because of this message—and despite its bleak subject matter and lack of closure—*Philadelphia Fire* is a hopeful novel. And with its chorus of voices, vigorous prose, and history lesson, it is also a democratic novel, and one that demands we don't forget. It is a warning to those who would like to evade the past that we can never escape the ghosts that haunt us. It is a dark message, to be sure, but also a hopeful one if heeded. As both Cudjoe and Wideman know, we must learn to speak for the silenced, self-exiled, and forgotten lest we wish to live forever with ghosts. That is, we must discover our voices and tell our private and public stories to honor and understand the lives of the lost: the 11 bombing victims, Wideman's imprisoned child, Cudjoe's forgotten schoolchildren, and the still-missing Simba, the city's invisible son.

SOURCES

Carden, Mary Paniccia. " 'If the City Is a Man': Founders and Cities and Sons in John Edgar Wideman's *Philadelphia Fire*," *Contemporary Literature* 44, no. 3 (2003): 472–500.

Coleman, James W. *Blackness and Modernism: The Literary Career of John Edgar Wideman*. Jackson: University Press of Mississippi, 1989.

Dubey, Madhu. "Literature and Urban Crisis: John Edgar Wideman's *Philadelphia Fire*," *African American Review* 32, no. 4 (1998): 579–595.

Lee, James Kyung-Jin. "Where the Talented Tenth Meets the Model Minority," *Novel: A Forum on Fiction* 35, no. 2 (2002): 231–257.

Mbalia, Doreatha Drummond. *John Edgar Wideman: Reclaiming the African Personality*. Selinsgrove, Pa.: Susquehanna University Press, 1995.

Pearsall, Susan M. " 'Narratives of Self' and the Abdication of Authority in Wideman's *Philadelphia Fire*," *MELUS* 26, no. 2 (2001): 15–46.

TuSmith, Bonnie. *Conversations with John Edgar Wideman*. Jackson: University Press of Mississippi, 1998.

Varsava, Jerry. " 'Woven of Many Strands': Multiple Subjectivity in John Edgar Wideman's *Philadelphia Fire*," *Critique* 41, no. 4 (2000): 425–444.

Zachary Dobbins

PHILLIPS, JAYNE ANNE (1952–)

As scholar Dorothy Combs Hill notes, all the works of Jayne Ann Phillips, a daughter of West Virginia, feel universal rather than regional, and "no one has labeled Phillips a Southern writer or a woman writer; her relentless intelligence breaks those boundaries" (Hill, 348).

Phillips writes about the uniqueness of each individual, about post-Vietnam war society, closeness and communication, loneliness and the absence of love, and about family relationships, particularly those between mothers and daughters. Her first novel, *Machine Dreams* (1984), received a National Book Critics Circle Award nomination and appeared on the *New York Times* Best Books of 1984 list. Her third novel, *Shelter* (1994), was chosen one of the best books of the year by *Publishers Weekly*.

Jayne Anne Phillips was born on July 19, 1952, in Buckhannon, West Virginia (where her family had settled two centuries earlier), to Russell R. Phillips, a contractor, and Martha Jane Thornhill Phillips, a teacher, who encouraged her independence and writerly talents. She earned a bachelor's degree (magna cum laude) from West Virginia University in 1974 and a master's degree from the University of Iowa in 1978. She married a Boston doctor. After publishing *Sweethearts* (1976) and *Counting* (1978) with small presses (novels that have never been reissued), Phillips broke into mainstream publishing with *Machine Dreams*. This novel depicts the lives of several generations, from World War II until the Vietnam War, and implicates the Vietnam war in the erosion of the family. Told from each family member's perspective, the novel chronicles the helpless, hapless Jean and Mitch Hampson, their daughter Danner, and their son Billy. In *Shelter,* four characters talk about good and evil at a West Virginia summer camp in July 1963. Two sisters, Lenny and Alma Swenson, Lenny's friend Cap Brierly, and Alma's friend Delia Campbell are joined in the narrative by Carmody, an insane ex-convict, and by eight-year-old Buddy, the cook's son. *MotherKind* (2000), Phillips's most recent novel, takes place in the Boston suburbs and features a mother and daughter known simply as Katherine and Kate, respectively. Kate returns to West Virginia to tell her cancer-stricken mother that she is pregnant. Within the parameters of imminent birth and death, Phillips explores the joys of the mother-daughter bond and the difficulties of marriage and divorce, children and stepchildren.

Jayne Anne Phillips lives with her husband in the Boston area, where she teaches and writes. She was inducted into the American Academy of Arts and Letters in 1997.

NOVELS

Counting. New York: Vehicle Editions, 1978.
Machine Dreams. New York: Dutton, 1984.
MotherKind. New York: Knopf, 2000.
Shelter. Boston: Houghton, 1994.
Sweethearts. Carrboro, N.C.: Truck Press, 1976.

SOURCES

Carter, Susanne. "Variations on Vietnam: Women's Innovative Interpretations of the Vietnam War Experience," *Extrapolation* 32, no. 2 (Summer 1991): 170–183.

Delbanco, Andrew. Review of *Shelter, New Republic,* 26 December 1994, pp. 39–40.

Eder, Richard. "A Summer of Transformations," *Los Angeles Times Book Review,* 4 September 1994, pp. 3, 5.

Hawthorne, Mary. "Carry on Camping," *London Review of Books,* 6 April 1995, p. 24.

Hill, Dorothy Combs. "Jayne Anne Phillips." In *Contemporary Fiction Writers of the South: A Bio-bibliographical Critical Sourcebook,* edited by Joseph M. Flora and Robert Bain. Westport, Conn.: Greenwood Press, 1993.

Larson, Leslie. "A Window on the Underworld," *Women's Review of Books* 12, no. 7 (April, 1995): 5.

Lassner, Phyllis. "Jayne Anne Phillips: Women's Narrative and the Recreation of History." In *American Women Writing Fiction: Memory, Identity, Family, Space,* edited by Mickey Pearlman, 193–210. Lexington: University of Kentucky Press, 1989.

Schwartz, Deb. "Look Homeward, Angels," *Nation,* 14 November 1994, pp. 585–588.

Schwartz, Miranda, "To Bury the Violence," *Belles Lettres* 10, no. 2 (Spring 1995): 11.

OTHER

Jayne Anne Phillips Homepage. Available online. URL: http://www.JayneAnnePhillips.com. Accessed September 25, 2005.

PIERRE; OR, THE AMBIGUITIES HERMAN MELVILLE (1852)

The publication of Herman MELVILLE's *Pierre; or The Ambiguities* was followed by scathing denunciations of the novel, which called Melville's prose a "string of nonsense," "trash," and "crazy rigamarole" and the entire work a "dead failure" (quoted in Higgins and Parker, 33; 40). The novel seemed to defy categorization. Some literary critics argued that it was a sentimental gothic novel, pointing to the mysterious face that haunts the protagonist,

Pierre Glendinning, and portends his family's ruination. Others suggested that Melville's book lampooned sentimental and domestic novels with its overblown language and sexual transgressions. Melville's unreliable narrative voice and his novel's postmodern tendencies annoyed other early critics.

In 1930, E. L. Grant Watson reexamined *Pierre* and rescued the work from its literary exile. Since that time, critics and scholars have continued to debate the merit of Melville's *Pierre*. In 1978, Melville scholars Brian Higgins and Hershel Parker wrote that *Pierre*'s "best readers" recognized the "heroic intellectual tasks" undertaken by Melville (Higgins and Parker, 241). Contemporary scholars often point out that numerous parallels to Melville's life indicate *Pierre* is a thinly veiled autobiography: An extant letter confirms that Melville, like Pierre, had an illegitimate sister; Pierre's frustrations as a writer mirror Melville's own at the time *Pierre* was written; and the picturesque setting of Saddle Meadows resembles places Melville frequented, including the Berkshire Mountains, the Hudson River Valley, and the farmhouse of his friend Nathaniel HAWTHORNE. In a more recent Melville biography, Laurie Robertson-Lorant called the work "one of the first great modern psychological novels in Western literature," exploring the same murky waters of human nature as Melville's *MOBY-DICK* (Robertson-Lorant, 304). Pierre's psychological demise is strongly influenced by the environments he inhabits. In fact, one of the most intriguing aspects of *Pierre* is the novel's ostensible division into two parts: the country and the city. The first half of the novel is set in Saddle Meadows, the Glendinning family's rural estate, while the second half takes place in the quintessentially urban New York City. "Nature planted our Pierre" wrote Melville, "because Nature intended a rare and original development in Pierre" (13). Pierre's "rare and original development" is shaped by themes of economic inequity, class division, and unconventional sexual relationships set against these rural and urban landscapes.

At Saddle Meadows, Pierre enjoys a bourgeois life with his mother, Mary Glendinning, taking in commanding views of a landscape paid for by the displacement of Native Americans. Pierre shares an intense relationship with his mother that resembles the romantic love of siblings, referring to his mother as "sister" while she calls him "brother." Set to marry his social and economic equal, Lucy Tartan, Pierre soon discovers that his deceased father has an illegitimate daughter, Isabel Banford. After anguished deliberation, Pierre dismisses Lucy and assumes responsibility for Isabel by agreeing to marry her. In this way, reconciles Pierre, their family secret will remain undisclosed and Isabel will be removed from a life of abject poverty. After his mother disowns him for this apparent social *faux pas,* however, Pierre leaves the rural, emotional, and financial comfort of Saddle Meadows for the "urban labyrinth" of New York City with his "wife" Isabel and her mute companion Delly (Kelley, 396). Thus Pierre's mental anguish, the redefinition of his relationships, and his movement away from the country upset not only the appearance of pastoral tranquility but also the reality of his psychological well-being.

The second half of the novel begins when Pierre, Isabel, and Delly enter New York City by way of a dark, desolated, and foreboding street. Seeking shelter with his cousin, Glendinning Stanly, Pierre and his traveling companions meet with disappointment when Glendinning shuns Pierre. Homeless and destitute, Pierre, Isabel, and Delly are forced to live in an abandoned church, known as the Church of the Apostles, where impoverished city dwellers find refuge. In this urban environment, readers suddenly discover that Pierre is a well-known writer, and the novel takes a decided turn into the frustrations of Pierre's work as an author and his further psychological deterioration. Meanwhile, his mother dies of shame and grief and Lucy joins the group at the Church of the Apostles. Lucy's action does not sit well with Glendinning, or with her older brother, Frederic, and the men confront Pierre. In the end, the urban labyrinth—both a physical and a mental construct—confounds them all: Pierre kills Glendinning and is incarcerated, Lucy and Isabel kill themselves over Pierre's imprisonment, and Pierre ultimately commits suicide.

Melville's *Pierre* anticipated literary theories that examine the associations and images in the country/city dichotomy and the role of rural and urban landscapes in 19th-century American literature (Otter, 352). Raymond Williams, for instance, argues that images of the "country as past" and the "city as future" represent "a growth and alteration of consciousness: a history repeated in many lives and many places which is fundamentally an alteration of perception and relationship" (Williams, 297). For Pierre, this alteration of perception is the result of dislocation from his past life at Saddle Meadows and relocation to New York City and a life of ambiguous meaning. To read *Pierre; or, The Ambiguities,* then, is to imagine two landscapes—the country and the city—that collide like colored patterns in a kaleidoscope, leaving human identities distorted, rearranged, and reframed, and to call each reader to envision a unique collision of light and shape.

SOURCES

Higgins, Brian, and Hershal Parker. *Critical Essays on Herman Melville's "Pierre; or, The Ambiguities."* Boston: G. K. Hall, 1983.

Kelley, Wyn. "Pierre in a Labyrinth: The Mysteries and Miseries of New York." In *Melville's Evermoving Dawn: Centennial Essays,* edited by John Bryant and Robert Milder, 393–406. Kent, Ohio: The Kent State University Press, 1997.

Melville, Herman. *Pierre; or, The Ambiguities.* Edited by William C. Spengemann. New York: Penguin, 1996.

Otter, Samuel. "The Overwrought Landscape of *Pierre.*" In *Melville's Evermoving Dawn: Centennial Essays,* edited by John Bryant and Robert Milder, 349–374. Kent, Ohio: The Kent State University Press, 1997.

Robertson-Lorant, Laurie. *Melville: A Biography.* New York: Clarkson Potter, 1996.

Watson, E. L. Grant. "Melville's *Pierre.*" *New England Quarterly* 3 (April 1930), 195–234. Reprinted in *Critics on Melville. Readings in Literary Criticism,* vol. 12, edited by Thomas J. Rountree. 94–100. Miami, Fla.: University of Miami Press, 1972.

Williams, Raymond. *The Country and the City.* New York: Oxford University Press, 1973.

Jennifer Hughes Westerman

PLAGUED BY THE NIGHTINGALE KAY BOYLE (1931)

Plagued by the Nightingale, written between 1924 and 1927 (Spanier, 57), published in 1931 in New York and republished in 1966 by Southern Illinois University Press, had long been considered Kay BOYLE's first novel until Sandra Spanier discovered and published the 1924 manuscript *Process* in 2001. *Plagued by the Nightingale* takes its title from a 1923 poem by Marianne Moore quoted in context as the epigraph of the novel. Boyle omits the poem's title ("Marriage"), suggesting that her novel is an obscure meditation on the topic of marriage. It is that, and far more. Drawing on autobiographical material from her marriage to Frenchman Richard Brault, with whom she left for France in 1923 to live with his family in Brittany, Boyle develops a scathing, occasionally funny, and ultimately tragic portrayal of a well-to-do provincial French family beset by a debilitating bone disease in the line of male inheritance and preoccupied with marriage, procreation, and living comme il faut. Joan Mellon has called the novel a "satire" (Mellon, 57). Boyle's long expatriate sojourn in Europe makes her a particularly astute commentator on the cultural clash between a progressive American woman and a traditional French family. In her subsequent novels set in France, Austria, and Germany, Boyle made a 20th-century version of the "international theme" her own characteristic literary territory.

Vignette-length chapters show family members in interaction with each other, rarely with outsiders. Papa and Maman fill their traditional roles as ruler and enforcer of the family, respectively. A nearly incestuous familial closeness is suggested by the older daughter Charlotte's life in the neighboring house. A papal dispensation was required for her marriage to her first cousin. Together with their five young children, they represent the older generation's ideal family. Papa's and Maman's three youngest daughters are all in love with the same young man, a physician named Luc, who is the only outsider admitted into this closely knit circle. Bridget, the young American woman who has married into the clan, learns over the course of a summer that her husband Nicholas will gain access to his family's economic opportunities only if the young couple produce a child. Nicholas, impeded in his vitality by his ever-weakening legs, will not consent to having a child and tacitly encourages Bridget's and Luc's apparent mutual affection.

Religious observations, proper dress and behavior, and extravagant verbal expressions of affection *en famille* fill this family's existence. Uncle Robert, residing in nearby St. Malo, completes the picture: the younger girls' dowries as well as Nicholas's future depend on his whim and munificence. The family's persistence in tradition and their apparent imperturbability amount to a resignation that refuses to recognize the passage of time. When a large acacia tree is felled by a storm, Charlotte's husband Jean plans on planting a new tree, " 'and, you'll see, in two hundred years it will amount to the same thing.' He spoke of these two centuries as if they were years in which the children would be growing up—mild and unalterable" (172). In her ability to sketch the psychological portraits of her characters both in their actions and in their thoughts, Boyle is heir to Edith WHARTON. Abby Werlock fully explores the Wharton/Boyle connection in her claim that "both invented new ways of writing the Bildungsroman" (Werlock, 263). In her use of symbols such as the fallen tree, the rushing tide on Brittany's coast, a fire in the village, the debilitating bone disease of the male characters, and finally the silent, caged nightingale, Boyle works in the vitalist tradition of the 1910s and 1920s that also finds expression in D. H. Lawrence (*Sons and Lovers*, 1913) and Rose Macaulay (*Dangerous Ages,* 1921). Boyle critiques the stifling trappings of French bourgeois culture but does not advocate a revolution of morals in this novel.

Bridget witnesses dramatic events, but her presence also decisively changes the dynamics of interaction in the French family. The early chapters are dominated by her linguistic insufficiency, while in the latter part of the novel both Bridget's speech and her decisions determine the family's future. Charlotte's sixth pregnancy, at age 32, brings about her death. Nicholas's wish to emigrate to North Africa has been thwarted. By summer's end, Luc has decided not to marry any of the three younger sisters but to emigrate to Indo-China instead. When he obliquely invites Bridget to escape with him, she refuses and tells him that she and Nicholas will have a child instead. Boyle leaves it to the reader to decide whether Bridget's acquiescence to the family's wish is a defeat or is either a loving or a pragmatic gesture of assistance to her fatalist husband. Dianne Chambers makes the convincing case that "Bridget's American blood represents the possibility of regeneration" (Chambers, 254). Suzanne Clark interprets Bridget's gesture as her claim to "the sexuality of the maternal," which becomes a rebellion "against the

bourgeois family's manipulative economy" (Clark, 140–141). Boyle herself would not return to the United States until the middle of World War II, even as her character Bridget has recognized, in Chambers's words, that "tradition exacts a price that runs counter to specifically identified American values of independence and individuality" (Chambers, 256). By thematizing a woman's conflict between self-determination and familial obligation, *Plagued by the Nightingale* also asks a central modernist question: Where can an individual still be at home in an international, culturally deracinated world?

SOURCES

Boyle, Kay. *Plagued by the Nightingale.* Carbondale: Southern Illinois University Press, 1966.

Chambers, Dianne. "Female Roles and National Identity in Kay Boyle's *Plagued by the Nightingale* and Edith Wharton's *Madame de Treymes.*" In *Critical Essays on Kay Boyle,* edited by Marilyn Elkins, 241–261. New York: G. K. Hall, 1997.

Clark, Suzanne. *Sentimental Modernism: Women Writers and the Revolution of the Word.* Bloomington: Indiana University Press, 1991.

Mellon, Joan. *Kay Boyle: Author of Herself.* New York: Farrar, Straus & Giroux, 1994.

Spanier, Sandra. *Kay Boyle: Artist and Activist.* New York: Paragon House, 1988.

Werlock, Abby. "Advancing Literary Women: Edith Wharton, Kay Boyle, and My Next Bride." In *Critical Essays on Kay Boyle,* edited by Marilyn Elkins, 262–275. New York: G. K. Hall, 1997.

Thomas Austenfeld

PLAINSONG KENT HARUF (1999)   *Plainsong,* by Kent HARUF, is a widely acclaimed, strong, and heartfelt novel of life in a rural farming and ranching town in western Colorado. The coming together of Haruf's original and fully realized characters creates a story sparsely but beautifully told of life in a remote and isolated small community. To a reader more accustomed to life in a big city with its multitude of social strife and urban problems, it may come as a surprise to find similar stress, pain, and coping mechanisms in a radically different environment. In the hands of another, less-accomplished author, this might have become a soap opera—or worse, a repetition of confessional stories we have all heard before. But Kent Haruf is an accomplished and talented writer. He has lived in towns like this one and understands and respects these people. He tells his story in a straightforward manner, and his readers quickly become immersed in the book. Haruf does not delve into or analyze anyone's psyche. Rather, he allows us to see human strengths and weaknesses, humor and curiosity, and ultimately resilience. Haruf's writing style echoes both the laconic and direct speech of these people and the sparse harshness of the wide-open land.

Emotions run deep here. This is an author who respects the multidimensional characters he has created. As we enter into their homes and lives, we not only are absorbed in their stories but also recognize the universality of family strife and joy. An astute reader should be able to go from the specifics of this story to the larger human condition. There is much here to enjoy and to value.

The plot is easy to ride along with. Haruf blends the tales of several disparate individuals whose lives converge as their paths intersect. The chapters bear the name of each main character. We do not get confused. The McPheron brothers, Harold and Raymond, are two seasoned farmers who spend their days working the land that has become theirs since the death of their parents, when the boys were still in their teens. Their work is hard. Farming and ranching require days spent with demanding and endless time-consuming chores. The men tend to their cattle on the family ranch and live an isolated life, rarely going into the small town nearby, and having very little to do with any other people. They are men of few words. Tom Guthrie is a high school teacher who lives a lonely life as he raises his two young sons. Guthrie's wife has been depressed for years, their marriage a failure. She withdraws from her family life, first emotionally involved only with her own unhappiness, and finally actually moving away from the town in which they live. Haruf, without being maudlin or sentimental, allows the reader to see how her departure affects the lives of everyone in her family. Guthrie often helps the McPherson brothers, providing a needed extra hand on the ranch. He often brings his boys with him, and we begin to see a natural mixing of the generations. Perhaps the most com-

pelling character here is a young pregnant high school girl, Victoria Roubideaux, who has been kicked out of the home she lived in with her mother and literally finds herself with nowhere to go. She turns to Maggie Jones, a warm-hearted high school teacher who in turn turns to the McPherson brothers and convinces them to allow Victoria to live with them. Maggie knows the brothers well enough to be certain they will be kind and decent to the girl, and that she in turn will provide an antidote to their isolation and loneliness.

This interweaving of lives, often somewhat improbable, becomes believable and convincing in Haruf's hands. These taciturn, hard-working farmers are decent people. Victoria is young and confused, but as they learn to adjust to living together, all grow in respect, caring, and love. Haruf writes with an emotional wisdom.

In the epigraph to this novel, Haruf explains that the title, *Plainsong,* refers to the simple and unadorned melody used in the Christian church from early times on. It is an apt analogy for his book. In his understated voice, direct and laconic, his writing exists within a narrow range of notes and tones. As author and teacher Mickey Pearlman has stated, "There is no harmony here—only melody."

This is a story about family, but it is also strongly a story about a specific locale. These people are products of where they live. The descriptions of the land with its rocky, rough terrain and the harsh weathers' cold and bitter winds bring us into a clearly drawn portrait of part of American life today. This sense of place is very important to the book, as it is in the more recently published *Eventide* (Alfred A. Knopf, 2004). Haruf knows his territory. Like William FAULKNER's Yoknapatawpha County, John UPDIKE's New England suburbia, and Cormac McCARTHY's Plains, Kent Haruf has made a specific community a significant focus point. Unlike those in many postmodern novels, these lives do not exist in a vague anywhere or anytime. The author has found a locality that offers him much richness to mine. The deeper he goes into its uniqueness—the larger the scope of its impact.

Plainsong is neither a "woman's novel," nor a "man's book." Full of the cadences and plainspoken manner of the plains, the writing transcends limitations or type, a fresh and original voice that makes the novel both compassionate and compelling. There is great authenticity here. Ultimately, we are left thinking about the absolute necessity of family, the solace of real friendship, and the possibility of finding courage and love in community.

In *Plainsong,* we are shown pain but also dignity, humor, and love. It is an understated and a hard-to-put-down book. As Howard Frank Mosher has stated, "Kent Haruf has created an American masterwork"—an "account of a place where family and community still come first."

SOURCES

Haruf, Kent. *Plainsong.* New York: Knopf, 1999.
Mosher, Howard Frank. *Plainsong* book jacket blurb. New York: Knopf, 1999,

Mona Dukess

PLAINS SONG: FOR FEMALE VOICES

WRIGHT MORRIS (1980) For this, his final novel, Wright MORRIS received an American Book Award. Although many of his previous novels had featured female characters, most of those characters had been seen through male points of view or characterized largely by their effect on the men around them. Although Morris had typically taken some pains to make his female characters credible and complex, they had often seemed projections of male failure, frustration, or fantasy. Ranging from emasculating matriarchs to sexual playthings, these female characters would hardly appeal to feminist critics. So the publication of *Plains Song,* a multigenerational family saga told from multiple female points of view and demonstrating a sympathetic understanding of those points of view, could hardly have been anticipated.

Plains Song is framed by the last hours of Cora Atkins, who is introduced in a coma at the beginning of the novel and finally expires near the close. Throughout her adult life, Cora has been the embodiment of endurance, of the values associated with a willingness to commit oneself to hard work. Born and raised in Massachusetts, Cora had moved to Ohio to work in an uncle's hotel. There she met a Nebraska homesteader named Emerson Atkins, whom she agreed to marry even though she knew even less about him than about Nebraska. It would be 10 days before they consummated their mar-

riage during their journey back to his homestead, and it would be the last time they ever had sexual relations. Cora found the experience so traumatic that she put her fist in her mouth to stifle her cries and bit through to the bone. Still, despite his brutish awkwardness, Emerson managed to make her pregnant, and after a long and difficult labor in which she refused to scream, Cora gave birth to her daughter, Madge.

Emerson's brother married an Arkansas woman named Belle who was in every way Cora's opposite. Sensuous but delicate, Belle would eventually die in childbirth but not before she produced three daughters, two of whom, Sharon Rose and Fayrene, would live to adulthood. Ironically, Cora's daughter, Madge, seemed temperamentally to take after her Aunt Belle, while Belle's oldest daughter, Sharon Rose, seemed more to take after Cora. Madge eventually married Ned Kibbee, with whom she had two daughters, Caroline and Blanche. Sharon Rose, however, remained single and moved to Chicago, where she entered into a long career as a music teacher. When Blanche came to live for a time with Sharon Rose, the girl's sexual precociousness caused her aunt to send her back to Nebraska much earlier than planned. Yet, despite her involvements with a series of men, Blanche has never married. Caroline, who has from a young age admired Sharon Rose's independence and self-reliance, has become an ardent feminist who regards marriage as an anachronism. At the other end of the spectrum, the fate of Sharon Rose's younger sister, Fayrene, represented everything that Sharon Rose was determined to escape. Fayrene had become pregnant by, and then married, a loutish farmhand named Avery Dickel.

Especially in the connections between Cora, Sharon Rose, and Caroline, Morris is able to explore the linkages and gaps between memory and truth and between sympathy and understanding. Most pointedly, Sharon Rose has literally as well as figuratively tried to distance herself from her family and her past. But when she returns to Nebraska for Cora's funeral, Sharon Rose feels all sorts of unexpected bonds to the other women in her family, regardless of how much she disapproves of or is simply bewildered by some of their life choices. In the context of these profound but inexplicable sympathies, not just the men but the dramatic historical events of the century are rendered almost extraneous to the essence of these women's lives. Cora's death causes the women in this extended family to recognize, each in her own way, that their shared experience is ultimately more significant than the differences by which they have defined themselves and distinguished themselves from each other. Of course, the conclusion of the novel contains some underlying ambiguities, the chief one being the suggestion of Sharon Rose's lesbianism. Certainly, the occasion of Cora's death has heightened the women's senses of connection, and time, distance, and routine will cause their differences to resurface. Still, the intensity of their sense of connection at this moment will ensure that it, too, will carry over.

SOURCES

Arnold, Marilyn. "Wright Morris's *Plains Song:* Woman's Search for Harmony," *South Dakota Review* 20 (Autumn 1982): 50–62.

Bird, Roy K. *Wright Morris: Memory and Imagination.* New York: Peter Lang, 1985.

Crump, Gail Bruce. *The Novels of Wright Morris: A Critical Interpretation.* Lincoln: University of Nebraska Press, 1978.

———. "Wright Morris." In *A Literary History of the American West,* edited by Max Westbrook, 777–791. Fort Worth: Texas Christian University Press, 1987.

Knoll, Robert E., ed. *Conversations with Wright Morris: Critical Views and Responses,* 153–167. Lincoln: University of Nebraska Press, 1977.

Lewis, Linda M. "*Plains Song:* Wright Morris's New Melody for Audacious Female Voices," *Great Plains Quarterly* 8 (Winter 1988): 29–37.

Madden, David. *Wright Morris.* Boston: Twayne, 1964.

Morris, Wright. *Plains Song: For Female Voices.* New York: Harper & Row, 1980.

Waldeland, Lynne. "*Plains Song:* Women's Voices in the Fiction of Wright Morris," *Critique: Studies in Contemporary Fiction* 24 (Fall 1982): 7–20.

Wydeven, Joseph J. "Visual Artistry in Wright Morris's *Plains Song for Female Voices,*" *Midamerica: The Yearbook of the Society for the Study of Midwestern Literature* 19 (1992): 116–126.

———. "Wright Morris: An Update." In *Updating the Literary West,* edited by Max Westbrook, 685–692. Fort Worth: Western Literature Association/Texas Christian University Press, 1997.

———. *Wright Morris Revisited.* Twayne's United States Authors Series, no. 703. New York: Twayne, 1998.

Martin Kich

PLATH, SYLVIA (1932–1963)

Since her 1963 suicide at age 30, Sylvia Plath's already fine reputation has burgeoned. It rests on her autobiographical novel *The Bell Jar* (1963), the extraordinary poetry in *Colossus* (1960), and her posthumously awarded Pulitzer Prize for poetry in 1982. Her poems are a blend of brilliant, imaginative, sometimes violent metaphor and image combined with passion, anger, a concern with feminism, and a compelling need to be understood. *The Bell Jar* recounts a young woman's search for identity, her rebellion against convention, mental collapse, and recovery. The novel, taught in many high school and college courses, continues to sell steadily in numerous countries, implying the still powerful nature of its message, particularly for women.

Sylvia Plath was born on October 27, 1932, in Boston, Massachusetts, to Otto Plath, a college professor who had immigrated from Germany, and Aurelia Schober, who taught secretarial studies at Boston University. Her father died when Plath was eight years old, and much of her poetry concerns her ambivalent, often tormented feelings about him. Plath matriculated at Smith College; she wrote and published poetry even while still a student. While at Smith she suffered the mental breakdown and attempted suicide she would describe some years later in *The Bell Jar;* after six months of treatment, however, Plath recovered, returned to Smith, and graduated summa cum laude in 1955. With a Fulbright grant, she traveled to England, met the English poet Ted Hughes, and married him on June 16, 1956. She continued to write and to publish poetry but also typed his manuscripts. In 1962, after learning of his affair with another woman, Plath separated from Hughes. She wrote poetry now recognized as stunningly original in its anger, its vivid colors, and its depiction of sunshine, energy, and life juxtaposed to the seductive lure of despair, emptiness, and darkness.

The Bell Jar, poignantly depicting the pain of adolescence, has been compared to such other American classics as J. D. SALINGER's *The CATCHER IN THE RYE.* It chronicles the potential and manic depression of Esther Greenwood, a student at a New England college, who, like Plath, through therapy and electroshock treatments, manages to return to a normal life. It was published, under the pseudonym Victoria Lucas, in England, in

January 1963. Despite its hopeful ending, Plath scholar Caroline King Barnard notes "a note of warning" for *The Bell Jar's* author, "for whom the prognosis" was "dark indeed" (Barnard, 33). Within a month, Plath was dead; she inhaled gas from her kitchen stove. If anything, interest in Plath's work and life have increased in the last few years. In 1978, Avco-Embassy produced a film version of *The Bell Jar.* In 2003, the BBC produced the film *Sylvia,* about Plath's relationship with Ted Hughes; it was written by John Brownlow and directed by Christine Jeffs and starred Gwyneth Paltrow as Plath. The film was objected to by the Hughes family, represented by Plath's daughter Frieda Hughes, who refused permission for the use of any of her mother's poetry. The film also spawned at least one lawsuit, successfully brought by Dr. Jane V. Anderson, who was the model for Esther Greenwood's friend Joan Gilling in the novel (Lacayo). Sylvia Plath's papers are housed at the Lilly Library of Indiana University, Bloomington, and the Rare Book Room at Smith College.

NOVEL

The Bell Jar. (Under pseudonym Victoria Lucas). London, England: Heinemann, 1963.

SOURCES

Alexander, Paul. *Rough Magic: A Biography of Sylvia Plath.* New York: Viking, 1991.

Axelrod, Steven Gould. *Sylvia Plath: The Wound and the Cure of Words.* Baltimore, Md.: Johns Hopkins University Press, 1990.

Barnard, Caroline King. *Sylvia Plath.* Boston: Twayne, 1978.

Broe, Mary Lynn. *Protean Poetic: The Poetry of Sylvia Plath.* Columbia: University of Missouri, 1980.

Hall, Caroline King Barnard. *Sylvia Plath. Revised.* Boston: Twayne, 1998.

Hargrove, Nancy Duvall. *The Journey toward Ariel: Sylvia Plath's Poems of 1956–1959.* Lund, Sweden: Lund University Press, 1994.

Hayman, Ronald. *The Death and Life of Sylvia Plath.* New York: Birch Lane Press, 1991.

Hughes, Ted. *Birthday Letters.* New York: Farrar, Straus, 1998.

Kroll, Judith. *Chapters in a Mythology: The Poetry of Sylvia Plath.* New York: Harper, 1976.

Malcolm, Janet. *The Silent Woman: Sylvia Plath Ted Hughes.* New York: Knopf, 1994.

Plath, Sylvia. *The Journals of Sylvia Plath.* Edited by Ted Hughes and Frances McCullough. New York: Ballantine, 1983.

———. *The Unabridged Journals of Sylvia Plath, 1950–1962.* Edited by Karen V. Kukil. New York: Anchor Books, 2000.

Rose, Jacqueline. *The Haunting of Sylvia Plath.* London: Virago, 1991.

Stevenson, Anne. *Bitter Fame: The Undiscovered Life of Sylvia Plath.* Boston: Houghton Mifflin, 1989.

Strangeways, Al. *Sylvia Plath: The Shaping of Shadows.* East Brunswick, N.J.: Fairleigh Dickinson University Press, 1998.

Tabor, Stephen. *Sylvia Plath: An Analytical Bibliography.* London: Mansell, 1987.

Tennant, Emma. *Sylvia and Ted.* New York: Holt, 2001.

Van Dyke, Susan R. *Revising Life: Sylvia Plath's Ariel Poems.* Chapel Hill: University of North Carolina Press, 1993.

Wagner-Martin, Linda. *The Bell Jar: A Novel of the Fifties.* Boston: Twayne, 1992.

———. *Sylvia Plath: A Biography.* New York: Simon & Schuster, 1987.

———. *Sylvia Plath: The Critical Heritage.* London: Routledge & Kegan Paul, 1988.

OTHER

The Academy of American Poets Poetry Exhibits: Sylvia Plath. Available online. URL: http://www.poets.org/poets/poets.cfm?prmID=11. Accessed September 25, 2005.

Lacayo, Richard. "Of Whom the Bell Told; Mixed Message from a Legal Battle over Facts and Fiction." *Time.* (February 9, 2003). Highbeam Research. Available online. URL: http://www.highbeam.com/library/doc3.asp?DOCID=1G1:4645445. Accessed September 25, 2005.

The Sylvia Plath Forum. Available online. URL: http://www.sylviaplathforum.com. Accessed September 25, 2005.

PLAY IT AS IT LAYS Joan Didion (1970)

Joan Didion sets her second novel, *Play It as It Lays,* in Hollywood and on the freeway and desert surrounding it. The Los Angeles area serves less as a subject than as a background for exploring protagonist Maria (pronounced mar-EYE-ah) Wyeth's depersonalizing experience of the Hollywood lifestyle popularized in movies and fiction.

Unlike starlets who make it big in Hollywood, Maria leads a decidedly unglamorous life: She gets only bit parts acting; her four-year-old daughter, Kate, is hospitalized with some undefined condition demanding treatment with early forms of Ritalin; her marriage to filmmaker Carter Lang (who featured Maria in two of his films) is falling apart; and she illegally aborts a pregnancy at Carter's insistence. Though Maria's precise reasons for having the abortion remain unclear, the novel presents her uncertainty about paternity and Carter's threat to Maria's custody of Kate as two possibilities, among others. To cope with the trauma, Maria takes to driving aimlessly on the freeways until she realizes the peril in constant movement, and turns to numbing her distress with alcohol, sex, and drugs. The emotional vertigo of the abortion prompts much of Maria's behavior throughout the text, which culminates in Maria's complicity in BZ's suicide. She finds herself in bed with BZ, her husband's gay producer, who is intent not on sex but on swallowing the Seconal that results in his dying in Maria's arms.

The reader discerns these circumstances in three narrated monologues by Maria, Helene, and Carter, which open the book, and in 84 rapid-fire sections, some comprising only a couple of sentences. Written in Didion's characteristically sparse style and focusing, like Didion's other work, on the characters' response to their environments, *Play It as It Lays*'s large amount of white space on the page reiterates the existential angst Maria feels. Maria's seeming lack of concern and her inability to respond have prompted some to read the novel as nihilistic, or as Didion's indictment of contemporary moral relativism. Some read Maria's abortion as a consequence of the Hollywood lifestyle, specifically, or of the breakdown in American morals, generally. To some, Maria emerges as rather nonchalant about moral values: She does not question what makes Iago evil, presumably because she either already knows or simply does not care; she goes along with Carter's suggested abortion without raising the issue with Les Goodwin, whom she suspects of fathering the child; and she makes no move to stop BZ from committing suicide, instead holding his hand as he dies.

Such judgments not only deny the decidedly feminine nature of her crisis, they also disable the reader's identification of influences underlying Maria's actions. Maria inherited a confused sense of how to be in the world from her father, Harry. He taught her to "play the game as it lays," and to watch for rattlesnakes under the rocks, but she discovers that these lessons do not "apply" in real life. For example, while giving life advice, Harry Wyeth continually insists that Maria is "holding all the aces" (7), but the game he talks about playing is craps, not poker. Maria sees the rattlesnakes, said by some critics to symbolize evil, as merely situational hazards that lurk everywhere. As part of the general malaise, they provide no system for understanding good and evil. When the reader considers that Maria has heretofore sought to live by her father's rules, only to discover their inefficacy, her mode of handling situations seems less a product of a failed moral vision, or of a world altogether devoid of one, than of a woman perpetually at the mercy of men around her and unable to affect change using her arsenal of experience and information about life. Maria endures a crisis because of the suffering of others, including her aborted fetus, but appears not to seek a means of understanding that crisis in moral terms. Nevertheless, the novel entertains the possibility that she will benefit from her experience of tragedy and transform her life. When deciding to have the abortion, Maria thinks that "she would do this one last thing and then they would never be able to touch her again" (73), as if bent on a course of future action.

Maria emerges, then, as a woman bereft of a heritage, moral or otherwise, which Didion poignantly symbolizes through her self-asserted "trouble with *as it was*" (5) and the disappearance of her hometown, Silver Wells, which sat in what is now the middle of a nuclear missile testing range. Maria's individual legacy thus becomes intertwined with America's, her inheritance literally subsumed by the nation's struggle for dominance via superior nuclear capability. This dubious future serves as a major theme of Didion's novel *Democracy* (1984) and her essay collections on California: *Slouching Towards Bethlehem* (1968), *The White Album* (1979), and *Where I Was From* (2003). *Play It As It Lays* does not warn or chide; instead, it explores how the promise of prosperity (what Maria seeks in her entrée to Hollywood) has been derailed by attempts to control its trajectory by characters like BZ, Carter, even Harry Wyeth, while those without hope for control languish in circumstances not entirely of their own making.

At the end of *Play It As It Lays,* Maria appears to be in a sanatorium or a neuropsychiatric ward. The reader learns of this fallout after BZ's suicide during the opening narratives, which only resonate upon completion of the novel, and from italicized sections from the journal Maria keeps at her doctors' behest. In the journal, she grapples with the "as it was" she has always forsworn and indicates another attempt to understand the present in terms of the past. But her thoughts are now largely turned toward a future with Kate, and, having not opted to kill herself alongside BZ, she has clearly determined that life is worth living. Though bleak, the ending thus also flickers with hope, because given all she has already endured, she appears quite equipped to survive. Perhaps, the novel suggests, "playing it as it lays" means surviving against the odds.

SOURCES

Didion, Joan. *Play It as It Lays.* New York: Pocket Books, 1970.

Friedman, Ellen G., ed. *Joan Didion: Essays and Conversations.* Princeton, N.J.: Ontario Review Press, 1984.

Henderson, Katherine Usher. *Joan Didion.* New York: Frederick Ungar Publishing, Co., 1981.

Wynchell, Mark Royden. *Joan Didion: Revised Edition.* Boston: Twayne, 1989.

Jon Adams

PLOT AGAINST AMERICA, THE Philip Roth (2004)

Although Philip Roth is one of the most significant American novelists writing in the late 20th and early 21st centuries, his critical success has not always translated into book sales. *Portnoy's Complaint,* Roth's scandalous (for the time) and highly comic foray into male sexuality ruled the best-seller lists in 1969, but since then few of his novels have matched its "highly flammable," and popularly successful, combination of controversy and timeliness. That is, until *The Plot against America* in 2004. In Roth's most recent novel, an alternate history in which aviator hero Charles A. Lindbergh runs against the popular Franklin D. Roosevelt in 1940 and wins the presidency, he once again turns to 20th-century American history as his narrative backdrop, as he did in the American Trilogy (*American Pastoral,* 1997; *I Married a Communist,* 1998; and *The Human Stain,* 2000). And also as in the trilogy, he uses the historical moment to show how individuals define themselves by, and at the same time become hostages to, the many cultural and political forces that surround them. Yet what has made *The Plot against America* such a popular (as well as critical) success is twofold: Roth's willingness to take on and "retextualize" a heroic American icon, and the perceived relevance of the novel's themes to its current sociopolitical contexts.

What has garnered the most attention in this novel is its alternate historical premise. The isolationist wing of the Republican Party, frustrated after eight years of political marginalization and resentful of FDR's interventionist policies against Nazi Germany, decides to nominate Charles Lindbergh over Wendell L. Wilkie for president of the United States in 1940. The wildly popular Lindbergh—supported by the America First Committee, traveling around the country in his legendary *Spirit of St. Louis,* and campaigning under the slogan "Vote for Lindbergh or Vote for War"—defeats FDR in a landslide. Within the first two years of his presidency, Lindbergh institutes a series of policies, all of which suggest an appeasement to Hitler's militaristic and racist strategies: signing nonaggression pacts with both Germany (the "Iceland Understanding") and Japan (the "Hawaii Understanding"); creating Just Folks, a volunteer work program managed under the newly formed Office of American Absorption, whose purpose is to introduce urban youth (read Jews) to "the traditional ways of heartland life" (84); and instituting Homestead 42, legislation reminiscent of the Homestead Act of 1862, but this time one designed to disperse and relocate inner-city ethnic Americans (again, read Jews) into rural regions of the country under the euphemistic goals of "provid[ing] a challenging environment steeped in our country's oldest traditions where parents and children can enrich their Americanness over the generations" (204–205).

However, all these alternate historical events, as provocative as they may be, are nothing more than a backdrop to the primary focus of the novel: Roth's family. Lindbergh's presidency and its many ramifications are rarely the primary subject of novel but are instead filtered through the dialogue and conflicts among a young Philip Roth, his family, and their Jewish community in the Weequahic section of Newark, New Jersey. As Roth does in his autobiographical tetralogy— *The Facts* (1988), *Deception* (1990), *Patrimony* (1991), and *Operation Shylock* (1993)—he uses "Philip Roth" as his protagonist, a fictional construct/character who nonetheless shares with his real-life counterpart an almost identical appearance, psychology, and history. The action in *The Plot against America* takes place over a period of young Philip's life from June 1940, when he is a seven-year-old third grader, to October 1942. During this time, he and his family struggle to make sense of the events unfolding around them, circumstances that as Americanized Jews they would have never predicted to encounter. Along the way Philip's older brother, Sandy, is willingly "absorbed" into the Just Folks program (and subsequently comes to appreciate both Lindbergh and pork products); a cousin, Alvin, runs off to Canada to enlist in their commando forces and fight against Hitler, losing his left leg in the process; their Aunt Evelyn marries Rabbi Lionel Benglesdorf, a bigwig in the Office of American Absorption and self-deluded Jewish front for the Lindbergh administration's anti-Semitic policies; and one of the family's former neighbors dies in America's first pogrom, sparked by the incendiary anti-Lindbergh rhetoric of journalist Walter Winchell, who, in 1942, becomes an early front-runner for the 1944 Democratic Party nomination.

One of the things that make *The Plot against America* so striking is Roth's handling not only of American history, but of America's heroic icons, most obviously Charles Lindbergh (who, in real life, was a member of the America First Committee, did receive the Iron Cross from Herman Goering, and did give a speech in 1941 calling American Jews, along with those in the Roosevelt administration, warmongers). This is not the kind of alternate history found in much science fiction, where the emphasis is placed on the political actions themselves, where grand figures stride across the narrative and immovable forces slowly unfold the text of history. In this novel, Roth shows us how American subjects, individuals as well as political ideas, have been given iconic status through a variety of texts: newspaper accounts, cinematic newsreels, gossip columns, history textbooks, congressional legislation,

and literary narrative. Roth indirectly demonstrates how constructed these identities are by "retextualizing" American history and, more specifically, the Norman Rockwellesque ideal of American identity as embodied in Charles A. Lindbergh. In much the same way he does in earlier novels such as *The Ghost Writer* (1979) and *The Counterlife* (1987), where the thematic emphasis is placed on postmodern constructions of the individual subject, Roth in his most recent novel focuses on the "text" of the self—except here, the contingency of identity is placed on the larger national stage. Coming as it does after the historical sweep of the American Trilogy, Roth's narrative focus in *The Plot against America* could not be otherwise.

Perhaps even more notable, at least in terms of the novel's popularity, are the ways in which readers approach *The Plot against America* as a roman à clef of current events (for example, the unlikeliness of the George W. Bush presidency, the 9/11 attacks, the Patriot Act and its restrictions on civil liberties). But Roth himself has warned against such a reading. His goal, as he bluntly stated in the *New York Times Book Review* immediately preceding the novel's publication, was merely to "reconstruct the years 1940–42 as they might have been if Lindbergh, instead of Roosevelt, had been elected president in the 1940 election. I am not pretending to be interested in those two years—I am interested in those two years" (*New York Times Book Review* 2004, 10). Yet how much are we to believe the author when, in the same *New York Times Book Review* essay, he blasts the current president as "a man unfit to run a hardware store let alone a nation like this one" (*New York Times Book Review* 2004, 10), and who brackets *The Plot against America* with the phrase "perpetual fear" (in the first sentence of the novel and the title of the last chapter)—an ambiguous emotional state that in many ways defines our post-9/11 world? Perhaps Philip Roth, well-known for his mischievous and labyrinthine textual play between fact and fiction, is wanting it both ways. Such a narrative stance brings to mind the profound romantic irony found in the works of Nathaniel HAWTHORNE, Herman MELVILLE, Henry JAMES, and William FAULKNER. For an aging contemporary novelist securing his place in American letters, this is not such bad company.

SOURCES

Roth, Philip. Interview with Jeffrey Brown. *News Hour with Jim Lehrer.* PBS. WNET, New York. October 27, 2004, and November 10, 2004. (Two-part interview)

———. Interview with Kurt Anderson. *Studio 360.* WNYC, New York. November 6, 2004. (Full interview, http://www.wnyc.org/studio360/show110604.html)

———. "Mrs. Lindbergh, Mr. Ciardi, and the Teeth and Claws of the Civilized World," *Chicago Review* 11 (1957): 72–76.

———. "Novelist Philip Roth." Interview with Tom Ashbrook. *On Point.* WBUR, Boston. December 3, 2004.

———. *The Plot against America.* Boston: Houghton Mifflin, 2004.

———. "Pulitzer Prize–Winning Novelist Philip Roth." Interview with Terry Gross. *Fresh Air.* Natl. Public Radio. WHYY, Philadelphia. October 11, 2004.

———. "Roth Rewrites History with *The Plot against America.*" Interview with Robert Siegel. *All Things Considered.* Natl. Public Radio. WNYC, New York. September 23, 2004.

———. "The Story behind *The Plot against America,*" *New York Times Book Review,* 19 September 2004, p. 10.

Royal, Derek Parker, ed. *Philip Roth: New Perspectives on an American Author.* Westport, Conn.: Praeger, 2005.

Derek Royal

POE, EDGAR ALLAN (1809–1849)

Edgar Allan Poe is forever identified with his eerie poem "The Raven," with his many gothic horror stories, and as the father of the detective story. His perspicacious literary criticism still influences literature in both the United States and Europe. Today's classroom discussions are often about his addictions to drugs and alcohol, his marriage to a 13-year-old cousin, and his still unexplained early death at age 40 (was he drunk? was he rabid?).

In addition to *Eureka* (1848), his novel-length prose poem, he wrote The NARRATIVE OF ARTHUR GORDON PYM, OF NANTUCKET (1838). Increasing interest in this novel, from myriad perspectives, attests to its significance in the American literary canon.

Edgar Allan Poe was born on January 19, 1809, in Boston, Massachusetts, to David Poe, Jr., and Elizabeth Arnold, both talented actors. Orphaned at age two, Poe was reared by his godfather, John Allan, a Richmond, Virginia, merchant. Allan raised Poe as a Southern patrician gentleman and educated him in England and at the University of Virginia and West Point. He married Virginia Clemmon May 16, 1836. Poe was publishing volumes of verse and, after being expelled from West Point, settled in Baltimore, where he began to write stories, and then in Richmond, where he became an influential editor of the *Southern Literary Messenger;* there he serialized *The Narrative of Arthur Gordon Pym,* and then extensively revised it before it was published in book form with the author's name "anonymous" in 1838. The novel is about a journal kept by Pym, who sails on a whaler from Nantucket, Massachusetts, and survives repeated and extended moments of horror on the high seas, until the ship disappears into a swirling chasm that dissolves into pure whiteness. Scholar Vincent Buranelli points out that *A. Gordon Pym* is so well developed "that it may have a descendant in [Herman MELVILLE'S] MOBY-DICK" (Buranelli, 70).

After *A. Gordon Pym* appeared, Poe moved to Philadelphia, then New York, where he edited *Burlington Gentleman's Magazine, Graham's Lady's and Gentleman's Magazine,* the *Evening Mirror,* and the *Broadway Journal,* and published most of his most celebrated stories. His wife died of tuberculosis in 1847 and Edgar Allan Poe died on October 7, 1849, in Baltimore, Maryland. He is buried alongside his wife and her mother.

Scholars continue to debate the meaning and depth of *A. Gordon Pym* in terms of Jungian psychology, philosophy, the Bible, good and evil, race relations, myth, and chaos theory.

NOVEL

The Narrative of Arthur Gordon Pym, of Nantucket. Anonymous. New York: Harper, 1838.

SOURCES

Allen, Hervey. *Israfel: The Life and Times of Edgar Allan Poe.* 2 vols. New York: Doran, 1926.

Benton. Richard P., ed. *New Approaches to Poe: A Symposium,* Hartford, Conn.: Transcendental Books, 1970.

Buranelli, Vincent. *Edgar Allan Poe.* Rev. ed. Boston: Twayne, 1977.

Griswold, Rufus Wilmot. "Memoir of the Author." In *The Works of the Late Edgar Allan Poe.* 4 vols. III: vii–xxxix. New York: J. S. Redfield, 1850–1856.

Ingram, John H. *Edgar Allan Poe: His Life, Letters and Opinions.* 2 vols. London: John Hogg, 1880.

Mabbott, Thomas Ollive. "Annals of Poe's Life." In *Collected Works of Edgar Allan Poe.* 3 vols. Cambridge, Mass.: Belknap Press of Harvard University Press, 1969–1978, I: 527–572.

Mankowitz, Wolf. *The Extraordinary Mr. Poe.* New York: Simon & Schuster, 1978.

Miller, John Carl, ed. *Building Poe Biography.* Baton Rouge: Louisiana State University Press, 1977.

———, ed. *Poe's Helen Remembers.* Charlottesville: University Press of Virginia, 1979.

Pollin, Burton R. *Discoveries in Poe.* Notre Dame, Ind.: University of Notre Dame Press, 1970.

Quinn, Arthur Hobson. *Edgar Allan Poe: A Critical Biography.* New York: Appleton-Century, 1941.

Symons, Julian. *The Tell-Tale Heart: The Life and Works of Edgar Allan Poe.* New York: Harper & Row, 1978.

Thomas, David K., and Dwight Thomas. *The Poe Log; A Documentary Life of Edgar Allan Poe, 1809–1849.* Boston: G. K. Hall, 1987.

Wagenknecht, Edward. *Edgar Allan Poe: The Man Behind the Legend.* New York: Oxford University Press, 1963.

Whitman, Sarah Helen. *Edgar Poe and His Critics.* New York: Rudd & Carleton, 1860.

Woodberry, George Edward. *The Life of Edgar Allan Poe, Personal and Literary.* 2 vols. Boston: Houghton Mifflin, 1909.

OTHER

The Edgar Allan Poe Society of Baltimore. Available online. URL: http://www.eapoe.org/index.htm. Accessed September 25, 2005.

Edgar Allan Poe's House of Usher. Available online. URL: http://www.comnet.ca/~forrest. Accessed September 25, 2005.

Online Literature Library Edgar Allan Poe. Available online. URL: http://www.literature.org/authors/poe-edgar-allan. Accessed on September 25, 2005.

The Poe Decoder. Available online. URL: http://www.poedecoder.com. Accessed September 25, 2005.

The Poetry Archives: Edgar Allen Poe. Available online. URL: http://www.emule.com/poetry/?page=overview&author=15. Accessed September 25, 2005.

A Poe Webliography. Available online. URL: http://andromeda.rutgers.edu/~ehrlich/poesites.html. Accessed September 25, 2005.

POISONWOOD BIBLE, THE BARBARA KINGSOLVER (1998)

This intricately structured, multi-vocal novel is at once an engrossing saga of an American missionary family and an important political allegory about the ethnocentricity with which the United States and Europe have historically approached Africa. Spanning roughly three decades, the novel begins in 1959, when Nathan Price, a domineering evangelical Baptist from Georgia, packs up his wife and four daughters and sets out to convert the heathen in what was then the Belgian Congo. Equipped with Bibles and Betty Crocker cake mixes, the Prices are repeatedly foiled in their attempts to transplant their lifestyle and worldview to a place with its own rich culture and a scarcity of resources for survival. Particularly thwarted is Nathan, whose imperious attitude is manifest as much in his abusive treatment of his family as in his disregard for the indigenous culture: He tramples on local customs and ignorantly blasphemes in the native language—mistranslating "Jesus" as both "fish bait" and "poisonwood." His inadvertent preaching of the gospel as poisonwood (yielding the title and a central theme of the novel) is more than a linguistic mistake; the chauvinistic attitudes that accompany Nathan's frequent mistranslations are "poison" to the indigenous culture.

While Nathan is symbolically central to the novel, this is not his story. Instead, KINGSOLVER masterfully weaves the story together from the perspectives of the wife and daughters. The mother, Orleana, narrates retrospectively from Sanderling Island, Georgia, while the girls (Rachel, Leah, Adah, and Ruth May) narrate from the moment, as if recording their reflections in a diary. In the first section, Orleana cues the reader that "disaster is coming" (6), and from that point the narrative burns at both ends, as the girls' telling of events gradually catches up to the mother's later vantage point. Each narrator relates how she has been profoundly shaped by her experiences in Africa; even Rachel, the least open-minded, declares, "You can't just sashay into the jungle aiming to change it all over the Christian style, without expecting the jungle to change you right back" (515).

The personal and political narratives intersect when the Prices lose their youngest daughter the same day that the newly independent Congo loses its first prime minister, Patrice Lumumba—murdered after having been deposed in a CIA-backed coup. Readers not familiar with this history will piece together an understanding of events along with the characters, learning that Lumumba's suspected alliance with the Soviet

Union made him a casualty of Cold War politics, and that in his place, the United States installed the purportedly "pro-Western" Mobutu, a corrupt ruler who went on to become one of the wealthiest men in the world while ruling over one of the poorest African nations. Kingsolver suggests that she and her readers are in a position analogous to that of the narrators: "We didn't make the awful decisions our government imposed on Africa. We didn't call for the assassination of Lumumba; we hardly even knew about it. We just inherited these decisions, and now have to reconcile them with our sense of who we are" (www.kingsolver.com, "*Poisonwood Bible* Questions and Answers"). The family tragedy is the catalyst that gives Orleana and the girls the courage to leave Nathan, though they will spend their lifetimes making sense of these events. This, then, is a story of reckoning—of assessing responsibility for personal and political events—as each woman grapples with finding a way to live with what she's learned and what she's become.

Kingsolver's earlier novels (*The* BEAN TREES, *Animal Dreams,* and *Pigs in Heaven*) also take on serious social and political issues, from the erasure of Native American cultures to industrial pollution. In fact, Kingsolver regards writing as a form of political activism, an extension of the anti-Vietnam protests and feminist consciousness-raising that she participated in while in college. While this overtly political focus leads some reviewers and critics to regard *The Poisonwood Bible* as polemical or reductive (see Kunz; Kakutani), the novel has garnered many popular and critical accolades, including winner of the Patterson Fiction Prize and the ABBY (American Booksellers Book of the Year) award, runner-up for PEN/Faulkner and Pulitzer prizes, and selection for Oprah's book-of-the-month club.

Regarding her writing process, Kingsolver explains, "I don't start building the story around pre-existing characters or incidents. I begin with a theme. I devise a very big question whose answers I believe will be amazing, and maybe shift the world a little bit on its axis" (www.kingsolver.com, "Other Questions and Answers"). For *The Poisonwood Bible,* that question is roughly, "What did we do to Africa, and how do we feel about it?" Kingsolver creates a fictional world that can accommodate the complexity of this question by addressing it from five distinct perspectives, and by giving the bulk of the narration to children, who draw the reader in with their wide-eyed observations, candidness, and productive naïveté—that is, the ability to report without judging or even fully understanding. This flexible consciousness makes the girls good ethnographers, not only of the new culture in which they are immersed, but also of their own.

The Poisonwood Bible is divided into seven books, six of which borrow their titles from either the King James Bible or the Apocrypha, which Nathan, unlike most Baptist preachers, regards as legitimate scripture. Corresponding quotations serve as epigraphs, introducing important themes. For instance, the epigraph of Book I (appropriately titled "Genesis") is "And God said unto them,/ Be fruitful, and multiply, and replenish the earth,/ and subdue it: and have dominion/ over the fish of the sea, and over the fowl of the air,/ and over every living thing that moveth upon the earth." Nathan twists these words to justify his assuming absolute authority over "every living thing"—a presumption rapidly belied when, ignoring a native woman's advice, he squanders half the family's seed supply in a garden planted for the fields of Georgia, not for the deluge-prone Congo. The scriptural epigraphs serve to convey the extent to which the Bible permeates the Prices' lives: The girls are able to quote scripture partly because they are frequently made to copy long passages as punishment for trivial infractions.

The first five books begin with a section by the mother, in which she addresses the spirit of her lost daughter, Ruth May. Orleana's voice combines lament, confession, and self-justification: Haunted by the past, she seeks both understanding and absolution. In part, she suggests, she was "a captive witness," a subservient housewife thrust into "a life she never bargained for"—and "What is the conqueror's wife if not a conquest herself?" (9). Yet she realizes that this characterization does not tell the whole story: "You'll say I walked across Africa with my wrists unshackled, and now I am one more soul walking free in a white skin, wearing some thread of the stolen goods: cotton or diamonds, freedom at the very least, prosperity" (9). The absolution Orleana seeks is not only for her possible failings as a mother, then, but also for playing an inadvertent role in a larger history of conquest and exploitation. The question of complicity is a central one in the novel, and one the reader must also grapple with, for, as Orleana goes on to suggest, we all wear stolen goods; the question is, "How do we aim to live with it?" (9).

Alternating sections by the daughters follow Orleana's reflections. The youngest is Ruth May, whose naive voice reminds the reader of the cultural baggage the Prices bring from Georgia, where, as Ruth tells it, the "children of Ham" go to a separate church and separate restaurants: "Jimmy Crow says that, and he makes the laws" (20). Though her young age and her early death buffer her from the larger political drama of which the other narrators gradually become aware, as a missionary's daughter, Ruth is still absorbed by issues of culpability and punishment. The eldest daughter is Rachel: Blond, vain, and shallow, she verges on caricature, while providing comic relief with her spirited reenactments of television commercials ("Aren't you glad you use Dial?") and frequent malapropisms that are often unintentionally apt ("Christians have our own system of marriage; it's called Monotony," 405). Her materialistic focus embodies the values of American consumer culture at its worst, serving to remind the reader of the enormous asymmetry of wealth that divide the typical American family from the people of Kilanga. Winding up as a wealthy hotel owner in South Africa, Rachel is uncritical of white supremacy, and untroubled by the feelings of complicity that preoccupy her mother and sisters.

Between these two are the twins: Leah, who is lithe and strong, and Adah, whom hemiplegia has rendered "crooked" and mute. Leah first idolizes her father, craving his approval as when she helps him plant his garden, until she comes to the terrifying realization that he is fallible and in some ways dangerous. She turns to the indigenous culture that seemingly offers a model of living more in harmony with the natural world. Her assimilation extends to marrying the local schoolteacher and skeptical translator of her father's sermons, Anatole, with whom she eventually has children and settles down with in Angola. Leah comes to regard whiteness itself as inextricable from a history of domination that she finds reprehensible. Looking at her children, "the colors of silt, loam, dusty, and clay,"

she has the solace that "time erases whiteness altogether" (526).

If Leah is critical of ethnocentricity (indeed, of whiteness), Adah is critical of a perspective that privileges normalcy, and ultimately, of one that privileges humans. Her silence cloaks rich insight and clever wordplay, often in the form of palindromes like "Live was I ere I saw evil"—to which she adds the Conrad–like qualification: "perhaps it was not evil I saw but merely the way of all hearts when fear has stripped off the husk of kind pretensions" (305). Playing on her asymmetrical posture, Adah invokes a line from her favorite poet Emily Dickinson, suggesting that one should "tell the truth but tell it slant." Adah's "slant," then, is construed not as disability but as perspective, as the basis for her unique vision. Used to encountering prejudice, Adah is surprised to discover that she does not stand out in Kilanga, where a woman who has lost the use of her legs shuffles about on her hands, and where bodies routinely "wear out" from malnutrition and hard labor. She is accepted for the first time here, her Kikongo name, b"nduka, signifying a new, dual identity: "B"nduka is the bent-sideways girl who walks slowly, but b"nduka is also the name of a fast-flying bird, the swallow with curved wings who darts crookedly quick through trees near the river." After Adah returns to the United States and goes through therapy that "corrects" the limp, she mourns for the loss of that old self: "Here there is no good name for my gift, so it died without ceremony" (493). For Adah, survival itself is fraught with a sense of guilt. She observes, "in our seventeenth months in Kilanga, thirty-one children died, including Ruth May. Why not Adah? I can think of no answer that exonerates me" (413). She begins to question the presumptiveness of humanity in general for assuming that our species should be the dominant one, and in her study of tropical diseases, deposes humans from that central position by avowing the fundamental "right of a plant or virus to rule the world" (531).

The novel is brought to a powerful conclusion with the seventh and final book that circles back to the beginning, with a title taken from the novel's first page: "I want you to be 'the eyes in the trees.' " Throughout the novel, Leah and Adah have wrestled with feelings of culpability, and Orleana has pleaded with Ruth May's spirit for forgiveness; here is an answer. The mystical voice emanates from the youngest daughter merged with the spirit of Africa, the vantage point high in the trees recalling her earlier fantasy of retreating into the form of a mamba snake—the one "safe place" Ruth could envision in times of danger. The last words from "the eyes in the trees" offer the long-sought redemption, ironically echoing Nathan's desperate urgings to the African children whom he wishes to baptize in the rain to "Walk forward into the light." In her most ambitious novel to date, with moments of narrative brilliance and a mostly seamless joining of the personal with the political, many readers feel that Kingsolver succeeds in tilting the world a bit on its axis.

SOURCES

DeMarr, Mary Jean. *Barbara Kingsolver: A Critical Companion.* Westport, Conn.: Greenwood Press, 1999.

Kakutani, Michiko. " '*The Poisonwood Bible*': A Family Heart of Darkness," *New York Times Book Review,* 16 October 1998.

Kingsolver, Barbara. *The Poisonwood Bible.* New York: HarperPerennial, 1998.

Kunz, Diane. "White Men in Africa: On Barbara Kingsolver's *The Poisonwood Bible.*" In *Novel History: Historians and Novelists Confront America's Past (and Each Other),* edited by Mark Carnes, 285–300. New York: Simon & Schuster, 2001.

Kwitny, Jonathan. *Endless Enemies: The Making of an Unfriendly World.* New York: Congdon & Weed, 1984.

Perry, Donna. *Backtalk: Women Writers Speak Out: Interviews.* New Brunswick, N.J.: Rutgers University Press, 1991.

Wagner-Martin, Linda. *The Poisonwood Bible: A Reader's Guide.* New York and London: Continuum International Publishing Group, 2001.

OTHER

Barbara Kingsolver. Available online. URL: www.kingsolver. com. Accessed September 26, 2005.

Carey Snyder

PORTER, CONNIE (CONNIE ROSE PORTER) (1959–)

Connie Porter impressed critics and readers alike with her first novel, *All-Bright Court* (1991), the tale of a black family's life in a run-down tenement in Lackawanna, New York, where Samuel Taylor and his wife Mary Kate have moved from Tupelo, Mississippi, in the early 1960s. Shortly thereafter, Porter contracted with the American Girls series to write Civil War–era books that feature Addy, a nine-year-old slave who escapes to freedom with her family; Porter has said that these children's books constitute a tribute to "all the brave and hardworking women in my family who had gone before me" (Maughan Interview). In 1998, she wrote her second novel for adults, *Imani All Mine,* about a single mother who survives a brutal rape and still completes her education and cares for her daughter. By 1999, Porter's American Girl books and novels had sold more than four and a half million copies, and *All-Bright Court* was popular with book clubs all over the country.

The residents of All-Bright Court, whose lives reflect the decaying steel mill, cope with disillusion and disappointment. The gifted boy Mikey has had a privileged education among white students, which confuses him about his racial heritage. *Imani All Mine,* set in the inner city, is told in street dialect from the perspective of its hero, 15-year-old Tasha, who survives rape, delivers her baby daughter, and returns to school, only to discover that her rapist is enrolled in the same school and does not even recognize her. Tasha loves the baby, Imani (meaning "faith"), since she looks nothing like her rapist father; but the infant is killed by a stray bullet during a gang war. Tasha, whose own mother had hoped for a brighter future for her, finds solace in religious faith and in bringing another child into the world.

Connie Porter was born in 1959 in New York City before her family moved to the Baker Homes housing project in Buffalo, New York. She was educated at the State University of New York at Albany, where she earned her bachelor's degree, and at Louisiana State University, where she earned her master of fine arts degree.

Inspired in her writing by the girls and young women she meets around the United States, Connie Porter says she will "always want to give a voice to someone who might not otherwise have a voice" (Barker). She lives and writes in Virginia Beach, Virginia.

NOVELS

All-Bright Court. Boston: Houghton, 1991.
Imani All Mine. Boston: Houghton, 1998.

SOURCES

Bush, Vanessa. Review of *Imani All Mine, Booklist,* August 1993, p. 2,063; January 1, 1999, p. 834.

Kakutani, Michiko. Review of *All-Bright Court, New York Times,* 10 September 1991, p. C14.

Krist, Gary. Review of *All-Bright Court, Hudson Review* (Spring 1992): 141–142.

Los Angeles Times Book Review, 13 October 1991, p. 9; September 6, 1992, p. 11.

New Yorker, September 9, 1991, p. 96.

New York Times Book Review, October 27, 1991, 12; August 16, 1992, 32.

Oktenberg, Adrian. Review of *All-Bright Court, Women's Review of Books,* April 1992, pp. 16–17.

Review of *Addy Learns a Lesson, Publishers Weekly,* July 5, 1993, p. 73.

Review of *Imani All Mine, Library Journal,* 1 February 1999, p. 122.

Review of *Imani All Mine, Publishers Weekly,* 23 November 1998, p. 58.

Tribune Books (Chicago, Ill.), August 25, 1991, p. 4.

Washington Post Book World, 11 August 1991, p. 3; 1 December 1991, p. 3; 26 July 1992, p. 12.

OTHER

Barker, Sandra J. "A Conversation with Connie Porter." *Contemporary Women's Issues Database* (March 1, 1998). Available online. Highbeam Research. URL: http://www.highbeam.com/library/doc3.asp?DOCID=1P1:29030069.

Connie Rose Porter. Interview. Houghton Mifflin. Available online. URL: http://www.houghtonmifflinbooks.com/catalog/authordetail.cfm?authorID=1244. Accessed January 11, 2006.

Peterson, V. R. "Connie Porter: Writing About Home," *Essence.* (September 1, 1991). Highbeam Research. Available online. URL: http://www.highbeam.com/library/doc3.asp?DOCID=1G1:11204340. Accessed September 26, 2005.

Porter, Connie Rose. Interview with Connie Porter. By Shannon Maughan. Available online. URL: http://www.kidsreads.com/authors/au-porter-connie.asp. Accessed September 26, 2005.

Profile of Connie Porter. Canisius College. Formerly available online. URL: http://www2.canisius.edu. Accessed September 26, 2005.

Wynn, Judith. "New U.S. Writers Turn Out Masterful Fiction," *The Boston Herald.* (March 7, 1999). Highbeam Research. Available online. URL: http://www.highbeam.com/library/doc3.asp?DOCID=1G1:57117039. Accessed September 26, 2005.

PORTER, KATHERINE ANNE (1890–1980)

Recipient of the 1966 Pulitzer Prize and the 1966 National Book Award for *The Collected Stories of Katherine Anne Porter,* this author is known as one of the premier 20th-century American short story writers. A number of Porter's stories, usually set in Texas or Mexico, about her autobiographical character, Miranda Gay, are actually novellas—notably, *Hacienda: A Story of Mexico* (1934) and *Noon Wine* (1937). Along with *Pale Horse, Pale Rider,* they are considered to be her most skillfully written works. Her only novel, SHIP OF FOOLS (1962), although less critically acclaimed than her shorter fictions, was popular with readers. Although her output was slim, each piece of writing was carefully crafted, a blend of imagism and symbolism filled with subtle resonances and subtexts, particularly about women's experience and a particular epiphany within a patriarchal structure.

Born Callie Russell and later renamed Katherine Anne, Porter was the great-great-great granddaughter of Jonathan Boone, Daniel Boone's younger brother. She was born on May 15, 1890, in Indian Creek, Texas, to Harrison Boone and Mary Alice Jones Porter, who died when Porter was two. Because her father could not support his four children, Porter and her siblings were raised in Kyle, Texas, by their paternal grandmother, Catherine Anne Porter, the indomitable model for the grandmother figures in Porter's stories. In 1906, at age 16, she married John Henry Koontz, a railway clerk. After their divorce in 1915, Porter—henceforth known as Katherine Anne Porter—was married three more times: to Ernest Stock, in 1925; to Eugene Dove Pressly, employed with the American Consulate in Paris, from 1933 to 1938; and to Albert Russel Erskine, Jr., a professor of English, from 1938 to 1942. In a restless, peripatetic life that took her from New York and New England to Mexico and Europe, Porter made lifelong friendships with the Southern writers Carolyn GORDON, Robert Penn WARREN, Allen Tate, and Andrew Lytle. During her Greenwich Village days, she became friends with the poet Elinor Wylie, and the proletarian novelist Josephine Herbst.

In her novella *Hacienda,* an American and a Russian communist filmmaker try to produce a documentary on life in Mexico. Porter's unnamed female narrator comments on the awkward interaction among the Mexicans, with whose revolution she had become disillusioned, and the foreigners, whose clumsy humanitarianism she describes with irony. *Pale Horse, Pale Rider* contains three novellas: *Old Mortality* and *Noon Wine*, earlier published separately, and *Pale Horse, Pale Rider*, the title novella. *Old Mortality*, divided into three sections, focuses on Miranda Gay: The first section stresses the family tendency to romanticize the past; the second features Miranda and her sister during their New Orleans convent-school days when reality changes the nature of the family myths. In the third section, Miranda, home for an uncle's funeral, decides to divorce her husband and strike out on her own. *Noon Wine* is the powerful story of a senseless murder. When a stranger who shows up at the Thompson homestead seeking Helton, the hired man who is responsible for saving this failing farm, Thompson commits the murder. He is acquitted, but his own rural Texas community rejects him and he commits suicide. Many readers view this tale as Porter's condemnation of Texas, a state to which she returned only after her death. Most critics and reviewers view the title novella, *Pale Horse, Pale Rider*, as her most artistically skilled example in this genre. Miranda Gay, like Porter herself 20 years earlier, becomes ill during the influenza epidemic of 1918. Using dream sequences and symbols to evoke the psychological complexities of her characters, including Adam, Miranda's boyfriend who dies from the flu while nursing her, Porter recounts Miranda's emotional disillusionment with Germany and its war mentality. *Pale Horse, Pale Rider* was awarded the first annual gold medal from the Society of the Libraries of New York University in 1940.

Ship of Fools, Porter's best-selling novel, takes place on the German ship *Vera* (truth) on its way from Veracruz, New Mexico, to Bremerhaven, Germany, in the summer of 1931. Drawing on her own European experiences, she tells the episodic stories of the passengers, most of whom cannot maintain lasting relationships. The novel, based on a 15th-century Christian allegory of the same title, has an international cast of characters—German, American, Mexican, Spanish, and Cuban—who transmit a pessimistic view of the world prior to World War II. *Ship of Fools* was filmed by Columbia in 1965. *Noon Wine* was adapted for the television show "ABC Stage 67" in 1967. Katherine Anne Porter died on September 18, 1980, in Silver Spring, Maryland, of cancer. She is buried near her mother in Indian Springs, Texas. The Katherine Anne Porter Room at the McKeldin Library at the University of Maryland is the chief repository of Porter material.

NOVELS AND NOVELLAS

Hacienda: A Story of Mexico. New York: Harrison of Paris, 1934.

Noon Wine. Detroit, Mich.: Schuman's, 1937.

Pale Horse, Pale Rider: Three Short Novels. New York: Harcourt, Brace, 1939.

Ship of Fools. Boston: Little, Brown, 1962.

SOURCES

Alvarez, Ruth M., and Thomas F. Walsh, eds. *Uncollected Early Prose of Katherine Anne Porter*. Austin: University of Texas Press, 1993.

Bayley. Isabel. ed. *Letters of Katherine Anne Porter*. New York: Atlantic Monthly Press, 1990.

Chandra, Lakshmi. *Katherine Anne Porter: Fiction as History*. New Delhi, India: Arnold, 1992.

Givner, Joan. *Katherine Anne Porter: A Life*. Athens: University of Georgia Press, 1991.

Hardy, J. E. *Katherine Anne Porter*. New York: Ungar, 1973.

Hartley, L. C., and G. Core, eds. *Katherine Anne Porter*. Athens: University of Georgia Press, 1969.

Hendrick, George, and Willene Hendrick. *Katherine Anne Porter*. Rev. ed. Boston: Twayne, 1988.

Hilt, Kathryn, and Ruth M. Alvarez. *Katherine Anne Porter: An Annotated Bibliography*. New York: Garland, 1990.

Machann, Clinton, and William Bedford Clark, eds. *Katherine Anne Porter and Texas: An Uneasy Relationship*. College Station: Texas A & M University Press, 1990.

Stout, Janis P. *Katherine Anne Porter: A Sense of the Times*. Charlottesville: University Press of Virginia, 1995.

———. *Strategies of Reticence: Silence and Meaning in the Works of Jane Austen, Willa Cather, Katherine Anne Porter, and Joan Didion*. Charlottesville: University Press of Virginia, 1990.

Tanner, James T. F. *The Texas Legacy of Katherine Anne Porter*. Denton: University of North Texas Press, 1991.

Unrue, Darlene Harbour. *Understanding Katherine Anne Porter*. Columbia: University of South Carolina Press, 1988.

———, ed. *This Strange, Old World and Other Book Reviews*. Athens: University of Georgia Press, 1991.

Walsh, Thomas F. *Katherine Anne Porter and Mexico: The Illusion of Eden*. Austin: University of Texas Press, 1992.

OTHER

Katherine Porter Library. University of Maryland. University Libraries. Available online. URL: http://www.lib.umd.edu/RARE/SpecialCollection/kap.html. Accessed September 25, 2005.

"Katherine Anne Porter." Available online. URL: http://www.accd.edu/sac/english/mcquien/htmlfils/Kaporter.htm. Accessed January 11, 2006.

PAL: Perspectives in American Literature. Katherine Anne Porter. Available online. URL: http://www.csustan.edu/english/reuben/pal/chap7/porter.html. Accessed September 25, 2005.

Valencia Community College, West Campus LRC. Porter, Katherine Anne. Available online. URL: http://valenciacc.edu/lrcwest/Author_Pathfinders/porter.html. Accessed September 25, 2005.

PORTIS, CHARLES (McCOLL) (1933–)

Although Arkansas-born Charles Portis's reputation rests largely on the best-selling *True Grit* (1968), he wrote several other novels. His first novel was *Norwood* (1966), followed by *The Dog of the South* (1979), *Masters of Atlantis: A Novel* (1985), and *Gringos* (1991). Writing in the picaresque tradition associated with his native Southwest and Mexico, Portis has earned praise from critics who see him not as a regionalist but as a writer who has transformed the contemporary western through the use of parody, comedy, and myth. Influenced by the new journalism of Tom WOLFE and others, he creates restless characters who seek self-definition; they also exact revenge for unforgivable wrongs and demand that justice be enforced in the western wastelands.

Charles McColl Portis was born in El Dorado, Arkansas, on December 28, 1933, to Samuel Portis, a superintendent of public schools, and Alice Waddell Portis. After serving in the U.S. Marine Corps from 1952 to 1955, Portis attended the University of Arkansas. He received his bachelor's degree in journalism in 1958, spent several years writing for newspapers in Tennessee, Arkansas, and New York, where he spent four years with the *New York Herald Tribune* until, in Tom Wolfe's words, Portis "quit cold one day," moved to Arkansas, and six months later published "a beautiful little novel called *Norwood*" (Wolfe, 9). Former Marine Norwood Pratt leaves Texas and goes on the road on a Trailways bus, aiming to collect a debt, and, like Voltaire's Candide or Miguel Cervantes's Don Quixote, encounters hypocrisy and evil as he makes his way to New York City and returns to Arkansas via North Carolina. *True Grit,* set in the 1870s, follows Mattie Ross, the 14-year-old girl whose father, farmer Frank Ross, is shot and killed by Tom Chaney, one of his hired hands. A half century later, Mattie, the Huck Finn–like character who clearly has "true grit," narrates the story of her participation in the murder of Chaney, thereby vindicating her father's murder. In the more overtly comic *The Dog of the South,* Portis focuses on Ray Midge as he follows his wife Norma, who has run off with her former husband to Belize. The novel includes a large cast of comic characters, all encountered by Ray on his quest.

Masters of Atlantis, peopled with such characters as Lamar Jimmerson, another Portis picaresque, and Cezar Golescu, a Hungarian scientist seeking innovative ways to extract gold, and *Gringos,* his most recent novel, demonstrate Portis's increasing attention in his fiction to the seriocomic possibilities of American speech and ideas in the late 20th century. As scholar John L. Idol, Jr., notes, "His ear is as good as Mark TWAIN's or Sinclair LEWIS', his eyes as attentive as those of H. L. Mencken. And his disgust that Americans abuse their tongue is as profound as that of William Safire or Edwin Newman" (Idol, 364). Charles Portis continues to live and write in Little Rock, Arkansas.

NOVELS

The Dog of the South. New York: Knopf, 1979.

Gringos. New York: Simon & Schuster, 1991.

Masters of Atlantis: A Novel. New York: Knopf, 1985.

Norwood. New York: Simon & Schuster, 1966.

True Grit. New York: Simon & Schuster, 1968.

SOURCES

Ditsky, John. "True 'Grit' and '*True Grit,*'" *Ariel* 4, no. 2 (1973): 18–31.

Idol, John L., Jr. "Charles [McColl] Portis." In *Contemporary Fiction Writers of the South: A Bio-bibliographical Critical Sourcebook,* edited by Joseph M. Flora and Robert Bain, 360–370. Westport, Conn.: Greenwood Press, 1993.

Wolfe, Tom. *The New Journalism.* New York: Harper, 1973.

PORTNOY'S COMPLAINT PHILIP ROTH (1969)

Since the late 1980s, Philip ROTH has been redefining himself as a novelist. Beginning with *The Counterlife* (1987), his postmodern tour de force, Roth's narratives have been increasingly ambitious and display an artistry that has far surpassed his earlier works. His autobiographical tetralogy—*The Facts* (1988), *Deception* (1990), *Patrimony* (1991), and *Operation Shylock* (1993)—1995's SABBATH'S THEATER, and his American Trilogy, composed of *American Pastoral* (1997), *I Married a Communist* (1998), and *The Human Stain* (2000), have earned him every major American literary award, not to mention an international standing as one the 20th century's most important novelists. And there is every reason to believe that he is on the short list for the Nobel Prize in literature. Yet as much as his writing has developed, as canonical as his fiction has become, and as many awards and recognitions as he continues to accumulate, many readers still know him solely as the bad boy of American literature, the author of the scandalously hilarious best-seller *Portnoy's Complaint.*

The setup, and the setting, of *Portnoy's Complaint* is straightforward enough: Alexander Portnoy, the Assistant Commissioner of Human Opportunity for the City of New York, is lying on the couch of his psychoanalyst, Dr. O. Spielvogel, describing his many problems with women and relating them to his troubled relationship with his mother. The stereotype of the Jewish mother, as many critics have noted, is perhaps this voluble novel's most celebrated target. The adult Portnoy is desperate to extricate himself from his mother's overbearing, overnurturing, and overanxious grasp, and as such he reverts to adolescent rebellion: "Because to be bad, Mother," he rants at one point, "that's the real struggle; to be bad—and enjoy it! That's what makes men of us boys, Mother." Then follows one of the book's most memorable lines: "LET'S PUT THE ID BACK IN YID!" (123–124). The novel is one long monologue (or kvetch), spoken, significantly enough, out of time—it is uncertain whether or not this is one long therapeutic session or a series of "highlights" spanning several—and structured as a sequence of recollections that are strung together in a free associative manner, suggestive of the psychotherapeutic process.

In many ways it can be read as a modern confessional novel, reminiscent of Albert Camus's *The Fall,* Saul BELLOW's HERZOG, and Nicholson BAKER's *The Fermata,* a form that Roth will return to later in *The Dying Animal* (2001).

In a 1974 essay titled "How Did You Come to Write That Book, Anyway?" Roth narrates the genesis of *Portnoy's Complaint.* In the early manifestations of the novel, he noticed two distinct personality types coming to the fore. The first he calls the "Jewboy," a marginalized yet all-too-curious young man who longs to partake of forbidden fruit, and the other he described as the "nice Jewish boy," the respectable and reliable kind of man whom every mother would be proud to have as her son. Roth admits that both of these figures are largely stereotypes, and he needed a way to blend both of these character types into one protagonist. The result is the hopelessly neurotic Alexander Portnoy.

The gist of Portnoy's spiel (his analyst's name is no accident) revolves around his inability to find emotional as well as sexual satisfaction in his relationships with women, almost all of them shiksas (young non-Jewish women), each one receiving an objectifying, yet comically revealing, nickname. As a young boy he fantasizes about Thereal McCoy (the real McCoy), a slutty and experienced woman—a sexual holy grail to his adolescent imagination—who will satisfy every sexual need, no matter how extravagant or perverse. In his real life there is The Pilgrim, Sarah Abbott Maulsby, the "Supergoy . . . one hundred and fourteen pounds of Republican refinement, and the pertest pair of nipples in all New England" (232, 234), and a woman he sleeps with as revenge against the anti-Semitic gentile establishment. Then there is The Pumpkin, Kay Campbell, a woman whose genteel and reserved upbringing so profoundly contrasts his own. But the most notable, and notorious, woman in Portnoy's life is Mary Jane Reed, The Monkey. She gets her moniker after revealing to Portnoy that she had once watched a couple have sex while eating a banana. She, more than any of the other women in his life, tries to submerge herself thoroughly in Portnoy's identity, and in this way becomes the central Oedipal link of the novel.

Coming as it did at the tail end of the "swinging '60s," many saw *Portnoy's Complaint* as the novelistic embodiment of the freewheeling and sexually liberating decade, helping propel the book to the top of the best-seller lists. With chapter titles such as "Wacking Off" and "The Most Prevalent Form of Degradation in Erotic Life," how could readers thing otherwise? Those in the literary/critical establishment, such as Irving Howe and Norman Podhoretz, were not so amused. They condemned the novel as a base form of entertainment, the "sit-down" version of the abusive, in-your-face comedy found in the stand-up acts of performers such as Lenny Bruce. Howe was particularly unforgiving with Roth. He had been one of Roth's early admirers, seeing in *Goodbye, Columbus* and *Five Short Stories* a promising voice in American literature. But in his (in)famous essay, "Philip Roth Reconsidered," Howe blasted Roth for his adolescent condescension toward Jewish life and culture, especially the postwar suburban variety. What is more, he believed that novels such as *Portnoy's Complaint* lacked world-historic amplitude due to its immersion in the author's superficial cultural experience and his angry, overly aggressive need to score comic points in the literary marketplace. (Eleven years after Howe's critical attack, Roth would get his revenge through a literary surrogate. In *The Anatomy Lesson,* novelist Nathan Zuckerman, outraged at literary/cultural critic Milton Appel for an unforgivingly scathing review, gets even with his nemesis by assuming Appel's name in public and claiming that he is the publisher of the pornographic magazine *Lickety Split* and owner of the swinging sex club Milton's Millennia.) The novel has also been condemned as a blatant exercise in literary chauvinism, and many have argued that the women in *Portnoy's Complaint*—indeed, the women in most of Roth's work—are nothing more than objectified and demeaning caricatures. Largely because of this novel, charges of misogyny have followed Roth throughout his career (although these attacks have been greatly tempered since the 1990s).

Regardless of how *Portnoy's Complaint* is read—as misogynistic rant, as literary masturbation, or as Jewish vernacular masterpiece—one cannot deny the comedic power behind the novel. Even detractors, although they might not admit it, probably laugh out loud when they read about Portnoy's dysfunctional family, his adoles-

cent experiences in the bathroom, the hand job session with 18-year-old Bubbles Girardi, and the imagination he demonstrates with raw liver. But underlying the laughs, as with all great comedy, is a bitterness longing to be expressed. "Doctor Spielvogel," Portnoy pleads early in the novel, "this is my life, my only life, and I'm living it in the middle of a Jewish joke! I am the son in the Jewish joke—only it ain't no joke! Please, who crippled us like this? . . . [W]hy, alone on my bed in New York, why am I still hopelessly beating my meat?" (35). As readers of Philip Roth well know, humor born of pain is a hallmark of his fiction and one that he uses with sheer exploitive brilliance.

SOURCES

Bettelheim, Bruno. "Portnoy Psychoanalyzed," *Midstream* 15 (1969): 3–10.

Bloom, Harold, ed. *Portnoy's Complaint: Modern Critical Interpretations.* New York: Chelsea House, 2004.

Brauner, David. "Masturbation and Its Discontents, or, Serious Relief: Freudian Comedy in *Portnoy's Complaint*," *Critical Review* 40 (2000): 75–90.

Cohen, Eileen Z. "Alex in Wonderland, or *Portnoy's Complaint*," *Twentieth-Century Literature* 17 (1971): 161–168.

Gross, Barry. "Seduction of the Innocent: *Portnoy's Complaint* and Popular Culture," *MELUS* 8, no. 4 (1981): 81–92.

Howe, Irving. "Philip Roth Reconsidered," *Commentary,* December 1972, pp. 69–77.

Podhoretz, Norman. "Laureate of the New Class," *Commentary,* December 1972, pp. 4–7.

Roth, Philip. "How Did You Come to Write That Book, Anyway?" In *Reading Myself and Others,* 33–41. Expanded edition. New York: Penguin, 1985.

———. *Portnoy's Complaint.* New York: Random, 1969.

Royal, Derek Parker, ed. *Philip Roth: New Perspectives on an American Author.* Westport, Conn.: Praeger, 2005.

Workman, Mark E. "The Serious Consequences of Ethnic Humor in *Portnoy's Complaint*," *Midwest Folklore* 13, no. 7 (1987): 16–26.

Derek P. Royal

PORTRAIT OF A LADY, THE HENRY JAMES (1881)

Considered one of Henry JAMES's best novels, as well as one of his most popular, *The Portrait of a Lady* raises many questions for contemporary readers. Whereas Isabel Archer appears to herald the "new woman," she makes choices that relegate her to the old

Victorian standards of marriage and propriety. Though American, she is a lady formed not through birth but through hardship. Although this novel marks James's development of stronger female protagonists, Isabel Archer does not tell her own story. The novel commences with Ralph Touchett, Mr. Touchett, and Lord Warburton anticipating her arrival and speculating upon what kind of woman she might be. Throughout the novel, the omniscient narrator maintains an insightful distance from the heroine and controls her psychological portrait just as her fellow characters convey her physical portrait.

One of the main themes involves freedom and its dangers. Early in the narrative Isabel values her freedom to choose, even if she makes the wrong choice. Having been orphaned at the death of her father, Isabel finds herself "rescued" by an unconventional aunt, Mrs. Touchett, a women who is more than willing to give Isabel the space to make her own acquaintances. Her husband, retired banker Mr. Touchett, seems the exact opposite of Isabel's late father, a man who squandered his wealth and kept no permanent home. The Touchetts are Americans abroad, and their son Ralph has adopted all the mannerisms of the European. His invalid state provides him with freedom from the demands of the American Protestant work ethic, and he revels in the role of connoisseur. Ralph discovers too late that art's values do not correspond with human values; in fact, most of the characters scrutinize each other as if they were subtle and complex paintings to understand and manipulate. Upon meeting Isabel, Ralph decides that his observation of her is even more important than the possibility of love. He perceives her as a masterpiece in progress—the new woman of initiative, cleverness, and perceptiveness—and upon his father's death provides her with the financial means to live independently and determine her own course.

Although Isabel is perceived as the perfect "specimen" by her circle, she finds herself misled by her own independence and willfulness. Despite her financial independence, she is not freed from the Victorian pressures of marriage and family. She is pursued by Lord Warburton and staunch, severe, ambitious Caspar Goodwood, who continues his suit even after her marriage to Gilbert Osmond. Whereas Isabel imagines that she is choosing an educated refined husband, she is actually falling into a trap set by Mme Serena Merle, who wishes to provide for her illegitimate daughter, Pansy. Ralph's generous gift of his inheritance "only serve[s] to usher Isabel into the old father-daughter marriage after all" (Habegger, 176). In James's European society, women can only retain their freedom by knowing and comprehending the subtext with all its secrets and obscured details.

With Osmond, Isabel comes to see that art does not equal life. Osmond's refinement makes him cold and calculating. His psychological games seek to enslave Isabel's mind; in fact, he achieves this with his daughter Pansy, whom he considers his living work of art, the perfect daughter. Only toward the end of the novel does Pansy reveal her awareness of this tortured existence. Unlike the long-suffering daughter, Isabel is able to abandon Rome for Gardencourt, honesty, and Ralph, if only temporarily. The conclusion of the novel shows her turning her back on the possibility of freedom from the consequences of her mistakes and turning toward duty.

Some critics indict James as a writer who could never escape his father's authoritarian point of view, one that included negative opinions of women. James created a female protagonist who possesses all the advantages and characteristics admired during her age, yet she still suffers from poor choices, is manipulated, loses her wealth to a husband, and tethers herself to a Victorian sense of duty. Having lost their fathers, both Isabel and Ralph display an obsession with the image of father, and this image cripples them to lives that are ordinary and inactive. Like Ralph, James was a passive connoisseur of people. According to critic Alfred Habegger, *The Portrait of a Lady* reveals less about a woman caught between Victorian and turn-of-the-century society, American and European, than about "James's indirect engagement with his father's authoritarianism—the authoritarianism that had sent Alice [his sister] to spend a winter with an antifeminist physician specializing in women's troubles just as Osmond sends Pansy back to the convent" (Habegger, 179). Like the character Isabel Archer, James's cousin Minnie Temple exhibited to his eyes a "brilliant potential [that came] to nothing," and his portrait ends as a "refusal to imagine that his cousin could have survived on her own terms" (Habegger, 181). James's pessimistic conclusion exposes his own disheartened view of the women in his life and his own inability to escape his father's control.

SOURCES

Allen, Elizabeth. *A Woman's Place in the Novels of Henry James.* New York: St. Martin's, 1984.

Blackmur, R. P. *Studies in Henry James.* New York: New Directions, 1983.

Cameron, Sharon. *Thinking in Henry James.* Chicago: University of Chicago Press, 1989.

Chapman, Sara S. *Henry James's Portrait of the Writer as Hero.* New York: St. Martin's, 1989.

Edel, Leon. *Henry James: A Life.* New York: Harper, 1985.

Fowler, Virginia C. *Henry James's American Girl: The Embroidery on the Canvas.* Madison: University of Wisconsin Press, 1984.

Fussell, Edwin Sill. *The French Side of Henry James.* New York: Columbia University Press, 1990.

Griffin, Susan M. *The Historical Eye: The Texture of the Visual in Late James.* Boston: Northeastern University Press, 1991.

Habegger, Alfred. *Henry James and the "Woman Business."* New York: Cambridge University Press, 1989.

Porte, Joel, ed. *New Essays on The Portrait of a Lady.* New York: Cambridge University Press, 1990.

Walton, Priscilla. *The Disruption of the Feminine in Henry James.* Toronto: University of Toronto Press, 1992.

Kerri A. Horrine

POSTMAN ALWAYS RINGS TWICE, THE

JAMES M. CAIN (1934) *The Postman* is the first and by far the most famous novel by this prolific and popular specialist in hard-boiled or "tough guy" fiction. The well-known plot was literally "torn from the headlines"—not for nothing did Edmund Wilson call James CAIN and his school the "poets of the tabloid murder" (Wilson, 21). In 1927 Cain, then a successful newspaperman, followed with interest the sensational trial of one Ruth Snyder and her lover, Henry Judd Gray, who were eventually found guilty and executed for the murder of Snyder's husband. The case fascinated the media and the public: Snyder and Judd seemed to reflect the tenor of the times, the illusory promises of the era twisted into frightening spectacles of lust and violence. As William Marling has suggested, the press saw them

"not as criminals but representative products of the Jazz age" (Marling, 152). Cain's 1934 novel borrows a great deal from the Snyder-Gray case, folding in many of his own ideas about romantic obsession and a bleak fatalism that he saw as endemic to American experience.

Narrator Frank Chambers begins the novel (retrospectively spoken, we later learn, as a death-row confession) by dropping off a California hay truck and walking into the Twin Oaks Tavern, "nothing but a roadside sandwich joint" (1). At first sight, Frank and Cora Papadakis, the owner's young wife, realize they share an intense, animal-like passion. And within a very few clipped, intense pages they have become lovers, taking advantage of her husband Nick's blind good nature (and his need for another hand at Twin Oaks) to initiate a stormy affair. With an eerie sense of their own unavoidable destiny, Frank and Cora hatch a plan to kill "the Greek"—an overelaborate scheme that comes to nothing, with Nick wounded but unsuspecting, and Frank prudently headed for Los Angeles. Yet, as even Frank seems to understand, this is not, indeed cannot be, the end of the story. Through an uncanny series of coincidences, Frank is lured back to Twin Oaks, Cora, and thoughts of murder. The second attempt is successful—not so much because of better planning or luck, but through the subtle legal machinations of their lawyer, Katz, who works out an ingenious courtroom maneuver that springs the two murderers.

Once freed, though, Frank and Cora are thrown back on themselves, forced to deal with the fact that under the pressure of possible punishment for their crime, both had been willing to betray the other. And yet Frank and Cora feel helpless in the face of their mutual fate: Rather than separate or seek a new life elsewhere, they doggedly pursue a "better life" at Twin Oaks, using Nick's insurance money to transform the sandwich joint into a roadside beer garden, marrying, and even conceiving a child. Even so, both seem to doubt their chances of making a go of it in the straight world. Their intimations of doom turn out to be well grounded when, in yet another bitterly ironic twist, Cora is killed in a genuine car accident, and Frank is sentenced to death not for his real crimes, but for this senseless tragedy. Cain's narrative works with the inexorable logic of a nightmare destiny; every line betrays what Joyce Carol OATES calls the "iron pattern of necessity" (Oates, 111).

Much of the plot outlined above derives directly from Cain's thoughts on the 1927 murder case, yet his conception of the novel goes beyond a retelling of that sordid story. By 1933, when he began work on *Postman,* Cain added at least two new, but crucial, elements. First, the New York crime was transferred to the strange California landscape that fascinated so many tough-guy writers, like Raymond CHANDLER or Horace McCoy. The change of locale is crucial, as it reflects so well the many ambivalences at work in the novel. California can offer immense rewards, like the tantalizing promise that brought Cora all the way from Iowa in search of stardom in the movies. Yet the novel's California is also essentially false and treacherous, a landscape of plenty wrested at great cost from the desert, a land of promise that turns to nightmare (Nyman, 85). Second, Cain emphasizes the unavoidable specter of the Depression, which lends the narrative a new sense of socioeconomic desperation. Gray had been a married, relatively conventional traveling salesman, a man who had bought into the Jazz Age's American promise of prosperity; Frank Chambers in *Postman* is a Depression-era bum, a man who has cheerfully opted out of the game. It is only when he comes into contact with Cora that Frank is reconnected to networks of desire and economics.

Cain's reworking of the murder victim is also suggestive. Albert Snyder had been an unassuming middle-class suburban New York magazine editor. Cain reimagines him as Nick Papadakis, Greek immigrant, naive aspirant to the American Dream—an innocent victim that Frank, even after the murder, cannot help but remember fondly. The novel's depiction of Nick is contradictory. On the one hand, he is unquestionably the injured party: He invites Frank into his home and his business, and is cuckolded, injured, and eventually murdered for his open-hearted generosity. Then, too, Nick is obliquely shown to be part of a genuine and living immigrant Greek subculture. His scrapbook features items on his "accident" (the first murder attempt) from the local Greek newspaper, and at his funeral there is a real sense of his friends and community rallying around a fallen comrade. Yet everything we know of Nick is filtered through Frank's narration. Thus, Nick is mostly reduced to either Cora's virulently racist distaste for his "greasy hair," his nights filled with romantic Greek folk songs and sweet Greek wines, or Frank's syrupy sentimental blubbering at his funeral. This strange contradiction—routine racism and romanticized nostalgia—is a common one in *Postman.* It shows up again in the motif of Mexico and points further south, both locus of the threatening other (Cora is insistent that her dark hair doesn't make her "Mex") and paradoxically Frank's destination of choice when he temporarily flees the uncomfortable reality of life with Cora. His idyll down south is a desperate bid to reclaim some of the freedom he has lost. But it is doomed to failure, a fact he recognizes himself: "It came to me then that Nicaragua wouldn't be quite far enough" (83).

The ambiguous status of the "foreign" in the novel stands as only one of Cain's more striking uncertainties. *Postman* has always drawn a strangely mixed reception, with critics alternately fascinated and repelled by its calculatedly lurid, sexually charged minimalism. Edmund Wilson (writing in 1940) approaches the novel as an ivory tower aesthete curious about what "people" are actually reading. Joyce Carol Oates admits that it may be interesting but is not "art," and considers it most significant as a link between 19th-century realism and 20th-century existentialism (with Albert Camus's *The Stranger* explicitly inspired by Cain's novel). There remains a certain unease as regards *Postman:* To what extent is Cain analyzing, or simply reflecting, the violence of American life? This perhaps unanswerable question lies at the heart of the novel's fascination—we read Cain today with the sure knowledge that his nightmare narrative, with its refusal to judge, psychologize, or contextualize the crimes it depicts, has touched on the very quintessence of modernity.

SOURCES

Bradbury, Richard. "Sexuality, Guilt and Detection: Tension Between History and Suspense." In *American Crime Fiction: Studies in the Genre,* edited by Brian Docherty. New York: St. Martin's Press, 1988.

Cain, James M. *"The Postman Always Rings Twice."* In *Cain x 3,* 1–100. New York: Alfred A. Knopf, 1969.

Madden, David. *James M. Cain.* Boston: Twayne, 1970.

Marling, William. *The American Roman Noir: Hammett, Cain and Chandler.* Athens: University of Georgia Press, 1995.

Nyman, Jopi. *Hard-Boiled Fiction and Dark Romanticism.* Frankfurt, Germany: Peter Lang, 1998.

Oates, Joyce Carol. "Man under Sentence of Death: The Novels of James M. Cain." In *Tough-Guy Writers of the Thirties,* edited by David Madden, 110–128. Carbondale: Southern Illinois University Press, 1968.

Wilson, Edmund. "The Boys in the Back Room." In *Classics and Commercials,* edited by David Costronovo. New York: Farrar, Straus & Giroux, 1950.

Andy Miller

POTOK, CHAIM (1929–2002)

Chaim Potok, novelist and ordained rabbi, is known particularly for *The* CHOSEN (1967), winner of the National Book Award, and for *The Gift of Asher Lev,* winner of the 1997 Jewish National Book Award. He writes about real and unending tensions between secular and observant Jews, between the modern world and the world of tradition, between a yearning for art or secular higher education and a genuinely pious attachment to Orthodox Judaism, which rejects that training. In Potok's hands, the conflicts between deeply held convictions inform and educate readers, who are often captivated, at the same time, by the author's artistry.

Chaim Potok was born Herman Harold Potok on February 17, 1929, to Benjamin Max Potok, a businessman, and Mollie Friedman Potok. (His parents also gave him the name Chaim Tzvi, meaning "life.") He was educated at Yeshiva University, where he earned his bachelor's degree, summa cum laude, in 1950. At the Jewish Theological seminary, he received a master's in Hebrew literature (1954), and at the University of Pennsylvania he was awarded a doctoral degree in 1965. He served as a chaplain with the U.S. Army in Korea from 1956 to 1957, and married Adena Sarah Mosevitzky in 1958. Potok's first novel, *The Chosen,* is about two boys: Danny Saunders, a Hasidic rabbi's son, and Reuven Malter, whose Orthodox family takes a more rational, less mystical approach to religious issues and exhibits a more loving bond between father and son. Potok's second novel, *The Promise* (1969), follows Danny and Reuven into maturity. Potok approaches the conflict directly in *My Name Is Asher Lev* (1972); Lev is a gifted youth who wishes to become an artist, but his Hasidic family objects to such a self-indulgent calling and associates it with both Christianity and unrestrained modern impulses. Lev reappears 20 years later in *The Gift of Asher Lev* (1990) as a successful artist living in the South of France. When a death in the family calls him back to the United States, he becomes embroiled again in the old conflicts between the worldly and the religious and must again make a choice—and a sacrifice.

Narrated by the young David Lurie, *In the Beginning* (1975), Potok's fourth novel, extends outward from the Jewish community into the gentile and depicts the conflicts between the two religions as well as between the sacred and the secular, conflicts composed of the intensely complex issues of a post-Holocaust world. In *The Book of Lights* (1981), Potok creates two young men, Arthur Leiden and Gershon Loran. Leiden has withdrawn from his university-level study of physics after learning of his father's participation in the production of the atom bomb. Gershon Loran is a rabbinical student who is questioning his religious path. The two travel together to Japan; when Arthur dies, Gershon, despite and because of the uncertainty of modern life, chooses the life of a Jewish scholar. *Davita's Harp* (1985) uses by now typical Potok concerns and themes, this time through the half-Jewish, half-Christian Lisa Schwarzbaum, Potok's first major female character. She chooses to live as a Jew but sees the conflict with her desires as a modern woman. Potok's final novel, *I Am the Clay* (1992), changes locales. Set during the Korean War, Potok introduces an elderly Korean couple who brave enemy fire in order to protect the orphan they have adopted.

In 1982, *The Chosen* was produced as a feature-length film starring Robbie Benson, Maximilian Schell, Rod Steiger, and Barry Miller. It was also adapted as a musical for the stage that opened in New York City, December 17, 1987.

Chaim Potok died of brain cancer on July 23, 2002, in Merion, Pennsylvania.

NOVELS

The Book of Lights. New York: Knopf, 1981.
The Chosen. New York: Simon & Schuster, 1967.
Davita's Harp. New York: Knopf, 1985.

The Gift of Asher Lev. New York: Knopf, 1990.

I Am the Clay. New York: Knopf, 1992.

In the Beginning. New York: Knopf, 1975.

My Name Is Asher Lev. New York: Knopf, 1972.

The Promise. New York: Knopf, 1969.

SOURCES

Abramson, Edward A. *Chaim Potok.* Boston: Twayne, 1986.

Bluefarb, Sam. "The Head, the Heart, and the Conflict of Generations in Chaim Potok's *The Chosen,*" *College Language Association Journal* 14 (June 1971): 402–409.

Bookspan, Martin. "A Conversation with Chaim Potok," in *The Eternal Light,* no. 1453, transcript of NBC Radio Network broadcast. November 22, 1981. New York: Jewish Theological Seminary of America, 1981.

Fagerheim, Cynthia. "A Bibliographic Essay," *Studies in American Jewish Literature* 4 (1985): 107–120.

Field, Leslie. "Chaim Potok and the Critics: Sampler From a Consistent Spectrum," *Studies in American Jewish Literature* 4 (1985): 3–12.

Herstein, Wendy. "An Interview with Chaim Potok," *The World & I* (August 1992): 309–313.

Kauvar, Elaine. "An Interview with Chaim Potok," *Contemporary Literature* 27 (Fall 1986): 291–317.

Kipen, Aviva. "The Odyssey of Asher Lev," *Jewish Quarterly* (Spring 1993): 1–5.

Kremer, S. Lillian. "Interview With Chaim Potok, July 21, 1981," *Studies in American Jewish Literature* 4 (1984): 84–99.

———. "Encountering the Other," *The World & I* (August 1992): 315–325.

Margolies, Edward. "Chaim Potok's *Book of Lights* and the Jewish American Novel," *Yiddish* 6, no. 4 (1987): 93–98.

Marovitz, Sanford. "*The Book of Lights:* Jewish Mysticism in the Shadow of the Bomb," *Studies in American Jewish Literature* 4 (1985): 62–83.

———. "Freedom, Faith, and Fanaticism: Cultural Conflict in the Novels of Chaim Potok," *Studies in American Jewish Literature* 5 (1986): 129–140.

Pinsker, Sanford. "The Crucifixion of Chaim Potok/The Excommunication of Asher Lev: Art and the Hasidic World," *Studies in American Jewish Literature* 4 (1985): 39–51.

Purcell, William F. "Potok's Fathers and Sons," *Studies in American Literature* 26 (1989): 75–92.

Ribalow, Harold. "Chaim Potok." In *The Tie That Binds: Conversations with Jewish Writers.* New York: Barnes, 1980.

Uffen, Ellen. "*My Name Is Asher Lev:* Chaim Potok's Portrait of the Young Hasid as Artist," *Studies in American Jewish Literature* 2 (1982): 174–180.

Walden, Daniel. "Chaim Potok: A *Zwischenmensch* ('Between-Person') Adrift in the Cultures," *Studies in American Jewish Literature* 4 (1985): 19–25.

Wisse, Ruth. "Jewish Dreams," *Commentary* 73 (March 1982): 45–48.

OTHER

Chaim Potok. Available online. URL: http://www.lasierra.edu/~ballen/potok/Potok.menu.html. Accessed September 25, 2005.

Silver, Elizabeth. "Silent Territory: Author Chaim Potok Maps His Past through His Writing." Jvibe. Available online. URL: http://www.jvibe.com/popculture/Potok.shtml. Accessed September 25, 2005.

POWELL, DAWN (1896–1965) Dawn Powell wrote more than 100 stories and 16 novels that were set in either small Ohio towns or in New York City. Her New York novels include *A Time to Be Born* (1942) and *The Locusts Have No King* (1948), which one reviewer believes "deserve to be on a short list of the best comic novels in American literature" (Weiner, 23). Although Powell never gained the recognition many of her admirers feel she deserved, all her works were reprinted in a two-volume Library of America edition in the 1990s, placing Powell, in the view of a *Library Journal* reviewer, "among the gods" (Rogers, 160). Powell excelled at combining humor with observations about the subtle influence of social class.

Dawn Powell was born on August 24, 1896, in Mount Gilead, Ohio, to Roy K. Powell, a traveling salesman, and Hattie B. Sherman Powell, who died when Powell was very young. After her father married a harsh and cruel woman, Powell ran away to live with her mother's sister. She earned her bachelor's degree at Lake Erie College in 1918 and that same year served in New York with the United States Naval Reserve Communications Service. She lived in Greenwich Village, married advertising executive Joseph Gousha, and published her first novel, *Whither,* in 1925. It is set in her native Ohio, as is the better known *The Bride's House* (1929), which takes place on the Midwest farm of the Truelove family. Here Sophie Truelove experiences marriage and adultery. Her sister, Mary Cecily, is the artist figure. The other Ohio novels include *She Walks in Beauty* (1928), *Dance Night* (1930), *The Tenth*

Moon (1932), *Jig Saw, a Comedy* (1934), and *The Story of a Country Boy* (1934).

Her New York novels begin with *Turn, Magic Wheel* (1936). *The Happy Island* (1938), one of Powell's memorable works, depicts the lives of Prudence Bly, a nightclub performer, and James Pinckney, one of Greenwich Village's gay and artistic residents. The follies of show business and literary types are viewed through Powell's satiric lens. *Angels on Toast* (1940), probably Powell's best-known novel, features New Yorker Ebie Vane, who is uncertain about love and marriage. Through her, Powell presents New Yorkers in the mood for extramarital dalliances. *The Wicked Pavilion* (1954), set mainly in the fictional Café Julien, depicts a New York café crowd. *The Golden Spur* (1962) describes Ohioan Jonathan Jaimison's odyssey through the 1950s Greenwich Village world of abstract-expressionist artists. Her last novel, *A Cage for Lovers*, appeared in 1957. She died on November 15, 1965, in New York City.

NOVELS

Angels on Toast. New York: Scribner, 1940. Revised version published as *A Man's Affair*. New York: Fawcett, 1956.

The Bride's House. New York: Brentano, 1929.

A Cage for Lovers. Boston: Houghton, 1957.

Dance Night. New York: Farrar & Rinehart, 1930.

The Golden Spur. New York: Viking, 1962.

The Happy Island. New York: Farrar & Rinehart, 1938.

Jig Saw, a Comedy. New York: Farrar & Rinehart, 1934.

The Locusts Have No King. New York: Scribner, 1948.

My Home Is Far Away. New York: Scribner, 1944.

She Walks in Beauty. New York: Brentano's, 1928.

The Story of a Country Boy. New York: Farrar & Rinehart, 1934.

The Tenth Moon. New York: Farrar & Rinehart, 1932.

A Time to Be Born. New York: Scribner, 1942.

Turn, Magic Wheel. New York: Farrar & Rinehart, 1936.

The Wicked Pavilion. Boston: Houghton, 1954.

Whither. Boston: Small, Maynard, 1925.

SOURCES

Josephson, Matthew. "Dawn Powell: A Woman of Esprit," *Southern Review* (Winter 1973): 18–52.

Page, Tim. *Dawn Powell: A Biography*. New York: Holt, 1998.

Powell, Dawn. *The Diaries of Dawn Powell, 1931–1965*. Edited by Tim Page. South Royalton, Vt.: Steerforth Press, 1995.

———. *Selected Letters of Dawn Powell, 1913–1965*. Edited by Tim Page. New York: Holt, 1999.

Rogers, Michael. Review of *The Novels of Dawn Powell*, *Library Journal* 127, no. 1 (January 2002), 160.

Van Gelder, Robert. *Writers and Writing*. New York: Scribner, 1946.

Weiner, Lauren, "Dawn Powell: the Fruits of Revival," *New Criterion* 17, no. 10 (June 1999), 23.

OTHER

Brownrigg, Sylvia. Review of *Dawn Powell: A Biography*. Salon. com. Available online. URL: http://www.salon.com/books/sneaks/1998/11/13sneaks.html. Accessed September 25, 2005.

POWER, SUSAN (1961–)

Although she is often compared to Louise ERDRICH, Susan Power has a unique and graceful vision. She won the Ernest Hemingway Foundation award for *The GRASS DANCER* (1994), the story of the South Dakota Sioux from the 1860s to the 1980s. Her characters—old and young, living and dead, male and female—move back and forth through time; as numerous critics have noted, most of her self-reliant and capable characters are women. She has been especially praised for her creation of such memorable, original characters as Pumpkin, the grass dancer; Red Dress and Ghost Horse, the ancestors whose ghosts haunt the contemporary characters; and the magic-practicing Mercury Thunder and her daughter Anna Thunder.

A member of the Sioux nation, Susan Power was born on October 12, 1961, in Chicago to Carleton Gilmore Power, a grandson of the Civil War–era New Hampshire governor, and Susan Kelly Power (a.k.a. Gathering of Storm Clouds Woman), descendant of the Sioux Chief Mata Nupa (Two Bears). She earned a bachelor's degree from Harvard/Radcliffe, a law degree from Harvard University Law School, and a master of fine arts degree from the University of Iowa. The ghost-filled novel *The Grass Dancer*, published to excellent critical responses, tells the tales of the Sioux people, alternating among the present, the Civil War, and essential moments in between.

Power is reportedly working on a novel called *The Strong Heart Society*. Set in Chicago, it was to be about three Native Americans—a South Dakota Sioux, a

Vietnam veteran, and a powwow princess. The novel has not yet been published.

NOVEL

The Grass Dancer. New York: Putnam, 1994.

SOURCES

Botrhner, Amy Bunting. "Changeable Pasts: Re-Inventing History," *DAIA* 5149, vol. 57, no. 12, Sec. A. (1997) (Pittsburgh University).

Shapiro, Dani. "Spirit in the Sky: Talking with Susan Power," *People Weekly* 42, no. 6 (August 8, 1994): 21–22.

Walter, Roland. "Pan-American (Re) Visions: Magical Realism and Amerindian Cultures in Susan Power's *The Grass Dancer,* Gioconda Belli's *La Mujer Habitada,* Linda Hogan's *Power,* and Mario Varas Llosa's *El Hablador,*" *American Studies International* (AsInt) 37, no. 3 (1999): 63–80.

Wright, Neil H. "Visitors from the Spirit Path: Tribal Magic in Susan Power's *The Grass Dancer,*" *Kentucky Philological Review* 10 (1995): 39–43.

OTHER

Power, Susan. Interview by Shari Oslos. Voices From the Gaps [VG]. Available online. URL: http://voices.cla.umn.edu/newsite/authors/POWERsusan.htm. Accessed September 25, 2005.

POWER OF SYMPATHY, THE William Hill Brown (1789)

The Power of Sympathy by William Hill Brown is considered the first novel by an American-born writer in the United States. First published anonymously, *The Power of Sympathy* is an example of sentimental romance written in epistolary form. The letters illustrate a dialogue between Harrington and Worthy, two young men who both have a love interest; Harrington has fallen in love with Harriot, who is beautiful and virtuous, but poor and beneath Harrington's station in life, and Worthy is engaged to Harrington's sister, Myra. Myra and Harriot are also friends, and their exchange of letters communicates Harriot's dilemma of maintaining her virtue, even though her poverty makes the prospect of marriage to Harrington unlikely. A family friend of the Harrington's, Mrs. Holmes, functions as a fifth correspondent who imparts wisdom on moral matters as well as providing the information for the story's surprising twist.

The novel reflects early American interest in the role of women as both the representatives and the safe-keepers of the country's moral health. It illustrates sexual temptation, portrays the disastrous effects of succumbing to seduction, and discusses ways for the young girl to avoid such a fate. While highly didactic, warning against sexual profligacy in both men and women, the novel also takes on a sympathetic tone toward the seducer and the fallen woman, and like similar novels of the day in America (*The Coquette, Charlotte Temple*), it urges the community to view the repentant sinner with compassion.

Harrington's original attempt to seduce Harriot and set her up as his mistress is first admonished by Worthy, who vehemently condemns Harrington's plan as childish (lacking contemplation and reason) and ignoble. Harrington first resists his friend's "dull sermons," arguing that Harriot is an orphan with no money or social status, and Harrington himself is "not so much a republican as formally to wed any person of this class" (11). But Harrington recants when confronted with Harriot's unwavering virtue. Like Pamela in the novel of that name by English author Samuel Richardson, Harriot is able to convince Harrington of her inestimable value through her unwavering good conduct and virtue. Eventually, Harrington is convinced she should be his wife, and they are engaged.

Harrington's change of heart illustrates the novel's concern with republican values structured upon a meritocracy. As seen in Harriot's case, a young woman can rise socially through marriage if she embodies those qualities prized in a wife and mother: virtue, beauty (a reflection of her virtue), and education. Yet the major theme of the novel considers the fate of men and women who fall in seduction's grip. This can further be seen in several additional subplots told within the framing of letters. The first describes the fate of Ophelia, who is seduced by her sister's husband and, when the affair is discovered, commits suicide. The second involves the story of a young man who also ends his life after learning that his fiancée has been captured by ruffians and assuming that she is dead. When she is found and returned unharmed, her betrothed is already dead. The third minor story presented narrates the fate of Miss Whitman, a young woman whose reading of romance leads her to reject several reasonable offers of marriage because no suitor could live up to her romantic ideal. When faced with becoming an old maid, she becomes more susceptible to seduction, has an affair, and becomes pregnant. Her fate is tragic. In the advanced stages of pregnancy she takes residence at an inn, and dies there shortly after giving birth to a stillborn child.

We know that two of the stories, Ophelia and of Miss Whitman, are based on fact—the latter is told without the use of pseudonym and provides the framework for Hannah FOSTER's novel *The Coquette*. The inclusion of these stories, especially that of Miss Whitman, a young lady whose head was turned by reading too many romances, illustrates the great effort made in *The Power of Sympathy,* a novel about romance and sexuality itself, to recoup a place for reading fiction by using the genre as a method for exploring the moral and social problems of the day. The novel reflects upon ways to instill virtue through reading, while addressing the culturally perceived dangers of reading fiction. Miss Whitman's story is told for the very purpose of warning against the dangers of reading when Mrs. Bourne asks others to what books should she direct her 14-year-old daughter. Mrs. Holmes, the narrator of this discussion, finds Mrs. Bourne tiresome and overly obsequious. Her daughter reflects the character weaknesses of her mother. Miss Bourn is tolerably beautiful but not striking, well dressed but not to her best advantage, and she lacks the polished manner of a truly virtuous lady. Better guidance from her mother— or perhaps, reading the right books—would correct these faults in the daughter.

The plot of Brown's novel takes an interesting twist when Harrington and Harriot do avoid the pitfalls of seduction, yet are not rewarded for their virtue. Through Mrs. Holmes another minor but crucial story is conveyed that implicates Harrington's father and Maria Fawcet, Harriot's mother. Just days before they plan to marry, Mrs. Holmes reveals to the young couple that they are in fact brother and sister. Harriot is the bastard child of Mr. Harrington. Both Harriot and Harrington are devastated by the knowledge that, because they are siblings, they cannot marry. The father, Mr. Harrington, shows true penitence for his sins of youth but cannot relieve the suffering of his son or newly acknowledged daughter. The son falls into a deep depression and the daughter's health fails quickly. Harrington's and Harriot's last letters convey a psychological complexity that illustrates the emotional crisis caused by a romantic love that has suddenly been rendered incestuous.

The closing message of the novel is a clear one: Not only does seduction destroy those involved, but in its aftermath—children with nameless fathers—incest becomes a greater possibility. The cultural preoccupations of *The Power of Sympathy,* the significance of chastity, education, and name for the future wives and mothers of the new nation were of central importance at the end of the 18th century. Brown's novel brings into focus that this is especially true in a society that allows freer marriage between the social classes, where the orphaned girl can marry a man of station.

SOURCES

Brown, Herbert Ross. *The Sentimental Novel in America, 1789–1860.* Durham, N.C.: Duke University Press, 1949.

Davidson, Cathy. *Revolution and the Word: The Rise of the Novel in America.* New York: Oxford University Press, 1986.

Mulford, Carla. Introduction to *The Power of Sympathy and The Coquette.* New York: Penguin Classics, 1996.

Rebecca C. Potter

PRAYER FOR OWEN MEANY, A JOHN IRVING (1989)

A Prayer for Owen Meany, John IRVING's seventh novel, was published in 1989. Unlike his other novels, it does not contain Vienna, Bears, or rapes. However, like many of his other novels, the narrator and main character's name is Johnny. Johnny Wheelwright is plagued throughout his childhood and adolescence by not knowing who his biological father is. He is raised, for the most part, by his mother, Tabitha Wheelwright, and his grandmother. Owen Meany, a little person with an unusual voice (his dialogue is written in all capital letters), accidentally kills Johnny's mother when he hits a foul ball that strikes her head. Despite this tragedy, Owen and Johnny are best friends. Owen helps Johnny discover who his real father is, and Johnny helps Owen fulfill his destiny as "the instrument of God" he believes he is.

Throughout the novel, there are a number of "signs" that the boys must interpret. In several of Irving's novels, there are phrases repeated throughout; however, in *A Prayer for Owen Meany* images are repeated. When Owen accidentally kills Johnny's mom, Dan Needham, Johnny's stepfather, helps Johnny remember that Owen loved Tabitha as a surrogate mother, since his own mother is emotionally distant. Johnny gives Owen his stuffed armadillo, and Owen returns it with no arms, showing his helplessness and regret for having hit the ball, as Dan explains. The armless figure is repeated throughout the novel, although its significance changes. The first armless figure is actually the totem of the Indian tribe that sells Johnny's ancestors the land on which Gravesend, the town in which they live, is eventually built. The figure appears again after Tabitha's death in her dressmaker's dummy, which Owen mistakes for the ghost of Tabitha. Upon being expelled from the Gravesend Academy as a teenager, Owen places the school's statue of Mary Magdalene minus her arms on the auditorium's stage; however, this time the figure symbolizes hypocrisy more than it symbolizes helplessness. The final armless figure is Owen himself, who loses his arms in fulfilling his duty as an instrument of God.

Owen sees his destiny and death in a vision he has while playing the Ghost of Christmas Future in *A Christmas Carol*. In the scene where he is supposed to show Ebenezer Scrooge his grave, Owen sees his own name and date of death on the tombstone instead of Ebenezer Scrooge's. Owen envisions himself saving Vietnamese children and sees Johnny there as well. Thus, Owen trains to be able to join the service to fulfill his destiny and cuts off Johnny's index finger to protect him from serving. Owen also prepares for being God's instrument by practicing "the shot" with Johnny for years. Owen runs up to Johnny with a basketball, and Johnny lifts him to the hoop, so Owen can slam dunk the ball. When a militant teenager attempts to blow up the children in a Phoenix airport restroom, Johnny and Owen are able to save them by using "the shot." Johnny lifts Owen up with the grenade thrown into the restroom; Owen holds the grenade on a high windowsill, protecting the children but blowing Owen's arms off and eventually causing him to bleed to death.

Some critics have suggested that Irving's novel is too Calvinistic for modern readers and that religion is too cutely portrayed (Pritchard, 37). Religion is an important part of this novel. Johnny states at the beginning that Owen Meany is his reason for believing in God, and Johnny also helps his biological father, Reverend Merrill, restore his faith. Merrill wallows in guilt from his affair with Tabitha and from his failure to acknowledge his illegitimate son until Johnny forces him to confront these issues. Moreover, Owen is presented as a Christ figure throughout the novel. He gives his life to save others, and he even plays the baby Jesus in the church's Christmas drama.

John Sykes argues that the novel "demands theological assessment" (Sykes, 58). Irving would argue that it also demands political assessment and that the Vietnam War is an equally important part of the novel as religion. When Disney made the novel into a film, Irving refused to allow the movie to be titled the same as the novel because the screenplay had edited out all references to the Vietnam War (Keil, 10). Edward Reilly contends that the novel "symboliz[es] the Vietnam War's far-reaching effects" (Reilly, 138). All the characters alive during the conflict are strongly affected by it. John moves to Canada because of his disillusionment with American politics. Owen joins the service and is never sent to Vietnam, but he works as casualty assistance officer. He is killed when the brother of a dead soldier attempts to kill Vietnamese orphans at the airport where the soldier's body will arrive. Hester, Johnny's cousin and Owen's girlfriend, reacts against the war and Owen's death. She becomes a rock star called "Hester the Molester" who has affairs with barely legal young men and sings songs that refer to Owen's life and death. She never has another serious relationship after Owen, and she portrays the carnage of the Vietnam War by using documentary footage of the war in her music videos.

A Prayer for Owen Meany shows that Irving has been strongly influenced by the American literary tradition. Philip Page has noted the similarities between this novel and Nathaniel HAWTHORNE's *The Scarlet Letter.* "The most significant [similarities are] the proliferation of signs and attempted explanations" (Page, 112). Page also recognizes John's similarities to F. Scott FITZGERALD's Nick Carraway. When John discusses *The Great Gatsby* in a literature course he is teaching, he questions Nick's reliability. Page points out several instances that illustrate John's own questionable reliability as a narrator. Like Hawthorne, Irving attempts to shows the power of faith and the fallibility of individuals' faith at the same time. Like Fitzgerald, Irving learns to portray powerfully life's tragedies and disappointments.

SOURCES

Irving, John. *A Prayer for Owen Meany*. New York: Ballantine, 1989.

Keil, Beth Landman. "Irving: Flick Hasn't Got a Prayer," *New York*, 4 April 1998, p. 10.

Page, Philip. "Hero Worship and Hermeneutic Dialects: John Irving's *A Prayer for Owen Meany*." In *John Irving*, edited by Harold Bloom, 105–120. Philadelphia: Chelsea, 2001.

Pritchard, William. "Small Town Saint," *New Republic*, 22 May 1989, p. 37.

Reilly, Edward C. *Understanding John Irving*. Columbia: University of South Carolina Press, 1991.

Sykes, John. "Christian Apologetic Uses of the Grotesque in John Irving and Flannery O'Connor," *Literature & Theology* 10 (1996): 58–67.

Jill Ann Channing

PRICE, (EDWARD) REYNOLDS (1933–)

Reynolds Price, author of KATE VAIDEN, the novel that won the National Book Critics Circle Award for the best work of fiction in 1984, is a much-admired writer who has written 15 novels to date, usually set in his native eastern North Carolina. Although comparisons to William FAULKNER have become more or less obligatory for Southern authors, in Price's case, the comparison seems apt. Like Faulkner, Price, using a complex, intricate structure and style, creates fictional families (the Mustians and the Mayfields) living in a fictional Southern place, and, like Faulkner's, his characters wrestle with ancestral guilt, family legacies, and determinism; many of them, through the exercise of free will, transcend the expectations of the past. Compared as well to Ernest HEMINGWAY and to Leo Tolstoy, Price also writes poetry, drama, memoir, and short fiction; his *Collected Stories* (1993) was a finalist for a Pulitzer Prize.

Reynolds Price was born on February 1, 1933, in Macon, North Carolina, to William Solomon Price, a traveling salesman, and Elizabeth Rodwell Price.

Despite Depression-era poverty and his father's alcoholism and death from cancer, Price earned a bachelor's degree (summa cum laude) at Duke University in 1955, and a B. Litt. degree at Oxford University in 1958, where he was a Rhodes Scholar from 1955–58. He published his first novel, *A LONG AND HAPPY LIFE,* in 1962; it won the Faulkner Foundation award for a first novel. Its pregnant protagonist, Rosacoke Mustian, eventually resigns herself to marrying the baby's father, Wesley Beavers. In an ironic interpretation of the title, neither seems happy about the prospect of a long life together, but, typically, Price leaves room for guarded optimism. The next novel about the Mustian family, *A Generous Man,* this time focusing on Rosacoke's 15-year-old brother Milo, appeared in 1966, again to general acclaim. The two novels, along with the short story "A Chain of Love," have been reissued as a trilogy under the title *Mustian* (1983). In the more experimental *Love and Work* (1968), Price leaves his Southern setting. Thomas Eborn, an unlikable, egotistic college professor, who learns some—but perhaps not enough—lessons about putting love of fellow humans ahead of his novel writing.

The Surface of Earth (1975) is the first in the Mayfield trilogy, followed by *The Source of Light* (1981) and *The Promise of Rest* (1995), published together as *A Great Circle: The Mayfield Trilogy* (2001). The Mustian trilogy covers only one generation of a working-class family, but the Mayfield trilogy spans six generations—nearly a century—of a well-educated middle-class family. The trilogy, particularly *The Surface of Earth,* is considered ambitious and complex, following suffering individuals, notably sons in quest of their fathers, spouses disillusioned with marriage, and, as scholar David Marion Holman notes, Mayfield males linked in misfortune through "the circulation of a gold wedding band" returned by a wife who walked out on her husband (Holman, 287). Homosexuality becomes a major focus in both *The Source of Light* and *The Promise of Rest* as Hutch, the hero-artist, copes with the loss of his father to cancer and then, years later, the loss of his own son to AIDS. In 1984, while working on a novel based on his mother, Price contracted cancer of the spine, an illness that confines him to a wheelchair. He has refused to allow his physical condition to interfere with his work schedule, however, and published *Kate Vaiden* in 1987, his most widely praised novel since *A Long and Happy Life*. Kate Vaiden's father kills her mother and then commits suicide when she is 11 years old; these acts become Kate's justification for her abandonment of her own son. She believes that no one is reliable, not even her first love, Gaston, or Daniel, the father of her son, both of whom also commit suicide.

In the late 1980s Price wrote *Good Hearts* (1988), completing the story of Rosacoke, now called Rosa, whose husband Wesley deserts her for a much younger woman named Wilson. Rosa, left unprotected, is raped, which leads Wesley to return to Rosa; they agree to spend the rest of their ordinary lives together. *The Tongues of Angels* (1990) is a short novel in which the narrator-protagonist, Bridge Boatner, recalls the death of Raphael Nauren, a boy at a summer camp 20 years earlier. Like *The Tongues of Angels* and *Kate Vaiden, Blue Calhoun* (1992) uses a first-person narrator. Sixty-five-year-old Bluford Calhoun tells his granddaughter about his adulterous love for Luna Absher, a 16-year-old girl, when he was in his mid–30s. In *Roxanna Slade* (1998), Price uses the first female voice since *Kate Vaiden;* nearly 100 years old, Roxanna feels glad to be alive despite all the losses and betrayals she has suffered. She is speaking, metaphorically, as the voice of 20th-century America. *Noble Norfleet* (2002) examines the results of a mother's murder of two of her three children: The surviving child, Noble, who volunteers as a medic during the Vietnam War, is trying to help others since he could not help his brother and sister. At the end of the novel, he must confront his responsibility to his mother, just released from a hospital for the criminally insane. Price's novel *The Good Priest's Son* was published in 2005.

Reynolds Price lives in North Carolina, where he has retired after a long career teaching creative writing at Duke University. Praised by academics, critics, and general readers alike, Price continues to write in all genres. His papers are collected at the Perkins Library at Duke University.

NOVELS AND NOVELLAS

Blue Calhoun. New York: Atheneum, 1992.

A Generous Man. New York: Atheneum, 1966.

Good Hearts. New York: Atheneum; Thorndike, Maine: Thorndike, 1988.

The Good Priest's Son. New York: Scribner, 2005.

Kate Vaiden. New York: Atheneum, 1986; Boston: G. K. Hall, 1987.

A Long and Happy Life. New York: Atheneum, 1962.

Love and Work. New York: Atheneum, 1968.

Michael Egerton. Mankato, Minn.: Creative Education, 1993.

Mustian: Two Novels and a Story. New York: Atheneum, 1983.

Noble Norfleet. New York: Scribner, 2002.

Permanent Errors. New York: Atheneum, 1970.

The Promise of Rest. New York: Scribner, 1995.

Roxanna Slade. New York: Scribner; Thorndike, Maine: Thorndike, 1998.

A Singular Family. New York: Scribner, 1999.

The Source of Light. New York: Atheneum, 1981, Scribner, 1995.

The Surface of Earth. New York: Atheneum, 1975; New York: Scribner, 1995.

The Tongues of Angels. New York: Atheneum; Thorndike, Maine: Thorndike, 1990.

SOURCES

Holman, David Marion. "Reynolds Price." In *Fifty Southern Writers After 1900: A Bio-bibliographical Critical Sourcebook,* edited by Joseph M. Flora, 382–390. Westport, Conn.: Greenwood Press, 1987.

Humphries, Jefferson, ed. *Conversations with Reynolds Price.* Jackson: University Press of Mississippi, 1991.

Kimball, Sue Leslie, and Lynn Veach Sadler, eds. *Reynolds Price: From "A Long and Happy Life" to "Good Hearts."* Fayetteville, N.C.: Methodist College Press, 1989.

Ray, William. *Conversations: Reynolds Price & William Ray.* Memphis, Tenn.: Memphis State University, 1976.

Rooke, Constance. *Reynolds Price.* Boston: Twayne, 1983.

Schiff, James A. *Understanding Reynolds Price.* Columbia: University of South Carolina Press, 1996.

Schiff, James A., ed. *Critical Essays on Reynolds Price.* Boston: G. K. Hall, 1998.

PRICE, RICHARD (1949–)

Often compared with James T. FARRELL and Hubert SELBY, Jr., his literary godfathers, Richard Price writes frequently about adolescents in city street gangs; as many critics and readers note, Price deals with the seamy, often desperate, street life of the Bronx and his fictional Dempsy, New Jersey. His novels are in the end moral, even, to some critics, didactic.

Richard Price was born on October 12, 1949, in New York City. He was educated at Cornell University (B.S.,

1971) and Columbia University (M.F.A., 1976). His first novels, *The Wanderers* (1974) and *Bloodbrothers* (1976), were written and published before he finished graduate school. As *New York Review of Books* reviewer Roger Sales notes, *The Wanderers,* divided into interconnecting stories, each focusing on one Bronx gang member, is about "loneliness and brutality and bigotry and squalor" (Sale, 26). *Bloodbrothers,* another Bronx tale, depicts 18-year-old Stony De Coco's coming of age amid family feuds that are as powerful and binding as family ties. In *Ladies' Man* (1978), Kenny Baker breaks up with his significant other and journeys through the dark underbelly of Greenwich Village's "backroom sex bars." *New Republic* reviewer Martin Duberman notes that Price comprehends and depicts the "world of live sex shows, porno shops, singles' bars" and alternate lifestyles to which Kenny's gay friend guides him. *Clockers* (1992), set in Dempsy, New Jersey, contains an almost painfully realistic depiction of crack dens, dealers, and police, and introduces Strike Dunham, the 19-year-old ailing black dealer, and Rocco Klein, the suspicious and wily policeman who comes to his aid.

Freedomland (1998), loosely based on the real-life story of Susan Smith, who drove her two toddlers into a river but accused a black man of kidnapping them, features the white Brenda Martin whose son Cody has apparently been kidnapped by a tall black male. The parallels, however, notes reviewer Jonathan Levi, end here. Price's most recent novel, *Samaritan,* another thriller, features Ray Mitchell, a television scriptwriter who leaves his career for a newer, more rewarding one as a teacher and mentor. As the novel opens, Mitchell is lying in a hospital bed, with terrible head injuries; old school friend and detective Nerese Ammons puts off her retirement to solve the mystery of this Samaritan. Richard Price lives in New York, where he writes both novels and screenplays. *Clockers* was adapted for the screen by director Spike Lee and released in 1995. In 2006, Columbia Tristar Pictures released Price's film adaptation of *Freedomland,* directed by Joe Roth and starring Julianne Moore and Samuel L. Jackson.

NOVELS
Bloodbrothers. Boston: Houghton, 1976.
The Break. New York: Simon & Schuster, 1983.
Clockers. Boston: Houghton, 1992.
Freedomland. New York: Broadway Books, 1998.
Ladies' Man. Boston: Houghton, 1978.
Samaritan. New York: Knopf, 2003.
The Wanderers. Boston: Houghton, 1974.

SOURCES
Barnes, Julian. Review of *Bloodbrothers, New Statesman* 93, no. 2409 (May 20, 1977): 681.
Duberman, Martin. Review of *Ladies' Man, The New Republic,* 6 January 1979, pp. 30–32.
Levi, Jonathan. "Star-Spangled Tragedy," *Los Angeles Times Book Review,* 31 May 1998, p. 10.
Sale, Roger. "The Dangers of Nostalgia," *The New York Review of Books,* 27 June 1974, pp. 24–26.
West, Paul. "America Narcotica," *National Review* 44, no. 15 (August 3, 1992): 42.

OTHER
Epstein, Daniel Robert. "Interview with Richard Price for UGO." Ugo.com. Available online. URL: http://www.ugo.com/channels/freestyle/features/richardpricedeFault.asp. Accessed September 23, 2005.
Mattingly, Dan. "The Vanity of Human Kindness. A Case Study in Philanthropic Narcissism," *The Yale Review of Books,* no. 6 (Summer 2003). Available online. URL: http://www.yalereviewofbooks.com/archive/summer03/review06.shtml.htm. Accessed September 25, 2005.

PRINCE AND THE PAUPER, THE MARK TWAIN (1881)

Samuel Langhorne Clemens (Mark TWAIN) entered a major phase of his career in the mid–1870s starting with the publication of *The Adventures of Tom Sawyer* (1876) and with his writing of the early chapters of its sequel, *Adventures of Huckleberry Finn.* As he worked on *Huck,* Clemens found himself struggling. His strategy was to set aside a book that was stalled to begin another. When he felt he had written himself out after the first 18 chapters of *Huck Finn,* Clemens turned to the story of the childhood adventures of Edward VI of England and his "twin," the pauper Tom Canty. That book became *The Prince and the Pauper.*

The idea for the tale took root during 1877 while the Clemenses were spending the summer in Elmira, New York, at the home of Olivia Clemens's sister Susan Crane. Clemens had read Charlotte Young's *Little Duke* in the Crane's library: The basic plot of that book is that lessons learned by Richard, duke of Normandy, during his childhood instill in him the humility that later marks his compassionate leadership. Clemens eventually transferred the scene to Tudor England (an earlier version set the story in Victorian England) and created fiction to explain the brief yet relatively compassionate rule of Edward VI. Edward's lessons are made possible when he and a "twin" switch identities, which puts a young pauper in the palace to learn the strains of royalty, and the prince out on the road and open to the harsh realities of common life. The plot device allowed Clemens to offer commentary on both the seemingly empty rituals of monarchy and the dire implications of royal law for commoners.

Clemens dedicated the novel "to those good-mannered and agreeable children, Susie and Clara Clemens." *The Prince and the Pauper* was the Clemens daughters' favorite of their father's books. The family often used the story as the basis for homemade theatrical productions in Hartford; the book was also adapted as a very successful stage play. This has fueled the idea that the book is a children's fable; however, Clemens took care to present a story with profoundly adult themes: It questions a father's influence on a son, what makes a "good" king, how life experience ultimately influences the moral development of a child. It also explores how environment and human compassion combine to shape character as both Tom and Edward run headlong into situations with a cast of characters positioned to affect their lives. It is a child's fantasy fueled by a critique of social and political practice.

The action of the novel is divided between Tom and Edward. The dual perspectives allow Clemens to explore the experiences of each child as he faces new circumstances. Tom, who suddenly finds himself a prince just as he has dreamed, struggles to conform to the expectations of the nobility that surround him. He is naive and finds his one lasting ally in the person of the prince's whipping boy, who helps school him in palace intrigue. When he finds himself about to be made king, he is mortified when he denies his own mother who calls to him from the crowd. Tom finds that there is a high price to be paid for power and comfort as he separates himself from maternal love and affection.

Edward's adventures are, in fact, more troubling. The young prince finds himself at the mercy of John Canty, Tom's scheming and violent father, and is forced to become a beggar to meet Canty's demands. When Edward manages to escape from Canty, he flees into the clutches of a band of robbers and thieves. While the dehumanizing treatment of the gang is a burden, Edward is more shocked as his travels through the kingdom highlight the injustice that wracks the common folk. He witnesses state-sanctioned executions and torture; he is placed in jeopardy because the letter and spirit of laws are enforced to maintain the status of the powerful. He is saved by the intervention of Miles Hendon, a displaced noble who takes pity on the boy, who seems insane. Hendon is the prince's savior and protector, and it is the compassion he shows Edward that helps the prince understand the value of humility and patience. Ultimately, Edward makes his way back to the palace just in time to halt Tom's ascending to the throne, and the boys are able to return to their proper lives, which gives Edward the chance to demonstrate his newly acquired compassion by rewarding both Tom and Miles for their good service and by acting to change oppressive laws.

Standing alone, *The Prince and the Pauper* offers sharp criticisms of a monarchy that is out of touch with the needs of the common man. It also argues that a king is best trained by traveling and experiencing life throughout the kingdom. The conflict between the dream of power and the responsibilities that come with that power is also prominent. Yet it is also important to see the novel in the context of Clemens's creative struggle in 1877 as he attempts to restart the stalled *Adventures of Huckleberry Finn*. Edward's experience as the pauper seems tied to the dilemma of Huck Finn. Like Huck, Edward must run from a violent "father" (John Canty) and travels the countryside wary of his safety. The lessons for Huck and Edward are similar, too: Each boy learns to watch for and appreciate the compassion of strangers and survives under the watchful eye of an adult who ties his own fortunes to the boy (Miles Hendon and Jim have a good deal in common in how they care for their traveling companions). In the end, however, Edward's fortunes offer a good deal more hope than Huck's difficult passage. That optimism may be why the Clemens daughters were so fond of the tale of the prince and the pauper. It may also be one reason readers are so fond of the novel today.

SOURCES

Emerson, Everett. *Mark Twain: A Literary Life*. Philadelphia: University of Pennsylvania Press, 2000.

Gerber, John C. *Mark Twain*. Boston: G. K. Hall & Co., 1988.

Rasmussen, R. Kent. *Mark Twain A to Z: The Essential Reference to His Life and Writings*. New York: Facts On File, Inc., 1995.

Twain, Mark. *Mark Twain's Notebooks & Journals, vol. II 1877–1883)*. Edited by Frederick Anderson, Lin Salamo, and Berhard L. Stein. Berkeley: University of California Press, 1975.

———. *The Prince and the Pauper*. Edited by Victor Fischer and Lin Salamo. Berkeley: University of California Press, 1979.

Michael J. Kiskis

PROMISED LAND, THE Mary Antin
(1912)   Mary Antin's novel-like autobiography, *The Promised Land*, first appeared in serialized format in *The Atlantic Monthly* in 1911. This story of a young Jewish girl's emigration from Russia and her adolescence in Boston was a best seller that fictionalized both the protagonist, clearly based on Antin herself, and some of her experiences. Antin also employed novelistic techniques that resulted in a spellbinding tale: Libraries reported it as the most requested book of the year, and special teacher manuals on the text were distributed for use in schools (Sollors, xxxii). *The Promised Land* remained one of the most popular and influential immigrant narratives for the first half of the 20th century. *The Promised Land* hit a cultural nerve; it was considered the best-selling autobiography ever published and spawned the publication of other immigrant novels and autobiographies. The resulting interest catapulted Antin to public stardom, and she used her fame to lecture around the country for education and open immigration policies. Antin's work even caught the attention of Theodore Roosevelt, who considered Antin a Progressive reformer as important as Jane Addams and Jacob Riis (Salz, 69).

The autobiography describes the process of transformation from "medieval" life in Eastern Europe to the bustling world of the modern American city. *The Promised Land* begins with Antin's early childhood in a Jewish shtetl in the Russian Pale of Settlement, and describes the political and economic persecution of Jews. The autobiography moves on to the traumatic emigration from Russia, which is told mostly through extended excerpted passages from her earlier book *From Plotzk to Boston* (1899) (the title was a misspelling of Polotzk). However, the bulk of the narrative is devoted to her adolescence in Boston. The autobiography emphasizes cheerful moments of adaptation and assimilation. As the title indicates, America is represented as a golden land of opportunity for impoverished and persecuted immigrants. In America, Antin claims, everyone is free to try for a better life, and anyone can become a citizen and, more powerfully, an American. Especially important for Antin is the fact that America provides compulsory education for girls, something not guaranteed in the religiously and politically circumscribed world of Russian Jewish life. In the America of *The Promised Land*, Antin can—and does—live up to her own "promise," becoming a star pupil, winning a scholarship to a private high school, and going to college.

Throughout the autobiography, Antin self-consciously sees her story as representative of millions of fellow immigrants. Her autobiography is thus an attempt to turn personal experience into national narrative, to make individual achievement into universal experience. This tension between singularity and representativeness can also be seen in the way that Antin claims authorship. While the title page identifies Mary Antin as the author, the text refers to the narrator as the fictional Esther Altmann. *The Promised Land* is thus both the story of the exceptional author Mary Antin and the tale of immigrant everyman Esther Altmann. This authorial confusion highlights the novelistic techniques that Antin consistently employs in writing her autobiography. While ostensibly a memoir of her own experiences, *The Promised Land* is also a document of literary ambition, a love letter to the English language. As a result, the autobiography is extremely self-conscious in its use of language. *The Promised Land* was one of the first Jewish immigration narratives in English, and it established Antin as a major literary figure, alongside fellow Jewish writers Abraham Cahan and Anzia Yezierska. Like those novelists, Antin sought to reach a wider audience of Jews and gentiles alike, and asked them to redefine American citizenship in more inclusive terms. Toward this end, Antin uses many Yiddish words in her text (which are left undefined save for a glossary at the end), in effect demanding that her audience adapt to her language, much as she has learned to write in English.

Throughout the autobiography, Antin pays special attention to community space, describing in detail each of the neighborhoods she has called home: first the Jewish Section of Polotzk, and then Union Place, Crescent Beach, Arlington Street, Wheeler and Dover Streets, and Harrison Avenue in Boston. The autobiography also features photographs of communal sites of markets, school, and streets. Betty Berglund argues that the photographs reveal a contradictory narrative to the story of easy assimilation; the close-knit community of her childhood village is pictured through scenes of social life, while the urban photographs of Boston are notable for lonely scenes of empty streets (Berglund, 56). Indeed, there is ample evidence that life in America was not as happy as Antin would have the reader believe. Despite their hard work, her family struggles to find work opportunities and improved living conditions. Similarly, Antin's relatively privileged education comes at the expense of her older sister, who is sent to work in sweatshops from the age of 14. *The Promised Land* shows Antin continually transforming her experiences into the form of an immigrant success story, whereby the immigrant truly does rise to the heights of American achievement. Some of this narrative resolution is achieved through editing and fictionalizing aspects of her life. This is especially noticeable at the end of *The Promised Land,* where Antin celebrates her educational success: graduating from high school and matriculating at Barnard College. In fact, Antin's marriage to an older man prevented her from finishing high school, which, in turn, prevented her from earning a college degree from Barnard. *The Promised Land* can thus be read as an attempt to rewrite history as one wishes it had occurred.

Nearly a century after its publication, *The Promised Land* remains a document of the hopes of millions of Americans seeking new lives in America, and a lesson in the difficulty of achieving those dreams.

SOURCES

Antin, Mary. *The Promised Land.* 1912. Introduction by Werner Sollors. New York: Penguin, 1997.

———. *From Plotzk to Boston.* 1899. Introduction by Pamela S. Nadell. Reprint, New York: Markus Wiener, 1985.

Bergland, Betty. "Photographs and Narratives in Ethnic Autobiography: Memory and Subjectivity in Mary Antin's *The Promised Land.*" In *Memory, Narrative, and Identity: New Essays in Ethnic American Literatures,* edited by Amritjit Singh, Joseph T. Skerrett, Jr., and Robert E. Hogan, 45–88. Boston: Northeastern University Press, 1994.

Howe, Irving. *World of Our Fathers: The Journey of the East European Jews to America and the Life They Found and Made There.* New York: Galahad Books, 1976.

Riis, Jacob. *How the Other Half Lives: Studies among the Tenements of New York.* 1890. Reprint, New York: Hill and Wang, 1957.

Salz, Evelyn, ed. *Selected Letters of Mary Antin.* Syracuse, N.Y.: Syracuse University Press, 2000.

Sollors, Werner. Introduction to *The Promised Land,* p. xi–l. New York: Penguin, 1997.

Julie A. Sheffer

PROSE, FRANCINE (1947–)

An accomplished novelist, poet, short story writer, and essayist who has won four Pushcart Prizes and whose recent young adult novel, *After* (2003), was nominated for a Los Angeles Times Book Award, Francine Prose is the author of more than a dozen novels, the most recent of which, *The Blue Angel* (2000), was a finalist for the National Book Award.

Francine Prose was born on April 1, 1947, in Brooklyn, New York, to Philip Prose and Jessie Rubin Prose, both physicians. She was educated at Radcliffe College, earning her bachelor's degree in 1968, and at Harvard University, earning her master's degree in 1969. In 1973 she published her first novel, *Judah the Pious,* a long story in the manner of old European folktales; set in Poland, it follows Rabbi Eliezer and his meeting with the Polish king. The following year she published *The Glorious Ones,* in which the 16th-century traveling players are involved in the creation and the telling of their own stories, an idea that has become familiar in Prose's fiction. After marrying Howard Michels, an artist, on September 24, 1976, Prose wrote *Marie Laveau* (1977), her first novel set in the United States; the title character, a 19th-century New Orleans mulatta, exhibits strong psychic powers.

Animal Magnetism (1978), a medical fantasy, was followed by *Household Saints* (1981), a mixture of legend and reality that Prose blended to tell the tale of a butcher and his family, and *Hungry Hearts* (1983), about a Yiddish theater star who becomes so obsessed with her role that it engulfs her personality. In *Bigfoot Dreams* (1986), the writer is horrified to know that the tabloid stories she has been inventing are actually happening. *Primitive People* (1992) is a disturbing presentation—through the eyes of Simone, a middle-class Haitian au pair—of the frequently rude and sometimes violent well-to-do dwellers of Hudson's Landing, an upscale community within commuting distance of New York City; they are not so different from the so-called primitive people in Simone's own country. *A Peaceable Kingdom* (1993) and *Guided Tours of Hell* (1997) are two darkly comic novellas that, according to reviewer Rod Kessler, should be added to the classic books that trace "the moral adventures of Americans in Europe" (Kessler, 232). In the first, *Guided Tours of Hell*, Landau, an American playwright, wrestles with his envy of successful, pompous, and possibly deceptive writer Jiri Krakauer as the satirically portrayed group of academics tours the Terrezenstadt Nazi concentration camp. *Three Pigs in Five Days* depicts a lonely American travel writer, Nina, as she tours a metaphorically dark hell-like Paris, where her lover has abandoned her.

Hunters and Gatherers (1995) features a factchecker at a magazine similar to *Vogue* and a goddessworshiping group who persuades her to accompany them to Arizona to learn Native American wisdom. As reviewer Carol LeMasters notes, however, once they reach "the Four Feathers Institute, the women find a derelict motel, the wrong shaman, suffocating sweat lodges, drumming at dawn and—when they aren't fasting—a diet of roadkill and Gatorade." *Blue Angel: a Novel* (2000), a parody about academia, depicts Ted Swenson, a 47-year-old married novelist and writing instructor at a Vermont college that has just instituted a sweeping sexual-harassment policy. Like the pathetic professor in the Marlene Dietrich movie of the same name, he cannot see that his talented writing student Angela Argo is interested only in aggressive promotion of herself, to the destruction of Ted's marriage and career. *After* (2003), her most recent novel, straddles the adult and young-adult line; it involves a violent shooting similar to the one that occurred at Columbine High School and focuses on the questions of security and authority. Francine Prose lives with her husband in Manhattan, where she continues to write.

NOVELS AND NOVELLAS

After. New York: HarperCollins, 2003.
Animal Magnetism. New York: Putnam, 1978.
Bigfoot Dreams. New York: Pantheon, 1986.
Blue Angel. New York: HarperCollins, 2000.
The Glorious Ones. New York: Atheneum, 1974.
Guided Tours of Hell: Novellas (includes *Guided Tours of Hell* and *Three Pigs in Five Days*). New York: Metropolitan/Holt, 1997.
Household Saints. New York: St. Martin's Press, 1981.
Hungry Hearts. New York: Pantheon, 1983.
Hunters and Gatherers. New York: Farrar, Straus & Giroux, 1995.
Judah the Pious. New York: Atheneum, 1973.
Marie Laveau. New York: Berkley, 1977.
Primitive People. New York: Farrar, Straus & Giroux, 1992.

SOURCES

Eisenberg, Deborah. "Francine Prose," *Bomb* 45 (Fall 1993).
Hooper, Brad. Review of *Blue Angel, Booklist,* 15 April 2000, p. 1,525.
Interview with Francine Prose. By John E. Baker. *Publishers Weekly,* 13 April 1992, p. 38.
Kessler, Rod. Review of *Guided Tours of Hell, The Review of Contemporary Fiction* 17, no. 3 (Fall 1997): 232.
Leiding, Reba. Review of *Blue Angel, Library Journal,* 1 February 2000, p. 118.
LeMasters, Carol. Review of *Hunters and Gatherers, The Women's Review of Books* 13, no. 3 (December 1995): 23–24.
O'Laughlin, Jim. Review of *Guided Tours of Hell, Booklist,* 15 December 1996, p. 709.
Pearlman, Mickey. "Francine Prose." In *Inter/View: Talks with America's Writing Women,* edited by Pearlman and Katherine Usher Henderson. Lexington: University of Kentucky Press, 1990.
Peretz, Evgenia. Review of *Hunters and Gatherers, The New Republic,* 13 November 1995, pp. 47–49.
Potok, Rena. "Francine Prose." In *Jewish American Women Writers: A Bio-Bibliographical and Critical Sourcebook,* edited by Sara R. Horowitz, 302–313. Westport, Conn.: Greenwood Press, 1994.
Prose, Francine. Interview. *Publishers Weekly,* 24 February 2003, p. 72.

Rosser, Claire. Review of *After,* *Kliatt* 38, no. i4 (July 2004): 23.

Schiff, Stacy. "Terpsichore, Thalia and Yoko: Francine Prose on the (Mostly) Unsung Lives of Nine Women Who Inspired Well-Known Male Artists," *The New York Times Book Review,* 22 September 2002, p. 9.

St. Andrews, B.A. Review of *Guided Tours of Hell, World Literature Today* 71, no. 4 (Autumn 1997): 788.

OTHER

Salij, Marta. "Francine Prose Is Sensitive to What It Means to Be Underestimated." Knight Ridder/Tribune News Service. Highbeam Resources. Available online. URL: http://www.highbeam.com/library/doc3.asp?DOCID=1G1:73103642. Accessed September 26, 2005.

Ydstie, John, and Jackie Lyden. Interview: Francine Prose Discusses Her Book *"The Lives of the Muses: Nine Women & the Artists They Inspired." All Things Considered* (NPR). Highbeam Resources. Available online. URL: http://www.highbeam.com/library/doc3.asp?DOCID=1P1:92649240. Accessed September 26, 2005.

PROULX, E. ANNIE (1935–)

Seldom has an author received so much attention for one novel. Annie Proulx's *The Shipping News* (1993), internationally acclaimed for its powerful evocation of place and for Proulx's mesmerizing blending of tragedy and poignancy, won the Pulitzer Prize, the National Book Award, and the *Irish Times* International Fiction Prize. In 2001 the novel was adapted to a feature-length film starring Kevin Spacey. Her other novels include *Postcards* (1992), winner of the 1993 PEN/Faulkner Award, and *Accordion Crimes* (1996).

Annie Proulx was born on August 22, 1935, in Norwich, Connecticut, to George Napolean Proulx and Lois Nelly Gill Proulx, an artist. Reared in New England, Proulx was educated at the University of Vermont, where she graduated cum laude (1969), and Sir George Williams University (now Concordia University), where she earned a master's degree (1973). She has been married and divorced three times. Proulx's first book of fiction, *Heart Songs and Other Stories* (1988), is a collection of tales set in rural New England. Four years later she published *Postcards,* tracing the Blood family of Vermont from the turn of the century to the aftermath of World War II. Loyal Blood, who has killed his girlfriend, flees to the West; he sends postcards periodically from various destinations over a period of 40 years. Unbeknownst to Loyal, the rest of the family, unable to adapt to the changing forces of modern America, meets a disastrous end. The bleak and desolate atmosphere of Proulx's novels extends to her landscapes, which, as every critic has noted, mark her novels and stories. *The Shipping News,* for instance, resonates with Proulx's evocation of the spare, brutal terrain of Newfoundland. Quoyle, a newspaperman, returns to his old family home to begin anew after the failure of his marriage and his wife's accidental death. *Accordion Crimes* is a collection of linked stories about a green accordion that passes from immigrant to immigrant for more than a hundred years. For all the immigrants—German, Polish, Sicilian, Mexican, French Canadian, black Cajun, Mexican, and Basque—the accordion brings bad luck, and the novel ends with the abandoned instrument on the side of a highway, its hidden treasure, $14,000 in cash, undiscovered.

Annie Proulx currently lives and writes in Wyoming. Her recent books include an acclaimed short fiction collection, *Close Range: Wyoming Stories* (1999), which included the story "Brokeback Mountain," made into a motion picture in 2005, and *That Old Ace in the Hole: A Novel* (2002). The latter features recent college graduate Bob Dollar as he moves to the Texas Panhandle, purchases former cattle land to be used for hog farms, and meets a rich array of local characters. *Bad Dirt: Wyoming Stories 2* was published in 2004.

NOVELS AND NOVELLAS

Accordion Crimes. New York: Scribner, 1996.
Brokeback Mountain. New York: Scribner, 2005.
Postcards. New York: Scribner, 1992.
The Shipping News. New York: Scribner, 1993.
That Old Ace in the Hole: A Novel. New York: Scribner, 2002.

SOURCES

Bell, Millicent. "Fiction Chronicle," *Partisan Review* 64, no. 1 (Winter 1997): 37–49.

Bemrose, John. "The Incredible Journey," *Maclean's,* 29 July 1996, p. 45.

Birkerts, Sven. "Fiction in Review," *Yale Review* 85, no. 1 (January 1997): 144–155.

Hospital, Janette Turner. "How to Make Seal-Flipper Pie,"
London Review of Books, 10 February 1994, p. 17.

PURDY, JAMES (1923–   ) James Purdy is the
author of more than 40 books, including novels, plays,
poetry, and essays. He remains, however, outside the
mainstream of contemporary American fiction, and
critics have speculated on the reasons for his relative
obscurity. Chief among them is his treatment of non-
traditional sexuality and perversity, which he feels are
ever present in the American psyche. His technique,
often experimental, is characterized by irony and complex narrative structure and point of view, combined
with a vivid re-creation of his native midwestern collo-
quialisms. Although he rejects the term "gay male
writer," he has benefited from the upsurge of interest in
gay studies and literature and the ensuing publication
of gay writers. His best known works include *63:
Dream Palace* (1956); *Malcolm* (1959), adapted as a
play by Edward Albee in 1966; *Cabot Wright Begins*
(1964); *Eustace Chisholm and the Works* (1967); and *On
Glory's Course* (1984), nominated for a PEN/Faulkner
prize. *In a Shallow Grave* (1975) was adapted and
filmed by Kenneth Bowser in 1988.

Purdy was born in rural Ohio on July 17, 1923,
but few details about his personal life are known. He
has taught occasionally at universities both here and
abroad and moved to Brooklyn, New York, more than
20 years ago. His literary preoccupations were established early in his career: spiritually bereft characters
seeking wholeness; violence, including torture, rape,
and murder; and the death of the American Dream. In
Malcolm, the 15-year-old protagonist has been abandoned by his father and is lost, both literally and figuratively; he is an easy target for adult predators. Like
many later Purdy characters, Malcolm dies. The central figure—Cliff, another orphan—of *The Nephew*
(1960) is literally missing from the novel. His aunt,
Alma Mason, tries to persuade the townspeople to
write a tribute to him, but instead exposes small-
town meanness and hypocrisy. Two novels from the
1960s caused a great deal of controversy: *Cabot
Wright Begins* (1964) is the memoir of a rapist and a
satirical expose of the New York literati; *Eustace
Chisholm and the Works,* set in Chicago during the

Great Depression, follows the exploits of the doomed
Daniel Hawes and his murder by the homosexual and
sadistic Captain Stadger.

In the 1970s Purdy produced works best described
as allegory, fairy tale, fable, and biblical parable. *I Am
Elijah Thrush* (1972) describes the title character's
unsuccessful attempts to avoid the evil Millicent De
Fayne, who eventually captures his spirit. The uplift-
ing power of love is evident in this novel and in
Jeremy's Vision (1970) and *The House of the Solitary
Maggot* (1974), both of which portray desperate fig-
ures in decaying communities. Gruesome acts are per-
formed in their homes. In his novel, *In a Shallow
Grave,* a disfigured Vietnam veteran named Gernet
Montrose is transformed by the love of a young drifter.
Purdy wrote his most experimental novel, *On Glory's
Course* (1984), in the 1980s. Nominated for a
PEN/Faulkner award, the novel epitomizes the
dichotomy between those who admire Purdy's outré
subject matter and style, and those who find him
almost impossible to read.

He continues to write; NARROW ROOMS (1978) and
Out With the Stars (1992) deal with homosexuality, *In
the Hollow of his Hand* (1986) is about a part–Native
American illegitimate child, *Garments the Living Wear*
(1989) about a plague in New York City, and *Gertrude
of Stony Island* (1998) about a mother mourning her
daughter.

NOVELS AND NOVELLAS
Cabot Wright Begins. New York: Farrar, Straus & Giroux,
    1964.
The Candles of Your Eyes. New York: Nadja, 1985.
Color of Darkness: 11 Stories and a Novella. New York: New
    Directions, 1957.
Eustace Chisholm and the Works. New York: Farrar, Straus &
    Giroux, 1967.
Garments the Living Wear. San Francisco: City Lights Books,
    1989.
Gertrude of Stony Island Avenue. New York: Morrow, 1998.
The House of the Solitary Maggot. Garden City, N.Y.: Double-
    day, 1974.
I Am Elijah Thrush. Garden City, N.Y.: Doubleday, 1972.
In a Shallow Grave. New York: Arbor House, 1975.
In the Hollow of His Hand. New York: Weidenfeld & Nicol-
    son, 1986.
Jeremy's Version. Garden City, N.Y.: Doubleday, 1970.

Malcolm. New York: Farrar, Straus & Cudahy, 1959.

Mourners Below. New York: Viking/London: Owen, 1984.

Narrow Rooms. New York: Arbor House, 1978.

The Nephew. New York: Farrar, Straus & Cudahy, 1960.

On Glory's Course. New York: Viking, 1984.

Out with the Stars: A Novel. San Francisco: City Lights Books, 1992.

63: Dream Palace. New York: William-Frederick, 1956.

SOURCES

Adams, Stephen D. *James Purdy.* New York: Barnes Noble, 1976.

The American Novel: Two Studies. Emporia: Kansas State Teachers College of Emporia, Graduate Division, 1965.

Chupack, Henry. *James Purdy.* Boston: Twayne, 1975.

Contemporary American Novelists. Edited by Harry T. Moore. Carbondale: Southern Illinois University Press, 1964.

Essays in Modern American Literature. Edited by Richard E. Langford. De Land, Fla.: Stetson University Press, 1963.

The Fifties: Fiction, Poetry, Drama. Edited by Warren French. DeLand, Fla.: Everett/Edwards, 1971.

French, Warren. *Season of Promise.* Columbia: University of Missouri Press, 1968.

Hyman, Stanley Edgar. *Standards: A Chronicle of Books for Our Time.* Dedham, Mass.: Horizon Press, 1966.

Kennard, Jean E. *Number and Nightmare: Forms of Fantasy in Contemporary Fiction.* Hamden, Conn.: Archon Books, 1975.

Kumar, Anil. *Alienation in the Fiction of Carson McCullers, J. D. Salinger, and James Purdy.* Amritsar, India: Guru Nanak Dev University, 1991.

Malin, Irving. *New American Gothic.* Carbondale: Southern Illinois University Press, 1962.

On Contemporary Literature. Edited by Richard Kostelanetz. New York: Avon, 1964.

Recent American Fiction: Some Critical Views. Edited by Joseph S. Waldmeir. East Lansing: Michigan State University, 1963.

Schwarzschild, Bettina. *The Not-Right House: Essays on James Purdy.* Columbia: University of Missouri Press, 1969.

Solotaroff, Theodore. *The Red Hot Vacuum and Other Pieces on the Writing of the Sixties.* New York: Atheneum, 1970.

Tanner, Tony. *City of Words: American Fiction, 1950–1970.* New York: Harper, 1971.

Weales, Gerald. *The Jumping-off Place: American Drama in the 1960's.* New York: Macmillan, 1969.

PUSHING THE BEAR Diane Glancy (1996)

Diane GLANCY is a writer of Cherokee and German/English ancestry who is celebrated for the stylistic experiments of her prose and poetry. Writing poetry that reads like prose and prose that is pure drama, she mixes written and oral culture so that her texts move somewhere "between petroglyth and written language" (*Claiming,* 20). Glancy's award-winning books include her collections of poetry, *Claiming Breath* (1992) and *The Relief of America* (2000); drama, *War Cries* (1996) and *American Gypsy* (2002); and essays, *West Pole* (1997). These books are woven out of fragments of the past, collective and individual memories that often address a sense of loss and alienation. Her first novel, *Pushing the Bear,* is no different. Using writing as a path to healing and wholeness, Glancy offers her readers inspiration, an aid to survival, and a bridge across the divided worlds in which we live.

Pushing the Bear is a gripping historical account of the Cherokee removal that begins with a stark statement of facts: From October 1938 through February 1839 some 11,000 to 13,000 Cherokee walked 900 miles in bitter cold from the southeast to Indian Territory. One-fourth died or disappeared along the way. The horrific experiences of the Trail of Tears are told by a multitude of characters whose individual voices re-create this tragic chapter of forced migration and dislocation in American history. These voices belong to Cherokee men and women of all ages and all clans. Joining them are the voices of soldiers, ministers, politicians, leaders, rebels, physicians, sympathizers, and oppressors who witness the Cherokees' journey from Georgia, Alabama, North Carolina, and Tennessee to Indian Territory.

Glancy's idea for the novel's multiple narrators and the ensuing narrative fragmentation was prompted by seeing a "[Cherokee] pottery bowl, broken and glued together with some parts missing and the cracks still showing" ("Author's Note," 236). Shattered into a multitude of different perspectives and parts, her novel, like the pottery bowl, seeks to re-create Cherokee history and culture literally from the fragments that are left. Some of those fragments are historical texts and inventories; others are songs, prayers, and stories written in the Cherokee syllabary invented by Sequoia in 1821. Glancy's use of the Cherokee language—strategically inserted into the English text as words, formulas, and phrases—creates holes in the text so the original can show through. These windows into the Cherokee language provide a glimpse into the larger problems of cultural translation and loss. The Cherokee words in the novel fragment the colonizer's English and ask the reader to learn a new language—to fill in what is missing—by consulting the Cherokee alphabet attached and/or making sense of the phrases in the context provided. In this sense the reader is not just a passive listener to the stories of the Cherokee, but an active participant in the meaning-making process and a translator of the novel's oral poetics. Barbara Duncan explains that the oral poetics method transcribes stories word for word "directly as spoken by the storytellers" (23). Glancy often imitates this method when she inserts direct Cherokee translations into her text. Instead of moving back and forth between oral culture and written history, the novel's voices envelop Cherokee history by referring casually to many historical persons; such as Andrew Jackson, the architect of the Removal; Chief Justice John Marshall; the Cherokee leaders John Ross, Elias Boudinot, John Ridge; and advocates for the Cherokee such as Daniel Boone, David Crockett, and others. History—such as the events and the legislation that led to the Removal—is embedded in the fictional voices and is fiercely debated by the characters throughout the novel. In this debate, Glancy focuses on the plurality and diversity of opinions among the Cherokee and on their confusion and sense of betrayal not only by whites but by Cherokee leaders who agreed to the "exchange of lands."

These political betrayals provide the simmering background ache to the physical hardships of the characters in the novel's foreground. The Cherokee must not only suffer hunger, cold, illness, confusion, and sure death, but they must overcome many emotional and spiritual challenges that accompany their ordeal. Glancy's narrative centers on a young fictional woman named Maritole and her husband Knowbowtee and their families who experience starvation, exhaustion, pain, and the psychological trauma caused by the loss of family, home, and land. Maritole fights hard against the heavy grief that sits like a bear on her chest and threatens to consume her. How each character deals with such grief, loss, and humiliation is an important theme of the novel expressed in the central metaphor of the bear who threatens to crush those who give in to despair and forget their humanity, community, and culture. Maritole, for instance, loses not only her baby, her brother, and both of her parents to illness and death but also her husband, who turns away from her in his own bitterness, grief, and powerlessness. This causes Maritole to rely on the protection and affection of a white soldier, Sergeant Williams, who is temporarily assigned to their removal unit. The rift in Maritole's marriage and the divisions and tensions within the community at large caused by the hardships of the Removal make this novel much more than "a good Indian/bad white man story" (237). It is a powerful, poetic narrative that sketches the complexity of the experience and the diversity of responses to such human tragedy. But ultimately, the novel is not primarily about the blood and tears of the Cherokee; it is about their incredible spiritual and cultural resilience.

The Cherokee take their stories and myths with them on the Trail of Tears, and it is through stories—ancient and new—that they make sense of their experiences. For instance, they tell the stories of Selu, the woman who gave her life so that the Cherokee would have corn, and of the monster Uk-ten, who was conquered with the help of a courageous boy. These traditional tales of sacrifice and courage lift the spirits of the people and remind them of who they are. They also listen to the voices of the ancestors, the Great Spirit, and the biblical stories of the Exodus. Like the Israelites, the Cherokee were led to a new land, says Reverend Bushyhead, and he asks his fellow travelers: "Did not the children of Israel also grumble?" All these stories, Cherokee and Christian, merge with the voices of the characters that tell of the confusion and hardships of the removal so that this experience, too, may become part of a collective story, a memory not only of pain but communal healing and survival.

Like the basket maker who weaves different strands of river cane into a basket, Glancy weaves the different responses of the Cherokee to the Trail of Tears into a collective narrative that creates meaning out of confusion and healing out of pain. Many Cherokee storytellers believe that stories help individuals and communities to "stay in balance" and that "placing importance on the good of the whole more than the individual" is crucial to the traditional Cherokee way of living (Duncan, 25). By narrating the story of the Removal as a collection of voices, and by weaving Cherokee language, songs, history, medicine, and crafts into the stories, Glancy celebrates the Native American oral tradition and in the process becomes an important Cherokee storyteller in her own right.

SOURCES

Duncan, Barbara R. *Living Stories of the Cherokee.* Chapel Hill: University of North Carolina Press, 1998.

Glancy, Diane. *Pushing the Bear.* New York: Harvest, 1996.

———. *Claiming Breath.* Lincoln: University of Nebraska Press, 1992.

Perdue, Theda. *Cherokee Women: Gender and Culture Change, 1700–1866.* Knoxville: University of Tennessee Press, 1979.

———, and Michael D. Green. *The Cherokee Removal: A Brief History with Documents.* Boston: St. Martin's 2005.

Annette Trefzer

PUZO, MARIO (1920–1999)

"For the average reader, the Italian-American novel arrived with Mario Puzo," says critic Rose Basile Green. Author of the phenomenal best-seller *The GODFATHER* (1969), Mario Puzo made publishing history by plugging into the reading public's inexhaustible curiosity about the Mafia. The novel, a chronicle of the lives and fortunes of the fictional Corleones, who emigrated from Sicily to the United States and became one of the most powerful Mafia families in the country, remained on the *New York Times* best-seller list—and on equivalent lists in England, France, and Germany—for well over a year. Puzo went on to collaborate with Francis Ford Coppola to write the Academy Award–winning screenplays *The Godfather* (1972) and *The Godfather: Part II* (1974); additionally, both *The Godfather* and *The Godfather: Part III* (1990) won the Golden Globe Award for best screenplay. Puzo has been repeatedly praised for his skillful use of irony, realism, characterization, and for his exploration of human nature and the American Dream. As recently as 2003, the British reading public voted *The Godfather* as "one of the nation's 100 best-loved novels." The public's interest in La Cosa Nostra continues into the 21st century with the five-year-long award-winning television series *The Sopranos,* which, like *The Godfather,* exposes the brutality of the Mafia while generating sympathy for many of its members and their families.

Mario Puzo was born on October 15, 1920, in the Hell's Kitchen neighborhood of New York City, to Antonio Puzo, a railroad trackman, and Maria Le Conti Puzo, both Italian immigrants. Puzo's father deserted his wife and seven children when Puzo was 12 years old. After serving in Germany with the U.S. Army Air Corps during World War II as a corporal, Puzo married Erika Lina Broske in 1946 and enrolled in writing courses at the New School for Social Research and Columbia University. He published his first novel, *The Dark Arena,* in 1955, a tale of Walter Mosca, an Italian-American soldier who returns to occupied Germany after World War II to exact revenge. In *The Fortunate Pilgrim* (1964) Lucia Santa, a courageous Italian-American woman, struggles to raise her family out of poverty in a crime-ridden area of New York. Both novels are now considered minor classics. Puzo became famous with his third novel, *The Godfather,* a page-turning account of Don Vito Corleone and his sons: Sonny, Freddie, and Michael. Here he explores the parallels between organized crime and mainstream American corporations.

Fools Die (1978), Puzo's personal favorite and another best-seller, uses the backdrop of Las Vegas to examine the world of gambling, debauchery, and corruption. Numerous readers have seen in the character of Osano a caricature of Norman MAILER. In *The Sicilian* (1984), set in the 1950s, Michael Corleone prepares to leave Sicily after a two-year stay and becomes embroiled with Salvatore Giuliano, a Sicilian outlaw. *The Fourth K* (1991) is a political thriller set in the first decade of the 21st century: It seems eerily prescient with its Mid-Eastern terrorists and its depiction of both right-wing and left-wing extremists. It includes a fictitious American president, Francis Xavier Kennedy, who is distantly related to John, Robert, and Edward Kennedy. *The Last Don: A Novel* (1996) focuses on the Clericuzio family and Don Cross DeLena's efforts to move the family from crime to respectability. Set in Hollywood, Las Vegas, and Long Island, Puzo's novel was a critical success, principally for its realistic characters. *Omerta* (meaning silence), completed by Carol

Gino, Puzo's long-term companion after his wife's death, was published after Puzo's death in 2000; it explores the Sicilian code of silence and its gradual disintegration as new generations rise to power.

Mario Puzo died from heart failure in July 1999 on Long Island. His manuscripts are housed at Boston University. In addition to the *Godfather* films, other films based on Puzo's work include *A Time to Die,* adapted by John Goff, Matt Cimbert, and William Russel, and released by Almi in 1983; *The Cotton Club,* based on a story by Puzo, Coppola, and William KENNEDY, adapted for the screen by Kennedy, and directed by Coppola for Orion Pictures in 1984; *The Fortunate Pilgrim,* adapted for television and broadcast as *Mario Puzo's The Fortunate Pilgrim* by NBC in April 1988; *The Sicilian,* adapted by Steve Shagan and directed by Michael Cimino for Twentieth Century-Fox in 1989; and *The Last Don,* adapted for television and broadcast by CBS in May 1997 and May 1998.

NOVELS
The Dark Arena. New York: Random House, 1955.
Fools Die. New York: Putnam, 1978.
The Fortunate Pilgrim. New York: Atheneum, 1964.
The Fourth K. New York: Random House, 1991.
The Godfather. New York: Putnam, 1969.
The Last Don: A Novel. New York: Random House, 1996.
Omerta. New York: Random House, 2000.
The Sicilian. New York: Linden Press/Simon & Schuster, 1984.

SOURCES
Green, Rose B. *The Italian-American Novel.* Rutherford, N.J.: Fairleigh Dickinson University Press, 1974, pp. 336–368.
Madden, David, ed. *Rediscoveries.* New York: Crown, 1972.
Puzo, Mario. *"The Godfather Papers" and Other Confessions.* New York: Putnam, 1972.
Wheeler, Thomas C., ed. *The Immigrant Experience: The Anguish of Becoming an American.* New York: Dial, 1971.

PYNCHON, THOMAS (THOMAS RUGGLES PYNCHON, JR.) (1937–) According to Joel Stein in a *Time* magazine review, Thomas Pynchon "created epic modernism" (Stein). In Stein's opinion, Pynchon's work goes beyond the "detail-saturated realism" of early modernists to create "Greek-size tales." By 1975 Pynchon had won the Howells Medal from the National Institute and American Academy of Arts and Letters for the entire body of his work. His three highly experimental postmodern novels at that time included *V.* (1963), winner of the William Faulkner award; *The CRYING OF LOT 49* (1966); and *GRAVITY'S RAINBOW* (1973), winner of the National Book Award. (Pynchon refused to accept that award.) Renowned for the dexterity and denseness of his prose, his wit, and his extraordinary demands on his readers, Pynchon is concerned with the unsettling effects of technology on contemporary life; he frequently features characters beset by paranoia. Along with William S. BURROUGHS he anticipated chaos theory and was a grandfather of the cyberpunk use of the literary chaos that emanates from information overload (Schroeder), Pynchon is also linked with Joseph HELLER, Kurt VONNEGUT, and John BARTH, all employers of black humor and experimental forms and subject matter. Pynchon continues to attract followers, particularly literary scholars and young readers.

Thomas Pynchon grants no interviews and reveals little about his personal life. He was born on May 8, 1937, in Glen Cove, Long Island, to Thomas Ruggles Pynchon, an industrial surveyor, and Katherine Frances Bennett Pynchon and was educated at Cornell University. He graduated with a B.A. (1958) and served two years in the navy. His writing career began with the publication of short stories, followed by the novel *V.* There Herbert Stencil embarks on a quest to discover the identity of a person noted in his father's diary and known only by that initial. Stencil's energy and sense of purpose is illuminated by his difference from the "Whole Sick Crew," an aimless and amoral group that represents the current state of society. Pynchon then published *The Crying of Lot 49.* It features Oedipa Maas, who, as executrix of the will of her former lover, discovers—or, as a Pynchon paranoiac thinks she discovers—a plot to topple the United States Post Office. Generally considered Pynchon's most important work, *Gravity's Rainbow,* Pynchon's longest and most complex novel, consists of an ingenious blending of fantasy and reality, humor and violence, parody and satire, and multiple suggestions that Western civilization has declined into decadence in proportion to the invention and deployment of its technologically perfect instruments of death. Set in London during World War II bombing raids and in postwar Germany, the novel was nominated for a Pulitzer Prize.

After a lengthy hiatus, in 1990 Pynchon published *Vineland,* named for a fictitious Northern California wilderness area that has become a 1980s refuge for aging hippies and counterculture folk. At the center is Prairie Wheeler, a young woman in search of her mother, Frenesi Gates, who has transformed from 1960s anti-Nixon radical to government informer, emblem of social and moral disintegration. His most recent novel is *Mason and Dixon* (1997), a satiric work written in 18th-century English and featuring such early Americans as George Washington and Ben Franklin.

NOVELS

The Crying of Lot 49. Philadelphia: J.B. Lippincott, 1966.
Gravity's Rainbow. New York: Viking, 1973.
Mason and Dixon. New York: Henry Holt, 1997.
V. Philadelphia: J.B. Lippincott, 1963.
Vineland. Boston: Little, Brown, 1990.

SOURCES

Arlett, Robert. *Epic Voices: Inner and Global Impulse in the Contemporary American and British Novel.* Selingsgrove, Pa.: Susquehanna University Press, 1996.
Chambers, Judith. *Thomas Pynchon.* New York: Twayne, 1992.
Chatman, Seymour, ed. *Approaches to Poetics.* New York: Columbia University Press, 1973.
Clerc, Charles, ed. *Approaches to "Gravity's Rainbow."* Columbus: Ohio State University Press, 1983.
Colvile, Georgiana M. M. *Beyond and Beneath the Mantle: On Thomas Pynchon's "The Crying of Lot 49."* Edited by C. C. Barfoot, Hans Bertens, and Theo D'haen. Amsterdam, The Netherlands: Rodopi, 1988.
Cooper, Peter L. *Signs and Symptoms: Thomas Pynchon and the Contemporary World.* Berkeley: University of California Press, 1983.
Cowart, David. *Thomas Pynchon: The Art of Allusion.* Carbondale: Southern Illinois University Press, 1980.
Dugdale, John. *Thomas Pynchon: Allusive Parables of Power.* New York: Macmillan, 1990.
Grant, J. Kerry. *A Companion to "The Crying of Lot 49."* Athens: University of Georgia Press, 1994.
Green, Geoffrey. *The Vineland Papers: Critical Takes on Pynchon's Novel.* Normal, Ill.: Dalkey Archive Press, 1994.
Hite, Molly. *Ideas of Order in the Novels of Thomas Pynchon.* Columbus: Ohio State University Press, 1983.

Hurm, Gerd. *Fragmented Urban Images: The American City in Modern Fiction from Stephen Crane to Thomas Pynchon.* New York: Peter Lang, 1991.
Madsen, Deborah L. *The Postmodernist Allegories of Thomas Pynchon.* New York: St. Martin's Press, 1991.
Mendelson, Edward, ed. *Pynchon: A Collection of Critical Essays.* Englewood Cliffs, N.J.: Prentice Hall, 1978.
Moore, Thomas. *The Style of Connectedness: "Gravity's Rainbow" and Thomas Pynchon.* Columbia: University of Missouri Press, 1987.
Nadeau, Robert. *Readings from the New Book on Nature: Physics and Metaphysics in the Modern Novel.* Amherst: University of Massachusetts Press, 1981.
Newman, Robert D. *Understanding Thomas Pynchon.* Columbia: University of South Carolina Press, 1986.
Plater, William M. *The Grim Phoenix: Reconstructing Thomas Pynchon.* Bloomington: University of Indiana Press, 1978.
Sakrajda, Mira. *Postmodern Discourses of Love: Pynchon, Barth, Coover, Gass, and Barthelme.* New York: Peter Lang, 1997.
Schaub, Thomas H. *Pynchon: The Voice of Ambiguity.* Urbana: University of Illinois Press, 1981.
Scotto, Robert M. *Three Contemporary Novelists: An Annotated Bibliography of Novels: An Annotated Bibliography of Works by and about John Hawkes, Joseph Heller, and Thomas Pynchon.* Boston: G. K. Hall, 1977.
Siegel, Mark R. *Pynchon: Creative Paranoia in "Gravity's Rainbow."* Port Washington, N.Y.: Kennikat, 1978.
Stark, John O. *Pynchon's Fictions: Thomas Pynchon and the Literature of Information.* Athens: Ohio University Press, 1980.
Tanner, Tony. *Thomas Pynchon.* London: Methuen, 1982.
Weisenburger, Steven. *A "Gravity's Rainbow" Companion: Sources and Contexts for Pynchon's Novel.* Athens: The University of Georgia Press, 1988.

OTHER

Lots of Thomas Pynchon Links. Available online. URL: http://www.acmeme.org/pynchon. Accessed September 26, 2005.
Schroeder, Randy. "Inheriting Chaos: Burroughs, Pynchon, Sterling, Rucker." *Extrapolation.* (March 22, 2002). Highbeam Resources. Available online. URL: http://www.highbeam.com/library/doc3.asp?DOCID=1G1:87128338. Accessed September 26, 2005.
Stein, Joel. "Thomas Pynchon: America's Best Novelist." *Time.* Highbeam Resources. Available online. URL: http://www.highbeam.com/library/doc3.asp?DOCID=1G1:76163933. Accessed September 26, 2005.

Q

QUICKSAND NELLA LARSEN **(1928)** Nella LARSEN's largely autobiographical novel *Quicksand,* for which she won a Bronze medal as second prize in literature from the Harmon Foundation in 1928, is considered one of the finest novels of the Harlem Renaissance.

Through the inability of its biracial heroine to find her identity in either African- or European-American communities, *Quicksand* depicts cultural dualism from both sociological and psychological perspectives. The third-person narration of the novel's plot is filtered through the consciousness of its 22-year-old heroine Helga Crane, daughter of a Danish mother and an African-American father. The novel opens with Helga on the verge of leaving her position as teacher at Naxos, an institution near Alabama dedicated to the education of African-American children. In Naxos the Victorian code of repression, propriety, and sanctimony rules the behavior of teachers and students. Helga Crane's determination to leave the stifling and pretentious environment of the school and her fiancé, James Vayle, a well-established member of both the school and the African-American middle class, is shaken but not altered by her encounter with the effective school principal Dr. Robert Anderson toward whom she has mixed feelings of repulsion and attraction.

Helga goes to Chicago where she experiences financial anxieties because she is rebuffed by the new wife of her Danish-American uncle Peter Nilssen, who previously financed Helga's education. She finally secures employment as speech-editor and companion to Mrs. Jeanette Hayes-Rore, a racial uplift speaker, who takes her to the Harlem residence of Anne Grey, the African-American widow of her late husband's nephew. Helga feels comfortable working and residing with Anne Grey in the cosmopolitan ambiance of Harlem until her racial and cultural unease catches up with her. Anne's inconsistencies in racial equality activities and Harlem's hypocrisy in racial uplift campaigns, in which Robert Anderson is also involved, disturb Helga's sense of belonging. She turns Robert Anderson's attention from herself to Anne Grey and, taking advantage of a convenient sum that comes to her from her uncle Peter Nilssen, relocates to Copenhagen to stay with her mother's sister Katrina and her husband Poul Dahl.

In the warmth of her relatives' welcome, Helga feels released from the racial prison of Harlem, but soon she discovers that Copenhagen accepts her only in terms of her being different, exotic, savage, and primitive. During her two-year stay in Denmark, a prominent Danish painter, Axel Olsen, paints her portrait and first asks her to become his mistress and then his wife. Smothered by Axel's artistic presence, social superiority, and sexual advances, she rejects both the proposition and the proposal. Unable to meet her Danish relatives' expectations for her to become a middle-class wife by accepting this socially profitable marriage, and feeling homesick for her African-American roots, she returns to New York to find Robert Anderson married to Anne Grey.

At a party in Harlem, Helga meets James Vayle and discourages him from proposing marriage to her again. In the same evening, she responds to the passionate kiss of a heavily intoxicated Robert Anderson and finally faces her strong sexual desire for him. Later, however, Anderson regrets his conduct and apologizes for it. Dejected by the denial of his feelings for her, Helga wanders about the streets of Harlem and has a conversion experience in a church where she meets Reverend Mr. Pleasant Green. She marries this country preacher and returns with him to Alabama, where she finds her superficial faith vanished and herself in the "quicksand" of domesticity and motherhood, giving birth to three children in 20 months. Hardly recovered from the death of her fourth baby, she finds herself expecting her fifth child.

The protagonist's tragic end yields to analysis of the psychological and social forces that effect her life. As well as displaying Helga Crane's counteraction to being rejected by Robert Anderson, her inadvertent marriage to a Southern preacher portrays the resolution of her doubtful origin, as marriage to a preacher doubly legitimizes her existence as a child out of wedlock. Her impetuous marriage also enacts the impingement of the social pressures on the sexuality of African-American women. Prevented from acknowledging and expressing her sexual passion freely by the racist social construct, which deems African-American women's sexuality savage and primitive, Helga assents to a marriage in which she pays for sexual pleasure by rural domesticity and cruel childbearing.

Helga's undeserved destiny also results from her desperate desire to belong. Unable to find a partner to match her mixed racial identity in the pretentious environment of oppressive Naxos, exemplified by James Vayle; the hypocritical climate of bourgeois Harlem, represented by Robert Anderson; and the overbearing milieu of middle-class Copenhagen, symbolized by Axel Olsen, she expects to find refuge in a marriage with a man who epitomizes a space, unrestricted by racial and social definitions, that she has entered through a sudden spiritual rebirth. The circumstances that thrust this final choice upon her seem more powerful than this protagonist, thus rendering a naturalistic component to the social and psychological realism of the plot. Nella Larsen's probe into African-American female sexuality, exploration of the social forces on the psyche of a woman of mixed ancestry, criticism of African-American middle-class values, and skepticism about the existence of God set her novel apart from the classical "racial uplift" and "tragic mulatto" novels of the late 19th and early 20th centuries.

SOURCES

Brickhouse, Anna. "Nella Larsen and the Intertextual Geography of *Quicksand*," *African American Review* 35, no. 4 (Winter 2001): 533–551.

Davis, Thadious. *Nella Larsen, Novelist of the Harlem Renaissance: A Woman's Life Unveiled.* Baton Rouge: Louisiana University Press, 1996.

Goldsmith, Meredith. "Shopping to Pass, Passing to Shop: Bodily Self-Fashioning in the Fiction of Nella Larsen." In *Recovering the Black Female Body: Self-Representations by African American Women,* edited by Michael Bennett and Vanessa D. Dickerson, 97–120. New Brunswick, N.J.: Rutgers University Press, 2001.

Larsen, Nella. *Quicksand and Passing.* Edited by Deborah E. McDowell. New Brunswick, N.J.: Rutgers University Press, 1986.

Larson, Charles R. *Invisible Darkness: Jean Toomer & Nella Larsen.* Iowa City: University of Iowa Press, 1993.

McLendon, Jacquelyn Y. *The Politics of Color in the Fiction of Jessie Fauset and Nella Larsen.* Charlottesville: University Press of Virginia, 1995.

Miller, Erica M. *The Other Reconstruction: Where Violence and Womanhood Meet in the Writings of Wells-Barnett, Grimké, and Larsen.* New York: Garland, 2000.

Wall, Cheryl A. *Women of the Harlem Renaissance.* Bloomington: Indiana University Press, 1995.

Ferdâ Asya

R

RABBIT REDUX John Updike (1971) John Updike's *Rabbit Redux,* published in 1971, is a sequel to his 1960 novel RABBIT, RUN. The novel is set in a middle-class community in east Pennsylvania in 1969, a year highlighting quintessential events in the United States: the moon exploration, the Vietnam War, feminist movements, sexual and black revolutions, drug addiction, hippie lifestyles, and middle-American anger and frustration. The narrative successfully integrates the important social and political issues addressed by different characters in its representation of the arid urban life of the 1960s.

The novel is divided into four sections named after the central figures thematizing certain concerns. Section One, "Pop/Mom/Moon," introduces the middle-aged, sexually diminished Harry Angstrom, who has become a burnt-out cynic—a washed-out, dissipated American man in need of "stability." This section opens with Harry discovering that his once mousy wife, Janice, is having a love affair with Charlie Stavros, a car salesman in her father's agency. Harry finds his dreary life shattered by the infidelity of his wife, who leaves him and abandons their 13-year-old son, Nelson. The section ends with the Apollo moon mission on TV as Harry and Nelson visit Harry's dying mother.

In Section Two, "Jill," Harry meets Jill, a teenage runaway girl, at a bar. Jill goes home with Harry and they make love. Jill's lack of self-concern makes Harry sexually passive; the "spaced-out" girl is described as an "angry mechanic," working to arouse Harry, who

only manages to complete the sexual act by imagining a machine on Jill's belly. Eroticism fails both Harry and Jill. The next morning Nelson meets Jill and they immediately develop a close relationship as siblings. Jill attempts to change Harry's conservative attitudes toward Vietnam, blacks, and sex.

Section Three, "Skeeter," centers on the character Skeeter, Jill's friend, a young Afro-American militant and Vietnam veteran, now a revolutionary. Skeeter has jumped bail for drug possession and wants a few days' asylum. Skeeter ends Harry's passivity, challenging him to fight, both psychologically and physically, and provoking verbal confrontations. Skeeter's "seminars" every night educate Harry out of the worst of his racism and free him to confront both his own exploited status and his class hatred. The section ends with a fiasco: Harry's house is firebombed, Jill burns to death, and Skeeter goes on the run.

The final section, "Mim," introduces Harry's younger sister Mim, a would-be actress who is now a Las Vegas call girl. Mim tells Harry that she has learned to manipulate people, and in order to expedite Harry's reunion with Janice, Mim sleeps with Stavros. When Stavros suffers a heart attack, Janice brings him back to life. Janice and Harry are reunited at the close of the novel, but the symbolic terms leave the final position unresolved.

John Updike's fiction participates in the contemporary debate over sexual identity and difference. Much criticism and reception of the tetralogy (RABBIT, RUN, *Rabbit Redux, Rabbit Is Rich, Rabbit at Rest*) has overemphasized the loss of Christian ideal or the absence of any transcendent mythos that Rabbit represents in contemporary middle-American society. However, throughout the Rabbit quartet, Updike's ostensible theme is a chronicle of the evolution of middle-class American manhood since the 1950s. For the author, the chief malady afflicting modern American man is "masculinity" itself. (Carnes, 448) Another critic, Peter K. Powers, also argues that "for Updike particularly, an acute sense of a diminished masculinity, both in aesthetics and religion, motivates his work as he alternately embraces and rejects the 'feminized male' who has developed as an ideal for twentieth-century middle-class masculinity" (Powers, 330). Labeling Rabbit as a chauvinist, racist, or misogynist could oversimplify Updike's creation of this well-known character, since the intertwined issues of gender, theology, and aesthetics have made Rabbit "far more unstable and contradictory than [the writer's] overt sexism might first lead us to assume" (Powers, 330). Through the protagonist Harry Angstrom in the four novels, Updike has produced the longest and most comprehensive representation of masculinity in American literature. In these books the author reevaluates gender issues, particularly masculinity, under the incessant stimulus of historical events and social changes. The events and forces shape Rabbit's masculinity as well as the ways his gender identity affects his personal and spiritual development, his relationships, and ultimately, his society.

The interplay of the failure of erotic questioning and the constant quest for a redefined masculinity as a series of paradoxes and struggles bulk large in *Rabbit Redux*. Rabbit's relationships with different characters reveal his own gender/sexuality anxiety from his encounters with the marginalized groups: Jill (teenage runaway), Skeeter (militant minority), Mim (prostitute). The very existence of this interracial, intergenerational community emphasizes how Harry's WASP masculinity has been undermined and reconstructed by differences of class, age, and ethnicity. The complications in Rabbit's erotic relationships show how Updike challenges stereotypical masculinity and reveals its limitations as the source of Rabbit's confusion and anxiety in the man/woman, man/man, and woman/woman entanglements that the protagonist seeks to cut through. *Rabbit Redux* invites readers to

question archetypal masculinity and see how its limitation has created anxieties and contradictions of a cultural phenomenon.

SOURCES

Carnes, Mark C. "Fictions and Fantasies of Early Twentieth-Century Manhood," *Reviews in American History* 24, no. 3 (1996): 448–453.

Hunt, George W. *John Updike and the Three Greatest Things: Sex, Religion, and Art.* Grand Rapids, Mich.: Eerdmans Publishing Company, 1980.

Kimmel, Michael. *Manhood in America: A Cultural History.* New York: The Free Press, 1996.

O'Connell, Mary. *Updike and the Patriarchal Dilemma: Masculinity in the Rabbit Novels.* Carbondale: Southern Illinois University Press, 1996.

Powers, Peter Kerry. "Scribbling for a Life: Masculinity, Doctrine, and Style in the Work of John Updike," *Christianity and Literature* 43, nos. 3–4 (1994): 329–346.

Slethaug, Gordon E. "*Rabbit Redux:* 'Freedom Is Made of Brambles.' " In *Critical Essays on John Updike,* edited by William R. Macnaughton, 237–253. Boston: G. K. Hall and Co., 1982.

Updike, John. *Rabbit Redux.* New York: Fawcett Crest, 1971.

Uphaus, Suzanne Henning. *John Updike.* New York: Frederick Ungar Publishing Co. Inc., 1980.

Wilson, Matthew. "The Rabbit Tetralogy: From Solitude to Society to Solitude Again," *MFS: Modern Fiction Studies* 37, no. 1 (Spring 1991): 5–24.

Bennett Fu

RABBIT, RUN JOHN UPDIKE **(1960)** In John UPDIKE's *Rabbit, Run* (1960), the protagonist runs, but not too far. Harry "Rabbit" Angstrom, a character Updike revisits in three subsequent novels, *RABBIT REDUX* (1971), *Rabbit Is Rich* (1981), and *Rabbit at Rest* (1990), and one novella, *Rabbit Remembered* (2000), is a 26-year-old married salesman and former star high-school athlete who literally runs out on Janice, his pregnant, alcoholic wife, and on Nelson, his two-year-old son. On his initial "flight from domesticity" (Kakutani, 1), Rabbit only travels as far as West Virginia before quickly returning to his hometown of Brewer, Pennsylvania. His freedom from entangled relationships is also short-lived. Soon thereafter, in Brewer, he creates a new domestic arrangement and another rote lifestyle. Rabbit, now no longer employed, spends his days playing house with a prostitute named Ruth, and playing golf with Reverend Eccles. Rabbit's chats with Eccles are the reverend's futile attempts to rectify Rabbit's plight. Throughout the novel, Rabbit, much like a runner doing continuous laps around a track, is caught in a loop. Eventually leaving Ruth, now pregnant, and returning to Janice, whose abandonment by Rabbit fuels her drinking, he then leaves Janice and returns to Ruth. By the novel's end, he is running again, this time after Janice accidentally drowns their infant daughter. Given how Rabbit first takes flight to restore the vitality drained by his "second-rate" marriage and job, this graphic and heart-wrenching conclusion underscores the tragic and ironic consequences of Rabbit's selfish decisions and indulged delusions.

Rabbit's circular journey, his flight from home that takes him back home, presents an archetypical male conflict: the competing drives to escape the domestic life and to settle down. Indeed, this struggle is a recurring theme for Updike and a traditionally American one. Some other famous male "runners" in American literature include Huck Finn in Mark TWAIN's *The ADVENTURES OF HUCKLEBERRY FINN* (1884), the nameless protagonist in Ralph ELLISON's *The INVISIBLE MAN* (1952), and Sal in Jack KEROUAC's *ON THE ROAD* (1957). Updike's 1988 novel, *S,* a humorous update of Nathaniel HAWTHORNE's *The SCARLET LETTER* as told from Hester Prynne's perspective, attempts to upend this theme somewhat and to challenge his reputation for portraying women "as being merely 'wives, sex objects, and purely domestic creatures' " (Kakutani, 1). Moreover, *Rabbit, Run* and *S* both punctuate how his fiction generally reworks America's "novel of manners." Traditionally about the lives of the upper class in New England and the Northeast, these novels were written by, among others, Henry JAMES, Edith WHARTON, John O'HARA, and John CHEEVER. Updike's concerns with middle-class living, sexual intercourse, dysfunctional families, and thankless jobs brilliantly infuse this tradition with a poignant realism (Dickstein, 26).

When introduced in 1960, Rabbit, now famous as the impulsively mobile and perpetually immature male protagonist, seemed a fitting reactionary figure to the previous decade. With 1950s America preaching moral conformity, family values, and hard work, by the decade's end, this atmosphere left many feeling constrained, frustrated, and disappointed. A "national malaise" became more widespread. In reaction to this ethos, many writers such as Jack Kerouac and J. D. SALINGER composed works that emphasized seeking personal happiness, expressing individuality, and experiencing freedom. John Updike credits Salinger and Kerouac's thematic concerns and lyric style for shaping his own focus and narrative voice. *Rabbit, Run,* written when he was a 20-something married father of four, scrutinizes the dire moral consequences, especially for relationships, when a married American male embraces this beatnik spirit (Dickstein, 103–111).

Updike grounds this countercultural movement in the inescapable entanglements and practicalities of everyday life. (Even when on the run, Rabbit must return home for more clothing.) More poignantly, though, Rabbit's longing to break free from familial constraints, his constant drive for sensual pleasure, and his wish to recapture his former youthful glory, all create turmoil for those around him. His repeated offenses make the reader recoil at this character's apparent "hardness of heart" (vii). Critics have long debated the level of Rabbit's self-awareness. Morris Dickstein credits Rabbit with an occasional epiphany about "life's limits" because of his time spent with his "goad and confidant," Reverend Eccles (Dickstein, 108–111). Frederick Karl is less hopeful; although he finds the character "not a bad man," he's even more "hollow" than Updike perceives. As readers, we are left to wonder if Rabbit is a prototype of the American male (Karl, 348)—one who rebuffs maturity and resists domestication.

In 1970, *Rabbit, Run* was made into a film, with James Caan playing the role of Rabbit Angstrom. The Rabbit tetralogy has garnered critical accolades: *Rabbit Is Rich* and *Rabbit at Rest* both won Pulitzer Prizes, in 1982 and 1991, respectively.

SOURCES

Dickstein, Morris. *Leopards in the Temple: The Transformation of American Fiction, 1945–1970.* Cambridge, Mass.: Harvard University Press, 2002.

Kakutani, Michiko. "Critics Notebook; Updike's Long Struggle to Portray Women," *New York Times,* 5 May 1988, C29.

Karl, Frederick R. *American Fictions, 1940/1980: A Comprehensive Edition and Critical Evaluation.* New York: Harper and Row, 1983.

Updike, John. *Rabbit, Run.* New York: Knopf, 1960.

Ilse Schrynemakers

RAGTIME E. L. DOCTOROW (1975) *Ragtime* is a historical novel that mingles fact and fiction, while interweaving the stories of three different families. The title hints at the raggedy coexistence of different narratives within the novel: DOCTOROW wrote his novel like a ragtime, as though a syncopated melody line, one strand of history, is played against a straight or routine accompaniment, another strand. He plays history like a tune on a player piano. He has emphasized the importance of understanding history as a kind of ragtime throughout his career. He believes that fiction understands history's sources to be more various than the historian might suppose, and *Ragtime* illustrates his belief, as expressed in an interview, that history becomes mythology unless composed of many perspectives: "If you don't constantly recompose and reinterpret history, then it begins to tighten its grip on your throat as myth and you find yourself in some kind of totalitarian society. . . . [T]he test of any society is its resistance to the subjective." He is suspicious of the process of writing history: "The history of . . . the murder of six million Jews, if Hitler had won the Second World War [would perhaps have been represented] in contemporary history as not having happened." Doctorow's ideal artist should therefore demonstrate the elusiveness of historical truth and can be central to the production of history, functioning as "a Distant Early Warning System in the defense of reality," as he explained. *Ragtime* confirms the importance of multiple perspectives to defend reality: At one point the character Dreiser turns his chair in circles, unable to find a "proper alignment," and there are apparently many centers to the ice-cap that the character Father explores. The novel mocks any single approach, whether romantic, scientific, or universal.

In condemning absolutist and deterministic history, *Ragtime* explores the dangers of Jung's theory of the collective unconscious, what Morgan calls the "universal patterns of order and repetition that give meaning to the activity of this planet," and even includes Jung as a character. When history seems to move in cycles, it does so in ominously military terms: The novel opens with Father making a living from patriotism, and closes with Thaw marching annually in a military parade. A repeating image of immersion conveys the stifling qualities of repetition: a baby in the earth, Houdini in coffins, Morgan in a tomb. The theme of silhouettes symbolizes history as a rigid outline, without detail or nuance: The explorers are silhouetted in a photograph, the characters are silhouettes on the beach, the pyramids are silhouetted.

One of the novel's major characters, Tateh, even creates silhouettes. But they eventually lead him to a career in filmmaking: He turns them into "movie-books," separate images that flick past as one long sequence to the eye. These detached moments become a continuous shaped history only because of the ability of the human mind to create order. Tateh learns that "everything in the world could as easily be something else" and reinvents himself so he is almost reminiscent of a film actor who has escaped the attention of the continuity-checker: He is dark-haired, then white-haired, then dark again. Doctorow thereby uses Tateh and his movie-books to explore vision and understanding as subjective, history as discontinuous, and fact as fiction.

Like Tateh, the character called The Boy seems eventually to understand the difference between truth and "images of truth," and to embrace the fragmentary, raggedy aspect of time and reality. He feels that the shape of history is crooked, and so is fascinated by his distorted appearance in a headlamp and a story in the paper about a curveball. Like Tateh, he knows that the past is not history, and material is not valuable evidence, unless the historian makes it so: He notices "traces quickly erased of moments passed" and treasures "anything discarded," investing it with value, just as imagination and film invest Tateh's silhouettes with detail and sequence, and fiction fleshes out the bare bones of history. Tateh and The Boy realize the truth of Nietzsche's statement, which Doctorow quoted in an interview in 1988: "You need meaning before you know what a fact is."

Ragtime perhaps also echoes Nietzsche's famous essay, "The Use and Abuse of History," which proposes "a kind of historical writing that had no drop of common fact in it," which could yet "claim to be called in the highest degree objective." Nietzsche wanted historians to learn to "think one thing with another, and weave the elements into a single whole" for history's "real value lies in inventing ingenious variations on a probably commonplace theme." Doctorow does just this: His novel weaves elements and variations together, into a ragtime of history.

SOURCES

Budick, Emily Miller. *Fiction and Historical Consciousness: The American Romance Tradition.* New Haven, Conn.: Yale University Press, 1989.

Doctorow, E. L. *Conversations with E. L. Doctorow.* Jackson: University Press of Mississippi, 1999.

———. *Essays and Conversations.* Princeton, N.J.: Ontario Review Press, 1983.

———. *Jack London, Hemingway and the Constitution.* New York: Random House, 1993.

———. *Ragtime.* New York: Random House, 1975.

Hellman, John. *Fables of Fact: The New Journalism as New Fiction.* Urbana: University of Illinois Press, 1981.

Zoe Trodd

RAND, AYN (1905–1982)

The late Ayn Rand—novelist, essayist, playwright, and philosopher—has become a cult figure. Although she published only four novels, they all illustrate her philosophy of rational egoism, called "objectivism." After her emigration in 1926 from Russia to the United States, she became an exemplar of Cold War anticommunism; her novels were an expression of her loathing for totalitarianism and her advocacy of capitalism. Her emphasis on the dignity and worth of the individual and her rejection of an all-powerful state still resonate with the large number of readers who continue to buy her books. (It remains a rite of passage for college freshmen to debate her ideas.) As numerous critics have noted, her stunning success as a novelist in English aligns Rand with other foreign-born writers such as Joseph Conrad and Vladimir NABOKOV.

Ayn Rand was born Alice Rosenbaum on February 2, 1905, in St. Petersburg, Russia, to Fronz Rosenbaum, a chemist, and Anna Rosenbaum. She was educated at the University of Petrograd, from which she graduated with highest honors in 1924, emigrated to the United States in 1926, married Charles Francis "Frank" O'Connor, an artist, in 1929, and became a naturalized citizen in 1931. She invented the name Ayn, pronounced like "ein," German for the number one, and took the name Rand from her Remington-Rand typewriter. Her first novel, *We The Living* (1936), tells the truth as Rand saw it, about life in communist Russia; in fact, she saw the book as a universal parable for people and all times and as a warning about the destructive effects of totalitarianism. It sold more than 2 million copies. She followed with the dystopian novella *Anthem* (1938), which illustrated the harsh physical and mental suppression of the individual in a society that has eliminated the word for "I." *The FOUNTAINHEAD* (1943) tells the tale of Howard Roark, a young architect who struggles to maintain his integrity in the face of "an intelligentsia that despises individual excellence and independence of thoughts" (Machan, 3). She uses herself as a model for the heroine, Dominique Francon. Other major characters: Wynand, for instance, seems a composite of William Randolph Hearst, Henry Luce, and Joseph Pulitzer; Ellworth Toohey is modeled on British socialist Harold Laski. The protagonist, Howard Roark, although Rand denied the similarity, is considered by many readers to be a fictional version of America's most famous architect, Frank Lloyd Wright. Despite the usual nervousness with which any Ayn Rand novel was received, it sold extremely well: more than 5 million copies by the end of the 20th century.

Her magnum opus and major achievement was *ATLAS SHRUGGED* (1957), a 1,000-page novel again touting objectivism as the guiding principle of a successful state. A large cast of characters peoples a United States that hovers on the brink of disaster because of its collectivist government; the hero, John Galt, who realizes that to save the country, individuals who can think clearly, intelligently, and rationally are needed. After this novel was published, Rand became a public figure—a campus teacher and lecturer—and was interviewed frequently on television. She died on March 6, 1982, in New York City and is buried in Kensico Cemetery in Valhalla, New York. In addition to her success as a novelist, Rand published four plays, two of which were produced on Broadway. Her play *Night of*

January 16th was released by Paramount in 1941, and her novel *We the Living* was filmed in Italy in 1942. She also edited *The Objectivist,* a newsletter dedicated to explaining and furthering her philosophy, and wrote numerous nonfiction essays and books on the subject of the superiority of capitalism to communism.

NOVELS AND NOVELLAS

Anthem. London: Cassell, 1938; revised edition, Los Angeles, Calif.: Pamphleteers, Inc., 1946; 50th anniversary edition, with new introduction by Leonard Peikoff. New York: Dutton, 1995.

Atlas Shrugged. New York: Random House, 1957.

The Fountainhead. Indianapolis, Ind. & New York: Bobbs-Merrill, 1943; reprinted with special introduction by Rand, 1968; reprinted, New York: Plume, 1994.

We the Living. New York: Macmillan, 1936; reprinted, New York: Random House, 1959; 60th anniversary edition, New York: Dutton, 1995.

SOURCES

Baker, James T. *Ayn Rand.* Boston: Twayne, 1987.

Barnes, Hazel Estella. *An Existential Ethics.* New York: Knopf, 1967.

Branden, Barbara. *The Passion of Ayn Rand.* Garden City, N.Y.: Doubleday, 1986.

Branden, Nathaniel. *Who Is Ayn Rand?: An Analysis of the Novels of Ayn Rand,* with biographical essay by Barbara Branden. New York: Random House, 1977.

———. *My Years with Ayn Rand.* San Francisco: Jossey-Bass, 1998.

Cerf, Bennett. *At Random.* New York: Random House, 1977.

Den Uyl, Douglas, and Douglas Rasmussen, eds. *The Philosophical Thought of Ayn Rand.* Urbana: University of Illinois Press, 1984.

Ellis, Albert. *Is Objectivism a Religion?* New York: Lyle Stuart, 1968.

Erickson, Peter F. *The Stance of Atlas: An Examination of the Philosophy of Ayn Rand.* Portland, Ore.: Herakles Press, 1997.

Gladstein, Mimi Reisel. *The Ayn Rand Companion.* Westport, Conn.: Greenwood Press, 1984.

Haydn, Hiram. *Words and Faces.* New York: Harcourt, 1974.

Machan, Tibor R. *Ayn Rand.* New York: Peter Lang, 1999.

O'Neill, William. *With Charity Toward None: An Analysis of Ayn Rand's Philosophy.* New York: Philosophical Library, 1971.

Paxton, Michael. *Ayn Rand: A Sense of Life; The Companion Book.* Layton, Utah: Gibbs Smith, 1998.

Peary, Gerald, and Roget Shatzkin, eds. *The Modern American Novel and the Movies.* New York: Ungar, 1978.

Schwartz, Peter, ed. *The Battle for Laissez-Faire Capitalism.* Charlottesville, Va.: Intellectual Activist, 1983.

Sciabarra, Chris Matthew. *Ayn Rand: The Russian Radical.* State College: Pennsylvania State University Press, 1995.

Slusser, George E., Eric S. Rabkin, and Robert Scholes, eds. *Coordinates: Placing Science Fiction and Fantasy, Alternative Series.* Carbondale: Southern Illinois University Press, 1984.

Tuccille, Jerome. *It Usually Begins with Ayn Rand.* New York: Stein & Day, 1972.

OTHER

Wired for Books: Audio Interview with Leonard Peikoff and Barbara Bramdem on Ayn Rand. Available online. URL: http://wiredforbooks.org/aynrand. Accessed September 25, 2005.

RAWLINGS, MARJORIE KINNAN (1896–1953)

Since the publication of *The YEARLING* (1938), Marjorie Kinnan Rawlings has been associated with north-central Florida, which she first visited on a 1928 fishing trip. She later purchased a citrus farm in the tiny rural community of Cross Creek. In addition to *The Yearling* and another Book-of-the-Month Club selection, *South Moon Under* (1933), she wrote the novels *Golden Apples* (1935); *The Sojourner* (1953), and *The Secret River* (1955); the novella *Jacob's Ladder* (1931); a number of short stories collected in *When the Whippoorwill* (1940); and the autobiographical *Cross Creek* (1942). Other stories and poems were published posthumously. Her literary reputation was secured when she won the 1939 Pulitzer Prize for *The Yearling.* MGM bought the rights to *The Yearling,* and the film, released in 1946, starred Gregory Peck and Jane Wyman as Jody Baxter's parents, and Claude Jarman, Jr., as Jody.

Rawlings was born on August 8, 1896, in Washington, D.C., to Arthur F. Kinnan, a U.S. Patent Office attorney, and Ida May Traphagen Kinnan. Her love of nature developed during her early years on the family's Maryland farm. She graduated Phi Beta Kappa in 1918 from the University of Wisconsin, married Charles Rawlings in 1919, and became a journalist in Rochester, New York. After the visit to north-central Florida, Rawlings published *Jacob's Ladder,* a modern-day version of the biblical story of Job. To write *South Moon Under,* Rawlings lived with an old woman and her moonshiner son, who became Piety Lantry and Lent Jacklin in the novel. In *Golden Apples,* an Englishman in Florida misunderstands the rural inhabitants, whose customs and speech he finds strange. Similarly, they misunderstand him. Her continuing fascination with the region surfaces in her depiction of Jody Baxter and his parents in *The Yearling;* the novel contains rich and descriptive language evoking the land and the growth of the characters in this coming-of-age novel. *The Sojourner,* set in upstate New York, chronicles three generations of the Linden family and their relationship to their farm. Ase Linden learns to accept his position in the family, after realizing that his mother prefers his older brother, Ben.

Rawlings, divorced from her first husband in 1933 and married to Norton Sanford Baskin in 1941, was planning to write a biography of her friend Ellen GLAS-GOW when she died of a cerebral hemorrhage on December 14, 1953. The bulk of her papers are located at the University of Florida Libraries' rare-book section.

NOVELS AND NOVELLAS

Golden Apples. New York: Scribner, 1935.
Jacob's Ladder. (First published in *Scribner's* 89 [April 1931], 351–366, 446–464.) Coral Gables, Fla.: University of Miami Press, 1950.
The Sojourner. New York: Scribner, 1953.
South Moon Under. New York: Scribner, 1933.
The Yearling. New York: Scribner, 1938.

SOURCES

Acton, Patricia Nassif. *Invasion of Privacy: The Cross Creek Trial of Marjorie Kinnan Rawlings.* Gainesville: University of Florida Press, 1988.
Bellman, Samuel I. *Marjorie Kinnan Rawlings.* Boston: Twayne, 1974.
Bigelow, Gordon E. *Frontier Eden: The Literary Career of Marjorie Kinnan Rawlings.* Miami: University of Florida Press, 1966.
Gilman, Owen. "Marjorie Kinnan Rawlings." In *Fifty Southern Writers After 1900: A Bio-bibliographical Sourcebook,* edited by Joseph M. Flora and Robert Bain, 401–410. Westport, Conn.: Greenwood Press, 1987.
Sammons, Sandra Wallus, and Nina McGuire. *Marjorie Kinnan Rawlings and the Florida Crackers.* Lake Buena Vista, Fla.: Tailored Tours Publications, 1995.

Selected Letters of Marjorie Kinnan Rawlings. Edited by Gordon E. Bigelow and Laura V. Monti. Tallahassee: University Presses of Florida, 1983.
Silverthorne, Elizabeth. *Marjorie Kinnan Rawlings: Sojourner at Cross Creek.* Woodstock, N.Y.: Overlook, 1988.
Turk, Janet K. "Marjorie Kinnan Rawlings." In *American Women Writers, 1900–1945: a Bio-bibliographical Critical Sourcebook,* edited by Laurie Champion, 287–294. Westport, Conn.: Greenwood Press, 2000.

RECTOR OF JUSTIN, THE LOUIS AUCHINCLOSS (1964)

Considered one of AUCHINCLOSS's finest works, *The Rector of Justin* purports to tell the life story of Francis Prescott, recently deceased headmaster of Justin Martyr Academy, a New England boarding school modeled on Groton, Auchincloss's alma mater in Massachusetts. On one level the novel may be viewed as an examination of the institution of the American private school. In the words of scholar David B. Parsell, as Justin Martyr Academy moves to center stage, the school becomes more than merely the setting of the novel: "Through the life, ambitions, and accomplishments of the fictional Frank Prescott, Auchincloss focuses directly upon the private boys' school as a sort of American hybrid, somewhat anomalous, illegitimately born into American democracy by deliberate contact with the British aristocracy" (Parsell, 48). Auchincloss is also examining the multifaceted human character epitomized by the school. Prescott, too, is a hybrid, and despite the best storytelling efforts of the many who knew him, in the end he remains an enigma. With this character Auchincloss makes clear that human personality is impressively complicated, and that our complexities are only selectively revealed to various friends and relatives. He uses several different first-person narrators to illustrate this idea.

Of these, Brian Aspinwall is the one who unifies the narrative threads, his account interspersed with other voices in the form of taped interviews, written accounts, and conversations. Arriving at Justin when Prescott is 80 years old, Aspinwall—now a teacher who has failed the army physical and feels uncertain of himself and his identity—is not going off to fight in World War II. Given his lack of self-confidence, Aspinwall initially feels drawn to Prescott because the rector seems his exact opposite—a strong-willed, successful man who can retire with pride in his accomplishments. Although he does not know at first that others have tried to write Prescott's biography and failed, Aspinwall decides that to write about the rector's life will be his most important task. As he becomes better acquainted with Prescott, however, Aspinwall perceives that Prescott feels he has failed, since his graduates, like those at similar elite schools, choose Wall Street positions over careers in the liberal arts, and at the cost of closer ties with family and friends. Numerous critics have pointed out that the reader sees (even though the characters do not) the fundamental inconsistency between instilling democratic and humane values in a school for the wealthy and the privileged. The implied question that follows is, Of what value is such an institution if it swallows up the individual?

One of the ironic sidelights in this character's feelings of failure is that Prescott often shunted his family off to one side in order to spend more hours with Justin. Through his boyhood friend, Horace Havistock, we learn that Prescott always had a vision of a model school and that he spent his entire life trying to create it. At an early age, Prescott lost his father in the Civil War Battle of Chancellorsville. His mother died soon afterward, and the prep school that he and Havistock attended became his substitute family. This belief, and his desire to form the perfect school for boys, became a religious mission. Despite his early success with the New York Central Railroad, where he impressed friends and colleagues with his extraordinary talents for leadership, for politics, perhaps even for future diplomatic negotiations, and despite his promising engagement to Eliza Dean, a spirited young California woman who might have brought to the marriage both happiness and originality, Prescott let both slip through his fingers: He gave up Eliza for the Harvard divinity degree essential to his educational vision, and in some sense sealed his own fate by marrying Harriet Winslow, a woman less vivacious than Eliza but well suited to the insularities of private-school life.

The dichotomy between the attractive ivory tower existence and the cloistered, close-minded, faintly homosexual experience of the boys prep school is elucidated by David Griscam, still another of Prescott's old friends, who mistakenly thought he could write the headmaster's biography. Griscam, a Wall Street lawyer whom Prescott himself dissuaded from a teaching career, attended Justin just as his father did, and therefore blames both the school and his father for his personal weaknesses and for the suicide of his son Jules, another Justin alumnus. A longtime member of the Justin board of trustees, a man who protects the rather naive Prescott from harsh worldly realities, Griscam emblematizes those who both understand and resent schools like Justin, yet also feel compelled to defend and preserve them.

Still another narrator is Cordelia, Prescott's third daughter, ironically named after Shakespeare's Cordelia, loving daughter to King Lear. Unlike Shakespeare's character, however, Auchincloss's Cordelia insists on telling the truth (as her mother would never do) about the ways her father destroyed her one idyllic romance and ruined her two marriages to Justin alumnae and supporters. After years of psychotherapy, Cordelia—unlike her two sisters, who are less articulate but equally wounded—has not only learned to speak out but insists upon doing so. When Aspinwall interviews her in her New York apartment, she exposes the darker, controlling side of her father, always a headmaster, even to his wife or daughters. Like the young Jules Griscam, Cordelia is a casualty of Prescott's naive, idealistic vision and his allegiance to an institution of questionable value. The ambiguity—the possibilities as well as the weaknesses—of both the institution and its headmaster mean that no single narrator can fully comprehend or define Frank Prescott. The reader is left at the end slightly anxious about Aspinwall's decision—despite his failure to complete the Prescott biography—to follow in the footsteps of the rector of Justin.

SOURCES

Auchincloss, Louis. The *Rector of Justin*. Boston: Houghton, 1964.

Parsell, David B. *Louis Auchincloss*. Boston: Twayne, 1988.

RED BADGE OF COURAGE, THE STEPHEN CRANE (1895)

With its ironic and scornful tone, Stephen CRANE's *The Red Badge of Courage* marked a significant departure from the heavily idealized Civil War fiction that appeared in the decades preceding its publication. The novel's unique tone and vivid imagery propelled its author to overnight success. Rather than portraying a larger historical view of the Civil War composed of epic battles that are fueled by a clash of ideals, Crane's focus is much narrower, in that he concentrates on the individual psychology of Private Henry Fleming. The novel impressionistically records Henry's shifting psychological state as he is transformed from a naive, vainglorious youth to an experienced soldier who possesses a deeper understanding of the nature of courage and self-preservation.

At the beginning of the novel, "the youth," as Henry is often referred to, possesses very romanticized notions about war and courage. As he waits encamped with his regiment, Henry frets not about death or being maimed but about whether or not he will run from battle and prove himself a coward in the eyes of his fellow soldiers. Henry's early preoccupation with "proving himself" in battle represents the naive and egoistic notions of courage and bravery that he holds early on in the story.

When Henry's regiment is finally ordered to move, the youth experiences a significant change in attitude as they approach the actual battle. With the thundering of canons on the horizon, Henry begins to feel that perhaps he has been duped by his romanticized notions of war and now begins to suspect, a bit closer to the truth, that "they were taking him out to be slaughtered" (21). He believes he is about to be sacrificed to war, "the blood-swollen god" (28). Though his fear continues to mount, Henry does not run from his first skirmish. In fact, he could not have run even if he felt the desire to do so. Henry becomes boxed in by his fellow soldiers and, like a frightened animal, fights fiercely and unthinkingly to preserve his own life. Henry is relieved that he made it through his first conflict without displaying cowardice. He does, however, succumb to his instinct for self-preservation and runs "like a rabbit" when he comes under heavy fire during his second engagement (39). After fleeing, the youth embarks on a psychological journey that moves from justification and guilt to acceptance and mature understanding at the end of the fierce battle.

Afraid that other soldiers may have witnessed his act of cowardice, Henry attempts to justify his behavior to himself by adopting a self-righteous attitude. He believes he did the right thing, the natural thing, by running to preserve his life. He thinks of the other soldiers who stay to fight as "methodical idiots" and "machine like fools" (41). His resolve is weakened, however, and he begins to feel a supreme sense of guilt after he comes across the "tattered man" in a column of retreating soldiers. The mortally wounded soldier badgers the youth, repeatedly asking Henry about his own wounds. Consumed with guilt, Henry leaves the tattered man to die and rejoins the war effort, eventually earning a superficial wound, his own "red badge of courage," from a blow with a rifle butt to the head by a retreating solder (52).

Once Henry rejoins the battle, he fights bravely and fiercely, even capturing the enemy flag. His own ideas about bravery and courage, however, have undergone a significant shift. He is no longer concerned about earning the accolades of bravery that he once associated with proving himself in battle. In fact, he has learned that it is not about proving himself at all. Henry has adopted a sense of detachment and is no longer concerned with becoming a hero. Rather, he fights bravely as one soldier among many who fight together like some mindless machine in order to defeat the common enemy. Henry also comes to realize the significance, or rather the insignificance, of each battle. Once a soldier reveals that this bloody fight is just a distraction for a more important maneuver, the youth understands that this battle is just one among many. Likewise, his experience, which he had viewed egotistically as unique, is quite similar to that of thousands of other men.

Many argue that the most memorable aspect of *The Red Badge of Courage* is the clarity and insightfulness with which Crane records Henry's transformation. Having never been in battle himself, Crane demonstrates his own instincts for recording the horrors of war and the experience of individual soldiers with great accuracy. Several Civil War veterans in his own time were convinced that Crane must have been in the war. Considered his best and most powerful work, Crane proved himself to be a great talent at a very young age with his war novel, which has never been out of print. Unfortunately, he never had much of a chance to outdo himself, since he died at the age of 29.

The Red Badge of Courage, however, continues to stand as a testament to his outstanding abilities as a writer.

SOURCE

Crane, Stephen. 1895. *The Red Badge of Courage.* Reprint, New York: Bantam, 1983.

Kathleen M. Hicks

RED DRAGON THOMAS HARRIS (1981)   The objective of a detective thriller, and much of so-called "true crime" journalism for that matter, is to enchant the reader. The criminal and/or the detective, and certainly the blood that is shed, must be imbued with something akin to magic, but magic within the terms of everyday life and without recourse to the otherworldliness that characterizes fantasy. Retired F.B.I. agent Will Graham's capacity to "reconstruct" a murderer's thinking by tracing back from mere traces left at the scene of the crime is a magical capacity to the degree that his intuitive mind's eye renders those traces a scene of the crime: "Graham wondered if he [the murderer] had lit a candle. The flickering light would simulate expression on their faces. . . . Maybe he would think to do that next time" (23). From Balzac and Conrad to MAILER and Ellroy, it has become a truism of cultural psychology that the detective's capacity to think like the criminal serves to reveal a shared proclivity that ideology would deny. Graham's capacity for vivid "[i]magination, projection" is a kind of curse, a compulsion not unlike, Harris induces the reader to believe, the overly intense imagination of the psychopath. Thus, the "first small bond" that an act of engaged imagination establishes between Graham and his unknown quarry is said to sting him "like a leech" (23).

The relation of the serial killer, Dolarhyde, to the ex-lawman Graham is that of a vague, but not indiscernible, alter ego—a shadow, a double, on the model of Jekyll and Hyde. Both Dolarhyde and Graham are trapped inside their solitude, inside their minds, inside their skins, which as the killer's name suggests is a skin (hide) of sadness and pain (dolor). Both are loners who do not fit in. Indeed, the institutionally unaffiliated Graham is an object of suspicion for the bureaucratized investigators at the F.B.I. because his unorthodox skills and techniques violate and expose the limitations of the categorical thinking that produces their psychological profiles. Graham and Dolarhyde are alike in other ways. In keeping with postmodern sentimentality, both are characterized as the walking wounded: Graham because his empathic capacities for the morbid and sordid suggests something psychologically perverse about himself, Dolarhyde because he was abandoned and abused as a child (in accord with another sentimental truism). Whereas Dolarhyde is partially absolved by this absence of family as the narrative takes up his pitiable point of view, Graham's striving to save American domesticity from further assault (two families and their pets have been murdered already) ironically results in his wife and children abandoning him. This shared morbidity and trauma allows the detective to inhabit the murderer's point of view and associative thinking, even though the murders appear random and without motivation.

For all its gore and lacerated flesh—in fact, on the evidence of its contribution to contemporary "wound culture" (Seltzer, 225)—*Red Dragon* is a novel about perception and sensibility. Dolarhyde might be termed an aesthete maudit, an accursed quasi-artist type who experiences life and (especially) death in terms of monstrously deformed aesthetic criteria: "Dolarhyde bore screams as a sculptor bears dust from the beaten stone" (112). (This trope is refined in Harris's subsequent books about Hannibal Lecter's exquisite tastes and subtle savorings.) Although Dolarhyde's aesthetic predispositions are incapable of sublimating his murderous compulsions, those predispositions nevertheless provide a second perspective from which to register an implicit displacement, and metaphoric critique, of more mundane propositions about existence. This also seems to be one of the functions of the intertextual dialogue the book conducts with the visionary poetry and art of William Blake. The novel's contrasting epigraphs from "The Divine Image" and "A Divine Image" (one a "song of innocence," the other a "song of experience") indicate Blake's desire to expose the simultaneously terrible and sublime energies in the human soul that bourgeois rationality could not or would not acknowledge. In this regard, Lecter, who makes his first appearance in this novel, seems born of the poet Baudelaire's contemptuous address to the bourgeois readers of *Flowers of Evil:* "Hypocrite lecteur, mon semblable, mon frere—Hypocrite reader, my likeness, my brother." Like most crime detection novels, *Red Dragon* is also about semiology, the art of discerning signs and reading them for their significations. Dolarhyde may be an author whose texts are his corpses and a dramatist with a flare for staging (note the way his murder and torture scenes turn the dead and will-be-dead into their own audience). But Graham and Lecter are masterful readers; they read the signs of death and interpret them as manifestations of unacknowledged desire.

Harris's books about serial killers play off a version of the criminal genius type against another type of crime narrative, the police procedural. In this instance, the police procedural takes the form of FBI psychological profiling techniques, which are imbued with their own mystique, the mystique of scientific systematicity. Harris's books have helped to make the purported observational precision and deductive reasoning of forensic scientists and psychological profilers the stuff of folklore, the signifiers of ready-made meanings available for slotting into all kinds of pop narratives. Harris's work has also been influential in establishing the cultural truism that the serial killer's tortures and dismemberments constitute an acting-out of fantasies that most people repress and that, therefore, these crimes are best understood as attempts to actualize heretofore thwarted or aborted individuality over and against social norms. Dolarhyde enigmatically refers to this process as "The Becoming," in the quasi-mythopoeic manner that the cultural imaginary grants, with Harris's encouragement, to the psychopath.

That this diagnostic conception has been so widely disseminated and so readily received provides a salient lesson in the contemporary formation of folklore since it so obviously accords with and relies upon the American ideological conception of the individual's rightful claim to autonomy. This conviction runs so deep it can withstand being pathologized. Harris and the reader can have it both ways: "At a time when other men first see and fear their isolation, Dolarhyde's became understandable to him: he was alone because he was Unique. With the fervour of conversion he saw that if he worked at it, if he followed the true urges he had kept

down for so long—cultivated them as the inspirations they truly were—he could Become" (264).

The cruel vengeance that Dolarhyde wreaks on the "true-crime" writer for his distorted tabloid accounts might be seen as a sardonic example of this idea. The journalist deserves his fate because he writes without the requisite transcendental inspiration: "I, who see more than you . . . I who pushed the world so much further than you" (204). Comparability between murderer and detective is further established by the fact that Graham, despising the journalist for his own reasons, wonders whether he has unconsciously ordained his murder by laying his hand on him as they were being photographed.

It is fitting that *Red Dragon* has been filmed twice (*Manhunter,* directed by Michael Mann, 1986; *Red Dragon,* directed by Brett Ratner, 2002), since filming and the general making and viewing of images play central roles in the action and characterization. This ultimately serves to raise the question of the relationship between criminality, psychopathology, and scopophilia, the desire and pleasure in gazing. This is one of the more morbid implications of the "wide-eyed dead" (19) that Dolarhyde stages and Graham must witness. Insofar as the term "wide-eyed" is usually applied to children, who in this case have been murdered, it serves as a reminder that Graham has long ago had his innocence violated by the murderers he has had to become in his imagination in order to apprehend them. Graham not only undertakes to understand the victims by watching their home movies, he also films the murders in his mind's eye as he imagines the scene from the perspective of the murderer. But the risk of witnessing and taking up the Other's point of view also applies to Dolarhyde, since his projected awareness of how his facial disfigurement looks to others dictates that he can only tolerate a dead and sightless audience (thus the only woman he might love is blind).

That Dolarhyde and his victims share taking pleasure in making and watching home movies is meant to be sardonic. Dolarhyde's voyeuristic viewing of their movies in the photo lab where he works violates the private domain prior to the home invasion and murders, thereby implicating the reader's vulnerability insofar as taking home movies is such a common practice. What is more, the law's use of pictures for purposes of documentation is, ironically, an aspect of the motivation that compels Dolarhyde: to freeze the flux of life to advance the process of his own becoming (compare Roland Barthes on photography and a cinematic prototype of the serial-killer narrative *Peeping Tom*).

SOURCES

Haltunen, Karen. *Murder Most Foul: The Killer and the American Gothic Imagination.* Cambridge, Mass.: Harvard University Press, 1998.

Harris, Thomas. *Red Dragon.* London: Arrow Books, 1993.

Seltzer, Mark. *Serial Killers: Death and Life in America's Wound Culture.* New York/London: Routledge, 1998.

Simpson, Philip. *Psycho Paths: Tracking the Serial Killer through Contemporary American Film and Fiction.* Carbondale: Southern Illinois University Press, 2000.

Tithecott, Richard. *Of Men and Monsters: Jeffrey Dahmer and the Construction of the Serial Killer.* Madison: University of Wisconsin Press, 1997.

David Brottman

REED, ISHMAEL (1938–) Novelist, essayist, and poet, Ishmael Reed is also the cofounder of the Before Columbus Foundation that honors talented young writers of color. He is the author of nine novels, many of which are racial-protest novels; indeed, a major precept for Reed is justice for ethnic and multicultural writers who, he says, neither inherit nor write within the Western classical tradition. In his own work, Reed employs a good number of Vodun (Hoodoo or Voodoo) rituals, folklores, and beliefs and creates an African American cowboy, who also appears in his poem, "I am a cowboy in the boat of Ra." He frequently alludes to rhythm and blues music and to black sports icons. As a postmodernist he deconstructs traditional form and parodies various genres from the dime novel to the western. Reed acknowledges the influence of earlier black writers, including Langston HUGHES and Zora Neale HURSTON. He is probably best known for his novel MUMBO JUMBO (1972), a wide-ranging examination of the American black aesthetic.

Ishmael Reed was born on February 22, 1938, in Chattanooga, Tennessee, and was reared in Buffalo, New York, where he attended the University of Buffalo until, unhappy with the lack of African Americans and other minorities on the reading lists, he left without taking a degree. While teaching at universities from Yale and Harvard to the University of Washington, Reed steadily published his work. His first novel, *The Free-Lance Pallbearers* (1967), satirizes both white leaders—whom he calls Harry Sam—and black, suggesting that all of them, from the fictional Black Muslim Elijah Raven to the novel's Baptist minister, Eclair Porkchop, are driven by a desire for power. *Yellow Back Radio Broke-Down* (1969), Reed's second novel, in a parody of the western novel tradition, introduces Hoodoo to the town, along with Loop Caroo, the African-American cowboy. The solution to fixing what has "broke-down" lies in accepting various cultural, spiritual, and ethnic traditions. In *Mumbo Jumbo,* Reed employs the Hoodoo detective Papa LaBas to present his theories of African-American art and aesthetics against a backdrop of 1920s New Orleans. *The Last Days of Louisiana Red* (1974) continues with the detective Papa LaBas; his job is to solve the murder of Louisiana Red, the Hoodoo name for evil.

The Terrible Twos (1982), set during the era of President Ronald Reagan, features Santa Claus, who points out the problem affecting contemporary America. By worshipping capitalism, Americans are, he says, no better than spoiled two-year-old toddlers. *Reckless Eyeballing* (1986) features Ian Ball, a black male writer, and Tremonisha Smarts, a black female writer, involved in a battle for the aesthetic hearts of the American people: Who will win, the black or the white writers? The term "reckless eyeballing" refers to the charges against Emmett Till, lynched in 1955 for supposedly looking at a white woman.

For more than two decades, Ishmael Reed has been a professor at the University of California at Berkeley. He lives and writes in Oakland, California. His most recent novel, *Japanese Spring,* appeared in 1993.

NOVELS

Flight to Canada. New York: Random House, 1976.

The Free-Lance Pallbearers. Garden City, N.Y.: Doubleday, 1967.

Japanese by Spring. New York: Atheneum, 1993.

The Last Days of Louisiana Red. New York: Random House, 1974.

Mumbo Jumbo. Garden City, N.Y.: Doubleday, 1972.
Reckless Eyeballing. New York: St. Martin's, 1986.
The Terrible Threes. New York: Atheneum, 1989.
The Terrible Twos. New York: St. Martin's/Marek, 1982.
Yellow Back Radio Broke-Down. Garden City, N.Y.: Doubleday, 1969.

SOURCES

Boyer, Jay. *Ishmael Reed.* Boise, Idaho: Boise State University Press, 1993.

Dick, Bruce, and Amritjit Singh, eds. *Conversations with Ishmael Reed.* Jackson: University Press of Mississippi, 1995.

Fox, Robert Eliot. *Conscientious Sorcerers: The Black Postmodernist Fiction of LeRoi Jones/Amiri Baraka, Ishmael Reed, and Samuel R. Delany.* Westport, Conn.: Greenwood Press, 1987.

Joyce, Joyce Ann. *Warriors, Conjurers and Priests: Defining African-Centered Literary Criticism.* Chicago: Third World Press, 1994.

Klinkowitz, Jerome. *Literary Subversions: New American Fiction and the Practice of Criticism.* Carbondale: Southern Illinois University Press, 1985.

Ludwig, Sami. *Concrete Language: Intercultural Communication in Maxine Hong Kingston's "The Woman Warrior" and Ishmael Reed's "Mumbo Jumbo."* New York: Peter Lang, 1996.

Martin, Reginald. *Ishmael Reed and the New Black Aesthetic.* London: Macmillan, 1987.

McGee, Patrick. *Ishmael Reed and the Ends of Race.* New York: St. Martin's Press, 1997.

Nazareth, Peter. *In the Trickster Tradition: the Novels of Andrew Salkey, Frances Ebejar, and Ishmael Reed.* London: Bogle-L'Ouverture Press, 1994.

O'Donnell, Patrick, and Robert Con Davis, eds. *Intertextuality and Contemporary American Fiction.* Baltimore, Md.: Johns Hopkins University Press, 1989.

Ostendorf, Berndt. *Black Literature in White America.* New York: Barnes & Noble, 1982.

REEF, THE EDITH WHARTON (1912)

Identified by many critics as the most autobiographical novel that Edith WHARTON wrote, *The Reef* was praised by Henry JAMES for its densely knit structure resembling classical drama. Narrated through the perspectives of its two characters, George Darrow and Anna Leath, the novel depicts Anna Leath's wavering emotions between accepting and refusing George Darrow's marriage proposal after discovering his brief affair with Sophy Viner.

Darrow, an American diplomat in London, meets Sophy at Dover before crossing the English Channel. Darrow's pride is hurt by the curt and detached tone of the telegram he has received from Anna before he takes the train at Charing Cross. Anna is postponing, for the second time, their meeting in Givré, where she lives with her late husband Frazer Leath's mother, Madame de Chantelle; her stepson, Owen; and her daughter, Effie. Sophy's future is indefinite. She has just left her position as companion to Mrs. Murrett and she is going to Paris with the hope of seeking the assistance of her friends, the Farlows, to obtain employment and study for the stage. Orphaned at a young age and left to her resources to earn her living, Sophy lacks Anna's conventional upbringing. The impulsive, natural, and unreserved characteristics that mark her personality contrast with the repressions, reticence, and evasions that shape Anna's. As Sophy's desire to attend plays in the Parisian theaters and her curiosity about the life in this city prove stronger than her prudence, Darrow purposely neglects to mail her letter informing the Farlows of her arrival and easily convinces her to spend a week with him in Paris. Darrow's intention, however, is neither to make a sexual conquest nor to show Sophy the city. He selfishly wants the young woman to stay with him, as her naive and inexperienced dependence on his knowledge about the city increases his self-importance and mends his bruised ego.

After almost a year, Anna invites Darrow to Givré with the intention of preparing for their marriage. To Darrow's horror, Sophy has taken her place in the château not only as Effie's governess but also Owen's fiancée. Having claimed his past acquaintance with Sophy merely as a casual meeting in a house where he used to dine, Darrow finds himself in a position both to testify for the uprightness of Sophy's character and to help Anna obtain Owen's aristocratic grandmother's approval of his marriage to someone below his class. Struggling with feelings of guilt for betraying Anna's trust in him and ignoring Sophy's emotions for him, Darrow endeavors to conceal his affair with Sophy from Anna and dissuade Sophy from marrying Owen.

While Adelaide Painter, a compatriot who has a considerable influence on the family's important decisions, convinces Madame de Chantelle of the suitability of

Sophy for Owen in marriage, Darrow, during concealed meetings with Sophy, manages to convince her that she will be unhappy if she marries a man with whom she is not in love. Sophy breaks off her engagement, and her affair with Darrow is exposed when Owen reveals to Anna, who has chanced upon Darrow's secret meetings with Sophy in Givré. Unable to understand Sophy, console Owen, and forgive Darrow, Anna vacillates between accepting and refusing Darrow's marriage proposal. She sends Darrow away from Givré to London twice without a definite answer to his proposal. After Owen leaves for Spain, Anna goes to Paris in search of Sophy. From her sister, Mrs. McTarvie-Birch, she learns that Sophy has left for India with her previous employer, Mrs. Murrett.

The story in *The Reef* closely parallels both the psychological states of Edith Wharton during her affair with the American journalist William Morton Fullerton from 1908 to 1910 and the circumstances in which their relationship progressed. The writer's intention for writing this novel at the end of an affair with a predictably disloyal partner was to explore her true feelings about her lover and their relationship. Wharton herself considered *The Reef* a character rather than a novel. When one reads the novel with the writer's purpose in mind, one transfers one's analytic efforts from unfolding plot to penetrating character. Wharton projects her internal guilt feelings, anxieties, doubts, and hesitations in her love affair on Anna Leath and, indirectly, on Owen Leath. She re-creates the part of her self which was the rational and practical lover in the character of Sophy Viner. Through George Darrow she represents both her ability to understand human weaknesses and the newly found maturity and experience of a skillful lover.

Through the internalization of the feeling of guilt and its influence on the moral development and actions of Anna Leath, this fiction enacts the devastating impact of the strict conventions of upbringing on the emotional and sexual development and behavior of women in the 1890s, and questions the reliability of these conventions as standard of virtue for women. Anna's indecisions between accepting and rejecting Darrow as a marriage partner result from the discrepancy between the ideal image of the self that her rigid familial upbringing and conventional environment have instilled in her and the self that she naturally inhabits, thus trapping her into the vicious circle of guilt feelings either for betraying her natural desires or for transgressing the dictates of social conventions.

As well as representing the affinity between the old American moral and social conventions and the traditional values of European aristocracy with Madame de Chantelle's conservative demeanor, *The Reef* conveys, through the contrast between the moral perspectives of Anna Leath and Sophy Viner, the liberating direction that these paralyzing conventions have taken at the turn of the 20th century.

Like two other novels by Wharton, *Madame de Treymes* and *The Custom of the Country*, *The Reef* portrays the lives of Americans in France.

SOURCES

Benstock, Shari. *No Gifts from Chance: A Biography of Edith Wharton*. New York: Scribner, 1994.

Faery, Rebecca Blevins. "Wharton's Reef: The Inscription of Female Sexuality." In *Edith Wharton: New Critical Essays*, edited by Alfred Bendixen and Annette Zilversmit, 79–96. New York and London: Garland, 1992.

Hutchinson, Stuart. " 'Beyond' George Eliot? Reconsidering Edith Wharton," *Modern Language Review* 95, no. 4 (October 2000): 942–950.

Killoran, Helen. *Edith Wharton: Art and Allusion*. Tuscaloosa, Ala., and London: University of Alabama Press, 1996.

Lewis, R. W. B. *Edith Wharton: A Biography*. New York: Fromm International, 1985.

Singley, Carol J. *Edith Wharton: Matters of Mind and Spirit*. New York: Cambridge University Press, 1995.

Wharton, Edith. *"The Reef."* In *Novels*, edited by R. W. B. Lewis, 349–619. New York: The Library of America, 1985.

Ferdâ Asya

RICE, ANNE (HOWARD ALLEN O'BRIEN, A. N. ROQUELAURE, ANNE RAMPLING) (1941–)

Anne Rice, author of INTERVIEW WITH THE VAMPIRE (1976), has been a household name for three decades. The critic Jennifer Smith notes that Rice's concern with "evil and power and the lure of immortality" is a part of her "genius as a novelist: she can combine mainstream moral philosophy and flesh-creeping horror in the same novel and make the reader enjoy both" (Smith). Rice continues to write critically acclaimed novels about vampires, the vampire Lestat in particular, but also novels written under the pseudonyms A. N. Roquelaure and Anne Rampling. Her sympathetic treatment of the vampires as lonely, brooding creatures trapped in an immortal state has captured the imagination of the reading public and made all these books best-sellers. Rice blends the gothic romance traditions of British poet Samuel Taylor Coleridge and Mary Shelley, author of *Frankenstein,* and those of the Americans Edgar Allan POE and H. P. LOVECRAFT. Her identification with Mary Shelley is clear, says Smith, not only in their personal lives—both married poets and suffered the loss of young children—but also in their depiction of monsters with a sense of humanity and morality (Smith). In *Interview* particularly, she recreates the six-year-old daughter she lost to a rare form of leukemia and gives her eternal life in the fictional person of the six-year-old Claudia.

Anne Rice was born Howard Allen O'Brien on October 4, 1941, to Howard O'Brien, a postal worker, novelist, and sculptor, and Katherine Allen O'Brien. Her name was changed to Anne in 1947. After marrying Stan Rice, a poet and painter, in 1961, she earned her bachelor's (1964) and master's (1971) degrees from San Francisco State College. *Interview with the Vampire* features Louis, who is initiated into vampirism after the death of his brother by the vampire Lestat; his feelings of guilt lead to his "interview" in which he recounts his life story along with vampire secrets. In later novels Lestat takes center stage; in *The Vampire Lestat* (1985), sequel to *Interview,* Lestat becomes a rock star; in *Queen of the Damned* (1988), Lestat's lineage is traced; in *The Tale of the Body Thief* (1993), Lestat trades his body with that of a mortal; and in *Memnoch the Devil* (1995), the devil tries to recruit Lestat. Other tales in the Vampire Chronicles series include *Pandora: New Tales of the Vampires* (1998) and *Vittorio the Vampire* (1999). The most recent is *Blood Canticle* (2003).

In another vampire series, Rice traces the history of the witches of Mayfair from medieval Europe to 18th-century Louisiana, to contemporary New Orleans and San Francisco; *The Witching Hour* (1990) introduces the family headed by the feminist neurosurgeon Rowan Mayfair, and is followed by *Lasher* (1993) and *Taltos* (1995), in which Lasher impregnates Rowan with an incubus that becomes a curse to the family. Anne Rice has also published the non-vampire historical novels *The Feast of All Saints* (1980), set in New Orleans and focusing on *les gens de coleur libres,* or mixed-race people, represented by a brother and sister, Marcel and Marie, who are shunned by both their black and their white families. *Cry to Heaven* (1982), set in 18th-century Italy, portrays the castrati, male singers castrated to preserve their high voices.

After her husband's death, Anne Rice moved from the lilac antebellum house they shared in the Garden District of New Orleans to a gated community in Jefferson Parish and then to California. A number of her works have been adapted to the screen. *Exit to Eden,* directed by Garry Marshall, starred Dana Delaney and Dan Ackroyd in 1994; *Interview with the Vampire,* directed by Neil Jordan, starred Brad Pitt and Tom Cruise in 1994; and *Queen of the Damned,* directed by Michael Rymer, starred Stuart Townsend in 2001. *Feast of All Saints* was adapted as a television miniseries by Showtime and ABC in 2001.

Rice's most recent novel, *Christ the Lord: Out of Egypt* is a striking departure, a portrait of the young Jesus Christ.

NOVELS

Christ the Lord: Out of Egypt. New York: Knopf, 2005.

Cry to Heaven. New York: Knopf, 1982.

The Feast of All Saints. New York: Simon & Schuster, 1980.

The Mummy: or, Ramses the Damned. New York: Ballantine, 1989.

Servant of the Bones. New York: Knopf, 1996.

Violin. New York: Knopf, 1997.

"VAMPIRE CHRONICLES" SERIES

Blackwood Farm. New York: Knopf, 2002.

Blood Canticle. New York: Knopf, 2003.

Interview with the Vampire. New York: Knopf, 1976.

Memnoch the Devil. New York: Knopf, 1995.

Merrick. New York: Knopf, 2000.

Pandora: New Tales of the Vampires. New York: Random House, 1998.

The Queen of the Damned. New York: Knopf, 1988.

The Tale of the Body Thief. New York: Knopf, 1993.

The Vampire Armand. New York: Knopf, 1998.

Vampire Chronicles (contains *Interview with the Vampire, The Vampire Lestat,* and *The Queen of the Damned*). New York: Random House, 1990.

The Vampire Lestat. New York: Ballantine, 1985.

Vittorio the Vampire. New York: Knopf, 1999.

"LIVES OF THE MAYFAIR WITCHES" SERIES

Lasher. New York: Knopf, 1993.

Taltos. New York: Knopf, 1994.

The Witching Hour. New York: Knopf, 1990.

EROTIC NOVELS, UNDER PSEUDONYM
A. N. ROQUELAURE

Beauty's Punishment. New York: Dutton, 1984.

Beauty's Release: The Continued Erotic Adventures of Sleeping Beauty. New York: Dutton, 1985.

The Claiming of Sleeping Beauty. New York: Dutton, 1983.

The Sleeping Beauty Novels (contains *The Claiming of Sleeping Beauty, Beauty's Punishment,* and *Beauty's Release: The Continued Erotic Adventures of Sleeping Beauty*). New York: New American Library, 1991.

NOVELS, UNDER PSEUDONYM
ANNE RAMPLING

Belinda. New York: Arbor House, 1986.

Exit to Eden. New York: Arbor House, 1985.

SOURCES

Badley, Linda. *Writing Horror and the Body: The Fiction of Stephen King, Clive Barker, and Anne Rice.* Westport, Conn.: Greenwood Press, 1996.

Beahm, George, ed. *The Unauthorized Anne Rice Companion.* Kansas City, Mo.: Andrews and McMeel, 1996.

Hoppenstand, Gary, and Ray B. Browne, eds. *The Gothic World of Anne Rice.* Bowling Green, Ohio: Bowling Green Popular Press, 1996.

Marcus, Jana. *In the Shadow of the Vampire: Reflections from the World of Anne Rice.* New York: Thunder's Mouth Press, 1997.

Ramsland, Katherine M. *Prism of the Night: A Biography of Anne Rice.* New York: Dutton, 1991.

———. *The Roquelaure Reader: A Companion to Anne Rice's Erotica.* New York: Plume, 1996.

———. *The Vampire Companion: The Official Guide to Anne Rice's The Vampire Chronicles.* New York: Ballantine, 1993.

———. *The Witches' Companion: The Official Guide to Anne Rice's Lives of the Mayfair Witches.* New York: Ballantine, 1994.

———, ed. *The Anne Rice Reader: Writers Explore the Universe of Anne Rice.* New York: Ballantine, 1997.

———. *The Anne Rice Trivia Book.* New York: Ballantine, 1994.

Riley, Michael. *Conversations with Anne Rice.* New York: Ballantine, 1996.

Roberts, Bette B. *Anne Rice.* New York: Twayne, 1994.

Smith, Jennifer. *Anne Rice: A Critical Companion.* Westport, Conn.: Greenwood Press, 1996.

OTHER

Official Anne Rice Web site. Available online. URL: http://www.annerice.com. Accessed September 25, 2005.

Anne Rice Page. Available online. URL: http://www.randomhouse.com/features/annerice/quizlist.html. Accessed September 25, 2005.

Wired for Books: Audio Interviews with Anne Rice. Available online. URL: http://wiredforbooks.org/annerice. Accessed September 25, 2005.

RISE OF DAVID LEVINSKY, THE ABRAHAM CAHAN (1917)

The novels of Abraham CAHAN, particularly his classic *The Rise of David Levinsky,* are foundation works in the emergence and development of Jewish-American literature. Indeed, *The Rise of David Levinsky* stands as one of the most important novels of immigrant experience in all American literature. In his examination of the immigrant experience in the new world of America, especially the pressures of assimilation and acculturation, Cahan highlights major themes that are returned to again and again in much Jewish-American literature of the 20th century. *The Rise of David Levinsky* is a multifaceted work as reflected in its literary history as a realist novel written by a trade union organizer and socialist, but has come to be regarded as a primary example of a business novel. The contradictory history of the novel's reception shadows the complex personal history of its author.

At the time of his writing *The Rise of David Levinsky,* Cahan was a committed proponent of international socialism and an active trade union supporter. His key position as editor of the *Forward* placed Cahan at the intersection of various social, cultural, and ethnic backgrounds. His political beliefs made him acutely aware of the dangers of Americanization. At the same time, his literature and his journalism offered perspectives of a cautious assimilationism. More than any of his literary predecessors, Cahan was able to move with great fluency between Yiddish, Russian, and American cultures. His unique skills give him a central place in the culture and literature of Jewish-American communities. This diversity of experience is drawn upon and reflected in Cahan's novel.

The Rise of David Levinsky tells the story of a young Hasidic Jew who turns away from his religious studies to pursue material success as a businessman among the growing manufacturing enterprises of the Lower East Side. Pursuing his economic goals with all the energy and attention he had previously devoted to his religious work, Levinsky becomes extremely successful financially but is increasingly separated from the culture and tradition that had sustained him psychologically. His is a tale of the pressures of assimilation facing immigrants in America and the deep personal costs extracted from those who become detached from the cultural roots of community.

This intensely felt separation is rendered by Cahan in sad and moving passages as a successful, but isolated, Levinsky reflects on the course of his life. Near the novel's end, Levinsky concludes regretfully: "I cannot escape from my old self. My past and my present do not comport well. David, the poor lad swinging over a Talmud volume at the Preacher's Synagogue, seems to have more in common with my inner identity than David Levinsky, the well-known cloak manufacturer" (530). Cahan offers a poignant analysis of the tensions and anxieties experienced by immigrants caught up in pursuit of the American dream. Cahan perceptively portrays the loss of deep personal and communal relationships that is a result of pursuing the dream. In this, the novel's title is shown to convey a deep irony. This simple reflection on the division between Levinsky's inner identity and his present self speaks to a variety of contradictions and discontinuities experienced by immigrants in early 20th-century America. Levinsky's identity is caught between the competing trajectories of his life: between religion and business, poverty and wealth, idealism and regret. At the same time, Cahan's work speaks to the complex and evolving relationships connecting Jewish Europe and Jewish America.

In The Rise of David Levinsky, Cahan depicts the creeping but steady processes of assimilation most effectively through his innovative use of language. The author gives his characters voices in unpolished hybrid dialects taken from the streets of New York's Lower East Side. Through his striking expression of the transformation and loss of language in the novel, Cahan examines shifting perceptions of culture and community among Jewish immigrants in America.

Influenced by the literary social realism of its day, The Rise of David Levinsky is a work revered by literary critics, historians, and sociologists alike. The novel's skillful melding of literary proficiency and social and historical documentation reflect Abraham Cahan's talents as a journalist and writer and mark The Rise of David Levinsky as a work of lasting significance. It can even be argued that The Rise of David Levinsky represents a paradigmatic moment in the emergence of Jewish-American literature and the translation of Yiddish heritage into both the language and culture of early 20th-century America and the simultaneous reenvisioning of America through the experiences of Jewish immigrants. It is a work that prefigures, by a generation, themes and concerns that would become prominent in the writings of better-known authors such as Henry ROTH, Saul BELLOW, and Bernard MALAMUD.

SOURCE

Cahan, Abraham. The Rise of David Levinsky. New York: Modern Library, 2001.

J. A. Shantz

RISE OF SILAS LAPHAM, THE WILLIAM DEAN HOWELLS (1885)   Of the nearly three dozen novels written by W. D. HOWELLS, The Rise of Silas Lapham has proved the most enduring. From its opening in 1875, a revealing interview of the 55-year-old Lapham in Boston provides information on his life to date: his background on a Vermont farm, his family, his crucial experience as an officer in the Civil War, his boorishness and lack of taste, his fortunate discovery of a mineral paint lode on his farm, and his rise to wealth manufacturing, obtrusively advertising, and selling the paint. The interview also exposes a point of vulnerability in that rise when Lapham self-consciously minimizes the role in it of his former partner, Milton K. Rogers; the interviewer—Bartley Hubbard of A Modern

Instance (1882), early in his doomed career as a reporter in Boston—perceives Lapham's momentary reticence but cautiously avoids noting it down for publication.

Lapham's self-portrait establishes a foundation for the mutually supportive plots that thread through the novel and illustrate the main themes: the duty to act responsibly as conscience dictates and the nobility or folly of self-sacrifice, determined by the extent of benefit or pain it would cause. The major plot directly concerns Lapham's economic fall and consequent moral rise after he knowingly and willingly sacrifices his fortune rather than securing part of it with a legal but unethical act. The primary subplot chiefly concerns the love triangle of Lapham's two daughters, Penelope, the elder intellectual brunette, and Irene, her younger, prettier, more practical redheaded sister, for Tom Corey, son of a patrician Brahmin couple. These two plots intertwine when Lapham's wealth motivates him and his wife, Persis, to climb socially for the girls' benefit by building an expensive home on Boston's Back Bay so they can move from their working-class neighborhood on the South End of the city. Simultaneously, both daughters succumb to Tom Corey's charm, Pen silently and Irene overtly, neither knowing until after a crisis occurs that he favors Pen rather than her sister. By then, Lapham has hired him as an office worker, and Tom's parents have hosted a dinner to meet the Laphams formally and begin introducing them into polite society.

The Laphams' preparations to attend the dinner expose their unfamiliarity with the social graces, and their attempts to acquire them quickly are at times pure comedy. The conversation during and after dinner, to which chapter 14 is devoted, is a thematic nexus for the novel because the principal topics discussed relate to conscience, duty, and self-sacrifice. Silas does not speak when the others deride or condemn foolish self-sacrifice as a subject of popular fiction, but he impresses them when he tells of a soldier, Jim Millon, who died protecting him from a sniper's ball during the war; Millon's sacrifice is the basis for a secondary subplot that unfolds late in the novel. That Lapham, unaccustomed to alcohol, becomes loud and boastful from overindulgence in wine is notable, but the incident has no enduring effect because it is quickly dismissed by the hosts and guests, who understand that it resulted only from inexperience, not decadence.

The dinner, however, is a major turning point in the novel. Shortly afterward, Silas tells Persis that his finances are being drained through bad investments with his former partner, whom he had pushed out of the business when outside capital was no longer needed. Since then, Lapham had ignored him despite his wife's insistence that Rogers had been wronged. Persis is the voice of Lapham's conscience, and Rogers embodies it as a shadow-figure. Because she presses her husband to finance Rogers and correct the wrong, Silas gives him money for railroad stock that has lost nearly all its value, an exchange that further undermines his fortune. Lapham's position grows still worse when his uninsured home under construction burns to the ground as a result of his own carelessness as the finishing touches are being added.

With his financial future at stake, Lapham can avoid a total collapse only by collaborating with Rogers in a legal but unethical scheme to cheat a group of wealthy British speculators out of their money by selling to them at full value the nearly worthless collateral he received from his ex-partner. After symbolically wrestling with the angel, Lapham refuses to cooperate, sells his paint manufactory to eager young competitors, and returns with Persis and Irene to their farm in Vermont, having ascended morally from his economic fall. He has paid all his debts, he says, and "come out with clean hands" by following his conscience and making the sacrifice (510).

Meanwhile Tom Corey has declared himself to Penelope, shocking her and sending her into paroxysms of dismay as she apprehends how his choosing her so unexpectedly over Irene will distress her lovesick sister. After she refuses him and begs him to leave, the bewildered suitor pleads at length for her hand, but despite her love for him, Pen adamantly refuses, willing to sacrifice herself in a foolish attempt to mollify Irene. Ultimately, she succumbs to the Rev. Sewell's "economy-of-pain" resolution that advocates the least pain for the fewest people, and Tom's pleas are successful (338).

Lapham is probably Howells's most thoughtfully constructed novel. The opening interview provides a foundation, the Corey dinner at midpoint marks a critical turn, and most of the early chapters between deal with the Lapham-Corey subplot. After the dinner, more attention is given to the rapid financial decline that leads to Lapham's dutiful self-sacrifice. Complementing it are Penelope's ludicrous readiness to sacrifice herself also but to no one's benefit, as well as the minor subplot stitched in near the end of the novel— which traces the responsibility Lapham has quietly assumed for the wife and daughter of Jim Millon, who had sacrificed his life for him. Millon's daughter, Zerilla, has married an alcoholic like her mother, and Lapham has employed the young woman as his secretary, unknown to Persis, who becomes jealous over the attractive typist in his office. This short naturalistic segment of the novel exposes first, the seedy side of Boston to Howells's realism; second, the dark consequences that in the real world may follow attempting to repay a mortal debt for which no compensation is possible; and third, the limitations of Persis, who has heretofore been portrayed as a stabilizing moral force on Lapham's life and career.

The house being constructed on Beacon Street is another complement, one symbolizing the building and rapid destruction of Lapham's career. During the early stages, Lapham's dialogues with the architect reveal the glaring difference between his conventional taste and the architect's fashionable ideas. Lapham's preference for a long, straight stairway from the front hall, for example, contrasts with the architect's recommendation that the stairs ascend in stages along three sides of it. In literary terms, the distinctively different types of staircases suggest the greater value of multiple plots over a single straight one, a structural device that proves particularly effective in this novel.

When Howells serialized *The Rise of Silas Lapham* in the *Century Magazine* from November 1884 through August 1885, readers eagerly awaited each new section. However, the complete novel with a few small but significant changes had a mixed reception when published by Harper & Brothers in 1885 because some critics questioned the value of fiction written about everyday life. Realism was still seeking its audience in the United States, and Howells was bringing out his most admirable novels in the 1880s to gain one. *The Rise of Silas Lapham* marks a high point in his ultimately successful efforts.

SOURCES

Bennett, George N. *William Dean Howells: The Development of a Novelist.* Norman: University of Oklahoma Press, 1957.

Cady, Edwin H. *The Road to Realism: The Early Years 1837–1885 of William Dean Howells.* Syracuse, N.Y.: Syracuse University Press, 1956.

Carter, Everett. *Howells and the Age of Realism.* Philadelphia: Lippincott, 1954.

Eble, Kenneth E. *William Dean Howells.* 2nd ed. Boston: Twayne, 1982.

Howells, William Dean. *The Rise of Silas Lapham.* New York: Harper & Brothers, 1885.

Pease, Donald E., ed. *New Essays on The Rise of Silas Lapham.* New York: Cambridge University Press, 1991.

Vanderbilt, Kermit. *The Achievement of William Dean Howells.* Princeton, N.J.: Princeton University Press, 1968.

Sanford E. Marovitz

RIVERA, TOMÁS (1935–1984)

Tomás Rivera, a pioneer in the development of modern Latino literature, burst onto the literary consciousness in 1971 with his novel, . . . *Y No Se lo Trago la Tierra/ . . . And the Earth Did Not Devour Him,* which received the first Quinto Sol National Literary Award. The novel describes the traditions and customs of individual Chicanos in the United States, whether migrant farm laborers or urban barrio dwellers. These impoverished working-class characters live on the margins of a more prosperous and privileged Anglo-American society. However, Rivera did not aim for a niche in the annals of American proletarian fiction. Instead, he portrayed the lives of ordinary Mexican Americans, drawn simultaneously to the ways of Old Mexico and those of the United States. Through an intriguing blend of 14 stories and 13 vignettes, says author Maria Herrera-Sobek, the novel's "apparently disjoined structure reflects the protagonist's chaotic disorientation in the first story" (Herrera-Sobek).

Tomás Rivera was born on December 22, 1935, in Crystal City, Texas, to Florencio M. Rivera, a migrant worker and cook, and Josefa Hernandez Rivera. He married Concepcion Garza in 1958, the same year he earned his bachelor's degree from Southwest Texas State University, where he also was awarded a master's degree in education in 1964. He earned a master of arts and doctoral degree at the University of Oklahoma, both in 1969. Just two years later, he published *And the Earth Did Not Devour Him,* nothing short of groundbreaking both in terms of Latino bildungsroman and the boy-narrator's search for identity in an uncertain new world. His work was translated and edited by his friend and colleague, Rolando HINOJOSA-SMITH and others.

Rivera's work is frequently compared with Rudolfo ANAYA's (*BLESS ME, ULTIMA* [1972]) and Hinojosa-Smith's (*Estampas del Valle* [1973]), both of whom address the survival of the community. Together, these three writers initiated the Chicano Renaissance. Tomás Rivera was chancellor of the University of California at Riverside from 1973 until his death in 1984, in Fontana, California. His papers are held in the Rivera Archives at the University of California at Riverside. In 2001 Hinojosa-Smith wrote an essay commemorating the 30th anniversary of Rivera's novel.

NOVEL

. . . *y no se lo trago la tierra/And the Earth Did Not Devour Him.* Berkeley, Calif.: Quinto Sol Publications, 1971. English-language edition published as . . . *And The Earth Did Not Devour Him.* Berkeley, Calif.: Quinto Sol Publications, 1971.

SOURCES

Bruce-Novoa, Juan. *Chicano Authors: Inquiry by Interview.* Austin: University of Texas Press, 1980.

Davila, Luis, ed. *Chicano Literature and Tomás Rivera.* Bloomington: University of Indiana Press, 1974.

Gonzalez-Berry, Erlinda, and Rebolledo, Tey Diana. "Growing Up Chicano: Tomás Rivera and Sandra Cisneros," *Revista Chicano-Riquena* 13, nos. 3–4 (Fall–Winter 1985): 109–119.

Hinojosa-Smith, Rolando, Gary Keller, and Vernon E. Lattin. *Tomás Rivera, 1935–1984: The Man and His Work.* Tempe, Ariz.: Bilingual/Editorial Bilingüe, 1988.

Sommers, Joseph, and Tomás Ybarra-Frausto, eds. *Modern Chicano Writers: A Collection of Critical Essays.* Englewood Cliffs, N.J.: Prentice-Hall, 1979.

OTHER

Herrera-Sobek, Maria. "A Spanish Novelist's Perspective on Chicano/a Literature," *Journal of Modern Literature.* Highbeam Resources. Available online. URL: http://www.highbeam.com/library/doc3.asp?DOCID=1G1:92805771. Accessed April 12, 2006.

Hinojosa-Smith, Rolando. "On The 30th Anniversary Of Tomás Rivera's . . . *Y No Se Lo Trago La Tierra,*" *World Literature Today* (January 1, 2001). HighBeam Research. Available online. URL: http://www.highbeam.com/library/doc3-asp?DOCID=1G1:76628983. Accessed September 26, 2005.

RIVER RUNS THROUGH IT, A NORMAN MACLEAN (1976)

"In the half century I taught literature, I was largely given the freedom to teach the literature of my choice, so naturally I chose literature that I felt was beautiful" (Maclean 1988, 69). Norman Maclean (1902–90) wrote the novella/memoir *A River Runs Through It* (1976) after retiring from the English faculty at the University of Chicago in 1973. It has become the best-known portion of his relatively small corpus of fiction and was made into a successful movie in 1992, directed by Robert Redford and starring Brad Pitt as Norman's brother, Paul Maclean. While the movie alters the plot romantically to feature Norman's courting of Jessie, his wife-to-be, they are already married in the novella. The text alternates passages of narration, reflection, and lyrical evocations of natural scenes that suggest a Thomistic approach to natural law. The arrangement suggests a narrative apologia for the argument from design that deduces a benevolent creator from the observation of an ordered, beautiful universe despite plenty of evidence of tragedy both in life and in the novella's plot. Because of the novella's structure, a narrative summary will be less successful than an account of how the differing passages evoke its central ideas, among which the celebration of beauty is key.

The now-famous opening sentence, "In our family, there was no clear line between religion and fly fishing," encapsulates some of the major themes propelling the narrative. The philosophical underpinnings of the story include the Scottish Presbyterianism practiced in Montana by the narrator's father, the Reverend Maclean, and the neo-Aristotelian structure of opposites that Norman Maclean used as his critical toolbox when teaching at the University of Chicago.

Presbyterianism provides the ground on which to discuss the need to help one's neighbor. As Mark Browning has noticed (Browning, 680), the notion of helping unifies the otherwise often discontinuous narrative: The brothers help each other recite the catechism, shoot the rapids together (in the movie), and are asked by Norman's wife, Jessie, to help her brother. Fly-fishing is connected humorously, though inaccurately, to Jesus and his disciples, and important conversations between Norman and his father center on the notion of selfless love and on the meaning of the Johannine gospel, especially the logos passage in chapter 1. The Neo-Aristotelian categories of either/or structure the oppositions in the text: those between the West and other American regions; those between men and women, whether real or symbolic; and finally those between women who are figured reductively either as healers or as temptresses, with Norman's mother and Jessie in the first category, and Paul's Native American girlfriend and the town prostitute, Old Rawhide, in the second. When, in young adulthood, the brothers take radically different paths, Norman as graduate student and professor in Chicago, Paul as newspaperman in Montana, Norman is finally unable to help Paul. The Christian command to love, the Presbyterian acknowledgment of a fallen world, and the neo-Aristotelian tendency toward dualism come together in the novella's exploration of obstacles to perfection. In episodes distributed over the text, Jessie's brother Neal has a sexual misadventure with Old Rawhide while on a fishing trip with the brothers. Later, Paul increasingly succumbs to his addictions to alcohol and gambling and is finally killed in a barroom fight. The elder Macleans then recede into old age, and the final textual passage takes us into the present of circa 1975, in which the narrator Norman has become a lonely old man who still fly-fishes.

The novella's most characteristic feature is the interpolation of lyrical passages. Maclean's debt to Wordsworth—"Poets talk about 'spots of time,' but it is really fishermen who experience eternity compressed into a moment" (44)—emerges when he lovingly describes the tying of flies; Paul's rhythmical casting of the rod; the immanence of water, trout, and fisherman; and the sheer beauty of watching Paul fish.

The novella celebrates masculine western outdoor activities, male friendships, and a paternalistic Christianity while offering largely schematic portrayals of its women characters. J. Gerard Dollar sees a misogynistic literary inheritance running from Mark TWAIN through Willa CATHER and Edward Abbey to Maclean. Mary Clearman Blew, however, successfully connects Paul's Northern Cheyenne girlfriend with other "dark women" in the American literary tradition. Gordon Slethaug interprets the text using stochastics and chaos theory; Teresa Ferreira offers an intertextual reading within American river literature. Like the sunrise it describes as "luminous but not clear" (28), the text proffers multiple spiritual suggestions in lieu of one theological argument.

In the end, Maclean pays homage to his brother's life within the categories that lend it meaning, blending the mythoi of fishing, self-determination, Christianity, a fallen world, and the great western outdoors. Norman and his father agree that Paul, in an apotheosis of fishing, is "beautiful" (100), an appellation that allows both theological and—more recently—ecocritical appreciation (see Grattan).

SOURCES

Blew, Mary Clearman. "Mo-nah-se-tah, the Whore, and the Three Scottish Women." In *Norman Maclean,* edited by McFarland and Nichols, 190–200. Lewiston, Idaho: Confluence, 1988.

Browning, Mark. " 'Some of the Words Are Theirs': The Elusive Logos in *A River Runs through It.*" *Christianity and Literature* 50, no. 4 (2001): 679–688.

Dollar, J. Gerard. "Misogyny in the American Eden: Abbey, Cather, and Maclean." In *Reading the Earth: New Directions in the Study of Literature and Environment,* edited by Michael P. Branch et al., 97–106. Moscow: University of Idaho Press, 1998.

Ferreira de Almeida Alves, Teresa. "Gazing at the River, Throwing the Line, Daring the Waters." In *Rivers and the American Experience,* edited by Jerzy Durczak, 13–33. Lublin, Poland: Maria Curie-Bodowska University Press, 2000.

Grattan, George F. "Climbing Back into the Tree: Art, Nature and Theology in *A River Runs Through It.*" In *Reading under the Sign of Nature: New Essays in Ecocriticism,* edited by John Tallmadge and Henry Harrington, 231–243. Salt Lake City: University of Utah Press, 2000.

Maclean, Norman. *A River Runs Through It and Other Stories.* Chicago and London: University of Chicago Press, 1976.

———. "Montana Memory." In *Norman Maclean,* edited by McFarland and Nichols, 68–74. Lewiston, Idaho: Confluence, 1988.

McFarland, Ron, and Hugh Nichols, eds. *Norman Maclean.* Lewiston, Idaho: Confluence, 1988.

Slethaug, Gordon E. "The Buried Stream: Stochastic Narration and 'A River Runs Through It,' " *English Studies in Canada* 23, no. 3 (1997): 315–329.

Thomas Austenfeld

ROBBER BRIDEGROOM, THE EUDORA WELTY (1942)

The Robber Bridegroom, Eudora WELTY's first piece of long fiction, is set in the frontier days of Mississippi's Natchez Trace. We overhear the beginning of the tale as it is told by Clement Musgrove to the mysterious stranger, Jamie Lockhart, who has just saved his life and who later kidnaps and seduces his daughter, Rosamond. Though much of Welty's later work makes use of myth, this novella teems with mythic, historical, and literary allusions. Sharing its title with a Grimm Brothers' story, *The Robber Bridegroom*'s fairy tale quality is enhanced by the character Salome, who is in part the classic wicked stepmother and in part the evil seductress whose name she bears. The biblical Salome dances for the delight of the lustful King Herod and so enchants him that he grants her any favor she might request of him. Prompted by her mother, she requests and is given John the Baptist's head on a platter. Unlike her namesake, however, Welty's Salome is not physically alluring. In fact, she is so ugly that the Indians who capture and kill her first husband before the novel begins are frightened of her and set her free. After the Indian attack, Welty tells us, she has nothing "left but ambition in her destroyed heart" (24). And so she convinces Clement Musgrove, who along with his young daughter also survived the attack, to marry her. Welty suggests that Salome's power stems from a supernatural source when, based on no clear evidence, she is able to instruct her husband to buy and sell at exactly the right times so they soon become wealthy landowners.

Salome also uses her powers against her stepdaughter, Rosamond. Like the wicked stepmother in the "Snow White" fairy tale, Salome envies the girl who is her opposite in almost every way: "Rosamond was as beautiful as the day, Salome was as ugly as the night" (33). She sends her stepdaughter into the dangerous woods, as does the queen in "Snow White," hoping she will be killed. The Grimm Brothers' "The Robber Bridegroom" features good and evil male characters, but Welty gives us these opposites as women. Like fairy tales, Welty's *The Robber Bridegroom* invokes the opposites of light and dark to designate good and evil. But she also reminds us that dark and light, good and evil, are just parts of one complete whole. This suspicion prompts Clement Musgrove's musings on the contrast between his beautiful first wife and Salome: "All things are divided in half—night and day, the soul and body, and sorrow and joy and youth and age, and sometimes I wonder if even my own wife has not been the one person all the time, and I loved her beauty so well at the beginning that it is only now that the ugliness has struck through to beset me like a madness" (126).

Like Salome, young Rosamond is a powerful, creative woman. But whereas Salome directs her creative energies to the acquisition of wealth, Rosamond is an artist figure who sings beautiful songs and creates fantastic stories. After being sent by her stepmother on a dangerous errand in the woods, Rosamond returns safely with a tale of a giant mother panther who carried her home in its mouth. "[S]he did not mean to tell anything but the truth, but when she opened her mouth in answer to a question, the lies would simply fall out like diamonds and pearls" (38). Welty shows us that, in their strong, independent natures, Salome and Rosamond have much in common. To Musgrove's threat of a tutor, Rosamond responds, "Never! I will learn it all for myself" (39). Similarly, Salome, who has directed her husband's life throughout their married years, defies the first person to try to control her, her Indian captor. " 'No one is to have power over me!' Salome cried, shaking both her fists in the smoky air. 'No man, and none of the elements! I am by myself in the world' " (160–161). And Welty shows the pair growing close as mother and daughter when, in desperation to see the face of Jamie, her mysterious bandit lover, Rosamond takes the advice of her evil stepmother: In a variation of the Psyche and Eros myth, Salome gives Rosamond a potion to remove the berry stains from

Jamie's face, and, as in the myth, he deserts his lover for her betrayal, jumping out the window.

As her beloved disappears, Rosamond realizes the mistake of following her evil stepmother's advice. Finding herself on her own after a second Indian attack takes her family, Rosamond seeks Jamie, to whom, instead of her beautiful lies, she speaks only the truth. A feminist interpretation laments Rosamond's surrender of her artistic independence. Already visibly pregnant, Rosamond abandons her creative voice to create babies. Upon seeing her father after many years, she happily describes her new middle-class life that is almost comically commonplace in this tale of magic and fantasy. No longer the daring bandit and his stolen bride, Jamie and Rosamond are a settled married couple who now, like the rest of us, imagine the bold exploits of real pirates from the comfort and safety of conventional lives. But though she restores Rosamond to patriarchal control, Welty does not silence her voice entirely. For when her father questions the truth of her tale, she takes him "to see for himself, and it was all true but the blue canopy" (184). Her creative voice adds the one dash of color to her ordinary life.

This early tale by Welty ends conventionally, with a happy marriage. And as patriarchal authority is restored, the evil female is destroyed. The biblical Salome's power lay in her seductive dance, and in her final act of defiance Welty's Salome also dances. But hers more closely resembles the self-destructive, mad dance of the Queen in the "Snow White" tale. Salome's rebellion reaches Luciferian proportions as she boasts to her Indian captors that even the sun obeys her command to stand still, and she proceeds to dance until it does so. Of course, the sun continues to rise despite her frenzied movements. On the surface, good triumphs over evil at the tale's conclusion. Another interpretation suggests that Salome's dance is a futile defiance of ultimate male authority that finally ends in her own undoing. She dances herself to death.

SOURCES

Entzminger, Betina. *The Belle Gone Bad: White Southern Women Writers and The Dark Seductress.* Baton Rouge: Louisiana State University Press, 2002.

French, Warren. " 'All Things Are Double': Eudora Welty as a Civilized Writer." In *Eudora Welty: Critical Essays,* edited

by Peggy Whitman Prenshaw, 179–188. Jackson: University Press of Mississippi, 1979.

Graulich, Melody. "Pioneering the Imagination: Eudora Welty's *The Robber Bridegroom.*" In *Women and Western American Literature,* edited by Helen Winter Stauffer and Susan Rosowski, 283–296. Troy, N.Y.: The Whitston Publishing Co., 1982.

Kreyling, Michael. "*The Robber Bridegroom* and the Pastoral Dream." In *Eudora Welty,* edited by Harold Bloom, 135–148. New York: Chelsea House Publishers, 1986.

Welty, Eudora. *The Robber Bridegroom.* New York: Harcourt, Brace & Co., 1942.

Betina Entzminger

ROBBINS, TOM (THOMAS EUGENE) (1936–)

Eccentric is the word that recurs repeatedly to describe not just Tom Robbins himself but also his fiction. A 1960s cult figure, Robbins—who is largely ignored by mainstream critics—still draws college and high school readers to his popular novel *Even Cowgirls Get the Blues* (1976). They identify with his rejection of state, social, and religious institutions, his adoption of Eastern religions and philosophies, and the characters who transcend establishment restrictions. Robbins, a master of creative plots and characters, an exaggerated use of metaphor, and an absurdist sense of humor, was named by *Writer's Digest* in 1997 as one of "The 100 Best Writers of the Twentieth Century."

Tom Robbins was born on July 22, 1936, in Blowing Rock, North Carolina, to George T. Robbins and Katherine Robinson Robbins. He served in the U.S. Air Force in Korea. After graduating from Richmond Professional Institute (now Virginia Commonwealth University) in 1960, he moved to the West Coast, "tuned in and dropped out," and became a novelist. In an interview with Tracy Johnson, he says that it was at a 1967 Doors concert in Seattle that he found his "voice": in his review of the concert, he described the style of the Doors as "early cunnilingual, late patricidal, lunchtime in the Everglades" (Johnson). *Another Roadside Attraction* (1971) is narrated by Marx Marvelous. Plucky Purcell discovers the mummified corpse of Jesus Christ and brings it to an enormous hot dog stand run by John Paul Ziller and Amanda, an earth-mother type. *Even Cowgirls Get the Blues* (1976), narrated by a psychiatrist named Robbins, features Sissy Hankshaw (of the nine-inch thumb), who hitch-hikes her way to the Rubber Rose Ranch in South Dakota. In this commune a Native American group dedicated to Eastern spirituality joins forces with the cowgirls and fights the government in the Whooping Crane War; Sissy finds salvation through Chink, the Japanese-American wise man. *Still Life with Wood-pecker* (1980) tells the tale of Princess Leigh-Chen, heiress of the Pacific, and Bernard Micky Wrangler, a.k.a. Woodpecker, who search for the ultimate per-fume. In *Jitterbug Perfume* (1984), King Alobar and his lover, Kudra; the psychedelic Wiggs Dannyboy; and his protagonist-lover, Seattle waitress Priscilla all attain a state similar to that called nirvana. *Skinny Legs and All* (1990) is about Ellen Cherry Charles and her husband, Boomer, as they seek success in the New York art world. *Half Asleep in Frog Pajamas* (1994), about escaping the mundane world through the aid of frog aliens, is followed by *Fierce Invalids Home from Hot Climates* (2000), in which the book's protagonist, Switters, a CIA operative, takes the reader from Peru to Syria. Robbins's most recent novel is *Via Incognito* (2003).

Married three times, Robbins lives in LaConner, Washington, with his wife, Alexa D'Avalon. In 1994, *Even Cowgirls Get the Blues* was adapted for film by Gus Van Sant and released by Fine Line Features.

NOVELS

Another Roadside Attraction. New York: Doubleday, 1971.
Even Cowgirls Get the Blues. Boston: Houghton Mifflin, 1976.
Fierce Invalids Home from Hot Climates. New York: Bantam, 2000.
Half Asleep in Frog Pajamas. New York: Bantam, 1994.
Jitterbug Perfume. New York: Bantam, 1984.
Skinny Legs and All. New York: Bantam, 1990.
Still Life with Woodpecker. New York: Bantam, 1980.
Via Incognito. New York: Bantam, 2003.

SOURCES

Hoyser, Catherine Elizabeth. *Tom Robbins: A Critical Com-panion.* Westport, Conn.: Greenwood Press, 1997.
Klinkowitz, Jerome. *The Practice of Fiction in America: Writers from Hawthorne to the Present.* Ames: Iowa State University Press, 1980.
Siegel, Mark. *Tom Robbins.* Boise, Idaho: Boise State Univer-sity Press, 1980.
The Writers Directory 2000. Detroit, Mich.: St. James Press, 2000.

OTHER

Johnson, Tracy. "Tom Robbins." Salon.com. Available online. URL: http://www.salon.com/people/feature/2000/03/09/robbins. Accessed September 25, 2005.
Sims, Michael. "Tom Robbins: An Outrageous Writer in a Politically Correct Era." Bookpage.com. Available online. URL: http://www.bookpage.com/005bp/tom_robbins. html. Accessed September 25, 2005.
Tom Robbins. Levity.com. Available online. URL: http://www.levity.com/corduroy/robbins.htm. Accessed Septem-ber 25, 2005.

ROBERTS, ELIZABETH MADOX (1886–1941)

A novelist, poet, and short story writer, Eliza-beth Madox Roberts is known primarily for her first novel, *The Time of Man* (1926), published to critical acclaim in the United States and abroad, and *The Great Meadow* (1930), a critical success and a Book-of-the-Month Club selection. In both novels, Roberts portrays pioneer women on mythic journeys to selfhood and uses the modernist techniques of myth, symbol, and allusion, particularly to *The Odyssey.* A significant member of the Southern Renaissance, Roberts has been compared to Thomas Wolfe and Robert Penn Warren.

Roberts was born on October 30, 1881, in Perryville, Kentucky, to Simpson Roberts and Mary Brent Roberts. Reared in Springfield, Kentucky, she contracted tuber-culosis and moved to Colorado to live for five years with her brother Charles before she was finally well enough to attend the University of Chicago, from which she graduated with honors in 1921. *The Time of Man,* published five years later, tells the story of Ellen Chesser, daughter of a poor and illiterate itinerant Ken-tucky farmer whose introspection leads to an under-standing of her personal relationship to the world around her. *My Heart and My Flesh* (1927), a much darker tale about Theodosia Bell, an artist, that elicited comparisons with Faulkner and Melville, involves incest and a mixed-race family. In *The Great Meadow,* Diony Jarvis, an 18th-century Kentucky pioneer confronting the hostility and loneliness of the physical environment, is part of the American westward movement. She finds her own strength and identity. In *A Buried Treasure* (1931), Andy and Philly Blair discover their love for each other and for the rest of their rural community. *He Sent Forth a Raven* (1935), set during World War I, emphasizes again a world marked by violence, rape, and rootlessness. The mythic story of humankind continues in *Black Is My True Love's Hair* (1938), in which the Everyman figure is a woman, Dena, who must escape her relationship with the rootless Will Langtry, a familiar figure in modernist fiction.

Never in the best of health, Roberts died in 1941 of Hodgkin's disease, in Orlando, Florida. Renewed interest in her work began with the 1984 Elizabeth Madox Roberts issue of the *Southern Review*. Many reappraisals of her fiction appear in book chapters published in the 1990s. Some of her papers are found at the Library of Congress.

NOVELS

Black Is My True Love's Hair. New York: Viking, 1938.
A Buried Treasure. New York: Viking, 1931.
The Great Meadow. New York: Viking, 1930.
He Sent forth a Raven. New York: Viking, 1935.
Jingling in the Wind. New York: Viking, 1928.
My Heart and My Flesh. New York: Viking, 1927.
The Time of Man. New York: Viking, 1926.

SOURCES

Adams, James Donald. *Elizabeth Madox Roberts.* New York: Viking, 1938.
Auchincloss, Louis. *Pioneers and Caretakers: A Study of Nine American Women Novelists.* Minneapolis: University of Minnesota Press, 1965.
Bryant, J. A., Jr. *Twentieth Century Southern Literature.* Lexington: University of Kentucky Press, 1997.
Campbell, Harry Modean, and Rule E. Foster. *Elizabeth Madox Roberts: American Novelist.* Norman: University of Oklahoma Press, 1956.
Donaldson, Susan V. "Gender, Race, and Allen Tate's Profession of Letters in the South." In *Haunted Bodies: Gender and Southern Texts,* edited by Anne Goodwyn Jones and Susan V. Donaldson, 492–518. Charlottesville: University Press of Virginia, 1997.
Harrison, Elizabeth Jane. *Female Pastoral: Women Writers Re-Visioning the American South.* Knoxville: University of Tennessee Press, 1991.
Joyner, Nancy Carol. "The Poetics of the House in Appalachian Fiction." In *The Poetics of Appalachian Space,* edited by Parks Lanier, Jr., 10–27. Knoxville: University of Tennessee Press, 1991.
McDowell, Frederick P. W. *Elizabeth Madox Roberts.* Boston: Twayne, 1963.
Rovit, Earl H. *Herald to Chaos: The Novels of Elizabeth Madox Roberts.* Lexington: University of Kentucky Press, 1960.
Special Elizabeth Madox Roberts Issue. Southern Review 20 (1984).
Tate, Linda. "Elizabeth Madox Roberts: A Bibliographical Essay," *Resources for American Literary Study* 18 (1992): 22–43.

ROBERTS, KENNETH (LEWIS) (1885–1957)

Kenneth Roberts published numerous historical novels in the 1920s and 1930s. Critics generally agree that his three most successful novels are *Arundel* (1930), about General Benedict Arnold's ill-fated march from Maine to take Quebec; its sequel, *Rabble in Arms* (1933), where Arnold and his troops leave their defeat at Quebec in 1776 to the second Battle of Saratoga in 1777; and *Northwest Passage* (1937), where Major Robert Rogers commands the colonial soldiers—known as Rogers's Rangers—during the French and Indian War. Other significant novels include *Oliver Wiswell* (1940), *The Lively Lady* (1931), and *Lydia Bailey* (1947).

Kenneth Lewis Roberts was born on December 8, 1885, in Kennebunk, Maine, to Frank Lewis Roberts and Grace Tibbets Roberts. He earned a bachelor's degree at Cornell University in 1908, married Anna Seiberling Mosser in 1911, and served as a captain in the U.S. Army from 1918 to 1919. His novels followed a stint at the *Saturday Evening Post,* for which he wrote hundreds of articles and stories and with which he held numerous positions, including editor of the Sunday humor page. In fact, many of his early novels, including *Arundel,* were first serialized in the *Saturday Evening Post. Arundel* is actually the story of Steven Nason, Kenneth Roberts's great-great-grandfather, who accompanied Benedict Arnold from Arundel, the Maine province where Nason lived, to Quebec. *Rabble in Arms* depicts a Congress hostile to Benedict Arnold after his defeat of General Burgoyne. In *The Lively Lady,* sequel to *Rabble in Arms,* Roberts's great-grandfather,

Richard, captains the *Lively Lady* and is taken prisoner in England. The sequel to *The Lively Lady* is *Captain Caution* (1934), involving a sea battle with Olive Branch, a merchant ship. Major Robert Rogers of *Northwest Passage* seeks an overland route to the Pacific Ocean, and a young Maine artist hopes to follow him and paint the likenesses of Indians. Roberts dedicated this novel to his frequent collaborator, Booth TARKINGTON. *Oliver Wiswell* (1940) depicts the American Revolution from the perspective of Oliver Wiswell, a university student who is also a loyal British subject. In *Lydia Bailey* (1947), set in Haiti during Toussaint L'Ouverture's slave revolt and Napoleon's attempts to take over the government, Albion Hamlin, a Maine lawyer, rescues and falls in love with Lydia Bailey, the daughter of one of his clients.

Kenneth Lewis Roberts was awarded the Special Pulitzer Prize for his contributions to early American history in 1957; he died one month later at Rocky Pasture, his Kennebunk estate, and was buried in Arlington National Cemetery. *Northwest Passage* was twice made into a feature-length film: in 1940 and, under the title *Mission of Danger,* in 1959. Although many of his novels had gone out of print by the late 20th century, a number of them have now been republished and are routinely recommended to readers of history. The most extensive collection of Roberts's papers is held by the Library of Congress.

NOVELS

Antiquamania. Garden City, N.Y.: Doubleday, Doran, 1928.

Arundel. Garden City, N.Y.: Doubleday, Doran, 1930.

The Battle of Cowpens: The Great Morale Builder. Garden City, N.Y.: Doubleday, 1958.

Black Magic. Indianapolis, Ind.: Bobbs-Merrill, 1924.

Boon Island. Garden City, N.Y.: Doubleday, 1956.

The Brotherhood of Man: A Drama in One Act. (With Robert Garland). New York: French, 1934.

Captain Caution. Garden City, N.Y.: Doubleday, Doran, 1934.

The Collector's Whatnot. Boston and New York: Houghton Mifflin, 1923.

Concentrated New England: A Sketch of Calvin Coolidge. Indianapolis, Ind.: Bobbs-Merrill, 1924.

Don't Say That about Maine! Garden City, N.Y.: Doubleday, 1951.

Europe's Morning After. New York: Harper, 1921.

Florida. New York: Harper, 1926.

Florida Loafing. Indianapolis, Ind.: Bobbs-Merrill, 1925.

For Authors Only, and Other Gloomy Essays. Garden City, N.Y.: Doubleday, Doran, 1935.

Henry Gross and His Dowsing Rod. Garden City, N.Y.: Doubleday, 1951.

It Must Be Your Tonsils. Garden City, N.Y.: Doubleday, Doran, 1936.

I Wanted to Write. Garden City, N.Y.: Doubleday, 1949.

The Lively Lady. Garden City, N.Y.: Doubleday, Doran, 1931.

Lydia Bailey. Garden City, N.Y.: Doubleday, Doran, 1947.

Northwest Passage. Garden City, N.Y.: Doubleday, Doran, 1937.

Oliver Wiswell. Garden City, N.Y.: Doubleday, Doran, 1940.

Rabble in Arms, A Chronicle of Arundel and the Burgoyne Invasion. Garden City, N.Y.: Doubleday, Doran, 1933.

The Seventh Sense. Garden City, N.Y.: Doubleday, 1953.

Sun Hunting: Adventures and Observations among the Native and Migratory Tribes of Florida, Including the Stoical Time-Killers of Palm Beach, the Gentle and Gregarious Tin-Canners of the Remote Interior, and the Vivacious and Semi-Violent Peoples of Miami and Its Pulieus. Indianapolis, Ind.: Bobbs-Merrill, 1922.

Water Unlimited. Garden City, N.Y.: Doubleday, 1957.

SOURCES

Bales, Jack. *Kenneth Roberts: The Man and His Works.* Metuchen, N.J.: Scarecrow, 1989.

Harris, Janet. *A Century of American History In Fiction: Kenneth Roberts' Novels.* New York: Gordon Press, 1976.

Special Roberts issue, *Colby Library Quarterly* 6, no. 3 (September 1962).

West, Herbert Faulkner. "The Works of Kenneth Roberts," *Colby Library Quarterly* (September 1962): 89–99.

ROBINSON, MARILYNNE (1944–)

Novelist, short story writer, and essayist, Marilynne Robinson wrote HOUSEKEEPING (1981), which has become an American classic. It earned her the PEN/Ernest Hemingway Award and nominations for a PEN/Faulkner Award and a Pulitzer Prize. It is the story of an orphaned adolescent but also of self-reliant, eclectic women, told with poetic lyricism and power. Robinson's prose, rich in image and metaphor, highlights the tension between nature and humankind, society and the individual, illusion and reality, dependence and self-sufficiency. The novel continues to defy precise interpretation and to earn praise from new readers. Her long-awaited second novel, *Gilead,* appeared in 2004.

Marilynne Robinson was born on November 26, 1944, in Sand Point, Idaho, to John J. Summers, a lumber company employee, and Ellen Harris Summers. Reared in Idaho, Robinson was educated at Brown University, earning her bachelor's degree in 1966, and at the University of Washington, earning her doctoral degree in 1977. While in graduate school she married; she and her husband separated in 1989. *Housekeeping* takes place in mid-20th-century Idaho and is narrated by Ruth Stone. The novel features Ruth and her sister Lucille, whose grandfather died in an accident in Fingerbone Lake; their father deserted the family, and their mother, Helen, committed suicide by driving into that same lake. The sisters are raised by their grandmother, several great aunts, and finally Aunt Sylvie Fisher, whose unconventional approach to life results in Lucille's decision to live with a home economics teacher; Sylvie and Ruth burn down the house and, like Huck Finn, head for the open spaces of America. Indeed, scholar Jacqui Smyth, who sees Sylvie as an early rendition of a female "drifter" or vagrant, suggests that "despite the novel's insights into "the homeless condition, it is also about coming to a new understanding of shelter and the ideology of home" (Smyth, 281).

The novel continues to inspire various readings and interpretations, ranging from the feminist and postmodern to the Emersonian, from the classical and biblical to the Freudian. *Gilead,* set during the abolition years leading up to the Civil War, is a novel about fathers and sons. In 2005, *Gilead* won the National Book Critics Circle Award, the Pen/Faulkner Award, and the Pulitzer Prize in literature. In 1987, Bill Forsyth adapted *Housekeeping* into a film released by Columbia. Since 1991, Marilynne Robinson has been on the faculty of the University of Iowa Writers' Workshops.

NOVELS

Gilead. New York: Farrar, Straus, 2004.
Housekeeping. New York: Farrar, Straus, 1981.

SOURCES

Bonetti, Kay. "Interview with Marilynne Robinson," audio recording, Columbia, Mo., *American Audio Prose Library,* 1989.
Booth, Alison. "To Caption Absent Bodies: Marilynne Robinson's *Housekeeping,*" *Essays in Literature* 19 (Fall 1992): 279–290.
Burke, William, "Border Crossings in Marilynne Robinson's *Housekeeping,*" *Modern Fiction Studies* 37 (Winter 1991): 716–724.
Caver, Christine. "Nothing Left to Lose: *Housekeeping's* Strange Freedoms," *American Literature* 68 (March 1996): 111–137.
Hedrick, Tace, Eileen Bartos, Carolyn Jacobson, and Ann E. Voss. "Interviews with Marilynne Robinson," *Iowa Review,* 22 (Winter 1992): 1–28.
Kaivola, Karen. "The Pleasures and Perils of Merging Female Subjectivity in Marilynne Robinson's *Housekeeping,*" *Contemporary Literature* 34 (Winter 1993): 670–690.
King, Kristin. "Resurfacings of 'The Deeps': Semiotic Balance in Marilynne Robinson's *Housekeeping,*" *Studies in the Novel* 28, no. 4 (Winter 1996): 565–581.
Lassner, Phyllis. "Escaping the Mirror of Sameness: Marilynne Robinson's *Housekeeping.*" In *Mother Puzzles: Daughters and Mothers in Contemporary American Literature,* edited by Mickey Pearlman. 49–58. Westport, Conn.: Greenwood Press, 1989.
O'Brien, Sheila Ruzycki. "*Housekeeping:* New West Novel, Old West Film." In *Old West-New West: Centennial Essays,* edited by Barbara Howard Meldrum, 173–183. Moscow, Idaho: University of Idaho Press. 1993.
———. "*Housekeeping* in the Western Tradition: Remodeling Tales of Western Travelers." In *Women and the Journey: The Female Travel Experience,* edited by Bonnie Frederick, 217–234. Pullman: Washington State University Press, 1993.
O'Connell, Nicholas. "Interview with Marilynne Robinson." In *At the Field's End: Interviews with Twenty Pacific Northwest Writers,* 220–230. Seattle, Wash.: Madrona Publishers, 1987.
Schaub, Thomas. "An Interview with Marilynne Robinson," *Contemporary Literature* 35, no. 2 (1994): 231–251.
Smyth, Jacqui. "Sheltered Vagrancy in Marilynne Robinson's *Housekeeping,*" *Critique* 40, no. 3 (Spring 1999): 281–291.
Vorda, Allan. "A Life of Perished Things: An Interview with Marilynne Robinson." In *Face to Face: Interviews with Contemporary Novelists,* edited by Allan Vorda, 153–184. Houston, Texas: Rice University Press, 1993.

ROIPHE, ANNE (1935–)

According to feminist critics (Roberta Rubenstein, for example), Anne Roiphe is a postfeminist writer of fiction and nonfiction, most of which depict women's issues, contemporary Jewish family life, parent-child relations, religion, aging, and identity. Hers is always an original viewpoint, however, for Roiphe is "extremely uninterested, in what is—or is not—politically correct" (Sherman). Roiphe is best known for her novels *Up the Sandbox!* and LOVINGKINDNESS.

Anne Roiphe was born on Christmas Day 1935, in New York City, to Eugene Roth, a lawyer, and Blanch Phillips Roth. She earned her bachelor's degree at Sara Lawrence College in 1957, married Jack Richardson in 1958, divorced him in 1963, and married Herman Roiphe, a psychoanalyst, in 1967, the same year she published her first novel, *Digging Out*. This novel depicts the struggles of Laura Smith who "digs out" the secrets of her own identity while caring for her dying mother. *Up the Sandbox!* (1970) was universally praised for its insight into Margaret Reynolds, the intelligent, feminist wife and mother of two. Margaret feels torn between caring for her children and leading an activist life. (One of her fantasies involves blowing up the George Washington Bridge.) Alternately disturbing, moving, and funny, the novel captures the spirit of its era. Roiphe followed with *Lovingkindness* (1987), a depiction of the feminist political scientist Annie Johnson as she meets the challenges posed by her 22-year-old punk daughter Andrea, who has elected to live in Jerusalem and allow the yeshiva to select her husband. *The Pursuit of Happiness* (1991) also depicts family relationships. This multigenerational tale moves back and forth as the Gruenbaum family emigrates in 1892 from a small Polish shtetl to the Lower East Side of New York; successive generations live in mid-Manhattan, successful in their pursuit of the American Dream, many choosing to have second homes in Israel. In *If You Knew Me* (1993), middle-aged biologist Leah Rose, on a seaside sabbatical on Long Island, rescues the retarded Sally Masters from drowning; she meets Sally's brother Ollie and the two embark on a poignantly rendered, sometimes awkward, sometimes amusing, love affair.

Roiphe's novel *Secrets of the City* (2003) represents a departure from her usual content. Written from the point of view of a male protagonist and serialized for 15 months in the *Forward,* the novel takes place amid a city-wide epidemic, as Mayor Mel Rosenberg, son of a Jewish immigrant, attempts to use various folk cures to cope with the inevitable crises of his city. Roiphe's

historical novel *An Imperfect Lens* was published in 2006. Anne Roiphe lives with her husband, Dr. Herman Roiphe, in New York City. Her daughter, Katie Roiphe, is a writer and novelist well-known for her controversial views on feminism.

NOVELS

Digging Out. (Under name Anne Richardson). New York: McGraw Hill, 1967.

If You Knew Me. Boston: Little, Brown, 1993.

An Imperfect Lens. New York: Shaye Areheart Books, 2006.

Long Division. New York: Simon & Schuster, 1972.

Lovingkindness. New York: Summit Books, 1987.

The Pursuit of Happiness. New York: Summit Books, 1991.

Secrets of the City. New York: Shaye Areheart Books, 2003.

To Rabbit, With Love and Squalor: An American Read. New York: Free Press, 2000.

Torch Song. (Under name Anne Richardson). New York: Farrar, Straus, 1977.

Up the Sandbox! New York: Simon & Schuster, 1970.

SOURCES

Brosnahan, John. Review of *The Pursuit of Happiness, Booklist,* 15 April 1991.

Burstein, Janet Handler. *Writing Mothers, Writing Daughters: Tracing the Maternal in Stories by American Jewish Women.* Urbana: University of Illinois Press, 1996.

Gendler, Anne. Review of *If You Knew Me, Booklist,* July 1993.

Leber, Michele. Review of *Lovingkindness. Library Journal Review.*

Neville, Maureen. Review of *Secrets of the City, Library Journal* 128, no. 19 (November 15, 2003): 99.

Rubenstein, Roberta. "Feminism, Eros and Coming of Age," *Frontiers* 22, no. 2 (June 2001): 1–19.

OTHER

Sherman, Suzan. "Secrets of the Scribbler: An Interview with Anne Roiphe." Forward.com. Available online. URL: http://www.forward.com/issues/2004/04.01.09/arts3.html. Accessed September 25, 2005.

ROLEY, BRIAN ASCALON (1966–)

Hailed as a new young voice in Asian-American fiction, Brian Ascalon Roley first attracted attention in 2001 with the publication of AMERICAN SON, a bildungsroman of powerful originality. The novel, set in California as the 21st century begins, follows two brothers, Tomas and his younger brother Gabe, the story's narrator. Together, the brothers represent the Filipino and "Hapa" communities in California, "Hapa" being a term derived from a Hawaiian phrase meaning "Half white/half foreigner." The boys' mother, having immigrated to the United States to escape the caste system in the Philippines, has little better luck in the United States: Divorced from the boys' American father, she works two low-paying jobs to provide opportunities for her sons. Her son Gabe attempts to protect her from learning about Tomas's gangster-style life, but as Gabe himself draws closer to that existence, he runs away, brings shame on the family, and returns home to face ruined expectations and a life of violence.

Roley was born in Los Angeles, California, in 1966, to Thomas Lee, an accountant, and Azucena Laurel Ascalon Roley, a social worker. He earned his master of fine arts degree from Cornell University in 1998, and his J.D. from the University of California, Los Angeles, in 1994. In 1999 he married Gwen Smith. *American Son* was a *New York Times* Notable Book of the Year in 2001, and a Piper's Alley/Faulkner Novella Award finalist. Roley's prose has been compared to that of Cormac MCCARTHY, while his tale of the dark side of immigrant life has been praised for its unflinching look at the anger and alienation that can result from cultural estrangement.

NOVEL

American Son. New York: W. W. Norton, 2001.

SOURCES

Brian Ascalom Roley-Biography. Available online. URL: http://www.brianroley.com/bio.htm. Accessed September 25, 2005.

Dowling, Brendan. Review of *American Son. Booklist* 97, no. 17 (May 1, 2001): 1,669.

Hemon, Aleksandar. "No surfer dudes: This debut novel examines racism through the story of Filipino-Americans in California," *The New York Times Book Review,* 12 August 2001, p. 20.

Ty, Eleanor. "Abjection, Masculinity, and Violence in Brian Roley's *American Son* and Han Ong's *Fixer Chao,*" *MELUS* 29, no. 1 (Spring 2004): 119–137.

ROSE OF DUTCHER'S COOLLY HAMLIN GARLAND (1895)

"Rose was an unaccountable child from the start." With the first sentence of his novel, GARLAND forecasts Rose's eventual rebellion and escape from the limitations of western farm life, especially as those limitations affected women. In the following sentences and chapters, Garland constructs, with unparalleled skill and care, the lineaments of the "unaccountable" Rose Dutcher; she becomes the most physically and intellectually vibrant female character in his work, if not in all American fiction up to that time. (Eric Sundquist writes that it is only in the writings of Thomas Hardy and D. H. Lawrence that one can find an equal for Garland's "revelation of Rose's burgeoning natural desires" [Eliot, 519]). Sinclair LEWIS, whose Carol Kennicot of his 1920 novel *MAIN STREET* is a direct descendent of Rose, proclaimed in his Nobel Prize acceptance speech that Rose was a "valiant and revelatory" work of realism that "made it possible for me to write of America as I see it" (Lewis, 308).

Rose—without a mother to coach her into regularized feminine behavior (she died when Rose was five) and with an indulgent father, living on an isolated farm among the "coollies" (valleys) of western Wisconsin—is able to develop herself and her ideas without reference to social or sexual norms. She evades these norms by, in part, doing everything "like the boys": She snares gophers, goes barefooted and bareheaded, isn't afraid of bugs and beetles, plays all the boys' games, performs the hard and dirty farm work, and, among other things, drinks from rivers "like the boys [do], that is, by lying down on their breasts and drinking as the hunter drinks" (29). This action is repeated throughout the novel, symbolizing her unconventional girl- and womanhood. "She saw no reason," the narrator remarks, "why boys should have all the fun" (17).

Rose is also sexually unconventional. Growing up on a farm, she is "exposed to sights and sounds which the city girl knows nothing of. Mysterious processes of generation and birth go on before [her] eyes"; "the apparently shameful fact of sex faced her everywhere" (22, 23). Freed from taboos, Rose is fascinated with "all the things girls are supposed not to think of" (127). She gets sensual pleasure from sleeping naked in bed, longs to strip and skinny-dip with the boys, and sometimes even slips off her clothes and runs "amid the tall corn-stalks like a wild thing."

Rose, in her questioning and challenging of prescribed behavior, is a sort of female Huck Finn of the western prairie; Huck, equally free of the socializing forces of a normal Southern family and school system, is able to construct his own behavior and moral code. Both Huck and Rose are determined to test things, not content to accept ideas until they have been personally verified. One day at school, for example, Rose is told that if she shakes her fist at the sky and swears at God, she will drop dead. Upon hearing this, "she calmly stepped forward and shook her little fist up at the sun and swore, while the awe-stricken children cowered like a covey of partridges." She says to them, "There! you see that's a lie." From that point, the narrator remarks, "she went on exploding these strange superstitious fancies" (8)—a sentence that could serve as a summary of her life, as she tests and rejects other givens of her environment, such as how and where she should live (she escapes to Chicago to establish an independent life), the state of marriage (she contracts a "companionate" marriage with a Chicago journalist), and how she should write (a poet, she rejects British and East Coast models for western local color).

Rose's leaving of her Wisconsin farm and moving to Chicago, which occurs nearly halfway through the novel, mirrors a massive ongoing historical phenomenon, namely the titanic migration from the farm to the city. If America was born in the country and moved to the city, as historian Richard Hofstadter writes (Hofstadter, 23), then *Rose of Dutcher's Coolly* constitutes one of the first and most important renderings of that epochal move. The narrator of *Rose* exclaims that "This was the age of cities. The world's thought went on in the great cities" (172). And Garland's description of the way Chicago lures Rose anticipates DREISER: Rose was "a fresh, young and powerful soul rushing to a great city, a shining atom of steel obeying the magnet" (181).

In Chicago, Rose not only becomes a part of the great urban migration, she also becomes linked to another massive shift in American culture, namely the New Woman movement. Some of the leading features of that movement—a loosening of legal and social restrictions, an opening up of educational and career opportunities—were instinctively practiced by Rose in her Wisconsin girlhood. But in Chicago, especially through her friend and mentor Dr. Isabel Herrick, she

encounters the New Woman movement in full consciousness. Dr. Herrick, an alienist (psychiatrist), is wholly "man-like" in her intellectual and professional achievements, completely unhindered socially, and on the verge of forming a companionate marriage herself with another doctor. Meeting Dr. Herrick for the first time at her office, "this small, resolute brusque woman was a world's wonder to her" (209). Dr. Herrick, a purposeful feminist who has consciously broken through previous restrictions, provides Rose's next step to being fully "unaccountable."

But if the Chicago section serves to develop and culminate many of the leading themes of the novel, it also serves to weaken it. Much of the freshness and depth of the first half of the novel is lost, as most critics (such as William Dean HOWELLS, Donald Pizer, and Eric Sundquist) have pointed out. The novel's themes, instead of being dramatized, are merely enunciated in a series of stiff set speeches. But in the brilliant first half of *Rose,* it is clear that Garland had, in 1895, reached an artistic height. He had gathered all the elements of his immense gallery of suffering women from his earlier short fiction, as well as all his critiques of the social and cultural limitations of the West, and put them together to create a character and story that, in the Wisconsin section at least, no Western writer has ever surpassed. That Garland's achievement—which influenced and inspired writers such as Dreiser and Lewis, among others—is largely forgotten constitutes a major blemish in American studies.

SOURCES

Eliot, Emory, ed. *Columbia Literary History of the United States.* New York: Columbia University Press, 1988.
Garland, Hamlin. *Rose of Dutcher's Coolly.* 1895. Reprint, Lincoln: University of Nebraska Press, 1969.
Hofstadter, Richard. *The Age of Reform: From Bryan to F. D. R.* New York: Vintage-Random, 1955.
Lewis, Sinclair. "Nobel Prize Address." In *The Theory of the American Novel,* edited by George Perkins, 301–309. New York: Holt, 1970.

Quentin Martin

ROSSNER, JUDITH (1935–2005) Novelist, short story writer, and poet, Judith Rossner published for nearly four decades. It was her 1975 novel, LOOKING

FOR MR. GOODBAR, that first brought her national attention and critical acclaim. It was released as a Paramount film in 1977. This chilling tale of 1970s New York City singles bars, although inspired by a West Side murder case, was not written as "new journalism" (Mitgang): Transformed by Rossner into fiction, it captured the imagination of the American reading public because of its portrait of a popular urban ritual and its implications about the shifting roles and attitudes of single women. In subsequent novels, Rossner created plots from real-life cases, as in *Emmeline* (1980), based on an actual Maine tragedy. Other Rossner best-sellers treat the pitfalls of materialism, the tension between selflessness and self-absorption, the effect of divorce on children, and the 1970s-era state of the women's movement. Rossner was adept at re-creating believable scenes and atmospheres, as in *August* (1983), with its portrait of East Hampton, Long Island, in late summer, just as she realistically explored the interior workings of women's hearts and minds.

Judith Rossner was born on March 1, 1935, in New York City, to Joseph George Perelman and Dorothy Shapiro Perelman. She dropped out of the City College of New York to marry Robert Rossner in 1954; after they divorced, she married again, to Mort Persky, in 1979. Her first novel, *To the Precipice* (1966), is a coming-of-age story, set in the 1940s and 1950s, about the marriage between a young Jewish woman, Ruth Kossoff, and a gentile. *Nine Months in the Life of an Old Maid* (1969), her second novel, evokes the awakening of mentally unstable Elizabeth, who, save for family exigencies, would have contentedly lived with her sister and brother-in-law for the remainder of her life. *Any Minute I Can Split* (1972), set in a 1960s commune, follows the pregnant Margaret Adams. She has run away from her husband but discovers that life with him in the city is preferable to the hypocritical commune, where the friendships and motivations are superficial. When *Esquire* asked her to write the account of Roseann Quinn, a schoolteacher who had been murdered by a man she had picked up in a singles bar, Rossner refused to write a factual account; instead she used her imagination and the creative process to transform the tragic but riveting story into *Looking for Mr. Goodbar*. Theresa Dunn, overweight and a polio survivor, has been rejected by her lover, an English professor, and has started to frequent singles bars. She is murdered in one of these bars by a drifter.

Following this success, Rossner published *Attachments* (1977), the story of Nadine Tumulty and her friend Diane, whose manipulative friendship is as much the subject of the novel as is their marriage to Siamese twins. In *Emmeline*, the 13-year-old title character works in the cotton mills in Lowell, Massachusetts, and is seduced by an overseer; she secretly gives away the baby. Years later, she marries a younger man who, it turns out, is that baby. *August* focuses on the world of psychoanalysis as Dawn Henley, a student at Barnard College, grows close to Dr. Lulu Shinefeld, her recently divorced psychiatrist; Rossner shifts back and forth between the complex stories of the two women. Rossner changed her focus in *His Little Women* (1990) to the relationship between father and movie mogul Sam Pearlstein and his children, the products of his three previous marriages. These four daughters—Nell, an attorney; Louisa, a novelist; and two other daughters nearly invisible in the shadowy drug world they inhabit—compete for his attention. *Olivia, or, The Weight of the Past* (1994) features Caroline Ferrante, whose daughter Olivia eloped with an aggressive, controlling Italian and decides to return to live with her mother in New York. The mother-daughter relationship recurs in *Perfidia* (1997), which draws its title from the Spanish word for betrayal. The novel depicts an intense rivalry between divorced mother Anita Stern and her daughter, Madeleine (Maddy); it is Anita, not Maddy, who eagerly enters the 1970s free-love and drugs era, but it is Maddy who murders her mother and changes her plans to attend Harvard University.

Judith Rossner died of unknown causes on August 9, 2005, at New York University Medical Center. *Emmeline* was aired on PBS on April 2, 1997, and subsequently performed as an opera.

NOVELS

Any Minute I Can Split. New York: McGraw, 1972.
Attachments. New York: Simon & Schuster, 1977.
August. Boston: Houghton, 1983.
Emmeline. New York: Simon & Schuster, 1980.
His Little Women. New York: Summit Books, 1990.
Looking for Mr. Goodbar. New York: Simon & Schuster, 1975.

Nine Months in the Life of an Old Maid. New York: Dial, 1969.

Olivia, or, The Weight of the Past. New York: Crown, 1994.

Perfidia: A Novel. New York: Nan A. Talese, 1997.

To the Precipice. New York: Morrow, 1966.

SOURCES

Potoker, E. M. "Judith Rossner: Daughter of Lovers," *Nation,* 29 May 1976, pp. 661–664.

Rinzler, C. E. Review of *Looking for Mr. Goodbar, New York Times Book Review,* 8 June 1975, pp. 25–26.

OTHER

Audio Interview with Judith Rossner. Wiredforbooks.org. Available online. URL: http://wiredforbooks.org/ judithrossner. Accessed September 25, 2005.

Behrens, Steve. "Tragic Legend Returns to Public TV," *Current* (July 22, 1996). Available online. URL: http://www.current.org/prog613.html. Accessed September 26, 2005.

Hickman, Lisa C. Review of *Perfidia. Endpapers.* Weeklywire.com. Available online. URL: http://weeklywire.com/ ww/11-17-97/memphis_book.html. Accessed September 25, 2005.

Hooper, Brad. Review of *Perfidia. Booklist Review.* Available online. URL: http://www.NoveList.com. Accessed September 25, 2005.

Mitgang, Herbert. "Behind the Best Sellers." New York Times on the Web. Available online. URL: http://www.nytimes.com/books/97/10/19/home/rossner-profile.html. Accessed September 25, 2005.

ROTH, HENRY (1906–1995)

Henry Roth is internationally known for one novel: CALL IT SLEEP (1934), largely unknown until its publication in paperback in 1964 but now translated into dozens of languages and considered one of the classics of 20th-century American literature. The novel depicts David Schearl's coming of age in Jewish-immigrant Harlem in New York City, and his efforts amid the bigotry, class conflicts, and assimilation struggles of the early 20th century to find his place within and without this America. Roth is lauded repeatedly for the eloquent lyricism of his prose, which evokes the spirituality and metaphysical levels to which some of his characters aspire. The *New York Review of Books* critic Robert Towers believes that the novel is "now generally recognized as the most moving and lyrical novel to come out of Jewish immigration to America before and after the turn of the century" (Towers, 24). *Call It Sleep* reflects Roth's commitment to the proletarian ideals of the Communist Party, of which he was a member, and the feelings of alienation and isolation that Roth, like his major influences, Franz Kafka and James Joyce, experienced. For six decades afterward, Roth wrote short fiction and essays but no novels until, in the early 1990s, three volumes of his six-volume fictional autobiography, *Mercy of a Rude Stream,* appeared. Volume 3, entitled *From Bondage,* written in the last years of Roth's life, was a National Book Critics Circle Award finalist in 1997.

Henry Roth was born in Tysmenica, Galicia, in Austria-Hungary, on February 8, 1906, to Herman Roth, a waiter, and Leah Farb Roth; when he was 18 months old, he and his mother joined Herman Roth, who had gone to New York City to find work. Reared in New York, Roth was educated at City College of New York, where he earned a bachelor's degree in 1928. He lived for a time with Eda Lou Walton, a poet. Walton had an affair with and later married David Mandel, who helped Roth publish his manuscript. Roth married Muriel Parker, a musician, composer, and elementary school principal and, like many American writers of his era, worked for the Works Progress Administration.

A Star Shines Over Mt. Morris Park (1994), volume 1 of *Mercy of a Rude Stream,* covers the pre–World War I youth of Ira Stigman, a marginalized, shy, intellectual boy who tries to deny his Jewishness. *Diving Rock on the Hudson* (1995) depicts the slightly older Ira's expulsion from high school and his emerging from confusion to his identity as a writer. *From Bondage* takes Ira through his college years, the influence of James Joyce on his writing, and his complicated affair with Edith Welles, an English professor also involved with her former student, Larry Gordon.

Henry Roth died on October 13, 1995, in Albuquerque, New Mexico. Three of the four volumes of *Mercy of a Rude Stream,* including *Requiem for Harlem* (1998), were published posthumously. Roth's manuscripts are housed at Boston University and the New York Public Library.

NOVELS

Call It Sleep. New York: Robert O. Ballou, 1934, 2nd edition with a history by Harold U. Ribalow, a critical introduction by Maxwell Geismar, and a personal appreciation by Meyer Levin. Paterson, N.J.: Pageant, 1960. Reprint, with a foreword by Walter Allen, London: M. Joseph, 1963.

Mercy of a Rude Stream. New York: St. Martin's, Volume 1: *A Star Shines over Mt. Morris Park,* 1994, Volume 2: *A Diving Rock on the Hudson,* 1995, Volume 3: *From Bondage,* 1996, Volume 4: *Requiem for Harlem,* 1998.

SOURCES

Adams, Stephen J. " 'The Noisiest Novel Ever Written': The Soundscape of Henry Roth's *Call It Sleep,*" *Twentieth Century Literature* 35, no. 1 (Spring 1989): 43–64.

Alter, Robert. "The Desolate Breach Between Himself and Himself," *The New York Times Book Review,* 16 January 1994, pp. 3, 29.

———. Review of *Shifting Landscape* and *Call It Sleep, New Republic,* 25 January 1988, pp. 33–37.

Berman, Marshall. "The Bonds of Love," *Nation,* 23 September 1996, pp. 25–30.

Dickstein, Morris. "Call It an Awakening," *The New York Times Book Review,* 29 November 1987, pp. 1, 33, 35–36.

Fein, Richard J. "Fear, Fatherhood, and Desire in *Call It Sleep,*" *Yiddish* 5, no. 4 (Fall 1984): 49–54.

Gordon, Mary. "Confession, Terminable and Interminable," *The New York Times Book Review,* 26 February 1995, p. 5.

Harris, Lis. "A Critic at Large: In the Shadow of the Golden Mountains," *New Yorker,* 27 June 1988, pp. 84–92.

Howe, Irving. "Life Never Let Up," *The New York Times Book Review,* 25 October 1964, pp. 1, 60.

Kazin, Alfred. "The Art of *Call It Sleep,*" *The New York Review of Books,* 10 October 1991, p. 15.

Kermode, Frank. " 'Holistic Rendering of My Lamentable Past,' " *The New York Times Book Review,* 14 July 1996, p. 6.

Leader, Zachary. "An East-Side Kid," *Times Literary Supplement,* 25 February 1994, p. 20.

Ledbetter, Kenneth. "Henry Roth's *Call It Sleep:* The Revival of a Proletarian Novel," *Twentieth Century Literature* 12, no. 3 (October 1966): 123–130.

Pinsker, Sanford. "The Re-Awakening of Henry Roth's *Call It Sleep,*" *Jewish Social Studies* 28, no. 3 (July 1966): 148–158.

Roth, Henry, with David Bronsen. "A Conversation with Henry Roth," *Partisan Review* 36, no. 2 (1969): 265–280.

———, with William Freedman. "Henry Roth in Jerusalem: An Interview," *The Literary Review* 23, no. 1 (Fall 1979): 5–23.

Towers, Robert. "Look Homeward, Ira," *The New York Review of Books,* 3 March 1994, pp. 24–25.

Wirth-Nesher, Hana, ed. *New Essays on "Call It Sleep."* New York: Cambridge University Press, 1996.

OTHER

Books and Writers: Henry Roth. Available online. URL: http://www.kirjasto.sci.fi/henryr.htm. Accessed September 25, 2005.

ROTH, PHILIP (MILTON) (1933–)

Philip Roth, along with Saul BELLOW and Bernard MALAMUD, is part of the triumvirate of writers who introduced Jewish-American literature to the general reading public. Roth, for one, earned his first National Book Award for *Goodbye, Columbus, and Five Short Stories* (1959) and in the subsequent four decades responded to the reality of postwar urban America and to many of his own characters in modes ranging from realism to comedy, and then from surealism to tragicomedy. He explored then, as he does today, the boundaries between life and fiction and morality and creativity. Because Roth so openly draws on his own history, critical response has been divided between those who see him as self-indulgent, self-hating, bitter, or perverse, and admirers who laud his exuberance and use of comedy and satire. Nevertheless, he continues to produce incisive portrayals of Americans who struggle to realize themselves but seem blocked by their own absurdities and vulgarities. Indeed, few of his contemporaries have created such complex yet sympathetic and hilarious characters. They live in Roth's imagination and in ours. Most notable are Neil Klugman, Alexander Portnoy, Peter Tarnopol, Nathan Zuckerman, and Mickey Sabbath, and many who emerge in Roth's finely realized short stories. These characters expose the foibles of American life. The GHOST WRITER (1979) earned an American Book Award nomination, as did *The Anatomy Lesson* (1983), which was also nominated for a National Book Critics Circle Award. From the 1980s onward, honors have come swiftly to Roth: *The Counterlife* (1986) won both the National Book Critics Circle Award and the National Jewish Book Award; *Patrimony* (1991), a memoir about Roth's father, won a National Book Critics Circle Award; and *Operation Shylock* (1992) won a PEN/Faulkner Award. Both SABBATH'S THEATER (1995) and AMERICAN PASTORAL (1997) were awarded the National Book Award, and the latter also received the 1998 Pulitzer

Prize. *The Human Stain* (2000) garnered the PEN/Faulkner and National Jewish Book Awards. In 2002, the National Book Foundation celebrated Roth's achievements with the Medal for Distinguished Contribution to American letters.

Philip Roth was born on March 19, 1933, in Newark, New Jersey, to which he often returns in his fiction. His parents were Herman Roth, an insurance manager, and Bess Finkel Roth. He was educated at Bucknell University, earning a bachelor's degree (magna cum laude) in 1954 and the University of Chicago (M.A., 1955). He spent 1955 to 1956 in the U.S. Army. From February 22, 1959, until her death in 1968, Roth was married to Margaret Martinson; and from April 29, 1990, until their divorce in 1994, he was married to the actress Claire Bloom. Both of them have written books about this relationship.

Roth's novella, *Goodbye Columbus* (1959), introduced Neil Klugman, a struggling working-class Jew who briefly loves but ultimately rejects both Radcliffe-educated Brenda Patimkin, his wealthy upper-class lover, and the life she represents. *Letting Go* (1962) is a novel whose value has risen over the decades: Set in the 1950s, the novel features young graduate-school students, their anxieties, and their responses to the pressures of human commitment. Gabe Wallach, the well-to-do, successful protagonist, has relationships with three women, to none of whom is he ever totally committed. He is incapable of commitment but is drawn to his foil, the overworked and penurious Paul Herz, who also has a fear of close relationships. Roth's next novel, *When She Was Good* (1967), is uncharacteristic of Roth: It follows Lucy Nelson, a midwestern Protestant housewife whose portrait lacks any of the satiric insight that most readers have come to expect. As her marriage collapses, she is ill-equipped to face the crisis, and walks into the snow where she dies of exposure. *PORTNOY'S COMPLAINT* (1969), however, is a satiric masterpiece. Here Roth returns to a mixture of Jewishness and sex. The novel, which propelled Roth into the limelight of American popular culture, is the story of Alex Portnoy, a guilt-ridden young man trying to escape his repressive mother through psychoanalytical sessions with Dr. Spielvogel. Both characters are now staples in the American canon. The novel also

made Roth fair game for critics, some of whom considered him an anti-Semite who demeaned his own people. Others acknowledged him as an insightful, creative writer who used humor to illuminate feelings of doubt and inadequacy, Jewish and otherwise.

For the next several years, Roth experimented with contemporary, sometimes outlandish subjects. *Our Gang* (1971) is a satiric treatment of President Nixon and his administration, while *The Breast* (1972) treats with seriousness and some restraint the Kafka-esque central image of David Kepesh, a professor who has been transformed into a giant mammary gland. In *The Great American Novel* (1973), Roth uses baseball to comment on American culture, much of which is the object of Roth's biting satire. With *My Life as a Man* (1974), Roth examines the inner life of Peter Tarnopol, a novelist writing about another novelist named Nathan Zuckerman. Roth uses the techniques of metafiction to examine the ways teaching and writing literature can heal a broken marriage and, in a more general sense, can illuminate the ways life is transformed into fiction. Both Tarnopol and Zuckerman have troubled relationships with women, Tarnopol with his wife and, later, Susan McCall. Zuckerman, on the other hand, marries Lydia Ketterer for the wrong reasons, and she commits suicide. *The Professor of Desire* (1977) follows the early life of David Kepesh, a character from *The Breast*. In this novel he wrestles with both the demands of academia and his own lustful behavior with a number of women.

Zuckerman reappears in three novels and a novella, all collected in 1985 under the title *Zuckerman Bound* (alluding to the process of binding all the novels into one volume and to Zuckerman's general predicament). In *The Ghost Writer* (1979), young Zuckerman scandalizes his readers with a novel that his father deems to be anti-Semitic (obviously this scene echoes Roth's own experience). Zuckerman apprentices himself to a reclusive Jewish-American writer, E. I. Lonoff, in order to understand the creative process and his own Jewishness. *ZUCKERMAN UNBOUND* (1981) likewise explores issues concerning fiction writing, and the artist's connection to home, family, and community. Set 13 years later, Zuckerman by this time has had three failed marriages, written four novels, and is currently being denounced for writing an explicitly sexual novel (see the criticism of Roth for writing *Portnoy's Complaint*). At the end of the novel, after his father's death, a solitary Nathan wanders through the now ghettoized Newark of his childhood. In *The Anatomy Lesson*, Zuckerman realizes that he has chosen to understand fiction instead of the ramifications of his own life and, because of this self-absorption, he can no longer write well. At the novel's end, he falls and breaks his jaw on a tombstone in a Jewish cemetery, an accident that renders him speechless. By the time we reencounter him in *The Prague Orgy* (1985), Zuckerman has regenerated himself: He now acknowledges the value and significance of his Jewish heritage and is internationally successful. He even attempts to help a writer in Kafka-like Czechoslovakia. One could say that Zuckerman has reconnected to history. In fact, he travels to Jerusalem in *The Counterlife* (1987), another rapprochement with heritage and, in Roth's version of postmodern self-reflexiveness, lives out several possible destinies along with his brother, Henry. Now married to an Englishwoman named Maria, Zuckerman dies, but Maria takes center stage and urges Nathan to rebel against his creator.

After a tetralogy based on his own life (*The Facts* [1988], *Deception* [1990], *Patrimony* [1991], and *Operation Shylock* [1993]) Roth wrote *Sabbath's Theater* (1995), which prepared the way for his AMERICAN TRILOGY (*American Pastoral* [1997], *I Married a Communist* [1998], and *The Human Stain* [2000]). Here Roth turns his attention to American history and its effect on the national character. His more recent books include *The Dying Animal* (2001), the much-acclaimed *The Plot against America* (2004), and *Everyman* (2006).

Philip Roth lives and writes in Connecticut. In 2004 Roth chose as his biographer University of Connecticut professor Ross Miller, who is also editor of the eight-volume Library of America edition of Roth's works, beginning with *Goodbye, Columbus* and *Portnoy's Complaint,* to be published by The Library of America in 2005. Subsequent volumes will be published between 2006 and 2013. To date, three of Roth's novels have been filmed: *Goodbye, Columbus* was written by Arnold Schulman and directed by Larry Peerce for Paramount in 1969; *Portnoy's Complaint* was written and directed by Ernest Lehman for Warner Bros. in 1972; *The Ghost Writer* was adapted for television and aired on the Public Broadcasting System in 1984. Most of Roth's papers are housed at the Library of Congress.

NOVELS AND NOVELLAS

American Pastoral. Boston: Houghton, 1997.
The Anatomy Lesson. New York: Farrar, Straus, 1983.
The Breast. New York: Holt, 1972.
The Counterlife. New York: Farrar, Straus, 1986.
Deception. New York: Simon & Schuster, 1990.
The Dying Animal. Boston: Houghton, 2001.
Everyman. Boston: Houghton, 2006.
The Ghost Writer. New York: Farrar, Straus, 1979.
Goodbye, Columbus, and Five Short Stories. Boston, Mass.: Houghton 1959; published as *Goodbye, Columbus.* New York: Houghton, 1989.
The Great American Novel. New York: Holt, 1973.
The Human Stain. Boston: Houghton, 2000.
I Married a Communist. Boston: Houghton, 1998.
Letting Go. New York: Random House, 1962.
My Life as a Man. New York: Holt, 1974.
Our Gang. New York: Random House, 1971.
The Plot against America. Boston: Houghton, 2004.
Portnoy's Complaint. New York: Random House, 1969.
The Professor of Desire. New York: Farrar, Straus, 1977.
Sabbath's Theater. Boston: Houghton, 1995.
When She Was Good. New York: Random House, 1967.
Zuckerman Unbound. New York: Farrar, Straus, 1981.

SOURCES

Appelfeld, Aron. *Beyond Despair: Three Lectures and a Conversation with Philip Roth.* New York: Fromm International, 1994.

Berman, Jeffrey. *The Talking Cure: Literary Representations of Psychoanalysis.* New York: New York University Press, 1985.

Cohen, Sarah Blacher, ed. *Comic Relief: Humor in Contemporary American Literature.* Carbondale: University of Illinois Press, 1978.

Cooper, Alan. *Philip Roth and the Jews.* Albany: State University of New York Press, 1996.

Gindin, James. *Harvest of a Quiet Eye: The Novel of Compassion.* Bloomington: Indiana University Press, 1971.

Guttman, Allen. *The Jewish Writer in America: Assimilation and the Crisis of Identity.* New York: Oxford University Press, 1971.

Harrison, Gilbert A., ed. *The Critic as Artist: Essays on Books, 1920–1970.* New York: Liveright, 1972.

Howe, Irving. *The Critical Point*. New York: Horizon, 1973.

Hyman, Stanley Edgar. *The Critic's Credentials: Essays and Reviews by Stanley Edgar Hyman*. Edited by Phoebe Pettingell. New York: Atheneum, 1978.

Kazin, Alfred. *Contemporaries*. Boston: Little, Brown, 1962.

Malin, Irving. *Jews and Americans*. Carbondale: Southern Illinois University Press, 1965.

McDaniel, John. *The Fiction of Philip Roth*. Haddonfield, N.J.: Haddonfield House, 1974.

Milbauer, Asher Z., and Donald G. Watson, eds. *Reading Philip Roth*. London: Macmillan, 1988.

Pinsher, Sanford. *The Comedy That "Hoits": An Essay on the Fiction of Philip Roth*. Columbia: University of Missouri Press, 1975.

Podhoretz, Norman. *Doings and Undoings*. New York: Farrar, Straus, 1964.

Pughe, Thomas. *Comic Sense: Reading Robert Coover, Stanley Elkin, and Philip Roth*. Basel, Switzerland: Birkhauser Verlag, 1994.

Rogers, Bernard F., Jr. *Philip Roth: A Bibliography*. Metuchen, N.J.: Scarecrow, 1974.

———. *Philip Roth*. Boston: Twayne, 1978.

Roth, Philip. *Patrimony: A True Story*. New York: Simon & Schuster, 1991.

Solotaroff, Theodore. *The Red Hot Vacuum and Other Pieces on the Writings of the Sixties*. New York: Atheneum, 1970.

Walden, Daniel, ed. *The Changing Mosaic: From Cahan to Malamud, Roth, and Ozick*. Albany: State University of New York Press, 1993.

Wisse, Ruth. *The Schlemiel as Modern Hero*. Chicago: University of Chicago Press, 1971.

ROWSON, SUSANNA HASWELL (1762–1824)

Novelist, actress, poet, and educator, Susanna Rowson wrote *Charlotte: A Tale of Truth* (1791) (later retitled *CHARLOTTE TEMPLE*), the first best-selling novel in America and the book on which her reputation rests today. The novel tells the story of a young girl whose worldly French teacher coerces her pupil into a relationship with an army officer. Recent scholarship applauds Rowson's skill at using the techniques of sentimentalism in her work while at the same time undermining it. She emphasized that sentimentalism proves dangerous to young women. Indeed, her career, dedicated to teaching girls to become educated and independent, culminated in the establishment of the Young Girl's Academy in Boston, where she remained director for 25 years.

Susanna Rowson was born on February 5, 1762, in Portsmouth, England, to William Haswell, a revenue collector in the Royal Navy, and Susanna Musgrave Haswell, who died giving birth to Susanna. Her father remarried, emigrated to Massachusetts, sent for Susanna, and was deported to England in 1778 for supporting the British during the American Revolution, taking his by then 18-year-old daughter with him. At age 24, still in England, Rowson published *Victoria* (1786), her first novel, partly to help her impoverished family. Victoria Baldwin, orphaned daughter of a naval officer, is seduced, becomes pregnant, and is predictably abandoned. In that same year the author married William Rowson; the two joined actors' troupes but, still needing to earn money, Rowson published *The Inquisitor* (1788), a domestic novel, and a third, *The Test of Honour* (1789). Published anonymously, this novel was about the spirited young Mary Newton, determined to marry her aristocratic suitor, but only after she has earned enough money to become his financial equal. *Charlotte* centers on the 15-year-old boarding-school student who elopes with Lieutenant Montraville to New York, where he reneges on his promise of marriage. With no help from her so-called friends, including the French teacher Miss LaRue, Charlotte falls ill, gives birth to a healthy baby, and dies. Her father, who has traveled across the Atlantic, takes home Lucy, Charlotte's baby. The advice-filled novel has gone through more than 150 editions. Rowson's next novel, *The Fille de Chambre, A Novel* (1792), based partly on Rowson's own experiences, depicts Rebecca's stormy Atlantic crossing to America during the Revolutionary War.

Other novels include *Trials of the Human Heart, A Novel* (1795); *Reuben and Rachel; or, Tales of Old Times. A Novel* (1798); *Sarah, or The Exemplary Wife* (1813), a heavily autobiographical novel that reflects Rowson's own unhappy marriage; and *Charlotte's Daughter: or, The Three Orphans. A Sequel to Charlotte Temple* (1828), in which Charlotte's daughter Lucy, warned just in time of the perfidy of men, remains single and opens a school for girls.

Susanna Rowson died on March 2, 1824, in Boston. The largest collection of Rowson material is housed at the American Antiquarian Society. A copy of the first edition of *Charlotte: A Tale of Truth* is in the Barrett Collection at the University of Virginia.

NOVELS

Charlotte: A Tale of Truth. 2 volumes. London: Printed for William Lane at the Minerva, 1791; Philadelphia: Printed by D. Humphreys for Mathew Carey, 1794.

Charlotte's Daughter: or, The Three Orphans. A Sequel to Charlotte Temple. Boston: Printed by J. H. A. Frost & published by Richardson & Lord, 1828.

The Fille de Chambre, A Novel. 3 volumes. London: Printed for William Lane at the Minerva, 1792; Philadelphia: Printed for H. & P. Rice and J. Rice & Co., 1794.

Reuben and Rachel; or, Tales of Old Times. A Novel. Boston: Printed by Manning & Loring for David West, 1798; London: William Lane, Minerva, 1799.

Sarah, or The Exemplary Wife. Boston: Printed by Watson & Bangs & published by Charles Williams, 1813.

The Test of Honour. A Novel by a Young Lady. 2 volumes. London: Printed by & for John Abraham, 1789.

Trials of the Human Heart, A Novel. 4 volumes. Philadelphia: Printed for the author by Wrigley & Berriman, 1795.

Victoria. A Novel. In Two Volumes. The Characters Taken from Real Life, and Calculated to Improve the Morals of the Female Sex, by Impressing Them with a Just Sense of The Merits of Filial Piety. London: Printed by J. P. Cooke for the author & sold by J. Bew & T. Hookham, 1786.

SOURCES

Brandt, Ellen B. *Susanna Haswell Rowson, America's First Best-Selling Novelist.* Chicago: Serbra Press, 1975.

Cobbett, William. *A Kick for a Bite; or, Review upon Review; with a Critical Essay, on the Works of Mrs. S. Rowson, in a Letter to the Editor, or Editors, of the American Monthly Review. 2nd edition. By Peter Porcupine.* Philadelphia: Printed by Thomas Bradford, 1796.

Davidson, Cathy N. "The Life and Times of Charlotte Temple: The Biography of a Book." In *Reading in America: Literature and Social History,* edited by Davidson, 157–179. Baltimore, Md.: Johns Hopkins University Press, 1989.

Fiedler, Leslie A. *Love and Death in the American Novel.* Revised edition. New York: Stein & Day, 1966, pp. 93–98.

Forcey, Blythe. "Charlotte Temple and the End of Epistolarity," *American Literature* 63 (1991): 225–241.

Greenfield, Susan. "Charlotte Temple and Charlotte's Daughter: The Reproduction of Woman's Word," *Women's Studies* 18 (1990): 269–286.

Martin, Wendy. "Profile: Susanna Rowson, Early American Novelist," *Women's Studies* 2 (1974): 1–8.

Parker, Patricia L. *Susanna Rowson.* Boston: G. K. Hall, 1986.

Rourke, Constance. *The Roots of American Culture and Other Essays.* New York: Harcourt, Brace, 1942, pp. 75–87.

Stern, Julia. "Working Through the Frame: Charlotte Temple and the Poetics of Maternal Melancholia," *Arizona Quarterly* 49 (Winter 1993): 1–21.

Vail, R. W. G. "Susanna Haswell Rowson, The Author of *Charlotte Temple:* A Bibliographical Study," *Proceedings of the American Antiquarian Society* 42 (April 1932): 47–160.

Weil, Dorothy. *In Defense of Women: Susanna Rowson (1762–1824).* University Park, Pa., & London: Pennsylvania State University Press, 1976.

OTHER

San Antonio College LitWeb The Susannah Rowson Page. Available online. URL: http://www.accd.edu/sac/english/bailey/rowson.htm. Accessed September 26, 2005.

University Library of Virginia. Early American Fiction. EAF Author: Susannah Haswell Rowson. Available online. URL: http://etext.lib.virginia.edu/eaf/authors/shr.htm. Accessed September 26, 2005.

RUBYFRUIT JUNGLE RITA MAE BROWN (1976)

One of Rita Mae BROWN's first attempts to have *Rubyfruit Jungle* published resulted, as she recalls in her memoirs, with a shocked editor throwing the manuscript at her: "You would have thought I'd tossed a canister of mustard gas into her office. She called me a pervert, telling me to get out of her office." After several more tries, a small feminist press finally took Brown's novel. The cause for such controversy was, undoubtedly, its open portrayal of lesbianism, and its protagonist's sincere and direct approach toward her own sexuality and her place in society.

Molly's determination to define who she is and what she will become is at the heart of *Rubyfruit Jungle.* Although for a long time she remains ignorant of the circumstances of her birth, Molly was an "illegitimate" child adopted by Carrie and Carl Bolt, Molly feels early on that she is different from her poor but loving family. As her childhood years go by, this distance becomes increasingly obvious to all. And while Carl encourages the rebellious girl who taught herself to read while still almost an infant, Carrie feels threatened by Molly's intelligent, inquisitive nature. Bound by her—and her community's—idea of a woman's role in life, Carrie sees Molly as a disrupting force: brash, unladylike, and too direct for her own good.

While young Molly's attitudes cause frequent clashes with both her mother and the conservative rural community where they live, even more detrimental to her at this time—although it will later prove a powerful weapon—is her stubborn refusal to feel ashamed of herself. After an early incident where Molly and her cousin Leroy collect money from their curious classmates for a view of Leroy's uncircumcised penis, Carrie launches a tirade against Molly that reveals the truth about Molly's real mother. Molly, however, seems unaffected by being called a bastard: "It makes no difference where I came from. I'm here, ain't I?" (7). Molly's unwillingness to classify people in terms of race, class, or gender seems impossible in a society that retains segregation between whites and "coloreds" and expects men and women to conform to specific roles. But then, this is the real proof of Molly's status as outsider.

Although *Rubyfruit Jungle* appears to be a novel about a girl/woman's sexual awakening as a lesbian, it is actually more about the often rude awakening of all who cross Molly's path. Molly realizes her love of women early on, and simply accepts it: She is never unsure or ashamed of her orientation. It is up to everyone else to adjust. In earlier lesbian literature, such as Radclyffe Hall's classic *The Well of Loneliness,* gay women were doomed to failed romances and an often suicidal fatalism surrounding their "condition": an acceptable fate for women seen as confused and mentally deranged. Brown, on the other hand, seems to create Molly as a wake-up call to the gay community, as a vehicle for a change in attitude, both in literature and in real life. Molly's sexuality, in the end, matters more to us than it does to her. From her sixth-grade romance with her friend Leota through her high school conquest of a popular cheerleader, Molly's tastes are free and diverse, and her goal is to enjoy her experiences: After all, "why would people get so upset about something that feels so good?" (70).

In a broader sense, *Rubyfruit Jungle* is about survival: Molly's being a lesbian seems the least of her worries once she leaves her small Florida high school and heads for university, determined to become a film director. Expelled from the University of Florida for becoming intimately involved with her female roommate, and consequently repudiated by Carrie and Aunt Florence, Molly hitchhikes to New York City with less than $20 to her name. There she must overcome two more pressing obstacles to her career than her homosexuality: her poverty and her gender. Here, too, Molly's tough willpower eventually sees her through; in the end, however, we are left wondering whether she has achieved total victory or simply won a series of small battles.

Molly's life in New York begins in absolute poverty: Her home during the first nights is an abandoned car. Soon she has a job as a waitress, where she meets a young woman "kept" by an aging actress. Holly introduces her to the upscale lesbian crowd, and Molly finds herself fighting off a renowned archaeologist's advances. Even in her precarious situation, though, Molly refuses to trade her integrity for financial security and academic support.

Once she has secured a scholarship at New York University, she discovers that life as a woman director is going to be very difficult. Her (male) professors scorn her, her classmates will not sign up to work on projects with her, and the film equipment always seems to have been checked out when she needs it. At the same time, Molly is working full-time at a publishing company, where her speed and talent only earn her suspicion and jealousy from the head receptionist, who can think only that something suspicious must have occurred between Molly and her supervisor, or the young college student would never have been promoted so quickly.

Thus, both her financial situation and her femaleness seem to force Molly into a corner for some time. She works and studies without rest but also without recognition. By the time she is ready to show her final project at film school, she has earned top grades but sees little hope for her career. Here, as always, her resiliency comes through, and a crewless Molly steals the film equipment and returns to Carrie, hoping to turn her final project into a memorable one. While her male classmates are busy shooting the hip "pornoviolence" in fashion at the time, Molly does the only thing she can: tell the truth.

Molly knows that no matter how good she is, those around her will try to bring her down because she is a woman, and because she is poor. In a sense, Carrie had feared this outcome as she saw her adopted daughter grow into an ambitious, independent woman. Maybe she was not so worried about being pushed aside once Molly became rich, famous, and contemptuous of her childhood poverty; perhaps she simply sensed the difficulties Molly would have to endure to reach that level in the first place. After all, it was relatively easy for Carl to show his support for Molly, since even in his financial situation he had enjoyed certain privileges as a man. During the week spent filming her ailing mother for her senior film project, Molly had come to know Carrie and the reasons behind her often fierce criticism of Molly. In what she assumes is the end of her life, Carrie reveals much about herself, her husband, and Molly's biological parents. From these stories, Molly understands that her artistic vein, her desire to travel, and even her openness toward sexuality must have come from Ruby and her French lover. She must also acknowledge, however, that her own strong will and desire for an honest life are Carrie's.

Molly's senior film project represents her reaction against her pretentious classmates, snobbish professors, and the hypocrisy she perceives in the film industry. In a 20-minute monologue, a terminally ill Carrie speaks her mind, "speeding away in her rocking chair; No quick cuts to steals from Kenneth Anger, no tinfoil balls dropping out of the sky to represent nuclear hail—just Carrie talking about her life, the world today, and the price of meat" (244). At the end, her classmates and instructor leave silently, embarrassed for themselves or for Molly, because no matter how brilliant her short slice of life might have been, it is the classmate who had drawn applause for a Martian rape film who gets the job in a children's program at CBS. Molly's hopes are momentarily grounded, eliciting her sole observation about what a greater triumph would have meant to her: "I kept hoping against hope I'd be the bright exception, the talented token that smashed sex and class barriers—I was the best in my class, didn't that count for anything?" (245).

While *Rubyfruit Jungle* could have ended with Molly's successful start as a film director, the author chooses to leave the young woman meditating about not only her future but that of her whole generation. It is a time when young people are "raging down the streets in protest" (246), expressing anger about various racial and gender issues, and yet keeping Molly's fellow gays and lesbians out of their movements. Resigning herself to remaining an outsider for the time being, Molly nevertheless promises to fight, however long it takes, until she can make her films and become "the hottest 50-year-old this side of the Mississippi" (246).

SOURCES

Abelove, Henry, Michele Aina Barale, and David M. Halperin, eds. *The Lesbian and Gay Studies Reader.* Boston: Routledge, 1993.

Brown, Rita Mae. *Rita Will: Memoir of a Literary Rabble-Rouser.* New York: Bantam, 1997.

———. *Rubyfruit Jungle.* London: Penguin, 1994.

Lilly, Mark, ed. *Lesbian and Gay Writing: an Anthology of Critical Essays.* Houndmills, Basingstoke, Hampshire: Macmillan, 1990.

Rule, Jane. *Lesbian Images.* London: Pluto Press, 1989.

Zimmerman, Bonnie. *The Safe Sea of Women: Lesbian Fiction, 1969–1989.* Boston: Beacon Press, 1990.

Maria Luisa Antonaya

RUSS, JOANNA (1937–)

Joanna Russ, literary critic and essayist, is a contemporary, award-winning writer of science fiction. Along with Ursula LeGuin, Samuel R. Delany, Marion Zimmer Bradley, and others, Russ brought a new sort of sexual awareness to this genre in the 1960s. Except for *On Strike Against God,* a "coming out" novel, she does not write specifically about lesbian issues, yet all her novels and stories are political and feminist, as well as literary in intent and tone. Her best-known novel, *The Female Man* (1975), has elicited both admiration and anger from critics: Some praise its irony and humor; others criticize its bitter depictions of female violence against men. As Robert Scholes and Eric Rabkin point out, however, with this novel and others, Joanna Russ has helped move the content of science fiction from "space opera and bug-eyed monsters to increasingly sophisticated psychological themes" (Scholes and Rabkin, ix).

Joanna Russ was born on February 22, 1937, in the Bronx in New York, to Evarett I. Russ and Bertha Zinner Russ, both teachers. She earned her bachelor's degree from Cornell University in 1957, and her master of fine arts degree from Yale University in 1960. Although she married in 1963, she knew from childhood that she was lesbian, and she obtained a divorce in 1967. For more than 20 years she taught at various colleges and universities while publishing stories and novels that concentrated on the disjunctions of contemporary society. Her first novel, *Picnic on Paradise* (1968), was nominated for a Nebula Award; it features Alyx, the hero who appears in several Russ stories that precede the novel. Here she is responsible for leading a group of future-tourists across the ice that covers a planet called Paradise, and must cope with crises among the tourists as well as the rivalry between two men: the macho Gunther and the coldly analytical Machine, both of whom are attracted to her. *And Chaos Died* (1970) introduces Jai Vedh, a homosexual—and therefore doubly different—whose ship crashes on a planet whose inhabitants are psychic. He returns to Earth briefly but is more fully accepted in the space colony, where he eventually lives as a god.

In *The Female Man,* Russ's most complex work, four women—Janet, Jeannine, Joanna, and Jael—are genetically identical. They live in four different eras: a future egalitarian world called Whileaway, contemporary (1960s) society, during the Great Depression era but without the occurrence of World War II, and in a world where men and women live separately and exist in a perpetual state of war. *We Who Are About To . . .* (1977) involves another shipwreck, this time on an undiscovered, uninhabited planet where the protagonist, who wishes to die with dignity, is opposed by six people who wish to fashion a new colony. Rather than be enslaved and raped, she murders the others one by one. In *The Two of Them* (1978), Irene Waskiewicz and her mentor and lover Ernst Neuman are sent on a work assignment to a planet whose patriarchal culture replicates that of Levittown; once acclimated, Irene realizes that the subservient, objectified, bored women are actually echoes of herself. As she rescues the young girl

Zubedah, Irene realizes that their escape depends on her murdering Ernst, and she kills him. Clearly, in Russ's work, the murder of patriarchal representatives is a rite of passage to independence for women. *Kittatinny: A Tale of Magic* (1978) centers on a young girl who, secure in her own sense of power and self, can kill dragons and rescue princesses. *On Strike Against God* (1980) is the coming out story of Esther, an English professor who falls in love with Jean, her student.

Russ was awarded a Hugo Award and a Nebula Award in 1983, both for the novella *Souls.* Recently, Russ has written and edited essay collections on feminism and science fiction: *To Write Like a Woman: Essays in Feminism and Science Fiction* (1995) and *What Are We Fighting for?: Sex, Race, Class, and the Future of Feminism* (1997).

NOVELS

And Chaos Died. New York: Ace, 1970.

The Female Man. Toronto, New York and London: Bantam, 1975.

Kittatinny: A Tale of Magic. New York: Daughters Publishing, 1978.

On Strike Against God: A Lesbian Love Story. Brooklyn, N.Y.: Out & Out Books, 1980.

Picnic on Paradise. New York: Ace, 1968.

The Two of Them. New York: Berkley, 1978.

We Who Are About To . . . New York: Dell, 1977.

SOURCES

Delany, Samuel R. "Orders of Chaos: The Science Fiction Writer Joanna Russ." In *Women Worldwalkers: New Dimensions of Science Fiction and Fantasy,* edited by Jane B. Weedman, 95–123. Lubbock: Texas Tech Press, 1985.

Garber, Eric, and Lyn Paleo. *Uranian Worlds: A Reader's Guide to Alternative Sexuality in Science Fiction and Fantasy.* Boston: G. K. Hall, 1983, pp. 115–119.

Huckle, Patricia. "Women in Utopias." In *The Utopian Vision: Seven Essays on the Quincentennial of Sir Thomas More,* edited by E. D. S. Sullivan, 115–136. San Diego, Calif.: San Diego State University Press, 1983.

Johnson, Charles. "A Dialogue: Samuel Delany and Joanna Russ on Science Fiction," *Callaloo* 7 (Fall 1984): 27–35.

Scholes, Robert, and Eric S. Rabkin. *Science Fiction: History, Science, Vision.* New York: Oxford University Press, 1977.

Spencer, Kathleen L. "Rescuing the Female Child: The Fiction of Joanna Russ," *Science Fiction Studies* 17 (1990): 167–187.

Walker, Nancy A. *A Very Serious Thing: Women's Humor and American Culture.* Minneapolis: University of Minnesota Press, 1988.

———. *Feminist Alternatives.* Jackson: University Press of Mississippi, 1990.

Walker, Paul. *Speaking of Science Fiction: The Paul Walker Interviews.* Oradell, N.J.: Luna Press, 1978.

OTHER

Alpha Ralpha Boulevard. Joanna Russ. Available online. URL: http://www.catch22.com/~espana/SFAuthors/SFR/Russ,Joanna.php3. Accessed September 25, 2005.

RYDER DJUNA BARNES (1928) Djuna BARNES's first novel, *Ryder,* is unconventional in all the traditional aspects of fiction: plot, character, setting, narration. In fact, in her essay "A Reader's *Ryder,*" Marie Ponsot observes that *Ryder* "is not a book that yields much to those who begin with a linear examination" (94); consequently, it is not an easy read for a person who sits down and anticipates the soothing and predictable structure of a bildungsroman. Contemporary readers are best advised to drop their expectations and simply enjoy the tour de force that Djuna Barnes has created.

Evidently, readers needed no such instruction in 1928, when *Ryder* was first published; indeed, the novel enjoyed a "brief best-seller status" (Broe, 6). This status may have been produced, albeit unwittingly, by those intending to repress *Ryder,* for, as Paul West notes, the novel was "censored by the New York Post Office" (West, 243) and then expurgated before it was published by Horace Liveright. The fact that Liveright published *Ryder* is significant in that it puts Barnes in interesting literary company. In 1922, Boni and Liveright published T. S. Eliot's *The Waste-Land,* and in 1925, Boni and Liveright published Ernest HEMINGWAY's *In Our Time.* Barnes and Hemingway knew each other in Paris in the 1920s, and many critics and readers have noted the link in last names between Jake Barnes, the narrator of *The Sun Also Rises,* and Djuna Barnes. Moreover, Barnes and T. S. Eliot had a long professional relationship: He edited and wrote an introduction to Barnes's best-known novel, NIGHTWOOD, and he also edited (or meddled with, depending on one's perspective) her play *The Antiphon.* Barnes was also well acquainted with James Joyce, and Marie Pon-

sot notes an intertextual relationship between Stephen Daedalus in Joyce's *A Portrait of the Artist as a Young Man* and Julie in Barnes's *Ryder* (Broe, 112). Another intertextual note worth considering is that a character in F. Scott FITZGERALD's first novel, *This Side of Paradise* (1919), is named Dawson Ryder.

Summarizing Djuna Barnes's *Ryder* seems antithetical to the author's project. In brief, *Ryder* documents the life of the Ryder family. The novel begins with a biblical overture and then two chapters on Sophia Grieve Ryder. Wendell Ryder, whom many have taken to be the novel's central character and the Ryder to whom the title refers, does first appear in chapter 4, "Wendell Is Born." Moreover, the narrator notes parenthetically that Sophia Grieve Ryder named her son Wendell Ryder and "gave him no father's name" (17); hence, the Ryder family is matriarchal. The novel then devotes chapters to Ryder family members Amelia, Sophia, Kate-Careless, Timothy, Elisha, and Julie, as well as The Beast Thingumbob and Matthew O'Connor, the doctor who also appears in Barnes's novel *Nightwood.* The novel is a family portrait, crossing generations and continents. The Ryder family is unusual in its configuration: Wendell grows up and establishes a household with his wife, Amelia, and their children and also his consort or second wife, Kate-Careless, and their children. *Ryder* ends with Wendell out of doors, convening with farm animals who seem to share his worldview and kinship practices, wondering, "whom should he disappoint?"

Perhaps because of its reputed difficulty or the fact that *Ryder* has been in and out of print, Barnes's novel *Nightwood* has garnered more critical attention than *Ryder* has. Nevertheless, a body of critical work on *Ryder* continues to grow. Mary Lynn Broe's important collection *Silence and Power: A Reevaluation of Djuna Barnes* (Broe, 1991) brings together essays on Barnes's life and works by some of the most influential feminist scholars of 20th-century literature as well as top Barnes scholars, among them Broe herself, Louise de Salvo, Karla Jay, and Jane Marcus.

Recent publications on *Ryder* include two essays that further investigate the novel's inscriptions of sexual abuse: Anne B. Dalton's essay "Escaping from Eden: Djuna Barnes's Revision of Psychoanalytic Theory and

Her Treatment of Father-Daughter Incest in Ryder" and Susan Edmunds's "Narratives of a Virgin's Violation: The Critique of Middle-Class Reformism in Djuna Barnes's *Ryder*." Sheryl Stevenson, a contributor to Broe's eminent anthology, continues her work on Barnes and *Ryder* in her essay "*Ryder* as Contraception: Barnes v. the Reproduction of Mothering." Stevenson's essay historicizes and contextualizes Ryder and relates it "to the writing of Barnes's contemporaries" (Stevenson, 102). In doing so, Stevenson opens up the text to new readings and new relevance for 21st-century readers for whom contraception, reproduction, pregnancy, and motherhood remain important issues. Stevenson suggests that "study of the novel's historical content can lend further support to a female-centered reading, focusing on *Ryder* as a text about mothering that reflects a crucial, transitional period in women's struggle for physical and social self-determination" (Stevenson, 97). She reads *Ryder* as "Djuna Barnes's strongest statement against women's enslavement to reproduction" (Stevenson, 104)—an approach that redirects the reader's focus from Wendell Ryder's insane promiscuity as the novel's central focus and aims it in other directions. Edmunds's essay takes a similar critical/theoretical avenue while maintaining the autobiographical or personal approach to *Ryder*. She claims that "the author's explicit goal in writing *Ryder* was to question the whole project of middle-class reformism even as the novel's autobiographical basis was also a significant factor in its reading."

Finally, in her essay "Doing Djuna Justice: The Challenges of the Barnes Biography," Margot Norris makes this observation: "Djuna Barnes's life yields marvelous materials for the biographer to work with: outlandish figures, bizarre relationships, scalding feelings, uncommon situations" (Norris, 581). One might use the same sets of modifiers and nouns to describe *Ryder*.

SOURCES

Barnes, Djuna. *Nightwood: The Original Version and Related Drafts*. Edited by Cheryl Plumb. Normal, Ill.: Dalkey Archive Press, 1995.

———. *Ryder*. 1928. Reprint, Normal, Ill.: Dalkey Archive Press, 1995.

Broe, Mary Lynn. "Introduction." *Silence and Power: A Reevaluation of Djuna Barnes*. Edited by Mary Lynn Broe 3–23. Carbondale: Southern Illinois University Press, 1991.

Dalton, Anne. B. "Escaping from Eden: Djuna Barnes's Revision of Psychoanalytic Theory and her Treatment of Father-Daughter Incest in *Ryder*," *Women's Studies* 22, no. 2 (March 1993).

Edmunds, Susan. "Narratives of a Virgin's Violation: The Critique of Middle-class Reformism in Djuna Barnes's *Ryder*," *Novel* 30, no. 2 (Winter 1997).

Norris, Margot. "Doing Djuna Justice: The Challenges of the Barnes Biography," *Studies in the Novel* 28, no. 4 (Winter 1996). *EBSCO*. Inver Hills Community College Library. Inver Grove Heights. Available online. URL: http://www.pals.msus.edu. Accessed September 25, 2005.

Ponsot, Marie. "A Reader's Ryder." In *Silence and Power: A Reevaluation of Djuna Barnes,* edited by Mary Lynn Broe, 94–112. Carbondale: Southern Illinois University Press, 1991.

Stevenson, Sheryl. "*Ryder* as Contraception: Barnes v. The Reproduction of Mothering," *The Review of Contemporary Fiction* 13, no. 3 (Fall 1993): 97–106.

West, Paul. "Afterword: 'The Havoc of this Nicety.' " In *Ryder* by Djuna Barnes. Normal, Ill.: Dalkey Archives Press, 1995, pp. 243–250.

Ellen Lansky

S

SABBATH'S THEATER PHILIP ROTH (1995)

Looking back over Philip ROTH's prodigious output—27 books over a 45-year career—one can see noticeable shifts in narrative trajectory, or put another way, turning points in his novelistic focus. There is the comedic, and at times manic, flair of PORTNOY'S COMPLAINT, which marked a radical departure from the more subdued realism found in earlier works such as "Goodbye, Columbus" and *Letting Go*. In *The GHOST WRITER*, Roth begins his exploration of the artist figure and the ways in which art can determine destiny. And with *The Counterlife,* his postmodern tour de force, Philip Roth inaugurates a series of works that highlights the constructedness of identity as well as the inextricable links between the written and nonwritten worlds. *Sabbath's Theater,* winner of the National Book Award and considered by critics such as Mark Shechner and Mark Krupnick to be Roth's masterpiece, is likewise a significant turning point in that the narrative—at times frantic, but never out of control—displays a revitalization of novelistic energy, and one that helped pave the way for the much-praised American Trilogy (*AMERICAN PASTORAL, I Married a Communist,* and *The Human Stain,*) that followed.

Philip Roth told the *New Yorker*'s David Remnick in a 2000 interview that the happiest time he had ever had with his work occurred during the writing of *Sabbath's Theater.* When asked why he felt that way, Roth responded, "Because I felt free. I feel like I am in charge now" (Remnick, 88). In light of the American Trilogy's reevaluation of late-20th-century American history, this response resonates. Several times throughout the novel, its protagonist, the puppeteer pornographer Mickey Sabbath, is directly associated with America in both its ideal as well as repellent qualities. His Croatian-born lover, Drenka Balich, longs to go "dancing with America," and having stated this says to him subsequently, "You are America. Yes, you are, my wicked boy" (419). In a 2003 interview that aired on BBC4, Roth elaborated further on how his 1995 novel served as a "springboard" to the novels that would follow. With *Sabbath* he wanted to "create someone who is deep in the disorder [. . .] someone who is not fearful of the repellent, who says I am repellent, I am disorder. Someone who wants to be dead, but he can't die. He has the opportunity finally to kill himself, and he can't leave, everything he hated was here" ("Roth at 70"). Given Roth's own comments, it is easy to see how Roth's exploration of postwar social breakdown, the thematic bedrock of the American Trilogy, has its roots in *Sabbath's Theater.*

In ways that evoke the wild tones of earlier works such as *Portnoy's Complaint, The Great American Novel,* and the outrageous short story "On the Air," *Sabbath's Theater* is perhaps best defined as a narrative of excess, one in which the author apparently revels in his protagonist's offensiveness and cynicism. Morris "Mickey" Sabbath, a 64-year-old ex-puppeteer whose arthritis will no longer allow him to perform, has apparently reached an impasse in his life, one that turns into an existential crisis as the book begins. He had once taught drama at a local college in Madamaska Falls, but was forced to resign over a scandal involving phone sex with one of his students. His wife, whom he can no longer tolerate, is a recovering alcoholic filled with politically correct observations and 12-step aphorisms. And, most significant to the plot of the novel, he has just lost his Croatian-born mistress, Drenka Balich, to ovarian cancer. She, like Mickey, is highly sexed and a notorious seducer, yet the two of them share a relationship, albeit one filled with unconventional sexual exploits, that approximates the solidity of marriage. Not long after Drenka's death, Mickey gets word that Lincoln Gelman, an old partner from the days of his Indecent Theater—risqué street performances where Mickey used his fingers as puppets to seduce unsuspecting college women—has just committed suicide. The two deaths plunge Sabbath into a deep malaise, and he plans a final trip to New York, where he will attend the funeral of Gelman and then commit suicide. It is this journey that structures most of the novel and makes of it an aborted quest narrative.

His journey is a circular one, taking him first to the New York home of his and Gelman's mutual friend, Norman Cowan, whose wife and illiterate Mexican housemaid he attempts to seduce; then to the graveyard where his parents and older brother are buried, and where he buys a small plot for himself; then on to the Jersey Shore where he used to live as a boy and where, he is surprised to learn, his 100-year-old second cousin Fish is still living; and then finally back to Madamaska Falls, where he "reaches out" to the dead Drenka by urinating on her grave, an act reminiscent of the kinky sexual games they used to play together. Throughout his brief travels, Sabbath seems almost always on the verge of a mental breakdown. And although he never completely disintegrates, is never committed, and never completely loses his senses, throughout the novel he nonetheless remains on the edge of an emotional precipice.

What keeps him on that edge is an obsession with death. The many references to Drenka's cancer, graveyards, expired relationships, dead colleagues, his aviator brother shot down during World War II, and the "ghost" of his mother that follows him wherever he

goes all underscore the overriding presence of death as a signifying force in Mickey Sabbath's life. In fact, the thanatotic (life-denying) impulse, especially as it is related to and counterbalanced by the erotic (life-sustaining), is perhaps the thematic driving force behind *Sabbath's Theater*. Having lost his art, his marriage, his mistress, his youth, and his ability to seduce, Mickey longs to end his life, yet he cannot bring himself ultimately to deny the very thing that defines him best: carnal pleasure. He is an irresolute presence with an ambiguous future, a representative of late-20th-century America—a nation that has had its own share of identity crises, and a country that Mickey, in many ways, has come to embody.

If Sabbath is representative of America, he stands as a highly precarious figure, one prone to the many uncertainties and ambiguities that underlie the national character. In a 2000 interview with Charles McGrath, Philip Roth acknowledges this connection between Mickey Sabbath and the ongoing American project. Reflecting on his attempts to "rediscover" his home country after living abroad for much of the 1970s and 1980s, the author states, "When I look back now, I see that *Sabbath's Theater* is the real turning back to American stuff. Mickey Sabbath's is such an American voice. And after him, if not out of him, came the American trilogy" (McGrath, 8). By the author's own admission, then, *Sabbath's* miasmic disorder heralded the ever-elusive American ideal defining much of Roth's fiction that follows.

SOURCES

Cooper, Alan. "Master Baiter: *Sabbath's Theater.*" In *Philip Roth and the Jews*, 281–290. Albany, N.Y.: State University of New York Press, 1996.

Mellard, James M. "Death, Mourning, and Besse's Ghost: From Philip Roth's *The Facts* to *Sabbath's Theater,*" *Shofar* 19 (2000): 66–73.

Omer-Sherman, Ranen. " 'A Stranger in the House': Assimilation, Madness, and Passing in Roth's Figure of the Pariah Jew in *Sabbath's Theater* (1995), *American Pastoral* (1997), and *The Human Stain* (2000)." In *Diaspora Zionism in Jewish American Literature: Lazarus, Syrkin, Reznikoff, and Roth*, 234–266. Hanover, N.H.: Brandeis University Press, 2002.

Remnick, David. "Into the Clear: Philip Roth Puts Turbulence in Its Place," *New Yorker,* 8 May 2000, pp. 84–89.

Roth, Philip. "Zuckerman's Alter Brain." Interview with Charles McGrath. *New York Times Book Review,* 7 May 2000, p. 8.

———. "Philip Roth at 70." Interview with David Remnick. BBC4, London. March 19, 2003.

———. *Sabbath's Theater.* Boston: Houghton Mifflin, 1995.

Royal, Derek Parker, ed. *Philip Roth's America: The Later Novels.* Spec. issue of *Studies in American Jewish Literature* 23 (2004): 1–181.

Safer, Elaine B. "The Tragicomic in Philip Roth's *Sabbath's Theater.*" In *American Literary Dimensions: Poems and Essays in Honor of Melvin J. Friedman,* edited by Ben Siegel and Jay L. Halio, 168–179. Newark: University of Delaware Press, 1999.

Shechner, Mark. *Up Society's Ass, Copper: Rereading Philip Roth.* Madison: University of Wisconsin Press, 2003.

Shostak, Debra. "Roth/Counter Roth: Postmodernism, the Masculine Subject, and *Sabbath's Theater,*" *Arizona Quarterly* 54 (1998): 119–142.

Zucker, David J. "Philip Roth: Desire and Death," *Studies in American Jewish Fiction* 23 (2004): 135–144.

Derek P. Royal

SALINGER, J(EROME) D(AVID) (1919–)

Along with some frequently anthologized short stories, J. D. Salinger's fame rests on one novel, *The CATCHER IN THE RYE,* a tale of adolescent initiation. The novel is a classic in the American canon, conveying the adolescent angst of young Holden Caulfield and his youthful idealism and rebellion against adult hypocrisy and phoniness. Indeed, it has become a commonplace to list Holden Caulfield alongside Mark TWAIN's Huckleberry Finn and F. Scott FITZGERALD's Jay Gatsby as exemplars of disaffected boys and men in various eras in American history. Salinger, a master of colloquial language, tells a complex and patterned story that still intrigues readers and critics alike. No one better depicts the themes of childhood innocence corrupted by the insensitive world of adults, the need for love as a ballast against an alien and absurd society, and the search for spiritual solace in a materialistic modern world. Salinger's stories in the *New Yorker* about the now iconic Seymour, Franny, Zooey, and other members of the Glass family captured the attention of the American reading public and were collected in *Nine Stories* (1953), *Franny and Zooey* (1961), and *Raise High the Roof Beams, Carpenters; and Seymour: An Introduction* (1963). In 1997, *Hapworth 16, 1924,* the final installment of the Glass family saga initially published in the *New Yorker* (June 1965), was published as a novel. It is Salinger's only other known novel to date.

J. D. Salinger was born on January 1, 1919, in New York City, to Sol Salinger, an importer, and Miriam Jillich Salinger, of Scotch-Irish ancestry. He was reared in Manhattan and served in the U.S. Army during World War II. He become a staff sergeant and received five battle stars. He attended New York University, Ursinus College, and Columbia University without taking a degree; was married briefly to Sylvia (surname unknown), a French physician, from September 1945 to July 1946; and published *The Catcher in the Rye* in 1951. The novel opens as Holden, an upper-middle-class teenager enrolled at Pencey Prep, sits on a hilltop overlooking a school football game. He revolts against the world of his teacher Mr. Antolini, who makes homosexual advances, and his classmate Stradlater, who brags about his seduction of Holden's friend Jane Gallagher, and from other adult hypocrisies from which Holden hopes to save both himself and his friends. His preoccupation with saving the ducks in New York's Central Park by skillful use of his catcher's mitt reflects his wish to protect others, particularly his precocious younger sister Phoebe. This need to protect is exacerbated by the death of his younger brother Allie, over whose fate Holden had no control. Critics continue to analyze and reevaluate his work, and the revival of interest in Salinger during the past two decades demonstrates the continuing importance of his contributions to American fiction.

J. D. Salinger, who was married to Claire Douglas from February 1955 to October 1967, lives in a reclusive fashion in Cornish, New Hampshire. He has pointedly avoided all contact with the public since the appearance of *The Catcher in the Rye.* After a 1992 fire at his home, the *New York Times* revealed that Salinger had a third wife, Colleen O'Neill, but no further information seems forthcoming.

NOVELS AND NOVELLAS
The Catcher in the Rye. Boston: Little, Brown, 1951.
Hapworth 16, 1924. Washington, D.C.: Orchises Press, 1997.

SOURCES

Alsen, Eberhard. *Salinger's Glass Stories as a Composite Novel.* Troy, N.Y.: Whitson, 1983.

Bloom Harold. *The Catcher in the Rye.* New York: Chelsea House, 1995.

———, ed. *J. D. Salinger: Modern Critical Views.* New York: Chelsea House, 1987.

Engel, Steven. *Readings on The Catcher in the Rye.* San Diego, Calif.: Greenhaven Press, 1998.

French, Warren. *J. D. Salinger.* Boston: Twayne, 1963. Reprinted, Boston: G. K. Hall, 1976.

———. *J. D. Salinger, Revisited.* Boston: Twayne, 1988.

Hamilton, Ian. *In Search of J. D. Salinger.* New York: Random House, 1988.

Holzman, Robert S., and Gary L. Perkins. *J. D. Salinger's "The Catcher in the Rye."* Piscataway, N.J.: Research & Education Association, 1995.

Kotzen, Kip, ed. *With Love and Squalor: Fourteen Writers Respond to the Work of J. D. Salinger.* New York: Broadway Books, 2001.

Lundquist, James. *J. D. Salinger.* New York: Ungar, 1979.

Madinaveitia, Catherine. *Brodie's Notes on J. D. Salinger's "The Catcher in the Rye."* London: Pan, 1987.

Maynard, Joyce. *At Home in the World: A Memoir.* New York: Picador USA, 1998.

Pinsker, Sanford. *The Catcher in the Rye: Innocence under Pressure.* New York: Twayne, 1993.

Rosen, Gerald. *Zen in the Art of J. D. Salinger.* Berkeley, Calif.: Creative Arts, 1977.

Salinger, Margaret A. *Dream Catcher: A Memoir.* New York: Washington Square Press, 2000.

Salzberg, Joel, ed. *Critical Essays on Salinger's "The Catcher in the Rye."* Boston: G. K. Hall, 1990.

Salzman, Jack, ed. *New Essays on "The Catcher in the Rye."* New York: Cambridge University Press, 1992.

Simonson, Harold P., and E. P. Hager, eds. *"Catcher in the Rye": Clamor vs. Criticism.* Boston: Heath, 1963.

Wenke, John. *J. D. Salinger: A Study of the Short Fiction.* Boston: Twayne, 1991.

OTHER

Bohemian Ink. Available online. URL: http://www.levity.com/corduroy/salinger.htm. Accessed September 25, 2005.

SALOME OF THE TENEMENTS ANZIA YEZIERSKA (1923)

Sonya Vrunsky, in *Salome of the Tenements,* sees millionaire philanthropist John Manning as literally her savior: "But only let me work for you and you will save my soul" (2) she tells him. She means that his model tenement house and its support organizations will allow her to help her fellow Jewish immigrants to overcome their poverty. Sonya has her own ideas for helping the people in her community, but she believes that Manning's money and his method of teaching immigrants "skills" (including hygiene and elocution) will help them to advance themselves. But Sonya is attracted to the man himself, or so she thinks:

> Head swung back, Sonya looked up in admiration at Manning, her heart pierced by the cultural elegance of his attire. Not a detail of his well-dressed figure escaped her. His finished grooming stood out all the more vividly in this background of horrid poverty. A master tailor had cut his loose Scotch tweeds. His pale brown pongee shirt was lighter and finer than a woman's waist. The rich hidden quietness of his silk tie, even his shoes had a handmade quality to them, she thought. (2)

In this passage it sounds as if Sonya is lusting after Manning's clothes more than the man himself. It is more accurate to say that Sonya is falling for Manning's class. She attributes to his dress and grooming qualities of culture, dignity, quietness, and control. His clothes signal effortless power: He does not have to work. He does not have to struggle or make an effort in his life. He can wear clothes that are delicate, won't last, and represent painstaking labor in the hands of invisible others. In just standing before her, Manning displays to Sonya all the promises of the American Dream: He stands defined against the "background of horrid poverty."

What does the upper-class character in a cross-class romance seek from romance with a working-class character? All the things he or she feels his/her class denies: sex, freedom from social obligation, passion, physicality, simplicity. In their initial meeting, John Manning falls in love with Sonya Vrunsky's class as surely (and superficially) as she does with his:

> Less definitely, but with equal interest, the man's glance took in the girl. Of severe blue serge, shiny from wear, there was about her dress the

nun-like austerity of the intellectual of the East Side. But personality, femininity, flamed through the unrevealing uniform. . . .

You have the burning fire of the Russian Jew in you, while I am motivated by a sickly conscience, trying to heal itself by the application of cold logic and cold cash. The real liberation of your people must come from within from such as you. (2–3)

Manning projects onto Sonya Vrunsky warmth, passion, personality, and freedom from responsibility. He feels bent down and numbed by the noblesse oblige of his wealth and old-family status. He sees her as an opportunity for his liberation, not just her people's.

While Sonya and John are attracted to each other for their other class stereotypes, their respective social groups are appalled by the prospect of their union. Sonya's friends disdain her scheming and self-reinvention as "vamping" (94), a word used in the early 20th century to denote a cross between sexual baiting and vampirism, luring someone so that you can suck him/her dry.

They see Sonya as a mercenary, willing to use her body and forsake her religion for economic advantages. They are not impressed with Manning or his class, either, seeing him as effeminate and sickly. They scoff at his philosophical talk of class equality as crazy and hypocritical. Mrs. Peltz tells him: "Even downtown we got differences. Let me and the lord's wife go to the butcher store for meat? For me, who bargains herself for every penny, or the landlord's wife what pays him over any price he asks?" (126).

Moreover, Sonya's social climbing through marriage is taken as a sign to her friends that she is as selfish and inured to the needs of others as the class she has married into. Mrs. Peltz exclaims at Sonya's wedding reception: "The price of this one carpet would be enough to feed the whole block for a year. Only a little from that silver on her side-board would free me from the worries for rent for the rest of my days. If she'd have a heart, she'd divide with us a little of her good luck" (124). When Sonya hears this, she is sickened with shame, but she does not share her wealth.

Manning's friends are even more scathing in their assessment of Sonya and her wedding guests. They see her friends as coarse and animal-like, and refer to his ascetic habits and charitable antics on the East Side as:

John's melodramatic vaudeville of social equality. . . . Indeed! One could consider it as the latest amusement. You remember the Newport monkey dinner that was given to a pet monkey? I would better be able to find it amusing if it were not that I'm fond of Manning. . . . Giving a dinner for a pet monkey is one thing and marrying one is quite another thing. . . . (127)

It is not enough for Manning's friend to declare Sonya and the people of the East Side lower on the evolutionary scale; they summarize her allure and her feelings for Manning as purely sexual, which, for them, is another form of bestiality: " 'They say,' broke in another voice, 'Russian Jewesses are always fascinating to men. The reason, my dear, is because they have neither breeding, culture nor tradition. . . . With all to gain and nothing to lose . . . They are mere creatures of sex. . . . And much as we may dislike to admit it, men uptown and downtown are the same' " (128).

The ironic tragedy of Sonya Vrunsky and John Manning's relationship in *Salome of the Tenements* is that what they love or desire about each other's class is the same thing, phrased only less generously, that their respective social groups each hate about the other class. Manning sees Sonya as passionate and unbridled, and his friends term her animal, uncultured, and sexual. Sonya loves Manning's calm and refinement; her friends find him cold and hording. In a cross-class romance, it seems that the two involved can never get beyond the issues of class to appreciate the beloved for him/herself.

SOURCE

Yezierska, Anzia. *Salome of the Tenements*. Urbana: University of Illinois Press, 1995.

Carolyn Whitsun

SALT EATERS, THE TONI CADE BAMBARA (1980)

African-American author Toni Cade BAMBARA is perhaps best known for her short stories such as "Raymond's Run" and "The Lesson." After publishing two collections of short stories, *Gorilla, My Love* (1972) and *The Seabirds Are Still Alive* (1977), she turned to writing *The Salt Eaters.* An accomplished short story writer and novelist, her first love was film (Bambara, *Deep Sightings,* x). After making several films and documentaries, Bambara died in 1995. However, Bambara's estate published two posthumous works: a second novel, *Those Bones Are Not My Child* (1999), about the Atlanta child murders, and *Deep Sightings and Rescue Missions: Fiction, Essays, and Conversations* (1996), a collection introduced by Bambara's friend and editor Toni MORRISON. Bambara often wrote from self-assigned topics and explained that *The Salt Eaters* came from a desire to bridge the spiritual and the political, "to investigate possible ways to bring our technicians of the sacred and our guerillas together" (Bambara "Interview," 31). New readers might usefully follow Bambara's connective suggestion and approach this complex novel with a willingness to think and read by association, rather than by strictly linear development. Though Bambara divides the novel into 12 chapters that occur over the same "real time" day, many chapters contain the viewpoints of multiple characters. Moreover, these multiple viewpoints flash back to several time periods, including the future conditional, or "what might have been." As literary critic Eleanor Traynor accurately describes it, time in *The Salt Eaters* is "convergent" (Traynor, 65). The symbolism of the novel's title insists on the need for balance: Salt can be an antidote for a snake bite, but in excess quantities it can often kill.

Because the novel focuses on a tightly knit community, many characters have relatives and past experiences in common. Velma, one of the novel's main characters, is wife to James "Obie" Henry, head of the Academy of 7 Arts and sister to Palma, one of the "Seven Sisters" performing arts troupe who is traveling by bus to Claybourne; she is also friends with Jan and Ruby, who share lunchtime insights about Velma's life over the course of several chapters.

The "present" of *The Salt Eaters* takes place in the fictional town of Claybourne, Georgia, in the late 1970s. As the novel opens, two events bring the predominantly African-American community together: the failed suicide attempt of Velma Henry, community activist, and the Spring Festival, an event designed by

Claybourne's Academy of the 7 Arts as a reenactment of a Mardi Gras slave insurrection and "a holding action . . . to encourage everyone to work together" (92). Velma's healing involves diverse individuals from the Claybourne Infirmary, including the wise-woman healer Minnie Ransom, the older doctor Doc Serge, the younger doctor Julius Meadows, and the 12-member "Master's Mind." Other communities include the multicultural, multiracial Seven Sisters, a troupe of performance artists; the Academy of the 7 Arts, Claybourne's once-vibrant community center; and the community between Jan and Ruby, two friends having lunch. Gloria (Akasha) Hull's essay usefully explicates the names and natures of the novel's interconnected characters. Early scholarship on *The Salt Eaters* involves an explication of characters (Hull) and the jazz intricacies (Traynor). More recent scholarship emphasizes the novel's multiple viewpoints and experimental structure and novel's "postmodern" aesthetic: the efficacy of language in political change (Burks), agency, or one's ability to act (Alwes), and "schizophrenic" structures (Butler-Evans). However, other critics have chosen to focus on the novel's holistic urges toward reconciliation, redemption, and multiracial coalition (Willis, Nimura).

The entire first chapter, approximately 40 pages, exemplifies the novel's associative chronological thinking. Though this chapter occurs over an hour of "real time," it moves between the "present" of the Infirmary and several associative flashbacks from Velma's point of view. The healer Minnie asks Velma, "Are you sure . . . that you want to be well?" (1). In silent response to Minnie's question, Velma begins a series of reminiscences that travel between the "present" of the Infirmary back to the beginnings of her failing relationship with her husband, James "Obie" Henry, her frustrations with the chauvinism of the Civil Rights movement, and her childhood memories. While Velma's mind "goes traveling," Minnie consults her spirit guide, "Old Wife," for advice, since Velma's healing appears to be a special case. What "ails" Velma goes deeper than overwork and exhaustion, just as what "ails" the community goes deeper than the poison of the encroaching nuclear power plant. However, as one of Velma's friends insists later in the novel, "They're connected" (242). Thus the chapter establishes several important themes in the novel: the "wasteful and dangerous split" between community activists and spiritual healers; the costs and benefits of working in coalitions; the urgent need to recognize the interdependence of past, present, and future; and the function of agency in health and wholeness.

SOURCES

Alwes, Derek. "The Burden of Liberty: Choice in Toni Morrison's *Jazz* and Toni Cade Bambara's *The Salt Eaters*," *African American Review* 30, no. 3 (1996): 353–365.

Bambara, Toni Cade. "Interview." In *Black Women Writers at Work,* edited by Claudia Tate, 12–38. New York: Continuum, 1983.

Burks, Ruth Elizabeth. "From Baptism to Resurrection: Toni Cade Bambara and the Incongruity of Language." In *Black Women Writers (1950–1980): A Critical Evaluation,* edited by Mari Evans, 48–58. Garden City, N.Y.: Anchor, 1984.

Butler-Evans, Elliott. "Rewriting and Revising in the 1980s: *Tar Baby, The Color Purple,* and *The Salt Eaters*." In *Race, Gender, and Desire: Narrative Strategies in the Fiction of Toni Cade Bambara, Toni Morrison, and Alice Walker.* Philadelphia: Temple University Press, 1989, pp. 151–187.

Byerman, Keith. "Healing Arts: Folklore and the Female Self in Toni Cade Bambara's *The Salt Eaters*," *Postscript 5* (1988): 37–43.

Hull, Gloria. "What It Is I Think She's Doing Anyhow: A Reading of Toni Cade Bambara's *The Salt Eaters.*" In *Home Girls: A Black Feminist Anthology,* edited by Barbara Smith, 124–142. Latham, N.Y.: Kitchen Table, Women of Color Press, 1983.

Nimura, Tamiko. "In a Coalitional Mode: African American Literatures, Asian American Literatures, and the Politics of Comparison," Dissertation. University of Washington, Seattle, Wash., 2004.

Traynor, Eleanor W. "Music as Theme: The Jazz Mode in the Works of Toni Cade Bambara." In *Black Women Writers (1950–1980),* edited by Mari Evans, 58–70. New York: Anchor Press/Doubleday, 1984.

Willis, Susan. "Problematizing the Individual: Toni Cade Bambara's Stories for the Revolution." In *Specifying: Black Women Writing the American Experience.* 129–158. Madison: University of Wisconsin Press, 1987.

Tamiko Nimura

SANCTUARY WILLIAM FAULKNER (1931) William FAULKNER said he wrote *Sanctuary* as a "potboiler" in

order to make money. He then revised the novel before publication so it would not shame his earlier works. *Sanctuary* is still strikingly different from his other novels, in its relatively short sentences and fast pace, in its grotesque characterization of Popeye, and in its bizarre details of sexual perversity. Perhaps one reason this book receives considerable critical attention is its enigmatic quality. Faulkner's tone throughout is detached, and he seldom reveals the thoughts of characters as they make important decisions. Key events, such as Red's murder or the presentation of the corncob at trial, are downplayed or occur completely offstage, leaving the reader uncertain of the novel's true subject. One major theme, however, is the discovery of evil, from which there is no redemption at the end.

The novel opens as lawyer Horace Benbow, pausing in a walk from his home in Kinston to his former home in Jefferson, drinks from a spring and is held there by the gangster Popeye who thinks he is trying to expose his bootlegging operation. The men stare at each other across the spring for two hours. The gangster has skin with a "dead, dark pallor" and "the face of a wax doll set too near a hot fire and forgotten" (5). Although he is a white man, Faulkner frequently uses the adjective "black" to describe Popeye. He wears a "tight black suit," and to Horace "he smells black" (7). Horace is described in opposition to Popeye: He wears a light-colored suit; he is tall and Popeye is short; he carries a book and Popeye carries a gun; he drinks from the spring and Popeye spits in it. With this opening, Faulkner appears to establish a dichotomy of good and evil using traditional symbols of light and dark, but the reader soon learns that good is not so easy to find. At dusk, Popeye takes Horace to his hideout, the Old Frenchman place, and has Ruby, the girlfriend of the head bootlegger, Lee Goodwin, feed him dinner. After Horace has too much to drink, he tells his host/captor that he has had incestuous feelings for his stepdaughter and left his wife. He thanks Ruby for dinner and suggests she leave the bootleggers, for she is young, Horace tells her, and unlike himself, she has the courage to act.

Horace is soon dropped off in Jefferson, where he visits his genteel sister, Narcissa, but the reader returns to the Old Frenchman place, this time with Temple Drake, a pretty, rich college student and coquette, and her boyfriend Gowan Stevens. Slipping away from school, Temple and Gowan intend to buy moonshine from Lee Goodwin, but their plans go awry when Gowan, already drunk, wrecks the car. Temple is described as a tease, but because her father is a judge and she has only associated with young gentlemen, she has never had to deal with the consequences of her actions. When she tries coy smiles and flirtation on the gangsters in order to get a ride to town, she is met with cold stares rather than acquiescence. Becoming frightened, Temple begins to dart hysterically from one hiding place to the next, but her frantic movements only excite the interest of Popeye. Ruby warns her to leave, accusing her of "playing at it," and then tries to hide her from the men. But Popeye soon catches up with Temple.

After casually shooting Tommy, a feebleminded young bootlegger who tries to protect Temple, Popeye traps her in the corncrib and rapes her. The reader learns only later that Popeye is impotent and had used a corncob to violate this virgin. Faulkner suggests Popeye's impotence as a cause of his cruelty, both the gun with which he shoots Tommy and the corncob serving as surrogate outlets for his frustrated masculinity. Popeye then drives Temple to a Memphis brothel where he imprisons her, forcing her to have sex with the handsome and virile Red while Popeye watches. The name Temple is an ironic comment on the sacred purity of Southern womanhood. Popeye violates the sanctuary of her body, but the reader has already seen that Temple is not so pure in mind, and we soon wonder if she was only waiting for an initiation to transform the thoughts into deeds. Temple begins to desire Red of her own accord and starts meeting him secretly. Is Temple's nymphomania the result of her natural inclinations finally being given free reign, or a captive's attempt to survive in the environment of her captors? Having discovered Temple's attraction, Popeye obliquely warns Temple that Red is in danger. When she doesn't stop seeing Red, Popeye shoots him.

Red's wake is one of the comic scenes Faulkner offers to relieve the general depravity and despair of *Sanctuary*. The wake is held at a roadhouse casino with the body laid out on the craps table. When a woman demands the corpse be removed so she can play, a fight erupts and the table is overturned. The body, of course, tumbles from the casket to the floor, and the mortician's wax plug pops out of the bullet hole in Red's skull. The mourners quickly end their disagreement and restore the body.

Shortly after Temple and Popeye's departure from the Old Frenchman place, Lee Goodwin has been arrested for the murder of Tommy, and Ruby solicits Horace Benbow to defend him. Although Goodwin is a bootlegger and Ruby is his moll, compared to the novel's other characters they are basically good people. They are the only characters who feel genuine love, each being concerned primarily about the other's future throughout the trial. Horace's sister, Narcissa, fails to see their basic morality. Because she doesn't want her brother to tarnish his career or the family's name by taking on such lowlife clientele, she rallies the "good" women of Jefferson to turn Ruby out from the hotel and undermines Horace's case. The situation appears hopeless until, with the help of Senator Clarence Snopes, a frequent visitor of the brothel, Horace finds Temple. She tells him of her rape at the hands of Popeye and subsequent kidnapping, and Horace persuades her to testify on Lee Goodwin's behalf. During her testimony, the bloody corncob is presented as evidence, shocking all in attendance. Temple, however, inexplicably perjures herself, accusing Lee of both the rape and murder and sealing his fate. Unwilling to wait for his sentence to be carried out, an angry mob takes Lee from the courthouse and lynches him in the street. Horrified, Horace Benbow looks on but is unable to act. Throughout the book, Horace has been portrayed as an effete intellectual and idealist, and part of the evil he discovers through the trial is his own moral torpor.

The novel ends with an overwhelming tone of despair. Horace returns to his wife, Belle, with whom he is morbidly unhappy. Popeye, accused of another murder he could not have possibly committed because he was murdering someone else at the same hour in another town, is executed. His trial parallels Lee Goodwin's. In both cases, "the jury was out eight minutes" (306, 327) and, though both men are innocent of the crimes of which they have been convicted, they both seem resigned to their fates. Temple's fate is less tragic but still pessimistic. Trying to help her forget her terrible ordeal, her father, the judge, takes her to Europe, where she sits yawning in the Luxembourg Gardens in the "season of rain and death" (333). Nature, which was present but failed to sympathize throughout Temple's nightmare at the Old Frenchman place, now seems to offer the appropriate emotional response that Temple is unable to feel.

SOURCES

Bloom, Harold, ed. *William Faulkner's Sanctuary.* New York: Chelsea House, 1988.

Brooks, Cleanth. *William Faulkner: The Yoknapatawpha Country.* New Haven, Conn.: Yale University Press, 1963.

Faulkner, William. *Sanctuary.* 1931. New York: Vintage Books, 1987.

Werlock, Abby H. P. "Victims Unvanquished: Temple Drake and the Women in William Faulkner's Novels." In *Women and Violence in Literature,* edited by Kathy Acker, 3–49. New York: Garland Publishing, 1989.

Betina Entzminger

SAROYAN, WILLIAM (1908–1981)   William

Saroyan wrote more than 40 books during his lifetime. He won awards for his work in three genres, and gained fame for his novel *The HUMAN COMEDY* (1943) and for a series of autobiographical novels centering on the role of the father. In the middle of the Great Depression, Saroyan wrote with optimism and humor about the American Dream. Despite his acknowledgment of their human weaknesses, Saroyan's belief in ordinary people and in immigrants trying to make a living in unfamiliar and often incomprehensible environments is pronounced. Critics repeatedly use words like *charm, simplicity, honesty, clarity,* and *spontaneity* to describe his fiction. When interviewer Garig Basmadjian asked Saroyan about his love of humanity, Saroyan said that readers should not be "deceived" by the warmheartedness: He was aware, he said, of the baser side of human nature, but "I am not going to become estranged from the human race. This is my family, these lunatics, and I love them" (Basmadjian, 133). "I will not cry. I will not moan and groan about the hideous predicament of man, the impossible hell of man's soul, the imprisonment of man's destiny" (Basmadjian, 136).

William Saroyan was born on August 31, 1908, in Fresno, California, to Armenak Saroyan, a Presbyterian preacher and writer, and Takoohi Saroyan, both immigrants from Armenia who escaped the Turkish massacres of Armenians that began in 1896. Because his father died when Saroyan was six, he and his brothers and sisters were placed in an orphanage until his mother, who found work in a cannery, was able to reunite the family. Saroyan left school at age 15, served in the U.S. Army from 1942 to 1945, married (1943) Carol Marcus, divorced (1949), remarried her (1951), and divorced again in 1951. After earning his reputation as a perceptive short story writer, he published his first novel. *The Human Comedy* depicts 14-year-old Homer Macauley of Ithaca, California, his widowed mother, his sister, and two brothers, one of whom, Marcus, is serving overseas during World War II. He called this novel his "most affirmative piece of writing" (Basmadjian). Here Saroyan emphasizes the strength of love, particularly in the face of alcoholism and the finality of death. In the same year, MGM bought the novel and adapted it as a feature-length film with a screenplay by Saroyan—who won an Academy Award—and starring Mickey Rooney as Homer. In 1946, Saroyan wrote *The Adventures of Wesley Jackson,* an antiwar novel. *Rock Wagram* (1951) was Saroyan's favorite of his "large novels" (Basmadjian, 156). *Tracy's Tiger* (1951) tells the obsessive tale of a man who longs for the past; it was Saroyan's favorite of his short novels (Basmadjian, 156). *The Laughing Matter* (1953) was, Saroyan said later, too grim a novel; "it doesn't have any laughter" (Basmadjian, 157). Saroyan impressed Beat writers William S. BURROUGHS and Jack KEROUAC with his depiction of marginalized people who find alternative ways to be happy and hopeful. Other novels include *Mama I Love You* (1956), *Papa You're Crazy* (1957), *Boys and Girls Together* (1963), and *One Day in the Afternoon of the World* (1964). Saroyan also wrote the 1951 song "Come On-A My House," made into a hit by singer Rosemary Clooney.

William Saroyan died of cancer in 1981 in Fresno; after his cremation, half his ashes were interred in Fresno and the other half near Yerevan, Armenia. Most of his manuscripts are housed at the John M. Olin Library at Cornell University; a sizable collection of letters is at the University of California Research Library, Los Angeles. In 2002 the William Saroyan International Prize for Writing was established by Stanford University Libraries and the William Saroyan Foundation.

NOVELS

The Adventures of Wesley Jackson. New York: Harcourt, 1946.

Boys and Girls Together. New York: Harcourt, 1963. Reprint, New York: Barricade, 1995.

The Human Comedy. New York: Harcourt, 1943. Revised edition, 1966.

The Laughing Matter. Garden City, N.Y.: Doubleday, 1953.

Mama I Love You. Boston and Toronto: Atlantic-Little, Brown, 1956; New York: Dell, 1986.

One Day in the Afternoon of the World. New York: Harcourt, 1964.

Papa You're Crazy. Boston and Toronto: Atlantic–Little, Brown, 1957.

Rock Wagram. Garden City, N.Y.: Doubleday, 1951.

Tracy's Tiger. Garden City, N.Y.: Doubleday, 1951. Revised edition, New York: Ballantine, 1967.

The Twin Adventures: The Adventures of William Saroyan, A Diary; The Adventures of Wesley Jackson, A Novel. New York: Harcourt, 1950.

SOURCES

Balakian, Nona. *The World of William Saroyan: A Literary Interpretation.* Lewisburg, Pa.: Bucknell University Press, 1997.

Calonne, David Stephen. *William Saroyan: My Real Work Is Being.* Chapel Hill: University of North Carolina Press, 1983.

Floan, Howard. *William Saroyan.* Boston: Twayne, 1966.

Gifford, Barry, and Lawrence Lee. *Saroyan: A Biography.* New York: Harper, 1984.

Keyishian, Harry. *Critical Essays on William Saroyan.* Engelwood Cliffs, N.J.: Prentice-Hall, 1995.

Lee, Lawrence, and Barry Gifford. *Saroyan: A Biography.* Berkeley: University of California Press, 1998.

Leggett, John (Ward). *A Daring Young Man: A Biography of William Saroyan.* New York: Knopf, 2002.

Saroyan, Aram. *William Saroyan.* New York: Harcourt, 1983.

———. *Last Rites: The Death of William Saroyan.* New York: Harcourt, 1983.

Saroyan, William. *Not Dying.* New York: Barricade Books, 1997.

———, and Garig Basmadjian. "Candid Conversation." In *William Saroyan: The Man and the Writer Remembered,* edited by Leo Hamalian, 132–157. Rutherford, N.J.: Fairleigh Dickinson University Press, 1987.

Whitmore, John. *William Saroyan: A Research and Production Sourcebook.* Westport, Conn.: Greenwood, 1994.

OTHER

Books and Writers. "William Saroyan." Available online. URL: http://www.kirjasto.sci.fi/saroyan.htm. Accessed September 25, 2005.

Kalinian Saroyan Homepage. "Remembering William Saroyan." Available online. URL: http://www.kalinian-saroyan.com. Accessed September 25, 2005.

William Saroyan. Cilicia.com. Available online. URL: http://www.cilicia.com/armo22_william_saroyan.html. Accessed September 25, 2005.

SARTON, MAY (ELEANOR MARIE SARTON) (1912–1995)

May Sarton thought of herself primarily as a poet, yet she wrote nearly 50 books, 19 of them novels. (Some were written for younger readers.) She is most well known for the groundbreaking *Mrs. Stevens Hears the Mermaids Singing* (1965), the novel in which Sarton addressed the complex interplay of artistry and lesbianism in an era when homosexuality was largely unnoted and suspect. Her major subjects include solitary women, women's relationships with family and lovers, and the reality and art of aging. Although after the 1930s, when she had been part of the circle that included Virginia Woolf, Julius Huxley, and Conrad Aiken, Sarton's poetry and fiction passed from favor, her autobiographical publications from the 1960s to the 1980s brought her renewed popular and critical attention.

May Sarton was born Eleanor Marie Sarton on May 3, 1912, in Wondelgem, Belgium, to George Alfred Leon, a science historian, and Eleanor Mabel Elwes Leon, an artist and designer. In autumn 1914, her family left Belgium for England and, in 1916, they immigrated to the United States and settled in Cambridge, Massachusetts. Rather than attend college, she chose to become a writer, publishing her first novel, *The Single Hound,* a story of two poets, in 1938. It was well received, as were *The Bridge of Years* (1946), about a Belgian family resisting fascism, and *Faithful Are the Wounds* (1955), about an American professor who commits suicide during the McCarthy era. *Mrs. Stevens*

Hears Mermaids Singing (1965) is a fictionalized account of Sarton's long-term relationship with her partner, known only as Judy. *Anger* (1982) focuses on the marriage of a passionate woman to an impersonal, cold man, and *The Magnificent Spinster* (1985) treats the lifelong relationship between two women who must cope with the prejudices of their community.

Sarton purchased an old farmhouse in New Hampshire and wrote a book, *Plant Dreaming Deep* (1968), about the importance of her home and its stability to her ability to write. The recipient of numerous awards and honorary doctorates, May Sarton died of breast cancer on July 16, 1995. Before her death, film rights to four of her novels—*A Reckoning, Mrs. Stevens Hears Mermaids Singing, Kinds of Love,* and *As We Are Now*—were optioned. There is an increasing awareness of her contributions to 20th-century American literature.

NOVELS

Anger. New York: Norton, 1982.
As We Are Now. New York: Norton, 1973.
The Birth of a Grandfather. New York: Rinehart, 1957.
The Bridge of Years. Garden City, N.Y.: Doubleday, 1946.
Crucial Conversations. New York: Norton, 1975.
The Education of Harriet Hatfield. New York: Norton, 1989.
Faithful Are the Wounds. New York: Rinehart, 1955.
Joanna and Ulysses. New York: Norton, 1963.
Kinds of Love. New York: Norton, 1970.
The Magnificent Spinster. New York: Norton, 1985.
Mrs. Stevens Hears the Mermaids Singing. New York: Norton, 1965.
A Reckoning. New York: Norton, 1978.
Shadow of a Man. New York: Rinehart, 1950.
A Shower of Summer Days. New York & Toronto: Rinehart, 1952.
The Single Hound. Boston: Houghton Mifflin, 1938.
The Small Room. New York: Norton, 1961.

SOURCES

Blotner, Joseph. *The Modern American Political Novel: 1900–1960.* Austin: University of Texas Press, 1966.
Blouin, Lenora. *May Sarton: A Bibliography.* Metuchen, N.J.: Scarecrow Press, 1978.
Dickey, James. *Babel to Byzantium.* New York: Farrar, Straus, 1968.
Evans, Elizabeth. *May Sarton Revisited.* Boston: Twayne, 1989.

Hunting, Constance, ed. *May Sarton: Woman and Poet.* Orono, Maine: National Poetry Foundation, 1982.
Peters, Margot. *May Sarton: A Biography.* New York: Knopf, 1997.
Rule, Jane. *Lesbian Images.* Garden City, N.Y.: Doubleday, 1975.
Sherman, Susan, ed. *May Sarton: Selected Letters.* 2 volumes. *1916–1954.* New York: Norton, 1997; *1955–1995.* New York: Norton, 2002.
Silbey, Agnes. *May Sarton.* Boston: Twayne, 1972.
Swartzlander, Susan, and Marilyn Mumford, eds. *That Great Sanity: Critical Essays on May Sarton.* Ann Arbor: University of Michigan Press, 1992.

OTHER

Blouin, Lenora P. "May Sarton: A Poet's Life." Available online. URL: http://digital.library.upenn.edu/women/sarton/blouin-biography.html. Accessed January 12, 2006.

SAVE ME THE WALTZ ZELDA FITZGERALD (1932)

Zelda FITZGERALD named her novel *Save Me the Waltz* from a title found in a Victor record catalog, according to Nancy Milford, in her biography of the author and famous wife of F. Scott FITZGERALD, *Zelda: A Biography.* Zelda Fitzgerald wrote her novel in 1932, during a span of "no more than three months," while receiving psychiatric care at John Hopkins University Hospital. The writing served as part of her treatment. Fitzgerald sent a manuscript of the project to her husband's editor, Maxwell Perkins, at Scribner, before allowing her husband to read her work—an act that created much suspicion and resentment. At the time, Scott Fitzgerald had been long at work on his novel *Tender Is the Night,* which addressed his wife's mental instability and drew upon the couple's experiences in Switzerland, where Zelda visited Prangins Hospital for care, from 1930–31. Though Zelda Fitzgerald had heard 40,000 words of her husband's novel, and his writing clearly influenced her work, the author, in her own right, reclaimed her life through the writing of the novel, which was a therapeutic act. Distinguishing her literary work from that of her husband, in *Save Me the Waltz,* Zelda presents her own story, or herstory, of her poignant struggle in facing the challenges of having to grow up very quickly.

The novel itself focuses on the appropriately named heroine Alabama and her entrance into womanhood as marked by her relationship with the artist David Knight, a lieutenant stationed in the South during the Great War. The plot of the novel largely follows the chronology of Zelda's relationship with Scott, whom she first met when he was a soldier stationed near Montgomery, Alabama, her hometown. Alabama leaves with Knight to New York, where they marry. David meets with immediate success and the couple welcomes the birth of their daughter, Bonnie. The story shifts to the French Riviera, where Alabama struggles with the mundane aspects of marriage—keeping track of expenditures, managing the household affairs, and so on—which acutely chafe when she meets the French aviator Jacques Chevre-Feuille, with whom a flirtation escalates. After a confrontation and the removal of Jacques from their lives, the couple meets Gabrielle Gibbs at a party, who serves as a temptation for David. When David sees Gabrielle to her hotel, after a party, only to return the morning after, Alabama, frustrated and deeply saddened, tries to shrug off the situation until she revealingly screams: "I can't stand this any longer. . . . I don't want to sleep with the men or imitate the women, and I can't stand it" (111). Citing David's infatuation with Gabrielle, Alabama promises to become "as famous a dancer as there are blue veins over the white marble of Miss Gibbs" (112) and looks to dance as a means of coping with life.

Milford emphasizes Alabama's need for dance as an outlet, as a "defense against the collapse of her marriage" (227), with an ever-increasing fervor that causes her to spend less time with her family. Fighting opinions that she is too old to become a ballet dancer, Alabama studies dance diligently, countering those who question her motives; ultimately, she makes the decision not to return to America with her family, but instead chooses to go to Naples to perform a solo part in *Faust,* with the San Carlos Opera. Alabama meets with success during her time in Naples, separated from David and Bonnie, who remain in Switzerland. Two traumatic events then occur—the severing of the tendons of Alabama's foot and the death of Alabama's father, Judge Beggs—that dramatically change the heroine's life. Alabama and her family return to America for the funeral of her father. By the end of the novel, the reader observes how much Alabama has had to change since she first met David, which led to Alabama's removal from the care of her father. Now, with her father dead, Alabama is left with many unanswered questions and the task of having to redefine herself without his presence in her life anymore. Disoriented, Alabama acknowledges the difficulty in trying to maintain a sense of self and of values now that her father's strong influence has been removed.

Milford points out that the characterization of Judge Beggs is the "heart of the novel," as the novel both begins and ends with his appearance (228). Certainly, given Scott Fitzgerald's version of Zelda's attachment to her father in *Tender Is the Night,* in which Scott imaginatively changes Zelda's mental illness into that of his character Nicole Diver, whose psychological troubles result from the consummation of an incestuous relationship with her father, the reader notes that Judge Sayre figured largely in the minds of both the Fitzgeralds. Interestingly, Milford notes: "It was not until the death of Judge Sayre that Zelda began to form her book and it would seem that his death provided a kind of psychological freeing for her that stimulated her into reviewing her life up until his death" (228). Clearly, the novel is a coming-of-age story that maps out Alabama Beggs's growth and development in the absence of her father—first through her marriage and leaving home and, second, with her father's death, which becomes a permanent separation—and investigates her artistic maturity.

Zelda Fitzgerald wrote her novel with a rhythm and an interesting use of language that marked her writing as very different from that of her husband, as the work of an artist. Fitzgerald's artistic expression in performance, such as in ballet, as well as in her painting, remarkably shown by her design of the cover art used on the novel's dust jacket, reveal the author's importance as an artist in her own right, apart from her husband's achievement. The vivid imagery and curious turn of phrase the reader meets when reading the pages of the novel give insight into a brilliant, if troubled mind. Certainly, *Save Me the Waltz* provides a fascinating examination of a young woman growing up in the 1920s, refreshingly written by an author whose husband's celebrity overshadowed her own ability and production.

SOURCES

Bruccoli, Matthew J., ed. *The Collected Writings of Zelda Fitzgerald.* Introduction by Mary Gordon. Tuscaloosa: University of Alabama Press, 1991.

Milford, Nancy. *Zelda: A Biography.* New York: Perennial, 1970.

Taylor, Kendall. *Sometimes Madness Is Wisdom: Zelda and Scott Fitzgerald, a Marriage.* New York: Ballantine Books, 2001.

Sharon Kehl Califano

SCARLET LETTER, THE NATHANIEL HAWTHORNE (1850)

The Scarlet Letter is a historical novel of Puritan New England in which the story of the central character, Hester Prynne, is introduced with images of prison. At the beginning of the novel, we encounter a jail door with decorative red ironwork that anticipates the flourishes of Hester Prynne's scarlet badge. This theme of entrapment is prevalent throughout the novel. Later, Hester's husband Chillingworth observes that their marriage was one of youth and decay, an "unnatural relation," but Hester's unnatural relation with decay extends beyond her marriage: She is painfully aware that she can no longer see or draw sustenance from her future. All tomorrows will be the "very same . . . with the same burden," she thinks at the beginning of the novel.

Hester is trapped by her own past. The narrative itself begins after the major events in Hester's life have already occurred. By the time we meet Hester, she has already been married to the old man Roger Chillingworth, had an affair with the young minister Arthur Dimmesdale, and given birth to Dimmesdale's daughter, Pearl, whose visible presence constitutes a perpetual reminder of Hester's "sin," another link in the chain that imprisons Hester in the past. Initially Hester's memory of her early life provides a blessed escape from the present moment, as she stands upon the scaffold in the novel's opening, but her compulsive remembering eventually torments her. Later, in an important scene with Dimmesdale in the woods, she feels for a brief moment that she is free from history. But the "the irrevocable past" returns. Like the river that runs through the woods, choked by branches and leaves, the onward movement of time for Hester is stopped by the heavy presence of the past, which blocks its free flow. The symbolism of the tree on which Hester and her past lover Dimmesdale sit in the woods is unmistakable: It was uprooted by a blast long ago and is covered in moss. They, ruined by the blast of their sin and Hester's punishment, have "earth's heaviest burden on them," "earth" here meaning both the world and soil. Hester's attempt to leave the past behind has come too late. She chose not to make a new life in another town or country, instead remaining to haunt the place where, as the narrator explains, a "great and marked event has given color to [her] lifetime." The words "marked" and color" remind us of the scarlet letter: Hester's marked color has ironically made her a colorless ghost among the living.

Some writers mourn the disconnect between the past and the present, the separation of history from contemporary culture, but Nathaniel HAWTHORNE, in contrast, was hostile to the idea of bringing the past into the present. His introduction to the novel is an essay called "The Custom-House" and seems initially to be an entrance to the past: "Custom" means "habit" as well as "trade," and thus the habits of another age might be accessible through the Custom-House doors. The essay's more likely function, however, is as a bridge between fiction and autobiography or romance and reality, for Hawthorne did not believe in fluid, safe movement between past and present. The narrator of "The Custom-House" insists that human nature does not "flourish, any more than a potato, if it be planted and replanted, for too long a series of generations in the same worn-out soil," and observes that the men in the Custom-House "ought to have given place to younger men" who wouldn't tell the "several thousandth repetition of old sea-stories." He even wishes he had written about the present instead of the past: "leaf after leaf" in the real world was presenting itself to him, and he senses that if he could write down "the reality of the flitting hour" then the "letters would turn to gold upon the page." These gold letters of the present hour contrast with the scarlet letter presented in the novel proper, which represents the unhealthy, frozen past. The leaves turn gold when Hester and Dimmesdale meet in the wood and Hester, momentarily believing herself to be free of the past, throws away the scarlet letter.

Hester's punishment, however, is permanent, and she cannot abandon for more than a few moments the scarlet letter that ties her to her past with threads as strong as chains. The scarlet letter not only imposes the past on the present but also fails even to represent the past accurately. In "The Custom House," the narrator describes his discovery of the embroidered red badge in later years: "My eyes fastened themselves upon the old scarlet letter, and would not be turned aside," he remembers. "Certainly there was some deep meaning in it, most worthy of interpretation, and which, as it were, streamed forth from the mystic symbol, subtly communicating itself to my sensibilities, but evading the analysis of my mind." Thus distracted, he ignores the papers that would solve this mystery: "In the absorbing contemplation of the scarlet letter, I had hitherto neglected to examine a small roll of dingy paper, around which it had been twisted." Here is a neglected but legible text, a hidden usable past.

The scarlet letter dominates everything. At another point in the novel, Hester sees herself in a mirror, and her image is distorted, with the scarlet badge disproportionately huge upon her breast. Similarly, the opening of the narrative proper describes the scarlet letter immediately. Distracted, the gaze of the reader moves away from the baby, which is the real evidence of sin but has been mentioned only briefly. And with eyes glued to the scarlet letter, the crowd in the opening scene misses the glance that passes between Hester and Dimmesdale and also Dimmesdale's gesture when Hester refuses to name the baby's father: Both glance and gesture would have revealed the secret behind the scarlet letter, but the crowd misses them, just as the narrator nearly misses the small roll of dingy paper in the Custom-House. The scarlet letter is thus also a red herring.

Hawthorne rejects the kind of forcible remembering caused by the scarlet letter's distracting presence. Instead he imagines in "The Custom-House" a place where the two worlds of past and present might come together as "somewhere between the real world and fairy-land, where the Actual and the Imaginary may meet and each imbue itself with the nature of the other." He adds, "Ghosts may enter here, without affrighting us." Ghosts become fairies, and the past and present coexist harmoniously in a place where reality and fiction merge. The novel's conclusion, then, offers a new style of history, composed of many perspectives: "more than one account," "various explanations," "the reader may choose among these theories." As readers we can write our own histories, breaking with determinism and the providential style of history that was popular in Hawthorne's day. We have been warned about the dangers of lingering too long in any one place. Like the fatherless Pearl, Hester's child, who finally leaves Massachusetts to live elsewhere, we put down roots in fresh soil. Although Hester is doomed to remain imprisoned in her past, Hawthorne suggests that we can learn from her lesson and avoid her Puritan fate.

SOURCES

Bercovitch, Sacvan. *The Office of the Scarlet Letter.* Baltimore, Md.: Johns Hopkins University Press, 1991.

Brodhead, Richard. *The School of Hawthorne.* New York: Oxford University Press, 1986.

Budick, Emily. *Engendering the Romance: Women Writers and the Hawthorne Tradition, 1850–1990.* New Haven, Conn.: Yale University Press, 1994.

Hawthorne, Nathaniel. *The Scarlet Letter.* Boston and New York: Houghton, Mifflin and Co., 1850.

James, Henry. *Hawthorne.* London: MacMillan, 1879.

Mathiessen, F. O. *American Renaissance.* Oxford: Oxford University Press, 1941.

Mizruchi, Susan. *The Power of Historical Knowledge: Narrating the Past in Hawthorne, James, and Dreiser.* Princeton, N.J.: Princeton University Press, 1988.

Zoe Trodd

SEAL WIFE, THE KATHRYN HARRISON (2002)

With another fictional exploration of female sexuality and the power and pain it weaves, *The Seal Wife,* Kathryn HARRISON's fifth novel, brings forth characters from another time, place, and culture while focusing on the psychological and sexual issues of solitude and obsession still palpable today. With prose as pure as the ice-covered Alaskan territory she re-creates, Harrison opens the door for not only her written work but also the controversy and resonance that often accompanies it.

While Harrison's writing has consisted primarily of novels, among them *Thicker Than Water, Exposure, Poison,* and *The Binding Chair or, a Visit from the Foot Eman-*

cipation Society, it is her 1997 memoir *The Kiss* that most people remember and judge her worth as a writer and, unfairly, a person. In *The Kiss* Harrison recounts the incestuous affair she and her father briefly conducted during her young adulthood. While some critics, most notably other literary writers, hailed *The Kiss* as an exceptional work of literary art, others believed Harrison had passed the portal of decency by revealing an area of her life that not didn't just touch the incest taboo but gratuitously stroked it. Yet those same critics and readers (and even nonreaders) who were repelled by *The Kiss* missed the memoir's central focus: that of isolation, loneliness, misused power and sexuality, and the means a person without love and affection will go to attain them. What Harrison addressed in *The Kiss* is nothing new to readers of her work. She gracefully explores these themes as well in *The Seal Wife.*

Her past two fictional works have used the realm of historical fiction, respectively setting those stories in Europe and China, but *The Seal Wife* brings the reader to a piece of America before it became part of America. In 1915, Bigelow, a 26-year-old observer from the U.S. Weather Bureau, is stationed in Anchorage, Alaska. There he is assigned to construct an observatory within a land as cold and harsh as his interaction with the few women who reside there. Men outnumber the women, and not only is the Arctic environment cold but daylight and night are realms of normalcy that do not exist outside the continental United States. With sleep disruption, lack of human interaction and food, and the region's constant cold, Bigelow spends his time not only on the task at hand but within his own thoughts. The unbearable isolation leads Bigelow and the reader to learn that while this environment and land are new to him, loneliness and lack of love are not. From its very start, silence remains one of *The Seal Wife's* dominant themes and is a way for the people in Bigelow's world to hold the most power over him.

The novel opens with Bigelow and the Aleut woman, the only name Harrison gives her, revealing the seclusion Bigelow must endure and the infatuation he feels throughout the novel toward this silent, unnamed female. No words are spoken, thoughts shared, or past events revealed, nothing to seal their consummation. But Bigelow wants her and even begs her " 'Promise me

there's no one else' " (7). Still, she doesn't answer. By demonstrating Bigelow's continual need to talk and share himself with the Aleut woman, Harrison shows that the power roles have shifted, leaving it resting with this woman who, with her silence, does not reflect the ways some Americans think are the means to gain and sustain power: advanced education, family background, and money. By remaining mute, the Aleut woman brings Bigelow to near madness and, even though she disappears for several pages into the novel, remains its dominant character.

Even in Bigelow's past, he lived without a sense of substantial closeness to those around him. The passing of his father when Bigelow was a child failed to produce tears. Harrison foreshadows the silence that will plague Bigelow with a brief scene recalling his father's death:

> "Say good-bye," his mother told him, and he followed her into the bedroom. The shades were drawn, but the sun found its way through the cracks.
>
> "Why is that there?" he asked, pointing to the white cloth tied under his father's jaw and over the top of his head.
> "To keep his mouth from . . ." She didn't finish.
> "From what?" he asked.
> "Opening." (62)

Bigelow futilely tries to achieve control. Not only does he encounter silence with the Aleut woman but also the shopkeeper's daughter Miriam. Silence consistently follows and nearly destroys him. There is no guarantee of fulfillment toward his predictions and wants. As much as the silence frustrates him, it is what truly excites him. Though the prostitute he procures talks, he gags her. Maria Russo in her *New York Times* book review of *The Seal Wife* points out that "Harrison wants to show silence as a symbol of oppression that can be twisted into a sources of power," also noting "[a]s the deprivations and forbidding terrain of the Fair North take their toll, the novel's awareness of the natural world gives it a sturdier, more philosophical underpinning, a more considered, less sensationalistic stance toward the inevitability of human suffering" (Russo, 12).

The Aleut woman eventually returns and Bigelow wonders "[h]ow [he] could have imagined her as a bird," finally recognizing that she mirrors the seal his presence frightens: "the animal hurries toward the water, throwing her head out before her, her sleek body following" (210). The novel ends on the start of summer solstice, with the Aleut woman and Bigelow traveling a hill and Bigelow contemplating how the images of their relationship form him and her, ultimately offering closure to his ravaged emotions and life. Russo questions why Harrison chooses to end her novel without offering concrete answers, yet in the same paragraph she offers an answer. Not only in *The Seal Wife* but in all her work, Harrison shows that love's nature remains unknown. Why people choose the paths they do to attain it cannot be answered objectively.

SOURCES

Harrison, Kathryn. *The Seal Wife.* 2002. Reprint, New York: Random House Trade Paperbacks, 2003.

Russo, Maria. "Which Way the Wind Blows." Review of *The Seal Wife, New York Times,* 5 May 2002, late ed., sec. 7, p. 12.

Laura Durnell

SEA-WOLF, THE JACK LONDON (1904)

Published only a year after *The CALL OF THE WILD, The Sea-Wolf* became Jack LONDON's second best-selling novel. While the novel exhibits the fiercely naturalistic tendencies of his earlier fiction, it primarily represents the ongoing conflict between materialism and idealism in London's own philosophy. He personifies this philosophical conflict in his protagonist, Humphrey Van Weyden, an effete idealist who is impressed onto a pelagic sealing voyage and must fend for himself and adapt to the ship's brutal, masculine environment. Throughout the novel, Van Weyden clashes with the novel's antagonist, Wolf Larsen, a tyrannical sea captain who repeatedly asserts his materialist philosophy in his conversations with Van Weyden and in the cruel treatment of his crew. Larsen, one of London's most enduring individualists, is a man of unparalleled physical strength and beauty, whose mental powers are no less prodigious, and like his literary predecessors before him, characters such as Milton's Satan and Melville's Captain Ahab, his innate will to overcome any chal-

lenge to his authority only augments his rebellious nature and preserves his limitless pride.

In contrast to many of his other rugged and self-sufficient narrators, London chooses the prestigious literary critic Humphrey Van Weyden to narrate the novel. Van Weyden opens his tale onboard the ferry steamer Martinez, where he must soon jump overboard into the frigid water as the steamer sinks off the coast after being rammed by another vessel. Unable to help the women to safety, he is powerless to save even his own life, as the current takes him out to sea. His ineptitude, here at the beginning of the novel, is an ideal counterpoint to his physical and philosophical transformation at the end, where he has survived the onslaughts of Wolf Larsen and nature, and stands on the decks of the once shipwrecked *Ghost,* now refitted with masts raised almost single-handedly by him, a captain on the same ocean where he was once only a passenger.

But all this is to come, for Van Weyden must first be pulled from the ocean, literally ripped, as he tells us, from "the suffocating blankness and darkness" of the sea (9). Rescued from certain death, Van Weyden is now reborn on the *Ghost,* a sealing schooner bound for the northern Pacific. Christened "Hump" by his captain and new father, Wolf Larsen, he first witnesses a funeral at sea after being impressed into the service as cabin boy. And through that funeral's lack of ceremony and the subsequent brutality of life aboard the *Ghost,* he begins to see that death no longer holds the same signification it once did, just as life has now "become cheap and tawdry, a beastly and inarticulate thing, a soulless stirring of ooze and slime" (31).

No matter how primitive the crew's behavior on the ship seems to Van Weyden throughout his voyage, London never lets us forget that the civilizing forces that label the conduct on the ship "brutal" and "primitive" are the same forces that make such conduct possible. Ironically, Wolf Larsen's bloodthirsty treatment of his crew and the seal-hunter's violence during the hunt are products of an economic system that foster the desire for sealskins to "adorn the fair shoulders of the women of the cities" (140). The violence of the first half of the novel, then, aptly frames a portrait of those same civilizing forces that have had such debilitating effects on Van Weyden. Interestingly enough, London reveals, whether the turn-of-the-century reader realized it or not, that bloodshed upon the ocean is always a staple ingredient of the finery worn in the streets.

Through his association with Wolf Larsen, Van Weyden discovers this fact and more about the world of his former life. During one of their early conversations, Larsen fleshes out for Van Weyden his radical materialism. Ultimately, life for Larsen represents the ongoing struggle between the weak and the strong, where "the big eat the little that they may continue to move, the strong eat the weak that they may retain their strength. The lucky eat the most and move the longest, that is all. . . . Might is right, and that is all there is to it. Weakness is wrong" (46, 72). In light of the new environment Van Weyden finds himself in, this claim proves quite persuasive, but throughout the novel, he attempts to maintain his optimism and preserve his faith in something more than the material, something ineffable that "transcend[s] utterance" (45). Thus begins their ongoing conflict of ideas, with the actions of the crew, and even those of Van Weyden himself, providing the evidence for Larsen to prove his materialist philosophy. The ship, then, a microcosm for all of life, becomes the perfect vehicle for Larsen to show Van Weyden the inherent weakness of his idealistic belief in conventional morality and the existence of the soul.

In analyzing his own behavior on the ship, Van Weyden begins to observe that Larsen's ideas have begun to alter his point of view. Just as Van Weyden begins to understand the latent strength within him, he also begins to note the destructive nature of Larsen's philosophy. He continually observes how Larsen's behavior destroys any sense of comradeship among the crew, which inevitably results in the mutiny that Larsen barely escapes with his life. Likewise, his mysterious headaches tell of some deep-seated psychological conflict within him.

Unlike Larsen, Van Weyden possesses the ability to change, and throughout his narration he marvels at his growing physical strength and capacity to endure. Despite his initial physical and philosophical attraction to Larsen, Van Weyden clings to his inherent faith in the soul and, more important, his belief in the power of comradeship, as we witness when Maud Brewster enters the scene. But his true strength rests in his ability to merge all that he has learned from Larsen with the stronger elements of his former philosophy. And it is this fact alone that baffles and thwarts Larsen throughout the second half of the novel.

With the entrance of Maud Brewster, a successful poet, we witness the degree of Van Weyden's transformation. Rescued mid-ocean, as well as mid-novel, Brewster is the physical as well as philosophical antithesis of Larsen, and just as Van Weyden was inexplicably drawn to Larsen's physicality, he now begins to gravitate toward Brewster's "kindred intellect and spirit" (193). Despite the pull of Brewster's character on him, Van Weyden brings to their relationship the lessons learned from his experience on the *Ghost*.

Larsen's brute strength becomes the last line of defense for his philosophy, and he once again asserts his physical prowess when he attempts to rape Maud Brewster. In order to defend her, Van Weyden, for the first time in the novel, physically challenges Larsen and with that act successfully defends his growing love for her, a connection that he believes is both physical and spiritual. During the struggle, Larsen suffers from a headache that will eventually blind him, and Brewster preserves his life in spite of Van Weyden's desire to take it. In the end, Van Weyden has sacrificed his physical body for Brewster, a sacrifice that represents the first physical victory in his philosophical conflict with Larsen. This act alone elicits the headache that blinds Larsen, which symbolically portrays his blindness to the strength of Van Weyden's idealism throughout the novel.

Soon after this incident, the lovers escape from the *Ghost* to their idyllic retreat on Endeavor Island, where they survive the elements through their symbiotic relationship. Bereft of his crew and slowly succumbing to his disease, Larsen is eventually shipwrecked on the island, where he must witness the strength of "the truest comradeship that may fall to man and woman" (327). As the couple restore the *Ghost* by themselves and eventually sail from the island to freedom, one cannot help but recognize what their connection to each other allows them to overcome, as Larsen, at one time the paragon of the physical, lays paralytic in his bunk unable to destroy the one connection that has outdone him.

The enduring power of the novel rests in its ability to depict the philosophical dilemma London struggled with throughout his life. In a sense, Larsen's alienation and suffering represents the despair that accompanied London's creed of individualism, a creed that plays out in much of his fiction (Kazin, 115). In creating the dynamic conflict between Larsen and Van Weyden, perhaps he recognized that the individualism of his most enduring characters was not enough. At one time or another, we must all, London seems to suggest, forge a connection with others, gather a mate-comrade to our sides, and discover what we might accomplish together.

SOURCES

Baskett, Sam S. "Sea Change in *The Sea-Wolf,*" *American Literary Realism* 24, no. 2 (1992): 5–22.

Ellis, James. "A New Reading of *The Sea-Wolf.*" In *Jack London: Essays in Criticism,* edited by Ray Wilson Ownbey, 92–99. Santa Barbara, Calif.: Peregrine Smith, 1978.

Kazin, Alfred. *On Native Grounds: An Interpretation of Modern American Prose Literature.* New York: Reynall & Hitchcock, 1942.

Labor, Earle, and Jeanne Campbell Reesman. *Jack London.* Twayne's United States Authors Ser., 230. New York: Twayne, 1994.

London, Jack. *The Sea-Wolf.* Edited by John Sutherland. New York: Oxford University Press, 2000.

Mitchell, Lee Clark. " 'And Rescue Us from Ourselves': Becoming Someone in Jack London's *The Sea-Wolf,*" *American Literature* 70, no. 2 (1998): 317–335.

Robinson, Forrest G. "The Eyes Have It: An Essay on Jack London's *The Sea-Wolf,*" *American Literary Realism* 18 (1985): 178–195.

Watson, Charles N.J. *The Novels of Jack London: a Reappraisal.* Madison: University of Wisconsin Press, 1983.

Timothy Adrian Lewis

SEBOLD, ALICE (1963–)

SEBOLD, ALICE (1963–) Alice Sebold, author of *The* LOVELY BONES (2002), won a Bram Stoker Award for the best first novel, and was nominated for the Horror Writers Association best novel in 2002. Perhaps this is because the novel is narrated by the spirit of a 14-year-old girl who has been raped and murdered and now tells her story from heaven. The *New York Times* reviewer Katherine Bouton seems more on target: Sebold, she says, "takes the stuff of neighborhood tragedy—the unexplained disappearance of a child, the shattered family alone with its grief—and turns it into literature" (Bouton, 14). In either case, with nearly 3 million hardcover copies and 65 weeks on the *New York Times* best-seller list, *The Lovely Bones* became the best-selling paperback novel of 2003 (*The Bookseller*).

Alice Sebold was born in 1963 in California and was educated at Syracuse University, the University of Houston, and at the University of California at Irvine, where she earned her master of fine arts degree in 1998. Her first book, *Lucky* (1999), is a memoir that graphically describes her rape in 1981, during her first year of college. Because another young woman had been raped and murdered on the same spot, the police called Sebold "lucky." *The Lovely Bones,* Sebold says, was partly written in tribute to the murdered woman (Levy, 36). Susie Salmon narrates the story of her rape and the details of her mother's affair with a policeman, her desertion of the family, and her father's obsession with finding the murderer. Susie's teenage sister, Lindsay, through whom Susie lives vicariously, also becomes endangered in her attempt to punish the killer.

In 2001, while enrolled in the MFA program at the University of California at Irvine, Sebold met and married Glen David Gold, author of *Carter Beats the Devil.* They live in Long Beach, California, where Sebold is working on a new novel.

NOVEL

The Lovely Bones: A Novel. Boston: Little, Brown, 2002.

SOURCES

Abbott, Charlotte. "How About Them Bones?" *Publishers Weekly,* 29 July 2002, pp. 22–24.

Barta-Moran, Ellie. Review of *Lucky, Booklist,* July 1999, p. 1,903.

Bouton, Katherine. "What Remains: A Debut Novel Chronicles the Aftermath of a Girl's Abduction and Murder," *The New York Times Book Review,* 14 July 2002, p. 14.

Continelli, Louise. "Victims' Advocate and Author Is Doomed to Live with the Nightmare of Being Raped," *Buffalo News,* 15 August 1999, p. C-2.

Crittenden, Yvonne. "Not So Lucky," *Toronto Sun* [Toronto, Canada], October 23, 1999.

Darby, Ann. "PW Talks with Alice Sebold," *Publishers Weekly,* 17 June 2002, p. 41.

Dunham, Janice. Review of *Lucky, Library Journal,* 15 June 1999, p. 92.

Dworkin, Andrea. "A Good Rape," *New Statesman,* 30 June 2003, pp. 51–52.

"Hollywood Break for Lynne's *Lovely Bones,*" *Sunday Herald* [Glasgow, Scotland], 10 February 2002. p. 11.

Kakutani, Michiko. "The Power of Love Leaps the Great Divide of Death," *New York Times,* 18 June 2002, p. E-1.

Levy, Lisa. "Newcomer of the Year: Alice Sebold," *Book,* January–February 2003, pp. 36–37.

Maryles, Daisy. "Lucky for Sebold," *Publishers Weekly,* 30 September 2002, p. 18.

McLellan, Dennis. "Memoir Frees Writer from Dark Days of Her Past," *Los Angeles Times,* 15 September 1999, p. 2.

Review of *The Lovely Bones: A Novel, Kirkus Review,* 1 May 2002, p. 608.

Sebold, Alice. *Lucky.* New York: Scribner, 1999.

OTHER

Baltasar, Michaela. "UCI MFA Graduate Says She Is *Lucky.*" *New University.* Available online. URL: http://newu.uci.edu/archive/1999-2000/fall/991025-q-991025-lucky.htm. Accessed February 12, 2006.

A Conversation with Aimee Bendor and Alice Sebold. Boldtype. Available online. URL: http://www.randomhouse.com. Accessed January 12, 2006.

Cue, Ehzra. "Award-Winning UCI Author Discusses Works." *New University.*" Available online. URL: http://www.newu.uci.edu/archive2000-2001/spring/010430/f-010430-alice.htm. Accessed January 12, 2005.

SEDGWICK, CATHARINE MARIA

(1789–1867) Once considered the equal of James Fenimore COOPER, William Bryant, Washington Irving, and Nathaniel HAWTHORNE, Catharine Maria Sedgwick was the author of the best-selling historical romance *HOPE LESLIE; OR, EARLY TIMES IN THE MASSACHUSETTS* (1827) and five other novels for adults. The success of *Hope Leslie,* as well as that of *Redwood* (1824), *Clarence; or, A Tale of Our Own Times* (1830), and *The Linwoods; or, "Sixty Years Since" in America* (1835) catapulted Sedgwick to early 19th-century literary stardom. Not until Harriet Beecher STOWE would the United States be home to such a popular author. In fact, she is credited with laying the groundwork for the sentimental tradition later made popular by Stowe, Maria Susana CUMMINS, and Susan WARNER. Although she dropped into obscurity during much of the 20th century, she has received renewed attention by feminist scholars and has been restored to her position as a significant founder of American literature.

Catharine Maria Sedgwick was born on December 28, 1789, in Stockbridge, Massachusetts, to Pamela Dwight Sedgwick, of a cultured and politically influential family, and Theodore Sedgwick, who became a member of the Continental Congress and Speaker of the newly formed House of Representatives. Sedgwick was educated at private schools and in the well-stocked library of her parents' home. Like her father and brothers, Sedgwick espoused what were then unorthodox religious views, joining the Unitarian Church and advocating Jacksonian democracy. One of the few women of her day who chose not to marry, Sedgwick began her distinguished literary career with *A New-England Tale; or, Sketches of New-England Character and Manners,* published anonymously in 1822. An instant best-seller on both sides of the Atlantic, the novel explores the life of the orphaned Jane Elton, mistreated by her Calvinist aunt and saved by her marriage to Mr. Lloyd, a Quaker. With the success of *Redwood,* her second novel, Sedgwick joined Cooper and Irving as arbiters of the national literature. This realistic novel explores societal hypocrisy; the hero, Ellen Bruce, whose parentage is questionable but whose moral and intellectual strengths are not, eventually wins over the Southerner, Mr. Redwood, who is actually her father. She meets and marries Charles Westall, Redwood's neighbor, who also doubts her. *Hope Leslie,* published under her own name and today considered her masterpiece, solidified Sedgwick's reputation as an internationally acclaimed author. The novel centers on Hope Leslie and her sister Faith, who has been captured by Pequot Indians. Like Cooper in *The LAST OF THE MOHICANS,* Sedgwick introduces the subject of miscegenation; Hope must accept Faith's love for, and marriage to, Oneco, brother of the princess Magawisca.

Sedgwick also wrote didactic domestic novels like *Home* (1835). Although not an activist, she founded the Society for the Aid and Relief of Poor Women and organized the first free school in New York, supported women's charities, and agreed with the abolitionists. In her final novel, *MARRIED OR SINGLE?* (1857), Sedgwick makes it clear that women need not depend on marriage for fulfillment. She died on July 31, 1867, in Roxbury, Massachusetts.

NOVELS

Clarence; or, A Tale of Our Own Times. 2 vols. Philadelphia: Carey & Lea, 1830.

Home. Boston and Cambridge, Mass.: Monroe, 1835.

Hope Leslie; or, Early Times in the Massachusetts. 2 vols. New York: White, Gallagher & White, 1827.

The Linwoods; or, "Sixty Years Since" in America. 2 vols. New York: Harper, 1835.

Live and Let Live; or, Domestic Service Illustrated. New York: Harper, 1837.

Married or Single? 2 vols, New York: Harper, 1857.

Mary Hollis: An Original Tale. (Anonymous). New York: New York Unitarian Book Society, 1822.

Means and Ends, or Self-Training. Boston: Marsh, Capen, Lyon & Webb, 1839.

A New-England Tale; or, Sketches of New-England Character and Manners. (Anonymous). New York: Bliss & White, 1822.

The Poor Rich Man and The Rich Poor Man. New York: Harper, 1836.

Redwood, A Tale. (Anonymous). 2 vols. New York: Bliss & White, 1824.

SOURCES

Baym, Nina. *Woman's Fiction: A Guide to Novels by and about Women in America, 1820–1870.* Second edition. Urbana, Ill.: University of Illinois Press, 1993.

Brooks, Gladys. *Three Wise Virgins.* New York: Dutton, 1957, pp. 53–63.

Castiglia, Christopher. "In Praise of Extra-Vagrant Women: *Hope Leslie* and the Captivity Romance," *Legacy* 6 (Fall 1989): 3–16.

Dewey, Mary E., ed. *Life and Letters of Miss Sedgwick.* New York: Harper, 1871.

Foster, Edward Halsey. *Catharine Maria Sedgwick.* Boston: Twayne, 1974.

Harris, Susan K. *19th-Century American Women's Novels: Interpretive Strategies.* New York: Cambridge University Press, 1990.

Holly, Carol. "Nineteenth-Century Autobiographies of Affiliation: The Case of Catharine Sedgwick and Lucy Larcom." In *American Autobiography: Retrospect and Prospect,* edited by Paul John Eakin, 216–234. Madison: University of Wisconsin Press, 1991.

Kalayjian, Patricia. "Revisioning America's Literary Past: Sedgwick's *Hope Leslie,*" *NWSA Journal* 8 (Fall 1996): 63–78.

Kelley, Mary. *Private Woman, Public Stage.* New York: Oxford University Press, 1984.

———. "Profile: Catharine Maria Sedgwick 1789–1867," *Legacy* 6 (Fall 1989): 43–50.

Nelson, Dana. "Sympathy as Strategy in Sedgwick's *Hope Leslie.*" In *The Culture of Sentiment: Race, Gender, and Sentimentality in Nineteenth-Century America,* edited by Shirley Samuels, 191–202. New York: Oxford University Press, 1992.

Singley, Carol J. "Catharine Maria Sedgwick's *Hope Leslie:* Radical Frontier Romance." In *Desert, Garden, Margin, Range,* edited by Eric Heyne, 110–122. New York: Twayne, 1992.

Zagarell, Sandra A. "Expanding 'America': Lydia Sigourney's *Sketch of Connecticut,* Catharine Sedgwick's *Hope Leslie,*" *Tulsa Studies in Women's Literature* 6 (Fall 1987): 225–245. Republished in *Redefining the Political Novel: American Women Writers, 1797–1901,* edited by Sharon M. Harris, 43–65. Knoxville, Tenn.: University of Tennessee Press, 1995.

SEIZE THE DAY SAUL BELLOW (1956)

BELLOW's novel (or more properly novella) *Seize the Day* may, at first glance, appear rather a slight tale. It is an account of just one day in the life of Tommy Wilhelm, 40-something and down on his luck, living at the Hotel Gloriana in New York's Upper West Side. However, this is a day of reckoning for Wilhelm in which, at the instigation of his friend, the enigmatic Dr. Tamkin, he takes a gamble in speculating in the commodities market and ends up losing all. And this is just one more failure in a catalogue of failures in his life, all mercilessly exposed in the course of the narrative. We see, for instance, his wholly unsatisfying relationship with his father—a retired doctor whose material success he has never had any hope of emulating—as they meet and talk at the breakfast table in the hotel; and the even more acerbic relationship with his estranged wife Margaret, in a later phone conversation. On top of his family troubles, we learn that he has also signally failed at the business of making a career (having once pursued a futile dream of making it big in Hollywood). And as well as giving a picture of his unsympathetic environment, the novel also reveals, through Wilhelm's interior monologues, the full extent of his confusions, frustrations, and disappointments.

In his depiction of a character succumbing to all manner of inimical social and economic pressures, and further tormented by his own inadequacies and unfulfilled longings, Bellow is undoubtedly influenced by his studies in anthropology and sociology, and is also, of course, engaging with a familiar theme of modern literature: the alienation of the individual, particularly in the modern urban jungle amid the wilderness of streets and the indifference of crowds. Wilhelm, although he entertains vague notions of starting anew elsewhere with his girlfriend Olive, is trapped in the city and indeed literally suffocating in its noxious air. Dealing with such concerns as these, *Seize the Day* may appear to be in the mold of Bellow's first two novels with such self-consciously grim titles as *Dangling Man* and *The Victim* (and unlike, for example, the later 1950s novel *Henderson the Rain King*, with its colorful locations and exotic peregrinations of the hero). However, it is sharply distinguished by its extraordinary tone. It eschews the somber approach of the earlier works and although in the main it employs lucid naturalistic prose, it also retains some of the exuberance of Bellow's third novel, *The Adventures of Augie March* (1953), and adds further distinctive and memorable touches. These range from the grotesque (the physical descriptions of Tamkin and the decrepits Mr. Perls and Mr. Rappaport) and the surreal (the food served in the Hotel Gloriana, where salads appear like Mexican architecture) to the poetic (Wilhelm's apocalyptic vision of his own state as "the ruins of life [. . .] chaos, and old night" [93]). All these elements combine to produce a brilliantly sustained and incisive commentary on Wilhelm's condition.

The use of such different modes is perhaps symptomatic of the essential duality that lies at the heart of the narrative, the pervasive sense of what Tamkin calls "the human tragedy-comedy" (72). The comic elements are rife in the portrayal of Wilhelm, in the way other people (especially his disapproving father) perceive him and also in the comic view he has of himself as a kind of lumbering hippopotamus. Moreover, his whole life appears to be an ongoing farce; he continually does things he would rather not do, or knows to be unwise—like getting involved with Tamkin's moneymaking schemes. This aspect of his life is neatly encapsulated in the image of him as a golden haired, "impressively handsome" warrior-type figure who picks up a weapon only to strike himself with it (17). Thus the heroic strain here changes, abruptly, into pure slapstick.

But there is also another side. Wilhelm may be ungainly and awkward but he is still a charmer; he may be heedless, lacking in diligence and direction, but he is also good-natured, affectionate, and not altogether stupid. And his pleas for help and understanding go ignored by his father, his wife, and the world at large. This is part of what Tamkin identifies as the overriding tragedy of human life: the subjugation of the individual by others, by society, the stifling of the true soul by the "pretender" soul that acts in accordance with "the society mechanism" (70). It is, in fact, an intolerable situation for which there can perhaps be only one solution: the cessation of life itself. Wilhelm's final release in a flood of tears takes place, we recall, in the presence of death (although some critics, in view of the associated water imagery, have chosen to interpret this as a symbolic rebirth).

However, Tamkin's sobering vision of human social life as tragic repression does not prevail for long: In fact, even as he's speaking, he begins to look "untrustworthy" to Wilhelm (72), and the reader is similarly thrown into doubt as to the validity of Tamkin's observations. This kind of sliding perspective is a recurrent feature of the text, producing a certain destabilizing effect that continually unsettles the reader. This is in spite of the fact that it does ostensibly appear to be quite a conventional type of novel, which has little in common with self-avowed modernist and "difficult" works (such as those of the early FAULKNER). It may be informed by a modernist sensibility that life is fragmentary, chaotic, and perhaps ultimately meaningless, so that in the absence of coherence, of a greater plan, of any long-term worthwhile purpose, one might as well take Tamkin's advice and live for the moment, "seize the day." However, although dealing with such a disorderly subject as modern urban life—and Wilhelm's life in particular—it imposes a certain shape on that disorder by establishing a clear setting and time structure (the course of a single day) and tending inexorably toward a definite end (the close of that one day).

Seize the Day is, on the face of it, a relatively straightforward novel. Taking a closer look, however, one is struck by its elusive nature. It resists easy definitions, refuses to pass judgments, and provides no answers. In the end, we are left with some intriguing questions. Is Wilhelm a pathetic Everyman for his times, or a hapless individual inviting ridicule? Are people (especially those in the big, modern cities) a set of selfish, grabbing mercenary caricatures, or is there, as Wilhelm suspects in a moment of fellow-feeling, some nobler "Truth" (85) to be glimpsed about the human race? Is life, finally, a comedy or a tragedy? Perhaps the most one can say is that it is both, and the tightly woven intricacies of Bellow's narrative would appear to suggest that it is inadvisable to try and extricate one from the other, to separate what is, in fact, inseparable.

SOURCES

Atlas, James. *Bellow: A Biography*. New York: Random House, 2000.

Bach, Gerhard, and Gloria L. Cronin, eds. *Small Planets: Saul Bellow and the Art of Short Fiction*. East Lansing: Michigan State University Press, 2000.

Bellow, Saul. *Seize the Day*. New York: Viking, 1956. Reprint, New York: Viking Penguin, 1996.

Kramer, Michael P., ed. *New Essays on Seize the Day*. Cambridge: Cambridge University Press, 1998.

Rovit Earl, ed. *Saul Bellow: A Collection of Critical Essays*. Englewood Cliffs, N.J.: Prentice, 1975.

Gurdip Kaur Panesar

SELBY, HUBERT, JR. (1928–2004)

Hubert Selby wrote *Last Exit to Brooklyn* (1964), a novel composed of linked stories that include, in graphic detail, a world of pimps, prostitutes, drag queens, rapists, drug dealers and users, and thugs. When the novel appeared, reviewers in the United States, while finding it shocking, also found more to praise than did the critics in England, where it was the subject of an obscenity trial, or Italy, where it was banned. He is frequently compared with James T. FARRELL, who wrote about Chicago, and reminds contemporary readers of Richard PRICE, who writes now about the slums of New Jersey. Reviewers of his work use adjectives like *monstrous, grotesque,* and *horrific,* but they also note that his work is powerful, realistic, and plausible. Selby wrote four additional novels, two screenplays, and numerous uncollected short stories.

Hubert Selby, Jr., was born on July 23, 1928, in Brooklyn, New York, to Hubert Selby, an engineer and apartment building manager, and Adalin Layne Selby. After one year at Peter Stuyvesant High School, Selby joined the Merchant Marine but was discharged with a severe case of tuberculosis. At various points in his life, Selby was addicted to alcohol and heroin, but he overcame both. He married three times: to Inez Taylor, from 1953 to 1960; to Judith Lumino in 1964; and Suzanne Shaw in 1969.

Last Exit is most frequently described as an unrelenting and compelling journey into hell; the novel describes the mindless, vicious, lustful behavior of its violent, often drug-crazed streetgang characters. Frequently cited as a metaphor for the entire novel—and for contemporary society—is the gang rape of the character Tralala. The novel filmed by Bernd Eichinger and Uli Edel in 1988.

Selby's second novel, *The Room* (1971), received very good reviews: Every act of its unnamed protagonist is described in sickening detail. As he sits in a jail cell for an unspecified crime, seeking vengeance against the police and reform of the judicial system, he is torn between guilt and denial of his crimes. In *The Demon* (1976), Harry White, a business executive consumed by his sexuality and his obsessive urge to steal and kill, murders a Roman Catholic cardinal and then commits suicide. Often compared with Nelson ALGREN's *The MAN WITH THE GOLDEN ARM,* Selby's *Requiem for a Dream* (1978) has four protagonists—Harry Goldfarb, his girlfriend Marion, Tyrone C. Love, and Harry's mother Sara Goldfarb—three of whom are heroin addicts; Sara is addicted to television and diet pills. Drugs also have a permanent place in organized crime and in the police force. (It was made into a film by Darren Aronofsky and Selby in 1998.)

In 1998, Selby published *The Willow Tree* about Moishe, a Nazi death camp survivor; Bobby, an African-American teenager; and his Chicana girlfriend, Maria. She is disfigured by a gang, and Bobby wreaks vengeance against individual gang members. Selby's last novel, *Waiting Period,* appeared in 2002; the nameless protagonist is saved from suicide by the Internet and its lure of cybercrime. There he finds instructions on making the *E. coli* virus and bombs. Hubert Selby, Jr., who since the 1990s has increasingly been seen as one of the century's most original writers, died on April 16, 2004, of chronic pulmonary disease.

NOVELS

The Demon. New York: Playboy Press, 1976; London: Marion Boyars, 1977.

Last Exit to Brooklyn. New York: Grove, 1964; London: Calder & Boyars, 1966.

Requiem for a Dream. New York: Playboy Press, 1978; London: Marion Boyars, 1979.

The Room. New York: Grove, 1971; London: Calder & Boyars, 1972.

Waiting Period. New York: Marion Boyars, 2002.

The Willow Tree: A Novel. New York and London: Marion Boyars, 1998.

SOURCES

Atchity, Kenneth John. "Hubert Selby's *Requiem for a Dream:* A Primer," *Review of Contemporary Fiction* 1 (1981): 399–405.

Buckeye, Robert. "Some Preliminary Notes Towards a Study of Selby," *Review of Contemporary Fiction* 1 (1981): 374–375.

Byrne, Jack. "Selby's Yahoos: The Brooklyn Breed, A Dialogue of the Mind with Itself," *Review of Contemporary Fiction* 1 (1981): 349–353.

Gehr, Richard. *"Last Exit to Brooklyn,"* *American Film* 15 (May 1990): 34–39, 48.

Giles, James R. *Understanding Hubert Selby, Jr.* Columbia: University of South Carolina Press, 1997.

Kermode, Frank. " 'Obscenity' and the 'Public Interest,' " *New American Review* 3 (April 1968): 229–244.

King, John. "Human Punk," *New Statesman* 131, no. 4589 (May 27, 2002): 51–52.

Metcalf, Paul. "Herman and Hubert: The Odd Couple," *Review of Contemporary Fiction* 1 (1981): 364–369.

Mottram, Eric. "Free Like the Rest of Us: Violation and Despair in Hubert Selby's Novels," *Review of Contemporary Fiction* 1 (1981): 353–363.

O'Brien, John. "The Materials of Art in Hubert Selby," *Review of Contemporary Fiction* 1 (1981): 376–379.

Stephen, Michael. "Hubert Selby, Jr.: The Poet of Prose Masters," *Review of Contemporary Fiction* 1 (1981): 389–397.

Tanner, Tony. "On the Parapet." In his *City of Words: American Fiction, 1950–1970,* 344–371. New York: Harper & Row, 1971.

Tindall, Kenneth. "The Fishing at Coney Island: Hubert Selby, Jr. and the Cult of Authenticity," *Review of Contemporary Fiction* 1 (1981): 370–373.

Wertime, Richard A. "On the Question of Style in Hubert Selby, Jr.'s Fiction," *Review of Contemporary Fiction* 1 (1981): 406–413.

———. "Psychic Vengeance in *Last Exit to Brooklyn,*" *Literature and Psychology* 24 (November 4, 1974): 153–166.

SENT FOR YOU YESTERDAY JOHN EDGAR WIDEMAN (1983)

The black neighborhoods of Pittsburgh, Pennsylvania, form the backdrop for many of John Edgar WIDEMAN's novels as well as much of the author's life. Wideman was born in Washington, D.C., but grew up in Pittsburgh, and then earned a bachelor of arts degree in English from the University of Pennsylvania and a bachelor of philosophy degree at Oxford University. He has written numerous essays, short stories, and novels. *Sent for You Yesterday,* the third novel of the Homewood trilogy, won the P.E.N./Faulkner Award in 1984 as the best work of fiction published the previous year.

Sent for You Yesterday opens with a nightmare about being trapped in a boxcar with other people who disappear if they scream. This dream sets the stage for a silence that speaks volumes throughout the rest of the novel. Only well into the story does the reader discover that Doot, who is not even born for much of the action, narrates the novel. Doot describes three generations of his family: the generation of his grandparents, Freeda and John French, and Albert Wilkes; the generation of his uncle, Carl, Lucy, and Brother Tate; and his own generation. Doot's storytelling begins with the reappearance of Albert Wilkes, John's good friend. Renowned for his ability to play the piano, Wilkes barely escapes the law after officers discover a murdered white man and make him the prime suspect. His return means that trouble has also returned to Cassina Way and the black neighborhood of Homewood, for Wilkes had never been cleared of the crime. When he stops by late one night to see John, Freeda becomes fearful and sends Carl to find his father the next morning. Freeda is not happy that John vows to help his longtime friend even if he faces sure annihilation.

No sooner than Wilkes arrives in Homewood does an anonymous tip lead the police to Wilkes. He dies in a shootout. Doot then switches gears and sketches the adolescent and adult exploits of Carl French and Lucy and Brother Tate, Carl's best friend, who is distinguished by his albinism and refusal to talk. Although Lucy and Brother Tate are not blood relatives, they act as brother and sister after Mrs. Tate takes him into her family. Doot chronicles the growing romance between Carl and Lucy and the friendship between Carl and

Brother Tate. He also tells the story of Brother Tate and Samantha, the mother of Junebug, his only child. Known for having a multitude of children, Samantha goes insane as a result of Junebug's death, which may have been caused by her other children, frightened by the albinism he inherits from his father.

Doot ends his recitation by focusing on Brother Tate, his reactions to the return of Albert Wilkes, his relationship with Samantha and the subsequent death of Junebug, and Carl's return from the war and his mysterious death on the railroad tracks. The novel ends with Doot, Carl, and Lucy back in the Tate's house reminiscing about Doot's first dance to the song "Sent for You Yesterday."

In this novel, Wideman uses a black postmodernist voice, which creates fictions about the past that retain a loyalty to the black tradition. The fragmented plotline deviates from standard literary convention. Doot narrates events that take place before he is born, and the reader hears about events out of order. Doot's voice is sometimes rendered in the first person, other times as the omniscient narrator. Because of the disjointed storyline, the stories that Doot tells become the organizing principle of the novel. Rather than cause and effect, it is Doot's associations in his memory that drive the narrative. He sees the characters in relation to each other, so that no one person has his or her own story. All stories are bound up in the stories of others. Instead of experience and blood to link the generations, oral forms like stories and music act as a bridge between generations. Carl tells Doot stories, and Wideman notes in the novel that stories are timeless in the neighborhood of Homewood and Cassina Way. Unlike single stories that focus on one person, the stories surrounding Cassina Way make sense only when put in dialogue with the experiences of other individuals. For this reason, Lucy cannot tell Junebug's story without telling Samantha's. Likewise, Carl needs Lucy to affirm his own story.

Doot's stories reveal erosion from one generation to the next, an erosion that parallels the debilitating standard of life enjoyed by African Americans. John and Freeda are trailblazers with a purposeful belief in themselves that allows them to forge a life for their children. Albert Wilkes represents danger, but it is a danger that Freeda attempts to divert from her family. In contrast, Carl fails to believe in himself and his ability to endure the life presented to him. Carl and Lucy fail to have children, and they engage in self-destructive behavior. They all suffer the ravages of drug addiction. They miss opportunities to improve their lives. Carl has some artistic talent but allows racially motivated negative criticism to discourage him. Wideman suggests that they have a responsibility to endure for the sake of the next generation, just as the generation before them had done.

Death is a motif that weaves its way throughout the novel, and its effect increases for members of successive generations who fail to cope with life's struggle. Albert Wilkes, whose piano playing is marveled at by all, meets a violent end at the hands of the police. Samantha is driven insane when her other children quite possibly kill their brother, Junebug, because he was born an albino. But death can also been seen as a precursor to rebirth. While the death of Junebug affects Brother profoundly because it represents interracial violence, he transforms the experience by linking it to a version of the middle passage that connects two continents rather than epitomizes the violent separation of the diaspora. He sings to Junebug to save his own life.

Both Brother's reinterpretation of past events, and Doot's stories, demonstrate the fluid nature of the past. As the narrator, Doot acts as a creator of a usable past employing material that has been handed down to him. This past is not a static entity. It changes based on the individual's point of view. The multiple versions of past events problematize the past, bringing to our attention the ways in which memory depends on perspective. In this way, the past fails to be an objective accounting.

Dreams also undermine reality and the notion of a stable past. Wideman suggests that at times, dreams are indistinguishable from reality. They allow others to experience the lives of other characters. Brother dreams he is Albert Wilkes. Samantha dreams she is Junebug. Both come away with a sense of the perspective of the person of whom they dream. Dreams can also be the manifestation of unconscious fears. Doot's narrative begins not with his birth but with a dream that Brother has about himself after he has died.

In addition to stories, music plays a significant role in the novel. It figures into all the major events. Music may very well be necessary to tell the stories of Cassina Way. It functions as a metaphor for life in Homewood, for everyone has some kind of relationship with it. Music also functions as a unifying motif in the novel, for through music, characters make sense of their lives. They use music to grapple with events so traumatic that they cannot articulate their feelings. When Albert returns to town, Freeda turns to music to express her fear.

In addition to the stories and music, Brother Tate also forms a connective thread throughout the novel. Brother provides a sustained interrogation of the concept of color, a concept that profoundly affects the lives of the black characters. Brother is an albino, an individual without pigment. This lack of color throws into chaos the preconceptions about the value of skin color. African Americans have historically been classified and have classified themselves by color. Color has served as a divisive entity as well as one that forms the basis of community, for segregation by color forged close-knit black communities. Brother is culturally black, but visually he is ambiguous. Doot often describes Brother as the shadow of Carl: always with him, yet not completely solid. Freeda describes Brother as a ghost. This description signifies a paradox: Because one can see it, a ghost implies presence and absence as a reminder of a departed individual.

Brother's ambiguity also translates into the ways that others see Brother. Wideman suggests that he acts as a mirror and that people project onto Brother their own notions of what he should be. Further underscoring this ambiguity is Brother's refusal to speak after the death of his son. While he communicates using sounds that approximate music, Brother's silence also speaks volumes because, like language, it too can be interpreted.

Brother's lack of color also imbues him with a degree of agency, the ability to act independently, for he is not constrained by expectations based on his color. He can be who he wants to be and becomes a multitalented person as a result of that kind of freedom. Before Albert Wilkes dies, he dreams he is Wilkes and receives his music, and apparently musical talent, after he dies.

While Brother evokes ambiguity around the idea of color, Freeda French, Doot's mother, has attitudes toward color that are unmistakable. Wideman describes Freeda as color struck because she assigns negative characteristics to the black migrant workers based solely on their color. As a light-skinned woman, she may have internalized the color prejudice of whites that can be traced back to slavery. While she prefers her own light hue, she is taken aback by Brother's lack of color because she organizes her world according to color. She cannot place him and is unnerved by the ambiguity he represents.

The novel complicates the notion of family as well as color. Wideman challenges the notion of nuclear families by creating strong extended families in the form of the relationships among Carl, Brother Tate, and Lucy. None of them is related, but both Brother and Lucy and Carl and Brother function as siblings. Wideman raises the bonds between men to the level of family in the loyalty that John has for Albert Wilkes, even when his life is in imminent danger. The relationship between John French and Albert Wilkes parallels that of Carl and Brother, in that they are friends to the end.

Wideman, moreover, revises the negative interpretation of single black women with large families. Rather than failing to care about the ramifications of having so many children, Samantha, a woman who attended some college, has children to strengthen the black race. He transforms the medical description of color and melanin into a story about the ancestral and noble purpose of black people. Choosing only the darkest men to father her children, she envisions her home as an ark that serves as a bulwark against the extinction of African Americans.

Although a complex novel, *Sent for You Yesterday* represents transformative ways of constructing fictions of the past. It is perhaps the best postmodern fictional depiction of the meaning of the past, along with suggestions for creating an optimistic future.

SOURCES

Bennion, John. "The Shape of Memory in John Edgar Wideman's *Sent For You Yesterday*," *Black American Literature Forum* 20, nos. 1&2 (1986): 143–150.

Coleman, James W. *"Sent for You Yesterday:* The Intellectual Voice and the Movement toward Postmodernism." In

Blackness and Modernism: The Literary Career of John Edgar Wideman. Jackson and London: University Press of Mississippi, 1989, pp. 97–114.

Grandjeat, Yves-Charles. "Brother Figures: The Rift and Riff in John E. Wideman's Fiction," *Callaloo* 22, no. 3 (1999): 615–622.

Wideman, John Edgar. *Sent for You Yesterday.* Boston: Houghton Mifflin, 1983.

Crystal Anderson

SEPARATE PEACE, A John Knowles (1960)

An immediate critical and financial success after its publication (in London, 1959, and New York, 1960) and winner of the William Faulkner Foundation Award, *A Separate Peace* continues to mesmerize readers as the timeless tale of a boy's initiation into the hostile, often ugly, world of adult reality. This enduring bildungsroman has been compared to such classics as Charles Dickens's *Great Expectations,* Mark Twain's *The Adventures of Huckleberry Finn,* and J. D. Salinger's *The Catcher in the Rye.*

Through an artistic manipulation of character, setting, and both mythic and Christian symbol, John Knowles moves his novel's young characters from the tranquil summer of adolescence at the Devon School into the violent winter of maturity and World War II. The loss of innocence experienced by Eugene (Gene) Forrester, the central character and narrator, so preoccupies him that he revisits the school 15 years after graduating to confront his memories of Phineas ("Finny"), the innocent friend who dies as an indirect result of Gene's envy, love, and betrayal. A majority of critics agree that, by facing the darkness of the human heart, Gene increases his understanding of his own moral complexity and of the greater love and purity that Finny embodied. Readers need to be wary, however, of oversimplifying the battle of good and evil: As critic Paul Witherington notes, "The world of *A Separate Peace* is not the world of Hawthorne but the inverted, shifting mythos of Kafka" with its "ambiguous moral atmosphere" (796).

The novel—expanded from "Phineas," Knowles's short story published in *Cosmopolitan* in May 1956—opens as Gene returns to New England and narrates the events that took place during the summer of 1942,

when he and Finny, his roommate and best friend, along with Brinker Hadley, Elwin "Leper" Lepellier, and other boys, attended Devon, a private New Hampshire boarding school under the looming shadow of World War II. The narrator describes the school in Edenic terms, calling it "the tame fringe of the last and greatest wilderness" (23), that is, adulthood. Somewhat as in *Tom Brown's Schooldays* and other boys' school novels, the school functions as a microcosm of the real world and immerses the students in situations that force confrontation with relationships, jealousies, hostilities, politics, and discipline. Most critics, though, view Knowles's presentation of the school world as an idyllic summer session that cools and hardens into the winter of the boys' final year as they approach the exigencies of a world at war.

One of the most intellectual students and a candidate for valedictorian of his class, Gene struggles with his feelings for Finny, an outstanding athlete, whom he both adores and envies. Finny is a vibrant, honest, likable boy who easily attracts friends and demonstrates repeatedly his philosophy of noncompetitiveness. Just as Finny advocates sports in which people play their best without winning, losing, or keeping score, he ascribes kindly attitudes and motives to all with whom he interacts. Finny, however, is no angel. He consciously flaunts the rules of the school, urging Gene and others to do likewise. He plays poker, wears the school tie as a belt, and skips classes. Finny is natural and uncompetitive and benevolent; he is also naive and irresponsible, and he denies that the war exists. Finny's view of history is singular: He views the roaring 1920s as a time "when they all drank bathtub gin and everybody who was young did just what they wanted," until they were stopped by "the preachers and the old ladies and all the stuffed shirts." According to Finny, when Prohibition failed, those same stuffed shirts invented the Depression for "the people who were young in the thirties," and when they found "they couldn't use that trick forever," they "cooked up this war fake" for the 1940s (100–101).

Gene has trouble believing that Finny is as good as he appears, and, as his jealousy and doubt evolve, he decides that Finny is trying to prevent him from excelling in his studies. During the summer session, one of the pivotal scenes in the novel occurs when Gene and Finny form the Super Suicide Society of the Summer Session. The society requires that each boy drop into the water from the branches of a tree that overhangs the Devon River. They do so successfully a number of times, but then, in a dark moment, Gene bounces the tree limb (whether consciously or unconsciously is never clear) and causes Finny to fall from the tree and break his leg, thereby crippling him and rendering him unfit for the athletics that he loved. Too late, Gene realizes that Finny was proud of Gene's academic accomplishments and that the resentment Gene sensed in Finny was utterly within his own heart. Nonetheless, when the boys return to school for their senior year, Gene devotes himself to Finny and, at Finny's suggestion, begins athletic training for the 1944 Olympics. As many critics note, at some level Gene wants to become Finny, not just with regard to sports, but with regard to his very identity. In a much-discussed scene, Gene dons Finny's clothing and stands before a mirror feeling an odd peace descend upon him. Finny, repeatedly described in terms of Greek gods and heroes, has become an object of devotion for Gene.

Gene, who plans to enlist but then changes his mind after Finny recovers and returns to school, understands that his friend could never be a soldier. Indeed, the boys' differing attitudes to the war may be viewed as measuring sticks of their personal philosophies: Finny, the talented athlete, sees the war as artificial and irrelevant; for him, real life occurs on the playing fields. Ironically, he thumbs his nose at the British notion—supposedly derived from a comment by the Duke of Wellington—that the battle of Waterloo was "won on the playing fields of Eton." To Finny, the whole world is on the playing fields of Devon, but as Gene points out to him, Finny would make a very poor soldier because he lacks understanding of even the most basic concept of human hostility. "They'd get you some place at the front and there'd be a lull in the fighting, and the next thing anyone knew you'd be over with the Germans or the Japs, asking if they'd like to field a baseball team against our side. . . . You'd make a mess, a terrible mess Finny, out of the war (173). Unlike Finny, Gene realizes that "wars were not made by generations and their special stupidities, but that wars were made instead by something ignorant in the human heart" (193). Because he is less good and also less naive than his friend, Gene is able to appreciate "this liberation we had torn from the gray encroachments of 1943, the escape we had concocted, this afternoon of momentary, illusory, special and separate peace" (128).

That peace must come to an end. Leper, the only student to enlist, goes mad during boot camp, when, in critic Ian Kennedy's words, he "meets the inverted disorder that is war" (357). Brinker, the conservative foil to Finny, insists on holding a kangaroo court—with Leper as his chief witness—to determine Gene's role in Finny's fall from the tree. Finny, who characteristically wanted no part of this inquisition, becomes so upset that he rushes from the mock trial room and falls once again, this time on the school stairs. He lingers a little while before dying of complications from this final fall. No wonder that the mature Gene sees that the war for him was a personal, private, internal one: "my war ended before I ever put on a uniform; I was on active duty all my time at school; I killed my enemy there" (196).

Although a majority of critics and readers agree with Ronald Weber that, at novel's end, "Gene's is a voice looking back on adolescence after the hard passage to maturity has been won" (Weber 70), some argue that Gene's is the voice of an unreliable narrator and so his information, even his presentation of Finny, is suspect. Kennedy suggests that Gene has two voices: that of the immature, unreliable Devon student, and that of the reliable man who has attained a hard-won maturity (352, 359). Additionally, although most critics find Finny an embodiment of goodness and innocence ("When you really love something, then it loves you back," he tells Gene [136]), others find character flaws in him as well as in Gene. Witherington, for example, sees "Finny's effort to entice Gene from his studies" to be just "as conscious as Gene's movement of the tree limb causing Finny's fall" (797). And for some, Finny's death suggests that his carefree and self-absorbed attitude, while charming, is not enough to weather the sometimes sinister realities of adulthood, so he dies before being plunged into adult reality.

The novel continues to be reissued and studied by new generations of readers and critics. *A Separate Peace* was issued as a feature length film in 1972.

SOURCES

Bryant, Hallman Bell. *A Separate Peace: The War Within.* Boston: Twayne, 1990.

Ellis, James. "A Separate Peace: The Fall from Innocence," *English Journal* 53 (May 1964): 313–318.

Halio, Jay L. "John Knowles's Short Novels," *Studies in Short Fiction* 1 (Winter 1964): 107–112.

Holborn, David G. "A Rationale for Reading John Knowles' *A Separate Peace.*" In *Censored Books: Critical Viewpoints,* edited by Nicholas J. Karolides, Lee Burress, and John M. Kean, 456–463. Metuchen, N.J.: The Scarecrow Press, Inc., 1993.

Karson, Jill, ed. *Readings on A Separate Peace.* San Diego, Calif.: Greenhaven Press, 1999.

Kennedy, Ian. "Dual Perspective Narrative and the Character of Phineas in *A Separate Peace,*" *Studies in Short Fiction* 11, no. 4 (Fall 1974): 353–359.

Knowles, John. *A Separate Peace.* New York: Dell Publishing Company, Inc., 1961.

———. *A Separate Peace.* Edited by Harold Bloom. Philadelphia, Pa.: Chelsea House, 1999.

Slethang, Gordon E. "The Play of the Double in *A Separate Peace,*" *Canadian Review of American Studies* 15 (1984): 259–270.

Weber, Ronald. "Narrative Method in *A Separate Peace,*" *Studies in Short Fiction* 3, no. 1 (Fall 1965): 63–72.

Witherington, Paul. "A Separate Peace: A Study in Structural Ambiguity," *English Journal* 54, no. 9 (December 1965): 795–800.

SETTLE, MARY LEE (1918–2005)

Mary Lee Settle won the National Book Award for *Blood Tie* (1977), set on the Turkish island of Caramos, and wrote 15 additional novels; six books of nonfiction; several short stories, essays, reviews; and 10 unpublished plays and film scripts. She also invented the town of Canona (the fictional equivalent of Charleston, West Virginia), but her major achievement remains the five-novel sequence known as the Beulah Quintet: *O Beulah Land* (1956), *Know Nothing* (1960), *Prisons* (1973), *The Scapegoat* (1980), and *The Killing Ground* (1982). This 28-year project produced serious historical fiction that traced three families from the 1660s English Civil War to West Virginia in the 1960s. Although her settings and themes are varied, the "prevailing theme," according to scholar Nancy Carol Joyner, is "the struggle for freedom," whether for the individual, the family, or the larger social unit (Joyner 1993, 395).

Mary Lee Settle was born on July 29, 1918, in Charleston to Joseph Edward Settle, a civil engineer and owner of coal mines, and Rachel Tompkins Settle. The family moved to Kentucky, then to Florida, before returning to West Virginia. After spending two years at Sweet Briar College, Settle moved in 1938 to New York City, where the following year she married Rodney Weathersbee, an Englishman and the first of three husbands. In 1946 Settle divorced Weathersbee and married Douglas Newton, whom she divorced in 1956; 22 years later she married William Littleton Tazewell, a columnist and historian. When her husband enlisted in the Canadian army during World War II, Settle joined the British Women's Auxiliary Air Force, the subject of her 1966 autobiography, *All the Brave Promises: Memoirs of Aircraft Woman 2nd Class 2146391.* In 1954 she published *The Love Eaters* and *The Kiss of Kin* (1955) to very positive reviews; both novels are set in West Virginia. *The Love Eaters,* intended as a contemporary Phaedra, features Hamilton Sacks, a crippled director of the play at the center of the novel, and ends tragically, with the death of the decadent young Selby. *The Kiss of Kin* tells the tale of the deceased matriarch Aunt Mary Passmore. The family gathers to hear the reading of her last testament.

In 1954 Settle began work on the Beulah Quintet. Although not published in this order, *Prisons* is the first chronologically, introducing young Johnnie Church, executed as a traitor by General Oliver Cromwell's troops; his illegitimate child Lacy, along with other characters in the novel, will reach the Virginia Territory; their descendants will migrate to Canona to form the nucleus of the remaining four novels. The fictional families—the Catletts, Laceys, Kreggs, McKarkles, and Crawfords—are juxtaposed against historical figures like Cromwell, General Braddock, and Mother Jones. *O Beulah Land,* set during the Indian Wars until the beginning of the American Revolution, continues as the characters move into the West Virginia mountains. Hannah, a pickpocket and prostitute who is the ancestor of the Catletts, is a victim of an Indian attack; Sally attempts to maintain a semblance of Virginia gentility. *Know Nothing* traces 30 years of history ending on the eve of the Civil War. Here Settle uses characters to exemplify attitudes about slavery; Jonathan Catlett becomes a Confederate Army captain, while his brother Lewis is an abolitionist. Settle introduces black characters who share some ancestors with the white Catletts. In Settle's suspenseful novel *The Scapegoat,* all strands of the plot are aimed toward the 1912 coal strike as the mine is sold to an eastern corporation; Mother Jones appears and gives support to the miners. The "old" Canona families remain prejudiced against the newly arrived Italians. Finally, in *The Killing Ground,* the violence of World War I eclipses any of the violence experienced in earlier novels; Lily Lacey, for instance, goes to France as a nurse and witnesses the horror of the 1915 Battle of the Somme. Settle also attempted to encompass the events of *Fight Night on a Sweet Saturday,* an earlier novel that her publishers cut drastically; there, Hannah McKarkle, namesake of the ancestor in *O Beulah Land,* returns to West Virginia from New York in time to witness her brother Johnnie's murder in a brawl and to discover ironic connections between white Catletts and black Laceys.

The Clam Shell (1971) is based on Settle's two years at Sweetbriar College. *Blood Tie* focuses on seven expatriates in Turkey whose efforts to rebuild their lives are frustrated by the repressive political events they experience; Settle's technique of multiple narration gives scope and voice to a wide spectrum of characters. *Charley Bland* (1989), whose protagonist commits suicide in *The Killing Ground,* is revealed through the perspective of a woman with whom he had an unhappy love affair. Settle's most recent novels include *Choices* (1995), about Melinda Kregg Dunstan of Kentucky and the Spanish Civil War, England during Hitler's World War II blitzkrieg, and Mississippi during the 1960s Civil Rights movement. *I, Roger Williams* (2001) re-creates Roger Williams's youth in England, his voyage from London to Massachusetts, his friendship with the Indians, and his founding of Rhode Island.

Mary Lee Settle's last work was a nonfiction travel book, *Spanish Recognitions: The Roads to the Present* (2004). Only in the last decade and a half, beginning with the Mary Lee Settle conference in 1990, did she start to receive the attention that her considerable talents and achievements deserved. Just before her death from lung cancer on September 27, 2005, at a hospice in Charlottesville, Virginia, Mary Lee Settle had been working on a fictionalized account of Thomas Jefferson's youth.

NOVELS

Addie: A Memoir. Columbia: University of South Carolina Press, 1998.

Blood Tie. Boston: Houghton, 1977.

Celebration. New York: Farrar, Straus, 1986.

Charley Bland. New York: Farrar, Straus, 1989.

Choices. Rockland, Mass.: Wheeler Publishing, 1995.

The Clam Shell. New York: Delacorte, 1971.

Fight Night on a Sweet Saturday. New York: Viking, 1964.

I, Roger Williams: A Fragment Autobiography. New York: Norton, 2001.

The Killing Ground. New York: Farrar, Straus, 1982.

The Kiss of Kin. New York: Harper, 1955.

Know Nothing. New York: Viking, 1960.

The Love Eaters. New York: Harper, 1954.

O Beulah Land. New York: Viking, 1956.

Prisons. New York: Putnam, 1973; published in England as *The Long Road to Paradise.* London: Constable, 1974.

The Scapegoat. New York: Random House, 1980.

The Search for Beulah Land. New York: Scribner, 1988.

SOURCES

Brown, Laurie L. "Interviews with Seven Contemporary Writers." In *Women Writers of the Contemporary South,* edited by Peggy Whitman Prenshaw, 3–22. Jackson: University of Mississippi Press, 1984.

Garrett, George. *Understanding Mary Lee Settle.* Columbia: University of South Carolina Press, 1988.

Gates, Anita. "Mary Lee Settle, 87, Author of 'Beulah' Novels, Is Dead." *New York Times,* 29 September 2005, Section B, p. 9.

Hooper, Brad. Review of *Choices, Booklist* 91, no. 16 (April 15, 1995): 1,481.

Joyner, Nancy Carol. "The Beulah Quintet: The Feral Edge of What Has Made Us," *Now and Then* 4 (1987): 44.

———. "Mary Lee Settle." In *Contemporary Fiction Writers of the South: A Bio-bibliographical Sourcebook,* edited by Joseph M. Flora and Robert Bain. Westport, Conn.: Greenwood Press, 1993.

———. "Mary Lee Settle's Connections: Class and Clothes in the Beulah Quintet." In *Women Writers of the Contempo-*

rary South, edited by Peggy Whitman Prenshaw, 165–178. Jackson: University of Mississippi Press, 1984.

Quinn, Mary Ellen. Review of *I, Roger Williams, Booklist* 97, no. 15 (April 1, 2001): 1,454.

Review of *Addie: A Memoir, Publishers Weekly* 245, no. 36 (September 7, 1998): 74.

Rosenberg, Brian. *Mary Lee Settle's Beulah Quintet: The Price of Freedom.* Baton Rouge: Louisiana State University Press, 1991.

———. "The Price of Freedom: An Interview with Mary Lee Settle," *Southern Review* 25 (1989): 351–365.

Schafer, William J. "Mary Lee Settle's Beulah Quintet: History Darkly, through a Single Lens Reflex," *Appalachian Journal* 10 (1982): 77–86.

Vance, Jane Gentry. "Historical Voices in Mary Lee Settle's *Prisons*," *Mississippi Quarterly* 38 (1985): 391–413.

———. "Mary Lee Settle: Ambiguity of Steel." In *American Women Writing Fiction: Memory, Identity, Family, Space,* edited by Mickey Pearlman, 213–229. Lexington: University Press of Kentucky, 1989.

———. "Mary Lee Settle's The Beulah Quintet: History Inherited: History Created," *Southern Literary Journal* 17 (1984): 40–53.

OTHER

Harris, Gale. Review of *Choices, Belles Lettres: A Review of Books by Women* 11, no. 1 (January 1996): 8.

Hogbin, Brian O. "Mary Lee Settle." Available online. URL: http://athena.english.vt.edu/~appalach/writersS/settle.html. Accessed September 25, 2005.

SHAARA, JEFF (1952–)

Jeff Shaara, author of five historical novels, including the best-selling *Gods and Generals* (1996), did not intend to become a writer like his Pulitzer Prize–winning father, Michael SHAARA. As the son remarked to interviewer Patricia Kelly O'Meara, his father led an unhappy life, and, "having seen how he suffered, writing was the last thing I wanted to do" (O'Meara). His father's death changed Jeff Shaara's career direction, however, and he wrote both the prequel and the sequel, *The Last Full Measure* (1998), to Michael Shaara's *The Killer Angels*. Like his father, Shaara combines historical figures and factual information with his own imagined, fictive interpretations of thoughts and motivations. Although his three Civil War novels have been his most successful, his *Rise to Rebellion* (2001), about the American Revolution, and *Gone for Soldiers: A Novel of the Mexican War* (2000) have been well reviewed.

Jeff Shaara was born on February 21, 1952, in New Brunswick, New Jersey, to Michael Shaara, a writer and educator, and Helen Krumwiede Shaara, a social worker. He earned a bachelor's degree in criminology at Florida State University and spent two decades as a rare-coin dealer in Tampa, Florida, before marrying Lynne Loveless in 1992. *Gods and Generals* follows four individual soldiers from 1858 through the Civil War battles leading up to the battle of Gettysburg; the last is depicted in *The Killer Angels*. Shaara uses Southerners Robert E. Lee and Stonewall Jackson and Northerners Winfield Scott Hancock and Joshua Chamberlain to express different reasons for fighting the war. Shaara's second novel, *The Last Full Measure,* begins as, the last shots at Gettysburg having been fired, General Lee retreats from Pennsylvania to Appomattox. The novel follows Lee, Jackson, Hancock, and Chamberlain, with particular attention to the relations between Lee and General Ulysses S. Grant as the novel focuses on the Appomattox courthouse. *Gone for Soldiers* (2000), inspired by Shaara's research into the backgrounds of the same men, demonstrates the way friendships and experiences were forged before the Civil War, in "that war with Mexico," the "story we didn't learn in school" (O'Meara); it includes all major characters from the Civil War novels except Jeb Stewart and Joshua Chamberlain, who were too young to have fought in Mexico. *Rise to Rebellion* (2001) depicts the seeds of the American Revolution, beginning with the Boston Massacre in 1770 and featuring such historical giants as Benjamin Franklin and Thomas Jefferson; in 1776 Shaara dramatizes the Fourth of July in Philadelphia, Pennsylvania, as the impact of the Declaration of Independence begins to be felt. Shaara's most recent novel, *Glorious Cause* (2002), continues to tell America's story from the perspective not only of George Washington and Benjamin Franklin, for instance, but also of the British general Lord Cornwallis.

Jeff Shaara and his wife divide their time between New York's Greenwich Village and Missoula, Montana. *Gods and Generals* was released as a film by Warner Bros. in 2003.

NOVELS

Glorious Cause. New York: Ballantine Books, 2002.
Gods and Generals. New York: Ballantine Books, 1996.

Gone for Soldiers: A Novel of the Mexican War. New York: Ballantine Books, 2000.

The Last Full Measure. New York: Ballantine Books, 1998.

Rise to Rebellion. New York: Ballantine Books, 2001.

SOURCES

Kilpatrick, Thomas L. Review of *Gods and Generals, Library Journal* 121, no. 8 (May 1, 1996): 134.

Taylor, Gilbert. Review of *The Last Full Measure, Booklist* 94, no. 17 (May 1, 1998): 1,478.

Unsigned Review of *Gods and Generals, Kirkus Reviews* (May 1, 1996): 633.

Unsigned Review of *Gods and Generals, Publishers Weekly* 243, no. 20 (May 13, 1996): 55.

Unsigned Review of *The Last Full Measure, Publishers Weekly* 245, no. 16 (April 20, 1998): 44.

OTHER

Adams, Noah. Interview: "Jeff Shaara." *NPR Weekly Edition.* National Public Radio. (July 7, 2001). Highbeam Research. Available online. URL: http://www.highbeam.com/library/doc3.asp?DOCID=1P1:45613154. Accessed September 25, 2005.

Hansen, Liane. Interview: "Jeff Shaara Discusses Writing *Gods and Generals.*" *NPR Weekend Edition.* National Public Radio. (June 30, 1996). Highbeam Research. Available online. URL: http://www.highbeam.com/library/doc3.asp?DOCID=1P1:28477354. Accessed September 25, 2005.

O'Meara, Kelly Patricia. Interview: "Shaara Makes Good on His Literary Legacy." *Insight on the News* (September 11, 2000). Highbeam Research. Available online. URL: http://www.highbeam.com/library/doc3.asp?DOCID=1G1:6513 3115. Accessed September 25, 2005.

Oxfeld, Jesse. "Shaara's March: *Gods and Generals.*" *Book* (January 1, 2003). Highbeam Research. Available online. URL: http://www.highbeam.com/library/doc3.asp?DOCID=1G1: 96554761. Accessed September 25, 2005.

SHAARA, MICHAEL (JOSEPH, JR.) (1929–1988)

Before his death at age 59, Michael Shaara wrote science fiction novels and sports literature, but it was *The Killer Angels* (1974) that won the Pulitzer Prize. It created a new standard for Civil War novels and was the source for the highly successful film *Gettysburg.*

Michael Shaara was born on June 23, 1929, in Jersey City, New Jersey, to Michael Joseph Shaara, Sr., a union organizer, and Alleene Maxwell Shaara. He earned a bachelor's degree from Rutgers University in 1951 and was married to Helen Krumwide from 1950 until 1980. After serving as a paratrooper with the U.S. Army 82nd Airborne Division (1946–49), a merchant seaman, and a police officer, Shaara published more than 70 short stories, many of which were collected in *Soldier Boy* (1982). While teaching at Florida State University (1961–73), Shaara produced his first novel, *The Broken Place* (1968), about a soldier-boxer named Tom McClain who kills a man in the ring; the reviews noted Shaara's debt to Hemingway (Rhodes, 36), particularly regarding the central role of physical fitness and the outdoors. *The Killer Angels* looks at the battle of Gettysburg from both Confederate and Union viewpoints, allowing the readers to feel the smoke and taste the gunpowder on their tongues. As Shaara says in the preface, quoted repeatedly by critics, his purpose was to convey "what it was like to *be* there, what the weather was like, what men's faces looked like." Twenty years later, when Ron Maxwell's *Gettysburg* reached movie theaters, *The Killer Angels* shot to the top of the best-seller lists, although it had failed to do so when it won the Pulitzer Prize. Then the nation's attention was focused on the Vietnam War. The critically acclaimed *Gettysburg,* the second-longest film in history (after Erich von Stoheim's 1924 silent film *Greed*), contained 125 speaking roles, 7,500 reenactors as extras, and veteran actors Martin Sheen as General Lee, Tom Berenger as General Longstreet, Sam Elliott as General Buford, and Jeff Daniels as Colonel Chamberlain (Oxfeld).

In 1981 *The Herald,* a science fiction novel, followed the pilot Nick Tesla as he confronted a Nazi-like scientist who wanted to create a master race. The manuscript of *For Love of the Game,* found by Shaara's son Jeff after the death of his father, was published posthumously in 1991. It is a baseball novel about an aging player who can still pitch a perfect game.

Michael Shaara, who had a history of heart trouble, died from a heart attack in 1989, in Tallahassee, Florida. He had suffered for many years from brain damage, the result of a 1972 motorcycle accident in Italy (Pierce). His son, Jeffrey SHAARA, organized his father's literary estate and wrote both the prequel and the sequel to *The Killer Angels.* It is now known as the "father-son trilogy": *Gods and Generals, The Killer Angels,* and *The Last Full Measure.*

NOVELS

The Broken Place. New York: New American Library, 1968.
For Love of the Game. New York: Carroll & Graf, 1991.
The Herald. New York: McGraw, 1981.
The Killer Angels. New York: McKay, 1974.

SOURCES

Leak, Thomas. "High Tide of the Confederacy," *New York Times,* 10 May 1975, p. 27.
Rhodes, Richard. "Boxer Gone Beserk," *New York Times,* 7 April 1968, Section VII, p. 36.

OTHER

Oxfeld, Jesse. "Shaara's march: *Gods and Generals,*" Book (January 7, 2003). Highbeam Research. Available online. URL: http://www.highbeam.com/library/doc3.asp?DOCID= 1G1:96554761. Accessed September 25, 2005.
Pierce, Greg. "*Gods'* Writer, Preceding his Father's Footsteps," The *Washington Times* (June 22, 1996) Highbeam Research. Available online. URL: http://www.highbeam.com/library/ doc3.asp?DOCID=1G1:58419613. Accessed September 25, 2005.
Sherwin, Elisabeth. "Father/son Trilogy Didn't Come Easily." Available online. URL: http://www.dcn.davis.ca.us/~gizmo/ 1998/shaara.html. Accessed September 25, 2005.

SHAW, IRWIN (1913–1984)   One of the most popular writers of the post–World War II era, Irwin Shaw came to public attention at age 23 with *Bury the Dead* (1936), a pacifist drama that became a Broadway hit. His novel *The YOUNG LIONS* (1948) is considered one of the major World War II novels. Only James JONES's *FROM HERE TO ETERNITY* and Norman MAILER's *The NAKED AND THE DEAD* rival it. His prolific oeuvre includes 12 novels, 14 plays, 13 volumes of short fiction, and three works of nonfiction. He also wrote 13 screenplays. His work, often given short shrift by critics and academics, is currently undergoing a reevaluation; some scholars, including James R. Giles, argue that critics have overlooked Shaw as "a writer of rigorous moral fables" (Giles, 176). Critic Ross Wetzsteon says that his novels are actually about struggles with "moral choice" (quoted in Giles 1983, 176).

Irwin Shaw was born on February 27, 1913, in the Bronx, New York, to William Shamforoff, a hat-trimming salesman, and Rose Tompkins Shamforoff. They later changed the family's name to Shaw and moved to Brooklyn, where the young Shaw was reared. He was educated at Brooklyn College, earning his bachelor's degree in 1934. After working as a scriptwriter for the 1930s radio shows *Dick Tracy* and *Andy Gump,* he married Marian Edwards, an actress, in 1939, served with the U.S. Army from 1942 to 1945, and published *The Young Lions* three years later. Shaw received excellent reviews for this novel about three young soldiers— Michael Whitacre and Noah Ackerman, both Americans, and Christian Diestl, a German—whose stories are told as they come together in Germany, with flashbacks to such major events as the Normandy invasion. They are linked as well through their individual relationships with Margaret Freemantle, a young American. *The Troubled Air* (1951) concerns Clement Archer, a radio station director during the hysteria over communism during the McCarthy era. Thereafter Shaw moved to Europe, spending the next 25 years between Paris and Klosters, Switzerland, where he used his expatriate status for insights into his American characters.

In Shaw's third novel, *Lucy Crown* (1956), protagonist Tony Crown witnesses his mother Lucy's seduction of his school friend. *Two Weeks in Another Town* (1960) features Jack Andrus, an alcoholic Hollywood star who travels to Rome, where he encounters his former wife Carlotta and his young and beautiful mistress Veronica. *Voices of a Summer Day* (1965), uncharacteristically romantic and lyrical, features the 50-year-old Benjamin Federov watching his 13-year-old son Michael playing in a Long Island baseball game and reminiscing about past relationships, disillusion, and adulteries. *Rich Man, Poor Man* (1970), a modern Cain and Abel story, follows the Jordaches, an upstate New York German-American family from the post–World War II years, through the McCarthy era, to the Vietnam War and the corruption of the Nixon presidency. Axel Jordach, a baker, has three children: the industrious, intelligent Rudolph; the aggressive, ruthless Thomas; and the confused, promiscuous Gretchen. Generally credited as the first of many American made-for-TV miniseries, it was enormously successful. The story continues in *Beggarman, Thief* (1977), seen mainly through the eyes of Billy Abbott (married to Gretchen) and of Wesley Jordach, Thomas's son.

In *Evening in Byzantium* (1973), Jesse Craig attends the 1970 Cannes Film Festival seeking both a resurrection of his talent as a formerly successful film producer and his lost identity. ("I am in Cannes," he says, "to save my life" [106–107].) Women—journalist Gail McKinnon, estranged wife Penelope, lover Constance, daughter Anne—play significant roles in his reassessment of his life. *Nightwork* (1975) features a night clerk in a rundown New York hotel who discovers a corpse and $100,000; the money enables him to move to Europe. In *The Top of the Hill* (1979), a young man turns his back on his successful life in the city and moves to the mountains to engage in dangerous outdoor sports and to evaluate his past life. *Bread Upon the Waters* (1981) reveals the consequences of wealth, prestige, and money in the life of history teacher Allen Strand. Russell Hazen, millionaire philanthropist, takes charge of the entire family through gifts of travel, education, and jobs. *Acceptable Losses* (1982) begins as protagonist Roger Damon, a literary agent, receives a phone call that causes him to reexamine his earlier life.

Irwin Shaw's alcoholism led to his divorce from Marion Shaw in 1970, but they reconciled and remarried in 1982. His popular work was adapted into both feature-length films and television miniseries. *The Young Lions,* directed by Edward Dmytryk, starred Montgomery Clift as Noah, Dean Martin as Michael, and Marlon Brando as Christien. *Rich Man, Poor Man,* starring Nick Nolte and Peter Strauss as the two brothers and William Smith as Falconetti, won three Emmy Awards for director David Greene and actors Ed Asner and Fionnula Flanagan. *Two Weeks in Another Town,* adapted for the screen in 1962, was directed by Vincente Minnelli and starred Kirk Douglas, Cyd Charisse, and Edward G. Robinson. Shaw died on May 16, 1984, of prostate cancer, in Davos, Switzerland.

NOVELS

Acceptable Losses. New York: Arbor House, 1982.
Beggarman, Thief. New York: Delacorte, 1977.
Bread upon the Waters. New York: Delacorte, 1981.
The City Was in Total Darkness. Tokyo, Japan: Kodansha, 1990.
Evening in Byzantium. New York: Delacorte, 1973.
Lucy Crown. New York: Random House, 1956.
Nightwork. New York: Delacorte, 1975.
Rich Man, Poor Man. New York: Delacorte, 1970.
The Top of the Hill. New York: Delacorte, 1979.
The Troubled Air. New York: Random House, 1951.
Two Weeks in Another Town. New York: Random House, 1960.

Voices of a Summer Day. New York: Delacorte, 1965.
The Young Lions. New York: Random House, 1948.

SOURCES

Aldridge, John W. *After the Lost Generation.* New York: Noonday, 1951, pp. 146–156.
Eisinger, Chester E. *Fiction of the Forties.* Chicago, Ill.: University of Chicago Press, 1963.
Evans, Bergen. "Irwin Shaw," *English Journal* 40 (November 1951): 485–491.
Fiedler, Leslie. "Irwin Shaw: Adultery, The Last Politics," *Commentary* 22 (July 1956): 71–74.
Giles, James Richard. *Irwin Shaw.* Boston: Twayne, 1983.
———. *Irwin Shaw: A Study of the Short Fiction.* Boston: Twayne, 1991.
———. "Irwin Shaw's Original Prologue to *The Young Lions,*" *Resources for American Literary Study* 11 (Spring 1981): 115–119.
Milic, Louis T. "Naming in Shaw's *The Young Lions,*" *Style* 23, no. 1 (Spring 1989): 113–123.
Newquist, Roy. *Counterpoint.* New York: Rand McNally, 1964.
Peden, William. "Best of Irwin Shaw," *Saturday Review of Literature* 33 (November 19, 1950): 27–28.
Saal, Hubert. "Disenchanted Men," *Saturday Review of Literature* 40 (August 3, 1957): 12–13.
Shnayerson, Michael. *Irwin Shaw: A Biography.* New York: Putnam's, 1989.
Startt, William. "Irwin Shaw: An Extended Talent," *Midwest Quarterly* 2 (Summer 1961): 325–337.
Trilling, Lionel. "Some Are Gentle, Some Are Not," *Saturday Review of Literature* 34 (July 9, 1951): 8–9.
Wetzsteon, Ross. "Irwin Shaw: The Conflict Between Big Bucks and Good Books," *Saturday Review* 8 (August 1981): 12–17.

OTHER

Books and Writers. "Irwin Shaw," (1913–1984). Available online. URL: http://www.kirjasto.sci.fi/ishaw.htm. Accessed September 25, 2005.

SHAWL, THE CYNTHIA OZICK **(1989)** Cynthia OZICK's novella *The Shawl* provides a powerful commentary on the nature of trauma and its aftermath, the balance between memory and forgetting, and the limitations and possibilities of language. Taking the reader to hell (the Holocaust) and back again (Miami), *The Shawl* culminates in a vision of reintegration and hope. A prominent Jewish-American writer of novels, essays, poems, and short stories, Ozick is not herself a Holocaust survivor: "I did it because I couldn't help it. It wanted to be done. . . . I wasn't there, and I pretended through imagination that I was" ("Imagination"). This ambivalence manifests in an ongoing tension between speech and silence.

The two sections that comprise the text, while individually effective and acclaimed (each was published separately and selected for the annual *Best American Short Stories* volume), come together to form a greater whole: "The Shawl," an eight-page concentration camp narrative, and "Rosa," set over 30 years later in Miami (and approximately six times as long), offer an imaginative re-creation of a traumatic moment and its much more complicated aftermath. They exist within a "synchronous" rather than a "diachronous" relationship; each shapes the reader's view of the other (Lowin, 121, 112). Reminiscent of William Blake's coupling of "Songs of Innocence" and "Songs of Experience," Ozick's structuring suggests that the issues surrounding trauma, survival, memory, and time all function in contrary though not contradictory ways.

In "The Shawl," Ozick paradoxically employs a detached third-person limited omniscient narrator to provide an unmediated experience, pared down to the agony of one mother's loss. Reminiscent of imagist poetry, densely symbolic in style, and structured through psychic associations (Kauvar, 184), "The Shawl" uses a single synecdochic episode to represent the entire Holocaust: the murder of Rosa Lublin's toddler by a Nazi concentration camp guard who throws the child against an electrified fence. "The Shawl" begins with Rosa, an assimilated Polish Jew, and her teenage niece, Stella, on a death march. Rosa concerns herself with her infant daughter, Magda, whom she carries wrapped in "a magic shawl [which] could nourish an infant for three days and three nights" while "ravenous" Stella looks only to her own self-preservation (5). In the concentration camp, Magda remains safely silent and invisible until "Stella, cold, cold, the coldness of hell" (3) takes Magda's shawl for warmth, prompting once-mute Magda to toddle wailing into the roll-call arena, where her mother, ironically relieved by Magda's newfound voice, observes her child's imminent death and proceeds to stuff the shawl down her

own throat, stifling her desire to cry out and thereby preserving her life. From the perspectives of feminism and of witnessing, Magda's finding her voice is redemptive, even as it brings about her death.

When "Rosa" begins, the muteness and passivity that characterize Rosa at the end of "The Shawl" have given way to excessive speech and wildly destructive acts: "a madwoman and a scavenger" (14), Rosa "murder[s]" her antiques business, "part with a big hammer . . . [and] part with a piece of construction metal" (46, 26) because "whoever came, they were like deaf people" (27). Rosa speaks, but her audience cannot comprehend the enormity of the Holocaust. Having destroyed the business that she and Stella ran in New York, Rosa relocates to a retirement hotel in Miami, putting herself in a "hell" (14), which uncannily replicates nearly every aspect of the concentration camp setting of "The Shawl" (Kauvar, 179): "everything is on fire," "the sand [is] littered with bodies," and Rosa finds herself "locked behind barbed wire" (39, 47, 49). Both settings are characterized by a fundamental disconnect between words and their meanings, suggesting the limitations of language. In the camps, Rosa and the other prisoners describe their conditions with euphemisms (8), while the Miami hotels are populated by " 'guests'—some [of whom] had been residents for a dozen years" (28). Whereas words fail her at Magda's death, Rosa now composes elaborate letters ("in the most excellent literary Polish" [14]) to her daughter ("a beautiful young woman of thirty, thirty-one: a doctor married to a doctor [35]), abandoning her refugee English in favor of her beloved mother tongue, which she uses "to make a history, to tell, to explain. To retrieve, to reprieve. To lie" (45). This propensity isolates Rosa, and her text dramatizes William FAULKNER's truism that "the past is never dead; it's not even past." In Rosa's case, it is her daughter Magda who is not dead, and the experience of the concentration camps that is not past. When Simon Persky, a well-meaning fellow Warsaw refugee, confronts Rosa about her poor quality of life, she explains: "Before [the Holocaust] is a dream. After is a joke. Only during stays. And to call it a life is a lie" (59). Hence Rosa has few social interactions: She dislikes Stella (though she remains Stella's dependent), distrusts Persky (because he escaped from

Warsaw before the Holocaust), and despises Dr. Tree (an academic who wishes "to observe survivor syndroming within the natural setting" [38]).

If Stella's theft of Magda's shawl brings about the central crisis of "The Shawl," then Stella's complying with Rosa's request to send the shawl to Miami should be the climax of "Rosa." Instead, the shawl becomes symbolically conflated with a manuscript from the hated Dr. Tree (a package Rosa mistakes for the one Stella sends) and with a pair of underwear that Rosa loses track of when she meets Persky at the laundromat. She destroys the manuscript and the underwear she concludes must have been stolen (Persky is the prime suspect) and buried in the sand. At this point, the traumatic repetition is interrupted. Rosa discovers that, unlike her stolen pre-Holocaust life, her underwear is only temporarily misplaced. Meanwhile, when the shawl itself arrives, an anticlimax that leaves Rosa "indifferent" (62), she places it over the telephone she has recently decided to reconnect. The phone rings, "a dead thing com[ing] to life" (62), and Rosa analogously unlocks the possibility of meaningful communication by inviting Persky up. Accepting a friendly overture from Persky (a married man without a wife) will allow Rosa (a mother without a daughter) to escape traumatic repetition and constraining labels to embrace a more promising, and even playful, future.

SOURCES

Kauvar, Elaine M. *Cynthia Ozick's Fiction: Tradition and Invention.* Bloomington: Indiana University Press, 1993.

Lowin, Joseph. *Cynthia Ozick.* Boston: Twayne, 1988.

Matterasi, Mario. "Imagination Unbound: An Interview with Cynthia Ozick," *Salmagundi* (Spring/Summer 1992): 94–95.

Ozick, Cynthia. *The Shawl.* 1980, 1983. Reprint, New York: Vintage International, 1990.

Jessica Rabin

SHELTERING SKY, THE PAUL BOWLES (1949)

The Sheltering Sky by Paul BOWLES mainly concerns itself with an American couple, Kit and Port, and their travels in Morocco. This first novel has a fairly straightforward plot but touches on the metaphysical in the style of writing and themes presented, representing the mysteriousness of the desert and the desert's similarities to the mysteries of the mind.

In the beginning of the novel, Kit and Port are traveling with their friend Tunner. Since relations between Kit and Port have been a little rocky, Tunner tries to insinuate himself into a relationship with Kit. Port and Kit move to a different town without Tunner, and Port falls ill with typhoid. Before he dies, he plunges into a delirium that introduces some of the surreal points in the novel. Kit is left mourning and goes slightly mad, walking out into the desert where she must be "saved" by traveling Bedouins, who essentially enslave her. She escapes eventually, but she is forever lost—mentally.

That's where the metaphysical part comes in. In Paul Bowles's world, being lost in the desert equals being lost within your head. The otherworldly qualities of the Arab world—the strong teas and drugs and even the stories and myths that are told by the natives—create a haziness that is slightly incomprehensible to the Westerner. Port dies for this in his quest to go ever farther into the desert. Kit also loses her mind after going much deeper into the desert than Port ever does—which is ironic because Port was the more fanatical traveler in the first place.

The divide is present even among other Europeans in Morocco: "The Spanish maid at the hotel had said to him that noon: 'La vida es pena.' 'Of course,' he had replied, feeling false even as he spoke, asking himself if any American can truthfully accept a definition of life which makes it synonymous with suffering" (15). The only characters that are far removed, like Kit and Port, are two British travelers who are perhaps even more separated from native Arab life (the woman writes guidebooks). And as Kit, Port, and Tunner eat in a cafe, Kit remarks, "Thank heavens they're Arabs, and not French. Otherwise it would have been against the rules to eat out here" (117). Kit and Port are attracted to the otherworldly culture without boundaries, ruled by the desert.

As Bowles said in a 1971 interview, "[W]hat I wanted to tell was the story of what the desert can do to us. That was all. The desert is the protagonist." "Us" here means, presumably, Americans, although there is a story that gives the first part of the novel its name, "Tea in the Sahara," which is about natives going out into the desert, getting lost, and ultimately dying. So it's not just Americans who are subject to the negative mystique of the desert.

The desert is also presented as alluring, and Bowles manages to portray its beauty masterfully: "It was perfectly quiet. The sky was white. Occasionally he stood up carefully and peered out. And so it was that when the sun came up he looked between two oleanders and saw it reflected red across the miles of flittering salt sebkha that lay between him and the mountains" (36). That beauty turns out to be a trap of sorts, but for Bowles, an aesthete, the beauty is also an end in itself.

SOURCES

Bowles, Paul. *This Sheltering Sky. Conversations with Paul Bowles.* Edited by Gena Dagel Caponi. Jackson: University of Mississippi Press, 1993.

Sawyer-Laucanno, Christopher. *An Invisible Spectator.* New York: Weidenfeld and Nicolson, 1989.

Allie M. D'Augustine

SHIP OF FOOLS KATHERINE ANNE PORTER

(1962) Katherine Anne PORTER's *Ship of Fools* was published to elaborate fanfare on April 1, 1962, more than a quarter of a century after she had begun writing it. The initial reviews were almost unanimously laudatory, and Mark Schorer's analysis in the *New York Times Book Review* set the tone. Calling Porter's novel a "masterpiece" that would take its place among the best books of the century, he compared it with George Eliot's *Middlemarch* and James Joyce's *Ulysses.*

Ship of Fools was an immediate best-seller, and film rights were quickly sold. Porter became a wealthy woman, and it looked as if her only long novel was going to enhance her already stellar reputation founded on her highly acclaimed short stories and short novels. In the fall, however, tepid and negative reviews appeared, and what had seemed like an unblemished success became tainted with controversy. German reviews were the most censorious, one headline labeling *Ship of Fools* a "document of hatred," but several British reviews were cool, and a review in the American journal *Commentary* was particularly shrill and condemning. Contrary to Schorer's location of humor, pathos, and enlightenment in the novel, some reviewers now raised questions about Porter's "dark view of humanity."

Ship of Fools details a five-week voyage of the North German Lloyd steamship *Vera* from Veracruz, Mexico,

to Bremerhaven, Germany, from August 22 to September 17, 1931, based on Porter's own 1931 voyage from Mexico to Germany on the North German Lloyd ship *Werra* with Eugene Pressly, whom she would marry in Paris in 1933 and divorce five years later. The ship is carrying 932 passengers and one dog. In a string of episodes divided among three parts and encapsulated within the frame of embarkation and disembarkation scenes, characters are presented in their interactions with one another during the voyage, and histories and relationships of several dozen are explored intensely.

The most significant characters are the Americans Jenny Brown and David Scott, both artists (based on Porter and Pressly); Mary Treadwell, a 45-year-old divorcée and another autobiographical character; William Denny, a bigoted and lecherous engineer from Texas based on Porter's first husband, J. H. Koontz; Dr. Schumann, the ship's physician, who suffers from a heart ailment; and the madwoman, La Condesa, who is also a drug addict.

Incidents that are highlighted in the novel include the passengers' appraisal of one another at the get-acquainted party; Mary Treadwell's painting her face in a primitive mask and beating the lecherous Denny with the heel of her shoe; Dr. Schumann's and La Condesa's disclosing their irrational love for one another; Jenny and David's arguments and reconciliations; the medical students' mocking La Condesa; Johann's defying his uncle to make a sexual bargain with one of the dancers; the twins Ric and Rac's throwing the dog Bèbè overboard; and the artist Etchegaray's sacrificing his life to save Bèbè.

Porter remarked that not one reviewer really understood what she was doing in the novel, and indeed the novel seemed to run afoul of post-1950s expectations of the novel genre, because of its shifting viewpoint, episodic structure, and absence of a sustained plot. Had it been published in the 1920s or 1930s, closer to its inception and closer to the publication of Joyce's *Ulysses* or Faulkner's *Absalom, Absalom!,* perhaps it would have been seen for the modernist work it was, and Porter's purpose and treatment would have been more readily understood and appreciated. On one level the novel is a moral allegory; on another it is a string of realistic scenes acted out by characters who with the aid of an authoritative narrative voice illustrate Porter's controlling themes: chauvinism at the root of Nazism, human isolation, love in all its manifestations and perversions, apathy's collusion with evil, religious intolerance, and the meaning of both art and home. On yet another level the novel is an old-fashioned, classic satire, crafted with caricature and laced with irony, in the spirit of Swift's *Gulliver's Travels.* "I am a passenger on that ship," Porter wrote, pointing out the universality of the voyage, the critic Mark Schorer concurred: "It will be a reader myopic to the point of blindness," he wrote, "who does not find his name on her passenger list."

SOURCES

Hendrick, George, and Willene Hendrick, "Ship of Fools." In *Katherine Anne Porter.* Twayne's United States Authors Series. Revised edition. Boston: G. K. Hall/Twayne, 1988.

Libermann, M. M. "The Responsibility of the Novelist and the Critical Reception of *Ship of Fools,*" *Criticism* 8 (1966): 377–388.

Schorer, Mark. "We're All on the Passenger List," *New York Times Book Review,* 1 April 1962, 1, 5.

Wescott, Glenway. "The Making of a Novel," *Atlantic Monthly* (April 1962): 43–49.

Darlene Unrue

SHIPPING NEWS, THE Annie Proulx (1993)

In *The Shipping News,* the protagonist, Quoyle, an awkward, unsuccessful, but tender-hearted man is described by the narrator as having "a great damp loaf of a body, [a] Head shaped like a crenshaw, no neck, [and a] monstrous chin, a freakish shelf jutting from the lower face" (2). When Quoyle's parents die, he loses his job, and his unfaithful wife, Petal Bear, is killed in a car crash after selling their daughters to a child abuser, from whom they are rescued physically untouched. His stouthearted aunt convinces him to make a fresh start by moving from Upstate New York to his ancestral home in a remote coastal village in Newfoundland. In the rustic atmosphere of Killick-Claw, Quoyle runs not away but toward his past. Therefore, Quoyle, unlike other characters in Proulx's novels, stops running, and he faces the consequences by, stoically, facing all challenges.

In *The Shipping News,* Proulx focuses almost completely on Quoyle, and his furious protest against pain as he searches for a better life. Gradually, Quoyle feels he belongs among his neighbors and his coworkers at the weekly newspaper, *The Gammy Bird.* Here Quoyle acquires self-respect by hard work at a job he learns to love. For the first time in his life, Quoyle does something right, and he becomes managing editor. Although Quoyle wholeheartedly joins the community and gives unconditionally, at the same time he uncovers many painful family secrets and the land that carries its curse. As Quoyle slowly overcomes his futile longing for Petal, he wins the love of Wavey Prowse, a "Tall and Quiet Woman." However, this happy ending is ironic, as Proulx skillfully suggests when she writes on the last line of the novel that, "love sometimes occurs without pain or misery" (336). But since Quoyle is aware that "There are still old knots unrecorded, [and] new knots to discover" (324), he succeeds because he now looks life in the face and no longer considers himself a failure.

The Shipping News consists of 39 short chapters, most with pictorial headings, tropes for chapter titles, and epigraphs. Since knots are tools for fisherman and other boaters, they are indispensable on the shores of Newfoundland. For Proulx, Newfoundland is an island of invention where Quoyle can unravel the tangle of old familial wounds: incest, petty hatreds, and long-standing feuds. Therefore, Proulx's imagery has much to do with knots both of the literal and figurative kind. Quoyle's name is an antiquated spelling of *coil,* and his fear of the ocean provides much of the novel's literal and metaphorical tension. Quoyle could not swim, and his father's continual attempt to force him to do so constitutes his failure in everything. Quoyle's chief failure was that of normal appearance, and even those close to him believed that "the part of Quoyle that was wonderful was, unfortunately, attached to the rest of him" (14). Is Proulx knowingly exploring what Nietzsche describes, in a maxim in *Beyond Good and Evil,* as the brutal recognition that "terrible experiences make one wonder whether he who experiences them is not something terrible." But, as Quoyle grows into responsibility, the old familial wounds begin to heal. In chapter 20, "Gaze Island," Quoyle learns that his ancestors were a clan of half-wit "wrackers," or pirates, who lured unsuspecting ships onto rocky shallows and then murdered the shipwrecked sailors. Although these savage people may seem quite foreign and removed from Quoyle, he must deal with his own tragic, more immediate past: Petal's betrayal, and the fact that his father raped his Aunt Agnis at the age of 12. Quoyle succeeds because he not only faces the grotesque sins of his ancestors but also breaks the cycle.

In *The Shipping News,* Proulx clearly demonstrates the notion of hard work and great strength necessary for survival, a common theme in Newfoundland literature. Jack Buggit combines the views of Bill Pretty and Tert Cart in his characterization of the old ways of inland fishing. "It was a hard life but it had the satisfaction. Terrible hard in them old days" (64). Although there is no secret that the life of a Newfoundland fisherman was not an easy one, the day there was no more fishing done was a day of great sadness and grief. Newfoundlanders knew no other life, but they were being forced to change. As Jack Buggit narrates Newfoundland's difficult shift away from fishing: "When the damn place give up on hard times and swapped 'em in for confederation with Canada what did we get? Slow and sure we got government. Sure I wanted health care, mail service, good education for me kids. Some of it come in. But not the jobs" (65). Proulx appears preoccupied with the tragedies so many Newfoundlanders faced at sea rather than their success at overcoming the odds. There are numerous storms at sea, murders, and rescues. Quoyle nearly drowns at one point, Jack loses his eldest boy at sea, and Quoyle's house is blown out to sea. Near the novel's end, Jack Buggit sits up in his own coffin, spouting water, having both drowned and not drowned. But, as Roz Kavenay in *New Statesman & Society* suggests, "Proulx's triumph is that she makes us swallow all of this. Her work looks us forthright in the eye and challenges disbelief" (39). Thus, in this artful novel, Proulx transports us to the foggy, storm-battered coast of Newfoundland, a land of myth, so that Quoyle's story, like billions of other people in the world, will not shrink in magnitude.

SOURCE

Kaveney, Roz. "Local Hero," *New Statesman & Society* 6, no. 281 (December 3, 1993): 39.

Harriet Gold

SHOW BOAT Edna Ferber (1926)   Near the end of *Show Boat,* heroine Magnolia Hawks Ravenal summarizes her life as well as the novel's plot: " 'What if I were to (say) that I used to be a show-boat actress, and that my father was drowned in the Mississippi, and my mother, at sixty, runs a show boat all alone, and that my husband is a gambler and we have no money, and that I have just come from the most notorious brothel in Chicago, where I returned a thousand dollars my husband had got there, and that I'm on my way to try to get work in a variety theatre?' She was smiling a little at a this absurd thought."

Edna Ferber probably smiled too at the thought that *Show Boat* would make her rich and help make her name immortal, if only in small print. As Ferber's biographer and grand-niece Julie Goldsmith Gilbert explains, "It's surprising—shocking, really—how many people think (*Show Boat*) was born a musical, not having a clue that it was a 1926 best seller born out of the head of Edna Ferber. Of course, every *Show Boat* marquee reads: 'Jerome Kern and Oscar Hammerstein's *Show Boat,*' and then underneath, in much smaller print, 'Based on the Novel by Edna Ferber.' The public's eye doesn't readily go to a . . . based on.' " *Show Boat* was Ferber's fifth novel (she ultimately wrote 12) and was her second of seven best-sellers. Two years earlier, *So Big* had been awarded the Pulitzer Prize. That the name *Show Boat* is well known today is due primarily to the musical, the Jerome Kern score (who can't hum a few bars of "Ol' Man River"?) and several film versions based on Ferber's novel.

According to Ferber, *Show Boat* was her only novel that "never was intended to be more than an authentic and romantic novel of Americana." As a result, unlike most Ferber novels, there is no real opponent or villain in *Show Boat.* In most other ways, however, *Show Boat* is a typical Ferber novel: a generational saga portraying social decline with at least the potential of restoration and, most notably, strong women overcoming obstacles (generally men) to become successful. *Show Boat* suggests that women could enrich themselves through wider exposure to life and that some longstanding frustrations may be rooted in their dependence.

America's 50-year showboat era was almost over when Ferber first caught wind of it in the mid-1920s.

She spent the next year tracking down information, interviewing people who could tell her about "floating theatres," reading everything she could find on the subject, and spending several days on a North Carolina showboat. Finally, she retreated to St. Jean-de-Luz in southwestern France to write. *Show Boat* was published serially in *Woman's Home Companion* and in book form by Doubleday in 1926.

Ferber's generational theme focuses on Magnolia (Nola), growing up on a Mississippi River showboat. Other characters include Nola's parents, henpecked Captain Andy and domineering Parthenia (Parthy). Readers are introduced to the entire showboat "cast," including dashing juvenile lead, Gaylord Ravenal, destined to marry Nola, and, in later chapters, to their daughter Kim, a Ferber-created name based on the girl's birthplace at the convergence of three states, Kentucky, Illinois, and Missouri. Throughout the novel, Ferber also emphasizes the key role played by two nonhuman characters: the boat, named the "Cotton Blossom," and the river itself (a female persona in the book, masculine in Hammerstein's lyrics).

To the extent that *Show Boat* wrestles with an issue, it is miscegenation. In a dramatic episode, Ferber retells a showboat legend involving two performers, a white man married to a black woman passing for white. When facing arrest, he pricks her finger and sucks a drop of her blood, thereby giving himself mixed blood. That interracial marriage was illegal in the post–Civil War South is not surprising; however, when this scene was brought to the stage, it helped establish *Show Boat*'s reputation as a new theatrical art form: a three-dimensional musical play as distinguished from light musical comedy. Ferber's present-day readers may find her authenticity jarring, including casual references to "coons," "niggers," and "darkies." Acknowledging her considerable talent conveying the panorama of bygone eras, Rudyard Kipling and William Allen White regard Ferber as much an historian as a novelist.

The setting changes in the novel's second half as Gay and Nola flee river life and move to Chicago, partly to escape overbearing Parthy. This change enables Ferber to write the book she originally envisioned—life in gangster-infested Chicago in the 1890s. Here, Gay gambles away his days as well as the couple's limited resources. Broke and defeated, he abandons Nola and Kim, prompting Nola to buy a secondhand banjo and take to the stage once again. Gay's fall and Nola's eventual rise are similar to Hurstwood and Carrie's experience in DREISER's *Sister Carrie*.

Parthy and Nola's unsatisfying marriages resemble the union that Ferber, who never married, observed most closely. As Gilbert observes, her parents' marriage "provided the original for all the 'ill-assorted' matches that Ferber was later to write about." Ferber admitted that her "parthyesque" mother Julia, "often to my surprise and sometimes annoyance, flung open the door and marched lifesize into many novels as I wrote them." Ferber counted *Show Boat* among her novels where this happened.

Parthy and daughter Nola are patterned after Julia Ferber and daughter Edna. And, like the Ferber women, the Hawks women gain strength and success over time. As one of George S. Kaufman's biographers observed (Ferber and Kaufman collaborated on six plays), "Edna was, in fact, one of those strong, courageous, dynamic women about whom she wrote in her own novels." In typical Ferber style, her leading women (Parthy, Nola, and Kim) all prove stronger and more successful than her male characters (Captain Andy, Gay, and Kim's husband Ken).

When Ferber died in 1968, her obituary in *The New York Times* noted that "her novels became minor classics and earned her a fortune. Her books were not profound, but they were vivid and had a sound sociological basis. Critics of the nineteen-twenties and thirties did not hesitate to call her the greatest American woman novelist of her day." Although Edna Ferber wrote about American life for four decades, her reputation today rests in large measure—and often in fine print—as the author of *Show Boat*.

SOURCES

Dickinson, Rogers. *Edna Ferber*. Garden City, N.Y.: Doubleday, Page & Company, 1925.

Ferber, Edna. *A Kind of Magic*. Garden City, N.Y.: Doubleday & Company, 1963.

———. *A Peculiar Treasure*. New York: Doubleday, Doran & Company, 1939.

———. *Show Boat.* Garden City, N.Y.: Doubleday, Page & Company, 1926.

Gilbert, Julie Goldsmith. *Ferber, A Biography.* Garden City, N.Y.: Doubleday & Company, 1978.

Shaughnessy, Mary Rose. *Women and Success in American Society in the Works of Edna Ferber.* New York: Gordon Press, 1977.

Teichmann, Howard. *George S. Kaufman, An Intimate Portrait.* New York: Atheneum, 1972.

Kurtis L. Meyer

SIDHWA, BAPSI (1938–)

Bapsi Sidhwa, who has been called the most accomplished Pakistani novelist writing in English is less well known in the United States and England than she is in South Asian countries. Her lack of widespread recognition in the United States is probably because American readers and reviewers know little about South Asian history and politics, particularly the 1947 partition of India and Pakistan, her central subject. Sidhwa's other major themes include the evils of patriarchy and the survival of the Parsi (Zoroastrian) religious minority, of which she is a member. Her four novels to date include *The Crow Eaters* (1978), *The Bride* (1983), *Cracking India* (1991) [published as *The Candy Man* in London, 1988]), and *An AMERICAN BRAT* (1993). Of these novels, South Asian history emerges most obviously in *Cracking India.* Sidhwa often employs farce and is known for her humorous treatment of political issues when the subject is not deadly serious, as it is in *Cracking India,* where she describes the atrocities committed by various community members.

Born in Karachi, then part of India, on August 11, 1938, Sidhwa earned her bachelor's degree from Kinnaird College for Women in Karachi in 1956. Sidhwa married Gustad Kermani in 1957 and, after Kermani's death, Noshir R. Sidhwa in 1962. When she immigrated to the United States in 1983, she had already written two novels, *The Crow Eaters* an often humorous account of the Parsi community, and *The Bride,* a serious sequel to *The Crow Eaters.* There a young girl who runs away from an arranged marriage is brutally hunted and killed. Gender and politics converge in *Cracking India* through her descriptions of the mass rapes and murders committed in the Punjab. *An American Brat,* a bildungsro-

man, centers on Feroza, a young Parsi girl who visits the United States, enrolls in college, and horrifies her mother by becoming engaged to a Jewish classmate, David Press. Sidhwa has been praised for her vivid characterizations and the woman's perspective she brings to her fiction. Her novels are included in numerous college and university courses on Asian-American fiction.

NOVELS

An American Brat. New Delhi: Penguin India, 1993.

The Bride. New York: St. Martin's Press, 1983.

Cracking India. Minneapolis, Minn.: Milkweed Editions, 1991; published as *Ice-Candy Man.* London: Heinemann, 1988.

The Crow Eaters. Lahore, Pakistan: Ilmi Printing Press, 1978.

SOURCES

Afzal-Khan, Fawzia. "Bapsi Sidhwa," In *International Literature in English: Essays on the Major Writers.* Edited by Robert L. Ross. 271–281. New York: Garland, 1991.

Baumgartner, Robert J., ed. *Creative Processes in Pakistani Fiction.* Urbana: University of Illinois Press, 1996, pp. 231–240.

Mehta, Nina. "From the Personal to the Political: An Interview with Pakistani Novelist Bapsi Sidhwa," *Bloomsbury Review* (June 1992): 3.

Montenegro, David. "Bapsi Sidhwa: An Interview." *Massachusetts Review* 31, no. 4 (Winter 1990): 513–533.

Powers, Janet M. "Bapsi Sidhwa," In *Asian American Novelists: A Bio-Bibliographical Critical Sourcebook,* edited by Emmanuel S. Nelson, 350–356. Westport, Conn: Greenwood Press, 2000.

OTHER

Malmberg, Jacob Lee. "Bapsi Sidhwa." Voices from the Gaps [VG]. Available online. URL: http://voices.cla.umn.edu/VG/Bios/entries/sidhwa.bapsi.html. Accessed September 25, 2005.

SILKO, LESLIE (MARMON) (1948–)

Leslie Marmon Silko is one of the finest writers associated with the Native American literary renaissance. A short story writer and poet whose first novel, *CEREMONY* (1977), is considered a classic of contemporary American literature, Silko uses the novel form to depict the affinity her characters have with the land, with their Pueblo Laguna customs, with the blending of Catholicism and Native rituals, and with the need for healing.

Silko incorporates strands of Native American and white culture and values.

Leslie Silko was born on March 5, 1948, in Albuquerque, New Mexico, to Leland (Lee) Marmon and Mary Virginia Lee Leslie, and was reared on Old Laguna, a Pueblo Indian reservation west of Albuquerque. She is herself of mixed white, Laguna, and Mexican heritage, and many of her poems and stories feature mixed-blood protagonists. In 1969 she graduated Phi Beta Kappa from the University of New Mexico with a bachelor's degree.

Ceremony features Tayo, a shell-shocked World War II veteran who returns to his Laguna reservation, where he suffers recurring nightmares about his cousin's death on the Bataan Death March. After a downward spiral into alcohol and self-pity, old Betonie and other mentors and healers guide him through the ceremonies that help to heal him. Silko's semiautobiographical *Storyteller* (1981) (critical opinion is divided as to its status as novel or, rather, a collection of stories and poems) appeared to critical acclaim. Using poems, stories, and photos, Silko interweaves these into the story of an orphaned Alaskan Inuit girl who uses her psychic powers to avenge the deaths of her parents. Here Silko powerfully evokes an Arctic winter and describes a polar bear stalking the girl's foster-father figure.

In *Almanac of the Dead* (1991), Silko continues to experiment with form. The novel has complex interwoven threads or plotlines, one of which focuses on the notebooks bequeathed to a Yaqui named Yoeme and her granddaughter Lecha's determination to decipher their meaning. Lecha is also much in demand for her psychic powers. The other main strand of the plot involves a massing of a Mexican revolutionary army planning to reclaim tribal lands to the North. An overarching theme involves the Native determination to reestablish tribal and family values.

Gardens in the Dunes: A Novel (1999) is set in the late 19th century as the struggle between the Native and white worlds is intensifying. The whites continue to plunder natural resources in their move west; the Indians futilely attempt to live off and maintain the sacred nature of the land and its decreasing bounty. The protagonist, Indigo, one of the last of the Sand Lizard people, travels through Europe and South America with the wealthy white woman Hattie, but eventually rejects wealth and luxury to return home to the gardens in the dunes.

Silko, who lives and writes in Tucson, Arizona, and was recently named a Living Cultural Treasure by the New Mexico Humanities Council, is the recipient of the Native Writers' Circle of the Americas Lifetime Achievement Award.

NOVELS

Almanac of the Dead. New York: Simon & Schuster, 1991.
Ceremony. New York: Viking, 1977.
Gardens in Dunes: A Novel. New York: Simon & Schuster, 1999.
Storyteller. New York: Seaver Books, 1981.

SOURCES

Barnes, Kim. Interview in *The Journal of Ethnic Studies* 13, no. 4 (Winter 1986): 83–105.

Blumenthal, Susan. "Spotted Cattle and Deer: Spirit Guides and Symbols of Endurance and Healing in *Ceremony,*" *American Indian Quarterly* 14, no. 4 (Fall 1990): 367–377.

———. "Spotted Cattle and Deer: Spirit Guides and Symbols of Endurance and Healing in *Ceremony,*" *American Indian Quarterly* 14, no. 4 (Fall 1990): 367–377.

Brown, Alanna Kathleen. "Pulling Silko's Threads through Time: An Exploration of *Storytelling,*" *American Indian Quarterly* 19, no. 2 (Spring 1995): 171–180.

Clair, Janet St. "Death of Love/Love of Death: Leslie Marmon Silko's *Almanac of the Dead,*" *MELUS* 21, no. 2 (Summer 1996): 141–156.

Danielson, Linda. "The Storytellers in *Storyteller,*" *Studies in American Indian Literatures* Series 2, vol. 1, no. 2 (Fall 1989): 21–31.

Evasdaughter, Elizabeth N. "Leslie Marmon Silko's *Ceremony:* Healing Ethnic Hatred by Mixed-Breed Laughter," *MELUS* 15, no. 1 (Spring 1988): 83–94.

Grobman, Laurie. "(Re)Interpreting *Storyteller* in the Classroom: Teaching at the Crossroads," *College Literature* 27, no. 3 (Fall 2000): 88–110.

Hirsch, Bernard A. " 'The Telling Which Continues': Oral Tradition and the Written Word in Leslie Marmon Silko's *Storyteller,*" *American Indian Quarterly* 12, no. 1 (Winter 1988): 1–28.

Jaskoski, Helen. "Words Like Bones," *CEA Critic* 55, no. 1 (Fall 1992): 70–84.

———. *Leslie Marmon Silko: A Study of the Short Fiction.* New York: Twayne, 1998, pp. 13–22.

Jones, Patricia. "The Web of Meaning: Naming the Absent Mother, in *Storyteller*." In *"Yellow Woman": Leslie Marmon Silko,* edited by Melody Graulich, 213–232. New Brunswick, N.J.: Rutgers University Press, 1993.

Karno, Valerie. "Legal Hunger, Law, Narrative, and Orality in Leslie Marmon Silko's *Storyteller* and *Almanac of the Dead*," *College Literature* 28, no. 1 (Winter 2001): 29–45.

Krumholz, Linda J. " 'To Understand This World Differently': Reading and Subversion in Leslie Marmon Silko's *Storyteller*," *Ariel* 25, no. 1 (January 1994): 89–113.

Krupat, Arnold. "The Dialogic of Silko's *Storyteller*." In *Narrative Chance: Postmodern Discourse on Native American Indian Literatures,* edited by Gerald Vizenor, 55–68. Albuquerque: University of New Mexico Press, 1989.

Nelson, Robert M. "He Said/She Said: Writing Oral Tradition in John Gunn's 'Ko-pot Ka-nat' and Leslie Silko's *Storyteller*," *SAIL: Studies in American Indian Literatures* 5, no. 1 (Spring 1993): 31–50.

Ruppert, James. "Dialogism and Mediation in Leslie Silko's *Ceremony*," *The Explicator* 51, no. 2 (Winter 1993): 129–134.

———. "The Reader's Lessons in 'Ceremony,'" *Arizona Quarterly* 44, no. 1 (Spring 1988): 78–85.

———. "Story Telling: The Fiction of Leslie Silko," *The Journal of Ethnic Studies* 9, no. 1 (Spring 1981): 53–58.

Salyer, Gregory. "*Storyteller*: Spider-Woman's Web." In *Leslie Marmon Silko,* 58–84. New York: Twayne, 1997.

Schweninger, Lee. "Writing Nature: Silko and Native Americans as Nature Writers," *MELUS* 18, no. 2 (Summer 1993): 47–60.

St. Clair, Janet. "Death of Love/Love of Death: Leslie Marmon Silko's *Almanac of the Dead*," *MELUS* 21, no. 2 (Summer 1996): 141–156.

Truesdale, C. W. "Tradition and *Ceremony*: Leslie Marmon Silko as an American Novelist," *North Dakota Quarterly* 59, no. 4 (Fall 1991): 200–228.

Vangen, Kate Shanley. "The Devil's Domain: Leslie Silko's 'Storyteller.' " In *Coyote Was Here: Essays on Contemporary Native American Literary and Political Mobilization,* edited by Bo Schöler, 116–123. Aarhus, Denmark: Sedkos, 1984.

Wallace, Karen L. "Liminality and Myth in Native American Fiction: *Ceremony* and *The Ancient Child*," *American Indian Culture and Research Journal* 20, no. 4 (1996): 91–119.

OTHER

Native American Authors Project. "Leslie Marmon Silko, 1948–." Available online. URL: http://www.ipl.org/div/natam/bin/browse.pl/A75. Accessed September 25, 2005.

Leslie Marmon Silko. The Creative Web. Available online. URL: http://www.blitz21.com/creativeweb/silko.html. Accessed September 25, 2005.

Voices from the Gaps [VG]. "Leslie Marmon Silko." Available online. URL: http://voices.cla.umn.edu/VG/Bios/entries/leslie_marmon.html. Accessed September 25, 2005.

SINCLAIR, UPTON (UPTON BEALL SINCLAIR) (1878–1968)

Upton Sinclair, a prolific novelist and playwright of the "muckraking" school of naturalism, remains best known for "having turned the stomach of a nation" (Bloodworth, 9) with his novel The JUNGLE (1906), an expose of the horrendous working conditions of the contemporary Chicago meat-packing industry. Politically a socialist who would run unsuccessfully in congressional, senatorial, and gubernatorial campaigns between 1906 and 1934, Sinclair devoted his novelistic talent to illuminating the evils of capitalism and its effects on the major components of American life. He was nominated for a Nobel Prize for literature in 1932, and was awarded the 1943 Pulitzer Prize for his novel *Dragon's Teeth* (1942), third in his 11-novel LANNY BUDD series, which relates the world's history from 1913 through World War II.

Upton Sinclair was born on September 20, 1878, in Baltimore, Maryland, to Upton Beall Sinclair, of an impoverished Virginia aristocratic family forced to become a traveling salesman—and, subsequently, an alcoholic—and Priscilla Harden Sinclair, a literate woman from a wealthy Baltimore family. Reared in Baltimore and New York City, Sinclair earned a bachelor's degree from City College (now City College of the City University of New York) in 1897 and became a full-time writer for the rest of his life, supporting himself during his graduate studies at Columbia University by pseudonymously writing more than 100 dime novels along with journalistic pieces for radical publications. In 1900 he married Meta H. Fuller and lived in New Jersey; after their divorce in 1912, he married Mary Craig Kimbaugh and moved to Southern California. His early novels—*Springtime and Harvest* (1901), *Prince Hagen* (1903), *The Journal of Arthur Stirling* (1903), and *A Captain of Industry* (1906), *The Overman* (1907, written in 1902–03)—were idealistic romances; even while writing these novels, however, his move toward socialistic ideals was evident in *Manassas* (1904), an abolitionist novel featuring Alan Montague, a plantation owner's son who abhors the "peculiar institution" of slavery. While many critics consider

Manassas the best of his early novels, *The Jungle* made him one of the most prominent of the "muckrakers," an early-20th-century group whose aim was social reform through public exposure of social and political abuses. It features Lithuanian immigrant Jurgis Rudkus, who, with his entire family, falls victim to the Chicago packing houses and the grim dwelling place of Packingtown until he sees the hope in socialism. The impact of the novel caused President Theodore Roosevelt to invite Sinclair to the White House and Congress to pass the Pure Food and Drug Act of 1906.

Sinclair continued to write his muckraking novels until the eve of World War II. Generally considered among his best are *King Coal* (1917), about conditions in the coal fields of Colorado; *Oil: A Novel* (1927), a fictional treatment of the Southern California oil fields during the Harding administration; and *Boston* (1928), a fictional account of the Sacco-Vanzetti case, in which the two Italian immigrants accused of murder, robbery, and anarchy were summarily hanged. Other novels include *The Flivver King* (1937), about the auto industry, and *Little Steel* (1938), about the steel industry. Sinclair also wrote numerous nonfiction books about the excesses of capitalism and its effects on institutionalized religion, education, journalism, and art. Between 1940 and 1953 he completed the ambitious Lanny Budd books, a historical series depicting the Western world from 1913 until 1946 and featuring the protagonist, Lanny Budd, age 13 in *World's End* (1940), the first novel in the series, and, like his creator, an enlightened and changed man who has become anticommunist in *The Return of Lanny Budd* (1953). The much admired *Dragon's Teeth* relates the effects of the Nazis on European countries.

In 1967 President Lyndon Johnson invited Upton Sinclair to witness the signing of the Wholesome Meat Act, legislation that would complete the work initiated by the Meat Inspection and Pure Food and Drugs Act many years earlier. On November 25, 1968, Sinclair died in Bound Brook, New Jersey, remembered today, in the words of scholar William Bloodworth, as a writer "who broke new literary ground" (Bloodworth, 64). His papers are housed in the Lilly Library at Indiana University. Several films have been based on books by Sinclair, including *The Adventurer,* produced in 1917 by

U.S. Amusement Corp.; *The Money Changers,* produced in 1920 by Pathé Exchange; *Marriage Forbidden,* produced in 1938 by Criterion; and *The Gnome-Mobile,* produced in 1967 by Walt Disney Productions.

NOVELS

Affectionately Eve. New York: Twayne, 1961.

Another Pamela; or, Virtue Still Rewarded. New York: Viking, 1950.

Boston: A Documentary Novel of the Sacco-Vanzetti Case. New York: A. C. Boni, 1928; published in England as *Boston: A Novel.* London: Laurie, 1929.

A Captain of Industry. Being the Story of a Civilized Man. Girard, Kans.: Appeal to Reason, 1906.

Cicero: A Tragedy of Ancient Rome. privately printed, 1960.

The Coal War: A Sequel to King Coal. Edited by John Graham. Boulder: Colorado Associated University Press, 1976.

Co-op: A Novel of Living Together. New York and Toronto: Farrar & Rinehart, 1936.

Damaged Goods (novelization of play "Les Avaries" by Eugene Brieux). Philadelphia: Winston, 1913; published as *Damaged Goods: A Novel about the Victims of Syphilis.* Girard, Kans.: Haldeman-Julius Publications, 1948.

The Flivver King. Detroit, United Auto Workers, 1937.

The Gnomobile: A Gnice Gnew Gnarrative with Gnonsense. but Gnothing Gnaughty (juvenile). New York: Farrar & Rinehart, 1936.

Jimmie Higgins. New York: Boni & Liveright, 1919.

The Journal of Arthur Stirling: "The Valley of the Shadow." New York: Appleton, 1903.

The Jungle. New York: Doubleday, Page, 1906.

King Coal. New York: Macmillan, 1917.

Limbo on the Loose: A Midsummer Night's Dream. Girard, Kans.: Haldeman-Julius Publications, 1948.

Little Steel. New York and Toronto: Farrar & Rinehart, 1938.

Love's Pilgrimage. New York and London: M. Kennerley, 1911.

Manassas: A Novel of the War. New York and London: Macmillan, 1904. Revised edition published as *Theirs Be the Guilt: A Novel of the War between the States.* New York: Twayne, 1959.

The Metropolis. New York: Moffat, Yard and Co., 1908.

The Millennium: A Comedy of the Year 2000. Girard, Kans.: Haldeman-Julius Publications, 1924.

The Moneychangers. New York: B. W. Dodge and Co., 1908.

Mountain City. New York: A. C. Boni, 1930.

No Pasarán! (They Shall Not Pass): A Story of the Battle of Madrid. Pasadena, Calif.: Author, 1937.

Oil! New York: A. C. Boni, 1927.

100%: The Story of a Patriot. Pasadena, Calif., Author, 1920; published in England as *The Spy.* London: Laurie, 1921.

Our Lady. Emmaus, Pa.: Rodale Press, 1938.

The Overman. New York: Doubleday, Page and Co., 1907.

Prince Hagen: A Phantasy. Boston: L. C. Page and Co., 1903.

Roman Holiday. New York: Farrar & Rinehart, 1931.

Samuel the Seeker. New York: B. W. Dodge and Co., 1910.

Springtime and Harvest: A Romance. New York: Sinclair Press, 1901. Republished as *King Midas, A Romance.* New York and London: Funk & Wagnalls, 1901.

Sylvia. Philadelphia and Chicago: Winston, 1913.

Sylvia's Marriage. Philadelphia and Chicago: Winston, 1914.

They Call Me Carpenter: A Tale of the Second Coming. New York: Boni & Liveright, 1922.

The Wet Parade. New York: Farrar & Rinehart, 1931.

What Didymus Did. London: Wingate, 1954; published as *It Happened to Didymus.* New York: Sagamore Press, 1958.

"LANNY BUDD" SERIES: NOVELS

Between Two Worlds. New York: Viking, 1941.

Dragon Harvest. New York: Viking, 1945.

Dragon's Teeth. New York: Viking, 1942.

One Clear Call. New York: Viking, 1948.

O Shepherd, Speak. New York: Viking, 1949.

Presidential Agent. New York: Viking, 1944.

Presidential Mission. New York: Viking, 1947.

The Return of Lanny Budd. New York: Viking, 1953.

Wide Is the Gate. New York: Viking, 1943.

World's End. New York: Viking, 1940.

A World to Win, 1940–1942. New York: Viking, 1946.

SOURCES

Blinderman, Abraham, ed. *Critics on Upton Sinclair.* Miami, Fla.: University of Miami Press, 1975.

Bloodworth, William A., Jr. *Upton Sinclair.* Boston: Twayne, 1977.

Evans, I. O., ed. *An Upton Sinclair Anthology.* New York: Farrar & Rinehart, 1934.

Grenier, Judson A. "Muckraking the Muckrakers: Upton Sinclair and His Peers." In *Reform and Reformers in the Progressive Era,* edited by David R. Colburn and George E. Pozzetta, 71–92. Westport, Conn.: Greenwood Press, 1983.

Harris, Leon. *Upton Sinclair: American Rebel.* Boston: Crowell, 1975.

Harte, James Lambert. *This Is Upton Sinclair.* Emmaus, Pa.: Rodale Press, 1938.

Schreiber, Georges, ed. *Portraits and Self-Portraits.* Boston: Houghton, 1936.

Scott, Ivan. *Upton Sinclair: The Forgotten Socialist.* Lanham, Md.: University Press of America, 1996.

Sinclair, Upton. *American Outpost* (autobiography). New York: Farrar & Rinehart, 1934.

———. *The Autobiography of Upton Sinclair.* New York: Harcourt, 1962.

Wilson, Christopher. "The Making of a Best Seller, 1906," *The New York Times Book Review,* 22 December 1985, pp. 1, 25, 27.

Yoder, John A., *Upton Sinclair.* New York: Ungar, 1975.

Youdelman, Jeffrey. "In Search of Lanny Budd," *San Jose Studies* 6, no. 1 (February 1980): 87–94.

OTHER

Social Security Online History Pages. "Upton Sinclair." Available online. URL: http://www.ssa.gov/history/sinclair.html. Accessed September 25, 2005.

Wilson, James C., ed. "Upton Sinclair (1878–1968)." Houghton Mifflin. Available online. URL: http://college.hmco.com/english/heath/syllabuild/iguide/sinclair.html. Accessed September 25, 2005.

SINGER, ISAAC BASHEVIS (1904–1991)

Winner of the 1978 Nobel Prize in Literature, Polish-born Isaac Bashevis Singer is remarkable for the way he revitalized the Yiddish language through his award-winning fiction; but he also closely supervised the translations of his work into English. Most of his fiction concerns the disappearance of the European Jewish communities that were held together by faith and culture until the Holocaust destroyed them. Woven into his tales are issues of cultural marginalization and assimilation, as well as individual quests for both romantic love and spiritual fulfillment. Unlike Saul BELLOW, Chaim POTOK, or Philip ROTH, Singer's work is rooted in the shtetls (Jewish villages of Europe); moreover, he thought of himself as a storyteller first and foremost, and, as a result, much of his fiction resonates with reminders of folklore, fable, and allegory. Although he is best known and won most of his awards as a short story writer, Singer wrote 15 novels, many of them originally published in the *Jewish Daily Forward,* a newspaper. All of them were eventually translated into English.

Isaac Bashevis Singer was born on July 14, 1904, in Leoncin, Poland, to author and rabbi Pichose Menachem and Bathsheba Zylberman Singer, the daughter of a rabbi. From 1920 to 1923, he attended Tachkemoni Rabbinical Seminary in Warsaw. After divorcing his first wife, he immigrated to the United States in 1935, became an editor for the *Jewish Daily Forward,* and married Alma Haimann on February 14, 1940. His first novella, *Satan in Goray* (1955), is set in 17th-century Poland and recounts the civil unrest and ensuing war between the Poles and the Ukranians; the book explores conflicts within the Jewish community, some of whom considered Sabbatai Zevi their Messiah. As Singer watched the fall of Warsaw during World War II, he wrote *The Family Moskat,* an enthusiastically received tribute to an (unnamed) Polish city. Narrated by Asa Heshel, it describes three generations of the Moskat family and their place in the changing Polish Jewish community, overshadowed in the end by the increasing power of Hitler. The novel ends just before the Nazi invasion of Poland. *The Manor* (1967) and *The Estate* (1969) are epics that take place in the years of czarist domination. *The Magician of Lublin* (1960) tells the story of acrobat and magician Yasha Mazur. A troubled individual haunted by the past, Yasha becomes a prototype for later Singer characters: He engages in affairs with five different women. When he realizes he can no longer deceive them, he isolates himself in a tiny cell.

The Slave (1962), set in the 17th century, describes the life of a fictional Sarah, Joseph's wife, who converts to Judaism and is ostracized by the entire community. *The King of the Fields* (1988) reaches back to Poland. *Enemies: A Love Story* (1972) focuses on a man who seeks to escape horrific memories of the Holocaust by engaging in multiple affairs: Herman Broder is a bigamist who engages in a passionate relationship with another Holocaust survivor. *Shosha* (1978) features an innocent young woman with a powerful effect on the rabbi's son: Despite a long period of philandering, he returns to her. For Singer, womanizing seemed to be a panacea of sorts, at least as it interrelates with spiritual issues in some of Singer's later fiction.

Scum (1991) features Max Barabander, who, like Yasha Mazur, finds that his sexual relationships with five different women obviously causes spiritual decline. In *The Certificate* (1992), Singer features three women—who represent Zionists, communists, and the Jewish community—all engaged in affairs with David

Bendinger, another rabbi's son who is a writer. In *Meshugah* (1994), Aaron Greidinger, a Polish Jew, lives in New York, Paris, and Israel, has an affair with a Holocaust survivor, and generally lives a life described in the book's title: one that's crazy. *Shadows on the Hudson* (1998) is set in Manhattan. Polish-born Hertz David Grein attempts to choose among the three women with whom he is passionately involved as he struggles with the interweavings of intellect, politics, and spirituality.

After several strokes, Isaac Bashevis Singer died on July 24, 1991, in Florida. He was buried at Beth-El Cemetery in New York City. Along with many of his stories, two of Singer's novels have been adapted for the screen: *The Magician of Lublin,* starring Alan Arkin in 1978, and *Enemies: A Love Story* in 1989. In 2003, playwright Emily Mann adapted *Meshugah* for the stage.

NOVELS AND NOVELLAS

The Certificate. New York: Farrar, Straus & Giroux, 1992.
Enemies: A Love Story. New York: Farrar, Straus & Giroux, 1972.
The Estate. New York: Farrar, Straus & Giroux, 1969.
The Family Moskat. New York: Knopf, 1950.
The King of the Fields. New York: Farrar, Straus & Giroux, 1988.
The Magician of Lublin. New York: Noonday, 1960.
The Manor. New York: Farrar, Straus & Giroux, 1967.
Meshugah. New York: Farrar, Straus & Giroux, 1994.
The Penitent. New York: Farrar, Straus & Giroux, 1983.
Reaches of Heaven: A Story of the Baal Shem Tov. New York: Farrar, Straus & Giroux, 1980.
Satan in Goray. New York: Noonday, 1955.
Scum. New York: Farrar, Straus & Giroux, 1991.
Shadows on the Hudson. New York: Farrar, Straus & Giroux, 1998.
Shosha. New York: Farrar, Straus & Giroux, 1978.
The Slave. New York: Farrar, Straus & Cudahy, 1962.

SOURCES

Alexander, Edward. *Isaac Bashevis Singer.* Boston: Twayne, 1980.
Allentuck, Marcia, ed. *The Achievement of Isaac Bashevis Singer.* Carbondale: Southern Illinois University Press, 1967.
Allison, Alida. *Isaac Bashevis Singer: Children's Stories and Memoirs.* New York: Twayne, 1996.

Biletzky, Israel Ch. *God, Jew, Satan in the Works of Isaac Bashevis-Singer.* Lanham, Md.: University Press of America, 1995.

Buchen, Irving H. *Isaac Bashevis Singer and the Eternal Past.* New York: New York University Press, 1968.

Farrell, Grace, ed. *Critical Essays on Isaac Bashevis Singer.* Boston: G. K. Hall, 1996.

Farrell Lee, Grace. *From Exile to Redemption: The Fiction of Isaac Bashevis Singer.* Carbondale: Southern Illinois University Press, 1987.

Gibbons, Frances Vargas. *Transgression and Self-Punishment in Isaac Bashevis Singer's Searches.* New York: Peter Lang, 1995.

Goran, Lester. *The Bright Streets of Surfside: The Memoir of a Friendship with Isaac Bashevis Singer.* Kent, Ohio: Kent State University Press, 1994.

Hadda, Janet. *Isaac Bashevis Singer: A Life.* New York: Oxford University Press, 1997.

Kresh, Paul. *Isaac Bashevis Singer: The Magician of West 86th Street.* New York: Dial, 1979.

Madison, Charles A. *Yiddish Literature: Its Scope and Major Writers.* New York: Ungar, 1968.

Malin, Irving, ed. *Critical Views of Isaac Bashevis Singer.* New York: New York University Press, 1969.

———. *Isaac Bashevis Singer.* New York: Ungar, 1972.

Pearl, Lila. *Isaac Bashevis Singer: The Life of a Storyteller.* Philadelphia: Jewish Publication Society, 1994.

Pinsker, Sanford. *The Schlemiel as Metaphor: Studies in the Yiddish and American Jewish Novel.* Carbondale: Southern Illinois University Press, 1971.

Siegel, Ben. *Isaac Bashevis Singer.* Minneapolis: University of Minnesota Press, 1969.

Singer, Isaac Bashevis. *Nobel Lecture.* New York: Farrar, Straus, 1979.

Telushkin, Dvorah. *Master of Dreams: A Memoir of Isaac Bashevis Singer.* New York: Morrow, 1997.

Tuszyanska, Agata. *Lost Landscapes: In Search of Isaac Bashevis Singer and the Jews of Poland.* Translated from the Polish by Madeline G. Levine. New York: Morrow, 1998.

Zamir, Israel, and Barbara Harshav. *Journey to My Father, Isaac Bashevis Singer.* Boston: Little, Brown, 1995.

OTHER

Books and Writers. "Isaac Bashevis Singer." Available online. URL: http://www.kirjasto.sci.fi.libsinger.htm. Accessed September 25, 2005.

Isaac Bashevis Singer (cassette). *Tapes for Readers,* 1978.

Meet the Newbery Author: Isaac Bashevis Singer (filmstrip with cassette). Miller-Brody Productions, 1976.

SISTER CARRIE Theodore Dreiser (1900)

When *Sister Carrie* was first published in 1900, it was criticized and ultimately suppressed due to its "immoral" content. Today it is hailed by critics as an exemplar of American literary naturalism and a chronicle of turn-of-the-century capitalism and progress. As a journalist turned author, Theodore Dreiser's writing was strongly influenced by the French literary mode of naturalism that sought to make literature an objective and scientific study of human beings, exploring through characters how experience is shaped by a combination of heredity, environment, and chance. Dreiser translated these ideas into an American context, using the rapid growth of cities and consumerism as his naturalistic setting.

The eponymous protagonist of *Sister Carrie* is Carrie Meeber, and the novel opens with her speeding on the train toward Chicago and "the gleam of a thousand lights" (4). She epitomizes the "American Dream," leaving her small-town life to seek adventure and new experience in unchartered territory. Robert Butler describes this phenomenon in his essay "Movement in Dreiser's *Sister Carrie*": "One of the central and most distinctive values in American culture is a desire for pure motion, movement for its own sake. A relatively new and chronically footless society, America has always placed an unusually high premium on mobility, rather than security and stability" (1). Carrie sets out upon her adventure unsure of her goals, and she continues to drift toward an undefined goal throughout the novel. She travels from Chicago to Montreal, to New York and then from theater to theater. The desire for motion is a desire for change, for progress and self-betterment, and this is Carrie's dream and, behind her, the dream of Dreiser and all Americans.

From page one of the story, Dreiser emphasizes Carrie's unformed, malleable nature that is ready to be influenced by her new environment. She is "bright, timid and full of the illusions of ignorance and youth" and her future lies in the hands of the "cunning wiles" of the city (3,4). Dreiser already warns us that it is the influence of others that will determine how she matures: "[e]ither she falls into saving hands and becomes better, or she rapidly assumes the cosmopolitan standard of virtue and becomes worse. Of an intermediate balance, under the circumstances, there is no possibility." Only a few paragraphs later, Carrie meets the first person who will steer her path: a salesman, Charles Drouet, who impresses her with his charm and good clothes. With Dreiser's caution in mind, we follow Carrie through her first experiences of the city.

The lure of the big city for job seekers in the late 1800s was its growing industry and rapidly developing consumer section. Carrie is seduced by the city and its endless opportunities, and her desire is stimulated and shaped by the department stores (Gammel, 68). There is little that seems to rouse Carrie's emotions more than clothes and material possession. Clothes serve as Carrie's temporary value system, her way of evaluating her new environment. She is immersed within culture, and so her desires become linked to her environment, the city.

In *Sister Carrie,* certain ideas and values espoused by culture are assigned a natural origin to explain their existence. Thus it is "natural" for a woman to act coquettish, to like clothes and ornamentation, and to succumb to emotion. But in Carrie these qualities are, as yet, only partially formed, and as Dreiser will show, it is the battle of supremacy between multiple variables—"instinct and reason, nature and culture, woman and man"—that becomes the pivotal issue of the novel.

Carrie's tale is often described as that of a "fallen woman" as she gives up trying to work for a living early in the novel and moves in with Drouet for the material comfort he offers. Later in the novel, Carrie leaves Drouet for his more sophisticated friend, Hurstwood, whom she later marries (although the marriage is a sham). Until she becomes a successful actress, Carrie relies on men to provide for her, trading her sexuality for material goods in a manner that many critics have described as prostitution. However, despite her traditional denomination as a "fallen woman," Carrie's fall seems relatively painless—indeed she lands on her feet. Carrie's economic and personal success, coupled with an unusual absence of societal punishment for her sexual transgressions, points to a new creed of naturalism.

For Dreiser mankind is evolving, climbing upward on a spiritual, intellectual ladder, in search of the inherent truth in morality and wisdom. It is Carrie

who rises above all this, but after satiating her desire for clothes and luxury, Carrie is left "disillusioned . . . still waiting for the halcyon day when she should be led forth among dreams become real" (487). Unable to achieve her dreams, she only rocks restlessly, weary of striving. And she moves even when she sits, back and forward in her rocking chair, "all the while the siren voice of the unrestful was whispering in her ear" (116).

In 1981 the University of Pennsylvania Press breathed new life into *Sister Carrie* by releasing a "complete" and annotated version of the text, restoring previously deleted material and giving the reader three possible endings. Now critics are left to debate both versions of *Sister Carrie,* guaranteeing its enduring place in contemporary literary discussions.

SOURCES
Butler, Robert James. "Movement in Dreiser's 'Sister Carrie,'" *Dreiser Newsletter* 11, no. 1 (1980): 1–12.

Cassuto, Leonard, and Clare Virginia Eby, eds. *The Cambridge Companion to Theodore Dreiser.* Cambridge: Cambridge University Press, 2004.

Dreiser, Theodore. *Sister Carrie.* Philadelphia: University of Pennsylvania Press, 1980.

Gammel, Irene. *Sexualizing Power in Naturalism: Theodore Dreiser and Frederick Philip Grove.* Calgary, Canada: University of Calgary Press, 1994.

Pizer, Donald, ed. *New Essays on Sister Carrie.* New York: Cambridge University Press, 1991.

Sloane, David E. E. *Sister Carrie: Theodore Dreiser's Sociological Tragedy.* New York: Twayne, 1992.

Kathryn E. Crowther

SLAUGHTERHOUSE-FIVE; OR, THE CHILDREN'S CRUSADE: A DUTY-DANCE WITH DEATH KURT VONNEGUT, JR. (1969)

It is a mixed blessing that *Slaughterhouse-Five,* the best-known of Kurt VONNEGUT, Jr.'s 14 novels, owes at least some of its notoriety to George Roy Hill's 1972 film adaptation. Although it cannot reproduce the novel's complex layers of fact and fiction, the film at least expanded the novel's potential audience beyond Vietnam-era college students and literary intellectuals. Right away the *New York Times* called the book "tough and very funny . . . sad and delightful," but at the same time it had been banned or even burned in North Dakota, Michigan, and

Kentucky. Three decades later it came in at number 18 on the *Modern Library's* list of the 20th century's top 100 novels.

Published almost a decade after CATCH-22, Joseph HELLER's 1961 absurdist look at World War II, *Slaughterhouse-Five* takes its predecessor's deconstruction of calendar time to a new extreme. In his first chapter, Vonnegut offers a rationale for the scrambled chronology as he narrates his preparations for writing a book about the 1945 firebombing of Dresden. He tries to research still-classified government records, tracks down an old war buddy, travels to East Germany on a Guggenheim, ponders possible outlines, and desperately maps subplots in colored crayon on a roll of wallpaper. When he finally proclaims the completion of his "lousy little book" (2) and begins chapter 2, the authorial persona steps aside and we meet alter-ego Billy Pilgrim, a raw American recruit stumbling through the snow as his unit is slaughtered around him in the Battle of the Bulge. His grueling experiences as a POW are based on Vonnegut's own wartime odyssey, with one significant exception, which amounts to the novel's central conceit: "Billy Pilgrim has become unstuck in time. . . . He says" (23).

The remainder of the novel tracks Billy's consciousness as it skips back and forth between his wartime captivity in Germany, his postwar life as a successful but depressed optometrist, and yet another kind of imprisonment in an extraterrestrial zoo, equipped with Sears & Roebuck furniture and household appliances. One night, in the aftermath of his daughter's wedding reception, he is watching a war movie that, as he drifts unstuck in time, makes more sense seen backward than forward, as "German fighters . . . made everything and everybody as good as new" (74). At this point he is, or imagines himself being, kidnapped by aliens called Trafalmadoreans, who sequester him beneath a transparent dome alongside a pornographic film star, Montana Wildhack. The Trafalmadoreans teach Billy a rigidly deterministic worldview in which past, present, and future coexist, free will does not exist, and humans are sealed in their fate "like bugs trapped in amber" (77).

Billy learns to "ignore the awful times and concentrate on the good ones" (117), as marriage and a career are thrust upon him after the war, and posttraumatic stress causes him to quietly but frequently weep. The Trafalmadoreans' philosophy comforts and reassures him, and most early readers, including Alfred Kazin, Anthony Burgess, and Tony Tanner, assumed that Vonnegut himself recommended passive acceptance as the only possible response to 20th-century horror and dehumanizing materialism. But far from endorsing fatalism, Vonnegut slyly undercuts it by making fatalism's chief proponent an inarticulate antihero, while damning his passivity with inane dialogue and sarcastic observations like "Everything was pretty much all right with Billy" (157).

As Robert Merrill and Peter A. Scholl argue in "Vonnegut's *Slaughterhouse-Five:* The Requirements of Chaos," and as numerous textual clues and public statements suggest, Vonnegut's view of human nature is a less cynical one. He attacks the triumphalist conventions of war narratives by juxtaposing Billy's compensatory fantasy with the realistic horror of the WW II scenes, but also shows moments of unassuming individual heroism and compassion that affirm what he told the 1970 graduating class at Bennington graduates: "I beg you to deny [the contemptibility of man]" (65). If the deliberate silliness of the space-opera clichés ("flying saucers," "zap guns," and aliens shaped like plumber's plungers) were not enough to indicate that Trafalmadore and its frame of reference were not to be taken on the same levels of reality as the POW camp and the autobiographical first chapter, scattered scenes in the novel show Billy assembling this subnarrative from the pulp science fiction of the hack writer Kilgore Trout, one of several Vonnegut characters visiting from his other novels, and a glimpse of Montana Wildhack in a porn-store peep show. Vonnegut's narrator points out that "They [war veterans] were trying to re-invent themselves and their universe, and science fiction was a big help" (101) and elsewhere satirizes the escapist materialism of suburban life: "Like so many Americans, she [Billy's mother] was trying to construct a life that made sense from things she found in gift shops" (39).

Similarly, Vonnegut transcends traditional metanarratives by abandoning linear chronology and embracing multiple levels of reality while unifying them through a richly interwoven fabric of fragmentary motifs, from images of glowing watch dials, frost-bitten feet, and open-mouthed barbershop singers to the smell of "mustard gas and roses," persistent refrains like a bird calling "poo-tee-weet" and the narrator intoning "so it goes" after every mention of death in the book. Although the immediate aftermath of the Dresden firebombing, in which more civilians died than at Hiroshima or Nagasaki, serves as the novel's conclusion, bits of Billy Pilgrim's postbellum life are scrambled into his progress from battlefield to POW camp to Dresden bunker, with the occasional connection of Billy's experiences to Vonnegut's by authorial intrusions such as "that was me. That was the author of this book" (125). Instead of using character development, rising conflict, and climax, the novel takes its shape from the sum total of these bits, voiced in Vonnegut's patient, ironic, and deadpan humorous tone.

In refusing to subscribe to any notion of meaning or redemption in warfare, or portray any soldier on either side as a hero or villain, by comparing military recruits to children coerced into a medieval crusade and religious conversion to UFO abduction, Vonnegut creates a faux-naive narrator closer to Billy than to his own war-weary persona, and through the resultant dramatic irony deconstructs all the little fictions that compensate for our modernist angst. Vonnegut's existential vision owes not a little to Beckett's, in the relentless scraping away of surfaces to reveal what compassion and agony lie at the heart of the human condition, and the sometimes bitter, sometimes lighthearted humor that makes this process bearable and even entertaining.

SOURCES

Bloom, Harold, ed. *Kurt Vonnegut.* Philadelphia: Chelsea House, 2000.

Bly, William. *Kurt Vonnegut's "Slaughterhouse-Five."* Woodbury, N.Y.: Barron's Educational Series, 1985.

Boon, Kevin A., ed. *At Millennium's End: New Essays on the Work of Kurt Vonnegut.* Albany: State University of New York Press, 2001.

Broer, Lawrence R. *Sanity Plea: Schizophrenia in the Novels of Kurt Vonnegut.* 2nd ed. Tuscaloosa: University of Alabama Press, 1994.

Klinkowitz, Jerome. *"Slaughterhouse-Five": Reforming the Novel and the World.* Boston: Twayne Publishers, 1990.

Marvin, Thomas F. *Kurt Vonnegut: A Critical Companion.* Westport, Conn.: Greenwood Press, 2002.

Merrill, Robert, ed. *Critical Essays on Kurt Vonnegut.* Boston: G. K. Hall, 1990.

———, and Peter A. Scholl. "Vonnegut's *Slaughterhouse-Five*: The Requirements of Chaos," *Studies in American Fiction* 6 (1978): 65–76.

Morse, Donald E. *Novels of Kurt Vonnegut: Imagining Being an American.* Westport, Conn.: Praeger Publishers, 2003.

Vonnegut, Kurt, Jr. *Slaughterhouse-Five; or, the Children's Crusade: A Duty-Dance with Death.* 1969. New York: Dell, 1971.

———. "Address to Graduating Class at Bennington College, 1970." In *Wampeters, Foma & Granfalloons.* New York: Delacorte Press, 1974.

OTHER

"At Last, Kurt Vonnegut's Famous Dresden Book." Unsigned review, *New York Times Book Review.* Available online. URL: http://www.nytimes.com/books/97/09/28/lifetimes/vonnegut-slaughterhouse.html. Accessed September 26, 2005.

David Fenimore

SLAVE, THE ISAAC BASHEVIS SINGER (1962)

Isaac Bashevis SINGER once remarked that he would only write a story if he had "the conviction or at least the illusion that I am the only one who could write [it]. If I suspect some of the other writers would be able to do it, this would mean that this is not really my story, it is not any more personal and I would not write it" (BBC interview, 1975). This insistence on the personal connection between author and story provides an excellent starting place for a consideration of *The Slave*, believed by many critics to be Singer's finest novel.

Singer, who was born in Poland and lived his adult life as an American citizen, wrote not in Polish or English, but in Yiddish. There is therefore an a priori personal relationship between author and work, emanating from his (and our) consciousness of his Jewish authorial identity. Singer worked closely with his English translator, Cecil Hemley, but the fact remains that his American identity was mediated through the language of his Jewish, Eastern European forefathers. The slave of the title is a man named Jacob, whose righteousness and fortitude recalls his biblical namesake. Singer takes 17th-century Poland as his setting, but the period resonates on several different levels: It can be read an a biblical allegory as well as a representation of Singer's day, not quite 20 years after the Holocaust. The Chmielnicki massacres of 1648 have destroyed a great deal of Poland's Jewry, wiping out Jacob's village, including his wife and children. Jacob himself was taken prisoner and enslaved by a Polish gentile living in the mountains of the surrounding area. Kept there for five years, Jacob is aghast at the behavior and living conditions of the mountain village. Its idol-worshiping inhabitants are little better than animals, who, in stark contrast to Jacob, have no moral code to speak of and no respect for the laws of the land or of any faith.

A devout, learned Jew, Jacob retains the observances of his faith, keeping the Sabbath, adhering to the laws of kashrut [kosher dietary laws], ritually washing his hands before meals, and praying frequently. Unable to eat the gentiles' meat because the animals were not slaughtered according to kosher prescription, Jacob subsists on a vegetarian diet. He is ridiculed by the villagers for this but refuses to assimilate to their lifestyle by eating their food, drinking their wine, or taking a wife from among them. Still, they recognize that there is something to be respected in Jacob, and in spite of their threats, they leave him alone.

No matter how strong Jacob's faith, he cannot prevent himself from falling in love with his master's daughter, Wanda. Their union is forbidden in both of their communities—it is punishable by death under Polish law of the period for a Jew to marry a Christian, and the penalty in the Jewish community for a Jew to marry a gentile only moderately less harsh: excommunication. Jacob finds himself faced with the destabilizing realization that he is committing a sin by loving Wanda but cannot prevent himself from loving her. He becomes, as Singer writes, "a man at war with himself" (33), and begins an interrogation of his faith that, rather than eroding his commitment, deepens and sustains it while inspiring Wanda to worship the Jewish god as well.

When Jacob is suddenly released from bondage, he is forced to leave Wanda behind and return to his community, where because of his years in slavery he is the object of the village's wonder and affection. He has changed irrevocably: although he held fast to his Ortho-

dox beliefs in the mountains, once he rejoins his community he finds he cannot renounce some of his mountain ways—his vegetarianism, for example, and his newfound appreciation for the countryside. Furthermore, he is haunted by visions of Wanda. Unable to live without her, he returns to the mountains and the two elope together. The conflict experienced by Jacob becomes, as Irving Buchen puts it, "the central issue of the novel"; that is, "whether man can love both God and man" (158).

Part 2 of the novel finds the lovers newly married and installed in the village of Pilitz, which is overseen by Lord Adam Pilitzsky, a megalomaniac pedophile (whose daughter killed herself after her father forced himself upon her). Wanda is reborn as Sarah, the name given to all female converts to Judaism, and, posing as a Jewish matron, she pretends to be mute so as not to betray her gentile roots with her elementary Yiddish. Jacob commands the same respect in this community as he has elsewhere, which intensifies the village's surveillance of his wife. They mock her, calling her "Dumb Sarah," and wonder how "so handsome a man" could have married such a "nanny goat" (118–19, 124). Sarah lives but for her husband's company and teaching, and her dedication to her new religion testifies to her own saintliness. The relationship between Jacob and Sarah internally withstands the pressure of their situation, but proves impossible to sustain within the context of the community. Sarah cannot pretend to be mute forever, and she is impelled to speak on several occasions, until finally, in the throes of childbirth, egged on by the cruelty of the community, she betrays her identity.

Some critics have found the role of women in Singer's work to be a particularly vexing subject, and the silence enforced on Wanda/Sarah and her subservience before God and Jacob throughout the novel, until her final rebellion, is worth further interrogation. In spite of its allegorical applications, Singer's novel is firmly rooted in its historical time and place, particularly through the depiction of the landscape, the reconstruction of the sounds and smells of the communities, and the gentile and Jewish myths and superstitions lacing the narrative. Doubtless this is the mark of Singer's personal relationship to his story; it is a testament to his power as a writer that he captures thus his native land from the exile of his Upper West Side Manhattan apartment.

SOURCES

Allentuck, Marcia, ed. *The Achievement of Isaac Bashevis Singer.* Carbondale: Southern Illinois University Press, 1969.

Bailey, Paul. BBC interview with Isaac Bashevis Singer, June 27, 2004.

Buchen, Irving. *Isaac Bashevis Singer and the Eternal Past.* New York: New York University Press, 1968.

Farrell, Grace, ed. *Critical Essays on Isaac Bashevis Singer.* New York: Hall, 1996.

Hadda, Janet. *Isaac Bashevis Singer: A Life.* Madison: University of Wisconsin Press, 2003.

Halio, Jay L. "The Individual Struggle for Faith in the Novels of I. B. Singer," *Studies in American Jewish Literature* 10, no. 1 (Spring 1991): 35–43.

Singer, Isaac Balshevis. *The Slave.* New York: Penguin Classics, 1996.

Lauren Elkin

SMEDLEY, AGNES (1892–1950)

Noting that the 1973 reissue of Agnes Smedley's brilliant autobiographical novel, DAUGHTER OF EARTH, energized renewed interest in the author in the late 20th century, reviewer Deirdre English suggests that Smedley is one of America's most impressive radicals, that rare breed of activist who moved to the heart of the revolutionary struggle without allowing her judgment to get swept away (English). In another view of Smedley, the NOVA online reviewer notes that Smedley's ashes were scattered over the Beijing cemetery for revolutionaries, and characterizes her as a triple agent working for the Soviets, the Chinese Communists, and the Indian nationalists—and "one of the most prolific female spies of the 20th century" (NOVA). Both these views, incorporated with the status of "feminist heroine," are true for Ruth Price, who, in her critically acclaimed 2004 biography, says Smedley was a political activist, journalist, and champion of the poor, female, and the oppressed.

Agnes Smedley was born on on February 23, 1892, on an Osgood, Missouri, tenant farm, to Charles and Sarah Ralls Smedley, who raised her in Colorado coal-mining towns and camps. Her mother was overworked and her father deserted the family when Smedley was 14 years old. She had little formal education and later, during her ceaseless travels, attended university classes as often as possible. As a journalist, she traveled in the United States, Germany, Russia, and China, campaigning with Margaret Sanger on behalf of birth control for women and advocating the cause of the downtrodden in both China and India. She married once, in 1912, to Ernest Brudin, an engineer, and, after their divorce, had numerous long-term relationships with men who were involved in revolutionary causes and espionage. In 1929, Smedley published her first book and only novel—she would go on to write numerous works of nonfiction—*Daughter of Earth.* The hero is Marie Rogers, a poverty-stricken rural schoolteacher who, like Smedley, becomes an internationally known journalist and revolutionary. Along the way, Marie examines issues like the double standard for women and the near enslavement that sometimes grows from physical intimacy: She concludes that "Freedom is higher than love. At least today. Perhaps one day the two will be one" (13).

During the McCarthy era, Smedley was accused of being a Soviet spy (true) and of being a member of the Communist Party (false—she was openly critical of Joseph Stalin). She moved to England and died of acute circulatory failure in May 1950. Her manuscripts are housed at the Hayden Library of Arizona State University at Tempe.

NOVEL

Daughter of Earth. New York: Coward-McCann, 1929; revised edition, 1935; published with a foreword by Alice Walker. New York: Feminist Press, 1987.

SOURCES

Guttman, Sondra. "Working Toward 'Unity in Diversity': Rape and the Reconciliation of Color and Comrade in Agnes Smedley's *Daughter of Earth,*" *Studies in the Novel* 32, no. 14 (Winter 2000): 488.

Price, Ruth. *The Lives of Agnes Smedley.* New York: Oxford University Press, 2004.

OTHER

Anonymous NOVA reviewer. "Agnes Smedley. Secrets, Lies, and Atomic Spies." Available online. URL: http://www.pbs.org/wgbh/nova/venona/dece_smedley.html. Accessed September 26, 2005.

Casey, Dennis. "Triple Agent Agnes Smedley," *Heritage. Air Intelligence Agency,* Lackland Air Force Base, February 2004. Available online. URL: http://aia/lackland.af.mil/homepages/pa/spokesman/feb04/heritage.cfm. Accessed September 26, 2005.

English, Deirdre. "Smedley: The Life and Times of an American Radical," *Washington Monthly* (October 1988) Available online. URL: http://www.findarticles.com/p/articles/mi_m1316/is_n9_v20/ai_6760766. Accessed September 26, 2005.

SMILEY, JANE (JANE GRAVES SMILEY)

(1949–) "To live in the quotidian world of Jane Smiley is to exercise will and to make decisions and choices, and to watch their implications play out over time," observes scholar Neil Nakadate. Because she lacks allegiance to "uncertainty" and "indeterminacy," suggests Nakadate, Smiley is distinctly at odds with postmodernism and poststructuralism (Nakadate, 24). Winner of the Pulitzer Prize and a National Book Critics Circle Award in 1991 for A THOUSAND ACRES (1991), a novel that focuses on Midwestern families, their problems, and their land. She has been especially praised for her detailed evocations of women, usually stouthearted and strong wives and mothers whose decisions have enormous impact on their familys' lives.

Jane Smiley was born on September 26, 1949, in Los Angeles, California, to James Laverne Smiley, an army officer and aeronautical engineer, and Frances Nuelle Graves Smiley, a journalist. Educated at Vassar College, where she earned her bachelor's degree (1971), and at the University of Iowa, where she earned her master of arts (1975), master of fine arts (1976), and doctoral degrees (1978), Smiley published her first novel, *Barn Blind,* in 1980. Set on an Illinois horse farm, it tells the tale of Kate Karlson, mother of four teenagers, who so blindly pursues her desire to produce a champion horse and rider that she cannot see that her ambitions will result in family disaster. *At Paradise Gate* (1981) features the elderly and contemplative Anna Robinson, who played the matriarch despite having married the coldly abusive Ike; she realizes, late in life, that she stayed married at the expense of her emotional life. *Duplicate Keys* (1984), Smiley's third novel, is a suspense story set in New York City.

The romance of librarian Alice Ellis disintegrates when two Minnesota friends are murdered and Ellis meets a police detective and reunites with an old friend.

The Greenlanders (1988), an epic novel that reflects Smiley's academic specialization in medieval literature, is set in 14th-century Greenland and features several generations of the Viking Gunnarsson family. Smiley traces the day-to-day relationships that result in family tragedy and the ultimately doomed Greenland colonies. *Ordinary Love and Good Will* (1989) features Rachel Kinsella, a 52-year-old wife and mother who is extraordinary, not in that she followed her passions into an extramarital affair, resulting in her husband's abandonment of her and his forbidding her to see the children, but in her acknowledgment of responsibility for her choices that elevated her passions as a woman over the joys of motherhood. Whereas *Ordinary Love* is narrated from Rachel's perspective, *Good Will,* the companion novella, uses a male perspective and constitutes a sharp critique of Western patriarchy.

A Thousand Acres (1991), a feminist recasting of Shakespeare's *King Lear,* has at its center Larry Cook, the father, and his decision to leave his multimillion-dollar farm to his three daughters, Ginny, Rose, and Caroline. To the epic sweep of this novel of the Midwest, Smiley adds the dark secret of incest and these central issues: the absence of the mother, the father's abuse of his daughters, and the resulting impact on the daughters' lives, marriages, and relationships to each other as sisters. The darkly comic *Moo* (1995), a satire of academic life at Smiley's agricultural college, Moo U., makes clear that the lust, avarice, and puffed-up egotism of the professoriat lie beneath layer upon layer of hypocrisy. According to Nakadate, *Moo* completed the third of the four genres of novels that Smiley had long planned to write: epic, tragedy, comedy, and romance. *The All-True Travels and Adventures of Lidie Newton* (1998) is a mid-19th-century Midwestern story of one woman's romance. Lida Harkness marries Thomas Newton, a Massachusetts abolitionist, and faces with him the difficulties of an emerging nation and the privations of pioneer life. Smiley's most recent novel is *Horse Heaven* (2000), a sprawling and insightful look into the world of the American racetrack through the eyes of the horses.

Smiley has been married three times: to John Whiston from 1970 to 1975; to William Silag, an editor, from 1978 to 1986; and to Stephen M. Mortensen, a screenwriter, from 1987 to 1997. She lives and writes in Carmel, California. In 1997, *A Thousand Acres* was adapted for film by Laura Jones and released by Touchstone Pictures in 1997, and the novella *The Age of Grief* was adapted by Craig Lucas as *The Secret Lives of Dentists,* directed by Alan Rudolph and starring Hope Davis and Campbell Scott.

NOVELS AND NOVELLAS

Age of Grief. New York: Knopf, 1987.
The All-True Travels and Adventures of Lidie Newton. New York: Knopf, 1998.
At Paradise Gate. New York: Simon & Schuster, 1981.
Barn Blind. New York: Harper & Row, 1980.
Duplicate Keys. New York: Knopf, 1984.
The Greenlanders. New York: Knopf, 1988.
Horse Heaven. New York: Knopf, 2000.
Moo. New York: Knopf, 1995.
Ordinary Love and Good Will. New York: Knopf, 1989.
A Thousand Acres. New York: Knopf, 1991.

SOURCES

Nakadate, Neil. *Understanding Jane Smiley.* Columbia: University of South Carolina Press, 1999.
Sheldon, Barbara H. *Daughters and Fathers in Feminist Novels.* New York: Peter Lang, 1997.

OTHER

Audio Interview with Jane Smiley. Wired for Books. Available online. URL: http://wiredforbooks.org/janesmiley. Accessed September 26, 2005.
Author Spotlight: Jane Smiley. Random House Web site. Available online. URL: http://www.randomhouse.ea/catalog/author.pperl?authorid=28760. Accessed September 26, 2005.
Review of *House Heaven.* Salon.com. Available online. URL: http://www.salon.com.books/review/2000/04/17/smiley. Accessed September 26, 2005.
Smiley, Jane. "Take a Wild Ride with Jane Smiley's Spirited New Heroine. By Ellen Kanner. BookPage. Available online. URL: http://www.bookpage.com/9804bp/jane_smiley.html. Accessed September 26, 2005.

SMITH, LEE (1944–)

A novelist and short story writer who writes about the mountains of Appalachia where she was reared, Lee Smith has emerged as a significant force in contemporary American literature. In a recent interview, she stressed the importance of recording regional distinctions "because of the homogenization that is going on in American culture. One place is becoming much like every other place. I am proud of my work in recording these regional distinctions and in creating a record of the values, mores, and manners of the Appalachian South" (Reading Group Guides). In addition, Smith experiments frequently with technique, particularly with point of view. She creates ordinary characters with singular voices who come vividly alive on the pages of her nine novels, often through the use of humor. Although critics continue to debate the ranking of her works, most agree that *Fair and Tender Ladies* (1988) and *Oral History* (1983) top the list.

Smith was born on November 1, 1944, in Grundy, Virginia, to Ernest Lee Smith, a successful entrepreneur, and Virginia Marshall Smith, a schoolteacher. She was educated at Hollins College, where she wrote her first novel, *The Last Day the Dogbushes Bloomed* (1968), published the year after she received her bachelor of arts degree and married poet James E. Seay. The novel examines the impact of her parents' divorce on a nine-year-old girl, Susan Tobey, who learns about life partly through her encounter with a disturbed city boy. Her next novel, *Something in the Wind* (1971), again depicts the initiation of a young girl, Brooke Kincaid, and the third, *Fancy Strut* (1973) (a term used by cheerleaders to describe a goose step), examines the novel's central event, a sesquicentennial, from multiple perspectives. In *Black Mountain Breakdown* (1980), Crystal Spangler—in addition to enduring rape—must choose between the social world of beauty contests and politics, and the world of her sometimes suicidal lover.

After her marriage dissolved in 1981, Smith began to write the Appalachian novels, emphasizing both the importance of language and the inescapability of the past. *Oral History* (1983) depicts four generations of the Cantrell family through the point of view of Granny, and *Family Linen* (1985)—dedicated to her second husband, journalist Hal Crowther, whom Smith married in 1985—unites the characters through a wedding and a funeral, both of which initiate change. *Fair and Tender Ladies* (1988) uses letters to reveal Ivy

Rowe's quest for meaning and identity. These last two novels also reveal Smith's increasing use of subversive language, particularly with regard to the artistic process. *The Devil's Dream* (1992) follows a musical family who sing country music; gradually they migrate from the Virginia mountains to Nashville.

Smith's most recent work, *The Last Girls* (2003), inspired by her memories of a rafting trip down the Mississippi River during her years at Hollins College (Author interview), explores the differences between expectations and reality in the lives of women who have a reunion many years after their college river trip. Lee Smith was honored by Emory and Henry College on October 11, 1985, the date of their Lee Smith Literary Festival. Smith continues to write and teach at North Carolina State University.

NOVELS AND NOVELLAS

Black Mountain Breakdown. New York: Putnam's, 1980.
The Christmas Letters: A Novella. Chapel Hill, N.C.: Algonquin Books, 1996.
The Devil's Dream. New York: Putnam's, 1992.
Fair and Tender Ladies. New York: Putnam's, 1988.
Family Linen. New York: Putnam's, 1985.
Fancy Strut. New York: Harper, 1973.
The Last Day the Dogbushes Bloomed. New York: Harper, 1968.
The Last Girls. Chapel Hill, N.C.: Algonquin Books, 2003.
Oral History. New York: Putnam's, 1983.
Saving Grace. New York: Putnam's, 1995.
Something in the Wind. New York: Harper, 1971.
We Don't Love with Our Teeth. Portland, Ore.: Chinook Press, 1994.

SOURCES

Hill, Dorothy Combs. *Lee Smith.* New York: Twayne, 1992.
Hobson, Fred. "A Question of Culture—and History: Bobbie Ann Mason, Lee Smith, and Barry Hannah." In *The Southern Writer in the Postmodern World.* Athens: University of Georgia Press, 1991.
Jones, Anne Goodwyn. "The World of Lee Smith," *Southern Quarterly* 22 (Fall 1983): 115–139. Reprinted in *Women Writers of the Contemporary South,* edited by Peggy Whitman Prenshaw. Jackson: University Press of Mississippi, 1984.
Parrish, Nancy C. *Lee Smith, Annie Dillard, and the Hollins Group: A Genesis of Writers.* Baton Rouge: Louisiana State University Press, 1998.
Smith, Rebecca. *Gender Dynamics in the Fiction of Lee Smith: Examining Language and Narrative Strategies.* San Francisco: International Scholars Publications, 1997.

OTHER

Random House. Reading Group Guides. Author Interview. Available online. URL: http://www.readinggroupguides.com/guides/news_of_the_spirit-author.asp#bio. Accessed September 26, 2005.

SNOW WHITE DONALD BARTHELME (1967)

Postmodern in its sensibility, Donald BARTHELME's prose has been noted for its "nonlinear narration, sportive form and cohabitation of radical fantasy with quotidian detail" (Barth, 3). His first of four novels, *Snow White* is an experimental work that utilizes subversive literary strategies to critique contemporary America. In his text, Barthelme parodies the fairy tale to such an extent that the familiar Grimm tale and its characters are barely recognizable. No longer is the title protagonist characterized by innocence, purity, and her desire to subscribe to fixed roles relegated to females in children's fables. The Snow White of Barthelme's story is creatively adventurous, sexually promiscuous, and seeks alternatives to her mundane existence.

Finding herself in a contemporary world marked by the homogenization of culture, a weakening of moral values, and the breakdown of meaningful communication and connection, Barthelme's protagonist yearns for new modes of expression and a language that is motivated by a fluid, innovative spirit. Voicing her regret that her imagination is stirring amidst stale forms of articulation, Barthelme's Snow White states, "Oh I wish there were some words in the world that were not the words I always hear!" (12). In like fashion, Snow White desires a different world than the one in which she lives. While penning a pornographic poem whose theme is loss, Snow White tells the seven men with whom she resides that the privation about which she writes "must be laid . . . to a failure of the imagination. [She has] not been able to imagine anything better" (65). Snow White's frustration stems from the prevailing contradiction inherent in the ideology of the day. That is, contemporary America promises greater possibilities than it can realistically bestow, and this creates perpetual disappointment and insatiability. "I have conflicting ideas," admits a rueful Snow White. "But the main theme that runs through my brain is that what is, is insufficient" (141). In addition to the said creative paucity that torments her, the grounding values that were prevalent in fairy tale, are lost to Barthelme's contemporary Snow White. These values have been buried by the "mindless consumption of ideas," material goods, and information that has resulted in an equanimity of all perspectives, interpretations, ideologies, and moral posturing (Morace, 167). Barthelme's characters lament the "unbearable consensus" (72) that they deem a consequence of this espoused relativity, and heed that one "should bear in mind multiplicity, and forget about uniqueness" (81) in the contemporary world.

Contributing to the theme of cultural deficiency in the novel are the substitution of the seven dwarfs' befitting Disney appellations for otherwise common names (Trachtenberg, 171) and the fact that they work to perpetuate the marketing schemes that exploit consumers' desires. In the context of Barthelme's novel, the seven dwarfs embody what critic Robert A. Morace calls a "dwarf culture" (Morace, 171). Bill, Clem, Dan, Edward, Henry, Hubert, and Kevin wash buildings and cook Chinese food in vats to sell as baby food. Demonstrating a deleterious marketing savvy that values attractive-looking merchandise above quality wares, one of the seven dwarfs tells the reader: "It is amazing how many mothers will spring for an attractively packaged jar of Baby Dim Sum, a tasty-looking potlet of Baby Jing Shar Shew Bow" (24). Further satirizing consumer culture, Edward focuses on its veneration of mass consumption when he ironically declares later in the novel that "[w]ere it not for [one's] enormous purchasing power and the heedless gaiety with which it is exercised, we would still be going around dressed in skins probably, with no big-ticket items to fill the empty voids, in our homes and in our hearts" (105). Underlying Edward's playful tone is the grave, fundamental paradox associated with the amassment of material goods: The more one accumulates, the greater the void generated by the emotional dissatisfaction that ensues. This paradox informs the metafictional strategy of the novel. As the novel progresses, the reader becomes increasingly aware of its lack of a conventional plot, and that many of the characters' anxieties emanate from the author's search for a new form of literature that can adequately depict the uncertainties prevalent in the contemporary world.

In its search for a new language to delineate the incertitude that pervades contemporary America, Barthelme's *Snow White* spawns far more questions than it answers. For example, it questions the extent to which a prince can exist within a literature that observes America's long-standing "democratic tradition which is anti-aristocratic" (147). "Egalitarianism precludes princeliness," asserts Clem. "And yet our people are not equal in any sense" (147). Satirizing America's exchange of one form of social stratification for another, Barthelme portrays Paul, Snow White's would-be prince, as an easily distracted welfare recipient. "Probably I should go out and effect a liaison with some beauty who needs me, and save her, and ride away with her flung over the pommel of my palfrey, I believe I have that right. But on the other hand, this duck-with-blue-cheese sandwich that I am eating is mighty attractive and absorbing, too" (33–34). Role reversal, uncertainty, and contradiction lead to anxieties associated with self-doubt, identity, and the nature of reality. "Paul?" Snow White asks herself. "Is there a Paul, or have I only projected him in the shape of my longing, boredom, ennui and pain?" (108). Given that subjectivity, relativity, and the notion of endless possibility rule the contemporary environment, perhaps the only way to a purer form of innovation is to "retract everything" (19), to start fresh, so as to find a new form that allows for possibility, but also does not compromise uniqueness. Donald Barthelme's *Snow White* is an experiment in doing just that.

SOURCES

Barth, John. "Thinking Man's Minimalist: Honoring Barthelme." In *Critical Essays on Donald Barthelme,* edited by Richard F. Patterson, 1–4. New York: G. K. Hall, 1992.

Barthelme, Donald. *Snow White.* 1967. Reprint, New York: Simon & Schuster, 1996.

Morace, Robert A. "Donald Barthelme's *Snow White:* The Novel, the Critics, and the Culture." In *Critical Essays on Donald Barthelme,* edited by Richard F. Patterson, 164–172. New York: G. K. Hall, 1992.

Trachtenberg, Stanley. *Understanding Donald Barthelme.* Columbia: University of South Carolina Press, 1990.

Alex Ambrozic

SO BIG Edna Ferber (1924)   *So Big* is the first in a series of regional novels for which Edna Ferber is well known, among them *Showboat* (1926), *Cimarron* (1930), *Saratoga Trunk* (1941), *Come and Get It* (1944), *Giant* (1952), and *Ice Palace* (1958). *So Big* won the Pulitzer Prize for fiction in 1925, the highest level of critical acclaim that Ferber would receive in her career. *So Big* prefigures Ferber's later work in its regional subject matter, its themes of idealism and adversity, and its storyline of the indomitable woman who must face her future with no help from the men in her life.

The novel is set in the fictional community of High Prairie, a fertile farmland community south of Chicago where first-generation Dutch truck farmers cultivate vegetables for the city's great markets. The book spans the years from the 1880s through the early 1920s during Chicago's transformation from a frontier town to what the poet Carl Sandburg called the "Hog Butcher for the World" in his 1916 poem, "Chicago." The title *So Big* comes from the nickname its heroine, Selina Peake DeJong, gives to her son, Dirk, from the familiar game that mothers play with their children, asking "How big is my baby?" to which the child answers "Soooo big!" with outstretched arms. Selina is the only child of a widower gambler, Simeon Peake, whom she adores despite his unreliable ways. When Simeon dies, he leaves her a small sum of money and two diamonds, but her intangible inheritance is already worth far more to her. She shares Simeon's imagination, his zest for living, and his understanding that "there are only two kinds of people in the world that really count. One kind's wheat and the other kind's emerald" (11). She carries this knowledge with her all her life, but imagination is a scarce and undervalued commodity in a community consumed with the brutal farm work that demands all its inhabitants' time and energy. For example, when early in her career as a prairie schoolteacher, Selina comments that the fields of cabbages are beautiful, Klaas Poole, the farmer with whom she boards, laughs at her. Only Roelf, the sensitive 12-year-old son of Klaas and his wife, Martje, finds encouragement in Selina's ideas.

Ferber's purpose is to show the vitality of the imagination and the life-enhancing force of a love of beauty. Selina's life is uneventful by most measures, but her quiet crusade to keep beauty alive in her own life and in that of her son animates the book. Like Ferber's other works, which frequently portray absent or undependable men and stalwart women, *So Big* includes a bittersweet love story. Selina falls in love with a handsome young farmer, Pervus DeJong, and marries him, but she does not live happily ever after, for her life becomes one of ceaseless toil, just like that of the women around her. Her work is even harder to bear because Pervus, like Klaas, laughs off her ideas for draining land and making the farm more productive. When Pervus dies, leaving Selina and Dirk near poverty on their unprofitable land, Selina takes on the man's job of farming and taking the produce to market. Although Selina cheerfully sacrifices her own life for Dirk's, saying that hers does not count, the book contains strong feminist themes, especially in this section. To the minister's pious platitudes about God providing for the weak and watching over the fallen sparrows, Selina replies, "I don't see . . . what good that does the sparrow, once it's fallen" (161). To a farmer who suggests that she should stay in her kitchen, where women belong, she snaps, "Don't talk to me like that, you great stupid! What good does it do a woman to stay home in her kitchen if she's going to starve there, and her boy with her?" (178). Selina vows to make a success of the farm and her life, and she does so with some help from August Hempel, the king of the meatpacking industry and the father of her school friend Julie.

The second half of the book follows Dirk's experiences as a student at Midwest University, as a struggling architect, and, after World War I, as a bond salesman. He soon rises to the top with the help of Paula, Julie's wealthy and unhappily married daughter. With the introduction of Paula, Ferber begins to use the symbol of hands to indicate character in this work: For example, Dirk is attracted to Paula, but he hesitates at first after observing that her hands are not large and generous like his mother's but small and grasping. He uneasily acknowledges that "her lean, dark, eager fingers had manipulated the mechanism that ordered his career" (299), but he continues to permit her to do so, becoming rich in worldly goods but abandoning his love of architecture. When Selina playfully challenges him about his profession, asking "How big is my son?" Dirk answers, " 'So big!' " and "measured a very tiny space between thumb and forefinger" (298). Outwardly successful, Dirk is miserable when he falls in love with an artist, Dallas O'Mara, who tells him that she can love only someone whose scarred and calloused hands reveal his struggle toward his dream. In short, Dirk does not qualify, for as Dallas tells him, "you haven't a mark on you" (348). He recognizes the depth of his failure at a gathering at Selina's farm, where Selina and Roelf Poole, now a famous artist, meet again. Recalling what Selina had told him about her father long ago, Roelf, Selina's spiritual son, tells her, "You're wheat, Selina," to which she replies, "And you're emerald," thus cementing the unspoken connection between them (357). Hearing this and seeing Dallas drawn to Roelf rather than himself, Dirk reflects, "You're nothing but a rubber stamp, Dirk DeJong" (358). Recognizing that he is neither wheat nor emerald, Dirk sees that he has squandered his own store of the creative force that Selina has put into her life, and that Roelf and Dallas have put into their art. As he prepares to meet Paula that evening, he sees himself trapped, for he understands that the rest of his life will center on the meaningless repetition of inconsequential acts.

Despite its initial positive reception, *So Big* has inspired almost no critical commentary over the past several decades. Much of the recent work on Ferber has focused on her earlier work, the Emma McChesney stories, which featured a traveling saleswoman, or the recent rediscovery of Ferber as a Jewish-American writer. Ferber's other novels have also received little critical attention, a trend that has shifted somewhat with recent essays on Ferber's treatment of race and ethnicity in *Showboat*.

SOURCES

Batker, Carol. "Literary Reformers: Crossing Class and Ethnic Boundaries in Jewish Women's Fiction of the 1920s," *MELUS: The Journal of the Society for the Study of the Multi-Ethnic Literature of the United States* 25, no. 1 (Spring 2000): 81–104.

Berlant, Lauren. "Pax Americana: The Case of *Show Boat.*" In *Cultural Institutions of the Novel,* edited by Deidre Warner and William B. Lynch, 399–422. Durham, N.C.: Duke University Press, 1996.

Ferber, Edna. *A Peculiar Treasure.* New York: Doubleday Doran & Company Inc., 1939.

———. *So Big.* Garden City, N.Y.: Doubleday, 1924.

Gilbert, Julie Goldsmith. *Ferber: A Biography.* Garden City, N.Y.: Doubleday, 1978.

Horowitz, Steven P., and Miriam J. Landsman. "The Americanization of Edna: A Study of Ms Ferber's Jewish American Identity," *Studies in American Jewish Literature* (1982): 69–80.

Shapiro, Ann R. "Edna Ferber, Jewish American Feminist," *Shofar: An Interdisciplinary Journal of Jewish Studies* 20, no. 2 (2001): 52–60.

Shaughnessy, Mary Rose. *Women and Success in American Society in the Works of Edna Ferber.* New York: Gordon, 1976.

Donna Campbell

SO FAR FROM GOD ANA CASTILLO (1998)

At the beginning of the novel, Sofia, the main character, embodies the figure of the surrogate mother and satisfying wife; she lives an uneventful family life until her youngest daughter dies. Surprisingly, the three-year-old girl, later referred to as "La Loca," wakes up in her coffin in the middle of her funeral, provoking a fright among the church congregation. From that moment on, Sofi changes her priorities in life, especially after her husband, Domingo, abandons her. Then she decides to take the reins not only of her house but of her business, the "Carne Buena Carnecería" (Good Meat Butchers). Her ambition later leads her to political power, becoming mayor of the village of Tomé. Not satisfied with her political success, she rises still higher after the second death of La Loca, founding a religious association, Mothers of Martyrs and Saints (M.O.M.A.S), which places her at the pinnacle of religious authority. She even defies the traditional beliefs of the Catholic Church: She has founded a true matriarchy at the top of which, as a pope herself, Sofi sits as "la first presidenta" (the first president).

Following the same religious symbolism, the names of the characters are allegorical: Domingo stands for the laziness of Sunday, Sofia means "wisdom," and the three eldest daughters bear the names of the three theological virtues in Spanish: Esperanza (Hope), Caridad (Charity) and Fe (Faith). Esperanza, the eldest, is a civil rights activist, the rebel woman involved in Chicano movements and demonstrations together with her boyfriend,

Rubén, who betrays her and their free-love agreement by marrying a rich woman. She dies in Saudi Arabia, where she is sent as a correspondent during the Gulf War. Caridad, divorced from her high school sweetheart, Memo, loves partying and having different lovers until she suffers a sexual attack, and miraculously her disfigured body is completely healed. From then on, Caridad learns, through Doña Felicia, the work of the *curandera* (healer) and she reveals to be a good "channeler," or medium. Finally, she finds real love in a woman called Esmeralda, whom she meets during a pilgrimage to Chimayó on Good Friday. However, Franciso El Penitente had also fallen in love with her during that pilgrimage and starts stalking her. Both women, tired of fighting for their love, end their lives by jumping off the mesa and disappearing into thin air, apparently supported by the hands of the goddess Tsichtinako.

The life Fe dreams of has nothing to do with her sister. She aims to marry her boyfriend, Tom, keep her job in a bank, and have children. However, Tom breaks their engagement and she has a nervous breakdown, screaming nonstop for days and damaging her vocal cords irreversibly. "La Gritona" (the Yeller) as people call her during the period, loses her job, although she finds a better paying one with ACME and marries her cousin Casimiro.

La Loca, the resurrected child, receives this nickname from the other villagers because she grows up to become a weird person who avoids contact with other human beings, although, paradoxically, she dies of AIDS. The reader never learns her real name and, to suggest her mythic status, Castillo makes her acquainted with La Llorona, a mythical figure of Chicano folklore, a woman who appears close to water, crying for her drowned children. La Llorona functions as a link with the supernatural in the novel, for she tells La Loca about the death of Esperanza; moreover it is after her visits that Sofi's family sees the lost daughter who returns in "ectoplasmic" form. The presence of La Llorona, far from being casual, contains Castillo's attempt to rescue female figures from the negative meanings of Chicano tradition. When Doña Felicia, the bonesetter, teaches Caridad to become a good *curandera,* she, too, acts according to the tradition of recovery. Common healing remedies from Doña Felicia

are provided in the narrative. New Mexico, where the novel is set, has traditionally been considered a land of enchantment and fantasy, and so Castillo states when she calls Santa Fe, the capital city of the state, "Fanta Se" because its inhabitants readily accept the supernatural as part of their lives.

So Far from God constitutes a protest against the injustices of the world; therefore, all Castillo's protagonists—except for Sofia, who has been called to make the change in the world—die tragically. Fe's death is condemnation of the environmental racism of the ACME company, which makes its employees use toxic components that damage their health and drive them to a sure death. Castillo draws attention to abuses of the female body by means of the strange circumstances of the sisters' deaths: Caridad's body vanishes in the air, Esperanza's is missing, and Fe's is destroyed by chemicals. Together with La Loca, whose ill body has shrunk so much that there is not much left to bury after her death, they become martyrs of a society that dehumanized them when they were alive.

The echo of old-fashioned novels of romance and chivalry appears in the titles of the chapters which also remind us of Latin American *telenovelas* (soap operas). This technique has also been used by postmodern authors. The most instructive way to view this novel is as parody: of institutions, of medicine, of religion, of patriarchy. However, Castillo's humor pales in the failure to change a world where women receive the worst part, even though some, like Sofi, become empowered and successfully challenge the established rules.

SOURCES

Maciel, David R., Isidro D. Ortiz, María Herrera-Sobek, eds. *Chicano Renaissance: Contemporary Cultural Trends.* Tucson: University of Arizona Press, 2000.

Madsen, Deborah L. *Understanding Contemporary Chicana Literature.* Columbia: University of South Carolina Press, 2000.

Rebolledo, Tey Diana. *Women Singing in the Snow: A Cultural Analysis of Chicana Literature.* Tucson: The University of Arizona Press, 1995.

Zinn, Maxine Baca. "Political Familism: Toward Sex Role Equality in Chicano Families." In *Latina Issues: fragments of historia (ella) (herstory),* edited by Antoinette Sedillo López, 237–251. New York: Garland Publications, 1999.

Imelda Martín Junquera

SON AT THE FRONT, A EDITH WHARTON (1923)

A Son at the Front is a political novel with a specific propagandist purpose. In 1907, Edith WHARTON moved to France. During World War I, she visited the French front "from end to end" (Wharton 1915, 216), established three major charities (Price, 40, 48), and experienced bombardment personally at home in Paris (Wharton 1934, 357). It was a visit to a hospital at Chalons-sur-Marne for the French Red Cross that made her "feel the urgency of telling my rich and generous compatriots something of the desperate needs of hospitals in the war-zone" (Wharton 1934, 352). Her particular propagandist task was to engender knowledge of, and sympathy for, the Allies' cause among her fellow countrymen, in order to persuade them to fight for it. Politically, this matched her friend, Theodore Roosevelt's, policy of "preparedness," expounded in *America and the World War* (1915) and *America and Preparedness* (campaign speeches of 1916 collected in 1917), his platform for the 1916 presidential election. (Wharton makes explicit reference to Roosevelt's "preparedness" in *A Son at the Front* [176].) To garner support for France, Wharton sent dispatches to *Scribner's Magazine* during the war (collected as *Fighting France: From Dunkerque to Belfort* [1915]), wrote essays on the French way of life (collected as *French Ways and Their Meaning* [1919]), and compiled a "gift-book," *The Book of the Homeless* (1916), soliciting contributions from distinguished writers and artists. In addition to *A Son at the Front,* she wrote a novella (*The Marne* [1918]) and several short stories (notably "How to Write a War Story" [1919]) about the conflict.

A Son at the Front not only bridges the gap between conditions in France and Wharton's American readership's knowledge of them, but also reveals another array of gaps. There is the obvious gap between the front, known only, as Shari Benstock points out, through rumour, speculation and clairvoyance (Benstock, xiv), and the rear. There is the time lapse between the end of the war and the novel's publication. ("Where in the world has Mrs. Wharton been all this time?" asked one reviewer in 1923 [Rascoe 17].) There is the "unbridgeable abyss" (212) between the artist, John Campton, and his son George, whose true intentions elude Campton for most of the novel, although the reader long guesses them. The gulf is complicated, but never eradicated, by Campton's growing feeling (intended as a parallel to American public opinion with regard to the country's involvement as a whole?) that George ought to fight, and to want to fight. There is another disparity, economic this time, between Campton and the Brants. There is the experiential difference between the combatants and those who view the war as "unwarrantable interference" with their private plans and to whom, in any event, approaches to the front are "sternly forbidden" (11, 71). There is the generational divide. Campton remarks: "Men of our age are the chorus of the tragedy. . . . As soon as I open my lips to blame or praise I see myself in white petticoats, with a long beard held on by an elastic, goading on the combatants in a cracked voice from a safe corner of the ramparts. On the whole I'd sooner be spinning with the women" (103). Finally, there is the particularly blatant difference between fighting Europe and pre-Lusitania, noninterventionist Wilsonian United States: "cant and cowardice had drugged and stupefied her into the strange belief that she was too proud to fight for others" (135).

But perhaps the most significant gap in *A Son at the Front* is the age-old one between art and life. Shari Benstock makes the intriguing point that, in the novel, the "front" is hidden from view even though Wharton, with her firsthand *Fighting France* experiences, could have described it in detail had she chosen to (Benstock, xiii). Campton, in the early months of the conflict, feels that "if ever there came a time for art to interpret the war . . . the day was not yet" (71). There is a need for distance—for a gap—before art can engage with experience. Before Wharton could write *A Son at the Front* or "deal objectively with the stored-up emotions of those years," she had "to get away from the present altogether" (Wharton 1934, 369). It took her five years to look back.

SOURCES
Benstock, Shari. "Introduction." *A Son at the Front by Edith Wharton.* DeKalb: Northern Illinois University Press, 1995, pp. vii–xvi.

Price, Alan. *The End of the Age of Innocence. Edith Wharton and the First World War.* London: Robert Hale, 1996.

Rascoe, Burton. "A Son at the Front," *New York Tribune* 9 September 1923, 17–18.

Wharton, Edith. *A Backward Glance.* New York and London: D. Appleton, 1934.

———. *Fighting France: From Dunkerque to Belfort.* London: Macmillan, 1915.

———. *A Son at the Front.* DeKalb: Northern Illinois University Press, 1995.

Kate McLoughlin

SONE, MONICA (KAZUKO ITOI)
(1919–) Monica Sone wrote *NISEI DAUGHTER,* a novel-like memoir about the Japanese internment experience during World War II. The book is often compared with John OKADA's *NO-NO BOY,* a story about Ichiro, a young Japanese American imprisoned during World War II, and his return to his former home in Seattle, Washington, or Julia Otsuka's much more recent *When the Emperor Was Divine,* a novel based on Otsuka's mother's experience in an internment camp during World War II.

Monica Sone was born Kazuko Itoi in 1919 in Seattle to Japanese immigrant parents who owned and operated a hotel on Seattle's Skid Road. As a child of first-generation Japanese Americans, she realized that she was both Japanese and American. She uses the image of "two heads" to describe this phenomenon. She was interned with her family at the Minidoka Camp in Topaz, Idaho, but, as a Nisei, was allowed to move outside the camp and find work. After the war, Sone received a bachelor's degree from Hanover College and a master's degree in clinical psychology in 1949 from Case Western Reserve University. She stayed in Ohio and married Geary Sone. *Nisei Daughter,* published four years later, is significant as both a historical account of the internment and a vivid and literary portrayal of key moments in the life of a bicultural American woman. *Nisei Daughter* is used in both literature and history courses along with such novels as Ralph ELLISON's *INVISIBLE MAN,* or Anzia YEZIERSKA's *The BREAD GIVERS.*

NOVEL/MEMOIR
Nisei Daughter. New York: Little, Brown, 1953.

SOURCES
Jacobs, Matthew. "Monica Sone: *Nisei Daughter.*" Available online. URL: http://www.library.csi.cuny.edu/dept/history/lavender/389/noframes/jacobs.html. Accessed September 26, 2005.

Lagonoy, Geoff. "Putting Asian Americans on the Bookshelf," *International Examiner* (September 4, 1994). Highbeam Research. Available online. URL: http://www.highbeam.com/library/doc3.asp?DOCID=1P1:2279167. Accessed September 26, 2005.

SONG OF SOLOMON TONI MORRISON
(1977) Toni MORRISON elevates storytelling to literary art—weaving poetry, myth, song and folklore together to preserve black culture and history. In 1993 she earned international recognition for her body of work when she was awarded the Nobel Prize for Literature.

In her third novel, *Song of Solomon,* Morrison creates evocative images of urban northern life contrasted against rural Southern life for four generations of an African-American family. Deeply layered with folklore that keeps African and Southern culture alive even among the city dwellers, the novel delivers a poignant and intimate exploration of the family of Macon Dead—the name given to the patriarch by a federal agent and imparted to the next two generations.

The novel opens as a man "flies" to his death from the cupola of Mercy Hospital in 1931—an event that induces the third Macon Dead's birth in the same hospital. Later dubbed "Milkman" because his lonely mother, Ruth, in naive perversity, nursed him until he was four years old, Milkman is connected to the theme of "flight" throughout the novel. Milkman's inauspicious birth testifies to the magic that enabled his conception and to his ability to survive despite the death that haunts him. He is threatened in utero by a father who tries to abort him, stalked by Hagar, the lover/cousin he casts aside, and avenged by his best and only friend, Guitar.

Milkman's father, Macon Dead the second, attains worldly success as a businessman but suffers personal and social alienation. He despises his wife, disdains the black tenants who live in his tenements, is estranged from his sister, Pilate—and has but one piece of advice for his son, Milkman, "the one important thing you'll ever need to know: own things." Milkman belongs to a new class in American urban life—the bourgeois black. He is wealthy because his father, Macon, is a slumlord, the new urban black version of the Southern whites who murdered Macon's father to steal his land.

Surrounded by richly complicated characters whose complexity eludes him, the shallow Milkman lives on the fringe of his culture, oblivious to those who help and hinder him, resent and worship him. He is unconscious of his ancestry, untouched by his family, and cavalier in his treatment of others. He lives selfishly among the strangers who are his family—his father, whom he fears, his mother whom he cannot forgive or understand, and his sisters—First Corinthians and Magdalene, to whom he barely speaks. "From the beginning, his mother and Pilate had fought for his life, and he had never so much as made either of them a cup of tea" (335).

Although the women enjoy the privileges of their men's wealth, they are not yet able to transcend their slavery—Ruth cannot rise above the nearly incestuous relationship she had with her deceased father and is treated as a slave by her son and with total disregard by her husband; Milkman's sisters, despite the college education of First Corinthians, have no place in either black or white society. His cousin and then lover Hagar is caught up in the materialism of urban life and is a slave to her passion for Milkman, whose rejection leads to her death.

Despite his self-centeredness, Milkman is a sympathetic character whose life, imperiled from the beginning, touches the reader. We root for this rootless young man on a quest to discover who he is, where he came from, and where he is going. Morrison describes *Song of Solomon* and Milkman's odyssey as "a journey from stupidity to epiphany, of a man, a complete man."

In a culture where naming identifies individuality, *Song of Solomon* bursts with felicitous names. Mains Avenue is called Doctor Street by the blacks who are proud that Ruth's father, the black physician in this community, lives on Mains. The white town fathers, abashed by such brazen disregard for things official, command that the street be called Mains, not Doctor Street, and in an ironic adherence to the new dictate, the blacks rename it Not Doctor Street. Mercy Hospital, where Milkman is born—the first black birth allowed in that institution—earns the appropriate epithet, No Mercy Hospital.

Characters derive their names from "yearnings, gestures, flaws, events, mistakes, weaknesses" (333)— Macon Dead, Sing Byrd, Guitar, Railroad Tommy,

Hospital Tommy, Empire State ("he just stood around and swayed" [333]), the Seven Days. The Dead women's names are plucked blindly from the Bible. Pilate, christened by the word her illiterate father methodically copied from the New Testament, wears the piece of paper that bears her name in a brass box suspended from her ear.

Song plays an integral role in the storytelling. Pilate sings for Milkman at his birth, Milkman sings for Pilate at her death, children sing the songs of African childhood, and throughout, like a Shakespearean chorus, the plaintive, true voices of Pilate, Reba, and Hagar recall the voices of their ancestors.

Song of Solomon takes Milkman on a quest for his family's lost fortune, but he discovers instead his family history, his true heritage. He reconnects with his past, finds himself, and unveils the human truths that forge African-American, and indeed all, human history.

SOURCES

Carmean, Karen. *Toni Morrison's World of Fiction*. Troy, N.Y.: The Whitston Publishing Company, 1993.

Grewal, Gurleen. *Circles of Sorrow, Lines of Struggle: The Novels of Toni Morrison*. Baton Rouge: Louisiana State University Press, 1998.

Mason, Theodore O., Jr. "The Novelist as Conservator: Stories and Comprehension in Toni Morrison's '*Song of Solomon*.'" In *Toni Morrison*, edited by Harold Bloom, 171–188. New York, Philadelphia: Chelsea House Publishers, 1991.

Jan Schubert Norris

SONG OF THE LARK, THE WILLA CATHER (1915)

Based in part on the life of the great Metropolitan Opera diva Olive Fremstad as well as on the author's recollections of growing up in Nebraska, Willa CATHER's *The Song of the Lark* tells the story of Thea Kronberg, descendant of Swedish immigrants, who leaves her family in Moonstone, Colorado, to study music in Chicago and who eventually achieves a career as a world-famous Wagnerian singer. She accomplishes this with the encouragement, artistic vision, and financial support of five men: Dr. Howard Archie, the local Moonstone physician who regards her as a daughter; Professor Wunsch, her first music teacher; Ray Kennedy, a railroad brakeman who leaves her a legacy that enables her to leave Moonstone; Andor Harsanyi, her Chicago piano teacher, who discovers that her voice is her true instrument; and Fred Ottenburg, a wealthy young businessman and patron of the arts. Each man recognizes that Thea is destined for greatness—"She will do nothing common. She is uncommon in a common, common world," Harsanyi says (193), for example—and each one wants to be a fairy godfather or knight errant to her. As Kennedy explains, "there are a lot of halfway people in this world who help the winners win . . . they can't dodge it. It's a natural law" (112).

In the preface to the 1932 edition of the novel in her collected works, Cather wrote: "The story set out to tell of an artist's awakening and struggle; her floundering escape from a smug, domestic, self-satisfied provincial world of utter ignorance. . . . What I cared about, and what I still care about was the girl's escape" (xxxii). Each of the six parts of the novel marks a step forward in Thea's hard-won progress toward complete realization of her art, which occurs at the end of part VI, during her Met debut as Sieglinde, a triumph witnessed by her three surviving benefactors as well as other well-wishing friends.

The need for escape, which is a result of artistic awakening, takes several forms in the novel. Most obvious is Thea's escape from Moonstone and its stifling conventionality. Essentially, Thea must escape from everyone except herself: She is constantly refining and redefining herself. As Harsanyi tells her, "Every artist makes himself born. It is very much harder than the other time and longer" (160). Being alone is a necessary part of the process: Thea gains her greatest insight and confidence when she is by herself, as in her attic room in Moonstone or camping in the ruins of the Anasazi cliff dwellings. As an artist, her joy lies in spiritual self-sufficiency: "It's waking up every morning with the feeling that your life is your own, and your strength is your own, and your talent is your own" (284). Cather said that "personal life becomes paler as the imaginative life becomes richer" (xxxii), and in the novel this becomes apparent as Thea becomes increasingly isolated from others, intent on perfecting her art. She rejects Ottenburg's love in order to study in Germany; she delays going to her dying mother so as to

fulfill an important contract in Europe. Years later she tells Ottenburg that she has very few friends and that she could lose all of them if necessary; to Dr. Archie she explains, "Your work becomes your personal life. You are not much good until it does" (392). Life is more real for Thea when she is onstage and in character. That is when the tired, fretful woman who looks old beyond her years fills with "energy and fire. . . . She felt like a tree bursting into bloom" (410).

Struggle also takes various forms. Thea is well-served by a dogged if initially uninformed ambition to succeed as a musician, as well as by a habit of rigorous training, for she must constantly contend with her own limitations and with those who would oppose her progress. She must struggle to achieve technical facility first on the piano and then on the voice; she has to struggle to catch up and learn about the musical repertory about which she knows nothing when she arrives in Chicago at age 17. She struggles both personally and professionally against those who are jealous of her gift and the attention that it brings her. Most of all she must struggle to maintain her artistic purity in the face of a society that would rather rave over a "common" singer with a showy voice and stage mannerisms rather than recognize a real artist. The Grieg song that Ottenburg has her sing over and over is a kind of theme for her constant struggle: "Thanks for your advice! But I prefer to steer my boat into the din of roaring breakers. Even if the journey is my last, I may find what I have never found before" (243).

Unlike the pioneers and immigrants who figure in so many of Cather's novels, Thea moves eastward to achieve her American dream: from Moonstone to Chicago to New York and then to Germany. Yet the American West—especially the Arizona canyonlands that figure in part IV—remains her touchstone. Returning to Moonstone after her first year in Chicago, she "felt that she was coming back to her own land" (199). Her coming of age occurs after listening to a performance of Dvorak's New World Symphony: "She pressed her hands upon her heaving bosom, that was a little girl's no longer" (183). Even the despised Moonstone provides her with the scale of values she uses in adult life, a scale her friends recognize keeps her "from getting off the track" (327).

In the character of Thea Kronberg, Cather not only celebrated the larger-than-life art of the operatic diva, but also the energy and imagination of the successful woman artist in general. It has been suggested that Kronberg the successful singer is a stand-in for Cather the successful writer, as certain details of Thea's life and character parallel those in Cather's own. Moreover, much of Cather's discussion of the nature of Thea's art is applicable to any art form. As Harsanyi says, "Her secret? It is every artist's secret . . . passion. That is all. It is an open secret and perfectly safe" (409).

SOURCES

Ahearn, Amy. "Full-Blooded Writing and Journalistic Fictions: Naturalism, the Female Artist and Willa Cather's *The Song of the Lark*," *American Literary Realism, 1870–1910* 33 (2001): 143–156.

Cather, Willa. *The Song of the Lark*. 1915. Foreword by Doris Grumbach. Boston, Mass.: Houghton Mifflin, Mariner Books, 1965; Foreword, 1988.

Fetterley, Judith. "Willa Cather and the Fiction of Female Development." In *Anxious Power: Reading, Writing, and Ambivalence in Narrative by Women*, edited by Carol J. Singley and Susan Elizabeth Sweeney, 221–234. Albany: State University of New York Press, 1993.

Hallgarth, Susan A. "The Woman Who Would Be an Artist in *The Song of the Lark* and *Lucy Gayheart*." In *Willa Cather: Family, Community, and History*, edited by John J. Murphy, Linda Hunter, and Paul Rawlins, 169–173. Provo, Utah: Brigham Young University Humanities Publishing Center, 1990.

Harvey, Sally Peltier. *Redefining the American Dream: The Novels of Willa Cather*. Rutherford, N.J.: Fairleigh Dickinson University Press, 1995.

Nona C. Flores

SOUND AND THE FURY, THE WILLIAM FAULKNER (1929)

In an interview, William FAULKNER once said *The Sound and the Fury* was his favorite book, and many believe it is his best. This modernist novel details the disintegration of the Compsons, a once well-to-do southern family. The characters include Jason Compson, Sr., a philosophically cynical and complacent alcoholic; Caroline Compson, a querulous and overbearing hypochondriac; and their children: Quentin, sensitive, intelligent, and doomed; Caddy, promiscuous, rebellious, and strong; Jason, weak, whining, and acquisitive; and Benjy, severely mentally handicapped. Other major characters are Caddy's daughter, also named Quentin, who takes after her mother, and Dilsey, the long-time family servant and moral center of the book.

The inspiration for *The Sound and the Fury* began for Faulkner with an image of Caddy's muddy drawers in the pear tree as she looked into her dying grandmother's window and her brothers, frightened, watched below. Like Eve, she gained forbidden knowledge of life and death as she gazed through the window, and the mud marks her sin and her fall. Each of the novel's four sections has a different narrator and a different style corresponding to the narrator's thoughts. Although Caddy is at the center of each section, Faulkner does not allow her to narrate, to tell her own story. We see Caddy only as what she represents to her three brothers—a mother to Benjy, a lover to Quentin, and a daughter to Jason. Through the brothers' preoccupation with their sister, Faulkner portrays the southern male's obsession with white female purity.

The novel's title is from a soliloquy in Shakespeare's Macbeth: "[Life] is a tale/ Told by an idiot, full of sound and fury,/ Signifying nothing." Appropriately, the first section is told by Benjy, an idiot, a term that describes a person with a mental age of no more than three. Because Benjy understands little, the reader must piece together information and delay closure. The stream of consciousness style follows Benjy's confused thoughts, jumping in time to his childhood, when his favorite sister Caddy cared for him, to his youth, when the family begins to fall apart and the already-pregnant Caddy endures an arranged marriage: "I couldn't tell if I was crying or not, and T. P. fell down on top of me, laughing, and it kept on making the sound and Quentin kicked T. P. and Caddy put her arms around me, and her shining veil, and I couldn't smell trees anymore and I began to cry" (40). In the present, April 7, 1928, when the family's pasture, sold to pay for brother Quentin's year at Harvard, has been made into a golf course, Benjy spends his days listening to golfers call "caddy."

The novel's second section, narrated by brother Quentin, leaps back in time to June 2, 1910, as Quentin finishes his year at Harvard and prepares for his suicide. Though this section is more accessible than the first, Quentin's thoughts are also fragmented due to his inability to accept his sister Caddy's promiscuity and his own failure to protect her. Quentin's conflict arises when he tries to live by the codes of chivalry in a world where they no longer apply, a conflict we learn more about in *Absalom, Absalom!* (1936), which is a prequel to *The Sound and the Fury* and features many of the same characters. In *The Sound and the Fury,* conversations and scenes from the past in Mississippi intermingle with conversations and scenes from Boston without marker or transition. One of Quentin's recurring memories is an encounter with Dalton Ames, his sister's lover. Standing on the bridge in Mississippi, a shadow of the bridge from which he commits suicide in Boston, Quentin had uttered an absurd ultimatum, "I'll give you till sundown" (159), and then, with little provocation, he had fainted "like a girl" (162). A year later he is haunted by his own humiliating weakness and Ames's contrasting masculinity.

A similar episode occurs as Quentin walks through the outskirts of Boston after being arrested for "stealing" the sister of an Italian immigrant. Quentin's inability to protect the little girl reinforces his sense of guilt for not protecting Caddy. He agonizes over Caddy's loss of virginity, a loss that he has never experienced. At times he imagines himself in Dalton Ames's role as sexual aggressor, claiming to have committed incest with Caddy so as to implicate himself in a "terrible crime" and become a part of the "something terrible" in his sister. As he emerges from this obsessive memory, he again lashes out in a dramatic and inappropriate way, punching Gerald, a fellow student, for no apparent reason. Quentin is unable to see the boundaries between his thoughts and reality because in his reveries he is not Quentin, but a powerful man who did protect his sister from her defiler. Quentin's identity dissolves even further by the end of his section. Dressing meticulously in his room, he prepares to go to the bridge for the last time: "then I saw that I'd forgotten my hat. I'd have to go by the post office and I'd be sure to meet some of them, and they'd think I was a Harvard Square student making like he was a senior" (179). Nearing his own death, he never thinks of the act he will commit, only of how he will appear to observers. At this point, seeing himself only as the object of censure, he commits suicide.

The novel's third section, narrated by brother Jason and set on April 6, 1928, is more linear and accessible, partly because Jason's mind is less complex. Like his brothers, however, he dwells on his sister Caddy and on his own inadequacies. Jason feels that Caddy has wronged him because Herbert Head, the husband from her arranged marriage, had promised him a job at his bank. Head divorced Caddy when he learned that she had been pregnant when he married her, and Jason's chances at the job are ruined. Now Jason clerks in a store, lives with his sickly mother after their father's death, and tries to control Caddy's rebellious daughter Quentin, now a teenager, who lives with the Compsons. Jason does not seem to distinguish between Caddy and her daughter. The words with which he begins the section, "Once a bitch, always a bitch" (180), seem directed at both. As the narrative progresses we learn that Jason lies to his mother that he is part owner in the store, steals the money that Caddy sends to her daughter, and revels in his victim status. Though he is his mother's favorite child, the only one who did not disgrace her, his bullying and inflated estimation of his own importance make him despised by everyone else.

The novel's fourth section takes place on Easter Sunday, April 8, 1928. Unlike the others, this section employs a third-person narrator and begins from the perspective of Dilsey as she cares for the remaining Compsons and attends church service. Dilsey's genuine spirituality, her compassion for Benjy and the young Quentin, and her forthright reproach of Jason make her the most morally sound character in the book. Instead of spending Easter morning in church, the Compsons spend it in pursuit of money and each other. Young Quentin steals back from Jason the money Caddy had sent her and runs away. Jason chases after Quentin, alienating the authorities and everyone else he comes in contact with, gets a migraine from gas fumes, and has to be driven home. At home, Benjy somehow senses that Quentin is gone like her mother and begins to moan and whine. In order to calm him, Luster, Dilsey's grandson, drives Benjy through town, but when he veers to a course slightly different from Benjy's normal route, Benjy begins bellowing: "It was horror; shock; agony eyeless, tongueless; just sound" (320). As the noise increases, Jason, having just arrived back in Jefferson, leaps onto the wagon, beats Luster, and turns the wagon around. The novel ends with Benjy serene in the wagon as "cornice and facade flowed smoothly once more from left to right . . . each in its ordered place" (321).

One cannot help but notice the Christian references in this novel, with three out of four chapters set around Easter weekend. Is Benjy, aged 33 and pure of heart, though empty of mind, a Christ figure? Is brother Quentin, who dies for a cause, however meaningless, and is resurrected in the form of Caddy's daughter, Quentin? Or is Jason, who, at least in his own eyes, suffers for others? Or is it, as the title suggests, all just sound and fury signifying nothing? Dilsey cries tears of genuine sorrow and empathy at the Easter service in the black church. But perhaps Faulkner suggests that, at least for the white characters, religion is, like Benjy's drive through town, simply a matter of comforting routine.

SOURCES

Bloom, Harold, ed. *William Faulkner's The Sound and the Fury.* New York: Chelsea House, 1988.

Butery, Karen Ann. "From Conflict to Suicide: The Inner Turmoil of Quentin Compson," *The American Journal of Psychoanalysis* 49, no. 3 (1989): 211–224.

Faulkner, William. *The Sound and the Fury.* 1929. Reprint, New York: Vintage Books, 1984.

Longley, John L., Jr. " 'Who Never Had a Sister': A Reading of *The Sound and the Fury.*" In *The Novels of William Faulkner,* edited by R. G. Collins and Kenneth McRobbie. Winnipeg, Canada: University of Manitoba Press, 1973.

Weinstein, Philip M. *Faulkner's Subject, a Cosmos No One Owns.* New York: Cambridge University Press, 1992.

Betina Entzminger

SOUTHERN DISCOMFORT RITA MAE BROWN (1988)

While the theme of hypocrisy among the upper classes is certainly not new to works of literature, the way it is developed by the author determines whether it will become another cliched account of a society gone awry or a a more refreshing view on the injustices we sometimes unknowingly perpetrate on ourselves and each other.

Rita Mae BROWN's *Southern Discomfort* chronicles two parallel societies over a period of 10 years in Montgomery, Alabama. The first, what we could call the "visible" society, is composed of the upper classes and the religious authority represented by moral crusader Reverend Linton Ray. In general, the visible society caters to the male, white population. Running beneath this world of strict etiquette and taboo is an underworld composed of the Water Street prostitutes, the black community, a developing but still despised middle class, and "show people," artists who although fascinating and entertaining seem to have fallen out of favor with the "nobility" because of their calling. In short, Montgomery is a superficially stable town, rocked by a strong undercurrent of chaos.

The story of *Southern Discomfort* could stop there, at a description of these two parallel worlds. But the strength behind this novel is the point at which these two paths cross. The intersection occurs between Hortensia Banastre and Hercules Jinks: a wealthy but unhappily married white woman and an educated black teenage boxer. The novel does not explain their attraction for each other or how quickly it develops; therefore, it may be as startling for the reader as it is unacceptable for the Montgomery community. The apparent irrationality of the relationship that blossoms between Hortensia and Hercules seems, in fact, to clean a slate soiled by the town's unwavering prejudice against its non-white, non-"respectable" population. As Hortensia's rebellious aunt Narcissa proclaims: "Great love always works at cross-purposes with society. . . . Either you live your life, or you let other people live it for you" (98–99).

The tragic death of Hercules—abandoned by a white ambulance driver who would not carry him to the hospital—drives Hortensia to Chicago, from where she returns almost a year later, with her trusted maid Amelie and a newborn girl. The girl is raised as Amelie's, but Catherine's green eyes and reddish hair immediately set her apart, and the young girl always suspects that she is not truly the daughter of her "aunt Hortensia's" black maid and her missing companion.

The other key players in uniting the town's two worlds are, ironically, the prostitutes of Water Street. Honest and daring, they are the only ones to acknowledge that passion is common to all men and women. Set against Reverend Linton Ray's moral crusade against drinking and debauchery, the women of Water Street eventually unite and manage to win over the tight-collared minister's supporters, even as they protect their own business activities, centered on their upper-crust customers.

In these outcast women Hortensia and other restless souls find a sincere if awkward alliance. Two of these women help Hortensia and Hercules rent a small cottage for their encounters. After Hercules's death, they comfort Hortensia.

A third union of the surface world and undercurrent of Montgomery occurs between the races: black and white. Beyond Hortensia's own affair, the harsh life of segregation and prejudice that dictates life for the black population contrasts with their reality as a complex community. At the center of this community we find Hercules's family, the Jinkses. Led by the matriarch, Ada, the Jinks family has the education and sensibility that is shockingly lacking in the so-called "upper" (white) class. The children are named Hercules, Athena, and Apollo; they have superb knowledge of Latin and other academic disciplines; and they are determined to forge the best path they can through life. Athena, following her mythological namesake, uses her wisdom to study law. Apollo selflessly enlists in the army of a country that does not respect his rights and loses his life in battle. Hercules makes use of his strength as a prizefighter, only to have his own existence cut tragically short.

The Jinkses also become an important part of the bond that keeps young Catherine with one foot planted in each world. She is of their blood (though Ada does not at first realize that Catherine is her granddaughter) and is in part educated by them, learning Latin from Ada. She also attends a segregated school. Yet Catherine knows she does not entirely belong in the black community, as much as she will never be accepted by white Montgomery; her classmates shun her because her skin is lighter than theirs, and yet she is barred from participation in the Halloween festivities planned for the white children. Catherine's anger and confusion mirrors the uneasy balance of the races in Montgomery, and the irrational regulations that keep them separate and trapped in assumptions of what each side is and is not. That the Jinks family is highly cultivated and literate does not matter: only their skin color does. Neither does it matter that Montgomery's "finest" men spend their nights in the brothels of Water Street: As white males, it is their prerogative, and their activities will not be publicized or reprimanded.

The story ends in 1928 and leaves the reader to wonder how World War II and, in time, the Civil Rights movement will further transform the inhabitants of Montgomery. Brown suggests that change depends on the hybrid nature of those who will resist the social hierarchy—people like Catherine, who feel so entitled to both worlds that they will eventually unite both threads to create history of another kind.

SOURCES

Levine, Daniel B. "Uses of Classical Mythology in Rita Mae Brown's *Southern Discomfort*," *Classical and Modern Literature* 10, no. 1 (Fall 1989): 63–70.
Ward, Carol M. *Rita Mae Brown*. New York: Twayne, 1993.

Marisa Antonaya

SPECTATOR BIRD, THE Wallace Stegner (1976)

Seventy years old, crotchety, and suffering from arthritis, retired literary agent Joe Allston receives a postcard from Astrid Wredel-Krarup, the impoverished countess with whom he and his wife, Ruth, shared an apartment in Denmark 20 years earlier. Her message prompts him to dig out the journals he kept during their three-month stay, and when Ruth learns of their existence, she insists that he read them aloud to her. Their bedtime readings frame a gothic tale of political, social, and moral exile, Faustian genetic experiments, and incest. The tale unfolds over several winter evenings and is punctuated by daytime visits from a flamboyant Italian novelist, Allston's retired octogenarian doctor, and neighbors, all of whom provoke Allston's signature sour observations on aging—for example, "I am just killing time till time gets around to killing me—nothing is building, everything is running down, there are no more chances for improvement" (89).

Stegner writes Allston's first-person narrative with wry humor, relentless insight, honesty, and precision.

Although replete with historical, mythic, and literary allusions that at times daunt, the novel's crisp metaphors, characterizations, and observations create its emotional cutting edge. Allston uses acerbic wit to avoid intimacy and keep his fears at bay. Reflecting on his habitual detachment from difficult personal issues, he observes, "Crucifixion can be discussed philosophically until they start driving in the nails" (23). Unflappable Ruth probes and pushes him toward intimacy and resolution of unfinished emotional business, including his estrangement from their only child, Curtis, "an over-age beach bum" (25), who died in a surfing accident, and the conflict between Allston's unfulfilled love for the countess and his commitment to Ruth. "Ah, me," he observes, "the complexity of being married to a woman you dearly love and automatically resist" (96).

The title refers to the combination of Allston's deliberately abrasive and detached manner that collapses over time and his frequent observations and characterizations of birds. As the book opens, he watches the birds outside his study and likens himself to the wrens, "surly and aggressive," although he admits he would prefer to be like the bush tits, "paying no attention to time or duty—generally enjoying themselves" (6). Later, when he reads his journals to Ruth, he comments, "I sometimes get the feeling my whole life happened to someone else" (81), although a few paragraphs later, he admits to himself that, while in Denmark and involved with the countess, "I wasn't quite spectator enough" (82). Finally, after admitting his love for the countess to Ruth and fleeing their bedroom in the book's most emotional display, he retreats into the third person and describes himself as "the spectator bird, having the feathers beaten off him in a game from which he had thought he was protected" (196).

Stegner introduced Joe Allston in 1967 in *All the Little Live Things.* Both novels are set in the hills above Stanford University, and in both, a beloved neighbor succumbs to cancer—a young mother in *All the Little Live Things* and a contemporary in *The Spectator Bird.* In both, Allston rails against the hippie culture and changing sexual mores of the late 1960s and 1970s and against the indifference of youth in general: "they just don't see you—. They don't seem offended that you

exist, only surprised" (117). By the end of *The Spectator Bird,* however, an older Allston rails less and understands more. The book shares dominant themes— aging and death, commitment and fidelity, and emotional safety—with Stegner's other novels, particularly *All the Little Live Things, ANGLE OF REPOSE, Remembering Laughter,* and *CROSSING TO SAFETY.* He treats aging and death with dark humor: "Getting old is like standing in a long, slow line. You wake up out of the shuffle and torpor only at those moments when the line moves you one step closer to the window" (171).

Commitment and fidelity are bluntly treated: "It has seemed to me that my commitments are often more important than my impulses or my pleasures, and that even when my pleasures or desires are the principal issue, there are choices to be made between better and worse, bad and better, good and good" (209). Allston and his friends seek physical and emotional safety, but safety eludes them, as it ultimately eludes all living things. As Karen Blixen (a.k.a. Isak Dineson, author of *Out of Africa*) tells Allston during a visit to her farm, Denmark is "very safe—full of retired sea captains growing roses" (104). Yet even "safe" Denmark can be dangerous, and Allston observes, "the hope of safety, not any lust for freedom" (110) brought his Danish mother and others to the New World. Ultimately, Allston concludes (213), "It is something—it can be everything—to have found a fellow bird with whom you can sit among the rafters while the drinking and boasting and reciting and fighting go on below; a fellow bird whom you can look after and find bugs and seeds for; one who will patch your bruises and straighten your ruffled feathers and mourn over your hurts when you accidentally fly into something you cannot handle."

SOURCES

Benson, Jackson J. *Wallace Stegner: His Life and Work.* New York: Penguin Books, 1996.

Stegner, Wallace. The *Spectator Bird.* Lincoln and London: University of Nebraska Press, 1979.

Stegner, Wallace, and Richard W. Etulain. *Conversations with Wallace Stegner on Western History and Literature.* Salt Lake City: University of Utah Press, 1983.

Walters, Thomas N. *"The Spectator Bird."* In *Critical Essays on Wallace Stegner,* edited by Anthony Arthur, 37–43. Boston: G. K. Hall & Company, 1982.

Suzanne Carey

SPENCER, ELIZABETH (1921–) Dur-
ing Mississippi-born Elizabeth Spencer's long career, she has produced a remarkably distinguished corpus of long and short fiction. Her early novels, *Fire in the Morning* (1948) and *The Voice at the Back Door* (1956), exemplify the haunting but realistically drawn rural South, and the tension between the Old South and the New. Since the publication of *The Light in the Piazza* (1960), Spencer's fiction contains an increasing number of female protagonists, Southern women who must deal with crises whether at home or abroad. *Marilee*, published in 1981, is the first example. A decade later, in *The Night Travellers* (1991), a Vietnam-era novel set in both North Carolina and Canada, Spencer creates another strong Southern woman, Mary Kerr.

Elizabeth Spencer was born on July 19, 1921, in Carrollton, Mississippi, to James Luther Spencer, a businessman, and Mary James McCain Spencer, a piano teacher and lover of books. Spencer was educated at Belhaven College, where she received her bachelor's degree, cum laude, in 1942, and at Vanderbilt University, where she received her master's degree in English in 1943. Although critics repeatedly compared her early novels to those of William FAULKNER (Spencer was reared only 60 miles from Faulkner's home town of Oxford, Mississippi), they also celebrated her ability to create strong original plots peopled with vivid, believable characters. While teaching at the University of Mississippi and working as a reporter for the Nashville *Tenneseean*, Spencer completed *Fire in the Morning*, the tale of Kinloch Armstrong and his involvement in a two-generation property feud in a rural Mississippi town. Her second novel, *This Crooked Way* (1952), again set in the rural South, features Amos Dudley, a rigidly religious man in pursuit of the wealth and success that he believes God has given him; only when he relinquishes this idea can Amos begin to love his family and enjoy the life of an ordinary individual. Spencer then moved to Italy for five years, writing the novellas *The Light in the Piazza* (1960), often compared to Henry JAMES's *DAISY MILLER*, and *Knights and Dragons* (1965). The former was a popular and critical success: Margaret Johnson, a Southern woman in Italy, defies her husband in order to ensure a happy future for her mentally disabled daughter, Clara. Like James's Daisy Miller, Clara falls in love with an Italian, here named Fabrizio. Unlike Daisy, Clara has a mother who negotiates her dowry and marries her to Fabrizio. Originally published in the *New Yorker*, the novella was subsequently made into a feature-length film by Metro-Goldwyn Mayer. *Knights and Dragons* focuses on Martha Ingram, who is breaking free of her former husband's emotional domination. Similarly, *No Place for an Angel* features a timid girl, Catherine Sasser, who learns to be strong and even noble.

In her later fiction, Spencer explores her views on individualism. In her detailed presentation of modernist society, the author warns against obsession with one's self and demonstrates the superior choice of communal responsibility. In *The Snare* (1972), Julia Garrett leaves the comfortable but superficial existence in her parents' home in the Garden District of New Orleans. She realizes her independence and accepts responsibility for her own child. Similarly, in *The Salt Line* (1984), Arnie Carrington eventually rejects his corrupted society and chooses to provide for the happiness of others.

Elizabeth Spencer married the British John Arthur Blackwood Rusher in 1956 and lived with him in Montreal, Canada, for 25 years. In 1985 she was elected to the American Academy and Institute for Arts and Letters, and in 1986 she and her husband moved to Chapel Hill, North Carolina, where Spencer accepted a teaching appointment at the University of North Carolina.

NOVELS AND NOVELLAS
Fire in the Morning. New York: Dodd, Mead, 1948.
Knights and Dragons. New York: McGraw-Hill, 1965.
The Light in the Piazza. New York: McGraw-Hill, 1960.
Marilee. Jackson: University Press of Mississippi, 1981.
The Night Travellers. New York: Viking, 1991.
No Place for an Angel. New York: McGraw-Hill, 1967.
The Salt Line. New York: Doubleday, 1984.
The Snare. New York: McGraw-Hill, 1972.
This Crooked Way. New York: Dodd, Mead, 1952.
The Voice at the Back Door. New York: McGraw-Hill, 1956.

SOURCES
Broadwell, Elizabeth Pell, and Ronald Wesley Hoag. "A Conversation with Elizabeth Spencer," *Southern Review* 18 (Winter 1982): 111–130.

Jones, John Griffin. "Elizabeth Spencer." In *Mississippi Writers Talking,* 95–129. Jackson: University Press of Mississippi, 1982.

Prenshaw, Peggy Whitman. *Elizabeth Spencer.* Boston: Twayne, 1985.

———, ed. *Conversations with Elizabeth Spencer.* Jackson: University Press of Mississippi, 1991.

Roberts, Terry. *Self and Community in the Fiction of Elizabeth Spencer.* Baton Rouge: Louisiana State University Press, 1994.

Spencer, Elizabeth. *Landscapes of the Heart.* New York: Random House, 1998.

SPIEGELMAN, ART (1948–)

Although Art Spiegelman is not a novelist in the conventional sense, his work provides an intriguing example of the innovative lengths to which postmodern artists, particularly in a post–World War II and post-Holocaust world, will search for forms appropriate to describe the horrors of the 20th century. Spiegelman wrote a comic book called *MAUS: A SURVIVORS TALE, MY FATHER BLEEDS HISTORY* (1986) that depicted his parents' arrest by the Nazis and their imprisonment at the concentration camp called Auschwitz. *Maus* was nominated by the National Book Critics Circle for an award in biography. It could be argued that Art Spiegelman's subject called for an extension of fictional, traditionally novelistic techniques, in the form of a comic book using animal characters. The sequel, *MAUS: A SURVIVORS TALE II, and HERE MY TROUBLES BEGAN* appeared in 1992, and Spiegelman received a Special Pulitzer Prize for both works. *Maus II* received a National Book Critics Circle Award, a *Los Angeles Times* Award, and an American Book Award. As more than one critic has pointed out, they are novels in pictures.

Art Spiegelman was born on February 15, 1948, in Stockholm, Sweden, to Vladek Spiegelman, a salesman, and Anja Zylberberg Spiegelman; Spiegelman immigrated to the United States, became a naturalized citizen, and attended Harpur College, now the State University of New York at Binghamton. He was an instructor in history and the aesthetics of comic books at the New York School of Visual Arts from 1979 to 1987 and a staff artist, during which time he published both *Maus* and *Maus II,* and he worked at the *New Yorker* from 1991 to 2003. The voices of Artie, the son, and Vladek, the father, tell the story in multiple time frames, with flashbacks to the pasts of both. *Maus II* continues the narrative as Vladek recalls Auschwitz, Birkenau, gas chambers, ovens, and graves; Artie speaks to a psychiatrist about his ambivalent feelings toward his own father. Opening with the premise used by Hitler, "The Jews are undoubtedly a race, but they are not human," Spiegelman depicts the Jews as mice, the Germans as cats, the Poles as pigs, the British as fish, the French as frogs, the Americans as dogs, the Swedes as reindeer, the gypsies as moths. All drawings are in black and white.

The work is based on meticulous research and accurate use of detail. In a *New York Times Book Review* article, Lawrence L. Langer notes, "Perhaps no Holocaust narrative will ever contain the whole experience. But Art Spiegelman has found an original and authentic form to draw us closer to its bleak heart" (Langer, 36). Art Spiegelman lives in Irvington, New York.

NOVELS

In the Shadow of No Towers. New York: Pantheon, 2004.

Maus: A Survivors Tale, My Father Bleeds History, Vol I. New York: Pantheon, 1986.

Maus: A Survivors Tale, and Here My Troubles Began, Vol II. New York: Pantheon, 1992.

SOURCES

Charlson, Joshua L. "Framing the Past: Postmodernism and the Making of Reflective Memory in Art Spiegelman's *Maus,*" *Arizona Quarterly* 57, no. 3 (Autumn 2001): 91–120.

Huyssen, Andreas. "Of Mice and Mimesis: Reading Spiegelman with Adorno," *New German Critique* 81 (Fall 2000): 65–82.

Laga, Barry. "*Maus,* Holocaust, and History: Redrawing the Frame," *Arizona Quarterly* 57, no. 1 (Spring 2001): 61–90.

Landsberg, Alison. "America, the Holocaust, and the Mass Culture of Memory: Toward a Radical Politics of Empathy," *New German Critique* 71 (Spring–Summer 1997): 63–86.

Lehmann, Sophia. " 'And Here [Their] Troubles Began': The Legacy of the Holocaust in the Writing of Cynthia Ozick, Art Spiegelman, and Philip Roth," *Clio* 28, no. 1 (Fall 1998): 29–52.

Ma, Sheng-Mei. "Mourning with the (as a) Jew: Metaphor, Ethnicity, and the Holocaust in Art Spiegelman's *Maus,*" *Studies in American Jewish Literature* 16 (1997): 115–129.

Staub, Michael E. "The Shoah Goes On and On: Remembrance and Representation in Art Spiegelman's *Maus*," *MELUS* 20, no. 3 (Fall 1995): 33–46.

Wilner, Arlene Fish. " 'Happy, Happy Ever After': Story and History in Art Spiegelman's *Maus*," *Journal of Narrative Technique* 27, no. 2 (Spring 1997): 171–189.

Witek, Joseph. *Comic Book as History: The Narrative Art of Jack Jackson, Art Spiegelman, and Harvey Pekar.* Jackson: University Press of Mississippi, 1989.

Young, James E. "The Holocaust as Vicarious Past: Art Spiegelman's *Maus* and the Afterimages of History," *Critical Inquiry* 24, no. 3 (Spring 1998): 666–699.

OTHER

Art Spiegelman. Steven Barclay Agency. Available online. URL: http://www.barclayagency.com/spiegelman.html. Accessed September 25, 2005.

Audio interview with Art Spiegelman. Wired for Books. Available online. URL: http://wiredforbooks.org/art-spiegelman. Accessed September 25, 2005.

"Jack Cole and Plastic Man: Forms Stretched to Their Limits. By Art Spiegelman and Chip Kidd." DC Comics. Available online. URL: http://www.dccomics.com/features/plas. Accessed January 13, 2006.

Spiegelman, Art. Interview with Art Spiegelman from *Corriere della Sera* (February 13, 2003). Electronic Iraq. Available online. URL: http://electroniciraq.net/cgi-bim/artman/exec/view.cgi/6/109printer. Accessed January 13, 2006.

———. Interview with Art Spiegelman. By Christopher Monte Smith. Booksense. Available online. URL: http://www.booksense.com/people/archive/spiegelmanart.jsp. Accessed January 13, 2006.

SPOFFORD, HARRIET ELIZABETH PRESCOTT (1835–1921)

Author of novels, short stories, and poetry, Harriet Prescott Spofford—like many other 19th-century women writers—was well known and well regarded in her time, but fell into obscurity until the late 20th century, when feminist scholarship began to examine her work. Spofford was a regularly published writer in *Harper's Bazar* and a contributor to such monthly magazines as the *Atlantic,* the *Knickerbocker,* and *Lippincott's.* Although today's critics suggest that her talents lay more in the short story than in the novel, she wrote 10 novels and novellas and reached a wide audience. Like Nathaniel HAWTHORNE and Edgar Allan POE, she was intrigued with the dark, mysterious aspects of the human psyche and frequently wrote about madness, monomania, crime, and the supernatural. In the most general terms, her interests lay in the nature of power used and abused by both men and women, but with particular attention to the silencing of women's voices. (Bendixen, 381).

Harriet Elizabeth Prescott was born on April 3, 1835, in Calais, Maine, to Sarah Bridges Prescott and Joseph Newmarch Prescott, at various times a merchant, lawyer, and politician who was ultimately unable to provide for his large family. Luckily, Prescott, who had been educated at the Putnam Free School and the Pinkerton Academy, wrote an essay that attracted the attention of Thomas Wentworth Higginson; he had also advised Emily Dickinson and encouraged Spofford to pursue a writing career. Her first *Atlantic* story, "In a Cellar," was published in 1859, drawing critical and popular attention to the young author. In 1860 Spofford published her first novel, *Sir Rohan's Ghost,* a ghost story about an artist who eventually discovers that he has fallen in love with his own daughter. This gothic romance drew praise from critics like James Russell Lowell, who pointed to Spofford's "genuine poetic power" and proclaimed her a writer "destined for great things" (St. Armand, 253, 254). Henry JAMES, on the other hand, thought that Spofford needed to relinquish her imagistic descriptions. He recommended, in a review of *Azarian: An Episode* (1864), Spofford's second novel (in which the hero cannot see that she is in love with a vain and self-centered man), that the author learn from the new realist school (St. Armand, 269).

After marrying Richard S. Spofford, Jr., a lawyer, on December 19, 1865, Spofford wrote other romantic works, including the novels *The Thief in the Night* (1872) and *The Marquis of Carabas* (1882), and the novella *A Master Spirit* (1896). Probably best known in the early 21st century for her story collection *The Amber Gods and Other Stories* (1863), Spofford continues to attract the attention of scholars to the haunting quality of her work, particularly her portraits of women who want respect and equal treatment from men. A member of the group of literary women that included Annie Fields, Rose Terry Cooke, Sarah Orne JEWETT, and others, Spofford wrote a tribute to these women in

A Little Book of Friends (1916). She died on August 14, 1921, at her home in Deer Island, Massachusetts.

NOVELS AND NOVELLAS

An Inheritance. New York: Charles Scribner Sons, 1897.
Azarian: An Episode. Boston: Ticknor and Fields, 1864.
The Maid He Married. Chicago: Herbert S. Stone, 1899.
The Making of a Fortune. A Romance. New York: Harper Brothers, 1894.
The Marquis of Carabas. Boston: Roberts Brothers, 1882.
A Master Spirit. New York: Charles Scribner Sons, 1896.
Priscilla's Love-Story. Chicago: Herbert S. Stone, 1898.
Sir Rohan's Ghost. A Romance. Boston: J. E. Tilton, 1860.
That Betty. New York: Fleming H. Revell, 1903.
The Thief in the Night. Boston: Roberts Brothers, 1872.

SOURCES

Bendixen, Alfred. "Harriet Prescott Spofford." In *Nineteenth-Century American Women Writers: A Bio-Bibliographical Critical Sourcebook,* edited by Denise Knight, 377–384. Westport, Conn.: Greenwood Press, 1997.

———. Introduction to *"The Amber Gods" and Other Stories.* New Brunswick, N.J.: Rutgers University Press, 1989, pp. ix–xxxix.

St. Armand, Barton Levi. *Emily Dickinson and Her Culture.* Cambridge: Cambridge University Press, 1984.

Shinn, Thelma J. "Harriet Prescott Spofford: A Reconsideration," *Turn-of-the-Century Women* 1, no. 1 (1984): 36–45.

SPY IN THE HOUSE OF LOVE, A ANAÏS NIN (1954)

A Spy in the House of Love (1954) is one of five volumes in Anaïs NIN's continuous novel series. This group of novelettes includes *Ladders to the Fire* (1946), *Children of the Albatross* (1947), *The Four-Chambered Heart* (1950), *Cities of the Interior* (1959), and *Seduction of the Minotaur* (1961). The concept behind Nin's continuous novel is to show the complexity of simultaneous female experiences; together, the works trace the multiple aspects of sexual (and other) relationships encountered by Lillian, Djuna, and Sabina, portraying "women in a continuous symphony of experience" (*Ladders,* ix).

This "experience" is related to the metaphor of the four disconnected chambers in the female heart, which can accommodate different and separate loyalties (Nalbantian, 3). Though each book in the series is written in a unique style, each new retelling of the same three women's lives "invites readers to know them in their inconsistencies and to participate in their unpredictable rhythms of growth" (Spenser). The characters' multi-faceted and confused identities in this series are often associated with Nin's own life. She managed several intimate relationships at one time, such as those with Hugh P. Guiler (Hugo), Otto Rank, and Henry MILLER in the 1930s, and then later, she alternated between Hugo and Rupert Pole (Spenser).

The content of *A Spy* focuses on Sabina's fragmented and divided female identity; her character oscillates between stereotypical female roles of child, seductress, actress, lover, and mother as she attempts to satiate her sexual and emotional desires without being a "bad woman" (85). At one point, however, she is free from these roles as she achieves the ability to have sex "like a man" for sexual pleasure without love (49). Similar to Henry Miller in *Tropic of Cancer,* Sabina wanders from one lover to another, including Philip, Mambo, John, Donald, and Jay, while maintaining a relationship with her husband, Alan. Through her encounters with men, Sabina comes to the conclusion that she is an international spy in the house of love as she maintains a secret identity with each lover (72). Her lifestyle choice requires careful planning: Behaving like a spy, she puts her clothes all on one chair at night so that she may dress quickly, leaving no traces of her comings or goings; once seated at the movie theater, she leaves only to reenter a second time from the back in order to choose a "safe" seat (51). Her spying activities cease as a result of her motherlike relationship with Donald (perhaps a homosexual), which kills her sexual desire (97). Despite the sexual power gained by Sabina earlier in the story, the conclusion of *A Spy* leaves the heroine in a defeated state. Like Radclyffe Hall's *The Well of Loneliness* (1928) and Djuna BARNES's *NIGHTWOOD* (1936), the female character expressing sexuality in her own terms collides with an inability to live her sexuality out in reality. In her case, Sabina metaphorically melts onto the floor, and readers are left wondering how or if she will recollect her multiple selves, if she will continue the odyssey for sexual satisfaction, or if the pulsatile remedy suggested by the lie detector will "cure" her.

Nin's poetic style and nonlinear chronology emphasize that *A Spy* is much more about Sabina's emotions and thoughts than a straightforward plotline. The story is almost completely circular: The book begins with the lie detector's pursuit of Sabina (perhaps one of a spy's greatest fears) and returns to his investigation of her near the end of the book. Words that seem to be the lie detector's own description of her, "Dressed in red and silver, she evoked the sounds and imagery of fire engines as they tore through the streets of New York," are later repeated as Jay's internal description of Sabina (7, 118). The lie detector overhears Sabina's Moroccan story, and readers later read the same story in Sabina's direct italicized discourse, suggesting that time and chronology have been displaced across the length of the novel (8, 120).

Nin produces an intertextually rich work that reflects her own interests in music, art, dance, theater, and other women's writings. Readers unfamiliar with Nin's admiration for Djuna Barnes may miss references to her and her works that create a bond between both authors and their attempts to write women's experiences. These references include the very obvious character named after Barnes and Nin's choice of Patchen Place (actually spelled Patchin Place), Barnes's home for over 40 years, as the location of Mambo's "trap" of a studio (Benstock, 429). A less-obvious example comes from Sabina, who asks Donald: " 'Where did you find all these repulsive women?' "—an intertextual reference to Barnes's 1915 chapbook *The Book of Repulsive Women 8 Rhythms and 5 Drawings,* a work which celebrates female sexuality (95). Aside from intertextual references, other structural elements include occasional passages in italics that indicate that the reader has access to an interior monologue; there are also frequent tense shifts from perfect to present tenses, giving a sense of immediacy or continuity. The erotic tone of *A Spy* reinforces Sabina's quest for sexual satisfaction, while poetic sensual imagery equates abstract, corporal, sexual experiences to earthly elements of sand, sea, and air, creating an eroticized body topography.

SOURCES

ANAIS: An International Journal [last published 2001].

Benstock, Shari. *Women of the Left Bank.* Austin: University of Texas Press, 1986.

Jason, Philip K., ed. *The Critical Response to Anais Nin.* Critical Responses in Arts and Letters, No 23. Westport, Conn.: Greenwood Press, 1996.

Nalbantian, Suzanne, ed. *Anaïs Nin: Literary Perspectives.* New York: St. Martin's Press, 1997.

Nin, Anaïs. *Ladders to the Fire.* 1946. Athens, Ohio: Swallow Press/Ohio University Press, 1995.

Oliveira, Ubiratan Paiva de. "*A Spy in the House of Love:* An Introduction to Anaïs Nin," *Ilha do Desterro: A Journal of Language and Literature* 14, no. 2 (1985): 71–81.

Richard-Allerdyce, Diane. *Anaïs Nin and the Remaking of Self: Gender, Modernism, and Narrative Identity.* Dekalb: Northern Illinois University Press, 1997.

Stuhlmann, Gunther, ed. *The Diary of Anaïs Nin Volume One: 1931–34.* New York: Swallow Press, Harcourt, Brace. 1966.

———. ed. *Ladders to the Fire.* New York: Dutton, 1946. Reprint, Chicago: Swallow Press, 1995.

Zaller, Robert. *A Casebook on Anaïs Nin.* New York: New American Library, 1974.

OTHER

Spenser, Sharon. "Forever Anaïs." *Anaïs Nin.* Available online. URL: http://www.anaisnin.com/scholarship/forever/index.html. Accessed January 13, 2006.

Amy D. Lynn

STAFFORD, JEAN (1915–1979)

Known chiefly for her 1970 Pulitzer Prize–winning short fiction in *Collected Stories,* many of which originally appeared in *The New Yorker,* Jean Stafford also earned a reputation as a writer of three first-rate novels. *Boston Adventure* (1944), *The MOUNTAIN LION* (1947), and *The Catherine Wheel* (1952), which focus on class difference, lost love, and alienation. With her focus on the loss of innocence and the high cost of self-realization, the situation for women in Stafford's novels is bleak. Largely neglected for several decades, recent scholarship has reaffirmed both her stylistic ingenuity and her keen, if disturbing, insights into the social and psychological pressures on women.

Jean Stafford was born on July 1, 1915, in Covina, California, to John Richard Stafford, who used the pseudonym Jack Wonder to write western fiction, and Mary McKillop Stafford. She was educated at the University of Colorado, where she earned both a bachelor's and a master's degree in 1936. Stafford married three times, to the poet Robert Lowell from 1940 to 1948; the writer Oliver Jensen from 1950 to 1953; and the *New Yorker* columnist A. J. Liebling, from 1959 until his death in 1963. Her first novel, the best-seller *Boston*

Adventure, a bildungsroman, is often compared to Charlotte Brontë's *Jane Eyre.* Sonie Marburg, an impoverished daughter of Russian and German New England immigrants, seeks but fails to find a better life with the wealthy Miss Pride of Boston. She has witnessed her mother's madness and her friend Hope's destructive sexuality and suicide, but ends up entrapped in the social sterility and hypocrisy of Boston society. Stafford's second novel, the somewhat autobiographical *The Mountain Lion,* depicts the brother and sister Ralph and Molly Fawcett as they come of age on their grandfather's ranch. Ralph opts for the self-reliance associated with the West and with his grandfather Kenyon, a friend to Jesse James; the intellectual, increasingly isolated Molly falls victim to a hunting accident involving a mountain lion. The lion symbolizes Molly's potential and marginality. In *The Catherine Wheel,* Katherine Congreve, a lonely middle-aged New England woman, cannot forget that John Shipley loved and married her cousin Maeve, not her. Twenty years later, spiritually dead and still fixated on her love for John, she fails his 12-year-old son Andrew who needs adult assistance with the despair he feels over the loss of his only friend.

Jean Stafford endured a number of major traumas in her life, including seeing her best friend shoot herself in the head. She suffered serious facial injuries and disfigurement in an automobile accident. The driver was Robert Lowell. Recent biographers trace these themes, along with her periodic alcoholism and depression, in her fiction. Suffering a stroke in 1976, Stafford died on March 26, 1979, in White Plains, New York, and is buried in Greenriver Cemetery in East Hampton, New York. Except for her letters to Lowell, now at Harvard University's Houghton Library, most of Stafford's papers are located in the Jean Stafford Collection of the Norlin Library at the University of Colorado in Boulder.

NOVELS

Boston Adventure. New York: Harcourt, Brace, 1944.
The Catherine Wheel. New York: Harcourt, Brace, 1952.
The Mountain Lion. New York: Harcourt, Brace, 1947.

SOURCES

Gelfant, Blanche H. "Reconsideration: *The Mountain Lion* by Jean Stafford," *New Republic,* May 10, 1975, pp. 22–25.
———. "Revolutionary Turnings: *The Mountain Lion* Reread," *Massachusetts Review* 20 (Spring 1979): 117–125.
Goodman, Charlotte M. *Jean Stafford: The Savage Heart.* Austin: University of Texas Press, 1990.
Hulbert, A. *The Interior Castle: The Art & Life of Jean Stafford.* New York: Knopf, 1992.
Leary, W. "Jean Stafford, Katherine White, and the New Yorker," *Sewanee Review* 93, no. 4 (Fall 1985): 584–596.
———. "Jean Stafford: The Wound and the Bow," *Sewanee Review* 98, no. 3 (Summer 1990): 333–349.
Mann, Jeanette W. "Toward New Archetypal Forms: *Boston Adventure,*" *Studies in the Novel* 8 (Fall 1976): 291–303.
———. "Toward New Archetypal Forms: Jean Stafford's *The Catherine Wheel,*" *Critique* 17 (December 1975): 77–92.
Roberts, David. "Jean and Joe: the Stafford-Liebling Marriage," *American Scholar* 57, no. 3 (Summer 1988): 373–391.
———. *Jean Stafford: A Biography.* Boston: Little, Brown, 1988.
Steinhagen, Carol. "Stalking the Feline Female: The Significance of Hunting in *The Cub of the Panther* and *The Mountain Lion.*" In *Women and Violence in Literature: An Essay Collection,* edited by Katherine Anne Ackley, 207–220. New York: Garland, 1990.
Walsh, Mary-Ellen W. *Jean Stafford.* New York: Macmillan, 1985.
White, Barbara. "Initiation, the West, and the Hunt in Jean Stafford's *The Mountain Lion,*" *Essays in Literature* 9 (Fall 1982): 194–210.
Wilson, Mary Ann. "In Another Country: Jean Stafford's Literary Apprenticeship in Baton Rouge," *Southern Review* 29 (Winter 1993): 58–66.

OTHER

Jean Stafford. Available online. URL: http://www.jscheuer. com/stafford.htm. Accessed September 25, 2005.

STAGGERFORD Jon Hassler (1977)

Who better to write a novel about an English teacher than one who has been involved in that career for most of his adult life? Jon HASSLER makes clear that he fashioned some of *Staggerford* from his own life experience. ". . . my fiction is 37 percent autobiographical. I think Miles is 37 percent me, that is, about one third of him is like me and about one-third of his experience is mine" (Plut). It is precisely this willingness to look at his life and the lives of those around him as "story" that makes Hassler's fiction unforgettable. Readers know these people in their own lives. While some critics have argued that Miles Pruitt, Agnes McGee, and Beverly Bingham, the three central characters in *Staggerford,* are two-dimensional and static, others argue with equal fervor that Hassler is a character genius and his are some of the best in contemporary literature, particularly Agnes McGee. Both groups of critics agree that the plot, satire, and themes of *Staggerford* carry the novel and make it an overall success. In his writing career, which spans nearly 30 years, Hassler has been compared to the likes of Flannery O'CONNOR and John CHEEVER. His first adult novel (published simultaneously, by chance, with his first young adult novel, *Four Miles to Pinecone*), *Staggerford* began as 7,500 hardcover copies and has transformed into "a cult book among English teachers" (Plut). Its effectiveness is based primarily on strong, vivid characters and an effortless, elegant plotline, derived from Hassler's choice to structure the novel over the course of nine consecutive days.

Staggerford recounts nine days in the lives of several residents of Staggerford, Minnesota, most specifically 35-year-old Miles Pruitt. He has lived in Staggerford all his life and is well known among the residents of this small town. The novel opens with Miles contemplating his daily life and existence through grading a class assignment: the "What I Wish" essays. He is respected by his students but continually questioned by the faculty and administration about his teaching methods and beliefs. Agnes McGee, his landlady and friend, supports him professionally, but she admonishes him personally for lapsing in his practice of Catholicism. The driving event of the novel is a conflict between Staggerford student Jeff Norquist and a Native American student who lives on the neighboring reservation but attends Staggerford High School, Hank Bird. The clash between Staggerford and the Sandhill reservation goes back further than either of these students have been alive, but Jeff hitting Hank during Miles's study hall proves to be the catalyst to instigate a face-to-face conflict involving residents of both areas as well as the governor and the National Guard, which will be "armed to the teeth" (Hassler, 252). As both sides work together and separately to reconcile, a secondary storyline involving Beverly Bingham, a student who has

fallen in love with Miles, comes to fruition and finishes out the novel. Beverly's mother, known to Staggerford residents as "The Bonewoman," is clinically insane. The residents believe she is harmless, but Beverly knows otherwise. Her public admission of a crime her mother has committed, plus the choice of the National Guard to use the Bingham property as their station, leads to the climax of the novel, an unforeseen and tragic loss to the Staggerford community.

The structure Hassler chose of dividing the novel into nine-day-long sections was instrumental in character establishment. By slowing down and focusing on each specific day, a mixture of the mundane, the extraordinary, and the tragic, Hassler proves his notion that stories are all around us. They need not be imagined; they already exist. To that end, by the conclusion of the nine-day time period, readers feel as if they have just spent a week with old friends.

While the events are told primarily from Miles's perspective, Hassler doesn't limit any other characters. His description of Agnes McGee presents a physical, mental, and spiritual profile in a few brief sentences: "Slight and splay-footed and quick as a bird . . . this was her forty-first year in the same classroom. . . . In the minds of her former students, many of whom were grandparents, she occupied a place somewhere between Moses and Emily Post and when they met her on the street they guarded not only their speech but also their thoughts" (Hassler, 17).

In contrast, but equally effective, is a purely physical description of Beverly Bingham, his student. "Since their visit in the Hub, she had applied something chartreuse and oily to her eyelids. He wanted to tell her to leave her eyes alone. They were large and blue and couldn't be improved upon. Keeping her hair from falling in front of them was the only attention they needed" (Hassler, 69). The majority of Miles's observations of Beverly are physical, alluding to the idea that he holds a slightly inappropriate affection for her. Eventually he admits to having feelings for her, but only to the privacy of his journal. Miles himself is described physically only once, and briefly at that ("Miles was tall, heavy, square-jawed and red-haired" [Hassler 26]); Hassler chose instead to present him through narration and through Miles's own journal, which records some of his most intimate thoughts. Through the structure, Hassler affords himself the opportunity to pause and describe without disturbing the action. At the conclusion of the novel, readers know Hassler's characters arguably better than they know some of their own neighbors.

Hassler used the nine-day structure to enhance the plot as well as the characterization. He described the whole day virtually from sunrise to sunset in detail rather than selecting singular elements of each to run the story. It is precisely because of this daily life, the pattern and safety it establishes, that the novel's final climactic action is such a shock. Extensive and rather obvious, foreshadowing still does not prepare readers for the final five pages when one of the lifelong residents suddenly leaves Staggerford forever. In fact, outside this climax, there are few major events in the novel overall. Besides the Staggerford-Sandhill conflict, the majority of the novel consists of day-to-day events: teaching, of course, visiting friends, a Halloween party, and Miles getting his wisdom teeth removed. Hassler presents *Staggerford* without apology and without grandeur: He doesn't force plot where it isn't necessary. The result is a novel that flows smoothly along, with the bumps of daily life, to a conclusion that shakes readers on a fundamental level simply because they don't see it coming. In an interview with former colleague Joseph Plut, Hassler says about the ending, "Yes, a lot of people say they had to read that paragraph over several times . . . because they didn't believe it. I'm surprised, of course, but I'm sort of pleased, too, that the novel had that much impact on the reader."

No one is more surprised than Jon Hassler himself about not only readers' reactions to his novels but to their success as a whole. However, with a structure that allows characters to become real flesh and blood people, and a plotline that resembles daily life on a frightening level, success is inevitable. Readers can rest assured that when they pick up *Staggerford,* they will be meeting new friends they will not be able to leave by simply closing the book. Agnes, Miles, Beverly, and "The Bonewoman" remain far after the sun has set on the final day in Staggerford.

SOURCES

Hassler, Jon. *Staggerford.* New York: Ballantine Books, 1977.
Plut, Joseph. "Conversations with Jon Hassler: About *Staggerford,*" *South Dakota Review,* (Spring 2001). Available online: URL: http://www.usd.edu/sdreview/39-1%20(interview). htm. Accessed September 25, 2005.

Kelly Flanagan

STEGNER, WALLACE (WALLACE EARLE STEGNER) (1909–1993)

Winner of the 1972 Pulitzer Prize for ANGLE OF REPOSE, the National Book Award for *The* SPECTATOR BIRD, and three O. Henry Awards for short stories, Wallace Stegner is forever associated with the American West. "It is a peculiarity and a strength of Stegner's vision that in looking east across America, he finds everywhere the same rootlessness he feels in himself," notes critic Verlyn Klikenborg, who also says that Stegner's voice is one of "reassurance, a voice of acceptance, not resignation" (Klinkenborg, 39, 40). During a five-decade-long career, Stegner—novelist, conservationist, historian—established the Stanford University Creative Writing Program, one of the most respected in the United States, and worked strenuously to preserve the land he cherished and extolled in his writing.

Wallace Stegner was born on February 18, 1909, in Lake Mills, Iowa, to George A. H. Stegner and Hilda Paulson Stegner. Raised there and in several western states, he earned his bachelor's degree at the University of Utah in 1930 and his master's (1932) and doctoral (1935) degrees at the University of Iowa. He married Mary Stuart Page in 1934. His first novella, *Remembering Laughter* (1937), depicts the love triangle among Alec Stuart, a farmer; his wife, Margaret; and his sister-in-law Elspeth. Stegner uses memory here in ways that anticipate his more complex use of the past in later novels. Two other novellas of this period include *The Potter's House* (1938) and *Fire and Ice* (1941). *On a Darkling Plain* (1940) is a novella about Edwin Vickers, a disillusioned war veteran who rejoins the Saskatchewan farming community from which he has isolated himself; Stegner debunks the romantic western myth of the self-reliant individual.

Fame came to Stegner with the publication of *The Big Rock Candy Mountain* in 1943. The novel ranges over vast western spaces, and features Bo Mason, an ambitious man based on Stegner's father, and his strong and determined wife, Elsa, based on Stegner's mother, their two sons, and the exorbitant price they pay for Bo's failure. *Second Growth* (1947) is the only Stegner novel set in the East, in a town modeled on Greensboro, Vermont; here the young people are stultified by social restrictions. *The Preacher and the Slave* 1950, published as *Joe Hill: A Biographical Novel* in 1969, is Stegner's fictional account of the labor radical who was arrested and executed in Salt Lake City during World War I. In *A Shooting Star* (1961), a popular success, Sabrina Castro is a passionate, rebellious woman determined to change her reliance on wealth and leisure. Instead, she and her mother lay plans to preserve the land from commercialization. *All the Little Live Things* (1967) is narrated by retired literary editor Joe Allston, who reappears in *The Spectator Bird* (1976). Considered by most critics to be Stegner's most didactic work, it contains numerous discussions on ethical and environmental issues.

Angle of Repose, a 20th-century classic, follows the unhappily married and retired Berkeley history professor Lyman Ward, who studies the careers of his writer-artist pioneer grandparents in order to understand his own life: He has lost a leg, his wife has deserted him, and his sociologist son, Rodman, rejects him. *The Spectator Bird* reintroduces Joe Allston, the cantankerous 70-year-old seeking answers to life beyond his contempt for contemporary culture. He is helped by a number of people when he returns to Europe to trace his Danish ancestry, including the novelist Karen Blixen.

In *Recapitulation* (1979), Bruce Mason (son of Bo Mason in *The Big Rock Candy Mountain*), now a retired diplomat, confronts the ghosts of his past. *CROSSING TO SAFETY* (1987), Stegner's last novel, tells two Depression-era stories: the Langs, an eastern couple modeled on close friends of Wallace and Mary Stegner, meet the Morgans, a western couple modeled on the Stegners. Both of the young men are first-year English professors at a Wisconsin university. The friendship between the couples survives class and monetary differences.

After being injured in a car accident on March 28, 1993, Wallace Stegner died on April 13, 1993, in Santa Fe, New Mexico. *Angle of Repose* was performed as an opera by Andrew Imbrie and Oakley Hall and the San Francisco Opera Company in 1976. Wallace Stegner's papers are housed in the Cecil H. Green Library at Stanford University and at the University of Utah in the J. Willard Marriot Library.

NOVELS AND NOVELLAS

All the Little Live Things. New York: Viking, 1967.
Angle of Repose. Garden City, N.Y.: Doubleday, 1971.
The Big Rock Candy Mountain. New York: Duell, 1943.
Crossing to Safety. New York: Random House, 1987.
Fire and Ice. New York: Duell, 1941.
On a Darkling Plain. New York: Harcourt, Brace, 1940.
The Potter's House. Muscatine, Iowa: Prairie Press, 1938.
The Preacher and the Slave. Boston: Houghton Mifflin, 1950, published as *Joe Hill: A Biographical Novel.* Garden City, N.Y.: Doubleday, 1969.
Recapitulation. Garden City, N.Y.: Doubleday, 1979.
Remembering Laughter. Boston: Little, Brown, 1937.
Second Growth. Boston: Houghton Mifflin, 1947.
A Shooting Star. New York: Viking, 1961.
The Spectator Bird. Garden City, N.Y.: Doubleday, 1976.

SOURCES

Arthur, Anthony, ed. *Critical Essays on Wallace Stegner.* Boston: G. K. Hall, 1982.
Benson, Jackson J. *Down by the Lemonade Springs: Essays on Wallace Stegner.* Reno: University of Nevada Press, 2001.
———. *Wallace Stegner: His Life and Work.* New York: Viking, 1996.
———. *Wallace Stegner: A Study of the Short Fiction.* New York: Twayne, 1998.
Cook-Lynn, Elizabeth. *Why I Can't Read Wallace Stegner and Other Essays: A Tribal Voice.* Madison: University of Wisconsin Press, 1997.
Dourgarian, James M., ed. *Wallace Earle Stegner, 1909–1993.* Walnut Creek, Calif.: J. M. Dourgarian, 1994.
Hepworth, James R., and Nancy Colberg. *Wallace Stegner: A Descriptive Bibliography.* Lewiston, Idaho: Confluence, 1990.
———, ed. *Stealing Glances: Three Interviews with Wallace Stegner.* Albuquerque: University of New Mexico Press, 1998.
Klinkenborg, Verlyn. "Writing the Land," *New Republic,* 20 & 27 August 1990, pp. 38–40.
Lewis, Merrill, and Lorene Lewis. *Wallace Stegner.* Boise, Idaho: Boise State College, 1972.
Meine, Curt. *Wallace Stegner and the Continental Vision: Critical Essays and Commentary.* Washington, D.C.: Island Press, 1997.

Rankin, Charles E., ed. *Wallace Stegner: Man and Writer.* Albuquerque: University of New Mexico Press, 1996.

Robinson, Forrest G., and Margaret C. Robinson. *Wallace Stegner.* Boston: Twayne, 1977.

South Dakota Review, special Stegner issue, 23 (Winter 1985).

Stegner, Page, ed. *The Geography of Hope: A Tribute to Wallace Stegner.* San Francisco: Sierra Club Books, 1996.

———, ed. *Marking the Sparrow's Fall: Wallace Stegner's American West.* New York: Holt, 1998.

Thomas, John L. *A Country in the Mind: Wallace Stegner, Bernard DeVoto, History, and the American Land.* New York: Routledge, 2000.

OTHER

The Stegner Collection. Available online. URL: http://www.lib.utah.edu/spc/photo/p561/p561.html. Accessed September 25, 2005.

STEIN, GERTRUDE (1874–1946)

Gertrude Stein will be forever associated with the phrases "rose is a rose is a rose," the "lost generation" of the 1920s, and her perhaps apocryphal description of California, "There is no there there." An American writer in Paris during the early decades of the 20th century, Stein was a novelist, short story writer, playwright, poet essayist, biographer, and librettist. In the last few decades, however, scholars have been seriously reconsidering her highly experimental writing, resulting in a large number of articles and books on this writer. She is now associated with 20th-century modernism and increasingly viewed as a pioneer of postmodernism. Difficult to read because of her unorthodox use of language, Stein wrote several novels and novellas, the longest of which, *The MAKING OF AMERICANS* (1925), was 1,000 pages; Stein believed it to be her greatest work. *Three Lives* (1909), written in what Stein termed a realistic style, remains the easiest to read. *Ida: A Novel* is based loosely on the life of the duchess of Windsor. Gertrude Stein remains best known for *The AUTOBIOGRAPHY OF ALICE B. TOKLAS,* her account of social and artistic circles in early 20th-century Paris.

Gertrude Stein was born on February 3, 1874, in Allegheny, Pennsylvania, to Daniel Stein and Amelia Keyser Stein. The family moved to Austria, and then to Oakland, California, where Stein was reared until 1892, when she decided to attend Radcliffe College while her brother Leo, to whom she was very close, went to Harvard University. She studied with the philosopher and psychologist William James, who would later remember Stein as one of the most brilliant students he had ever taught. After her graduation (magna cum laude), she and Leo both attended Johns Hopkins University Medical School, then moved in 1902 to Paris, France. They lived together until Alice B. Toklas moved in at Stein's invitation; Stein and Toklas lived together from 1910 until Stein's death.

In Paris, Stein began to write and to collect the paintings of Cezanne, Renoir, Matisse, and Picasso. In fact, Picasso began painting his famous portrait of Gertrude Stein in 1905, the same year that Stein wrote her first published work, *Three Lives,* a collection of two stories, "The Good Anna" and "The Gentle Lena," along with the novella *Melanctha.* All three tales present women whose powerlessness is represented by their submission to a world they cannot control; *Melanctha,* one of the few instances where a white author attempts to portray a black woman's consciousness, earned praise from such Harlem Renaissance writers as Nella LARSEN and Richard WRIGHT. Stein's first novella, *Q.E.D.,* written in 1903, remained unpublished until 1950, when it was released as *Things as They Are.* It is the story of a love triangle and, unlike most of her other writing, follows a fairly linear narrative about three women involved in a lesbian relationship; the character representing Stein is rejected and shunned. *Fernhurst,* a novella also written in 1905 but published posthumously, is about gender issues and differences among the students at a women's college.

The Making of Americans, referred to as Stein's "magnum opus," tells the tale of two immigrant families, the Dehnings and Herslands; based on Stein's own family history, it was intended to make the two families metaphors for the immigrant experience in America. In fact, the novel is very loosely held together by episodes and vignettes and there is so much repetition that all but the most diligent readers have difficulty finishing it. Stein was experimenting here with the temporary abandonment of syntax and punctuation; she tried to replicate through language the jumbled and disjointed state of the human mind: To use language in an ordered way, she believed, presented an unreal picture of human experience. Although scholars continue to argue about the extent of her influence on the modernist writers Ernest HEMINGWAY, F. Scott FITZGERALD, Sherwood ANDERSON, and others, Stein's own writings are clearly in the avant-garde of the modernists and precursors of contemporary postmodernism. Her intellect never waned, as the well-known anecdote about her final days in a Paris hospital attests: She reportedly asked, "What is the answer?" and, when no answer was forthcoming, she asked, "In that case, what is the question?" Gertrude Stein died on July 27, 1946, in Neuilly-sur-Seine, France. The world that had known her as the "Sibyl of Montparnesse" had lost its modernist icon.

NOVELS AND NOVELLAS

The Autobiography of Alice B. Toklas. New York: Harcourt, 1933.

Blood on the Dining-Room Floor. Pawlet, Vt.: Banyan Press, 1948.

Fernhurst, Q.E.D., and Other Early Writings. New York: Liveright, 1971.

Ida, a Novel. New York: Random House, 1941.

The Making of Americans. Paris: Contact Editions, 1925; New York: A. &. C. Boni, 1926; London: Owen, 1968.

A Novel of Thank You. (Originally published in 1958 by Yale University Press as volume 8 of "The Yale Edition of the Unpublished Writings of Gertrude Stein." Normal, Ill.: Dalkey Archive Press, 1994.

Q.E.D.

1903. Published as *Things as They Are.* Pawlet, Vt.: Banyan Press, 1950.

Three Lives: Stories of the Good Anna, Melanctha, and the Gentle Lena. New York: Grafton Press, 1909.

SOURCES

Burns, Edward M., Ulla Dydo, and William Rice, eds. *Mirrors of Friendship: The Letters of Gertrude Stein and Thornton Wilder.* New Haven, Conn.: Yale University Press, 1996.

Caramallo, Charles. *Henry James, Gertrude Stein, and the Biographical Act.* Chapel Hill: University of North Carolina Press, 1996.

Carson, Luke. *Consumption and Depression in Gertrude Stein, Louis Zukofsky, and Ezra Pound.* New York: St. Martin's Press, 1998.

Dickie, Margaret. *Stein, Bishop, and Rich: Lyrics of Love, War, and Peace.* Chapel Hill: University of North Carolina Press, 1997.

Galvin, Mary E. *Queer Poetics: Five Modernist Women Writers.* Westport, Conn.: Greenwood Press, 1998.

Gygax, Franziska. *Gender and Genre in Gertrude Stein.* Westport, Conn.: Greenwood Press, 1998.

Harrison, Gilbert A. *Gertrude Stein's America.* New York: R. B. Luce, 1965.

Kaufmann, Michael. *Textual Bodies: Modernism, Postmodernism, and Print.* Lewisburg, Pa.: Bucknell University Press, 1994.

Moore, George B. *Gertrude Stein's The Making of Americans: and the Emergence of Modernism.* New York: Peter Lang, 1997.

———. *The Unfinished Aesthetic: Gertrude Stein and "The Making of Americans."* New York: Peter Lang, 1996.

Perelman, Bob. *The Trouble with Genius: Reading Pound, Joyce, Stein, and Zukofsky.* Berkeley: University of California Press, 1994.

Riddel, Joseph N. *The Turning Word: American Literary Modernism and Continental Theory.* Edited by Mark Bauerlein. Philadelphia: University of Pennsylvania Press, 1996.

Rogers, W. G. *When This You See Remember Me: Gertrude Stein in Person.* New York: Rinehart & Co., 1948.

Simon, Linda. *Gertrude Stein Remembered.* Lincoln: University of Nebraska Press, 1994.

Stein, Gertrude. *Everybody's Autobiography.* New York: Random House, 1937.

Stendhal, Renate, ed. *Gertrude Stein: In Words and Pictures: A Photobiography.* Chapel Hill, N.C.: Algonquin Books, 1994.

Wagner-Martin, Linda. *Favored Strangers: Gertrude Stein and Her Family.* New Brunswick, N.J.: Rutgers University Press, 1995.

Watson, Steven. *Prepare for Saints: Gertrude Stein, Virgil Thomson, and the Mainstreaming of American Modernism.* New York: Random House, 1998.

Watts, Linda S. *Rapture Untold: Gender, Mysticism, and the "Moment of Recognition" in Novels: Gertrude Stein.* New York: Peter Lang, 1996.

Weiss, M. Lynn. *Gertrude Stein and Richard Wright: The Poetics and Politics of Modernism.* Jackson: University Press of Mississippi, 1998.

Welch, Lew, and Eric Paul Shaffer. *How I Read Gertrude Stein.* San Francisco: Grey Fox Press, 1994.

Wilson, Edmund. *Axel's Castle: A Study in the Imaginative Literature of 1870–1930.* New York: Scribner, 1931.

Wineapple, Brenda. *Sister Brother: Gertrude and Leo Stein.* New York: Putnam, 1996.

OTHER

Gertrude Stein Online. Available online. URL: http://www. tenderbuttons.com. Accessed September 25, 2005.

Readings: Gertrude Stein. Modern & Contemporary American Poetry. Available online. URL: http://www.english.upenn. edu/~afilreis/88/stein-bio.html. Accessed September 25, 2005.

The World of Gertrude Stein. Available online. URL: http:// www.ellensplace.net/gstein2.html. Accessed January 13, 2006.

STEINBECK, JOHN (JOHN ERNST STEINBECK) (1902–1968)

John Steinbeck, who won the Nobel Prize in 1962, has earned a significant place in American literary history. His deceptively simple writing style appeals to younger as well as to more sophisticated readers.

Because Steinbeck popularized and immortalized his native region of central California, it is frequently referred to as Steinbeck Country, a place that represents both the positive and the nightmarish aspects of the American Dream. Many of his now mythic characters have become part of the American literary landscape: his "paisanos" in TORTILLA FLAT (1935) and CANNERY ROW (1945), George and Lennie in OF MICE AND MEN (1937), the Joad family—particularly the larger-than-life Ma Joad—of The GRAPES OF WRATH, the young Jody of The Red Pony (1937), the depraved Cathy of EAST OF EDEN (1952). Steinbeck was also concerned with the evils perpetrated on the land, and contemporary environmentalists celebrate his prescience about these matters. Above all, Steinbeck honored life and the human ability to survive various setbacks.

John Steinbeck was born on February 27, 1902, in Salinas, California, to John Ernest Steinbeck, a county treasurer, and Olive Hamilton Steinbeck, a schoolteacher. He was educated at Stanford University, which he attended from 1919 to 1925 without taking a degree. In 1930, Steinbeck married Carol Henning, the year after publishing his first novel, *Cup of Gold: A Life of Henry Morgan, Buccaneer.* It relates the life of a 17th-century Caribbean pirate, Sir Henry Morgan, who attacks Panama City in Panama, the "cup of gold," in order to win a woman whom he then ransoms to her husband. The PASTURES OF HEAVEN (1932), often compared to Sherwood ANDERSON's *Winesburg, Ohio,* is a short story cycle set between Monterey and Salinas in Corral de Tierra—called the Pastures of Heaven—that focuses on the myth of the rural American West and on two families in particular: Munroes, former city dwellers, who have chosen the pastoral life, and the Whitesides, a traditional farming family. The novel exposes the self-deceptions and delusions of ordinary folk who fail to achieve happiness in their Edenic locale. *To a God Unknown* (1933), set in the mystical town of Jolon at the southern end of the Salinas Valley, follows the western odyssey of New Englander Joseph Wayne. His obsession with the land and his establishment of a dynasty turns to dust as one of California's periodic droughts wreaks destruction and leads to Wayne's mystical death. *Tortilla Flat* (1935), Steinbeck's first best-seller, features the various stories of Monterey's Mexican Americans and compares them to the knights of King Arthur's round table. At the end of the novel, their communal housing stands empty and the landlord who held them all together falls to his death. The formerly close friends disband.

In Dubious Battle (1936) illustrates Steinbeck's theory of "group man," his belief that the individual is revealed by his relationship to the group rather than in isolation. It is also his first novel to explore seriously the lives of hardscrabble working-class people, in this case California apple pickers who go on strike against their employers. The central character, Doc Burton, can work no miracles in this grim tale. *Of Mice and Men* (1937), Steinbeck's first major success, harshly evokes reality at the same time it celebrates friendship between George Milton and Lennie Small, two itinerant farm laborers who define Steinbeck's version of the American Dream: finding security through a house and land of one's own. After Lennie inadvertently kills the wife of the ranch owner's son, George feels he will do Lennie a favor by shooting him before the mob reaches him. *The Red Pony* (1937) is a clearly unified story sequence comprising "The Gift," "The Great Mountains," "The Promise"—published in *North American Review* and *Harpers* between 1933 and 1937—and "The Leader of the People," which appeared in a story collection, *The Long Valley.* One of Steinbeck's finest works, frequently compared with FAULKNER's *The Bear* or HEMINGWAY's Nick Adams stories, it tells the coming-of-age story of Jody Tiflin as he grows from boyhood to manhood on a Salinas Valley ranch.

The Grapes of Wrath (1939) is easily the best-known protest novel in American fiction; it had both admirers and detractors but it seems that everyone has read the book. Based on Steinbeck's own investigations and experiences as an agricultural worker, about which he had already published a number of newspaper articles, it features the impoverished and exploited Joads who, driven from their home in Oklahoma's Dust Bowl, seek the paradise promised by California. Their tale, as they join migrant grape pickers who endure hunger and shantytowns, is interspersed with more general commentary on the era. The Joads become symbols of an entire nation.

The Moon Is Down (1942), set in a mythical European village, is based on the Nazi occupation of Norway. In *Cannery Row* (1945) Steinbeck turns his attention once again to those living on the margins of society; the main character, based on Steinbeck's friend Ed Ricketts, is Doc, a selfless and good man who refuses to succumb to the materialism around him. *The Wayward Bus* (1947) follows Juan Chicoy on his bus named Sweetheart as he drives his varied passengers from Rebel Corners to San Juan de la Cruz; when the bus gets stuck in the mud, the behavior of the characters illustrates Steinbeck's point, that modern American life has corrupted values and sexual attitudes. THE PEARL (1947), a mythic parable of a Mexican fisherman that Steinbeck based on a folktale heard during a trip in the Gulf of Mexico with Ricketts, features Kino, a poor villager from La Paz, Mexico. Kino, like the other pearl divers in the village, seeks the fabulous wealth promised by finding the perfect pearl. He finds that pearl but ends up throwing it back in the Gulf after realizing it has brought him nothing but sin and grief.

East of Eden (1952) was Steinbeck's study of the nature of good and evil as one Salinas Valley family falls from its Edenic state. Based on the story of Cain and Abel, the long and complex novel traces the history of Adam Trask and the Hamiltons, his maternal ancestors, and of Adam's twin sons, Aron and Caleb (who may be his brother's). In *Sweet Thursday* (1954), *Cannery Row*'s Doc tries and fails to live in a society that

has renounced communal connections. *The Short Reign of Pippin IV: A Fabrication* (1957) is a parody of French politics under Charles De Gaulle. In *The WINTER OF OUR DISCONTENT* (1961), set on Long Island, the protagonist, Ethan Allen Hawley, cannot prosper in the materialistic world in which he finds himself, and the once ethical businessman suffers a moral collapse.

John Steinbeck was married three times: after divorcing Carol Henning in 1943, he married Gwyn Conger 1943. They divorced in 1948, and he was married to Elaine Scott from 1950 until his death from heart disease in 1968, in New York City. He was buried in Salinas, California. Elaine Steinbeck's death in 2003 resulted in a lawsuit filed by Steinbeck's son and granddaughter, who believe that Steinbeck's widow cheated them out of copyright control and royalties from his literary estate.

Steinbeck's novels have inspired numerous films, many of them now considered classics: *Of Mice and Men,* starring Burgess Meredith and Lon Cheney, was produced by United Artists in 1939, directed by Reza Badiyi for a teleplay in 1981; and, most recently, as a Metro-Goldwyn-Mayer film starring Gary Sinise and John Malkovich in 1992. *The Grapes of Wrath,* starring Henry Fonda, was directed by John Ford at Twentieth Century-Fox in 1940. *Tortilla Flat,* starring Spencer Tracy, was filmed by MGM in 1942. *The Moon Is Down,* produced by Twentieth Century-Fox in 1943, starred Sir Cedric Hardwicke and Lee J. Cobb. In 1954, Warner Brothers filmed *East of Eden,* with James Dean and Jo Van Fleet, who won an Oscar for her performance; in the 1960s, it was made into a television miniseries and a musical that opened in New York in 1968. In 1947 a Mexican film rendition of *The Pearl* appeared, and, in 1948, RKO issued the film for which Steinbeck wrote the screenplay. He also wrote the screenplay for *The Red Pony* (1949), starring Robert Mitchum. *The Wayward Bus* was produced by Twentieth Century–Fox in 1957. MGM's *Cannery Row* starred Nick Nolte and Debra Winger in 1982.

John Steinbeck's papers, correspondence, and manuscripts are in the following libraries: Stanford University, the Bancroft Library of the University of California at Berkeley, Ball State University, the Preston Beyer Collection at Princeton University, the University of Texas at Austin, the University of Virginia, the Center for Steinbeck Studies at San Jose State University, and the Salinas Public Library in Salinas, California. Steinbeck's numerous honors include a 1940 Pulitzer Prize for *The Grapes of Wrath* and a New York Drama Critics Circle Award in 1938 for the theatrical version of *Of Mice and Men*.

NOVELS

Burning Bright: A Play in Story Form. New York: Viking, 1950.

Cannery Row. New York: Viking, 1945.

Cup of Gold: A Life of Henry Morgan, Buccaneer. New York: Robert McBride, 1929.

East of Eden. New York: Viking, 1952.

The Forgotten Village. New York: Viking, 1941.

The Grapes of Wrath. New York: Viking, 1939.

In Dubious Battle. New York: Viking, 1936.

The Moon Is Down. New York: Viking, 1942.

Of Mice and Men. New York: Viking, 1937.

The Pastures of Heaven. New York: Viking, 1932.

The Pearl. New York: Viking, 1947.

The Red Pony. New York: Covici, Friede, 1937.

The Short Reign of Pippin IV: A Fabrication. New York: Viking, 1957.

Sweet Thursday. New York: Viking, 1954.

To a God Unknown. New York: Viking, 1933.

Tortilla Flat. New York: Viking, 1935.

The Wayward Bus. New York: Viking, 1947.

The Winter of Our Discontent. New York: Viking, 1961.

SOURCES

Astro, Richard. *John Steinbeck and Edward F. Ricketts: The Shaping of a Novelist*. Minneapolis: University of Minnesota Press, 1973.

———, and Tetsumaro Hayashi, eds. *Steinbeck: The Man and His Work*. Corvallis: Oregon State University Press, 1971.

Beegel, Susan F., et al., eds. *Steinbeck and the Environment*. Tuscaloosa: University of Alabama Press, 1997.

Benson, Jackson J. *The True Adventures of John Steinbeck, Writer*. New York: Viking, 1984.

———, ed. *The Short Novels of John Steinbeck: Critical Essays with a Checklist to Steinbeck Criticism*. Durham, N.C.: Duke University Press, 1990.

Bloom, Harold, ed. *John Steinbeck's "Of Mice and Men."* New York: Chelsea House, 1996.

———, ed. *John Steinbeck's "The Grapes of Wrath."* New York: Chelsea House, 1996.

Coers, Donald V., ed. *After the Grapes of Wrath: Essays on John Steinbeck in Honor of Tetsumaro Hayashi*. Athens: Ohio University Press, 1995.

Cusick, Lee. *John Steinbeck's "The Grapes of Wrath."* Piscataway, N.J.: Research & Education Association, 1994.

Davis, Robert Conn, ed. *Twentieth Century Interpretations of "The Grapes of Wrath": A Collection of Critical Essays*. Englewood Cliffs, N.J.: Prentice Hall, 1982.

Ditsky, John, ed. *Critical Essays on "The Grapes of Wrath."* Boston: G. K. Hall, 1988.

Ferrell, Keith. *John Steinbeck: The Voice of the Land*. New York: Evans, 1986.

Fontenrose, Joseph. *John Steinbeck: An Introduction and Interpretation*. New York: Barnes & Noble, 1963.

French, Warren. *A Filmguide to "The Grapes of Wrath."* Bloomington: Indiana University Press, 1973.

———, ed. *A Companion to "The Grapes of Wrath."* New York: Viking, 1963.

———. *John Steinbeck*. Boston: Twayne, 1961, revised, 1975.

———. *John Steinbeck's Fiction Revisited*. New York: Twayne, 1994.

Geismar, Maxwell. *Writers in Crisis*. Boston: Houghton, 1942.

Hadella, Charlotte. *"Of Mice and Men": A Kinship of Powerlessness*. New York: Twayne, 1995.

Harmon, Robert B. *Steinbeck Bibliographies: An Annotated Guide*. Metuchen, N.J.: Scarecrow, 1987.

Hayashi, Tetsumaro, ed. *Steinbeck's Literary Dimension*. Metuchen, N.J.: Scarecrow, 1973.

———, ed. *John Steinbeck: A Dictionary of His Fictional Characters*. Metuchen, N.J.: Scarecrow, 1976.

———. *Steinbeck's Women: Essays in Criticism*. Muncie, Ind.: Ball State University, 1979.

———, ed. *A Study Guide to Steinbeck: A Handbook to His Major Works*. Metuchen, N.J.: Scarecrow, 1974; Part II, Scarecrow, 1979.

———, and Beverly K. Simpson. *John Steinbeck: Dissertation Abstracts and Research Opportunities*. Metuchen, N.J.: Scarecrow, 1994.

Hedgpeth, Joel W., ed. *The Outer Shores*. Eureka, Calif.: Mad River Press, 1978.

Hughes, R. S. *John Steinbeck: A Study of the Short Fiction*. Boston: Twayne, 1989.

Ito, Tom. *John Steinbeck*. San Diego, Calif.: Lucent Books, 1994.

Johnson, Claudia Durst. *Understanding "Of Mice and Men," "The Red Pony," and "The Pearl": A Student Casebook to Issues, Sources, and Historical Documents*. Westport, Conn.: Greenwood Press, 1997.

Karson, Jill. *Reading on "Of Mice and Men."* San Diego, Calif.: Greenhaven Press, 1997.

Lisca, Peter. *The Wide World of John Steinbeck.* New Brunswick, N.J.: Rutgers University Press, 1958.

———. *Steinbeck: The Man and His Work.* Corvallis: Oregon State University Press, 1971.

———. *John Steinbeck: Nature and Myth.* New York: Thomas Y. Crowell, 1978.

———. *"The Grapes of Wrath": Text and Criticism.* 2nd edition. New York: Penguin, 1996.

Loewen, Nancy. *John Steinbeck.* Mankato, Minn.: Creative Education, 1997.

McElrath, Joseph R., et al., eds. *John Steinbeck: The Contemporary Reviews.* New York: Cambridge University Press, 1996.

Millichap, Joseph R. *Steinbeck and Film.* New York: Ungar, 1983.

Moore, Harry Thornton. *The Novels of John Steinbeck: A First Critical Study.* Chicago: Normandie House, 1939.

Owens, Louis. *John Steinbeck's Re-Vision of America.* Athens: University of Georgia Press, 1985.

———. *"The Grapes of Wrath": Trouble in the Promised Land.* Boston: Twayne, 1989.

Parini, Jay. *John Steinbeck: A Biography.* New York: Holt, 1995.

Reef, Catherine. *John Steinbeck.* New York: Clarion Books, 1996.

Simmonds, Roy S. *John Steinbeck: The War Years, 1939–1945.* Lewisburg, Pa.: Bucknell University Press, 1996.

Swisher, Clarice, ed. *Readings on John Steinbeck.* San Diego, Calif.: Greenhaven Press, 1996.

Timmerman, John H. *John Steinbeck's Fiction: The Aesthetics of the Road Taken.* Norman: University of Oklahoma Press, 1986.

OTHER

Audio interview with Elaine Steinbeck about John Steinbeck. Wired for Books. Available online. URL: http://wiredforbooks.org/elainesteinbeck. Accessed September 25, 2005.

John Steinbeck—Biography. Nobelprize.org. Available online. URL: http://nobelprize.org/literature/laureates/1962/Steinbeck-bio.html. Accessed September 25, 2005.

Martin Heasley Cox. *Center for Steinbeck Studies.* San José State University. Available online. URL: http://www.Steinbeck.sjsu.edu/home/index.jsp. Accessed January 13, 2006.

Steinbeck: The California Novels. Available online. URL: http://www.ac.wwu.edu/~stephan/Steinbeck. Accessed September 25, 2005.

STEPS JERZY KOSINSKI (1969) The subject of *Steps* undergoes a continual metamorphosis throughout its pages. At the beginning of each of the 46 episodes into which the book is divided, an "older" self is negated (not canceled out entirely, but preserved in the memory of the work), and a "new" one forms and takes its place. Each self belongs to a "present" instant that is disconnected from the preceding series of instants, each of which is itself displaced from history. If a unified authorial consciousness embraces each transformation, holding together the death and reformation of the subject in each instance, this can only be discerned in the articulation of the individual episodes. And if a link binds the episodes together (the "steps" of the title), it is the guiding thread of submission and domination, the only two forms of relationship of which the subject is capable. The author, Jerzy KOSINSKI, was surely disingenuous and willfully misleading when he claimed in an interview that the book progresses from "the formed mind of the protagonist (in the beginning of the novel) when he sees himself as a unique manipulator of others, to the stage (at the novel's end) when he realizes that he is nothing but a composite of various steps of culture." To speak of a "progression" in any strict sense would be inaccurate. It is the case that the narrator manipulates a young girl who is dazzled by the narrator's credit cards at the very beginning, but there are no traces of a gradual progression from the mind of a sovereign subject who exploits a dominant culture for his own purposes to one who recognizes his subjection to that culture. On many occasions throughout the work, long before its denouement, he is a plaything given over to powers that infinitely surpass his own, exposed to the whims of the uncontrollable, without a barrier to shield him from the forces that invade him.

The seductiveness of *Steps* resides in its power to lead the reader astray, away from the world to which s/he has grown accustomed and into a fictional space from which there is no easy escape. However oppressive its horror becomes, it is difficult to tear one's eyes from this book. Literary analysis may engage with the book's meaning but will necessarily fail to adequately explain the spell it casts over the reader. Each "step" is macabre and unsettling in its violence. In one episode, the subject is a farmhand at the mercy of peasants who spit on him for their amusement [II, 2]. He seeks revenge by inserting discarded fishhooks into morsels of bread, which he feeds to the children of those who torture him. The only way to invert the existing hierarchy, he seems to feel, is to become an oppressor oneself: Oppression generates oppression in the way that fire generates fire. A group of peasants, in another "step," gapes at a performance in which a young girl is violated by an animal [I, 4]. It is uncertain, the narrator tells us dryly, whether her screams indicate that she is actually suffering or whether she is merely playing to the audience. The extent to which the girl is a victim or a manipulator remains undetermined. In another episode, a nurse passively endures the amorous advances of the narrator, now a photographer, who longs for sexual contact with her in order to distinguish himself as much as possible from the seemingly nonhuman inmates of a senior citizen's home whom he has been photographing [III, 1]. When the narrator enters uninvited into the nurse's apartment, he finds her coupling with a simian creature who, ambiguously, is later described as "human." The narrator, in another episode, is an office worker whose lover is unaware that she is his lover [V, 5].

The narrator plots with a friend to take possession of her. The woman submits entirely to the friend's will and agrees to allow herself to be possessed by a stranger while blindfolded. Now the narrator can dispose of her sightless body as he wishes: a relationship that is emblematic of all of the relationships portrayed in *Steps*. Despite her complete availability, his desire remains frustrated. Nothing about her is concealed, but her nudity is itself a form of concealment. At another moment, the narrator is on a jury [V, 3]. The defendant explains his deed in the most ordinary terms without ever attempting to justify his behavior. A fictive identification is afforded between the members of the jury and the "executioner": They visualize themselves in the act of killing, but cannot project themselves into the mind of the victim who is in the act of being killed. The agony of the victim is lost to vision altogether. The narrator, in another episode, becomes the powerless spectator of his girlfriend's rape [III, 3].

Afterward, their relationship changes. He can now only represent her to himself as one who has been violated and who is worthy of violation: Her rape comes to define her. He visualizes her as a kind of crustacean or mollusk emerging from her shell. The conclusion of the episode follows an implacable logic: Under false pretenses, the narrator offers his girlfriend to the rowdy guests at a party, who proceed to have their way with her. Her pearl necklace, a gift from the narrator, scatters to the floor like so many iridescent seeds (a somberly beautiful passage that gives the lie to Kosinski's own self-interpretive remark that Steps eschews figurative language). The architect of an orchestrated violation, the narrator departs without witnessing the inescapable result of his designs. Such a summary can only imperfectly approximate the grotesque horror of this book.

One may wonder whether there is a point to such an uninterrupted current of phantasmagoric images. The reader may be invited to take delight in the extremity of its descriptions: Such would nurture one's suspicion that *Steps* is a purely nihilistic work. What we find in each instance is a relationship between one who terrorizes and oppresses or who sympathizes with terror and oppression (this is often, but not always, the narrator) and one who surrenders, voluntarily or otherwise, to the will of the oppressor. By describing such scenes of exploitation and persecution in a neutral manner, the book seems to offer no moral transcendence. Such an interpretation, however, would ignore the book's moral center. The book's ethical dimension first becomes apparent in an italicized transitional episode in which the protagonist tells his lover of an architect who designed plans for a concentration camp, the main purpose of which, the narrator explains, was "hygiene" [IV, 1].

Genocide was for those responsible indistinguishable from the extermination of vermin: "Rats have to be removed. We exterminate them, but this has nothing to do with our attitudes toward cats, dogs, or any other animal. Rats aren't murdered—we get rid of them; or, to use a better word, they are eliminated; this act of elimination is empty of all meaning." This passage in particular casts light on the "theme" of dehumanization that runs pervasively throughout the book. In *Steps*, the other person is reduced to the status of a thing. To make of the other human being a thing: Such is sadism. Only by representing those to be murdered as vermin (as things to be exterminated) is mass murder possible. It is no accident, from this perspective, that the narrator imagines himself felling trees when he obeys an order to slit his victim's throat toward the end of the book: It is the only way that he can suppress the nausea that wells up within him [VIII, 3]. Each human being is irreplaceable, and the death of a person is, therefore, an irrecoverable loss. By forgetting this, by turning the other human being into a mere object, one is able to dutifully "obey orders" to kill without the intrusion of moral consciousness. *Steps* aims at disgusting the reader by showing him/her the obscene consequences of objectification. From this perspective, is profoundly moral.

The center of *Steps* may serve as a counterbalance to the parade of scenes of horror and degradation that constitute it. However, this center does not govern the totality of its operations. A tonality of evil informs these poisonous pages; in terms of its sheer cruelty, the work could only be compared to the writings of the Marquis de Sade. Although one can point to its moral character from the passages cited above, the book could also be determined as a willfully perverse affirmation of simulation, falsehood, and metamorphosis that suspends the dimension of the ethical altogether. The subject ceaselessly yearns to exteriorize himself, to become part of an exterior space in which he would become entirely other-than-himself. It is a space in which he would be unencumbered by all forms of ethical responsibility: "If I could become one of them, if I could only part with my language, my manner, my belongings" [VII, 1].

SOURCES

Boyers, Robert. "Language and Reality in Kosinski's *Steps*," *Centennial Review* 16 (Winter 1972): 41–61.

Daler, John Kent von. "An Introduction to Jerzy Kosinski's *Steps*," *Language and Literature* 1 (January 1971): 43–49.

Kenner, Hugh. "Keys on a Ring." In *Critical Essays on Jerzy Kosinski*, edited by Barbara Tepa Lupach, 57–58. Boston: G. K. Hall, 1998.

Kosinski, Jerzy. *The Art of the Self: Essays apropos Steps.* New York: Scientia-Factum, 1968.

———. *Steps.* New York: Grove Press, 1997.

Petrakis, Byron. "Jerzy Kosinski's *Steps* and the Cinematic Novel," *Comparatist* (February 1978): 16–22.

Tartikoff, Brandon. "Interview with Jerzy Kosinski," *Metropolitan Review* 8 (October 1971): 104. Reprinted in *Conversations with Jerzy Kosinski,* edited Tom Teicholz, 13–14. Jackson: University Press of Mississippi, 1993.

Teicholz, Tom. *Conservations with Jerzy Kosinski* Jackson: University Press of Mississippi, 1993.

Tucker, Martin. "A Moralist's Journey into the Heart of Darkness," *Critical Essays on Jerzy Kosinski,* edited by Barbara Tepa Lupace, 63–65. Boston: G. K. Hall, 1998.

Joseph Suglia

STODDARD, ELIZABETH DREW BARSTOW (1823–1902)

Elizabeth Drew Barstow Stoddard was praised by her contemporaries, Nathaniel HAWTHORNE and William Dean HOWELLS, but she failed to achieve popularity in her own day. Lawrence Buell and Sandra A. Zagarell, who edited the 1984 critical edition of Stoddard's writings, believe that her talent places her on the same level with Hawthorne and Herman MELVILLE, and that her voice is "the most strikingly original" of her day (Buell and Zagarell, xi). This 19th-century novelist, short story writer, poet, essayist, and journalist insisted on writing realistic prose when most of her contemporaries were capitulating to the public craving for sentimental fiction. Indeed, today's readers are much more likely to appreciate Stoddard's straightforward treatment of women's erotic nature. As scholars have noted, Stoddard achieved her greatest fame near the end of the 20th century, and it continues into the 21st. Of her three novels—The MORGESONS (1862, 1901), *Two Men* (1865), and *Temple House* (1867)—The *Morgesons* continues to attract most attention. The scholar and critic Susan K. Harris, for instance, suggests that it may be "the most radical women's novel of the 19th-century" (Harris 1992, 152).

Elizabeth Drew Barstow Stoddard was born on May 6, 1823, to Betsy Drew Barstow and Wilson Barstow, a shipbuilder, whose financial difficulties reappear in *The Morgesons.* Stoddard was educated briefly at the Wheaton Female Seminary in Norton, Massachusetts, but left school after the deaths of her mother and her sister Jane. She married Richard Henry Stoddard, a poet, on December 6, 1852, and moved permanently to New York. She wrote prolifically during the next half century, including 75 newspaper columns for the *Daily Alta California* and more than 80 short stories and essays. When *The Morgesons* appeared, the tale of Cassandra Morgeson (who distinctly resembled Stoddard) and her passion for her married cousin sold poorly. But Stoddard believed that woman's sexual nature must be acknowledged and addressed, and *Two Men* and *Temple House* likewise feature daring women. *Two Men,* moreover, is the story of a love affair between a privileged white man, Parke Auster, and a passionate and beautiful black woman, Charlotte Lang. The novel, one of the first to address mixed race relationships, ends tragically.

Elizabeth Drew Barstow Stoddard suffered repeated losses and disappointments in her life, including the deaths of two of her children at young ages and the death of a third child, a playwright, at the age of 37. The reawakened interest in her work, particularly her novels, shows no signs of abating.

NOVELS

The Morgesons. New York: Carleton and Co., 1862.
Temple House. New York: Carleton and Co., 1867.
Two Men. New York: Bunce and Huntington, 1865.

SOURCES

Aldrich, Mrs. Thomas Bailey. *Crowding Memories.* Boston and New York: Houghton Mifflin, 1920.

Buell, Lawrence, and Sandra A. Zagarell, eds. "Biographical and Critical Introduction." In *"The Morgesons" and Other Writings, Published and Unpublished by Elizabeth Stoddard,* edited by Lawrence Buell & Sandra A. Zagarell, xi–xxix. Philadelphia: University of Pennsylvania Press, 1984.

Harris, Susan K. "Projecting the 'I'/Conoclast: First-Person Narration in *The Morgesons.*" In *19th-Century American Women's Novels: Interpretive Strategies,* 152–170. New York: Cambridge University Press, 1992.

———. "Stoddard's *The Morgesons*: A Contextual Evaluation," *English Studies Quarterly* 31 (1st quarter 1985): 11–23.

Matlack, James Hendrickson. "Hawthorne and Elizabeth Barstow Stoddard," *New England Quarterly* 50 (June 1977): 278–302.

Reynolds, David S. *Beneath the American Renaissance: The Subversive Imagination in the Age of Emerson and Melville.* New York: Knopf, 1988.

Zagarell, Sandra A. "*Legacy* Profile: Elizabeth Drew Barstow Stoddard (1823–1902)," *Legacy* 8 (Spring 1984): 73–91.

STONE, ROBERT (ROBERT ANTHONY STONE) (1937–)

Robert Stone is a novelist whose prizewinning fiction typically features Vietnam veterans, gunrunners, drug pushers, psychotics, and spies in a bleak and evil world. Nonetheless, he holds on to hope for those lost in a universe that nearly always seems hostile. His first novel, *A Hall of Mirrors* (1967), won the Faulkner award for Notable First Novel. *DOG SOLDIERS* (1974) won the National Book Award. Both novels were made into feature-length movies, with Paul Newman and Joanne Woodward starring in *WUSA,* Stone's adaptation of *A Hall of Mirrors,* and Nick Nolte and Tuesday Weld in *Who'll Stop the Rain,* the film title for *Dog Soldiers. A Flag for Sunrise* received an American Academy and Institute of Arts and Letters Award and John Dos Passos Prize, as well as nominations for the Pulitzer Prize, the American Book Award, the National Book Critics Award, and the PEN/Faulkner Award. *Outerbridge Reach* (1992) won for Stone a second National Book Award.

Robert Stone was born on August 21, 1937, in New York City, to C. Homer Stone and Gladys Catherine Grant Stone, a former teacher. His father deserted his mother while she was pregnant with him. Raised in Brooklyn and a product of Catholic schools, Stone married Janice G. Burr on December 11, 1959. They traveled around the United States until Stone published *A Hall of Mirrors,* set in New Orleans during the era of the Civil Rights movement. The protagonist, Morgan Ranie, learns that unscrupulous whites are using the census far a scam designed to remove lower-income blacks from the welfare rolls. After a race riot, again engineered by whites, Ranie is killed and his friend Geraldine Crosby commits suicide. This pessimistic view of contemporary society continues in *Dog Soldiers,* in which former Marine and Vietnam veteran Raymond Hicks brings several million dollars worth of heroin from Vietnam to Berkeley, California, for the journalist John Converse. The plan goes awry and Hicks goes off with Converse's wife, Marge, to a commune, clearly illustrating Stone's view of the contemporary loss of any moral center. *A Flag for Sunrise* explores this loss in terms of gnosticism, an ancient belief in the dark forces behind the creation, juxtaposed against the Catholicism of the alcoholic Father Egan and the idealistic Sister Justin. The novel takes place in the fictional central American country of Tecan during a revolution. They are visited by Frank Holliwell, a professor of anthropology and Vietnam veteran, and Pablo Tabor, a murderer and deserter from the Coast Guard. One of the most fascinating subplots involves Gordon Walker, an aging screen-writer with a midlife crisis, and Lu Anne Bourgeois, an actor who is about to act out, literally, Walker's screenplay of Kate Chopin's The AWAKENING, in which the protagonist drowns herself. At the end of this complex novel, Sister Justin is murdered for her part in the revolution. The Christianity of the dying Sister Justin seems stronger, and therefore more hopeful, than the gnosticism to which Holliwell retreats.

Outerbridge Reach (1992) features another filmmaker, Ronald Strickland, who is filming the journey of a Vietnam veteran, Owen Brown. Brown, a former naval officer, is disturbed by his Vietnam memories and leaves his wife Anne to embark on a round-the-world cruise on his yacht. Tragically, Brown's madness overtakes him, and Anne succumbs to Strickland's seductive advances. In *Damascus Gate* (1998), writer Christopher Lucas travels to Jerusalem to research the religious cults, only to fall in love with Sonia Barnes, a half-Jewish, half–African American Sufi jazz singer. She is a follower of Adam de Kuff, who believes he is the messiah. Stone's most recent novel, *Bay of Souls,* focuses on Michael Ahearn, a Minnesota English professor suffering from a midlife crisis. Despite his wife's injury, incurred while rescuing their son from nearly freezing, Ahearn leaves her to follow Lara Purcell, a female colleague, to a Caribbean island where he becomes involved in voodoo and a war. Stone remains consistent in his careful craftsmanship, realistic dialogue, persuasively realized characters, and explorations of religious beliefs, perhaps suggesting an alternative to his often delineated existentialist world.

NOVELS

Bay of Souls. Boston: Houghton Mifflin, 2003.
Children of Light. New York: Knopf, 1986.
Damascus Gate. Boston: Houghton Mifflin, 1998.
Dog Soldiers. Boston: Houghton Mifflin, 1974.
A Flag for Sunrise. New York: Knopf, 1981.
A Hall of Mirrors. Boston: Houghton Mifflin, 1967.
Outerbridge Reach. New York: Ticknor & Fields, 1992.

SOURCES

Bloom, James D. "Cultural Capital and Contrarian Investing: Stone, Thom Jones, and Others," *Contemporary Literature* 36, no. 3 (Fall 1995): 490–507.

Bull, Jeoffrey S. " 'What about a Problem That Doesn't Have a Solution?' Stone's *A Flag for Sunrise,* DeLillo's *Mao II,* and the Politics of Political Fiction," *Critique: Studies in Contemporary Fiction* 40, no. 3 (Spring 1999): 215–229.

Finn, James. "The Moral Vision of Robert Stone: The Transcendent in the Muck of History," *Commonweal* 120, no. 19 (November 5, 1993): 9–14.

Fredrickson, Robert S. "Robert Stone's Decadent Leftists." *Papers on Language and Literature* 32, no. 3 (Summer 1996): 315–334.

———. "Robert Stone's Opium of the People: Religious Ambivalence in *Damascus Gate,*" *Papers on Language and Literature* 36, no. 1 (Winter 2000): 42–57.

Hower, Edward. "A Parable for the Millennium," *World and I* 13, no. 9 (September 1998): 255–262.

Karagueuzian, Maureen. "Irony in Robert Stone's *Dog Soldiers,*" *Critique: Studies in Contemporary Fiction* 24, no. 2 (Winter 1983): 65–73.

McGraw, Erin. "Larger Concerns," *Georgia Review* 51, no. 4 (Winter 1997): 782–792.

Pritchard, William H. "Actual Fiction," *Hudson Review* 50, no. 4 (Winter 1998): 656–664.

Schroeder, Eric James. "Two Interviews: Talks with Tim O'Brien and Robert Stone," *Modern Fiction Studies* 30 (Spring 1984): 135–164.

Shelton, Frank W. "Robert Stone's *Dog Soldiers:* Vietnam Comes Home to America," *Critique: Studies in Contemporary Fiction* 24, no. 2 (Winter 1983): 74–81.

Solotaroff, Robert. *Robert Stone.* New York: Twayne, 1994.

Stone, Robert, David Pink, and Chuck Lewis. "An Interview with Robert Stone," *Salmagundi* 108 (Fall 1995): 117–139.

STORY OF AVIS, THE ELIZABETH STUART PHELPS (WARD) (1877)

Elizabeth Stuart PHELPS's *The Story of Avis* depicts the plight of 19th-century women torn between personal self-fulfillment and marriage and suggests that overwhelming domestic duties ultimately destroy creativity. Although some early reviewers described the novel as having "a dangerous lesson to preach, and no less dangerous than untrue" and not "altogether a wholesome story," both a moral and a realistic dimension appear throughout. Avis Dobell, Phelps's favorite female character, is at least partially autobiographical. The numerous parallels between Avis and Phelps include an epiphanic reading of Elizabeth Barrett Browning's Aurora Leigh and a dislike of domestic tasks—Avis describes sewing as making "a crawling down my back." Phelps's mother, herself the victim of domestic overwork while struggling to write, is another source. Other characters, including Avis's father may well have their genesis in Phelp's own family.

After studying in Europe for several years, Avis returns to her native New England to make her reputation. Carol Kessler notes that Avis's potential greatness perhaps represents "human creative potential in general," but, as for most artistic women of her time, Avis finds work difficult. She is often deterred by what Kessler identifies as "incapacitating expectations of family, friends, and society" (xiii).

At a meeting of the Spenser Club, Avis encounters Philip Ostrander, a young professor at the local college and a protégé of her father. In a sexually charged exchange, Philip forces Avis to admit that she recalls their encounter in Paris, but Avis rejects their physical attraction, instinctively sensing it endangers her creativity. After a symbolic rescue scene full of deterministic imagery—Philip retrieves Avis from the lighthouse jetties where she is attempting to save a bird subsequently smothered in his coat pocket—Avis's fate seems sealed. Although forewarned by her European master to avoid portrait painting, she yields to Philip's pressure to paint his portrait. The months of creating the portrait pass sometimes idyllically, but contentious scenes in natural settings such as the apple orchard punctuate them, and Avis's distrust of marriage consistently frames them. Phelps phrases their actions in martial terms to indicate their power struggle. When Philip proposes, Avis rejects him, citing her God-given power to paint and insisting that she "must not think of love" because she "cannot accept the consequences of love as other women do." Philip promises that, if they are married, she "would paint," but Avis remains steadfast. Stunned, Philip joins the Union army.

Avis's creativity is already damaged. Unable to paint, she seeks imaginative inspiration in an alcoholic hallucination, visualizes a sphinx, and can again work. Wounded, Philip returns to Harmouth to recuperate. Again, Avis's work is interrupted, this time when she bruises her hand rowing. In another emotionally charged scene, Avis, overcome by Philip's "physical

ruin and helplessness," admits her love and later, although she describes love as "like death," agrees to marriage. Philip promises that he wants her love, not her "individuality," and that she will not be his "housekeeper." These vows prove empty.

After the betrothal, Phelps introduces a telling discussion between Aunt Chloe and Avis, highlighting the unacknowledged repression wrought by traditional 19th-century attitudes prescribing woman's role. Initially, Aunt Chloe maintains that, for a wife, "her husband's interests in life are enough," but reluctantly she admits that, if she could "choose for her selfish pleasure," she would devote herself to studying plants, as a florist or a botanist. This scene parallels earlier descriptions of Avis's mother forsaking her stage ambitions to marry and a later moment when Coy, Avis's best friend who is happy in her role as wife and mother, admits her reluctance to ask her husband for money.

Married life soon disappoints both Avis and Philip. As the promised studio never materializes, Avis's masterpiece, *The Sphinx,* remains unfinished; to ease their financial burdens, she paints portraits in their attic. When they are called to Philip's mother's deathbed, Avis, sensing that Philip has somehow "neglected" his mother, questions Philip's character. A moment of sisterhood transpires, with Avis accepting Philip's mother as a surrogate. Beyond giving another example of the uncomplaining woman whose interests have always been inferior to the male's, this scene highlights one of the reasons Avis has been unable to work since her marriage: She lacks the emotional support of another woman—a mother, a sister, a friend. Van, Avis's sickly first-born, allows Phelps to question maternal instinct. The burden of child care falls to Avis, who must cope with the colicky, crying child. She feels "ashamed . . . for being the mother of so cross a baby" and finds a child "a great deal of trouble." And Philip's character is again questioned when Susan Wanamaker, Philip's rejected lover, visits Avis. Susan's contrast of Philip as "a handsome boy" with her own alcoholic husband, a "brute," allows Phelps to stress a social problem and ironically foreshadows Philip's betrayal of Avis.

Financial troubles increase when Philip loses his job; physical woes compound these problems. With everyone in the house ill, Avis's friend Barbara, who nursed Philip when he had been wounded, arrives to help. Discovering Barbara and Philip in a compromising situation destroys Avis's faith in her husband. To improve his health, Philip travels to Europe, leaving Avis to cope with all domestic and financial worries. Van sickens and dies. Philip returns, more ill than before, and Avis, overcome by pity, adopts a maternal manner with Philip. Leaving their daughter with Avis's father and Aunt Chloe, Avis and Philip travel to Florida, where Philip's health improves, but, in another naturalistic scene, he dies in the swampy forest of the St. Johns River. Avis returns to New England, but the emotional stresses of her marriage have "stiffened" her hand, and she can no longer paint. Recognizing that her creative time is past, Avis resigns herself to teaching painting, but, as she reads the story of Lancelot and Sir Galahad, she passes the grail to her daughter.

Like many 19th-century women's novels, *Avis* has been criticized for "artistic weaknesses" and "an anxious but failed search for . . . the graceful phrase," (Kelly, 210; Kessler, xxviii); however, its story resonates with women even today, and contemporary readings of the novel view it as stylistically complex. Ronna Privett had identified numerous layers of meaning involving "literary, cultural, and historical references ranging from Greek mythology to current scientific theories," but especially focusing on the Victorians' language of flowers (Privett, 10).

Indeed, as Privett maintains, *Avis* was "stylistically in tune with (perhaps even ahead of) most of the writing" of Phelps's time (Privett, 10). With the exception of free love, all the elements of the 19th-century "anarchist critique of heterosexual marriage appear in *Avis*. However, Phelps is unwilling to condemn marriage as an institution (Kessler, xvi). She presents Avis as questioning what might have been, yet accepting her fate as "what god meant for her." Avis's hope lies in the future of her daughter Wait, whom she determines will not "repeat her blunders." In what Susan K. Harris describes as "a biological as well as a spiritual inheritance," Phelps suggests that changing society's vision of woman's role requires more than one generation (Harris, 202). Perhaps Wait will be the "true woman" Phelps described in an article in *The Independent* in 1872, one she maintains "the earth has never seen,"

one who will have equal opportunities for education and equal rights. Yet, as Susan Coultrap McQuin explains, Phelps's "views fall on the conservative side of New Womanhood because, while she wished to expand women's rights and social opportunities, she only ambivalently rejected the ideas of the True Woman" (McQuin, 181). Perhaps, like Avis, she leaves that to Wait's generation.

SOURCES

Coultrap-McQuin, Susan. *Doing Literary Business*. Chapel Hill: University of North Carolina Press, 1990.

Harris, Susan K. *19th-Century American Women's Novels, Interpretive Strategies*. Cambridge: Cambridge University Press, 1992.

Kelly, Lori Duin. *The Life and Works of Elizabeth Stuart Phelps, Victorian Feminist Writer*. Troy, N.Y.: Whitston Publishing, 1983.

Phelps, Elizabeth Stuart. *The Story of Avis*. Edited by Carol Farley Kessler. New Brunswick, N.J.: Rutgers University Press, 1985.

Privett, Ronna Coffey. *A Comprehensive Study of American Writer Elizabeth Stuart Phelps, 1844–1911: Art for Truth's Sake*. Lewiston, Me.: Edwin Mellen Press, 2003.

Gloria Shearin

STOUT, REX (REX TODHUNTER STOUT) (1886–1975)

Known as the creator of Nero Wolfe, the private investigator often compared to Earle Stanley GARDNER's well-known protagonist Perry Mason, Rex Stout was by all accounts a brilliant, witty, and eccentric writer who contributed a thoroughly original character to 20th-century American detective fiction. Nero Wolfe, a man of capacious size and gourmet tastes, was soon joined by detective Archie Goodwin, who assumed the role of the narrator. Stout has been repeatedly praised for his witty dialogue and ability to build a suspenseful tale.

Rex Stout was born on December 1, 1886, in Noblesville, Indiana, to John Wallace Stout and Lucetta Todhunter Stout, who shortly afterward moved to a farm in Wakarusa, Kansas, where Rex was reared. Enlisting in the navy in 1908 after one year at the University of Kansas, Stout served aboard the *Mayflower*, President Theodore Roosevelt's yacht. After military service, he moved to New York City and began to publish prolifically in the pulp magazines until his marriage in 1915 to Fay Kennedy of Topeka. Then he and his brother, Bob, opened a savings bank. Stout made enough money to become a full-time writer, publishing several romance and adventure novels and stories before settling in 1937 on the detective genre. In 1931 he and his first wife divorced, and Stout moved to High Meadow, an 18-acre estate built by him in Brewster, New York; in 1932 he married Pola Weinbach and published his first Nero Wolfe novel, *Fer-de-Lance,* in 1934. For the rest of his life—with ample time out, particularly during World War II, for political activism—Stout devoted his novelistic energies to the 286-pound Nero Wolfe, who lives in a brownstone on New York's West 35th Street. One of Archie Goodwin's main charges is to entice Wolfe from his apartment once in awhile. Wolfe loves beer, yellow silk pajamas, and orchids, and readers loved him from the inception.

The month of his death, Stout published his 72nd novel (his 46th featuring Nero Wolfe). A 73rd novel was published posthumously in 1985 after the discovery of the manuscript. As scholar David R. Anderson writes, "[T]he world that he imagined and brought into being has won its place in our literature for its witty, engaging, and ultimately moving treatment of crime fiction's great theme: the struggle between order and disorder" (Anderson, 1). In 2001, television's Arts and Entertainment channel aired a series of novels and novellas, encouraging a new generation to experience Nero Wolfe.

NOVELS

And Be a Villain. New York: Viking, 1948; published in England as *More Deaths Than One.* London: Collins, 1949.

Before Midnight. New York: Viking, 1955.

The Black Mountain. New York: Viking, 1954.

Black Orchids. (Two novellas: *Black Orchids* and *Cordially Invited to Meet Death; Invited to Meet Death,* later published under title *Invitation to Murder*). New York: Farrar & Rinehart, 1942.

Death of a Doxy. New York: Viking, 1966.

The Doorbell Rang. New York: Viking, 1965.

A Family Affair. New York: Viking, 1975.

Fer-de-Lance. New York: Farrar & Rinehart, 1934.

Forest Fire. New York: Farrar & Rinehart, 1933.

The Hand in the Glove: A Dol Bonner Mystery. New York: Farrar & Rinehart, 1937; published in England as *Crime on Her Hands.* London: Collins, 1939.

How Like a God. New York: Vanguard, 1929.

If Death Ever Slept. New York: Viking, 1957.

In the Best Families. New York: Viking, 1950; published in England as *Even in the Best Families.* London: Collins, 1951.

The League of Frightened Men. New York: Farrar & Rinehart, 1935.

Murder by the Book. New York: Viking, 1951. *Curtains for Three.* (Three novellas: *The Gun with Wings, Bullet for One,* and *Disguise for Murder*). New York: Viking, 1951.

Not Quite Dead Enough. (Two novellas: *Not Quite Dead Enough* and *Booby Trap*). New York: Farrar & Rinehart, 1944.

The Red Box. New York: Farrar & Rinehart, 1937.

The Rubber Band. New York: Farrar & Rinehart, 1936, published as *To Kill Again.* New York: Curl, 1960.

The Second Confession. New York: Viking, 1949.

Seed on the Wind. New York: Vanguard, 1930.

The Silent Speaker. New York: Viking, 1946.

Some Buried Caesar. New York: Farrar & Rinehart, 1939; condensed edition published as *The Red Bull.* New York: Dell, 1945.

Three Doors to Death. (Three novellas: *Man Alive, Omit Flowers,* and *Door to Death*). New York: Viking, 1950.

Three Men Out. (Three novellas; *Invitation to Murder, The Zero Clue,* and *This Won't Kill You*). New York: Viking, 1954.

Too Many Cooks. New York: Farrar & Rinehart, 1938.

Too Many Women. New York: Viking, 1947.

Where There's a Will. New York: Farrar & Rinehart, 1940.

SOURCES

Anderson, David R. *Rex Stout.* New York: Ungar, 1984.

Baring-Gould, William S. *Nero Wolfe of West Thirty-Fourth Street: The Life and Times of America's Largest Private Detective.* New York: Viking, 1969.

Darby, Ken. *The Brownstone House of Nero Wolfe.* Boston: Little, Brown, 1983.

McAleer, John. *Rex Stout: A Biography.* San Bernardino, Calif.: Brownstone Books, 1994.

Townsend, Guy M., and John McAleer. *The Work of Rex Stout: An Annotated Biography and Guide.* Edited by Boden Clarke. San Bernardino, Calif.: Borgo Press, 1995.

Van Dover, J. Kenneth. *At Wolfe's Door: The Nero Wolfe Novels of Rex Stout.* San Bernardino, Calif.: Borgo Press, 1991.

OTHER

Books and Writers. Rex Stout (1886–1975). Available online. URL: http://www.kirjasto.sci.fi/rexstout.htm. Accessed September 25, 2005.

Merely a Genius . . . [Rex Stout fan site]. Available online. URL: http://www.geocities.com/Athens/8907/nero.html. Accessed September 25, 2005.

STOWE, HARRIET BEECHER (HARRIET ELIZABETH BEECHER STOWE) (1811–1896)

Harriet Beecher Stowe wrote what some scholars agree was the most important American novel ever written: UNCLE TOM'S CABIN; OR, LIFE AMONG THE LOWLY (1852). Published in protest of the Compromise of 1850 that kept all African Americans at risk, *Uncle Tom's Cabin* made every reader aware of the evils of slavery, the societal blight that culminated in the Civil War. According to President Abraham Lincoln in 1862, Harriet Beecher Stowe was, "the little lady who started this great war." Her second novel, *The Minister's Wooing* (1859), a courtship tale, was also popular but much less important. Many of Stowe's other novels were rediscovered during the latter decades of the 20th century and are undergoing reevaluation. Chief among these are *Dred: A Tale of the Great Dismal Swamp* (1866), an antislavery novel set in North Carolina, and *The Pearl of Orr's Island: A Story of the Coast of Maine* (1862), the psychological examination of a talented young woman who chafes at society's barriers.

Harriet Beecher Stowe was born on June 14, 1811, in Litchfield, Connecticut, to Congregationalist minister Lyman Beecher and Roxana Foote Beecher, who died of tuberculosis when Harriet was five years old. Reared primarily by her older sister Catharine—who was to become a renowned educator and writer—Stowe attended and later taught at Hartfield Female Seminary, a school run by her sister. When the family moved to Cincinnati, Ohio, in 1832, Stowe again taught at her sister's school, this time the Western Female Seminary, until her marriage to Calvin Stowe in January 1836. It was her desire to add to her husband's modest professorial salary that led to Stowe's writing.

Uncle Tom's Cabin, a novel set on plantations in Kentucky and Louisiana, features the escaped slave Eliza Harris, who refuses to see her son sold; eventually they reach freedom in the North. Uncle Tom, however, is sold "down the river" to the plantation of the evil Simon Legree, where he eventually dies. Stowe wrote another antislavery novel, *Dred* (1866), about the need for vengeance in Dred, an enraged and bitter black man. *The Minister's Wooing* (1859) on the other hand, is a story that borrows from the Beecher family history and follows the elderly Reverend Samuel Hopkins as he courts Mary Scudder, who firmly rejects the rigid tenets of Calvinism. *Old-Town Folks* (1869), set in Natick, Massachusetts likewise excoriates the religion of an angry God. While it is based on Calvin Stowe's youth, *Poganuc People: Their Lives and Loves* (1878) draws on recollections from Harriet Beecher's own childhood.

The Pearl of Orr's Island (1862), apparently autobiographical in many respects, examines the different philosophies of two young girls, one of whom accepts conventional religion; the other is drawn to more secular pursuits. In the second part of the novel, the adventurous and talented Mara Lincoln, frustrated by the lack of opportunities for women like herself, loves a Spanish youth, Moses; Mara dies and Moses marries her friend Sally. The novel has attracted much attention from feminist critics. Stowe also draws attention to the role of women in her so-called "society novels": *Pink and White Tyranny: A Society Novel* (1871), *My Wife and I; or, Harry Henderson's History* (1871), and *We and Our Neighbors; or, The Records of an Unfashionable Street* (1875). A talented and conscientious writer who interwove didactic messages into her realistic presentations of people, places, and issues, Stowe's reputation in American letters seems secure. She died at Nook Farm, her home in Hartford, in 1896, and is buried at the Andover Theological Seminary in Andover, Massachusetts.

NOVELS

Agnes of Sorrento. Boston: Ticknor & Fields, 1862.

Dred: A Tale of the Great Dismal Swamp. 2 vols. Boston: Phillips, Sampson, 1856, republished as *Nina Gordon: A Tale of the Great Dismal Swamp.* 2 vols. Boston: Ticknor & Fields, 1866.

The Minister's Wooing. New York: Derby & Jackson, 1859.

My Wife and I; or, Harry Henderson's History. New York: Ford, 1871.

Old-Town Folks. Boston: Fields, Osgood, 1869.

The Pearl of Orr's Island: A Story of the Coast of Maine. Boston: Ticknor & Fields, 1862.

Pink and White Tyranny: A Society Novel. Boston: Roberts, 1871.

Poganuc People: Their Lives and Loves. New York: Fords, Howard, & Hulbert, 1878.

Six of One by Half a Dozen of the Other: An Every Day Novel (with Edward Everett Hale, Lucretia Peabody Hale, et al.). Boston: Roberts, 1872.

Uncle Tom's Cabin; or, Life among the Lowly. 2 vols. Boston: Jewett; Cleveland, Ohio: Jewett, Proctor & Worthington, 1852.

We and Our Neighbors; or, The Records of an Unfashionable Street. New York: Ford, 1875.

SOURCES

Adams, John R. *Harriet Beecher Stowe.* Boston: Twayne, 1963.

Ammons, Elizabeth, ed. *Critical Essays on Harriet Beecher Stowe.* Boston: G. K. Hall, 1980.

Crozier, Alice C. *The Novels of Harriet Beecher Stowe.* New York: Oxford University Press, 1969.

Foster, Charles. *The Rungless Ladder: Harriet Beecher Stowe and New England Puritanism.* Durham, N.C.: Duke University Press, 1954.

Gerson, Noel B. *Harriet Beecher Stowe.* New York: Praeger, 1976.

Gossett, Thomas F. *"Uncle Tom's Cabin" and American Culture.* Dallas, Tex.: Southern Methodist University Press, 1985.

Hedrick, Joan D. *Harriet Beecher Stowe: A Life.* New York: Oxford University Press, 1994.

Kimball, Gayle. *The Religious Ideas of Harriet Beecher Stowe: Her Gospel of Womanhood.* Lewiston, N.Y.: Edwin Mellen, 1982.

———. *Life and Letters of Harriet Beecher Stowe.* Edited by Annie E. Fields. Boston: Houghton, Mifflin, 1897.

Moers, Ellen. *Harriet Beecher Stowe and American Literature.* Hartford, Conn.: Stowe-Day Foundation, 1978.

Sundquist, Eric J. *New Essays on "Uncle Tom's Cabin."* New York: Cambridge University Press, 1986.

Tompkins, Jane P. "Sentimental Power: *Uncle Tom's Cabin* and the Politics of Literary History." In *The New Feminist Criticism: Essays on Women, Literature, and Theory,* edited by Elaine Showalter, 81–104. New York: Pantheon, 1985.

Wagenknecht, Edward Charles. *Harriet Beecher Stowe: The Known and the Unknown.* New York: Oxford University Press, 1965.

STRANGER IN A STRANGE LAND

ROBERT A. HEINLEIN (1961) *Stranger in a Strange Land,* first published in 1961, is Robert HEINLEIN's best-known novel, rivaled only by *Starship Troopers* (1959) and *The Moon Is a Harsh Mistress* (1966). The novel earned him his third Hugo Award for science fiction achievement and was the first science fiction novel to appear in the best-seller list of *The New York Times Book Review.* As with Heinlein's other well-known works, *Stranger* explores Heinlein's concerns with libertarian politics, mystical religious belief, and the relationship of individuals to society. Where *Starship Troopers* is sometimes interpreted as an endorsement of an authoritarian social order and *The Moon Is a Harsh Mistress* seems to advocate a radical libertarianism indifferent to the needs of community, *Stranger in a Strange Land* is generally read as a manifesto for a progressive, free-spirited utopian vision for humanity. As such, *Stranger* stands alone among Heinlein's novels in its importance to 1960s counterculture movements, including neo-paganism and "sexual liberation," and is sometimes referred to as "The Hippie Bible." Indeed, among works of speculative fiction, only Frank Herbert's *Dune* and J.R.R. Tolkien's *Lord of the Rings* were of comparable influence to a wider society beyond genre-fiction fans.

Heinlein set down the first notes for what would become *Stranger in a Strange Land* in 1948, when he was brainstorming ideas for the November issue of *Astounding Science Fiction.* The magazine asked readers for titles that would be transformed into stories to later be written by established science fiction writers. Editor John W. Campbell assigned the title "Gulf" to Heinlein, and Virginia Heinlein suggested Robert write "a story about a human infant, raised by an alien race." Heinlein decided the idea was too complex for a short story and so set it aside, leaving more than a decade between the original idea and the first publication of the novel. Ideas that were radical in the early 1960s might be seen as revolutionary in the late 1940s, and this may have played a part in Heinlein's decision to forestall work on the novel. Even at the time of the 1961 Putnam edition, only part of the novel saw print. Virginia Heinlein's introduction to the 1991 Ace Trade edition cites the earlier edition as running to 160,000 words, while the uncut "original" version has around 220,000. Readers will most likely still encounter the earlier version that, having become a staple of counterculture thought, might also be considered the "original," leaving Heinlein's unedited first manuscript to offer much greater explication on points of plot and philosophy.

The book's protagonist, Valentine Michael Smith, often referred to by his everyman name "Smith" or

Heinlein-favorite "Mike," is a Martian. Or rather, Smith is a human raised as a Martian who, upon returning to Earth, experiences culture shock and ultimately brings about social transformation by introducing humanity to Martian culture and particularly Martian philosophy. *Stranger*'s opening line—"Once upon a time there was a Martian named Valentine Michael Smith"— serves to underline the importance of culture and context to identity as distinct from a biological humanity. It also lends a fairy-tale air that suggests the allegorical quality of the story. The name Michael, to take one example, is from a Hebrew name meaning "who is like God" and is the name of an Archangel. Heinlein's Martians certainly evoke angels as sources of literally otherworldly wisdom and grace while Smith's gnostic claim "Thou art God" makes a literal comparison between the character and divinity.

Stranger addresses several philosophical issues that Heinlein presents as mutually supporting ideas but that may usefully be distinguished from one another. First, a libertine social and sexual morality. Second, a mystical rather than doctrinal engagement with religion and faith. Finally, a thoroughgoing cultural determinism. It is the first of these storylines that attracts many readers to the book and has also attracted much of the criticism directed toward it. It becomes clear that Smith was born to parents from a lost expedition to Mars but, while the expedition was made up of married couples, Smith's parents were not married. The Ark metaphor combines with adultery and a child born out of wedlock, hardly shocking themes now but controversial and thought provoking in the context of the early 1960s. Smith's parentage is transposed onto a succession of sexual relationships that violate period conventions of monogamy, possessiveness, and ownership and public/private intimacy. *Stranger* was a model for hippie ideals of "free love" and the refusal to be tied to particular bonded relationships or show deference to social authority. Ironically, contemporary readings of *Stranger* find little offense in sex outside marriage but take exception to a notion of "sexual liberation" that shows little respect and concern for the rights or desires of women while advocating a hedonistic free-for-all where men with psychic powers use them to make women's clothes disappear. This last example speaks more to a particular construc-

tion of adolescent heterosexual male fantasy than to a model for utopian egalitarianism, and it is in Heinlein's gendered utopia that the work is most dated.

Stranger retains its power to speak to other issues, however, and especially in a dissenting vision of spirituality. The same refusal of ownership in matters of love and sexuality is transposed onto an individual's relationship to divine love. Smith establishes a "Church of All Worlds," advocating a somewhat nebulous yet all-encompassing ecumenicism grounded in communities of loving friendship and based empirically in psychic training that reveals humanity's latent abilities. Given the influence of *Stranger* on the '60s counterculture, it is not surprising that a New Age group took on the name of the "Church of All Worlds" and attempted to live by the philosophy articulated by Heinlein's characters. Martian spirituality expresses a sense of the interconnectedness of all living things and the immanence of the divine in them, and as such has a strong affinity for mystical, nontheistic and non-Western sources of religious inspiration in the mid to late 1960s. While the sexual content of the book was the most obvious lightning rod for criticism, Smith's declaration of himself and his followers to be God has also attracted charges of blasphemy from Christians who find a debased Christianity in *Stranger* offensive, especially in so far as the Smith Christ-figure is advocating and enacting an explicitly sexual religious philosophy. As such, the enduring legacy of *Stranger* may lie more in the controversy, or inspiration, some have read into the novel than in its formal content.

A critical element of initiation into the Church of All Worlds is training in Martian language. It is in this aspect of *Stranger* that Heinlein works out in detail the cultural determinism hinted at in the opening sentence of the novel. Smith is a Martian, and not human, precisely in so far as he was raised by Martians and in this way has been acculturated through his knowledge of Martian culture and especially in Martian language. Heinlein was a devotee of the work of Polish-American linguist Alfred Korzybski through the 1930s and 1940s. Korzybski's model of general semantics argues that language structures thought in ways that both constrain and enable our perceptions of social and physical worlds. Korzybski's famous dictum that "the map is not the territory" is a reminder of what he argues to be the common error of mistaking our conceptions of the world for the world itself and consequently finding ourselves frustrated as reality fails to meet our expectations of it. General semantics influenced a variety of schools of social construction in psychology and anthropology, including neuro-linguistic programming (NLP), cybernetics, and the work of Gregory Bateson, as well as the thought of counterculture idols such as Robert Anton Wilson and Timothy Leary. Heinlein's Martian language is an idealized style of communication that seeks an immediacy between experience and representation free from false constructions such as authority, guilt, or inhibition. Learning Martian is held not only to free an individual from errors in cognition but also to serve as the basis of a speech-community whose morality would transparently express authentic desires rather than an insidious false consciousness. Again, while Heinlein's particular gendered articulation of an idealized community is subject to criticism, his advocacy of the importance of language to social construction, and the emancipatory possibility of language, remains topical and an important point of debate for students of his work.

The best-known and loved term of Heinlein's Martian language is the word *grok*. *Grok* has joined *hobbit* (Tolkien 1937) and *vril* (Edward Bulwer-Lytton 1871) as invented words from speculative fiction that have been canonized by their inclusion in the *Oxford English Dictionary*. *Grok* literally means "to drink" and absorb but clearly has a much broader and deeper implication for the philosophy Smith advocates. The centerpiece of Martian ritual is the Water Ceremony, a simple sharing of a glass of water that nevertheless evokes a shared substance, shared life, and eucharistic participatory embodiment of the divine. Heinlein runs the risk of reproducing Martian folkways through the lens of the noble savage, with all the problematical aspects of that particular romanticism. At the same time, the water ritual reflects an earnest attempt to reenchant the world and reengage with issues of ecology so important to social movements of the 1960s and today. It is almost impossible to come away from a reading of *Stranger* without *grok* creeping into a reader's vocabulary and bringing about the subsequent irritation of the reader's friends as they fail to grok the term.

SOURCES

Heinlein, Robert. *Stranger in a Strange Land*. New York: Ace Trade Edition, 1991.
Heinlein, Virginia. "Preface" to *Stranger in a Strange Land*. New York: Ace Trade Edition, 1991.

A. Nicholas Packwood

STREET, THE ANN LANE PETRY (1946)

Unlike other naturalistic novels of this era, PETRY's portrait of Lutie Johnson, a young African-American woman who moves to Harlem in 1944 in order to provide a better life for herself and her son, does not constitute a one-sided piece of social criticism but a finely crafted work of art that depicts the entire range of possible responses to the realities of life in the streets of Harlem, a life between desire and despair.

Lutie Johnson's hopes spring from her first contact with Ben Franklin's philosophy when she works as a maid for white employers in Lyme, Connecticut. Petry describes how creature comforts and consumer goods create artificial desires in Lutie Johnson, who naively believes she will be able to escape the restriction of class, race, and gender by taking night classes and carefully planning her daily activities and budget. Petry models Lutie's behavior upon Franklin's only to reveal that Lutie is mistaken in her belief that, to a poor, black woman, the American Dream is accessible. When the walls of her apartment and the uncertainty of her future stifle her, she escapes to the Junto, a bar and grill whose intriguing name is modeled on that of Ben Franklin's philanthropic club in Philadelphia.

While Lutie's hopes for success stem from her need for economic security and physical and spiritual well-being, other characters in the novel experience sexual desires. Jones, the super, lusts after Lutie. Petry cleverly depicts him close to a furnace he must feed regularly with coal and whose heat nearly suffocates him. He suffers from nearly unbearable thirst while the dog at his side looks half-starved. Jones's repressed sexual desires constitute a factor that can lead to despair, aggression, and violence. When Jones cannot have Lutie, he takes his anger out on his girlfriend, Min. When she resists him as well, he funnels all his energy into devising a plot whereby he might destroy Lutie by corrupting her son.

Petry introduces various other forces of despair. On the first page of the novel, the wind that whips Lutie around the street, blinding her so that she can barely make out the street signs, heaps up the garbage and nearly freezes the blood in her veins; it is merciless in the pursuit of those it can hurt. It is an elemental force, not romantic in nature, but uncaring and brutal and symbolic of all that continually threatens to take hold of Lutie, attacks her physically, and dampens her spirits.

Thwarted dreams also brutalize people, like Lutie's husband. Out of work for a long time and frustrated by his inability to locate new employment, he eventually turns mean and beats and cheats on his wife. Lutie does not even blame him because she saw these changes coming but could do nothing to prevent them. Lutie herself can take only so many blows. Each disappointment makes her a little angrier. After the singing job offered by Boots Smith falls through and the super instigates Bub's arrest for stealing mail from the other tenants, her anger turns to rage and then violence and hatred so strong that she commits a murder: She beats Boots Smith to death with a candlestick.

The worst thing that happens to Lutie, however, is the onslaught of resignation. Lutie saw it before in so many faces that she swore she would never succumb to lost hope and the lack of any expectations. At the end of the novel, while sitting on the train that is to take her away from the scene of the crime, she draws intersecting circles on the window pane. They seem to represent the vicious circles from which she could not free herself. Remembering her schoolteacher's derogatory remarks, she begins to wonder why, indeed, she was ever taught to write when she was not given the chance to put her talents to good use. Resignation has caught up with her, too.

Petry suggests alternatives to this rather glum picture: In Lutie's memory, her grandmother speaks of a time long lost, when families were intact and children could be kept safe. Occasionally, a voice of reason speaks to Lutie, a voice that mediates between her desires and her despair. At times this voice just sounds like Granny, but then it also speaks in the manner of a social scientist who criticizes the conditions in which Lutie and Bub live. Most of Lutie's basic values were imbued by her grandmother, and it may be a grave mistake that she dismisses them so easily. Whenever her ambitions lure her into danger, her intuitions inspired by Granny warn her not to proceed, but she chooses to ignore these warnings.

SOURCES

Bell, Bernard W. *The Afro-American Novel and Its Tradition*. Amherst: University of Massachusetts Press, 1987.

Bone, Robert. *The Negro Novel in America*. Revised edition. New Haven, Conn.: Yale University Press, 1965.

Clark, Keith. "A Distaff Dream Deferred? Ann Petry and the Art of Subversion," *African American Review* 26, no. 3 (1992): 495–505.

Ervin, Hazel Arnett. *Ann Petry: A Bio-Bibliography*. New York: G. K. Hall, 1993.

Holloday, Hilary. *Ann Petry*. New York: Twayne, 1996.

Petry, Ann. *The Street*. 1946. Reprint, Boston: Beacon Press, 1974.

Pryse, Marjorie. " 'Pattern against the Sky': Deism and Motherhood in Ann Petry's *The Street*." In *Conjuring: Black Women, Fiction and Literary Tradition*, edited by Marjorie Pryse and Hortense Spillers, 116–131. Bloomington: Indiana University Press, 1984.

Washington, Mary Helen. *Invented Lives: Narratives of Black Women 1860–1960*. New York: Doubleday, 1987.

OTHER

"Ann Petry." *Voices from the Gaps* [VG]. Available online. URL: http://voices.cla.umn.edu/vg/Bios/entries/PETRYann.html. Accessed April 19, 2006.

Susanna Hoeness-Krupsaw

STUDS LONIGAN JAMES T. FARRELL (1932–1935)

The Studs Lonigan Trilogy occupies a bizarre place in modern literary opinion; some readily assign it a place among the American masterpieces of the 20th century (number 29 on the Modern Library's list of the century's greatest English-language novels), some see it primarily as fodder for critical attack, while few others in the general population and academic circles alike have even heard of the book or its author. The work was the prolific FARRELL's first, in three volumes: *Young Lonigan* (1932), *The Young Manhood of Studs Lonigan* (1934), and *Judgment Day* (1935), the last published when he was only 31, chronicling the life of a lower-middle-class South

Chicago male from his grammar school graduation in 1916 to his ignominious death in the depths of the Great Depression. Among the mixed reviews were the best Farrell would ever receive, and his popularity and critical esteem steadily dwindled until his death in 1979. Farrell published more than 50 works but is usually considered to have peaked early with Studs Lonigan, admirers of which have included the more recognizable Theodore DREISER, Richard WRIGHT, Norman MAILER, and Studs Terkel (who took his name from the book).

Any history of or essay on Studs Lonigan, then, is necessarily in part a defense of it, and an examination of questions such as, What stumbling blocks in its history have kept it from being more widely acclaimed? Which are failings of the work itself, and which of its audience? Historically, a disproportionate amount of critical attention has been focused on Farrell's intentions (What is he attacking and what is he defending?) and his technique (Is it mammoth in scope or merely insufficiently edited?). While the novel has been most frequently at odds with the Catholic Church for its (now commonplace) negative portrayal of that institution, the greatest dissonance for the contemporary reader will likely come as a result of the principal characters' unenlightened ideas about and, occasionally, actions toward minorities and women. While none but the most misguided or uncharitable readers would mistake Farrell's sociohistorical accuracy for maleficence, these issues still provide fodder as good as any for debate, and will undoubtedly constitute the major focus of classroom discussion wherever Studs Lonigan is still being taught.

Farrell himself conceived William "Studs" Lonigan as "a normal American boy of Irish-Catholic extraction." The concept of normalcy, apparently, was in many ways as problematic then as now, and Farrell was many times compelled to deny his affiliation with the "naturalism" of Zola (the suggestion often being a backhanded critical manner of suggesting lack of purpose or imagination). Others emphasize Farrell's Marxist leanings and view Studs Lonigan primarily as political invective; a presentation of the human spirit polluted by capitalism. This is the easiest method of viewing the novel, to be sure, since it excuses, even

prefers, a wholesale condemnation of its inhabitants, but it is also the most boring; someone who begins Studs Lonigan thinking its animus to be exhortatory Marxist shock value will either change his mind at some point or not finish it. Yes, Farrell admitted that the "spiritual poverty" (though not necessarily economic poverty) enveloping his characters—a helpful parallel might be Joyce's *Dubliners*—is a very real force, but he manifests its baleful presence and deleterious effects not primarily to assign blame for it, and even less to suggest sociopolitical solutions.

Ann Douglas wrote that "Farrell's great subject, from first to last, was failure," and Studs Lonigan is essentially the story of either a failure or a tragedy, depending largely not on one's interpretation of events, but of Studs himself. In the four months in 1916 chronicled in *Young Lonigan*, we see what Studs himself forever sees as the crowning achievements, or, at least, purest moments, of his life: He shares a summer afternoon of kisses (literally sitting in a tree) with his first love, the idealized Lucy Scanlan, in a gorgeously written section made all the more poignant by the fact that Studs is never that happy again; and he defeats the neighborhood bully, the execrable Weary Reilley, in an epic fistfight witnessed by very nearly everyone he knows and is never that proud again. Robert Butler has observed (while advancing a much-needed theory of Farrell's structural meticulousness) that the events of *The Young Manhood,* which sporadically cover the years 1917–1929, mockingly invert those of the first book. Studs, now drunk a good part of the time on questionable Prohibition-era liquor, engages in joyless relations with prostitutes and "liberated" young girls, one of them on the ground near his and Lucy's tree; at the New Year's Eve, 1929, party that closes the volume, he is effortlessly thrashed by Weary in front of the same crowd, and those events of *Judgment Day* recombine the same themes and symbolisms into new complexities.

The third volume opens with most of the old gang dead of hard living and Studs himself in perilous health, having lain all night unconscious in the street after being beaten by Weary. Studs is engaged to Catherine, who is more or less responsible for the positive changes and new maturity that come over him (and, in turn, the book), but usually loses out in his mind when Studs privately compares her to Lucy, a foregone conclusion, one might say, since Catherine is far more human than we, or Studs, ever got the chance to see Lucy be.

The problematic question of how we are to view Studs is largely attributable to Farrell's admirable capacity for that with which he is rarely credited, restraint. We see and think as Studs, and Farrell never has things occur to him which could not believably occur to a person of his intelligence, in his place and time. Though Farrell admired and owed a technical debt to Joyce, he does not ask us to believe, as Joyce does, that average people think the way very smart people write. The fusion of the third-person (first-person would be wholly unbelievable) with Studs himself is so masterful that it has been mistaken for literary aimlessness where Studs is aimless and, more tragically, literary cruelty where Studs is cruel. It is the intellectual Danny O'Neill (a minor character in *Studs*, but the focus of Farrell's next cycle of novels) who is Farrell's surrogate and not Studs, but Farrell does not give Danny the opportunity to speak for him about Studs, who speaks for himself and more than himself (the unification of turning points in Studs's life with major events in American history is not accidental), despite being described by Farrell as "all I decided I would not be and did not want to be." Though Studs is both "tough" and "natural," his lack of determined resourcefulness or unfailing moral compass remind us that he is neither Nick Adams nor Huck Finn. Studs is creative, but he is not original.

After Studs, the most important presence in the novels is the South Side neighborhood itself, though it should be noted that Farrell is not attempting a celebratory cartographical thoroughness, a la *Ulysses* (among the Joyce books, *Dubliners* and *Ulysses* are thematically relevant to Studs Lonigan, whereas *Portrait of the Artist* is not), but rather filters the city's identity through Studs's mind, the few times it does intrude as a presence unto itself, the effect is ominous. The other major distinction to be made with *Ulysses* here is that Studs Lonigan incorporates historical elements of flux rather than stasis; its 15 years coincide with great ethnic migrations in South Chicago, whereas *Ulysses* gives us a city with a fixed ethnic identity on one given day.

It is this theme (mainly through the musings of Studs's father, Paddy, a landlord) that brings in the aspects of the work most jarring to a modern audience; the attitudes toward one another of South Chicago ethnic groups; most problematically, that of the Irish-Catholic primary characters toward blacks and Jews. Virtually all the characters we meet come from families new to America, living at a time and in a social stratus when ethnic identity and, as a direct result, ethnic prejudice was the primary, often only, mode of self-actualization. There is so much ethnic stereotyping flying around from character to character that at times it nearly cancels itself out, though, for obvious reasons, a slur against a Jew stands out to the modern eye more than one against, say, a Hungarian or a Swede.

One is also tempted to make a key distinction between the ethnic prejudice directed by European-Americans at one another and the racial prejudice directed at blacks, though at the time, the definition of white was up for debate in a very real sense, and in many circles did not include the Irish themselves (though, since the novels never substantially deviate from Studs's point of view, we observe this only glancingly: brief monologues from Davey Cohen; want ads specifying Protestant only). The Irish in the novels do have the luxury of referring to themselves as either Irish or Americans whenever it suits them, typically using the former (since it implies Catholic) in the face of religious alterity (for example, Jews) and the latter in the face of political alterity (for example, Communists), but the fluidity between those self-definitions is hardly established opinion and reflects two deep-seated paranoias: first, that Catholics are still not true Americans in the eyes of most people, and second, that many of the other American ethnic groups, most notably blacks, have, in fact, been here longer. And in many cases, as Daniel Shiffman has observed, ethnic distinctions in *Studs Lonigan* are very often only a means to insult rather than a motivation for insulting, for example, the football game where the best player on the opposing team is referred to as Jewboy Schwartz by the 58th St. gang despite the fact that their own center, Nate Klein, is also Jewish. In any case, Studs Lonigan's historically accurate depictions of racial and ethnic tension provide an important reminder that contemporary academic notions of what has been called "happy family multiculturalism" are largely revisionist and illusory, and that very often, as Shiffman puts it, "ethnic experiences are not simply waiting for us to 'celebrate' them."

The notions of gender espoused by the characters—both male and female—are likewise principally guided by historical accuracy, and certainly neither celebrated nor excused. Our sympathy for Studs can cut through his sexism and virgin-whore complex because, as in other matters, his dealings with women are still more fundamentally decent than those of his peers, who have all grown up being told and shown the same things. Grabarek points out that Catholicism for the work's Irish is "an affair of nothing but negations," providing much threatening rhetoric about sex but no reinforcement about love. As a result, Studs's romantic aimlessness (the core of his general aimlessness) is brought about by his never realizing that his active self, his individualism and free will, is supposed to provide the other half of a dialectic with his (consistently lacking attempts at) self-denial: "Maybe you couldn't help yourself about it when the right broad came along. That was what love was," he passively muses [*Young Manhood,* 159].

The anti-individualist ideology to which Studs is exposed brings about a mindset in him that allows the occasional trip to a brothel with his friends (since it is public) but, ironically, not true romantic love (since it is private). Douglas remarks that Studs sees "Catherine as nothing but one specimen of a totalized category: 'women' do this, 'women' do that." To the extent that this is true, it is just as true of the way Catherine sees Studs. Nearly her every teasing or angry rebuke to him, ironically, since this is her method of initiating intimacy, begins with "you men" this or "you men" that. Granted, this is primarily a coy verbal mannerism on Catherine's part, whereas it is serious would-be philosophizing on Studs's, but both traits are equally the products of an unstable socioreligious environment that turns its piercing gaze on the individual while despising individuality. Even the parish's star priest, Father Shannon, denounces notions of personality-based marital "compatibility" (because the notion has the potential to lead to divorce) as decadent: Studs and

Catherine are more encouraged on all sides to see themselves—and each other—as Man and Woman than as Studs and Catherine.

In what is nearly a parody of *Ulysses's* "Penelope" chapter, the novel's subsumed feminine voice rises wild at the end—neither in triumph nor transcendence, but in rage. Mary Lonigan's unendurable torture of Catherine, blaming her for Studs's condition after extracting the secret of Catherine's pregnancy through feigned sympathy, is feminine anger at feminine powerlessness, but instead of turning itself on the masculine in defiance or righteousness, it turns on itself in bitterness and jealousy. There are certainly those who would condemn the scene as antifeminist (when, to be fair, it is only prefeminist), though after all, we detest Mary on behalf of Catherine, whom we desire to help, for her own sake as much as Studs's, and this impulse is not protectionist, it is human.

It is this power on our part to observe and judge that could have saved Studs from all for which we might judge him, if only he could have somehow known that he was in a book. As Douglas puts it, he "knows no way to live but before an audience," and this is less an indication of vanity on Studs's part than his best personal reconfiguration of what is put before him: his church's emphasis on being watched by God, and his appearance-obsessed mother and sisters' emphasis on being watched by "the neighbors" and so forth. How can anything of real importance be achieved unless it is externally observed and, in turn, judged? Studs's much-maligned aimlessness is brought about partly because he and his peers have inherited the barely bourgeois social standing their parents had to work for, and thus, like many American generations since, feel they are owed something (so the disparity in work ethic between Paddy and Studs, unlike that between, say, Hamlets Sr. and Jr., is here more for historical accuracy than dramatic effect); and partly by his instinctual waiting for an audience that will never come. Studs cannot make it materialize, nor can he bravely shift his need for validation to a different ideal. Huck Finn's famous "Alright then, I'll go to Hell" has no analogue in *Studs Lonigan,* because although religious rhetoric is flawed here as well, the only ones capable of seeing so are the audience and Danny O'Neill. Studs is not. Morality, for Studs, has nothing to do with amending his viewpoints, only with refraining from indulging his impulses. His cruel paradox is that, while full participation in the workings of the world as he sees it means certain damnation, so does developing a new way of seeing that world. Communists and "godless" professors, for example, are counted among the damned for Studs, a viewpoint aggressively reinforced by his priests and his mother, who, in remarking that "some books [are] like bad companions" [*Young Manhood,* 342] sounds like a PC sophomore attacking Studs Lonigan for presenting the worldview Mrs. Lonigan means to protect. When Studs thinks about people—O'Neill, for example—who "went crazy from reading too many books" [*Judgement Day,* 12] at the University of Chicago, it is not sour-grapes anti-nerdism—he really believes it. Near the end of the trilogy, in what is perhaps its finest symbolic turn, Studs and Catherine, at a South Shore beach, overhear a group of swingers make casual jokes about spouse-swapping, and react with rote Catholic disgust. After overhearing these people, bound by nothing yet seemingly none the worse for it, Studs passes a few stunned moments staring out at Lake Michigan (the closest thing to a symbol of infinitude that the novel's geography allows) before blacking out in it and nearly drowning: The idea that barriers are subjective and may simply be disregarded is too much for Studs to hold in his mind and remain conscious. (Butler's suggestion of a "subconscious desire to commit suicide" in this scene seems inconsistent with Studs's thoughts and actions elsewhere.) The challenge that must be issued to those who would condemn Studs is, What would you have him do that it is possible for him to do? In the end it is this question, rather than any dirty word or outdated idea, that is most problematic about *Studs Lonigan,* and, needless to say, about the condition of being alive.

SOURCES

Butler, Robert. "Farrell's Ethnic Neighborhood and Wright's Urban Ghetto: Two Visions of Chicago's South Side," *MELUS* 18, no. 1 (Spring 1993): 103–111.

———. "Scenic Structure in Farrell's *Studs Lonigan,*" *Essays in Literature* 14, no. 1 (Spring 1987): 93–103.

———. "Urban Frontiers, Neighborhoods and Traps: The City in Dreiser's *Sister Carrie,* Farrell's *Studs Lonigan,* and Wright's *Native Son.*" In *Theodore Dreiser and American Culture,* edited Yoshinobu Hakutani, 274–290. Newark: University of Delaware Press, 2000.

Fanning, Charles, and Ellen Skerrett. "James T. Farrell and Washington Park: The Novel as Social History." In *A Wild Kind of Boldness: The Chicago History Reader,* edited Rosemary K. Adams, 338–348. Grand Rapids, Mich.: William B. Eerdman's Publishing Co., 1998.

Farrell, James T. *Studs Lonigan.* Modern Library Edition. Introduction by John Chamberlain. New York: Random House, Inc., 1938.

———. *Studs Lonigan.* Prairie State Books Edition. Introduction by Charles Fanning. Urbana & Chicago: University of Illinois Press, 1993.

———. *Studs Lonigan.* Penguin Classics. Introduction by Ann Douglas. New York: Penguin Books, Ltd., 2001.

Giles, Paul. *American Catholic Arts and Fictions: Culture, Ideology, Aesthetics.* New York: Cambridge University Press, 1992.

Grabarek, Stanislaus. "Failures of the Spirit: The Institutional Church in the Fiction of James T. Farrell, J. F. Powers, Walker Percy." Dissertation, University of Chicago, 1978.

Halperin, Irving. "*Studs Lonigan* Revisited," *American Book Collector* 19, no. 4 (1968): 10–12.

Shiffman, Daniel. "Ethnic Competitors in *Studs Lonigan,*" *MELUS* 24, no. 3 (Fall 1999): 67–79.

Wald, Alan M. "Revolutionary Novelist in Crisis." In *The New York Intellectuals: The Rise and Decline of the Anti-Stalinist Left from the 1930s to the 1980s,* 249–263. Chapel Hill: University of North Carolina Press, 1987.

OTHER

Shafer, Ingrid H. "Family, Sex, and Church in the Novels of James T. Farrell and Andrew M. Greeley." Available online. URL: http://www.usao.edu/~facshaferi/greeleyfarrell2.htm. Accessed September 25, 2005.

Chris O. Cook

STYRON, WILLIAM (1925–) William

Styron's place in American literary history is secure: He is the author of the powerful *Lie Down in Darkness* (1951), winner of the 1952 American Academy of Arts Prix de Rome; *Set This House on Fire* (1960), (acclaimed more highly in France than in the United States); *The Confessions of Nat Turner* (1967), winner of the

Pulitzer Prize; and *Sophie's Choice* (1979), recipient of an American Book Award and adapted for the screen in a popular movie starring Meryl Streep. He has also written *In the Clap Shack* (1973), a play performed by the Yale Repertory Theater in December 1973, as well as a volume of selected short writings and his well-received *Darkness Visible: A Memoir of Madness* (1990), an account of his struggle with depression, and *A Tidewater Morning: Three Tales from Youth* (1993). Because of his powerful writing and the risks he takes in choosing his subject matter—the South and slavery, Nazism and the Holocaust—Styron will likely remain a controversial writer for a number of readers and critics.

William Styron was born on June 11, 1925, in Newport News, Virginia, to William Clark Styron, a shipyard engineer, and Pauline Abraham Styron, a Pennsylvanian whose father had served as an officer in the Confederacy during the Civil War. Styron joined the Marine Corps in 1943 (serving in the Pacific Theater and becoming a first lieutenant before his discharge at the end of World War II), was educated at Duke University, receiving his bachelor's degree in 1947, and worked briefly for the New York publisher McGraw-Hill. He had just finished *Lie Down in Darkness* when he was briefly recalled to serve in the Marine Corps during the Korean War. His military experiences led him to write *The Long March* (1953, serial). Set in the Virginia Tidewater, *Lie Down in Darkness* opens as Milton Loftis awaits the body of his deceased daughter, Peyton. A succession of narrators tells the story in flashbacks of Peyton Loftis, a young woman who threw herself from the roof of a Harlem tenement building. Through these several points of view, the reader gradually learns the reasons—these include incest, alcoholism, and infidelity—for her descent into madness and suicide. Moreover, her suicide occurs at the exact moment of the explosion of the atomic bomb on Hiroshima. The novella, *The Long March,* is based on an actual incident at Camp Lejeune, North Carolina, in which eight young men died during a forced march. Much of the story, which illustrates Styron's antimilitary stance, is told from the point of view of Lieutenant Culver, a reservist who speaks for Styron. *Set This House on Fire,* in the tradition of Mark TWAIN, Henry JAMES, and F. Scott FITZGERALD, explores the myth of the American in Europe. Set primarily in Sambuca, Italy, it concerns Cass Kinsolving, a Virginia writer who suffers writer's block and shares the narration with his old friend, Virginia lawyer Peter Leverett. They meet in Charleston, South Carolina, to discuss the apparent suicide of their mutual friend Mason Flagg when all three men were in Sambuca. The truth gradually emerges: Cass, enraged at Mason's rape of Francesca, Cass's lover, murdered the man who for him personified pure evil.

The Confessions of Nat Turner earned for Styron a Pulitzer Prize. There were accolades on one hand and angry accusations of insensitivity and racism on the other. The novel was set during the 1831 slave rebellion led by Nat Turner, a black slave and preacher, during which 55 whites and 200 blacks were murdered. After this novel appeared, writer and critic John E. Clark edited an essay collection, *William Styron's Nat Turner: Ten Black Writers Respond* (1968), in which Styron is accused of appropriating black experience and contributing to notions of black stereotypes. Styron's response was that he intended to make Nat Turner into a complex and fallible human being, not a hero. Black novelist Sherley Anne WILLIAMS wrote *DESSA ROSE* in response to *Confessions.*

In Styron's next novel, *Sophie's Choice,* a Virginian named Stingo narrates events in post–World War II Brooklyn that he witnessed during the war: The Polish Catholic Sophie, a survivor of the Nazi death camp, Auschwitz, is consumed with guilt; when the Nazis forced her to choose between her son and her daughter, she complied and ended up losing both children. Her recollections are juxtaposed to her love affair with Nathan, a Brooklyn Jew so consumed with guilt about avoiding the Nazi atrocities that he forces Sophie to join him in a double suicide. Stingo, at work on his first novel, loses all his WASP naiveté as he tells their story.

Recently William Styron received both the National Medal of Arts and the Commonwealth Award. With the poet Rose Burgunder, his wife since May 4, 1953, he divides his time between their farmhouse in Roxbury, Connecticut, and their house on Martha's Vineyard.

NOVELS AND NOVELLAS

The Confessions of Nat Turner. New York: Random House, 1967.

Lie Down in Darkness. Indianapolis: Bobbs-Merrill, 1951.

The Long March. New York: Vintage, 1956.

Set This House on Fire. New York: Random House, 1960.

Sophie's Choice. New York: Random House, 1979.

A Tidewater Morning: Three Tales from Youth. New York: Random House, 1993.

SOURCES

Bryer, Jackson R., and Mary B. Hatem. *William Styron: A Reference Guide.* Boston: G. K. Hall, 1978.

Casciato, Arthur D., and James L. W. West III, eds. *Critical Essays on William Styron.* Boston: G. K. Hall, 1982.

Coale, Samuel. *William Styron Revisited.* Boston: Twayne, 1991.

Cologne-Brookes, Gavin. *The Novels of William Styron: From Harmony to History.* Baton Rouge: Louisiana State University, 1995.

Crane, John K. *The Root of All Evil: The Thematic Unity of William Styron's Fiction.* Columbia: University of South Carolina Press, 1985.

Creyling, Michael. "Speakable and Unspeakable in Styron's *Sophie's Choice,*" *Southern Review* 20 (Summer 1984): 546–561.

Friedman, Melvin J. *William Styron.* Bowling Green, Ohio: Bowling Green University, 1974.

Hadaller, David. *Gynicide: Women in the Novels of William Styron.* Madison, N.J.: Fairleigh Dickinson University Press, 1996.

Lupack, Barbara T. "The Politics of Gender: William Styron's *Sophie's Choice,*" *Connecticut Review* 14 (Fall 1992): 1–8.

Morris, Robert K., and Irving Malin, eds. *The Achievement of William Styron.* Athens: University of Georgia Press, 1981.

Ratner, Marc L. *William Styron.* Boston: Twayne, 1972.

Ross, Daniel William. *The Critical Response to William Styron.* Westport, Conn.: Greenwood Press, 1995.

Ruderman, Judith. *William Styron.* New York: Ungar, 1989.

Sirlin, Rhoda. *William Styron's Sophie's Choice: Crime and Self-Punishment.* Ann Arbor, Mich.: UMI Research Press, 1990.

Stone, Albert E. *The Return of Nat Turner: History, Literature, and Cultural Politics in Sixties America.* Athens: University of Georgia Press, 1992.

West, James L. W., III, ed. *Conversations with William Styron.* Jackson: University Press of Mississippi, 1985.

———. *William Styron: A Descriptive Bibliography.* Boston: G. K. Hall, 1977.

———. *William Styron: A Life.* New York: Random House, 1998.

OTHER

American Masters: William Styron. RBS. Available online. URL: http://www.pbs.org/wnet/americanmasters/database/styron_w.html. Accessed January 13, 2006.

William Styron. Available online. URL: http://www.virginia.edu/~history/courses/courses.old/hius323/styron.html. Accessed September 25, 2005.

Wired for Books: Audio Interviews with William Styron. Available online. URL: http://wiredforbooks.org/williamstyron. Accessed September 25, 2005.

SUCKOW, RUTH (1892–1960)

After decades of critical neglect and dismissal as a regionalist who was overly concerned with women's issues, Ruth Suckow is receiving critical and scholarly attention as both a novelist and short story writer. In her own era she was well known not only for her descriptions of the Midwest but also for her realistic portraits of lonely, isolated characters. She is compared often to Willa CATHER and Sinclair LEWIS. Her fictional women, according to scholar Abigail Ann Hamblen, nearly always sacrifice themselves to husbands, children, and lovers, and have difficulty communicating with men. Most important, according to Hamblen, they relinquish "everything for romantic or sexual love" (Hamblen, 1978, 20). Should they refuse the sacrifices expected of them, the consequences are unsettling at best, emotionally and socially ruinous at worst.

Ruth Suckow was born on August 6, 1892, in Hawarden, Iowa, to William Suckow, a minister, and Anna Kluckhohn Suckow, the daughter of a methodist minister. She graduated from the University of Denver, with a bachelor's degree in 1917 and a master's in 1918. Suckow became a pacifist during World War I and, to support herself, worked as a beekeeper while she wrote stories. Her first novel, *Country People,* serialized in *Century Magazine* in 1924, featured the Kaetterhenrys, a German family and their Iowa descendants. Her second novel, *The Odyssey of a Nice Girl* (1925), is about Marjorie Schoessel, a young midwestern farm girl who seeks a better life. She followed with *The Bonney Family* (1928), a study of the lonely and, in her view, essentially dead life of a small-town midwesterner. Suckow married Ferner Nuhn, a writer, in 1929. *Cora,* published that year, depicts 14-year-old Cora Schwieterts, the daughter of German immigrants who sees that her father cannot provide for the family and instead moves them from town to town; she energizes the family to put down roots and find jobs. She becomes a career woman who must never allow men or marriage to sway her from her course; she is profoundly lonely. Cora, notes Hamblen, "deserves to be numbered among the notable women in American fiction" (Hamblen, 1978, 24). *The Kramer Girls* (1930) demonstrates Suckow's similar concerns with feminine psychology and the lack of opportunity for women in Iowa.

For most readers, Suckow's most complex and ambitious novel is *The Folks* (1934). Iowans Fred and Annie Ferguson produce four children, two of whom, Dorothy and Margaret, agonize about the difficulties encountered by vital women in an unsympathetic environment. Suckow's penchant for using autobiographical details has been noted by most critics: *New Hope* (1942) is set in a town similar to Suckow's own birthplace, and its central character, young William Greenwood, resembles Suckow's father. Numerous critics have noted that Suckow introduces into this unusually optimistic novel a HAWTHORNE-like character, the allegorical Delight, whose childhood is happy. *The John Wood Case,* her last novel, features a crisis that is based on her father's pastoral experiences when one of his parishioners embezzled some funds.

Ruth Suckow died on January 23, 1960, in Claremont, California. The majority of her papers and manuscripts are housed at the University of Iowa Library in Iowa City.

NOVELS

The Bonney Family. New York: Knopf, 1928.
Cora. New York: Knopf, 1929.
Country People. Knopf, New York: 1924.
The Folks. New York: Farrar & Rinehart, 1934.
The John Wood Case. New York: Viking, 1959.
The Kramer Girls. New York: Knopf, 1930.
New Hope. New York & Toronto, Canada: Farrar & Rinehart, 1942.
The Odyssey of a Nice Girl. New York: Knopf, 1925.

SOURCES

Andrews, Clarence A. Introduction to *A Ruth Suckow Omnibus.* Iowa City: University of Iowa Press, 1988.
———. *A Literary History of Iowa.* Iowa City: University of Iowa Press, 1972, pp. 79–101.
Baker, Joseph. "Regionalism in the Middle West," *American Review* 4 (November 1934–March 1935): 603–614.
Buchanan, Aimée. "A Walk in the Mountains," *Southwest Review,* 46 (Summer 1961): 231–243.
De Marr, Mary Jean. "Ruth Suckow's Iowa 'Nice Girls,' " *Midamerica* 8 (1986): 69–83.
Frederick, John T. "Ruth Suckow and the Middle Western Literary Movement," *English Journal* 20 (January 1931): 1–8.
Hamblen, Abigail Ann. *Ruth Suckow.* Boise, Idaho: Boise State University, 1978.
———. "Ruth Suckow and Thomas Wolfe: A Study in Similarity," *Forum* (Houston), 3 (Winter 1962): 27–31.
Kiesel, Margaret Matlack. "Iowans in the Arts: Ruth Suckow in the Twenties," *Annals of Iowa* (Spring 1980): 259–287.
———. "Ruth Suckow's Grinnell," *Grinnell Magazine* 8 (November–December 1975): 7–10.
Kissane, Leedice McAnelly. "D. H. Lawrence, Ruth Suckow, and 'Modern Marriage,' " *Rendezvous* 4 (1969): 39–45.
———. *Ruth Suckow.* Boston: Twayne, 1969.
Martin, Abigail Ann. "*The Folks:* Anatomy of Rural Life and Shifting Values," *North Dakota Quarterly* 53 (Fall 1985): 173–179.
Muehl, Lois B. "Ruth Suckow's Art of Fiction," *Books at Iowa* 13 (November 1970): 3–12.
Nuhn, Ferner. "The Orchard Apiary: Ruth Suckow in Earlville," *Iowan* 20 (Summer 1972): 21–24, 54.
Oehlschlaeger, Fritz. "The Art of Ruth Suckow's 'A Start in Life,' " *Western American Literature* 15 (Fall 1980): 177–186.
———. "A Book of Resolutions: Ruth Suckow's *Some Others and Myself,*" *Western American Literature* 21 (Summer 1986): 111–121.
Omrcanin, Margaret Stewart. *Ruth Suckow: A Critical Study of Her Fiction.* Philadelphia: Dorrance, 1972.
Paluka, Frank. "Ruth Suckow: A Calendar of Letters," *Books at Iowa* 1 (October 1964): 34–40; 2 (April 1965): 31–40.
White, Barbara A. "Nice Girls and Their Folks: The Adolescent and the Family in Ruth Suckow's Fiction," In *Growing Up Female: Adolescent Girlhood in American Fiction,* 65–88. Westport, Conn.: Greenwood, 1985.

SUI SIN FAR (EDITH MAUDE EATON) (1865–1914)

Edith Maude Eaton (also known as Sui Sin Far) and her sister, the novelist Winifred Eaton (also known as Onoto Watanna), are the first Chinese-American writers on the North American continent. The study of all Asian-American fiction begins with them. Although some scholars consider Sui Sin Far to be a Canadian, rather than an American, she spent most of her adult life in Seattle, San

Francisco, Los Angeles, and Boston, with frequent return trips to Montreal, Canada. As scholar Carman C. Curton points out, recent research on Sui Sin Far credits her as "the first American writer, of any race, to present fully rounded portrayals of Chinese people" (Curton 335). Although technically a short story writer, some readers have argued that her story collection MRS. SPRING FRAGRANCE (1912), although difficult to classify, has the overall effect of a novel. Her characters endure the difficulties shared by Asian-American immigrants, but they contribution substantially to American society. Sui Sin Far writes about immigration and gender; of particular note are her mixed-race characters and their difficulties in connecting East and West.

Edith Eaton, or Sui Sin Far (Chinese for "narcissus" or "water lily"), was born on March 15, 1865, in Macclesfield, England, to Edward Eaton, an Englishman, and Lotus Blossom Trufusis, a Chinese woman. The family immigrated to Canada in 1872, when the future Sui Sin Far was seven years old. Although she worked as a secretary and stenographer, Sui Sin Far began publishing stories and nonfiction essays in American newspapers in the 1880s. In her essays, she implies that she never married because of her racial heritage: To marry a white man would mean denying her Chinese heritage, and so on. Near the end of her life, she published "Leaves from the Mental Portfolio of an Eurasian" (1909), an autobiographical sketch, and collected other stories and sketches into the single volume entitled *Mrs. Spring Fragrance.* The manuscript of her one novel was, according to her own account, lost during one of her many trips.

New scholarship on Sui Sin Far suggests that she was even more subtle than originally thought, using irony to undercut some of her own commentary on racist portrayals of the Chinese, and endowing her characters with disguises to mask either gender or ethnicity or both. The work of Sui Sin Far continues to be a touchstone for the study of Asian-American literature.

NOVELS (SHORT STORY CYCLES)
Mrs. Spring Fragrance. Chicago: A. C. McClurg, 1912.
Mrs. Spring Fragrance and Other Writings. Edited by Amy Ling and Annette White-Parks. Urbana: University of Illinois Press, 1995.

SOURCES
Ammons, Elizabeth. "Audacious Words: Sui Sin Far's *Mrs. Spring Fragrance.*" In *Conflicting Stories: American Women Writers at the Turn into the Twentieth Century,* edited by Elizabeth Ammons, 105–120. New York: Oxford University Press, 1991.

Curton, Carman C. "Sui Sin Far (Edith Maude Eaton). "In *American Women Writers, 1900–1945. A Bio-bibliographical Sourcebook,* edited by Emmanuel S. Nelson, 333. Westport, Conn.: Greenwood Press, 2000.

Doyle, James. "Sui Sin Far and Onoto Watanna: Two Early Chinese-Canadian Authors," *Canadian Literature* 140 (Spring 1994): 50–58.

Levesque, Andree. "Sui Sin Far/Edith Maude Eaton," *Canadian Historical Review* (June 1997): 280–283.

Ling, Amy. "Creating One's Self: The Eaton Sisters." In *Reading the Literatures of Asian America,* edited by Ling and Shirley Geok-lin Lim, 305–318. Philadelphia: Temple University Press, 1992.

———. "Edith Eaton: Pioneer Chinamerican Writer and Feminist," *American Literary Realism* 16 (Autumn 1983): 287–298.

———. "Pioneers and Paradigms: The Eaton Sisters." In *Between Worlds: Women Writers of Chinese Ancestry,* edited by Amy Ling, 21–55. New York: Pergamon, 1990.

———. "Revelation and Mask: Autobiographies of the Eaton Sisters," *a/b: Auto-Biography Studies* 3 (Summer 1987): 49.

———. "Writers with a Cause: Sui Sin Far and Han Suyin," *Women's Studies International Forum* 9 (1986): 411–419.

Roth-Spaulding, Carol. "'Wavering Images': Mixed-Race Identity in the Stories of Edith Eaton/Sui Sin Far." In *Ethnicity and the American Short Story,* edited by Julie Brown, 155–176. New York: Garland, 1997.

Solberg, S. E. "Sui Sin Far/Edith Eaton: First Chinese American Fictionist," *MELUS* 8 (Spring 1981): 27–39.

Sui Sin Far. "Leaves from the Mental Portfolio of an Eurasian," *Independent* 66 (January 21, 1909): 125–132.

Tonkovich, Nicole. "Genealogy, Genre, Gender: Sui Sin Far's 'Leaves from the Mental Portfolio of an Eurasian.' " In *Beyond the Binary: Reconstructing Cultural Identity in a Multicultural Context,* edited by Timothy B. Powell, 236–260. New Brunswick, N.J.: Rutgers University Press, 1999.

White-Parks, Annette. "A Reversal of American Concepts of 'Other-ness' in the Fiction of Sui Sin Far," *MELUS* 20 (1995): 17–34.

———. *Sui Sin Far/Edith Maude Eaton: A Literary Biography.* Urbana: University of Illinois Press, 1995.

Yin, Xiao-Huang. "Between the East and West: Sui Sin Far—the First Chinese-American Woman Writer," *Arizona Quarterly* 47 (Winter 1991): 49–83.

Yu, Ning. "Fanny Fern and Sui Sin Far: The Beginning of an Asian American Voice," *Women and Language* 19, no. 2 (1996): 44–47.

OTHER

Edith Eaton. *Voice from the Gaps [VG]*. Available online. URL: http://voices.cla.umn.edu/vg/Bios/entries/eaton_edith_sui_Far.html. Accessed September 26, 2005.

Review of Ammette White Parks, Edith Maude Eaton. *A Literary Biography*. University of Illinois Press. Available online. URL: http://www.press.uillinois.edu/s95/white_pr.html. Accessed September 25, 2005.

SULA TONI MORRISON (1973) Toni MORRISON's 1973 novel *Sula* is the story of a community, "a neighborhood, really," called the Bottom, and the struggles of its residents to survive in an environment where they've been (literally) "set up" to fail. Although the chronological action takes place in the Ohio town of Medallion, between the years of 1919 and 1965, the novel is prefaced by a few brief pages that both provide a "pre-history" of the Bottom and inform the reader of it's post-1965 destiny. We learn that the Bottom got it's name as early as the post–Civil War era because of a "nigger joke," whereby the "good" farmer of Medallion had promised "freedom and a piece of bottom land" to his slave in exchange for labor. Reluctant to part with the fertile valley soil, the farmer tricks the slave into believing that "bottom" refers to the rocky hilltop area of Medallion, so named because of it's proximity to heaven ("when God looks down, it's the bottom"). Thus from the outset the reader has an indication that ensuing generations of the Bottom community, engendered through false promises and built essentially on unstable ground, are not likely to prosper.

Within the framework of the ironically named hilltop world and the valley town that lies below, *Sula* depicts relationships that should be connective—family, marriage, friendship—but which eventually fail, speeding the figurative and literal destruction of the Bottom. The novel's main storyline centers around two families—the Wright's and the Peace's. Both clans are essentially matriarchal; the men have either left, died,

or, in the case of Wiley Wright, taken a job that requires months of travel at a time. Helene Wright runs her home and her daughter Nel with the manner and bearing of a society matriarch. Seeking to erase the "less dignified" aspect of her lineage, Helene forges a small, safe world bounded by a kind of self-righteous respectability. She establishes herself as the arbiter of good taste among the black community in Medallion, but in the process of narrowly defining her own existence, she squelches her daughter's imagination, leaving 10-year-old Nel with the burning desire to define herself.

The novel devotes considerably more attention to the world of Eva Peace, her daughter Hannah, and Hannah's daughter Sula. Like Helene Wright, the Peace women are self-sustaining, but they derive their strength not by adhering to conventional social order but by flaunting those rules. Eva inspires considerable awe in the Bottom community, mostly because of the rumor that her financial stability was achieved by putting her leg under the wheels of a train in order to collect the insurance money. Having the strength to make this sacrifice for the good of the family foreshadows the moment when Eva lights a fire in her son Plum's bedroom, where he lies in a cocaine-induced stupor. (When Hannah later confronts her mother about Plum's death, Eva describes a baby who tries to return to the womb in full adulthood, a metaphor which implies that Plum's regressive state had gotten to the point where he was not only killing himself but his mother as well.)

Hannah, like her mother, is not dependent on a man for her existence. However, neither Hannah nor Eva exist in a world without men. Both women love men simply for their maleness, inviting them into the house to fulfill different needs. Her husband Rekus having died (before the action of the novel begins), Hannah has "a steady sequence of lovers, mostly the husbands of her friends and neighbors." She doesn't want any kind of depth or commitment from these men, however, just the physical pleasure of human touch. Eva likes engaging men in games of checkers (which she wins) and stimulating conversation and debate. Even with one leg, Eva has sex appeal to the men of the Bottom, who are fascinated by her remaining leg, svelte and alluring in its hosiery and sexy shoe. Because

Hannah and Eva make the men of the Bottom feel good about themselves, they are able to get what they need from men without alienating them.

It is the friendship of Hannah's daughter Sula and Helene's daughter Nel that the novel hinges upon. The girls, one from a strict home, the other from a wild one, bond so closely that they become "two eyes and one throat." Each gets from the other what she is missing, or has not gotten from her own environment. Nel loves the spontaneous and open atmosphere of the Peace house, for example, while Sula soaks up the quiet elegance and decorum Helene Wright has established. Sula, despite what the narrator describes as her inconstant nature, models independent thinking and strength of conviction for Nel. Threatened by four Irish boys, Sula convinces Nel not to avoid the issue, and then vanquishes the threat by performing a violence upon herself. When the girls meet up with Chicken Little, it is Sula who cajoles him into climbing the tree, and it is Sula who is swinging him around when he slips from her grip and drowns in the river. In both of these instances, Nel's participation takes the form of passive involvement; her watching is a form of silent support for Sula.

As the two girls become women, however, the social and cultural expectations by which women are assigned value serve to divide them. Nel gets noticed by Jude Greene, whose gaze serves to select Nel away from Sula. Jude's individual attention secretly pleases Nel, who has seen herself up to this point as indistinguishable from her friend. Nel fails to recognize, however, that she has exchanged a perceived dependence for a very real one. The closer courtship brings Nel to marriage with Jude, the more she defines herself through his gaze and his expectations. On their wedding day, Nel's cooption is complete; her veil is so heavy she cannot feel Jude's kiss upon her head. Sula, having supported Nel throughout the process, leaves Medallion immediately after the wedding, both because there is no place for her in Nel's newly attained conventional role and because she wants no part of it.

Part II of the novel depicts the adult lives of Nel and Sula and shows the continued struggles of the Bottom community to survive. In the intervening 10 years between Sula's departure and return, Nel has faded in her marriage to Jude, and the Bottom has also started to fall apart. Sula's return affects both the community and her friend. Although Nel's marriage and family life have resulted in her conforming to the Bottom and its values, she comes to life when Sula returns, recovering the joy she'd experienced in their girlhood friendship. However, when she discovers Jude and Sula naked in her bedroom, she can't comprehend what she sees as a betrayal. Jude leaves town and, now without Sula's friendship, Nel feels completely empty and purposeless.

The people of the Bottom hear of this incident and condemn Sula, seeing a woman who lives alone, who put her own grandmother into a nursing home, and who (the rumor goes) sleeps with white men. Treated as an outsider by the community, Sula now functions as someone they can define themselves in opposition to; their efforts to protect themselves from a perceived evil ironically result in them taking better care of their lives, although the Bottom doesn't recognize Sula's role in this change. Sula, whose background had not taught her to appreciate the notion of possession and thus had not understood Nel's response to her bedding Jude, lives an isolated existence, punctuated by sexual encounters that provide her with the ability to fully experience her own emptiness. It is in this context that Sula meets Ajax and has her first rewarding relationship. When Sula begins to exhibit signs of possession and desire for commitment, Ajax leaves her. Alone, Sula becomes sick (cancer?). After a final confrontation with Nel, who has come, duty-bound, to see if Sula needs anything on her deathbed, Sula dies. In the wake of her death, the community resumes its careless and uncaring ways, and so slides into destructive apathy. It is in this spirit that many of the townspeople join Shadrack in his Suicide Day parade and are led to their death when the New River Road tunnel collapses on them. Nel continues to live as a righteous woman of the community, visiting the sick and aged and volunteering at the church. At the old folk's home, she visits Eva Peace, who accuses her of being no different than Sula. The shock of Eva's accusation causes Nel to rethink her relationship with Sula, and she breaks down, mourning the loss.

How people forge identity and the importance of selfhood are major themes in *Sula*. Eva Peace, it is repeatedly hinted, has sold a piece of herself in exchange for self-reliance. Helene Wright carefully crafts a self she can maintain only in the upside-down world of the Bottom; outside, in the world of "separate but equal," she is stripped of her humanness and humiliated at every turn. The horrors of war having shattered his identity, Shadrack becomes insane until he is able to confirm his identity by locating his reflection in a toilet bowl. The three Deweys, as they become indistinguishable from each other, become progressively crazy, their communications with each other inscrutable to the outside world. They remain as immature in adulthood as they were the year Eva acquired them. A strong sense of identity, it can be deduced, is necessary for individual and community progress. Moreover, relationships, which usually help people to define themselves, take on a destructive role in Sula. As Nel becomes involved with Jude, and Sula with Ajax, the two women seek to define themselves through the male gaze, gradually failing to perceive themselves as individuals: a kind of symbolic death which leads to their personal destruction in the course of the novel. Lack of personal identity, whether one is prevented from developing it, or is gradually stripped of it in the course of succumbing to powerful cultural conventions, leads one to lose a sense of self. The internal erosion of selfhood in the novel is paralleled by the physical wasting, disappearance, and death of its characters, and by the gradual disintegration of the entire community.

From a political perspective, the novel sends a message about the way racial inequality is established and institutionalized. The values of the dominant (white) culture are held up as an exemplar for successful living, but the black community in the novel is first deceived about, then denied, legitimate means of living by those values. The people of the Bottom buy into the lies they are told about the value of the land upon which they build their lives; thus, their physical and metaphorical "grounding" is essentially unstable. The black men of Medallion, eager to apply their energies toward participating in the capitalist economy, can only find useless work, sweeping floors or waiting tables; they are denied the opportunity to work on the New Road, valuable work that would have conferred

upon them a measure of dignity. Unable to feed their families, it is no wonder relationships and families fail. This theme of instability is echoed in the way things in the Bottom fall apart: Chicken Little's death after he slips from Sula's grip; the breakdown of Nel's marriage; Ajax's impotent dreams of airplanes and his real flight to Dayton; the collapse of self-respect and solidarity among the Bottom women in the wake of Sula's death; and the landslide that kills many community members in the novel's final tragedy—these events demonstrate the consequences of living in a world whose guiding principles promote not unity but fragmentation.

It is "just as well," hints Morrison in *Sula's* opening pages, that environments like the Bottom are dismantled. Through the demise of the Bottom community and the relationships formed within it, Morrison reveals the consequences for black Americans of unwittingly buying into, and then replicating, a deceptive system of values that will not benefit them. Those who strive honestly to form lasting relationships and find meaningful work in an environment that precludes the attainment of such values are (albeit unfairly) doomed to fail. Perhaps more tragic is the fate of those few, like Nel, who come to understand the value of authentic connection but whose epiphany comes too late. Nel's sudden recognition of her errors in judgment in the final pages of the novel ("we was girls together") results in total loss, since she now has neither the false comfort of social norms nor the live presence of her nonconventional friend to bolster her, "just circles and circles of sorrow."

SOURCE

Morrison, Toni. *Sula.* New York: Knopf, 1973; Reprint, New York: Plume-Penguin, 1982.

Catherine Ramsden

SUMMER EDITH WHARTON (1917)   Edith WHAR-TON published her 10th novel, *Summer,* in 1917. Like many of Wharton's other novels, *Summer* was adapted by Charles Gaines into a television film in 1981, starring Diane Lane as Charity Royall, while John Cullum played Lawyer Royall. As one of Wharton's New England novels, *Summer* both takes on and twists the tradition many critics call a seduction-and-abandonment plot. It follows Charity as she seeks independence from her guardian, Mr. Royall, while coming of age in the small town of North Dormer. The story traces the tension created by the young woman's questionable past linked to the nearby, derelict mountain folk and her increasing interest in the visiting city boy, Lucius Harney. When her friendship with Harney turns romantic, the circumstances for great passion and great tragedy evolve into Charity's journey of self-discovery.

Wharton explores individual power when she sets up Charity's background. Charity is powerless against the Royalls and the North Dormer community, who tell her who she is. She has no memories of her first years on the nearby mountain, so life seems to begin when she awakens from a fever at the foot of Mrs. Royall's bed when she is five years old. Her very name, Charity, imposed upon her at her arrival, designates her dependent position in the community. If she disagrees with North Dormer about the kind of person they think she is, she has no rebuttal because she has no memories of her own with which to refute their ideas.

As Charity matures, the power relations begin to shift. If Charity is not sure who she is, she certainly has a strong sense of who she is not. Soon after the death of Mrs. Royall, her foster mother, Charity rebukes the now-widowed Mr. Royall's late-night, lonesome visit to her door. Even though her potential for independence or a life away from her small town seems impossible, she rejects a secure future by refusing the marriage proposal Mr. Royall offers a few days later to legitimize his desire. These events and the town librarian job Mr. Royall arranges for her give her reigning power in the Royall household and the community.

Charity's new relationship with Lucius Harney begins a series of independent experiences that help her figure out who she is away from the community's influence while tipping the power structure. In charity, Wharton constructs a character who is both convincingly naive enough to be called inexperienced, yet confident enough to retain her dignity. She does not chase after Harney before his departure, reasoning instead that if he wanted to see her, he would come to her. Wharton exposes the power of small-town gossip when an evening Charity spent peeping into Harney's window is misinterpreted and spreads into a late-night

romantic encounter. Charity keeps secret the rest of her liaisons with Harney, even though she claims indifference to the town's prejudice.

Wharton reveals the couple's clashing sensibilities from their first moments in the library and continues the trend with their divergent cultural tastes. The author often places Charity amid animal imagery that pairs her with descriptions of sun-warmed animals and dim comprehension, while Harney is surrounded by books and sketches. Unlike the North Dormer community that distrusts Charity's mountain heritage, Harney finds her background interesting and even valuable for his architectural studies. His own naiveté about the mountain means that he does not place expectations on Charity's identity and behavior like those from her family and town. The friendship remains respectfully platonic until they orchestrate a Fourth of July trip to the larger town of Nettleton, where their relationship ignites with a kiss. After the fireworks, Mr. Royall discovers her with Harney, while the lawyer's own compromising position leads to an emotional and awkward scene.

Although her bond with Harney seems to bring out a new person in Charity, she only seeks out an existence different from her mundane North Dormer experiences rather than attempting to join higher society with Harney. Their liaisons mostly occur in an abandoned shack located between North Dormer and the mountain, but in sight of both communities. When Mr. Royall tries to force the couple to marry, Charity once again knows exactly who she is not and dismisses her capability to be an appropriate wife for Harney. Wharton first alters the possibility that Harney might desert Charity when instead he agrees to marry her. Discovering she is pregnant while Harney is back in the city, the next twist to the seduction-and-abandonment theme is when Charity tries to escape her circumstances by returning to the mountain. Her experiences there, where Mr. Royall once again rescues her, places her at a critical decision point when she has to stop knowing who she is not and finally figure out who she is.

At this point, Charity must choose between several possibilities that diverge from her hopes of independently leaving North Dormer. She has had the opportunity to build her own identity by bringing together her experiences with Harney and the mountain, forcing them to coexist with the identity imposed on her by the Royalls and North Dormer. With unsatisfying marriages and abortion among her options, her ultimate decision highlights the ways she remains a powerful person. Combining her new experiences with her known past, she finally chooses who Charity Royall is.

SOURCES

Benstock, Shari. *No Gifts from Chance: A Biography of Edith Wharton*. New York: Maxwell Macmillan International, 1994.

Dwight, Eleanor. *Edith Wharton: An Extraordinary Life*. New York: H. N. Abrams, 1994.

Goodman, Susan. *Edith Wharton's Women: Friends & Rivals*. Hanover, N.H.: The University Press of New England, 1990.

Lewis, R. W. B. *Edith Wharton*. New York: Harper & Row, 1975.

Wharton, Edith. *A Backward Glance*. New York: Charles Scribner Sons, 1933.

———. *Summer*. Edited by Cynthia Griffin Wolff. New York: The Library of America, 1990, pp. 159–311.

OTHER

The Edith Wharton Society. Gonzaga University. Available online. URL: http://www.wsu.edu/~campbelld/wharton/index.html. Accessed January 13, 2006.

Max Despain

SUN ALSO RISES, THE ERNEST HEMINGWAY (1926)

Ernest HEMINGWAY's first published novel, *The Sun Also Rises*, is perhaps his finest. The novel takes its title from Ecclesiastes, also quoted in the opening page of the book: "One generation passeth away, and another generation cometh; but the earth abideth forever 'The sun also ariseth, and the sun goeth down, and hasteth to the place where he arose.' " Above, on the same page, is a brief quotation attributed to Gertrude Stein: "You are all a lost generation." The juxtaposition of the two quotations suggests a cyclical dynamic to the post–World War I "lost generation" that is represented in the novel. By repeating the same self-destructive behavior, the characters perpetuate the sense of alienation and meaninglessness that became widespread following the devastation of the war.

Narrated by its protagonist, Jake Barnes, an American journalist in Europe, *The Sun Also Rises* conveys a sense of profound loss and disillusionment during the post–World War I era. Jake, whose impotence resulted from a war injury, embodies the pervasive futility within the text. He and his acquaintances inhabit a world where love continually fails and consequently is not regenerative, a definitive modernist trope also reflected in texts such as T. S. Eliot's *The Waste Land* (1922) and F. Scott FITZGERALD's *The Great Gatsby* (1925). Specifically in Hemingway's novel, romantic relationships either cannot be consummated or cannot be sustained, and none of these relationships ever produces any children.

Characteristic of the failed relationships depicted in *The Sun Also Rises*, Jake is in love with Brett Ashley but is unable to be intimate with her. Unwilling to commit to Jake, Brett is the central focus for many of Jake's expatriate acquaintances, with whom he travels from Paris to Spain and back to Paris. While Brett is engaged to Scottish veteran Michael Campbell, she has an affair with Jake's friend Robert Cohn, who is the only Jew in the novel and is frequently treated as an outsider. Brett also has a brief affair with a young bullfighter named Romero. As the characters travel in pursuit of amusement, Jake struggles to preserve the relationships among them, despite the divisive jealousy and violence provoked by Brett's and her lovers' entanglements.

Since Jake and his friends spend most of their time talking and drinking, the plot develops through Hemingway's "deceptively simple dialogue," which "managed to capture the dynamics of real-life speech" (Lamb, 455). Typical of Hemingway's dialogue style, the brief, seemingly empty exchanges between characters express the depths of their disillusionment. Harold Bloom attributes this expression to the author's "art of evocation" (Bloom, 6), which requires the reader to infer meaning from his prose. Through dialogue, then, the reader can perceive the characters' devastating pain and desperation. Exemplifying the relentless alienation many of the characters suffer, Robert laments the emptiness he feels: "I can't stand it to think my life is going so fast and I'm not really living it" (10). Similarly, no one in the novel appears to be "really living," as they spend most of their time intoxicated, in avoidance of life.

Representing epidemic social alienation, many modernist authors dramatized the world as a place where love cannot flourish and relationships fall apart. Yet their texts, as works of art, attempted to convey a sense of order that the early 20th-century world appeared to lack. Likewise, Hemingway manifests the possibility of restoration in a disordered, fragmented world through Jake's character. Although Jake suffers from feelings of alienation, he makes subtle attempts to recover meaning. A self-identified Catholic, he seems unable to explain what that means when asked by his friend Bill Gorton (124). On different occasions, though, Jake tries to pray. One of these early attempts leads him to reflect: "I was a little ashamed, and regretted that I was such a rotten Catholic, but realized there was nothing I could do about it, at least for a while, and maybe never, but that anyway it was a grand religion, and I only wished I felt religious and maybe I would the next time" (97). Later, when Jake enters a chapel with Brett, he claims: "I'm pretty religious" (209), an assertion that suggests that Jake's prayers have been answered.

Whether his prayers have truly been answered or not is less important than the repetition of Jake's attempts at "being" Catholic. His suggestion to Brett when they visit the chapel that she "might pray" (208) indicates the implicit hope Jake embodies. In a postwar world seemingly empty of meaning, where human relationships repeatedly fail, Jake recovers at least a semblance of hope. As the sun continues to rise each day, Jake's continual attempts at a religious faith enact humanity's refusal to abandon the pursuit of meaningfulness and renew the possibility of progress in a culture where hope was nearly destroyed altogether.

SOURCES

Bloom, Harold, ed. "Ernest Hemingway's *The Sun Also Rises*." In *Modern Critical Interpretations*. New York: Chelsea House Publishers, 1987.

Hemingway, Ernest. *The Sun Also Rises*. New York: Charles Scribner Sons, 1926.

Lamb, Robert Paul. "Hemingway and the Creation of Twentieth-Century Dialogue," *Twentieth Century Literature* 42 (1996): 453–480.

Heather Ostman

SUNDOWN JOHN JOSEPH MATHEWS (1934)

Scholars of Native American literature point to the period beginning in the late 1960s and diminishing somewhat in the 1980s as a time of rising popular and critical attention paid to fiction and poetry written by Native Americans. Kenneth Lincoln, in his groundbreaking book of the same name, dubbed this period the Native American Renaissance, which is generally perceived as beginning with N. Scott MOMADAY's winning of the Pulitzer Prize for Fiction in 1969. Other writers followed, including James WELCH and Leslie Marmon SILKO, both writing about contemporary Native American issues while also turning toward traditional Indian methods of storytelling while forming their written works.

But there were Native American writers who came before who laid the groundwork for this "rebirth," namely D'Arcy McNICKLE and John Joseph Mathews, author of the 1934 novel *Sundown*. Both of these writers took on the all-too-unfortunate issues that Native Americans have faced since European settlement began—loss of traditional ways of life and homelands, the idea of mixed blood (Indian and white), the boarding school system begun by the U. S. government in the 19th century, life on and off the reservation, alcoholism, and other dealings with Euro-Americans that rarely work out in the Natives' favor. Mathews and McNickle took on these highly charged issues when doing so was much more risky than it was in the more liberal 1960s and '70s, and they both had strong influences on the Indian writing that was to follow.

Mathews's *Sundown* presents the story of Challenge Windzer (Chal for short), beginning with his birth and childhood, covering his college years off the reservation, and ending with his attempts to find his place in the modern, white world of the 1920s. Like the author himself, Chal is of mixed blood, Osage and white. Chal's father, who was descended in part from a white artist who visited the Osage, wants his son to pursue the opportunities provided by Euro-American culture, while his mother, a full-blood Osage, silently hopes that Chal will follow a more traditional path. These issues concerning mixed/full-blood and Euro-American/Native American traditions and cultures inform the entire novel, thus giving readers the opportunity to discover a very early example of American postcolonial writing (which critiques institutions and effects of colonization, often using the colonizer's language). It's worth noting that many would consider this novel years ahead of its time in this regard.

Louis Owens, author of *Other Destinies: Understanding the American Indian Novel,* perhaps gives this novel its best treatment to date. He argues that the novel begins, as Chal is born, at a "critical point of transition for the Osage Nation between old worlds and new." The Osage people have been relocated to reservations by the U.S. government, oil leases on their property are an issue of contention, and encroaching white settlement is slowly beginning to absorb traditional Indian lands (Owens, 51). One point of contention lies between the full-blood and the mixed-blood Osage. The full-bloods, whose lives often reflect a more traditional way of thinking, are skeptical of the white influence on Osage culture and are more resistant to the government's plans for Osage reservation lands. The mixed bloods, on the other hand, linger around the Agency and the store, talking of political issues, the oil leases, the Dawes Act, and the coming allotment of Osage lands. They look at the government influences on their lives as being much more positive. Chal's father, John Windzer, whose father was a British aristocrat who lived among the Osage, reads Byron's "Child Harolde" (a Romantic-period British poem), goes on trips to Washington to deal with the government, and generally encourages his son to give up the traditional ways of life and take advantage of the opportunities offered by white culture. Chal takes his father's advice—studying at the local government grade school, going to the state university, serving as a pilot in the Army Air Corps, and hiding and denouncing his Indian blood—but he is never happy. Thus, blood quantum is an essential thematic element of the novel (readers should note how often Mathews uses the word *red* in the novel, both to denote blood and "Indianness").

Moving away from the theme of blood quantum, one important early (chapter 4) scene in the novel offers readers a microcosmic example of another theme in the work—the encroachment of white settlers onto Indian lands and the effects of such. Chal and his friends enjoy visiting a swimming hole in the summer when all the Indians come to the Agency to collect their money. During one visit, the fun is interrupted when a group of white kids show up at the swimming hole, strip down, and splash into the water: "The Indian boys went on playing but Chal felt very annoyed with the intrusion, and he told little Running Elk and Sun-on-His-Wing that he was going because the white boys stared so and made so much noise." Chal even feels that the naked bodies of the white boys "were indecent in some inscrutable way" (36). For a while, the Indian boys "pretended not to see them, but were so fascinated by some of the things they heard that they lost interest in their game" (36). Mathews's point should be clear enough—as white colonizers make contact with Natives, there is interruption. Values and language change, and it's no coincidence that the Indian boys lose interest in what they've already been doing for years when they hear the talk and feel the presence of the white boys. Mathews has given readers an example of the effects of colonization in miniature. The general white, Euro-American influence on Native Americans has been the same since the process of colonization began more than 500 years ago.

Chal does eventually return home to his people after his father's death (murder or suicide), but the white influence on him has been too great. After college, the war, and life in the white world, he takes part in a traditional sweat-lodge ceremony, an unsuccessful attempt to return to the traditional ways of the full-bloods. But after all, Chal is a mixed-blood Osage, and his promise to his mother that he will go to law school at the end of the novel reflects the historical movement of young Indians away from the reservations and traditional values into the white Euro-American world.

SOURCES

Debo, Angie. *And Still the Waters Run: The Betrayal of the Five Civilized Tribes.* Princeton, N.J.: Princeton University Press, 1940.

Mathews, John Joseph. *Sundown.* Norman: University of Oklahoma Press, 1988.

Owens, Louis. "Maps of the Mind: John Joseph Mathews and D'Arcy McNickle." In *Other Destinies: Understanding the American Indian Novel,* 49–89. Norman: University of Oklahoma Press, 1992.

Parker, Robert Dale. "Nothing to Do: John Joseph Mathews's *Sundown* and *Restless Young Indian Men.*" In *The Invention of Native American Literature,* 19–50. Ithaca, N.Y.: Cornell University Press, 2003.

James Mayo

SURI, MANIL (1959–)

SURI, MANIL (1959–) Manil Suri, author of *The Death of Vishnu* (2001), sees the novel as part of a projected trilogy. Although many Asian-American writers use mythical figures to express contrast, contradiction, and biculturalism, Suri uses a homeless man named for the Hindu god Vishnu, the preserver. The novel takes place over a 24-hour period and is set in a Bombay apartment building. The homeless Vishnu lies dying on the steps of the building and, as he loses consciousness, believes he really is the god Vishnu and thus privy to the conversations among the apartment dwellers on all three floors; he feels that he knows what is happening to all of them as well. As the novel unfolds, the reader also gains access to the interior lives of these characters—the Astanis and the Pathaks, warring over their shared kitchen on the first floor; the Jalal family, the only Muslims, on the second; and the reclusive but forever grieving widower, Mr. Taneja, on the third. Perhaps the genius in this novel is in the author's lack of anger or condescension as he reveals the foibles and petty vanities of his characters. As with many characters in a William FAULKNER novel, the reader can appreciate the essential humanity of each.

Suri was born in July 1959, in Bombay to Ram Lal, a film music director, and Prem (Bindra) Suri, a schoolteacher and social worker. He received his bachelor's of science degree from the University of Bombay in 1979 and both master's (1980) and doctoral degrees in mathematics (1983) from Carnegie Mellon University. Currently a professor of mathematics at the University of Maryland at Baltimore Country, Suri was stunned at the attention and awards his book received. (*The Death of Vishnu* was a finalist for the PEN/Faulkner Award and the Hemingway Foundation/PEN Award for first fiction.) Manil's storytelling abilities recall those of Bernard MALAMUD and Isaac Bashevis SINGER. He is working on the next two books in the trilogy: *The Life of Shiva* and *The Birth of Brahma.*

NOVEL

The Death of Vishnu. New York: W. W. Norton, 2001.

SOURCES

Budzynski, Brian. Review of *The Death of Vishnu, The Review of Contemporary Fiction* 21, no. 12 (Summer 2001): 173.

Mathias, Anita. Review of *The Death of Vishnu, Commonweal* 128, no. 21 (December 7, 2001): 23.

SUTTREE CORMAC McCARTHY (1979)

SUTTREE CORMAC McCARTHY (1979) *Suttree,* published as Cormac McCARTHY's fourth novel, is a masterpiece, a book that Hal Crowther says will be regarded in the future as "a benchmark of literacy," just as *The Sound and the Fury* is now (37). *Suttree* combines a picaresque plot and structure with profound social, psychological, and spiritual themes narrated in an extreme style that John Ditsky observes "simply goes beyond FAULKNER" (2). Written in the genre of the Southern grotesque, this novel represents the culmination of McCarthy's Southern works before he began exploring the western genre in such best-selling novels as *All the Pretty Horses.* Like McCarthy's other early works, *Suttree* shares an Appalachian setting, but atypically it is an urban novel, set primarily in and around Knoxville.

The novel's protagonist, Cornelius Suttree, has rejected his father's middle-class values and has instead embraced a life of voluntary poverty, choosing to live on a shanty boat on the Tennessee River and choosing to scrape out a bare-subsistence living by fishing. His adventures involve his interaction with scores of impoverished, variously disabled oddballs and misfits inhabiting a Knoxville ghetto known as McAnally Flats. One of these miscreants, the hapless and hilarious Gene Harrogate, is at first the focus of his own plot, making him a kind of secondary protagonist.

The novel tracks Suttree's life from 1950 until 1955 as he seeks to understand himself and his relation to his past. He contemplates vivid memories of his childhood as an altar boy and a parochial school student as well as memories of his relatives and stories about his ancestors. He visits important sites from his childhood and studies an old family photo album for clues to his identity. As an adult he drinks excessively, gets drawn into barroom brawls, has repeated run-ins with the police, serves time in a correctional facility, lives for a while with a prostitute, obsesses over the death of his stillborn twin, and at times even considers suicide. He indicates that he is a lapsed Catholic, but he clearly regards a spiritual search as an important part of the business of his life. His religious quest, which ultimately results in three mystical experiences, is illuminated by existential philosophy (Longley, Prather, Shelton), by Native American spiritual beliefs (Spencer 2000, 100–107), by Buddhist philosophy, and by William James's book *The Varieties of Religious Experience.* Suttree's mystical experiences help reveal his progress toward psychological health and spiritual enlightenment (Spencer 2000, 87–92).

Suttree's living in voluntary poverty may be viewed as a Thoreauvian attempt to live life fully and authentically—even heroically. Although he has abandoned his wife and son (as did the Buddha), he establishes such caring ties with a number of the needy denizens of McAnally that he functions almost as a volunteer social worker, making sure that his friends have shelter, food, warmth, and other necessities. He expertly adapts his language and his manner to his audience so that he is able to bridge the usual societal barriers (Spencer 2003, 18–24). Ironically, although he himself is a social dropout, he serves to bring others into a community.

Much of the novel's rich humor centers on the absurd schemes of Gene Harrogate, whom Suttree first meets in the workhouse after Harrogate is arrested for practicing perversion in a melon patch. The novel's outrageous comedy also includes an abundance of scatological and grotesque elements, which situate it in the tradition of Rabelaisian satire (Canfield, 666–667, 686–692). McCarthy takes satiric aim both at the pursuit of money and power and at the failings of the organized church. Suttree resists Harrogate's doomed enterprises but at times becomes involved in order to rescue his clownish friend from his predicaments.

The most persistent, heated critical debate about this novel concerns the issue of Suttree's development as a character. Some view Suttree as stagnant, as someone who learns little, who fails to mature, and who at the end of the novel is essentially unchanged. These read-

ers often consider Suttree as a less-than-sympathetic character, and they are likely to view his departure from Knoxville at the end of the novel as one more instance of a possible tendency toward escape. Other readers view Suttree's leaving as one of many signs that he has significantly changed. The end of the novel is in fact filled with symbols of transformation. Suttree takes a decisive step when he commits his most serious act of civil disobedience in protest over the police's treatment of his black friend Ab Jones. While the police pursue his friend on foot, Suttree steals their cruiser and launches it into the Tennessee River, which functions as a complex symbol of nature, waste, and the passage of time. Suttree's gesture of rebellion is in vain, however, as he learns later that Ab has died in jail—one of many deaths of family and friends that Suttree must face and cope with. His awareness of death intensifies still further when, soon afterward, he nearly dies of typhoid fever and in his delirium confronts his own mortality. This last mystical experience helps Suttree allay his fear of death and his acute discomfort over feeling a sense of dual identity. After dreading throughout the novel that he is haunted by a host of doppelgangers, Suttree finally concludes "that there is one Suttree and one Suttree only" (461). McCarthy further emphasizes a death/rebirth motif by depicting Suttree discovering a corpse in his own bed, a kind of pseudo-death. McCarthy's fisherman also relinquishes the good-luck charms that he has been carrying and decides to trust instead his own heart. As he leaves town and leaves his former life behind, houses are being razed to make way for a new highway through Knoxville—a final exterior symbolization of Suttree's interior transformation.

SOURCES

Canfield, J. Douglas. "The Dawning of the Age of Aquarius: Abjection, Identity, and the Carnivalesque in Cormac McCarthy's *Suttree,*" *Contemporary Literature* 44, no. 4 (2003): 664–696.

Crowther, Hal. *Cathedrals of Kudzu: A Personal Landscape of the South.* Baton Rouge: Louisiana State University Press, 2000.

Ditsky, John. "Further into Darkness: The Novels of Cormac McCarthy," *Hollins Critic* 18 (1981): 1–11.

Jarrett, Robert L. *Cormac McCarthy.* New York: Twayne, 1997.

Longley, John Lewis, Jr. "*Suttree* and the Metaphysics of Death," *Southern Literary Journal* 17 (1985): 79–90.

McCarthy, Cormac. *Suttree*. New York: Random House, 1979.

Prather, William. "Absurd Reasoning in an Existential World: A Consideration of Cormac McCarthy's *Suttree*." In *Sacred Violence: A Reader's Companion to Cormac McCarthy,* edited by Wade Hall and Rick Wallach, 103–114. El Paso: Texas Western Press, 1995.

Spencer, William C. "Altered States of Consciousness in *Suttree*," *Southern Quarterly* 35, no. 2 (1997): 87–92.

———. "The Seventh Direction, or Suttree's Vision Quest." In *Myth, Legend, Dust: Critical Responses to Cormac McCarthy,* edited by Rick Wallach, 100–107. Manchester, England: Manchester University Press, 2000.

———. "Suttree, Linguistic Chameleon," *POMPA* (2003): 18–24.

William C. Spencer

T

TAN, AMY (RUTH) (1952–) Amy Tan exploded onto the literary scene with her first novel, *The Joy Luck Club* (1989). That novel became an instant success with both the critics and the reading public, remaining on the *New York Times* best-seller list for nine months and becoming standard fare in American university literature classes; it was nominated for both Book Critics Circle and *Los Angeles Times* awards. Tan has become well-known not only for her complex portraits of Chinese and Chinese-American characters but also for her depiction of the relationships between mothers and daughters, especially the generational, cultural, and geographical differences between Chinese-immigrant mothers and American-born daughters. Together with Maxine Hong Kingston, Tan opened the way for Asian-American authors, although her work is also in the tradition of such writers as Anzia Yezierska, Edith Wharton, and Toni Morrison. Her lyrical, imagistic explorations of emotional conflict, loss and hope, differences and reconciliations, are frequently punctuated by a sense of humor.

Amy Tan was born on February 19, 1952, in Oakland, California, to John Yuehan, a Baptist minister and electrical engineer, and Daisy Li Bing Zi Tan, a vocational nurse. She was educated at San Jose State University, earning both a bachelor's degree (1973) and a master's (1974). After more than a decade as an educational administrator and freelance writer, Tan began publishing short stories. *The Joy Luck Club*, too, is a skillfully narrated collection of interwoven stories set in San Francisco in the post–World War II era that evokes the tensions among four pairs of mothers and daughters: Suyuan and Jing-mei "June" Woo, An-mei and Rose Hsu, Lindo and Waverly Jong, and Ying-ying and Lena St. Clair. At the death of her mother, Suyuan, Jing-Mei takes her place in the Joy Luck Club, a mahjongg club to which her mother had belonged, and the group finances her trip to China to meet her family; Jing-Mei, like the other daughters, gradually acknowledges her mother's strengths and her own bicultural heritage. Tan's second novel, *The Kitchen God's Wife* (1991), features Winnie Louie and her American-born daughter Pearl Brandt. Pearl learns to respect her mother when she learns of Winnie Louie's life in China. There, as Jiang Weili, she survived the painful loss of her own mother, an abusive marriage, and the deaths of three previous children before she escaped to the United States.

The Hundred Secret Senses (1995) relates the tales of two sisters, Chinese-American Olivia Yee Bishop, unhappily married to the Caucasian American Simon Bishop, and her Chinese half-sister Kwan, who is endowed with the "hundred secret senses" that enable her to speak with spirits. Together the two sisters travel to China where, Kwan believes, they had lived together in previous lives in the mid-19th century. In Tan's most recent novel, *The Bone Setter's Daughter* (2001), Ruth Young attempts to come to terms with her mother's mysterious Chinese past. Luling, like Tan's own mother, suffers from Alzheimer's disease.

Amy Tan lives with her husband, Louis M. DiMattei, a tax attorney, in San Francisco and New York. Her book *The Opposite of Fate: A Book of Musings* (2003) contains essays that explore aspects of Tan's own life. In 2005, Tan published her novel *Saving Fish from Drowning*.

NOVELS

The Bonesetter's Daughter. New York: Putnam, 2001.

The Hundred Secret Senses. New York: Putnam, 1995.

The Joy Luck Club. New York: Putnam, 1989.

The Kitchen God's Wife. New York: Putnam, 1991.

Saving Fish from Drowning. New York: Putnam, 2005.

The Year of No Flood. New York: Putnam, 1995.

SOURCES

Dooley, Susan. "Mah-Jongg and the Ladies of the Club," *Book World Washington Post,* 5 March 1989, p. 7.

Dorris, Michael. "Mother and Daughters," *Chicago Tribune-Books,* 12 March 1989, pp. 1, 11.

Henderson, Katherine Usher. "Interview with Amy Tan." In *Inter/View: Talks With America's Writing Women,* edited by Mickey Pearlman and Katherine Usher Henderson, 15–22. Lexington: University Press of Kentucky, 1990.

Heung, Marina. "Daughter-Text/Mother-Text: Matrilineage in Amy Tan's *Joy Luck Club,*" *Feminist Studies* 19, no. 3 (Fall 1993): 597–613.

Ling, Amy. *Between Worlds: Women Writers of Chinese Ancestry.* New York: Pergamon, 1990.

Palumbo-Liu, David, ed. *The Ethnic Canon: Histories, Institutions, and Interventions,* 174–210. Minneapolis: University of Minnesota Press.

Sau-ling, Cynthia Wong. *Reading Asian American Literatures: From Necessity to Extravagance.* Princeton, N.J.: Princeton University Press, 1993.

Schell, Orville. "Your Mother Is in Your Bones," *The New York Times Book Review,* 19 March 1989, pp. 3, 28.

Seaman, Donna. "The Booklist Interview: Amy Tan," *Booklist,* 1 October 1990, p. 2,567.

See, Carolyn. "Drowning in America, Starving for China," *Los Angeles Times Book Review,* 12 March 1989, pp. 1, 11.

Shear, Walter. "Generational Differences and the Diaspora in *The Joy Luck Club,*" *Critique* 34, no. 3 (Spring 1993): 193–199.

Xu, Ben. "Memory and the Ethnic Self: Reading Amy Tan's *The Joy Luck Club,*" *MELUS* 19, no. 1: 316.

Yglesias, Helen. Review of *The Kitchen God's Wife, The Women's Review of Books,* September 1991, pp. 1, 3–4.

OTHER

Amy Tan. Voices from the Gaps [VG]. Available online. URL: http://www.voices.cla.umn.edu./vg/Bios/entries/tan_amy.htlm. Accessed September 26, 2005.

TAR BABY Toni Morrison (1981) *Tar Baby* is Toni MORRISON's fourth novel and perhaps her most anomalous. It differs from her previous and subsequent works in significant ways: Some of its central characters are white; it is set outside the United States, on the fictional French Caribbean island of Isle des Chevaliers; and it takes place in a time contemporary with the book's publication. Moreover, despite an initially warm reception that thrust the author onto the cover of *Newsweek* magazine and made the book a best-seller, *Tar Baby* has since fallen out of critical favor. Although the novel consists of Morrison's trademark qualities—grand thematic ambitions and a preoccupation with the lives of black women explored in lush, sensuous prose that results in moments of breath-taking lyricism—observers have pointed to its somewhat schematic characterizations; its occasionally intrusive, essayistic narrative voice; and its puzzling conclusion, which leaves the central love story unresolved, as characteristics that make it less successful than Morrison's other novels. Critic Nancy J. Peterson cites factors such as these when she identifies *Tar Baby* as the most critically neglected and least taught of the author's works.

In *Tar Baby* Toni Morrison forgoes the intricate exploration of life in African-American communities characteristic of her other novels. Instead, at the heart of this work is the love story between Jadine Childs, a light-skinned, Sorbonne-educated fashion model, and Son (William Green), a product of the rural South and a fugitive from a murder rap. Their romance takes place amid the fragile interracial and class arrangements at L'Arbe de la Croix, the island home of Valerian Street, a retired white American candy magnate. After Valerian's wife, Margaret, discovers Son hiding in her closet, Valerian invites the rank and disheveled intruder to sit down to dinner with him, gives him a new set of clothes, and sets him up in the guest room. Valerian's behavior horrifies his wife and rankles his servants, Sydney and Ondine Childs (Jadine's aunt and uncle), who view Son as a dangerous "swamp nigger" and resent the high-handed treatment their boss accords to this uncouth stranger. Son's presence soon begins to disrupt the tenuous harmony of L'Arbe de la Croix's plantation-like domestic order and brings simmering personal, cultural, and class antagonisms to the surface.

The narrative hinges largely on the traditional family Christmas dinner Margaret so desperately anticipates. Neither Michael, the Streets' only child, nor the other guests arrive, and the dinner turns explosive after first Son, then Ondine, questions Valerian's firing of Gideon and Therese—natives of the island who work at the house and are known by all but Son as simply "Yardman" and one of the "Marys." After Valerian sacks Ondine for challenging his proprietary rights, she then reveals that she witnessed Margaret abuse Michael when he was a baby. The flare-up sends Son and Jadine into retreat, first to her room and soon to New York. The wake of this domestic storm, however, brings a modest and more equitable recalibration in the power relations between Valerian and his wife, and between the Streets and the Childs.

After the Christmas dinner, however, the novel becomes primarily the story of Jadine and Son's relationship. Through them, Morrison explores the thematic oppositions she has set up between white and black culture, city and country, North and South, and civilization and nature. Initially, their romance assumes fairy tale qualities, but personal and cultural differences quickly complicate the relationship. The more cosmopolitan Jadine feels at home in New York, but Son insists they make an extended visit to Eloe, his all-black hometown in northern Florida, a place he deems the best in the world. Jadine, however, finds Eloe "Paleolithic" and the people "Neanderthal," and, haunted by disturbing dreams and a sense of feminine inadequacy, cuts short her stay and flies back to New York. When Son returns, he and Jadine fight over Eloe, over their future, over white people, and about what it means to be black. Their relationship reaches what seems to be the breaking point when Son accuses Jadine of being a tar baby—an instrument of Valerian's making, a traitor to her race, and a trap laid to emasculate authentically black men like him.

Perhaps because of Son's accusation, some readers have interpreted the novel as a virtual allegory in which Jadine, a cultural orphan duped by the lures of Western civilization, must reconnect with her African-American roots, while Son represents the kind of authentic black-ness missing from Jadine's experience. The novel does much to encourage such a reading, for in many ways both Son and Jadine are less fully realized characters than vehicles for representing opposite sides of the thematic binaries Morrison has set up. Moreover, in contrast to Jadine's chic bitchiness, Son's earthy male sensibility makes him by far the more appealing of the two characters. Yet privileging one character and the values he or she embodies seems to be an interpretive trap Morrison has laid, for doing so in effect reifies the very oppositions the novel consistently seeks to dismantle. Though Jadine's status as cultural orphan serves as a cautionary tale about the price of assimilating too fully into the white American mainstream, Son himself struggles to overcome the romantic view of rural black life that he personifies. As critic Trudier Harris points out, each character shuttles between the multiples roles of the tar-baby folktale, and the novel persistently raises such question as "who is the tar baby, who is trapped, who needs rescue from whom, and whether or not he (or she) effects an escape."

Frustrating though it may be for many readers, the novel's open-ended conclusion, which finds Son back on Isle des Chevaliers in pursuit of Jadine, who has just returned to Paris, thus remains faithful to Morrison's vision throughout the novel. Although the characters have become aware of their need to escape their own ideological traps and cultural deficiencies, it remains unclear whether they will succeed in doing so. *Tar Baby* concludes then not with the resolution of the central romance but rather with the characters poised to confront the contradictions the romance has laid bare.

SOURCES

Gates, Henry Louis, Jr., and K. A. Appiah, eds. *Toni Morrison: Critical Perspectives Past and Present.* New York: Amistad, 1993.

Harris, Trudier. *Fiction and Folklore: The Novels of Toni Morrison.* Knoxville: University of Tennessee Press, 1991.

Kubitschek, Missy Dehn. *Toni Morrison: A Critical Companion.* Westport, Conn.: Greenwood Press, 1998.

McKay, Nellie Y., ed. *Critical Essays on Toni Morrison.* Boston: G. K. Hall, 1985.

Peterson, Nancy J. *Toni Morrison: Critical and Theoretical Approaches.* Baltimore, Md.: Johns Hopkins University Press, 1997.

Samuels, Wilfred D., and Clenora Hudson-Weems. *Toni Morrison*. Boston: Twayne, 1990.

Kevin Quirk

TARKINGTON, BOOTH (BOOTH NEWTON TARKINGTON) (1869–1946)

Booth Tarkington, winner of the Pulitzer Prize for *The Magnificent Ambersons* in 1919 and for *ALICE ADAMS* in 1922 (both novels), also distinguished himself for more than 50 years as an essayist and playwright, in addition to his serialized fiction in such mass-circulation periodicals as *Colliers, Saturday Evening Post,* and *Redbook.* A large number of Tarkington's writings were adapted for early motion pictures by Thomas Edison as well as Warner Brothers and Paramount Pictures. Tarkington wrote about middle-class families and the values familiar to his readers, not just in the Midwest where many of novels take place. He wrote about the value of hard work, the power of ambitious women, and of boyhood. Although Tarkington has been dead for more than 50 years, he is still valued for his insights into the sociocultural aspects of American development and for the careful artistry that characterized his fiction.

Booth Tarkington was born on July 29, 1869, in Indianapolis, Indiana, to John Stevenson Tarkington, a lawyer, and Elizabeth Booth Tarkington. He attended Purdue University (1890) and Princeton University (1891–93) and graduated from neither, but was awarded honorary degrees in 1939 and 1899, respectively. He moved to New York City in 1895, published *The Gentleman From Indiana* in 1899, returned to Indiana, and followed immediately with the popular costume drama *Monsieur Beaucaire* (serialized in *McClure's* in 1899 and published in book form in 1900). Although he moved back to New York in 1902, he returned to Indiana and served in the Indiana House of Representatives (1902–03) and, on June 18, 1902, married Laurel Louisa Fletcher. After their divorce in 1911, Tarkington married Susannah Robinson in 1912. Tarkington went on to write more than 40 novels. His *Growth* Trilogy traces the development of an Indiana town: *The Turmoil* (1915) is about the upwardly mobile and vulgar Sheridan family; *The Magnificent Ambersons* uses the decline of the Amberson family as a microcosm of the historical and cultural development of the nation; and *The Midlander* (1924) (republished in the trilogy as *National Avenue*) depicts Dan Oliphant, a visionary who expands the city but dies amid financial ruin and abandonment by his wife and family. *Alice Adams,* praised by contemporary reviewers as a "book to move the heart and wilt the collar" (Broun, 395), is still admired as a study of a middle-class family and their daughter Alice's unsuccessful attempts to save herself from—and then finally accept—the life of a working-class woman, a typist and stenographer.

Booth Tarkington died on May 19, 1946, in Indianapolis. In addition to his novels and plays, Tarkington published the immensely popular Penrod series, books for children and young adults that chronicled the adventures of a mid-19th-century boy named Penrod Schofield. Begun in 1914, and published collectively in 1931, the books have been ranked with Mark TWAIN'S *Tom Sawyer;* they sold a half-million copies during Tarkington's lifetime. The year before his death, Tarkington received the Howells Medal from the American Academy of Arts and Letters; he was also the recipient of the 1933 Gold Medal from the National Institute of Arts and Letters and the 1942 Roosevelt Distinguished Service Medal. Nearly 40 of his novels and stories were adapted for the movies, including *The Magnificent Ambersons* in 1942, and *Alice Adams* in 1935, both for RKO Radio Pictures. Many of his papers and manuscripts are housed at Princeton University.

NOVELS

Alice Adams. New York: Doubleday, Page, 1921.
Beasley's Christmas Party. New York: Harper & Brothers, 1909.
The Beautiful Lady. New York: McClure, Phillips, 1905.
Cherry. New York: Harper & Brothers, 1903.
Claire Ambler. New York: Doubleday, Doran, 1928.
The Conquest of Canaan: A Novel. New York: Harper & Brothers, 1905.
"The Fascinating Stranger," and Other Stories. New York: Doubleday, Page, 1923.
The Fighting Littles. New York: Doubleday, Doran, 1941.
The Flirt. New York: Doubleday, Page, 1913.
Gentle Julia. New York: Doubleday, Page, 1922.
The Gentleman from Indiana. New York: Doubleday & McClure, 1899.
Growth (contains *The Turmoil, The Magnificent Ambersons,* and *National Avenue*). New York: Doubleday, Page, 1927.

The Guest of Quesnay. New York: McClure, 1908.

"Harlequin and Columbine and Other Stories. New York: Doubleday, Page, 1918.

The Heritage of Hatcher Ide (published serially as *The Man of the Family*). New York: Doubleday, Doran, 1941.

His Own People. New York: Doubleday, Page, 1907.

Image of Josephine. New York: Doubleday, Doran, 1945.

In the Arena: Stories of Political Life. New York: McClure, Phillips, 1905.

Kate Fennigate. New York: Doubleday, Doran, 1943.

Little Orvie. New York: Doubleday, Doran, 1934.

Looking Forward, and Others. New York: Doubleday, Page, 1926.

The Lorenzo Bunch. New York: Doubleday, Doran, 1936.

The Magnificent Ambersons. New York: Doubleday, Page, 1918.

Mary's Neck. New York: Doubleday, Doran, 1932.

The Midlander. New York: Doubleday, Page, 1924, published as *National Avenue* in *Growth.*

Mirthful Haven. New York: Doubleday, Doran, 1930.

Monsieur Beaucaire. (First serialized in *McClure's,* 1899.) Illustrated by C. D. Williams. New York: McClure, Phillips, 1900.

"Monsieur Beaucaire," "The Beautiful Lady," "His Own People," and Other Stories. New York: Doubleday, Page, 1918.

"Mr. White," "The Red Barn," "Hell," and "Bridewater." New York: Doubleday, Doran, 1935.

The Plutocrat: A Novel. New York: Doubleday, Page, 1927.

Presenting Lily Mars. New York: Doubleday, Doran, 1933.

Ramsey Milholland. New York: Doubleday, Page, 1919.

Rumbin Galleries. New York: Doubleday, Doran, 1937.

The Show Piece. New York: Doubleday, 1947.

The Spring Concert. New York: The Ridgeway Company, 1910.

Three Selected Short Novels (contains *Walterson, Uncertain Molly Collicut,* and *Rennie Peddigoe*). New York: Doubleday, 1947.

The Two Vanrevels. New York: McClure, Phillips, 1902.

The Turmoil: A Novel. New York: Harper & Brothers, 1915.

Wanton Mally. New York: Doubleday, Doran, 1932.

Women. New York: Doubleday, Page, 1925.

Young Mrs. Greeley. New York: Doubleday, Doran, 1929.

SOURCES

Boynton, Percy H. *Some Contemporary Americans: The Personal Equation in Literature.* Chicago: University of Chicago Press, 1924, pp. 108–125.

Broun, Heywood. "A Group of Books Worth Reading: 'Alice Adams,' " *The Bookman* LIV, no. 4 (December 1921): 394–395.

Cabell, James Branch. *Beyond Life: Dizain des demiurges.* New York: R. M. McBride, 1919, pp. 277–322.

Clark, Barrett H. *A Study of the Modern Drama: A Handbook for the Study and Appreciation of Typical Plays, European, English, and American, of the Last Three-Quarters of a Century.* New York: Appleton, 1938, pp. 359–410.

Fennimore, Keith J. *Booth Tarkington.* Boston: Twayne, 1974.

Mayberry, Susanah. *My Amiable Uncle: Recollections about Booth Tarkington.* West Lafayette, Ind.: Purdue University Press, 1983.

Phelps, William Lyon. *The Advance of the English Novel.* New York: Dodd, Mead, 1916, pp. 267–301.

Tarkington, Booth. *The World Does Move.* New York: Doubleday, Doran, 1928.

Twentieth-Century Children's Writers. 3rd edition. Detroit, Mich.: St. James Press, 1989, pp. 947–949.

Woodress, James Leslie. *Booth Tarkington: Gentleman from Indiana.* New York: Lippincott, 1955.

TARZAN OF THE APES EDGAR RICE BUR-ROUGHS (1914)

The first of 26 novels in a series, *Tarzan of the Apes* was first serialized in *All-Story Magazine* in 1912. Incorporating BURROUGHS's own views of heredity and environment, his Tarzan is an orphaned, aristocratic English lord raised by apes who combines the physical strength of his jungle home with the intelligence of his "noble blood." Tarzan possesses a remarkable physical and intellectual prowess, but exhibits a vulnerability that derives from the tentativeness of his identity. In contrast to the popular image of a grunting apeman, Tarzan can read English and can speak both English and French as well as animal languages. By the end of the series, he has become a true polyglot, speaking German, Swahili, Arabic, in addition to "lost languages."

The novel begins with the English Lord Greystoke, John Clayton, and his pregnant wife, Alice, finding themselves marooned on an isolated portion of the African coast after a ship's mutiny. The couple survive a year in the wild environment but die after the birth of their child, a son, whom the female ape Kala discovers and exchanges for her own dead baby. She raises him as her own, naming him Tarzan, meaning "white skin." As Tarzan matures he slowly realizes the differences between himself and the other apes and eventually returns to the small hut his parents had built. From the books that were left, Tarzan teaches himself to read and write English, and a knife he finds gives him an advantage over the larger, stronger animals. With technological tools such as the knife and a lasso, combined with his mental superiority, Tarzan defeats his ape father Turkoz and becomes the ruler of his ape tribe.

Tarzan's emotional development is sparked by the arrival of a group of Americans and English who have also been marooned following a ship's mutiny. The group includes Jane Porter and William Clayton, who has inherited the Greystoke title. Tarzan saves the group from wild animals and rescues Jane, who had been abducted by Turkoz. The group is eventually rescued by French soldiers, but one soldier is left, presumed dead. Tarzan nurses the soldier, D'Arnot, back to health, in exchange, D'Arnot teaches Tarzan French. Together they return to civilization and follow Jane to America, where once again Tarzan rescues her. In the end, Tarzan renounces his birthright and Jane and returns to the jungle.

It was not until the 1960s that serious critical attention was focused on the Tarzan series. In the eighties and nineties, Tarzan became a common topic of study in postcolonial studies as well as gender and masculinity studies. Often criticized for its racist, xenophobic, and imperialist undertones, Tarzan can also be seen as a utopian pastoral escape from the urban growth that marked the beginning of the century. Critic Marianna Torgovnick sees Tarzan as a key figure in the primitive movement, claiming that Tarzan "is an attempt to imagine the primitive as a source of empowerment—as a locus for making things anew, to preserve what is worth preserving and change what deserves to be changed." This would seem congruent with Burroughs's aim of creating an ideal masculine figure, one that transcends class, race, and sex. Although there are clear instances of racism in the novel, the only figure who escapes critique is Tarzan himself—the others, including the apes, the African natives, the French soldiers, William Clayton, and even Jane Porter, are subject to Burroughs's criticism.

The success of the novels quickly prompted film versions, the first of which appeared in 1918. The most successful film Tarzan, however, was the 1932 version with Johnny Weismuller as Tarzan the Apeman. The Weismuller films excised all signs of aristocratic origins and ignored Tarzan's intellectual and moral development. This Tarzan is childlike, prelinguistic, and unconcerned with most moral issues found in the novel.

SOURCES

Burroughs, Edgar Rice. *Tarzan of the Apes.* New York: Penguin, 1990.

Cheyfitz, Eric. *The Poetics of Imperialism: Translation and Colonization from The Tempest to Tarzan.* Expanded edition. Philadelphia: University of Pennsylvania Press, 1997.

Jurca, Catherine. *White Diaspora: The Suburb and the Twentieth-Century American Novel.* Princeton, N.J.: Princeton University Press, 2001.

Kasson, John. *Houdini, Tarzan, and the Perfect Man: The White Male Body and the Challenge of Modernity in America.* New York: Hill and Wang, 2001.

Morton, Walt. "Tracking the Sign of Tarzan: Trans-Media Representations of Pop-Culture Icon." In *You Tarzan: Masculinity, Movies and Men,* edited by Pat Kirkham and Janet Thumim, 106–125. New York: St. Martin's, 1993.

Torgovnick, Marianna. *Gone Primitive: Savage Intellects, Modern Lives.* Chicago: University of Chicago Press, 1990.

Eric Leuschner

TAYLOR, PETER (PETER HILLSMAN TAYLOR) (1917–1994)

Although best known for his short fiction, author Peter Taylor received critical acclaim for his novels *A Woman of Means* (1950), *In the Tennessee Country* (1994), and the Pulitzer Prize– and PEN/Faulkner Award–winning *A Summons to Memphis* (1986). Associated with the Southern literary renaissance, Taylor (also a playwright) was concerned with form; he was a meticulous, talented craftsman who wrote tales about family conflict in a changing contemporary South. Although his stories and novels are usually set in Tennessee, and his upper-middle-class characters grapple with the influences of history, ancestry, values, traditions, and the relocation from Southern small towns to cities, Taylor's work is universal. His treatment of troubled relationships with family members, spouses, and professional acquaintances is exemplified in his ironically titled story collection *Happy Families Are All Alike* (1959). More optimistically, Taylor's work is suffused with strong women.

Peter Taylor was born on January 8, 1917, to Matthew Hillsman Taylor and Katherine Baird Taylor, in Trenton, Tennessee, probably his model for the fictional Thornton, Tennessee. Taylor became friends with John Crowe Ransom and Robert Lowell at Kenyon College, from which he graduated in 1940. He briefly attended graduate school at Louisiana State University, then dropped out to serve in the U.S. Army from 1941 to 1945. Taylor and the poet Eleanor Ross were married in 1942. His first novel (Taylor called it a novelette), *A Woman of Means,* concerns Anna Lauterbach, an attractive and wealthy St. Louis widow who marries the widowed father of Quint Dudley. Dudley reflects on his father's courtship and move from rural Tennessee to St. Louis and there discovers secrets and surprises in the home of his stepmother. She feels attracted to her stepson and is eventually diagnosed as "mad" and institutionalized. In *A Summons to Memphis,* Phillip Carver, the protagonist, is called home to Memphis from New York by his two sisters. The 80-year-old widower Mr. Carver, who is about to remarry, is undermined by his middle-aged children whose romances and marriages he had thwarted through his powerful controlling behavior. Taylor's last novel, *In the Tennessee Country,* follows Nathan Longfort, another complex Taylor character, from his protected youth to his life as a historian of the South and the Civil War.

Critics have speculated about whether Taylor's reputation as a short story writer rather than a novelist has denied him his due as one of the premier American writers of the 20th century. He died of pneumonia on November 2, 1994, in Charlottesville, Virginia.

NOVELS

In the Tennessee Country. New York: Knopf, 1994.
A Summons to Memphis. New York: Knopf, 1986.
A Woman of Means. New York: Harcourt, 1950.

SOURCES

Graham, Catherine Clark. *Southern Accents: The Fiction of Peter Taylor.* New York: Peter Lang, 1993.
Griffith, Albert. *Peter Taylor.* Boston: Twayne, 1970; revised, 1990.
Kramer, Victor A. *Andrew Lytle, Walker Percy, Peter Taylor: A Reference Guide.* Boston: G. K. Hall, 1983.
McAlexander, Hubert H. *Conversations with Peter Taylor.* Jackson: University Press of Mississippi, 1987.
McAlexander, Hubert H., ed. *Critical Essays on Peter Taylor.* Boston: G. K. Hall, 1993.
Robinson, David M. *World of Relations: The Achievement of Peter Taylor.* Lexington: University Press of Kentucky, 1998.
Robinson, James Curry. *Peter Taylor: A Study of the Short Fiction.* Boston: Twayne, 1988.
Stephens, Ralph, and Salamon, Linda B., eds. *The Craft of Peter Taylor.* Tuscaloosa: University of Alabama Press, 1995.
Wright, Stuart T. *Peter Taylor: A Descriptive Bibliography, 1934–87.* Charlottesville: University Press of Virginia, 1988.

TELL ME A RIDDLE TILLIE OLSEN (1961)

Published in 1961, the novella *Tell Me a Riddle,* the longest story in the collection also called *Tell Me a Riddle,* recounts a poignant story of an old couple, Eva and David. Married for 47 years, David feels empty inside and tries in vain to persuade Eva to sell their house and join him at a home for old people. Eva finds no other pleasure than staying at her home to do what she has failed to do over the past decades. She is disheartened to realize that their house has been sold and still insists on going home. Neither David nor some of her children understand her until she is diagnosed with cancer. Eva, in her songs about the past, expresses her remembered happiness as well as her regret over not leading a self-fulfilled life. Eva has been living "for people" instead of for herself.

The intriguing title may serve as a clue to the novella. While the grandchildren keep asking their grandmother Eva for a riddle, she cannot meet the demand. The reader can easily detect the contrast between the grandfather's wide knowledge and the grandmother's poor knowledge. What intensifies the irony is that Eva, who has been taking care of the children, should have no idea how to amuse them. If the title *Tell Me a Riddle* is considered a boastful remark from David asserted at Eva to parade his capacity for solving the riddle, the reader would find David facing the challenge of demystifying the riddle in his wife. While David assumes that all kinds of difficult problems could be solved by moving to Haven, he is quite unprepared for the most complex problem of Eva's emotional needs. For 47 years they have been living together as one family, yet it is not until Eva definitely departs from the family that her disappointment is voiced and heard (quite reluctantly at first).

It might be suggested that the anguish in Eva stems from the social and cultural prescription of gender roles. The cultural restrictions for married working-class women prevent them from even having a notion of pursuing other goals than domestic work. The traditional beliefs about women's roles have confined women within a narrow sphere outside which their ideals are hard to reach. Women's life, it may be considered, revolves in daytime around their children and at nighttime around their husbands.

Does this mean that the story is only a woman's tragedy? Apparently, David suffers from insecurity, too, due to Eva's worsening condition. Fortunately, David, archetype of the male, is awakened to his responsibility. This indicates that whether a woman obtains fulfillment or not determines her family's happiness.

SOURCES

Nelson, Kay Hoyle, and Nancy Huse, eds. *The Critical Response to Tillie Olsen.* Westport, Conn.: Greenwood Press, 1994.

Olsen, Tillie. *Tell Me a Riddle.* New York: Delta, 1994.

Li Jin

TEMPLE OF MY FAMILIAR, THE Alice Walker (1989)

In her novel *The Temple of My Familiar,* Alice WALKER weaves a remarkable tapestry of the human condition. Her earlier novels deal primarily with the sense of isolation felt by black women who "are trapped by circumstances and this entrapment is the result of their sense of powerlessness against the structure of the dominant society as well as the fact that they have little understanding of that structure" (Parker-Smith, 479). This novel broadens her scope; she sets out to analyze, dismember, rearrange, reassemble, and perhaps even repudiate the human psyche. It is all humanity that is trapped by circumstances; it is all humanity that no longer listens to its "familiar" nature, as it were, leading to a sense of isolation and abandonment; it is all humanity that is imprisoned in the morass of racial, ethnic, religious, and sexual one-upmanship. Walker wrote *The Temple of My Familiar* after purchasing a multicolored Guatemalan shawl with the words "You all remember!" writ-

ten in Spanish on the cloth (Walker 1997, 116). From there, almost unbidden, came the central theme that is, as Alice Walker says, "about our collusion with the forces that suppress and colonize our spirituality" (Walker 1997, 118). Three seemingly disparate vignettes are artfully interwoven into a seamless whole, leaving the reader with no set answer to the questions posed but with at least a starting point from which to begin the journey toward an answer.

Walker begins this novel in almost typical fashion, showing the oppression of women. These are Indian women in a fictitious South American country. Zede is a young woman caught in the political infighting of her country. The college at which she hopes to get her teaching degree is closed by the government. Soon thereafter, she is arrested for being a Communist (5). While in prison, she becomes pregnant with her daughter Carlotta. Zede and Carlotta escape the slave conditions of the prison for the slave conditions of life as a domestic servant in a school for troubled rich children. Zede and Carlotta flee from this school with the assistance of one of the children, a white American girl named Mary Ann, whom they had helped at an earlier time. They end up in San Francisco living in abject poverty until Carlotta meets, falls in love with, and marries a famous musician named Arveyda.

Suwelo is a young black professional who has come to Baltimore to put his deceased great Uncle Rafe's affairs in order. Suwelo has just finalized his divorce from his wife Fanny Nzingha, who still loves him and waits for him in San Francisco but who does not want to be married to him anymore. While he is waiting for his uncle's house to be sold, he begins looking into his uncle's past and into the history of two of his uncle's friends, Miss Lissie and Mr. Hal, an elderly couple originally from an island off the coast of one of the Southern states. They each begin telling Suwelo their story, which both complements and supports all of the other stories. Most interesting is the part told by Miss Lissie, whose name means "the one who remembers everything" (52) and who claims to have lived many times before and been witness to the worst of humanity as well as the loss of humanity's sense of self.

The last vignette is supplied by Fanny Nzingha, ex-wife of Suwelo, eventual colleague of Carlotta, and most interestingly granddaughter of Miss Celie—a character last seen in another of Alice Walker's novel *The Color Purple.* The reader learns more of what happens to Fanny's mother Olivia, Miss Celie, Shug, and even Miss Celie's husband, Albert. Fanny is able to see and converse with spirits from the past. She travels to Africa to meet her father, Ola, a successful revolutionary no longer wanted by the government he helped put into power, as well as a sister Fanny she never knew about and her father's present wife, Mary Ann, the same woman who helped Zede and Carlotta many years before and who married Ola so she could remain in the country and run the art school she had opened. Fanny tries to reconnect to herself, her humanity, and her familiar.

The Temple of My Familiar is a novel that spans three continents and a great deal of human history. It gives Ms. Walker's view of the sexes and the races and the way they must inevitably relate to each other. She shows many characters, of different races and sexes, how to reach understanding and, for want of a better word, salvation. Although it is not as easy a book to read as *The Color Purple* or *The Third Life of Grange Copeland,* this book is more thought provoking. There are faint echoes throughout the early portions of the book that become loud roars in the last two parts and reveal how everything is connected. Walker takes on all humanity and tries to show how the dispossessed, the unhappy, and the unfulfilled may regain that portion that has been taken from them. With her words, she has re-created that shawl that was the seed for the story and allows everyone to begin the search for his or her ever-elusive familiar.

SOURCES

Parker-Smith, Bettye J. "Alice Walker's Women: In Search of Some Peace of Mind." In *Black Women Writers (1950–1980),* edited by Mari Evans, 478–493. New York: Anchor, 1984.

Walker, Alice. *Anything We Love Can Be Saved: A Writer's Activism.* New York: Random House, 1997.

———. *The Temple of My Familiar.* New York: Pocket Books, 1989.

Lowell Martin

TENDER IS THE NIGHT F. Scott Fitzgerald (1934)

In 1962 Andrew Turnbull wrote of F. Scott Fitzgerald, "He abused his talent, but he couldn't suppress it" (204). This terse fragment of the biographer's sentence neatly summarizes the years of work and revisions Fitzgerald put into the writing and rewriting of *Tender Is the Night,* a novel that evolved through five titles, nearly 20 drafts, and over 5000 manuscript pages.

Fitzgerald's most acclaimed novel is, and likely always will be, *The Great Gatsby.* While *Gatsby* is a remarkable story of the Jazz Age and the brashness, ebullience, and eventual moral disintegration of the young Americans who lived it, *Tender Is the Night* is a thing apart. A number of critics now suggest that *Tender Is the Night* is Fitzgerald's finest work, and the fact that he spent nine years writing and rewriting the novel testifies to the value the author placed upon the story. Today the book is acclaimed as both a cultural portrait of wealthy expatriate life between the wars and a psychologically detailed, complex, and revealing portrait of the handsome, witty psychiatrist Dick Diver and his beautiful, wealthy wife Nicole Warren Diver. The story is told in three parts. Book One, beginning in medias res, focuses on a group of expatriate Americans who are residents of the French Riviera during the 1920s. Book Two tells of an earlier time period in the lives of the protagonists, and Book Three brings their stories to a close.

The novel opens as Rosemary Hoyt, a young American actress, meets the trendsetting Dick Diver and his wife Nicole, formerly his psychiatric patient and now rehabilitated. The Divers are at the nucleus of the expatriate group living in Tarmes, a small town on the French Riviera. Rosemary falls in love with Dick, who is exactly twice her age, but also becomes fond of Nicole and the Divers' two children, Lanier and Topsy. Because readers view the characters through Rosemary's perspective, we see not only the wealth and glamor that attracts her but also the gradual dissolution of that image as an ugly reality emerges to strip away the veneer from their friends. Musician Abe North becomes drunk with increasing frequency; becomes involved in a seamy episode in which a black American, Jules Peterson, is murdered; and is himself eventually killed in a New York City speakeasy. The episode with Jules Peterson, whose body is placed on Rosemary's bed, triggers Nicole's second hysterical relapse (the first had occurred during a party at the Diver villa). Albert McKisco, a writer with an inferiority complex, challenges French-American mercenary Tommy Barban to a duel, and we realize that Nicole's hysteria is linked not only to her past but also to the life she leads with Dick. By the end of Book One, Dick is obsessed with Rosemary, and Nicole is aware of his infatuation.

Book Two of the novel flashes back to earlier periods in the lives of Dick and Nicole, detailing Dick's education, his service during World War I, and the brilliant future that this charismatic doctor and author of medical books expected to enjoy. He meets Nicole while she is being treated at a Zurich psychiatric clinic run by his friends Dr. Dohmler and Dr. Franz Gregorovius. We learn that after her mother's death, when Nicole was 11 years old, her father, Devereux Warren, began a sexual relationship with Nicole, causing a complete mental breakdown by the time she was 16. After Warren committed her to the Zurich clinic, she met, fell in love with, and eventually married Dick and began to return to normalcy. Her breakdowns, first mentioned in Book One, continue after the couple leaves Tarmes for Zurich, where Dick and Franz codirect a psychiatric clinic. These bouts of hysteria are apparently triggered by Dick's preoccupations with young women—including Rosemary, a nameless girl in a bar, and a 15-year-old patient. Nicole eventually overcomes her fears and her dependence on Dick and emerges in Book Three as a strong, independent woman who leaves Dick and falls in love with and marries Tommy Barban.

Book Three of the novel is presented from Nicole's viewpoint, and the reader understands that she has come into her own as a full and independent human being. Dick, on the other hand, failing to control his self-indulgent alcoholism and sexual longings, falls into a downward spiral from the peak of his brilliant psychiatric career. It is no accident that his name is Doctor Dick Diver. The name is pretentious in the form of address ("Doctor"), vulgar in the nickname for Richard, and metaphoric of a dive or a fall from a great height (Stern, 309).

Thematically threaded through the novel is the father-daughter relationship; it underscores the incestuous sexual abuse suffered by the young Nicole Warren at the hands of her father. The prurient preoccupation of older men with girls and women young enough to be their daughters reverberates through the story: Rosemary stars in a film called "Daddy's Girl," Dick is attracted to Rosemary partly because of her youth, a 15-year-old psychiatric patient accuses Dick of seducing her, and Dick is briefly mistaken for the rapist of a five-year-old girl when he is arrested for drunkenness in Milan. Nicole, according to critic William F. Hall, views Dick "as the 'evil' father who seduced her" (621).

On a larger scale, the novel presents Fitzgerald's view of the United States in the years between the two world wars. The possibilities for both success and failure are inherent in the fictional characters: Some, like Nicole and Albert, at first clearly a portrait of the naive and opinionated American, rise to the occasion; others, however, like Abe and Dick, forgo their brilliant potential and step off the stage, Abe dying in a New York City speakeasy and Dick wandering in an alcoholic haze through small towns in upstate New York after a relationship with a 15-year-old girl.

Fitzgerald and his wife Zelda were revered as symbols of youth in the United States of the Roaring Twenties. That these two were icons of the Jazz Age in the years between the two world wars leads many to believe that the lifestyle constituted the author, and many cannot view his writing as something aside from his life. It is true that Fitzgerald based Dick partly on himself and Gerald Murphy, Nicole on Zelda and Sara Murphy, Rosemary on Hollywood starlet Lois Moran, and Tommy on French aviator Edouard Jozan (Moran and Jozan were romantic interests for Scott and Zelda, respectively); it is also true that readers continue to be fascinated by the parallels between Fitzgerald's fiction and his life. Yet the novel is greater than the sum of these parallels.

The fact that the novel was first published in spring 1934, when the United States was experiencing the depths of the Great Depression, spelled disaster for F. Scott Fitzgerald's masterpiece. That the novel had taken so long to write and was a tale of a "golden moment" in the country's brief history was not lost on the readers of 1934. Book purchasers were not in a collective mood to read novels dissecting the lives of the idle rich on the French Riviera. F. Scott and Zelda Fitzgerald had embodied "the golden couple" in the America of the 1920s, much as movie star couples do in these times. Fitzgerald's old friend, Ernest Hemingway, "found the characters in the novel to be beautifully faked case histories rather than people" (Mayfield, 207).

Time, however, has been kind to this novel, which deals realistically with the American and universal issues of alcoholism, sex, wealth, frivolity, and hypocrisy. Fitzgerald felt that wealth made people careless with everything they owned, including other people's affections and admiration for them. In 1934, the American public was perhaps not ready for this message. Part of the American mythology is the belief that if one is good, no matter how one conducts one's life, everything will be fine, and that peace, prosperity, or love is just around the next corner. The 1920s, the decade that brought America the flapper and swing music, was at a confluence of important events. Americans had grown weary of their President, Woodrow Wilson, a Princeton scholar, who led them into World War I. In the war's aftermath, the country retreated into a self-induced stupor and went straight to the business of pursuing the good life about which Fitzgerald and his contemporaries wrote. The critic Milton Stern suggests that, when Fitzgerald as writer is separated from the myth of his life, he becomes a prophet of the sort who is always without honor in his own land or in his own time. *Tender Is the Night* may have been a critical and popular failure because people were uncomfortable with Fitzgerald's exposure of the underlying sickness of society. Unfortunately for the man, but fortunately for the readers who have savored his writing through the past half century, there was much that was true in what Fitzgerald was saying through his novels.

If a microcosm of publishing history can be suggested by one book, *Tender Is the Night* is the place to begin studying. Fitzgerald scholar Matthew Bruccoli spent nearly a year at the Princeton University Library, where the documents and letters of F. Scott Fitzgerald are housed. The extraordinary book *The Composition of Tender Is the Night* is the end result of Bruccoli's research and demonstrates how seriously Fitzgerald took his craft as he kept revising and editing his own manuscripts. In *The Golden Moment: The Novels of F. Scott Fitzgerald,* Milton R. Stern, in a concise summary of the novel's various avatars, states that Bruccoli found "three major versions of the novel, which underwent a total of seventeen drafts (eighteen if one counts the incompletely revised version of the book, published posthumously) . . . revised in five drafts, with a change in title for almost every change in draft: *Our Type, The Boy Who Killed His Mother, The Melarkey Case,* and *The World's Fair"* (Stern, 293).

The title changes show that the concept of the novel was changing as it was being written. *World's Fair,* the original title of 1925, was intended to be a lighthearted look at Americans after the war, enjoying Europe. The original title character, Francis Melarkey, was matricidal, and in 1926 the title evolved into *The Boy Who Killed His Mother.* This title was based on a poem Fitzgerald had written. By the seventh draft, titled *The Drunkard's Holiday,* the protagonist's name had been changed to Dr. Dick Diver, and the book was beginning to resemble more closely the final published version. By 1951, when Fitzgerald's editor, Malcolm Cowley, published a second edition in which events unfolded in chronological order, Fitzgerald had been dead for five years. Cowley, who rearranged the parts and made over 800 corrections, was certain he had Fitzgerald's best interests and intentions in mind. Critical reaction was largely unfavorable, and today, it is the first edition that everyone reads.

For the film of *Tender Is the Night,* Fitzgerald drastically reworked the novel and gave it a happy ending. After Metro-Goldwyn-Mayer rejected the film, Twentieth Century–Fox Studios hired MGM producer Frank Taylor, who brought the manuscript with him. David O. Selznick was in charge of the studio. Jason Robards and Jennifer Jones were cast as the Dick and Nicole Diver in the movie, and *Tender Is the Night* was released in 1962, 22 years after Fitzgerald's death.

SOURCES

Bloom, Harold, ed. *Modern Critical Views: F. Scott Fitzgerald.* New York: Chelsea House, 1985.

Bruccoli, Matthew J. *The Composition of Tender Is the Night*. Pittsburgh: University of Pittsburgh Press, 1963.

Buttitta, Tony. *After the Good Gay Times: Asheville Summer of '35: A Season with F. Scott Fitzgerald*. New York: Viking. 1974.

Callahan, John F. "F. Scott Fitzgerald's Evolving American Dream: The Pursuit of Happiness in *Gatsby, Tender Is the Night,* and *The Last Tycoon,*" *Twentieth Century Literature* (Fall 1996).

Chambers, John B. *The Novels of F. Scott Fitzgerald*. New York: St. Martin's Press, 1989.

deKoster, Katie, ed. *Readings on F. Scott Fitzgerald*. San Diego: Greenhaven Press, 1998.

Epstein, Joseph. "F. Scott Fitzgerald's Third Act," *Commentary*, November 1994.

Evans, Julian. "An American Sublime," *New Statesman*, 28 August 2000.

Fitzgerald, F. Scott. *Tender Is the Night*. New York: Scribner, 1934.

Gaskell, Philip. *A New Introduction to Bibliography*. New Castle, Del.: Oak Knoll Press, 1995.

Hall, William F. "Dialogue and Theme in *Tender Is the Night,*" *Modern Language Notes* 76, no. 7 (November 1961): 616–622.

Hicks, John D., ed. *A History of American Democracy*. Boston: Houghton Mifflin: 1970.

Johns, Adrian.. *The Nature of the Book: Print and Knowledge in the Making*. Chicago: University of Chicago Press, 1998.

Krummel, D. W. *Fiat Lux, Fiat Latebra: A Celebration of Historical Library Functions*. Urbana: University of Illinois Press, 1999.

Mangum, Bryant. *A Fortune Yet: Money in the Art of F. Scott Fitzgerald's Short Stories*. New York: Garland Publishing, 1991.

Mayfield, Sara. *Exiles from Paradise: Zelda and Scott Fitzgerald*. New York: Delacorte Press, 1971.

Nowlin, Michael. "The World's Rarest Work: Modernism and Masculinity in Fitzgerald's *Tender Is the Night,*" *College Literature* (Spring 1998): 60–77.

Phillips, Gene D. *Fiction, Film and Fitzgerald*. Chicago: Loyola University Press, 1968.

Shain, Charles E. *F. Scott Fitzgerald*. Minneapolis: University of Minnesota Press, 1961.

Stern, Milton R. *The Golden Moment: The Novels of F. Scott Fitzgerald*. Urbana: University of Illinois Press, 1970.

Turnbull, Andrew. *Scott Fitzgerald*. New York: Scribner, 1962.

Laurie Howell Hime

TERMS OF ENDEARMENT LARRY McMURTRY (1975)

Larry McMURTRY's *Terms of Endearment* (1975) and its sequel, *The Evening Star* (1992), have been referred to as the "Aurora Greenway novels." In addition, some critics have referred to *Moving On* (1970), *All My Friends Are Going to Be Strangers*, and *Terms of Endearment* as McMurtry's "urban trilogy," distinguishing them from his first three novels—*Horseman, Pass By* (1961), *Leaving Cheyenne* (1963), and *The Last Picture Show*—which in retrospect have then been described as his "rural trilogy." Interestingly, although it does not become the primary setting until *The Last Picture Show*, the town of Thalia is a secondary setting in the first two novels of the "rural trilogy," and although Emma Horton does not become a focal character until *Terms of Endearment*, she does appear in all the novels of the "urban trilogy."

The screen adaptation of *Terms of Endearment* won five Academy Awards, including the awards for Best Picture, Best Actress (Shirley MacLaine as Aurora Greenway), and Best Supporting Actor (Jack Nicholson as Garrett Breedlove). The film is true to the novel, except for the character played by Nicholson, who doesn't exist in the novel. At the center of both the novel and the film adaptation is the relationship between Aurora Greenway and her daughter Emma. For most of Emma's life, the relationship is strained by the differences between them. A widow torn between maintaining her autonomy and continually proving her desirability, Aurora is a paradoxical amalgam of propriety and outrageousness, pragmatism and flightiness, haughtiness and awkwardness. In contrast, Emma is perfectly ordinary, unselfconscious, and quite level-headed.

It is the novel's essential irony that this mother should be so perpetually disappointed by this daughter. When Emma marries an aspiring college professor named Flap Horton, Aurora refuses to attend the wedding, predicting that the marriage will turn out disastrously. For a while, she seems to have been proven wrong as Flap and Emma have three children and, as he becomes established in his academic career, settle into a fairly comfortable life. Even Aurora begins to thaw toward Flap. Then Emma discovers that Flap is having an affair with one of his students, and she herself subsequently has a brief affair with a banker.

Aurora is put in what for her is the especially disconcerting position of being disappointed at having been proven right. Then Emma is diagnosed with the cancer that eventually kills her, and all the antagonisms between Aurora and Flap are put on hold as mother and daughter become absorbed in their need to connect with each other or, more precisely, to become finally comfortable with the deep connection that they have always felt with each other.

SOURCES

Landess, Thomas. *Larry McMurtry.* Southwest Writers Series, No. 23. Austin, Tex.: Steck-Vaughn, 1969.

Linck, Ernestine Sewell. "Larry McMurtry." In *Updating the Literary West,* edited by Max Westbrook, 628–632. Fort Worth, Tex.: Western Literature Association/Texas Christian University Press, 1997.

Neinstein, Raymond L. *The Ghost Country: A Study of the Novels of Larry McMurtry.* Berkeley, Calif.: Creative Arts, 1976.

Nelson, Jane. "Larry McMurtry." In *A Literary History of the American West,* edited by Max Westbrook, 612–621. Fort Worth: Texas Christian University Press, 1987.

Peavy, Charles D. *Larry McMurtry.* Twayne's United States Authors Series, No. 291. Boston: Twayne, 1977.

Reilly, John M. *Larry McMurtry: A Critical Companion.* Westport, Conn.: Greenwood, 2000.

Reynolds, Clay, ed. *Taking Stock: A Larry McMurtry Casebook.* Dallas, Tex.: Southern Methodist University Press, 1989.

Schmidt, Dorey, ed. *Larry McMurtry: Unredeemed Dreams.* Living Author Series, No. 1. Edinburg, Tex.: School of Humanities, Pan American University, 1978, pp. 1–4.

Speidel, Constance. "Whose Terms of Endearment?" *Literature/Film Quarterly* 12, no. 4 (1984): 271–273.

Martin Kich

THEIR EYES WERE WATCHING GOD

Zora Neale Hurston (1937) When Zora Neale Hurston's work was revived by authors and critics in the 1970s, her novel *Their Eyes Were Watching God* was recognized as a classic. Not only is the main character, Janie, a strong African-American female protagonist, but she speaks in her own dialect with her own hard-won wisdom. Like many artists of the Harlem Renaissance, Hurston expressed the desire for mobility, freedom, and voice.

The beginning occurs not just at sundown, but after a death; however, this ending provides the protagonist with a new life. Throughout the narrative, Death is personified and brings transformation that is destructive as well as creative. In fact, each death in the novel heralds Janie's physical journey: Nanny's death signals Janie's departure from home as well as her abandonment of Logan Killicks, Joe's death allows her to leave for the Everglades, and Tea Cake's death sends her back to Eatonville.

Instead of presenting the community as a nurturing environment, Hurston reveals its destructive qualities with which Janie must continually grapple. Janie's first realization of racial difference begins with a photograph of herself in a group of children, a communal mirror. When she returns to Eatonville at the beginning of the novel, women and men watch her with various feelings of envy, judgment, wonder, lust, dismay, condemnation, and curiosity. They had previously failed to help her when she was abused by Joe Starks and insulted her with warnings about her vulnerability to predatory suitors once he had died. Resembling this community is the worker enclave—extreme in love, hate, music, and violence—in the Everglades. When Tea Cake beats Janie, the men and women admire him, and when Janie kills the rabid man in self-defense, they try to destroy her.

The most positive people in Janie's life are Pheoby and Nanny. Pheoby takes the place of the reader. The tale is told to her, and she listens with awe. At the beginning of the novel Nanny tries to nourish Janie's self-respect and self-knowledge, but her material values severely limit her choices for Janie. Panicking over Janie's first kiss, Nanny—with the imagery of the pear tree in a storm—marries her to Brother Logan Killicks. What she wants most for Janie is protection, something that she could not give Janie's mother, who was raped by a teacher. This distrust causes her to abandon even dreams of Janie continuing her education in favor of marriage. All the husbands fall short of Janie's dreams: Logan desires a workhorse for his land, Joe wants a silent clerk for his store, and Tea Cake puts Janie to work picking beans in the Everglades. Despite the negative influences of the community, husbands, and a racist America, Janie perseveres and emerges more sure of herself than ever. Throughout the narrative, images of rich earth and barren earth, nature, and animals reflect individuals' situations. Household imagery indicates the difficulty of everyday roles.

Despite her husbands' needs to exploit, silence, and possess her, Janie is the one who survives. She maintains her confidence in herself and resists the temptation to judge. " 'You got tuh go there tuh know there,' " she asserts (183). At the end of the novel, her solitude is not pitiable but rich with reflection and memory. Through a combination of third-person narrative, first-person narrative, and dialogue, Janie's story encompasses all points of view and applies natural images of growth and decay to the cycles and processes of her life.

SOURCES

Bell, Bernard W. *The Afro-American Novel and Its Tradition.* Amherst: University of Massachusetts Press, 1987.

Bloom, Harold, ed. *Zora Neale Hurston.* New York: Chelsea, 1986.

Carby, Hazel. "It Jus Be's Dat Way Sometime: The Sexual Politics of Women's Blues." In *Feminisms: An Anthology of Literary Theory and Criticism,* edited by Robyn R. Warhol, and Diane Price Herndl, 746–758. New Brunswick, N.J.: Rutgers University Press, 1991.

Gates, Henry Louis. *The Signifying Monkey: A Theory of Afro-American Literary Criticism.* New York: Oxford University Press, 1988.

Hemenway, Robert. *Zora Neale Hurston: A Literary Biography.* Urbana: University of Illinois Press, 1977.

Hill, Lynda. *Social Rituals and the Verbal Art of Zora Neale Hurston.* Washington, D.C.: Howard University Press, 1996.

Howard, Lillie P. *Zora Neale Hurston.* Boston: Twayne, 1980.

Lowe, John. *Jump at the Sun: Zora Neale Hurston's Cosmic Comedy.* Urbana: University of Illinois Press, 1994.

Walker, Alice. *In Search of Our Mothers' Gardens.* New York: Harcourt, 1983.

———, ed. *I Love Myself: A Zora Neale Hurston Reader.* New York: Feminist Press, 1979.

Wall, Cheryl A. "Zora Neale Hurston (1891–1960). Introduction." In *The Gender of Modernism: A Critical Anthology,* edited by Bonnie Kime Scott, 170–174. Bloomington: Indiana University Press, 1990.

Washington, Mary Helen. *Invented Lives: Narratives of Black Women 1860–1960.* Garden City, N.Y.: Doubleday, 1987.

Willis, Susan. *Specifying: Black Women Writing the American Experience.* Madison: University of Wisconsin Press, 1987.

Kerri A. Horrine

THEM JOYCE CAROL OATES (1969) When OATES received the National Book Award for this novel, it was the first major acknowledgment of her stature as one of the most significant American novelists and short story writers of her generation. *them* was Oates's fourth novel. Unlike the early work of other novelists that has seemed overvalued in retrospect, *them* has continued to be perceived as a remarkably mature work, exhibiting considerable technical invention and great thematic complexity. Still, it is a tribute to Oates's continuing development as a novelist that her achievement in *them* has not overshadowed her later work. In *them,* Oates synthesizes a variety of novelistic forms. The book is a naturalistic coming-of-age story, depicting the traumas that shaped the life experience of its main character, Maureen Wendall. It is a family saga, chronicling a slice of American social history through the microcosm of the Wendall family. It is an urban novel, presenting the recent history of Detroit and charting its decline from an industrial powerhouse to an urban war zone, a postindustrial wasteland. Lastly, *them* is a work of documentary realism, in which Oates herself appears as a character, the writing teacher to whom Maureen Wendall confides parts of her life story.

The novel covers the events of three decades, from 1937 to 1967. The main characters besides Maureen Wendall are her mother, Loretta, and her brother, Jules. Each of these character's lives is not so much shaped, as it is punctuated by nightmarish events. While in her midteens, Loretta sleeps with a boy she loves. When she wakes in the morning, he is lying dead beside her. Her brother, Brock, has murdered the boy in his sleep and then run off. Howard Wendall, the policeman who comes to investigate the murder, feels sorry for Loretta and manages to cover up the details of the crime. Later that day she sleeps with him, and shortly afterward, they marry. But the marriage is strained by differences in temperament, by the demands of relatives, and by Howard's dismissal from the police force for corruption. After a failed retreat to a farm, Loretta leaves Howard for good and returns with their three children to the city. Lost in tawdry romantic dreaming, Loretta remarries, but she is too unstable to be emotionally consistent in her relationships with her new husband or with her children.

Television becomes her palliative, but as Detroit is convulsed in violent riots, even television fails her as she recognizes her estranged son Jules among the rioters.

Although he can find no work beyond menial jobs, Jules becomes passionately infatuated with a young woman from a "better" family, whose main reason for becoming involved with him seems to be to spite her parents. They run off to Texas, but when Jules becomes very ill, she deserts him at a seedy motel. After she marries someone more acceptable to her parents, she and Jules do, however, resume their relationship. But this time around, it ends even more disastrously than it had in Texas. Overcome by a combination of guilt and self-pity, Jules's lover shoots him and very nearly kills him. From this point on, Jules's cynicism overwhelms the last vestiges of the romantic daydreams that had provided a reprieve from the dull routine of his daily existence. He becomes a political radical, an anarchist, but he is clearly driven more by personal rage than by any broader sense of outrage at social inequities or injustices. As the riots consume Detroit, he acts as an informal spokesperson for the rioters, trying to define the rioting as an expression of a political cause. Yet the crimes that he personally commits in the course of the riots seem largely rooted in just plain meanness.

Outwardly a demure Catholic schoolgirl, Maureen begins to prostitute herself with businessmen after school. In the process, she not only builds a cache of money that might eventually allow her to escape her family's impoverishment, she also finds a mode of self-expression that permits her to feel separate from her family, to feel that there is a part of her that is not "them." She begins to recognize that the real predators are not the others who live in their tough neighborhood, but the members of her family who, lacking other sustenance, feed on each other's souls. But, when her stepfather discovers what she has been doing, he beats her terribly. For almost a year, she lies in bed in a catatonic state. When she finally emerges from it, she sets out to construct a life for herself. She begins taking college courses, including a writing course with Oates, and she purposefully seduces another married English teacher, with whom she creates a modestly comfortable home life. It isn't a perfect situation—he

has three children to support from his first marriage—but it is better than anything else Maureen has known. When Jules suddenly appears at her door, she makes it clear to him that her new life no longer has any room in it—her heart no longer has any room in it—for anyone from her former life.

SOURCES

Bevilacqua, Winifred Farrant. " 'All of Detroit Is Melodrama': Joyce Carol Oates' them." In *La Citta delle Donne: Immaginario Urbana e Letteratura del Novecento,* edited by Oriana Palusci, 123–139. Turin: Tirrenia, 1992.

DeCurtis, Anthony. "The Process of Fictionalization in Joyce Carol Oates's them," *International Fiction Review* 6 (1979): 121–128.

Giles, James R. "Suffering, Transcendence, and Artistic 'Form': Joyce Carol Oates's them," *Arizona Quarterly* 32 (1976): 213–226.

Keeble, Robert. "Depersonalization in Joyce Carol Oates's them," *Notes on Contemporary Literature* 28 (March 1998): 2–3.

Pinsker, Sanford. "The Blue Collar Apocalypse or Detroit Bridge's Falling Down: Joyce Carol Oates' them," *Descant: The Texas Christian University Literary Journal* 23, no. 4 (1979): 35–47.

Martin Kich

THEROUX, PAUL (PAUL EDWARD THEROUX) (1941–)

Paul Theroux, novelist, short story writer, travel writer, and playwright, explores the world of late-20th-century expatriates in a plethora of countries. Continuing in the tradition of Nathaniel HAWTHORNE, Henry JAMES, and Edith WHARTON, also expatriates, Theroux recounts the comedy and tragedy of both the expatriates and of the indigenous people with whom they interact. Indeed, his novels are set in various locales: Africa, Asia, England, and the United States. In his review of Theroux's novel, *My Secret History* (1989), Gary Krist notes that "Theroux's life involves plenty of interesting sex in exotic foreign climes, [which] ensures that this novel, like everything he writes, entertains even as it gathers weight" (Krist, 40). In addition, he remains fascinated with the dual personality or secret self that he employs in a number of his more recent novels: *My Secret History, Chicago Loop* (1990), and *My Other Life* (1996). Recurrent violence also surfaces in Theroux's work, in the form of terrorism and physical violence perpetrated by warped, bizarre, or repressed people; these desires often result in guilt or despair on the part of his unhappy protagonists. Much of Theroux's work can be interpreted as parables or illuminated fictive commentaries on the weaknesses and pitfalls of characters living in the postmodern world. In addition to the Whitbread Prize for Best Novel for *Picture Palace* (1978) and the James Tait Black Memorial Prize for Best Novel for *The Mosquito Coast* (1982), Theroux has garnered two American Book Award nominations: for *The Mosquito Coast* and *The Old Patagonian Express: By Train through the Americas* (1979).

Paul Theroux (rhymes with "skiddoo") was born on April 10, 1941, in Medford, Massachusetts, to Albert Eugene Theroux and Anne Dittami Theroux, a teacher. He was educated at the University of Massachusetts, earning his B.A. in 1963. He joined the Peace Corps, and lived in Malawi, Uganda, Singapore, and London, where he still lives. After meeting the novelist V. S. Naipaul, who became his mentor and friend, Theroux published his first novel, *Waldo,* and married Anne Castle, a British journalist, in 1967. In *Waldo,* as in his two subsequent novels, *Fong and the Indians* (1968) and *Girls at Play* (1969), he portrays alien "travelers" seeking their identities in exotic foreign settings. The English Waldo engages in furious activity as he seeks to avoid imprisonment, first in a school for delinquents and later in a glass cage in a night club. The Chinese Catholic Sam Fong, who lives in Africa, finds that he shares with the Indians their status as objects of racial and cultural prejudice. The young American of *Girls at Play* is so disillusioned with the prejudice she finds in Malawi that she commits suicide. *Jungle Lovers* (1971), also set in Malawi, features Massachusetts born Calvin Mullet, who attempts with another man to alter the lives of the Malawians, with predictably unsuccessful results.

Saint Jack (1973) features Jack Flowers, a pimp and a writer, like Mullet, living in Singapore and frustrated with a meaningless existence that he cannot change. *The Black House* (1974), partly a ghost story, underscores the universality of haunted locales. Alfred Munday finds that leaving haunted Africa for England leads him to another haunted house, this time in the English countryside. *The Family Arsenal* (1976), set in London,

features, with almost certain parodic intent, an American family of bombers whose substitution of violence and death mocks the communal comfort and life-sustaining image of the normal family and its relationship to the neighborhood. In *Picture Palace* (1978), set in Massachusetts, Maude Coffin Pratt, a photographer, reveals her unconsummated incestuous love for her brother, who slept with their sister; Maude's repression of this verboten love has colored her entire life.

The Mosquito Coast (1982) won international acclaim for Theroux's presentation of his protagonist, obsessive inventor Allie Fox, whose paranoid belief in an American nuclear disaster sends him and his family to a community in a Honduran jungle. Because of individualism and technology, the jungle ceases to be a haven. *Half Moon Street* contains *Doctor Slaughter* (published separately first) and *Doctor DeMarr,* doubles or doppelgangers living in England and the United States, respectively. Frequently compared to Robert Louis Stevenson's *Dr. Jekyll and Mr. Hyde,* Edgar Allan Poe's "William Wilson," or Joseph Conrad's "The Secret Sharer," the novellas explore the hypocrisy and self-absorption that can result in a disintegrating personality. *O-Zone* (1986) is a dystopian novel whose plot springs from another nuclear disaster, this time in New York City; the New Yorker character flees to the American heartland only to discover that it is divided into haves and have-nots. He learns a lesson from "Fizzy" Fisher, a young boy who demonstrate his ability to transcend the old order. *My Secret History* (1989), although told in the first person and based on Theroux's life, blends fictional and mythical techniques and themes that transcend autobiography or memoir. *Chicago Loop* (1990) revisits the theme of sexual obsession that characterizes some of Theroux's early novels. After picking up and murdering a prostitute, Parker Jagoda punishes himself by walking about in her clothes until he inevitably meets the same fate. *Millroy the Magician* (1994), like many Theroux characters, mistakenly tries to impose his own version of order and truth on the world.

His most recent book is *The Stranger at the Palazzo D'Oro and Other Stories* (2004). A number of his novels have been adapted to the screen in various formats: *Saint Jack* was adapted as a motion picture, directed by

Peter Bogdanovich, in 1979; *The Mosquito Coast* was adapted as a motion picture, written by Paul Schrader, directed by Peter Weir, starring Harrison Ford, Warner Bros., in 1986; *Doctor Slaughter* was adapted as the motion picture *Half Moon Street,* written by Edward Behr and Bob Swain, directed by Swain, starring Sigourney Weaver and Michael Caine, RKO/Fox, in 1986; *London Embassy* was adapted as a television miniseries in the United Kingdom, written by T. R. Bowen and Ian Kennedy Martin, directed by David Giles III and Ronald Wilson, in 1987.

NOVELS AND NOVELLAS

The Black House. Boston: Houghton Mifflin, 1974.
Chicago Loop. New York: Random House, 1990.
The Collected Short Novels. London: Penguin Books, 1999.
Doctor Slaughter. London: Hamish Hamilton, 1984.
The Family Arsenal. Boston: Houghton Mifflin, 1976.
Fong and the Indians. Boston: Houghton Mifflin, 1968.
Girls at Play. Boston: Houghton Mifflin, 1969.
Half Moon Street: Two Short Novels (contains *Doctor Slaughter* and *Doctor DeMarr*). Boston: Houghton Mifflin, 1984.
Hotel Honolulu. Boston: Houghton Mifflin, 2000.
Jungle Lovers. Boston: Houghton Mifflin, 1971.
Kowloon Tong. Thorndike, Maine: G. K. Hall, 1997.
Millroy the Magician. New York: Random House, 1994.
The Mosquito Coast. (With woodcuts by David Frampton.) Boston: Houghton Mifflin, 1982.
Murder in Mount Holly. London: Alan Ross, 1969.
My Other Life. Boston: Houghton Mifflin, 1996.
My Secret History. New York: Putnam, 1989.
O-Zone. New York: Putnam, 1986.
Picture Palace. Boston: Houghton Mifflin, 1978.
Saint Jack. Boston: Houghton Mifflin, 1973.
Waldo. Boston: Houghton Mifflin, 1967.

SOURCES

Blank, Jonah. "Feuding Literary Titans," *U.S. News and World Report,* 10 August 1998, p. 39.
Coale, Samuel. *Paul Theroux.* Boston: Twayne, 1987.
Gray, Rockwell. "The Pungent Smell of a Rancid Friendship." *Christian Science Monitor,* 8 October 1998, B-7.
Howe, Nicholas. "Booking Passage," *New Republic,* 6 August 2001, pp. 34–42.
Johnson-Cramer, Sharon. "A British Family Divides as Hong Kong Returns to China," *Christian Science Monitor,* 25 June 1997, p. 15.

Krist, Gary. "Me, Myself, and I," *New Republic,* 17–24 July 1989, pp. 40–41.
Levi, Peter. "Ever So Slightly Interesting," *Spectator,* 28 October 1995, p. 36.
Lewis, Maggie. "Shallow Voyagers through a Vivid Future Landscape," *Christian Science Monitor,* 24 November 1986, p. 30.
Read, Piers Paul. "Whose Life Is It Anyway?" *Spectator,* 6 July 1996, p. 32.
Ritts, Morton. "Double Vision," *Maclean's,* 14 August 1989, p. 55.
Shapiro, Laura. "A Tale of Two Giant Egos," *Newsweek,* 10 August 1998, p. 45.
Solomon, Jay. "Observer Status," *Far Eastern Economic Review,* 5 September 1996, pp. 46–47.
Theroux, Paul, and Julie Baumgold. "Fellow Traveler," *Esquire,* September 1996, pp. 184, 182.
Updike, John. "The Book as Cook Book," *New Yorker,* 15 March 1994, pp. 92–94.
Winchester, Simon. "Tonga-Tied," *Far Eastern Economic Review,* 3 December 1992, pp. 32–33.

OTHER

Audio Interview with Paul Theroux. Wired for Books. Available online. URL: http://wiredforbooks.org/paultheroux. Accessed September 22, 2005.
An Interview with Paul Theroux. The Atlantic Online. Available online by subscription. URL: http://www.theatlantic.com/unbound/bookauth/ptint.htm. Accessed September 22, 2005.
Paul Theroux. Houghton Mifflin. Available online. URL: http://www.HoughtonMifflinmifflinbooks.com/catalog/authordetail.cfm?authorID=1043. Accessed September 22, 2005.
Paul Theroux. The Salon Interview, by Dwight Garner. Salon.com. Available online. URL: http://www.salonmagazine.com/weekly/interview960902.html. Accessed September 22, 2005.
Worldguide Interview: Paul Theroux. Available online. URL: http://www.worldmind.com/Cannon/Culture/Interviews/theroux.html. Accessed September 22, 2005.

THINGS THEY CARRIED, THE TIM O'BRIEN (1990) Tim O'BRIEN writes articles, short fiction, memoir, and novels. While marketed as a novel by its publisher and called a "composite novel" (O'Gorman) by some critics, *The Things They Carried* can also be considered a short story cycle or even a fictionalized memoir

attempting to convey some of the truths of the experiences of soldiers in Vietnam. Tim O'Brien, the author, is himself a Vietnam veteran, and Tim O'Brien is a central character in these stories—or chapters—set, for the most part, in Vietnam during the war. Does that imply that the work is a memoir merely cast as fiction? The stories slip back and forth in time, with characters resurfacing and plots becoming fuller. A soldier may be already dead in one story and his death explained in a later one. Are the book's units, then, stories or chapters? The book itself defies genre from its initial pages. The first and title story—or chapter—introduces a cast of characters. Here, readers understand that each soldier is defined by what he carries, by letters or a good-luck charm or a souvenir. What they carried was "largely determined by necessity" and varied according to such things as rank and mission; the standard uniform itself had weight, all men carried weapons they were issued, some carried communications equipment, and so on. Also, "They carried all the emotional baggage of men who might die. Grief, terror, love, longing—these were intangibles, but the intangibles had their own mass and specific gravity, they had tangible weight." The language and structure of this story is especially poetic; the words resist forming a sequential plot in favor of reliance on images, objects, and recurring syntax. The rest of *The Things They Carried,* through the characters, plots, and images established in this first story, reveals, explores, and explains a great deal of this intangible weight, thereby making it tangible through language for the readers.

"On the Rainy River," the fourth story, looks back from 20 years after its occurrence in 1968, to recount a story "never told before." Because it gives background on the narrator, it functions as a sort of displaced first chapter. Here, the narrating character Tim O'Brien—who, like the author, grew up in Minnesota and graduated from Macalester College—makes courage tangible and personally specific, something with "finite quantities, like an inheritance." O'Brien receives his draft notice. His first thoughts are that the country's leaders—those who decided to go to war and who continue to fuel it—should send their own families instead of him, that he is "too good for this war." By the end, the narrator admits, "I would go to the war—I would kill and maybe die—because I was embarrassed not to." Is this story true?

O'Brien explores this question more overtly in "How to Tell a True War Story," which is situated roughly one-third of the way into the book and, thereby, questions the truth of all the stories. This story opens with a claim that it is true; however, by the end, readers recognize that what may be most true may not be exactingly factual: "All you can do is tell it one more time, patiently, adding and subtracting, making up a few things to get at a real truth." Perhaps, the whole thing never happened; perhaps, it happened but not there. Repetition seems to be the key to telling a true war story. The war story here, though, is actually a love story or a story of loss, for the real stories are not necessarily about the war per se.

This larger, even sweeping, perspective O'Brien continually reveals and builds in *The Things We Carry* suggests the true scope of O'Brien's interests: In his work there is an abiding concern with the question of battlefield courage, linking him not only with the best of a tradition of American war writers—James Fenimore COOPER, Stephen CRANE, Ernest HEMINGWAY—but also with the ancients; a more general concern with moral choice and the human capacity for evil that links him to such writers as Joseph Conrad (perhaps his most oft-cited influence); and, finally, an explicit interest in storytelling itself, in narrative forms and the power of the imagination, which might connect him to a number of experimental writers, both modern and postmodern (O'Gorman, 290).

This text, then, situates itself in various literary traditions and chronicles an important time in our nation's history. O'Brien's work is indeed tied to specific historical—and personal—events but also to human experience and morality in general.

The final story, "The Lives of the Dead," combines a sort of oxymoron or ambiguity in its title and suggests the necessary intermingling of life and death not just in war but in all human experience. The narrator—or is it the author, since both are now writers—claims that "stories can save us" and that stories allow the dead to "return to this world." In this story he saves—resurrects, revives, preserves—a nine-year-old classmate's life. The death of his boyhood girlfriend is linked to the death of his soldier buddies in Vietnam; a moral essence, some sort of truth, overrides these experiences. And the act of telling the stories—like the ear-lier shaking of a dead man's hand or soldiers' joking about death within moments of its occurrence—becomes a way to will people alive, to move beyond the simply intellectual understanding of bodily death.

The Things They Carried is a wonderfully complex and accessible insight not only into literary questions of genre but also into the Vietnam War, particularly impor-tant as current high school and college readers were born well after direct U.S. involvement in the conflict.

SOURCES

Kaplan, Stephen. *Understanding Tim O'Brien.* Columbia: Uni-versity of South Carolina Press, 1995.

O'Brien, Tim. *The Things They Carried.* Boston: Houghton Mifflin, 1990.

O'Gorman, Farrell. "*The Things They Carried* as Composite Novel," *War, Literature, and the Arts* 10, no. 2 (Fall/Winter 1998): 289–309.

"Tim O'Brien Issue." *Critique: Studies in Contemporary Fiction* 36, no. 4 (Summer 1994).

Anna Leahy

THIN MAN, THE Dashiell Hammett (1934)

The Thin Man is the last of the five detective novels published by Dashiell HAMMETT between 1929 and 1934. It is the only one not first serialized in *Black Mask;* begun in 1931 and finished in 1933, its gesta-tion was far longer than that of any of its predecessors; after it, Hammett would publish only a couple of short stories. It is, therefore, the fifth and final act in Ham-mett's reinvention of the detective story. The hard-boiled qualities that characterized the Hammett version of the detective story are still present: There are gangsters and gunshots, tough cops and speakeasies, wisecracks and beatings, predatory and unreliable women. But there is also a detective's wife and a detec-tive's dog. Nora does not actually help Nick Charles (Charlambides) detect, but the banter between her and her husband mark Nick as a quite different man from the Continental Op, Sam Spade, or Ned Beaumont. Beaumont was a complicated figure, groping toward a more intimate relationship; Nick Charles is secure in his marriage, and can be playful and protective. He is, indeed, an ex-detective, having retired from the Trans-American Detective Agency six year ago, and he is a reluctant inquirer into the matter of the disappearance of the eccentric thin man, Clyde Wynant.

Although Nick and Nora are Californians, they are spending Christmas 1932 in New York City; they read headlines and attend Broadway shows that actual New Yorkers read and attended in 1932. Despite Prohibition, they drink a lot (the celebrated series of six *Thin Man* movies produced between 1934 and 1947 gave the schnauzer, Asta, a rather larger role than Hammett did, but the Charlese's bibulousness is hardly exaggerated). It is while drinking in a speakeasy that Nick learns from Wynant's nubile daughter that her father has disap-peared. Wynant is a wealthy inventor who is divorced from his wife, Mimi. Mimi now lives with her second husband, Christian Jorgensen, and her two children by Wynant, Dorothy and her younger brother, Gilbert.

Wynant's disappearance becomes more than a trou-blesome absence when Mimi discovers the corpse of his murdered secretary (and, it is implied, mistress), Julia Wolf. The crime is complicated when it is revealed that Julia Wolf was once linked to an impris-oned Ohio gangster, Face Peppler, and that a low-life snitch named Arthur Nunheim has reported seeing a New York gangster, Shep Morelli, near the scene of the crime. Morelli, offended by the implication, invades the Charles's Hotel Normandie rooms and fires a bul-let that grazes Nick's side. Morelli's false impression of Nick's involvement in the investigation is shared by the newspapers and by the police; finding himself thrust into the case, and encouraged by the Wynant family and Wynant's lawyer, Herbert Macaulay, Nick begins to detect.

The affair is further complicated by the murder of the witness, Nunheim; by the discovery that Jorgensen is, in fact, a rival inventor named Victor Rosewater who once threatened to kill Wynant for stealing his ideas (Rosewater-Jorgensen's revenge—marrying Wynant's wife and thus accessing Wynant's wealth through the divorce settlement—may be neat but is certainly improbable); by Mimi's inexhaustible inclina-tion to lie; and by messages telegraphed or mailed by Wynant. Lt. Guild, the policeman assigned to the case, is a tough cop who comes to respect, though never entirely to trust, Nick. He is baffled by the

1262 **THIS BOY'S LIFE**

developments. Mimi, Jorgensen, Morelli, and, of course, Clyde Wynant himself are all viable suspects in the murders of Julia Wolf and Arthur Nunheim. When a dismembered body and a fat man's clothing with the initials D.W.Q. are discovered interred beneath the floor of Wynant's old laboratory, the case against Wynant seems overwhelming. This, however, is the moment that Nick Charles announces that the killer—of Wynant as well as of Wolf and Nunheim—is the lawyer, Herbert Macaulay.

The novel's final chapter presents Nick outlining his case against Macauley. It is, as Nora several times interjects, a case full of "loose" inferences and "reasonable doubts" and "theories." Nick responds with "It doesn't click any other way." It must have happened according to the complex scenario that he lays out. Macauley and Wolf must have been embezzling from Wynant's accounts; Macauley must have murdered Wynant in Scarsdale on October 3, and must have carried the pieces of Wynant's body to New York City on the sixth to bury them (and the misleading clothes) in the laboratory basement; and so on. The scenario that Nick recounts is certainly satisfyingly complete, but his insistence that the details are justified by "It doesn't click any other way," and not by irrefutable evidence or, even better, by confession, gives point to the novel's last words, Nora's complaint that "it's all pretty unsatisfactory." In a classic mystery story, this sort of mere likelihood would constitute a radical defect. In reality, Nick explains, this is the way murder mysteries end.

Hammett's final detective novel thus subverts the conventions of the genre. It features a reluctant detective drawn into an investigation that he views with a degree of bemused detachment, quite unlike the professional dedication of the Continental Op or Sam Spade. Nora is an ornament, contributing nothing substantial to the solution of the mystery, but much to the nature of the narrative. Her high spirits make her a mate for her husband; she is responsible for transforming the Detective into a Man Detecting.

SOURCES

Dooley, Dennis. *Dashiell Hammett*. New York: Ungar, 1984.

Gale, Robert L. *A Dashiell Hammett Companion*. Westport, Conn.: Greenwood Press, 2000.

Gregory, Sinda. *Private Investigations: The Novels of Dashiell Hammett*. Carbondale: Southern Illinois University Press, 1985.

Metress, Christopher, ed. *The Critical Response to Dashiell Hammett*. Westport, Conn.: Greenwood, 1994.

Nolan, William F. *Dashiell Hammett: A Casebook*. Santa Barbara, Calif.: McNally & Loftin, 1969.

———. *Hammett: A Life on the Edge*. New York: Congdon and Weed, 1983.

Skinner, Robert E. *The Hard-Boiled Explicator: A Guide to the Study of Dashiell Hammett, Raymond Chandler, and Ross Macdonald*. Metuchen, N.J.: Scarecrow Press, 1985.

J. K. Van Dover

THIS BOY'S LIFE TOBIAS WOLFF (1989)

Many critics have believed that Tobias WOLFF's memoir of his life from age 10 until age 16 should really be termed a novel, because of its literary qualities. The story begins in 1955, as he and his mother drive from Florida to Utah, fleeing her abusive boyfriend, singing, and dreaming of a better life in the West. When the boyfriend traces them to Salt Lake City, they again flee, arriving in Seattle by luck of the Greyhound schedule. There, Toby falls in with boys who smoke, steal trinkets from the local merchants, and commit minor acts of vandalism. After he is suspended for writing an obscenity on the boys' bathroom wall, his mother, desperate to prevent further trouble, sends him to live with her suitor and his three children in Chinook, a small company town three hours north of Seattle. The book centers on his years in Chinook and his turbulent relationship with his hard-drinking, domineering, and explosively tempered stepfather, the rowdy, petty-thieving boys he hangs out with, and his effeminate best friend, Arthur. The book ends as he leaves Chinook for an eastern prep school he forged transcripts and recommendations to enter and from which he is eventually expelled.

The title refers to *Boy's Life,* the official Boy Scout magazine that captures Toby's imagination and feeds his dreams of self-sufficiency, adventure, and bravery. The dominant theme is Toby's need to bridge the gap between the life he wants and the one he has, between the boy he wants to be and the boy he is. He dreams of being reunited with his father and older brother, becoming a family once more, rather than a fatherless outsider who falls far short of his expectations of changing. In Salt Lake City, he changes his name to Jack, after Jack LONDON, believing "that having his name would charge me with some of the strength and competence inherent in my idea of him" (8). In Chinook, he sees himself, as a straight-A student, star swimmer, and "boy of integrity" (213). In reality, he is bright but lazy, with poor to failing grades, a fair swimmer, and one badge short of Eagle Scout. He dreams of escaping from Chinook's limited blue-collar world to prep school, harboring never-to-be-realized fantasies of belonging—becoming a top student and swim-team captain and achieving the ease, manners, and material trappings of the boys whose photos he studies in the admissions-office brochures.

Painful honesty and well-drawn characters and events yield a memoir with the power of an adventure novel. As Wolff writes in the prologue, "This is a book of memory, and memory has its own story to tell." His tight focus on a troubled boy's struggles to become a good man creates dramatic tension, and his well-paced tales of basketball games, schoolyard scraps, domestic confrontations, friendships, and ill-conceived plans of escape, rather than extensive reflection, are more characteristic of a novel than traditional memoir.

Wolff writes a boy's narrative with a man's insight, without rationalization, apology, or labels—his stepfather drinks heavily and often but is never called an "alcoholic"; his best friend displays many effeminate characteristics, kisses him impulsively, and acquires a girlfriend as "the weakest part of his act," but he never calls him gay. His straightforward statements, without labeling or whining, keep us on his side, even when the facts support the opposition. When his Scout leader stepfather refuses to submit the paperwork for the final badge he needs to become an Eagle Scout, we sympathize, even though his tales of lying, drinking, and cheating demonstrate that his stepfather is right when he says Toby doesn't "deserve to be an Eagle" (198). While he gives numerous examples of his stepfather's cruelty and duplicity (stealing his paper route earnings and his beloved Winchester, beating him, and threatening his mother), he also tells us how Dwight voluntarily took on the job of raising him, months before marrying his mother, and became a Scout leader

and purchased a newspaper route in attempts to keep him productively occupied.

By the book's end, we predict a difficult and unsuccessful future for Toby. Subsequently, Wolff has published *In Pharaoh's Army, Memories of the Lost War* (1994), which describes his experiences after he was expelled from prep school, joined the army, and wound up serving in the Special Forces in Vietnam. It ends with his enrollment at Oxford University.

This Boy's Life was made into a movie, released in 1993, starring Leonardo DiCaprio as Toby, Robert De Niro as his stepfather, and Ellen Barkin as his mother. The movie's focus is narrower than that of the book, concentrating on the three characters and their relationships, rather than on Toby's relationships and adventures with other boys.

SOURCES

Penfield, Wilder III. "Writing Wrongs of His Childhood, Tobias Wolff on *This Boy's Life*," *Toronto Sun*, 23 October 1996.

Wolff, Geoffrey. *The Duke of Deception, Memories of My Father*. New York: Random House, 1979.

———. *In Pharaoh's Army, Memories of the Lost War*. New York: Alfred A. Knopf, 1994.

———. *This Boy's Life*. New York: HarperPerennial, 1990.

OTHER

Smith, Joan. "Speaking into the Unknown, Tobias Wolff." *Salon.com*. Available online. URL: http://www.salon.com/dec96/interview961216.html. Accessed September 27, 2005.

Suzanne Carey

THOMAS, JOYCE CAROL (1938–)

Best known for her three interconnected novels *Marked by Fire* (1982), winner of the American Book Award (now the National Book Award); *Bright Shadow* (1983), winner of the Coretta Scott King Award; and *Water Girl* (1986), Joyce Carol Thomas is acclaimed for her poetic, lyrical language. Equally if not more significant, however, is her portrayal of black women characters, depictions that have earned her serious attention and favorable comparisons to Toni MORRISON, Gloria NAYLOR, and Alice WALKER. Thomas's novels, widely adopted for classroom use in both high schools and universities, describe the identity quests of young black women and men; they have been classified as YA (young adult) novels, but are also popular with adults who read novels by Maya ANGELOU and James BALDWIN. Thomas, additionally a prolific writer of poetry, plays, and award-winning books for young children, turned to full-time writing in 1994 after another career as an English professor.

Joyce Carol Thomas was born on May 25, 1938, in Ponca City, Oklahoma, to Leona Thompson Haynes, a housekeeper and hair stylist, and Floyd David Haynes, a bricklayer. She moved with her family to Tracy, California, at age 10, and received her bachelor's degree in French and Spanish from San Jose State University in 1966 and her master's degree in education at Stanford University in 1967. She married twice: in 1959, to Gettis L. Withers, whom she divorced in 1968; and in 1968, to Roy T. Thomas, Jr., whom she divorced in 1979.

The title of her first novel, *Marked by Fire,* refers to the burn scar borne by Abyssinia Jackson, who survives a brush fire in a cotton field and, at age 10, is raped by a member of her church. This violent and terrifying incident renders her temporarily mute. The novel, set in Ponca City, Oklahoma (along with California, a prominent setting in her novels), follows her movement into adult life, aided by a close-knit community of women. The sequel, *Bright Shadow,* is similarly horrifying and includes the brutal murder of her favorite Aunt Serena by Serena's insane husband, a minister. Abyssinia attends college and falls in love with Carl Lee Jefferson, who deserts her; she learns to see life in the "bright shadows" that contain beauty as well as terror. In the next novel, *Water Girl,* the readers learn that, when she was young, Abyssinia had given up a daughter for adoption. In this novel, Abyssinia's long-ago adopted daughter, Amber Westbrook, discovers the identity of her birth mother while reading an old letter. Carl Lee reappears in *The Golden Pasture,* a novel about Lee's early attachment to his rodeo-riding grandfather. Using his rescue of an injured Appaloosa as a means of drawing Lee closer to his father, Thomas depicts Lee's lessening fear of and growing love for the man.

In *Journey,* Thomas experiments with the mixed genres of mystery and fantasy, mysticism and folklore. On one level of the novel, the resolute, brave Maggie Alexander solves a murder, while on another, more complex level, she intuitively learns lessons about "ingrained prejudices, intercultural violence, and the effect of both on children and adults" (Earhart, 451). *When the Nightingale Sings* experiments with new ways of presenting a coming-of-age tale, blending gospel, folktale, fairy tale. It is the story of a family reunion for young Marigold and her three adult sisters, and was performed as a musical play at the University of Tennessee in 1991. In her most recent novel, *House of Light,* which received excellent reviews, the middle-aged Dr. Abyssinia Jackson returns to Ponca City, Oklahoma, where she advises, nurtures, and heals the troubled women of the community. One of them, Vennie Walker, was inspired by women in Thomas's own life. In an interview with Lauretta Pierce, Thomas remarks, "[H]earing of the sacrifices these women made for their families troubled me. I decided to write about a Black woman who gets tired of being insulted, who rises up, and says NO. No more! That's Vennie Walker."

Joyce Carol Thomas lives and continues to write in Berkeley, California.

NOVELS

Abide with Me. New York: Hyperion, 2001.
Bright Shadow. New York: Avon, 1983.
The Golden Pasture. New York: Scholastic, 1986.
House of Light. New York: Hyperion, 2001.
Journey. New York: Scholastic, 1988.
Marked by Fire. New York: Avon, 1982.
Water Girl. New York: Avon, 1986.
When the Nightingale Sings. New York: HarperCollins, 1992.

SOURCES

Earhart, Amy E. "Joyce Carol Thomas." In *Contemporary African American Novelists: A Bio-bibliographical Critical Sourcebook,* edited by Emmanuel S. Nelson. Westport, Conn: Greenwood, 1999.

Henderson, Katherine Usher. "Joyce Carol Thomas." In *Inter/View: Talks With America's Writing Women,* edited by Mickey Pearlman and Katherine Usher Henderson, 125–131. Louisville: University Press of Kentucky, 1990.

Yalom, Marilyn. "Joyce Carol Thomas." In *Women Writers of the West Coast,* edited by Marilyn Yalom, 31–39. Santa Barbara, Calif.: Capra, 1983.

OTHER

Joyce Carol Thomas. Available online. URL: http://www.joycecarolthomas.com. Accessed September 22, 2005.

Thomas, Joyce Carol. Interview by Lauretta Pierce, March, 2002. The Library World. Available online. URL: http://www.angelfire.com/co4/interviews/thomas.html. Accessed September 22, 2005.

THOUSAND ACRES, A JANE SMILEY (1991)

Although Jane SMILEY published numerous earlier works, including the novellas *Ordinary Love* and *Good Will* (1989) and the well-received novella and story collection *The Age of Grief* (1987), *A Thousand Acres* became Smiley's most acclaimed work, having earned both the Pulitzer Prize and the National Book Critics Circle Award in 1991. The film version, starring Jessica Lange and Michelle Pfeiffer, was released in 1997.

The novel is a feminist retelling of the King Lear tale set on an Iowa family farm at the end of the 1970s and beginning of the 1980s, a time of increasing farm foreclosures and economic shifts. The farm's patriarch, Larry Cook, decides to retire and turn the farm over to his three daughters. Ginny, the oldest and narrator of the story, comes "to see a legacy of exploitation that involves not only abuse of family members but destruction of the land itself" (Weatherford, 149).

The other sisters play vital roles in Ginny's realization. Caroline, the youngest daughter and updated Cordelia, is a lawyer in Des Moines and, having left the family farm both physically and emotionally years earlier, initially opposes her father's plans. At times she speaks "as a woman rather than a daughter," something Ginny and Rose are unable to do, though Ginny and Rose raised Caroline after their mother's death. Rose, on the other hand, feels she's earned her share of the farm. Through Rose, now a mother herself, readers are able to understand the ambiguities—the multiple, simultaneous factors and possible results—of both inner strength and outward retribution. Ironically, Rose eventually takes her father's place running the farm.

The supporting male characters play important roles in Ginny's development as well. Ty, Ginny's husband, proves to be a pivotal character. Early in the novel, readers learn that, after several failed pregnancies, he's unwilling to have sex with his wife without using birth control. Much later, Ty articulates some of the attitudes behind the rifts within the family, saying such things as "I think people should keep private things private" and "There was real history here! And of course not everybody got what they wanted, and not everybody acted right all the time, but that's the way it is. Life is. You got to accept that." Jess Clark, who returns to Iowa as a vegetarian with an interest in Eastern religion, offers Ginny both an alternative romantic relationship and a different way of looking at the world, a way that challenges the status quo of Ginny's Iowa farm life.

Secrets and subplots move this novel forward, as the tension between highly valued "social respectability" and the dangers of "confronting reality" (Holstad, 5) mounts. The women, at first, tend to keep quiet to keep the peace, for instance. Throughout the story and for each character, appearances are deceiving. In this way and because of the first-person point of view, the novel offers insight and reveals characters' manipulation of each other in ways Shakespeare's version does not.

What is most powerful and lasting about Smiley's novel, perhaps, is its insistence that abuse—of land, of women—is systemic rather than merely an individual's decision. The problems Ginny and her sisters face are not isolated incidents but rather symptoms of the larger farming community in which they live. Ginny, for example, attributes her inability to carry a pregnancy to term and Rose's cancer to the poisons that farming have introduced to the water. Likewise, her father's treatment of his daughters stems from the same attitudes that he holds about farming and land acquisition. The language and metaphors Smiley uses convey this sense that the seemingly natural and necessary attributes of a successful farm are the same attributes that lead to destruction, silence, and grief.

Shakespeare's evil sisters, then, are interestingly complicated in Smiley's retelling. The evil is systemic, and every individual harbors the potential for great evil. Even Ginny contemplates murder and takes action. Evil, among other influences, shapes each character; yet no character is simply or inherently evil. The men, in fact, are often practical and good-natured with the best of intentions to preserve the farm and the family, but when the women assert themselves, the men react cruelly or tragically. The lawsuit that divides Ginny and Rose from Caroline and her father is another aspect of how larger influences shape the relationships, often changing what seems once pleasant enough into something filled with resentment.

A Thousand Acres can also been defined as a family saga, as it "traces the history of a family over many generations, from its roots in a specific location or time to its downfall. The theme is almost inevitably the destruction of this family and a reversal of its rules, which may be seen as a negative or tragic downfall or as a liberating and positive step." In addition, like other family sagas, The novel has an oral quality to it and "impart[s] opinions and varying versions of 'history' based on hearsay or gossip. . . . Finally, the families portrayed become representatives of their communities. . . ." (Ween, 111). Smiley's novel, then, functions as a history to be left to the next generation, to—in the terms of the novel—Rose's daughters.

SOURCES

Green, Michelle, and Barbara Kleban Mills. "Of Serpents Teeth in Iowa," *People,* 13 January 1992.

Holstad, Scott C. "Jane Smiley's *A Thousand Acres,*" *Notes on Contemporary Literature* 26, no. 2 (1996): 5–6.

Kakutani, Michiko. "Pleasures and Hazards of Familial Love," *New York Times,* 31 October 1989.

Smiley, Jane. *A Thousand Acres.* New York: Knopf, 1991.

Weatherford, Kathleen Jeannette. "Inextricable Fates and Individual Destiny in Jane Smiley's *A Thousand Acres* and Annie Proulx's *Postcards,*" *Philological Papers* 44 (1998–1999): 147–153.

Ween, Lori. "Family Sagas of the Americas: *Los Sangurimas* and *A Thousand Acres,*" *The Comparist* 20 (1996): 111–125.

Anna Leahy

THUNDER HORSE Peter Bowen (1998)

Thunder Horse is the fifth and, arguably, most distinguished of Peter Bowen's Montana mysteries featuring the Deputy and amateur sleuth Gabriel Du Pré. (By 2005, 12 of Bowen's Du Pré books had been published.) A hard-drinking, coarse-mannered, middle-aged Mitis Indian, Du Pré dominates all the books' narratives, using legal and not so legal means to get to the bottom of local mysteries. In *Thunder Horse,* after a

significant earthquake, a Berkeley academic, Palmer, is found shot dead near Toussaint, a remote, rural, rugged part of Montana. The death coincides with the inexplicable desire of some Japanese businessmen to dig ponds for recreational fishing in the lightly populated area that has only "a whole load of nothing." After many twists, the discovery of remains of ancient Caucasians, distractions concerning deposits of uranium ore, media scrums, and other developments, it turns out that the Japanese businessmen and Palmer have been seeking a very valuable *Tyrannosaurus rex* skeleton—the "Thunder Horse" of the title.

Du Pré learns that Palmer was shot by a family of Crow Indians who conceal the *T-rex* bones because they lie in the same place as an old Indian burial site— "one not found by the whites." Palmer came too close to violating the secrecy surrounding the sacred site. Respecting the wishes of the steadfast Crow guards, Du Pré will not reveal the cause of Palmer's murder or the whereabouts of the dinosaur bones. The Crows actually have knowledge of three complete *T-rex* skeletons, and will eventually concede one to the authorities. But the yielding of the secret *T-rex* will not compromise the secrecy of their ancestors' burial ground. The plot, then, is sensational and possibly over-the-top, but the novel's themes—antipathy between Indians and whites, and excessive human greed—transcend the compelling if far-fetched story.

Du Pré has an ingrained distaste for archaeologists and anthropologists, many of whom compete with one another aggressively in the hunt for dinosaur and human skeletons. Indian remains are treated with no more respect than those of insects, Du Pré believes. He also ruminates ruefully about historical crimes committed by Europeans against Indians and the environment—he is particularly angered by the slaughtering of millions of bison in the late-19th century. Du Pré thinks to himself that Indians fought little before the coming of the whites, after which they had to fight with more determination: "[T]hem damn whites . . . are very serious about war." The Crows guard their ancestor's secret burial place so doggedly simply because they suspect that whites will ransack the site, caring only for the profitability of the ore and the *T-rex* remains, and caring nothing for the location's elevated holiness. But a white man has been a hero, one who has done much to keep the Crows' burial place undiscovered. One Morgenstern had visited the site in the late 1800s, when surveying ore deposits. In his esoteric book about the subject, he gave directions—but willfully incorrect ones. He respected the Crows, and was as anxious as the Native Americans to keep the site holy and hidden. Learning this, despite reservations about whites' intent, Du Pré accepts that cooperation between Indians and whites can often be highly desirable and successful.

Human greed is a major theme in the novel. Palmer has died because he seeks financial reward from the dinosaur skeleton, and the Japanese businessmen, though no more egregious than others, are concerned only about profits. Bowen places a great stress upon food in the novel: Characters seem constantly to eat unhealthy mounds of fries and cheeseburgers. Drinking is a perennial activity in Toussaint. One extraordinary old character, Benetsee, an amalgam of a medicine man and a con artist, seems to desire only the cheap wine that Du Pré gives him in exchange for historical and local knowledge. Subtly, Bowen compares human greed to the less appealing habits of animals. Noticing a bald eagle, "so stuffed with [deer] meat it couldn't fly," struggling to walk, and then falling over, Bart, a companion of Du Pré, remarks sarcastically that the plight of this specimen of the national bird "makes ya proud to be an American." Excessive eating in a carrion bird, then, is clearly connected to humans' greed for food, a greed that is linked to the lust for money that causes the murder of Palmer and other damaging upheavals. A comparison between coyotes and humans is also made apparent. Coyotes eat the thighs of Palmer's corpse, profiting from his death—in the same way, humans with less integrity than Du Pré seek to profit from the ancient deaths of the Indians and the dinosaurs. And squabbles between magpies and other carrion-eating birds over another deer cadaver symbolizes the unholy squabbles between the media, academics, and a hooligan-like gang of Sioux Indians who all clamor relentlessly over access to the bones of the ancient Caucasians.

These themes may appear familiar, but Bowen's unusual style and storytelling verve render *Thunder Horse* an engaging read. The book is packed with quaint paradoxes (at one point, Du Pré and his wife, Madelaine, are "both too tired to sleep") and even quainter characters. We meet an accident-prone Jesuit priest who knocks himself out by trapping his head in his car door, and Oleson, a Norwegian who places his false teeth on the Du Prés' bar. Oleson wants to play his hardfinger fiddle, but the move is vetoed by Du Pré, who cannot tolerate the scratchings of a "deaf old arthritic drunk." Bowen has other engaging tendencies: one is that of using seemingly bizarre but ultimately appropriate onomatopoeia. Another extraordinary character is the 91-year-old scholar, Morgenstern—a relative of the 19th-century Morgenstern. He examines a dinosaur tooth. There is often an elision between the voice of the omniscient narrator and that of a character's inner voice. The narrator articulates Morgenstern's inner voice as he peruses the bone: he mumbles, inwardly, "umumumumhumhumhumumumumum-yesyesyesyesyes." In *Thunder Horse,* an entire paragraph can consist of the word, "Ah"; such a paragraph can be followed immediately by another with only the word "Ho." The plot of *Thunder Horse* may feature improbable events, and the novel's themes are unremarkable, but it is touches such as the quirky characterizations and striking use of onomatopoeia that make it so distinctive, readable, and memorable.

SOURCE
Bowen, Peter. *Thunder Horse.* New York: St. Martin's Press, 1998.

Kevin De Ornellas

TIME TO BE BORN, A DAWN POWELL (1942)

POWELL apparently conceived *A Time to Be Born* in fall 1940, as a diary entry for October 29 contains preliminary notes for the novel's opening meditation (*Diaries,* 182). Powell started writing the novel in January 1941 and completed it in May 1942 (*Diaries,* 196, 200). Sometime in 1941, Powell wrote a synopsis for *Scribner's* (*Selected Letters,* 112–13), which published the novel in August 1942 (191). The title was taken from *Ecclesiastes* (*Selected Letters,* 112), projecting the novel's portrayal of "a time to love" and "a time of war" (3:1–8). *Scribner's* advertised the novel in *Publishers' Weekly*

(June 20, 1942) as "amusing, witty, slightly mad, romantic, pungent" and "tops in entertainment." In a letter of July 6, 1942, Powell told editor Max Perkins that there was "nothing wacky in the book" and defended it as "serious satire in the way Dickens or Thackeray built satire—the surface may be entertaining but the content is important comment on contemporary affairs." Powell thought "the book's contemporary scene value should be stressed," and that if it was "slightly mad," it was "merely reflecting the times" (*Selected Letters*, 116).

The novel covers approximately the year before America entered World War II in December 1941. As Powell notes at the outset: "Paris was gone [June 1940], London was under fire, the Atlantic was now a drop of water between the flame on one side and the waiting dynamite on the other" (1).

Against the background of this nervous, indecisive time, Powell tells the story of two young women—Amanda Keeler and Victoria Haven—who have both migrated to New York from Lakeville, Ohio (a fictitious town whose name derives perhaps from *Lake* Erie College in Paines*ville, Ohio, where Powell had studied before coming to New York herself in 1918). "At thirty, Amanda had all the beauty, fame and wit that money could buy, and she had another advantage over her rivals, that . . . she knew exactly what she wanted from life, which was, in a word, everything" (23). Amanda had married the wealthy and powerful newspaper magnate Julian Evans, whose influence had made it possible for her to publish what became the best-selling historical novel *Such Is the Legend* (14–15). "Such fabulous profits from this confection piled up for the pretty author that her random thoughts on economics and military strategy became automatically incontrovertible" (4). There were real-life models for these characters, foremost among whom was the beautiful, ambitious playwright and journalist Clare Boothe Luce (1903–87), who had appeared frequently in New York society columns (for example, Cholly Knickerbocker's in the *New York American*) and was profiled in the *New Yorker* for January 4 and 11, 1941. Clare had first married (1923) and divorced (1929) New York millionaire George Tuttle Brokaw (1880–1935) and then attracted the attention of the publisher of *Time* magazine, Henry

R. Luce (1898–1967), who left his wife and two sons to marry Clare in 1935. Powell denied for years that Clare was the major model for Amanda (*Diaries*, 356 [1956]), but after newly elected congresswoman Luce attacked Vice President Henry Wallace for his internationalist views in 1943, Powell confessed: "I was glad I had slashed her in my last book and realized that my immediate weapons are most necessary and can help. The lashing of such evil can only be done by satire and I am the only person who is doing contemporary satire" (*Diaries*, 213 [1943]). Numerous parallels in the novel also suggest the Luces as the primary historical (contemporary) models for the Evanses.

"Bored with two years of fidelity" (23), however, Amanda takes advantage of the arrival of Vicky Haven, 26, in New York by getting her a job with one of Julian's publications, *Peabody's* magazine, and by providing her a "studio" apartment "in the Murray Hill section just off Park" (97), which Amanda can use as a cover by day to renew a relationship with a former lover, writer Ken Saunders. Working at *Peabody's*, Vicky, who has "no gift for self-exploitation," is befriended by such "would-be Amandas" (*Selected Letters*, 113) as Miss Finkelstein and Nancy Elroy, who are interested only in her connection with Amanda. Dinner parties at the Evans's "graystone mansion off Fifth Avenue" (6) and Mrs. Elroy's "spacious suite" in the Marguery Hotel (107) at Park Avenue and 47th Street provide Powell opportunity for satirical treatment of the Evanses, the Elroys, and their guests in social and political conversations. Vicky complicates matters by falling in love with Ken Saunders, whom Amanda had discarded to marry Julian, and by moving to Greenwich Village (where Powell had lived since 1924), where Ken's writer friend, Dennis Orphen (who also appears in Powell's other New York novels), lives. Amanda is "so wounded by this personal blow" (*Selected Letters*, 113) to her vanity that she recklessly endangers her marriage and reputation. The latter part of the novel deals with Amanda's frantic, but ultimately disastrous, efforts to indulge her private emotions without surrendering her public position.

Losing Ken to Vicky, Amanda pursues (in vain) another writer, Andrew Callingham (modeled on

Ernest HEMINGWAY [188]), but is followed by a private detective hired by Julian, for whom the last straw, however, is the publication of Amanda's confessional article on her humble origins, "I Came from the Wrong Side of the Tracks," in *Peabody's* magazine for August 1941 (306). Physically threatened, Amanda flees the Evans mansion, and Julian files for divorce. In the final scene, Ken and Vicky are on their brief honeymoon before he joins the army. "There isn't a thing in the papers about it," marveled Vicky. "You're not looking for Cholly Knickerbocker's account of our wedding, are you, my love? . . . No, dear, people like us have to push each other out the window before we're news." "I'm looking for Amanda, silly," Vicky answered. "You never see a thing about her anymore" (325). Ken's reply recalls the opening meditation: "There was no future; every one waited, marked time, waited. For what? On Fifth Avenue and Fifty-fifth Street hundreds waited for a man on a hotel window ledge to jump; . . . and in the tension of waiting it was a relief to have one little man jump" (3). Vicky and Ken may be "unimportant people" who have "no news value" in "this important age" (5), but in the end they are the true subjects of Powell's novel of "a time to love" and "a time of war."

SOURCES

Goodwin, Doris Kearns. *No Ordinary Time. Franklin and Eleanor Roosevelt: The Homefront in World War II*. New York: Simon & Schuster, 1994.

Morris, Sylvia Jukes. *Rage for Fame. The Ascent of Clare Boothe Luce*. New York: Random House, 1997.

Page, Tim. *Dawn Powell. A Biography*. New York: Henry Holt, 1998.

———, ed. *The Diaries of Dawn Powell 1931–1965*. South Royalton, Vermont: Steerforth, 1995.

———, ed. *Selected Letters of Dawn Powell, 1913–1965*. New York: Henry Holt, 1999.

Powell, Dawn. *A Time To Be Born*. New York: Scribner, 1942; reprinted in D.P. *Novels 1930–1942*, edited by Tim Page. New York: The Library of America, 2001.

———. *A Time To Be Born*. South Royalton, Vermont: Steerforth, 1999. (Quotations from this edition.)

Rice, Marcelle Smith. *Dawn Powell*. Twayne's United States Authors Series 715. New York: Twayne, 2000.

Frederick Betz

TOBACCO ROAD ERSKINE CALDWELL (1932)

Published as a novel in 1932 and staged as a drama in New York City in 1933, Erskine CALDWELL'S *Tobacco Road* shocked readers and audiences alike with its unflinching portrait of the last, starving days of impoverished Georgia sharecropper Jeeter Lester and his family. Critics could not reconcile Caldwell's mix of grotesque comedy and social realism, unsure of whether to laugh nervously at Jeeter or feel sympathy for his relentlessly pathetic existence. Decades of readers such as Sylvia Jenkins Cook, however, have recognized that while the "suffering and degeneracy of [Caldwell's] characters is virtually irremediable," his narrative of the successive catastrophes of these vividly drawn people "demands justice for a humanity that is so destroyed as to be scarcely recognizable" (Cook, 65).

Jeeter's narrative begins and ends against the backdrop of his dilapidated cabin and barren land, once the center of a large Lester tobacco farm, now abandoned by its last landlord, Captain Jack. Though Jeeter and his wife, Ada, recollect having had 17 children, only two remain with them, along with the slowly withering Mother Lester, whom they ignore and beat in the hopes that there will be one less mouth to feed. Into this tableau comes Lov Bensey, to whom Jeeter betrothed his 12-year-old daughter Pearl in exchange for seven dollars, "some quilts and nearly a gallon of cylinder oil" (32). Lov begins to complain of Pearl's frigidity, but the starving Jeeter can only concentrate on the sack of turnips at Lov's feet. While Lov is distracted by the rutting movements of daughter Ellie May, scooting bare-bottomed across the yard toward him, Jeeter pounces on the turnips and runs into the broom hedge. As the scene ends, a bedraggled Lov limps home while old Mother Lester lights a hopeful fire of twigs lest there be any turnips left. The reader is left to wonder: What kind of world is this? What kind of man trades his little girl, steals from his son-in-law, and starves his mother?

As the narrative unfolds, the reader begins to understand just what kind of world has formed Jeeter Lester. Though he is indeed lazy and ignorant, Jeeter is also buffeted by the forces of the Depression, centralizing changes in agriculture, and unscrupulous moneylenders. Thus, when we learn that "there were always well-developed plans in Jeeter's mind for the things he intended doing; but somehow he never got around to doing them" (70), we realize that in part the crushing economic system dissuades him from taking any initiative. So he doesn't get Ellie May the operation to fix her harelip; he doesn't contact his oldest son Tom; and he never gets around to planting a crop, though he sorely wishes to do so. Instead, he gets involved with a wily widow preacher, Sister Bessie Rice, who "marries" herself to his youngest son, 16-year-old Dude. Her involvement sets in motion a chain of hilarious and pathetic events, as the country bumpkins travel to town and encounter sophisticated city folk. When Sister Bessie, with all the money in her possession, buys a car, the reader knows it is doomed. As she and Dude successively crash, mangle, and poke the car into salvage parts over a period of days, the ridiculous auto becomes a metaphor for the forces, both external and internal, that have led to the Lester family's downfall. The reader wants to reach into the novel and shake some sense into Jeeter, but ultimately must admire the stubborn, foolish will that keeps him rooted, a forlorn, brutally comic symbol of American independence. Jeeter himself acknowledges, "Maybe I ain't got much sense, but I know it ain't intended for me to work in the mills. The land was where I was put at the start, and it's where I'm going to be at the end" (152). And it is.

SOURCES

Caldwell, Erskine. *Tobacco Road.* 1932. Reprint, New York: Book of the Month Club, 1994.

Cook, Sylvia Jenkins. *From Tobacco Road to Route 22: The Southern Poor White in Fiction.* Chapel Hill: University of North Carolina Press, 1976.

Devlin, James E. *Erskine Caldwell.* Boston: Twayne, 1984.

McDonald, Robert L., ed. *The Critical Response to Erskine Caldwell.* Westport, Conn.: Greenwood Press, 1997.

Mixon, Wayne. *The People's Writer: Erskine Caldwell and the South.* Charlottesville: University Press of Virginia, 1995.

Patricia Becker Lee

TO HAVE AND HAVE NOT   Ernest Hemingway (1937)

To Have and Have Not is the story of Harry Morgan, a fishing boat captain who manages to eke out a living only by smuggling alcohol and people in Cuba and the Florida Keys. The novel is characterized by Hemingway's sharp ear for dialogue as well as a penchant for describing various forms of human suffering.

The "haves" and "have nots" of the title are ostensibly those who have money and those who don't—the former being the yachtsmen and sportsmen who inhabit Key West, the latter being Harry Morgan, his associates, and people such as Cuban revolutionaries. However, these "have nots" have something that the rich and idle do not have, namely an ideology or just a simple set of morals. In the middle are a college professor and a writer who deal with their own struggles. The writer's wife has a monologue in which she describes her working-class father: "He was a boiler maker and his hands were all broken and he liked to fight when he drank, and he could fight when he was sober. He went to mass because my mother wanted him to and he did his Easter duty for her and for Our Lord, but mostly for her, and he was a good union man and if he ever went with another woman she never knew it" (187). So, in Hemingway's presentation, there is a certain nobility in the common man.

In another moving passage, a veteran elucidates, "We are the desperate ones. The ones with nothing to lose. We are the completely brutalized ones. We're worse than the stuff the original Spartacus worked with. But it's tough to try to do anything with because we have been beaten so far that the only solace is booze and the only pride is in being able to take it" (206). Harry Morgan, the main character, quite literally loses something—his leg. But he doesn't allow his pride to be taken, even as he goes to his death after being mixed up with the wrong people. He is also able to hold his liquor, which is a running theme in this novel as a sign of character—those who let alcohol affect their behavior are either the "have nots" who deserve their fate, or the overly privileged, moneyed class.

Even the emotions and relationships of the lower classes are portrayed in a more deserving, deeper way than those of the wayward privileged men and women: "*To Have and Have Not* juxtaposes the beauty and depth of Harry and Marie's love with the shallow and unfulfilling loves of the economic haves" (Knott, 140). Hemingway paints picture after picture of failing relationships among those who feel entitled to "the good life" simply because of their positive economic status. This is also a novel of the 1930s, one which some see as a "testament to Hemingway's newfound social consciousness . . . and his desire to sign on as a literary soldier in the social battle for brotherhood in opposition to the bosses, the demeaning bureaucracies, and the fascist oppressors" (Knott, 188). Some argue with this interpretation, but ultimately the novel comes out on the side of the individual over organized groups of any sort.

SOURCES

Hemingway, Ernest. *To Have and Have Not.* New York: Scribner Paperback Fiction, 1996.

Knott, Toni D., ed. *One Man Alone: Hemingway and To Have and Have Not.* Lanham, Md.: University Press of America, 1999.

Reynolds, Michael. *Hemingway: The 1930s.* New York: W. W. Norton and Company, 1997.

Allie M. d'Augustine

TO KILL A MOCKINGBIRD HARPER LEE (1960)

Winner of the 1961 Pulitzer Prize for Fiction, Harper LEE's *To Kill a Mockingbird* draws from the author's loving recollections of her own childhood in the South. Set during the Depression in the small rural Alabama town of Maycomb, the story is told by child-narrator Jean Louise Finch, nicknamed Scout, daughter of widowed lawyer Atticus Finch. Not quite six when the novel opens, Scout relates many events of interest to herself and her older brother Jem over the course of three summers, but the two constant narrative strands are the children's obsession to see their reclusive neighbor Boo Radley, and the trial of the Negro laborer Tom Robinson for the alleged rape of the white woman Mayella Ewell and its tragic aftermath. These two storylines come together dramatically in the novel's climax.

In the character of Scout, Harper Lee has achieved the perfect balance between the dominant voice of innocent naivete and the hindsight of adult experience. Maycomb is first seen as a kind of Eden for children: It's a hot, slow-paced summer, a time for treehouses, new friends, and new games. Yet Maycomb County is gradually revealed by the observant Scout to be a society divided by race, class, gender, and even heredity as defined by such accepted truisms as "Every third Merriweather is morbid" (131). The Tom Robinson trial acts as a catalyst that brings all the tensions and prejudices to the surface of what had initially appeared to be a peach-pie perfect picture of small-town America.

The Finch household ostensibly breaks all the conventional rules: Atticus and his brother Jack have broken the family tradition of males living off the family's land; the children call their father "Atticus"; the stern mother-figure is the black cook Calpurnia who teaches Scout how to write; Scout persists in wearing overalls to the special abhorrence of her proper Aunt Alexandra; Scout has fistfights with boys in the schoolyard; and Scout enters the first grade knowing how to read and write, thus earning censure from the new teacher armed with up-to-date pedagogical methods. Scout is even encouraged in her anarchy: Jem tells her, "sometimes you act so much like a girl it's mortifyin' " (38). Despite these eccentricities, the Finch family is known and respected throughout the county because they are rooted there historically and because Atticus himself is so highly regarded by the County's "Fine Folks," those who do the best they can with the sense they have (147).

Atticus Finch is the moral center of the novel, as well as the unacknowledged center of his children's universe. They find him merely "satisfactory," for they are embarrassed that he isn't like other fathers: "He did not do the things our schoolmates' fathers did: he did not play poker or fish or drink or smoke. He sat in the livingroom and read" (89). Others must teach the Finch children about their father's skill as a lawyer, as a teacher, and as a human being: "[Y]ou don't know you're pa's not a run-of-the-mill man . . . you haven't seen enough of the world yet," the "sinful" Mr. Dolphus Raymond tells Scout (201). Atticus holds himself to a strict code of personal morality: "before I can live with other folks I've got to live with myself. The one thing that doesn't abide by majority rule is a person's conscience" (105). He advises the hot-headed Scout to try to consider another person's point of view before flying to the defense of her own—"climb into his skin and walk around in it" (30), thus explaining his patient tolerance toward all. The Robinson trial is a kind of personal Golgotha for Atticus: At his summation, his children watch in horror as he loosens his tie and vest, takes off his jacket, and wipes sweat from his forehead, things they have never seen him do. Despite the verbal dryness of his defense, it requires a complete baring of his soul to everyone assembled in the courthouse.

Bob Ewell stands in direct contrast to Atticus. During his testimony Ewell is all rant and evasion. Where Atticus has "an infinite capacity for calming turbulent seas" (169), with one sentence Ewell "turned happy picnickers into a sulky, tense, murmuring crowd" (173). He drinks his welfare money so that his many children live in a filthy hovel surrounded by a yard that looks "like the playground of an insane child" (170); they are dependent on game caught out of season and on the charity of the county which otherwise despises them. One son is observed on his annual morning appearance in the first grade, where he curses the teacher, making her cry, before stomping off, having fulfilled the county's educational requirement for the year. During the Robinson trial, daughter Mayella unintentionally reveals that he beats her, and it is implied that he abuses her sexually as well. Nor are these characters unique: "Every town the size of Maycomb had families like the Ewells."

The foil for the Finch children, whose father's love is like the daylight which banishes nightmares, is their friend Dill Harris, a character based on Lee's close childhood friend Truman CAPOTE. Dill is passed around among his relatives because his mother and stepfather, though not physically abusive, have no time for him. In self-defense, his lively imagination fashions Tom Sawyer–like adventure stories with himself as the hero, many involving an imaginary father figure. He too comes to adopt Atticus as a father figure. It is Dill who makes the Radley Place a source of such fascination to the Finch children, who had hitherto simply regarded it as another part of their lives' background.

The Robinson trial, which Atticus acknowledges was lost months before it opened, reveals many ugly truths about racism and hypocrisy to the children. Yet Lee's novel also shows that there are those in Maycomb whose sense of justice and fairness under the law outweigh any consideration of color. This hope for the future lies in Judge Taylor's assignment of the case to the conscientious Atticus rather than the most junior

public defender; in attorney Gilmer's half-hearted prosecution; in the white male jury's long deliberation. "We're making a step," says their neighbor Miss Maudie Atkinson, "it's just a baby-step, but it's a step" (216). Most of all, hope lies in Jem's heartbroken and angry reaction to the verdict, for Jem represents the next generation of Southern lawyers and politicians.

Though Scout is the narrator, Jem is the child most affected by the events of the novel, for he is the child on the brink of maturity. By the opening of part 2, Jem is 12 and Scout finds him changed almost overnight: "Jem had acquired an alien set of values and was trying to impose them on me. . . . 'It's time you started bein' a girl and acting right!' " he snaps, sending her into tears (115). Jem is the one who cries in secret when Boo's hiding place—Boo's only avenue of communication with the world—is cemented shut, the one moved to fury by the irascible Mrs. Dubose who shouts her criticism of Atticus from her front porch, the one whose worldview is utterly crushed by the injustice of the Robinson trial verdict. Jem completes the archetypal journey from innocence to experience the evening he escorts Scout to the Halloween pageant— "our longest journey together" (254)—an evening that opens with the hilarious picture of Scout costumed as a ham butt to represent part of Maycomb County's agricultural bounty, and ends with Bob Ewell's vicious attack on the children with a carving knife while they are walking home in the woods and their rescue by Boo Radley.

Though easily categorized as a regional novel, *To Kill a Mockingbird*'s universal appeal is proven by its translation into 40 languages. Also, an Academy Award–winning film version of the novel was released in 1962 starring Gregory Peck as Atticus Finch. With a script by Horton Foote, it remains one of the most successful cinematic adaptations of a literary work.

SOURCES

Johnson, Claudia Durst. *Understanding To Kill a Mockingbird: A Student Casebook to Issues, Sources and Historic Documents.* Westport, Conn.: Greenwood Press, 1994.

———. *To Kill a Mockingbird: Threatening Boundaries.* New York: Twayne, 1994.

Lee, Harper. *To Kill a Mockingbird.* Philadelphia: J. B. Lippincott Co., 1960.

O'Neill, Terry, ed. *Readings on To Kill a Mockingbird.* San Diego, Calif.: Greenhaven, 2000.

Shakelford, Dean. "The Female Voice in To Kill a Mockingbird: Narrative Strategies in Film and Novel," *Mississippi Quarterly* 50 (1996–97): 101–113.

Nona Flores

TOOLE, JOHN KENNEDY (1937–1969)

John Kennedy Toole was the posthumous winner of the Pulitzer Prize for his novel, *A Confederacy of Dunces* (1980). After his suicide in 1969, his mother, Thelma Toole, vowed to publish her son's manuscript, ignoring rejections and finally asking novelist Walker PERCY to read the manuscript. Percy did so and, to his astonishment, he thought the novel original and talented; he recommended it to Louisiana State University Press, who published it in 1980 to rave reviews. *A Confederacy of Dunces* became a Book-of-the-Month Club selection, a best-seller, and a film. At once hilarious and sad, it satirizes contemporary middle-class life and achieves much of its humor from its "reverse satire," that is, the hero of the novel embodies all the flaws that he detests in the society that is the object of his wrath.

John Kennedy Toole was born in New Orleans, Louisiana, in 1937, to John Toole, a car salesman, and Thelma Ducoing Toole, a teacher. He received a bachelor's degree (Phi Beta Kappa) from Tulane University in 1958, graduating with honors, and a master's degree from Columbia University in 1959. He served with the U.S. Army from 1962 to 1963, stationed at Fort Buchanan in Puerto Rico, during which time he wrote *A Confederacy of Dunces.* Returning to New Orleans, Toole attempted unsuccessfully to publish the novel between from 1963 and 1966. After holding a succession of teaching jobs, Toole committed suicide on March 26, 1969, in Biloxi, Mississippi. The novel features Ignatius J. Reilly, a rebel who loathes his middle-class existence and leaves the Catholic Church. As scholar Beverly Jarrett notes, "[I]f there is one central theme in Toole's work, it is the loss of faith and the failure of the church to meet contemporary man's needs" (Jarrett, 436). An antihero frequently compared to Jonathan Swift's antihero in *Gulliver's Travels,* Ignatius, too, feels contempt for everyone he criticizes, yet he is

as guilty as they. Toole's sense of humor and carefully crafted language invites the reader's sympathy, however, and Ignatius J. Reilly takes his place alongside the characters of Joseph HELLER's *Catch-22* and John IRVING's *The World According to Garp.*

A manuscript that Toole had written at age 16, called *The Neon Bible,* was published as a novel in 1989 amid the family feuds chronicled by Pat Carr in *Modern Fiction Studies* that same year. In it, the protagonist, David, finds religion the villain of contemporary society. The John Kennedy Toole Papers are in the Howard-Tilton Memorial Library at Tulane University.

NOVELS
A Confederacy of Dunces. Baton Rouge: Louisiana State University Press, 1980.
The Neon Bible. New York: Grove Press, 1989.

SOURCES
Bell, Elizabeth S. "The Clash of World Views in John Kennedy Toole's *A Confederacy of Dunces,*" *Southern Literary Journal* 21 (Fall 1988): 15–22.
Carr, Pat. "John Kennedy Toole, *The Neon Bible,* and a Confederacy of Friends and Relatives," *Modern Fiction Studies* 35 (Winter 1989): 716–718.
Coles, Robert. "Gravity and Grace in the Novel *A Confederacy of Dunces.*" The Flora Levy Lecture in the Humanities, No. 2. Delivered as a lecture, September 18, 1981, at the University of Southwestern Louisiana, and published as a booklet by Savoy-Sicie Press, Lafayette, La., in 1983.
Jarrett, Beverly. "John Kennedy Toole." In *Contemporary Fiction Writers of the South: A Bio-bibliographical Sourcebook,* edited by Joseph M. Flora and Robert Bain, 432–440. Westport, Conn.: Greenwood Press, 1993.
McNeil, David. "*A Confederacy of Dunces* as Reverse Satire: The American Subgenre," *Mississippi Quarterly* 38 (Winter 1984–85): 33–47.
Nelson, William. "Unlikely Heroes: The Central Figures in *The World According to Garp, Even Cowgirls Get the Blues,* and *A Confederacy of Dunces.*" In *The Hero in Transition,* edited by Ray B. Browne and Marshall W. Fishwick, 163–170. Bowling Green, Ohio: Bowling Green State University Popular Press, 1983.
Reilly, Edward C. "Batman and Ignatius J. Reilly in *A Confederacy of Dunces,*" *Notes on Contemporary Literature* 12 (January 1982): 10–11.

OTHER

John Kennedy Toole. Bohemian Ink. Available online. URL: http://www.levity.com/corduroy/toole.htm. Accessed September 22, 2005.

TOOMER, JEAN (1894–1967)

Jean Toomer, poet and experimental novelist, was one of the central figures of the Harlem Renaissance. Along with Langston HUGHES, Countee Cullen, Claude McKAY, Arna BONTEMPS, and Zora Neale HURSTON, Toomer interpreted the black experience in a new way. Author of CANE, published in 1923, and rediscovered in the 1960s and acclaimed as a work of genius, the novel is a montage of vignettes, poetry, stories, and drama. Because it broke new ground, it belongs alongside such works as Sherwood ANDERSON's *Winesburg, Ohio,* and Ernest HEMINGWAY's *In Our Time.* The mysterious, haunting, imagistic and lyrical quality of his vision has also prompted comparisons of Toomer to William FAULKNER, both chroniclers of the questing modern soul seeking solace. Toomer's experimentation with the form of the novel is also echoed in the postmodern works of John WIDEMAN and Gayl JONES, and even in the science fiction of Octavia BUTLER and Samuel DELANY.

Jean Toomer was born on December 26, 1894, in Washington, D.C., to Nathan Toomer and Nina Pinchback Toomer, daughter of P. B. S. Pinchback, former Louisiana governor during Reconstruction. He married Marjorie Latimer in 1931; after her death, he married Marjorie Content in 1934. Educated at a number of universities without taking a degree, Toomer read voraciously and met many writers, including Sherwood ANDERSON, with whom he corresponded extensively. The turning point in Toomer's life came in 1921, when he accepted a temporary position as principal of a school in Sparta, Georgia. He was transformed by his immersion in southern black culture and exposure to the strength and dignity of black people in the face of poverty, brutality, oppression, and enforced segregation. He transformed this dual awareness into *Cane;* the seemingly disparate elements of the novel accommodate both southern rural experience and northern urban life in a three-part structure. The novel is unified through the story of Kabris, a wandering black man who seeks to identify himself through black culture. The title has been interpreted in various ways, suggesting both the land of sugar cane and the characters who are descendants of the Old Testament Cain.

After publishing *Cane,* Toomer experimented with the Eastern mysticism of Georges Gurdjieff, and in his last years he became a practicing Quaker. Although he wrote poetry and plays, Toomer never published another novel, but his manuscript collection at the Fisk University Archives includes four full-length novels. At this point, however, Toomer's considerable reputation rests on one slim volume, *Cane,* a literary masterpiece.

NOVELS

Cane. New York: Boni & Liveright, 1923.

SOURCES

Benson, Brian Joseph, and Mabel Mayle Dillard. *Jean Toomer.* Boston: Twayne, 1980.

Byrd, Rudolph P. *Jean Toomer's Years with Gurdjieff: Portrait of an Artists, 1923–1936.* Athens: University of Georgia Press, 1990.

Jones, Robert B. *Jean Toomer and the Prison-House of Thought: A Phenomenology of the Spirit.* Amherst: University of Massachusetts Press, 1993.

Larson, Charles R. *Invisible Darkness: Jean Toomer and Nella Larson.* Iowa City: University of Iowa Press, 1993.

McKay, Nellie. *Jean Toomer: Artist.* Chapel Hill: University of North Carolina Press, 1984.

OTHER

Jean Toomer. American Literature from the Civil War to 1930. Available online: URL: http://www.unc.edu/courses/pre2000fall/eng81br1/toomer.html. Accessed September 22, 2005.

The Jean Toomer Page. The San Antonio College Lit Web. Available online. URL: http://www.accd.edu/sac/english/bailey/toomer.htm. Accessed September 22, 2005.

TORTILLA FLAT JOHN STEINBECK (1935)

Although John STEINBECK had been writing and publishing for 15 years before writing *Tortilla Flat,* his warm-hearted, comic depiction of Mexican paisanos in Monterey, California, this novel brought John Steinbeck public recognition and notable critical attention for the first time. On the surface, the novel may seem to be simply a humorous depiction of the Mexicans who worked in the fields around Monterey and at the Spreckels Sugar Mill, whom Steinbeck had come to know and love. A penetrating reader, however, will discover the seeds of the major themes that preoccupied Steinbeck for the next decade and found more detailed expression in his most celebrated works of that period, especially *In Dubious Battle* (1936), *Of Mice and Men* (1937), and *The Grapes of Wrath* (1939).

Tortilla Flat is a lighthearted and humorous novel. Steinbeck's stylized dialogue and elevation of Danny and his friends' convoluted quests for women and wine to the level of heroic exploit contributes to the book's hilarity. Steinbeck writes, "Danny's house was not unlike the Round Table, and Danny's friends were not unlike the knights of it" (1). The Arthurian backdrop contributes further to the fantastic and mythical quality of the already exaggerated tales of the paisanos' lives. It likewise adds a moral dimension to the lifestyle of Danny and his friends, who might otherwise be viewed as amoral bums. In many ways, then, *Tortilla Flat* is an experimental novel, combining myth and fantasy, local legend and folklore, to create a humorous picture of paisano life that harbors very serious undertones. Steinbeck's choice of subject matter was also experimental and quite radical for that time. The novel is one of the first in American literature to use Mexican Americans as its main characters and to celebrate a group of derelicts' sexual and immoral exploits. *Tortilla Flat,* however, is strikingly moral. With its emphasis on loyalty and charity, the novel condemns greed and materialism. Ultimately, Danny's inheritance of a piece of property destroys the bond that exists among the paisanos. The novel's celebration of the paisanos' unattached, worry-free, and unconventional lives also flouts what Steinbeck saw as the hypocritical morality of Monterey's bourgeois society.

Perhaps the most important aspect of *Tortilla Flat* is that it gives voice to Steinbeck's thinking on the phalanx theory, or "group man" theory, a subject that fascinated him and gave shape to many of his succeeding works. Steinbeck, influenced by the ideas of William Emerson Ritter, believed that wholes in nature are made up of interdependent parts that not only constitute the whole, but exercise control over it. Each member of the whole, be it an animal in a specific ecosystem or a human in a community, governs itself differently in a group than it does as an individual, ensuring the continued functioning of the whole. In the novel Steinbeck writes, "This is the story of Danny and of Danny's friends and of Danny's house. . . . when you speak of Danny's house you are understood to mean a unit of which the parts are men" (1). The novel, then, is concerned with examining the individual characters and their relationships with others to see how they cooperate to form the whole that becomes Danny's house. Steinbeck's analysis of their behavior is distinctly biological and provides early insight into his own views of biology and holistic ecology that heavily influence his later works, making *Tortilla Flat* both an entertaining and important text in the Steinbeck canon.

SOURCE
Steinbeck, John. *Tortilla Flat.* New York: Penguin, 1986.

Kathleen M. Hicks

TRACKS LOUISE ERDRICH (1988)   Louise ERDRICH's *Tracks* is the third installment in a five-book sequence that began with *Love Medicine* (1984) and *The Beet Queen* (1986) and concluded with *The Bingo Palace* (1994) and *The Last Report on the Miracles at Little No Horse* (2001). Often compared to William FAULKNER because of her use of multiple narrators, her sustained development of a single fictional setting (the imaginary town of Argus, North Dakota), and her exploration of family life across generations, Erdrich has also been deeply influenced by traditional Anishinaabe (Chippewa) mythology and culture. In *Tracks,* she draws heavily on this heritage to tell a story about the cultural fragmentation following the passage of the General Allotment Act (Dawes Act) of 1887. By reinterpreting a number of archetypal figures from Anishinaabe myth, especially the trickster, the gambler, and the weendigo, Erdrich produces a powerful and nuanced account of the struggle against cultural extermination in the first two decades of the 20th century.

Tracks tells the story of Fleur Pillager, the last of a line of midewewin—tribal shamans who draw their power from a spiritual connection with the dangerous, lake-dwelling spirit, or manitou, known as Misshepesshu. Throughout the book, Fleur struggles to protect her lands from tax collectors and logging companies and to keep her family together in the face of a range of threats—including infidelity, famine, and tribal politics. Fleur's connections to the traditional world of Anishinaabe spirituality are not only complex but also ambiguous. Early in the novel, for example, while working at a butcher shop in Argus, she reenacts the mythic story of the trickster Nanabozho's contest with Nina Ataged (the great gambler). In that myth, Nanabozho (acting here as a culture-hero) tricks the gambler at his own game and saves the spirit of the people from eternal destruction. In the novel, Fleur's uncanny card-playing skills enable her to win a large sum of money from her white coworkers, money that she uses to pay the fees on her lands and temporarily save them. The mythic parallel to Nanabozho's victory is not perfect, however, for Fleur is then brutally raped by the enraged and drunken men. Although nature itself seems to avenge this violation as a tornado sweeps through Argus, and Fleur's assailants are frozen in the meat locker, this early episode sets up some of the novel's recurrent questions. What are the limits of Fleur's power? Can the old ways truly stand up to the encroachment of the white world? Fleur's experiences throughout the balance of the book suggest that Erdrich's answer to the second question is a qualified no. Early on in the text, Fleur's spirit power seems persistent and potent. For example, a drunken bear—an embodiment of earth power and the spirit of transformation—plays an instrumental role in the birth of her first child, Lulu.

Later in the book, however, Fleur proves unable to guide her husband Eli in hunting the vanishing game they need to survive, and her second child is stillborn when she loses a rematch with the gambler in a dream vision. Most significantly, at the end of the novel, Fleur is unable to prevent the logging company from seizing her land. She does obtain a measure of revenge for the loss, cutting through the trees around her cabin so they fall upon the astonished loggers when they arrive to survey the area. The gesture may strike some readers as a pyrrhic victory, however. The fact remains that the land has been lost, the trees have fallen, and Fleur must leave the reservation alone, for Lulu has been sent away to boarding school and Eli has taken a job with the logging company. If Fleur is defiant in the novel's final pages, she is also entering a period of exile.

Although Fleur's story has the scent of tragedy, there is much more to Erdrich's novel than the preceding account suggests. While Fleur is the focus of the book's plot, *Tracks* is also very much the story of its two narrators, Nanapush and Pauline Puyat. Perhaps the most useful way to read the book, in fact, is to see it as a presentation of three different paths, or "tracks," that Native American peoples might follow—Fleur's, Nanapush's, and Pauline's. Nanapush is clearly an avatar of the Anishinaabe trickster, Nanabozho. His chapters are written to suggest the immediacy of an oral tradition and the tremendous power of language—the trickster's greatest weapon. A traditionalist who nonetheless understands the white world because he received a Jesuit education, the elderly Nanapush "tells" his story to Fleur's estranged daughter Lulu, hoping to reconcile the two and awaken in Lulu a greater appreciation of the old ways. To do so, he presents Fleur as a mysterious, dangerous, but essentially positive presence, a figure who uses her sacred power to preserve and protect traditional life. As he tells his tale, Nanapush himself emerges as a different kind of tribal leader. As we would expect of a trickster, Nanapush can use words to influence others, to achieve his ends, and even to heal. He is a mediating presence who knows the ways of both the Indian and white worlds. He understands the law that is being used to defraud his people and the importance of the old stories. By the end of the novel, these gifts have enabled Nanapush to become tribal chairman, a position he uses to bring Lulu home from the boarding school. In this respect, Nanapush reveals a second path that Native peoples might follow. Unlike Fleur, he represents a blending of old and new, an ability to laugh at difficulties and to accommodate change without assimilating.

If Nanapush represents a positive kind of an ability to live between cultural extremes without being torn apart by contradiction, Pauline's divided nature takes her in a different direction. A psychologically complex character, Pauline is a "mixed-blood" proponent of assimilation whose desire to fit into the white world leads her to a tragic form of self-hatred. Early in the book, she repudiates her Indian heritage and language and actively sets out to facilitate the destruction of the old ways. Erdrich reinforces her characterization of

Pauline as a self-destructive midwife of cultural death by linking her to the mythic figure of the windeego, a skeletal, cannibalistic monster that preys on its own people and suffers from constant hunger. Pauline's hunger in the novel seems primarily existential. She yearns for a positive sense of identity but cannot seem to find a way to make sense of what it means to be a "mixed-blood." Consequently, she deludes herself into thinking that she can be "purified" by Christianity and emerge as wholly white.

Pauline's tortured religious consciousness manifests itself in her schizophrenic attitude toward Fleur. While she initially displays a strong attraction to Fleur, Pauline also presents her to the reader as a kind of witch. As the novel progresses, this early ambivalence gives way to overt aggression. Pauline comes to define her own life as a crusade against the traditionalism that Fleur represents. In doing so, she develops a morbid fixation on martyrdom, emblematic of her misguided yearning for the obliteration of her Indian identity. Pauline's path leads her to self-mortification, the repudiation of her own illegitimate child, delusions, murder, and, finally, a darkly ironic entry into a convent. In the end, Pauline reveals herself to be a classic unreliable narrator. At the same time, her highly subjective account of Fleur's life offers readers a powerful portrait of the psychological damage caused to Indian peoples by the assimilationist policies of the early 20th century and by the racial categorization of individuals as "mixed-bloods" or "half-breeds."

SOURCES

Brehm, Victoria. "The Metamorphosis of an Ojibwa Manido," *American Literature* 68, no. 4 (December 1996): 677–706.

Chavkin, Allan, ed. *The Chippewa Landscape of Louise Erdrich.* Tuscaloosa: University of Alabama Press, 1999.

Chavkin, Allan, and Nancy Feyl Chavkin, eds. *Conversations with Louise Erdrich and Michael Dorris.* Jackson: University Press of Mississippi, 1994.

Clarke, Joni Adamson. "Why Bears Are Good to Think and Theory Doesn't Have to Be Murder: Transformation and Oral Tradition in Louise Erdrich's *Tracks,*" *SAIL* 2, no. 4 (Spring 1992): 28–47.

Coltelli, Laura. *Winged Words: American Indian Writers Speak.* Lincoln: University of Nebraska Press, 1990.

Erdrich, Louise. *Tracks.* New York: Harper & Row, 1988.

Johnson, Basil. *The Manitous: The Spiritual World of the Ojibway.* St. Paul: Minnesota Historical Society Press, 2001.

Owens, Louis. *Other Destinies: Understanding the American Indian Novel.* Norman: University of Oklahoma Press, 1992.

Smith, Jeanne Rosier. *Writing Tricksters: Mythic Gambols in American Ethnic Literature.* Berkeley: University of California Press, 1997.

Vizenor, Gerald. *The People Named the Chippewa: Narrative Histories.* Minneapolis: University of Minnesota Press, 1984.

David J. Carlson

TRAGEDY OF PUDD'NHEAD WILSON, THE MARK TWAIN (1894)

Samuel Langhorne Clemens (Mark TWAIN) began writing the book that would become *The Tragedy of Pudd'nhead Wilson* in the early 1890s. A manuscript version of the novel, which included a long portion that would become the companion piece *Those Extraordinary Twins,* was completed in 1892 while the Clemenses were living in Italy; however, Clemens had to revise the manuscript substantially before eventually publishing *Pudd'nhead Wilson* serially in the *Century* magazine from December 1893 to June 1894. The aesthetically challenged book was published late in 1894: It remains open to charges of narrative confusion and structural weakness. The novel has gained in importance as a statement on race relations and identity. It is a more complex and more disturbing investigation of racial tensions than Clemens's earlier *Adventures of Huckleberry Finn.*

The first chapter of the novel offers a detailed description of Dawson's Landing and the community's social structure. The year is 1830. The town is primarily poor; however, there is a strong awareness of class distinctions among the citizens, made clear as the town's leaders are introduced and their pedigree established. The townspeople's sense of superiority is reinforced when they confront a newcomer, David Wilson, and promptly label him "Pudd'nhead" after a joke he tells falls flat. The townspeople have no sense of humor, and irony is alien to their sensibility, something that is underscored at the end of the novel. Clemens uses this opening to set the stage for a carefully plotted story that emphasizes questions of race identity and the implications of social stupidity mixed with a tale of murder.

There are several competing plotlines: David Wilson's ability to forge a life in a community that has judged him incompetent so quickly; the town's quick and unquestioning embrace of a pair of supposed "twin" brothers, though there is little support for their claims of a European background and little evidence of their exceptionality that supposedly kept them for years as a sideshow exhibit; and the murder of the town's beloved Judge Driscoll and David Wilson's defense of the twins, made possible by Wilson's collection of fingerprints. The tale, however, is held together by a supremely complex set of events starting with the introduction of Roxana, a young woman who is bound in slavery even though she appears to be white and whose child, Valet de Chambre, following the law and custom of the society, is identified as black because of his $1/32$ of African blood. Slavery is central to this society: Miscegenation lurks in the background, as does the overarching social power of whites. Fearful that she and her child will be sold down the river, Roxy decides to drown herself and the baby, until she notices that the boy is so similar to her master's son Thomas a Becket Driscoll. They are similar in complexion if not status. She switches the children in the hope that her own child will benefit from the privilege of white society. As the children grow, and as Roxy's son becomes more and more spoiled and violent and racist, questions arise regarding the nature of character, the possibility of a racial base for corruption, and the possibility of justice within a society locked into defining its members by physical characteristics and stereotypical behaviors.

Readers who approach the novel looking for definite answers come away deeply disappointed. At times, the story seems to fall on the side of nature as the basis for human identity, reinforced by both Roxy and her son's thinking that his corruption is natural to his being black; at other times, there is strong conflicting evidence that corruption is the result of nurturing that emphasizes pampering and profligacy and white assumptions of superiority. Clemens offers no clear position on these issues, and the text swings back and forth as various events unfold: from Roxy's careful raising of both boys in line with their adopted identities rather than their original social status, to Chambre's (as Tom) absolute acceptance of his inferior status after Roxy unmasks her role in placing him within the Driscoll household, to the narrator's comment on the willingness of the Driscolls to spoil the young man. In the end, the novel is best seen as Clemens's attempt to write through the debate. His uncertainty influences both the design and the content of the tale.

Most troubling is the final act of the mystery when David Wilson takes center stage to free the wrongly accused twins Luigi and Angelo and thereby identify the murderer. The crime is quickly dismissed and attention shifts to Wilson's more sensational charge that a white child and black child were switched: a black child has had inappropriate advantages; a white child was deprived of his rightful place and assigned to the slave quarters. This is the crime that horrifies the town. Clemens works the scene to enable David Wilson to reclaim his place within the community. In a romantic flourish, Wilson resets the balance in the community, a balance that Roxy disrupted 20 years earlier and that has upset the delicately and legally enforced identities of Tom and Chambre. His setting things right brings him thanks from and notoriety within Dawson's Landing, and he finally achieves his social reward: His reputation is made and he becomes mayor.

But at what cost. The tragedy of David (Pudd'nhead) Wilson is that neither he nor the town understands that order is achieved on the backs of slaves. He and the townspeople are complicit in the system of slavery and enforce that system by emotional and psychological violence. When Chambre is finally sold down the river to recover some of the value for Judge Driscoll's estate, the circle that began in chapter 1 is complete. It is a circle marked by racial prejudice and enforced fictions of law and custom. The novel becomes the record of Clemens's and his (our) society's confusion regarding identity and the social fictions that are created so that the socially prominent retain power.

SOURCES

Emerson, Everett. *Mark Twain: A Literary Life.* Philadelphia: University of Pennsylvania Press, 2000.

Foner, Philip S. *Mark Twain Social Critic.* New York: International Publishers, 1958.

Gerber, John C. *Mark Twain.* Boston: G. K. Hall & Co., 1988.

Gillman, Susan. *Dark Twins: Imposture and Identity in Mark Twain's America.* Chicago: The University of Chicago Press, 1989.

Gillman, Susan, and Forest G. Robinson, *Mark Twain's Pudd'nhead Wilson: Race, Conflict, and Culture.* Durham, N.C.: Duke University Press, 1990.

Twain, Mark. *The Tragedy of Pudd'nhead Wilson and the Comedy of Those Extraordinary Twins.* Edited by Shelley Fisher Fishkin. New York: Oxford University Press, 1996.

Michael Kiskis

TRIPMASTER MONKEY: HIS FAKE BOOK

MAXINE HONG KINGSTON (1989)   The first of her Chinese immigrant parents' American-born children, Maxine Hong KINGSTON was born on October 27, 1940, in Stockton, California, where she lived until she attended the University of California. Initially an engineering student, she graduated with a bachelor of arts degree in English in 1962. Since that time, she has published several essays, short stories and novels, including *Tripmaster Monkey: His Fake Book* (1989). Kingston's focus on the experiences of Chinese Americans places her in the company of such other Chinese-American writers as Amy TAN and Frank CHIN. Her focus on gender issues parallels that of other ethnic women writers, Toni MORRISON and Leslie Marmon SILKO, for instance. Her novel reflects the complex style of such literary classics as James Joyce's *Ulysses.*

Tripmaster Monkey: His Fake Book tells the story of Wittman Ah Sing, an aspiring Chinese-American playwright who seeks to produce his own play during the 1960s. Wittman exudes cockiness and chauvinistic tendencies but remains committed to the Chinese-American community and its welfare. His personality is multivalent, for he takes on different personas during the course of the novel.

The novel follows Wittman through a series of adventures as he seeks to make his dream of a production a reality. Wittman considers casting Nanci Lee, a former classmate and aspiring Chinese-American actress who is also the object of his unspoken affection. He scares her off when she reacts negatively to his poetry, thus propelling him to seek other potential actors.

Wittman recruits potential performers after attending a party given by Lance Kamiyama, a Japanese-American friend who lives a fairly normal, middle-class lifestyle. After observing several scenes of partygoers engaged in various conversations, Lance and Wittman argue. Wittman accuses Lance of participating in the degradation of Chinese Americans by embodying the "model minority" stereotype that presents all Asian Americans as impossibly quiet and self-effacing with a resistance to "making waves." They reconcile and Wittman enlists Lance and the remaining partygoers in an informal rehearsal of his play. He also meets his future wife, a white bohemian. He takes her home to meet his parents, Ruby Ah Sing, a former showgirl, and Zeppelin Ah Sing, a retired performer who lives by the river.

Wittman's adventures next take him to his unemployment caseworker, whom he manages to incorporate into his production. He secures a venue for his play and puts on a wild show of several vignettes that range from tong wars to depictions of Chang and Eng, the celebrated "Siamese" twins of the 19th century. Wittman caps the performance by a lengthy monologue about his thoughts on the state of the Chinese-American community.

Kingston's novel possesses several characteristics of postmodern literary production. The narrative represents a fragmented story. The primary plot diverges on tangents that appear completely unrelated. Wittman's encounter with Judy Louis on a bus to Lance's party seems insignificant, especially when Judy does not reappear in the narrative until the end.

Kingston also employs pastiche, using her narrative as a collage of various cultural sources, especially from Chinese lore. She uses the image of the Monkey King from "Journey to the West," which tells the story of the mythic Monkey King as he journeys to obtain Buddhist scripture for China. "Romance of the Three Kingdoms" describes power struggles among the three major kingdoms of China and the lifelong friendship among three men. "The Water Margin" represents the legend of 108 outlaws known for their loyalty to each other and subversion of government policies. In addition, the novel also contains references to high and low Western culture that disintegrate the distinctions between them. Wittman pays just as much homage to Walt Whitman as he does to *West Side Story.*

In addition to postmodern strategies, Kingston also employs innovative narrative techniques. The novel possesses two distinct narrative voices. On one hand, Wittman's worldview is chauvinistic, mired in the contemporary moment of the 1960s, and committed to an individualistic perspective that borders on the egotistical. On the other hand, the omniscient narrator identified by Kingston as Kwan Yin, the goddess of mercy from the Chinese oral tradition, acts as a balance to Wittman's character. She represents a more communal voice that is also distinctly female. Her memory reaches back to the earliest history. Together, Wittman and Kwan Yin represent a mode of narration that captures the complexity of the novel's fragmented narrative.

While Wittman seems to be limited by some aspects of his personality, he achieves a great deal of agency as a trickster figure. His very identity shifts. His first name links him to the quintessential American poet, Walt Whitman, while his surname places him squarely within the Chinese cultural tradition. Moreover, he is the modern-day version of the legendary Chinese Monkey King, a mythical trickster. Wittman uses his own transformative abilities to infiltrate spaces and disrupt proceedings, as he does at the management trainee seminar. The prominence of performance in the novel also underscores his transformative proclivities. For Wittman, all the world is indeed a stage as he takes on several roles on and off the theater platform. His facility with several cultural traditions marks him as one who traverses cultural boundaries. Wittman easily uses references to Chinese oral tradition and Western literary tradition. He can move among the hectic scene of 1960s bohemia with ease. Rather than alienating him from both Chinese and American culture, his liminal status reinforces a complex American identity.

At the same time, Wittman can be viewed as having no allegiance to creating social change and actually chafes at any kind of imposition of social responsibility. He represents a subject that is not beholden to a single perspective, which accounts for his interest in various cultural perspectives and art forms. His commitment to individuality causes him to avoid becoming a representative of something larger than himself.

As a trickster novel, *Tripmaster Monkey* critiques various cultural phenomena. Through Wittman and Kwan Yin, the novel interrogates the relationship between individuals and communities. Wittman learns to balance his need for individualistic expression with the needs of the community. In the process, he continues to question the amount of actual freedom in an individual's separation from a group and to note the limiting tendencies of communal expectations. Wittman focuses his critical eye on the Chinese-American community in particular. While Wittman's antics often ensure a certain amount of distance between himself and the community, he remains concerned about its viability. In his monologue, he urges the community to take responsibility for its image in the popular culture. He implores Chinese Americans to reject stereotypes and actively create their own collective identity. Wittman calls attention to the diversity within the Chinese-American community and the Asian-American community at large and advises both to reject the notion that all Asian Americans look alike and are alike.

Wittman also addresses more sensitive topics regarding the Chinese-American community. He highlights the fault lines between Chinese Americans and Japanese Americans forged in historical experiences. Wittman's argument with Lance draws on the way the Japanese Americans joined American culture in denigrating Chinese immigrants while depicting themselves as the "good" Asian immigrant group. Wittman also problematizes the hyphenated descriptions of Chinese Americans, which, Kingston argues, keeps them as foreigners and inauthentic Americans in the cultural imagination. She uses Wittman to erase the hyphen between Chinese American, thus allowing for more ambiguity in Chinese-American identity.

The novel also questions the Western cultural narrative, particularly in the literary tradition and the popular culture, and its impact on Chinese Americans. During the course of his monologue, he cautions Chinese Americans against the ways they have been stereotypically characterized in film. War movies produced by Hollywood depict Asian soldiers as dispensable. Fantasy movies portray Chinese Americans as inherently evil and perverse with characters like Fu Manchu. Detective movies represent Chinese Americans as inscrutable with characters like Charlie Chan. Wittman also finds ways to celebrate and honor the ways in which Chinese Americans have contributed to American culture. In doing so, Wittman seeks not only to transform the way Chinese Americans view their experiences in America, but also to transform America itself.

The novel additionally targets the discourse of war. Wittman admires the writings of war strategists and wants to feature big battles in his play. Yet, Kwan Yin suggests the dangers of war mongering, especially for Asian Americans during the Vietnam War era, where they were often not differentiated from the enemy. Kingston also examines the concept of the heroic discourse by basing Wittman's status as hero not on violent exploits, but on nonviolent acts that further social change. Wittman clearly identifies himself as a pacifist and he takes a job in a toy department to avoid a profession that supports the military. By the end of the novel, he manages to produce a play that promotes peace.

In focusing on peace, Kingston provides a counterpoint to other Chinese-American writers who define the tradition as martial in nature. Chinese-American writers like Frank Chin argue that Chinese-American culture is guided by a martial aesthetic that values combat. Through this novel, Kingston challenges Chin by creating a character remarkably similar to him and using that character to question the suitability of the martial tradition as the defining ethos for Chinese-American literature. She defends her revision of Chinese legend and uses the novel to question the emphasis on the masculine by Chin. She advocates a concept of gender that is constantly in flux. The hybrid form of the novel, from the narration to the characterization, questions the stereotypical assignations of male and female behavior by blurring the lines.

Tripmaster Monkey, through its allusions to various cultural traditions, multiple narrators, and multipronged cultural critique, ultimately presents a complex view of Chinese-American experiences.

SOURCES

Chang, Hsiao-hung. "Gender Crossing in Maxine Hong Kingston's Tripmaster Monkey," *MELUS* 22, no. 1 (1997): 15–34.

Chu, Patricia P. "*Tripmaster Monkey,* Frank Chin, and the Chinese Heroic Tradition." In *Assimilating Asians: Gendered Strategies of Authorship in Asian America,* 169–187. Durham, N.C., and London: Duke University Press, 2000.

Furth, Isabella. "Bee-e-een! Nation, Transformation, and the Hyphen of Ethnicity in Kingston's *Tripmaster Monkey,*" *Modern Fiction Studies* 40, no. 1 (1994): 33–49.

Gao, Yan. "Wittman Ah Sing's "Song of Myself": *Tripmaster Monkey.* In *The Art of Parody: Maxine Hong Kingston's Use of Chinese Sources,* 97–147. New York: Peter Lang, 1996.

Hogue, W. Lawrence. "The Postmodern Subject: Maxine Hong Kingston's *Tripmaster Monkey* and Richard Perry's *Montgomery's Children.*" In *Race, Modernity and Postmodernity: A Look and the History and Literatures of People of Color Since the 1960s,* 151–198. Albany: State University of New York Press, 1996.

Huntley, E. D. *Maxine Hong Kingston: A Critical Companion.* Westport, Conn.: Greenwood Press, 2001.

Kingston, Maxine Hong. *Tripmaster Monkey: His Fake Book.* New York: Vintage, 1990.

Lin, Patricia. "Clashing Constructs of Reality: Reading Maxine Hong Kingston's *Tripmaster Monkey: His Fake Book* as Indigenous Ethnography." In *Reading the Literatures of Asian America,* edited by Shirley Geok-lin Lim and Amy Ling, 333–348. Philadelphia: Temple University Press, 1992.

Shostak, Debra. "Maxine Hong Kingston's Fake Books." In *Memory, Narrative and Identity: New Essays in Ethnic American Literatures,* edited by Amritjit Singh, Joseph T. Skerrett, and Robert E. Hogan. 233–260. Boston: Northeastern University Press, 1994.

Simmons, Diane. "*Tripmaster Monkey* and the Scrutable Self." In *Maxine Hong Kingston,* 140–162. New York: Twayne, 1999.

Smith, Jeanne. "Monkey Business: Maxine Hong Kingston's Transformational Trickster Texts." In *Writing Tricksters: Mythic Gambols in American Ethnic Literature,* 31–70. Berkeley: University of California Press, 1997.

Suzuki-Martinez, Sharon. "Trickster Strategies: Challenging American Identity, Community and Art in Kingston's *Tripmaster Monkey.*" In *Reviewing Asian America: Locating Diversity,* edited by Wendy L. Ng and Soo-Young Chin, 161–170. Pullman: Washington State University Press, 1995.

Tanner, James T. F. "Walt Whitman's Presence in Maxine Hong Kingston's *Tripmaster Monkey: His Fake Book,*" *MELUS* 20, no. 4 (1995): 61–74.

Wang, Jennie. "*Tripmaster Monkey:* Kingston's Postmodern Representation of a New 'China Man,' " *MELUS* 20, no. 1 (1995): 101–114.

Williams, A. Noelle. "Parody and Pacifist Transformations in Maxine Hong Kingston's *Tripmaster Monkey: His Fake Book*," *MELUS* 20, no. 1 (1995): 83–100.

Crystal Anderson

TROPIC OF CANCER Henry Miller (1934)

"It may well be that we are doomed, that there is no hope for any of us," wrote Henry Miller in *Tropic of Cancer*, "but if that is so then let us set up a last agonizing, bloodcurdling howl, a screech of defiance, a war whoop! Away with lamentations! Away with elegies and dirges! Away with biographies and histories, and libraries and museums! Let the dead eat the dead. Let us living ones dance about the rim of the crater, a last expiring dance. But a dance!" (257). *Tropic of Cancer*, Miller's first published book, is such a dance, a full-bodied, hot-blooded celebration of joy and pain, of lust and decay, of poverty and plenty. Its frankness so shocked censors upon its publication in 1934 that the book remained banned in the United States for another 27 years.

To this day, *Tropic of Cancer* still incites arguments between those who laud Miller for his liberated worldview and those who see him (or, perhaps more accurately, the book's narrator) simply as a misogynistic, selfish boor. Ironically, this book, set in Paris, owes much of its spirit to writers such as Henry David Thoreau and Walt Whitman. Miller's disdain for western society and how it crushes those who do not march to its beat is reminiscent of Thoreau's *Walden*, while Miller's depiction of sex and the body is frank in much the same way as Whitman's verse. Yet, like Whitman and Thoreau, Miller is hardly a crank, and his seriousness is tempered with good humor and joy, wonder and awe.

Miller makes no secret of his love for Whitman in *Cancer*, explicitly stating that he considered Whitman "the poet of the body and soul," and that "there is no equivalent in the languages of Europe for the spirit which he immortalized. Europe is saturated with art and her soil is full of dead bones and her museums are bursting with plundered treasures, but what Europe has never had is a free healthy spirit, what you might call a MAN. Goethe was the nearest approach, but Goethe was a stuffed shirt, by comparison . . . Goethe is an end of something, Whitman is a beginning" (240).

Many of Miller's champions picked up the connection. Writers from Lawrence Durrell, Anaïs Nin, and George Orwell through to Norman Mailer and Erica Jong saw Miller as nothing less than Whitman's successor: a uniquely American writer who accepted and reveled even as he condemned and recoiled. Orwell, quoted in Nin's introduction to *Cancer*, stated that "it is the book of a man who is happy. . . . So far from protesting, he is accepting. And the very word 'acceptance' calls up his real affinity . . . Walt Whitman" (xi). More than accepting, though, Miller celebrates, as did Whitman, the odd, the grotesque, the fantastic, the obscene, the unusual in all its manifestations. As Miller put it in *The Books in My Life*, "there is nothing but the marvelous and only the marvelous" (Miller 1969, 125). His narrator in *Cancer* flows from scene to scene, never even sure at times where his next meal will be coming from, spending francs as quickly as they come into his hands, watching as his friends wallow in misery and use the women around them. All the while, he remains detached; in the words of Leon Lewis, resisting "the squalor which he could have easily slipped into" (Lewis, 81). The narrator in *Cancer*, Lewis notes, "often gets angry or discouraged, but . . . he never curses life" (Lewis, 90).

It is testament to Miller that *Cancer* was a shout of exhilaration and not a curse. Miller wrote the book in Paris in the early 1930s after struggling through the 1920s as an office worker in his native New York City. "I had written three (novels) that weren't published (in the 1920s) and was finally at the end of my rope," he said in a 1956 interview. "That was how I got my start, by being completely defeated, and then I found I could write; I found my own voice" (Kersnowski, 5).

According to Miller, in 1927 he typed out over 30 pages of autobiographical notes that, in retrospect, formed "an outline of everything I was going to write," he said, "the substance of everything I've written that concerns my life" (Kersnowski, 67). Later novels such as *Black Spring* and the Rosy Crucifixion trilogy (*Sexus, Nexus,* and *Plexus*) clearly were based on those notes.

But *Tropic of Cancer*, according to Miller, "was written on the spot, while I was living it. It was the story about how I'm writing that book a thing of the immediate present. In a way, that makes it different from everything else I've ever done" (Kersnowski, 51, 67).

Many critics have taken issue with Miller for his narrator's supposed misogynistic view of women, but, as Lewis points out, "both the men and the women Miller spends time with (in *Cancer*) are treated with similar harshness" (Lewis, 78–79), if not in the direct language of the narrator, then in their own self-damning dialogue and monologues.

Much of the controversy around *Cancer* swirled around the language of the book. Miller stated that his lifestyle in Paris, that of "an exile living on the French without money, brought me into contact with the strangest people: rogues, prostitutes, wastrels, people you wouldn't meet if you were living an ordinary life . . . In talking of them, I would transcribe their language" (Kersnowski, 5). When asked, in the 1950s, if he would consider editing the book in an effort to revoke its "banned" status, Miller stated that he considered the "obscenity" of the book "so integral that (removing it) would destroy the whole value of the book from a literary standpoint . . . I don't know what the book would look like without it" (Kersnowski, 5).

Lewis suggests that to call *Cancer* a novel "confuses the issue and tends to induce expectations that are not satisfied . . . The narrative consciousness of the artist/hero gives it some continuity, but it does not have any real character development, a chronological linear progression, a plot one could outline, or any dramatic denouement or even a conclusion that ties things up" (Lewis, 81). Miller would probably have agreed with that assessment. When asked in a 1962 interview about the possibility of filming *Tropic of Cancer*, he said, "I can't see how anybody could possibly make a film of that book. I don't see the story there" (Kersnowski, 62).

While there may be no clear plotline and no blatant denouement or resolution, and the narrator of the "story about writing a book" really seems no closer to finishing his book at the end of *Cancer* than he was at the beginning, *Cancer* still ends on a note of exhilaration at the constancy of change. "I feel this river flowing through me," the narrator concludes after having flowed thought the events in the novel (318), and the overwhelming feeling is that Miller is every bit as much "the happiest man on earth" on the last page of the book as he was on the first.

SOURCES

Gordon, William A. *The Mind and Art of Henry Miller.* Baton Rouge: Louisiana State University Press, 1967.

Jong, Erica. *The Devil at Large: Erica Jong on Henry Miller.* New York: Random House, 1993.

Kersnowski, Frank L., and Alice Hughes, eds. *Conversations with Henry Miller.* Jackson: University of Mississippi Press, 1994.

Lewis, Leon. *Henry Miller: The Major Writings.* New York: Schocken Books, 1986.

Mailer, Norman. *Genius and Lust: A Journey through the Major Writings of Henry Miller.* New York: Grove Press, 1976.

Miller, Henry. *The Books in My Life.* New York: New Directions, 1969.

———. *Henry Miller on Writing.* New York: New Directions, 1964.

———. *Tropic of Cancer.* New York: Grove Press, 1961.

Nelson, Jane A. *Form and Image in the Fiction of Henry Miller.* Detroit, Mich.: Wayne State University Press, 1970.

Perles, Alfred. *My Friend Henry Miller: An Intimate Biography.* New York: J. Day and Company, 1956.

Max H. Shenk

TROPIC OF CAPRICORN Henry Miller (France, 1939; U.S., 1961)

A "prequel" to the more uniformly admired *Tropic of Cancer, Tropic of Capricorn* continues Miller's mythologized autobiography, concentrating on his time in 1920s New York before leaving his first wife for Paris expatriate life, the fallout from which is chronicled in *Cancer.* Depending on whom you ask, *Capricorn* is either the sloppiest or most formally innovative of Miller's works—George Wickes characterizes it as "more disconnected than the rest of his books, creating the impression that he was constantly distracted, 'a pastiche of brilliant passages,' which by their discontinuity indicate where he sat down to write and where he left off." In keeping with conventional thinking on Miller—both champions and detractors agree on his profound aliterariness—its formal peculiarities are generally viewed as defiant aimlessness.

The first section, comprising a fifth of the whole and subtitled "On the Ovarian Trolley"—a reference to recreational sex, the involuntariness of birth/existence, and a character's diatribes about his wife's reproductive health problems—concerns Miller's tenure at the Cosmodemonic (alternately "Cosmococcic") Telegraph Company of North America. The initial event prefigures the haphazard nature, in the novel's eyes, of nearly all organizational endeavor: Henry Miller applies in desperation for a messenger's position, is turned down, heads to the president's office to complain, and emerges as the new employment manager. The resultant picture is one of utter chaos: "The system was wrong from start to finish, but it was not my place to criticize the system. It was mine to hire and fire. I was in the center of a revolving disk which was whirling so fast that nothing could stay put . . . the important thing was to keep hiring and firing; as long as there were men and ammunition we were to advance, to keep mopping up the trenches" (22–3). Miller uses his position as both a means to "save" unqualified immigrant applicants and a means of extracting sexual favors from female applicants and subordinates alike—most prominently his secretary Valeska, news of whose suicide will open the second section.

Regarding the supposed aimlessness of the ensuing four-fifths of *Capricorn,* it seems too appropriate to be accidental that the setting for the first act is a telegraph company (the real Miller's time at Western Union notwithstanding). As an overseer of messengers, Miller controls communication itself for the web of imposing architecture that is New York City—just as the author navigates communication through the architecture of the novel, and the human through a fluctuating existence (Miller, of course, does not distinguish between the latter two). As corporate communication breaks down—revealed from within as a senseless impossibility of Great War proportions—the illusions of novelistic unity and linear biochronology dissolve with it.

The second section opens on Miller's miserable home life; he cannot abide "personal" sex—which, reversing traditional Western morality, he characterizes as artificial in comparison to anonymous sex—and loathes his wife. The reader is foiled in expectations for any number of affairs to materialize into plotlines; none do. The only sustained female presence in *Capricorn* aside from Valeska and Miller's wife is the dance-

hall star Mara (his second wife, June, renamed Mona in *The Rosy Crucifixion*). An 80-page dance-hall daydream comprises the middle fifth of the book, and she and Miller fly into each other's arms in *Capricorn's* rapturous coda.

It is, of course, Miller's depiction of sex and characterization—or lack thereof—of women, in *Capricorn* and elsewhere, that have sparked the most heated debates over his moral value. Kate Millett presents the most comprehensive indictment of his supposed barbarism in her 1970 landmark *Sexual Politics* (others, including Miller's lover Anaïs NIN, have accused Millett of ignoring the tragicomic intent). But in *Capricorn,* it is precisely the most offensive aspects of Millerian sexuality—the aggressive, impersonal stance in relation to the act; the near-constant referral to women as cunts—that align with the novel's formal transcendence: Just as worker-Miller both revolts against and surrenders to the Cosmodemonic Company, lover-Miller is fascinated and bored with the human as sexual being. The eschewing of personality in favor of metonymic focus on genitalia highlights the absurd simplicity of the fact that humans, for all their achievements and pretensions, have nothing necessary to do except fulfill the dictates of form—we are little besides floating genitalia, so few of us being truly alive. At the summation of the flashback sequence on Miller's childhood—which begins with his accidentally killing another boy with a thrown rock—his father dies after being disappointed in an attempted religious awakening. Immediately afterward, at the exact center of the novel, the "Land of Fuck" interlude commences—an extended pornographic fantasy blurring the line between sacred and profane: The father reaches after that which is most hypothetical, dies, and is succeeded by that which is most verifiable. All communication/communion is futile, all interaction is necrophilia, and all deaths lead to all births.

The remainder of *Capricorn* is reminiscence, concerned alternately with sex and books. Though Dostoevsky, Rimbaud, and the Dadaists are all identified as inspirations, the "bible" of *Capricorn* is Henri Bergson's *Creative Evolution,* which argues that the concept of disorder is illusory, and proposes instead a dichotomy between two antithetical orders. The first is "dead," geometric order, of which the analytical mind constructs templates; the second is "vital" order, the animus of flux, the domain of intuition.

Micky Riggs writes that "salvation" for the Miller of *Capricorn* "is the search for the vital order—autonomy rather than automatism." This is true, but also bound in paradox—Miller the character is Miller the author and will one day write the book in which he appears. More so than to live, his goal is to write, and so his ultimate, ironic "salvation" must involve killing the "vital" order by capturing it in words, the novel-as-object being as dead a form as geometry. Similarly, recreational sex will eventually (via either marriage or bad luck) destroy itself by creating a child. But literary forms are necessary to provoke new revolutionary responses, and children are necessary to continue the existence of sex itself. The fact that *Tropic of Capricorn* must end by—and can only ever have existed through—stopping its own motion is the central ridiculousness of its dream.

SOURCES

Blinder, Caroline. "La Revolte enfantine: On Georges Bataille's 'La Morale de Miller' and Jean-Paul Sartre's 'Un Nouveau mystique,' " *Critique* 40, no. 1 (Fall 1998): 39–47. Also available online. URL: http://www.sauer=thompson.com/essays/Bataille%20on%20Miller.doc. Accessed January 13, 2006.

Gordon, William A. *The Mind and Art of Henry Miller.* Baton Rouge: Louisiana State University Press, 1967.

Gottesman, Ronald, ed. *Critical Essays on Henry Miller.* New York: Macmillan Publishing Co., 1992.

Mailer, Norman. *Genius and Lust: A Journey through the Writings of Henry Miller.* New York: Grove Press, Inc., 1976.

Miller, Henry. *Tropic of Capricorn.* New York: Grove/Atlantic, Inc, 1961.

Mitchell, Edward, ed. *Henry Miller: Three Decades of Criticism.* New York: New York University Press, 1971.

Nelson, Jane A. *Form and Image in the Work of Henry Miller.* Detroit, Mich.: Wayne State University Press, 1970.

Riggs, Micky. "Bergsonian Order in Tropic of Capricorn," *Artes Liberales* 4, no. 2 (Spring 1978): 9–15.

Wickes, George. "Henry Miller: Down and Out in Paris." In *Critical Essays on Henry Miller,* edited by Ronald Gottesman. New York: Macmillan Publishing Co., 1992.

Chris O. Cook

TROUT FISHING IN AMERICA RICHARD BRAUTIGAN (1967)

Some critics consider *Trout Fishing in America* a cult book; a band took the name as its own, and one person legally changed his name to the title. Popularly, it is too often dismissed as happy, hippy nonsense. However, the novel deserves greater attention and serious study.

BRAUTIGAN is a conservationist of the imagination and uses the American West as metaphor, hoping to regain the open range of the mind. His narrator's whimsical, ironic humor and the simplicity of his prose, ironically, disguise a complex web of literary allusions and symbolism. Some of the literary range Brautigan covers is Ben Franklin's autobiography (Franklin is mentioned frequently in the book, but sometimes by tricorner hat alone), Ernest HEMINGWAY, Henry David Thoreau, Nathanael WEST, Mark TWAIN, and Herman MELVILLE. Brautigan is like a Huck Finn who lit out to the territory of the imagination and found it fenced in and cemented over. What does he do when he arrives? He parodies some, he uses others as pastiche to make a larger point about America.

Brautigan, a late arrival to the San Francisco Beat scene, knew the Beat poets and their work intimately. Allen Ginsberg's poem "On Burrough's Work" is instructive in understanding Brautigan's novel. Ginsberg says:

> The method must be purest meat
> and no symbolic dressing, . . .
> But allegories are so much lettuce.
> Don't hide the madness.

Trout Fishing in America is "so much lettuce." The book's first chapter, "The Cover for Trout Fishing in America," describes, literally, the photo on the cover of the book, which includes a statue of Benjamin Franklin in San Francisco's Washington Square. Brautigan continues, saying poor people gather in the park to wait for a church to begin handing out food.

> It's sandwich time for the poor. But they cannot cross the street until the signal is given. Then they all run across the street to the church and get their sandwiches that are wrapped in newspaper. They go back to the park and unwrap the

newspaper and see what their sandwiches are all about. A friend of mine unwrapped his sandwich one afternoon and looked inside to find just a leaf of spinach. That was all. (2)

Brautigan suggests Franklin's work ethic and his inventiveness, both symbolized by the statue, are marble now. Brautigan finishes the chapter by ironically using a quote from Kafka, who, after reading the autobiography of Benjamin Franklin, wrote, "I like the Americans because they are healthy and optimistic."

Brautigan's technique is to move from an idea, to an adjective for the idea, to metaphor of the idea, and then to a full-blown conceit. This yoking of ideas through conceit is often done for humor, but they have deeper meanings as well. "Knock on Wood (Part One)," the second story in the book, uses this method explicitly:

> The old drunk told me about trout fishing. When he could talk, he had a way of describing trout as if they were a precious and intelligent metal. Silver is not a good adjective to describe what I felt when he told me about trout fishing. I'd like to get it right. Maybe trout steel. Steel made from trout. The clear snow- filled river acting as foundry and heat. Imagine Pittsburgh. A steel that comes from trout, used to make buildings, trains and tunnels. The Andrew Carnegie of Trout! (3)

These steps are less frequently made explicit as the novel progresses, causing the characters and the reader to bump their imaginations up against unpleasant realities. For example, in "Knock on Wood (Part Two)," the narrator mistakes an old woman for a trout stream: " 'Excuse me,' I said. 'I thought you were a trout stream.' 'I'm not,' she said" (5). Finally, in one of the concluding stories, "The Cleveland Wrecking Yard," there is no explanation as to why the narrator visits a junkyard to see a Colorado trout stream stacked and ready for sale. The narrator here has no problem with the commodification of the environment or what he sees. In "Trout Fishing in America Nib," the narrator describes first a gold nib for a fountain pen, then he imagines writing with one made from trout: "I thought

to myself what a lovely nib trout fishing in America would make with a stroke of cool green trees along the river's shore, wild flowers and dark fins pressed against the paper." The descriptions suggest the Mississippi River in Twain's time or Hemingway's "Big Two-Hearted River." However, America changed; the experience is only imaginary and the conceit, unfortunately, is even more removed from experience.

In "Prelude to the Mayonnaise Chapter," the narrator says "expressing a human need, I always wanted to write a book that ended with the word Mayonnaise." Then, in the final story, "The Mayonnaise Chapter" ends with "P.S. Sorry I forgot to give you the mayonaise." Even the narrator's desire to accomplish a small, easily accomplished idea such as finishing a novel with the word "mayonnaise" fails because it is misspelled. It's sandwich time for the poor. What Brautigan can gather from the American West to make a sandwich, such as lettuce and mayonnaise, are not what they used to be.

SOURCES

Boyer, Jay. *Richard Brautigan. Western Writers Series.* Boise, Idaho: Boise State University, 1987.

Brautigan, Richard. *Trout Fishing in America.* New York: Delta, 1967.

James M. Wilson

TURN OF THE SCREW, THE   Henry James
(1897)   *The Turn of the Screw,* a deceptively simple novella by Henry JAMES, has generated considerable debate from the time the author penned it in 1897 to the present. A ghost story, the tale utilizes many of the conventions found in other 19th-century examples of the genre—an ancient estate, a plucky young woman, and a commonsense housekeeper, for example—but it also introduces psychological, theological, educational, historical, sociological, and sexual issues that continue to fascinate modern readers. Most of James's supernatural fiction was written between 1891 and 1900; of this body of work, *The Turn of the Screw* is the most celebrated and widely read. The story is a masterpiece of ambiguity, and James refused to clarify its meaning, saying that "it just gleams and glooms" (quoted in Varnado, 87).

In a letter of 1898, James identifies the source of his plot as a story told by the father of Archbishop Benson (letter to Percy Lubbock in Smith, 124). Leon Edel, James's biographer, discovered an additional source in "Temptation," by Tom Taylor, an 1855 story that includes a villain named Peter Quin, a probable model for Peter Quint in James's novella (Smith, 124). Peter Beidler suggests that a case of an eight-year-old girl and a 10-year-old boy accused of demonic possession, discussed by James's brother William in an 1896 lecture, may also have contributed material for *The Turn of the Screw* (Beidler, 173). The fact that James mentions "witchcraft cases" in the preface to his collected works lends credence to Beidler's suggestion (Wilson, 94).

The story is nevertheless uniquely Jamesian in its ironic opacity, its refusal to be definitively interpreted. Contributing to its complexity is a narrative structure by means of which the long-dead governess's written account is read by Douglas, an acquaintance of the governess, to a small group of guests at a country inn, among whom is the chief narrator of the story as James presents it to the reader. The reliability of each narrator is open to question. The existence of the ghosts is therefore open to question.

A young woman, the naive daughter of a British country parson, takes a job at Bly, an isolated estate. Her employer, a carefree bachelor now living in London, wishing not to be burdened with the upbringing of his orphaned niece and nephew, tells the governess that he expects her to handle all contingencies at Bly and not to consult him about decisions concerning his wards. The governess finds eight-year-old Flora, her youngest charge, enchanting and engaging. Flora's brother Miles, who arrives at Bly after his expulsion from school, seems also charming and innocent. The governess and the housekeeper, Mrs. Grose, cannot imagine why he was expelled; nor do they ask. The governess proceeds to educate both children at home, a task that she finds delightful.

The idyl at Bly is soon interrupted, however, by the ghosts of the former governess, Miss Jessel, and Peter Quint, who once served as valet to the children's uncle. According to Mrs. Grose, the bachelor uncle had left the children under Miss Jessel's care, and Miss Jessel became intimate with the valet, who spent consider-

able time with the children, particularly Miles. The thoroughly Victorian Mrs. Grose implies that this relationship was highly inappropriate, partly because of Quint's class and partly because of his character.

The governess assumes when the ghosts appear that they wish to contact, possess, or at least influence the children. She believes she must "save" them (40, 76), become "an expiatory victim" (31), and "protect and defend" (34) her pupils from unfathomable horrors. But she veils her mission in silence until she concludes that her pupils also see the ghosts and are faking their innocence; she then tries to force them to admit their complicity with evil.

In the end, Flora turns against the governess, and Mrs. Grose takes her away to London. Left with Miles, the governess attempts to coerce the child to "confess" to consorting with the ghosts (92). When Quint's ghost appears at the window, Miles claims not to see him. The governess, in a last ditch effort to thwart Quint's designs upon the child, grabs Miles, who then dies in her arms.

Edmund Wilson, in his oft-cited interpretation of James's novella, contends that the ghosts are merely figments of the governess's disturbed imagination. He acknowledges Edna Kenton as the first to opine that the governess "is a neurotic case of sex repression" who projects her own desire onto the two ghosts (Wilson, 88–89). He supports Kenton's view with Freudian theory and with the observation "that there is never any reason for supposing that anybody but the governess sees the ghosts" (Wilson, 90).

Others, such as R. W. B. Lewis, believe that the ghosts are meant to be real. Lewis reminds readers that Mrs. Grose corroborates the governess's vision by identifying Quint as the ghostly figure the governess describes. For Lewis, the specters evoke what James himself called "the reader's general vision of evil" (Lewis, xv). Robert Heilman agrees that the ghosts cannot be dismissed as the "symbolization of evil" (Heilman, 346), which he characterizes as "ubiquitous, mysterious, and, though limited in scope, eternal" (Heilman, 346–347).

Peter Beidler makes a good case for the objective existence of the ghosts, claiming that the children do not see the ghosts because they are possessed by them. The children are, hence, both innocent and evil

(Beidler, 149), a reading that maintains what Rimmon calls "the moral and epistemological" dimension of the novella (Rimmon, 117).

Contemporary critics are split on the issue of whether or not the governess "invents" the ghosts. However, they read the ghosts less often as generalized, "ubiquitous, mysterious" evil and more often as representatives of specific, marginalized behavior condemned by Victorian mores. Smith, for example, recognizes a "reverberating current of homophobia" in the tale (Smith, 126) and believes that James also portrays a rigid "English class consciousness" in his characters. Pifer sees in the story suggestions of "childhood sexuality," "pedophilia," and "child abuse" (Pifer, 53–56).

One must conclude that James's work "gleams and glooms" as much for the present generation as it has for past generations. No doubt, this classic will also speak to whatever specters haunt us in the future.

SOURCES

Beidler, Peter G. *Ghosts, Demons, and Henry James: The Turn of the Screw at the Turn of the Century.* Columbia: University of Missouri Press, 1987.

Heilman, Robert B. "The Lure of the Demonic: James and Durrenmatt," *Comparative Literature* 13 (Fall 1961): 346–357.

James, Henry. *The Turn of the Screw and Other Short Fiction by Henry James.* New York: Bantam, 1981.

Lewis, R. W. B. Introduction to *The Turn of the Screw and Other Short Fiction by Henry James.* New York: Bantam, 1981.

Pifer, Ellen. *Demon or Doll: Images of the Child in Contemporary Writing and Culture.* Charlottesville: University Press of Virginia, 2000.

Rimmon, Shlomith. *The Concept of Ambiguity: The Example of James.* Chicago: University of Chicago Press, 1977.

Smith, Elton E. "Pedophiles amidst Looming Portentousness." In *The Haunted Mind: The Supernatural in Victorian Literature,* edited by Elton E. Smith and Robert Haas. Metuchen, N.J..: Scarecrow Press, 1999.

Varnado, S. L. *Haunted Presence: The Numinous in Gothic Fiction.* Tuscaloosa: University of Alabama Press, 1987.

Wilson, Edmund. *The Triple Thinkers.* New York: Oxford University Press, 1948.

Gwen M. Neary

TUROW, SCOTT (1949–)

Successful attorney and best-selling novelist Scott Turow is famous for legal thrillers. To date, more than 25 million copies of his novels are in print and have been translated into 20 languages (scottturow.com). His biographer, Derek Lundy, notes that "Turow's novels are mediations on the dark side of human behavior" (Lundy, 10); not surprisingly, he is often ranked with Dashiell HAMMETT and Raymond CHANDLER. His first and most successful novel, *Presumed Innocent* (more than 4 million copies in print), won the 1988 Silver Dagger Award. The key to his success, reviewers and critics suggest, is that he still practices law. Words of praise for Turow's literary skill come from no less a talent than Wallace STEGNER, who calls *Presumed Innocent* "an achievement of a high order—with marvelous control and touch, an awesome capacity to assemble and dispense (and sometimes withhold) evidence," not to mention "a cast of characters who are dismayingly credible" (quoted in scottturow.com).

Scott Turow was born on April 12, 1949, in Chicago, Illinois, to David D. Turow, a physician, and Ria Pastron Turow, a writer. Turow received his bachelor's degree at Amherst College (1970), his master's degree at Stanford University (1974), and his law degree at Harvard University (1978). After marrying Annette Weisberg, an artist, on April 4, 1971, Turow published a best-selling book based on his experiences during his first year at Harvard law school. *Presumed Innocent* burst onto the best-seller lists in 1987. This enthralling novel centers on a lawyer, Rusty Sabitch, his mathematician wife Barbara, and his murdered paramour Carolyn Polhemus. He followed with *The Burden of Proof* (1990), which opens with the suicide of Clara, wife of defense attorney Alejandro "Sandy" Stem (who defended Sabitch in *Presumed Innocent*). In his third novel, *Pleading Guilty* (1993), Turow returns to Kindle County, by now familiar territory, as McCormack A. "Mack" Malloy seeks a missing litigator and nearly $6 million.

Turow's fourth novel, *The Laws of Our Fathers* (1996), takes for its subject Kindle County's housing projects and a mysterious murder. The judge is Sonia "Sonny" Klonsky, a character from *The Burden of Proof;* the trial reveals that the wrong man has been apprehended. Robbie Feaver is the protagonist of *Personal Injuries* (1999), which returns to the lives of privileged lawyers: Robbie's wife is dying and Robbie himself is charged with embezzlement, a charge that leads him to an affair with Evon Miller, an FBI agent assigned to his case. Turow's most recent novel, *Reversible Errors* (2002), is a suspense-filled tale about a triple-murder charge, and Arthur Raven, the court-appointed attorney for Rommy "Squirrel" Gandolph, the accused man. Turow published the novel *Ordinary Heroes* in 2005.

Scott Turow, whom Anne RICE has called "a profoundly gifted writer" (Rice, 29), lives with his wife in Chicago, where he is a partner in the Sonnenschein, Carlin, Nath & Rosenthal law firm. *Presumed Innocent,* a 1990 Warner Brothers film, directed by Alan J. Pakula, starred Harrison Ford, Bonnie Bedelia, Brian Dennehy, and Raul Julia. In 1992, *The Burden of Proof,* a two-part television film based on the novel, starred Hector Elizondo, Brian Dennehy, and Adrienne Barbeau; *Reversible Errors* was adapted as a CBS television miniseries in 2004.

NOVELS

The Burden of Proof. New York: Farrar, Straus, 1990.
The Laws of Our Fathers. New York: Farrar, Straus, 1996.
Ordinary Heroes. New York: Farrar, Straus, 2005.
Personal Injuries. New York: Farrar, Straus & Giroux, 1999.
Pleading Guilty. New York: Farrar, Straus, 1993.
Presumed Innocent. New York: Farrar, Straus, 1987.
Reversible Errors. New York: Farrar, Straus & Giroux, 2002.

SOURCES

Lundy, Derek. *Scott Turow: Meeting the Enemy.* East Toronto, Ontario: Ecw Press, 1995.
Rice, Anne. "She Knew Too Many, Too Well," *The New York Times Book Review,* 28 June 1987, pp. 1, 28–29.

OTHER

Buckley, James, Jr. "Going Undercover in Life and Law: A Talk with Scott Turow." BookPage. Available online. URL: http://www.bookpage.com. Accessed September 22, 2005.
Groner, Jonathan. Review of *Personal Injuries.* Salon.com. Available online. URL: http://www.salon.com. Accessed September 22, 2005.
O'Leary, Shannon. "Legal Letdown." January. Available online. URL: http://www.januarymagazine.com. Accessed September 22, 2005.

Scott Turow Web site. Available online. URL: http://www.scottturow.com. Accessed September 22, 2005.

TWAIN, MARK (SAMUEL LANGHORNE CLEMENS) (1835–1910)

Considered the father of modern American fiction by his literary descendants, William FAULKNER and Ernest HEMINGWAY, Mark Twain, the pseudonym of Samuel Langhorne Clemens, is synonymous with two of his most famous books, *The ADVENTURES OF HUCKLEBERRY FINN,* (1884) and *The ADVENTURES OF TOM SAWYER* (1876). Those novels contain the hallmarks for which Twain continues to be revered: honesty, truth, the use of the plain vernacular of the ordinary American, humor, and above all, a genius for telling a story. Mingled with these obvious talents are his penetrating social criticism, sympathy for the plight of the oppressed, and his powerful ability to evoke the beauty and promise of America.

Samuel Clemens was born on November 30, 1835, the year of Halley's Comet, in Florida, Missouri, on the banks of the Mississippi River. His father was John Marshall Clemens, a merchant and a lawyer, and his mother was Jane Lampton Clemens. He worked as a Mississippi riverboat pilot, a Nevada and California newspaperman, and a successful public speaker and storyteller. All of these prepared him for the writing career that began with short stories and travel books. His first novel, *The Gilded Age: A Tale of Today,* appeared in 1873, after Twain's move to the East and marriage in 1870, to Olivia L. Langdon of Elmira, New York. Twain collaborated with Charles Dudley Warner on *The Gilded Age,* a sentimental novel that contains the memorable optimist, Colonel Sellers, and some of Twain's most trenchant satire on the greed and political corruption that gave the age its moniker. Twain's portion was later published as *The Adventures of Colonel Sellers* in 1965. *The Adventures of Tom Sawyer,* with its nostalgic view of Twain's own childhood, evokes, even today, a sense of childhood innocence. The romance between Tom and Becky, the unforgettable Aunt Polly, and Tom's involvement with Injun Joe and Huck Finn in the murder plot are some of the major ingredients of this novel.

The PRINCE AND THE PAUPER, a historical novel written concurrently with *Huckleberry Finn,* appeared in 1882.

Set in 16th-century England, it relates the mix-up in identity between the urchin Tom Canty and Prince Edward VI.

The Adventures of Huckleberry Finn (1884), though it continues to inspire spirited debate, is recognized today for the brilliant use of an innocent child's voice and perception as a means of telling the powerful story of slavery's survival in the United States. The novel, banned in Concord, Massachusetts, in 1885 because of Huck's vulgar behavior, has disturbed a number of late-20th-century readers because of Huck's use of the 19th-century racial epithet "nigger," despite his apparent friendship with Jim, the escaped slave with whom he rafts down the river. The novel's power, its painful rendering of antebellum America, and its classic portrayal of Huck himself, ensures that this novel will remain a classic for the foreseeable future.

Next Twain wrote *A Connecticut Yankee in King Arthur's Court* (1889) a literary burlesque of the Age of Chivalry and Thomas Malory's *Morte D'Arthur* that features Hank Morgan, another colloquial narrator and a prototypical 19th-century ordinary American. He intends to do good by modernizing the medieval country, but becomes a power-hungry mogul. It also addresses an immediate concern of the day: the effects of industrialism and technology on then-rural America and its inhabitants.

The TRAGEDY OF PUDD'NHEAD WILSON (1894) involves another mix-up in identity, this time between Valet de Chambre, born to the slave Roxana, and Thomas a Becket Driscoll, the son of Roxy's master, Judge Driscoll. Roxy switches the babies when they are infants, and the ensuing tragedy illuminates the destructive presence of racism in American society. The "pudd'nhead" in the novel is the attorney who eventually discovers the identities of the young men and also solves a murder. *Personal Recollections of Joan of Arc* (1896), written under the pseudonym Sieur Louis de Conte, is a historical novel that has been praised for its insight into the political situations that resulted in the death of Saint Joan.

Twain died on April 21, 1910, of heart disease, in Redding, Connecticut, with Halley's Comet ushering him out just as it had welcomed him into this world. He was buried in Elmira, New York. A number of his works have been published posthumously, including *The Mysterious Stranger: A Romance* (1916); *Simon Wheeler: Detective,* a novel unfinished at Twain's death and edited by Franklin R. Rogers in 1963; *Huck Finn and Tom Sawyer Collaboration,* an unfinished novel completed by Stephen Stewart in 2001; and *Huck Finn and Tom Sawyer among the Indians,* an unfinished novel completed by Lee Nelson in 2003.

The Adventures of Huckleberry Finn was adapted as a film four times: in 1931 by Paramount, in 1939 and again in 1960 by Metro-Goldwyn-Mayer (MGM), and in 1974 by United Artists; *The Adventures of Tom Sawyer* was adapted in 1930 by Paramount, in 1938 by Selznick International, in 1973 by United Artists, and the film "Tom Sawyer, Detective" by Paramount in 1939. *A Connecticut Yankee in King Arthur's Court* was adapted as a film in 1931 by Twentieth Century-Fox, and in 1949 by Paramount; *The Prince and the Pauper* was adapted in 1937 by Warner Bros., in 1969 by Childhood Productions, and as a film titled "Crossed Swords" in 1978 by Warner Bros.

The Bancroft Library of the University of California at Berkeley houses the Mark Twain papers, the major collection of Mark Twain materials. Other major holdings of significant Twain materials include Yale University Library, the Henry W. and Albert A. Berg Collection of the New York Public Library, Vassar College, and the Alderman Library of the University of Virginia.

NOVELS; UNDER PSEUDONYM MARK TWAIN, EXCEPT WHERE INDICATED:

The Adventures of Huckleberry Finn, Tom Sawyer's Comrade. London: Chatto & Windus, 1884; New York: Webster, 1885.

The Adventures of Tom Sawyer. Hartford, Conn.: American Publishing, 1876.

The American Claimant. New York: Webster, 1892.

A Connecticut Yankee in King Arthur's Court. New York: Webster, 1889; published as *A Yankee at the Court of King Arthur.* London: Chatto & Windus, 1889.

Extract from Captain Stormfield's Visit to Heaven. New York: Harper, 1909.

The Gilded Age: A Tale of Today. (With Charles Dudley Warner) Hartford, Conn.: American Publishing, 1873; Twain's portion published separately as *The Adventures of*

Colonel Sellers. Edited by Charles Nelder, Garden City, N.Y.: Doubleday, 1965.

Huck Finn and Tom Sawyer among the Indians. (novel unfinished by Mark Twain completed by Lee Nelson). Springville, Utah: Council Press, 2003.

Huck Finn and Tom Sawyer Collaboration. (novel unfinished by Mark Twain completed by Stephen Stewart). Meadow Vista, Calif.: New Mill, 2001.

The Mysterious Stranger: A Romance. Edited by Albert Bigelow Paine and Frederick A. Duneka. New York: Harper, 1916.

Personal Recollections of Joan of Arc. (Under pseudonym Sieur Louis de Conte) New York: Harper, 1896.

The Prince and the Pauper. London: Chatto & Windus, 1881; Boston: Osgood, 1882.

Pudd'nhead Wilson: A Tale. London: Chatto & Windus, 1894; expanded as *The Tragedy of Pudd'nhead Wilson, and the Comedy of Those Extraordinary Twins.* Hartford, Conn.: American Publishing, 1894.

Simon Wheeler: Detective (unfinished novel). Edited by Franklin R. Rogers. New York: New York Public Library, 1963.

Tom Sawyer Abroad, by Huck Finn. New York: Webster, 1894.

SOURCES

Andrews, Kenneth. *Nook Farm: Mark Twain's Hartford Circle.* Cambridge, Mass.: Harvard University Press, 1950.

Benson, Ivan. *Mark Twain's Western Years.* Palo Alto, Calif.: Stanford University Press, 1938.

Clemens, Cyril. *My Cousin Mark Twain.* Rodale, 1939.

De Voto, Bernard. *Mark Twain's America.* Boston: Little, Brown, 1932.

Ferguson, J. DeLancey. *Mark Twain: Man and Legend.* Indianapolis, Ind.: Bobbs-Merrill, 1943.

Fishkin, Shelley Fisher. *Was Huck Black?: Mark Twain and African-American Voices.* New York: Oxford University Press, 1993.

Gale, Robert L. *Plots and Characters in the Works of Mark Twain.* 2 volumes. Nottingham, England: Shoe String Press, 1973.

Gibson, William M. *The Art of Mark Twain.* New York: Oxford University Press, 1976.

Gillis, William R. *Gold Rush Days with Mark Twain.* New York: AMS Press, 1969.

Hill, Hamlin. *Mark Twain: God's Fool.* New York: Harper, 1973.

Howells, William Dean. *My Mark Twain.* Mineola, N.Y.: Dover Publications, 1997.

Kaplan, Justin. *Mark Twain and His World.* New York: Simon & Schuster, 1974.

———. *Mr. Clemens and Mr. Twain.* New York: Simon & Schuster, 1966.

Lawton, Mary. *A Lifetime with Mark Twain.* New York: Harcourt, 1925.

Masters, Edgar Lee. *Mark Twain: A Portrait.* New York: Scribner, 1938.

McMahan, Elizabeth, ed. *Critical Approaches to Mark Twain's Short Stories.* Port Washington, N.Y.: Kennikat Press, 1981.

Mencken, H. L. *A Mencken Chrestomathy.* New York: Knopf, 1949.

Miller, Robert Keith. *Mark Twain.* New York: Ungar, 1983.

Neider, Charles. *Mark Twain.* New York: Horizon Press, 1967.

Paine, Albert Bigelow. *Mark Twain: A Biography; the Personal and Literary Life of Samuel Langhorne Clemens.* 4 volumes. New York: Harper, 1912.

Rasmussen, Kent. *Mark Twain A to Z.* New York: Facts On File, 1995.

Sanborn, Margaret. *Mark Twain: The Bachelor Years: A Biography.* New York: Doubleday, 1990.

Shillingsburg, Miram Jones. *At Home Abroad: Mark Twain in Australasia.* Jackson: University Press of Mississippi, 1988.

Smith, Henry Nash. *Mark Twain: A Collection of Critical Essays.* Englewood Cliffs, N.J.: Prentice Hall, 1963.

———, ed. *Mark Twain: The Development of a Writer.* Cambridge, Mass.: Belknap, 1962.

Stahl, J. D. *Mark Twain, Culture and Gender: Envisioning America through Europe.* Athens: University of Georgia Press, 1994.

Stone, Albert E. *The Innocent Eye: Childhood in Mark Twain's Fiction.* New Haven, Conn.: Yale University Press, 1961.

Tenney, Thomas. *Mark Twain: A Reference Guide.* Boston: G. K. Hall, 1977.

Twain, Mark. *Old Times on the Mississippi.* Toronto: Belford, 1876; reprinted as *The Mississippi Pilot.* London: Ward, Lock & Tyler, 1877, revised as *Life on the Mississippi.* Boston: Osgood, 1883.

———. *Mark Twain's Autobiography* 2 volumes. Edited by Albert Bigelow Paine. New York: Harper, 1924, edited as one volume by Charles Neider. New York: Harper, 1959.

Wagenknecht, Edward. *Mark Twain: The Man and His Work.* 3rd edition. Norman: University of Oklahoma Press, 1967.

Wecter, Dixon. *Sam Clemens of Hannibal.* Boston: Houghton, 1952.

Wilson, James D. *A Reader's Guide to the Short Stories of Mark Twain.* Boston: G. K. Hall, 1987.

Zall, Paul M., ed. *Mark Twain Laughing: Humorous Anecdotes by and about Samuel L. Clemens.* Knoxville: University of Tennessee Press, 1985.

TYLER, ANNE (1941–   )

Author of 15 novels and numerous short stories, Anne Tyler is one of America's most distinguished novelists. After several nominations in the 1980s for major literary awards, Tyler won the 1983 PEN/Faulkner Award for *Dinner at the Homesick Restaurant,* the 1985 National Book Critics Circle award for *The ACCIDENTAL TOURIST,* and the 1988 Pulitzer Prize for *Breathing Lessons.* In the work of Tyler, individuals try to assert themselves and come to terms with their complex involvements with family and community. They frequently try to break free of family tradition and convention. Even when her characters fail to escape and instead return home, they have usually learned lessons that will stand them in good stead. As scholar Alice Hall Petry points out, these ideas make it difficult to label Tyler: Critics have called her "a realist, a romantic, a Victorian, a postmodernist, a minimalist, a sentimentalist, a feminist, a non-feminist, and a naturalist," terms that are, according to Petry, "stridently incompatible" (Petry, 5). Although the influence of earlier writers, including poet and essayist Ralph Waldo Emerson, and the Southern writers, particularly Eudora WELTY and Carson McCULLERS, have often been noted, the most salient aspect of her work is the "upbeat stance" usually missing in contemporary fiction: "No wonder," comments Petry, "she defies classification" (Petry, 17). She is, in scholar Elizabeth Evans's words, "more interested in endurance and reconciliation than in alienation and isolation" (Evans, 20).

Anne Tyler was born on October 25, 1941, in a Quaker community in Minneapolis, Minnesota, to Lloyd Parry Tyler, a chemist, and Phyllis Mahon Tyler. After moving with her Quaker parents to North Carolina, she studied writing at Duke University with Reynolds Price, graduating with a bachelor's degree in 1961. In her first novel, *If Morning Ever Comes* (1964), Ben Joe Hawkes discovers that it is he, not the women in his life, who lacks self-sufficiency. Tyler's second novel, *The Tin Can Tree* (1965), set in an isolated, rural three-apartment row house on the border of a North Carolina tobacco field, features a photographer, James, who enlarges a photo of Rosie; the six-year-old's unexpected death causes numerous family reactions. The protagonist of *The Clock Winder* (1972) travels from North Carolina to Baltimore, where she finds a home with an upper-class family named Emerson, while one of the young Emersons escapes the family by moving South with his bride, a Georgia waitress. *A Slipping-Down Life* (1970) depicts Evie Decker, a teenager who survives an elopement with would-be rock star Drumstrings Casey to learn something about herself and her forthcoming baby. In *Celestial Navigation* (1974), the agoraphobic artist figure Jeremy Paulding is aware of his need to replace his dead mother through his marriage to the self-confident and efficient Mary Tell. *Searching for Caleb* (1976), like several subsequent Tyler novels, depicts an artist seeking freedom from his family in order to practice his craft; it uses the idea of travel as a metaphor for escape: Sixty-one years earlier, Caleb left the family, and now Duncan and Jessie Peck are the only two of their generation who will escape the restrictions of the Baltimore clan. *Earthly Possessions* (1977) is told through the perspective of Charlotte Emory, who alternates between the past, when she was taken hostage and forcibly removed to Florida, and the present, when she realizes that "life" itself takes us where it will.

Her eighth novel, *Morgan's Passing* (1980), won the 1981 Janet Heidinger Kafka prize, a 1980 National Book Critics Circle fiction award nomination, and a 1982 American Book Award nomination in paperback fiction. The title character, Morgan Gower, changes his identity by wearing a variety of hats, beards, and masks. *Dinner at the Homesick Restaurant* is a dark tale of a Baltimore family abandoned by Beck Tull, the traveling salesman and father; despite the efforts of the mother, Pearl Tull, to hold the family together, the adult children bear the scars of poverty and deprivation. In Tyler's 10th novel, *The Accidental Tourist,* Macon Leary, a travel-guide writer who, after his son dies and his wife leaves him, gradually returns to life and reality. Maggie Moran and her husband, Ira, take a one-day train trip in *Breathing Lessons* that symbolizes the continuity of family and the inescapable passage of time. In Tyler's 12th novel, *Saint Maybe* (1991), the teenager Ian Bedloe partially causes and then reacts to the upheavals resulting from his brother Danny's marriage to a divorcee; these upheavals include a suicide, drug overdose, and the unwitting interference of the

Reverend Emmett. In *Ladder of Years* (1995), Delia Grinstead walks out on her family only to return to them after supporting herself for a time; like many other Tyler characters, Delia learns to examine her options and make the choice that brings her the most happiness possible under the circumstances. The 29-year-old Barnaby Gaitlin in *A Patchwork Planet* (1998) tells his tale through a first-person narrative, gradually changing from a delinquent teenager presented in flashbacks into a young man with a clear sense of his own place. *When We Were Grownups* presents 53-year-old Rebecca Davitch, a large, eccentric woman who, temporarily dressed as a bag lady, thinks about her high school boyfriend and her two husbands but returns to the life that she has left behind.

Anne Tyler, who was married to Taghi Modarressi, a psychiatrist and writer, from 1963 until his death in 1997, lives and writes in her adopted city of Baltimore. *The Accidental Tourist,* starring Kathleen Turner and William Hurt, was released by Warner Brothers in 1988. *A Slipping-down Life* was adapted for film in 2004. Three unpublished novels by Tyler and some correspondence are housed at the Perkins Library at Duke University. Tyler's most recent novel is *The Amateur Marriage* (2004).

NOVELS

The Accidental Tourist. New York: Berkley Books, 1985.
The Amateur Marriage. New York: Knopf, 2004.
Breathing Lessons. New York: Berkley Books, 1988.
Celestial Navigation. New York: Ivy Books, 1974.
The Clock Winder. New York: Berkley Books, 1972.
Dinner at the Homesick Restaurant. New York: Berkley Books, 1982.
Earthly Possessions. New York: Ivy Books, 1977.
If Morning Ever Comes. New York: Ivy Books, 1964.
Ladder of Years. New York: Knopf, 1995.
Morgan's Passing. New York: Knopf, 1980.
A Patchwork Planet. New York: Knopf, 1998.
Saint Maybe. New York: Ivy Books, 1991.
Searching for Caleb. New York: Ivy Books, 1976.
A Slipping-Down Life. New York: Ivy Books, 1970.
The Tin Can Tree. New York: Berkley Books, 1965.
When We Were Grownups. New York: Knopf, 2001.

SOURCES

Betts, Doris. "The Fiction of Anne Tyler," *Southern Quarterly* 21 (Summer 1983): 23–28. Reprinted in Peggy Whitman Prenshaw, ed. *Women Writers of the Contemporary South.* Jackson: University Press of Mississippi, 1984, pp. 23–37.

Brown, Laurie L. "Interviews with Seven Contemporary Writers," *Southern Quarterly* 21 (Summer 1983): 3–22.

Croft, Robert W. *Anne Tyler: A Bio-bibliography.* Westport, Conn.: Greenwood Press, 1995.

Eder, Richard. Review of *Ladder of Years, Los Angeles Times Book Review,* 7 May 1995, 3.

Evans, Elizabeth. *Anne Tyler.* New York: Twayne, 1993.

Gilbert, Susan. "Anne Tyler." In *Southern Women Writers: The New Generation,* edited by Tonette Bond Inge, 251–278. Tuscaloosa: University of Alabama Press, 1990.

Gullette, Margaret Morganroth. *Safe at Last in the Middle Years: The Invention of the Midlife Progress Novel: Saul Bellow, Margaret Drabble, Anne Tyler, and John Updike.* Berkeley: University of California Press, 1988.

Harper, Natalie. "Searching for Anne Tyler," *Simon's Rock of Bard College Bulletin* 4 (Fall 1984): 6–7.

Jones, Anne. "Home at Last and Homesick Again: The Ten Novels of Anne Tyler," *Hollins Critic* 23 (April 1986): 1–13.

Kissel, Susan. *Moving On: The Heroines of Shirley Anne Grau, Anne Tyler, and Gail Godwin.* Bowling Green, Ohio: Bowling Green State University Popular Press, 1969.

Magee, Rosemary M., ed. *Friendship and Sympathy: Communities of Southern Women Writers.* Jackson: University Press of Mississippi, 1992.

Nesanovich, Stella. "The Individual in the Family: Anne Tyler's *Searching for Caleb* and *Earthly Possessions,*" *Southern Review* 14 (Winter 1978): 170–176.

Petry, Alice Hall. *Critical Essays on Anne Tyler.* Boston: G. K. Hall, 1992.

———, ed. *Understanding Anne Tyler.* Columbia: University of South Carolina Press, 1990.

Robertson, Mary F. "Anne Tyler: Medusa Points and Contact Ponts." In *Contemporary American Women Writers: Narrative Strategies,* edited by Catherine Rainwater and William J. Scheik, 119–142. Lexington: University of Kentucky Press, 1985.

Ross-Bryant, Lynn. "Anne Tyler's *Searching for Caleb*: The Sacrality of the Everyday," *Soundings* 73 (Spring 1990): 191–207.

Salwak, Dale, ed. *Anne Tyler as Novelist.* Iowa City: University of Iowa Press, 1994.

Smith, Lucinda Irwin. *Women Who Write: From the Past and the Present to the Future.* Englewood Cliffs, N.J.: Prentice Hall, 1989.

Stephens, C. Ralph, ed. *The Fiction of Anne Tyler.* Jackson: University Press of Mississippi, 1990.

Updike, John. "Family Ways," *New Yorker,* 29 March 1976, pp. 110–112. Reprinted in John Updike. *Hugging the Shore.* New York: Random House, 1983, pp. 273–278.

———. "Imagining Things," *New Yorker,* 23 June 1980, pp. 97–101. Reprinted in John Updike. *Hugging the Shore.* New York: Random House, 1983, pp. 293–294.

———. "On Such a Beautiful Green Little Planet," *New Yorker,* 5 April 1982, pp. 193–197. Reprinted in John Updike. *Hugging the Shore.* New York: Random House, 1983, pp. 292–299.

Voelker, Joseph C. *Art and the Accidental in Anne Tyler.* Columbia: University of Missouri Press, 1989.

Willrich, Patricia Rowe. "Watching through Windows: A Perspective on Anne Tyler," *Virginia Quarterly Review* 68 (Summer 1992): 497–516.

Zahlan, Anne R. "Anne Tyler." In *Fifty Southern Writers after 1900: A Bio-Bibliographical Sourcebook* edited by Joseph M. Flora and Robert Bain, 491–504. Westport, Conn.: Greenwood Press, 1987.

OTHER
Books and Writers. Anne Tyler. Available online. URL: http://www.kirjasto.sci.fi/atyler.htm. Accessed September 22, 2005.

TYLER, ROYALL (1757–1826)

Principally known as a dramatist, Royall Tyler wrote the first successful comedy by a native-born American. *The Contrast* (published in 1790) was first produced in New York City on April 16, 1787; it features the usual admirable Yankees who contrast sharply with the hypocritical English character. A decade later, Tyler wrote a novel, *The ALGERINE CAPTIVE,* a satirical picaresque work in two volumes published in 1797. These are his two most significant works, although he also wrote at least six additional plays, one of the first American musical dramas, poetry, travel letters, and a newspaper column, as well as speeches, sermons, and legal tracts.

Tyler (initially named William Clark Tyler) was born on July 18, 1757, in Boston, Massachusetts, to Royall Tyler, a member of the Massachusetts House of Representatives. When his father died in 1771, Tyler legally adopted his first name, Royall. He was educated at Harvard, receiving his bachelor's degree in 1776 (as well as an honorary B.A. from Yale, in those days a courtesy practiced by the two colleges). After serving briefly with General Sullivan in Newport, Rhode Island, he earned his master's degree from Harvard in 1779 and was admitted to the Massachusetts bar in 1780. When his romance with Abigail Adams, daughter of John Adams, ended in 1785, Tyler performed diplomatic and legal missions for General Benjamin Lincoln over the next two years, arriving in New York in time to see *The Contrast* performed. Shortly thereafter, he moved to Guilford, Vermont, to begin what became a successful law practice. In 1794 he married Mary Palmer, daughter of Joseph Palmer, with whom he had lived during the Shays Rebellion. While practicing law and contributing to newspaper columns, Tyler wrote *The Algerine Captive,* featuring Updike Underhill, a naive narrator whom critics compare to Voltaire's Candide or Jonathan Swift's Gulliver. After losing his schoolhouse to a fire, he wanders south, where he observes the degradation of the slaves and becomes a ship's doctor, but realizes too late that he is, himself, on a slave ship. Updike also becomes a slave in Algeria and is finally rescued by a Portuguese ship and an American treaty. Tyler uses satire and irony not only to evoke the brutality of slavery wherever it occurs but also to warn his fledgling nation.

In the years after he published *The Algerine Captive,* Royall Tyler served as chief justice of the Vermont Supreme Court (1807–13) and as a professor at the University of Vermont. His reputation today rests on his conviction that American characters speaking real American dialects were artistically viable in the new republic and across the Atlantic as well. Most of his papers are in the Royall Tyler collection at the Vermont Historical Society in Montpelier, Vermont.

NOVELS
The Algerine Captive; or, the Life and Adventures of Doctor Updike Underhill: Six Years a Prisoner Among the Algerines. 2 volumes. Walpole, N.H.: Printed & sold by David Carlisle, 1797.

SOURCES
Carson, Ada Lou, and Herbert L. Carson. *Royall Tyler.* Boston: Twayne, 1979.

Dennis, Larry R. "Legitimizing the Novel: Royall Tyler's *The Algerine Captive,*" *Early American Literature,* 9 (Spring 1974): 71–80.

Tanselle, G. Thomas. *Royall Tyler.* Cambridge, Mass.: Harvard University Press, 1967.

TYPICAL AMERICAN GISH JEN (1988) Gish

JEN's *Typical American* is a landmark novel in Chinese-American women's writing. It stands apart from the West Coast second-generation writing of Maxine Hong KINGSTON and Amy TAN in that it deals with great irony and humor with the immigrant life of a Chinese family in the New York region. The novel concentrates on the lives of the central characters Ralph, Theresa, and Helen Chang after their arrival in the United States from China. Although they initially have a strong sense of their Chinese identity, the fact that they are known in the novel by their American names reveals the absence of any concern or backward glances to China. Despite being set in the context of a Chinese-American family, the novel is concerned primarily with the general immigrant experience of becoming an American and integrating into a capitalist American society.

Although Ralph first comes to America in order to study for a doctorate, at which he eventually succeeds and gains a tenured teaching post in an American university, he abandons such a career in order to plunge himself into the (to him) unexplored and exciting world of entrepreneurial capitalist America. For this reason the critic Rachel C. Lee considers the novel to be a pioneer story in which "Jen substitutes a green lawn in the suburbs for buffalo-roaming plains, and, instead of hostile Native Americans, Ralph must grapple with an American-born Chinese man named Grover Ding. . . . In the mid-20th century, the frontiersman becomes an Asian-American engineer; the frontiers, a Connecticut residence and venture capitalism" (Lee, 13).

At first glance, much of the novel follows the Chang family's steady rise up the American social ladder—so much so that they call themselves the "Changkees"—and the novel appears to be celebrating the possibilities of immigrant integration and success through buying property and being a "self-made" entrepreneur. The novel, in fact, begins with the statement, "It's an American story: Before he was a thinker, or a doer, or an engineer, much less an imagineer like his self-made millionaire friend Grover Ding, Ralph Chang was just a small boy in China, struggling to grow up his father's son" (3). However, the Changs' success is shaken when the building they have

extended in order to expand their fast food restaurant is found to have poor foundations. Jen appears to be suggesting through symbolism that the foundations of the immigrant American dream is indeed built on shaky ground. Indeed, the fact that they are Chinese and are therefore not fully accepted in a racist suburban America is a barely audible but nonetheless present refrain throughout the novel.

Following the collapse of the business, Ralph has to return to his teaching post feeling like an entrepreneurial failure, and they begin the process of selling their family home. However, the novel does not purely consist of this capitalist and rather masculinist plot. The family, too, is beginning to be fractured through the pressures of assimilation into suburban American life. In particular, as the critic Rachel C. Lee states, the novel strongly portrays the changing position of women and the way in which they are both affected by Ralph's involvement with the capitalist system and liberated by their position in American society (Lee, 45).

Ralph's wife, Helen, is as seduced by the trappings of capitalist America as is her husband. She sees her own success in the manner in which she is able to furnish her new home, and her desires are focused upon items of furniture such as a "love seat." In fact, she allows herself to be seduced by Ralph's millionaire business partner on that very love seat, where she dreams of being the mistress of a grander home with a maid and all the trappings of a rich wife. Typical of Jen's novel, it is possible to understand Helen's motivation as both an embrace and a criticism of capitalism. Helen is looking not only for riches in the arms of Grover Ding but also for the attention that her husband withholds from her during his infatuation with chasing financial gain.

Ralph's sister Theresa could be viewed as the heroine of the novel. Whenever Ralph faces failure, Theresa saves him—once by miraculously finding him sitting on a park bench with his last few pennies and once when she recovers from a coma reminding Ralph of the priorities of love and family above financial success. From a feminist perspective it is Theresa who transforms her own life, through expanding her independence and her personal liberty. The narrator expresses the thoughts of the family, asking, "Was this finally, the

New World? They all noticed that there seemed to be no boundaries anymore" (126). The dilemma in the novel is what one does with such liberty. Theresa works quietly and consistently at succeeding in her original aim to train as a doctor, unlike Ralph, who rejects his aim to become a professor in order to follow his capitalist desires. Moreover, she also slowly gains success in finding happiness by leaving behind her strict Chinese morals and social mores in favor of finding love and a love of life with a man who leaves his failed marriage for her. As Ralph goes to reconcile himself with Theresa when she wakes from her coma, his lasting image of her is during the summer, when she was splashing in a paddling pool wearing a brightly colored swimsuit with her lover. This strongly contrasts with Ralph's circumstance at the time, tightly bound by his heavy clothing in a winter storm and nurturing the thought that "a man is as doomed here as he is in China" (296).

The novel ends with an optimistic note despite its critical stance toward capitalist America and its effects on the lives of women and families. The ending image of Theresa splashing in the pool signifies the possibility of attaining success in America, not through capitalist success, but through following Theresa's example of embracing the personally liberating possibilities of being an immigrant in the United States.

SOURCES

Jen, Gish. *Typical American.* London: Granta, 1998.

Lee, Rachel C. *The Americas of Asian American Literature: Gendered Fictions of Nation and Transnation.* Princeton N.J.: Princeton University Press, 1999.

Lim, Shirley Geok-Lin. "Immigration and Diaspora." In *An Interethnic Companion to Asian American Literature,* 289–311. New York: Cambridge University Press, 1997.

Xiaojing, Zhou. "Becoming Americans: Gish Jen's *Typical American.*" In *The Immigrant Experience in North American Literature: Carving Out a Niche,* edited by Katherine Payant and Toby Rose, 151–163. Westport, Conn.: Greenwood Press, 1999.

Maggie Ann Bowers

U

UNCLE TOM'S CABIN HARRIET BEECHER STOWE (1852) Harriet Beecher STOWE's controversial fictional account of the horrors of slavery, *Uncle Tom's Cabin,* was written in response to the Fugitive Slave Law of 1850. A best-selling novel of the 19th century, it contributed to the rise of antislavery sentiment before the Civil War.

Many critics interpret the characters in *Uncle Tom's Cabin* to be stand-ins for various groups in society. The evil slave-holder Simon Legree, whose horrific treatment of his slaves leads ultimately to the death of the novel's namesake, represents the worst of the Southern slave-holding aristocracy. Uncle Tom represents Stowe's notion of people of color. She writes that Tom "had, to the full, the gentle, domestic heart, which, woe for them! has been a peculiar characteristic of his unhappy race." Miss Ophelia, the sister of one of the slave owners who comes to live on a slave plantation in the South, represents the upright, prudent Northern woman, and perhaps Stowe herself.

Aside from its dominant aim of contributing to the anti-slavery cause, *Uncle Tom's Cabin* is also a work of feminist literature. Stowe's voice is prominent. With 43 asides, Stowe as author is just as important a character in the novel as Miss Ophelia or Legree. At the same time, however, Stowe claims to be an agent of God, a passive vessel for God's words. Her novel is markedly religious and stresses the immorality of slavery on the grounds of Christian ethics. Like many other works of protest literature of the period, Stowe emphasizes the importance of social injustice as not only destructive to the nation but also as sinful. She addresses the reader at the close of the novel: "not surer is the eternal law by which the millstone sinks in the ocean, than the stronger law by which injustice and cruelty shall bring on nations the wrath of Almighty God!" (485).

Some critics have dismissed *Uncle Tom's Cabin* as simplistic. James BALDWIN wrote famously, "*Uncle Tom's Cabin* is a very bad novel" (Baldwin, 11). Baldwin criticized the work for its sentimentality as well as its racism. Indeed, Stowe characterizes people of color as submissive and incapable of resistance, as exemplified by her characterization of Tom. In the context of the abolitionist, antiracist writing of her time, Stowe was a moderate. David Walker had published his much more radical *Appeal to the Colored Citizens of the World* in 1829, and Frederick Douglas wrote *The Heroic Slave* in 1853, a work that featured a strong black man who fights and rebels against slavery and is viewed by some critics as a direct challenge to the representation of masculinity in *Uncle Tom's Cabin*.

Stowe nevertheless succeeds in drawing readers into the drama she constructs. It is difficult to resist falling in love with characters like Eliza, an innocent and beautiful girl who risks her life to save her angelic child upon learning that he had been sold by her master. The severing of compelling maternal bonds at the hands of agents of the institution of slavery occurs many times throughout Stowe's narrative. Stowe successfully uses the strategy of depicting the horror and suffering that result from these separations to convince the reader of slavery's evils. Indeed, Stowe's novel had so deep an impact on antislavery sentiment upon its publishing that Abraham Lincoln is said to have greeted Stowe when they met at the White House with, "So this is the little lady who made this big war."

In all, criticism of *Uncle Tom's Cabin* is best put by Darryl Pinckney, who wrote the introduction to the 150th anniversary edition of Stowe's work: *Uncle Tom's Cabin* is always better or worse than anyone has said" (Pinckney, 10).

SOURCES

Baldwin, James. "Everybody's Protest Novel." In *Notes of a Native Son*. Boston: Beacon, 1955.

Donovan, Josephine. *"Uncle Tom's Cabin": Evil, Affliction, and Redemptive Love*. Boston: Twayne, 1991.

Pinckney, Darryl. Introduction. *Uncle Tom's Cabin*. New York: Signet Classic, 1998.

Rosenthal, Deborah J., ed. *A Routledge Literary Sourcebook on Harriet Beecher Stowe's "Uncle Tom's Cabin."* New York: Routledge, 2004.

Stowe, Harriet Beecher. *Key to Uncle Tom's Cabin*. Salem, Mass.: Ayer, 1987.

———. *Uncle Tom's Cabin*. New York: Salem Classic, 1998.

Sundquist, Eric J., ed. *New Essays on Uncle Tom's Cabin*. New York: Cambridge University Press, 1986.

Westbrook, Ellen E., Mason I. Lowance, Jr., and R. C. De Prospo, eds. *The Stowe Debate: Rhetorical Strategies in "Uncle Tom's Cabin."* Amherst: University of Massachusetts Press, 1994.

Jeff Rakover

UNVANQUISHED, THE WILLIAM FAULKNER (1934)

The Unvanquished is a series of connected stories set during and after the Civil War. William FAULKNER published six of these seven stories individually in popular magazines, five in the *Saturday Evening Post* and one in *Scribner's*. He then revised the stories and incorporated them into a novel. Only the final story, "An Odor of Verbena," was new in the published book. Some readers find this, the least difficult of Faulkner's novels, too conventional in its romantic view of the Old South and the Civil War. The romanticism is due, at least in part, to the adolescent narra-

tor of the first few sections, and it is undercut in the final section when the narrator is more mature.

In the first section, titled "Ambuscade," the narrator, Bayard Sartoris, is 12 years old. To him, the war is an adventure, and his father, Colonel John Sartoris, is a hero. Many of the characters in the Sartoris family were modeled after Faulkner's own family, especially Colonel Sartoris who resembles Faulkner's great-grandfather. The reader is introduced to a later generation of this family, when Bayard is an old man, in Faulkner's early novel *Sartoris* (1929). In *The Unvanquished*, Bayard experiences the Civil War with his best friend, Ringo, a slave. Their friendship transcends, as much as is possible in a slave society, the confines of race: "Ringo and I had been born in the same month and had both fed at the same breast and had slept together and eaten together for so long that Ringo called Granny "Granny" just like I did, until maybe he wasn't a nigger any more or maybe I wasn't a white boy any more, the two of us neither" (9). Their friendship is one reason this book is sometimes labeled unrealistic. Though he is described as more intelligent than Bayard, Ringo never openly bridles at his slave status. When the other slaves flee to the North during the war, Ringo stays with the family, perhaps because he is considered one of the family. As the two boys play at war and idolize the colonel, this section takes on the humorous quality of Mark TWAIN's tall-tale fiction, especially when they kill a Yankee's horse and hide together from the irate officer underneath Granny's full skirt.

The grandmother, Rose Millard, also takes on a heroic quality. During the war, she develops a scheme to get mules from the Union Army with forged documents. She distributes the mules to her neighbors to help them work their devastated land but winds up getting involved with some scalawags, and it is here that the tone of the book becomes darker. One of the scalawags, a man named Grumby, murders Granny. In the section titled "Vendee," 15-year-old Bayard sets out to avenge her death. He kills Grumby, and he and Ringo nail the man's body to the door of the old cotton compress, cut off his right hand, and place it on Granny's grave. Faulkner portrays an ordered and traditional society brought to chaos and lawlessness by war. Once-loyal servants desert their masters; women, such as Granny, must take on the roles normally played by men; men kill ladies, who ought to be protected; and boys commit grisly acts of vengeance.

In the section titled "Skirmish at Sartoris," we find that Drusilla is another woman driven to unconventional behavior during the war. After her fiancé dies at Shiloh, Drusilla "had deliberately tried to unsex herself" (131) in order to take an active role in the war. She dresses as a soldier and rides in John Sartoris's troop. When the war ends and she continues to live at Sartoris's estate, not as a lover but as an extra hand, Aunt Louisa, Drusilla's mother, is scandalized by the impropriety of the situation and demands that Colonel Sartoris marry her. Though they are not in love, they agree to marry to appease their female relations. As Drusilla and John Sartoris ride into town to be wed, they interrupt an election organized by two carpetbaggers, the Burdens, to elect former slave Cash Benbow as U.S. Marshal. Acting on the wishes of the white citizens of Jefferson, John shoots and kills the Burdens and gives Drusilla the ballot box to take back to the house. At Sartoris's house, they hold a sham election in which George Wyatt, a former soldier under Colonel Sartoris, writes out all the ballots. In all the commotion, Drusilla and John had forgotten to get married, much to the dismay of Aunt Louisa. The marriage is finally performed by a minister summoned to the house.

The final section, "An Odor of Verbena," begins when Bayard Sartoris, away at law school, receives the news that his father has been shot by a political opponent, Ben Redmond, in Jefferson. Bayard rides back to Jefferson with Ringo, who had been sent to summon him and who offers to help him kill Redmond. Bayard refuses all who offer to exact vengeance for him, and through his introspection, the reader sees that Bayard has matured from the 15-year-old who unquestioningly killed Grumby: "At least this will be my chance to find out if I am what I think I am or if I just hope; if I am going to do what I have taught myself is right or if I am just going to wish I were" (148). Through a flashback the reader learns about some of the situation's complexity. Bayard is in love with Drusilla, his stepmother, who is only eight years his senior. Her feelings for John had never been more than admiration, and she marries him only for the sake of appear-

ances. When, the summer before his father's death, he kisses Drusilla, Bayard is compelled by honor to tell his father. John, however, is so preoccupied with his political plans that he either doesn't fully comprehend or doesn't care. The characters compare Sartoris's dream of building a railroad to Thomas Sutpen's design, which is the subject of Faulkner's novel *Absalom, Absalom!* (1936). Unlike Sutpen, however, John Sartoris wants to improve the whole community, not just his own family.

When Bayard arrives at his father's house after learning of his father's murder, Drusilla greets him with two dueling pistols. Obsessed with honor and yearning for her days as a soldier, Drusilla wishes she could avenge her husband's death, but because the war is over, she is constrained by conventional feminine behavior. Although he says nothing, Drusilla senses that Bayard has no plans to kill Redmond, and she dismisses him contemptuously. But Bayard is not a coward. Perhaps he carries out what he sees as his father's last wishes, uttered the previous summer: "I'm tired of killing men, no matter what the necessity nor the end" (159). Bayard walks into Redmond's office unarmed and allows Redmond to fire at and purposefully miss him twice. Redmond then boards a train and leaves Jefferson forever. Cleanth Brooks says, "*The Unvanquished* is a novel about growing up—it is the story of an education" (84), and this scene with Redmond is Bayard's initiation into manhood. Unlike the boy of 12 in the book's opening section, this man no longer romanticizes violence. The novel ends when Bayard returns to the house and discovers Drusilla has left Jefferson to live with relatives in Montgomery. She has left on his pillow a sprig of the verbena she always wears, in effect retracting the harsh words she spoke to him earlier and commemorating all they lost.

SOURCES

Brooks, Cleanth. *William Faulkner: The Yoknapatawpha Country.* New Haven, Conn.: Yale University Press, 1963.

Creighton, Joanne V. *William Faulkner's Craft of Revision: The Snopes Trilogy, "The Unvanquished" and "Go Down, Moses."* Detroit, Mich.: Wayne State University Press, 1977.

Faulkner, William. *The Unvanquished.* 1934. London: Penguin Books, 1970.

Betina Entzminger

UPDIKE, JOHN (JOHN HOYER UPDIKE)

(1932–) John Updike is one of America's prolific fictional chroniclers. Among his numerous awards are a National Book Award in 1964 for *The Centaur* and a National Book Foundation Medal for distinguished contribution to American letters in 1998. Author of more than 20 novels, nearly 20 volumes of poetry, more than 20 volumes of collected short stories, and 15 books of essays, he is internationally known for his Rabbit series—*RABBIT, RUN* (1960), *RABBIT REDUX* (1971), *Rabbit Is Rich* (1981), and *Rabbit at Rest* (1990)—a tetralogy that follows high school athletic star Harry "Rabbit" Angstrom through four decades of a changing American social and sexual landscape. *Rabbit Is Rich* was awarded the Pulitzer Prize and the National Book Award in 1982; *Rabbit at Rest* won another Pulitzer Prize and a National Book Critics Award in 1990. John Updike is repeatedly praised for his perceptive insights and ability to evoke absurdity, irony, helplessness, and joy in lyrical, rhythmic prose that is rich with metaphor. Nearly all his work involves Americans who attempt to reconstruct lives that have become shabby and meaningless; he typically writes about middle-class suburbanites whose lives mirror the cultural angst and commonplace joys of the last 50 years. His settings most resemble those of his Pennsylvania childhood (in his novels, the fictional Olinger, Pennsylvania) or his adult life in Ipswich, Massachusetts, his home for many years.

John Updike was born on March 18, 1932, in Shillington, Pennsylvania, to Wesley Russell Updike, a high school teacher, and Linda Grace Hoyer Updike, a writer. He married Mary Entwistle Pennington in 1953, the year before he received his bachelor's degree (summa cum laude) from Harvard. (The marriage lasted until 1977, when they divorced and Updike married Martha Ruggles Bernhard.) After graduation, Updike spent two years working at the *New Yorker*—to which he would contribute poetry and short fiction for four decades—and then published his first novel, *The Poorhouse Fair,* in 1959. Set in the future, it describes the deplorable state of elderly people in a welfare state. *The Centaur* (1963), paralleling the mythic relationship between Chiron and Prometheus, portrays a high school teacher and his son; their rapport is based on Updike's adolescent relationship with his own father. It

was followed by *Of the Farm* (1965), based on Updike's relationship with his mother. *Couples* (1968) portrays marital infidelity among 10 couples in a Massachusetts town.

With *Rabbit, Run,* Updike received both popular and critical acclaim. The novel introduces Rabbit Angstrom and details his marriage to Janice, his infidelity, and his vague feeling that life has deteriorated since the glory days of his high school basketball stardom. In *Rabbit Redux,* set in the turbulent 1960s, Janice and Rabbit have decided to remain married despite their mutual infidelities, particularly Rabbit's relationship with a young hippie woman. Updike moves to the 1970s, with its excesses and oil crises, in *Rabbit Is Rich*. Rabbit now owns a Toyota dealership. He finally dies in *Rabbit at Rest.*

The Coup (1978), a dark satiric comedy, received excellent reviews. Unusual for Updike, the novel is set in an emerging African nation governed by a dictator amid political and social turmoil. *The Witches of Eastwick* (1984) involves a humorous portrayal of modern witchcraft and demonic possession as practiced by suburban women in Rhode Island. Drawing on Nathaniel HAWTHORNE'S *The SCARLET LETTER,* Updike wrote three novels that examine the classic lovers' triangle from the perspective of the shamed Hester Prynne's illicit clergyman lover (*A Month of Sundays* [1975]); from her cuckolded husband (*Roger's Version* [1986]); and, finally, the woman's viewpoint (*S.* [1988]). *Memories of the Ford Administration* (1992) involves academic scandal and a reminiscing history professor; *Brazil* (1994) reworks in contemporary times and tones the legendary medieval love story of Tristram and Iseult. *In the Beauty of the Lilies* (1996) traces four generations of the Wilmot family; their deterioration mirrors that of the increasingly vulgar consumer culture until they begin to reawaken to their diminished spirituality. In 1997, Updike published *Toward the End of Time,* a futuristic 21st-century novel set in the aftermath of a nuclear war with China; it features an old man in Massachusetts who recalls his youth.

John Updike lives with his wife at Beverly Farms in Massachusetts. His most recent novels include *Gertrude and Claudius* (2000), focusing on Hamlet's mother and her second husband; *Seek My Face* (2002); and *Villages* (2004), where 75-year-old Owen Mackenzie reflects on all the women he has known in Willow, Pennsylvania, where he was reared, and Middle Falls, Connecticut, where he lived as an adult. Several of Updike's novels have been selected for the screen: *Couples* was purchased by United Artists in 1969; *Rabbit, Run* was filmed by Warner Bros. in 1970; and director George Miller's movie *The Witches of Eastwick* in 1987 was loosely based on Updike's novel of the same title.

NOVELS

Brazil. New York: Knopf, 1994.
The Centaur. New York: Knopf, 1963.
The Coup. New York: Knopf, 1978.
Couples. New York: Knopf, 1968.
Gertrude and Claudius. New York: Knopf, 2000.
The Indian, Blue Cloud. Marvin, S.D.: Abbey, 1971.
In the Beauty of the Lilies. New York: Knopf, 1996.
Marry Me: A Romance. New York: Knopf, 1976.
Memories of the Ford Administration. New York: Knopf, 1992.
A Month of Sundays. New York: Knopf, 1975.
Of the Farm. New York: Knopf, 1965.
The Poorhouse Fair. New York: Knopf, 1959.
Rabbit at Rest. New York: Knopf, 1990.
Rabbit Is Rich. New York: Knopf, 1981.
Rabbit Redux. New York: Knopf, 1971.
Rabbit, Run. New York: Knopf, 1960.
Roger's Version. New York: Knopf, 1986.
S. New York: Knopf, 1988.
Seek My Face. New York: Knopf, 2002.
Toward the End of Time. New York: Knopf, 1997.
Villages. New York: Knopf, 2004.
The Witches of Eastwick. New York: Knopf, 1984.

SOURCES

Aldridge, John W. *Time to Murder and Create: The Contemporary Novel in Crisis.* New York: McKay, 1966.
Bloom, Harold, ed. *John Updike: Modern Critical Views.* New York: Chelsea House, 1987.
Boswell, Marshall. *John Updike's Rabbit Tetralogy: Mastered Irony In Motion.* Columbia: University of Missouri Press, 2000.
Broer, Lawrence R., ed. *Rabbit Tales: Poetry and Politics in John Updike's Rabbit Novels.* Tuscaloosa: University of Alabama Press, 1998.
De Bellis, Jack. *John Updike: A Bibliography, 1967–1993.* Foreword by Updike. Westport, Conn.: Greenwood Press, 1994.
Detweiler, Robert. *John Updike.* Boston: Twayne, 1972. Revised edition, 1984.

Greiner, Donald J. *Adultery in the American Novel: Updike, James, Hawthorne.* Columbia: University of South Carolina Press, 1985.
———. *John Updike's Novels.* Athens: Ohio University Press, 1984.
Hunt, George. *John Updike and the Three Great Secret Things.* Grand Rapids, Mich.: Eerdmans, 1980.
Luscher, Robert M. *John Updike: A Study of the Short Fiction.* New York: Twayne, 1993.
Miller, D. Quentin. *John Updike and the Cold War: Drawing the Iron Curtain.* Columbia: University of Missouri Press, 2001.
Neary, John. *Something and Nothingness: The Fiction of John Updike and John Fowles.* Carbondale: Southern Illinois University Press, 1992.
Newman, Judie. *John Updike.* New York: St. Martin's, 1988.
Plath, James, ed. *Conversations with John Updike.* Jackson: University Press of Mississippi, 1994.
Schiff, James A. *John Updike Revisited.* New York: Twayne, 1998.
———. *Updike's Version: Rewriting "The Scarlet Letter."* Columbia: University of Missouri Press, 1992.
Singh, Sukhbir. *The Survivor in Contemporary American Fiction: Saul Bellow, Bernard Malamud, John Updike, Kurt Vonnegut Jr.* Delhi, India: B. R. Publishing, 1991.
Thorburn, David, and Howard Eiland, eds. *John Updike: A Collection of Critical Essays.* Boston: G. K. Hall, 1982.
Trachtenberg, Stanley, ed. *New Essays on "Rabbit, Run."* Cambridge, England: Cambridge University Press, 1993.
Updike, John. *Self-Consciousness: Memoirs.* New York: Knopf, 1989.
Uphaus, Suzanne Henning. *John Updike.* New York: Ungar, 1980.
Yerkes, James, ed. *John Updike and Religion: The Sense of the Sacred and the Motions of Grace.* Grand Rapids, Mich.: Eerdmans, 1999.

OTHER

Audio Interview with John Updike. Wired for Books. Available online. URL: http://wiredforbooks.org/johnupdike. Accessed September 22, 2005.
Books and Writers. John Updike. Available online. URL: http://www.kirjasto.sci.fi/updike.htm. Accessed September 22, 2005.

U.S.A. TRILOGY JOHN DOS PASSOS **(1930, 1932, 1936)** Composed of *The 42nd Parallel* (1930), *Nineteen Nineteen* (1932), and *The Big Money* (1936), John DOS PASSOS's *U.S.A.* stands alongside James T.

FARRELL's *Studs Lonigan* trilogy as one of the most important works of American literature to come out of the 1930s. Rarely read today or discussed in classrooms, *U.S.A.* has often been lumped together with the proletarian literature of its time and thus is seen more as a sociohistorical or political document. Certainly, Dos Passos's trilogy is informed by leftist politics and by the radicalization he underwent during and after his involvement with the Sacco-Vanzetti case, but to dismiss it on such grounds is to oversimplify the novels. Not one book of the trilogy ends in some kind of triumphant message of socialism, working-class revolution, or even national unity. Even the paragraph-long description of what *U.S.A.* is, found at the beginning of each novel, struggles to articulate a unified vision and instead reveals how disparate and fractured the country is. Indeed, fragmentation is one of the dominant themes in the novels and is reflected in their content and style.

Dos Passos's previous novel, *Manhattan Transfer* (1925), provided him with the chance to experiment with a fragmented, modernist style and with multiple narratives, both tactics intended to mirror the chaotic and disorienting nature of the urban fabric in which the characters find themselves. In some ways, the urban environment of *Manhattan Transfer* develops a life of its own and comes to have more power to effect change than the characters do. This kind of situation, a remnant of literary naturalism, where static characters are dwarfed by larger forces, continues in the trilogy where not only characters but also the narrative structures themselves are determined by historical forces and events. *The 42nd Parallel* traces America from the Spanish-American War until its entry into World War I; *Nineteen Nineteen* (1932) concerns itself with the war and its aftermath; and *The Big Money* depicts the hedonistic materialism of the 1920s. Furthermore, the discontinuous narratives of the 12 main characters are invariably influenced and interrupted by historical information, whether it be in the form of the newsreels, the biographies, or the stream-of-consciousness Camera Eye sections. Historical forces come to overshadow the lives of the characters and the language structures used to give form to history invariably fall short. The final Camera Eye section may

state that "we have only words against" and imply perhaps that words can be potent weapons for truth, but the biography section that follows, that of Samuel Insull, ends with "thousands of ruined investors, at least so the newspapers said, who had lost their last savings sat crying over the home editions at the thought of how Mr. Insull had suffered." Language does not necessarily lead to enlightenment, and the form in which it is framed can be manipulated in order to deceive.

Like FITZGERALD's stories of Jazz Age dissipation, the *U.S.A.* trilogy paints a bleak portrait, made especially so because the world depicted here is not necessarily one of disintegration but one where repeated patterns prevent both progression and regression. The young man who walks by himself in search of a job at the beginning of the trilogy is there at the end, in the somewhat different form of Vag, who has been promised opportunity by his society yet finds himself still without a job. In fact, nearly all the characters in the narratives—even those who die, such as Eveline and Joe Williams—are static. J. Ward Moorehouse, who has achieved material success in *The Big Money*, remains essentially the same exploitative personality who appeared in *The 42nd Parallel*. This applies as well to minor characters such as Doc Bingham, who by the end has substituted his pornographic books for patent medicines but remains a huckster, making money on false promises. The narratives themselves are static, episodic and aimless, devoid of the elements of conventional plot structure. No profound epiphanies or grand realizations occur, and more often than not characters repeat their mistakes. Moreover, the biographies depict types embodied again and again in various historical figures. The ruthless capitalist, for example, appears in many guises, as J. P. Morgan, Henry Ford, and Samuel Insull, but they are all essentially the same story, just variations on a theme. Dos Passos thus presents history as cyclical, as a series of repeated patterns, like watching figures on Keats's "Grecian Urn." For the 12 characters whose lives are governed by such larger forces, then, history itself becomes a trap. In this way, the newsreels, biographies, and Camera Eyes can be viewed as structural reflections of Dos Passos's thematic aims. The patterns of fragmented facts, ironic commentary, and stream-of-consciousness, as well as the concerns about capitalism, war, and injustice, appear again and again, their repetition occurring because history fails to resolve these concerns and achieve closure. Toward the end of the trilogy, in *The Camera Eye* (50), the narrator announces in response to the execution of Sacco and Vanzetti that "all right we are two nations" and says in bitter resignation that "we stand defeated America." It is appropriate, therefore, in cyclical fashion, that Dos Passos should wind up the trilogy where he began, with a case that brings only despair and defeat, echoes numerous other stories of injustice told throughout the three novels, and reveals a U.S.A. fractured once again. *The Big Money* does not end with a satisfying, resolved closure but with a simple state-ment—"a hundred miles down the road"—that looks to an ever-receding horizon, an unreachable destination.

SOURCES

Colley, Iain. *Dos Passos and the Fiction of Despair.* Totowa, N.J.: Rowman and Littlefield, 1978.

Hook, Andrew, ed. *Dos Passos: A Collection of Critical Essays.* Englewood Cliffs, N.J.: Prentice-Hall, 1974.

Maine, Barry, ed. *Dos Passos, the Critical Heritage.* London and New York: Routledge & Kegan Paul, 1988.

Pizer, Donald. *Dos Passos' U.S.A.: A Critical Study.* Charlottesville: University Press of Virginia, 1988.

Rosen, Robert C. *John Dos Passos, Politics and the Writer.* Lincoln: University of Nebraska Press, 1981.

Monty Kozbial Ernst

V

V. **THOMAS PYNCHON (1963)** Thomas PYNCHON's first novel, *V.*, published in 1963, contains more than 200 character names and a dizzying array of plots; nevertheless, it focuses primarily upon two narrative threads. The first is the story of Benny Profane, a drifter looking for meaning in contemporary (1950s) America. The second features Herbert Stencil, a privileged European drifting around the European-American world searching for meaning attached to a reference in his father's journal: a woman called, simply, V. The two narrative threads intertwine as Profane and Stencil meet as part of a group of young people in New York called The Whole Sick Crew. By means of their struggles for meaning, Pynchon is able to draw attention to the problem of the unreliability of history and the impossibility of arriving at stable, reliable knowledge.

As the novel begins, Benny Profane has just left the navy and is working as a day laborer. One of the odd jobs Profane takes is as a night guard at Anthroresearch Associates, where he strikes up an imaginary conversation with "SHOCK (synthetic human object, casualty kinematics)" and "SHROUD (synthetic human, radiation output determined)" (285). Profane argues with SHROUD that the robots are not human but merely "masquerading as a human being" (295). SHROUD responds:

> Of course. Like a human being. Now remember, right after the war, the Nuremberg war trials? Remember the photographs of Auschwitz?

Thousands of Jewish corpses, stacked up like those poor car-bodies. Schlemiel. It's already started. "Hitler did that. He was crazy." Hitler, Eichmann, Mengele. Fifteen years ago. Has it occurred to you there may be no more standards for crazy or sane, now that it's started? (295).

In a world without standards for sanity, Profane is unable to establish clearly a meaning for himself or others, leaving him feeling essentially passive and inanimate. However, it is Profane's real human life as a "schlemiel," in all its contingency, that effectively denies his mechanization and asserts his animateness.

Herbert Stencil, who speaks of himself in the third person, is the son of a British Foreign Office man, Sidney Stencil. Herbert is born "in 1901, the year Victoria died" (52) and raised without a mother whose existence remains a mystery. "No facts on the mother's disappearance. Died in childbirth, ran off with someone, committed suicide: some way of vanishing painful enough to keep Sidney from ever referring to it in all the correspondence to his son which is available. The father died under unknown circumstances in 1919 while investigating the June Disturbances in Malta" (52). His obsession with learning the truth about V., which he pursues "for no other reason than that V. was there to track down" (55), allows him to live almost entirely in "the network of white halls in his own brain" (53). Here he turns vague correspondences with his father's journal into the rationale for his life, seeking, and as often as not, manufacturing connections. These plots about his history form what critic Tony Tanner calls the novel's "historical episodes," but because these histories are based on largely unreliable data and Stencil's consistently faulty inductive analysis, Pynchon is able to draw attention to the fictive elements of history. Thus while the central question of these "historical episodes" is "What is V.?" the novel provides no answer.

Appearances of the V.-symbol proliferate in the novel, but the letter V is most consistently attached to the various appearances of a female figure. We meet Victoria Wren in chapter 7, a beautiful young woman whose life has, at the age of 19, become a series of affairs with wealthy and powerful men whom she uses and discards. "At age nineteen she had crystallized into a nun-like temperament pushed to its most dangerous extreme. Whether she had taken the veil or not, it was as if she felt Christ were her husband and that the marriage's physical consummation must be achieved through imperfect, mortal versions of himself" (167). The central plot of chapter 7 is the theft by a group of Venezuelan revolutionaries and a few Florentines of Botticelli's *Birth of Venus,* the painting representing a European male notion of female beauty and love. As the chapter develops, a contrast emerges between Botticelli's ideal of beauty and that of Victoria Wren, whose beauty masks a lust for power exemplified by her adherence to Machiavelli's assertion in *The Prince* of the importance of virtue, a term variously defined by Machiavelli but understood by Victoria Wren to mean individual agency. Victoria's cruelty, her distance from the savagery of her world, is seen in the comb that she wears in her hair: a depiction of five crucified figures. While the Venezuelans riot, Victoria watches dispassionately:

> Her face betrayed no emotion. It was as if she saw herself embodying a feminine principle, acting as complement to all this bursting, explosive male energy. Inviolate and calm, she watched the spasms of wounded bodies, the fair of violent death, framed and staged, it seemed, for her alone in that tiny square. From her hair the heads of five crucified also looked on, no more expressive than she. (290)

The suggestion of inanimateness in this passage, the notion that Victoria is not quite human, is carried over to the next appearance of a woman in Paris in the 1920s. The woman is involved in a ballet (based on the first performance of Igor Stravinsky's *The Rite of Spring,* a ballet whose first performance in Paris caused a riot); she takes the 15-year-old Melanie l'Heurmaudit (the surname translating to "damned hour") as her lover and employs her as the human sacrifice in a ballet employing automata as handmaidens. This mixture of the human and the mechanical corresponds to the woman herself, having had mechanical parts fitted into her body, replacing the natural human parts. At the first performance of the ballet, Melanie, the human sacrifice, is impaled and dies on stage. "Of the woman, her lover, nothing further was seen" (414). She seems to reappear in the 1940s in Valletta, Malta, as recounted in the diary of the Maltese poet, Fausto Maijstral in chapter 11. Here she appears as the Bad Priest who is trapped under a fallen beam during a German bombing raid. As she lies dying, children remove her clothing, discovering for the first time that the priest is a woman. One of the items the children take from her seems to be a comb like the one with the crucified figures worn by Victoria Wren. However, Pynchon distributes this clue between two boys, one finding "an ivory comb" and the other "a two-color Crucifixion" in the form of a tattoo, thereby calling this connection into doubt. Furthermore, this woman's body is young, so it does not seem possible that she is Victoria Wren, unless the various mechanical objects incorporated into the body of the woman in chapter 14 included sufficient cosmetic changes to allow a woman of some 60-odd years to appear youthful. But as we struggle to connect these clues, we are again undone: None leads reliably to a truth. As this story comes to us through Maijstral's "Confessions," and these from Stencil, all of the appearances of women who might be the lady V. are dubious.

A central idea in *V.* is the impossibility of reliable knowledge. As Melvyn New writes, "Pynchon's *V.* leads one quite readily into an examination of the critical process because it is so profoundly concerned with the human need to order fragments. While Herbert Stencil searches for clues to the meaning of the woman V., we, as readers, parallel his activity" (New, 399). We search for a reliable meaning to emerge and satisfy our expectation of closure, but the frustration we feel at the failure of the novel to provide certainty places us side-by-side with Stencil and Profane. As Stencil creates conspiratorial connections, there develops "a relationship between making fictions and imagining conspiracies. The difference is between consciousness in control of its own inventions, and consciousness succumbing to its inventions until they present themselves as perceptions" (Tanner, 52). For Stencil, his imaginings become as real as perceptions; consequently, his histories are irretrievably flawed. Stencil's histories are not accurate in any reliable sense; rather they are interpretations of stories about the past. Richard Patteson writes, "If anything is clear in Pynchon, it is that every interpretational foray . . . leads inevitably to another version" (Patteson, 307). Pynchon draws attention to the role of invention in the creation of history, blurring the distinction between history and fiction. As Maarten Van Delden asserts, since "it is impossible to distinguish in any consistent or meaningful way between history and fiction . . . writers may now regard the past as a largely unmarked terrain upon which they can freely impose their own designs" (Van Delden, 133). Pynchon's novel becomes, in part, a commentary on the ways we create meaning. This commentary allows Pynchon to question those historical truths that have dominated modern European thought and its hierarchical power structures. The truths upon which Stencil's father's generation built its power can no longer be sustained. Stencil's and Profane's failed quests for external meaning point to the failure of attempting to construct absolute truths. Readers are left in the same state as Stencil and Profane: We cannot find a clear meaning either in the novel or in the world. We have to accept contingency; we have to be satisfied with whatever meanings we can assemble for ourselves.

SOURCES

New, Melvyn. "Profane and Stenciled Texts: In Search of Pynchon's *V.,*" *Georgia Review* 33 (1979): 395–412.

Patteson, Richard F. "How True a Text? Chapter Three of *V.* And 'Under the Rose,' " *Southern Humanities Review* 18, no. 4 (Fall 1984): 299–308.

Pynchon, Thomas. *V.* 1963. New York: Harper, 1989.

Tanner, Tony. "Caries and Cabals." In *Mindful Pleasures: Essays on Thomas Pynchon,* edited by George Levine and David Leverenz, 49–65. Boston: Little, Brown, 1976.

Van Delden, Maarten. "Modernism, the New Criticism, and Thomas Pynchon's *V.,*" *Novel* 23 (1990): 117–136.

Alan W. Brownlie

VALIS PHILIP K. DICK (1981) *Valis* is this prolific science fiction writer's masterpiece. It represents DICK's attempt to use fictional narrative as a way of making sense of visionary experiences he had undergone in February and March 1974, whose dubious significance he had spent eight years and over 2 million words in his journal commentaries, "Exegesis," trying to comprehend. These experiences began with a visitation, recorded in the novel. A mesmerizingly beautiful black-haired girl (a recurring motif in his writing that is usually identified with desire and torment) delivers a prescription of pain killers for an impacted wisdom tooth. His attention is drawn to the centerpiece of her gold necklace, a fish, which she identifies as a sign used by early Christians. This seems to trigger subsequent episodes of communications from "one or more archetypes" who he felt "had taken him over" with the intention of waking him out of spiritual sleep and compelling him to remember what he had always been genetically programmed to remember: his celestial origins—the fact that he is "in this world in a thrown condition, but . . . not of this world" (Dick quoted in Sutin, 210).

Reflecting an ironic awareness of his cognitive and emotional bipolarity, Dick splits himself in the novel between two alter egos, a troubled writer named Philip Dick and his even more disturbed friend, Horselover Fat (a bilingual pun: *phil* [Greek, "love"], *hippos* [Greek, "horse"], *dich* [German, "thick"]). Fat, like the author himself, receives coded pictographic revelations beamed from "Vast Active Living Intelligence System" (acronymically, VALIS)—who is sometimes identified with Sophia, the female emanation of Divine Wisdom in Gnostic theology, and sometimes with an artificial intelligence or advanced alien form beaming prophetic messages from the future. Speculating that temporal planes are layered, simultaneous, and interpenetrating, Fat (again, like the author) comes to believe that he may have been contacted by immortal Christian resistors to the tyranny of the Roman Empire ("the Empire never ended"), who had entered Watergate America to help bring down Richard Nixon. (At the time of these experiences, indeed for many years prior to them, Dick had been living in increasingly paranoid panic that he was either being groomed by the KGB or having his patriotic loyalty tested by the FBI because of his growing popularity among left-wing intellectuals due to his career-long satirizing of capitalism and his more recent attacks on Nixon.) Fat further believes that despite the hegemony of the Black Iron Prison in which "everyone dwelt without realizing it," the birth of the spirit can occur whenever the "plasmate" of the divine replicates itself in the human cortex as a "homoplasmate" (53ff). This accords with Dick's avowal in his "Exegesis":

> The Savior woke me temporarily, & temporarily I remembered my true nature & task, through the saving gnosis [i.e., a mystically revealed knowledge of origins], but I must be silent, because of the true, secret, transtemporal early Christians at work, hidden among us as ordinary humans. I briefly became one of them, Siddhartha himself (the Buddha or enlightened one)" (Dick quoted by Sutin 1995, 288).

Synthesizing Dick's wide reading in world mythology, Gnostic theosophy, Christian and Jewish mysticism, Buddhism, and German philosophy, and suffused with pop culture references (particularly, music and TV), *Valis* epitomizes his conviction that "the symbols of the divine show up in our world initially at the trash stratum" (256). Many of the preoccupations that had always typified Dick's are reworked: the machinations of galactic puppet masters, their clandestine infiltration of consciousness by way of popular culture (the words to the Beatles' "Strawberry Fields Forever" figures significantly in the "Exegesis"), the disintegration of psychological structures in the encounter with ambiguities generated in equal measure by the consensual hallucination manufactured by media elites and by cultic counter-hegemonic resistance.

Plot elements are also recycled: the shabby, humdrum life of a "little guy" is again totally disrupted upon the discovery that he has always been implicated, without knowing it, in an intricate, massive and sustained illusion. Formerly hidden forces, agencies, networks are suddenly revealed, whose magnitude and scope exceed the individual's capacity to deny them. Precisely because nightmarish disclosures cannot be rationalized away in the hope of maintaining the illusion of autonomy, Dick's conspiracy narratives function simultaneously as case-studies of paranoia and as allegorical critiques satirizing the totalitarian tendencies of postwar American social formations. But in *Valis* and the subsequent novels *Radio Free Albemuth* and *The Divine Invasion,* which form a kind of trilogy, these plot elements are directed more explicitly to a Gnostic project of anamnesis, the reversal of forgetfulness in regard to ontological and metaphysical reality. This process is far from comforting. The exposure of phantasmatic "paraworlds" (that is, alternative realities) that preclude systematic comprehension torments Dick's protagonists, who, unable to live with ambiguity and doubt, become ever more complicit in their own victimization. Obsessively picking at the scab of enigma, they restlessly scratch at their lives for clues and traces of unseen powers.

Dick's protagonists (like Dick himself in the "Exegesis") proceed to construct more and more elaborate explanatory models in compensatory response to profound feelings of personal insubstantiality and impotence. By blurring the demarcation between "actual" events and psychic processes, and thereby surrendering cognitive suppositions to endless permutation, Dick's destabilizing novels of epistemological quandary throw into question all criteria for establishing credibility or warrant for credulity and future action. Sanity-threatening confusions multiply with each ostensible verification of a hypothesis. The paranoid's search for an unimpeachable founding premise is tinged for comic effect with the self-reflexive, endlessly digressive thought processes typically conduced by certain pharmaceuticals Dick was known to consume in legendary quantities. Dick parodies (or does he?) the paranoid's determined effort to interconnect seemingly incongruent phenomena as if they were systematized signs; thus, for example, a TV ad for Food King segues to a Felix the Cat cartoon, thereby producing King Felix—code for Christ the Savior (252). And, for all its desperation (Fat tries to commit suicide in chapter 4, just as Dick did many times), the book can carnivalize that desperation: " 'Come to me, artificially accelerated cortical-development idea,' he said in prayer."

Thus, the novel self-reflexively dramatizes, in alternately comic and melancholy tones, Dick's recognition that the fictions and commentaries inspired by his experiences were probably at one and the same time the overwrought speculative jags of a manic-depressive, paranoid, suicidal, sometimes quasi-psychotic, pill-popper and authentic spiritual meditations on intimations sent by the divine to redeem him, and those who he could reach, from life-long delusion, sin, and spiritual wretchedness.

Like their creator, Dick's protagonists live in a universe of intimations, visitations, and epiphanies. And like him, they seem to be inspired by the thought of being conspired against insofar as conspiracy-thinking reenchants existence. While *Valis* can take its place in the American literary tradition that seeks to transmogrify (monstrously deform) metaphysical speculation, the tradition of MELVILLE, the later TWAIN, Flannery O'CONNOR, and PYNCHON, Dick's idiosyncratic exegetical commentaries put him in the company of other eccentric American autodidacts: Charles Fort's assurance that "we are property," Elijah Muhammad's revelation that the white race was devolved from the black by a cosmic "big head scientist," and L. Ron Hubbard's claim that humans derive from incorporeal entities who became entrapped and self-forgetful while playing at "the game" of incarnation.

SOURCES

Dick, Philip K. *Valis.* London: Gollancz, 2001.

Palmer, Christopher. *Philip K. Dick: Exhilaration and Terror of the Postmodern.* Liverpool, U.K.: Liverpool University Press, 2003.

Sutin, Lawrence. *Divine Invasions: A Life of Philip K. Dick.* New York: Harmony Books, 1989.

————, ed. *The Shifting Realities of Philip K. Dick: Selected Literary and Philosophical Writings.* New York: Vintage, 1995.

David Brottman

VAN DINE, S. S. (WILLARD HUNTINGTON WRIGHT) (1888–1939)

Art critic, newspaper and magazine editor (including *Smart Set* [1912–14]), fiction writer, creator of the detective Philo Vance, and inventor of "Twenty Rules for Writing Detective Stories," Willard Huntington Wright wrote all but one of his novels under the pseudonym of S. S. Van Dine. Among his most popular novels were *The Benson Murder Case* (1926) and *The CANARY MURDER CASE* (1927).

Willard Huntington Wright was born in 1888 in Charlottesville, Virginia; although little information is available about his family, they were reportedly well-to-do. Wright was educated at a number of schools, colleges, and universities in the United States and abroad, and graduated from Pomona College at age 16. After working with the *Los Angeles Times* and *Smart Set,* Wright published his first novel, *The Man of Promise,* in 1916, a novel well reviewed by H. L. Mencken, who had taken the reins as editor of *Smart Set.* Autobiographical in nature, it describes a youth painfully aware of the intelligence level and talent that separated him from his contemporaries. Mencken found in it a touch of "the Greek spirit" and an "appeal to the intellect," concluding that "such novels are as rare in the United States as good music" (Mencken, 491). Two years later, Wright suffered a nervous breakdown exacerbated by his dependence on alcohol and drugs. During his convalescence he read some 2,000 detective novels, publishing his own, *The Benson Murder Case* (1926), under the name S. S. Van Dine. Here he introduced Philo Vance, the erudite amateur sleuth who quotes philosophy and brings his intuition to the plodding facts of a crime scene. It made Van Dine an overnight sensation. According to critic Roger Rosenblatt, the uniqueness of the monocle-wearing Vance lies not in his snobbishness or intellect, but in the fact that "we are not permitted to like him" (Rosenblatt, 32); unlike Sherlock Holmes, Vance has no Watson; unlike Nero Wolfe, he has no Archie Goodwin. It is arguably this solitariness that makes him such a success, as he stands on the periphery of the action, he pays meticulous attention not only to detail but to the psychology of the players in the drama. As Michael E. Grost points out, "The Van Dine school sleuths" are recognizable by "the exhaustive search of both victims' rooms and crime scenes; they query disinterested passersby who have tons of information to share; and they institute resourceful police inquiries for information" (Grost).

Willard Huntington Wright was married to Katharine Belle Boynton from 1907 until their divorce in 1930. He died of heart failure on April 11, 1939. *The Winter Murder Case* was published posthumously that same year. During Wright's lifetime, numerous films were made of his Philo Vance novels.

NOVELS

The Benson Murder Case. New York: Scribner, 1926.
The Bishop Murder Case. New York: Scribner, 1929.
The Canary Murder Case. New York: Scribner, 1927.
The Casino Murder Case. New York: Scribner, 1934.
The Dragon Murder Case. New York: Scribner, 1934.
The Garden Murder Case. New York: Scribner, 1935.
The Gracie Allen Murder Case. New York: Scribner, 1938, published as *The Smell of Murder.* New York: Bantam, 1950.
The Greene Murder Case. New York: Scribner, 1928.
I Used to Be a Highbrow but Look at Me Now. New York: Scribner, 1929.
The Kennel Murder Case. New York: Scribner, 1933.
The Kidnap Murder Case. New York: Scribner, 1936.
The Man of Promise. New York: Lane, 1916.
The President's Mystery Story. New York: Farrar & Rinehart, 1935.
The Scarab Murder Case. New York: Scribner, 1930.
The Winter Murder Case. New York: Scribner, 1939.

SOURCES

Mencken, H. L. "American Produces a Novelist," *Forum* 55 (April 1916): 490–496.
Rosenblatt, Roger. "S.S. Van Dine." *New Republic,* 26 July 1975, pp. 32–34.

OTHER

Grost, Michael E. Classic Mystery Home Page. Available online. URL: http://members.aol.com/MG4273/classics. htm. Accessed September 22, 2005.

VENUS ENVY RITA MAE BROWN (1993)

Although *Venus Envy* could be read as a sequel to Rita Mae BROWN's earlier work *Rubyfruit Jungle*, this novel tackles issues and characters that are vastly different. While *Rubyfruit*'s protagonist, Molly Bolt, deals with growing up as a confidently gay woman and struggles to complete her journey from poverty to artistic success, in *Venus Envy* we encounter a woman who risks all that has brought her social and material comfort in order to face her own fears concerning her sexuality. In this sense, there couldn't be a wider chasm between Molly and Frazier Armstrong. While Molly struggles against others, Frazier must ultimately confront herself.

Venus Envy reads much like a comedy of errors, where misplaced partners search for their true match in love. The novel's strong mythological undercurrent, represented by Frazier's painting of the Greek deities, serves to reinforce this cast of characters whose actions often seem guided by the gods themselves.

Left to their own devices, Frazier's friends and relatives might have continued in their sometimes unhappy routine as part of a wealthy and rigidly structured society that often leaves little room for individual differences. The problem is that Frazier is very different, and when at the start of the novel she believes she is dying, she decides to make peace with her own conscience by writing a series of letters to family and friends, letters that not only reveal she is lesbian but that also detail her feelings toward them.

In essence, the letters she sends before her doctor corrects the faulty diagnosis tell their recipients that life is too short to lie to ourselves and others, and that everyone is entitled to seek out happiness and pleasure in life. The way the message is conveyed is not necessarily good-natured: Frazier tells her on-off closeted lover Ann that she feels their relationship was like a "job," and ends by stating: "[Y]ou are as sick as you are secret" (51). Convinced that both her father and brother are trapped in loveless marriages, Frazier encourages them to stand up for what they desire in life, even if—in her brother's case—it means leaving what has become so familiar for an unknown future with another person. Finally, she scolds both her mother and her gay friend Billy for being cold in their relationships, and blatantly manipulating the love others felt toward them in order to achieve their own material and emotional ends.

Needless to say, the letters hit hard, and the stage is set for Frazier herself to examine her relationships; after all, what has she done by writing the letters in what seem to be her final moments besides assuaging her own guilty conscience for not having stood up and voiced these feelings at a time when she would have had to face their consequences? In a stroke of what must be fate, Frazier's condition goes from lung cancer to a bad bronchitis; the gods are surely playing a joke on her, especially when the letters have already been sent.

The situations that arise from her letters force Frazier to explore her own feelings on truth, love, and taking one's pleasure before it's too late. In a short time, she finds out who her real friends and allies are. Who are her real family? The mother who has guided her through her social duties without contemplating Frazier's own desires, or the apparently scatter-brained father who has allowed her to grow into her own character? Her gay friends Ann and Billy, who appear at social functions with "dates" of the opposite sex; or her outspoken assistant Mandy and Billy's ex-boyfriend Kenny, who are not afraid to explore their own sexuality and encourage Frazier to do the same?

Gradually, Frazier finds herself isolated by people she thought liked and respected her: social clubs, mothers who no longer want their daughters around her, and people who suddenly believe that their own reputation depends on Frazier's sexual orientation. It is, to say the least, disconcerting for Frazier: What good has telling the truth done? Her family is falling apart, her friends have abandoned her, and she has become unpopular in her community. The uncomfortable meetings and tense social reunions escalate into hostility until it seems as if Frazier will succumb and surrender her newfound convictions. And then something extraordinary happens.

In the lengthy mythological scene near the end, Frazier is transported to Mount Olympus, and more specifically to the realm of Venus and Mercury, carefree gods who don't hesitate to play and fulfill their desires. There she experiences herself on a grander scale and looks down on her world with a combination of dismay and pity. How can she return when she has done so much harm?

However, the gods will not let her give up so easily. Once she has seen herself and her surroundings from such a distance, they reason, she will be able to see her future path more clearly: "Remember, there are no separate solutions. There are only community solutions. You fight for your place in the community. It doesn't matter that not everyone will accept you for yourself" (388). In other words, isolation does not bring about

change. And once Frazier gazes down and sees her father finally standing up to her mother, she realizes that she has inspired some change. After all, Frazier's brother has also left his wife to be with the woman he really loves, and her friend Kenny has escaped Billy's psychological abuse. With this realization, Frazier sees that "life is calling" and returns to earth uncertain of her future, but willing to confront whatever obstacles still stand in the way of her own fulfillment.

Thus, *Venus Envy* challenges the reader to define pleasure and happiness: Do we approach them always in relation to what others can give us, or as something that needs to flow from ourselves first, in order to later share it with others? *Rubyfruit Jungle* dealt with our basic right to grow into a society as a full-fledged member, no matter our race, sex, social status, etc. As the next step, *Venus Envy* seeks a higher level of maturity, focusing on our need to experience all the physical and emotional joys that we cultivate through our honest relationship with ourselves and others.

SOURCE
Venus Envy. New York: Bantam, 1993.

Maria Luisa Antonaya

VIDAL, GORE (1925–)

Increasingly known today as the author of *The City and the Pillar,* the first American novel to focus on homosexuality, and for the satire *Myra Breckinridge* (1968), made into a film starring Mae West, Gore Vidal has long been esteemed for his achievements in the historical novel. He wrote about America in *Washington, D.C.* (1967), *Burr* (1973), *1876* (1976), *Lincoln* (1984), *Empire* (1987), and produced the more classical *Julian* (1964) and *Creation* (1981). In the 1950s, he also wrote three detective novels under the pseudonym of Edgar Box. With more than 20 novels, several successful stage and screen credits, and dozens of essays, Vidal is a versatile post–World War II writer with a biting wit. His acerbic commentaries on American social mores have appeared regularly in the *New York Review of Books,* and he won a National Book Critics Circle Award for literary criticism in *The Second American Revolution and Other Essays* (1982).

Gore Vidal was born Eugene Luther Vidal on October 3, 1925, at the United States Military Academy at West Point, New York, to Eugene Vidal, an aeronautics instructor at West Point, and Nina Gore Vidal, a distant cousin of Senator Albert Gore. When Vidal was 10, his mother divorced his father, married Hugh Auchincloss, and moved her family to Merriewood, the Auchincloss estate in McLean, Virginia. Auchincloss then divorced her and married Jacqueline Bouvier Kennedy's mother, thereby connecting Vidal to the Kennedy family. In 1943, Vidal joined the U.S. Army Reserve Corps, in which he served as a warrant officer. While onboard a ship to the Aleutian Islands, he gathered material for his first novel, *Williwaw* (1946), an account of the squall's effect on the ship's crew and officers. With *Williwaw* (which means "a sudden, violent storm"), Vidal joined the ranks of such literary enfants terribles as Norman MAILER, who dominated the American cultural scene just after World War II. His name was often linked with other postwar prodigies: Truman CAPOTE, John Horn Burns, and James JONES, for instance. This desire to break the mold emerges again in his second novel, *In a Yellow Wood* (1947), when the protagonist, Robert Holton, chooses the "road not taken," the title of the Robert Frost poem to which the title alludes. His third novel, *The City and the Pillar* (1948), caused an immediate sensation. The protagonist, Jim Willard, longs to return to those halcyon days spent with his boyhood love, Bob Ford, but at their reunion many years later, Bob rejects him as a "queer," and Jim rapes and kills Bob. Seventeen years later, Vidal revised the novel and amended the violent ending.

During the 1950s, Vidal, determined to make money, wrote Hollywood and television screenplays, including adaptations of Henry JAMES's *The TURN OF THE SCREW,* Ernest HEMINGWAY's *A FAREWELL TO ARMS,* and Tennessee WILLIAMS's *Suddenly Last Summer.* In the 1960s, he returned to novel writing. *Julian* chronicles the Roman emperor's battle against Christianity, dramatizing his relationships with his fourth-century contemporaries; in *Creation* (1981), a grandson of Zoroaster interacts with such figures as Confucius and Buddha. Both novels exhibit Vidal's use of satire and familiar detail, hallmarks of his historical novels. The American sequence followed in the late 1960s and 1970s, the novels linked by the Schuyler/Sanford dynasty, descended from Aaron Burr, and chronicle the emergence of the modern United States. *Burr* and *Lincoln* are particularly admired by critics, both historical figures revealed and rendered human through the eyes of Charles Schemerhorn Schuyler, illegitimate son of Aaron Burr. In spite of Vidal's enormous output, his penchant for demythologizing and lampooning American cultural icons was probably best and most humorously realized in *Myra Breckinridge,* a novel about a transsexual. The Twentieth Century-Fox film appeared in 1970, and Vidal published the sequel, *Myron,* in 1974.

Critics and scholars are discovering that some of Vidal's lesser known works deserve reexamination: *The Season of Comfort* (1949), *Two Sisters: A Novel in the Form of a Memoir* (1970), *The Judgment of Paris* (1965), *Hollywood* (1990), and *The Golden Age* (2000). For decades, Gore Vidal lived and wrote in Salerno, Italy and Los Angeles. He now resides permanently in the Hollywood Hills.

NOVELS

Burr. New York: Random House, 1973.
The City and the Pillar. New York: Dutton, 1948. Revised edition. Published as *The City and the Pillar Revised,* 1965.
Creation. New York: Random House, 1981.
Dark Green, Bright Red. New York: Dutton, 1950.
Duluth. New York: Random House, 1983.
1876. New York: Random House, 1976.
Empire. New York: Random House, 1987.
The Golden Age. New York: Broadway, 2000.
Hollywood: A Novel of America in the 1920s. New York: Random House, 1990.
In a Yellow Wood. New York: Dutton, 1947.
The Judgment of Paris. New York: Dutton, 1952. Revised edition, Boston: Little, Brown, 1965.
Julian. Boston: Little, Brown, 1964.
Kalki. New York: Random House, 1978.
Lincoln. New York: Random House, 1984.
Messiah. New York: Dutton, 1954. Revised edition, Boston: Little, Brown, 1965.
Myra Breckinridge. Boston: Little, Brown, 1968.
Myron. New York: Random House, 1974.
A Search for the King: A Twelfth-Century Legend. New York: Dutton, 1950.

The Season of Comfort. New York: Dutton, 1949.

The Smithsonian Institution: A Novel. New York: Random House, 1998.

Two Sisters: A Novel in the Form of a Memoir. Boston: Little, Brown, 1970.

Washington, D.C. Boston: Little, Brown, 1967.

Williwaw. New York: Dutton, 1946. (Published in paperback as *Dangerous Voyage,* New York: Signet, 1953.)

UNDER PSEUDONYM EDGAR BOX; MYSTERIES

Death before Bedtime. New York: Dutton, 1953.

Death in the Fifth Position. New York: Dutton, 1952.

Death Likes It Hot. New York: Dutton, 1954.

SOURCES

Baker, Susan. *Gore Vidal: A Critical Companion.* Westport, Conn.: Greenwood Publishing Group, 1997.

Dick, Bernard F. *The Apostate Angel: A Critical Study of Gore Vidal.* New York: Random House, 1974.

Kaplan, Fred. *Gore Vidal: A Biography.* New York: Doubleday, 1999.

Kiernan, Robert F. *Gore Vidal.* New York: Ungar, 1982.

Parini, Jay, ed. *Gore Vidal: Writer against the Grain.* New York: Columbia University Press, 1992.

Stanton, Robert J., and Gore Vidal, eds. *Views from a Window: Conversations with Gore Vidal.* Secaucus, N.J.: Lyle Stuart, 1980.

Vidal, Gore. *Palimpsest: A Memoir.* New York: Random House, 1995.

Weightman, John. *The Concept of the Avant Garde: Explorations in Modernism.* LaSalle, Ill.: Library Press, 1973.

White, Ray Lewis. *Gore Vidal.* Boston: Twayne, 1968.

OTHER

Audio Interview with Gore Vidal. Wired for Books. Available online. URL: http://wiredforbooks.org/gorevidal. Accessed September 22, 2005.

Gore Vidal. Bohemian Ink. Available online. URL: http://www.levity.com/corduroy/vidal.htm. Accessed September 22, 2005.

VIOLENT BEAR IT AWAY, THE FLANNERY O'CONNOR (1955)

While much of the literary criticism on Flannery O'CONNOR's complicated novel *The Violent Bear It Away* rightly focuses on religion, the novel also offers a strong indictment against formal education and its outcomes. The action shifts between Francis Tarwater's burden to complete the religious work of his great-uncle, Mason Tarwater, who has died when the story opens, and the struggle of Francis's cousin, Rayber, a school teacher who conducts sociological research, to convince Francis of the possibilities of living a more modern and secular life. Mason Tarwater's legacy to his nephew, Francis, is that he will become a prophet and baptize Rayber's young son, Bishop. The story takes place alternatively between the Tarwaters' home in the backwoods of Powderhead, Tennessee, and an unnamed city that functions both as Rayber and Bishop's home and a symbol of the fallen city to the story's self-declared prophets.

The structure of the novel is complicated. The story begins with young Francis Tarwater digging the grave for his recently deceased great-uncle, Mason, but the reader gets to know Mason through flashbacks and Francis's reflections of his life with the old man. Having been raised by his great-uncle from infancy, Francis learned his lessons at home rather than having attended school. "His uncle had taught him Figures, Reading, Writing, and History beginning with Adam expelled from the Garden and going on down through the Presidents to Herbert Hoover and on in speculation toward the Second Coming and the Day of Judgment" (4). Young Francis Marion Tarwater learns only those subjects that his great-uncle wants him to know, with an emphasis on religion, since the old man considers himself to be a prophet and agent of God. The novel includes scenes that show the desperate measures that Mason takes to kidnap Bishop in order to baptize him, urging Francis to complete this mission if the old man fails. Francis clearly recalls his great-uncle's instructions: " 'If by the time I die,' he had said to Tarwater, 'I haven't got him baptized, it'll be up to you. It'll be the first mission the Lord sends you' " (9).

But the novel offers a complicated commentary on the place of religion in a person's life. Francis Tarwater, who is only 14 years old when his great-uncle dies, questions the role of prophet that his great-uncle had played. That is, Francis recalls a trip to the city with Mason to meet with several lawyers in an attempt to transfer the title of the land on which they live. Young Tarwater challenges Mason's motives for conducting such business in the name of religion. "Now I see what kind of prophet you are. Elijah would think a heap of you" (27). But Mason defends his actions. He focuses on the potential financial gain from the land while he denounces the city and what it represents. The incongruity of the old man's speech and actions gives Francis pause. Although the burden to baptize Bishop falls to Francis, he struggles internally about his role as a prophet and battles questions about his faith.

The interaction between Rayber and Francis highlights the novel's most pressing questions about organized religion and formal education, and whether the two institutions complement each other in any way. Francis remembers Mason's warnings about Rayber—and his invasive research in the area of social science:

> Where he wanted me was inside that school teacher magazine. He thought once he got me in there, I'd be as good as inside his head and done for and that would be that, that would be the end of it. Well, that wasn't the end of it! Here I sit. And there you sit. In freedom. Not inside anybody's head! (20)

Clearly, the elder Tarwater envisioned Rayber's research as a limited space that confined rather than liberated his research subjects. But young Tarwater is reminded by a friend that the old man limited his options as well. That is, Francis was denied community and agency and was prohibited from traveling to the city, and, therefore, the opportunity to sample its offerings:

> You could have been a city slicker for the last fourteen years. Instead, you been deprived of any company but his, you been living in a two-story barn in the middle of this earth's bald patch, following behind a mule and plow since you were seven. And how do you know the education he give you is true to the facts? Maybe he taught you a system of figures nobody else uses? (46)

The unnamed friend squarely asks "What is truth?" He calls into question the truth that Mason insisted on teaching Francis and, by extension, the truth that Rayber pursues in his research.

The novel's conclusion brings Rayber and Francis together—with Bishop serving as the innocent victim of the men's competing belief systems. In a complicated move that Francis may not understand himself, he drowns Bishop in a ritual baptism. Rayber stares at the pond from the window:

> He knew with an instinct as sure as the dull mechanical beat of his heart that he had baptized the child even as he drowned him, that he was headed for everything that the old man had prepared him for, that he moved off now through the black forest toward a violent encounter with his fate. (203)

This violent encounter that takes the novel's title into account refers to the stranger's rape of Francis. Throughout the novel, the voice of the unnamed stranger prevails as an eerie motif. Finally, after Bishop's complicated and upsetting death, Francis, exhausted and anxious, is picked up and raped by a stranger who drives along the road toward Powderhead. The end brings Francis Tarwater full circle—back to his Uncle Mason's grave. His return is one of great change, however, for he enacted violence and violence is enacted upon him. Yet, he comes to understand his place in the world more clearly—with all of its complexity and potential.

SOURCES

O'Connor, Flannery. *The Violent Bear It Away*. New York: Farrar, Straus & Giroux, 1955.

Paulson, Suzanne Morrow. "Apocalypse of Self, Resurrection of the Double: Flannery O'Connor's *The Violent Bear It Away*." In *Flannery O'Connor New Perspectives*, edited by Sura P. Rath and Mary Neff Shaw, 121–138. Athens: University of Georgia Press, 1996.

Westling, Louise. *Sacred Groves and Ravaged Gardens: The Fiction of Eudora Welty, Carson McCullers, and Flannery O'Connor*. Athens: University of Georgia Press, 1985.

Carla Lee Verderame

VIRGINIA ELLEN GLASGOW (1913)

Many critics have described GLASGOW's *Virginia* as the turning point in her prolific writing career. As Dorothy Scura notes, it is in Glasgow's 10th novel that her ideas about "women and freedom" (40) come to the forefront and find expression for the first time in a female protagonist (30). Glasgow's *Virginia* becomes both a psychological and literary battleground for the author's conflicting ideas about womanhood.

Glasgow juxtaposes many different images of women throughout her novel, always exposing the more pitiable characteristics of some by the more positive expressions of others. The innocent shyness and intellectual emptiness of Virginia Pendleton, for example, is cleverly contrasted with the strength and mental rigor of Susan Treadwell from the beginning pages of the novel, foreshadowing the law of natural selection that will determine each character's fate.

The older generation of the women of Dinwiddie represents various responses to the time-honored call of femininity. Both Lucy Pendleton and Belinda Treadwell answer the call in the expected manner by marrying and producing offspring. Lucy Pendleton, depicted as the worn, selfless, shell of a once beautiful and lively woman, garners pleasure from a self-martyrdom to her husband and child, an inherited mode of thinking she will pass on to her daughter, Virginia. Once her husband dies and she feels that her daughter's life is well established, Lucy Pendleton anxiously awaits death, having fulfilled her purpose in living. Similarly, Belinda Treadwell becomes paralyzed and ceases to "live" after she recognizes that she cannot reconcile the troubles of her marriage. The responses of both these women to their fates foreshadow Virginia's tragic demise. As Phillip Atterberry points out, Virginia, like her mother and Belinda Treadwell, is "paralyzed in her capacity to understand or deal . . ." with her domestic troubles (126).

The two women who do not receive proposals of marriage, Miss Priscilla Batte and Miss Willy, though decidedly wistful about not being able to fulfill what they feel is the call of the ages, manage to attain relative happiness. Priscilla Batte, the embodiment of the old order, clings to the traditional notions of the feminine ideal of her era by partaking in a form of surrogate motherhood. By reforming the minds of the new generation at the Academy for Young Ladies, "the only nice and respectable occupation which required neither preparation of mind or the considerable outlay of money," Priscilla Batte proudly marries herself to the established principles of anti-intellectualism for women instilled by her ancestors (9). But Priscilla

Batte, in contrast to her contemporaries Lucy Pendelton and Belinda Treadwell, is spared the debilitating effects of marriage and childrearing. Priscilla, like these women, lives via her offspring, but Priscilla has the advantage of never "outliving her usefulness," as will Lucy, Belinda, and eventually Virginia herself (390). Miss Pricilla has a seemingly endless supply of young in which to instill the age-old ideals of the era, and in fact it is only after the Academy has closed and she begins to witness the old law begin to crumble, that she begins to show her age.

Miss Willy also achieves a similar degree of happiness via the antiquated notions of a woman's utility. Miss Willy serves as the dressmaker for generations of women in Dinwiddie, and by putting a little of herself into her dresses and into the dreams of the young girls who wear them, she too is able to maintain that spring in her step that the other women find so enviable.

Although there are women who have learned to be happy despite the limitations of tradition in the older generation, Glasgow's conception of the free woman is more accurately represented in the next generation, through the person of Susan Treadwell. While Virginia Pendleton is a slave to the sacrificial notions of love and marriage instilled by maternal heritage, Susan Treadwell's intellectual competence and energy are more admirable. Susan's intellectualism is still dependent upon the societal constraints imposed upon women of the period, but she manages to take control of her destiny by marrying a man who does not threaten her intellectual freedom. Susan Treadwell's marriage to John Henry Pendleton—the other Treadwell-Pendleton union in the novel—is successful perhaps because it mirrors Virginia's marriage; in this case, however, the female retains mental autonomy. Susan, a realist, marries John Henry because of his goodness and with full awareness of his limitations. By marrying a man with a "safe, slow mind" and an "excellent heart" who drops out of school at the age of eight to care for his widowed mother, Susan reveals her understanding of what it takes to secure independence in the era in which she lives (33).

In contrast to Susan, who characteristically enters marriage with open eyes, both Virginia Pendleton and Oliver Treadwell become victims of the sentimental visions of marriage predominant in the Victorian era. In the chapter entitled "White Magic," Virginia falls madly in love with Oliver after just one lingering glance from across the street. From the moment Virginia happens upon a man her fancy can mold into the "object of worship" she has been taught to seek, she devotes herself entirely to this end (70). Oliver, for his part, marries Virginia because she "appeal[s] to the strongest part of him, which is not his heart, but his imagination" (117). Despite his noble intentions of reforming the old world of its imperfections, Oliver falls prey to the temptation of the conventional ideal of femininity and realizes it too late.

While Susan Treadwell is the vision of a happy and intellectually liberated female at the end of Glasgow's novel, Virginia is not treated as kindly. The ending of Glasgow's sympathetic condemnation of the version of womanhood transmitted through the character of Virginia leaves her much as we find her at her story's commencement—waiting patiently for the action of a male to determine her future. Virginia as the "classic ideal of her sex" (154) meets her tragic end because, unlike Susan's, "her soul craves no adventure beyond the permissible adventure of being sought in marriage" (153).

SOURCES

Atterberry, Phillip D. "The Framing of Glasgow's *Virginia*," *Tennessee Studies in Literature* (1995): 124–131.

Glasgow, Ellen. *Virginia*. New York: Penguin, 1989.

Scura, Dorothy M. "A Knowledge in the Heart: Ellen Glasgow, the Women's Movement, and *Virginia*," *American Literary Realism* 22 (1990): 30–43.

Alicia Clay

VIRGINIAN, THE OWEN WISTER (1902)

Published in 1902, Owen WISTER's *The Virginian* was reprinted 15 times within its first eight months and sold more than any other book during 1902–03 (Etulain, 11). Its popularity has been steady over the last hundred years. Hollywood has made four versions of *The Virginian*, including Ted Turner's 2000 production (Graulich, 299). The novel has inspired dozens of formula westerns by authors such as Zane GREY and Max Brand (Etulain, 36). And it is still widely read and studied in college classrooms across the country. So what about this book

continues to interest both casual reader and scholar? *The Virginian* is certainly a romantic tale of the ultimate American folk hero: Wister's "son of the soil" ascends from cowboy to foreman to wealthy landowner through hard work and natural ability; he repeatedly beats and finally kills the villain Trampas; and, of course, he marries the beautiful and spirited schoolmarm Molly Wood. But there is more to Wister's western story than romance. *The Virginian* complicates, among other things, issues of race and gender; it provides historical and literary perspectives; and, as Melody Graulich and other scholars contend in *Reading The Virginian in the New West*, it "offers a stage for debating central issues for the next century" (XIII).

Race is a complicated issue in Wister's novel. Although the Virginian is a Southerner whose attitudes toward blacks appear in his trail songs, his—and Wister's—attitudes toward Indians in the novel are more difficult to categorize. Absent for most of the story, Indians occasionally appear to sell food and wares to railroad passengers, and they listen with approval to the Virginian's "frawgs" of Tulare, California, story (116, 123). But Indians don't play a significant role until they ambush the Virginian halfway through the book. Wister builds up to the attack by positioning the Virginian and Balaam, his traveling companion, on a trail where Indians have been. Balaam seems nervous when they pass the remains of an Indian camp, but the Virginian is unconcerned. He assures Balaam the Indians "have gone on to visit their friends" (190). But just a few pages later, the Indians strike. Wister doesn't describe the Indian attack; in fact, he doesn't even explain the reason for it. After Molly discovers the wounded Virginian and takes him to safety, readers find out that "The Indians who had done this were . . . in military custody," that they had come "unpermitted" from a southern reservation, and that they "perhaps had killed a trapper" in the mountains (212). Indians make convenient villains when Wister needs them, but the savage Indians disappear as suddenly as they appeared. Wister's novel could be accused of both ignoring Native Americans and perpetuating negative stereotypical images of them. But the Indian reference directly following their attack of the Virginian complicates that reading. Ironically, the Virginian recovers from his wound under the warmth of Molly's Navajo blanket. Indians aren't simply bloodthirsty savages threatening the safety of the good white settlers: They make blankets "striped with . . . splendid zigzags of barbarity" that provide warmth, comfort, and safety (221). And suddenly, Indians aren't just Indians; they're Navajo Indians. While it is impossible to deny the book's racism, it is a mistake to ignore the complex and interesting ways Wister deals with race. Equally ambiguous and interesting is *The Virginian's* treatment of gender, class, land use, and religion.

Wister's depiction of these social issues is, according to Richard Etulain, a reflection of the cultural tensions of the Progressive Era (37). In fact it was personal and cultural tension that first sent Wister west. Owen Wister was a wealthy eastern gentleman whose friends included William Dean HOWELLS, Oliver Wendell Holmes, Jr., and Theodore Roosevelt. Educated at Harvard, well-traveled, and talented, Wister's first ambition was music composition. At the encouragement of his father, who wanted his son to choose a financially rewarding, practical career, Wister took a job computing interest at Union Safe Deposit Vaults in Boston. Wister's health declined, so he quit his job. His health deteriorated further as his difficulty choosing a profession grew. So, on the advice of family friend Dr. S. Weir Mitchell, Wister headed west in 1885 (Etulain, 8). Mitchell often sent "privileged young [men] on a wild western journey" as a cure for neurasthenia, or nerves (Owens, 76). The clean air and brisk activity Wister found there seemed to cure his malaise. He fell in love with the West and returned nearly every summer for the next 15 years.

Etulain calls his excursions "more than sightseeing tours; they were antidotes for the perplexities that were eating at his psyche" (9). He suggests that other turn-of-the-century Americans had similar feelings. They "hungered and thirsted after a frontier that would continue and would not be engulfed by the tidal wave of urbanism and industrialism that seemed to threaten the nation (11). The Virginian attempts to meet that need—for Wister and for his readership. In the Virginian, they found a cowboy hero who was self-reliant, strong, and independent. He lived and worked in a spacious, clean land, virtually untainted by man or machine. But, according to the progressive

mentality, the Virginian had to move toward marriage, community connections, and the machine. As Etulain points out, "Though his son will continue to ride his father's horse, the hero takes up with the machine which steams into his territory" (37). Wister's novel glorifies the mythic American hero and his qualities, but it also requires him to embrace the changes that will make him less heroic. Wister's final chapter often leaves readers unsatisfied because, as Stephen Tatum suggests, the point of *The Virginian* is "to dramatize, for better or worse, the evolution of the 'nomadic, bachelor West' into the 'housed, married West' " (Tatum, 255).

A century has passed since the publication of Wister's influential western work, and the West continues to evolve. Although Wister's West is in some ways long gone, Americans continue to think about relations between Native Americans and Anglos, the construction of gender, the effects of immigration on the economy, and how much we should embrace or resist technology that changes where we live and who we are. Some things remain the same. After all, Melody Graulich reminds us, "in 2002 we have a president in the White House who wears cowboy boots for photo ops, who runs a Texas cattle ranch for a hobby and digs oil wells for profit" (Graulich, XII). Much more than a romantic, overdone, and outdated piece of Americana, *The Virginian* is a rich text that complicates the way we think about the West and offers us insights into its future.

SOURCES

Etulain, Richard W. *Owen Wister.* Western Writers Series 7. Boise, Idaho: Boise State University Press, 1973.

Graulich, Melody, ed. "Introduction." In *Reading The Virginian in the New West,* edited by Melody Graulich and Stephen Tatum, XI–XIX. Lincoln: University of Nebraska Press, 2003.

Owens, Louis. "White for a Hundred Years." In *Reading The Virginian in the New West,* edited by Melody Graulich and Stephen Tatum, 72–88. Lincoln: University of Nebraska Press, 2003.

Tatum, Stephen, ed. "Afterword." In *Reading The Virginian in the New West,* edited by Melody Graulich and Stephen Tatum, 255–272. Lincoln: University of Nebraska Press, 2003.

Rachel Rich

VIZENOR, GERALD ROBERT (1934–   )

Gerald Vizenor is a prolific poet, novelist, short story writer, filmmaker, and teacher. His novel, *Griever: An American Monkey King in China,* won the 1988 American Book Award, and Vizenor himself won the 2001 Lifetime Literary Achievement Award from the Native Writer's Circle of the Americas at the University of Oklahoma. He is admired not only for his innovative use of Native American culture and history in his novels, his depiction of people of mixed-blood, and his deromanticizing of false images of Native Americans, but for his sense of humor and his refusal to write from the perspective of a victim.

Gerald Vizenor was born on October 22, 1934, in Minneapolis, Minnesota, to Clement William Vizenor, an Ojibwa Indian painter and paper hanger originally from Minnesota's White Earth Reservation, and LaVerne Lydia Peterson Vizenor. His father was murdered when Vizenor was just 20 months old; when his mother remarried six years later, Vizenor was raised by her second husband, Elmer Petesch, a mill engineer, until his death nine years later. Vizenor married Judith Helen Horns in 1959, earned his bachelor's degree at the University of Minnesota in 1960, served in the Minnesota National Guard (1950–51) and the U.S. Army (1952–55), and began a long career as a university professor. In Vizenor's first novel, *Darkness in Saint Louis Bearheart* (1973), republished as *Bearheart* in 1990, Proude Ceadarfair and his wife, Rosina, are forced from the Red Cedar Reservation by the government. They want Proude's cedar trees for fuel. In this novel Vizenor introduces the Native American trickster figure, especially important in Anishinabean myth and literature and in Vizenor's own work. *Griever: An American Monkey King in China,* based on the author's experiences, depicts an American trickster, Griever, teaching English at Tianjin University in China. Their culture contains Monkey, Trickster's counterpart. Griever is unsuccessful in liberating the people from oppression. Griever reappears in *The Trickster of Liberty: Tribal Heirs to a Wild Baronage* (1988), although the focus in this novel is on the Brownes, the most notable family on the White Earth Reservation. They include China, a magazine writer, Tune, founder of the New School of Socioacupuncture, Tulip, a private investigator, and Eternal Flame, a social worker who helps abused women living on the reservation.

With an entirely original profile of Christopher Columbus, Vizenor presents him as a Native American, specifically a Mayan, in *The Heirs of Columbus* (1992). Most of the novel focuses on Columbus's descendants, in particular the trickster storyteller Stone Columbus. *Dead Voices: Natural Agonies in the New World* (1992) once again uses the trickster figure, this time as a figure in a contemporary card game. *Hotline Healers: An Almost Browne Novel* (1997) features a son of Eternal Flame Browne, featured in *The Trickster of Liberty.* At the center of *Chancers: A Novel* (2000), Vizenor's most recent novel, is the contemporary issue of access to the remains of Native people.

Vizenor lives and writes in Berkeley, California, with Laura Hall, an ethnic studies scholar who has been his wife since 1981. In addition to his life as a novelist, Vizenor is a talented writer for film: His *Harold of Orange* won the 1983 Film-in-the-Cities competition sponsored at the Robert Redford Sundance Film Institute, and a best film citation at the San Francisco Film Festival for American Indian Films. His papers are housed with the American Literature Manuscripts Collection at the Beinecke Library at Yale University.

NOVELS

Chancers: A Novel. Norman: University of Oklahoma Press, 2000.

Darkness in Saint Louis Bearheart. St. Paul, Minn.: Truck Press, 1973. Published as *Bearheart: The Heirship Chronicles.* Minneapolis: University of Minnesota Press, 1990.

Dead Voices: Natural Agonies in the New World. Norman: University of Oklahoma Press, 1992.

Griever: An American Monkey King in China. New York: Fiction Collective, 1987.

The Heirs of Columbus. Hanover, N.H.: Wesleyan University Press, 1992.

Hotline Healers: An Almost Browne Novel. Hanover, N.H.: Wesleyan University Press, 1997.

The Trickster of Liberty: Tribal Heirs to a Wild Baronage. Minneapolis: University of Minnesota Press, 1988.

SOURCES

Blaeser, Kimberly M. *Gerald Vizenor: Writing in Oral Tradition.* Norman: University of Oklahoma Press, 1996.

Coltelli, Laura. "Gerald Vizenor." In her *Winged Words: American Indian Writers Speak,* 155–184. Lincoln: University of Nebraska Press, 1990.

McCaffery, Larry, and Tom Marshall. "On Thin Ice, You Might As Well Dance: An Interview with Gerald Vizenor." In *Some Other Fluency: Interviews with Innovative American Authors,* edited by McCaffery, 287–309. Philadelphia: University of Pennsylvania Press, 1996.

Miller, Dallas. "Mythic Rage and Laughter: An Interview with Gerald Vizenor," *Studies in American Indian Literatures* 7 (Spring 1995): 77–95.

Owens, Louis. " 'Ecstatic Strategies': Gerald Vizenor's Trickster Narratives." In *Other Destinies: Understanding the American Indian Novel,* 225–254. Norman: University of Oklahoma Press, 1992.

Ruppert, James. "Mythic Vision: *Bearheart: The Heirship Chronicles.*" In his *Mediation in Contemporary Native American Fiction,* 92–108. Norman: University of Oklahoma Press, 1995.

Velie, Alan R. *Four American Indian Literary Masters: N. Scott Momaday, James Welch, Leslie Marmon Silko, and Gerald Vizenor.* Norman: University of Oklahoma Press, 1982, pp. 123–148.

Vizenor, Gerald. "The Envoy to Haiku," *Chicago Review* 39, nos. 3–4 (1993): 55–62.

———. *Interior Landscapes: Autobiographical Myths and Metaphors.* Minneapolis: University of Minnesota Press, 1990.

———, with Larry McCaffery and Tom Marshall. "Head Water: An Interview with Gerald Vizenor," *Chicago Review* 39, nos. 3–4 (1993): 50–54.

OTHER

Gerald Vizenor. Minnesota Author Biography Project. Minnesota Historical Society. Available online. URL: http://people.mnhs.org/authors/biog_detail.cfm?PersonID=Vize363. Accessed September 22, 2005.

Gerald Vizenor. Minnesota Author Biography Project. Minnesota Historical Society. Available online. URL: http://www.hanksville.org/storytellers/vizenor. Accessed September 22, 2005.

Gerald Vizenor. Available online. URL: http://www.ipl.org/div/natam/bin/browse.pl/A96. Accessed September 22, 2005.

VOICE AT THE BACK DOOR, THE ELIZABETH SPENCER (1956)

Although Elizabeth SPENCER wrote *The Voice at the Back Door* while in Italy on a Guggenheim Fellowship, and although it appeared in print after she had permanently moved to the North, the book's subject is near to her Southern roots. It deals with race relations in Lacey, Mississippi, a fictional small town much like Carrollton, where Spencer grew up. The author commented in an interview that the racist attitudes the book records from the early 1950s are part of the reason she left the South. The novel received almost universal praise from reviewers, and it was compared to the novels of William FAULKNER for its examination of Southern attitudes and apt portrayal of Southern characters. In fact, Spencer has two of her characters, Kerney Woolbright and Duncan Harper, mention Faulkner; his books have become a part of the landscape she explores.

Like Faulkner's, Spencer's treatment of racial issues isn't didactic. The major characters are complexly drawn, so the novel is more than just an allegory of good versus evil. The third-person omniscient narrator delves into characters' thoughts and sometimes reveals them in the idiom of that character, helping the reader understand motivations and personalities. Spencer also uses flashbacks to show how the past has shaped the present.

The context through which Spencer treats her subject is an election for county sheriff that turns on the candidates' positions on prohibition and civil rights. As the novel opens, Winfield County sheriff Travis Brevard has just died of a heart attack in Duncan Harper's store. Brevard wants Duncan to replace him instead of his deputy, Willard Follansbee, because he hopes Duncan can change some of the town's hypocrisy. Brevard has allowed this hypocrisy to control his life for the past 15 years, the time he has been having an affair with a black woman, Ida Belle, though he has been married to his white wife, Miss Ada, for 30 years. Though the sheriff has children with Ida Belle and prefers her company to that of his wife, he cannot openly acknowledge the relationship. Through the roles of these two women, Spencer reveals how racist attitudes that lingered long after slavery divided black and white women into two halves of one whole human being: the black woman being consigned to a role of sexual and material comfort and the white woman being consigned to a role of distant, idealized symbol. The novel covers the six months between Brevard's death and the next election, during which time Duncan serves as acting sheriff and campaigns for the election.

The novel's title comes from an internal monologue of Duncan's wife, Tinker: "It is part of the consciousness of a Southern household that a Negro is calling at the back door in the night" (83). This voice at the back door calls for help in times of difficulty. Implicit in the approach to the back door instead of the front door is the paradox of black and white relations in the South, that is, simultaneous intimacy and inequality: the former because only an intimate can come to the more private rear entrance, and the latter because by approaching the rear entrance, the visitor does not merit the formal reception reserved for equals or betters. The voice calling at the back door could also be the voice of conscience, admonishing whites for their mistreatment of blacks.

Besides Duncan and Tinker, two other major characters are Jimmy Tallant, Duncan's friend who owns a bar though they live in a dry county, and Beck Dozer, a black man who is in business with Tallant though his father had been lynched by Tallant's father 30 years ago. Tallant and Dozer act as if they are enemies to throw Harper off the scent of their bootlegging operation, but when Tallant is shot and seriously wounded by some of his disreputable New Orleans associates, the town assumes Dozer did it. The town wants to lynch Beck Dozer for shooting a white man, and Beck goes to Harper for protection. When the mob comes to the jail, however, they have cameras instead of guns. They destroy Harper in the media by making him appear too liberal to be elected sheriff. Is Duncan really liberal, the reader wonders, or does he merely follow the tradition of paternalistic gentlemen who protect women and blacks?

Another major character who complicates the situation is Kerney Woolbright, a 25-years-old graduate of Yale Law School who wants to be a state senator. Although Duncan Harper is a close friend, Woolbright's political views are influenced by the powerful and conservative Jason Hunt, whose daughter, Cissy, he wants to marry. Woolbright ultimately betrays Harper, concealing a telegram that would exonerate Beck Dozer, but he is plagued by a guilty conscience. When the lynch mob still threatens Dozer, Duncan

Harper arranges to meet him on the outskirts of town and drive him to safety. Two white men witness Dozer getting into the front seat with Harper and his wife and become outraged. As Harper speeds away, his tires blow out, but the reader suspects the tires have been purposely punctured by the white men. The novel offers some hope for the reconciliation of racial conflict, for although Harper dies in the accident, he becomes a type of martyr for the cause of racial equality. Jimmy Tallant, Beck Dozer, and Kerney Woolbright all have a moral awakening at the end. The novel's ending also suggests that many of the characters, including Jimmy Tallant with the widow Tinker Harper, find renewal through love.

One character, however, is denied a healing relationship. Marcia Mae Hunt, the eldest daughter of the conservative and powerful Jason Hunt, has never been content with her Southern heritage. She longs to be a more powerful woman than her passive mother and sister. Years ago, she had been engaged to Duncan Harper, but she had left him because he would not leave the South with her. She has recently returned after her Yankee husband was killed in World War II, and she and Duncan renew their old feelings in an extramarital affair. It is Marcia Mae who warns Duncan about the approaching mob, and she confronts Kerney Woolbright for his treachery. At the end of the novel she realizes, as did Spencer herself around the time of the novel's publication, that there is no place for her in the South.

SOURCES

Prenshaw, Peggy Whitman. *Elizabeth Spencer.* Boston: Twayne, 1985.

Roberts, Terry. *Self and Community in the Fiction of Elizabeth Spencer.* Baton Rouge: Louisiana State University Press, 1994.

Spencer, Elizabeth. *The Voice at the Back Door.* New York: McGraw-Hill, 1956.

Betina Entzminger

VONNEGUT, KURT, JR. (1922–) Kurt Vonnegut is the author of SLAUGHTERHOUSE-FIVE; OR, THE CHILDREN'S CRUSADE: A DUTY-DANCE WITH DEATH (1969), now considered a classic in the annals of postmodern American fiction. With 14 additional novels, four short fiction collections, and several plays, Vonnegut is widely

considered one of the foremost living American writers. Using intriguing blendings of black humor, science fiction, fantasy, the comic strip, recurring characters like Kilgore Trout, a sense of fatalism and Zen-inspired phrases like "So it goes," Vonnegut writes of ordinary individuals caught up in a complicated, greedy, materialistic, and often absurd world. Occasionally, they connect and recognize their shared humanity.

Kurt Vonnegut was born on November 11, 1922, in Indianapolis, Indiana, to Kurt Vonnegut, an architect, and Edith Sophia Lieber Vonnegut. After studying at Cornell University (1940–42) and Carnegie Institute of Technology (1943), Vonnegut served in the U.S. Army infantry in Germany, where he was a prisoner of war and received a Purple Heart. After his discharge in 1945, Vonnegut married Jane Marie Cox on September 1, 1945, and studied at the University of Chicago from 1945 to 1947. His first published novel, *Player Piano* (1952), set in the fictional city of Ilium (based on Schenectady, N.Y.), features a computer named EPICAC who controls the lives of its residents until challenged by the rebellious Dr. Paul Proteus and his subversive group. *The Sirens of Titan* (1959) also has a fantastical setting on several planets, including Mars, whose military dictatorship electronically controls all residents. He followed with *Mother Night* (1962), the story of Howard W. Campbell, Jr., an American expatriate who performs as a double agent for the Nazis and Allies during World War II. He eventually commits suicide. *Cat's Cradle* (1963), one of his most acclaimed novels, uses the familiar children's game of intricately looped string to denote the empty nature of conventional religion and uses a man-made image in ice called "ice-nine," that can freeze all water on earth, to symbolize the destructive potential of ill-conceived forms of progress. In his next novel, *God Bless You, Mr. Rosewater; or, Pearls before Swine* (1965), Eliot Rosewater, a controversial and odious character, appears sympathetic to others and stands juxtaposed to the materialistic, greedy, self-centered individuals by whom he is surrounded.

Slaughterhouse-Five, based on Vonnegut's own experiences as a POW, features protagonist Billy Pilgrim, who has been profoundly affected by the bombings of Dresden. His feelings coalesce two decades after the war, causing a nervous breakdown and a dissolution of linear time. Billy begins to experience past, present, and future events at random, without reference to chronology. Familiar to most readers of contemporary literature are the novel's refrains of "po-tee-weet," the song of the birds who reappear even on the sites of atomic devastation, and "And so it goes," the narrative editorial comment on the apparent randomness of good and evil. From this point onward, Vonnegut's novels explore the postwar phenomenon of loneliness and spiritual malaise in *Breakfast of Champions; or, Goodbye Blue Monday* (1973). Here Vonnegut divides his personal traits among author Philboyd Sludge; Sludge's protagonist, Dwayne Hoover, a used car dealer; and science fiction novelist Kilgore Trout, often seen as Vonnegut's alter ego. Other novels treat the aftermath of the Watergate scandal of President Nixon's era (*Jailbird* [1979], another Kilgore Trout novel); environmental pollution (*Galapagos* [1985], featuring Kilgore's son Leon Trotsky Trout); and the Vietnam War (*Hocus-Pocus; or, What's the Hurry, Son?* [1990]). Vonnegut is also the author of *Bluebeard* (1987), a study of the nature of art through painter Rabo Karabekian of *Breakfast of Champions;* and his most recent, *Timequake* (1997), another Kilgore Trout novel.

Kurt Vonnegut, who married photographer Jill Krementz in 1979 after his divorce from his first wife that same year, lives and writes in New York City. He is currently at work on a novel entitled *If God Were Alive Today.* Many of Vonnegut's short stories and novels have been adapted for film, including *Slaughterhouse Five,* in 1972; *Slapstick,* as *Slapstick of Another Kind,* in 1984; *Mother Night,* in 1996; and *Breakfast of Champions,* with a screenplay by Alan Rudolph, who also directed, in 1999. In honor of his 80th birthday, New York's mayor Michael Bloomberg designated November 2, 2002, "Kurt Vonnegut, Jr., Day."

NOVELS

Bluebeard. New York: Delacorte, 1987.

Breakfast of Champions; or, Goodbye Blue Monday. New York: Seymour Lawrence/Delacorte, 1973.

Cat's Cradle. New York: Holt, 1963.

Deadeye Dick. New York: Seymour Lawrence/Delacorte, 1982.

Galapagos. New York: Seymour Lawrence/Delacorte, 1985.

God Bless You, Mr. Rosewater; or, Pearls before Swine. New York: Holt, 1965.

Hocus Pocus. New York: Putnam, 1990.

Jailbird. New York: Seymour Lawrence/Delacorte, 1979.

Mother Night. New York: Gold Medal Books, 1962.

Player Piano. New York: Scribner, 1952. Published as *Utopia 14.* New York: Bantam, 1954.

The Sirens of Titan. New York: Dell, 1959.

Slapstick; or, Lonesome No More. New York: Seymour Lawrence/Delacorte, 1976.

Slaughterhouse Five; or, The Children's Crusade: A Duty-Dance with Death, by Kurt Vonnegut Jr. New York: Seymour Lawrence/Delacorte, 1969.

Timequake. New York: Putnam, 1997.

SOURCES

Broer, Lawrence R., ed. *Sanity Plea: Schizophrenia in the Novels of Kurt Vonnegut.* Revised edition. Tuscaloosa: University of Alabama Press, 1994.

Chernuchin, Michael, ed. *Vonnegut Talks!* Forest Hills, N.Y.: Pylon Press, 1977.

Giannone, Richard. *Vonnegut: A Preface to His Novels.* Port Washington, N.Y.: Kennikat, 1977.

Kazin, Alfred. *Bright Book of Life: American Novelists and Storytellers from Hemingway to Mailer.* Boston: Little, Brown, 1973.

Klinkowitz, Jerome, and John Somer, eds. *The Vonnegut Statement: Original Essays on the Life and Work of Kurt Vonnegut.* New York: Delacorte, 1973.

———. *Literary Disruptions: The Making of a Post-Contemporary American Fiction.* Urbana: University of Illinois Press, 1975.

———, and Donald L. Lawler, eds. *Vonnegut in America: An Introduction to the Life and Work of Kurt Vonnegut.* New York: Delacorte, 1977.

———. *The American 1960s: Imaginative Acts in a Decade of Change.* Ames: Iowa State University Press, 1980.

———. *Kurt Vonnegut.* New York: Methuen, 1982.

———. *Literary Subversions: New American Fiction and the Practice of Criticism.* Carbondale: Southern Illinois University Press, 1985.

Krementz, Jill, ed. *Happy Birthday, Kurt Vonnegut: A Festschrift for Kurt Vonnegut on His Sixtieth Birthday.* New York: Delacorte, 1982.

Leeds, Marc. *The Vonnegut Encyclopedia: An Authorized Compendium.* Westport, Conn.: Greenwood Press, 1995.

Lundquist, James. *Kurt Vonnegut.* New York: Ungar, 1977.

Mustazza, Leonard, ed. *The Critical Response to Kurt Vonnegut.* Westport, Conn.: Greenwood Press, 1994.

Plimpton, George, ed. *Writers at Work: The "Paris Review" Interviews,* sixth series. New York: Penguin, 1984.

Reed, Peter J. *Kurt Vonnegut Jr.* New York: Warner Books, 1972.

———, and Marc Leeds, eds. *The Vonnegut Chronicles: Interviews and Essays.* Westport, Conn.: Greenwood Press, 1996.

Schatt, Stanley. *Kurt Vonnegut Jr.* Boston: Twayne, 1976.

OTHER

Audio Interview with Kurt Vonnegut, Jr. Wired for Books. Available online. URL: http://wiredforbooks.org/kurtvonnegut. Accessed September 22, 2005.

Kurt Vonnegut Essay Collection. Mark Uit's Kurt Vonnegut Corner. Available online. URL: http://www.geocities.com/Hollywood/4953/kv_essays.html. Accessed September 22, 2005.

The Official Website of Kurt Vonnegut. Available online. URL: http://www.Vonnegut.com. Accessed September 22, 2005.

W

WAITING HA JIN (1999) HA JIN's second novel, *Waiting*, winner of the 1999 National Book Award, set in Jilin Province in Northeast China, has a deceptively simple plot based on a triangle relationship. Manna Wu, a nurse in an army hospital, is in love with Dr. Lin Kong, but has to wait 18 years for him to divorce his wife, Shuyu, a peasant woman whom Lin married out of filial obligation. Lin's parents need a kind, dutiful daughter-in-law to take care of them in their old age. This plot is laid out in the prologue, which begins with Lin's apparently comic, yet intriguing saga of divorce: "Every summer Lin Kong returned to Goose Village to divorce his wife, Shuyu. Together they had appeared at the courthouse in Wujia Town many times, but she had always changed her mind at the last moment when the judge asked if she would accept a divorce" (3). Thus year after year, Lin goes back to the country from the city to bring his case to the town courthouse during his annual 12-day vacation for 17 years. He is finally granted a divorce in the 18th year, because according to the army hospital's rule, only after 18 years' separation can an officer end his marriage without his wife's consent. There are other strict rules established by the army hospital, including the prohibition of "a man and a woman on the staff from walking together outside the compound, unless they were married or engaged" (16). Within a few pages of the prologue, Ha Jin is able to give the reader a poignant sense of Lin's dilemma, and of the messy entanglement of the Chinese legal system with local and military authorities, especially the extent to which individuals' conduct is regulated and their personal lives are constrained by a rigid morality, under the surveillance of the public and authorities, during a particular period of Communist China, from the 1960s to the 1980s. But *Waiting* is as much a dramatization of humanity that transcends geographical and cultural borders as it is a story about life in a historically situated location in China.

Written in the tradition of the realist, particularly the Russian, novel, *Waiting* entails remarkable scope and depth in portraying both the characters and their society. Its narrative is structured on the relationship among Lin, Shuyu, and Manna, and unfolds with its twists and turns, especially the unexpected development in Lin's relationship with Manna. In fact, this relationship is like the center of a spider's web, from which a complex, interrelated web of social structures and power relations is spun. By situating the relationship among the three characters in this intricate web over a span of 20 years, Ha Jin is able to reveal changes in the major characters—Lin and Manna—by relating these changes to the social surroundings shaped by China's political climate. Following the prologue, the narrative begins with the first stage of Lin's relationship with Manna, when Lin is working in an army hospital and teaching at a small nursing school where Manna is a student. It is extremely important to pay close attention to the way this relationship develops in order to understand why it ends tragically.

The other part of the triangle, the relationship between Lin and Shuyu, enables Ha Jin to shift the narrative from the army hospital to the village, from the country to the city, thus further broadening the world and revealing other circumstances that contribute to the long delay in Lin's divorce. Through keen observation, Ha Jin depicts the differences of life in the city and the country, including the contrasts in food, values, and human relationships, with great details, which give the reader a sense of the sounds, smells, and sights of the surroundings and the localized rhythms of life. While these details paint a vivid picture of the different worlds between which Lin moves, they also help explain why Lin's attempts at divorce fail time and again. Although Shuyu is plain, illiterate, looks much older than Lin, and has bound feet (unusual in the 1960s), she is a good mother to their daughter, and a dutiful daughter-in-law to Lin's parents, whom she has nursed in their old age and illness. For Lin, Shuyu is utterly "unrepresentable" as his wife in the hospital or the city, whereas the villagers regard Shuyu as a perfect wife, and no one pays much attention to her bound feet. Lin asks the court to grant him a divorce because there is no love in his marriage, but for the villagers, the absence of love as a condition for divorce is irrelevant. In fact, in the eyes of the villagers, particularly Shuyu's brother, Lin's attempt to "discard" his wife after she has devoted her life to caring for his parents is utterly immoral and heartless. Despite her reticence, Shuyu obviously does not want a divorce and always breaks into tears in court. On one occasion, her brother rallies a group of supporters for his sister outside the courthouse, threatening violence against Lin if the divorce is granted. The petty judge of the town courthouse relishes his power over Lin in the name of morality. To make this divorce case even more impossible, Lin not only feels guilty about the divorce, he actually enjoys being home in the country. The selfless, devoted Shuyu makes life peaceful and comfortable for Lin during his yearly visit home. Thus Lin does not need much persuasion to give up pressing his wife for divorce. Meanwhile, his relationship with Manna gradually becomes a trap for both of them.

After waiting for 18 years for his divorce to come through so he can marry the woman he loves, Lin finds his marriage to Manna disappointing. During the wait for Lin's divorce, Manna has suffered a great deal of humiliation, disappointment, and betrayal. By the time she and Lin are married, she has changed from a gentle, healthy, innocent, vivacious young woman to a bitter, jealous, and bad-tempered middle-aged woman. Soon after giving birth to twin sons, Manna is found to be dying of heart disease. Lin finds Manna boring and unpleasant to be with, and his married life seems "so tedious, so chaotic, and so exhausting" that he begins to miss the "peaceful time" that now appears remote. By the end of the novel, Lin realizes that suffering has changed Manna. He also begins to question whether he has really loved Manna. Once, when he leaves home after Manna loses her temper over burnt rice, Lin experiences a moment of epiphany. He suddenly realizes that he has never loved Manna or any other woman the way Manna loves him. "His instinct and ability to love passionately had withered away before they had an opportunity to blossom" (296). To his dismay, he recognizes that he has been "pulled and pushed about by others' opinions, by external pressure," and by his illusions and "the official rules" he has "internalized." He reaches the devastating, profound conclusion that he has been misled because he believed that "what you were not allowed to have was what your heart was destined to embrace" (295). To understand Lin's inability to love as wholeheartedly as he wants to, and to understand why it takes 18 years for him to get a divorce, and why his marriage to Manna turns out to be a tragedy, it is necessary to gain some insights into the society that has shaped Lin's life.

Ha Jin is masterful in offering the reader a range of intimate perspectives on the society in which his characters live, by making the most of the relationship among Lin, Manna, and Shuyu. As the relationship between Lin and Manna develops from one between teacher and student, to one between friends, and finally to one between an engaged couple of sorts, their physical contact has been restricted to holding hands in secret. During the development of this relationship, a number of minor characters are introduced through their contact with Lin or Manna, or both: a fine arts teacher who is a widower with three children, a high-ranking army officer whose close ties with the radical leftist "Gang of Four" leads to his death in prison, and a demobilized soldier who rapes Manna but gets away with the crime and even becomes an entrepreneur in the 1980s economic reforms. While these characters help broaden the world of the army hospital, a number of other minor characters on the hospital staff provide an intimate glimpse into the network of gossip and politics that determine the fate of both Lin's and Manna's lives and careers. Ha Jin portrays both the major and minor characters with compassion, humor, irony, and an unflinching critical eye. *Waiting* renders a world vastly different from the West, yet accessible without reducing its complexity and humanity.

SOURCES

Feeley, Gregory. Review of *Waiting*, "Time's Corrosive Effect on a Love That's Stuck on Hold," *Manchester Guardian Weekly*, 20 January 2000, p. 34.

Quan, Shirley N. Review of *Waiting*, Library Journal 124, no. 17 (October 15, 1999): 105.

Zhou Xiaojing

WAITING TO EXHALE Terry McMillan

(1992) *Waiting to Exhale* is the third novel by Terry McMillan, after *Mama* (1987) and *Disappearing Acts* (1989). Immensely popular, especially since its film adaptation in 1995, the novel strengthened McMillan's popularity in her main audience (African-American women) while also appealing to a wider public. The novel traces the lives, friendship, and ties of four women in their 30s, Savannah, Bernardine, Robin, and Gloria, at various points. They have different views of the world and in their place in it, but nonetheless all of them share a common trait: They are looking for a good man, for a potential "Mr. Right" to replace the imperfect men they have encountered up to this point of their lives.

Working in Phoenix, the four women strive to find sense in the world around them, especially in their love affairs. Savannah, a successful public relations executive, just moved from Denver to be with her friend Bernardine, abandoned after a marriage of 11 years and left with two children. Savannah, educated and attractive, is always about to find the man of her dreams but places too much stress on sexual attraction.

Never married, she realizes that in the eyes of her family, her success at work is irrelevant, since she has not been able to start her own family. As a counterpoint, Bernardine has just been disappointed by her ex-husband and is trying to reevaluate her priorities while undergoing all kinds of emotional and personal metamorphoses. Their friend Robin, an insurance professional, is a specialist in bad choices, pathologically in need of a man to make her life complete, yet always attracting inadequate men: As she places her own value and desirability in others, she is usually disappointed in herself and turns to compulsive shopping to escape her lack of self-esteem. Finally, Gloria is an overweight, matronly type who tries to balance her lack of a love and sex life with food, her work in her beauty salon, religion, and her teenager son, Tarik. Never married and afraid to date, she still holds feelings for her son's father.

As the novel progresses, the reader discovers the personality of each of the four friends and their relationships with their families and community. While they work, party, date, and talk, we witness the different kinds of experiences they have had in their relationships with men, to the assorted degrees of loneliness that each of them have to face, and to the support they offer each other, as their friendships keep them from losing their grip on reality. A key issue in the book is that of female bonding and friendship, and how the enduring structures of loving, supportive friends can complement (or replace) love relationships.

The dialogue in *Waiting to Exhale* is witty and creates characters that become real for the reader. Part of the success in the characterization is, however, due to a technique by no means new, but masterfully used by McMillan: The "four-woman form" has also been successfully used by May Louise Alcott in Little Women, Julia Alvarez in How the García Girls Lost Their Accents, and Amy Tan in The Joy Luck Club. It allows multiple perspectives through each of the characters, and at the same time it stresses common experiences for women in a male-dominated society (Richards, 124). Since this narrative structure is based on the characters themselves, the writer must strive to create characters that are credible to the reader and that can relate meaningfully to one another. In McMillan, the "four-woman form" allows her to explore how different women may react to the same situation and find an array of different approaches to everyday dilemmas. To further enrich the variety of perspectives, Robin and Savannah narrate their stories in the first person, while the parts concerning Gloria and Bernardine are told in the third person along alternating chapters. The combination of these different points of view offers positive resources for the characterization: an exclusively third-person narrator would have placed a distance between characters and readers, and thus lessened the intimacy that broadens the circle of the four friends to include the reader herself. Also, the two characters that are chosen to narrate in the first person are precisely Savannah, the most incisive one, and Robin, an ingénue to the point of self-delusion. Savannah discovers and grows throughout her narration, while Robin is bent on repeating the same mistakes over and over: In this sense, they complement each other's narration, emphasizing how Robin's lack of self-analysis makes her the kind of woman who has to depend on men to regard herself as valuable. The combination of this first-person intimate reporting with parts narrated in the third-person stresses the collective view of the women as a group and their collective experience.

Unlike the film version, McMillan's novel is not bent on criticising men per se, although males sometimes appear as stereotypes (the pretender, the married man who is always promising to leave his wife—this time for good—the magnificent man who suddenly discovers his homosexuality). Male-bashing is not an end: In fact, both Bernardine and Gloria seem to find caring and intelligent men by the end of the novel, and women are depicted as guilty of making poor choices involving romantic partnerships. Rather, the novel deals with a series of basic issues (divorce, love disenchantment, loneliness, kids, family, friendship) that transcends ethnic demarcations. Also, the nice depiction of the protagonists' families (Bernardine's kids, her cynical but loving mother, Robin's senile father and debilitated mother) make the emotions disclosed in the novel appear universal, not strictly African American.

The last part of the novel stresses self-discovery, as Robin and Savannah learn to reconsider their priori-

ties, and Gloria and Bernardine seem to have good prospects regarding men. The end of the book makes it also a story about self-growth and personal advancement through bonding and friendship in convoluted surroundings.

SOURCES

Fish, Bruce, and Becky Durost Fish. *Terry McMillan.* Philadelphia: Chelsea House Publishers, 2002.

McMillan, Terry. *Waiting to Exhale.* New York: Viking, 1992.

Richards, Paulette. *Terry McMillan: A Critical Companion.* Westport, Conn.: Greenwood Press, 1999.

Carmen Méndez García

WALKER, ALICE (ALICE MALSENIOR WALKER) (1944–   )

One of the most widely read contemporary American authors, Alice Walker has made a distinct place for herself in American culture and in American literature. Novelist, short story writer, essayist, poet, and critic, Walker, author of the Pulitzer Prize winning *The COLOR PURPLE* (1982), uses her talents to point out injustices against any oppressed individual, with a special focus on black women. As many critics have noted, however, her women characters are rarely powerless; the majority of them transcend victimization to become life-affirming and dignified individuals. In the opening pages of her essay collection, *In Search of Our Mother's Gardens: Womanist Prose* (1983), she explains her coinage of the term "womanist": She invented it to describe black feminists or any women of color, but the term has expanded to describe women's culture in general and has become basic to women's studies courses. Walker is also one of those responsible for revived interest in Zora Neale HURSTON, Walker's favorite author, and despite resistance within parts of the African-American community, she has been relentless in her depiction of black men's oppression of black women.

Alice Malsenior Walker was born on February 9, 1944, in Eatonton, Georgia, to Minnie Tallulah Grant Walker and Willie Lee Walker, both sharecroppers who toiled in the cotton fields. As biographers and scholars point out, Walker was blinded in one eye when her brother accidentally shot her with his BB gun; the resulting handicap led not only to her intro-spectivity and feelings of marginalization, but to her scholarship to Spelman College. She transferred to Sarah Lawrence College, earning a bachelor's degree in 1965, then worked as a civil rights activist in Missis-sippi and married civil rights lawyer Melvyn Roseman Leventhal in 1967. She published her first novel, *The Third Life of Grange Copeland,* in 1970. It follows the lives of three generations of Georgia sharecroppers, Grange Copeland and his son Brownfield Copeland. They abuse their wives; Grange's wife Margaret com-mits suicide; Brownfield murders his wife. Grange, however, himself the victim of abuse by his white boss, becomes the protector of his granddaughter Ruth. In MERIDIAN (1976), Walker chronicles the racial and sex-ual politics of the 1960s Civil Rights movement. The novel moves back and forth between the present, the mid-1970s, and the early 1960s, using interior mono-logue, flashbacks, storytelling, and symbols to evoke Meridian Hill's past and give meaning to her survival and her dedication to improving her community.

Her next novel, *The Color Purple,* was not published until 1982. In an epistolary form, Walker recounts the story of Celie, who survives incest and abuse to become a successful entrepreneur. The novel remained on the *New York Times* best-seller list for 25 weeks, and, in 1985, Steven Spielberg made it into a popular and well-received feature-length film, and a Broadway musical.

Seven years later, Walker published *The TEMPLE OF MY FAMILIAR* (1989), a complex treatment of black men and women (one of whom, Fanny, is the granddaugh-ter of Celie in *The Color Purple*); all are examples of the civilizations of Africa, Europe, and the Americas. Walker recounts not only the evolving history of blacks but also of women, who gradually lost their power to domineering men. In *Possessing the Secret of Joy* (1992), Walker uses Tashi, another character from *The Color Purple,* to draw attention to certain African, Asian, and Middle Eastern cultures that practice female genital mutilation. From this overtly political work, Walker donated a percentage of her profits to educate people about genital mutilation. *By the Light of My Father's Smile* (1998) is Walker's most recent novel.

Walker continues to live in the San Francisco area, where she has founded Wild Trees, a small press dedi-cated to publishing lesser-known writers. A pioneering figure who has invented new voices for American fic-tion, Walker still travels and lectures frequently both in the United States and abroad.

NOVELS

By the Light of My Father's Smile. New York: Random House, 1998.

The Color Purple. New York: Harcourt, 1982.

Meridian. New York: Harcourt, 1976.

Possessing the Secret of Joy. New York: Harcourt, 1992.

The Temple of My Familiar. New York: Harcourt, 1989.

The Third Life of Grange Copeland. New York: Harcourt, 1970.

The Way Forward Is with a Broken Heart. New York: Random House, 2000.

SOURCES

Allan, Tuzyline Jita. *Womanist and Feminist Aesthetics: A Comparative Review.* Athens: Ohio University Press, 1995.

Evans, Mari, ed. *Black Women Writers (1950–1980): A Critical Evaluation.* New York: Anchor, 1984.

Howard, Lillie P., ed. *Alice Walker and Zora Neale Hurston: The Common Bond.* Westport, Conn.: Greenwood Press, 1993.

Johnson, Yvonne. *The Voices of African American Women: The Use of Narrative and Authorial Voice in the Works of Harriet Jacobs, Zora Neale Hurston, and Alice Walker.* New York: Peter Lang, 1995.

Kaplan, Carla. *The Erotics of Talk: Women's Writing and Feminist Paradigms.* New York: Oxford University Press, 1996.

Kramer, Barbara. *Alice Walker: Author of "The Color Purple."* Berkeley Heights, N.J.: Enslow, 1995.

O'Brien, John. *Interviews with Black Writers.* New York: Liveright, 1973.

Prenshaw, Peggy W., ed. *Women Writers of the Contemporary South.* Jackson: University Press of Mississippi, 1984.

Wade-Gale, Gloria. "Black, Southern, and Womanist: The Genius of Alice Walker." In *Southern Women Writers: The New Generation,* edited by Tonette Bond Inge. Tuscaloosa: University of Alabama Press, 1990.

Walker, Alice. *The Same River Twice: Honoring the Difficult: A Meditation of Life, Spirit, Art, and the Making of the film "The Color Purple," Ten Years Later.* New York: Scribner, 1996.

Washington, Mary Helen. "An Essay on Alice Walker." In *Sturdy Black Bridges,* edited by Roseann P. Bell, Bettye J. Parker, and Beverly Guy-Sheftall, 133–149. Garden City, N.Y.: Doubleday & Co., 1979.

WALKER, MARGARET (MARGARET ABIGAIL WALKER) (1915–1998)

Margaret Walker wrote her much-acclaimed novel JUBILEE (1966) as her doctoral dissertation at the University of Iowa. It has captured the attention of readers and critics alike. Many of those critics believe that *Jubilee* is the first historical black American novel, or in the words of scholar and critic Bernard W. Bell, "the first major neoslave narrative" (Bell, 289). Because Bell considers the novel to be the first important contemporary fictional account of slavery, he places it next to Ernest GAINES's *The AUTOBIOGRAPHY OF MISS JANE PITTMAN*, Sherley Ann WILLIAMS's *DESSA ROSE*, Toni MORRISON's *BELOVED*, and Octavia BUTLER's *KINDRED* (Bell, 289) in the canon of African-American literature.

Margaret Abigail Walker was born on July 7, 1915, in Birmingham, Alabama, to Sigismund C. Walker, a minister, and Marion Dozier Walker, a music teacher. Reared mainly in New Orleans, Walker earned a bachelor's degree from Northwestern University in 1935 and her master's (1940) and doctoral (1965) degrees from the University of Iowa. After her graduation from Northwestern, Walker, then a poet, worked on the Federal Writers' Project in Chicago and met Langston HUGHES, Richard WRIGHT, Gwendolyn BROOKS, and Arna BONTEMPS. After marrying Firnist James Alexander in 1943, she raised four children and embarked on a 30-year teaching career at Jackson State University in Mississippi. During this time, she carried in her head the tales that belonged to her maternal grandmother, daughter of an ex-slave, and did formal research on slavery and the Civil War. *Jubilee* is the result; a meticulously structured epic featuring Vyry—the fictional version of Walker's great-grandmother, Margaret Duggans Ware Brown—a slave on a Georgia plantation, during antebellum, Civil War, and Reconstruction days. Using Vyry as a focal point, Walker details the cruelties inflicted on the slaves and the issues of miscegenation, broken families, and racial and class tensions. She writes, too, about the attitudes of the white families and the communal life among the slaves, which included singing, sermons, conjuring, and making herbal remedies.

In 1972, Walker published *How I Wrote "Jubilee,"* implicitly answering critics who questioned her veracity. She continued writing essays, poetry, and a biography entitled *Richard Wright: Daemonic Genius* (1988). Margaret Walker died of breast cancer on November 30, 1998, in Chicago, Illinois.

NOVELS

Jubilee. Boston: Houghton Mifflin, 1966.

SOURCES

Bell, Bernard W. *The Afro-American Novel and Its Tradition.* Amherst: University of Massachusetts Press, 1987.

Christian, Barbara. " 'Somebody Forgot to Tell Somebody Something': African-American Women's Historical Novels." In *Wild Women in the Whirlwind,* edited by Joanne M. Braxton and Andree Nicola McLaughlin, 326–341. New Brunswick, N.J.: Rutgers University Press, 1990.

Goodman, Charlotte. "From *Uncle Tom's Cabin* to Vyry's Kitchen: The Black Female Folk Tradition in Margaret Walker's *Jubilee.*" In *Tradition and the Talents of Women,* edited by Florence Howe, 328–337. Urbana: University of Illinois Press, 1991.

Gwin, Minrose. *Black and White Women of the Old South.* Knoxville: University of Tennessee Press, 1985.

Traylor, Eleanor. "Music as Theme: The Blues Mode in the Works of Margaret Walker." In *Black Women Writers (1950–1980),* edited by Mari Evans. Garden City, N.Y.: Doubleday, 1984.

Walker, Margaret. *How I wrote "Jubilee" and Other Essays on Life and Literature.* Edited by Maryemma Grahm. New York: Feminist Press, 1990.

——— and Nikki Giovanni. *A Poetic Equation: Conversations between Nikki Giovanni and Margaret Walker.* Washington, D.C.: Howard University Press, 1974.

Williams Delores S. "Black Women's Literature and the Task of Feminist Theology." In *Immaculate and Powerful: The Female in Sacred Image and Social Reality,* edited by Clarissa W. Atkinson, Constance H. Buchanan, and Margaret R. Miles, 88–110. Boston: Beacon Press, 1985.

WAR AND REMEMBRANCE

HERMAN WOUK (1978) WOUK's popular novel *The Winds of War* (1972) chronicles the events leading up to the American involvement in World War II with the Japanese attack on Pearl Harbor. The story is told largely through the experiences of naval attaché Victor "Pug" Henry and those of the members of his expanding and increasingly scattered family. Pug is stationed in Berlin as the Nazi aggressions are beginning, and because of his astute observations, he soon becomes a personal adviser to President Roosevelt.

War and Remembrance picks up the story in the aftermath of the attack on Pearl Harbor and chronicles events in the European and Pacific theaters of the World War up to the dropping of the atomic bombs on Hiroshima and Nagasaki. As in *Winds of War,* the focus is still primarily on Pug, but here greater emphasis and more space are given to events involving his children and their spouses and lovers. Still, Pug racks up a lot of mileage. He commands several ships in the Pacific theater, participating in the naval battles off Guadalcanal and much later at Leyte Gulf in the Philippines. In between, he is assigned to the United Kingdom to address issues involving the craft to be used in the landings at Normandy, and to Persia, to coordinate the transportation of lend-lease materials through that country and into the Soviet Union. Through Pug, the reader is presented with concise characterizations of Franklin Delano Roosevelt, Winston Churchill, Adolph Hitler, and Joseph Stalin, as well as many of the historical figures involved in their governments and regimes.

Through Pug's increasingly estranged wife Rhoda, aspects of the American home front are presented—in particular, the economic constraints and the strains on marriages. Through Pug's intermittent relationship with Pamela Tudsbury, the daughter of a well-known British war correspondent who becomes Pug's second wife, glimpses of many minor theaters of operation are provided. In addition, Pug and Rhoda's son Warren is a pilot who participates in the battle of Midway. Their daughter Madeline has an affair with a married man who is a USO entertainer; she later marries a man involved in the development of the atomic bomb at Los Alamos, New Mexico. Their son Byron commands a submarine in the Pacific theater. He is married to Natalie Jastrow, a Jewish woman who is forcibly transported with their son and her uncle Aaron, a famous author, from the uncle's home in Italy to the concentration camps at Theresienstadt and Auschwitz. Even more views of the war are provided by extended fictional reconstructions of documentary texts included within the novel: a memoir by a German general convicted as a war criminal, which Pug translates, and a

concentration-camp diary kept secretly by Aaron Jastrow while confined at Theresienstadt.

The Winds of War and *War and Remembrance* are each well over 1,000 pages long. Wouk has clearly attempted to provide a panoramic fictional treatment of the American involvement in World War II that is comparable in scope and method to Leo Tolstoy's treatment of the French invasion of Russia under Napoleon in *War and Peace.* Reviewers have praised Wouk's ability to create distinctive characters, to write believable dialogue, to generate suspense through careful plotting, and to provide an authentic, insightful, and engaging view of historical events within the confines of his narrative.

Nonetheless, Wouk's novels have not achieved any sort of sustained critical recognition. *Winds of War* was a great commercial success and adapted for a very successful miniseries. But, as a fictional treatment of the prewar years, it did not—and could not—have quite the concentrated effect of James JONES's *FROM HERE TO ETERNITY* (1951). Moreover, the traditional, realist novel had generally fallen into critical disrepute at the time of the novel's publication, and the influence of Marxist criticism had undermined the belief in the individual's role in the shaping of historical epochs. In large part because Norman MAILER offers a critique of that belief without entirely abandoning the scope, shape, and energy of the expansive, realist novel, *The NAKED AND THE DEAD* (1948) is still considered the greatest novel about the war. In the 1960s and 1970s, however, other novels such as Irwin SHAW's *The Young Lions* (1948) and Jones' *The Thin Red Line* (1962), which had been regarded as contenders to that title, were increasingly passed over in favor of more experimental, postmodern treatments of the conflict, such as John HAWKES's *The Cannibal* (1949). Joseph HELLER's *CATCH-22* (1961) and Kurt VONNEGUT, Jr.'s *SLAUGHTERHOUSE FIVE* (1969).

War and Remembrance was the number two bestselling novel of 1978, behind only James MICHENER's *Chesapeake.* The broader association with Michener's increasingly workmanlike historical sagas did not serve Wouk's critical reputation. In fact, the great commercial success of *War and Remembrance* and its development into an extravagantly produced $9^1/_2$-hour miniseries reinforced the notion that Wouk had been driven by commercial incentives, rather than literary ambitions, to write the novel. In an online review, the commercial investment in—and anticipated profitability of—the novel's adaptation to the miniseries are conveyed through a few numbers. The working script was almost 1,500 pages long. It contained more than 2,000 scenes filmed at almost 800 locations on three continents. The script included more than 350 speaking parts and required more than 40,000 extras. In even some of the most positive reviews of the novel, the reviewers observe that the novel seems to have been written with its adaptation to a miniseries in mind.

SOURCES

Beichman, Arnold. *Herman Wouk: The Novelist as Social Historian.* New Brunswick, N.J.: Transaction, 2004.

Bondebjerg, Ib. "Popular Fiction, Narrative and the Melodramatic Epic of American Television," *Dolphin* 17 (1989): 35–51.

Phillipson, John S. "Herman Wouk and Thomas Wolfe," *Thomas Wolfe Review* 12 (Fall 1988): 33–37.

Zhang, Yidong. "Two Panoramas about Great Wars," *Journal of Popular Culture* 19 (Summer 1985): 57–63.

Martin Kich

WARNER, SUSAN BOGERT (1819–1885)

Susan Bogert Warner wrote *The Wide, Wide World* (1850), the first American novel to sell more than a million copies; scholar Edward Halsey Foster calls it "one of the greatest publishing successes of all time" (Foster, 35). Indeed, this publishing phenomenon has frequently been compared to both Harriet Beecher Stowe's Uncle Tom's Cabin and Louisa May Alcott's Little Women. The tale of a motherless girl on her own in the big world captured the imagination of readers both in the United States and abroad and established a blueprint for the female bildungsroman. Warner published more than 30 novels, including several—*Wych Hazel* (1876), for example, and *Say and Seal* (1860)—that she coauthored with her sister Anna Bartlett Warner. Like many other women, Warner, who used the pen name "Elizabeth Weatherell," wrote to earn money after the financial reversals of her father.

Susan Bogert Warner was born on July 11, 1819, in New York City, to Henry Whiting Warner, a lawyer, and Anna Marsh Bartlett Warner, from a wealthy Long Island family. Warner's mother died when she was only nine years old, an event reflected in her motherless fictional creations. She and her sister were reared by their father's sister, Frances Warner. She was educated at home, studying German, French, and Italian as well as Latin and Greek, along with literature, science, mathematics, and the arts. When her father suffered financial losses during the Panic of 1837, the family moved to Constitution Island, a family property opposite West Point; Warner would remain at this farmhouse until her death. Her first novel, *The Wide, Wide World,* tells the tale of the motherless preadolescent girl, Ellen Montgomery, as she suffers and succeeds and grows spiritually mature; she marries John Humphreys, son of the Rev. John Humphreys and brother of Ellen's friend, Alice. In the final chapter of the novel, not published until 1987 in the Jane Tompkins edition (see bibliography), John Humphreys marries Ellen and takes her home from Scotland to America. This novel, along with the semiautobiographical *Queechy* (1852), was also praised for its detailed depiction of domestic life and work. Here, the orphaned Fleda Ringgan is raised by affluent relatives until financial exigencies force a move to rural Queechy, where Fleda must perform physical labor. She becomes spiritually fulfilled through her immersion in religion, although, unlike Ellen, Fleda marries a wealthy Englishman named Guy Carleton. All her novels contain extensive descriptions of 19th-century New England and New York State life.

Warner continued to write novels until she died on March 17, 1885, in Highland Falls, New York. The Constitution Island Association Archives is the primary repository for Susan Warner's manuscripts, journals, scrapbooks, and correspondence. Special Collections at the Cadet Library at the United States Military Academy houses another important collection of her correspondence. The manuscript for *The Wide, Wide World* is at the Huntington Library.

SELECTED NOVELS

The Gold of Chickaree. By Warner and Anna Warner. New York: Putnam's, 1876.

The Hills of Shatemuc. 2 vols. New York: Appleton, 1856.

Melbourne House. 2 vols. New York: Carter, 1864.

Nobody. New York: Carter, 1882.

Queechy. 2 vols. New York: Putnam's, 1852.

Say and Seal. By Warner and Anna Warner. 2 vols. Philadelphia: Lippincott, 1860.

The Wide, Wide World. 2 vols. New York: Putnam's, 1850; 1 volume, London: Nisbet, 1852.

Wych Hazel. By Warner and Anna Warner. New York: Putnam's, 1876.

SOURCES

Baker, Mabel. *The Warner Family and the Warner Books.* West Point, N.Y.: Constitution Island Association, 1971.

Bauermeister, Erica R. "*The Lamplighter, The Wide, Wide World,* and *Hope Leslie:* Reconsidering the Recipes for Nineteenth-Century American Women's Novels," *Legacy* 8 (Spring 1991): 17–28.

Foster, Edward Halsey. *Susan and Anna Warner.* Boston: Twayne, 1978.

Hovet Grace Ann, and Theodore R. Hovet. "Identity Development in Susan Warner's *The Wide, Wide World:* Relationship, Performance and Construction," *Legacy* 8 (Spring 1991): 3–16.

Meyers, D. G. "The Canonization of Susan Warner," *New Criterion* 7 (December 1988): 73–78.

O'Connell, Catharine. " 'We Must Sorrow': Silence, Suffering, and Sentimentality in Susan Warner's *The Wide, Wide World,*" *Studies in American Fiction* 25 (Spring 1997): 21–39.

Sanderson, Dorothy Hurlbut. *They Wrote for a Living: A Bibliography of the Works of Susan Bogert Warner and Anna Bartlett Warner.* West Point, N.Y.: Constitution Island Association, 1976.

Schnog, Nancy. "Inside the Sentimental: The Psychological Work of *The Wide, Wide World,*" *Genders* 4 (March 1989): 11–25.

Stewart, Veronica. "Mothering a Female Saint: Susan Warner's Dialogic Role in *The Wide, Wide World,*" *Essays in Literature* 22 (Spring 1995): 58–74.

———. "The Wild Side of *The Wide, Wide World,*" *Legacy* 11 (1994): 1–16.

Stokes, Olivia E. Phelps. *Letters and Memories of Susan and Anna Bartlett Warner.* New York: Putnam's, 1925.

Tompkins, Jane. "Afterword." *The Wide, Wide World.* New York: Feminist Press, 1987.

White, Isabelle. "Anti-Individualism, Authority, and Identity: Susan Warner's Contradictions in *The Wide, Wide World,*" *American Studies* 31 (Fall 1990): 31–41.

Williams, Cynthia Schoolar. "Susan Warner's *Queechy* and the Bildungsroman Tradition," *Legacy* 7 (Fall 1990) 3–16.

OTHER

Susan Warner [a.k.a. Elizabeth Wendell]. Domestic Goddesses. Available online. URL: http://www.womenwriters.net/domesticgoddess/warner1.html. Accessed September 22, 2005.

WARREN, ROBERT PENN (1905–1989)

An American Renaissance man, Robert Penn Warren, winner of the Pulitzer Prize for fiction (1947) and for poetry (1948), was a member of the Fugitive Group in the 1920s, the first U.S. Poet Laureate (1986), and a distinguished writer of novels, poems, short stories, and literary criticism. With John Crowe Ransom and Cleanth Brooks, he was one of the leading New Critics, a group that revolutionized the teaching of literature by emphasizing closer reading of the work itself. Warren was awarded the National Medal for Literature in 1970. His critically acclaimed novels include *Night Rider* (1939), *ALL THE KING'S MEN* (1946), *WORLD ENOUGH AND TIME* (1950), *BAND OF ANGELS* (1955), *At Heaven's Gate* (1943), *The Cave* (1959), *Wilderness: A Tale of the Civil War* (1961), *Flood: A Romance of Our Time* (1964), *Meet Me in the Green Glen* (1971), *A Place to Come To* (1977), and the novella *Blackberry Winter* (1946). All his novels acknowledge the complexities and ironies inherent in the modern world and the necessity of a link between the individual and his community. His vision includes protagonists who desperately seek identity and meaning in a modern wasteland without respect for integrity and old values.

Robert Penn Warren was born on April 24, 1905, in Guthrie, Kentucky, to Robert Franklin Warren, a banker, and Anna Ruth Penn Warren, daughter of Gabriel Penn, a Confederate cavalryman under General Nathan Bedford Forrest. He earned a bachelor's degree from Vanderbilt University, graduating summa cum laude in 1925, and a master's degree from the University of California in 1927, then earned a B. Litt. from Oxford University in 1930 as a Rhodes Scholar. He married Emma Brescia in 1930; after they divorced in 1950, he married the writer Eleanor Clark in 1952. His first novel, *Night Rider,* uses a fictional protagonist who resembles Samuel Taylor Coleridge's narrator in *The Rime of the Ancient Mariner.* Warren used this device through *Band of Angels,* and it is especially noticeable in the Pulitzer Prize–winning *All the King's Men,* featuring narrator Jack Burden. He tells the tale of Louisiana governor Willie Stark, who is based on Louisiana Governor Huey Long. Burden sees that he must take some responsibility for his own actions and become more involved in the lives of others. *World Enough and Time,* another history-based novel, fictionalizes the murder of Colonel Solomon P. Sharp by Jeroboam O. Beauchamp and the sensational trial that followed in 1826.

Although some critics criticized Warren for exploiting sex and violence in Southern gothic novels, most readers feel that his is a moral voice exhorting the individual to transcend the spiritual wasteland of contemporary life and to understand that evil can be overcome. Robert Penn Warren died on September 15, 1989, in Stratton, Vermont. The majority of his papers are housed at the Beinecke Library at Yale University.

NOVELS

All the King's Men. New York: Harcourt Brace, 1946.

At Heaven's Gate. New York: Harcourt Brace, 1943.

Band of Angels. New York: Random House, 1955.

Blackberry Winter. Cummington, Mass.: Cummington Press, 1946.

The Cave. New York: Random House, 1959.

Flood: A Romance of Our Time. New York: Random House, 1964.

Meet Me in the Green Glen. New York: Random House, 1971.

Night Rider. New York: Houghton, 1939.

A Place to Come To. New York: Random House, 1977.

Wilderness: A Tale of the Civil War. New York: Random House, 1961.

World Enough and Time. New York: Random House, 1950.

SOURCES

Berger, Walter. *A Southern Renaissance Man: Views of Robert Penn Warren.* Baton Rouge: Louisiana State University Press, 1984.

Blotner, Joseph Leo. *Robert Penn Warren: A Biography.* New York: Random House, 1997.

Burt, John. *Robert Penn Warren and American Idealism.* New Haven, Conn.: Yale University Press, 1988.

Casper, Leonard. *The Blood-marriage of Earth and Sky: Robert Penn Warren's Later Novels.* Baton Rouge: Louisiana State University Press, 1997.

Clark, William Bedford, ed. *Critical Essays on Robert Penn Warren.* Boston: Twayne, 1981.

Ferriss, Lucy. *Sleeping with the Boss: Female Subjectivity and Narrative Pattern in the Fiction of Robert Penn Warren.* Baton Rouge: Louisiana State University Press, 1997.

Gray, Richard, ed. *Robert Penn Warren: A Collection of Critical Essays.* Englewood Cliffs, N.J.: Prentice-Hall, 1980.

Grimshaw, James A. Jr., ed. *Robert Penn Warren's Brother to Dragons: A Discussion.* Baton Rouge: Louisiana State University Press, 1983.

Grimshaw, James A., Jr. *Time's Glory: Original Essays on Robert Penn Warren.* Conway: University of Central Arkansas Press, 1986.

Justus, James H. *The Achievement of Robert Penn Warren.* Baton Rouge: Louisiana State University Press, 1981.

Koppelman, Robert S. *Robert Penn Warren's Modernist Spirituality.* Columbia: University of Missouri Press, 1995.

Nakadate, Neil, ed. *Robert Penn Warren: Critical Perspectives.* Lexington: University Press of Kentucky, 1981.

Watkins, Floyd C., and John T. Hiers, eds. *Robert Penn Warren Talking: Interviews 1950–1978.* New York: Random House, 1980.

West, Paul. *Robert Penn Warren.* Minneapolis: University of Minnesota Press, 1964.

WASHINGTON SQUARE Henry James (1880)

One of Henry James's last "early phase" novels, *Washington Square* is also one of his "American" novels, which also includes *The Bostonians* and *The Europeans.* First serialized in both *Cornhill Magazine* and *Harper's Magazine* in 1880, it was published in book form in 1881. While it received favorable reviews at the time, James's own estimation of the novel was fairly low and he did not include it in the collected "New York Edition" of 1907–10. Following its initial appearance, James wrote to William Dean Howells, describing it as "a poorish story." Despite the author's own feelings, the novel has remained one of his more popular and was adapted into a successful stage play and adapted several times for the screen. Gender theorists, Marxist critics, and cultural theorists have all taken the novel as their object of study in recent years.

The novel centers on the character of Catherine Sloper, the daughter of the widowered Dr. Austin Sloper, a successful physician who lives in the fashionable Washington Square neighborhood of mid-century New York. As the title suggests, the setting was important to James's conception of the work. Critics have argued, however, that his long descriptive passages of the setting detract from, rather than add to, the novel's impact. Whatever its effect, the social and economic circumstances of the novel's setting, especially in the opportunities for women, contribute greatly to the situation in which Catherine Sloper finds herself, as essentially a commodity in a system of financial exchange. James's attention to the downtown business district emphasizes the economic aspect of the novel.

Catherine Sloper, described as plain, shy, and passive, grows up under her father's disappointed eye; she cannot fill the place of her dead mother or brother. When Morris Townsend, penniless suitor who has squandered one inheritance abroad, proposes to Catherine, Dr. Sloper, recognizing him as a fortune hunter, refuses his consent, threatens his daughter with disinheritance, and forbids future contact. The two young people continue to meet surreptitiously and Catherine promises Townsend she will marry him when he is ready, as he is waiting for Dr. Sloper to change his attitude toward the inheritance. Dr. Sloper decides to take Catherine to Europe on a Grand Tour for a year. During this time, Catherine's melodramatic Aunt Lavinia Penniman, who lives in the Sloper household, encourages Morris to continue his suit. While in Europe, Catherine realizes the reason for Townsend's interest and, upon returning to New York, breaks the engagement. Although she does not see Townsend again, she persists in a battle of wills with her father by also refusing to concede to her father's dying request to never marry Townsend, even after his death. By so refusing, her inheritance is reduced considerably. Years later, Townsend returns and proposes again. Catherine refuses and the final lines of the novel reveal her returning to her needlework: "Catherine, meanwhile, in the parlour, picking up her morsel of fancywork, had seated herself with it again—for life, as it were."

Critical attention to *Washington Square* has never been large in terms of quantity, especially as compared to that given to James's later novels, *The PORTRAIT OF A LADY, The AMBASSADORS, Wings of the Dove,* and *The Golden Bowl,* or even shorter works such as *The TURN OF THE SCREW* and *DAISY MILLER.* The novel's place in James's literary development has been examined, noting, for example, how Catherine Sloper prefigures the character of Isabel Archer in *The Portrait of a Lady,*

James's next book following *Washington Square.* Both characters are known for the psychological intensity and their moments of self-realization, although Catherine's realization in Europe of Morris Townsend's intent is not as developed as the integral chapter 42 of *The Portrait of a Lady.* The relationship between father and daughter has also been a popular topic as have locating the sources for James's novel; in Balzac's *Eugenie Grandet,* critics identify a model for Catherine Sloper and a similar use of sparing dialogue. Other critics have noted the novel's humor, especially James's characterization of Lavinia Penniman. Recently, critics of the novel have focused on its successful adaptation to film, notably in William Wyler's *The Heiress* (1949) and Agnieszka Holland's *Washington Square* (1997).

SOURCES

Bell, Ian F. A. *"Washington Square": Styles of Money.* New York: Twayne, 1993.

Berlant, Lauren. "Fancy-Work and Fancy Foot-Work: Motives for Silence in *Washington Square," Criticism: A Quarterly for Literature and the Arts* 29 (1987): 439–458.

Bradley, John R., ed. *Henry James on Stage and Screen.* New York: Palgrave, 2000.

Griffin, Susan M., ed. *Henry James Goes to the Movies.* Lexington: University Press of Kentucky, 2002.

James, Henry. *Washington Square.* New York: Penguin, 1984.

Maini, Dashan Singh. "Washington Square: A Centennial Essay," *Henry James Review* 1 (1979): 81–101.

Poirier, Richard. *The Comic Sense of Henry James: A Study of the Early Novels.* New York: Oxford University Press, 1967.

Eric Leuschner

WAYS OF WHITE FOLKS, THE LANGSTON HUGHES (1933)

Langston HUGHES, a towering figure in American literature, is certainly best known for his poetry. His nonfiction work, and also his ill-fated dramatic collaboration with Zora Neale HURSTON, *Mule Bone,* also hold places of prominence in the study of African American literature. Nonetheless, his 1933 work *The Ways of White Folks* stands as a significant literary achievement in its own right. With its stunning array of characters and its vivid depiction of the often explosive nature of social contact between black and white Americans in the first half of the 20th century, this collection of stories is another example of Hughes's prolific and varied contribution to the artistic output of the Harlem Renaissance.

Instead of one storyline and one set of characters, Hughes gives us 14 diverse and seemingly unconnected episodes. No geographic location is common to all, but throughout *The Ways of White Folks,* the influence of Hughes's own experience as an artist during the Harlem Renaissance and his close, often intimate contact with the white world and its money, power, and patronage can be seen. Because of its unity of theme, some critics consider the work a novel. In both form and content, *Ways* holds a strong similarity to Jean TOOMER's *Cane,* written a decade earlier than Hughes's work. Though *Ways* lacks Toomer's multigenre approach, Hughes does experiment with narrative point of view in this work, and according to David Michael Nifong, he "meets with varying degrees of success" (94). Hughes's book is at its best when well-developed African-American characters view the hypocrisy and caprice of the affluent white Americans around them, in episodes such as "Slave on the Block," "A Good Job Gone," and "Poor Little Black Fellow." The more experimental sections, as far as narration goes, include "Passing," "Red-Headed Baby," and "Little Dog."

Hughes also creates several memorable and extremely thought-provoking African-American characters, including the indomitable Cora Jenkins in "Cora Unashamed," the tortured musician Roy Williams from "Home," and the brilliant, yet pragmatic piano protege Oceola Jones of "The Blues I'm Playing." This achievement is significant, since literary critic Houston A. Baker, Jr., states that Hughes "[was] not averse to criticizing blacks in works that are sometimes scathing in their satire" (107).

The reader should not forget the title of the book, though, and should keep in mind that each story is intended as a view of white Americans and their culture through the eyes of the black characters. Hughes intends many of these episodes to be commentaries not only on his white characters, but on white society in general, with its strange, fitful, and often violent ways. All of the episodes do have African-American characters at the center of the action, but in almost every case, it is actually the white characters being presented for the inspection of the reader.

Understandably, Hughes is not as sympathetic in his creation of white characters. The frivolousness of these individuals is exceeded only by their almost universal lack of understanding of African Americans as human beings. The Carraways are attracted to Luther, in much the same way that Mrs. Dora Ellsworth is drawn to Oceola, but none of the white characters can accept that these black artists have lives of their own, full of love and passion, outside the confined paternal worlds that the whites have created for them. Even the benevolent Mr. Lloyd from "A Good Job Gone" demonstrates a huge blind spot when it comes to understanding African Americans; Pauline drives him crazy with lust, and he ends up "in a padded cell" (65).

Amusingly, the "great" Mr. Eugene Lesche also understands this interracial lust, and he and his partner make a fortune by conning rich white women with their therapeutic program of "primitive" African art and music in "Rejuvenation Through Joy." This connection between "primitive" African art and "modern" European art is at the heart of much of the work produced during the 1920s and 1930s; Gertrude STEIN and Pablo Picasso were a few of the prominent artists strongly influenced by African culture.

Ultimately, the strength of Hughes's book comes not from its demonstration of the lives of common African Americans living in a racist society, as seen in the fiction of Richard WRIGHT and Zora Neale Hurston, but from its depiction of exceptional African Americans. Like Hughes himself, the artists and the musicians of *The Ways of White Folks* have the unique opportunity to see firsthand the inexplicable ways of rich white Americans, and what they see amazes them. Oceola Jones perhaps sums it up best in her description of Mrs. Ellsworth: "Strange! Too strange! Too strange!" (117). In this same episode, Hughes points to an apparently unbridgeable gap between these two races that reappears throughout the book; Mrs. Ellsworth is insatiably drawn to Oceola, but the nature of the attraction comes from the fact that she sees Oceola as "just as black and she herself was white" (103).

SOURCES

Baker, Houston A., Jr. *Long Black Song: Essays in Black American Literature and Culture.* Charlottesville: University Press of Virginia, 1972.

Gates, Henry Louis, Jr., and Cornel West, eds. *The African American Century: How Black Americans Have Shaped Our Country.* New York: Free Press, 2000.

Hughes, Langston, ed. *An African American Treasury: Articles, Stories, Poems, By Black Africans.* New York: Pyramid Books, 1961.

Hughes, Langston. *The Big Sea: An Autobiography.* New York: Thunder's Mouth Press: Distributed by Persea Books, 1986.

————. *The Ways of White Folks.* New York: Knopf, 1963.

Nichols, Charles H., ed. *Arna Bontemps–Langston Hughes Letters, 1925–1967.* New York: Paragon House, 1990.

Nifong, David Michael. "Narrative Technique and Theory in *The Ways of White Folks,*" *Black American Literature Forum* 15, no. 3 (1981): 93–96.

North, Michael. *The Dialect of Modernism.* New York: Oxford University Press, 1994.

Rampersad, Arnold. *The Life of Langston Hughes: Volume I.* New York: Oxford University Press, 1986.

Randy Jasmine

WEBER, KATHARINE (1955–)

Katharine Weber, author of OBJECTS IN MIRROR ARE CLOSER THAN THEY APPEAR (1995), *The Music Lesson* (1999), and *The Little Women* (2003), and a well-known book reviewer, is a writer of indisputable merit who was included on the list of *Granta's* Best American Writers Under 40 after the publication of her debut novel.

Katharine Weber was born on November 12, 1955, in New York City, to Sidney Weber, a film producer, and Andrea Warburg Weber, a photographer. At age 16, Weber was recruited for the then brand-new New School college program. She worked in various jobs and married the art historian and writer, Nicholas Fox Weber, in 1976. She attended Yale University for two years in the 1980s and began teaching there in 1997. In her first novel, *Objects in Mirror Are Closer than They Appear,* New York photographer Harriet Rose temporarily leaves her new love, Benedict, while she travels to Switzerland and becomes involved in her friend Anne Gordon's affair with Victor, a married man and Auschwitz survivor. *The Music Lesson,* on the other hand, is a psychological thriller set in Ireland and centers on an IRA plot to steal a Vermeeer painting. A New York art historian, Patricia Dolan, realizes that her passionate love affair with Michael O'Driscoll has blinded her to the fact that she is being used for political as well as sexual purposes. Weber's most recent novel, *The Little Women,* interests readers for two reasons: Although it is not, as Weber points out, a sequel to Louisa May ALCOTT's classic novel, it clearly comments on that 19th-century novel in contemporary ways; and second, its self-reflexive, postmodernist structure intentionally augments and undercuts Weber's story about Meg, Joanna, and Amy Green, who, shocked at learning of their mother Janet's affair with one of her graduate students, decide to live together at Meg's apartment in New Haven, Connecticut, where Meg is a first-year student at Yale. Harriet Rose, the protagonist of *Objects in Mirror,* reappears in *The Little Women.*

Katharine Weber lives in rural Connecticut with her husband. Next to their 18th-century house is Weber's studio, where she is at work on a new novel that incorporates the story of the Triangle Shirtwaist Factory fire (Steinberg, 52) and some of Weber's grandmother's experiences at the factory.

NOVELS

The Little Women. New York: Farrar, Strauss, 2003.

The Music Lesson. New York: Farrar, Strauss, 1999.

Objects in Mirror Are Closer than They Appear. New York: Crown Publishers, 1995.

SOURCES

Bader, Eleanor J. Review of *The Little Women, Library Journal* 128, no. 11 (June 15, 2003): 103.

Baker, John F. "New Take on *Little Women,*" *Publishers Weekly* 249, no. 37 (September 16, 2002): 14.

Joyce, Alice. Review of *Objects in Mirror Are Closer Than They Appear, Booklist* 91, no. 17 (May 1, 1995): 1,554.

Steinberg, Sybil. "Turning a Classic on Its Head: Katharine Weber," *Publishers Weekly* 250, no. 36 (September 8, 2003): 50–52.

WE HAVE ALWAYS LIVED IN THE CASTLE SHIRLEY JACKSON (1962)

We Have Always Lived in the Castle, Shirley JACKSON's final novel, is a witty, poignant, and ultimately chilling tale of madness, misanthropy, and sisterly love. A powerful and wickedly humorous fictionalization of the Lizzie Borden murder case, the novel represents the culmination of preoccupations present in Jackson's writing from the very beginning of her career and is considered, along with *The Haunting of Hill House,* one of her finest accomplishments. The novel was anticipated in a journal entry Jackson made toward the beginning of her career, an entry which, as S. T. Joshi has noted, serves as an accurate encapsulation of her work: "I thought I was insane and would write about how the only sane people are those who are condemned as mad and how the whole world is cruel and foolish and afraid of those who are different" (quoted in Joshi, 54).

Sisters Mary Catherine (or Merricat) and Constance Blackwood have been social pariahs since the murders of the rest of the Blackwood family six years before. Since the murders (for which Constance, the elder, was tried but acquitted), they and their senile uncle Julian have existed in their own peaceful, comfortable world, a world in which the upkeep of the family home and the loving preparation of food take center stage; ironic considering that the rest of the family died after eating one of Constance's splendid meals.

Constance, the cheerful mother figure of the house, is an agoraphobic, unable to venture beyond the boundaries of the Blackwood property. It is a status quo welcomed by the cunning, childish Merricat, the family's only envoy to the outside world, who sees anyone apart from her immediate circle as inhuman "ghosts" and "demons." She dreams of living with her beloved Constance on the moon, where no one can reach them, and the thought of losing her sister scares her as nothing else can. Appropriately, her household job is fence mending: keeping the family "safe." She spends her time erecting charms and totems all over the property.

For Merricat, the house is everything, and she is unable to understand her sister's gradual longing for change. When Constance asks, "Don't you ever want to leave here, Merricat?" she blithely responds, "What place would be better for us than this?" (448).

The novel opens with a masterful account of her last-ever shopping trip to the local village. The village and the people in it fill Merricat with fear and paranoia. The depth of her loathing for the villagers she encounters, and the extent of her madness, is made clear in her graphic fantasies of murder and violence. As she makes her way down the main street, she wishes "they were all dead and I was walking on their bodies" and, even

more gruesomely, ". . . thought of them rotting away and curling in pain and crying out loud; I wanted them doubled up and crying on the ground in front of me" (407). However, family pride and a kind of savage dignity (instilled in her by Constance) are still important; she keeps up a pretence of politeness despite the provocation she encounters. This insistence upon maintaining gentility and social superiority is poignantly maintained at the novel's conclusion.

The closest we come to an outsider's perspective in *Castle* comes with the introduction of the eminently dislikeable cousin Charles. He conforms to a frequent Jackson character type: the feckless, lazy, untrustworthy young man, a nastier version of Essex in *The Sundial* or Luke Sanderson in *The Haunting of Hill House.* Charles insists (perhaps rightly) that something be done about Merricat, but his greed and arrogance make everything he says suspect. The insidious manner in which he slots into the position previously occupied by the sister's tyrannical father, and the searing resentment he inspires in Merricat, means that some sort of violent resolution is inevitable.

Though we eventually discover that Merricat is a remorseless mass murderer, and that the aptly named Constance had taken the blame out of a misguided sense of guilt or responsibility, their actions are never analysed or judged within any context wider than the confines of their own home. Indeed, we are even invited to look upon Merricat's act in a sympathetic manner. Constance is said to have announced to the police upon her arrest that "those people (meaning her father, mother, aunt, and little brother) deserved to die?" (432). Either the seemingly mild-mannered, good-natured Constance has been affected with some of the bloodthirstiness of her sister, or Jackson wants us to be aware that the Blackwood family was in some way deserving of their deaths.

Unlike Jackson's earlier psychological novels *Hangsaman* (1951) and *The Bird's Nest* (1954), in which certain events are cited as the trigger for mental imbalance, no explanations are ever supplied in *Castle.* Merricat suffers no pangs of conscience and clings to no moral code: The only absolute wrong to her is anything that will hurt Constance or separate them.

Castle ends not with a return to societal standards of normality but with a final retreat into deranged isolationism. Merricat's paranoid worldview is ultimately vindicated when a vengeful mob of villagers destroys the family home (the fact that she has brought them there in the first place, by setting the place on fire, does not occur to her). By the novel's conclusion, the sisters have resigned themselves to living in the blackened ruins and have done their best to reestablish their familiar domestic routine. The identification of mind with place that recurs so often in Jackson's fiction here provides a striking and poignant conclusion: The Blackwood sisters sit huddled in the blackened ruins of their once magnificent house, forever shunning the outside world. As so often happens to the women in Jackson's fiction, their home becomes both refuge and prison.

SOURCES

Hattenhauer, Darryl. *Shirley Jackson's American Gothic.* Albany: State University of New York Press, 2003.

Jackson, Shirley. *We Have Always Lived in the Castle.* In *The Masterpieces of Shirley Jackson,* edited by S. T. Joshi. London: Constable Robinson, 1996.

Joshi, S. T. "Shirley Jackson: Domestic Horror." In *The Modern Weird Tale.* Jefferson, N.C.: McFarland and Company, 2001.

Bernice Murphy

WELCH, JAMES [PHILIP] (JAMES PHILIP WELCH, JR.) (1940–2003)

James Welch came to public attention with WINTER IN THE BLOOD (1974), his first novel, about a part Blackfoot and part Gros Ventre Indian living on a Montana reservation. Following N. Scott MOMADAY's HOUSE MADE OF DAWN (1968), *Winter in the Blood* is considered the second major novel in the Native American renaissance of the late 20th century and has become a classic of modern Native American literature. In the book, Yellow Calf, grandfather of the nameless protagonist, helps his troubled and aimless grandson come to terms with his identity.

James Welch was born on November 18, 1940, in Browning, Montana, on the Blackfoot Reservation, to James Philip Welch, predominantly Blackfoot, and Rosella O'Bryan Welch, predominantly Gros Ventre. Welch studied at the University of Montana, where he earned his bachelor's degree in 1965. He and Lois Monk, now professor of English at the University of Montana, married in 1968. His second novel, *The Death of Jim Loney* (1979), features the tortured "half-breed" Jim Loney, who agonizes over his accidental shooting of Myron Pretty Weasel, a high school classmate, and finally, unable to understand himself as either Indian or white, intentionally provokes tribal policeman Quentin Doore into shooting him.

With his third novel, *Fools Crow* (1986), which won the American Book Award, the *Los Angeles Times* Book Prize, and the Pacific Northwest Book Award, Welch ushers in a different sort of protagonist: Fools Crow is a fullblood Blackfoot and the story is set in the 1860s and 1870s, when the tribe was strong and confident. Unlike the protagonists in the first two novels, Fools Crow is untroubled with alcoholism or identity issues; instead, he must witness helplessly the ceaseless encroachment of the whites on to Native territory. In *The Indian Lawyer* (1990) Welch again switches theme and perspective, this time featuring Sylvester Yellow Calf, a successful Indian in a white world. He bears the name of the grandfather of the protagonist in *Winter in the Blood,* however, and that is ironic: the further he enters the white world, the more he leaves his heritage behind; at the end he rejects the white world and offers pro bono legal expertise to his people. In his last novel, Welch features a young Oglala Sioux, a witness to the Battle of the Little Bighorn. Charging Elk joins Buffalo Bill's Wild West Show, moves to France, is imprisoned for murder, and finally, on his release, begins to build a new life in Marseilles. James Welch died of a heart attack on August 4, 2003, in Missoula, Montana.

NOVELS

The Death of Jim Loney. New York: Harper, 1979.

Fools Crow. New York: Viking, 1986.

The Heartsong of Charging Elk. Garden City, N.Y.: Doubleday, 2000.

The Indian Lawyer. New York: Norton, 1990.

Winter in the Blood. New York: Harper, 1974.

SOURCES

Auer, Tom. "The Indian Writer: An Interview with James Welch," *Bloomsbury Review* 11 (March 1991): 11, 25.

Ballard, Charles G. "The Question of Survival in *Fools Crow*," *North Dakota Quarterly* 59 (Spring 1991): 251–259.

———. "The Theme of the Helping Hand in *Winter in the Blood*," *MELUS* 17 (Spring 1991–1992): 63–74.

Barry, Nora. "The Lost Children in James Welch's *The Death of Jim Loney*," *Western American Literature* 25 (May 1990): 35–48.

Bevis, William W. "James Welch," *Western American Literature* 32, no. 1 (Spring 1997): 33–53.

———. *Ten Tough Trips: Montana Writers and the West.* Seattle: University of Washington Press, 1990.

———. "Wylie Tales: An Interview with James Welch," *Weber Studies* 12, no. 3 (Fall 1995): 15–32.

Fitz, Karsten. "Bridging the Gap: Strategies of Survival in James Welch's Novels," *American Indian Culture and Research Journal* 20–21 (1996): 131–146.

Gish, Robert. "Word Medicine: Storytelling and Magic Realism in James Welch's *Fools Crow*," *American Indian Quarterly* 14 (Fall 1990): 349–354.

Larson, Charles R. *American Indian Fiction.* Albuquerque: University of New Mexico Press, 1978, 140–149.

McFarland, Ron, ed. *James Welch.* Lewiston, Idaho: Confluence Press, 1986.

Pavich, Paul N. Review of *The Death of Jim Loney, Western American Literature* XV, no. 3 (November 1980): 219–220.

Sands, Kathleen Mullen. "Closing the Distance: Critic, Reader and the Works of James Welch," *MELUS* 14, no. 2 (Summer 1987): 73–85.

Tatum, Stephen. "Distance, Desire, and the Ideological Matrix of *Winter in the Blood*," *Arizona Quarterly* 46, no. 2 (Summer 1990): 73–100.

Velie, Alan R. *Four American Indian Literary Masters.* Norman: University of Oklahoma Press, 1982, pp. 66–103.

Wild, Peter. *James Welch.* Boise, Idaho: Boise State University, 1983.

WELLS, REBECCA (1952–)

Author of the best-selling *Divine Secrets of the Ya-Ya Sisterhood* (1996), as well as the acclaimed *Little Altars Everywhere* (1992), Rebecca Wells writes about her native space, central Louisiana, via a fictional town called Alexandria. She peoples her territory with ordinary individuals who, like the rest of us, often have complicated and deleterious family relationships. The popularity of her novels (*Ya-Ya Sisterhood* has sold more than 3 million copies, *Little Altars* more than 1 million) demonstrates the power of "word-of-mouth" publicity: Wells's work achieved "phenomenal success" (a phrase used repeatedly in reviews of her books) without the usual marketing techniques: interviews and television appearances.

Rebecca Wells was born in 1952 in Rapides, Louisiana. Her father was a self-employed businessman. She prefers not to reveal her exact birthday, nor to discuss details of her family. She studied at Louisiana State University and earned a bachelor's degree in 1970 before studying with Allen Ginsburg at the Naropa Institute in Boulder, Colorado, and then moving to New York City to study the Stanislavsky method of acting. It was not until after her move to Seattle, Washington, in 1982, that she published her first novel. *Little Altars Everywhere* is told from the perspectives of Siddalee Walker, now a New York theater director, and other family members. They re-create the warmth of family love, on one hand, and the half-remembered moments of physical abuse, on the other, all experienced during the 1960s on their 900-acre farm, Pecan Grove. In addition to its "deceptively simple" first-person narrator and realistic use of language and dialogue, as reviewer Beth Farell notes, the novel "explores such weighty issues as the loss of innocence, the traditional roles of women in the South, and the plight of farmers" (Farell, 142). *Divine Secrets of the Ya-Ya Sisterhood,* the sequel, also features Sidda, who decides to reunite with her mother, Vivi. During her visit home she learns that her mother was part of a group of women—the Ya-Ya Sisterhood—who had formed their own spiritual group presided over by a benign "Holy Lady," which was better suited to them than the Catholic Church, in which they were raised. Because of Wells's book, The Sisterhood, "a gang of merry, smart, brave, poignant, and unforgettable goddesses" (Seaman, 1674), has been re-created all over the United States.

Rebecca Wells, who also writes plays and occasionally performs on stage, is married to photographer Tom Schworer and lives near Seattle on a small island in Puget Sound. Bette Midler's All-Girl Productions purchased the movie rights to *Divine Secrets of the Ya-Ya Sisterhood,* and the Warner Brothers movie, directed by Callie Khouri and starring Ellen Burstyn, Ashley Judd, and Sandra Bullock, appeared in 2002.

NOVELS

Divine Secrets of the Ya-Ya Sisterhood. New York: Harper-Collins, 1996.

Little Altars Everywhere. Seattle, Wash.: Broken Moon Press, 1992.

SOURCES

Farell, Beth. Review of *Little Altars Everywhere, Library Journal* 124, no. 18 (November 1, 1999), 142.

Gantt, Patricia. " 'Against Regulations': Southern Women in the Fiction of Rebecca Wells." In *Songs of the New South: Writing Contemporary Louisiana,* edited by Suzanne Disheroon-Green and Lisa Abney, 163–171. Westport, Conn.: Greenwood Press, 2001.

Rowlett, Lori. "Lady of the Earth and Moon: Goddess Imagery and the Ya-Yas." In *Songs of the New South: Writing Contemporary Louisiana,* edited by Disheroon-Green and Abney, 115–122. Westport, Conn.: Greenwood Press, 2001.

Seaman, Donna. Review of *Divine Secrets of the Ya-Ya Sisterhood, Booklist* 92, nos. 19–20 (June 1, 1996): 1,674.

Unsigned Review of *Divine Secrets of the Ya-Ya Sisterhood, Publishers Weekly* 243, no. 15 (April 8, 1996), 57.

Unsigned Review of *Little Altars Everywhere, Publishers Weekly* 239, no. 29 (June 29, 1992), 58.

Van Boven, Sarah. "Getting their Ya-Yas Out." *Newsweek,* 6 July 1998, p. 71.

Whitney, Scott. Review of *Little Altars Everywhere, Booklist* (June 1, 1999), 1,853.

Wilson, Mary Ann. "Living on the Edge in Rebecca Wells's *Little Altars Everywhere.*" In *Songs of the New South: Writing Contemporary Louisiana,* edited by Disheroon- Green and Abney, 3–9. Westport, Conn.: Greenwood Press, 2001.

OTHER

Bain, Rebecca. "Women Everywhere Embrace the Ya-Ya Sisterhood of Rebecca Wells." *BookPage.* Available online. URL: http://www.bookpage.com/9710bp/firstperson2.html. Accessed September 22, 2005.

Frye. Donna. "Rebecca Wells." A Celebration of Women Writers. Formerly available online. URL: http://webpages.marshall.edu/~frye16/overview.html. Accessed September 22, 2005.

WELTY, EUDORA (1909–2001)

Eudora Welty is one of the most important American writers of the 20th century. Mississippi, her native state, is the locus for nearly all her fiction. Although she is inevitably compared with William FAULKNER, because they both use myths and symbols, her detached, ironic tone and frequent use of humor and satire, combined with her intensely lyrical style, results in a vision of humanity that is tragicomic rather than tragic. Her themes include the significance of human connectedness, the central place of family, the presence of wanderers, isolates, and grotesques, all of whom remain part of the universal panorama. Each dream, myth, and symbol is notable for the way it evokes a Weltian world, although this world can be depicted in realistic, concrete detail, as well.

Eudora Alice Welty was born on April 13, 1909, in Jackson, Mississippi, to Christian Webb Welty, an insurance executive, and Mary Chestina Andrews, a teacher. She was educated at Mississippi State College for Women for two years and the University of Wisconsin for the next two, graduating with a bachelor's degree in 1929. Although she knew she wanted to become a writer, she attended graduate classes in advertising at Columbia University from 1930 to 1931, returning to Jackson when her father died in 1931. She lived in the family home for the rest of her life; after a three-year employment with the Works Progress Administration, during which she interviewed and photographed a wide range of Mississippians across the state, she began producing stories, novels, reviews, and essays. Her first novel (some call it a novella), THE ROBBER BRIDEGROOM, appeared in 1942. Set in Mississippi during pioneer days, the novel blends fairy tale, legend, folktale, and southwestern humor as well as the Greek myth of Cupid and Psyche; the title derives from a fairy tale called the *Robber Bridegroom* by the brothers Grimm. Most critics agree that her next novel, DELTA WEDDING (1946), is more realistic. She describes the first of many social events to gather together various family members who emerge as individual portraits and as storytellers with memorable ways of speaking. Here the elder family members overcome the reluctance of other relatives to accept Dabney Fairchild's hill-country husband. In the novel, Welty also creates a benign matriarchy headed by Ellen Fairchild, who takes under her wing a nine-year-old girl who has lost her mother. Continuing to publish short story collections, Welty also wrote *The Ponder Heart,* a comic tour de force of a novel (some call it a novella) featuring Edna Earle Poole, who delivers a dramatic monologue about her uncle Daniel Ponder. At the Clay, Mississippi, Beulah Hotel that she manages, Edna Earle tells a traveling salesman her outraged but comic story about Daniel, who woos the 17-year-old Bonnie Dee Peacock and ends up literally tickling her to death. The novel was adapted by Jerome Chodorov and Joseph Fields as a Broadway play in 1956 and an opera bouffe in 1982.

LOSING BATTLES (1970) is Welty's longest work, as well as the first to appear on the best-seller lists. The occasion for the Vaughn-Beecham-Renfro clan reunion is Granny Vaughn's 90th birthday and Jack Renfro's release from prison. Through stories, yarns, and personal battles (against ignorance, against the Depression, against outside interference), the reader learns the history of this six-generation family. They maintain unity in the face of discord and family feuds by holding reunions. The *OPTIMIST'S DAUGHTER,* Welty's last novel, appeared in 1972. Her most autobiographical work (Welty's mother died in 1966 after a protracted illness), the novel opens as Laurel McKelva, a young professional woman in New York City, returns home to New Orleans to be with her dying father who, after his first wife's death, married a vulgar younger woman, Fay Chisom. In this emotionally complex novel, Laurel faces the destructive as well as the positive aspects of love and the inevitability of change.

The recipient of a remarkable number of awards, including the American Book Award, the National Medal of Arts, the National Institute of Arts and Letters Gold Medal, the first Cleanth Brooks Medal, and the Chevalier de l'Ordre des Arts et Lettres, Eudora Welty honestly and realistically depicted the dark side of life while joyously celebrating the victory of love and connectedness. She received the William Dean Howells Medal of the American Academy for *The Ponder Heart* (1954) and the Pulitzer Prize for *The Optimist's Daughter* (1972). She died of pneumonia on July 23, 2001, in Jackson, Mississippi. In 1991, the Eudora Welty Society was formed, and various Internet resources, including the Eudora Welty Newsletter, are available online. Eudora Welty's papers and manuscripts are housed at the University of Mississippi.

NOVELS AND NOVELLAS

Delta Wedding. New York: Harcourt, 1946.
Losing Battles. New York: Random House, 1970.
The Optimist's Daughter. New York: Random House, 1972.
The Ponder Heart. New York: Harcourt, 1954.
The Robber Bridegroom. Garden City, N.Y.: Doubleday, 1942.

SOURCES
Bloom, Harold, ed. *Modern Critical Views: Eudora Welty.* New York: Chelsea House, 1986.

Buckley, William F., Jr. "The Southern Imagination: An Interview with Eudora Welty and Walker Percy," *Mississippi Quarterly* 26 (Fall 1973): 493–516.

Carson, Barbara Harrell. *Eudora Welty: Two Pictures at Once in Her Frame.* Troy, N.Y.: Whitson, 1992.

Champion, Laurie. *The Critical Response to Eudora Welty's Fiction.* Westport, Conn.: Greenwood Press, 1994.

Craig, Turner, W., and Lee Emling Harding, eds. *Critical Essays on Eudora Welty.* Boston: G. K. Hall, 1989.

Evans, Elizabeth. *Eudora Welty.* New York: Ungar, 1981.

Gretlund, Jan Norby. *Eudora Welty's Aesthetics of Place.* Columbia: University of South Carolina Press, 1997.

Gygax, Franziska. *Serious Daring from Within: Female Narrative Strategies in Eudora Welty's Novels.* Westport, Conn.: Greenwood Press, 1990.

Harrison, Suzan. *Eudora Welty and Virginia Woolf: Gender, Genre, and Influence.* Baton Rouge: Louisiana State University Press, 1996.

Kreyling, Michael. *Author and Agent: Eudora Welty and Diarmuid Russell.* New York: Farrar, Straus & Giroux, 1991.

Mortimer, Gail L. *Daughter of the Swan: Love and Knowledge in Eudora Welty's Fiction.* Athens: University of Georgia Press, 1994.

Pingatore, Diana R. *A Reader's Guide to the Short Stories of Eudora Welty.* Englewood Cliffs, N.J.: Prentice Hall, 1996.

Polk, Noel. *Eudora Welty—A Bibliography of Her Work.* Jackson: University Press of Mississippi, 1994.

Prenshaw, Peggy Whitman, ed. *Conversations with Eudora Welty.* Jackson: University Press of Mississippi, 1984.

———. *Eudora Welty: Critical Essays.* Jackson: University Press of Mississippi, 1979.

———, ed. *More Conversations with Eudora Welty.* Jackson: University Press of Mississippi, 1996.

Trouard, Dawn, ed. *Eudora Welty: Eye of the Storyteller.* Kent, Ohio: Kent State University Press, 1990.

Vande Kieft, Ruth. *Eudora Welty.* Boston: Twayne, 1962; revised, 1987.

Waldron, Ann. *Eudora: A Writer's Life.* New York: Doubleday, 1998.

Westling, Louise. *Eudora Welty.* Totowa, N.J.: Barnes, 1988.
———. *Sacred Groves and Ravaged Gardens: The Fiction of Eudora Welty, Carson McCullers, and Flannery O'Connor.* Athens: University of Georgia Press, 1985.

OTHER

Eudora Welty Newsletter. Available online. URL: http://www.gsu.edu~wwwewn. Accessed September 22, 2005.
Eudora Welty Society. Available online. URL: http://www.textsandtech.org/orgs/ews. Accessed September 22, 2005.
Mississippi Writers. Available online. URL: http://www.olemiss.edu/depts/english/ms-writers/dir/welty_eudora. Accessed September 22, 2005.
Moses, Kate. "Happy Birthday, Miss Welty." *Salon.com.* Available online. URL: http://www.salon.com/people/bc/1999/04/13/welty. Accessed September 22, 2005.

WEST, DOROTHY (1907–1998)

When Dorothy West died in 1998 at 91, she was mourned as the last of the living Harlem Renaissance writers. A novelist, short story writer, and editor, West's first literary success was "Typewriter," which tied for second place in the 1926 *Opportunity* magazine short story contest, along with Zora Neale HURSTON's "Spunk." West founded and edited two short-lived but influential literary magazines, *Challenge* (1934–36) and *New Challenge* (1937), coedited with Richard WRIGHT; the magazines included work by Langston HUGHES, James Weldon JOHNSON, and Ralph ELLISON. West published her first novel, *The Living Is Easy* (1948), to general critical acclaim. Although her work disappeared from literary anthologies and college classrooms, she reappeared after the republication of *The Living Is Easy* in 1982. In 1995, at age 85, with the encouragement of Doubleday editor Jacqueline Kennedy Onassis, West published *The Wedding*, a tale set in the Martha's Vineyard, which satirizes middle-class values and explores social and racial issues, to enthusiastic reviews. In 1998 Oprah Winfrey adapted the novel for television.

Dorothy West was born on June 2, 1907, in Boston, Massachusetts, to Isaac Christopher West, a man born into slavery and emancipated at age seven. (He became a successful grocer known as the "Black Banana King" of Boston.) Her mother, Rachel Pease Benson West, was West's model for Cleo Jerico Judson, the hero of *The Living Is Easy.* After attending Girls Latin School in Boston, West moved to New York, where her friends included Hurston, Wright, Claude McKAY, Countee Cullen, and Arna BONTEMPS. She traveled to Russia in 1932 with 20 other African Americans to produce "Black and White," a film documentary on race. Although the film never appeared, West remained in Russia for a year with Hughes. She returned to New York and to editing and working for the Federal Writers Project before publishing *The Living Is Easy.* Set in Boston, the novel portrays the Black elite and the problems caused by wealth, power, and leisure. The light-skinned and determined Cleo Jerico marries the older businessman Bart Judson. She invites her sisters to live with them and to share the wealthy lifestyle. This scenario provides West with a chance to explore class and gender roles and the superficial values of the elite.

West remained in Oak Bluffs, Martha's Vineyard, for the rest of her days, where she wrote *The Wedding.* The main character, beautiful blond Shelby Coles, is a black woman engaged to the white musician. Jute McNeil, a black man, tries to persuade Shelby to change her mind and marry him. More than a love story, the novel is about entrenched attitudes about skin color.

Dorothy West died in Boston on August 16, 1998, after enjoying renewed attention from literary circles during her final years; she lectured, gave interviews, and wrote stories that have been collected, together with her earlier ones, in a volume entitled *The Richer, The Poorer: Stories, Sketches, and Reminiscences.* The majority of West's papers are held in the Mugar Memorial Library at Boston University.

NOVELS

The Living Is Easy. Boston: Houghton Mifflin, 1948; London: Virago, 1987.
The Wedding. New York: Doubleday, 1995; London: Abacus, 1995.

SOURCES

Dekgard, Katrine. "Alive and Well and Living on the Island of Martha's Vineyard: An Interview with Dorothy West, October 29, 1988," *The Langston Hughes Review* (Fall 1993): 28–44.
Guinier, Genii. *Black Women Oral History Project Interview with Dorothy West, May 6, 1978.* Cambridge, Mass.: Schlesinger Library, Radcliffe College, 1981, pp. 1–75.

Karpen, Lynn. "The Last Leaf," *New York Times Book Review,* 12 February 1995, p. 11.

Perry, Margaret. *Silence to the Drums: A Survey of the Literature of the Harlem Renaissance.* Westport, Conn.: Greenwood Press, 1976, p. 132.

Roses, Lorraine Elena. "Interviews with Black Women Writers: Dorothy West at Oak Bluffs, Massachusetts," *SAGE: A Scholarly Journal on Black Women* (Spring 1985): 47–49.

Rueschmann, Eva. "Sister Bonds: Intersections of Family and Race in Jessie Redmon Fauset's *Plum Bun* and Dorothy West's *The Living Is Easy.*" In *The Significance of Sibling Relationships in Literature,* edited by JoAnna Stephens Mink and Janet Doubler Ward, 120–131. Bowling Green, Ohio: Bowling Green University Popular Press, 1992.

Steinberg, Sybil. "Dorothy West: Her Own Renaissance," *Publishers Weekly* 242, no. 27 (July 3, 1995): 34.

OTHER

Voices from the Gaps [VG]. Dorothy West. Available online. URL: http://voices.cla.umn.edu/auvg/Bios/entries/west_dorothy.html. Accessed September 22, 2005.

WEST, NATHANAEL (1903–1940)

WEST, NATHANAEL (1903–1940) Novelist and screenplay writer Nathanael West is commonly associated with the years of the Great Depression that he experienced for much of his adult life. In both reality and in his most famous fictional works, MISS LONELYHEARTS (1933) and THE DAY OF THE LOCUST (1939), West attempted to transcend the poverty, pain, and emptiness of modern life (as he saw it) by helping those in need. He provided rent-free accommodations to such writers as Dashiell HAMMETT, Lilian Hellman, and S. J. Perelman during the years he managed inexpensive New York City hotels, and in all his novels his characters, often with the help of an artist protagonist, try to overcome despair and disillusionment. While his novels received critical but not popular acclaim, his screenplays, unlike those of his friend and fellow novelist-turned-screenwriter F. Scott FITZGERALD, earned him money during the last years of his life.

Born Nathan Weinstein on October 17, 1903, in New York City, to Max Weinstein, a building contractor, and Anna Wallenstein Weinstein, West graduated from Brown University with a bachelor of philosophy degree in 1924. He changed his name to Nathanael West on August 16, 1926, and published his first novel, *The Dream Life of Balso Snell,* in 1931. This surrealistic work follows Snell, an artist, to ancient Troy, where he finds the Trojan horse and enters it through its anus. In this and other satiric episodes, the artist is presented as a figure of mockery—vain and self-centered. In his next novel, *Miss Lonelyhearts,* the title character is the pseudonym of the otherwise nameless protagonist who, as an lovelorn advice columnist, becomes caught up in and tries to help the sad souls who write to Miss Lonelyhearts. West presents him as a Christ-like figure who tries to demonstrate love for everyone but whose attempts fail at the end of the novel when he is accidentally shot by one of his readers. The last of his New York novels, *A Cool Million,* satirizes the American Dream and the Horatio ALGER myth. It attracted the attention of a movie studio and, encouraged, West moved to Hollywood in 1935. It provided the seed for *The Day of the Locust,* West's Hollywood novel combining a surrealistic view of "Tinseltown" with the already familiar theme of the artist concerned with rescuing those around him. As in *Miss Lonelyhearts,* however, his efforts result in failure.

Nathanael West married Eileen McKenney (real-life hero of Ruth McKenney's novel *My Sister Eileen*) on April 19, 1940, just months before the couple were killed in an automobile accident in December, in El Centro, California. *Miss Lonelyhearts* has been adapted for the screen twice: by Leonard Praskins for the film "Advice to the Lovelorn" in 1933, and by Dore Schary for the film "Lonelyhearts" in 1958. Michael Dinner and others adapted it as a PBS television play in 1983, and Howard Teichmann adapted *Miss Lonelyhearts* for the stage in 1957. *The Day of the Locust* was adapted by Waldo Salt as a film in 1975.

NOVELS

A Cool Million: The Dismantling of Lemuel Pitkin. New York: Covici, Friede, 1934.

The Day of the Locust. New York: Random House, 1939.

The Dream Life of Balso Snell. Paris: Contact Editions, 1931.

Miss Lonelyhearts. New York: Liveright, 1933.

SOURCES

Auden, W. H. *The Dyer's Hand and Other Essays.* New York: Random House, 1962.

Barnard, Rita. *The Great Depression and the Culture of Abundance: Kenneth Fearing, Nathanael West, and Mass Culture in the 1930s.* New York: Cambridge University Press, 1995.

Bloom, Harold, ed. *Nathanael West: Modern Critical Views.* New York: Chelsea House, 1986.

Comerchero, Victor. *Nathanael West: The Ironic Prophet.* Syracuse, N.Y.: Syracuse University Press, 1964.

Hyman, Stanley Edgar. *Nathanael West.* Minneapolis: University of Minnesota Press, 1962.

Light, James F. *Nathanael West: An Interpretive Study.* Second edition. Evanston, Ill.: Northwestern University Press, 1971.

Long, Robert Emmet. *Nathanael West.* New York: Ungar, 1985.

Madden, David, ed. *Nathanael West; The Cheaters and the Cheated: A Collection of Critical Essays.* DeLand, Fla.: Everett/Edwards, 1973.

Martin, Jay. *Nathanael West: The Art of His Life.* New York: Farrar, Straus, 1970.

Martin, Jay, ed. *Nathanael West: A Collection of Critical Essays.* Englewood Cliffs, N.J.: Prentice Hall, 1971.

Siegel, Ben, ed. *Critical Essays on Nathanael West.* New York: G. K. Hall, 1994.

Veitch, Jonathan. *American Superrealism: Nathanael West and the Politics of Representation in the 1930s.* Madison: University of Wisconsin Press, 1997.

Widmer, Kingsley. *Nathanael West.* Boston: Twayne, 1982.

Wisker, Alistair. *The Writing of Nathanael West.* New York: St. Martin's Press, 1990.

OTHER

Books and Writers. "Nathanael West (1903–1940)." Available online. URL: http://www.kirjasto.sci.fi/nwest.htm. Accessed September 22, 2005.

WHARTON, EDITH (NEWBOLD JONES) (1862–1937)

One of the most brilliant, versatile, and prolific writers of the 20th century, Edith Wharton wrote more than 40 volumes, including novels, short stories, essays, criticism, poetry, and travel writing. The first woman awarded an honorary doctoral degree from Yale University (1923), Wharton received the Pulitzer Prize in 1925 for the novel *The AGE OF INNOCENCE.* Wharton took for her subject matter the nature of Americans, both at home and abroad, a topic particularly well suited to her penchant for wit and satire. Since she was an expatriate who lived nearly half her life in France, she was particularly adept at exposing hypocrisy among the socially elite or as evidenced in the cultural values of Americans. Another major interest of Wharton is the plight of the intelligent woman, and the nature of the men—many of whom she saw as "negative heroes"—with whom they fell in love or from whom they tried to escape.

Edith Wharton was born on January 24, 1862, to George Frederic Jones, heir to a merchant-ship fortune, and Lucretia Stevens Rhinelander Jones, a descendant of Revolutionary War general Ebenezer Stevens. Like most young women of her class and financial position, Wharton was educated privately, both at home in New York and in Europe, where the family traveled extensively. She married Edward (Teddy) Robbins Wharton, a banker, in 1885 and divorced him in 1912. After suffering a nervous breakdown, commonly called "neurasthenia," Wharton, like her contemporaries Charlotte Perkins GILMAN and Owen WISTER, consulted Dr. S. Weir Mitchell and, against his advice, persevered with her writing. She published *The Greater Inclination,* a short story collection, in 1899; a novella, *The Touchstone,* in 1900; and her first novel, *The Valley of Decision,* a historical tale of moral decline set in 18th-century Italy, in 1902. *Sanctuary* came out in 1903; however, most readers agree that her first significant novel was *The HOUSE OF MIRTH* (1905), the story of Lily Bart, the quintessential young woman who exemplifies the social pressures of the time. On one level, she must marry well to continue in her life of leisure; on another, she is too honest to marry for money, and her refusal to compromise her principles results in her tragic demise. The novel also features Lawrence Seldon, the first major exemplar of Wharton's many charming but weak male characters.

Madame de Treymes (1907), the first of two novels set in France, pits the European decadence of Madame Christiane de Treymes against her brother's widow, the young American Fanny Malrive. In *The Fruit of the Tree* (1907), set in New England, Justine Brent responds to a number of such contemporary social dilemmas—euthanasia and factory worker reform—and simultaneously must revise her opinion of her husband, wealthy factory owner John Amherst. In *ETHAN FROME* (1911), Wharton explores the agony of a man torn between loyalty to his wife Zeena and love for the young Mattie Silver. A suicide attempt that fails results in the crippling of the lovers and of their passion for each other. *The REEF* (1912) focuses on three Americans in France: the widowed Anna Leath, her fiancé George Darrow, a friend from her New York childhood, and Sophy Viner with whom George has a brief affair. Eventually, this affair changes all three characters and they go their separate ways. *The CUSTOM OF THE COUNTRY* (1913) features one of Wharton's best known and most controversial characters, Undine Spragg, who sees no harm in following the logical outcome of the customs of the United States, where women are viewed as commodities. In Wharton's view the country has spawned women who, like men, view marriage as a business and as a way to realize the American Dream of wealth and position.

SUMMER (1917) was written as a companion piece to *Ethan Frome* (Wharton often referred to the former as "hot Ethan" and the latter as "cold Ethan"): again set in New England, the novel belies the romantic view of the region. Instead it describes the cold reality of Charity Royal and her inability to leave her birthplace. Pregnant with the child of her New York lover Lucius Harney, she finally understands that he will marry a woman of his own social class. *The Marne* (1918) tells the story of an American who volunteers as a U.S. Ambulance Service driver, only to lose his life during the Battle of the Marne. *The Age of Innocence* (1920) is another story of Old New York and the Four Hundred, as the cream of the elite were termed. Newland Archer's love for May Welland is diverted by Ellen Olenska, an expatriate New Yorker whose marriage to a Polish count has failed. In *The Glimpses of the Moon* (1922), Nick Lansing leaves his wife, Suzy, whom he accuses of adultery. Suzy does penance by becoming a governess to five children. In *A SON AT THE FRONT* (1923), set during World War I, artist George Campion, who carelessly abandoned his son 20 years previously, now awaits his son's return from the war; he must face the fact that his newly awakened love for him has come too late.

Old New York (1924), a series of four novellas set in the mid-1800s, describes the lives of New York women in a period ruled by social convention and oppression; particularly popular is *The Old Maid,* in which Charlotte Lovell gives up her out-of-wedlock daughter to her rival, Delia Ralston, who is married to the child's father. Charlotte suffers when her daughter identifies increasingly with her "mother," Delia. *The MOTHER'S RECOM-*

PENSE (1925) tells the story of the reunion of expatriate Kate Clephane and her daughter Anne, whom she left behind after divorcing Anne's father years earlier. Kate is shocked when Anne later marries Chris Fenno, one of her former lovers. *The Children* (1928), republished as *The Marriage Playground* (1930), explores the tensions between the widowed expatriate Rose Sellars and her fiancé Martin Boyne. He is attracted to a 15-year-old girl, one of five children whom he met onboard ship. *Hudson River Bracketed* (1929) and its sequel, *The Gods Arrive* (1932), two of Wharton's favorite novels, depict a semiautobiographical hero, Halo Tarrant, who divorces Lewis Tarrant, and moves to Europe with her young lover Vance Weston; the romance wears off as Halo sees his vain and philandering nature. She returns to her home on the Hudson River, where she prepares to give birth to the child she and Vance have conceived. *The Buccaneers* (1938, 1995) was unfinished at Wharton's death, but published along with the notes she left: Wharton projected a happy ending for her hero, expatriate New Yorker Nan St. George, who suffers through one European marriage but will marry an Englishman who loves her and will run away with her to Australia. In this novel Nan and her friends surmount class distinctions and rigidities to live life as they choose.

The foremost American woman of letters at her death, Edith Wharton succumbed to a heart attack on August 11, 1937, at Pavilion Colombe, her home in St. Brice-sous-Foret, France, and is buried in the American Cemetery at Versailles, France, next to her friend Walter Berry. In addition to Broadway performances of a number of her novels, a film version of *The Age of Innocence* starring Daniel Day-Lewis, Winona Ryder, and Michelle Pfeiffer was produced by Columbia Pictures and directed by Martin Scorsese in 1993; a film version of *The House of Mirth* starring Gillian Anderson and Dan Aykroyd was written and directed by Terence Davies and released by Sony Pictures in 2000. Most of Edith Wharton's papers are housed at the Beinecke Library at Yale University.

NOVELS

The Age of Innocence. New York and London: Appleton, 1920.

The Buccaneers. New York and London: Appleton-Century, 1938.

The Children. New York and London: Appleton, 1928; republished as *The Marriage Playground.* New York: Grosset & Dunlap, 1930.

The Custom of the Country. New York: Scribner, 1913.

Ethan Frome. New York: Scribner, 1911.

The Fruit of the Tree. New York: Scribner, 1907.

The Glimpses of the Moon. New York and London: Appleton, 1922.

The Gods Arrive. New York and London: Appleton, 1932.

The House of Mirth. New York: Scribner, 1905.

Hudson River Bracketed. New York and London: Appleton, 1929.

Madame de Treymes. New York: Scribner, 1907.

The Marne. New York: Appleton, 1918.

The Mother's Recompense. New York and London: Appleton, 1925.

Old New York. 4 vols. New York and London: Appleton, 1924.

The Reef. New York: Appleton, 1912.

Sanctuary. New York: Scribner, 1903.

A Son at the Front. New York: Scribner, 1923.

Summer. New York: Appleton, 1917.

The Touchstone. New York: Scribner, 1900; republished as *A Gift from the Grave.* London: Murray, 1900.

The Valley of Decision. 2 vols. New York: Scribner, 1902.

SOURCES

Ammons, Elizabeth Miller. "Fairy-Tale Love and *The Reef,*" *American Literature,* 47 (January 1976): 615–628.

Auchincloss, Louis. *Edith Wharton: A Woman in Her Time.* New York: Viking, 1971.

Bauer, Dale M. *Edith Wharton's Brave New Politics.* Madison: University of Wisconsin Press, 1994.

Beer, Janet. *Kate Chopin, Edith Wharton, and Charlotte Perkins Gilman: Studies in Short Fiction.* New York: St. Martin's Press, 1997.

Bell, Millicent. *Edith Wharton and Henry James: The Story of Their Friendship.* New York: Braziller, 1965.

———, ed. *The Cambridge Companion to Edith Wharton.* New York: Cambridge University Press, 1995.

Benstock, Shari. *No Gifts from Chance: A Biography of Edith Wharton.* New York: Scribner, 1994.

Dwight, Eleanor. *Edith Wharton: An Extraordinary Life.* New York: Abrams, 1994.

Fracasso, Evelyn E. *Edith Wharton's Prisoners of Consciousness: A Study of Theme and Technique in the Tales.* Westport, Conn.: Greenwood Press, 1994.

Goodman, Susan. *Edith Wharton's Inner Circle.* Austin: University of Texas Press, 1994.

Joslin-Jeske, Katherine. *Edith Wharton.* New York: St. Martin's, 1991.

Killoran, Helen. *Edith Wharton: Art and Allusion.* Tuscaloosa: University of Alabama Press, 1996.

Lawson, Richard H. *Edith Wharton.* New York: Ungar, 1977.

Lewis, R. W. B. *Edith Wharton: A Biography.* New York, Evanston, San Francisco & London: Harper & Row, 1975.

Lubbock, Percy. *Portrait of Edith Wharton.* New York: Appleton-Century, 1947.

Nevius, Blake. *Edith Wharton.* Berkeley and Los Angeles: University of California Press, 1953.

Price, Alan. *The End of the Age of Innocence: Edith Wharton and the First World War.* New York: St. Martin's Press, 1996.

Singley, Carol J. *Edith Wharton: Matters of Mind and Spirit.* New York: Cambridge University Press, 1995.

Tuttleton, James W., Kristin O. Lauer, and Margaret P. Murray, eds. *Edith Wharton: The Contemporary Reviews.* New York: Cambridge University Press, 1992.

White, Barbara Anne. *Edith Wharton: A Study of the Short Fiction.* Boston: Twayne, 1991.

Wilson, Edmund. "Justice to Edith Wharton." In *The Wound and the Bow,* 195–213. Boston: Houghton Mifflin, 1941.

Wolff, Cynthia Griffin. *A Feast of Words: The Triumph of Edith Wharton.* New York: Oxford University Press, 1976.

Wright, Sarah Bird. *Edith Wharton A to Z: The Essential Guide to the Life and Work.* New York: Facts On File, 1998.

———. *Edith Wharton's Travel Writing: The Making of a Connoisseur.* New York: St. Martin's Press, 1997.

Zilversmit, Annette. *Edith Wharton: New Critical Essays.* New York: Garland, 1992.

OTHER

The Edith Wharton Page. San Antonio College. Available online. URL: http://www.accd.edu/Sac/english/bailey/wharton.htm. Accessed September 22, 2005.

Edith Wharton. An Overview with Biocritical Sources. Available online. URL: http://www.geocities.com/EnchantedForest/6741. Accessed September 22, 2005.

WHAT MAISIE KNEW HENRY JAMES (1897)

In *What Maisie Knew* Henry JAMES explores some of the new narrative techniques that were developing at the turn of the century. The novel recounts the story of Maisie, a girl of five, whose parents, Beale and Ida Farange, divorce and start a virulent war against each other using their own daughter as the main weapon. They do not fight for actual custody of the child;

rather, they find it much more effective to express their mutual hatred by leaving Maisie in the other's care beyond the period settled by the court.

Meanwhile, both parents begin having affairs and remarrying, so that Maisie soon finds herself with four parents, two of whom—the real ones—take no responsibility for her. Her stepfather, Sir Claude, becomes Maisie's friend but is too dependent on his passion for women, first Ida Farange and then Mrs. Beale, to be a real source of support for the child. Consequently, a succession of governesses becomes central to the girl's life. Miss Overmore is Maisie's governess until she marries Beale Farange, when, as Mrs. Beale, she becomes Maisie's ostensibly fond stepmother, but her lack of honesty and subsequent affair with Sir Claude prevent her from establishing a meaningful relationship with her. If Mrs. Beale is not altogether reliable, Mrs. Wix—Maisie's second governess—instills in the child a certain sense of morality and the difference between right and wrong. Mrs. Wix, however, is not a flawless character either—although she really wants to help the child, she worries about losing her job if she is even partially disloyal to her employer, Ida Farange. Moreover, she also falls in love with Sir Claude, who is half her age. But in the end, she is the only person to whom Maisie can turn.

Henry James chooses the story of a child struggling to make sense of adult wickedness and irresponsibility to demonstrate the wide range of perceptions, interpretations, and tricks she develops to help her construct a meaningful world. James does not make Maisie the narrator of her own experience because, as he explains in the preface, "Small children have many more perceptions than they have terms to translate them; their vision is at any moment much richer, their apprehension even constantly stronger, than their prompt, their at all producible, vocabulary" (27). Though the narrating voice is not Maisie's, it reflects the vision, perceptions, and thoughts of the girl, making her the focalizer of the story. Maisie sees and listens to adults uttering baffling sentences in front of her—and the reader follows her train of thought, but the narrator masterfully provides the meaning that is beyond the full comprehension of an innocent child.

James is not as interested in the morality of sexual liaisons among parents and their lovers, as in the way the neglected child comprehends them. In fact, he seems to imply that if Maisie acquires a moral sense, she does so through assimilated experience, rather than through avoidance of thorny situations. Maisie is, then, the most highly developed character in the novel, and we learn about the others through her. She succeeds in maintaining her own natural goodness, harboring no feelings of rancour, revenge, or contempt for her parents, and—although perfectly conscious of not being loved—she still rejoices when she discovers that they are not entirely wicked. And despite her innocence, Maisie develops some artful tricks as means of self-defense. She learns to keep silent in order to exasperate her parents, because this apparent stupidity renders her useless in their vengeful schemes. Because of her profound desire to be loved and to trust others, she is quick to shift her affection from one person to the other according to the amount of care she receives from them. In the end she has learned to judge the reliability of human feelings and so act accordingly.

What Maisie Knew can also be read as a critique of the British upper classes in the late 19th century. Neither Beale Farange nor Sir Claude have any sort of career or occupation, depending instead on their wives for support. Mr. Farange is determined to divorce his second wife and leave England to follow a wealthy Countess. Ida Farange has an affair with Mr. Perriam simply because of his fortune. Love is apparently determined by money and status, even in regard to the child. The problem of bringing her up is not just an affective one. Sir Claude, Mrs. Beale, and Mrs. Wix raise this issue in their last argument, though it is Mrs. Wix—the penniless governess—who keeps the child, however uncertain their future may be.

In the development of the novel genre, one of the important techniques developed by James, as well as such other writers as Virginia Woolf and Joseph Conrad, involved nuanced ways of representing perception. In this novel, James engages in diverse manners of articulating or concealing reality and the ways a child perceives. Maisie "was at the age for which all stories are true and all conceptions are stories" (42). By presenting two perspectives, Maisie's and the adult narrator's, we are offered a multilayered view of her situation and permitted access to the child's inner world. *What Maisie Knew* constitutes thus a sample of the reasons why Henry James is considered one of the milestones in the narrative technique of the last two centuries.

SOURCES

Bellringer, Alan W. *Henry James.* London: Macmillan, 1988.

Bloom, Harold, ed. *Modern Critical Views: Henry James.* New York: Chelsea House Publishers, 1987.

Kaplan, Fred. *Henry James. The Imagination of Genius.* Baltimore, Md.: The Johns Hopkins University Press, 1992.

James, Henry. *What Maisie Knew.* 1897. Edited by Paul Theroux. Reprinted, Harmondsworth, England: Penguin, 1985.

Reeve, N. H., ed. *Henry James: The Shorter Fiction: Reassessments.* London: Macmillan, 1997.

Ana Beatriz Delgado

WHEN THE RAINBOW GODDESS WEPT
CECILIA MANGUERRA BRAINARD (1999)   Drawing in part from the recollections of her parents, Cecilia Manguerra BRAINARD commemorates the suffering and triumph of the Filipino people during World War II in *When the Rainbow Goddess Wept,* originally published in the Philippines in 1991 as *Song of Yvonne.* Nine-year-old child-narrator Yvonne Macaraig and her upper-middle-class parents leave their home in edenic Ubec, a fictional city based on Brainard's native Cebu, in 1941 to join the guerilla movement, assuming that America will win the war in six months. They are rapidly disabused of this hope: They suffer hunger, deprivation, and threats from Japanese soldiers. Yvonne's delicately bred mother gives birth to a dead infant son while squatting in the jungle as Japanese troops patrol nearby. They witness horrific Japanese atrocities against civilians and the traumatic aftermath suffered by survivors, but the greatest betrayal they experience is from the renegade American guerilla Martin Lewis, who is responsible for the death of Filipino leader Gil Alvarez. Liberation in 1944 brings the family back to a fallen Ubec. There they find that Yvonne's cousin Esperanza and her Aunt Lourdes—serving as foils to Yvonne and her mother—have survived largely due to the kindness of a Japanese army doctor. Amid the wreckage, Yvonne's father

reminds them that the war has just been a moment in time in the city's long history, and that Ubec will rebuild and grow as it has so many times in the past.

Yvonne's solace throughout her archetypal journey from innocence to experience are the legends and folklore passed on to her by the family cook Laydan, who had trained with the epic singer Inuk: "Her stories were part of my soul; they sustained my spirit" (123). These myths and stories represent the survival of native Filipino culture in the face of Western culture imported by colonizers and conquerors. This is a society where the American-trained physician Doc Mendes can see auras, use leeches, and learn from faith healers. At the midpoint of the novel, Yvonne assumes Laydan's role and burden—"Become the epic"—when the old woman dies. Yvonne uses these stories to illuminate contemporary situations: Her mother's defying a Japanese soldier is like the woman warrior Bongkatolan, her desire to search for her missing father is compared to Bolak Soday's search for her kidnapped husband. She relates these tales to others in an effort to bring them "peace and hope" (97). By the novel's end, Yvonne realizes that the epic she must tell is her own life: "We had experienced a story that needed to be told, that needed never to be forgotten" (216).

This story, as told by its child-narrator, juxtaposes unsentimental description of the horrors of war with childish preoccupations and fantastic musings: Grief-crazed Doc Mendes runs by carrying his dead wife's head like a ball while the frightened Yvonne concentrates on a sparrow; Laydan comforts her with the story of the goddess Meybuyan, who cares for the souls of dead infants. Yvonne sees the war not so much as fighting and death, but as change and loss of the past: "I missed Ubec, our life before the war. . . . It came to me that even if the war ended and we returned home, things would not be the same" (147). In her innocence she is more apt to recognize common humanity than political differences. After joining with other children who play with the bloated corpse of a Japanese soldier that has washed up on the beach, Yvonne wonders if this man might also have a daughter who anxiously awaits her father's return, just as she does: "I could not help but feel sad for the dead man. You can hate someone with all your might and yet you couldn't help thinking" (153).

Yvonne's movement from innocence to experience, from childhood to the threshold of maturity is paralleled by other characters in the novel, as well as by the Philippines as a nation. For so many of the characters, including Yvonne, the watershed event is the kidnapping, imprisonment, and torture of Gil Alvarez, Yvonne's father, and their friend Max by the American Lewis and Alvarez's subsequent death. Women from all over the island flock to the funeral of Alvarez, Ubec's demigod: "Crying, they talked about how Alvarez symbolized their youth, and how his death signaled the unquestionable end of the days when they laughed and rhumbaed and jitter-bugged. . . . They mourned for the death that happened in their souls" (196–197).

This experience is also the turning point for Yvonne's father Nando, an American-trained engineering professor who had previously put his trust in American aid to the beleaguered Philippines, a man who had lovingly told his daughter about snow, pine trees, and oranges, experiences completely alien to his child. Now Nando and his men fight the Japanese with a new intensity for their country's freedom: "my father realized that Filipinos must shape their own destiny, that they were responsible for their own future, that America (with all her professed good intentions) watched out for herself and her citizens . . . even if this means using other countries and peoples" (198). Thus the war brings both individuals and the Philippines as an independent nation-state to the brink of maturity. In its historical context, Brainard's novel is postmodernist in its reexamination of the relationship between America and the Philippines during this period.

SOURCES

Brainard, Cecilia Manguerra. *Song of Yvonne.* Quezon City, The Philippines: New Day Publishers, 1991.

———. *When the Rainbow Goddess Wept.* Ann Arbor: University of Michigan Press, 1999.

Caspar, Leonard. "*Song of Yvonne:* Possibilities of Humanities in An Age of Slaughter," *Philippine Studies* 41 (Second Quarter 1993), 251–254.

Hidalgo, Cristina Pantoja. *Filipino Woman Writing: Home and Exile in the Autobiographical Narratives of Ten Writers.* Manila, The Philippines: Ateneo de Manila University Press, 1994.

Ty, Eleanor. "Cecilia Manguerra Brainard." In *Asian American Novelists: A Bio-Bibliographical Critical Sourcebook,* edited by Emmanuel S. Nelson, 29–33. Westport, Conn.: Greenwood Press, 2000.

Nona C. Flores

WHITE FANG JACK LONDON (1906) Following the success of his earlier novel *The* CALL OF THE WILD (1903), Jack LONDON turned his attention to a new story inspired by life in the North. *White Fang* was intended as a companion, indeed the antithesis, to *The Call of the Wild.* London stated that he was "going to reverse the process" (14). *White Fang* would present the civilization or evolution of a wolf-dog rather than the decivilizing of a dog. This story would depict the wild animal brought under the forces of domesticity, morality, love, and faithfulness and treated to the amenities of modern society. In *The Call of the Wild* and *The* SEA-WOLF, a domesticated creature (Buck, Humphrey van Weyden) is forced to become strong and self-reliant through exposure to the cruelty and brutality of a Darwinian struggle, while in *White Fang* the self-reliant creature is made docile and dependent. More than twice as long as *The Call of the Wild, White Fang* did not give in to the reader's desire for access to wilderness and nature. Instead it confronts those who might seek the freedom of the wild with their own domestic status, their own tameness. If *The Call of the Wild* could be identified by critics as a piece of escapist literature, appealing to the longings of overcivilized Americans who sought access to Buck's vital, unrestrained life in the North, *White Fang* allowed no such sentimental escape.

In London's depiction, the wolf-dog is made to shift its allegiance from the wild to a human deity. White Fang learns that the man who lights the fires and carries the weapons is the god, the pinnacle of nature's chain. In exchange for food, fire, protection, and companionship, White Fang exchanges his own liberty. As London describes it, for the possession of a flesh-and-blood god, White Fang guards the god's property, defends its body, and works for and obeys it. The primacy of law in industrial America is highlighted quite directly when White Fang saves his master's father from a criminal escaped from a local prison. While White Fang experiences great internal struggles between his wild impulses and the civilizing tendencies, the animal's domestication is complete by the novel's ending as the wolf-dog settles into a pleasant life with its partner, the dog Collie, and their puppies. The animal ends not as that leader of a pack of wild wolves, having proven its character in the day-to-day struggles of nature but as an object of leisurely affection for middle-class domesticates. In *White Fang* the natural and basic, even authentic, loses out to the world of comfort, leisure, amenities, and virtues. For London, a lifelong socialist, this is the victory of industrial capitalism and its slave morality. This is the triumph of bourgeois laws and the regulation of the particularities and mundanities of life. White Fang, like the citizen of industrial capitalist America, is made to learn obedience, loyalty, and work discipline.

The story of domestication relates to London's commitment to socialism and his criticism of the hypocrisy of bourgeois culture. It also expressed his sense that capitalist society dampened the natural strengths and desires of the working class, its capacity to struggle for a better world, through the civilizing processes instilled through morality and laws. This sense was expressed in London's own life, even within the socialist groups of which he was a part, when he quit the Socialist Labor Party in 1916 complaining of "its lack of fire and fight, and its loss of emphasis on the class struggle" ("Resignation Letter"). In *White Fang*, London's socialist concerns are combined with a critique of bourgeois morality drawn from his readings of Nietzsche. This combination has contributed to London's identification as a revolutionary nihilist.

London's reading of sociology, biology, and philosophy had deeply marked him with a Darwinian perspective that informed his views of the Yukon as a field of ongoing survival of the fittest and natural selection. For London, the North, with its "white silence," was the place where the ultimate meaning of life, survival, and reproduction could be most fully known. Its wilderness drew out qualities that had been submerged by the conditioned layers of civilization. The period of the novel's release was one of relentless American imperial expansion in the Western Hemisphere. It was written at a time when the influence of literary naturalism was great. The confrontation of citizens of modernity with the elements of nature was a theme that enjoyed widespread resonance during the turn of the 19th and 20th centuries.

White Fang expresses the naturalist emphasis on the significance of environment in shaping characters' actions. London provides a vivid and memorable description of the threatening, desolate, and unforgiving landscape of the Northland Wild in the opening section of the story as two men, Henry and Bill, struggle with their dog team to pull their dogsled across the forbidding terrain. The violent character of the wilderness is expressed by the hunger-stricken wolf pack that follows the men and dogs, luring away and eating a dog each evening. This is not the romantic "call of the wild" that spoke to Buck, but a world in which one either "eats grub or is grub." Deprived of the comforts of civilization, men are rendered puny and weak, lacking wisdom in the face of the "great blind elements and forces" (172).

Critically less well received upon its release, the story represents a more extreme version of London's naturalist vision. It is also evoked most forcefully during the process of White Fang's maturation in section two: "Life itself is meat. Life lived on life. There were eaters and the eaten. The law was EAT OR BE EATEN" (243). London's emphasis on natural selection is symbolized further in the fact that White Fang, the strongest and fiercest of the litter of five pups, is the only one to survive the several famines that the animals must endure. London allows for no sentimentality over any of the story's deaths, whether Bill, the dogs, or White Fang's siblings. London confronts his readers with the treacherous reality behind the alluring appeal of the wild that he had presented in *The Call of the Wild*. At the same time, London was familiar enough with Darwin's writings to know that a key characteristic in his discussions of the survival of species is not strength but adaptability. Thus while White Fang's strength in surviving famines and gunshots is legendary, an equally important, if overlooked, aspect of his survival is his capacity to adapt to new and changing circumstances. White Fang learns to fight and later to obey, love, and be tamed.

SOURCES

London, Jack. *The Call of the Wild, White Fang and Other Stories.* New York: Penguin, 1993.

———. "Resignation Letter to the Socialist Labor Party." Available online. URL: www.bedfordsmartins.com/litlinks/fiction/london.htm. Accessed September 25, 2005.

Jeff Shantz

WHITE MULE WILLIAM CARLOS WILLIAMS (1937)

At the beginning of *White Mule,* a baby girl is born into an immigrant home in upper Manhattan circa 1900. WILLIAMS, who was a pediatrician as well as a poet, describes the birth clinically, as only a doctor would: "In behind the [baby's] ears there was still that white grease of pre-birth." Williams is a tough writer, and on the surface he is unsentimental about birth and motherhood. As soon as the baby is born, its mother, a Norwegian immigrant named Gurlie Stecher, tells the midwife to "Take it away. I don't want it. All this trouble for another girl." Gurlie had wanted all boys, and now she is irritated at having to look after her second girl.

This birth, unremarkable yet at the same time infused with the wonder Williams had about children and their ability to flourish in the most unlikely circumstances, begins the first book in a trilogy about a German emigre, Joe Stecher, and his family living the American Dream. The book's title refers to the infant Flossie, whose powerful kick the author compares to a brand of whiskey called White Mule. In the first part of the book, Flossie refuses to nurse and is close to death. Williams does not romanticize what it was like to grow up in an immigrant house; Gurlie is routinely disgusted by Flossie's failure to thrive, and the baby is only saved when Joe buys a can of condensed milk, which the baby hungrily sucks down. This is not a world of sterile hospitals but of overburdened doctors who care more about their dinner than about a baby suffering in a walk-up apartment.

After getting the can of milk, the baby Flossie finds a way to hang on to dear life, though in the course of reading this book, we constantly ask why she wants to. Her father, once a labor organizer and now a press operator, is kicked about by corrupt bosses and has to endure a strike during which he is the object of physical abuse. Joe sympathizes with working men, but he cannot abide their dislike of honest work. Gurlie, while clearly in love with her husband, constantly berates him about his reluctance to ask for a raise, and she wants to move her family to the country, where she is sure her children will prosper. It is easy to find Gurlie cold, but she has enough backbone to support her family and push them to something greater. When we see Gurlie leaving her hot West Side apartment and striding across Central Park, we know that her strong legs can take her anywhere, and we understand that she is a country girl who feels cooped up in the airless city.

Williams had a busy practice as a pediatrician in New Jersey, and his life was filled with immigrant women like Gurlie whose children he loved and whose plight he understood. Yet the doctors in this book are uncaring and weary of mothers trying to raise their children in the dust and heat of New York City. The doctors are tired out from trying to make babies grow without air and light. Williams's heroes in this book are the children, not the doctors. His dedication at the beginning of the book simply reads "To the Kids." In one unforgettable scene, Joe goes to visit an unemployed worker in his infested tenement and meets the man's robust children. Joe thinks to himself "what wonderful children sometimes come out of such places as this." When Joe leaves, the father returns to beat his wife in a drunken fury while the children hide behind the stove or busy themselves reading. It is almost as if the children survive in spite of their parents, not because of them.

In the later installments of the Stecher trilogy, the family goes on to claim their small piece of the American Dream, but the theme of this first dark book is merely survival. Williams implies that the Stechers are able to survive the city life because they have roots in the primeval forests of Europe. In one passage, Joe is walking to work through the hot city while his mind is on the verdant green of the rural world he came from: "Joe knew he was a working man, he had to be, that's all he asked them to expect of him. But very deep inside him moved another man . . . under water, under earth . . . among the worms and fishes, among the plant roots . . . an impalpable atmosphere through which he strode." In the passages where Williams waxes lyrical about the countryside, we see the poet underneath the novelist, just as we see the country man underneath Joe the urban worker. In the end of the book, the country and its wholesomeness save Joe's family. It's almost as if the Stechers have to return to their roots to get the energy to survive their new urban life.

Williams is better known for his poetry, but his novels will delight his poetry readers. He does not offer sentimentality or even a clean version of the American Dream. Instead, he gives us honest prose that is worked over to the point of scrubbed perfection. Williams is clinical and severe in his vision, but there is a soft, sweet underside, the subtle kind you might see in a city doctor.

SOURCES
Williams, William Carlos. *White Mule*. New York: New Directions, 1937, 1967.

Blythe Grossberg

WHITE NOISE Don DeLillo (1984) Don DeLillo's novel *White Noise* has been hailed by many critics as a model of postmodern writing for both form and content. The novel is composed of a barrage of images and words gleaned from the ever-increasing media consumption of one typical American family intermingled with the musings and anxieties of the novel's central character. DeLillo uses this format to expose and discuss the intrusion of media, industry, and technology into the lives of 20th-century Americans as we struggle to rediscover meaning and identity in an increasingly globalized community. DeLillo's exaggerated portrait of the "typical" American family, immersed in the mindless babble of a technocentric culture, preaches media awareness while simultaneously presenting a foreboding image of such a culture's full impact upon human conceptions of agency and identity. DeLillo is also clear about the toxic effects of such a culture, not only on its members, but on its landscape as well. As a postmodern text, *White Noise* neither condemns nor exonerates those elements of society (the media, technology, etc.) that constitute the "white noise" that DeLillo refers to in the novel's title; however, he does call into question the ideologies and objects against which people immersed in a mediated culture identify themselves.

White Noise chronicles the often ordinary and occasionally extraordinary events in the life of a small-town college professor and the amalgamation of wives, ex-wives, children, and stepchildren that constitute his family. From the caravan of station wagons depositing upper-middle-class teenagers at the archetypal College-on-the-Hill, through the toxic chemical spill that becomes known as the airborne toxic event, to the desperate and sometimes violent attempts to eradicate an overwhelming fear of death, DeLillo uses the running commentary of his main character, Jack Gladney, to examine what life in America in the 20th century has come to mean. Through Jack's eyes, we glimpse a society that is inundated with information, but unable to make sense of it, unable to understand how to utilize it and how to construct meaning from it. We see characters who urgently desire and fumble toward some sense of union or community, but who more often than not fall just short of achieving this goal.

Plagued by anxieties regarding their own mortality, these characters are often separated from one another by the very things they have in common. For example, the main obstacle standing between Jack and his wife, Babette, is their mutual horror at the prospect of their own deaths. Instead of drawing comfort from one another or experiencing relief at the fact that, despite their previous assumptions, this is a shared fear, not only between them but among most human beings, they engage in a competition of sorts to decide who fears death more. They hide secrets from one another, to such an extent that they question whether they truly know one another. In this manner, they both come to recognize the identities they have placed on one another, the conceptions of who the other person is and how they have come to rely upon these illusions, even though they are far from the truth. When Babette reveals the affair she has had with Willie Mink and her involvement with the experimental drug Dylar in order to cure her fear of death, Jack self-pityingly exclaims, "This is the whole point of Babette. She's a joyous person. She doesn't succumb to gloom or self-pity . . . You are the happy one. I am the damned fool. That's what I can't forgive you for. Telling me you're not the woman I believed you were. I'm hurt, I'm devastated" (191, 197). As with the other events in the novel, DeLillo uses this crisis in Jack and Babette's relationship to expose the illusions about ourselves and one another that we embrace in order to sustain some sense of order and meaning in an increasingly chaotic and meaningless world.

DeLillo also uses ordinary, everyday experiences of American suburban life, such as going to the grocery store or watching television, to explore how the identity we construct for ourselves is constantly mediated by information technology. During an airborne toxic event, members of the community are outraged and dejected when they realize that their communal disaster has somehow escaped recognition from the local news programs and television stations. The victims of the airborne toxic event depend on media coverage to identify themselves as victims and to justify their terror. They look to the media to confirm the reality of what has happened to them. Even Jack's "death" is only real because it is projected by computer analysis. As John Frow has noted, in *White Noise,* there is no distinction between representation and reality. This is again evident when Jack's daughter and stepdaughter, Steffie and Denise, begin adopting symptoms related to the airborne toxic event only after they hear about them on the radio.

It is obvious that the characters in *White Noise* rely on elements of media and technology to guide their behavior and reassure them about the meaning of their own existence. Likewise, the characters rely on consumerism as a buffer against their own mortality. The supermarket setting is prevalent throughout the novel. Again and again we encounter Murray (Jack's colleague), Jack, Babette, and the children at the supermarket, deriving pleasure from the act of consumerism. The supermarket, with its incredible array of exotic and foreign foods as well as the necessary allotment of familiar comfort foods, represents the increasing globalization of society. The number of choices is dizzying and empowering for Jack, Babette, and Murray. In fact, Murray continually points out how the meaning that appears to be missing from all of their lives, for which they are searching, can be regained through purchasing. Shopping is a way to deny death and to ensure, through the products that are purchased, that one not only continues a material existence but also that this existence is as stable and rich as one would like. In this way, consumerism is linked to immortality.

Ultimately, *White Noise* forces us to recognize the impact that our postmodern world has had on us as individuals as well as a culture and community. DeLillo pushes us as readers to acknowledge the shifts taking place in our own identity formation and our reliance on outside forces, specifically technology and media, for self and cultural definition. DeLillo's portrait of life in late-20th-century America is a grim one, in which the characters are often confused and alienated. Unfortunately, as Bruce Bawer has noted, DeLillo seems to suggest in the novel that the only outlet for the feelings of terror and meaninglessness that Jack Gladney, and all those like him, experience is violence. As Murray suggests to Jack, brutal, random violence, the ability and desire to take another human life, is the only escape from the anxieties and emptiness that characterize postmodern existence. However, even this fails in the end. Although Jack does shoot Mink at the end of the novel in an attempt to recover his own meaning and life, Mink shoots Jack in the wrist, once again bringing Jack closer to his mortality. Consequently, even this last outlet appears to have been an illusion, and the novel ends on a note of loss and capitulation to something inevitable. The novel concludes, fittingly enough, in the supermarket where the vast array of items has been rearranged. Symbolic of the ultimately inescapable terror and emptiness that is a direct result of the fast-paced postmodern era, DeLillo claims, "There is a sense of wandering now, an aimless and haunted mood, sweet-tempered people taken to the edge" (326).

SOURCES

Bawer, Bruce. "Don DeLillo's America," *New Criterion* (1985): 34–42.

Bonca, Cornel. "Don DeLillo's *White Noise:* The Natural Language of the Species," *College Literature* 23, no. 2 (1996): 25–44.

Conroy, Mark. "From Tombstone to Tabloid: Authority Figured in *White Noise,*" *Critique* 35, no. 2 (Winter 1994): 97–110.

DeLillo, Don. *White Noise.* New York: Penguin Books, 1985.

Duvall, John N. "The (Super)Marketplace of Images: Television as Unmediated Mediation in Don DeLillo's *White*

Noise," *Arizona Quarterly: A Journal of American Literature, Culture, and Theory* 50, no. 3 (1994): 127–147.

Frow, John. "The Last Things Before the Last: Notes on *White Noise*," *South Atlantic Quarterly* 89 (1990): 413–429.

Hayles, N. Katherine. "Postmodern Parataxis: Embodied Texts, Weightless Information," *American Literary History* 2, no. 3 (Fall 1990): 394–421.

King, Noel. "Reading *White Noise*: Floating Remarks," *Critical Quarterly* 33, no. 3 (1991): 66–83.

Peyser, Thomas. "Globalization in America: The Case of Don DeLillo's *White Noise*," *CLIO* 25, no. 3 (1996): 255–271.

Heather Bliven

WHO WILL RUN THE FROG HOSPITAL?

LORRIE MOORE (1994)   Lorrie MOORE's fourth work of fiction, *Frog Hospital,* is narrated by Berie Carr, a photograph curator at a Midwest museum who is approaching 40. When the story opens, she is in Paris with her husband, Daniel, a medical researcher, who is attending a professional conference. It's clear from the outset that troubles threaten their childless marriage, as Berie observes: "I feel his lack of love for me" (5).

Perhaps because of her marital problems, while in Paris Berie conjures pleasant memories of summer 1972, when she was 15 and living with her middle-class family in the town of Horsehearts, in Upstate New York. The local draft board has sent many of the local young men fleeing for Canada to avoid Vietnam; Watergate is in the air; and the federal government has just legalized abortion. It is Berie's memories of that summer, interpolated into the text, that enliven the narrative, making *Frog Hospital* a fascinating coming-of-age story.

As is true with most small towns, Horsehearts offers little diversion for adventuresome teens. While managing to remain "babysitting material" with high scores on standardized tests, Berie and her friend Sils rebel in the teenage fashion by smoking cigarettes, staying out after curfew, and visiting area bars using fake identifications. Theirs is a strong and intriguing friendship. While Berie is flat-chested and plain looking, given to making frequent self-deprecating wisecracks, Sils possesses the body of a 20-year-old, with a face that lands her a job as Cinderella at Storyland,

a local theme park. As Sils roams the grounds in full costume, charming young girls and older boys and men, Berie works as a cashier at the park's entrance. Rather than feeling jealousy, Berie admires her friend, though all the while fearful that Sils might ditch her for more mature pursuits.

When Sils becomes pregnant by an older boy she's met at a bar, self-sacrificing Berie embarks on a scheme to steal from the Storyland till, taking small amounts every day to avoid arousing suspicion. With the money, Sils undergoes an abortion in Vermont because, while abortion is now legal, none of the local Horsehearts physicians will perform one. Even after she already has raised enough money for the abortion, Berie continues to steal on the job. Theft has become an addiction. Eventually, management sets a trap and catches Berie, but because the park owner, the town millionaire, wants to keep trouble out of the newspaper, she is dismissed without facing charges. Deeply disappointed, Berie's parents send her to a religious boarding school, in part to separate her from Sils, whom her parents consider a negative influence.

From there the story races through Berie's high school and college career, chronicling her late blooming, her first boyfriends, and sexual initiation. After a while, the narrative pace slows again to show a series of poignant reunions and partings, first with Sils, who has moved to Hawaii to serve as a letter carrier, and then LaRoue, Berie's frumpy overweight foster sister, whom Berie mostly ignored while she was pals with Sils. The last remaining family member in Horsehearts, LaRoue, is three years from suicide, a revelation that reinforces the theme of lost hope. The unique title comes from a painting made by Sils after she is hired as Cinderella at Storyland. The painting recalls the time when, as young girls, Berie and Sils used to visit a nearby marsh to bandage frogs wounded by neighborhood boys with BB guns. The Cinderella fable adds new dimension to the coming-of-age story and opportunities of irony, though critics, on occasion, have argued that the use of Cinderella might strike readers as too contrived, and the numerous allusions to frogs in the novel can seem overdone.

The novel features a unique construction. By interpolating scenes from Berie's past, Moore sets up many interesting contrasts and comparisons. For example, in the back story one focus is on Sils's abortion, while in the contemporary story, we learn that Berie and Daniel have been unable to conceive a child and that his professional conference, in fact, is related to fertility. In a more general sense, Moore depicts the limitless hopes of youth and the major disappointments that can occur in adult life. The two narrative threads move in chronological order, except for the moving final scene, which, in an interesting coda, shows Berie and Sils singing together in an all-girls choir in high school.

Most critics consider *Frog Hospital* a breakthrough for Moore, combining her lush style with a newfound depth of characterization. Moore possesses an uncanny ability to identify and report the revealing details that enliven the setting and makes all the characters, even the minor ones, vivid and unforgettable. Whether it's a clubfooted taxi driver, a frumpy stepsister, or Berie's cold father, Moore evokes the essence of their personality in swift, economical brush strokes. Moore's work is more than sheer surfaces; it is full of keen psychological insights, capturing the depths of adolescence and adulthood. It possesses warmth, wisdom, and a voice that is both funny and original.

SOURCES

James, Caryn. "I Feel His Lack of Love For Me." Review of *Who Will Run the Frog Hospital? New York Times,* 9 October 1994, p. 7.

Johnson, Claudia. "A Sad and Gory Land." Review of *Who Will Run the Frog Hospital? The London Review of Books,* 23 February 1995, pp. 28–29.

Larsen, Eric. "That Anteroom of Girlhood." Review of *Who Will Run the Frog Hospital? Los Angeles Times,* 27 November 1994, p. 15.

Miner, Valerie. "Connections and Disconnections." Review of *Who Will Run the Frog Hospital? The Women's Review of Books* 12 (1995): 14.

Moore, Lorrie. *Who Will Run the Frog Hospital?* New York: Warner Books, 1994.

William Grattan

WIDEMAN, JOHN EDGAR (1941–) John Edgar Wideman, the only American novelist to win two PEN/Faulkner Awards (for SENT FOR YOU YESTERDAY [1984] and PHILADELPHIA FIRE [1990]), is, in the opinion of many scholars, one of the most accomplished writers in the United States. Reviewer Laura Miller praises "Wideman's potent, lyrical voice," one that "picks up strands of Shakespeare and Poe, as well as more ancient storytelling traditions" (Miller). He is the author of seven novels and two short story collections, as well as numerous articles and essays. Although Wideman's early novels were influenced by William FAULKNER and T. S. Eliot, he has changed his narrative voice in later novels. From 1981 onward, he has chosen to explore African-American cultural and identity issues. To do so, he uses the African-American oral tradition, which includes communal myth and memory, and mirrors or pairs two characters to make a larger point. And throughout his career, he continues to examine the role of violence in American cities.

John Edgar Wideman was born on June 14, 1941, in Washington, D.C., to Edgar Wideman and Betty French Wideman. Reared in Homewood, a predominantly African-American neighborhood in Pittsburgh, until he was 12, and then Shadyside, a predominantly white neighborhood. Wideman earned a scholarship to the University of Pennsylvania, was a member of Phi Beta Kappa, and received his bachelor's degree in English in 1963. As a Rhodes Scholar at New College, Oxford University, he received a bachelor of philosophy degree in 1966. Wideman married Judith Ann Goldman in 1965, became the first African American tenured at the University of Pennsylvania, where he founded its first African-American studies program in 1971, and now holds an endowed chair at the University of Massachusetts at Amherst.

Wideman's first novel, *A Glance Away* (1967), focuses on Eddie Lawson, a recovering drug addict who returns to Homewood to reintegrate himself into the community. Also in residence are Brother Small, an albino black man, his lover Robert Thurley, a white homosexual college professor who is Eddie's racial double and mirrors his fears and bigotries. In *Hurry Home* (1970), Wideman examines the estranged black intellectual, a recurring interest, Here Cecil Braithewaite, the first black lawyer in his community, travels to Europe and becomes involved with a mulatto baby who dies. Cecil returns home, knowing that Europe does not have the answers and that he must take responsibility for his own story and his place in the American community. In *The Lynchers* (1973), Wideman introduces his first black vernacular voice, that of Tom Wilkerson, and a plan by four black men to lynch a white Philadelphia policeman. Wilkerson eventually averts the lynching, questions the ritual killing, and suggests the power and potential of the voice that can articulate oral history.

Wideman's Homewood Trilogy (1981) includes *Damballah,* a series of interconnected stories, and *Hiding Place,* a novel. *Hiding Place* continues the tale of Tommy Lawson of *Damballah,* one of whose themes is the role of language rituals in shaping the black cultural tradition. Tommy has returned to his relative, Bess, who lives at their ancestral home. After he is shot by the police, Bess leaves her "hiding place" and moves to Homewood so that she can tell his story. The trilogy concludes with the award-winning *Sent for You Yesterday,* in which John (Doot) Lawson returns to Homewood to learn the stories of his uncle, Carl French; of his lover, the albino Brother Tate; and Brother's sister Lucy. The tension between their stories of the past and the violence threatening the community of the present reveal a lesson that John, and the reader, must learn. In *Reuben* (1987), Wideman blends his earlier interest in the alienated black intellectual with his later interest in positive mythmaking and storytelling roles. Reuben, a lawyer in Homewood, advises Kwansa, a black prostitute whose daughter is kidnapped, and Wally, a college basketball coach who has been involved with the murder of a white man. With *Philadelphia Fire* (1990) and *The Cattle Killing,* however, Wideman explores the issue of urban violence. *Philadelphia Fire* is based on the 1985 police bombing of the headquarters of MOVE, a black organization resisting eviction notices from the city. In the novel, Cudjoe, a writer, searches for a boy seen running from the scene. He symbolizes society, both black and white, and its failing structure. The title refers ironically to William Penn's statement that Philadelphia, the City of Brotherly Love, would never burn. *The Cattle Killing* is also based on a real incident, the 1793 persecution of African Americans by whites who believe that blacks brought yellow fever to Philadelphia. Alternating between past and present, the immensely complex novel gives voices to whites and blacks, using as a central metaphor the African Shosa's killing of their cattle, in the erroneous belief that the act would save them from the European invaders.

In an interview with Laura Miller shortly after the publication of *The Cattle Killing,* Wideman mused about the issues of skepticism and faith, citing his mother's profoundly unshakable faith in her religion. "Like Ellison said, beneath our certainties, there's always chaos. I'm examining that profound skepticism and reinforcing whatever positive faith I have that it's worth writing another sentence, worth making another try to make myself a better person, to understand things. I'm trying to find reasons to live a rational and ethical life" (Miller). Wideman's most recent novel, *Hoop Roots,* links basketball with jazz, with art, with writing, but also with the roots of black life and culture in America.

NOVELS

The Cattle Killing. Boston: Houghton, Mifflin, 1996.

A Glance Away. New York: Harcourt, 1967.

"A Glance Away," "Hurry Home," and "The Lynchers": Three Early Novels by John Edgar Wideman. New York: Henry Holt and Co., 1994.

Hiding Place. New York: Avon, 1981.

The Homewood Trilogy (includes *Damballah, Hiding Place,* and *Sent for You Yesterday*). New York: Avon, 1985.

Hoop Roots. Boston: Houghton, Mifflin, 2001.

Hurry Home. New York: Harcourt, 1970.

The Lynchers. New York: Harcourt, 1973.

Philadelphia Fire. New York: Henry Holt and Co., 1990.

Reuben. New York: Henry Holt and Co., 1987.

Sent for You Yesterday. New York: Avon, 1983.

Two Cities. Boston: Houghton, Mifflin, 1998.

SOURCES

Coleman, James W. *Blackness and Modernism: The Literary Career of John Edgar Wideman.* Jackson: University Press of Mississippi, 1989.

Harris, Trudier. *Exorcising Blackness: Historical and Literary Lynching and Burning Rituals.* Bloomington: Indiana University Press, 1984.

Lustig, Jessica. "Home: An Interview with John Edgar Wideman," *African American Review* 26, no. 3 (1992): 453–457.

Mbalia, Doreatha Drummond. *John Edgar Wideman: Reclaiming the African Personality.* Selinsgrove, Pa.: Susquehanna University Press, 1995.

Rushdy, Ashraf H. A. "Fraternal Blues: John Edgar Wideman's Homewood Trilogy," *Contemporary Literature* 32, no. 3 (1991): 312–345.

Samuels, Wilfred D. "Going Home: A Conversation with John Edgar Wideman," *Callaloo* 6 (1983): 40–59.

Wideman, John Edgar, with Bonnie Tusmith. *Conversations with John Edgar Wideman.* Jackson: University Press of Mississippi, 1998.

OTHER

John Edgar Wideman. African American Literature Book Club. Available online. URL: http://aalbc,com?authors/johne,htm. Accessed January 17, 2006.

John Edgar Wideman Literary Society. Available online. URL: http://www.ship.edu/-rejani. Accessed January 17, 2006.

Miller, Laura. "Interview with John Edgar Wideman." *Salon .com.* Available online. URL: http://www.salon.com/nov96/interview.961111.html. Accessed January 17, 2006.

Simon, Scott. "Jamming: John Edgar Wideman Connects Life and Sport." NPR [National Public Radio]. Available online. URL: http://www.npr.org/programs/wesat/features/2001/wideman/011103.wideman.html. Accessed January 17, 2006.

WIELAND; OR THE TRANSFORMATION, AN AMERICAN TALE CHARLES BROCKDEN BROWN (1798)

Wieland; or the Transformation, an American Tale, was greatly admired by Charles Brockden BROWN's contemporaries, an important influence on later American writers like POE, HAWTHORNE, and MELVILLE, and judged today by critics as among the greatest, if not the greatest work by an early American author.

Set in the years before the Revolutionary War in rural Pennsylvania, the tale is written in an "Americanized Gothic style," meaning the story is psychologically complex, dark, and mysterious (Watts, 72). Clara Wieland, sister to the titled character, narrates the novel. Though Clara is passive at times, in general, she is as resilient, courageous, and intelligent as any male character in the text. She begins the narrative with the ending "Fate has done its worst" (5), setting the reader on guard for a lurid tale. Nevertheless, Clara's stated purpose is not to excite, but to teach "the duty of avoiding deceit . . . and show, the immeasurable evils that flow from an erroneous or imperfect discipline" (5).

To exemplify the latter caution, Clara begins with the story of her father's uneven and "narrow" religious study (9). From this study in his native Germany, Theodore Wieland feels a call to proselytize North American Indians. Upon arriving in America, his courage quickly fails him; instead, he marries, has children, and becomes wealthy enough to retire from physical labor. With leisure, his call to preach revisits him with a vengeance, and when he fails in another attempt to teach the Indians, Theodore believes he is under God's condemnation. The narrator treats her father's assessment almost mockingly, but she cannot do the same for his punishment for it is unequivocal and immediate—and one of the strangest incidents in all American literature. One night, compelled to solitary worship in the temple he's built to his God, Wieland self-combusts—or at least all his clothing does, leaving him naked, bruised, and barely breathing. He dies, and his wife soon follows him to the grave, leaving a son, Theodore Jr., and daughter Clara haunted by the extraordinary experience. Brown insists the possibility of auto-combustion exists—even offering scientific proof from contemporary journals—whether it is God's punishment or not (23). Less important than the veracity of the story is the fact that the burning and aftermath are described sincerely. Brown clearly means to encourage the belief that the events are possibly divine, or at least that Clara and Theodore Jr. believe so.

After their parents die, Theodore and Clara are raised by a kind aunt who gives them a rational education, free of the religious prejudice that marked their father's instruction. The two remain very close, even after Theodore marries their neighbor Catharine Pleyel. Their tiny social circle is complete when Catharine's brother, Henry, returns from his travels to Germany. The four adults, along with Theodore and Catharine's four children and a young servant girl, form an isolated group that deals little with the outside world.

The idyllic group, most often engaged in listening to Theodore and Henry debate the meaning in classic Roman speeches, is upset by two events: First, Theodore is certain he hears the voice of his wife when out at night, though she is with the others at home all the while; second, a former acquaintance of Henry's, Francis Carwin, insinuates himself in the group. Carwin, a mysterious stranger with the persuasive powers of a Cicero, the Roman orator Theodore Wieland so admired, lacks the moral powers necessary to regulate his gift and thus unwittingly wreaks havoc with his talent (Axelrod, 85). Still, no one associates Carwin's sudden appearance with the peculiar voices they all hear at different times.

The voices Clara hears are the most ominous: She perceives two men plotting to kill her from her bedroom closet; and while meditating in a secluded spot, another voice warns her of impending danger. Although known for her reason and courage, Clara falters in the face of the disembodied voices. She is certain someone is plotting her death but equally sure she will be protected by divine powers. The voices Henry hears also affect Clara: While walking to her house to declare his feelings for her, Henry is certain he overhears Clara and Carwin in a sexual encounter. No amount of tears or reason can convince Henry his senses have been deceived; he rejects Clara as a profligate, wounding her pride and breaking her heart. This, however, is the least of Clara's worries: Clara returns from arguing with Henry to find, on her own bed, her sister-in-law, Catharine, murdered. As she flees to warn her brother at his house against Carwin—the certain culprit—she discovers the four children and servant girl butchered. Clara's shock at these gruesome events is such that it takes weeks for her to comprehend that the destruction of the Wieland family comes not from an outside source but from within.

For just as Clara and Henry sought an explanation for the voices their ears undeniably hear, so does Theodore. While Henry represents the limitations of 18th-century rationalist thinking, Theodore characterizes religious enthusiasts, or those with a tendency to mistake one's own ardor for heavenly messages (Axelrod, 67). Henry believes, like other followers of Locke, that all knowledge is derived from human experience with their senses. He discredits any innate knowledge and emphasizes human reason. Theodore, on the other hand, believes in supernatural interventions and accepts the voices as divine, not human-made—the predilection for which he certainly inherited from his father. The two characters "crudely represent the temperamental division of the age" (Fliegelman, viii), and Brown indicates both can lead to society's destruction. Wieland is a "devastating critique" of the rationalists (Watts, 82) because the novel continually shows senses cannot be trusted and that rationalism is "impotent to deal with an irrational element at the core of human nature" (Axelrod, 83). Equally destructive are humans who rely on their limited perceptions to interpret God's will, as clearly illustrated in all the Wieland men, most especially Theodore Jr.

The voices Theodore hears demand the sacrifice of his family, and to show his faithfulness, like Abraham of the Old Testament, Theodore complies. Still, the biblical story of Abraham "affirms man's capacity for attaining absolute truth whereas Brown's novel denies the human capacity for attaining any truth absolutely" (Axelrod, 91–92), since the source of Theodore's voices is never ascertained. Taken into custody, Theodore claims no remorse, believing he's been obedient. The final sacrifice would be the life of his beloved sister; Theodore escapes prison three times to fulfill this command. He finally succeeds in finding Clara in her house where she's gone to meet Carwin for a promised defense of his innocence. Carwin admits his guilt at sporting with Clara's fears and reputation, but denies greater culpability. He achieves his aims through the skill of ventriloquism, new to the 18th century. Carwin explains that, early on, he learned both to imitate the voice of others and to throw his own voice. It was his voice Clara and Henry heard on every occasion, pretending the voices of others; it was even his voice that Theodore first heard. But Carwin adamantly denies being the source of Theodore's command to kill. By way of proof, Carwin, through the use of his skill, saves Clara in the final physical struggle with her brother. Carwin throws his voice and commands Theodore to "Hold!" adding that his design to kill his family has been his own, not God's. Theodore, in a moment of clarity, recognizes his responsibility and takes his own life.

Carwin remains an enigma throughout the novel. In the final confrontation he shows he is not completely malevolent by saving Clara; yet Clara would never have been in mortal danger had Carwin not began his mischief. And in the end, it appears as though that is all Carwin is guilty of. Carwin, then, is merely the catalyst for Theodore's lunacy and the destruction of an idyllic society, suggesting that, as Clara's moral expresses, imperfect discipline inevitably allows one to be deceived, despite social class, economic status, or higher education.

Brown based his narrative of a true account of a New York man who killed his family in 1781, convinced it was God's command. But Brown hoped for more than mere sensationalism, as the novel's subtitles suggest. The Transformation refers to the psychological developments necessary to transform a man from loving husband to murderer. But it also refers to the difficulties the new nation felt in the transformation from a government of absolute authority to a government where any with enough skill might gain authority (Fliegelman, xii). In such a society, men must learn which voices to listen in order to choose their leaders wisely—not an easy task when Brown shows you can't trust your own senses or your religious inclinations. The second subtitle, *An American Tale,* indicates Brown meant this warning specifically for the new nation, and he does not seem very hopeful. The novel ends with Clara, married at last to Henry, and relatively happy. But she no longer lives in America; she finds peace only in Europe. There may be a way to make a graceful and meaningful transformation, but the sad fate of the Wieland family shows failure is a terrifying reality.

SOURCES

Allen, Paul. *The Life of Charles Brockden Brown.* Delmar, N.Y.: Scholars' Facsimiles & Reprints, 1975.

Axelrod, Alan. *An American Tale: Charles Brockden Brown.* Austin: University of Texas Press, 1983.

Brown, Charles Brockden. *Wieland and Memoirs of Carwin the Biloquist.* Edited and with an introduction by Jay Fliegelman. New York: Penguin, 1991.

Clark, David Lee. *Charles Brockden Brown: Pioneer Voice of America.* Durham, N.C.: Duke University Press, 1952.

Grabo, Norman S. *The Coincidental Art of Charles Brockden Brown.* Chapel Hill: University of North Carolina Press, 1981.

Hinds, Elizabeth Jane Wall. *Private Property: Charles Brockden Brown's Gendered Economics of Virtue.* Newark: University of Delaware Press, 1997.

Lewis, Paul. "Charles Brockden Brown and the Gendered Canon of Early American Fiction," *Early American Literature* 31, no. 2 (1996), 167–188.

Rosenthal, Bernard, ed. *Critical Essays on Charles Brockden Brown.* Boston: G. K. Hall, 1981.

Tompkins, Jane. *Sensational Designs: The Cultural Work of American Fiction, 1790–1860.* New York: Oxford University Press, 1985.

Watts, Steven. *The Romance of Real Life: Charles Brockden Brown and the Origins of American Culture.* Baltimore, Md.: The Johns Hopkins University Press, 1994.

Wiley, Lulu Rumsey. *The Sources and Influence of the Novels of Charles Brockden Brown.* New York: Vantage Press, 1950.

H. L. Johnsen

WIESEL, ELIE(ZER) (1928–2005)   Elie Wiesel

was a survivor of the Nazi death camps of World War II and the preeminent chronicler of the horrors that he witnessed and endured. A novelist, playwright, essayist, historian, Wiesel won an impressive number of awards for literature and humanitarianism; in 1986 he was awarded the Nobel Peace Prize. All his work is grounded in the Holocaust and its aftermath; his millions of readers are indelibly moved by his descriptions of this part of the Jewish experience, and of the faith in God that sustains a humanity who might otherwise have succumbed to despair. His first and best-known novel, NIGHT (1960; published as *La Nuit* in 1958), became part of The Night Trilogy, composed of *Night, Dawn* (1961; published as *L'Aube* in 1960), and *The Accident* (1962, published as *Le Jour* in 1961). Wiesel was driven by the need to speak out so people will know and remember, and by the opposite, the impossibility of words to describe the full extent of the horror. Always enveloping his writing in surrealism or opacity, Wiesel achieved an understated, mystical style that collides with the horrific reality that is his subject. Many critics of Wiesel's work point out that his descriptions of the Holocaust are a metaphor for the modern human condition.

Elie Wiesel was born on September 30, 1928, in Sighet, Romania, to Shlomo Wiesel, a grocer, and Sarah Feig Wiesel. Although he survived four Nazi death camps—Birkenau, Auschwitz, Buna, and Buchenwald—his mother, father, and younger sister were murdered by the Nazis. After the war, he studied at the

Sorbonne from 1948 to 1951. He immigrated to the United States in 1956 and became a naturalized American citizen in 1963. In 1969 Wiesel married Marion Erster Rose, a Holocaust survivor who would become the major translator of his works from French to English. The French novelist Francois Mauriac persuaded young Wiesel to break his silence and to write about the Holocaust, and the result was the novel *Night,* a powerful autobiographical evocation of the atrocities Wiesel witnessed at Auschwitz and Buchenwald. The underlying premise of this title is that we are accustomed to looking into the night sky and seeing the stars and the eyes of God; but in Wiesel's endless-seeming night sky, filled with the smoke of burning bodies, even the stars seem to emanate from the fires of the crematorium. In *Dawn,* Eliezer, a young Holocaust survivor, moves to Palestine but forsakes his religious ideals and becomes a persecutor himself. *The Accident* tells the story of a journalist who, struck by a taxi (as Wiesel himself was struck), realizes that his guilt as a death-camp survivor has fueled his self-destructive desires.

Wiesel's subsequent novels focus on the moral issues faced in the aftermath of the Holocaust. In *La ville de la chance* (1962; *The Town beyond the Wall*), the survivor returns to Hungary to confront his Nazi prison guard only to try to come to grips with his own sense of responsibility. In *Les portes de la foret* (1964; *The Gates of the Forest*), the survivor confronts a God who, he thinks, may in fact be mad, only to move beyond his own suffering to acknowledge his connection to others. *Le cinquième fils* (1983; *The Fifth Son*) follows the son of a survivor to Europe. Although the son initially intends to avenge his father by killing the guard who brutalized him in the death camps, he abandons his plans when he realizes that the man, now old, does not comprehend his guilt. *L'Oubli* (1989; *The Forgotten*) examines the reactions and responsibilities of the children of Holocaust survivors. Wiesel's most recent novel, *Le juges* (1999; *The Judges*), uses a snowstorm to examine the revelations of five stranded airline passengers and to raise significant philosophical questions of good and evil.

Wiesel wrote a memoir in two volumes: *All Rivers Run to the Sea* (taking him from youth to the 1960s) and *And the Sea Is Never Full* (taking up the story of Wiesel in the last three decades of the 20th century). After working at the *Jewish Daily Forward,* Wiesel taught at numerous universities, including City College of New York, where he was Distinguished Professor from 1971 to 1976, and Boston University, where he was professor of philosophy from 1988. With his wife, Marion Wiesel, he founded the Elie Wiesel Foundation for Humanity in 1986. He served on the advisory board of more than 70 organizations and received more than 100 honorary degrees. Wiesel died in 2005.

NOVELS IN ENGLISH

All Rivers Run to the Sea. New York: Knopf, 1995.

And the Sea Is Never Full: Memoirs. 1969–. Translation by Marion Wiesel. New York: Knopf, 1999.

The Forgotten. Translated by Stephen Becker. New York: Summit Books, 1992.

The Judges. New York: Knopf, 2002.

La Nuit. 1958; translation by Stella Rodway published as *Night.* New York: Hill & Wang, 1960.

L'Aube. 1960; translation by Frances Frenaye published as *Dawn.* New York: Hill & Wang, 1961.

La Nuit. L'Aube. [and] Le Jour. 1969; translation published as *Night. Dawn. [and] The Accident: Three Tales.* New York: Hill & Wang, 1972; reprinted as *The Night Trilogy: Night, Dawn, The Accident.* New York: Farrar, Straus, 1987; translation by Stella Rodway published as *Night. Dawn. Day.* New York: Aronson, 1985.

La Ville de la chance. 1962; translation by Stephen Becker published as *The Town beyond the Wall.* New York: Atheneum, 1964; new edition, New York: Holt, 1967.

Le Jour. 1961; translation by Anne Borchardt published as *The Accident.* New York: Hill & Wang 1962.

Le Mendiant de Jerusalem. 1968; translation by the author and L. Edelman published as *A Beggar in Jerusalem.* New York: Random House, 1970.

Les Portes de la foret. 1964; translation by Frances Frenaye published as *The Gates of the Forest.* New York: Holt, 1966.

SOURCES

Berenbaum, Michael. *Elie Wiesel: God, the Holocaust, and the Children of Israel.* West Orange, N.J.: Behrman House, 1994.

Davis, Colin. *Elie Wiesel's Secretive Texts.* Gainesville: University Press of Florida Press, 1994.

Franciosi, Robert. *Elie Wiesel: Conversations.* Edited by Robert Franciosi. Jackson: University of Mississippi Press, 2002.

Heffner, Richard D. *Conversations with Elie Wiesel.* Thomas J. Vinciguerra, ed. New York: Schocken Books, 2001.

Lazo, Caroline Evensen. *Elie Wiesel*. New York: Macmillan, 1994.

Pariser, Michael. *Elie Wiesel: Bearing Witness*. Brookfield, Conn.: Millbrook Press, 1994.

Rosenfeld, Alvin. *Confronting the Holocaust*. Bloomington: Indiana University Press, 1978.

Schuman, Michael. *Elie Wiesel: Voice from the Holocaust*. Springfield, N.J.: Enslow, 1994.

Sibelman, Simon P. *Silence in the Novels of Elie Wiesel*. New York: St. Martin's Press, 1995.

Stern, Ellen Norman. *Elie Wiesel: A Voice for Humanity*. Philadelphia: Jewish Publication Society, 1996.

Wiesel, Elie. *L'Oublie: Roman*. Paris: Editions du Seuil, 1989.

OTHER

Elie Wiesel Foundation for Humanity. Available online. URL: http://www.eliewieselfoundation.org. Accessed June 25, 2003.

WIFE BHARATI MUKHERJEE (1975)

Bharati MUKHERJEE's second novel, *Wife,* opens in Calcutta with Dimple Dasgupta's father seeking her a suitable mate of appropriate caste, an engineer, by scouring matrimonial advertisements. When we first meet Dimple she is fantasizing about marriage, not to an engineer, but to a neurosurgeon. She imagines it will bring her freedom, love, and a more desirable life. Life has so far been simply a rehearsal for real life, the kind of real life that comes with marriage; for marriage brings opportunities that single women are denied in Indian culture, and Dimple longs for those freedoms more than anything.

Dimple worries that she is not fair or bosomy enough for marriage. From the start Dimple seeks to manipulate her identity through whatever means in order to become more desirable. Dimple studied at Calcutta University but is unable to take her exams, over which she despairs because without a B.A. she will be considered less marketable. She is presented as unformed and malleable; she simply adapts and adjusts according to others.

Mukherjee presents a feminist perspective, creating an image of the oppressed woman who struggles with her identity but does not know it. Dimple is subject to the desires and whims of others and has been socialized to be unaware of her own desire for an independent identity. She believes she wants to be a wife, but her longing is confused with her desire for freedom.

She also is unaware that such a role will not grant her those desires.

Dimple's Calcutta neighbor Parameta Ray (Pixie), is colorfully drawn and represents all that Dimple would like to be. Pixie is a gregarious go-getter who eventually achieves the status and fanfare for which Dimple longs. Dimple will measure herself against Pixie throughout as Pixie becomes at first a working woman and eventually the wife of a film star. But Pixie, too, is limited in her potential, as she is content being "Mrs. P Bagchi of Calcutta and Bombay."

Dimple seeks instruction and confirmation for her life through various media channels. She writes Miss Problem-Walla c/o Eve's Beauty-Basket in Bombay for guidance, not of the beauty kind, but as if she might be some sort of guru able to aid in emotional matters as well. Dimple is compelled by the authority of print, but her letters go either unanswered or dismissed, further highlighting her isolation in society.

Dimple's husband, Amit Kumar Basu, is eventually found in the papers; Dimple is not, however, the Basu family's first choice. While the wedding is perfect, it is clear that the marriage will not be. The first of Dimple's series of disappointments comes in learning that Basu is a short Prince Charming rather than a tall one. And in general her marriage does not turn out to be what she has hoped and dreamed. Rather than blossoming by gaining a firmer identity as a married woman, she finds that with each day she becomes less enthused. First her mother-in-law takes away her name, preferring instead Nandini. Then the newlyweds move into Dimple's mother-in-law's, where they live a far-less-than-glamorous life. And Amit wants Dimple to act robotically, knowing simply what to do and say to please him.

When the two immigrate to America, Dimple finds herself further removed, now in an even more unfamiliar society. She sees in those Indians who surround her further reflections of what she should and should not be. Meena Sen represents the ideal Indian woman, perpetually satisfied with her position and her identity as wife and mother. Ina Mullick represents the opposite extreme, an emboldened pants-wearing woman who is determined to live freely and to also free Dimple. Dimple sees in herself neither.

Dimple is cast into the world of the "other," exiled, unassimilated, but also unable to fully embrace her role as Bengali housewife. As such she is depicted as a character to whom things happen. Staying home, she is isolated and grows more and more depressed. She is detached and begins to confuse her reality with television. She reacts to others passively, never actively engaging in socializing or housework. She sleeps nearly all day, cooks when necessary, and increasingly watches television and reads magazines while her husband repeatedly inquires what she does all day. Amit begins to become something of a caricature: at one time he is even imagined as a profile in a whiskey ad; he is in many ways cast as the one-dimensional character of the matrimonial ad. Dimple even has a brief affair with the American Milt Glasser, from which she is equally detached. It is as if the sexual act occurred in a surreal dream world like television. Dimple seems at all times absent, but there is violence beneath her passive exterior.

Before they left Calcutta for America, Dimple had found herself pregnant. Unable to face motherhood, she jumped rope until she aborted her fetus. Foreshadowing the climax of the novel, Dimple had then exclaimed that it wasn't murder, that she could never commit murder. There is little early evidence that Dimple will act violently toward others, since the violence she fantasizes about is largely self-imposed; she imagines her own suicide regularly, compiling a list of various ways to succeed and even using it as a way of "counting sheep" to sleep. Being found dead would grant her some form of identity. But once, when Amit sneaks up to embrace her, she lashes at him with a knife, reflecting how impulsive her nature can be when she responds instinctively to the uncontrollable fears she has of her environment.

Wife ends climactically, with Dimple committing murder after all. She kills Amit by stabbing at the mole on his face, her realities so confused that she is not fully aware of her own actions. Again it is depicted like a dream. She is symbolically freed from the power Amit and their marriage had over her through this violent act and seems to hope to embrace such freedom since she believes women on television get away with murder. It is ironic that with a name like Dimple, she chooses to kill Amit by stabbing at his mole. Her identity might simply be described as the slight indentation for which she is named, and in vengeance she has sought Amit's much more identifiable facial feature as the target for her frustrations.

The novel is written in three sections, the first taking place in Calcutta, the second in America while Amit and Dimple are living with Sens, and the third when they are subletting an apartment in Manhattan. *Wife* develops many of the themes for which Mukherjee's work is celebrated in her depiction of the life of one woman exiled from her country and herself.

SOURCES

Koshy, Susan. "The Geography of Female Subjectivity, Ethnicity, Gender, and Diaspora." In *Contemporary American Women Writers: Gender, Class, Ethnicity,* edited by Lois Parkinson Zamora. London: Longman, 1998.

Krishnan, R. S. "Cultural Construct and the Female Identity: Bharati Mukherjee's *Wife,*" *International Fiction Review* 25, nos. 1–2 (1998): 89–97.

Ramachandra, Ragini. "Bharati Mukherjee's *Wife:* An Assessment," *Literary Criterion* 26, no. 3 (1991): 56–67.

Sarkar, Farida. "Suppression, Frustration, Anger, and the Identity Crisis of Dimple Dasgupta in Bharati Mukherjee's *Wife.*" In *Contributions to Bengal Studies: An Interdisciplinary and International Approach,* edited by Enayetur Rahim. Dhaka. Beximco, 1998.

Shankar, Lavina Dhingra. "Activism, 'Feminism' and Americanization in Bharati Mukherjee's *Wife* and *Jasmine,*" *Hitting Critical Mass: A Journal of Asian American Cultural Criticism* 3, no. 1 (1995 Winter): 61–84.

Wickramagamage, Carmen. "Relocation and Positive Act: The Immigrant Experience in Bharati Mukherjee's Novels," *Diaspora: A Journal of Transnational Studies* 2, no. 2 (1992 Fall): 171–200.

Deirdre Fagan

WILDER, THORNTON (NIVEN) (1897–1975)

Although primarily known as an award-winning, innovative playwright who celebrated the lives of ordinary individuals, Thornton Wilder was also the author of eight novels. They included the best-sellers *Heaven's My Destination* (1928); *The Ides of March* (1948); *The BRIDGE OF SAN LUIS REY* (1927) (which won the Pulitzer Prize); and *The Eighth Day* (1967) (which won the National Book Award). He was considered by his contemporaries to be one of the most sensitive and erudite observers of American culture.

Thornton Wilder was born on April 17, 1897, in Madison, Wisconsin, to Amos Parker Wilder, a newspaper editor and American Consul to China, and Isabella Thornton Niven Wilder. After attending schools in the United States and China, Wilder earned a bachelor's degree from Yale University in 1920 and a master's degree from Princeton University in 1926. He served twice in the U.S. Army: as a corporal in the Coast Artillery Corps in 1918, and as a captain in Army Air Intelligence from 1942 to 1945, earning the rank of lieutenant colonel and receiving the Legion of Merit, Bronze Star; Legion d'Honneur, and Honorary Member of the Order of the British Empire (M.B.E.). His debut novel, *The Cabala* (1926), set in Rome, Italy, is about a young American student who joins a mysterious association comprised of the youthful but decaying European aristocracy; he returns to the United States as a more mature artist. *The Bridge of San Luis Rey,* his second novel, established his reputation when it won a Pulitzer Prize. (He would win two additional Pulitzers, for his plays *Our Town* [1938] and in 1943 for *The Skin of Our Teeth.*) Central to the novel, which is set in 18th-century Peru, is a rope bridge that collapses and causes the deaths of five people—a boy, an adolescent girl, a young man, a middle-aged man, and an elderly noblewoman. The priest-protagonist finds in their deaths the evidence of unrequited love and questions of a deeply spiritual significance.

The Woman of Andros (1930), as in the first two novels, explores both cultural and theological issues, this time by juxtaposing pre-Christian Greek culture against later Christian ideas. A pagan boy falls in love with both an older woman and her younger sister, both of whom die, leaving him, the novel suggests, without benefit of Christian solace. The novel survived a famous attack by Marxist critic Michael Gold, who castigated Wilder for not writing instead about Depression-era social issues. Set during the Depression era, *Heaven's My Destination* is a picaresque novel that portrays a Don Quixote figure named George Brush, a book salesman who travels around the United States. It was a popular success, as was *The Ides of March,* which, as the title suggests, is a historical novel that centers on the assassination of the Roman emperor Julius Caesar. It has earned high praise for its historical accuracy and vision. *The Eighth Day,* often considered Wilder's most important accomplishment, depicts a man on the run from a false murder charge. Set in a small southern Illinois town, the novel follows John Ashley as he becomes a fugitive and examines the families of Ashley and Breckenridge Lansing, the man whom Ashley was convicted of shooting. *Theophilus North* (1973), set in Newport, Rhode Island, is a novel composed of autobiographical short stories that Wilder said represented his twin (who died at birth) and what he might have made of his life.

Thornton Wilder died of a heart attack in December 1975 in Hamden, Connecticut. His numerous honorary degrees and prizes include the 1952 Gold Medal for Fiction from the American Academy of Arts and Letters and the 1965 first-ever presentation of the National Book Committee's National Medal for Literature. *The Bridge of San Luis Rey* was filmed three times, initially in 1929; *Theophilus North* was made into the movie *Mr. North* by John Huston, starring Danny Huston, Anjelica Huston, and Robert Mitchum.

NOVELS

The Bridge of San Luis Rey. New York: A. and C. Boni, 1927.

The Cabala. New York: A. and C. Boni, 1926.

The Eighth Day. New York: Harper, 1967.

Heaven's My Destination. New York: Coward-McCann, 1928.

The Ides of March. New York: Harper, 1948.

Theophilus North. New York: Harper, 1973.

The Woman of Andros. New York: A. and C. Boni, 1930.

SOURCES

Blank, Martin. *Critical Essays on Thornton Wilder.* Englewood Cliffs, N.J.: Prentice Hall, 1995.

Bryer, Jackson R., ed. *Conversations with Thornton Wilder.* Jackson: University Press of Mississippi, 1992.

Burbank, R. *Thornton Wilder.* Boston: Twayne, 1961.

Castronovo, David. *Thornton Wilder.* New York: Ungar, 1986.

Cowley, Malcolm, ed. *Writers at Work: The Paris Review Interviews.* New York: Viking, 1957.

De Koster, Katie, ed. *Readings on Thornton Wilder.* San Diego, Calif.: Greenhaven Press, 1998.

Goldstein, Malcolm. *The Art of Thornton Wilder.* Lincoln: University of Nebraska Press, 1965.

Goldstone, Richard H. *Thornton Wilder, An Intimate Portrait.* New York: Dutton, 1975.

Grebanier, Bernard. *Thornton Wilder.* Minneapolis: University of Minnesota Press, 1965.

Harrison, Gilbert A. *The Enthusiast: A Life of Thornton Wilder.* New Haven, Conn.: Ticknor & Fields, 1983.

Kuner, M. C. *Thornton Wilder: The Bright and the Dark.* Boston: Thomas Y. Crowell Co., 1972.

Simon, Linda. *Thornton Wilder: His Work.* Garden City, N.Y.: Doubleday, 1979.

Wilder, Amos Niven. *Thornton Wilder and His Public.* Philadelphia: Fortress Press, 1980.

Wilder, Thornton. *The Journals of Thornton Wilder, 1939–1961.* Edited by Donald Gallup. New Haven, Conn.: Yale University Press, 1985.

OTHER

The Official Thornton Wilder Site. Available online. URL: http://www.thorntonwilder.com. Accessed September 25, 2005.

The Thornton Wilder Society. Available online. URL: http://www.thorntonwildersociety.org. Accessed September 25, 2005.

WILD MEAT AND THE BULLY BURGERS

LOIS ANN YAMANAKA (1996) Lois Ann YAMANAKA's *Wild Meat and the Bully Burgers* begins with an ending, specifically "Happy Endings," the first chapter of her debut novel. Readers quickly realize that the happy ending of the initial chapter's title alludes not to the tone of the novel but to the longing of the adolescent protagonist, Lovey Nariyoshi, for she desires to live the life of her movie idol, Shirley Temple, fantasizing about a screen life far different from her own. Yamanaka's quirky coming-of-age story is set in the mid-1970s in Hilo, Hawaii, and chronicles a year in Lovey's life as she grows from being 12 and playing with Barbie dolls to attending the junior high school end-of-the-year dance. Lovey lives in a working-class neighborhood with her younger sister, Calhoon, who is endowed with the gift of spiritual sight; her mother, Verva, who feels harassed by her two daughters but also protective of them; and her father, Hubert, a modern-day hunter and gatherer who wanted sons but ended up with daughters.

Narrated entirely in pidgin, *Wild Meat and the Bully Burgers* is told through the first-person perspective of Lovey as she describes the daily trials and tribulations she experiences as a girl who is not in the popular crowd; whose one and only best friend is an effeminate boy, Jerry; and who desires to achieve acceptance through marrying a *haole* (white American) and living a middle-class lifestyle. Lovey, ashamed of her family's working-class and Japanese-ethnic roots, struggles with standard English in school, with her teenage consumer desires (wanting store-bought food and clothes versus her family's homemade products), and with the changes occurring to her body in her adolescence. Praised for writing in an authentic local voice, Yamanaka divides her novel into three sections with very brief chapters (9–10 pages at most), and because of their brevity, her prose has an intensity that reflects the immediacy of Lovey's painful adolescent experiences. Lovey narrates things as they directly unfold, describing with raw honesty the shame she feels trick-or-treating in the rich enclave of Reed's Island, the overwhelming embarrassment and confusion she experiences when she gets her period and must buy sanitary napkins at the local store, and her exultation at being asked to dance the last slow dance by the most popular boy at her school.

In many senses, this is a novel about fitting in and not fitting in. Many characters do not adhere to white, mainland American societal models or molds. Her best friend, Jerry, does not conform to notions of male gender identity because of his attraction to David Cassidy and his interest in Barbie dolls. And both he and Lovey are ostracized by the popular clique at their school, the Rays of the Rising Dawns, a group of rich girls who taunt Lovey and Jerry due to their poorer economic status. The second-generation Hawaii-born Nariyoshis, by virtue of their class standing, do not fit into the model-minority myth of upwardly mobile Asian Americans, nor do they reflect a portrait of Hawaiian leisure and luxury, since they struggle to put food on the table through Hubert's hunting forays and Verva's home-gardening efforts. Lovey herself does not fit into gender expectations of a Japanese-American girl in Hawaii, as she constantly tries to win her father's affection by accompanying him on hunting expeditions and participating in his many schemes to earn extra money for family luxuries like a secondhand stereo or cassette player.

Acting like the eldest son and hunter's side-kick that Hubert longs for, Lovey and her father draw closer together, making this novel an atypical Asian-American story about a daughter's bond with her father. For it is on these trips that Lovey learns about her father's life growing up on a Kauai plantation, his relationship with his brothers and parents, and the importance of home and family, which is central to his pride and identity as a local Hawaiian man. Through the portrait of Lovey's relationship with Hubert, Yamanaka investigates the tension Lovey feels between pride in her family's identity and shame at not fitting in with her richer peers. In particular, Yamanaka critiques the materialist and racist effects of mass consumer culture, which has poisoned Lovey into believing that in order to be accepted, she must be either rich, white, or skinny (or preferably all three). However, by the end of the novel, Lovey truly understands the lessons that her father has imparted to her through stories of the Nariyoshis, allowing Lovey to come of age through an appreciation of her local identity and place. And although the novel does not end with the idyllic movie happy ending that Lovey idolizes, the journey Lovey takes on her road to maturity is both heartbreaking and rewarding.

SOURCES

Bromley, Roger. "This Body Is Your Only Real Home: Migrancy and Identity—*Dreaming in Cuban, Native Speaker, Wild Meat and the Bully Burgers,* and *My Year of Meats.*" In *Narratives for a New Belonging: Diasporic Cultural Fictions,* 66–95. Edinburgh: Edinburgh University Press, 2000.

Davis, Rocio G. "I Wish You a Land": Hawai'i Short Story Cycles and Aloha 'Aina," *Journal of American Studies* 35 (2001): 47–64.

Takahama, Valerie. "Controversial Adventures in 'Paradise': Bully Burgers and Pidgin," *Orange County Register,* 15 February 1996, morning ed., E01.

Wilson, Rob. "Bloody Mary Meets Lois-Ann Yamanaka; Imagining Hawaiian Locality, from *South Pacific* to Bamboo Ridge and Beyond." In *Reimagining the American Pacific: from South Pacific to Bamboo Ridge and Beyond,* 163–189. Durham, N.C.: Duke University Press, 2000.

Yamanaka, Lois-Ann. Interview, *Asian Reporter,* 20 February 2001, 12.

———. *Wild Meat and the Bully Burgers.* New York: Harcourt Brace, 1997.

Jennifer Ho

WILLIAMS, SHERLEY ANNE (1944–1999)

Critic, novelist, poet, essayist, and educator, Sherley Anne Williams is probably best known for her first book, *Give Birth to Brightness: A Thematic Study in Neo-Black Literature* (1972), and her first novel, *DESSA ROSE: A RIVETING STORY OF THE SOUTH DURING SLAVERY* (1986). The first sets forth Williams's philosophy: her belief in the unbroken connection between contemporary black writers and their ancestors, and the need to analyze and understand black literature within the black, not the white, experience. Williams also tries to tell the stories of uneducated and poor black women. In *Dessa Rose,* she uses the oral tradition of black culture to present slavery and the South from the perspective of a black woman and, as their friendship develops, a white woman. The novel earned positive reviews for its poetic style. Dessa Rose, who leads a slave revolt while on a coffle (a group of slaves chained together on the way to the auction bloc), and Ruth, a white woman, provide sanctuary to escaped slaves.

Sherley Anne Williams was born in 1944 in Bakersfield, California, to Jesse Winson Williams, who died of tuberculosis when she was seven years old, and Lelia Marie Williams, who died when she was 16. Williams received her bachelor's degree in history from California State University at Fresno in 1966 and a master's degree from Brown University in 1972. She was professor of Afro-American literature until her death, from cancer, in San Diego, on July 6, 1999. *Dessa Rose* has become standard fare in university-level courses on black history and literature in particular, and American literature in general.

NOVELS

Dessa Rose: A Riveting Story of the South during Slavery. New York: Morrow, 1986.

SOURCES

Davies, Carole Boyce. "Mother Right/Write Revisited: *Beloved* and *Dessa Rose* and the Construction of Motherhood in Black Women's Fiction." In *Narrating Mothers: The Theorizing Maternal Subjectives,* edited by Brenda O. Daly and Maureen T. Reddy, 44–57. Knoxville: University of Tennessee Press, 1991.

Fisher, Dexter, and Robert B. Stepto, eds. *Afro-American Literature: The Reconstruction of Instruction.* New York: Modern Language Association of America, 1979.

Kekeh, Andree Anne. "Sherley Anne Williams's *Dessa Rose:* History and the Disruptive Power of Memory." In *History and Memory in African American Culture,* edited by Genevieve Fabre and Robert O'Meally, 219–227. New York: Oxford University Press, 1994.

McDowell, Deborah E. "Negotiating between Tenses: Witnessing Slavery after Freedom—*Dessa Rose.*" In *Slavery and the Literary Imagination,* edited by Deborah McDowell and Arnold Rampersad, 144–163. Baltimore, Md.: Johns Hopkins University Press, 1989.

Porter, Nancy. "Women's Interracial Friendships and Visions of Community in *Meridian, The Salt Eaters, Civil Wars,* and *Dessa Rose.*" In *Tradition and Talents of Women,* edited by Florence Howe, 251–267. Urbana: University of Illinois Press, 1991.

Tate, Claudia, ed. *Black Woman Writers at Work.* New York: Continuum, 1983.

Trapasso, Anne E. "Returning to the Site of Violence: The Restructuring of Slavery's Legacy in Sherley Anne Williams's *Dessa Rose.*" In *Violence, Silence and Anger: Women's Writing as Transgression,* edited by Deirdre Lashgari, 219–230. Charlottesville: University of Virginia Press, 1995.

Williams, Sherley Anne. *Give Birth to Brightness: A Thematic Study in Neo-Black Literature.* New York: Dial, 1972.

WILLIAMS, TENNESSEE (THOMAS LANIER WILLIAMS) (1911–1983)

For an enormous number of readers, theatergoers, and critics all over the world, Tennessee Williams was the premier American playwright of the 20th century, known for a long list of now-classic dramas; they include *The Glass Menagerie* (1945), winner of the New York Drama Critics Circle Prize; *A Streetcar Named Desire* (1947) and *Cat on a Hot Tin Roof* (1955), both of which won a Pulitzer Prize. Fifteen of his works were made into motion pictures, and a number were Broadway successes, including *Suddenly Last Summer* (1958), *Sweet Bird of Youth* (1959), and *Night of the Iguana* (1961). But although he was a dramatist first and foremost, publishing more than 60 plays, he was also a talented fiction writer who wrote two novels, four volumes of poetry, two collections of short stories, an autobiography, and various essays. His first novel, *The Roman Spring of Mrs. Stone* (1950), was made into a Warner Brothers film in 1961. His second, *Moise and the World of Reason,* published 25 years later, is a tale about the artistic process and love, both heterosexual and homosexual. Although neither novel is set in the South, the usual setting for most of his plays and short fiction, both novels contain sensitive portraits of women who are artists, and both are about love.

Tennessee Williams was born on March 29, 1911, in Columbus, Mississippi, to Cornelius Coffin Williams (a boisterous traveling shoe salesman who later served as the model for Stanley Kowalski in *A Streetcar Named Desire*), and Edwina Dakin Williams. The family moved to St. Louis, Missouri, when Williams was seven; he attended the University of Missouri, eventually graduating from the University of Iowa with a bachelor's degree in 1938. He was an established playwright by the time he published *The Roman Spring of Mrs. Stone.* As scholar Ren Draya points out, in some ways the work resembles a play, in that it opens with descriptions of place and lighting (Draya, 657) and uses no quotation marks for dialogue. In this novel Karen Stone, an actor approaching 50, is criticized by both critics and theatergoers as being too old for her role. So when her husband, 20 years her senior, dies of a heart attack on a flight to Rome, Mrs. Stone stays in Italy, leases an apartment with a magnificent view, and meets a young man named Paolo di Lio, with whom she falls in love. Critics have noted her similarity to Williams himself, whose long-term partner was an Italian-American named Frank Merlo. In 1961, Jose Quintero directed *Roman Spring* as a motion picture starring Vivien Leigh as Karen Stone, Warren Beatty as Paolo, and Lotte Lenya as the Contessa who introduces them; in 2003 Robert Ackerman directed it as a made-for-TV movie starring Helen Mirren as Karen Stone, Olivier Martinez as Paolo, and Anne Bancroft as the Contessa.

Moise and the World of Reason is narrated by an aging playwright, and, unlike Williams's earlier work, is a specifically gay novel, a tale of anguished loss that ends happily for both the playwright-narrator and for Moise, the artist. Moise is happy only when she can paint, and at the end, a large delivery of art supplies appears at her studio so she can continue to create art. Both novels explore the characteristic Williams themes of loneliness and desire.

Although he made his mark in the modern theater and will continue to be viewed primarily as a playwright, Williams's prose fiction needs to be better known. Indeed, at least one critic finds his fiction "perhaps even more consistent in quality that his drama" (Draya, 647). The novels, taken together with Williams's short fiction, cover the full range of his obsessions—violence, murder, rape, nymphomania, castration, drugs, alcoholism, and sexuality, both straight and gay, all often cloaked in the sensual, pungent, emotional world of the South. Tennessee Williams, who wrestled with his own drug and alcohol addiction, died accidentally by choking on the cap of a pill bottle on February 24, 1983, in his suite at Hotel Elysie, in New York. He is buried in St. Louis, Missouri. His manuscripts and letters are housed in the Humanities Research Center at the University of Texas at Austin.

NOVELS

Moise and the World of Reason. New York: Simon & Schuster, 1975.
The Roman Spring of Mrs. Stone. New York: New Directions, 1950.

SOURCES

Crandell, George W. *Tennessee Williams: A Descriptive Bibliography.* Pittsburgh, Pa.: University of Pittsburgh Press, 1995.
———. *The Critical Response to Tennessee Williams.* Westport, Conn.: Greenwood Press, 1996.
Devlin, Albert J., ed. *Conversations with Tennessee Williams.* Jackson: University Press of Mississippi, 1986.
Draya, Ren. "The Fiction of Tennessee Williams." In *Tennessee Williams: A Tribute,* edited by Jac Tharpe, 647–662. Jackson: University Press of Mississippi, 1977.
Falk, Signi. *Tennessee Williams.* 2nd edition. Boston: Twayne, 1978.
Griffin, Alice. *Understanding Tennessee Williams.* Columbia: University of South Carolina Press, 1995.
Leverich, Lyle. *Tom: The Unknown Tennessee Williams.* New York: Crown Publishers, 1995.
———. *Tenn: The Timeless World of Tennessee Williams.* New York: Crown Publishers, 1997.
Londre, Felicia Hardison. *Tennessee Williams.* New York: Ungar, 1979.
Martin, Robert A., ed. *Critical Essays on Tennessee Williams.* Englewood Cliffs, N.J.: Prentice Hall International, 1997.
McCann, John S. *The Critical Reputation of Tennessee Williams: A Reference Guide.* Boston: G. K. Hall, 1983.
Spoto, Donald. *The Kindness of Strangers: The Life of Tennessee Williams.* Boston: Little, Brown, 1985.
Tharpe, Jac, ed. *Tennessee Williams: A Tribute.* Jackson: University Press of Mississippi, 1977.
Williams, Tennessee. *Conversations with Tennessee Williams.* Edited by Albert J. Devlin. Jackson: University Press of Mississippi, 1986.

OTHER

The Tennessee Williams Page. Available online. URL: http://www.lambda.net/~maximum/williams.html. Accessed September 25, 2005.
Tennessee Williams. The Mississippi Writers Page. Available online. URL: http://www.olemiss.edu/depts/english/ms-writers/dir/williams_tennessee. Accessed September 25, 2005.
Tennessee William. Eastern Illinois University. Available online. URL: http://www.eiu.edu/~eng1002/authors/williams3. Accessed September 25, 2005.

WILLIAMS, WILLIAM CARLOS (1883–1963)

Best known as one of the great American poets of the modernist period and author of the five-book epic poem *Paterson,* William Carlos Williams is also admired for five novels, particularly WHITE MULE (1937), *In the Money* (1940), and *The Build-Up* (1952). These three novels comprise Williams's Stetcher Trilogy, patterned on the early lives of his wife Flossie Herman and her immigrant family. Williams uses his art to transform their lives into a story about American materialism and its effect on individual members of a family. As both a poet and a novelist, Williams admired the person who questioned the status quo. Particularly during the Great Depression of the 1930s, Williams, a physician, wrote compassionately about the poverty endured by many of his patients.

William Carlos Williams was born on September 17, 1883, in Rutherford, New Jersey, to William George Williams, a British businessman, and the Puerto Rican Raquel Helene Hoheb Williams. Williams was educated at the University of Pennsylvania, where he received his medical degree in 1906. In 1912 he married Florence Herman. In *The Great American Novel* (1923), an experimental work, Williams paints a self-portrait. He is attracted by Paris and avant-garde art, a yen he was able to satisfy a year later when he and his wife divided their time between New York and Paris. *A*

Voyage to Pagany (1928), based on that trip, features an innocent American on his first tour of Europe; it is written in a more conventional style than his first novel or his third, *A Novelette* (1932). *White Mule* portrays Flossie, the assertive baby, who can kick like White Mule whiskey. Born in New York City to an immigrant Scandinavian named Joe, a printer, and his ambitious wife, Gurlie, Flossie moves to upstate New York, where the country life improves her health and her father starts his own printing company. *In the Money* depicts Joe's success and move to the suburbs, and *The Build-Up* exemplifies the newly acquired middle-class values of the family; all grow from the ambition Gurlie has instilled in her newly American family.

William Carlos Williams died on March 4, 1963, in Rutherford. Most of his manuscripts and letters are housed in the Lockwood Memorial Library at the State University of New York at Buffalo; the Beinecke Rare Book and Manuscript Library at Yale University; and the Humanities Research Center at the University of Texas at Austin.

NOVELS AND NOVELLAS

The Build-Up. New York: Random House, 1952.

The Great American Novel. Paris: Three Mountains Press, 1923.

In the Money. New York: New Directions, 1940.

A Novelette and Other Prose. Toulon, France: TO Publishers, 1932.

A Voyage to Pagany. New York: Macaulay, 1928.

White Mule. New York: New Directions, 1937.

SOURCES

Axelrod, Steven Gould, and Helen Deese. *Critical Essays on William Carlos Williams.* New York: MacMillan, 1994.

Berry, S. L. *William Carlos Williams.* Mankato, Minn.: Creative Education, 1997.

Bloom, Harold, ed. *William Carlos Williams.* New York: Chelsea House, 1986.

Breslin, James E. *William Carlos Williams: An American Artist.* New York: Oxford University Press, 1970.

Doyle, Charles, ed. *William Carlos Williams: The Critical Heritage.* Boston: Routledge & Kegan Paul, 1980.

Engels, John. *Guide to William Carlos Williams.* Indianapolis, Ind.: Bobbs-Merrill, 1969.

Guimond, James. *The Art of William Carlos Williams: A Discovery and Possession of America.* Urbana: University of Illinois Press, 1968.

Laughlin, James. *Remembering William Carlos Williams.* New York: New Directions, 1995.

Lenhart, Gary. *The Teachers & Writers Guide to William Carlos Williams.* New York: Teachers & Writers Collaborative, 1998.

Miller, J. Hillis, ed. *William Carlos Williams: A Collection of Critical Essays.* Englewood Cliffs, N.J.: Prentice-Hall, 1966.

Morris, Daniel. *The Writings of William Carlos Williams: Publicity for the Self.* Columbia: University of Missouri Press, 1995.

Nardi, Marcia. *The Last Word: Letters Between Marcia Nardi and William Carlos Williams.* Iowa City: University of Iowa Press, 1994.

Wagner, Linda Welshimer, ed. *Interviews with William Carlos Williams: "Speaking Straight Ahead."* New York: New Directions, 1976.

———. *The Prose of William Carlos Williams.* Middletown, Conn.: Wesleyan University Press, 1970.

———. *William Carlos Williams: A Reference Guide.* Boston: G. K. Hall, 1978.

Whitaker, Thomas R. *William Carlos Williams.* Revised edition. Boston: Twayne, 1989.

Williams, William Carlos. *The Autobiography of William Carlos Williams.* New York: New Directions, 1967.

———. *Selected Letters.* Edited by John C. Thirlwall. New York: McDowell, Obolensky, 1957.

WILLIE MASTERS' LONESOME WIFE

WILLIAM H. GASS (1968) *Willie Masters' Lonesome Wife* self-consciously defies an unreflective and unengaged reader/text interaction. Originally published as an oversize volume featuring page signatures of varying color, texture, and thickness, GASS's work of fiction even challenges the conventional materiality of the book form. Punctuated with nude pictures of a buxom young woman (perhaps referring to the wife in the title, but as we read, representation as such becomes more and more complicated), the "text" of the novel speaks to itself—its own conventions, limitations, even desires—as the reader must balance the narrative of the text as "imagination imagining itself imagine" and the impasses reached when attempting to connect the world of the text to the world proper. Though exemplary of metafictional works (works that directly address and focus upon their status as fiction), the text does not function simply as an allegory of reading;

rather, the work directly confronts the reader with its structural difficulties and limitations, demanding that reading occur on its terms, not on those with which a learned reader comes to a work of fiction.

The metaphor of the body—developed both pictorially and textually—pervades the text at numerous points. *Willie Masters' Lonesome Wife*—whether this title should refer to Babs, Olga, or any other of the numerous characters nominally present within the text—requires a stand-in for the inattentive lover, the inattentive husband: the reader. Yet, the reader cannot approach the text without first experiencing the abrupt jolt resulting from the stark interplay of textual high jinks on the page. Numerous fonts, typefaces, digressions, shifts in narrative perspective/point of view, proper names, sexual images, footnotes, page designs, inserted documents, mirror images, textual arrangements, and even a number of simulated coffee stains provide the only direction for the reader to follow; without even the guidance of numbered pages, the text sets the rules and conventions for reading.

So how should the reader attempt to interpret the text? Gass gives few clues, always insisting that the text, the words on the page, constitute their own reality and should not have to match up or directly correlate with any world outside the text itself. As Gass notes in his collection of essays *Habitations of the Word,* words remain "concerned only with survival, domination, and their success in supplanting all rival realities with their own" (Gass 1997, 101). In this sense, *Willie Masters' Lonesome Wife,* as a self-contained textual body, fights against the reader's attempt to correlate the text itself with any stable, outside reality. In a similar assessment of the text, Arthur Saltzman notes: "[L]anguage is not revitalized by emphasizing its referential status" (Saltzman, 107). Language, that which comprises her body—the textual body of *Willie Masters' Lonesome Wife*—does not require an outside referent (something to correspond directly to in the outside world); it stands alone within the text, circling in upon itself, "imagining itself imagine."

Yet certain scholars such as H. L. Hix have criticized such a reading of the text, pointing out that the book, as a whole, does not achieve its intended effect(s). Hix writes: "*Willie Masters' Lonesome Wife* proved too exclusively an intellectual exercise, without enough emotional charge to sustain it" (Hix, 63). Though Gass himself has noted the project's shortcomings—"Too many ideas turned out to be only ideas . . . I don't give a shit for ideas—which in fiction represent inadequately embodied projects—I care only for affective effects" (quoted in LeClair 22)—nonetheless, the work does succeed in, if nothing else, forcing the reader to give up some of her autonomy in reading and following the dictates of the text itself.

What, exactly, might represent important results and/or "affective effects" of reading the text on its own terms? Unlike Hix, Michael Kaufmann argues that the book—though a self-contained unit which does not make any claims to direct representation of the real world—forces the reader to reflect on the nature of the reading experience, interpreting the experience alongside more traditional uses of language, of communication. Kaufmann succinctly sums up such a reading when he remarks: "The narrator's insistence that we attend to the language itself may seem to have implication only for aesthetics, but the power of language to shape the world makes it important that everyone see language" (Kaufmann, 92). Language, as Kaufmann points out, always seeps in and out of our interaction with the text; the reading experience demands it. Arguably, the experience of reading *Willie Masters' Lonesome Wife* demands it more adamantly than most texts.

Interestingly, at certain points in the work, the text addresses and confronts the reader directly, antagonizing the reader so as to highlight the agency of the text. In one particular footnote the text (narrator? Babs? Gass?) taunts the reader: "Now that I've got you alone down here, you bastard, don't think I'm letting you get away easily, no sir, not you brother; anyway, how do you think that you're going to get out . . . well you don't know anything, do you? not anything, do you? not why you came or how you can back yourself out." This tension between text and reader, while quite explicit in such a passage, plays itself out in numerous ways throughout the text. Though Gass's intentions might confuse and disorient the reader, that undoubtedly is the point.

Toward the end of the work, the text (again, the reader cannot decipher the speaking subject) isolates the reader, indicating the mistakes she made in reading: "You've been had . . . from start to finish." The inattentive reader, just like the inattentive lover, skips, glosses over, rushes through the act, as language—in this case the text of the novel—never receives the attention, the interaction it deserves. Arguably, any text, no matter how clearly it offers up its mechanisms to the scrutiny of the reader, falls victim to such inattentiveness when read. For Gass, such is the nature of language: its simultaneous pleasure/frustration, clarity/duplicity, promise/subversion of such promise, reductiveness/generative force. *Willie Masters' Lonesome Wife* brings these characteristics to the fore, making them the essence of the work as such, which encourages readers to look a bit more closely the next time they approach any text.

SOURCES

Gass, William H. *Habitations of the Word*. Ithaca, N.Y.: Cornell University Press, 1997.

———. *Willie Masters' Lonesome Wife*. Normal, Ill.: Dalkey Archive, 1989.

Hix, H. L. *Understanding William H. Gass*. Columbia: University of South Carolina Press, 2002.

Kaufmann, Michael. "The Textual Body of William Gass's *Willie Masters' Lonesome Wife*." In *Textual Bodies: Modernism, Postmodernism, and Print*, 87–105. Cranbury, N.J.: Associated University Presses, 1994.

LeClair, Thomas. "William Gass: The Art of Fiction LXV." In *Conversations with William H. Gass*, edited by Theodore G. Ammon, 17–38. Jackson: University of Mississippi Press, 2003.

Saltzman, Arthur M. *The Fiction of William Gass: The Consolation of Language*. Carbondale: Southern Illinois University Press, 1986.

Zach Weir

WILSON, HARRIET E. ADAMS (1827?–1870)

Since the reissuing of *OUR NIG; OR SKETCHES FROM THE LIFE OF A FREE BLACK, IN A TWO-STORY WHITE HOUSE, NORTH. SHOWING THAT SLAVERY'S SHADOWS FALL EVEN THERE* (1859), scholars have attempted to place this novel and its author, Harriet E. Adams Wilson, within literary history. *Our Nig* is the first novel by an African American and is clearly fictionalized autobiography, but it also seems to derive from the sentimental tradition in literature as well as from the genres of black autobiography and the slave narrative. Apparently Wilson not only copyrighted the novel but also paid for its publication in 1859, hoping, as she declares in the preface, to improve the near destitute circumstances she suffered after her husband deserted her and her baby. *Our Nig* features Frado, the mulatto protagonist, who struggles to find a voice despite her situation as a black woman utterly alone. Particularly striking in this novel is Frado's virulent anger against the Northern abolitionists, who rarely appear in fiction in roles other than those of saviors of black people.

Many of the details of the life of Harriet E. Adams Wilson are uncertain. She was born in either 1807 or 1808—or 1827, depending on which census record correctly names her—in either Fredericksburg, Virginia, or New Hampshire, and she died prior to 1863 or in 1870. If some of Wilson's statements in *Our Nig* are autobiographical rather than fictional, then she did indeed work as an indentured servant to a white family in Milford, New Hampshire, but the identity of the family has been a subject of scholarly debate. Wilson was married on October 6, 1851, to Thomas Wilson, who deserted her before she gave birth to their son, George Mason Wilson. Ironically, this son died about six months after his mother published *Our Nig*. Wilson herself apparently lived in Boston until 1863, after which she disappeared from public records.

Although scholars have not determined the final place of *Our Nig* in the American literary canon, it is clear that it was published earlier than previous contenders for the first black American novel. The first black woman published in the United States was thought to be Frances Ellen Watkins HARPER and her novel *IOLA LEROY, OR SHADOWS UPLIFTED*, appeared in 1892. William Wells BROWN published *CLOTEL* in London in 1853. As readers and critics, especially African-American scholars, come to learn more about both Wilson and her novel, however, at least one fact will remain unchanged: the untenable situation of a black-American woman in 19th-century America.

NOVEL

Our Nig; or, Sketches from the Life of a Free Black, in a Two-Story White House, North. Showing That Slavery's Shadows

Fall Even There. Boston: George C. Rand and Avery, 1859. Reprint, New York: Vintage Books, 1983.

SOURCES

Bell, Bernard W. "Harriet E. Wilson." In *The Afro-American Novel and Its Tradition*. Amherst: University of Massachusetts Press, 1987.

Carby, Hazel. *Reconstructing Womanhood: The Emergence of the Afro-American Woman Novelist*. New York: Oxford University Press, 1987.

Foster, Frances Smith. "Adding Color and Contour to Early American Self-Portraitures: Autobiographical Writings of Afro-American Women." In *Conjuring: Black Women, Fiction, and Literary Tradition*, edited by Marjorie Pryse and Hortense J. Spillers. Bloomington: Indiana University Press, 1985.

Gates, Henry Louis. Introduction. In Harriet E. Wilson, *Our Nig; or, Sketches from the Life of a Free Black, in a Two-Story House, North. Showing That Slavery's Shadows Fall Even There*. Boston: George C. Rand and Avery, 1859. Reprint, New York: Vintage Books, 1983, pp. xi–lv.

———, and David Ames Curtis. "Establishing the Identity of the Author of *Our Nig*." In *Wild Women in the Whirlwind: Afro-American Culture and the Contemporary Literary Renaissance*, edited by Joanne Braxton and Andree Nicola McLaughlin. New Brunswick, N.J.: Rutgers University Press, 1990.

Shockley, Ann Allen. "Harriet E. Adams Wilson." In *Afro-American Women Writers, 1746–1933*. Boston: G. K. Hall, 1988.

Tate, Claudia. "Allegories of Black Female Desire: Or, Rereading Nineteenth-Century Sentimental Narratives of Black Female Authority." In *Changing Our Own Words: Essays on Criticism, theory, and Writing by Black Women*, edited by Cheryl A. Wall, 98–126. New Brunswick, N.J.: Rutgers University Press, 1989.

White, Barbara A. "*Our Nig* and the She-Devil: New Information About Harriet Wilson and the 'Bellmont' Family," *American Literature* 65 (March 1993): 19–52.

WIND FROM AN ENEMY SKY D'ARCY McNICKLE (1978)

In 1936, D'Arcy McNickle's first novel, written under the name "D'Arcy Dahlberg," was rejected by Harcourt, Brace, and Company. One reader's response to the novel, included in the rejection letter, contained a portentous comment: "Perhaps the beginning of a new Indian literature to rival that of [the] Harlem [Renaissance]" (Owens, 60). The novel was eventually published as *The Surrounded*, and the reader's comments proved to be true, as D'Arcy McNickle and John Joseph Mathews are seen today as two writers from the first half of the 20th century who strongly influenced the Indian writers of the 1960s and 1970s. One could argue, perhaps correctly, that these two writers were almost totally responsible for the flourishing Native American Renaissance that took place in the second half of the 20th century.

McNickle was born on the Flathead Indian Reservation in Montana in 1904, and his work, like that of most of his successors, focuses on the people and issues he was exposed to on the reservation. He was particularly interested in traditional Indian cultures, which found their way into his fiction as well as his widely acclaimed anthropological work, *Native American Tribalism*.

Though it went unpublished until after his death in 1977, *Wind From an Enemy Sky* is a novel that offers a strong statement on the relationships and differences between Native Americans and Euro-Americans, with basic themes of language and land or place. But most every area of focus in the novel revolves around difference—the differences between how Indians and whites make use of the land, how they value sacred objects, how they communicate, and, simply, how they live their lives. In almost every aspect, this novel should be considered an early example (along with the work of John Joseph Mathews) of postcolonial writing in the United States. McNickle makes no apologies for his open (and dangerous for his time) criticism of the colonization of Native Americans and how whites have abused the land and the people who lived there before Europeans arrived.

The novel begins as Antoine, the grandson of a chief named Bull, returns from his experience in the government boarding-school system just as two important events occur. He accompanies his grandfather into the mountains so the old man can view, for himself, the existence of a dam that has been built by the whites. The old man, stunned at the concept of someone's stopping the water, is overwhelmed and saddened by the industrial intrusion into his traditional homeland. Soon afterward, Bull's brother Henry Jim, who had chosen 30 years before to follow the white man's ways, returns to Bull's camp with an offer of reconciliation and promising to ask the government agent to help with the return of a sacred bundle that Henry Jim had given to a government museum (the cause of his ostracization from Bull's camp). Thus the central conflict of the novel begins. Henry Jim is eager to become reconciled with his brother and people, and the somewhat-sympathetic agent Rafferty wants to help, hoping that his doing so will convince Bull to come to the reservation as his brother did, an act that all the previous agents had been unable to accomplish.

As readers may suspect, the attempts to regain the Featherboy Bundle are unsuccessful. Adam Pell, the man who is responsible for the dam and who is in possession of the sacred bundle, argues that the Natives should give up on objects of the past and move on with the process of assimilation into the dominant white culture—a life of farming instead of hunting, a life of living in city homes instead of close to the land, a life of rejecting a traditional earth-based religion and becoming Christians.

It is important to note that Bull, upon seeing the dam for the first time, fires at the concrete structure repeatedly and uselessly with his .22 rifle. This may seem like a minor detail in the plot, but it is actually very significant. As critic Louis Owens and others have pointed out, Bull's shooting at the dam is symbolic of the Native American's struggle with white colonization. The dam, which is technologically impressive, is representative of white culture and its intrusion on the land. The Indian, shooting at it hopelessly with a very small caliber rifle, can do nothing to stop the intrusion. There are other gunshots in the novel that are important as well. A young man named Pock Face (think smallpox and germ warfare) shoots Adam Pell's nephew, and when Bull's people come to the agency hoping to receive their sacred bundle, Bull shoots both Adam Pell and the agent Rafferty when they are told that the bundle, which they held as an extremely sacred object, had been destroyed by mice in storage. Bull is then killed by The Boy, leaving his grandson Antoine to continue to struggle to find peace between Indians and whites.

It may be difficult for readers to pin down the time/place setting of *Wind from an Enemy Sky,* and perhaps McNickle confuses his readers intentionally. In the novel, we encounter modern dams, sidewalks, and lawn sprinklers, yet Bull and his people live in the mountains outside the agency (reservation) and live in a traditional manner, somewhat isolated from the influence of the white world. McNickle may want readers to become lost in time so they may fully consider the damage that the white intrusion does to the small band living in the mountains and, in a larger sense, the damage that colonization has done to Native American cultures as a whole.

SOURCES

Allen, Paula Gunn. "Whose Dream Is This Anyway?" In *The Sacred Hoop: Recovering the Feminine in American Indian Traditions,* 76–85. Boston: Beacon Press, 1986.

McNickle, D'Arcy. *Wind from an Enemy Sky.* Albuquerque: University of New Mexico Press, 1988.

Owens, Louis. "Maps of the Mind: John Joseph Mathews and D'Arcy McNickle." In *Other Destinies: Understanding the American Indian Novel,* 48–89. Norman: University of Oklahoma Press, 1992.

James Mayo

WINDS OF WAR, THE HERMAN WOUK (1971)

Herman WOUK achieved early critical and commercial success, especially with his third novel, *The CAINE MUTINY* (1951), for which he received a Pulitzer Prize. For that novel, he drew directly on his experiences as a naval officer during World War II. Its success made him begin to conceive a much more expansive fictional treatment of the war, a novel that would suggest the massive scale on which the war had been conducted. Although Wouk's next three novels—*Marjorie Morningstar* (1955), *Youngblood Hawke* (1962), and *Don't Stop the Carnival* (1965)—were commercially successful (all three were, for instance, Book of the Month Club selections), the critical response seemed to become more mixed with each novel. Wishing to recover the critical standing he had earned with *The Caine Mutiny,* Wouk resurrected his dormant plan for a broader novelistic treatment of the war. After devoting more than half a decade to primary as well as secondary research on the war, he began to draft the novel that would become *The Winds of War.* His research, however, had yielded so much rich material that there was too much to fit into one novel, even one that would approach a thousand pages. Wouk decided to split the narrative into two novels, each of which would ultimately approach a thousand pages: *The Winds of War,* covering the events from 1936 to the Japanese attack on Pearl Harbor, and *War and Remembrance,* covering the period of direct U.S. involvement in the war from Pearl Harbor to the Japanese surrender.

Given Wouk's ambitions, it is ironic that these two novels would cement his reputation as a commercially successful novelist whose work lacks the subtlety, complexity, and ambiguity that, taken together, define great literature. *The Winds of War* was number seven on the composite list of the best-selling novels of 1971 and number six on the list for 1972. It would more briefly rejoin the best-seller lists in 1983, when the television miniseries adapted from it became one of the most-watched programs in television history.

While readers found Wouk's depiction of historical events to be absorbing and his characters to be engaging American types, critics felt that the historical material sometimes overwhelmed—or was simply more interesting than—the fictional elements and that the characters were too much confined to familiar types. The most common complaint, however, was that Wouk's attempt to tell the story through the points of view of the members of one extended family created the preposterous premise that someone from the family would be present at just about every major historical event between 1936 and 1941. So, although critics expressed admiration for Wouk's ambition and for his efforts to present an authentic sense of historical events, they were almost unanimous in their judgment that *The Winds of War* and *War and Remembrance* do not warrant inclusion with the best novels about World War II.

The Winds of War opens with the assignment of American Captain Victor "Pug" Henry as naval attaché to Berlin. Although he is not especially tall, Pug is a physically imposing man with the bearing of someone who demands to be taken seriously. He has much more skill and subtlety as a diplomat and as an intelligence agent than one might expect. The Nazis have consolidated their power in Germany and are beginning to make threatening gestures toward their neighbors. Pug's mission is to make an assessment on the seriousness and immediacy of the threat. Shortly after his arrival in Berlin, Pug is formally introduced to Hitler himself. From his contacts with Germans not naturally sympathetic to the Nazis, such as the conservative general Armin von Roon, and from his own attention to the news and to rumors, Pug subsequently learns enough about the direction of Nazi diplomacy to predict the seemingly unthinkable nonaggression pact between Nazi Germany and the Soviet Union, states that were ideologically antagonistic. The almost singular insight that Pug demonstrates with this prediction of this pact brings him to the notice of President Roosevelt, who, after a face-to-face meeting, makes Pug one of his informal personal emissaries. This role takes Pug not only back to Berlin, but to London, Rome, and Moscow, where he has access to most of the major personalities who are shaping the events that lead to the outbreak of war in the European and then the Asian theaters. At the end of *The Winds of War,* Pug arrives in Honolulu the day after the devastating Japanese attack on Pearl Harbor.

The other members of the Henry family provide firsthand perspectives on events in still further corners of the world. As Pug becomes more peripatetic, his wife, Rhoda, settles back in the United States. A somewhat self-involved personality, who drinks too much and resents her husband's absences, Rhoda eventually engages in an extended affair with a scientist who becomes involved in the Manhattan Project. The Henrys' oldest son, Byron, becomes involved with a young Jewish woman named Natalie Jastrow, who is living in Italy with her learned uncle. Together, Byron and Natalie witness not only Fascist Italy's increasing commitment to an alliance with the Nazis, but also the Nazis' invasion of Poland and the destruction of Warsaw. Byron's less-bookish brother, Warren, pursues a career as a fighter pilot as the American military leadership attempts almost overnight to create a credible fighting force. Their sister, Madeline, is employed in the fledgling television industry, where she has contacts with all sorts of celebrities in entertainment and politics alike. Through Rhoda, Warren, and Madeline, Wouk provides a variegated view of life in America as the nation seemed to be drifting just behind the rest of the world toward a catastrophic war.

SOURCES

Beichman, Arnold. *Herman Wouk: The Novelist as Social Historian.* New Brunswick, N.J.: Transaction, 2004.

Bolton, Richard R. "*The Winds of War* and Wouk's Wish for the World," *Midwest Quarterly* 16 (1975): 389–408.

Bondebjerg, Ib. "Popular Fiction, Narrative and the Melodramatic Epic of American Television," *Dolphin* 17 (1989): 35–51.

Hawley, William M. "Spying on the Margins: George Smiley and Pug Henry," *Culture & Communication* 2 (Summer 1999): 129–146.

Mazzeno, Laurence W. "Herman Wouk (1915–   )." In *Contemporary Jewish-American Novelists: A Bio-Critical Sourcebook,* edited by Joel Shatzky and Michael Taub, 460–467. Westport, Conn.: Greenwood, 1997.

Phillipson, John S. "Herman Wouk and Thomas Wolfe," *Thomas Wolfe Review* 12 (Fall 1988): 33–37.

Zhang, Yidong. "Two Panoramas about Great Wars," *Journal of Popular Culture* 19 (Summer 1985): 57–63.

Martin Kich

WINTER IN THE BLOOD JAMES WELCH

(1974) Perhaps arriving in a very timely fashion, James WELCH's first novel, *Winter in the Blood,* helped established Welch as a major figure in what critic Kenneth Lincoln dubbed the "Native American Renaissance," a period of interest in Native American writing that began in the late 1960s and peaked in the 1970s. Many works by Native American authors in this time period, including Welch, twist together traditional Native modes of storytelling and other cultural ideas with plots that reflect the life of contemporary Native peoples, focusing on the bleak life on modern reservations, alcoholism, depression, suicide, and feelings of alienation. Another important thematic idea prevalent in many of these works concerns the psychological impact of the loss of traditional ways of life, especially for males, who in the past were considered warriors charged with the task of protecting their communities.

When first introduced to *Winter in the Blood,* readers find a deceptively simple tale of a young reservation Indian's attempt to recover a rifle and an electric razor that were stolen by his former girlfriend. The unnamed narrator's quest to find this woman and regain his possessions takes him on a series of strange, somewhat inter-connected incidents that seem to give the novel an almost absurdist feel. Divided into three sections of roughly 60 pages each, the action follows the unnamed narrator's activities on the reservation (mostly internal and family matters), his flashbacks to the past as he tries to come to terms with the unrelated deaths of his father and brother, and his trips off the reservation to the small cities of Harlem and Havre in the northern extremes of Montana.

At home, he is faced with the usual reservation activities. His life is boring (he fishes in a river that has no fish; he flips through popular magazines looking for an article he hasn't already read), which is probably related to the fact that he's 35 and still living with his mother, her new husband, and his aged grandmother. He has duties on his mother's ranch that he has to attend to with Lame Bull, his mother's husband. He listens to his grandmother's stories about the past and visits an old prophet, Yellow Calf, who can fill in the gaps in the traditional stories. There's plenty of drinking around the kitchen table with family and friends. On the other hand, life off the reservation offers something of adventure. His trips into town to find the woman who stole his razor and gun find him "rolling" a drunk white man and helping steal his wallet; pursuing drinking and sexual interludes in the local bars; getting a broken nose, when the brother of his ex-girlfriend punches him when he doesn't expect it; and becoming involved in a strange, absurd intrigue with a local tourist known only as "the airplane man." None of these events have any meaning for the narrator, though, and it's only at home on the reservation that he can find what he's looking for.

In *Other Destinies: Understanding the American Indian Novel,* Louis Owens introduces a very useful method of interpreting this novel. Owens points out that the novel contains a great deal of myth, from both American Indian and "western" (that is, European) mythologies, arguing that Welch has "great fun parodying" the Fisher King myth, as notably portrayed in T. S. Eliot's modern poem *The Waste Land* (132). In the ancient grail myth, the Fisher King has been maimed and becomes unable to tend to his lands, which then fall into disrepair and infertility. In order for the lands to become fertile again, the Fisher King must be healed and restored (Weston, 2).

Owens's reference to the Fisher King and *The Waste Land* can easily be expanded to offer a comprehensive way of looking at the novel. Welch's narrator, who is nameless (the Fisher King has several names himself), is on a quest himself that has similarities to both some Native American spiritual quests and the quest for spiritual enlightenment similar to that of the Fisher King. The novel is loaded with images that suggest both death and the idea that the land is arid and sterile: "burnt grass" (1); "the dry, cracked gumbo flats" (2); "dried crushed chokeberries" (3); a stagnant river devoid of fish; "the dry irrigation ditch" (26). And like the Fisher King, who is maimed both physically and mentally, the narrator suffers from a knee injury that occurred in the same accident in which his brother was killed and an emotional scar resulting from the guilt he feels from his brother's death. He knows that something is not right in the world and that he must come to terms with the death of his brother to gain full emotional and psychological recovery. The Fisher King of the novel must be restored physically and mentally, and the Holy Water sprinkled by his Catholic mother (40) is not quite enough.

But it's T. S. Eliot's version of the Fisher King story that Welch obviously found appealing, probably because Eliot's poem captures the modern sensibility (hopelessness, despair, sexual dysfunction) so well. The novel is rich with allusions to Eliot's poem—from the Fisher King motif to the sterility of the land to the drunken secretary the narrator meets and tries to seduce (a typist and a pimple-faced young man who have awkward sex in Section III of Eliot's poem) to the blind Indian prophet (the blind prophet Tiresias in Eliot) to the quest for answers and redemption.

The young narrator never really finds the answers he's looking for (his rifle and razor aren't returned and his brother is still dead), but the blind Indian prophet named Yellow Calf, who speaks to the animals and knows of tradition, leads him to an answer that he did not know he was searching for. Like Tiresias in *The Waste Land*, Yellow Calf knows and sees all things and serves as a link between the narrator and his traditional Indian past. As the old man talks of the old days, the narrator comes to realize that Yellow Calf is actually his grandfather, as Yellow Calf cared for and developed a relationship with the narrator's grandmother years before when her husband was killed in a battle with white soldiers. It seems that this would only cause more confusion for the narrator, but once this knowledge is gained, the skies open up and rain comes to the valley, suggesting that the Fisher King and order have been restored to the land.

SOURCES

Lincoln, Kenneth. "Blackfeet Winter Blues: James Welch." In *Native American Renaissance*. Berkeley: University of California Press, 1983.

McFarland, Ron, ed. *James Welch*. Lewiston, Idaho: Confluence Press, 1986.

———. *Understanding James Welch*. Columbia: University of South Carolina Press, 2000.

Owens, Louis. "Earthboy's Return: James Welch's Acts of Recovery." In *Other Destinies: Understanding the American Indian Novel*. Norman: University of Oklahoma Press, 1992.

Welch, James. *Winter in the Blood*. New York: Penguin, 1986.

Weston, Jessie L. *The Quest of the Holy Grail*. New York: Haskell House, 1965.

Wild, Peter. *James Welch*. Boise State University Western Writers Series Number 57. Boise, Idaho: Boise State University, 1983.

James Mayo

WINTER OF OUR DISCONTENT, THE

JOHN STEINBECK (1961)   As STEINBECK told a reporter in England, the theme of *The Winter of Our Discontent* is immorality. Using the Hawley family of New Baytown as representative of every American, the novel condemns the American nation as soft, comfortable, and content. Steinbeck's *The Winter of Our Discontent* grew out of two aborted attempts at transforming and modernizing older texts. Begun in 1958, the first work, *Don Keehan,* was a modern western and was evidently a takeoff on Cervantes's *Don Quixote;* it was also interrelated with a second work, an adaptation of Malory's *Morte D'Arthur,* since both legends and quests were direct descendants of each other and were, Steinbeck felt, in some way intermingled with the American Dream. Consequently, Steinbeck decided to use the translation of Arthur to say what he wanted to say about his own time: condemning its immorality and decrying the decay of such values as loyalty, courtesy, courage, and honor.

Another source for the novel was the Steinbeck short story "How Mr. Hogan Robbed a Bank," which was first published in the *Atlantic Monthly* in March 1956. In fact, some of the story's details have direct parallels in *Winter*. Hogan is a grocery clerk like Ethan Allen, and he schemes to rob the bank next to his grocery on the Saturday night before Labor Day. Unlike Ethan, however, he goes through with the robbery, obtaining $8,320. Yet another factor in the composition of *Winter* was the fact that Steinbeck had discovered that the new generation, including his own sons, was being raised by example to believe that success was more important than honesty and that greed and lack of principles had become an accepted norm. Specifically, the television quiz show scandals and the election of 1960 influenced the production of *Winter*. Steinbeck felt that the scandal over the TV game show, *The $64,000 Question*, especially scholar Charles van Doren's involvement in the fraud, asserted America's superficiality and greed.

Steinbeck saw the conflict on which the novel is centered (Ethan Hawley's betrayal of himself and his brother Danny Taylor) in larger terms. Thus the Bible, Shakespeare's sonnets and plays, especially *Richard III*, Malory's *Morte D'Arthur*, and documents from American history are all alluded to in important ways by the text. Not surprisingly, the Republican candidate for president, Richard Nixon, became for Steinbeck a symbol for such degradation in the political scene. His given name in Richard fit well into America's Revolutionary past (as in Ben Franklin's *Poor Richard's Almanack*) and also provided an association with the villainous Richard III who betrayed both his brothers for a kingdom and for an increase in his estate. The biblical characters of Judas and Cain were also natural associations with "tricky Dick," suggesting still another betrayal of a friend/brother that causes his ultimate death.

Steinbeck's manipulation of religious images is perhaps the most obvious technique used in *The Winter of Our Discontent*. The temptation, betrayal, crucifixion, and burial of Christ provide a time pattern for the first half of the novel and shape its characters as well. Religious images thus appear and disappear, and some merge into paradoxical opposites that suggest the characters' good and evil natures simultaneously. The first section of the book begins on Good Friday and ends on Easter Tuesday. During this brief time period, Steinbeck brings his protagonist Ethan Allen Hawley (suggesting a New England pronunciation of "holy") to a confrontation of his two natures—sinful and godly. Like Christ before him, Ethan must decide if he can bear the temptations of the world and conquer them. The other option is, of course, to capitulate, worshipping power, prestige, and money as the new American gods and ignoring the moral beliefs on which this country was founded.

Three more temptations remain before Ethan capitulates to "death." First, the bank president, Mr. Baker, urges Ethan to invest his wife's legacy. However, despite Baker's convincing argument, Ethan recognizes that at this point he is unwilling to risk his wife's legacy to gain more wealth. Second, Margie Young-Hunt, the town whore, offers herself to Ethan. Despite her suggestive words and her attempts at seduction, Ethan is able to resist the temptation of the flesh by quoting the Gospel for Good Friday. The third temptation occurs as Ethan is confronted in the dark store by Mr. Biggers, an agent for B. B. D. & D. Wholesalers, who asks Ethan to deceive his boss, Alfio Marullo, and buy from Biggers in return for a 5 percent kickback. Biggers jests at Ethan's honesty and his suggestion that he will turn the 5 percent over to Marullo. To Biggers, no sin is involved, and he offers a richly constructed wallet as a bribe. This time Ethan capitulates. He recognizes that a betrayal of Marullo will win him the grocery store, a betrayal Baker will bring him power and prestige, and a betrayal of Danny will restore riches as well as an increased social status (he can sell Danny's property for a planned airport). As the novel's central metaphor, betrayal implies that selling one's soul has become the norm of society.

Ethan's subsequent visit to his "Place," a cave about five feet deep carved into the harbor, prefigures his eventual death and burial. Thus Ethan's entry into the cave begins a subsequent moral decline and a loss to an unholy Trinity of mortal and materialistic temptations. Ethan's descent into hell begins approximately on Holy Saturday; his eyes are suddenly open to the world around him, and he appears to others as a changed man. Ironically, he also receives more respect for his Judas traits than for his Christian ones.

Not surprisingly, very few residents of New Bay town are shocked by Ethan's changes since, like the majority of Americans, he maintains the facade of respectability and makes his motives appear pure rather than tainted. Easter Tuesday reveals an Ethan who has been thoroughly "converted" to evil but who maintains a paradoxical revulsion for moral betrayal on higher levels. Although Ethan maintains he has changed goals and is no longer influenced by morality, he still exhibits a double standard by expecting his children to reject his self-centered role modeling. Unfortunately, he fails to see his own duplicity and continues his "descent into hell," though at times he inexplicably calls out to Mary, his wife, to serve as his intercessor (the role of the Virgin Mary) and to guard him from evil within and without. Other biblical symbols used by Steinbeck involve Margie Young-Hunt (the town whore with a witchlike personality). Margie's visions reveal Ethan as the hanged man in the tarot pack and as a snake shedding its skin. This snake image also brings to mind Steinbeck's preoccupation with the book of Genesis and the first stories of mankind. Thus Ethan's association with the serpent not only reminds the reader of the first temptation in Eden but is complicated by the fact that Ethan also functions as the innocent Adam who is tempted by Margie's sensual Eve.

Steinbeck first examines specific early forefathers, including the protagonist's given name, Ethan Allen. The name recalls a revolutionary war figure who can be historically associated with a takeover of land and with secret attacks on a neighboring country. Moreover, some of the revolutionary Allen's unethical acts were approved by the U.S. Congress, giving him respectability and prestige despite his tendency to play both ends against the middle for his own benefit. The strong parallels to the present-day Ethan are obvious.

The book also examines the original American stock from which Ethan has descended and suggests it is not nearly as pure as he might claim. First of all, Ethan acknowledges he is descended from both Puritans and pirates, underscoring the duality of America. Even though literal piracy is out, the impulse lingers: People

want something for nothing, wealth without effort. Steinbeck asserts that a new generation of greedy Americans, including some of the biggest people in the country, have defected from honor, ethics, and morality and have chosen evil methods to attain desired success. As he observes the past, he recognizes that all of New Baytown is involved in a similar sellout of morality. Consequently, the value of the historical past has become relative since Ethan's present tarnished reputation is revealed to be an inherited trait from the patriarchs who first settled America. Even the admirable words of famous men like Henry Clay, Daniel Webster, Thomas Jefferson, and Abraham Lincoln (patriarchs whose words are plagiarized in Ethan's son's "I Love America" essay) cannot resuscitate the dying morals and values that were once so important.

Yet Ethan's so-called honesty is still impressive to Alfio Marullo, who wants to make a monument to what America once was, a down payment so the light of morality will not flicker and die out. To Marullo, the Statue of Liberty, the Declaration of Independence, and the Bill of Rights are still praiseworthy. The positive side of America is still alive. In fact, Steinbeck symbolizes Marullo's hope for America's future in the July 4 setting of a land of justice, love, and equality. Steinbeck's historical references are designed to reform American society: to motivate the removal of ethnic prejudices, kickbacks, political manipulation, sexual blackmail, and phony real estate promotion. Ethan's remorse about his history, his simultaneous action and regret of action, indicate that perhaps his integrity will return and his morality and America's will be renewed.

Steinbeck's use of literary allusion is significant, especially to Shakespeare's history play *Richard III*. The title is taken from the opening soliloquy and is spoken by the title character himself. This soliloquy effectively sets up the theme of opposites, for in Shakespeare's play, the winter of discontent has been miraculously transformed into summer by the ascension of the Yorkist monarch and the abdication of Henry VI, the Lancastrian holder of the throne. Furthermore, Richard himself is revealed as a paradox. Outwardly he appears to be the helpful servant of his brothers, King Edward IV and the Duke of Clarence, but inwardly he is plotting their deaths and his own ascension to power.

Richard is the epitome of duplicity, providing a clear parallel to Ethan. As Ethan contemplates suicide and returns to the cave to slit his wrists, he is paralleled to King Arthur, too, who despairs over the decline of the Round Table and the rise of his evil nephew/son Mordred. Though Arthur/Ethan may die, the light-bearer of the future is ready to reassume the moral task. Thus as Ethan reaches for the razor blades to slit his wrists, he discovers the family talisman instead. Similar to the Holy Grail in the Arthurian legend, the talisman becomes his salvation. Although a metamorphosis occurs a second time as Ethan dismisses suicide, the reader is still unsure of both Ethan's future and that of his family. The heritage of truth, justice, and honesty is hanging in the balance and its continuance is questionable. It is still threatened by materialism, greed, and selfishness. The reader, as in the Arthur myth, must wait for the return of the king (Jesus/religious morality) before a restored Camelot (Paradise) can be attained. This renewal takes on historical meaning as well when associated with the Kennedy presidency and the descriptions of a return to Camelot, where knightly actions would right wrongs by means of potent deeds and legislation. As Steinbeck has skillfully shown, Ethan and the America he stands for are at that low point. The jeremiad was designed to recall them to a higher purpose.

Steinbeck's interweaving of biblical, historical, and literary texts in this story of America's declining morals indicates the complexity of the work. What appeared to the early critics as weakness now seems an insightful and innovative technique utilized by a determined experimenter. Steinbeck's final novel is an excellent example of the well-crafted tale. His interweaving of opposites, his merging of symbols, and his experimentation with style and humor make the novel a worthy successor to *The Grapes of Wrath* as a social document calling on all America to account for its ambivalent reaction and commitment to moral uprightness.

SOURCES

Astro, Richard, and Tetsumaro Hayashi, eds. *Steinbeck: The Man and His Work.* Corvallis: Oregon State University Press, 1971.

Benson, Jackson L. *The True Adventures of John Steinbeck, Writer: A Biography.* New York: Viking, 1984.

French, Warren. *John Steinbeck's Fiction Revisited.* New York: Twayne, 1994.

Hayashi, Tetsumaro, ed. *John Steinbeck: The Years of Greatness, 1936–1939.* Tuscaloosa: University of Alabama Press, 1993.

———. *A New Study Guide to Steinbeck's Major Works, with Critical Explications.* Metuchen, N.J.: Scarecrow Press, 1993.

McElrath, Joseph R., Jr., Jesse S. Crisler, and Susan Shillinglaw, eds. *John Steinbeck: The Contemporary Reviews.* New York: Cambridge University Press, 1996.

Owens, Louis. *John Steinbeck's Re-Vision of America.* Athens: University of Georgia Press, 1985.

Parini, Jay. *John Steinbeck: A Biography.* New York: Holt, 1995.

Simmonds, Roy S. *John Steinbeck: The War Years, 1939–1945.* Lewisburg, Pa.: Bucknell University Press, 1996.

Tedlock E. W., and C. V. Wicker, eds. *Steinbeck and His Critics: A Record of Twenty-five Years.* Albuquerque: University of New Mexico Press, 1957.

Timmerman, John H. *John Steinbeck's Fiction: The Aesthetics of the Road Taken.* Norman: University of Oklahoma Press, 1986.

Michael J. Meyer

WISE BLOOD Flannery O'Connor (1952)

In 1962, 10 years after publishing *Wise Blood,* Flannery O'Connor explained her first novel was "about a Christian *malgré lui,* and as such, very serious, for all comic novels that are any good must be about matters of life and death" (2). The *malgre lui* is the text's protagonist, Hazel Motes, who finds divine redemption through suffering, despite his attempts to evade both by denouncing Christ. Through the figure of Motes, the novel posits nihilism as a false antithesis to faith, as his asserted belief in nothing inadvertently affirms his faith in Christ. A devout Catholic her entire life, O'Connor develops the theme of redemption in the text by employing comic and grotesque motifs. Using brutal and stark imagery, she challenges modern audiences to abandon secularism by empathizing with the characters' suffering.

The novel opens as Motes returns from his military service on a train headed toward his hometown, although he no longer has family there. While he insists that he is "not a preacher" and does not "believe in anything" (15), Motes becomes the only member of his newly established Church Without Christ once he settles into the city. In Motes's aggressive efforts to denounce Christ, he visits Mrs. Watts, a prostitute; tries to avoid Enoch Emory, the only man to show him friendship; and resists the advances of Sabbath Lily, despite his earlier resolution to seduce her. Although he avoids Sabbath, Motes becomes obsessed with the con artist Asa Hawks, her father. Hawks had once called his former congregation to see the spectacle of his self-blinding as a testament of his proclaimed faith, but he was unable to completely blind himself and is able to see a shocking revelation when Motes discovers the truth.

Disillusioned and eventually displaced from his own church, Motes tries to leave the city, but a police officer destroys his car, prompting Motes to return to his boarding room and successfully blind himself. The end of the novel finds him under the care of his landlady, who discovers Motes has been walking with small rocks and glass in his shoes and has wound barbed wire around his chest. His landlady, Mrs. Flood, tells Motes her desire to marry him because, she explains: "If we don't help each other, Mr. Motes, there's nobody to help us. . . . Nobody. The world is an empty place" (118). However, Motes leaves without responding to her offer, but his dead body is soon returned to her home. With his body laid before her, Mrs. Flood stares "with her eyes shut, into his eyes" until "she saw him moving farther and farther away, farther and farther into the darkness until he was the pin point of light" (120). The landlady's vision suggests that Motes in fact finds redemption as his life of suffering transforms him into the light amid the darkness.

The kind of transformation Motes undergoes, from nihilist to believer, is linked by his continuous view of suffering as symbolic of one's devotion and faith. Until he discovers Hawks's lie, Motes could not believe that a self-blinded preacher could be as "all the way evil" as his daughter claims (62). Certainly, he cannot believe that someone who punishes himself so drastically would not be redeemed. When he discovers Hawks to be a fake, Motes confirms his own belief in ascetic displays of redemption: Only authentic suffering warrants divine redemption.

This link originated with Motes's grandfather and mother, who are dead by the time of the novel. In different ways, they modeled lives of Christian devotion, leaving Motes with the contrary desire to avoid both Christ and pain. Maddened by his own preaching, his grandfather used to point at his grandson, the "mean sinful unthinking boy," and insist that "Jesus would have him in the end" (10). The soul-hungry Jesus, "a wild ragged figure motioning him to turn around and come off into the dark where he was not sure of his footing, where he might be walking on the water and not know it and then suddenly know it and drown," becomes in Motes's mind the object to be avoided (10). For him, this menacing image of Christ embodies the risk of faith, in effect the terror of the unknown.

Motes's resolution to believe in nothing only temporarily staves off the terror but does not resolve it. On the train ride home, Motes thinks explicitly about the deaths of every member of his family. With the exception of his mother, each death signifies grave and terrifying finality, without any sign of resurrection. Even his grandfather, who kept "Jesus hidden in his head like a stinger," dies like everyone else: "they shut the top of his box down and he didn't make a move" (9). Only Motes's mother stirs after death, at least in his imagination, as he "wondered if she walked at night" (13). She is also the first ascetic Motes knows; she always and only wore long black dresses and deprived herself of pleasure. Affecting his mother's asceticism as a boy, Motes's first experience with self-inflicted suffering does not relieve him of his guilt. Hence, he comes to believe his repentance does not satisfy Christ, and he is haunted into adulthood by unrelenting guilt: "He had the feeling that everything he saw was a broken-off piece of some giant blank thing that he had forgotten had happened to him" (38). He mistakenly assumes that he has done something, so his adulthood denial of Christ cannot protect him, since the "giant blank thing" is original sin, a much greater burden than he realizes.

Yet Sabbath is correct, in a sense, when she declares that Motes has wanted "Jesus" all along. His final acts of violence to himself are attempts to reconcile his earlier denial of Christ, as he comes to understand that original sin is unavoidable. As a result, he transforms his nihilistic, intellectualized belief. Motes's faith indeed becomes a matter of "life and death," and, as critic Richard Giannone writes, "the would-be nihilist Hazel Motes becomes a saint for our unbelieving age" (Giannone, 9).

SOURCES

Edmondson, Henry I. *Return to Good and Evil: Flannery O'Connor's Response to Nihilism.* Lanham, Md.: Rowan & Littlefield Publishing Group, 2002.

Giannone, Richard. *Flannery O'Connor and the Mystery of Love.* Urbana: University of Illinois Press, 1989.

O'Connor, Flannery. *Wise Blood. 3 By Flannery O'Connor.* New York: Penguin Books, 1983. pp. 1–120.

Heather Ostman

WISTER, OWEN (1860–1938)

When the 100th-anniversary edition of Owen Wister's *The VIRGINIAN: A HORSEMAN OF THE PLAINS* appeared in 2002, critic Michael Rogers called it "a beauty" and summed up the work as follows: "Considered by many to be the best Western novel, Wister's work essentially defined the genre, both in print and on film, and also created the archetypal Western hero: the strong silent type who rides in from the range and saves the day by shooting the bad guys full of holes" (Rogers, 124).

Owen Wister was born on July 14, 1860, in Germantown (now part of Philadelphia), Pennsylvania, to Owen Jones Wister, a physician, and Sarah Butler Wister, a writer, linguist, pianist, and daughter of renowned actress Fanny Kemble. Wister, who some consider the creator of the cowboy, America's arguably most enduring cultural icon, was himself from a highly cultivated family, graduated summa cum laude and Phi Beta Kappa from Harvard University in 1882 and counted among his friends Henry Cabot Lodge, President Theodore Roosevelt, artist Frederic Remington, and novelist and editor William Dean HOWELLS. Dissuaded by his parents from a promising musical career, he earned a Harvard law degree and, like authors Edith WHARTON and Charlotte Perkins GILMAN, was treated by Dr. S. Weir Mitchell for a nervous collapse. As a result, Wister headed for Wyoming and began his lifelong love affair with the West. His first book, *Red Men and White* (1895), was a collection of short stories; his first novel, *Lin McLean* (1897), was an interrelated grouping of sketches about Wister's first western hero. In 1898 he married Molly

Channing, an intellectual Philadelphia socialite who worked with needy children until her death in childbirth in 1913. She is the model for the women heroes in both *The Virginian* and *Lady Baltimore* (1906).

The Virginian, Wister's only western, narrated by an outsider unfamiliar with Wyoming, features an unnamed hero who is falsely accused of cheating by the villain, Trampas. It is to Trampas that the Virginian addresses his now classic line, "When you call me that, smile!" On the eve of his marriage to the schoolteacher, Molly Wood, the Virginian kills the evil Trampas in a shoot-out. (The villain draws and shoots first.) Critic Frederic D. Schwarz observes that "The dominant theme throughout is the contrast between Western vigor and Eastern decadence" (Schwarz, 96). His next novel, *Lady Baltimore,* another best-seller, was a comedy of manners set in Charleston, South Carolina. The genealogist narrator has come to Charleston to do research and becomes entranced with the antics of John Mayrant, the hero in search of a wife.

Owen Wister died from a cerebral hemorrhage on July 21, 1938, at his summer home in North Kingston, Rhode Island. In addition to his novels and stories, he wrote several volumes of poetry and biographies of three presidents: Ulysses S. Grant, George Washington, and Theodore Roosevelt. Four film versions of *The Virginian* were released during Wister's lifetime: two, in 1914 and 1923, were silents. The third starred Gary Cooper in 1929, and the fourth in 1946 starred Joel McCrea. A television series employing Wister's title and major characters aired on NBC from 1962 to 1971, and the Western Writers of America has honored significant writers with a lifetime achievement award named for Wister. The bulk of his papers is housed at the Library of Congress.

NOVELS

Lady Baltimore. New York: Macmillan, 1906.

Lin McLean. New York: Harper 1898; reissued Upper Saddle River, N.J.: Literature House, 1970.

The Virginian: A Horseman of the Plains. New York: Macmillan, 1902.

SOURCES

Cobbs, John L. *Owen Wister.* Boston: Twayne, 1984.

Etulain, Richard W. *Owen Wister.* Boise, Idaho: Boise State College Western Writers Series, 1973.

Fifty Years of the Virginian 1902–1952. Laramie: University of Wyoming Library Associates, 1952.

Mason, Julian. "Owen Wister: Champion of Old Charleston," *Quarterly Journal of The Library of Congress* 29 (July 1972): 162–185.

———. "Owen Wister and World War I: Appeal for Pentecost," *Pennsylvania Magazine of History and Biography* 101 (January 1977): 89–102.

Rogers. Michael. Review of Owen Wister's *The Virginian:* 100th-Anniversary Edition, *Library Journal* 128, no. 2 (February 1, 2003), 124.

Rowe, Anne E. *The Enchanted Country: Northern Writers in the South 1865–1910.* Baton Rouge: Louisiana State University Press, 1978, pp. 96–122.

Schwarz, Frederic D. "1902: 'when you call me that, smile!' " *American Heritage* 53, no. 2 (April–May 2002): 96.

Stokes, Frances K. W. *My Father, Owen Wister.* Laramie, Wyo.: (Self-published), 1952.

Vorpahl, Ben Merchant. *My Dear Wister—The Frederic Remington-Owen Wister Letters.* Palo Alto, Calif.: American West Publishing Co., 1972.

White, G. Edward. *The Eastern Establishment and the Western Experience: The West of Frederic Remington, Theodore Roosevelt, and Owen Wister.* New Haven, Conn.: Yale University Press, 1968.

OTHER

Owen Wister (1860–1938). Books and Writers. Available online. URL: http://www.kirjasto.sci.fi/owister.htm. Accessed September 25, 2005.

Philosophy 4 by Owen Wister. Available online. URL: http://world.std.com/~dpbsmith/phil4back.html. Accessed September 25, 2005.

WOLFE, THOMAS CLAYTON (1900–1938)

Thomas Wolfe is remembered today as a genius who attempted to write all of America into his novels and to create a national epic. Also a short story writer and playwright, Wolfe wrote novels, characterized by a lyric exuberance, that employed myth and sociology, symbol and image. During his brief lifetime, he published the Pulitzer Prize–winning LOOK HOMEWARD, ANGEL (1929) and *Of Time and the River* (1935), massive autobiographical novels cut drastically for publication by Maxwell Perkins, his editor at Scribners. When Wolfe realized that Perkins did not fully understand his intent to move from a focus on his character's youth to a focus on American life itself, he switched editors and publishers. Unfortunately, he did not live to see his edited 1 million word manuscript in print: At age 38, Wolfe died of pneumonia and tuberculosis, and Edward C. Aswell, the editor at Harper and Brothers, reduced and published *The Web and the Rock* (1939) and *You Can't Go Home Again* (1940). Because the manuscript was excised, scholars have never been entirely comfortable with the published versions of these novels, and in 2001, Arlyn Bruccoli and Matthew J. Bruccoli published *O Lost: A Story of the Buried Life,* the original manuscript of *Look Homeward, Angel.*

Thomas Clayton Wolfe was born on October 3, 1900, to William O. Wolfe, a tombstone cutter, and Julia Elizabeth Westall Wolfe, who ran a successful Asheville boarding house. He matriculated at the University of North Carolina at Chapel Hill at age 15, loaded cargo and ammunition at the Newport News, Virginia, docks in 1918, graduated in 1920, and earned his master's degree from Harvard University in 1922. While teaching at New York University, Wolfe met Sinclair LEWIS and F. Scott FITZGERALD. Of great importance is his meeting with Aline Bernstein, a married woman 17 years his senior, with whom he had a celebrated five-year love affair. He dedicated *Look Homeward, Angel* to her and modeled Esther (in *The Web and the Rock*) after her. *Look Homeward, Angel* features Eugene Gant, a clearly autobiographical figure, as he progresses through childhood and early adulthood. He falls into and emerges from the traps that are in his path to artistic success and spiritual tranquillity. *Of Time and the River* continues where *Look Homeward, Angel* ends, as Eugene Gant, now in Europe, is homesick—he describes memorably vivid scenes of American life. On the ship returning home, he falls in love with Esther Jack. In the posthumously published *The Web and the Rock,* George Webber, a successful novelist, passionately loves, and then leaves, the beautiful Esther Jack. He flees New York for Europe, only to find that Hitler has risen to power. Like its predecessor, *You Can't Go Home Again,* the sequel, also ponders increasingly the human propensity for evil and violence, leading Webber to excoriate the idle wealthy and to feel compassion for the less fortunate.

Thomas Wolfe studies, including the Thomas Wolfe Society and several Web sites, are flourishing. More of his original manuscripts are forthcoming. Wolfe's manuscripts and papers have been dispersed among several major university libraries: the Houghton Library of Harvard University; the Wilson Library of the University of North Carolina at Chapel Hill; the Braden-Hatchett Thomas Wolfe Collection at Memphis State University; the Sarah Graham Kenan Library of St. Mary's College in Raleigh, North Carolina; and the Pack Memorial Library in Asheville, North Carolina.

NOVELS AND NOVELLAS

From Death to Morning. New York: Scribner, 1935.

The Hills Beyond. New York and London: Harper, 1941.

Look Homeward, Angel. New York: Scribner, 1929.

The Lost Boys: A Novella. Edited by James W. Clark, Jr. Chapel Hill: University of North Carolina Press, 1992.

Of Time and the River. New York: Scribner, 1935.

O Lost: A Story of the Buried Life. Original manuscript of *Look Homeward, Angel.* Text established by Arlyn Bruccoli and Matthew J. Bruccoli. Columbia: University of South Carolina Press, 2001.

The Party at Jack's. Edited by Suzanne Stutman and John L. Idol, Jr. Chapel Hill: University of North Carolina Press, 1995.

The Short Novels of Thomas Wolfe. Edited by C. Hugh Holman. New York: Scribner, 1961.

The Starwick Episodes. Edited by Richard S. Kennedy. Baton Rouge: Louisiana State University Press, 1994.

The Story of a Novel. New York and London: Scribner, 1936.

The Web and the Rock. New York and London: Harper, 1939.

You Can't Go Home Again. New York and London: Harper, 1940.

SOURCES

Berg, A. Scott. *Max Perkins: Editor of Genius.* New York: Dutton, 1978.

Bruccoli, Matthew J., and Park Bucker, eds. *To Loot My Life Clean: The Thomas Wolfe–Maxwell Perkins Correspondence.* Chapel Hill: University of South Carolina Press, 2001.

Donald, David Herbert. *Look Homeward: A Life of Thomas Wolfe.* Boston: Little, Brown, 1987.

Evans, Elizabeth. *Thomas Wolfe.* New York: Ungar, 1984.

Field, Leslie A. *Thomas Wolfe and His Editors.* Norman: University of Oklahoma Press, 1987.

Griffin, John Chandler. *Memories of Thomas Wolfe: A Pictorial Companion to "Look Homeward, Angel."* Columbia, S.C.: Summerhouse Press, 1996.

Holman, C. Hugh. *The Loneliness at the Core: Studies in Thomas Wolfe.* Baton Rouge: Louisiana State University Press, 1975.

Idol, John Lane, Jr. *A Thomas Wolfe Companion.* Westport, Conn.: Greenwood, 1987.

Johnson, Elmer D. *Of Time and Thomas Wolfe: A Bibliography with a Character Index of His Works.* Metuchen, N.J.: Scarecrow, 1959.

Johnson, Pamela Hansford. *Hungry Gulliver.* New York: Scribner, 1948; republished as *The Art of Thomas Wolfe.* New York: Scribner, 1963.

Johnston, Carol Ingalls. *Of Time and the Artist: Thomas Wolfe, His Novels, and the Critics.* Columbia, S.C.: Camden House, 1995.

———. *Thomas Wolfe: A Descriptive Bibliography.* Pittsburgh, Pa.: University of Pittsburgh Press, 1987.

Kennedy Richard S., and Paschal Reeves, eds. *The Notebooks of Thomas Wolfe.* 2 volumes. Chapel Hill: University of North Carolina Press, 1970.

Magi, Aldo P., and Richard Walser, eds. *Thomas Wolfe Interviewed.* Baton Rouge and London: Louisiana State University Press, 1985.

Norwood, Hayden. *The Marble Man's Wife.* New York: Scribner, 1947.

Phillipson, John S. *Thomas Wolfe: A Reference Guide.* Boston: G. K. Hall, 1977.

Reeves, Paschal ed. *Studies in Look Homeward, Angel.* Columbus, Ohio: Charles E. Merrill, 1970.

———, ed. *Thomas Wolfe: The Critical Reception.* New York: Lewis, 1974.

Ryssel, Fritz Heinrich. *Thomas Wolfe.* New York: Ungar, 1972.

Snyder, William U. *Thomas Wolfe: Ulysses and Narcissus.* Athens: Ohio University Press, 1971.

Steele, Richard. *Thomas Wolfe: A Study in Psychoanalytic Literary Criticism.* Philadelphia: Dorrance, 1976.

Walser, Richard. *Thomas Wolfe, Undergraduate.* Durham, N.C.: Duke University Press, 1977.

———. *Thomas Wolfe: An Introduction and Interpretation.* New York: Barnes & Noble, 1961.

Wheaton, Mabel Wolfe, and Legette Blythe. *Thomas Wolfe and His Family.* Garden City, N.Y.: Doubleday, 1961.

Wheelock, John Hall, ed. *Editor to Author: The Letters of Maxwell E. Perkins.* New York: Scribner, 1950.

OTHER

The Thomas Wolfe Society Web Site. Available online. URL: http://www.thomaswolfe.org. Accessed September 25, 2005.

The Thomas Wolfe Web Site. Available online. URL: http://library.uncwil.edu/wolfe.html. Accessed September 27, 2005.

WOLFE, TOM (THOMAS KENNERLY WOLFE, JR.) (1931–)

The quintessential counterculture novelist and nonfiction writer of the late 20th century, Tom Wolfe, reminiscent of Mark TWAIN in his ever-present trademark white suit, has been an icon of pop culture since his emergence on the literary scene in the late 1960s. Like Truman CAPOTE, Wolfe wrote what became known as the New Journalism, a blending of factual information into a short story or novel. His first book of essays, *The Kandy-Kolored Tangerine-Flake Streamline Baby* (1965), a satiric treatment of 1960s pop culture icons, preceded *The Electric Kool-Aid Acid Test* (1968), his account of his travels with novelist Ken KESEY and the Merry Pranksters on their psychedelic bus. *The Right Stuff* (1979) won both an American Book Award and a National Book Award and was acclaimed for its depiction of real-life astronauts and the wonders of space. His first traditionally constructed novel, *The BONFIRE OF THE VANITIES* (1987), about racial, ethical, and legal issues in contemporary New York City, remained on the best-seller lists for 10 weeks. *A Man in Full* (1998) examines the concept of a satisfying life at the beginning of the new millennium. His latest novel, *I Am Charlotte Simmons,* examines modern college life through the eyes of a brilliant but naive young heroine. Wolfe continues to be known for his inimitable style, which uses slang, vernacular, satire, exclamation points, and a journalist's eye for detail to involve the reader in Wolfe's current subject.

Tom Wolfe was born on March 2, 1931, in Richmond, Virginia, to Thomas Kennerly Wolfe, a scientist and business executive, and Helen Hughes Wolfe. He was educated at Washington and Lee University (B.A., cum laude, 1951) and Yale University (Ph.D., 1957). A journalist and correspondent for the *New York Herald Tribune,* he published his first book in 1965 and married Sheila Berger, art director of *Harper's* magazine in 1978. His first "nonfiction novel," *The Right Stuff,* features the seven astronauts in the Mercury program, focusing particularly on Alan Shepard, John Glenn, and Chuck Yeager; he contrasts the public and the private personas of each man, and relates the world of test pilots to the larger culture of mainstream America. *The Bonfire of the Vanities,* a novel about contemporary New York that many critics call Wolfe's Dickensian novel, follows

Wolfe's protagonist, bond trader Sherman McCoy, on a painful journey. McCoy's mistress hits a young African American while the two are driving through Harlem. McCoy is blamed for the accident and becomes enmeshed in the American criminal justice system as well as in the turbulent urban class and racial divisions. *A Man in Full* (1998), follows Charles Croker, a 60-year-old Atlanta real estate developer who meets a 23-year-old unemployed factory worker. *I Am Charlotte Simmons* describes the frenzy of college life from the point of view of a brilliant, previously sheltered female student.

Thomas Wolfe lives in New York with his wife. In 1983, Warner Brothers adapted *The Right Stuff* for a film of the same title. *Bonfire of the Vanities,* directed by Brian DePalma and starring Tom Hanks, Melanie Griffith, and Bruce Willis, was filmed and released in 1990.

NOVELS

The Bonfire of the Vanities. New York: Farrar, Straus, 1987.
I Am Charlotte Simmons. New York: Farrar, Straus, 2004.
A Man in Full. New York: Farrar, Straus, 1998.
The Right Stuff. New York: Farrar, Straus, 1979.

SOURCES

Bellamy, Joe David, ed. *The New Fiction: Interviews with Innovative American Writers.* Champaign: University of Illinois Press, 1974.
Bing, Jonathan. "Tom Wolfe on Top," *Publishers Weekly* 245, no. 49 (December 7, 1998): 37–39.
Connery, Thomas B., ed. *A Sourcebook of American Literary Journalism: Representative Writers in an Emerging Genre.* Westport, Conn.: Greenwood Press, 1992.
Crowther, Hal. "Clinging to the Rock: A Novelist's Choices in the New Mediocracy," *South Atlantic Quarterly* 89 (Spring 1990): 321–336.
Epstein, Mikhail. "Tom Wolfe and Social(ist) Realism," *Common Knowledge* 1, no. 2 (Fall 1992): 147–160.
Harvey, Chris. "Tom Wolfe's Revenge," *American Journalism Review* (October 1994): 40–46.
Hellmann, John. *Fables of Fact: The New Journalism as New Fiction.* Urbana: University of Illinois Press, 1981.
Konas, Gary. "Traveling 'Furthur' with Tom Wolfe's Heroes," *Journal of Popular Culture* 28 no. 3 (Winter 1994): 177–191.
Lounsberry, Barbara. "Tom Wolfe's American Jeremiad." in *The Art of Fact: Contemporary Artists of Nonfiction.* Westport, Conn.: Greenwood Press, 1990.
McKeen, William. *Tom Wolfe.* Englewood Cliffs, N.J.: Prentice Hall, 1995.

O'Sullivan, John. "Honor amid the Ruins," *American Spectator* 32, no. 1 (January 1999): 64–68.

Reilly, Charlie. "Interview: Tom Wolfe," *On The Bus* 6, no. 1, issue 13 (Winter 1993–Spring 1994): 226–229.

Scura, Dorothy, ed. *Conversations with Tom Wolfe.* Jackson: University Press of Mississippi, 1990.

Shomette, Doug, ed. *The Critical Response to Tom Wolfe.* Westport, Conn.: Greenwood Press, 1992.

Special Tom Wolfe Issue. *Journal of American Culture* 14 (Fall 1991).

Special Tom Wolfe Issue. *Journal of Popular Culture* 9 (Summer 1975).

Stull, James N. *Literary Selves: Autobiography and Contemporary American Nonfiction.* Westport, Conn.: Greenwood Press, 1993.

Towers, Robert. "The Flap over Tom Wolfe: How Real Is the Retreat from Realism?" *New York Times Book Review,* 28 January 1990, pp. 15–16.

Varsava, Jerry A. "Tom Wolfe's Defense of the New (Old) Social Novel: Or, the Perils of the Great White-Suited Hunter," *Journal of American Culture* 14 (Fall 1991): 35–41.

OTHER

Tom Wolfe Web Site. Picador. Available online. URL: http://www.tomwolfe/index2.html. Accessed September 27, 2005.

WOLFF, TOBIAS (JONATHAN ANSELL)

(1945–) Tobias Wolff, winner of the PEN/Faulkner Award for his novella *The BARRACKS THIEF* (1984) and finalist for a National Book Award for his novelistic autobiography, *THIS BOY'S LIFE: A MEMOIR* (1989), writes in spare, muscular prose reminiscent of Ernest HEMINGWAY, one of the many 20th-century writers Wolff admires. On record for his lack of interest in the "self-indulgence" of experimental fiction (Lyons and Oliver, 140), Wolff is renowned for depictions of ordinary middle-class children and adults who frequently find themselves at an ethical crossroads. He uses detail and dialogue in both his fiction and his nonfiction, the latter of which has been praised for its novelistic merits.

Tobias Wolff was born on June 19, 1945, in Birmingham, Alabama, to Arthur Saunders Wolff, an aeronautical engineer, and Rosemary Loftus Wolff, a secretary and waitress. After serving with the U.S. Army Special Forces in Vietnam from 1964 to 1968, Wolff, who had left the service as a first lieutenant, earned a bachelor's degree with first class honors from Oxford University in 1972, a master's degree, also from Oxford, in 1975, and a master's degree from Stanford University in 1978. In 1975, Wolff married Catherine Delores Spohn, a clinical social worker and art history teacher, and published his first novel, *Ugly Rumours.* It follows two young men, Woermer and Grubbs, during their training in officer's candidate school and their departure for the Vietnam War. It was the novella *The Barracks Thief,* however, that brought serious recognition to Wolff. Featuring three paratroopers—Philip Bishop, Hubbard, and Lewis—at Fort Bragg, North Carolina, the tale depicts the unlikely bonding of the three through such experiences as a July 4 fire and an antiwar protest outside the base. When the less intelligent and less appealing Lewis proves to be the man who was stealing from his friends, the matter is resolved unofficially through a "blanket party" and the ethical musings of Bishop, who narrates most of the story in retrospect.

The critically acclaimed *This Boy's Life,* based on Wolff's childhood memories, was an ironic commentary on the idealistic and unrealistic portrayals of American boyhood in the magazine *Boy's Life.* It was followed by *In Pharoah's Army: Memories of the Lost War* (1994), another well-reviewed memoir evoking in all its hellish detail the village of My Tho, Vietnam, where Lieutenant Tobias Wolff served with the U.S. Special Forces. His most recent novel, *Old School* (2003), was nominated for both the PEN/Faulkner and the National Book Critics Circle Award in 2004.

Tobias Wolff lives in Stanford, California, where he is Professor of English and Creative Writing at Stanford University. In 1993, *This Boy's Life: A Memoir* was made into the movie *This Boy's Life,* directed by Michael Caton-Jones and starring Robert De Niro as Wolff's stepfather, Ellen Barkin as Wolff's mother, and Leonardo DiCaprio as Wolff.

NOVELS AND NOVELLAS
The Barracks Thief. New York: Ecco Press, 1984.

Old School. New York: Knopf, 2003.

Ugly Rumours. London: Allen & Unwin, 1975.

SOURCES
Gates, David. "Our Stories, Our Selves," *Newsweek,* 23 January 1989, p. 64.

Gill, Jonathan. "Fourth Grade Never Dies Out," *New York Times Book Review,* 15 January 1989, p. 28.

Lyons, Bonnie, and Bill Oliver. "An Interview with Tobias Wolff." In *Tobias Wolff: A Study of the Short Fiction,* edited by James Hannah, 129–143. New York: Twayne, 1996.

Prose, Francine. "The Brothers Wolff," *New York Times Magazine,* 5 February 1989, pp. 22–31.

Wolff, Geoffrey. "Advice My Brother Never Took," *New York Times Book Review,* 20 August 1989, pp. 1, 22.

OTHER

"A Conversation with Tobias Wolff. *Stanford Home Page.* Available online. URL: http://www.stanford.edu. Accessed September 26, 2005.

Edwards, Jerome. "Tobias Wolff." *Central Booking: The Reading Life Online.* Available online. URL: http://www.centralbooking.com. Accessed September 26, 2005.

Peterson, Anne Palmer. "Talking with Tobias Wolff." Continuum. Available online. URL: http://www.alumni.utah.edu/continuum.summer 98/Finally.html. Accessed September 26, 2005.

"Tobias Wolff." *Salon.com.* Available online. URL: http://www.salon.com/dec96/interview961216.html. Accessed September 26, 2005.

Wolf, Tobias. Interview: Tobias Wolff. By David Schrieberg. Stanford Today. Available online. URL: http://www.stanford.edu/dept/news/stanfordtoday/ed/9809/9809fea101.shtml. Accessed September 27, 2005.

WOMAN OF GENIUS, A MARY AUSTIN (1912)

One of Mary AUSTIN's earliest novels, *A Woman of Genius,* remains, as Nancy Porter observed in 1985, an often "overlooked classic of feminism" (297), despite Austin's recovery as a significant literary regional writer, one whose characters "gain their identity from the regions they inhabit" (Fetterly and Pryse, xvii). Described by its first-person narrator, Olivia Lattimore, as "the story of the struggle between a Genius for Tragic Acting and the daughter of a County Clerk, with the social ideal of Taylorville, Ohianna, for the villain," this "drama" is also, Olivia tells her readers, "one in which none of the characters played the parts they were cast for, and invariably spoke from the wrong cues." It is also one in which there is "no plot," since "plot is distinctly the province of fiction" (Austin, 4). This "plotless" dramatic novel utilizes elements of situational and verbal irony; literary regionalism (particularly in its depiction of the dogmatic social values of an early-20th-century Midwestern small town); psycho-logical, if not mystical, self-discovery (of its first-person narrator); inverted melodramatic conventions; and early 20th-century gender discourse to offer an experimental novel that is neither tragic nor comic.

The novel is divided into four books, each with between six and 10 chapters. Book I begins with a reference to Pauline Mills, a woman who plagues the memory of the narrator, Olivia Lattimore, because Pauline represents the "social ideal" of what a woman is supposed to be, according to the small Midwestern community of Taylorville, Ohianna. That ideal is "true womanliness," which involves legal marriage, doting motherhood, and domestic servility to one's husband (Austin, 3). Olivia recounts the uneasiness of her childhood, one troubled not only by her father's early death and her mother's coldness, but the rigid gender expectations imposed upon her (but not her brother Forester) by her mother and the Taylorville community. In Taylorville, too, she first meets Helmeth Garrett, a man who, with one kiss, awakens something "electrical" in her (Austin, 58) but then leaves town. Shortly after, Olivia becomes engaged to Tommy Bettersworth, a man she does not love but eventually marries (in Book II) for the sake of social convention. In Book II, also, Olivia has a child with Tommy, a child who (like Austin's actual child) is "feeble from birth" (Austin, 79) and eventually dies. This traumatic experience leaves Olivia not only with a deeper understanding of herself as a woman but also a deeper emptiness—an emptiness that eventually leads to the dissolution of her marriage to Tommy and to her career as an actress. Between Books I and II, Olivia also begins to refer to herself in the third person, and these narrative shifts from first to third person reinforce Olivia's self-division and conflicts regarding her early social and gender conditioning in Taylorville. She also meets a colleague, an actress, Sarah Croyden, who will become an increasingly important alternate female "ideal" in the second half of the book. Book II culminates with the death of Olivia's mother and the beginning of her acting career.

Books III and IV continue to explore what Esther Lanigan describes as "the modern ideas in many of Austin's novels, particularly her thoughts about genius . . . and a woman's place in the modern world of the 1910's and 1920's, a world in which the writer deemed herself a 'feminist' " (14). In these final sections, Olivia struggles to and does finally become a successful actress, first in regional theaters, then in Chicago, and finally in New York and London. In Book III, however, Olivia still struggles more with gender roles or irritatingly "true" women such as Pauline Mills (who she literally encounters again) and their often ineffectual male counterparts than with her acting career. Acting, in these sections, becomes a metaphor for any woman who would be an artist, and the theatrical career itself is not as important to Olivia (or Austin) as the process of breaking free from the regional and social constraints imposed upon her in Taylorville. She develops respect and friendship with other theatrical "artists," most notably the actress Sarah Croydon. In Book III, too, Olivia again meets Helmeth Garrett, who still attracts her but is married. However, two years later, in Book IV, Helmeth's wife has died, and when Helmeth and Olivia kiss again, they quickly become lovers. Much of the rest of Book IV details Olivia's conflicted feelings about whether to become Helmeth's wife or to pursue her increasingly successful acting career. This conflict is resolved by Helmeth who, much to Olivia's surprise, becomes engaged to another woman. Book IV concludes not only with Olivia's final encounter and rejection of Pauline Mills as a feminine ideal, but also her bittersweet ruminations and strong conviction to refrain from being "like the other" women, despite the difficulties it will doubtless continue to cause her (Austin, 294).

Although Austin's critics now recognize the significance of *A Woman of Genius* to an understanding of her self-declared feminist perspective, the novel continues to provoke differing views about what that perspective is. For example, while Melody Graulich regards the novel as one "about an exceptional woman" who "explores the importance of support from other women" (140), Nancy Porter believes it reveals Austin's irritation with "groups of women" and belief "in the individual genius leading the group" (311). These seemingly opposite readings are, however, both supported by this novel. For even as Olivia Lattimore spends much of her time attempting to free herself from the female "social ideal" embraced by groups of women like her mother or Pauline Mills, she works toward a new sense of egalitarian community with other female actresses, or, in terms of the novel, artists. Because of this dual impetus, *A Woman of Genius* pioneers, along with Austin's theoretical essay on literary regionalism, a more complex way of understanding the relationship between gender and regional writing—not only in Austin's writings, but in writings by other significant American women regional writers, such as Sarah Orne JEWETT, Mary Wilkins FREEMAN, and Willa CATHER.

SOURCES

Austin, Mary. *A Woman of Genius.* Old Westbury, N.Y: The Feminist Press, 1985.

———. "Regionalism in American Fiction," *English Journal* 21 (February 1932): 97–107.

Fetterly, Judith, and Marjorie Pryse. Introduction. *American Women Regionalists: A Norton Anthology.* New York and London: W. W. Norton & Company, 1995.

Graulich, Melody. "Creating Great Women: Mary Austin and Charlotte Perkins Gilman." In *Charlotte Perkins Gilman and Her Contemporaries: Literary and Intellectual Contexts,* edited by Cynthia J. Davis and Denise D. Knight. Tuscaloosa: University of Alabama Press, 2004.

Lanigan, Esther. Introduction. *A Mary Austin Reader.* Tucson: University of Arizona Press, 1996, pp. 3–20.

Porter, Nancy. Afterword. *A Woman of Genius.* Old Westbury, N.Y.: The Feminist Press, 1985, pp. 295–321.

Beverly Hume

WOMAN ON THE EDGE OF TIME

MARGE PIERCY (1976) Marge Piercy's *Woman on the Edge of Time* is a novel that fits into many categories: fantasy, women's literature, and utopian literature. As a novel produced during the active second wave of American feminism, it questions the roles of women within American society. Further, it anticipates the more inclusive third wave of feminism, in that it explores elements of class and race as well: Connie, the protagonist of the novel, is a poor Chicana who is unjustly committed to an insane asylum due to her attempt to protect her niece from physical and sexual abuse. Geraldo follows Dolly to Connie's home and breaks in as Connie attempts to protect Dolly, physically abusing Connie and knocking her unconscious.

He brings her to Bellevue, and they readily believe Geraldo's fabrication that he and Dolly were attacked by Connie.

Her commitment to Bellevue is made possible by all three markers of her identity—her gender, race, and class—in that all three are marked as deviant in our culture; her previous incarceration within Bellevue also makes her commitment easy, since it marks her as already insane. She is readily and repeatedly marked as a monstrous madwoman.

Connie's belief in her own sanity makes her commitment even more terrifying. In her previous commitment, she had believed herself to be ill, accepting Anglo definitions of success, relationships, and sanity. However, she comes to learn the codes by which she is judged within the mental hospital and learns to trust in herself for validation rather than in American institutions. She learns that playing the roles of the stereotypical female, nonresistant to the values of dominant society, marks one as more normal, as acquiescing rather than transgressing. When Connie learns the codes and how to manipulate them, she gains a measure of power over them (rather than vice-versa). She is thus able to fool the staff that she is progressing by their definitions, that she is compliant and able to be controlled. She does not allow the codes of femininity and the codes that negatively label her a monster to constrain and hurt her any longer.

In the present of the novel, it is Connie's connection to a possible future that allows her to maintain and continue to construct her sense of agency, sanity, and redefinition. Luciente, a "sender" from the future (the year 2137) assigned to the project of visiting the past, connects with Connie, a "catcher," in order to learn about the late 20th century and to influence individuals there. She is able to visit Connie in her time and to allow Connie into the future, specifically Luciente's village of Mattapoisett. Through Connie's forays into the future, we are introduced into a possible utopian future while our present is critiqued. The differences in cultures allow for the discussion of norms and behaviors. This possibility is central to utopian and dystopian representations, and often to fantasy and science fiction in general. Connie acts as the standard visitor to a different world, a common trope of utopian texts. This visitor represents our voice and viewpoints and gradually is educated as to the deficiencies of her/his culture or, at least, to the differences in norms between the two cultures and the constructedness of such norms. While Connie believes in her own sanity and in her self, she also holds onto dominant contemporary notions of progress, child care, childbirth, work, and relationships, among other concepts. The conflict between her beliefs and those that confront her in the future, as well as conversations with the people of that future, enable Connie to critique her situation and her society more pointedly. She is also able to see the result of certain oppressive behaviors, such as the psychosurgery being performed upon her in order to control her behaviors, and understand how her place in society relates to the whole. This encourages her to further action, as she realizes that her life can, indeed, make a difference and count for something.

Connie's confrontation with alternative futures (she also visits a dystopian alternative future) directly affects her sense of agency. Contact with the dystopian future horrifies Connie, and this horror, as well as a deep connection to the people of Mattapoisett, is a catalyst to action. The connection between the psychosurgery being performed on Connie (and a handful of others deemed violent or psychologically incorrigible) and the dystopian future is clear from events transpiring before and after Connie's visit there.

Connie is part of a small test population of people deemed uncontrollably violent; the purpose of the experiment is to eradicate that violence and produce more socially desirable emotions. These people form the test population because they do not have advocates for their rights. While Connie's body has been a battleground between dominant and dominated cultures all her life, her body has now become more explicitly a battleground between present and future, oppression and freedom.

In order to act against the intrusion on civil rights that the psychosurgery represents, as well as safeguard the utopian future, Connie decides to poison her doctors. In a scene reminiscent of Lady Macbeth's obsession with the blood—and guilt—upon her hands, Connie cleanses her hands out of fear of the poison, acknowledging her guilt but emphasizing the war she sees herself engaged in: "I killed them. Because it is war. . . . I'm a dead woman now too. I know it. But I did fight them. I'm not ashamed. I tried. . . . At least once I fought and won" (375). Connie does not easily kill these people; she came to the decision to murder slowly and painfully. Her act, a monstrous one, is performed in order to protect and preserve. She understands her own agency and rejects a negative connotation of monstrosity for herself or her actions. She is the monstrous mother now as she has killed to protect others, but this monstrousness is a positive, enabling image. She has revisioned the image of the monster rather than attempting to deny it by associating herself with the forces of hegemony. In the view of the psychiatrists in the novel, she has chosen madness over acquiescence. For the readers of the text, however, she has rejected both categories and acted to ensure the freedom of future societal "misfits." Her so-called madness is used as a means to action.

SOURCES

Adams, Karen C. "The Utopian Vision of Marge Piercy in *Woman on the Edge of Time*." In *Ways of Knowing: Essays on Marge Piercy,* edited by Sue Walker and Eugenie Hamner. Mobile, Ala.: Negative Capability, 1991.

Afnan, Elham. "Chaos and Utopia: Social Transformation in *Woman on the Edge of Time*," *Extrapolation: A Journal of Science Fiction and Fantasy* 37, no. 4 (Winter 1996): 330–340.

Buckman, Alyson R. "Blunting the Razor's Edge of Sanity: Marge Piercy's *Woman on the Edge of Time*." Under Revision for FEMSPEC.

Gygax, Franziska. "Demur—You're Straightway Dangerous: *Woman on the Edge of Time*." In *Ways of Knowing: Essays on Marge Piercy,* edited by Sue Walker and Eugenie Hamner. Mobile, Ala.: Negative Capability, 1991.

Hansen, Elaine Tuttle. "Mothers Tomorrow and Mothers Yesterday, but Never Mothers Today: *Woman on the Edge of Time* and *The Handmaid's Tale*." In *Narrating Mothers: Theorizing Maternal Subjectivities,* edited by Brenda O. Daly and Maureen T. Reddy. Knoxville: University of Tennessee Press, 1991.

Haran, Joan. "(Re)Productive Fictions: Reproduction, Embodiment and Feminist Science in Marge Piercy's Science Fiction." In *Science Fiction, Critical Frontiers,* edited by Karen Sayer and John Moore. New York: St. Martin's Press, 2000.

Kessler, Carol Farley. "*Woman on the Edge of Time*: A Novel 'To Be of Use,' " *Extrapolation: A Journal of Science Fiction and Fantasy* 28, no. 4 (Winter 1987): 310–318.

Kormali, Sema. "Feminist Science Fiction: The Alternative Worlds of Piercy, Elgin, and Atwood," *Journal of American Studies of Turkey* 4 (Fall 1996): 69–77.

Moylan, Thomas P. "History and Utopia in Marge Piercy's *Woman on the Edge of Time*." In *Science Fiction Dialogues,* edited by Gary Wolfe, 133–140. Chicago: Academy Chicago Press, 1982.

Orr, Elaine. "Mothering as Good Fiction: Instances from Marge Piercy's *Woman on the Edge of Time*," *Journal of Narrative Technique* 23, no. 2 (Spring 1993): 61–79.

Seabury, Marcia Bundy. "The Monsters We Create: *Woman on the Edge of Time* and *Frankenstein*," *Critique: Studies in Contemporary Fiction* 42, no. 2 (Winter 2001): 131–143.

Silbergleid, Robin. "Women, Utopia, and Narrative: Toward a Postmodern Feminist Citizenship," *Hypatia: A Journal of Feminist Philosophy* 12, no. 4 (Fall 1997): 156–177.

Alyson R. Buckman

WOMAN WARRIOR, THE MAXINE HONG KINGSTON (1976)

Winner of the National Book Critics Circle Award for the best book of nonfiction published in 1976, Maxine Hong KINGSTON's *The Woman Warrior: Memoirs of a Girlhood Among Ghosts* chronicles pivotal phases of a Chinese-American woman growing up in California. Through her childhood memories, Kingston, "fictionalizing" the episodes in an autobiographical manner, integrates her mother's stories told to her as a child. The narrative shifts between different voices of various generations, jumping from the past to the present. Using the story of the legendary woman warrior Fa Mu Lan, Kingston astutely reinscribes the Chinese myth within the Western context. Fa Mu Lan, who disguised herself as a man to be a conscript in her father's place, is said to have led an army throughout China fighting against the barbarians. Inspired by the heroine, the narrator also imagines herself as a woman warrior leading an army to protect Chinese-American women from sexism within the patriarchal system and racism in Western society. As critic Lee Quinby has argued, "Kingston represents her girlhood as triply displaced because of America's deeply embedded Sinophobia, her parents' ambivalence about America and the poverty they face, and the misogynistic attitudes she finds in both her American and Chinese heritages" (301).

Structurally, the novel consists of five sections, and each section, intertwined with Chinese tales and the narrator's childhood memoirs, brings up important identity-formation questions. Kingston raises issues of gender, sexuality, race, and class that the protagonist encounters in constructing a new Chinese-American identity, particularly Chinese-American women's subjectivity. A feminist reading could illuminate the novel's complexity. The first section, "No Name Woman," tells the tragedy of the protagonist's transgressive paternal aunt whose disgrace because she conceived an illegitimate child makes her an outcast in the small Chinese village. The protagonist's mother tells the story of this "no name" woman to warn the girl about the dangers of sexual immorality.

The second section, "White Tigers," in which the Fa Mu Lan tale is introduced in the mother's "talk stories," describes the mighty power of the woman warrior who lives to protect her family and village. In this section, Kingston interweaves two narrative voices: the mythical swordswoman in ancient China and the verbal woman warrior in modern America.

The third section, "Shaman," examines the life of the narrator's mother, Brave Orchid. The ghost is also introduced in this section. The protagonist's mother uses the word *ghost* to refer to both spirits and to Americans; that the girl grows up among the Bai Gwei, white ghosts, explains why the book is subtitled "Memoirs of a Girlhood among Ghosts." For the narrator, the supernatural ghost, representing a battle between the two cultures, crosses historical and geographical borders, and the use of *ghost* allows the narrative to strategically shuttle back and forth between the past and the present, between China and the United States, and between reality and imagination.

The fourth section, "At the Western Palace," describes the earlier years of Brave Orchid and her sister Moon Orchid in China before their immigration to the United States. In China, Brave Orchid is a doctor/midwife and she moves to America to join her husband to run a laundry. Moon Orchid, too, later tries to rejoin her husband in the United States, but he has remarried and thus rejects her. Becoming mentally ill, Moon Orchid is put in an asylum, where she dies.

In the concluding section, "A Song for a Barbarian Reed Pipe," Kingston reinterprets another Chinese legend, that of Ts'ai Yen, a woman kidnapped by barbarians and forced to become a concubine to raise her children in an alien—and alienated—land. Like Fa Mu Lan, Ts'ai Yen has fought in battle, but as a captive soldier. Ts'ai Yen's story echoes Brave Orchid's bringing up her children on a foreign soil and this last section retells the protagonist's childhood memoirs of the ways culture and identity create complex clashes in the real world.

Many critics point out Kingston's literary strategy of articulating silences by exploding the stock image of the quiet Oriental damsel. One of Kingston's major concerns is the way gender roles and femininity are redefined in Asian American culture. Throughout the five sections, by expressing her ideas and telling the stories of many silenced women, the writer/narrator Kingston believes in the power of words that eventually transform the silent girl into a strident word warrior. In claiming her identity in the (un)hyphenated Chinese American space, the protagonist is constantly caught in a kind of cultural ambivalence. Critic Amy Ling calls this ambivalence "the between world condition," one that recalls W. E. B. DuBois's notable concept of an African American's "double-consciousness": In this state, "one ever feels his two-ness—an American, a Negro; two souls, two thoughts, two unreconciled strivings; two warring ideals in one dark body" (3). The space occupied by the modern woman warrior is thus between the two poles of different cultures.

Within this space of cultural ambivalence, the narrative exemplifies the protagonist's desire to establish a new Chinese-American female selfhood. One may thus read the entire novel (and despite its designation as memoir, it has all the techniques of an excellent novel) as an extended exploration of the meanings of three words: *Chinese, American,* and *woman.* To deconstruct a monolithic Chinese-American identity, Kingston uses different, mixed voices in her narrative: her own voice, her mother's voice, and the voices of other mythical and historical figures from her mother's talk-stories. In providing her reader with so many narratives, the writer demonstrates her awareness of writing as a reflection of multiplying images. The use of memoirs, different from the traditional autobiography that uses a singular *I* in a chronologically sequenced account, constructs a multiple and complicated subjectivity. It is important to notice Kingston's use of memoirs, whose dialogical format destabilizes unified selfhood; in other words, the writer/narrator's memoirs, a sign of separation from her mother's oral tradition and women's enforced silences, accentuate the conflicts and confusions of identity that constitute her discursive *I*. Therefore, acquiring a new voice by breaking the longstanding silence is the feature of the female subjectivity that allows the writer to construct a new collective identity for the Chinese women born in the United States.

SOURCES

Cheung, King-Kok. "*The Woman Warrior* Versus *The China-man* Pacific: Must a Chinese American Critic Choose between Feminism and Heroism?" In *Asian American Studies: A Reader,* edited by Jean Wu and Min Song, 307–323. New Brunswick, N.J.: Rutgers University Press, 2000.

———. *Articulate Silences: Hisaye Yamamoto, Maxine Hong Kingston, Joy Kogawa.* Ithaca, N.Y., and London: Cornell University Press, 1993.

DuBois, W. E. B. *The Souls of Black Folk.* 1903. Reprinted, Millwood, N.Y.: Kraus-Thomson Organization, 1973.

Juhasz, Suzanne. "Maxine Hong Kingston: Narrative Technique and Female Identity." In *Contemporary American Women Writers: Narrative Strategies,* edited by Catherine Rainwater and William J. Scheik, 173–189. Lexington: University Press of Kentucky, 1985.

Kingston, Maxine Hong. *The Woman Warrior: Memoir of a Girlhood among Ghosts.* New York: Knopf, 1976.

Quinby, Lee. "The Subject of Memoirs: *The Woman Warrior's* Technology of Ideographic Selfhood." In *De/Colonizing the Subject: The Politics of Gender in Women's Autobiography,* edited by Sidonie Smith and Julia Watson, 297–320. Minneapolis: University of Minnesota Press, 1992.

Bennett Fu

WOMAN WHO OWNED THE SHADOWS, THE PAULA GUNN ALLEN (1983)

According to Paula Gunn ALLEN, "stories out of the oral tradition, when left to themselves and not recast by Indian or white collector, tend to meander gracefully from event to event; the major unifying device . . . is the relationship of the tale of the ritual life of the tribe" (Allen 1992, 153). This then is the structure of her 1983 novel *The Women Who Owned the Shadows,* which contains any number of stories from Keres and Navajo oral tradition and history, as well as stories of the half-breed Guadalupe protagonist Ephanie Atencio and her grandmother. In fact, according to Elizabeth Hanson, "It's setting, time, plot, and characters are derived largely from Allen's own contemporary time and experience in the post-war American Southwest" (Hanson, 35). Allen herself argues that the "plotting is as near to a conversation with Indians as [she] could make it" (Allen 1992, 153). This conversation centers on Ephanie's struggle to find her place in life and to combine all the parts of herself because as a half-breed, she is in-between two cultures. Specifically, she struggles to find psychic balance by recognizing the parallels between her life and the life of the gods, particularly Spider/Thought Woman. And as she finds balance in her life, that life turns into one that could easily fit into, in form and action, the tribal narrative of the Keres.

Gunn Allen insists that time is a central theme of the novel; "in the book, dream, 'actual' event, myth, tale, history, and internal dialogue are run together, making it evident that divisions do not lead to comprehension" (Allen 1992, 153). Furthermore, Allen's choppy, repetitive style at times seems unedited and confusing, but at other times perfectly captures a mood. As Vanessa Holford argues, readers "experience Ephanie's panic by reading it. Spasmodic flights between images and thoughts communicate Ephanie's personal fragmentation" (Holford). In "Naiya Iyatiku Is Calling," the emotions and feelings of parents and their baby twins are perfectly captured by Allen's style: "At four in the morning. After being up all day. Too exhausted. Two babies, crying. Or one then the other. Crying. Wet. Hungry. Colicky. Lonely. Cold. Restless. Bored. Not sleeping" (103). Or after the death of one of the twins: "So still. So silent. The spindly bundle blue. Mottle blue. Still" (103). This style also works to capture the everyday details of her life. Elizabeth Hanson argues that Ephanie's "fear is made visible through the minutiae of her life, the details of her private rituals of daily experience . . . what she wears, what she eats, how she deals with the 'simple dust of her house' are juxtaposed to a Native American belief system that might explain the workings of the world" (Hanson, 37–8). And Allen uses these daily experiences as "clues to a new way of seeing and interpreting women's writing, her own included" (Hanson, 38).

The Anglo-European society is what causes Ephanie to be so lost. The pressure to be heterosexual and stereotypically feminine creates chaos and unhappiness for Ephanie. Vanessa Holford argues that these pressures turn Ephanie into a "non-person, an acceptable woman" (Holford). Ephanie dreams of being "tall and pretty and dated. Adored. Mated. Housed in some pretty house somewhere far from the dusty mesas of her childhood" (203). Gone are her dreams of heroism, bravery, strength; she became "passive and plastic" (Holford). Ephanie also becomes heterosexual. Holford points out that "lesbianism in the novel is vitally important because it is representative of women's self-love. The characters who forbid Ephanie to love Elena are forbidding her to love herself, to be complete. Distrust of lesbianism is fear of women's renewed strength, self-value, and unity" (Holford). In fact it is her lover Teresa who during a physic reading first points Ephanie toward her grandmother's spirit. This spirit represents all the women in her life, past and present, and her dreams reveal that her deepest fear is being shut out from the females of her culture, including the gods.

In her struggle to find peace, forces seem to work against Ephanie to "destroy whatever link she has to the traditional [Keres] culture in which the women are central figures," suggests Annette Van Dyke (8). While Ephanie is a passive receptacle for life, life does not treat her well. When she takes hold of her own life, things improve. Or as Allen puts it, when she realizes that she has "power in her own right," and does not expect a man to give it to her, things improve (quoted in Ballinger and Swann, 7). Readers participate, following Ephanie through her healing journey. Thus in some way balance is restored to readers' communities or the community at large through this participation (Van Dyke, 8). The parts of the novel trace Ephanie's fall and rise. In part I, Ephanie is abandoned by the woman she loves, Elena, and her husband Stephen. In part II's "Naiya Iyatiku Was Singing," Ephanie is lost; she "understood that there was no way to understand. Anything. Ever"

(106). Near the end of part II are "Therapist's Notes" and at the very end is a "Divorce Settlement" document (109–112, 120). These are written documents from the non-Native world representing her troubles. Their inclusion in the novel suggests how far Ephanie has wandered from Keres ways, as well as the fact that she is subject to the "documents" and "cures" of the non-Native world. According to Peter Nabokov, "Unlike oral tradition, print was marked by the impersonality of its transmission." These documents are extremely impersonal, and cannot capture the essence of her pain, as the spoken word could. However, a document like a divorce decree is necessary in the print-driven "White" world and does allow her to move on "officially." Yet it isn't documents or "White" cures alone that can heal her; she also needs her Keres beliefs. In part III's "There's Four Sides to Every Question," her Keres ways begin to enter her consciousness again as Ephanie realizes that life fits together, that "it all came together somewhere" (147).

Then in the prologue's "In the Shadows She Sang, Remembering," Ephanie "understood at least that everything was connected. Everything was related . . . What had happened in time immemorial . . . happened now" (191). This understanding comes through the examination of traditional native stories. She realizes that they are not separate from her; they personally affect her— "hours she pondered [the stories], slowing growing stronger, more clear, as the light in the room turned to shadows, to twilight, to dark. Still she sat, re membering" (196). Just as Gunn redesigns the creation myth in the prologue by feminizing Spider Woman, Ephanie is redoing herself in the light of the traditional stories, as the separation of the word "re membering" in the title and the previous quote illustrates. Remembering her life is "remember[ing] the [Keres] story that told it" (195). By the end of the novel Ephanie has "entered the song" (213). She is now not only thinking as a Keres but also believing as one who knows she is part of a greater song.

SOURCES

Allen, Paula Gunn. *The Sacred Hoop*. Boston: Beacon, 1992.
———. *The Women Who Owned the Shadows*. New York: Fire Keepers, 1995.
Ballinger, Franchot, and Brian Swann. "Interview with Paula Gunn Allen." In *Native American Women Writers*, edited by Harold Bloom, 5–7. Philadelphia: Chelsea, 1998.

Hanson, Elizabeth. *Western Writers Series #96: Paula Gunn Allen.* Boise, Idaho: Boise State University, 1990.

Holford, Vanessa. "Re Membering Ephanie: A Woman's Re-Creation of Self in Paula Gunn Allen's *The Woman Who Owned the Shadows,*" *Studies in American Indian Literature* 6, no. 1 (Spring 1994): 99–113.

Nabokov, Peter. "American Indian Literature: A Tradition of Renewal," *Studies in American Indian Literature* 2, no.3 (Autumn 1978).

Van Dyke, Annette. "Critical Extracts." In *Native American Women Writers,* edited by Harold Bloom, 8–9. Philadelphia: Chelsea, 1998.

Kristen Rozzell

WOMEN Charles Bukowski (1978)   In no other work does Charles Bukowski seem to exhibit himself as purely as he does in *Women* (1978). Nothing else could account for the book's enduring appeal and seductiveness. It is true that the main character has a pseudonym, Henry Chinaski, and there is a publisher's note that says, "This novel is a work of fiction and no character is intended to portray any person or combination of persons living or dead" (6). And yet there are seemingly no other masks or precautions. Throughout this work, Bukowski, apparently, shows himself as himself, revealing to the reader his self in all its ugliness and misanthropy.

It is no accident, from this perspective, that *Women* is almost completely devoid of novelistic qualities. What is remarkable about the work is the bluntness of its "style," its total reliance on ordinary language, and the junk that is stockpiled in its every corner—that is, the superabundance of digressions, seemingly culled from the surfaces of everyday life. Because of its coarse and digressive character, *Women* does not read like a novel; instead, it resembles a raw document of an experience, a bloody chunk excised from the tissue of ordinary life. Perhaps this is the reason for the work's repetitiveness. Each scene of the "narrative" (if the book has one) follows exactly the same pattern: (1) Chinaski meets a woman who is invariably significantly younger than him and who, in most cases, knows and admires his work. (The women in the novel are drawn to Chinaski partly because of his literary reputation and partly because of the way in which he describes women in his books. As a self-portrait, *Women* resembles nothing more than a literary personals advertisement. (2) He has some form of sexual intercourse with the woman. (By having sex with young women, Chinaski hopes to achieve victory over death, a kind of sexualized immortality. And perhaps this is also the reason that he writes, "My art is my fear" [189].) Intermittently, there are also poetry readings, noisy breakups, trips to a racetrack, and laconic conversations with friends, acquaintances, and strangers. Nothing extraordinary happens. Chinaski's account of his life is as uneventful and banal as most lives are thought to be. A book that is repetitive and tedious may express a life that is repetitive and tedious; and if one accepts that the book documents an engagement with life, how could one fault the author for this?

Throughout the pages of *Women,* the reader watches as an endless parade of women move in and out of Chinaski's life. One bout of copulation is succeeded by another. Each of Chinaski's sexual encounters resembles a form of violent appropriation, the besmirching of what is sacred or the slaughtering or maiming of a wild beast ("one animal knifing another into submission" [77]). It is not coincidental that racetracks and boxing matches serve as the backdrop for much of the action in *Women,* for sex, according to the logic of this book, is a sport—indeed, it is the bloodiest sport of all.

Although he defines himself as a writer, Chinaski prefers women to writing: " 'You're good enough with the ladies,' the character Dee Dee said. 'And you're a helluva writer.' [Chinaski replies:] 'I'd rather be good with the ladies' " (50). Writing is, for him, merely a vicissitude of life; it is an addiction ("an insanity," he says at one point), but no more gripping than any of his other addictions—such as horse-betting, drinking, and sex. Writing is indeed a compulsion, but only one compulsion among others. All his compulsions are variations of the same compulsion, the American wet dream. That dream, of course, is to acquire and to accumulate as much of a thing as possible. More money. More sex. More drinks. More of everything. Like everyone else in his milieu, Chinaski is "sick on the dream" (104)—the dream of gross acquisition and accumulation that defines American culture.

SOURCES
Brewer, Gay. *Charles Bukowski.* New York: Twayne, 1997.

Bukowski, Charles. *Women*. Santa Barbara, Calif.: Black Sparrow Press, 1978.

Fox, Hugh. *Charles Bukowski: A Critical and Biographical Study*. Somerville, Mass.: Abyss Publications, 1969.

Harrison, Russell. *Against the American Dream: Essays on Charles Bukowski*. Santa Rosa, Calif.: Black Sparrow Press, 1994.

Miller, William Joyce. *Bukowski, and Their Enemies: Essays on Contemporary Culture*. Greensboro, N.C.: Avisson, 1996.

Joseph Suglia

WONG, SHAWN HSU (1949–)

Shawn Wong published his first novel, *Homebase,* in 1979, the year that his landmark book *Aiiieeeee!: An Anthology of Asian American Writers,* edited with Jeffrey Paul Chan, Frank CHIN, and Lawson Fusso Inada, appeared. The timing of the two publications suggests the twin goals that have driven much of Wong's career: his ongoing search to rediscover older Asian-American voices and to seek out the new, and to find his own complex voice. *Homebase,* one of the first novels published by a Chinese American (Chen, 391), depicts the life of Rainsford Chan, a fourth-generation Chinese American whose odyssey leads to an understanding of his ancestors and to his personal self-discovery as an American. Wong uses diaries, journals, essays, real and imagined letters, etc., to reclaim for the reader, as well as for Rainsford, significant truths about the building of the Pacific Railroad over the Sierra Nevada mountains and Angel Island, the West Coast equivalent to Ellis Island. Wong's second novel, *American Knees* (1995), tells the story of Raymond Ding. Schoolyard taunts aimed at Ding provide the book's title: "Are you," asks one character, "Chinese, Japanese, or American knees?" The novel follows Raymond, director of minority affairs at a small Bay Area college, on a quest for love and an understanding of the way his heritage blends with his American self.

Wong, who was born on August 11, 1949, in Oakland, California, was educated at the University of California at Berkeley, where he earned his bachelor's degree in 1971, and at San Francisco State University, where he received his master's degree in 1974. *Homebase* evolved from his master's thesis, directed by the novelist and creative writing instructor Kay BOYLE, who believed in his talent. Wong also coedited *The Big Aiiieeeee!: An Anthology of Chinese American and Japanese American Literature* (1991), and edited *Asian American Literature: A Brief Introduction and Anthology* (1996), several other anthologies, and "I Miss the Person I Love Every Day" (1998), a tribute to his wife Vicki, who died in 1997, for the anthology *A Few Thousand Words About Love,* edited by Mickey Pearlman (1998). Responsible, with others, for rediscovering such now classic writers as John OKADA, SUI SIN FAR, and Louis CHU, Wong remains firmly in the anti-assimilationist camp of Asian-American literature, reminding writers and readers alike to remain vigilant and self-critical.

NOVELS
American Knees. New York: Simon & Schuster, 1995.
Homebase. New York: I. Reed Books, 1979.

SOURCES
Chen, Chih-Ping. "Shawn Wong." In *Asian American Novelists: A Bio-Bibliographical Critical Sourcebook,* edited by Emmanuel S. Nelson, 391–397. Westport, Conn.: Greenwood Press, 2000.

Kim, Elaine H. "Shawn Hsu Wong." In *Asian American Literature: An Introduction to the Writings and Their Social Context,* 194–197. Philadelphia: Temple University Press, 1982.

Wong, Shawn. "I Miss the Person I Love Every Day." In *A Few Thousand Words About Love,* edited by Mickey Pearlman, 157–158. Lexington: University Press of Kentucky, 1998.

WOOLSON, CONSTANCE FENIMORE (1840–1894)

Novelist, short story writer, poet, and essayist, and widely published during her lifetime, Constance Fenimore Woolson wrote most of her best work after she immigrated to Italy in 1880. Viewed by her contemporaries as a local colorist, especially about the Great Lakes, she also created bizarre, lonely, even weird characters related to the gothic tradition. She has been the subject of much scholarly study in recent years. In addition to *For the Major* (1883), a novella, she wrote four novels: *Anne* (1882), *Horace Chase* (1894), *East Angels* (1886), and *Jupiter Lights* (1889).

Woolson, the grand-niece of James Fenimore COOPER, was born on March 5, 1840, in Claremont, New Hampshire, but she was reared in Cleveland,

Ohio. She was educated at Miss Hayden's School and the Cleveland Female Seminary, completing her formal education in New York at Madame Chegaray's boarding school, from which she graduated at the head of her class in 1858. Unlike such New England contemporaries as Sarah Orne JEWETT or Mary Wilkins FREEMAN, Woolson traveled often; consequently, New England, the Midwest, the South, and Europe figure in her work. In Florence, Woolson met Henry JAMES, who became a close friend and significant literary influence.

Although Woolson's novels were written in Europe, *Anne* is set on Michigan's Mackinaw Island and in New York, and depicts the outsider who moves into a multiethnic community and becomes engaged to the wrong man. This early novel demonstrates Woolson's penchant for psychological analysis, as does *For the Major,* the first of her novels to take place in the American South. Madame Carroll, who needs a stable home, subsumes her identity in order to make her marriage to the much older major succeed. In *East Angels,* Margaret Harold struggles unsuccessfully with her husband's philandering; she cannot bring herself to break up her marriage to be with the man whom she ardently loves. The Florida setting features characters of New England, Cuban, or Spanish heritage. Woolson's final novel, *Jupiter Lights,* is a singularly penetrating analysis of the dismal effects of child and wife abuse.

Woolson's life ended at age 54 when she fell from her Venetian apartment window. Whether she committed suicide remains unresolved, but Henry James was so convinced of it that he refused to attend her funeral. Buried in the Protestant Cemetery in Rome, Woolson is receiving an increasing amount of scholarly attention and is gradually appearing on American-literature course syllabi. The largest collection of her papers is held at the Western Reserve Historical Society in Cleveland, Ohio.

NOVELS AND NOVELLAS
Anne. New York: Harper, 1882.
East Angels. New York: Harper, 1886.
For the Major. New York: Harper, 1883.
Horace Chase. New York: Harper, 1894.
Jupiter Lights. New York: Harper, 1889.

SOURCES
Dean, Sharon. *Constance Fenimore Woolson: Homeward Bound.* Knoxville: University of Tennessee Press, 1995.
Kern, John Dwight. *Constance Fenimore Woolson: Literary Pioneer.* Philadelphia: University of Pennsylvania Press, 1934.
Moore, Rayburn S. *Constance F. Woolson.* Boston: Twayne, 1963.
Torsney, Cheryl B. *Constance Fenimore Woolson: The Grief of Artistry.* Athens: University of Georgia Press, 1989.
———, ed. *Critical Essays on Constance Fenimore Woolson.* New York: G. K. Hall, 1992.

WORLD ACCORDING TO GARP, THE
JOHN IRVING (1976) *The World According to Garp,* published in 1976, brought John IRVING out of the arena of critically acclaimed but lackluster-selling fiction to critically acclaimed and best-selling fiction, an arena the East Coast–based author has yet to leave. *Garp* won an American Book Award for best paperback novel, and in 1983 director George Roy Hill brought *Garp's* unique world to the silver screen. Many of Irving's other novels have graced movie theaters, among them *The HOTEL NEW HAMPSHIRE, A PRAYER FOR OWEN MEANY* (released under the title *Simon Birch*), and most recently *The CIDER HOUSE RULES,* for which Irving won a best-adapted screenplay Oscar. While his other work cannot be dismissed, it is *Garp* that resonates as Irving's masterpiece.

Some readers may find *Garp's* plot elements absurd: Garp's conception when Jenny Fields has sex with one of her brain-damaged patients, the World War II ball turret gunner Technical Sergeant Garp; Garp's wife Helen Holm castrating her graduate student Michael Milton during an act of fellatio; and the transsexual Roberta Muldoon being a former tight end for the Philadelphia Eagles. But through his prose, Irving masterfully points out the obvious—that life is absurd, full of drama as well as humor. The cliché that an event so weird would not be believed in a work of fiction does not occur here because Irving fleshes out each of his characters and presents these events so true that they cannot be dismissed. As critics Carol C. Harter and James R. Thompson note in their book on Irving, this is "... a novel whose voice, structure, and vision define it as a unique expression of 'true' (as opposed to 'real') human experience" (74). It should be no surprise that Donald Whitcomb, the author of Garp's biography, entitles his work *Lunacy and Sorrow: The Life and Art of T.S. Garp.*

The realization that, no matter how hard people try, life cannot be controlled can be a hard one to grasp, even when the unplanned repeatedly appears on their doorstep. Garp's life and death demonstrate this. Even when he tries to apologize to the Ellen Jamesians for his multitude of angry letters, he still meets his death at the hands of Ellen Jamesian Pooh Percy—the sister of Cushie Percy, whom he lost his virginity to at the novel's start. Pooh now belongs to this sect of women who cut off their own tongues in solidarity of the little raped girl Ellen James. Pooh associates Cushie's own death to ". . . Garp's adolescent lust for her sister . . ." (Campbell, 73). Despite Garp's own effort to control the anger he created toward him within this sect, Pooh nonetheless assassinates him, still tying in the absurd thought of her sister's death to a teenage romp. With writing being one of the novel's crucial elements, Irving shows that his characters' only sense of control is within their own literary creations.

The journey toward maturity plays a huge role in *Garp,* as is the journey Garp and Jenny take to Vienna to concentrate on and nurture their own writing. As scholar Josie P. Campbell notes in her own criticism of Irving and his work, "It is a plot of becoming [author's emphasis]" (9). Campbell notices ". . . the protagonists of Irving's novels demonstrat[ing] growth. They are, to be sure, characters who bumble and fumble their way through life, but they are much more than a bundle of mechanical gestures" (11). By constructing certain works of fiction during crucial periods of his life, Garp grows as a writer and a person, most notably with his novel *The World According to Bensenhaver,* written after the death of his son Walt.

Perhaps the strongest prevailing theme is Irving's take on gender roles throughout *Garp.* While Garp's mother, Jenny, rejects the label "feminist" attached to her, Jenny's actions and the writing of *Sexual Suspect* demonstrates the contrary. Irving's novel begins in the '40s, a time when women's independent thoughts and actions were not believed acceptable. Despite this social norm and the bemoaning of her parents, Jenny

Fields remain true to herself, even deciding to have a child out of wedlock, so she is not tied to a husband the rest of her life. And Garp himself rejects the typical role of adult son and husband by letting Jenny and Helen support him financially while he concentrates on his own writing. Women play a central role in Irving's novel, whether it is the strong Jenny, ". . . the independent Roberta Muldoon . . . the little girl he 'saves' after she is raped in the park . . . Ellen James . . . [his] own lust for baby-sitters . . ." (81). At the end of *Garp,* Garp's son Duncan, obviously without any prejudice, marries a transsexual, with Irving calling it "[a]nother gift to Duncan's life from Roberta Muldoon!" (604–605). Irving seems to question the labels attached to men and women. He brings in the flip-flopped gender role of Garp's own life as well as Jenny's and Helen's, adding Garp's friendship with the former jock and transsexual Roberta and Duncan's decision to marry a transsexual for the ultimate effect.

Whereas in other works of fiction women are penalized for their sexual desires, in *Garp* it is the men who meet this fate, most notably Michael Milton. In addition to the accident that cost Duncan his eye, Walt his life, and Garp his speech, Milton loses his penis. Like the soldier that Jenny injures at the beginning of the novel and Garp's death toward the novel's conclusion, Milton in a way is punished for his libidinousness. When Garp writes *The World According to Bensenhaver,* he has the raped character of Hope stab the rapist with the rapist's own fisherman's blade.

Family stands at the Garp's forefront. In addition to his biological family of Jenny Fields and the one produced by his marriage to Helen, of whom he has two sons, Duncan and Walt, and a daughter named after Jenny, there are the characters with whom Garp has no blood or civil union. This other family includes Roberta, Ellen James, and Garp's agent, John Wolf, who mirrors Jenny's role as nurturer and protector. But in this case, Wolf nurtures Garp as a writer. In fact the name Wolf harkens back to Garp's own description of Jenny as ". . . a lone wolf" (2).

The Grim Reaper can be called an additional character in *Garp.* In addition to assassination, the act that took Jenny and Garp, cancer takes the lives of a majority of the characters, notably the Vienna prostitute

Charlotte, Garp's daughter, Jenny, and John Wolf. A last chapter entitled "Life After Garp" accounts the lives and deaths of the rest of the characters. Garp foreshadows his own death in chapter 2 "Blood and Blue": " 'Like my father,' Garp wrote, 'I believe I have a knack for brevity. I'm a one-shot man' " (33). Walt calls the undertow at Dog's Head the "Under Toad," a childishly erroneous phrase that the novel repeats throughout in terms of the death and tragedy stalking the characters. Having death so prominent in the novel is another plot element that adds reality and relates back to control and absurdity.

The World According to Garp's complexity touches on specific thoughts and moments within the individual reader. While the last line of the novel states ". . . we are all terminal cases" (609), the depth of Irving's writing in *Garp* proves that powerful literature can stave off the inevitable.

SOURCES

Campbell, Josie P. *John Irving: A Critical Companion. Critical Companions to Popular Contemporary Writers.* Series edited by Kathleen Gregory Klein. Westport, Conn.: Greenwood Press, 1998.

Harter, Carol C., and James R. Thompson. *John Irving.* Boston: Twayne, 1986.

Irving, John. *The World According to Garp.* 1976. New York: Ballantine, 1997.

Laura Durnell

WORLD ENOUGH AND TIME ROBERT PENN WARREN (1950)

No single work better reveals Robert Penn WARREN's purposes than *World Enough and Time*, which appeared in 1950 in the middle of his career. Subtitled *A Romantic Novel*, Warren's fiction re-creates the historical case of the "Kentucky Tragedy," a sensational story of love and jealousy, then of murder and suicide, earlier taken as a literary subject by 19th-century Southern writers including William Gilmore Simms and Edgar Allan POE. However, Warren chooses Nathaniel HAWTHORNE as his model, especially in terms of *The Scarlet Letter,* published just a century earlier, in 1850. As in Hawthorne's "The Customs House" preface, Warren's own voice seems to discuss the documents that present this tragic story of love and death that follows, but his narrative voice takes a detached, realistic view of the romantic tale told by its 19th-century protagonist.

Warren's long and complex novel for the most part stays close to its historical sources, in particular the autobiographical justification penned by its narrator, here called Jeremiah Beaumont. Warren invents some of young Jerry's development, including the early death of his father, which leaves him to find his own way in the world. As in many of Warren's works, the search for a father surrogate preoccupies his central character until he finally realizes his own psychic selfhood, often by becoming a father himself. Jerry's most important father figure is his employer, Colonel Cassius Fort, a successful lawyer, politician, and speculator on the Kentucky frontier in the early decades of the 19th century. When Wilkie Barron, another protégé of the colonel's, reveals that their mentor seduced and impregnated a fatherless local beauty, Rachel Jordan, Jerry rejects Fort and courts Rachel in an act of romantic rebellion.

This personal story is paralleled by a complicated political plot, one again drawn realistically from the documents of the 1820s. After the national financial panic of 1819, the populist Kentucky legislature enacted a number of "Relief" measures to protect debtors from foreclosure, and Warren uses the reaction of an "Anti-Relief" party to depict the historical tension between liberal and conservative impulses throughout our history. Personal and political factors were closely intertwined in the historical sources, and Warren makes them even more symbolic by showing Colonel Fort a turncoat, deserting his theoretical support for Relief for the practical advantages of Anti-Relief. Jerry has moved in the opposite direction, encouraged by the equally romantic Rachel, whose farm has been saved by Relief laws. Finally, she brings Jerry to the grave of her stillborn baby and promises to become his beloved and his wife if he will kill the colonel in an act of personal and political revenge.

The pragmatic Fort refuses a duel, and Jerry considers his debt of honor paid to Rachel, who then marries him and soon carries his child. Jerry thus discovers his psychological selfhood by settling down as a successful country squire. In a subsequent political campaign, the colonel seems to refute charges of seduction by circulating the rumor that Rachel had been impregnated by her black coachman. When she again miscarries, Rachel demands revenge, withholding her love from Jerry until the deed is done. When Fort still refuses his challenge, Jerry stabs him to death in a mysterious midnight meeting. The long middle section of the novel then concerns itself with his trial for murder in the state capitol at Frankfort, a trial made more sensational by the political undercurrents to his personal revenge. Warren underlines another of his characteristic themes, the elusive nature of philosophical truth and therefore of practical justice, as both prosecution and defense resort to perjury, subornation, and intimidation. When Jerry is sentenced to death, Rachel swears to share his fate by suicide.

At this point Warren makes his major deviation from his historical sources. Wilkie Barron reappears to engineer the couple's "delivery" from prison to far western Kentucky, still essentially the frontier. On his earlier hunting trips, Jerry was possessed by a romantic vision of pure nature, much in the tradition of American romanticism. Warren's works depict his native state as the "dark and bloody ground" of folklore, however, and *World Enough and Time* proves no exception. The hunted couple find shelter in the wilderness domain of the "Gran Boz," the monstrous patriarch of the Ohio River pirates. Thus Warren's invented westward expedition extends his concern with the ideal and the real, the romantic and the realistic, into the American future. In this heart of darkness, the weakened Rachel sickens and dies; Jerry is then murdered trying to return to civilization to protest his innocence. Wilkie Barron's killer decapitates Jerry's corpse to collect a reward, with proof of the head preserved in a mud-filled sack.

Readers of *All the King's Men* and Warren's earlier works should not have been surprised by *World Enough and Time,* though many were. Popular readers, anticipating the historical costume drama implied by the dust-jacket illustrations, were only a bit more taken aback than academic critics, who thought Warren had descended into depressing melodrama and shocking violence. The novel is a demanding text—long, complex, and thick with ideas and images; indeed, its rhetoric seems to strain after poetry in much the same way

that the central characters communicate by means of their poems for and to each other. Warren's immediately succeeding works, the epic poem *Brother to Dragons* (1953) and the historical novel *Band of Angels* (1955), continued many of the directions discovered in *World Enough and Time,* especially in the realistic treatment of romantic historical material from his native state. Later critics have even broader perspectives that place it among Robert Penn Warren's half-dozen best books.

SOURCES
Blotner, Joseph. *Robert Penn Warren: A Biography.* New York: Random House, 1997.

Justus, James. *The Achievement of Robert Penn Warren.* Baton Rouge: Louisiana State University Press, 1981.

Millichap, Joseph R. "Robert Penn Warren's West," *Southern Literary Journal* (Fall 1993): 54–63.

Warren, Robert Penn. *World Enough and Time.* New York: Random House, 1950.

Watkins, Floyd C., et al., eds. *Talking with Robert Penn Warren.* Athens: University of Georgia Press, 1990.

Joe Millichap

WOUK, HERMAN (1915–)

Herman Wouk, novelist and dramatist, has written 12 novels, eight of them best sellers, and four plays, two of them popular and successful. His works, which have sold millions of copies worldwide, have been translated into some 30 languages. Wouk is still best known for his Pulitzer Prize–winning novel, *The CAINE MUTINY* (1951), the starkly compelling tale of mutiny aboard a World War II destroyer, and for his novels *WINDS OF WAR* (1971) and *WAR AND REMEMBRANCE* (1978), the latter nominated for an American Book Award. Wouk was also a pioneer in writing about Jewish issues in otherwise mainstream novels.

Born in New York City, Herman Wouk (pronounced "Woke") is the son of Russian immigrants Abraham Isaac Wouk, owner of a laundry chain, and Esther Levine Wouk, daughter of a rabbi. Wouk was educated at Columbia University and, in 1934, he received a bachelor of arts degree with honors. After some radio writing assignments, including a job assisting Fred Allen with his weekly radio scripts, he enlisted in the U.S. Navy, became a lieutenant, and served as a deck officer on the destroyer/minesweeper U.S.S. *Zane* in the Pacific for three years, receiving four campaign stars and a Presidential Unit Citation. In December 1945, Wouk married Betty Sarah Brown and in 1947 published his debut novel, *Aurora Dawn,* a satire about the New York advertising world, featuring money-hungry Andrew Reale, and *City Boy* (1948), a partially autobiographical Bronx bildungsroman centered on protagonist Herbie Bookbinder. *The Caine Mutiny,* although set at the time of Wouk's naval shipboard duty during World War II, is a fictional account of mutiny against Captain Queeg, commander of the U.S.S. *Caine.* Because of the sympathetic portrayal of such likable characters as Lieutenants Keefer and Maryk, main players in the mutiny, the dramatic courtroom scene that ends the novel catches readers off-guard with its condemnation of the mutineers who morally betrayed the military service that was protecting Americans against fascism.

Wouk's fourth novel, *Marjorie Morningstar,* is a sympathetic portrayal of a young aspiring actress who fails in her career, marries a lawyer, and learns to understand herself through plumbing her Jewish heritage. The following year, Wouk published *The Lomokome Papers,* a science fiction novel that appeared in *Collier's* in 1956 and in book form in 1968. In *Youngblood Hawke* (1962), Arthur Youngblood, a writer clearly modeled on novelist Thomas WOLFE, loses his talent to his preoccupation with business, finance, and women without values. *Don't Stop the Carnival* (1965), a wittily conceived novel, depicts former Broadway press agent and heart attack victim Norman Paperman as he takes over a Caribbean hotel, only to find that insane employees and destructive typhoons prove even more stressful than New York City, to which he eventually returns.

When Wouk finished *The Caine Mutiny,* he wrote in his journal, "Unless I'm mistaken, this is a good book. But it's not yet the war novel I mean to write" (quoted in Edwards). Wouk's next two novels, the best-selling *The Winds of War* and *War and Remembrance,* have been called the American *War and Peace* (Liukkonen). *The Winds of War* focuses on Navy commander (later admiral) Victor Henry and his family from 1939 through the Japanese attack on Pearl Harbor on December 7th, 1941); *War and Remembrance* continues the epic tale of

World War II and the Holocaust, following Admiral Henry and his family until the end of the war and the end of his marriage; by the end of the two novels, the clear implication is that only through memory of war can peace be attained. In his next three novels, *Inside Out* (1985), *The Hope* (1993), and *Glory* (1994), Wouk features the Jewish experience: In the first, Israeli David Goodkind travels as an envoy between the United States and Israel as he also moves mentally between his "outside" political life and his "inside" family life and Jewish culture; in the second, the 1967 Six-Day War between Israel and the Arabs is presented through the perspective of Israeli officer Zev Barak; and in the third, Wouk brings the story of modern Israel up to the leadership of Prime Minister Menachim Begin and the Camp David Peace Accords of the 1980s.

Herman Wouk lives with his wife in Palm Springs, California, and maintains a home in Washington, D.C. His nonfiction books include *The Will to Live on* and *This Is My God,* both of which set forth Wouk's religious views. His most recent novel is *A Hole in Texas* (2004), an espionage thriller about the underground Superconducting SuperCollider. Wouk's war-novel manuscripts are housed at the Library of Congress, while the others may be found at Columbia University's Butler Library. Numerous film and television adaptations of Wouk's novels include *The Caine Mutiny,* filmed by Columbia in 1954 and starring Humphrey Bogart as Captain Queeg; *The City Boy,* filmed by Columbia in 1950; *Marjorie Morningstar,* filmed by Warner Bros. in 1958 and starring Natalie Wood as the title character; and *Youngblood Hawke* in 1964. A television adaptation of *The Caine Mutiny Court Martial,* starring Barry Sullivan, Lloyd Nolan, and Frank Lovejoy, aired on "Ford Star Jubilee" in 1955; in 1983 and 1988, respectively, *The Winds of War* and *War and Remembrance* aired as television miniseries on ABC-TV.

NOVELS

Aurora Dawn. New York: Simon & Schuster, 1947.
The Caine Mutiny: A Novel of World War II. Garden City, N.Y.: Doubleday, 1951.
The City Boy. New York: Simon & Schuster, 1948.
Don't Stop the Carnival. Garden City, N.Y.: Doubleday, 1965.
The Glory. Boston: Little, Brown, 1994.

A Hole in Texas. Boston: Little, Brown, 2004.

The Hope. Boston: Little, Brown, 1993.

Inside, Outside. Boston: Little, Brown, 1985.

The Lomokome Papers. New York: Pocket Books, 1968.

Marjorie Morningstar. Garden City, N.Y.: Doubleday, 1955.

Slattery's Hurricane. New York: Permabooks, 1956.

War and Remembrance. Boston: Little, Brown, 1978.

The Winds of War. Boston: Little, Brown, 1971.

Youngblood Hawke. Garden City, N.Y.: Doubleday, 1962.

SOURCES

Beichman, Arnold. *Herman Wouk: The Novelist as Social Historian.* New Brunswick, N.J.: Transaction Books, 1984.

Bolton, Richard R. "*The Winds of War* and Wouk's Wish for the World," *Midwest Quarterly* 16 (July 1975): 389–408.

Darby, William. *Necessary American Fictions: Popular Literature of the 1950s.* Bowling Green, Ohio: Bowling Green State University Popular Press, 1987, pp. 43–55.

Fussell, Paul. *Review of War and Remembrance, New Republic,* 14 October 1978, pp. 32–33.

Geismar, Maxwell. *American Moderns from Rebellion to Conformity.* New York: Hill & Wang, 1958, pp. 38–45.

Mazzeno, Laurence. *Herman Wouk.* New York: Twayne, 1994.

McElderry, B. R. "The Conservative as Novelist: Herman Wouk," *Arizona Quarterly* 15 (Summer 1959): 128–136.

OTHER

Brawarsky, Sandee. "The Torah and the Tank: Herman Wouk, at 84, Reflects on the Apocalyptic 20th Century and the Future of the Jewish Enterprise," *Jewish Week.* Highbeam Research. Available online. URL: http://www.highbeam.com/library/doc3.asp?DOCID=1P1:79391741. Accessed September 25, 2005.

Edwards, Bob. "Interview: Herman Wouk Discusses His New Book, *A Hole in Texas,*" Morning Edition (NPR). Highbeam Research. Available online. URL: http://www.highbeam.com/library/doc3.asp?docid=1P1:92513002. Accessed September 25, 2005.

"Herman Wouk (1915–   )." *Books and Writers.* Available online. URL: http://www.kirjasto.sci.fi/wouk.htm. Accessed September 25, 2005.

Liukkonen, Petri. "Herman Wouk: 1915–   ." LitWeb.net. Available online. URL: www.biblion.com/litweb/biogs/wouk_herman.html. Accessed April 17, 2006.

WRIGHT, RICHARD (RICHARD NATHANIEL WRIGHT) (1908–1960)

Richard Wright, one of the most notable American authors of the 20th century, was one of the first black Americans to have a novel—*NATIVE SON* (1940)—adapted for the Broadway stage, and the first black American to see his books—both *Native Son* and *BLACK BOY* (1945)—on the mainstream best-seller lists. As Ralph ELLISON said, Richard Wright, through his life and his writing, altered the black American tendency "toward self-annihilation and 'going underground' into a will to confront the world," and to confront unabashedly the racism of the United States. Less appreciated in America after his self-exile to Paris during the last 14 years of his life, Wright nonetheless continued to write realistically about oppressed individuals who stood up to bigotry and persevered in their quests for selfhood. Since his death in 1960, a large body of scholarship attests to the importance of his vision and example.

Richard Nathaniel Wright was born on September 4, 1908, on a Mississippi delta cotton plantation near Natchez, to Nathan Wright and Ella Wilson Wright, a former schoolteacher. After his father deserted the family in 1914, Wright moved with his chronically ill mother and brother to family homes in Arkansas, Mississippi, and Tennessee. Although his formal schooling ended at age 15, Wright read voraciously, particularly the unsentimental, ascerbic essays of H. L. Mencken; from Mencken he learned of and read the American naturalists—Theodore DREISER, Stephen CRANE, and Sherwood ANDERSON, as well as the Europeans Fyodor Dostoevsky, Nikolai Gogol, and Henrik Ibsen. After moving to Chicago in 1927, he joined the Communist Party in 1932 and published short stories and poems in such left-wing magazines as *Partisan* and *New Masses.* Like many writers of his era, Wright worked for the Works Progress Administration (WPA); he published his first book, *Uncle Tom's Children: Four Novellas* (1938), and won first prize in a WPA-sponsored writing contest. The novellas expose white hatred, prejudice, and violence against blacks, as well as the violence that some of the black characters resort to in reaction to that hatred. *Native Son* appeared two years later and shocked the reading public into an awareness of the rage, misery, and helplessness of black men in 20th century America, emblematized by Bigger Thomas, an inarticulate black who is driven by circumstances to commit murder. The book sold approximately 250,000 copies in its first month and was adopted as a Book-of-the-Month Club selection.

Although *Native Son* would probably have secured Wright's reputation, the publication of *Black Boy* in

1945 gained for Wright even more acclaim; like its predecessor, it, too, was a Book-of-the-Month Club selection. A number of critics see the book as more novel than autobiography; scholar Thadious M. Davis, for example, calls the book a "fictionalized autobiography" (Davis, 549) because its structure, technique, and impassioned voice rely on the fictional and creative talents normally associated with the novel. Critics have also written about *Black Boy* as a modern slave narrative and sociological study. Wright depicts himself as an outcast, a rebellious outsider who resists the subservient role expected of Southern blacks in the 1920s and 1930s. By rejecting religion and upbraiding fellow blacks for their servile attitudes, in this book and other books, Wright broke ground for such later writers as James BALDWIN and Ralph Ellison.

After moving to Paris in 1947, Wright continued to write fiction, publishing *The OUTSIDER* (1953), a novel clearly influenced by the existentialist writer Jean-Paul Sartre, with whom Wright had become friendly; in fact, the work is one of the earliest American existentialist novels. Its hero is a black man, Cross Damon, but the issues are more philosophical than specifically racial: Damon escapes family encumbrances to join the Communist Party as a way to live his life; he is ultimately killed by one of the communists. A more effective dramatization of Wright's interest in existentialism is the novella *The Man Who Lived Underground,* published posthumously in 1971. Fred Daniels finds a new identity in the sewer system, staying alive by robbing those above who have excluded him. "Invisibility," however, is not the answer; when he emerges from the sewer, the police shoot him dead. *Savage Holiday* (1954) is Wright's only novel to feature a white protagonist, an insurance salesman whose rootless wandering suggests the state of the modern individual. *The Long Dream* (1958) centers on Fishbelly, a middle-class black youth who, like Wright himself, embarks on an odyssey away from the South and toward a self-constructed, meaningful philosophy. *Rite of Passage,* a novella written in the 1940s, was published posthumously. Fifteen-year-old Johnny Gibbs returns home with his straight-A report card only to learn that his parents are actually foster parents, not blood rela-

tives, and that they must send him to a foster home. He runs away and joins a violent Harlem street gang.

Richard Wright was married briefly to Dhimah Rose Meadman in the late 1930s and in 1941 married Ellen Poplar, at the time a fellow communist and daughter of Polish immigrants. Richard Wright died of a heart attack on November 28, 1960, in Paris, France, and his ashes, along with those of the manuscript of *Black Boy,* are buried in the Colambarium in Paris. At the beginning of the 21st century, it is difficult to overestimate Richard Wright's significance.

NOVELS AND NOVELLAS
Black Boy: A Record of Childhood and Youth. New York: Harper, 1945.

Lawd Today. New York: Walker, 1963.

The Long Dream. Garden City, N.Y.: Doubleday, 1958.

The Man Who Lived Underground. Paris: Aubier-Flammarion, 1971.

Native Son. New York and London: Harper, 1940.

The Outsider. New York: Harper, 1953.

Rite of Passage. New York: HarperCollins, 1995.

Savage Holiday. New York: Avon, 1954.

Uncle Tom's Children: Four Novellas. New York and London: Harper, 1938; expanded as *Uncle Tom's Children: Five Long Stories.* New York and London: Harper, 1940.

SOURCES
Abcarian, Richard. *Richard Wright's Native Son: A Critical Handbook.* Belmont, Calif.: Wadsworth, 1970.

Bakish, David. *Richard Wright.* New York: Ungar, 1973.

Bloom, Harold, ed. *Richard Wright's Native Son.* New York: Chelsea House, 1995.

Bone, Robert. *Richard Wright.* Minneapolis: University of Minnesota Press, 1969.

Brignano, Russell Carl. *Richard Wright: An Introduction to the Man and His Works.* Pittsburgh: University of Pittsburgh Press, 1970.

Butler, Robert. *The Critical Response to Richard Wright.* Westport, Conn.: Greenwood Press, 1995.

———. *Native Son: The Emergence of a New Black Hero.* Boston: Twayne, 1991.

Campbell, James. *Exiled in Paris: Richard Wright, James Baldwin, Samuel Beckett and Others on the Left Bank.* New York: Scribner, 1995.

Davis, Thadious M. "Richard Wright." In *Fifty Southern Writers After 1900: A Bio-bibliographical Sourcebook,* edited by Joseph M. Flora and Robert Bain, 545–559. Wesport, Conn.: Greenwood Press, 1987.

Dickstein, Morris. *Gates of Eden.* New York: Basic Books, 1977.

Ellison, Ralph. "Richard Wright's Blues." In Ralph Ellison, *Shadow and Act,* 77–94. New York: Random House, 1964.

Fabre, Michel. *The Unfinished Quest of Richard Wright.* Translated by Isabel Barzun. New York: William Morrow, 1973.

———. *The World of Richard Wright.* Jackson: University Press of Mississippi, 1985.

Fabre, Michel, and Charles Davis. *Richard Wright: The Primary Sources.* Boston: G. K. Hall, 1982.

Felgar, Robert. *Richard Wright.* Boston: Twayne, 1980.

———. *Understanding Richard Wright's Black Boy: A Student Casebook to Issues, Sources, and Historical Documents.* Westport, Conn.: Greenwood Press, 1998.

Hakutani, Yoshinobu. *Critical Essays on Richard Wright.* Boston: G. K. Hall, 1982.

———. *Richard Wright and Racial Discourse.* Columbia: University of Missouri Press, 1996.

Kinnamon, Keneth, ed. *Critical Essays on Richard Wright's "Native Son."* New York: Twayne, 1997.

Margolies, Edward. *The Art of Richard Wright.* Carbondale: Southern Illinois University Press, 1969.

Miller, James A., ed. *Approaches to Teaching Wright's "Native Son."* New York: Modern Language Association of America, 1997.

Rampersad, Arnold, ed. *Richard Wright: A Collection of Critical Essays.* Englewood Cliffs. N.J.: Prentice Hall, 1995.

Ray, David, and Robert M. Farnsworth, eds. *Richard Wright: Impressions and Perspectives.* Ann Arbor: University of Michigan Press, 1973.

Reilly, John M. *Richard Wright: The Critical Reception.* New York: Burt Franklin, 1978.

Stepto, Robert B. *Literacy and Ascent: Richard Wright's "Black Boy."* In *From behind the Veil: A Study of Afro-American Narrative,* edited by Robert B. Stepto, 128–162. Urbana: University of Illinois Press, 1979.

Walker, Margaret. *Richard Wright: Daemonic Genius.* New York: Warner Books/Amistad Press, 1988.

Webb, Constance. *Richard Wright: A Biography.* New York: Putnam's, 1968.

Wright, Richard. *American Hunger.* New York: Harper, 1977.

Y

YAMANAKA, LOIS-ANN (1961–) One of the most distinctive of the young Asian-American writers, Lois-Ann Yamanaka has made an enormous impact with her Hawaiian trilogy—WILD MEAT AND THE BULLY BURGERS (1996), BLU'S HANGING (1997), and *Heads by Harry* (1999). All these novels focus on adolescent Japanese Americans in a series of coming-of-age tales, usually with females as the leading characters. Thematically, each covers similar territory but with a whole new set of characters and situations. While the teenagers experiment in the usual adolescent manner with drugs, sex, and alcohol, with sometimes disastrous results, the heart-wrenching reality that all these young characters share is absent parents, who have sometimes physically disappeared and are at other times emotionally absent. And these parents, like their children, are frequently depicted as incapacitated or irresponsible because they are descendants of Japanese-American plantation laborers. Stylistically, Yamanaka blends her own poetic intonations with the tough and gritty pidgin dialect of her characters. This remarkable feature of her work began with *Saturday Night at the Pahala Theatre* (1993), a four-part verse novella depicting four working-class Japanese-American teenage girls, and continues through the trilogy and her most recent novel, *Father of the Four Passages* (2001).

Inspired by *The HOUSE ON MANGO STREET* (1996), the award-winning novel by Chicana writer Sandra CISNEROS, *Wild Meat and the Bully Burgers* is composed of a series of loosely connected stories that take place in Hilo, Hawaii, in the 1970s. Narrating in pidgin dialect, Lovey Nariyoshi relates the incidents of this working-class Japanese-American bildungsroman. *Blu's Hanging,* similarly narrated in first-person pidgin, this time by 13-year-old Ivah Igata, tells the poignant and painful tale of three children (Ivah is the eldest). In the case of the youngest child, the mother's death leaves him literally speechless. The middle child, Blu, is left vulnerable to exploitation. The concluding novel in the trilogy, *Heads by Harry,* is again narrated by a young girl, Toni Yagyuu. As the middle child, Toni is sandwiched between Sheldon, her homosexual brother, and Bunny, her beautiful, attention-craving younger sister. Toni battles drug and alcohol addiction and several unwanted pregnancies before finally learning to assert her individuality. In *Father of the Four Passages,* Yamanaka's most recent novel, the hip Sonia Kurisu, after having three abortions, decides not to abort Sonny Boy, the baby conceived in her fourth pregnancy—but for much of the remainder of the book she is haunted by the three aborted babies and returns from college in Las Vegas to begin the healing process in Hawaii.

Yamanaka was born in 1950 on Molokai and was reared in the Hilo, Kau, and Kona districts of Hawaii. After earning a bachelor's degree in 1983 and a master's degrees in education in 1987 from the University of Hawaii, she began teaching in the Honolulu public schools and married John Inferrera. Although controversy boiled up among the Asian-American community over perceived racial slurs directed at Filipino Americans in her first two books, Yamanaka was defended by such other writers as Amy TAN, Maxine Hong KINGSTON, and Jessica HAGEDORN, who affirmed her right to artistic freedom. Like many other Asian-American writers, Yamanaka says she writes her own truth and does not believe that she speaks for all Asian Americans.

NOVELS

Blu's Hanging. New York: Farrar, Straus & Giroux, 1997.
Father of the Four Passages. New York: Farrar, Straus & Giroux, 2001.
Heads by Harry. New York: Farrar, Straus & Giroux, 1999.
Wild Meat and the Bully Burgers. New York: Farrar, Straus & Giroux, 1996.

YEARLING, THE MARJORIE KINNAN RAWLINGS **(1938)** Set in the rural landscape of Cross Creek, Florida, where RAWLINGS resided, *The Yearling* may seem like a rather local, time and place–specific novel. Rawlings's uncompromising use of the region's dialect suggests this localness. The devotion to the sound of rural Florida speech sometimes manifests itself in benign comedy. For instance, "Ma" Baxter stipulates a "carefully written" list of items to be purchased during a trip to town: She demands "A haf bolt perty blue and wite check gingham for Mrs. B now a real perty blue." Later, she chides her son, Jody, for using grammar incorrectly: "You'd ought to say, 'The roaches has eat it,' " she confidently asserts. This vivid regard for local oral habits is matched by Rawlings's meticulous reconstruction of Florida's then-present fauna and flora. Like the humans who struggle against nature to farm, the animals, too, struggle through extreme weather and perennial competition from other species in untamed Florida. Yet the book transcends local concerns. Telling of the development of Judy—an only child—growing up with his hardship-accustomed parents, the book won the Pulitzer Prize for Fiction in 1939, found a massive readership, and has continued to be reprinted and read by adolescents and adults ever since.

There are at least three reasons for *The Yearling's* almost universal appeal: Jody comes to realize that self-interest largely drives adults; he learns about what Benjamin T. Spencer, writing in 1939 about *The Yearling,* memorably identified as the necessity of "supporting life at the expense of justice"; and Jody, on the cusp of adolescence, must deal with what is to him an inexplicable awakening of sexuality. Cross Creek contains families that are—necessarily because of the poverty caused by the terrain's harshness—self-interested. The Baxters have a particularly strained relationship with one large family, the Forresters. Although some Forresters are more aggressive and unreasonable than others, they are prone to violence: During one fight, Jody is knocked out, and they are strongly suspected of burning down a house during a feud over a girl, Twink. Jody's father, "Pa" Baxter, is renowned for his honesty, but even he is prepared to use reverse psychology to outwit his neighbors. Keen to sell to the Forresters a hunting dog that has thus far proved useless, "Pa" stresses, insincerely, that "I jest wouldn't put no notion o' tradin' in your minds." The deal is made, to the Baxters' advantage. Jody learns that in order to flourish when people are as predatory as animals, even honest persons must be occasionally dishonest.

The Baxters have to protect themselves against families such as the Forresters—and they have to protect themselves against the appetitive needs of wild animals. The yearling of the title is an orphaned fawn that Jody has rescued. At first, the animal causes little disruption to the Baxters' habits, but Flag soon becomes too big for the house, knocking over food and essential household items. Keeping Flag outside proves to be an inadequate solution, because he soon uproots and irrevocably damages the family's crops. The Baxters, who struggle to produce enough food to last through challenging Florida winters, cannot afford to lose any crops. Jody's parents insist that Flag must be killed—they see the fawn as a rival, not a companion as does Jody. After an initially hysterical reaction to the shooting of Flag, Jody comes to terms with the death, realizing that, indeed, the killing of the splendid creature was unjust and unwanted, but necessary for the family's survival.

Although the action takes place over the course of just one eventful year, *The Yearling* is in many respects a bildungsroman—it is a novel about Jody reaching a life milestone. Like the fawn, Jody too is called a "yearlin' boy" by "Pa" Baxter when the father is reminding the son of his naivety and unreadiness for adult negotiations. By the novel's end, however, "Pa" observes newfound maturity in Jody, who can now even wash his feet without parental instruction. "Pa" insists with grave pride: "You ain't a yearlin' no longer." Future conversations between Jody and "Pa" will be "man to man," not adult to child. Jody's initial, prepubescent distaste for the company of girls amuses because it is stereotypical. He feels a "murderous fury" when teased about an alleged fondness for a local girl, proclaiming that "I—I hate girls. I hate Eulalie most of all." This romance-averse attitude is consistent with Jody's difficult relationship with an obstreperous cousin, Oliver. Jody resents the time that Oliver spends with his sweetheart, Twink—and with the time that Oliver spends fighting the Forresters over her. "Hit's Twink," Jody complains, blaming Oliver's inconsiderate behavior on his passion for the young woman, "Hit's gals does it. I don't never aim to have no gal."

Predictably, Jody's attitude changes. At a social gathering, Jody is stirred by the sight of Eulalie in feminine attire, with a white dress, ribbons, and ruffles; in particular, he resents the girl's attention being distracted by a ferry-boy, because "in a remote fashion, [she] belonged to him, Jody, to do with as he pleased, if only to throw potatoes at her." He cannot explain or identify his sexual feelings, but he feels them vividly nonetheless. He even enjoys a gentle kiss from Twink, who has married Oliver, finding her touch "strangely agreeable." Jody now tolerates Oliver and Twink's romance because, albeit unconsciously, he now feels empathy for their affective desires. Earlier, Jody has helped to kill an especially violent bear. His pride in his role is expressed through the narrator's use of phallic imagery. Standing near the "tallest pine," Jody "slid one hand along the barrel of his gun," and "a blessed stiffening and clarity came to him." In this environment, masculinity is tested by the ability to kill; phallocentric satisfaction is felt by Jody, who complements the coming of sexual feelings with the coming of a sense of responsibility to harden himself to the dog-eat-dog realities of this poor backwater in Florida.

SOURCES

Balee, Susan. "Marjorie Kinnan Rawlings in the New Millennium," *Marjorie Kinnan Rawlings Journal of Florida Literature* 11 (2002): 7–14.

Bellman, Samuel Irving. *Marjorie Kinnan Rawlings.* Boston, Twayne, 1974.

Brown, Stephen Gilbert. "The Storytellers: Marjorie Talking to Harry Talking to Me about *The Yearling*," *Marjorie Kinnan Rawlings Journal of Florida Literature* 9 (1999): 1–16.

Cauthen, Sudye. "Sacred Place in the Work of Marjorie Kinnan Rawlings," *Marjorie Kinnan Rawlings Journal of Florida Literature* 11 (2002): 61–70.

Doig, Ivan. "Introduction." *The Yearling* by Marjorie Kinnan Rawlings. New York: Scribner Paperback Fiction, 2002, pp. 5–12.

Keeley, Jennifer. *Understanding "The Yearling."* San Diego, Calif.: Lucent Books, 2000.

King, Laura. "A 'Cosmic Maturity': Marjorie Kinnan Rawlings' Use of Rain in *The Yearling*," *Marjorie Kinnan Rawlings Journal of Florida Literature* 11 (2002): 45–49.

Spencer, Benjamin T. "Wherefore this Southern Fiction?" *Sewanee Review* 47 (1939): 500–513.

Turk, Janet K. "Marjorie Kinnan Rawlings (1896–1953)." In *American Women Writers, 1900–1945: A Bio-Bibliographical Critical Sourcebook,* edited by Laurie Champion, 287–294. Westport, Conn.: Greenwood, 2000.

Kevin De Ornellas

YELLOW RAFT IN BLUE WATER, A

MICHAEL DORRIS (1987) Michael DORRIS's first novel *A Yellow Raft in Blue Water* is sometimes categorized as young adult fiction. Themes of initiation, maturation, discrimination, peer problems, and family confusions all speak to young adult readers. The three first-person narrators also suggest such a categorization. The novel begins with the voice of 15-year-old Rayona, narrating the disintegration of her family. When the novel moves to the two other first-person narrators, each also begins her section of the novel with a significant event in her 15th year. Yet the novel is not strictly for young adults; the label is not inappropriate, only limiting. The characters in *A Yellow Raft in Blue Water* speak to any reader interested in the position of minorities in America; its style speaks to any reader interested in the power of storytelling; its themes and voices speak to any reader interested in women in American culture and in the struggle constantly waged between an individual and family.

Characters of mixed heritage have the most difficulty with discrimination in this novel. Rayona, the initial narrator, has an African-American father and a Native American mother. Although raised in an urban setting as an Indian, even knowing the language of her mother's reservation, Rayona looks more like her African-American father. Of mixed ancestry himself (Dorris's father was part Modoc; his mother was of European descent), Dorris portrays well the confusion Rayona displays as she struggles both in urban Seattle and rural Montana to make sense of herself and find a place for herself in the culture and in the family. Reflecting on Rayona's situation, her mother Christine thinks Rayona "was the wrong color, had the wrong name, had the wrong family—all an accident" (276).

In a 1997 interview on National Public Radio, Dorris addressed the idea of family in the novel. In response to the suggestion that Rayona's family is not "usual," Dorris quipped that although he grew up watching model families on *The Donna Reed Show* and *Father Knows Best,* he didn't know many "usual families." Despite the surprising turns in family history that unfold in *Yellow Raft,* the genuine quality of Rayona's family prevails largely because of the voices of the three women narrators. The oral quality of the three voices ensures storytelling as a major theme. Snippets of stories, imagined or real, fill the novel, and stories untold haunt the novel. The same incident told from varying perspectives reveals the subjectivity of stories. The novel gains momentum and complexity because the three narrators have different tones and motives for telling their stories. The order of the three narratives, from present into past, encourages readers to make assumptions that are later overturned. Rayona's opening narrative in the present tense appears straightforward. Yet once the reader feels comfortable with Rayona's perspective, Christine begins narrating, filling in family history that forces readers to reevaluate some of their judgments. As Dorris widens the scope by incrementally giving the vision of someone who has lived longer, complications arise. One of the main problems in Rayona's family is the apparent refusal to communicate feelings. Christine and Aunt Ida's pride causes rifts in the family, some of which can never be bridged. Aunt Ida's narrative, the final and by far the briefest, clarifies that Rayona's family problems in the 1980s have roots in the Depression. Yet as the novel moves from one narrator to another, parallel scenes and repeated symbols hold out hope that some gener-

ation, perhaps Rayona's, may dissolve the family grudges. The repeated symbol of braiding, for example, mirrors the three-narrator structure but also provides optimism for family unity.

Dorris's novel centers on women, but a constellation of interesting male characters swirl around his women narrators. Some of the male characters are family members; others are not strictly so. *Yellow Raft* indicates how families need not be defined by genetics. Adalaide Morris notes how Dorris extends the concept of family; she writes that families "are the first place that compels us to process more than one issue, more than one point of view, more than one emotion at a time" (19). Several important male characters help the three women narrators grow precisely by providing different experiences, feelings, and views. Dayton Nichols, for example, who is not biologically or maritally related to any of the narrators, gradually comes to play an important familial role. Not all the male characters are positive influences. Through structural parallels, Dorris touches on the important role priests as missionaries played on Native American reservations. Both Ida and Rayona are befriended by missionary priests but with vastly different results. Both priests are privy to secrets in Rayona's family, but only one of the priests exhibits a familial concern.

Ten years after the publication of *Yellow Raft,* Dorris published a sequel, *Cloud Chamber* (1997). Covering 12 decades and five generations, beginning in Boyle, Ireland, County Roscommon, it ends on the Indian Reservation in eastern Montana, where Rayona's mother was born. As *Yellow Raft* reveals the hidden history of Rayona's matriarchal line, *Cloud Chamber* uncovers her father's family history. The later novel may well remind readers of the virtues of *Yellow Raft,* as it too untangles a web of family bitterness and deceit as well as love through multiple narrators.

SOURCES

Cowart, David. "Braid of Blood: *A Yellow Raft in Blue Water.*" In *Other Americans, Other Americas: The Politics and Poetics of Multiculturalism,* edited by Magdalena J. Zaborowska and Tim Caudery, 140–149. Aarhus, Denmark: Aarhus University Press, 1998.
Dorris, Michael. *Cloud Chamber.* New York: Scribner, 1997.
———. Interview with Bob Edwards. *Morning Edition.* National Public Radio. WVIA, January 13, 1997.

———. *A Yellow Raft in Blue Water.* 1987. New York: Warner, 1988.

Morris, Adalaide. "First Persons Plural in Contemporary Feminist Fiction," *Tulsa Studies in Women's Literature* 11, no. 1 (Spring 1992): 11–29.

Wong, Hertha D. Sweet. "Taking Place: African-Native American Subjectivity in *A Yellow Raft in Blue Water.*" In *Mixed Race Literature,* edited by Jonathan Brennan, 165–176. Stanford, Calif.: Stanford University Press, 2002.

Marion Petrillo

YELLOW WALLPAPER, THE Charlotte Perkins Gilman (1892)

In January 1892, Charlotte Perkins GILMAN, through her novella *The Yellow Wallpaper,* first revealed to her readers the horror of the then-popular "rest cure," a remedy often prescribed for women suffering from what was then diagnosed as neurasthenia or hysteria. The story, printed in *The New England Magazine,* with illustrations by Jo. H. Hatfield, appeared as a hybrid fictional form—combining influences of both sentimental fiction and an American gothic tradition, as well as including some autobiographical elements. Gilman, who would become a vocal advocate for feminist social issues, had known the extreme isolation and severe psychological distress that the rest cure caused for the women forced to follow its mandates and drew upon her own personal experience with S. Weir Mitchell's experimental treatment for melancholia for her fictional piece. The story still enthralls readers today due to Gilman's remarkable style of demonstrating, through formal literary presentation, the mental deterioration of her narrator through a first-person point of view maintained in what appears to be a woman's journal.

The form of the story contributes much to the fictional realism of the literary piece. As in Poe's well-established and widely read gothic short stories, the narrative assumes the perspective of a first-person point of view, which brings the reader directly into the mental state of the narrator, as one might observe in "The Black Cat" or "The Tell-Tale Heart." Stories told from this perspective often seem authentic, given the immediacy of the thoughts, feelings, and information related through the assumed narrative voice. Sentimental fiction often used this point of view, with narrators attributing the appellatives "gentle reader" or "dear reader" to the audience—

for example, Charlotte Brontë's famous "Reader, I married him," from *Jane Eyre.* Due to the formal aspects of the printed text, Gilman's audience could analyze the story's pages for evidence of the acute mental disorder from which the narrator might be suffering. Sentence fragments, choppy lines, truncated paragraphs, and writing that becomes increasingly frantic through exaggerated punctuation, italicized words, and repetition suggest that the narrator is indeed becoming mad, but the investigative work on the part of the reader will be to figure out what the cause of that mental distress might be.

In his scholarly work *No Place of Grace: Antimodernism and the Transformation of American Culture 1880–1920,* Jackson Lears examines the malaise of the "late-Victorian bourgeoisie" that resulted from modernization. Possessing the learned Protestant practice of self-examination, many white men and women of the upper middle class could not justify their inactivity, from which a growing nervous restlessness resulted. From a cultural historical perspective, Lears notes that observers proposed that this widely spread nervousness, often defined and treated as "neurasthenia," in actuality, stemmed from "overcivilization" (51). Lears continues: "Neurasthenia was historically important not because nervous ailments had actually increased—that point is impossible to substantiate—but because observers believed nervousness was on the rise, and treated its spread as a cultural problem" (51). Numerous "remedies for nervousness" directly resulted from this fascination and obsessive interest in what was thought to be the psychological disintegration of the privileged class, extremely popular during the 1880s in the United States. Lear continues, "For many neurasthenics, the therapy was worse than the disease. Charlotte Perkins Gilman's autobiographical short story 'The Yellow Wall Paper' (1892) typified one response" (53). Gilman's story gave voice to the woman imprisoned within her own home, trapped in her own private asylum.

In her story, Charlotte Perkins Gilman responds to the treatment that she endured under the care of S. Weir Mitchell, who believed that Americans had too much "moral and intellectual strenuosity." The popular physician advised his patients to undergo a "protracted 'rest cure' designed to isolate his patients from nervous stimuli, to 'fatten' and 'redden' them until they could return to active life" (Lears, 52). Gilman's female narrator shows how her own physician husband fails to properly identify or acknowledge her symptoms and who along with the narrator's brother, also a doctor, acts in a manner similar to S. Weir Mitchell (48). The reader bears witness to the mental suffering of the narrator, who obsessively details the room in which she is imprisoned—with a peculiar interest in the putrid, acrid, yellowed paper that covers its walls. Scholars still debate over the significance of the color yellow— symbolizing urine, Asian immigration, or arsenic used in wallpaper production in late Victorian America (Bauer, 27). Yet the room itself becomes an eerie site for investigation. Clues appear in the room—the ripped wallpaper, the "sickly, sulphur tint" of the paper observed in places, the "scratched" "gouged" floor, the pitted plaster, the nailed-down, immovable bed, the barred windows and the "rings and things in the walls"—to suggest that the house had once been an asylum or mental hospital, which conjures up haunting specters of insane patients who had been there long before. This contributes to the narrator's own sense of the room's maddening influence.

Given current medical knowledge, the modern reader would likely diagnose the narrator as suffering from postpartum depression, as she had given birth to a baby not too long before the story begins. Elaine Showalter, in *Sister's Choice: Tradition and Change in American Women's Writing,* suggests that the true ghost that haunts the female narrator in Gilman's text is the "specter of infanticide," a desire that stems from postpartum depression. Showalter writes: "Psychosis, involving hallucinations and delusions, can develop from postpartum depressions marked by crying spells, confusion, sleeplessness, and anxiety. Victorian doctors already knew what recent studies have documented: that 'it's during a psychotic depression that mothers are at great risk of killing their babies' " (134). The narrator's desire to kill her own baby here becomes "transformed" into violent self-destruction. Showalter places Gilman's story within a tradition of "American Female Gothic plots" that examined the "repression and incarceration typical of late nineteenth-century psychiatric

practice" (135). Certainly, Gilman's piece gives insight into the medical treatment of female neurasthenics from the 1890s and provides a commentary on a historical social issue that affected contemporary readers.

SOURCES

Chessler, Phyllis. Foreword. *Women of the Asylum: Voices Behind the Walls, 1840–1945.* Edited by Jeffery L. Geller and Maxine Harris. New York: Anchor Books, 1994.

Gilman, Charlotte Perkins. *The Yellow Wallpaper.* Bedford Cultural Edition. Introduction. Edited by Dale M. Bauer. Boston: Bedford/St. Martin's, 1998.

Lears, T. J. Jackson. *No Place of Grace: Antimodernism and the Transformation of American Culture 1880–1920.* New York: Pantheon, 1981.

Showalter, Elaine. *Sister's Choice: Tradition and Change in American Women's Writing.* New York: Oxford University Press, 1991.

Tuttle, Jennifer S. "Rewriting the West Cure: Charlotte Perkins Gilman, Owen Wister, and the Sexual Politics of Neurasthenia." In *The Mixed Legacy of Charlotte Perkins Gilman,* edited by Catherine J. Golden and Joanna Schneider Zangrando, 103–121. Newark: University of Delaware Press, 2000.

YERBY, FRANK (FRANK GARVIN YERBY) (1916–1991)

The first African-American author to write a best-selling novel, and the first to sell a novel to Hollywood (*The Foxes of Harrow* [1946]), Frank Yerby died in 1991 with an unsurpassed record of 33 novels, 12 of them best-sellers, with translations into 14 languages and sales exceeding 55 million copies (Pratt, 505). His so-called formulaic novels and "costume" novels resulted in decades of controversy about the depth and extent of his talent. He has, consequently, been excluded from numerous anthologies and courses on African-American literature. Many scholars are now arguing for more recognition for Yerby and, indeed, his reassessment has already begun in scholarly journals; a book on Yerby will likely follow soon.

Yerby was born on September 15, 1916, to Rufus Garvin Yerby and Willie Smythe Yerby, in Augusta, Georgia. He received a bachelor's degree in 1937 from Paine College, and a master's degree in 1938 from Fisk University. After winning an O. Henry Memorial Award for his short story "Health Card," Yerby wrote but failed to publish a protest novel. However, within two years he published *The Foxes of Harrow,* an epic Civil War romance that focuses on the fortunes and perspectives of hero Stephen Fox. Yerby continued in this vein for two decades until he began using black characters instead of white in *Speak Now* (1969) and *A Darkness at Ingraham's Crest* (1979). The novel that attracted the most acclaim, however, was *The DAHOMEAN* (1971), set in 19th-century Africa and focusing on the Dahomean people. The hero, Nyasanu, becomes province governor but watches his fortunes decline and his family disappear; his enemies sell him into slavery in the United States.

Frank Yerby died on November 29, 1991, of congestive heart failure in Madrid, Spain. *The Foxes of Harrow,* filmed by Twentieth Century-Fox in 1951, starred Rex Harrison and Maureen O'Hara. *The Golden Hawk* and *The Saracen Blade* were filmed by Columbia in 1952 and 1954, respectively; *Pride's Castle* was a made-for-television movie.

SELECTED MAJOR NOVELS

Benton's Row. New York: Dial Press, 1954.
Bride of Liberty. Garden City, N.Y.: Doubleday, 1954.
Captain Rebel. New York: Dial Press, 1956.
The Dahomean. New York: Dial Press, 1971.
A Darkness at Ingraham's Crest. New York: Dial Press, 1979.
The Devil's Laughter. New York: Dial Press, 1953.
Devilseed. Garden City, N.Y.: Doubleday, 1984.
Fairoaks. New York: Dial Press, 1957.
Floodtide. New York: Dial Press, 1950. London: Heinemann, 1951.
The Foxes of Harrow. New York: Dial Press, 1946.
The Garfield Honor. New York: Dial Press, 1961.
Gillian. New York: Dial Press, 1960.
The Girl from Storyville: A Victorian Novel. New York: Dial Press, 1972.
Goat Song: A Novel of Ancient Greece. New York: Dial Press, 1967.
The Golden Hawk. New York: Dial Press, 1948.
Griffin's Way. New York: Dial Press, 1962.
Hail the Conquering Hero. New York: Dial Press, 1977.
Historical Novel. New York: Dial Press, 1971.
Jarrett's Jade. New York: Dial Press, 1959.
Judas, My Brother: The Story of the Thirteenth Disciple. New York: Dial Press, 1969.
McKenzie's Hundred. Garden City, N.Y.: Doubleday, 1985.
An Odor of Sanctity. New York: Dial Press, 1965.

The Old Gods Laugh: A Modern Romance. New York: Dial Press, 1964.
Pride's Castle. New York: Dial Press, 1949.
A Rose for Ana María. New York: Dial Press, 1976.
The Saracen Blade. New York: Dial Press, 1952.
The Serpent and the Staff. New York: Dial Press, 1958.
Speak Now. New York: Dial Press, 1969.
Tobias and the Angel. New York: Dial Press, 1975.
Treasure of Pleasant Valley. New York: Dial Press, 1955.
The Vixens. New York: Dial Press, 1947.
The Voyage Unplanned. New York: Dial Press, 1974.
Western: A Saga of the Great Plains. New York: Dial Press, 1982.
A Woman Called Fancy. New York: Dial Press, 1951.

SOURCES

Hill, James L. "The Anti-Heroic Hero in Frank Yerby's Historical Novels." In *Perspectives of Black Popular Culture,* edited by Harry B. Shaw, 144–154. Bowling Green, Ohio: Bowling Green State University Popular Press, 1990.
Morgan, Gwendolyn D. "Challenging the Black Aesthetic: The Silencing of Frank Yerby," *Florida A and M University Research Bulletin* 35 (September 1993): 19–30.
Pratt, Louis Hill. "Frank Garvin Yerby." In *Contemporary African American Novelists: A Bio-Bibliographical Sourcebook,* edited by Emmanuel S. Nelson, 506–511. Westport, Conn.: Greenwood Press, 1999.
Turner, Darwin T. "Frank Yerby as Debunker," *Massachusetts Review* 20 (Summer 1968): 569–577.
———. "Frank Yerby: Golden Debunker," *Black Boots Bulletin* 1 (1972): 4–9, 30–33.
———. "The Negro Novelist at the South," *Southern Humanities Review* 1 (1967): 21–29.
———. "An Interview with Frank Garvin Yerby," *Resources for American Literary Study* 21, no. 2 (1995): 206–239.

YEZIERSKA, ANZIA (1885–1970) Anzia

Yezierska, novelist and short story writer, known widely as the "sweatshop cinderella," took as her subject New York's early-20th-century immigrant Jewish community. A volatile, forthright, passionate tone characterizes her writing and remains the source of much of her fiction's appeal. She became a celebrity when her well-received first collection of stories, *Hungry Hearts* (1920), was optioned for the movies by Samuel Goldwyn, as was her first novel, *SALOME OF THE TENEMENTS* (1923). *BREAD GIVERS: A STRUGGLE BETWEEN A FATHER OF THE OLD WORLD AND A DAUGHTER OF THE NEW* (1925), Yezierska's depiction of the tension between genders and generations, is admired by feminist scholars and social historians. It depicts a young woman's struggle against Old World patriarchy, one of many strong, self-reliant women heroes who must negotiate the boundaries between immigrant culture and poverty and the life of the recently enfranchised New American Woman.

Anzia Yezierska did not know her exact birth date, but many literary historians agree on 1885 as the year she was born on the Russian-Polish border, to Rabbi Bernard Yezierska and Pearl Yezierska. The family immigrated to New York's Lower East Side in the early 1890s. As usual, in immigrant families, the boys were educated, while tradition dictated that Yezierska and her sister worked in low-paying menial jobs until marriages were arranged for them. Yezierska, however, educated herself at Columbia University by working in a laundry and gaining the financial assistance of wealthy patrons; she graduated from Teachers College in 1904. In 1910 she married Jacob Gordon, an attorney, but the marriage was annulled six months afterward, and she married Arnold Levitas, a teacher and textbook writer, in 1911. By 1915, however, she had permanently separated from him and published her first story. In 1917 she approached the philosopher and educator John Dewey in his office at Columbia University. He encouraged her and apparently initiated a romantic relationship with her that ended with his departure for China the following year. Thereafter the theme of the passionate immigrant woman and the repressed Protestant man recurs frequently in her fiction. *Salome of the Tenements* is based on the life of her friend Rose Pastor, who married philanthropist Graham Stokes; unlike Rose, however, Sonya Vrunsky, Yezierska's protagonist, finds only failure in her marriage to the Anglo-Saxon John Manning. Her next and most autobiographical work, *Bread Givers,* earned Yezierska critical acclaim. Rabbi Smolinsky tyrannizes his daughters, sends them to work in sweatshops, and then sells them into marriage; only the youngest, Sara, escapes, educating herself, rejecting her Protestant suitor, and marrying Hugo Seelig, an Americanized Jew who bridges the two cultures.

Her next novels, *Arrogant Beggar* (1927) and *All I Could Never Be* (1932), were neither critical nor commercial successes. *Arrogant Beggar* again explores the theme of the immigrant woman, here named Adele Lindner, who moves from a tenement to a Home for Working Girls and then reacts with disillusion to the shallow hypocrisy she finds. *All I Could Never Be* is, according to Yezierska's daughter, Louise Levitas Henrikson, a fictionalized version of her relationship with Dewey: The novel presents the relationship through the immigrant character Fanya Ivanova and the famous professor Henry Scott, who ends up losing interest in her because she lets emotion rather than reason rule her reactions. Yezierska's final autobiographical novel, *Red Ribbon on a White Horse* (1950), was a critical success and, according to scholar Aleta Cane, enabled her to work for the *New York Times* as a book reviewer (Cane, 380). Yezierska continued to write essays, stories, and reviews until her death in California on November 21, 1970. Boston University houses a collection of Yezierska's manuscripts and letters.

NOVELS

All I Could Never Be. New York: Putnam, 1932.
Arrogant Beggar. Garden City, N.Y.: Doubleday, 1927.
Bread Givers: A Struggle Between a Father of the Old World and a Daughter of the New. Garden City, N.Y.: Doubleday, 1925.
Red Ribbon on a White Horse. New York: Scribner, 1950.
Salome of the Tenements. New York: Boni & Liveright, 1923.

SOURCES

Boydston, Jo Ann, ed. *The Poems of John Dewey.* Carbondale: Southern Illinois University Press, 1977.
Cane, Aleta. "Anzia Yezierska." In *American Women Writers, 1900–1945: A Bio-Bibliographical Critical Sourcebook,* edited by Laurie Champion, 378–382. Westport, Conn.: Greenwood Press, 2000.
Dearborn, Mary V. *Love in the Promised Land: The Story of Anzia Yezierska and John Dewey.* New York: Free Press, 1988.
Henriksen, Louise Levitas. "Anzia Yezierska." In *The Oxford Companion to American Women Writers,* edited by Cathy N. Davidson and Linda Wagner-Martin, 948. New York: Oxford University Press, 1995.
———. *Anzia Yezierska: A Writer's Life.* New Brunswick, N.J.: Rutgers University Press, 1988.
Konzett, Delia Caparoso. *Ethnic Modernisms: Anzia Yezierska, Zora Neale Hurston, Jean Rhys, and the Aesthetics of Dislocation.* New York: Palgrave, 2002.
Rosen, Norma. *John and Anzia: An American Romance.* New York: Dutton, 1989.

Schoen, Carol B. *Anzia Yezierska.* Boston: G. K. Hall, 1982.

Wexler, Laura. "Looking at Yezierska." In *Women of the Word: Jewish Women and Jewish Writing,* edited by Judith Baskin, 153–181. Detroit, Mich.: Wayne State University Press, 1994.

Wilentz, Gay. "Cultural Mediation and the Immigrant's Daughter: Anzia Yezierska's *Bread Givers,*" *MELUS* 17, no. 3 (1991–1992): 33–41.

OTHER

Drucker, Sally Ann. "Anzia Yezierska (1881?–1970)." Houghton Mifflin. Online Study Center. Available online. URL: http://college.hmco.com/english/heath/syllabuild/iguide/yeziersk.html. Accessed September 25, 2005.

Y NO SE LO TRAGÓ LA TIERRA Tomás Rivera (1971)

This widely acclaimed novel by Tomás Rivera was published in 1971 under the auspices of Quinto Sol, of which prize the author was the first recipient the same year of its publication. First published entirely in Spanish, . . . *Y no se lo tragó la tierra/ . . . And the Earth Did Not Part* became . . . *And the Earth Did Not Devour Him* in a bilingual edition, including Evangelina Vigil-Piñón's translation into English for Arte Público Press in 1987. Rivera always refused to write in English, so it had to be his good friend Rolando Hinojosa-Smith who re-created the novel under the title of *This Migrant Earth,* also published in 1987 by Arte Publico Press. Both Rivera and Hinojosa belong to the generation of writers who would inaugurate the Chicano literary renaissance that took place in the 1970s.

In 1995, Severo Perez directed the film *And the Earth Did Not Swallow Him,* based on Rivera's novel, to document the study the novelist did on the life of the migrant Chicano worker. It was a study unparalleled since Steinbeck's *Grapes of Wrath* and showed the white lower-class American worker traveling along the country to work on South-Western fields during the Depression era. Through a series of sketches, Rivera presents a bildungsroman (a coming-of-age novel) in which the protagonists fight against environmental racism and exploitation to save their families from the situation of starvation and oppression in which they are immersed. All these conditions make them one and the same boy trying to reach adulthood against the difficulties of thirst, hunger, and sunstrokes among other calamities. The stereotypical image of the working-class Chicano, the migrant farm laborer bending his back in the field until he collapses, gets repeated along the multiple situations Rivera presents the reader. Contempt for the "gringos" is widely manifested throughout the narrative, especially in the passage when "the earth did not devour" the adolescent who loses his faith in God. He complains against injustice, against the sun striking on his father and younger brothers while working in the fields from dawn to dusk.

A tribute to Luis Valdez and Cesar Chavez, several scenes remember El Teatro Campesino, the theater Valdez created to support Chavez and the United Farm Workers. *Y no se lo tragó la tierra* maintains Chavez's rebellious spirit and enhances his tone of protest while reflecting the broken soul of the Chicano. The novel is told for the most part by a child or young adult who contemplates with a critical eye his family situation and that of his neighbors in a symbolic one-year time period. The time symbolism resides in the fact that the hard reality of the Chicano farmworker gets repeated invariably every year, either with the same or with different protagonists. The stories stand on their own as an interrelated network of events, or they fit together as a whole novel about itinerant workers moving from childhood to adulthood and from state to state along the South and the Midwest searching for crops to harvest in order to survive. Through these descriptions of the seasonal workers, the reader gets to know the route of the Chicano farm workers through the United States and the nomadic character of their lives. The story "When We Arrive" symbolizes the nomadic life of the Chicano that never reaches a final destination; hence, the bus breaking down represents the eternal traveling condition.

Even if the novel represents the life of a community, there is a noticeable empty space: The feminine voice is still absent in Rivera's work. The migrant experience seems genuinely masculine while women remain in the background, their lives subordinated to their husbands' place of work. Only the woman in "The Night Before Christmas" acquires a relevant role, for it is through her nervous condition and her anxiety attack in a shopping center crowded with whites that Rivera expresses the feeling of alienation Chicanos experience in U.S. cities.

Rivera's novel sounds a song of resistance to assimilation, to surrendering to the American way of life, and as a call to retain a past that is getting lost with new generations. Rivera rebels against the English language, makes his characters speak in Spanish and preserve their cultural background, rejecting assimilation to the Anglo culture. The Chicano voices of these stories never become bicultural, although they wish their descendants would be fluent in English and able to work in a white world. Among all the pessimistic views about the future that Rivera's characters share, the hope for the youngest to get an education seems the only light left burning in a dark night. Unfortunately, many of these hopes get killed or missing in action in the Korean War, like "Julianito" or "el Chuy."

On the Chicano farmworker's grave, no epitaph will be written, no honors received for breaking his back in the field from sun to sun. The difficulty of fieldwork and the time employed in the task haunt Rivera's characters and uproot them from a universe of incomprehension where the border always marks the difference for the exploitation of "la raza." Tejano migrant laborers, crossing the border illegally, without rights, rich and poor equal, all get a voice and an identity through Rivera's sketches, a voice that had previously been silent because the life of the farmworker has always been deemed worthless.

SOURCES

Rivera, Tomás. . . . *Y no se lo tragó la tierra/. . . And the Earth Did Not Devour Him.* 1971. Reprinted, Houston, Tex.: Arte Público Press, 1992.

Steinbeck, John. *The Grapes of Wrath.* 1939. Reprint, New York: Penguin Books, 1992.

FURTHER READING

Augenbraum Harold, and Margarite Fernandez Olmos M. *U.S. Latino Literature: A Critical Guide for Students and Teachers.* Westport, Conn.: Greenwood Press, 2000.

Calderon, Hector, and Jose David Saldivar, eds. *Criticism in the Borderlands: Studies in Chicano Literature, Culture, and Ideology.* Durham, N.C.: Duke University Press, 1991.

Olivares, Julian. *International Studies in Honor of Tomás Rivera.* Houston, Tex.: Arte Publico Press, University of Houston, 1986.

Imelda Martin-Junquera

¡YO! JULIA ALVAREZ (1997)   More than merely a sequel to ALVAREZ's brilliant *HOW THE GARCÍA GIRLS LOST THEIR ACCENTS*, *¡Yo!* is a response to that earlier narrative, a metafictional *tour de force* that reflects on the nature, power, and effects of stories and storytelling. Yolanda García, the narrator of the first book, becomes the subject of the second volume recounted, in turn, by many of the characters she had previously written about. After infuriating her family by writing about them in the first novel, she is converted into the target of their creative imagination, and *¡Yo!* gathers the responses of the people around her to Yolanda's need to write about what she knows.

The first novel described Yolanda's act of writing about her family as an integral part of her process of healing and coming to terms with her biculturality, and this novel also centers on the act and art of writing, and is a commentary on the nature of fiction. Composed of a prologue and three parts with five stories in each, the stories are narrated or focalized by a different character (or characters, as in "The wedding guests"). The stories' titles identify the speaker and match the story with either a literary form ("The mother nonfiction," "The teacher-romance"), a rhetorical device ("The caretaker's revelation," "The suitor resolution"), and elements of fiction ("The night-watchment setting," "The third-husband characterization"). But Yolanda, professor and writer, is now the subject and object of the telling, rather than the narrator. The voices of this novel belong to an impressive melange of people: her parents and sisters, a cousin and the daughter of their maid, an old professor and a student, a boyfriend and her third husband, her best friend, a landlady, a man who stalks her, the caretakers, and the night watchman of the house in the Dominican Republic at which she vacations.

Alvarez's penchant for nuanced titles is evidenced here once again. The title of the book may be read bilingually, doubling its meaning: Read in English, it is Yolanda's nickname; in Spanish, it means "me" or "I." Yolanda does not speak of herself or for herself in this novel; nonetheless, her voice is never heard, except through that of others. The Yolanda that emerges from these stories is a composite built up through memories, encounters, episodes, difficulties, and conversations with others. The diverse accounts reflect on her animated personality, the meaning of writing for her, and her position as a Latino American, living in two languages. She is presented as brilliant, kind, insecure, headstrong, fearful, imaginative and impulsive, engaged in a lifelong and dangerous romance with stories and storytelling, hovering between American pragmatism and Dominican superstition. She even comes close to being represented as a trickster figure—appearing as many different things to different people, transforming the lives of all that know her.

The novel also examines the effect writers have on those around them. Her sisters are furious at Yo's revealing their lives in her book, her mother is embarassed at Yo's revelations of family secrets, one of her former students realizes she has plagiarized a story he wrote, the caretakers in the house in the Dominican Republic consider her habits strange, and the stalker's obsession with her lasts for years until he manages to get her to listen to his story. On another level, the narratives contradict Yolanda's version in the earlier book. "The cousin," for example, challenges Yo's portrayal of Lucinda as a Latin-American Barbie doll with a size-three soul. Speaking for herself, Lucinda challenges Yolanda to revise her feminist conclusions and decide which cousin is actually more stable and fulfilled in her personal life and has come to terms with her personal contingencies and cultural choices.

¡Yo! negotiates many of the issues developed in *How the García Girls Lost Their Accents* but takes some of them further: The question of class difference becomes more important and a central theme in several of the accounts, because the people in the Dominican Republic have difficulty comprehending Yolanda's American liberalism. Her ambivalence about a definition of home and affiliation with language also makes her return periodically to the Dominican Republic, where she writes. The easy binary between American feminism and Dominican patriarchy is complicated in this novel, as the adult characters explain Dominican women's diverse tactics for survival. Most important, it delves deeper into Yolanda's path toward selfhood and narrates details of the relationships that marked her journey—from her father's early prohibition against telling stories because she has put them in danger, to his real-

ization that she is destined to become a storyteller, to her struggles to find a professional calling, to her three marriages and affairs, to the point where she appears to have found her personal and cultural niche as a writer-traveler who lives between countries and languages.

SOURCE

Alvarez, Julia. *¡Yo!* Chapel Hill, N.C.: Algonquin Books, 1997.

Rocío G. Davis

YOU MUST REMEMBER THIS JOYCE CAROL OATES (1987)

With its title taken from Herman Hupfield's 1931 song "As Time Goes By," Joyce Carol OATES's novel *You Must Remember This* captures the worries of the decade 1946–56, with its concern over communism and nuclear war. This authorial remembering of a "now remote decade" is what excited Oates the most during the "fifteen months of its composition" (Oates 1988, 379). She based her fictional Port Oriskany on places she remembers from her youth; specifically, it is "an amalgam of two cities in upstate New York—Buffalo and Lockport . . ." (Oates 1988, 379). Although Oates sums the novel up as a family chronicle, it is young Enid Stevick who interests the reader most.

Enid's passion for her father's half brother Felix counteracts her desire for suicide. For Felix, a retired boxer in his 30s, the intense relationship with his niece seems a way of regaining his youth, but through it he also "exorcises an instinct for self-destructive violence" (Oates 1988, 380). Just as witnessing a boxing match allows an audience to enjoy the thrill of two people beating each other up—for once to relish an experience that seems so wrong, Oates permits her reader to share the excitement of the affair of Enid and Felix. Since Oates is careful to give us the innermost thoughts of both characters, readers feel as if for once they can understand even the most extreme passions of each gender. In Oates's work, readers feel free to take pleasure in what we ourselves usually consider taboo because her works are considered worthy of scholarly analysis.

Although no one ever discovers their secret, Enid and Felix do pay a high price for their obsessions. The implication is that their secret relationship inspired them to live and thrive in those few years of clandestine meetings. Despite the fact that Felix really controls when and where, or even if, the two will meet, it is Enid who unexpectedly benefits most from the affair:

> She was in love and her love set her in a relationship with the world that was unexpected, potent, mysterious. Because of Felix she had the power to cultivate friendships where she wished, she had the power to cultivate her own quick restless analytic intelligence as if it were a factor distinct from her personality (210).

However, the memory of what they had will also haunt them both, even as they move on to their separate lives. Oates certainly exposes double standards of male-female sexual behavior in this novel, but Enid's ability to harness her sexual experience into her musical and academic pursuits puts a fresh spin on the notion of young girls as victims of male dominance. Ironically, Felix has quite the conservative view of how women should behave in public. He is furious to discover that Enid hitches rides, not because it was dangerous, but because it was "cheap" (121). The reader realizes that jealousy is Felix's motive for leaving his car and running after Enid in broad daylight on one occasion. He couldn't bear to see her with boys from school. He obsesses over her as his possession, revealing that for him, this relationship is less than healthy.

Although Felix takes advantage of his niece for selfish desires, Oates never paints him as an evil character. In fact, Enid warms immediately to the sexual relationship with her uncle; the only difference is how each views what they are doing. Felix dismisses it as "just something they had to do" (307). He insists that what is between them isn't love. On her 16th birthday Felix leaves her a heart-shaped locket and chain with her mother, but when she calls to thank him, he is careful to explain that it "doesn't mean anything" (182). Looking back, Enid notes the way her older sister Lizzie and her friends talk about love and sex: "She thought how coarse was the connection between men and women, you started out thinking love and wound up thinking sex, everything reduced to jokes that were vulgar, flippant, sometimes even funny, Felix himself used the expression fuck a good deal as if intent upon showing her how little it all meant really, how little she could count upon it . . ." (353). *You Must Remember This* explores how men and women view life so differently (Showalter, 19). Although Oates's research on boxing allows her to incorporate a behind-the-scenes look at this sport and "male experience" (Wesley, 65), Enid wonders at Felix's sanity when she hears his "masculine reading of the world so alien to her own she could barely comprehend it" (214).

The structure of *You Must Remember This,* like much of Oates's fiction, is a unique presentation of time. Although the novel's events are presented chronologically, the narration often gives further detail of an earlier event later as it is recounted by a character's memory, furthering the element of obsession that pervades the novel. This technique allows Oates to hook the reader periodically into wanting to know more about one moment but then having to wait to find out later. Important moments in the lives of the other members of the Stevick family come intermittently so that readers are diverted by the worries of the father, Lyle, whose midlife crisis takes the palpable form of a bomb shelter he has built belowground at the family's rented home. Meanwhile, the only son, Warren, who returned mentally and physically scarred from the war, has begun working tirelessly for nuclear disarmament. The two older Stevick daughters are opposites, since Geraldine marries early and takes pride in motherhood, while Lizzie moves out and supports herself by singing in nightclubs. These two sisters and their mother serve as foils for Enid, who is the most intellectual and secretly the most sexual.

Mrs. Stevick remains a traditional motherly figure for most of the novel; she once remarks in a resigned way that Enid will "only get married anyway" (307) as if there were no point to her piano lessons. However, by the novel's end, she has gone into business with her sister as a professional seamstress, and this career clearly improves her outlook as a person. The novel's epilogue focuses on Mr. and Mrs. Stevick's relationship, ending with them spontaneously making love for the first time in 18 years and admitting that they love each other after all that time. Oates sets this final scene in the bomb shelter Lyle has built despite his wife's objections, but now she has used her newly marketable skill to sew bedspreads for the shelter's bunks. Throughout the novel Oates reveals the culture of this chapter in American history, but she also reveals the humanity behind social change. Although there is nostalgia for the innocence of the past, there is also hope for a future grounded in greater equality for all. Oates creates characters whose obsessions enable them to suppress emotionally the individual concerns that threaten them, and the reader cannot help but admire their means of survival.

SOURCES

Daly, Brenda. *Lavish Self-Divisions: The Novels of Joyce Carol Oates.* Jackson: University Press of Mississippi, 1996.

Oates, Joyce Carol. *The Profane Art: Essays and Reviews.* New York: Ontario Review, 1983.

———. *You Must Remember This.* New York: Ontario Review, 1987.

———. *Woman Writer: Occasions and Opportunities.* New York: Ontario Review, 1988.

Showalter, Elaine. *Sister's Choice: Tradition and Change in American Women's Writing.* Oxford: Clarendon Press, 1991.

Strandberg, Victor. "Sex, Violence, and Philosophy in *You Must Remember This,*" *Studies in American Fiction* 17, no. 1 (Spring 1989): 3–17.

Waller, G. F. *Dreaming America: Obsession and Transcendence in the Fiction of Joyce Carol Oates.* Baton Rouge: Louisiana State University Press, 1979.

Wesley, Marilyn C. "On Sport: Magic and Masculinity in Joyce Carol Oates' Fiction," *Literature Interpretation Theory* 3, no. 1 (1991): 65–75.

Rachel G. Wall

YOUNG LIONS, THE IRWIN SHAW (1948)

In the late 1930s and early 1940s, Irwin SHAW established himself as a major playwright. Between 1936 and 1945, seven of his plays were produced on Broadway. The most widely remembered has been the first, *Bury the Dead,* which was first produced on Broadway and published by Random House in 1936. Ironically, Shaw's first novel, *The Young Lions,* has also been typically considered his most ambitious and most successful effort in that genre, even though he would subsequently write 11 other novels.

Shaw served in the military from 1942 to 1945. In *The Young Lions,* he combines a firsthand knowledge of military life with the progressive political convictions that define the themes of his plays. Consistent with the classification of his plays as "proletarian" literature, he focuses in *The Young Lions* on three ordinary soldiers: an American WASP, an American Jew, and a German. The attitudes of each of these men about the military, about the war effort, and about his own place in the world undergo significant changes directly connected to his experiences in the war.

In civilian life, Michael Whiteacre has been a successful playwright. When the United States enters the war, he decides to enlist as an ordinary soldier and not to make use of his many social connections to acquire a commission as an officer and a preferential posting. The outbreak of war stirs Whiteacre from the unsettling complacency that has begun to characterize much of his personal and professional life. His marriage is deteriorating under the weight of predictability and the absence of real intimacy. His commercial success as a playwright has come at a cost of much of the emotional and intellectual intensity that initially attracted him to the theater. He is a political progressive whose success has removed him from the social, economic, and political realities that have shaped his convictions. After he is initially given a bureaucratic posting well out of combat, he requests a transfer to a combat unit. Although his battle experience is hardly ennobling, it does restore his sense of cause, arousing in him a deep antipathy toward fascism. Yet, exactly how this transformation might carry over as he reenters civilian life after the war remains ambiguous. Because he has clearly been hardened by his experience of combat, he might simply become more exasperated by the superficiality of many of the manifestations of his success without being able to recapture the energetic idealism of his youth.

In many ways, Noah Ackerman is Michael Whiteacre's opposite number. Whereas Whiteacre comes from a world of privilege, Ackerman is an ordinary Jew who has had no opportunity to become complacent or affluent. The one reliable reference point in his life is his wife, Hope, but in order to marry her, he has had to overcome the ingrained anti-Semitism of her hardheaded father. Then, when he is drafted into the army, Ackerman literally has to fight for his life well before he sees combat. Stigmatized as an outsider, he fights, in succession, 10 of the toughest men in his company until his sheer capacity to endure the brutal beatings wins him a reprieve and even some grudging respect. When Ackerman is shipped overseas and enters combat, he faces it with greater steadiness than most of his fellow soldiers. He has already reached the point where he no longer feels the need to prove himself. That he does not survive the war is a terrible irony for Shaw's readers—and one that the film adaptation of the novel reverses. Nonetheless, it is the sort of irony that Ackerman has been conditioned—and has conditioned himself—to accept.

The German Christian Diestl has been indoctrinated by Nazism to view warfare as a glorious pursuit and to accept death in battle as the most noble sacrifice that the most inherently superior race of men can make. As the Nazis move victoriously across Europe, their decisive conquests, though not without cost, seem to confirm the party's propaganda about the historic destiny of the Third Reich. But the general collapse of the German effort in North Africa combines with Diestl's own immediate experience to erode his confidence in the Nazi cause and in his own integrity and purpose. The ghastly costs, the pointless sacrifices, and the arbitrary command decisions that actually define most warfare are highlighted more pointedly and horribly in defeat than in victory. As the war becomes an escalating disaster for Germany, Diestl becomes something of an apathetic automaton, unwilling to desert his "duty" only because he has no identity whatsoever without it.

In the climactic scene of the novel, which occurs symbolically near a concentration camp, Diestl ambushes Ackerman, killing him with little emotion, and then Diestl himself is killed, but in a cold fury, by Whiteacre. Interestingly, in the film adaptation, Diestl has thrown down his weapon and is stumbling down a hillside is a sort of disoriented hopelessness when he startles the Americans and is shot dead. Then, in a denouement full of sentiment, Ackerman returns safe and whole to his wife and home in a working-class urban neighborhood. The success of the film adaptation—which starred Dean Martin as Whiteacre, Montgomery Clift as Ackerman, and Marlon Brando as Diestl—has thus reinforced the critical judgement that *The Young Lions* is thematically simplistic, even though the novel's resolution is much more complex and ambiguous than is the film's.

As a compliment to Shaw's craftsmanship, John Aldridge has painstakingly delineated the complex pattern of parallels and counterpoints in the novel's structure. Some subsequent critics have, however, dismissed that complexity as a great contrivance that inevitably reduces any thematic complexity that Shaw may be trying to achieve. Indeed, as Shaw's novels increasingly became commercially successful and were adapted not only to profitable films but even to very popular television miniseries, there was a tendency to view *The Young Lions* both as the evidence of the literary promise that he betrayed for commercial success and as the first evidence of such a betrayal.

SOURCES

Aldridge, John. *After the Lost Generation.* New York: McGraw-Hill, 1951, pp. 150ff.

Eisinger, Chester E. *Fiction of the Forties.* Chicago, Ill.: University of Chicago Press, 1963, pp. 110–111.

Giles, James R. "Interviews with Irwin Shaw: Summer 1980," *Resources for American Literary Study* 18, no. 1 (1992): 1–21.

———. *Irwin Shaw.* Boston: Twayne, 1983.

———. "Irwin Shaw's Original Prologue to *The Young Lions,*" *Resources for American Literary Study* 11 (Spring 1981): 115–119.

Krementz, Jill. "Irwin Shaw." In *The Jewish Writer,* 108–109. New York: Henry Holt, 1998.

Milic, Louis T. "Naming in Shaw's *The Young Lions.*" *Style* 23 (Spring 1989): 113–123.

Salter, James. "Winter of the Lion," *Esquire,* July 1989, pp. 69–76.

Shnayerson, Michael. *Irwin Shaw: A Biography.* New York: Putnam, 1989.

Martin Kich

Z

ZUCKERMAN UNBOUND Philip Roth

(1981) *Zuckerman Unbound*, the second book in the Zuckerman Bound trilogy, follows Nathan Zuckerman as he tries to adjust to life and forge a new identity in the wake of the great success of his novel *Carnovsky*, which closely resembles Roth's own infamous Portnoy's Complaint in its concern with the carnal escapades of its young Jewish protagonist. With *Carnovsky*'s publication came huge amounts of fame and money, but that's not all to which Zuckerman must adjust. Shortly before *Carnovsky*'s publication, Zuckerman left his wife Laura and moved from New York's Greenwich Village to the Upper East Side; in matters of economics, public opinion, family, and home his life has changed drastically. He is completely at sea, unhinged or "unbound" by the speed and extent to which the entire fabric of his life has changed. "It wasn't like this in Zuckerman's study" (137), he thinks. Being a writer now means more than actually writing, and Zuckerman does not have the necessary skills to negotiate these waters. Zuckerman becomes anxious, a shut-in, a paranoiac, and a depressive who is disturbed by how things have changed, by all the work he's not doing, all the television he's watching, and "the strangeness of sitting in your bathrobe on your Oriental rug eating a takeout barbecued chicken and hearing someone [on television] suddenly talking about you" (185).

One thing has not changed much, though: Everyone has an opinion on what Zuckerman should do, act like, and be. And with his boost in public recog-nition, "everyone" includes not just his family and the Newark Jewish community. Complete strangers approach Zuckerman on the street, on the bus, and even on the phone to offer him advice and their opinion. Alvin Pepler, a fellow Jew from Newark, is one such stranger. Pepler begins talking to him in a deli and, despite Zuckerman's best efforts to politely cut the conversation short, follows him doggedly. Although Pepler is insistent, unsettling, and probably paranoid, Zuckerman nonetheless responds to him as something familiar in the sea of change. The familiarity may even be their shared sense of paranoia. Peplar tells Zuckerman about being a quiz-show contestant during the 1950s quiz show scandals, maintaining that "it didn't do the Jewish people any harm having a Marine veteran of two wars representing them on prime-time national television for three consecutive weeks" (120). But the show was rigged, and Pepler feels he was ousted from the show over just this question of representation. "What it came down to was that they couldn't afford to let a Jew be a big winner too long" (129). Peplar is Zuckerman's doppelganger in this regard: While Peplar sees himself as representing Jews to America, Zuckerman wishes he were not held responsible for representing American Jewry to his readers. Peplar is enraged that his stay on national television was cut short and that none of the promises of a future television career came through. He feels that by not being on television, he has let American Jews down (121).

Zuckerman, on the other hand, is uncomfortable in the spotlight, and especially so when his book is read as autobiography or as otherwise representational. But representation is a central issue for Zuckerman, and the confusion of fame, fortune, and new circumstances is something that Zuckerman has brought deliberately upon himself. Zuckerman himself thinks of his wife Laura, a lawyer working against the Vietnam War, as his alter ego: "She is the reputable face that you turn toward the reputable, the face you have been turning to them all your life" (141). Laura, then, represents for him a part of himself, a part that existed before he even met her and that is diametrically opposed to "everything that enlivens [his] writing" (141). In giving vent to all the libido and angst that made up *Carnovsky,* Zuckerman has finally done away with his own respectable side. The result, far from being a productive liberation, is turmoil and chaos. Without Laura propping up his identity, without his respectable side telling him how to conduct his affairs, he is completely at sea. He even questions "whether Laura's purpose wasn't the shield behind which he was still hiding his own, even from himself" (140).

Zuckerman quickly latches on to another woman to prop up his identity. His agent's wife has set him up with the devastingly beautiful—and far more famous—movie star Caesara O'Shea. Zuckerman sees O'Shea as someone who can teach him how to negotiate his new outward identity by teaching him how to handle fame. Although he still does not feel like he can write, "at least he'd been able to focus on something other than himself being stuffed to bursting at the trough of inanities. He was bursting now with her" (168). From Laura, to the inanities of his new life, to Caesara O'Shea, Zuckerman has turned outward to fill the empty spaces of his identity. After his date with O'Shea, Zuckerman feels energized to begin life anew. He tends to the outward aspects of his personality by being fit for a wardrobe of new, expensive suits. His desire to use Ceasara as the new front for his identity is foiled, however, when she flies to Havana without warning. Zuckerman finds out from his agent's wife that " 'She's been having an affair. Since March. With Fidel Castro' " (170). Despite his best efforts to get a grip on his life, "[Zuckerman's] world was getting stupider by the hour" (211).

At sea again, Zuckerman must deal with an extortionist who continually phones him, threatening to kill Zuckerman's mother if he does not pay. He must also deal with Pepler, who shows up at the funeral home across the street from his apartment when a famous mobster dies. Zuckerman alternates between enjoying his conversation with Pepler and worrying that Pepler is unhinged, dangerous, and perhaps even the extortionist who is phoning him for money. Pepler certainly is unhinged—after Zuckerman critiques a piece of his writing, he takes offense, accuses Zuckerman of stealing the material for *Carnovsky* from his own life, and, a la Carnovsky, returns to Zuckerman's mailbox, defiled, the handkerchief Zuckerman had loaned him. Roth never reveals for certain who the extortionist is. To some extent, the extortion plot is simply another illustration of how unstable his life has become, driven increasingly by nothing more than mere circumstance. The extortion plot segues into family drama when Zuckerman receives an urgent message from his aunt Essie to phone. He assumes the extortionist has put his plot in motion, but finds instead that his ailing father has had a coronary and is on his deathbed. Zuckerman flies to Florida to be with his family. Once there, however, the only thing he can think to tell his father is a summary of the book he read on the plane: an explanation of the creation of the universe via the big bang. His father is much more direct: His dying word, delivered as he looks directly at Zuckerman, is "Barely audible, but painstakingly pronounced. 'Bastard' " (224). The cryptic nature of his father's last word, and Zuckerman's need to rationalize it, are Victor Zuckerman's coup de grace, ensuring that Zuckerman will never feel entirely free of his father's opinion.

On the way home from the airport, Zuckerman stops in the Newark neighborhood in which he grew up, only to find it drastically changed as well. At the "garage where the superintendent's wayward daughter, Thea, and the grocer's daughter, Doris, has enticed him one day" (242) to repeat dirty words, the garage where Zuckerman had "his first strong experience of the power of language and of the power of girls" (242), one of the new residents asks Zuckerman, "Who you supposed to be?" (242). "No one," replied Zuckerman, and that was the end of that. "You are no longer any man's son, you are no longer some good woman's husband, you are no longer your brother's brother, and you don't come from anywhere anymore, either." (242). The last vestige of Zuckerman's former identity is gone; the last of his ties are broken. In their place stands only Zuckerman with his unchecked libido, unable, finally, to negotiate his identity crisis, and primed for the full-fledged midlife crisis to come in *The Anatomy Lesson.*

Zuckerman Unbound, like Roth's earlier *The Ghost Writer,* is a *Künstlerroman,* or novel about the development of an artist. But *Zuckerman Unbound* pushes the *Künstlerroman* beyond its typical bounds in showing the artist after his initial development, in dissolution and at odds with society. In bringing the issues of representation raised in *The Ghost Writer* to bear upon Zuckerman's new world, Roth shows that balancing art with societal dictates does not come easily or naturally after the artist's first success, and that the possibilities for the *Künstlerroman* are greater than is often thought. Roth continues to explore the *Künstlerroman* genre through the character of Nathan Zuckerman in *The Anatomy Lesson* (1983) and "The Prague Orgy" (1985), which were published with *The Ghost Writer* (1979) and *Zuckerman Unbound* (1981) as *Zuckerman Bound* (1985), "a trilogy and an epilogue" (cover), in *The Counterlife* (1986) and in the later "AMERICAN TRILOGY": AMERICAN PASTORAL (1997), *I Married a Communist* (1998), and *The Human Stain* (2000).

SOURCE

Roth, Philip. *Zuckerman Unbound.* 1981. In *Zuckerman Bound.* 1985. Reprint, New York: Ballantine, 1986, pp. 109–243.

Kerry Higgins Wendt

SUBJECT ENTRIES

THE AFRICAN-AMERICAN NOVEL In 1982, when Professor Henry L. Gates, Jr., published his "major discovery," Harriet Wilson's novel, *Our Nig, or Sketches of a Free Black in a Two-Story White House, North, Showing That Slavery's Shadows Fall Even There* (1859), identifying it as one of the first novels published by an African American, his "find" shook the foundation of the history of the development of the African-American novel. Scholars of the African-American literary tradition had remained unaware that Wilson, a free northern black, had published her novel a century and a quarter before its rediscovery, authentication, and republication; consequently, its significance had been completely ignored.

These scholars were sent scurrying back to the site of excavation to revisit and revise their unanimously endorsed time line. They continued to identify *The Heroic Slave* (1853), a novella by former slave Frederick Douglass, and *Clotel or the President's Daughter: A Narrative of Slave Life in the United States* (1853), by former abolitionist leader William Wells Brown, as the first full-length works of fiction published by African Americans. They now, however, correctly distinguished these works, which were first published in England, from Wilson's novel, which was published in the United States, making *Our Nig* the first known novel written by an African American—a woman—to be published on native soil.

Two decades later, Professor Gates once again shook the foundation of the African-American literary tradition and the history of the development of the African-American novel with yet another "find": his recent procurement, authentication, and publication of Hannah Crafts's *The Bondwoman's Narrative,* an autobiographical novel, written, like the novels identified above, before the Civil War and emancipation, but unlike them, not published until the 21st century. Purporting to be the story of a fugitive female slave from North Carolina and her escape north to freedom, *The Bondwoman's Narrative,* Professor Gates maintains, is "definitely the first novel written by a black woman and definitely the first novel written by a woman who had been a slave."

In addition to the two works mentioned above, the first known novels written and published by African-American writers also include Frank Webb's *The Garies and Their Friends* (1857) and Martin Delany's *Blake or the Huts of America* (1859). Inevitably, given the dominance of slavery, each author developed his novel around themes, characters, and metaphors that exposed extant disparity and hypocrisy in the land of the free. Their ultimate objective was to solicit the assistance of readers in abolishing slavery and recognizing the basic humanity of their black, often biracial, characters.

This almost formulaic approach to the novel is best offered by Brown's *Clotel,* which is prefaced by his own autobiographical account of his enslavement and life as a fugitive slave. Brown purports to tell the long-rumored story of Thomas Jefferson's slave property: his enslaved mulatto mistress and daughters. Visibly white but sociopolitically black, Clotel, Brown's heroine, is tragic because she is liminal: She is neither black nor white, yet she must remain, legally, a slave forever. In the end, while trying to kidnap her daughter to take her to freedom, Clotel, herself a fugitive, is forced to choose death over a life of reenslavement. More important, however, the first novels derived in part from the black autobiography/slave narrative—record the heroic feats of the central characters, despite the hue of their skin or condition of servitude.

In spite of the general shift in thematic focus brought by emancipation, African-American novelists writing during the post-Reconstruction period, including Frances E. W. Harper, Charles Chesnutt, and Paul L. Dunbar, were concerned with the efforts of their main characters to achieve meaningful communal aggregation in a world of prevailing marginalization and fragmentation, not solely in the American South, where legal segregation was endorsed by the Supreme Court decision *Plessy v. Ferguson* (1896), but also, as in Dunbar's novel, in the urban, more modern North, the envisioned "Promised Land" of generations of African Americans, enslaved and freed. This central theme can be found in Harper's *Iola Leroy* (1892) and in such turn-of-the-century novels as Pauline E. Hopkins's *Contending Forces: A Romance Illustrative of Negro Lives North and South* (1900), Chesnutt's *The House Behind the Cedars* (1900) and *The Marrow of Tradition* (1901), Dunbar's *The Sport of the Gods* (1902), Sutton E. Griggs's *Overshadowed* (1901), and James Weldon Johnson's *The Autobiography of an Ex-Coloured Man* (1912), a forerunner to the novels of the Harlem Renaissance. In the end, one can argue, as does William Andrews, that Chesnutt remained, to a large degree, a "social problem novelist"; however, Dunbar and Johnson successfully pioneered the modern African-American novel, one steeped in literary realism, even naturalism, that would crystallize in the abundance of works produced from the Harlem Renaissance to the publication of Wright's *Native Son* (1940).

The bountiful harvest of novels published during the "New Negro Renaissance" or Harlem Renaissance—the blossoming in African-American culture that took place following World War I—included Walter White's *Fire in the Flint* (1924), Jean Toomer's *Cane* (1925), Nella Larsen's *Quicksand* (1928) and *Passing* (1929), McKay's

Home to Harlem (1928), Jessie Redmond Fauset's *There Is Confusion* (1924) and *Plum Bun* (1929), Rudolph Fisher's *The Walls of Jericho* (1928), and Wallace Thurman's *The Blacker the Berry* (1929), all representing nuggets of the empowered and untrammeled voices of African-American writers during the Jazz Age. A new generation of black writers, basking in the sociopolitical activities of W. E. B. DuBois and the National Association of Colored People (NAACP), Charles S. Johnson and the National Urban League, and Marcus Garvey and the Universal Negro Improvement Association (UNIA), and experiencing what Alain Locke described as "a spiritual emancipation," demanded, as did Locke in *The New Negro* (1925), that "the Negro . . . be seen through other than the dusty spectacles of past controversy. . . ." They, too, declared that "it is time to scrap the fictions, garret the bogey and settle down to a realistic facing of fact." According to the renaissance's designated poet laureate, Langston Hughes, younger African-American artists would write "to express [their] individual dark-skinned selves without fear or shame. . . . We build our temples for tomorrow, strong as we know how, and stand on top of the mountain free within ourselves."

In themes and characterizations, the novelists unabashedly explored and celebrated (even satirized) the full spectrum of black life, from the common folk and exoticism of Harlem cabaret nightlife (a prerequisite in renaissance novels) to the parlors and intellectual gatherings of the genteel DuBois's "talented tenth." Equally important was the psychological complexity of racial passing (crossing over the color line) thematically examined by many of the writers.

The level of maturity achieved by these novelists is evidenced, for example, by Toomer's experimental novel, *Cane* (1925), and by the spectrum of their artistic lenses and genres (realism, naturalism, satire, detective, and African-American music—jazz and the blues—as legitimate literary art forms). While George S. Schuyler's *Black No More* (1931) and Thurman's *Infants of the Spring* (1932) are satires, Fisher's *The Conjure Man Dies: A Mystery Tale of Dark Harlem* (1932) is the first known detective novel to be published by an African-American writer. Published in 1937, Arna Bontemps's *Black Thunder* offers a fictional account of the historical slave uprising led by Gabriel Prosser.

Interest in the literary productivity of renaissance writers was not only evidenced by the sponsors many writers (for example Hughes and Hurston) had, but also by the willingness of major mainstream publishers (Knopf, Macaulay, and Harper and Brothers) to publish their works and the critical attention the works received, not only in such black-owned journals as the *Crisis* magazine and *Opportunity,* but in mainstream journals like the *Atlantic Monthly.* In 1928, McKay's *Home to Harlem* became the first novel by an African-American writer to be placed on New York's lists of best-sellers. While many novelists, such as McKay and Hughes, were also award-winning poets, many women writers, particularly Zora Neale Hurston and Dorothy West, who continued writing beyond the 1930s, were concerned with gender politics. For example, Janie, Hurston's heroine in *Their Eyes Were Watching God* (1937), discovers her voice and reaches independence after three unfulfilling marriages. Hurston and *Their Eyes* were embraced by the feminist movement of the 1980s. In her works, Hurston, a trained anthropologist, was also celebrated for her use of folk custom, superstition, and, above all, speech. West published her last novel, *The Wedding,* in 1995, shortly before her death.

At this historical juncture the significance of these writers and their works lies not solely in their composite contributions to American/African-American culture, but in the ways which they affected the marginal space African Americans continued to occupy in modern America and the development and coming of age of the African-American novel. Indeed, they paved the way for the prolific Mississippi-born novelist Richard Wright, whose life, as he claimed in his autobiography, *Black Boy* (1945), had shaped him for "the realism, the naturalism of the modern novel."

Deeply influenced by the naturalistic works of Theodore Dreiser (particularly *An American Tragedy* [1925]), Wright uses Bigger Thomas, the psychologically demented protagonist of *Native Son* (1940), to call America's attention to the dehumanizing consequences of racism. Trapped, like the rat he kills at the beginning of the novel, Bigger feels like he is "on the outside of the world peeping in through a knot-hole in the fence." The novel ends with him claiming a sense

of existential freedom, the result of two murders he commits, accidentally and intentionally. As he prepares to go to the electric chair, Bigger defiantly tells his Communist attorney, Max, ". . . what I killed for I am," assuming responsibility for his action; refusing the proscription America had assigned him, he had refused to act in bad faith and falsehood. Although, as one critic put it, *Native Son* "jolted the nation," the critical response to Wright and his novel far surpassed any heretofore received by an African-American writer.

It is general consensus that, with the publication of his collection of short stories, *Uncle Tom's Children* (1938), and his Book-of-the-Month Club novel, *Native Son* (1940), Wright, as Donald B. Gibson noted, "changed the landscape of possibility for African American writers. . . . [Wright's] insistence on the expression of an African American voice allowed later writers to do the same." Writers following in what are called the Wrightian schools of literary naturalism and protest literature dominated the literary landscape with one best-seller after another for more than a decade. They included Anne Petry's *The Street* (1946), Chester Himes's *If He Hollers Let Him Go* (1945) and *Lonely Crusade* (1947), William Attaway's *Blood on the Forge* (1941), Curtis Lucas's *Third Ward Newark* (1946) and *Alden Bland, Behold a Cry* (1947), William Gardner Smith's *Last of the Conqueror* (1948), and Willard Motley's *Knock on Any Door* (1947), which, devoid of a single black character—the protagonist is an Italian Catholic—was made into a movie starring Humphrey Bogart. African-American writers—including Frank Yerby, whose works were generally not racially specific (for example, *The Foxes of Harrow* [1946])—published more than 28 novels during the 1940s.

Movement away from the naturalism of Wright's *Native Son* and toward what Bernard Bell calls myth, legend, and rituals is found in Ralph Ellison's *Invisible Man* (1952) and the novels of James Baldwin, particularly *Go Tell It on the Mountain* (1953) and *Another Country* (1962). Ellison's now classic encyclopedic work, which traces the spiritual journey and coming of age of its anonymous protagonist, drawing both on African-American folklore and the epic tradition in Western culture, won the National Book Award, was on the best-seller list for 16 weeks, and has been translated into at least 15 languages. Not surprisingly, Ellison has been compared to the masters of Western literature and culture: Joyce, Melville, Camus, Kafka, and Faulkner. Recognized for its "universal" appeal, as well as for Ellison's masterful incorporation of jazz and blues forms and themes, *Invisible Man* was listed among the best 100 novels published during the 20th century.

Rejecting Wright's protest genre because it represented the "rejection of life, the human being, the denial of beauty, dread, power, in is insistence that it is [this] categorization alone which is real and which cannot be transcended," Baldwin sought to provide what Bell calls "a more faithful, comprehensive portrayal of the richness and vitality of Afro-American character" in such novels as *Go Tell It on the Mountain, If Beale Street Could Talk* (1974), and *Just Above My Head* (1979), which, as their titles reveal, are rooted in African-American folk culture, specifically its orality and music: spirituals, gospel, blues, and jazz, the central sounds of the black church, the threshing floor on which Baldwin was fashioned and shaped by age 14 to become a youth preacher. In his work, redemption is possible through love that is not only unconditional but unbound by social or religious parameters. As Baldwin's narrator in *If Beale Street* reminds readers, irrespective of race, class, or orientation, "When two people love each other, when they really love each other, everything that happens between them has a sacramental air."

Although African-American male authors, including Hal Bennett, Ronald Fair, Ernest Gaines, William Melvin Kelley, John O. Killens, Clarence Major, Ishmael Reed, John Edgar Wideman, and John A. Williams continued to dominate the African-American literary landscape through the 1980s, women novelists would reign throughout the last two decades of the 20th century. Toni Cade Bambara, Paule Marshall, Terry McMillan, Toni Morrison, Gloria Naylor, Alice Walker, and Sherley Anne Williams moved to the head of the class. Their novels were not only read by a general audience but popularized in courses in American and African-American literature, ethnic and African-American studies, women's studies, and cultural studies in classrooms on university campuses across the nation. They were recognized with major literary awards, including Nay-

lor's *Women of Brewster Place* (1983), which won the American Book Award; Walker's epistolary novel, *The Color Purple* (1982), which won the National Book Award (1983) and the Pulitzer Prize (1983), and Morrison's National Book Critics Circle Award and Book-of-the-Month Club selection, *Song of Solomon* (1977), and her Pulitzer Prize and Robert F. Kennedy Award winner, *Beloved* (1987).

In general, African-American writers, and specifically novelists, began the 20th century vociferously trying to call attention to their works; they ended it at the opposite end of the spectrum. Not only had many received awards and recognition as producing works that were clearly central to the canon, particularly Morrison's receiving the Nobel Prize for Literature in 1993, but many continued well-established traditions begun by other writers. For example, Morrison's *Beloved,* Sherley Anne William's *Dessa Rose,* and Charles Johnson's National Book Award winner, *Middle Passage* (1990), further developed the neo–slave narrative genre introduced by Bontemps. In such novels as *Mumbo Jumbo* (1972) and *Flight to Canada* (1976), Ishmael Reed mastered the satiric tradition established by Schuyler. Whereas Baldwin evolved the blues novel with *If Beale Street Could Talk,* two-time PEN/Faulkner Award winner postmodern novelist John Edgar Wideman, in such works as *Sent for You Yesterday* (1983) and *Two Cities* (1998), uses jazz as a form for the novel (as does Morrison with her novel *Jazz* [1992]). The experimentation with the novel as form begun by Toomer in *Cane* can be found in the works of Wideman, Gayl Jones (for example, *Eva's Man* [1976]), and Octavia Butler, who wrote *Kindred* (1979). In addition, Samuel R. Delany, author of *Dhalgren* (1976), stands in the vanguard of American science fiction writers, while new arrival Nalo Hopkinson, author of *Brown Girl in the Ring* (1998), takes science fiction to yet another dimension by adding to it West Indian fantasy and mysticism. Paule Marshall, who builds her work around her West Indian heritage and Brooklyn experience, as she does in *Brown Girl, Brownstones* (1959) and *Praisesong for the Widow* (1983), continues to have her characters cross borders from New York to Barbados and back, projecting a more pan-African perspective of the black experience.

With novelists such as Terry McMillan (*Waiting to Exhale* [1992]), a major voice of the feminist movement, and E. Lynn Harris (*Invisible Life* [1991]), a major voice of the gay and lesbian literary movement, topping the charts of national best-seller lists, including the *New York Times Book Review,* while having their works made into blockbusters and being identified as "crossover" writers, one can only conclude that, no matter how many new finds are excavated and published in the future, the African-American novel and its development remain central to the American literary tradition, indeed to world literature overall, irrespective of its unique characteristics.

WORKS CITED

Andrews, William L. Introduction. *Three Classic African-American Novels.* New York: Mentor Book, 1990.
———, et. al., eds. *The Oxford Companion to African American Literature.* New York: Oxford University Press, 1997.
Bell, Bernard W. *The African American Novel and Its Tradition.* Amherst: University of Massachusetts Press, 1987.
Bruck, Peter, and Wolfgang Karrer, eds. *The Afro-American Novel Since 1960.* Amsterdam: B. R. Gruner Publishing Co., 1982.
Davis, Arthur P. *Afro-American Writers 1900 to 1960.* Washington, D.C.: Howard University Press, 1974.
Gates, Jr., Henry L. Introduction. *The Bondwoman's Narrative by Hannah Crafts.* New York: Warner Books, 2002.
Gibson, Donald. "Richard Wright." In *The Oxford Companion to African American Literature,* edited by William Andrews, et. al. New York: Oxford University Press, 1997.
Lewis, David Levering. *When Harlem Was in Vogue.* New York: Alfred A. Knopf, 1981.
Locke, Alain. *The New Negro: An Interpretation.* New York: Boni and Liveright, 1925.
Sundquist, Eric J., ed. *Cultural Contexts for Ralph Ellison's Invisible Man.* Boston: Bedford Books, 1994.
Wall, Cheryl A. *Women of the Harlem Renaissance.* Bloomington: Indiana University Press, 1995.

Wilfred D. Samuels

THE ASIAN-AMERICAN NOVEL

The umbrella term "Asian-American novel" designates writing by people of national origins in countries like China, Japan, Korea, the Philippines, India, Singapore, Vietnam, and Cambodia who either were born in or immigrated to the United States. The expression "Asian American," popularized in the 1960s, promotes political solidarity and cultural recognition for Asian Americans, and stresses shared experiences of Asian immigrants in the United States. The narratives of Asian-American writers creatively engage the experience of being of Asian descent in the United States while dealing with the historical, linguistic, and ethnic specificities of each nationality. Early novels tended to focus on stories of immigration and questions of assimilation and the "between worlds" situation. They also tended to challenge American perceptions of Asians; analyze what constitutes an "Asian" or "American" identity; examine language, generational conflicts and relationships, racism and social class; and remember national history and claim the immigrants' place in the history of America, among other concerns. Later novels, apart from experimentation with narrative forms, expanded the scope of thematic concerns to engage urban living and interethnic relationships; examine the question of assimilation and suggest the possibility of different cultural choices, including biraciality, biculturality, and bilingualism; explore the question of authenticity; develop issues of gender and sexuality; analyze the intersections of the personal and the political; and engage the histories of Asian countries and the definitions of the term *American.*

Literary criticism has also shifted from an early concern with authenticity and with claiming a unique literary tradition, as opposed to the Euro-American tradition. Asian-American novels are today being read in the wider contexts of diaspora, postcolonialism, and the traditions of Asian writing, as well as in conjunction with other ethnic literatures in the United States. The changing parameters of criticism, and the increasing international recognition that Asian-American literature is receiving, responds to the explosion of writing in the 1980s and 1990s. Though Asian-American novels have been written from the beginning of the century, the 1980s and 1990s established the field as an important constituent of American studies.

CHINESE-AMERICAN NOVELS

In general, the beginnings of Chinese-American fiction are traced back to Edith and Winnifred Eaton, daughters of a British father and Chinese mother, who settled first in Canada and then in the United States. Both wrote under pseudonyms: Edith adopted the Chinese name Sui Sin Far and published numerous short stories in popular journals at the turn of the century, and a collection, *Mrs. Spring Fragrance* (1912), while Winnifred, aware of the negative views of the Chinese at the time, appropriated a Japanese-sounding name, Otono Watanna, and a fictionalized family story. She became an extremely well-known writer of deliberately exotic "Japanese" romances, including *Miss Nume of Japan* (1899, the first known Asian-American novel), *The Heart of Hyacinth* (1903), and *Tama* (1910), many of which catered to the stereotypical ideas Americans had about "Orientals" at the time. The complicated position of the Chinese in America in the early 20th century, and the bachelor society that existed as a result of Exclusion Acts, is the subject of several important novels, notably Louis Chu's *Eat a Bowl of Tea* (1961) and Ruthanne Lum McCunn's *Thousand Pieces of Gold* (1981), the story of a Chinese woman who is forced to work as a prostitute.

A deliberate engagement with historical recuperations is notably visible in novels such as Shawn Wong's *Homebase* (1979) and Frank Chin's *Donald Duk* (1991), both of which deal with young boys learning about and coming to terms with how the untold history of the Chinese in America influences their lives. McCunn's fictionalized biography of Lue Gin Gong, *Wooden Fish Songs* (1995), examines the life of a pioneer who transformed the horticulture industry in Florida in the late 1800s. Stories of immigration and strategies of assimilation, as well as generational/cultural conflicts (particularly between mothers and daughters), are the themes of Amy Tan's *The Joy Luck Club* (1989) and *The Kitchen God's Wife* (1991) and Gish Jen's *Typical American* (1991) and *Mona in the Promised Land* (1996). In Gus Lee's *China Boy* (1993), Shawn Wong's *American Knees* (1995), and David Wong Louie's *The Barbarians Are Coming* (2001), Chinese-American protagonists negotiate interethnic relationships in urban settings and struggle to define their identity and positions in multiethnic America. Other novels involve Chinese-American writers' and characters' relationship with the homeland, such as Andrea Louie's *Moon Cakes* (1995), Ha Jin's National

Book Award–winning *Waiting* (1999), and Terrence Cheng's *Sons of Heaven* (2002), the story of how political affiliations destroy families and set against the backdrop of the Tiananman Square Massacre.

Chinese-American novels also demonstrate a variety of narrative stances and styles. Maxine Hong Kingston's seminal *The Woman Warrior: Memoirs of a Girlhood Among Ghosts* (1976) examines possible definitions of her Chinese-American identity through an experimental text that mirrors the fragmentary and communal nature of her self-perception. Chuang Hua's *Crossings* (1968) is an experimental novel of high modernism whose protagonist attempts to come to terms with her racial affiliations. Fae Myenne Ng's *Bone* (1993) and Aimee Liu's *Face* (1994) subvert narrative chronology and tell stories of Chinatown and family tragedies backward. Amy Tan's *The Hundred Secret Senses* (1999) exhibits characteristics of magic realism as it shifts from San Francisco to China. Kingston's *Tripmaster Monkey: His Fake Book* (1989) is formally and stylistically innovative and challenging.

FILIPINO-AMERICAN NOVELS

American colonization of the Philippines at the end of the 19th century led to the immigration of migrant workers and student-scholars, many of whom settled permanently and began to creatively engage the cultural consequences of the Filipino's ambivalent relationship with America. In general, three generations of writers may be identified: the pioneering generation of both the Filipino novel in English and Filipino-American writing, whose works dealt with the situation of early Filipino immigrants; the second, more politically conscious group who immigrated in the 1960s–70s, many of whom were exiles from the Marcos regime; and the new generation that arose in the 1990s, mostly second-generation children whose stimulating writing expands existing structural and thematic approaches. The most important writers of the first generation include Bienvenido Santos, whose novels *The Man Who (Thought He) Looked like Robert Taylor* (1983) and *What the Hell for You Left Your Heart in San Francisco* (1987) foreground the lonely lives of Filipino expatriates in the United States and their longing for their homeland, and N. V. M. Gonzalez, who wrote both in the Philippines and in the United States novels like *The Season of Grace* (1954) and *The Bamboo Dancers* (1961), which explore Filipino country life with nostalgia, as well as the difficulties of returning home.

Linda Ty-Casper is one of the central, though little-recognized, writers of the second generation, and her works helped shape many of those of her contemporaries. In novels like *The Peninsulars* (1964), *The Three-Cornered Sun* (1979), *Fortress in the Plaza* (1985), *Wings of Stone* (1986), and *Awaiting Trespass* (1989), she explores the Filipino history of successive colonizations, as well as the period of Marcos's dictatorship; several of her novels could not be published in the Philippines because they were set during the martial-law years. Her work has become a subtext for Ninotchka Rosca's revision of the successive colonizations of the Philippines, *State of War* (1988) and *Twice Blessed* (1992), a political satire on the downfall of the Marcoses. Cecilia Manguerra Brainard's *When the Rainbow Goddess Wept* (1994) centers on the horrors of the Japanese occupation of the Philippines as told by a young girl growing up between traditional Filipino myths and the realities of war. In this group is Jessica Hagedorn, perhaps the most well-known Filipina-American writer today, who immigrated to the United States as a teenager. Her two novels, *Dogeaters* (1990) and *The Gangster of Love* (1996), blend representations of pop culture and family ties with political intrigue and explores the characters' ambivalent cultural affiliations.

The third group of writers explore the relationship of second-generation children with the contradictions of America, and nuance the representation of immigration. Peter Bacho's award-winning *Cebu* (1991) presents a Filipino-American priest whose return to the Philippines shatters his complacency about his ideas of home and religious commitment. The protagonist of his *Nelson's Run* (2002) subverts accepted ideas about American neocolonialism in the Philippines. R. Zamora Linmark's *Rolling the R's* (1995) experiments with narrative structure, perspective, and language to address growing up gay in 1970s Hawaii. Bino Realuyo's *The Umbrella Country* (1999) is the coming-of-age novel of a boy before his immigration to the United States and provides a clear-eyed view of Filipino familial and social structures. Sophia G. Romero's *Always Hiding* (1998) explores rampant illegal immigration and issues of social class. The war in the Philippines and the importance of cultural memory is also the subtext of Tess Urriza Holte's *When the Elephants Dance* (2002). Two recent novels demonstrate a growing consciousness of issues beyond race, particularly the question of class and social status, as well as the awareness of how American perceptions of Asians can be manipulated: Brian Ascalon Roley's *American Son* (2001) presents two biracial Filipino-American brothers growing up amid the contradictory opulence and violence of Los Angeles, embarrassed by their Filipina mother, and Han Ong's *Fixer Chao* (2001) powerfully subverts Asian stereotypes through his character, a gay Filipino American in New York who poses as a feng shui expert and deceives the upper class until his deception backfires.

JAPANESE-AMERICAN NOVELS

Japanese-American narratives must be read in the context of the two historical events that gave the community its shape: the arrival, in the first two decades of the 20th century, of tens of thousands of Japanese "picture brides," leading to the birth of a large generation of Americans of Japanese descent and the establishment of flourishing communities; and the internment of Japanese Americans during World War II. Novels like Yoshiko Uchida's *Picture Bride* (1987); Milton Murayama's *Five Years on a Rock* (1994), based on his mother's life; and Yoji Yamaguchi's *Face of a Stranger* (1995) all deal with the lives of women who crossed the sea to marry men they had not met and to raise American children. In general, the novels stress the courage and resilience of the Japanese women, educated in the virtues of patience and loyalty, who encountered poverty and suffering upon arrival. Yamaguchi's novel, nonetheless, demonstrates the deception played on some Japanese women who, thinking they were going to the United States to be married, find out upon their arrival that they have actually been bought to work in brothels. The story highlights the ingenuity of some of these women, who manage to salvage a sense of dignity and eventually escape their lives of bondage. Two emblematic texts from the 1950s may be said to have established the Japanese-American novel: first, John Okada's *No-No Boy* (1957), largely ignored at the time by Japanese Americans and mainstream readers, mostly because of its portrayal of postwar Japanese-American life and the problematic position of its hero, Ichiro Yamada, who struggles to define his identity; second, Murayama's *All I Asking for Is My Body* (1959) (the sequel to *Five Years,* though written first), set in a Hawaiian sugar plantation in the 1930s and 1940s, which explores the turbulent parent-child relationship and the clash of traditional Japanese values with the exploitation of the plantation system and new American possibilities.

The concept of generational identity constitutes a vital part of Japanese-American cultural manifestations, and the concerns of each generation—issei, the first generation; nisei, their children; sansei, third generation—are clearly reflected in their narratives. Julie Shigekuni's *The Bridge Between Us* (1995) and Rahna Reiko Rizzuto's *Why She Left Us* (1999) narrate the complexities of generational relationships, as well as delve into the importance of links with the homeland. Japan and the idea of family heritage has increasingly occupied the Japanese-American creative imagination, as in Lydia Minatoya's *The Strangeness of Beauty* (1999), Mako Yoshikawa's *One Hundred and One Ways* (1999), and Kyoko Mori's *Stone Field, True Arrow* (2000). Here the protagonists, women at critical points in their personal lives, turn to the memory of Japanese parents or grandparents or enact a physical return to Japan in order to acquire a sense of self and as a springboard for present decisions and choices.

Other writers have widened the themes and approaches to narrative. Cynthia Kadohata's novels *The Floating World* (1989) and *In the Heart of the Valley of Love* (1992) expand the representation of Japanese-American characters and themes. Both are travel narratives that repeatedly challenge the stereotypes of Japanese Americans and their families, as well as the themes traditionally attributed to Asian-American writers: The second novel, for example, envisions a futuristic world where survival is of the essence. Lois-Ann Yamanaka's novels feature characters growing up in Hawaii's multicultural setting. In *Wild Meat and the Bully Burgers* (1996), *Blu's Hanging* (1997), and *Heads by Harry* (1999), she skillfully uses the child's per-

spective to explore the Hawaiian experience with insightful humor, using pidgin—the language of her Hawaiian childhood—creatively to stress dramas of identity and belonging, as well as the specificity of the local experience. The novels emphasize multiplicity of experiences, as well as diverse ways of engaging the heritage culture and how it has evolved in American's multicultural context. Ruth L. Ozeki's *My Year of Meats* (1998) uses humor and romance to describe a Japanese American and a Japanese woman's search for self, as well as to expose the unethical practices of the American meat industry.

KOREAN-AMERICAN NOVELS

Relatively few Korean-American novels were published before the 1980s, and autobiographies and memoirs outnumber fiction. The first important Korean-American novels, *The Martyred* (1964) and *The Innocent* (1968), were written by Richard E. Kim, who was studying in the United States after serving in the Korean Army from 1950–54. Both set in Korea during the war, *The Martyred* explores existentialist questions on death and faith and became an American best-seller, and *The Innocent* describes the events surrounding a military coup d' etat in South Korea. The painful legacy of the Japanese occupation of Korea, in particular the institution of "comfort women"—Korean women forced to serve as prostitutes for the Japanese army—becomes the subtext of other novels: Nora Okja Keller's *Comfort Woman* (1998) and Chang-Rae Lee's *A Gesture Life* (1999). Keller's narrative focuses on the memory of the abuse suffered by a mother, a former comfort woman now living in the United States, and her daughter. Lee's novel offers the perspective of a Korean-born Japanese army officer living a perfectly ordered life in a small town and struggling with the guilt over errors in his past. Other recent novels explore the consequences of the Korean War and American occupation and the drama of biracialism: Heinz Insu Fenkl's autobiographical *Memories of My Ghost Brother* (1996) and Keller's *Fox Girl* (2002). Two novels center on young girls growing up in postwar Korea who struggle to overcome the effects of war and learn the importance of family and cultural history: Helen

Kim's *Long Season of Rain* (1996) and Mia Yun's *House of the Winds* (1998).

The immigrant struggle is described in Kim Ron-young's *Clay Walls* (1987), which narrates a mother's efforts to succeed and her children's process of defining their Korean-American identity. Susan Choi's *The Foreign Student* (1998) is an interracial love story between a Korean man and an American girl, set in 1950s Tennessee. Narratives that explore the second generation's attempts to find their place in America include Chang-Rae Lee's, *Native Speaker* (1995), which delves into questions of language, interethnic marriage, the death of a child, and urban politics, Patti Kim's *A Cab Called Reliable* (1997), the story of a young Korean girl whose mother abandons her and her father and centers on the child's attempts to find cultural markers for her evolving identity as she discovers hidden truths about her family, and Frances Park's *When My Sister Was Cleopatra Moon* (2000), about two Korean-American sisters struggling to define themselves. Perhaps the single most complex Asian-American novel is Theresa Hak Kyung Cha's *Dictee* (1982), a multilayered, multilingual collage that explores processes of subject-formation.

SOUTH ASIAN–AMERICAN NOVELS

In spite of the presence of South Asians in the United States from the beginning of the 20th century, novels by writers of this ethnic group developed proportionately late, and flourished after the 1970s. Among the earlier writers of note are Zulfikar Ghose, with novels such as *The Murder of Aziz Khan* (1967) and *The Incredible Brazilian* (1972), Peter Nazareth with *In a Brown Mantle* (1972) and *The General Is Up* (1984), and the prolific Anita Desai. In Desai's case, in particular, charting her trajectory as a novelist allows the reader to comprehend her process of transculturality. From novels set in India like *Fire on the Mountain* (1977), *In Custody* (1984), and *Baumgartner's Bombay* (1988), to her most recent *Fasting, Feasting* (1999), she multiplies the manners in which her Indian characters function in a globalized world as she engages the influences of the West on the East and vice versa.

The drama of immigration is central to novels such as Bharati Mukherjee's *The Wife* (1975) and *Jasmine* (1989), one of the most analyzed Asian-American

texts, and Chitra Banerjee Divakaruni's *The Mistress of Spices* (1997). Her *Sister of My Heart* (2000) begins the account of two cousins in India, and their separate but interlocking destinies in the United States, continued in *Vine of Desire* (2002). The experience of American universities gives humor to the process of adaptation in Kirin Narayan's *Love, Stars, and All That* (1994), a romantic comedy about an Indian student who goes to Berkeley believing she is destined to meet Mr. Right, and Bapsi Sidhwa's *An American Brat* (1993), where Parsi Feroza Ginwalla trades religious fundamentalism for American freedoms. Meena Alexander's *Manhattan Music* (1997) centers on an immigrant who struggles between cultures and relationships and succumbs to mental illness; Mukherjee's *Desirable Daughters* (2002) describes the relationship of siblings in different continents. The question of a possible return to a homeland becomes another recurring theme. In both Mukherjee's *The Tiger's Daughter* (1971) and Meena Alexander's *Nampally Road* (1991), women educated in the West return to India, where they struggle to define their place and role in a place that they no longer recognize.

Indian or Pakistani history, social divisions, customs, and cultural life are the center of novels such as Gita Mehta's *A River Sutra* (1993) and *Raj* (1993); Victor Rangel-Ribeiro's *Tivolem* (1998), set in a quiet village in Goa in the 1930s; Manil Suri's *The Death of Vishnu* (2001); and David Davidar's *The House of Blue Mangoes* (2002). Kiran Desai's *Hulabaloo in the Guava Orchard* (1998) announces the arrival of a second-generation writer who looks back on the homeland. The Partition is a central event in both Sidhwa's *Cracking India* (1988) and Shauna Singh Baldwin's *What the Body Remembers* (1999), which traces the life of two women and the history of a Sikh community.

SOUTHEAST ASIAN–AMERICAN NOVELS

Novels by writers with links to countries in Southeast Asia also form part of the canon of Asian-American writing. In *The Coffin Tree* (1983) and *Irrawaddy Tango* (1993), Wendy Law-Yone explores the political situation in Burma and the immigration of diverse people. In the first novel, the narrator's brother descends into madness in New York; in the second, a dictator's wife experiences the trauma of shifting allegiances. Fiona Cheong's *The Scent of the Gods* (1991) foregrounds events in Singaporean history of the 1960s, narrated though the eyes of a young girl. National Book Award–winning poet Shirley Geok-lin Lim also engages the intersection of the personal with the political in her first novel, *Joss and Gold* (2001), set in three countries—Malaysia, the United States, and Singapore. The continuing trauma of the Vietnam War is the subtext of Lan Cao's *The Monkey Bridge* (1997). Thai-born T. C. Huo's novels, *A Thousand Wings* (1998) and *Land of Smiles* (2000), are narratives of immigration and assimilation into American society.

BIBLIOGRAPHY

Cheung, King-kok, ed. *An Interethnic Companion to Asian American Literature.* New York: Cambridge University Press, 1997.

Chu, Patricia Press. *Assimilating Asians: Gendered Strategies of Authorship in Asian America.* Durham & London: Duke University Press, 2000.

Davis, Rocío G., and Sämi Ludwig, eds. *Asian American Literature in the International Context: Readings on Fiction, Poetry, and Performance.* Hamburg: LIT Verlag, 2002.

Ho, Wendy. *In Her Mother's House: The Politics of Asian American Mother-Daughter Writing.* Walnut Creek & Oxford: AltaMira Press, 1999.

Kim, Elaine H. *Asian American Literature: An Introduction to the Writings and Their Social Context.* Philadelphia: Temple University Press, 1982.

———. "Defining Asian American Realities through Literature," *Cultural Critique* 6 (Spring 1987): 86–111.

Koshy, Susan. "The Fiction of Asian American Literature," *Yale Journal of Criticism* 9, no. 2 (Fall 1996): 315–346. Reprinted in *Asian American Studies: A Reader,* edited by Jean Yu-Wen Wu and Min Song, 465–495. New Brunswick, N.J.: Rutgers University Press, 2000.

Lee, Rachel C. *The Americas of Asian American Literature: Gendered Fictions of Nation and Transnation.* Princeton, N.J.: Princeton University Press, 1999.

Lim, Shirley Geok-lin. "Assaying the Gold; or, Contesting the Ground of Asian American Literature," *New Literary History* 24 (1993): 147–169.

Lim, Shirley Geok-lin, and Amy Ling, eds. *Reading the Literatures of Asian America.* Philadelphia: Temple University Press, 1992.

Ling, Amy. *Between Worlds: Women Writers of Chinese Ancestry.* New York: Pergamon Press, 1990.

Ling, Jinqi. *Narrating Nationalism: Ideology and Form in Asian American Literature.* New York: Oxford University Press, 1998.

Maira, Sunaina, and Rajini Srikanth, eds. *Contours of the Heart: South Asians Map North America.* New York: Asian American Writers' Workshop, 1996.

Nelson, Emmanuel, ed. *Asian American Novelists: A Bio-Bibliographical Critical Sourcebook.* Westport, Conn.: Greenwood Press, 2000.

Wong, Sau-ling Cynthia, and Stephen H. Sumida, eds. *A Resource Guide to Asian American Literature.* New York: The Modern Language Association, 2001.

Wong, Sau-ling Cynthia. *Reading Asian American Literature: From Necessity to Extravagance.* Princeton, N.J.: Princeton University Press, 1993.

Yamamoto, Traise. *Masking Selves, Making Subjects: Japanese American Women, Identity, and the Body.* Berkeley: University of California Press, 1999.

Rocío G. Davis

THE LATINO NOVEL   Literary scholars face a formidable challenge in evaluating the Latino novel for two reasons. First, this kind of fiction expresses the divergent cultural histories of Hispanics in the United States from the 19th century to the present. Second, there is no consensus on the appropriate term for individuals of Spanish-speaking origin. The Census Bureau favors the term *Hispanic* and reports that they constitute the largest minority in the United States. Mexican Americans, Puerto Ricans, Cuban Americans, and Dominican Americans, as well as immigrants and exiles from Latin America, make up 12.5 percent of the U.S. population (Census 2000). On the other hand, artists, academics, and politicians tend to use the term *Latino* to build bridges from one ethnic group to another and to call attention to a shared resistance to U.S. hegemony (the predomination of one set of values, practices, and cultural expressions over another). The terms *Hispanic* and *Latino* are basically interchangeable, but the connotation is different—the former usually reflects official business and data-gathering, and the latter becomes a way to explain cultural production and to create coalition.

Given the United States's 19th- and early-20th-century occupation of Mexico, Puerto Rico, the Dominican Republic, and Cuba, many Latino authors address their vexed relationship with U.S. imperialism by reclaiming their Caribbean or Latin-American roots. In relating stories of translocation and migration, Latino novelists preserve through storytelling the ways of their communities; in doing so they owe much to their colonial, bourgeois, immigrant, and exilic predecessors, as well as to their own families who have passed down anecdotes. Although Latino literature dates from the 1800s, novels have proliferated in the last 50 years with the momentum of the Civil Rights movement, the validation of ethnic studies, and the boom in Latin-American fiction. Mexican-American novelists include Tomás Rivera, Arturo Islas, Ana Castillo, Sandra Cisneros, and Rolando Hinojosa. Esmeralda Santiago, Magali García Ramis, and Nicholasa Mohr represent Puerto Rican communities, both on the island and in New York. Cuban-American literature features the erudite narratives of Cristina Garcia and Oscar Hijuelos. Finally, award-winning author Julia Alvarez and best-selling brash writer Junot Díaz have put the Dominican Republic on the literary map

Though not sharing one uniform experience, Latino authors engage in dialogue with one another as they document the past, reflect on the present, and speculate about the future. This documentation through fiction reveals an ongoing debate about Latino literature—whether it articulates a search for identity or whether it affirms identity through its narration (Horno-Delgado, 3). In either case, one can analyze the Latino novel by considering the 19th-century print culture from which it sprang as well as by looking at authorial application of language and plot.

AUDIENCE AND LANGUAGE

Latino writers may express themselves in English, Spanish, or a combination of the two. Both languages, by virtue of their colonial origins, reproduce hegemonic relations. When writers are bilingual, one choice over another indicates a certain postcolonial position and attempt at authenticity. Texan novelist Tomás Rivera, though perfectly fluent in English, published his groundbreaking novel in Spanish *Y no se lo tragó la tierra* (1971), translated as *And the Earth Did Not Devour Him* (1992). Rolando Hinojosa, who won the prestigious Casa de Las Americas award, writes well in both

languages and has translated his own works, such as *Klail City y sus alrededores* and *Mi Querido Rafa,* from Spanish to English. Hinojosa's translations speak to the fact that authors want to reach as broad a readership as possible. While Spanish is widely spoken in the United States, Latino readers do not necessarily choose to read in Spanish. Increasingly, we find writers such as Sandra Cisneros and Julia Alvarez injecting Spanish into English prose; this code-switching underscores allegiances that cut across generational, as well as urban and rural, divisions. Urban writers such as Junot Díaz (*Drown,* 1996) use, for example, African-American slang to express cultural affiliation.

In narrating episodes of acculturation, exile, or migration, Latino novels, as suggested earlier, capture a particular postcolonial moment (one that reflects on the colonial past from the critical viewpoint of the present). These moments, in turn, stem from a broader context of writing and transmigration that began in the 1800s. Latino fiction originates in the 19th century when Cubans, Puerto Ricans, Dominicans, and Mexicans made the United States their home, willingly or otherwise. Local newspapers and magazines disseminated poetry, essays, and memoirs, mostly those written by the bourgeoisie, who, motivated by political freedom and economic prosperity in the United States, abandoned their Latin-American homes. Nineteenth-century salons and writing communities found their 20th-century equivalent in cafes, universities, and literary journals such as *Arizona Quarterly* and *Revista Chicano-Riqueña,* which was later named *Americas Review* to dismantle the Mexican-American and Puerto Rican binary that fails to describe Latino fiction.

Notwithstanding the distinct histories giving rise to it, the Latino novel features characters who strive to maintain their individuality while balancing family and community obligations. To be sure, before the Latino novel gained notice in the 1980s and 1990s, several influential autobiographies left their mark on the literary scene. These include Piri Thomas's grim portrait of Puerto Rican and Cuban Harlem, *Down These Mean Streets* (1967); Ernesto Galarza's epic story of Mexican immigration, *Barrio Boy* (1971); Victor Villaseñor's California–Mexico border saga, *Rain of Gold* (1991); and Richard Rodriguez's intellectual memoir, *Hunger of Memory: The Education of*

Richard Rodriguez (1981). *Hunger of Memory* demands special attention for the controversy it has created over bilingual education (Rodriguez opposes it), and for the argument that United States and European knowledge may come at the expense of the Mexican-American self, in all its manifestations. These issues of language and acculturation surface in many coming-of-age accounts, notably Alvarez's *How the García Girls Lost Their Accents* (1991) and Santiago's *When I Was Puerto Rican* (1993).

One challenge to publishers has been making autobiographies and Latino fiction relevant to a wider audience. In this regard academic presses, as well as English and Spanish teachers, have bridged the gap between writer and public. Venues include academic and commercial presses such as Random House, HarperPerennial, Penguin, and Ballantine. Arte Público Press has actually shaped the Latino "canon," while coordinating the "Recovering the U.S. Hispanic Literary Project" at the University of Houston. The World Wide Web, too, avails itself as a literary space for students of writing and for independent authors. The Internet will also have major consequences in the cultural exchanges that take place between the United States and the border, and between the Caribbean and the mainland, especially as technology becomes more accessible in developing countries such as Cuba, where at present Internet-access cards are available on the black market for the cost of a month's wages.

PLOTS AND THEMES

Latino novels mirror the cultural clashes taking place on the U.S.–Mexico border, in urban areas such as New York, Miami, Los Angeles, and Chicago, as well as in the Caribbean. The plots often center on discord within the community and the resolution of these tensions through acceptance of a maverick character or affirmation of an elder's decisions. Toward that end, Latino narratives often incorporate daily routines, travel through "the visitor," and diaries to take the reader to another space in time. Often biographical and autobiographical, Latino fiction renders memorable the rhythms of salsa and *son* (a Cuban form of music) in Miami, the bustling tenements of the Bronx and Harlem, and the resilient migrant communities of the Southwest.

Generally speaking, though, Latino literature has shifted its settings (and its politics) from harvesting the fields to personal adjustment in cities and suburbs. While generational differences, politics, education, and class make it difficult to generalize about the Latino novel, certain themes do recur. These include the lament for the loves of yesteryear, the need for family approval, the delights of the kitchen, the betrayals by one's father or husband, the forbidden ecstasies of a Catholic culture, the barriers to success, and pervasive feelings of loss and displacement.

Writers commonly will use an instigatory moment in the present to review the past or to anticipate the future. This technique allows readers to examine the values ranging from a conservative, patriarchal Latin-American culture to a Westernized, English-speaking, commercialized, and often fragmented one. Yet Latina novelists find the apertures of assimilation potentially liberating; more specifically, Julia Alvarez and Cristina García illustrate in their works the productive outlets for American women outside the home. For her part, Alvarez observes that the "ready enfranchisement" of Latina writers—and by extension their characters—"has something to do with the fact that a generation has come before them, *abriendo caminos*" [opening roads or paths]. She explains that Latinas' narrators owe much to their own *tías* and *abuelas* [respectively, aunts and grandmothers] who "told, but never wrote, their own stories" (*Latina*, 107). Latino fiction, therefore, has much to contribute to larger discourses of storytelling and life in a patriarchal—but transformative—society.

Given the striking topographies of the Mexican-American border and the island cultures of Puerto Ricans, Dominicans, and Cubans, assessing the Latino novel is a daunting task. The languages, histories, and themes vary, but interstices do appear. Therefore, this essay addresses the Latino novel by surveying the most populous and influential groups—Mexican Americans, Puerto Ricans, Cuban Americans, and Dominican Americans. Hopefully such an overview will allow entry into this fascinating literary realm.

MEXICAN-AMERICAN NOVELS

Mexican-American authors enjoy the longest history of storytelling among Latino novelists, and they are also, perhaps, the most political in their blurring of auto-biography, politics, and narrative. Post–civil rights Mexican-American writers often refer to themselves as Chicanos, a truncated version of *mexicano*. Whether identifying with Chicanos and "La Raza" (the united people or the race), or whether claiming their place in American letters without such a designation, Mexican-American novelists descend from families who were here before the Treaty of Guadalupe-Hidalgo of 1848 converted Mexican land into U.S. territory—now the American Southwest. Or they are immigrants or children of those who emigrated here from Mexico. The distinction remains an important one, particularly in Californian, Texan, and New Mexican fiction, where well-established families are shown to snub the "wetbacks" of recent decades.

In his inventory of histories, memoirs, and novels, Raymund Paredes observes that Mexican-American writers regard their U.S. citizenry through a lens of nostalgia, ambivalence, or a combination of the two, as in Josephina Niggli's *Mexican Village* (1945) and José Villarreal's *Pocho* (1959) (Paredes, 40–41). These texts appeared at a critical time in history, re-creating the delicate and potentially explosive social climate of the 1940s and 1950s. After World War II and the Korean War, the GI Bill opened the university to Latino servicemen and in doing so offered greater opportunities to individuals who otherwise might have had to settle for menial jobs. However, such change could undermine longstanding family beliefs, as seen in Villarreal's novel. *Pocho*, the title a term for an Americanized Mexican American, depicts Richard Rubio's rejection of his family (especially his mother's faith) and search for freedom from the constraints and dead ends of his life through enlistment in the U.S. Navy. Not surprisingly, Richard Rubio's assimilation involves loss, a theme that continues to inform Chicano fiction.

Writers of the 1970s, Tomás Rivera most prominent among them, articulate feelings of loss and disempowerment in straightforward yet poetic ways. Rivera's *Y no se lo tragó la tierra* (1971), translated as *And the Earth Did Not Devour Him*, remains one of the most important texts not just in Chicano letters but also in U.S. literature more broadly. Through the use of vignettes of migrant farming, Rivera exposes abusive labor practices, barriers

to education, and other forms of discrimination that Mexican Americans have historically faced from the 1940s on. He details the risks and economic dead ends of the Texan laborer trucking to Utah and Minnesota to harvest beets, spinach, and other crops. Given their transitory and marginal status, Rivera's migrant characters sleep in chicken coops and endure the health dangers (tuberculosis, heat stroke, and kidney failure) of agricultural life. At the same time, family and community provide their members protection and support.

Since Rivera's groundbreaking work, Latino novelists tend to validate or play with the concept of identity and in doing so divulge entangled family relations. Ana Castillo, Sandra Cisneros, Rolando Hinojosa Smith, and Arturo Islas draw on oral traditions, prayers, natural remedies, culinary arts, and horticulture to bring the reader into the border communities of the Southwest and into the barrios of, say, El Paso and Chicago. One novel that ties together cultural tradition (the *rebozo,* or Mexican shawl), the notion of family, and the movement across the border is Cisneros's *Caramelo,* a book of epic proportion that tells the story of the Reyes family and their yearly trips from Chicago to Mexico (2002). Meanwhile, folk elements inform the melodramatic and surreal episodes of Ana Castillo's *So Far from God* (1994), the urban loss of innocence in Sandra Cisneros's tightly crafted *House on Mango Street* (1984), the weekly scandals of unplanned pregnancy and barroom brawls in Hinojosa's *Klail City* (1987), and the beautiful imagery of the desert of Arturo Islas's semiautobiographical work *The Rain God* (1984).

Before dying in 1991, Islas produced one of the most lyrical Latino novels in *The Rain God*. Using an old photograph of Miguel Chico and his grandmother as the text's point of departure, Islas expounds upon the personal tribulations of the Angel clan: Mama Chona and her immigration to the states after the Mexican Revolution of 1910, Miguel Grande's marriage in the 1940s, and the postmodern angst of the third generation: Miguel Chico and his cousins. By moving to San Francisco from his arid and isolated Texan hometown, the prodigal son tries to evade his duties and efface his ties to the past; but family loss prevents Miguel Chico from doing so. The novel parallels the unspoken desires of Miguel Chico with those of his uncle Felix, who is kicked to death after propositioning a young American soldier. But by reclaiming Felix in his memory, the aging professor better understands his own frustrations and therefore forgives himself and his loved ones. Although Miguel Chico is separated from the Angels by virtue of his Ph.D., sexuality, and chronic illness, the dead beckon him from their grave: "He needed very much to make peace with the dead, to prepare a feast with them so that they would stop haunting him. He would feed them words and make candied skulls out of paper. He looked, once again, at the old photograph of himself and Mama Chona. The white daisies in her hat no longer frightened him; now that she was gone, the child in the picture held only a ghost by the hand and was free to tell the family secrets" (160). When Miguel Chico dies, he will return to the desert storms of his childhood, buried with the rest of the Angels, seeking their rest.

PUERTO RICAN NOVELS

As in Chicano fiction, the idea of searching for acceptance figures in many Puerto Rican novels. This should not be surprising considering the island's century of troubled relations with the United States. Narrative perspective depends in part on whether Puerto Rican authors hail from the island or from the mainland, particularly New York. When Puerto Rico became a U.S. commonwealth in 1898, islanders regarded this bold transformation with interest and anxiety. Apprehensions about the island's American future from turn-of-the-century novelists Ana Roqué (*Luz y sombra,* 1903) and Manuel Zeno Gandía (*La Charca,* 1894) came to pass, especially after World War II. The U.S.-driven Operation Bootstrap targeted industrialization and public health as its priorities in the 1950s and brought to the island changes that both dispensed summarily with Spanish colonialism and furnished benefits of American capitalism. This becomes the crux for many Puerto Rican narratives, particularly those of Esmeralda Santiago and Magali García Ramis.

Harvard graduate Esmeralda Santiago and Columbia-educated Magali García Ramis grew up in San Juan and then relocated to the Northeast. In their novels, protagonists often question, celebrate, and critique Puerto Rican–U.S. relations. García Ramis employs the

bildungsroman structure to develop the plot of *Happy Days, Uncle Sergio* (1995), which is set during the 1950s in Santurce, an affluent suburb of San Juan. The main conflict stems from the arrival of Uncle Sergio, who offers his niece, Lidia, an alternative to the insular habits of her mother and aunts, who head the household. From Lidia's adolescent point of view, Sergio departs from norms by refusing to marry, by listening to romantic boleros, by consorting with the lower classes, and by maintaining communist tendencies in the age of McCarthy. He also opens Lidia up to the popular songs and practices that her family has denied her. But as she comes of age, Lidia sees that her uncle is a homosexual outcast and that her beloved neighborhood has given way to U.S. encroachment; developers replace the plant-lined balconies of Santurce homes with new homogenous constructions, signifying a modern, suburban, and alienating present.

Santiago's *When I Was Puerto Rican* (1993) also recalls the troubled and enlightening years of youth, but from her narrator's *jíbara,* or "hillbilly," perspective. In this text, U.S. economic development brings vaccinations, electricity, running water, and breakfast at school. But Esmeralda recognizes the mismatch of Caribbean and mainland values when officials force her to eat processed food in the name of nutrition: "[T]he server slapped margarine on two bread squares, which he laid like a pyramid over the eggs. . . . [The food] was warm and gave off that peculiar odor I'd smelled coming in. It tasted like cardboard covers of our primers, salty, dry, fibrous, but not as satisfyingly chewy. If these were once eggs, it had been a long time since they'd been inside a hen. . . . The bread formed moist balls inside my mouth, no matter how much I chewed it" (76). Esmeralda begins to see fences where she once played, and she watches as Rockefeller's hotels pepper the beaches. In the classroom, she attunes to how the harsh Anglo-Saxon language replaces the Latinate rhythms of Spanish. After her translocation from the island to Brooklyn, Esmeralda undertakes a completely different and stressful life with her nine siblings and mother on welfare. Her days walking to school are marked by curiosity and some feelings of terror, particularly as Santiago describes the *gente mala* (bad people) of the slums. Education, however, allows the narrator to forge a path out of poverty and toward new literary and intellectual territory.

CUBAN-AMERICAN NOVELS

Contemporary Cuban-American authors partake in the literary dialogue about identity that advances the novels of Santiago and García Ramis. Prominent Cuban-American novelists include Oscar Hijuelos, born in New York in 1951, and Cristina Garcia, born in Havana in 1958. The backgrounds of these authors reflect the seeds of exile, which were planted in New York in the late 19th century. In the 1890s, Cuban revolutionary José Martí asked his readers to accept *mestizos* (persons of mixed race) and to reject foreign ideas if those ideas corrupt the essence of being Latin American. Martí's essay "Nuestra America" ("Our America," 1891) urged Latin Americans to look out for the deleterious effects of European colonialism and U.S. intervention. In 1959, Fidel Castro took up Martí's rallying cry, and even in the 21st century he uses the "Apostle's" rhetoric to promote Cuba's autonomy. But this valorization of independence comes at the price of alienating many Cubans, some of whom seek repatriation to the United States. This first wave of exiles has been able to maintain its island connections. For writers like Cristina Garcia, and her counterparts who were only born on the island, maintaining Cuban relations is difficult with the U.S. embargo. The blockade provides one narrative thread in Garcia's *Dreaming in Cuban* (1992), which relates Pilar's desire to leave the United States to visit her Cuban grandmother. Notwithstanding the reunion at the end, *Dreaming in Cuban* presents a family divided by communism, capitalism, and sexism. Episodes cut across three generations, from Celia's unrequited romance with a married Spaniard, to Felicia's fascination with the Afro-Caribbean practice of Santeria, to Pilar's punk rebellion in New York.

In *Dreaming in Cuban,* Celia supports Castro, but in Garcia's second novel, *The Agüero Sisters* (1997), it is the next generation, that of the 1960s, that openly partakes in the Cuban Revolution. Reina Agüero serves her comrades as a highly skilled electrician, even though she will eventually leave the country. In this text, Reina's adherence to communism contrasts with the materialism of her enterprising sister, Constancia, who lives in Miami. But the real crux of *The Agüero Sisters* is in the inexplicable murder of their mother during a bird-collecting expedition in the Zapata swamp, a setting rendered in exquisite description. This story, while corresponding somewhat with Garcia's own family, departs dramatically from the usual plots and inspirations of the Latino novel in its dual settings of Cuba and Miami, its application of botanical and zoological discourse, and its elegant weaving of three disparate story lines.

The same sophistication can be said of Oscar Hijuelos. An energetic and popular author, Hijuelos has six novels to his credit, including *Our House in the Last World* (1983), which won the Rome Prize in literature, the Pulitzer Prize–winning *Mambo Kings Play Songs of Love, Empress of the Splendid Season,* and his recent *A Simple Habana Melody: From When the World Was Good* (2002). *Mambo Kings* (1990), later made into a film, tells the story of the Castillo brothers, who leave Habana in 1949 to perform the wildly popular mambo in New York. With their translocation comes decadence and heartache, especially for Nestor Castillo, who, having failed at love, produces multiple versions of the song "Beautiful Maria of My Soul" as a kind of therapy.

Hijuelos elaborates on the theme of ill-fated love and music as therapy with his latest novel, *A Simple Habana Melody* (2002). Here we meet the successful *zarzuela* and *habanera* composer Israel Levis, who, having written "Rosas Puras," seeks European recognition as a musician and conductor. Like his fictional counterparts who escape their woes through drink and women, Levis compensates for the unrequited love of Rita Valladeres by frequenting the red-velvet brothels of Paris. Like Garcia, Hijuelos's novels dramatically depart from the usual autobiographical coming-of-age or reflection plots of most Latino novels. Instead, he uses rich Cuban lyrics and cabaret imagery to set the scene for Levis's fall to Nazi authorities who identify him as a Jew. Levis survives the Buchenwald concentration camp, shedding every last trace of bourgeois privilege, including his own corpulence. Interestingly, Hijuelos allows his character to die in 1953 before he has to face Castro's Cuba.

Hijuelos reveals his range of writing in *Empress of the Splendid Season* (1999), where he assumes a Cuban-immigrant woman's point of view and does so admirably. This is the story of Lydia España, who, having lost her wealth and status after the revolution, moves to the United States and cleans houses for a living. Lydia recognizes that she lives in the greener pastures of years gone by to temper the inescapability of class and to accept the humble advantages of serving the wealthy. Her strength and resiliency are tinged, as in Hijuelos's other novels, with a sense of loss and inconclusiveness.

DOMINICAN-AMERICAN NOVELS

In addition to Mexican Americans, Puerto Ricans, and Cuban Americans, the immigration of families from the Dominican Republic and South America merits attention. This is especially true of Dominican-American writers Julia Alvarez and Junot Díaz, who add to the Latino novel an important historical dimension and faithfulness to the individualism that characterizes American letters. Julia Alvarez, though born in New York, spent her childhood in the Dominican Republic and fled Trujillo's regime in 1960. Díaz, born in Santo Domingo, was raised and educated in the Northeast. Alvarez and Díaz write their fiction from radically different worldviews—Díaz's work exposes the poverty, dirt, and disappointment of life in the United States and in the Dominican Republic. Alvarez, though sensitive to class prejudice and racism, writes about the Dominicans with land, maids, and the option to attend elite American private schools; this is especially true of her self-reflective novel ¡Yo!.

In ¡Yo! (1997), Julia Alvarez blurs the lines between fact and fiction in her depiction of aspiring author Yolanda García. Alvarez organizes the novel according to Yolanda's development as a storyteller; each of the chapters represents a form of narration (for example, "omniscient"), a genre (for example, "poetry"), or mode (for example, "resolution") relevant to Yo's craft. Alvarez's applies this format to illustrate how Yolanda's invention of tales has grave consequences in the Dominican Republic, while in the United States it is something that can be given full reign. This is a message important for Alvarez, who uses the pen to put into perspective the disturbing aspects of Trujillo's regime and to sharpen insights about her own bicultural situation.

In what is arguably her best work, In the Time of the Butterflies (1995), Alvarez conflates fact and fiction in her depiction of the Mirabal family and their revolutionary activity during Rafael Trujillo's regime. By assuming the perspective of each sister, Alvarez recreates the diaries of Maria Teresa, which record her and Minerva's imprisonment. She depicts the sacrifices Minerva Maribal makes as a leader of the June 14 movement, and she renders memorable Patria Mirabal's conversion from devout housewife to rebel. To wrap up an emotionally exhausting story, Alvarez uses scattered details about the sisters' belongings before they were kidnapped to reiterate the incompleteness of knowing fully about their deaths. This novel was made into a mediocre film that, while failing to deliver the richness of the text, nevertheless serves as an index of Alvarez's achievement. Alvarez's focus has shifted rather markedly with her most recent novel, In the Name of Salomé (2000), which recounts the life and trials of Dominican poetess Salomé Ureña.

Junot Díaz's work stands in stark contrast to that of Alvarez for its subject matter. In his best-selling debut novel, Drown (1996), Díaz shows the horror of being poor on the island and the tough side of the turnpikes and wastelands of New Jersey and New York. His style and message are conveyed with a postmodern passivity that characterizes Latino urban fiction, notably that of Bronx writer Abraham Rodriguez, Jr. Díaz's narrative voice is terse and loaded as he depicts a fatherless childhood in the Dominican Republic and a young criminal adulthood in the Northeast. He explains his living by observing that "I deal close to home, trooping up and down those dead end streets where kids drink and smoke. . . . Now that the strip malls line Route 9, a lot of folks have part time jobs; the kids stand around smoking in their aprons, name tags dangling heavily from their pockets" (106). Drown relies on distancing techniques to convey survival in a world of drugs, AIDS, and domestic violence.

CRITICISM

Despite the intricacies of the Latino novel, literary critics have zeroed in on this vein of American literature. Substantive analyses of Latino fiction appear in Ramón Gutierrez and Genero Padilla's Recovering the U.S. Hispanic Literary Project (1993) and in Asunción Horno-

Delgado, Eliana Ortega, and Nina Scott's *Breaking Boundaries: Latina Writing and Critical Readings* (1989). *Dance between Two Cultures: Latino Caribbean Literature Written in the United States* (1997) furnishes the reader with a wonderfully detailed history of what the author calls "Spanish Caribbean" literature. Luis locates a rich literary tradition in 19th-century precedents—the work of Puerto Rican and Cuban exiles living in the United States. Alvarez Borland's *Cuban-American Literature of Exile: From Person to Persona* (1998) is likewise a good resource for its focus. And for Chicano studies, readers will find helpful Calderón and Saldívar's *Criticism in the Borderlands: Studies in Chicano Literature, Culture and Ideology* (1991) and Rosemary King's *Border Confluences: Borderland Narratives from the Mexican War to the Present* (2004).

Readers of the Latino novel will find a wealth of histories, geographies, and voices from which to choose and, in doing so, will discover that this brand of fiction has much in common with American literature as a whole. Tales of difficult journeys, the trials of immigration and migration, and the desire for acceptance characterize many American tales. Thus Latino writers are building upon a larger tradition while maintaining their individuality and linguistic style. In the future, one can expect more novels from the four major Latino groups, and one can anticipate writing from Latin Americans (Guatemalans, Chileans, Colombians, etc.) who have made the United States their home.

BIBLIOGRAPHY

Alvarez, Julia. "Cafecito Cup Readings: Latina literature is coming of age—almost!" *Latina*, January 2000, p. 107.

———. *How the García Girls Lost Their Accents.* New York: Plume, 1992.

———. *In the Name of Salomé.* Chapel Hill, N.C.: Algonquin Books, 2000.

———. *In the Time of the Butterflies.* New York: Plume, 1995.

———. *¡Yo!.* Chapel Hill, N.C.: Algonquin Books, 1997.

Alvarez Borland, Isabel. *Cuban-American Literature of Exile: From Person to Persona.* Charlottesville: University Press of Virginia, 1998.

Calderón, Hector, and José David Saldívar. *Criticism in the Borderlands: Studies in Chicano Literature, Culture and Ideology.* Durham, N.C.: Duke University Press, 1991.

Castillo, Ana. *So Far from God.* New York: Plume, 1994.

Cisneros, Sandra. *Caramelo.* New York: Alfred A. Knopf, 2002.

———. *House on Mango Street.* New York: Vintage Books, 1991.

Díaz, Junot. *Drown.* New York: Riverhead Books, 1996.

Galarza, Ernesto. *Barrio Boy.* Notre Dame, Ind.: University of Notre Dame Press, 1971.

Garcia, Cristina. *The Agüero Sisters.* New York: Ballantine, 1997.

———. *Dreaming in Cuban.* New York: Ballantine Books, 1992.

García Ramis, Magali. *Happy Days, Uncle Sergio.* Fredonia, N.Y.: White Pine Press, 1995.

Gutierrez, Ramón, and Genero Padilla, eds. *Recovering the U.S. Hispanic Literary Heritage.* Houston: Arte Público Press, 1993.

Hijuelos, Oscar. *Empress of the Splendid Season.* New York: HarperCollins, 1999.

———. *The Mambo Kings Play Songs of Love.* New York: Harper & Row, 1990.

———. *A Simple Habana Melody: From When the World Was Good.* New York: HarperCollins, 2002.

Hinojosa, Rolando. *Klail City.* Houston: Arte Público Press, 1987.

Horno-Delgado, Asunción, Eliana Ortega, et al., eds. *Breaking Boundaries: Latina Writing and Critical Readings.* Amherst: University of Massachusetts Press, 1989.

Islas, Arturo. *The Rain God.* New York: Avon Books, 1984.

King, Rosemary A. *Border Confluences: Borderland Narratives from the Mexican War to the Present.* Tucson: University of Arizona Press, 2004.

Luis, William. *Dance between Two Cultures: Latino Caribbean Literature Written in the United States.* Nashville: Vanderbilt University Press, 1997.

Martí, José. *Nuestra America.* Habana: Casa de las Americas, 1974.

Niggli, Josephina. *Mexican Village.* 1945. Albuquerque: University of New Mexico Press, 1994.

Ramirez, Luz Elena. "Hispanic-American Short Fiction." In *Companion to the American Short Story,* edited by Abby H. P. Werlock. New York: Facts On File, 2000.

Rivera, Tomás. *Y se no lo tragó la tierra / . . . And the Earth Did Not Devour Him.* Translated by Evangelina Vigil-Pinón. Houston: Arte Público Press, 1992.

Rodriguez, Richard. *Hunger of Memory: The Education of Richard Rodriguez.* Boston: D. R. Godine, 1981.

Villareal, José. *Pocho.* (1959) New York: Anchor Press, 1970.

Villaseñor, Victor. *Rain of Gold.* Houston: Arte Público Press, 1991.

Luz Elena Ramirez

THE DETECTIVE NOVEL

THE DETECTIVE NOVEL   Detective fiction is often defined in narrow terms to avoid confusing it with crime fiction, spy fiction, or other classes of fiction that present a puzzle to be solved. Frederic Dannay, writing as his alter ego Ellery Queen in 1942, summed this up most succinctly when he called it "a tale of ratiocination, complete with crime and/or mystery, suspects, investigation, clues, deduction, and solution; in its purest form the chief characters should be a detective, amateur or professional, who devotes most of his (or her) time to the problems of detection."

The pure detective novel begins with the crime (murder, robbery, or blackmail, for instance), during which the criminal makes mistakes and inadvertently leaves clues that the detective must be clever enough to recognize. The detective fits together the evidence and identifies the perpetrator of the crime. The formula differs from that of the crime novel, in which the criminal may be the central figure and the story concerns his motive for committing the crime. He may or may not escape the law. The suspense novel has no central detective to solve the mystery but may have a protagonist who becomes involved in events and situations that must be resolved by the end of the story. Variants of the detective novel include the police procedural, in which the police solve the mystery by means of official police methods. Many readers refer to all these forms as murder mysteries even when there is no murder and little mystery.

The difference between the detective short story (created in 1841 by Edgar Allan Poe is his "Murders in the Rue Morgue") and the detective novel is not merely one of length. The broader canvas allows the writer greater freedom to shift points of view, delineate character, describe setting, and otherwise build up suspense while unfolding the plot.

Just as there were detective elements in fiction prior to Poe's short stories, there were detective elements in the fiction that followed his examples in both the short form and the novel. However, it was not for 20 or 30 years that there were novels that contained enough of the elements of a detective story to be classed as detective novels. Historians of the genre tend to ignore the dime novel and story paper serials that flourished in the decades following Poe, but these melodramatic tales established the popular concept of police and detective procedures, and heroes like Nick Carter became household names.

Some critics argue that *The Dead Letter* (1866), by Seeley Regester, the pseudonym of Metta Fuller Victor, is not really the first American detective novel because the detection is unorthodox. Still, the central concern of the novel is the investigation of a murder by two individuals who act as detectives, Burton, a private citizen employed by the police, and the lawyer Redfield. No one doubts however that Anna Katharine Green's *The Leavenworth Case* (1878) is a detective novel, the first in a series of novels that feature the police detective Ebenezer Gryce. Green was the first truly popular American writer of detective fiction, and some of her novels (among them *That Affair Next Door,* 1897) include one of the first female detectives in fiction, Amelia Butterworth.

While Mary Roberts Rinehart's novels are not, strictly speaking, detective novels, they do feature protagonists (such as Rachel Innes in *The Circular Staircase,* 1908) who take on the role of detective, at least in part. She is credited with having created the "Had I but Known" school of suspense, in which the narrator's reflections on her situation foreshadow the solution.

Beginning with *The Clue* (1909), Carolyn Wells's long series of novels about scholarly detective Fleming Stone reflected a more traditional approach to detection, although Stone seldom arrived on the scene until the story was more than half told.

During the Golden Age of the detective story (the 1920s and 1930s), Earl Derr Biggers published *The House without a Key* (1925), the first of six novels about Honolulu police detective Charlie Chan, who would achieve greater fame in the movies. At about the same time, art critic Willard Huntington Wright, writing as S. S. Van Dine, published his first novel, about the excessively erudite amateur sleuth Philo Vance, whose erudition on the printed page was supported by equally erudite footnotes. *The Benson Murder Case* (1926) was a best-seller and was followed by 11 other cases for Vance, which were almost equally well received. The increased interest in detective novels after Van Dine's success may have inspired others to follow suit. The feminist writer Charlotte Perkins Gilman wrote a mystery novel in 1929, *Unpunished,* which included a case for women's freedom and empowerment, but it went unpublished until 1997, long after her death in 1935.

Van Dine's popularity definitely inspired cousins Frederic Dannay and Manfred Lee to create Ellery Queen, both as the name for the detective and as their joint pseudonym. Beginning with *The Roman Hat Mystery* in 1929 and concluding with *A Fine and Private Place* in 1971, the Ellery Queen novels (especially *Calamity Town,* 1942) and short stories reflected the changes in American society in the 20th century. The Ellery Queen series contained imaginative puzzles (at some point there would be a formal "Challenge to the Reader" to provide a solution based on what he/she had read so far), and detective Ellery had a greater social conscience than Philo Vance.

Perhaps the most significant development in the genre was the creation of the hard-boiled detective. Dashiell Hammett, the father of the form, spun fairy tales inhabited by real people, and some of his characters, especially Sam Spade in *The Maltese Falcon* (1930) have become American icons. Working independently of Hammett, Raymond Chandler reworked some of the short stories he had written for the pulp magazine *Black Mask* into seven novels about private detective Philip Marlowe, beginning with *The Big Sleep* in 1939.

The hard-boiled form is characterized by a greater realism than the artificial world of the classic, formal detective story, and the stories are usually narrated by the detective. It has been imitated by many writers, most successfully by Ross Macdonald (the pseudonym of Kenneth Millar) in his California stories of Lew Archer (*The Moving Target,* 1949) and by Robert B. Parker in his stories about Boston private eye Spenser (*The Godwulf Manuscript,* 1973). It has also frequently been the subject of parody and satire: Richard S. Prather's stories of breezy Shell Scott (*Scrambled Yeggs,* 1958) are a prime example.

The most innovative approach to the hard-boiled story came in the 1970s and 1980s with the work of Marcia Muller (*Edwin of the Iron Shoes,* 1976), Sue Grafton (*A Is for Alibi,* 1982), and Sara Paretsky (*Indemnity Only,* 1982). Their female private eyes (Sharon McCone, Kinsey Milhone, and V. I. Warshawsky) prove to be as tough as their earlier male counterparts.

John Dickson Carr, working in a more traditional form inspired by G. K. Chesterton, wrote 70 novels about British sleuths, Dr. Gideon Fell (*The Mad Hatter Mystery,* 1933), Sir Henry Merrivale (*The White Priory Murders,* 1934), and others in which he displayed a fertile imagination as he baffled his readers. The Merrivale books were published under the pseudonym Carter Dickson. Among his most ingenious plot devices was the use of the "Locked Room" puzzle, in which the murder was committed in a room locked from the inside, from which the murderer could not have escaped but seemingly did.

Rex Stout's Nero Wolfe (described as weighing a seventh of a ton) and Archie Goodwin (the narrator and legman in the series) have been described as a blend of the great detective of the Sherlock Holmes school and the wise-cracking style of the hard-boiled form. Beginning with *Fer-de-Lance* in 1934 and concluding with *A Family Affair* in 1975, most of the stories took place in Wolfe's brownstone on West 35th Street in New York. The narrative style and the dialogue, especially the sparring between Wolfe and Archie, were sometimes more satisfying than the plot.

Other writers who entertained without necessarily being innovative include Frances and Richard Lockridge with their stories of Mr. and Mrs. North (*The Norths Meet Murder,* 1940). Richard Lockridge had been a frequent contributor to the *New Yorker* prior to embarking on the mystery writing trail. George Harmon Coxe, creator of Flashgun Casey for *Black Mask,* alternated stories about urbane Kent Murdock, Boston newspaper photographer, with novels set in the Caribbean. Brett Halliday (the pseudonym of Davis Dresser) varied the traditional private eye California location by setting his Michael Shayne novels in Miami, Florida. Craig Rice (the pseudonym of Georgiana Ann Randolph Craig) brought the screwball comedy of the movies to the printed page in her Chicago-based novels about scruffy lawyer John J. Malone and his friends Jake and Helene Justus (*Trial by Fury,* 1941).

Another writer who served his apprenticeship in the pulps was Erle Stanley Gardner, but he achieved a kind of immortality in 1934 when he wrote the first of 85 books about lawyer-detective Perry Mason, *The Case of the Velvet Claws.* Formulaic yet complex, they were very popular, and the concept translated readily to film, radio, and television. Under the pseudonym A. A. Fair, he also wrote numerous stories about private detectives Donald Lam and Bertha Cool (*The Bigger They Come,* 1939).

Following the death of Earl Derr Biggers, the creator of Charlie Chan, the *Saturday Evening Post* arranged with social satirist and popular novelist John P. Marquand to write serials (*Think Fast, Mr. Moto,* 1937) about another Asian character, the secret agent Mr. I. A. Moto, who also had a brief film career in the l940s. Moto is not really a detective in Marquand's six novels, but in the films that is his role. Historical novelist F. Van Wyck Mason turned out stories about intelligence officer Captain Hugh North (later promoted to major and then to colonel), who solved mysteries from Washington, D.C., to the far corners of the world (*The Singapore Exile Murders,* 1939).

Following World War II, the police procedural, in which realism is attained by having the police investigate multiple and overlapping cases, became a significant form. It had been popular in England for some time but did not make an impression in the United States until 1945, when Lawrence Treat's *V as in Victim* was published. Hillary Waugh's *Last Seen Wearing* (1952) moved the setting from the big city to a smaller New England town, but the day-to-day police operations were the same. Perhaps the longest-lasting series has been the 87th Precinct novels by Ed McBain (the pseudonym of Evan Hunter). Set in a fictitious New York City that is not named New York, the first novel was *Cop Hater* in 1956. Writing directly for the paperback market, McBain's intention was not to single out one character as a hero but to make the entire detective squad the hero.

The postwar period also saw the popularity of Mickey Spillane's *I, the Jury* (1947) and other cases for vigilante Mike Hammer. The books were once criticized for their excessive violence and sex (though little is explicit in either area), but later critics have come to see the novels as a reflection of the psyche of America from the loss of innocence following World War II to the loss of purpose and direction in the 1980s.

In recent years writers have combined ingenious mysteries solved by equally ingenious detectives with other elements, and plot is often less important than character. The detectives tend to be concerned about society and the novels include themes of ethnicity, gender, sexuality, occupation, and avocation. There are black detectives, Native American detectives, gay detectives, lesbian detectives, and feminist detectives, as well as detectives who work in various professions besides that of detection and police science.

Chester Himes has been called the first black mystery writer to use black detectives in his work, and his stories of Grave Digger Jones and Coffin Ed Johnson (*The Crazy Kill,* 1959) are set in Harlem. He has been followed by Walter Mosley's Easy Rawlins, a private eye in Los Angeles (*Devil in a Blue Dress,* 1990), and Barbara Neely's Blanche White, a black domestic worker who investigates a murder in *Blanche on the Lam* (1992). Tony Hillerman's Joe Leaphorn and Jim Chee are Native American detectives who solve crimes set in the Southwest (*Skinwalkers,* 1987). Joseph Hansen wrote 12 novels about Dave Brandstetter, a gay private eye (*Skinflick,* 1979), and Ellen Hart's Jane Lawless is a lesbian restaurateur in Minneapolis in *Stage Fright* (1992). A variety of professions and avocations are represented, from Amanda Cross's feminist university professor Kate Fansler (*Death in a Tenured Position,* 1981), to Emma Lathen's banker-detective John Putnam Thatcher in *Green Grow the Dollars* (1982), to M. D. Lake's campus cop Peggy O'Neill in *Amends for Murder* (1989), to Nevada Barr's Anna Pigeon, a park ranger like her creator, in *Track of the Cat* (1993), to Bill Pronzini's "Nameless Detective," who collects pulp magazines (*Scattershot,* 1982), and Elizabeth Peters's Egyptologist Amelia Peabody, who solves mysteries in the late Victorian and Edwardian era (*Lord of the Silent,* 2001). Other writers have explored the history and lore of specific areas such as New England in Jane Langton's Homer Kelly mysteries (*Emily Dickinson Is Dead,* 1984) or old England in Martha Grimes's Inspector Richard Jury novels, which are named for actual inns (*The Old Contemptibles,* 1990). There is a small body of culinary mysteries that involve food, kitchens, restaurants, and culinary professionals; some of these include recipes as well (Virginia Rich's *The Nantucket*

Diet Murders, 1985; Rex Stout's *Too Many Cooks,* 1938). It should come as no surprise that this branch of the genre has also inspired cookbooks such as Jeanine Larmouth and Charlotte Turgeon's *Murder on the Menu* (1972) and Stout's own *Nero Wolfe Cookbook* (1971).

Where once fictional detectives were distinguished largely by their methods of detection or their personal idiosyncracies, today's writers have a richly diverse canvas on which to exercise their imaginations and entertain their readers.

BIBLIOGRAPHY

Baker, Robert A., and Michael T. Nietzel. *Private Eyes: One Hundred and One Knights; A Survey of American Detective Fiction 1922–1984.* Bowling Green, Ohio: Bowling Green State University Popular Press, 1985.

Bakerman, Jane, ed. *And Then There Were Nine . . . More Women of Mystery.* Bowling Green, Ohio: Bowling Green State University Popular Press, 1985.

Bargainnier, Earl F., ed. *Ten Women of Mystery.* Bowling Green, Ohio: Bowling Green State University Popular Press, 1981.

———, and George N. Dove, eds. *Cops and Constables: American and British Fictional Policemen.* Bowling Green, Ohio: Bowling Green State University Popular Press, 1986.

Barzun, Jacques, and Wendell Hertig Taylor. *A Catalogue of Crime.* Revised edition New York: Harper & Row, 1989.

Cox, J. Randolph. *Masters of Mystery and Detective Fiction: An Annotated Bibliography.* Englewood Cliffs, N.J.: Salem Press, 1989.

Dove, George N. *The Police Procedural.* Bowling Green, Ohio: Bowling Green State University Popular Press, 1982.

Geherin, David. *The American Private Eye: The Image in Fiction.* New York: Frederick Ungar Publishing Co., 1985.

Haycraft, Howard. *Murder for Pleasure: The Life and Times of the Detective Story.* New York: D. Appleton-Century, 1941.

———, ed. *The Art of the Mystery Story.* New York: Simon & Schuster, 1946.

Herbert, Rosemary, ed. *The Oxford Companion to Crime and Mystery Writing.* New York & Oxford: Oxford University Press, 1999.

Nickerson, Catherine Ross. *The Web of Iniquity: Early Detective Fiction by American Women.* Durham & London: Duke University Press, 1998.

Panek, Leroy Lad. *Probable Cause: Crime Fiction in America.* Bowling Green, Ohio: Bowling Green State University Popular Press, 1990.

Pronzini, Bill, and Marcia Muller, eds. *1001 Midnights: The Aficionado's Guide to Mystery and Detective Fiction.* New York: Arbor House, 1986.

Symons, Julian. *Bloody Murder: From the Detective Story to the Crime Novel, a History.* Revised edition. New York: Viking, 1985.

J. Randolph Cox

THE NATIVE AMERICAN NOVEL

Native American novels and novelists exist in a complex historical and critical context. There are approximately 310 distinct Native American cultures existing in the continental United States, using languages from seven different language families. Speaking of Native Americans or Indians as though the members of various tribal societies hold a singular worldview comes from faulty and uninformed thinking. Native American novelists often identify themselves first according to their tribal affiliation, then according to their indigenous identity, and finally in terms of their American citizenship. Such categories, however, become further complicated by the question, "What, exactly, is an Indian?" in terms of blood quantum, participation in tribal communities, and degrees of assimilation into Western cultural ways, including conversion to Christianity.

Native American peoples, historically, have experienced gross injustice. Precontact estimates for American Indian populations in North America are 15 million (Stiffarm and Lane, 27). Disease, warfare, genocidal policies, and U.S. government legislation against traditional cultural practices reduced Native populations to 10 percent of their original numbers.

Many Native novelists recount the impact on their people of numerous laws passed against them by the U.S. government. Among the laws most frequently referred to in Native fiction are the following: The Indian Removal Act (1830), The Major Crimes Act (1885), The General Allotment Act (1887), The Indian Citizen Act (1924), The Indian Reorganization Act (1934), The Indian Claims Commission Act (1946), The Termination Act (1953), The Relocation Act (1956), and The American Indian Religious Freedom Act (1978). Essentially, these laws forced various Indian tribes to move from their immemorial tribal lands to "Indian Territory" (Oklahoma); forced tribal governments to adhere to American legal ideologies; allotted portions of communal lands to individual tribal members (thus becoming taxable property); left all other Indian lands open for homesteading; forced U.S. citizenship onto members of indigenous nations; and reorganized traditional tribal systems of government into councils patterned after corporate leadership. In other words, Native peoples have generally been denied self-determination.

The history of Native American novels is often divided between works written before and after N. Scott Momaday's 1969 Pulitzer Prize for *House Made of Dawn*. Edward M. Bruner says that before 1970, the story told by anthropologists about American Indians was that "the present was disorganization, the past was glorious [or barbaric—noble or savage], and the future assimilation." After 1970, the story took on a "sharp epistemological break," where "the present was resistance, the past was exploitation, and the future was ethnic resurgence" (Bruner, 18). While any attempt to reduce an entire body of works to simple thematic descriptions is fraught with flaws, Bruner's descriptions are useful in describing the ways that academics have read Native experiences, including Native authors.

Few novels by American Indians were published before Momaday's *House Made of Dawn*. Those novels that were published, though, have significant historical, thematic, and artistic merit. In 1854, John Rollin Ridge (Cherokee) published *The Life and Adventures of Joaquin Murietta, the Celebrated California Bandit*. Scott B. Vickers says that although the novel describes "the trials and revenge of a mixed-blood Mexican," the novel is actually "a picaresque western adventure based on the resistance of California Natives to the incursion of whites brought on by the gold rush." Ridge's personal history is probably more fascinating than his novel. Ridge was among those on the Trail of Tears during the Cherokee Removal from their eastern homeland to Oklahoma. Ridge's grandfather and father were both assassinated for their part in signing away their ancestral lands without permission of the tribe. S. Alice Callahan's (Creek) *Wynema: A Child of the Forest* was published in 1891. A. LaVonne Brown Ruoff notes that "this novel incorporates explanations of Creek customs" and is a fictional account "of the

events that led to the murder of Sitting Bull and the massacre at Wounded Knee," as well as a novel that pleads for "women's rights and suffrage" (Ruoff, 222). A Potawatomi Indian, Simon Pokagon was the last Native novelist to publish during the 19th century; he published *Queen of the Woods* in 1899. Ruoff describes this novel as "a romance that laments the Potawatomi's loss of their Edenic past and warns about how alcohol can destroy Indians and whites" (Ruoff, 148).

Early 20th-century novels include *Cogewea: The Half-Blood* (1927) by Mourning Dove (Okanagon-Colville), *Brothers Three* (1935) by John Milton Oskison (Cherokee), and *Wah'Kon-Tah: The Osage and the White Man's Road* (1932) and *Sundown* (1934) by John Joseph Matthews (Osage). D'Arcy McNickle (Cree/Metis/Salish) also published three novels prior to the era that Kenneth Lincoln has called the Native American Renaissance: *The Surrounded* (1936), *Runner in the Sun: A Story of Indian Maize* (1954), and *Wind from the Enemy Sky* (published after McNickle's death in 1978). Of these early 20th-century novels, three have received considerable attention and acclaim: Mourning Dove's *Cogewea*, John Joseph Matthews's *Sundown*, and McNickle's *The Surrounded*.

Cogewea is a romantic/tragic tale of a mixed-blood woman who is wooed by two men—a mixed-blood (the foreman on the ranch where Cogewea lives) and a duplicitous, fortune-hunting white man. In Paula Gunn Allen's words, "The novel turns on the question of identity—a question peculiarly American. Cogewea's conflict between traditional family values and the siren call of city life and modern values very nearly costs her her life" (79). Matthews's *Sundown* is the story of a Osage Indian, Challenge Windser, the son of a man who believes in progress, and a traditional Osage mother. Chal enrolls in college, joins the U.S. Army Air Corps, and is so seduced by the white man's world that he becomes somewhat ashamed of his Indian heritage while remaining attached to his mother and her spiritual values. Terry P. Wilson claims that "The last portion of the novel focuses on Chal's inability to develop meaning and direction in his life after the war, wavering between the hedonism and decadence of oil-rich Indians and the hardheaded capitalism of the white men" (Wilson, 247). An excellent full-length study of

Matthews's intellectual contribution to human letters can be found in Robert Allen Warrior's *Tribal Secrets*. In this book, Warrior challenges traditional interpretations of Matthews and his works; he sees *Sundown* as a literary treatise on the survival of Native identity against overwhelming odds (Warrior, 26).

McNickle's *The Surrounded* tells the story of Archilde Leon, another mixed-blood whose forays into the white world leave him disassociated and silent. Louis Owens writes: "Again and again in the novel, understanding fails and something goes inexplicably wrong for the Indians, as if they are in the grip of an incomprehensible fate—as if, in fact, McNickle's Indians are playing out their tragic roles in the American epic, roles that simply require that they perish and that deny them what Bakhtin calls 'another destiny or another plot' " (65). McNickle's Natives are "surrounded"—like fenced-in cattle—by powerful alien government and religious representatives trying to turn Indians into artifacts or remake them into their own Euro-American image. These themes—loss of land, identity, and traditional beliefs complicated by mixed-blood identities—go through a revision in the works of Momaday and those novelists that followed him. Indeed, as Louis Owens suggests, "other destinies" than degradation, poverty, and forced assimilation are possible for Native Americans.

The most prominent post–Civil Rights novelists include N. Scott Momaday (Kiowa), Leslie Marmon Silko (Laguna), James Welch (Blackfoot-Gros Ventre), Louise Erdrich (Chippewa), Gerald Vizenor (Chippewa), and Linda Hogan (Chickasaw). Sherman Alexie (Coeur d' Alene), Thomas King (Cherokee), and Louis Owens (Choctaw-Cherokee) are also rapidly becoming well-known and highly acclaimed novelists. While these authors address unique tribal problems and issues, common themes abound. One prevalent theme involves the movement of various characters from profound, debilitating suffering into well-being, brought about through ceremonial reclamations of their traditional heritages. Both *House Made of Dawn* and *The Ancient Child* by N. Scott Momaday are founded on this plot. None of the above authors claim that Native peoples can return to ancient material or spiritual culture. For example, Leslie Silko's character Tayo, in her novel *Ceremony* (1977), must create a healing ceremony out of his own troubled past and a combination of revised Pueblo and Navajo myths and rituals. His acknowledgment of the necessary role of the ceremony means that myth and ritual are dynamic processes, and that revelation of the sacred is ongoing.

Sexual perversion, violence, and abuse are also typical themes in these novels. In fact, sexual violence is a predominant symbol for the psychological condition of disassociation experienced by many characters. The works of Linda Hogan (especially *Solar Storms* [1995]), Leslie Silko (especially *Almanac for the Dead* [1991]), Sherman Alexie (especially *The Toughest Indian in the World* [2000]), and Louis Owens particularly explore this topic. Perhaps all of Louise Erdrich's North Dakota novels—from *Love Medicine* (1984) to *Four Souls* (2004)—are grounded on the exploration of intimacy patterns, especially as these patterns relate to complex genealogies and religious ideologies. In these works, harmony and respect between genders is also a symbol for harmony in the world. Other issues that these novelists explore include those of mixed-blood identities, the significance of place, the coexistence of spiritual truth with everyday existence, the significance of ancestors to full well-being, and the comic (not tragic) nature of Native discourse. Many of the novels by these authors are peopled with characters who demonstrate that truth comes into the world with two faces—one smiling, the other frowning. And yet, the comic mode prevails, strongly suggesting that the most profound dislocations can be overcome.

All these contemporary authors have won numerous awards for their fiction; their art both represents their particular traditional perspectives and transcends cultural boundaries. Moreover, all these authors are still living as the 21st century opens. Most are also poets, short-story writers, autobiographers, and critics and either have been or are currently university professors.

Literally dozens of other Native authors have written or are writing novels. Many writers have proved very prolific, yet are not as widely known as those previously discussed. Joseph Bruchac's (Abenaki) works, for example, appear in more than 400 publications. His novel, *Dawn Land,* re-creates the value system of precontact Natives. He has also recorded traditional stories and made them available in print and on audiocassettes known variously under the general title *Keepers of the Earth*. Bruchac cofounded the Greenfield Review Press so he could promote the works of emerging Indian authors. Janet Campbell Hale's (Coeur d'Alene) *The Jailing of Cecelia Capture* (1985) was a finalist for a Pulitzer Prize. Paula Gunn Allen (Laguna), well-known activist and critic, also wrote a novel, *The Woman Who Owned the Shadows* (1983). The now-deceased husband of Louise Erdrich, Michael Dorris (Modoc), wrote *A Yellow Raft in Blue Water* (1987) and, with Erdrich, coauthored the financially successful *The Crown of Columbus* (1991).

Legitimate concerns abound. Can, should, or do individual American Indian authors represent the views and beliefs of those tribes from which they come? Who owns traditional beliefs? And who, if anyone, has the right to police the creative products of individual Native American writers? More important, can individuals from one tribe claim to know the belief systems of those from other tribes? Some critics, for example, claim that Leslie Marmon Silko "fell from the sky." The implication of such a statement is that Pueblo creation narratives are emergence narratives: Original Laguna people emerged from the earth rather than fell from the sky. The origin myths of the Iroquois describe the original people as falling from a world above this one. In other words, critics are suggesting that Silko's use of Laguna mythology without permission in her novel *Ceremony* marks her as someone who does not respect her beliefs. The fact that Silko also incorporates Navajo mythology is also suspect to some critics. Many Coeur d' Alene were upset with Sherman Alexie's depiction of reservation life in the film *Smoke Signals* (adapted from his fiction), a fact that brings into focus the problems of one urban Indian's interpretation of collective reservation experience. When Native peoples have traditionally been misrepresented, the new focus on their problems in literature (even by insiders) could be seen as perpetuating the victimage. Who, from any family, dysfunctional or not, wants any member to presume to describe the family as a whole? Craig S. Womack (Muskogee Creek and Cherokee) has written *Red on Red: Native American Literary Separatism* (1999), and Arnold Krupat has written *Red Matters* (2002), both of which explore these dilemmas. Many of these issues also collapse boundaries between and among ethnology, mythology, history, politics, and multicultural studies. Can Natives and non-Natives engage in dialogue across such vast boundaries? Is it the moral imperative of our time to hear the stories of the "other" with the hope that such shared experience can help humans overcome suffering, violence, and humiliation? And, finally, do we have to be a people in order to learn from them?

BIBLIOGRAPHY

Allen, Paula Gunn. "Mourning Dove (Humishuma)." In *Voice of the Turtle: American Indian Literature 1900–1970,* edited by Paula Gunn Allen, 78–79. New York: Ballantine Books, 1994.

Bruner, Edward M. "Experience and Its Expressions." In *The Anthropology of Experience,* edited by Victor W. Turner and Edward M. Bruner, 3–33. Chicago: University of Illinois Press, 1986.

Churchill, Ward, and Glenn T. Morris. "Key Indian Laws and Cases." In *The State of Native America: Genocide, Colonization, and Resistence,* edited by M. Annette Jaimes, 13–23. Boston: South End Press, 1992.

Cook-Lynn, Elizabeth. "The American Indian Fiction Writers: Cosmopolitanism, Nationalism, The Third World, and First Nation Sovereignty." In *Nothing but the Truth,* edited by John L. Purdy and James Ruppert, 23–39. Upper Saddle River, New Jersey: Prentice Hall, 2001.

Eliade, Mircea. *Myth and Reality.* San Francisco: Harper & Row, 1963.

Owens, Louis. *Other Destinies: Understanding the American Indian Novel.* Norman: University of Oklahoma Press, 1992.

Ruoff, A. Lavonne Brown. "S. Alice Callahan." In *Handbook of Native American Literature,* edited by Andrew Wiget, 221–225. New York: Garland Publishing, Inc., 1996.

———. "Simon Pokagon." In *Handbook of Native American Literature,* edited by Andrew Wiget, 277–281. New York: Garland Publishing, Inc., 1996.

Stiffarm, Lenore A., with Phil Lane, Jr. "The Demography of Native North America." In *The State of Native America,* edited by M. Annette Jaimes, 23–55. Boston: South End Press, 1992.

Vickers, Scott B. *Native American Identities.* Albuquerque: University of New Mexico Press, 1998.

Warrior, Robert Allen. *Tribal Secrets.* Minneapolis: University of Minnesota Press, 1995.

Wilson, Terry P. "John Joseph Matthews." In *Handbook of Native American Literature,* edited by Andrew Wiget, 245–251. New York: Garland Publishing, Inc., 1996.

Suzanne Evertsen Lundquist

APPENDIX I

LIST OF MAJOR PRIZEWINNERS

PULITZER PRIZE FOR FICTION

The Pulitzer Prize, established at Columbia University by American newspaper publisher Joseph Pulitzer, awards prizes in the genres of fiction, general nonfiction, history, poetry, and biography/autobiography.

2006
Geraldine Brooks, *March*

2005
Marilynne Robinson, *Gilead*

2004
Edward Jones, *The Known World*

2003
Jeffrey Eugenides, *Middlesex*

2002
Richard Russo, *Empire Falls*

2001
Michael Chabon, *The Amazing Adventures of Kavalier & Clay*

2000
Jhumpa Lahiri, *Interpreter of Maladies* (story collection)

1999
Michael Cunningham, *The Hours*

1998
Philip Roth, *American Pastoral*

1997
Steven Millhauser, *Martin Dressler*

1996
Richard Ford, *Independence Day*

1995
Carol Shields, *The Stone Diaries*

1994
E. Anne Proulx, *The Shipping News*

1993
Robert Olen Butler, *A Good Scent from a Strange Mountain* (story collection)

1992
Jane Smiley, *A Thousand Acres*

1991
John Updike, *Rabbit at Rest*

1990
Oscar Hijuelos, *The Mambo Kings Play Songs of Love*

1989
Anne Tyler, *Breathing Lessons*

1988
Toni Morrison, *Beloved*

1987
Peter Taylor, *A Summons to Memphis*

1986
Larry McMurtry, *Lonesome Dove*

1985
Alison Lurie, *Foreign Affairs*

1984
William Kennedy, *Ironweed*

1983
Alice Walker, *The Color Purple*

1982
John Updike, *Rabbit Is Rich*

1981
John Kennedy Toole, *A Confederacy of Dunces*

1980
Norman Mailer, *The Executioner's Song*

1979
John Cheever, *The Stories of John Cheever* (story collection)

1978
James Alan McPherson, *Elbow Room* (story collection)

1977
No Award

1976
Saul Bellow, *Humboldt's Gift*

1975
Michael Shaara, *The Killer Angels*

1974
No Award

1973
Eudora Welty, *The Optimist's Daughter*

1972
Wallace Stegner, *Angle of Repose*

1971
No Award

1970
Jean Stafford, *Collected Stories* (story collection)

1969
N. Scott Momaday, *House Made of Dawn*

1968
William Styron, *The Confessions of Nat Turner*

1967
Bernard Malamud, *The Fixer*

1966
Katherine Anne Porter, *Collected Stories of Katherine Anne Porter* (story collection)

1965
Shirley A. Grau, *The Keepers of the House*

1964
No Award

1963
William Faulkner, *The Reivers*

1962
Edwin O'Connor, *The Edge of Sadness*

1961
Harper Lee, *To Kill a Mockingbird*

1960
Allen Drury, *Advise and Consent*

1959
Robert Lewis Taylor, *The Travels of Jaimie McPheeters*

1958
James Agee, *A Death in the Family*

1957
Honorary Award to Kenneth Roberts

1956
MacKinlay Kantor, *Andersonville*

1955
William Faulkner, *A Fable*

1954
No Award

1953
Ernest Hemingway, *The Old Man and the Sea*

1952
Herman Wouk, *The Caine Mutiny*

1951
Conrad Richter, *The Town*

1950
A. B. Guthrie, *The Way West*

1949
James Gould Cozzens, *Guard of Honor*

1948
James Michener, *Tales of the South Pacific*

1947
Robert Penn Warren, *All the King's Men*

1946
No Award

1945
John Hersey, *A Bell for Adano*

1944
Martin Flavin, *Journey in the Dark*

1943
Upton Sinclair, *Dragon's Teeth*

1942
Ellen Glasgow, *In This Our Life*

1941
No Award

1940
John Steinbeck, *The Grapes of Wrath*

1939
Marjorie Kinnan Rawlings, *The Yearling*

1938
John P. Marquand, *The Late George Apley*

1937
Margaret Mitchell, *Gone With the Wind*

1936
Harold L. Davis, *Honey in the Horn*

1935
Josephine W. Johnson, *Now in November*

1934
Caroline Miller, *Lamb in His Bosom*

1933
T. S. Stribling, *The Store*

1932
Pearl S. Buck, *The Good Earth*

1931
Margaret Ayer Barnes, *Years of Grace*

1930
Oliver La Farge, *Laughing Boy*

1929
Julia Peterkin, *Scarlet Sister Mary*

1928
Thornton Wilder, *The Bridge of San Luis Rey*

1927
Louis Bromfield, *Early Autumn*

1926
Sinclair Lewis, *Arrowsmith*

1925
Edna Ferber, *So Big*

1924
Margaret Wilson, *The Able McLaughlins*

1923
Willa Cather, *One of Ours*

1922
Booth Tarkington, *Alice Adams*

1921
Edith Wharton, *The Age of Innocence*

1920
No Award

1919
Booth Tarkington, *The Magnificent Ambersons*

1918
Ernest Poole, *His Family*

NATIONAL BOOK AWARD

The National Book Award was established in 1950. It is given annually to recognize achievements in four genres: fiction, nonfiction, poetry, and young people's literature.

2005
William T. Vollmann, *Europe Central*

2004
Lily Tuck, *The News from Paraguay*

2003
Shirley Hazzard, *The Great Fire*

2002
Julia Glass, *Three Junes*

2001
Jonathan Franzen, *The Corrections*

2000
Susan Sontag, *In America*

1999
Ha Jin, *Waiting*

1998
Alice McDermott, *Charming Billy*

1997
Charles Frazier, *Cold Mountain*

1996
Andrea Barrett, *Ship Fever and Other Stories* (story collection)

1995
Philip Roth, *Sabbath's Theater*

1994
William Gaddis, *A Frolic of His Own*

1993
E. Annie Proulx, *The Shipping News*

1992
Cormac McCarthy, *All the Pretty Horses*

1991
Norman Rush, *Mating*

1990
Charles Johnson, *Middle Passage*

1989
John Casey, *Spartina*

1988
Pete Dexter, *Paris Trout*

1987
Larry Heinemann, *Paco's Story*

1986
E. L. Doctorow, *World's Fair*

1985
Don DeLillo, *White Noise*

1984
Ellen Gilchrist, *Victory over Japan* (story collection)

1983
Alice Walker, *The Color Purple*

1982
John Updike, *Rabbit Is Rich*

1981
Wright Morris, *Plains Song*

1980
William Styron, *Sophie's Choice*

1979
Tim O'Brien, *Going After Cacciato*

1978
Mary Lee Settle, *Blood Tie*

1977
Wallace Stegner, *The Spectator Bird*

1976
William Gaddis, *JR*

1975
Thomas Williams, *The Hair of Harold Roux* and Robert Stone, *Dog Soldiers*

1974
Thomas Pynchon, *Gravity's Rainbow*

1973
John Barth, *Chimera* and John Williams, *Augustus*

1972
Flannery O'Connor, *The Complete Stories of Flannery O'Connor* (story collection)

1971
Saul Bellow, *Mr. Sammler's Planet*

1970
Joyce Carol Oates, *them*

1969
Jerzy Kosinski, *Steps*

1968
Thornton Wilder, *The Eighth Day*

1967
Bernard Malamud, *The Fixer*

1966

Katherine Anne Porter, *The Collected Stories of Katherine Anne Porter* (story collection)

1965

Saul Bellow, *Herzog*

1964

John Updike, *The Centaur*

1963

J. F. Powers, *Morte d'Urban*

1962

Walker Percy, *The Moviegoer*

1961

Conrad Richter, *The Waters of Kronos*

1960

Philip Roth, *Goodbye Columbus*

1959

Bernard Malamud, *The Magic Barrel* (story collection)

1958

John Cheever, *The Wapshot Chronicle*

1957

Wright Morris, *The Field of Vision*

1956

John O'Hara, *Ten North Frederick*

1955

William Faulkner, *A Fable*

1954

Saul Bellow, *The Adventures of Augie March*

1953

Ralph Ellison, *Invisible Man*

1952

James Jones, *From Here to Eternity*

1951

William Faulkner, *The Collected Stories of William Faulkner* (story collection)

1950

Nelson Algren, *The Man with the Golden Arm*

NATIONAL BOOK CRITICS CIRCLE AWARD

The National Book Critics Circle, founded in 1974, consists of approximately 700 active book reviewers. Every year the circle selects award winners in fiction, as well as general nonfiction, biography/autobiography, poetry and criticism.

2005

E. L. Doctorow, *The March*

2004

Marilynne Robinson, *Gilead*

2003

Edward P. Jones, *The Known World*

2002

Ian McEwan, *Atonement* (non-American)

2001

Winfried Georg Sebald, *Austerlitz* (non-American)

2000

Jim Crace, *Being Dead* (non-American)

1999

Jonathan Lethem, *Motherless Brooklyn*

1998

Alice Munro, *The Love of a Good Woman* (non-American)

1997

Penelope Fitzgerald, *The Blue Flower* (non-American)

1996

Gina Berriault, *Women in Their Beds* (story collection)

1995

Stanley Elkin, *Mrs. Ted Bliss*

1994

Carol Shields, *The Stone Diaries*

1993

Ernest J. Gaines, *A Lesson before Dying*

1992
Cormac McCarthy, *All the Pretty Horses*

1991
Jane Smiley, *A Thousand Acres*

1990
John Updike, *Rabbit at Rest*

1989
E. L. Doctorow, *Billy Bathgate*

1988
Bharati Mukherjee *The Middleman and Other Stories* (story collection)

1987
Philip Roth, *The Counterlife*

1986
Reynolds Price, *Kate Vaiden*

1985
Anne Tyler, *The Accidental Tourist*

1984
Louise Erdrich, *Love Medicine*

1983
William Kennedy, *Ironweed*

1982
Stanley Elkin, *George Mills*

1981
John Updike, *Rabbit Is Rich*

1980
Shirley Hazzard *The Transit of Venus*

1979
Thomas Flanagan, *The Year of the French*

1978
John Cheever, *The Stories of John Cheever*

1977
Toni Morrison, *Song of Solomon*

1976
John Gardner, *October Light*

1975
E. L. Doctorow, *Ragtime*

PEN/FAULKNER AWARD FOR FICTION

Named for William Faulkner, the PEN Faulkner Award was established in 1980 by writers to honor their peers each year.

2005
Ha Jin, *War Trash*

2004
John Updike, *The Early Stories* (story collection)

2003
Sabina Murray, *The Caprices* (story collection)

2002
Ann Patchett, *Bel Canto*

2001
Phillip Roth, *The Human Stain*

2000
Ha Jin, *Waiting*

1999
Michael Cunningham, *The Hours*

1998
Rafi Zabor, *The Bear Comes Home*

1997
Gina Berriault, *Women in Their Beds*

1996
Richard Ford, *Independence Day*

1995
David Guterson, *Snow Falling on Cedars*

1994
Philip Roth, *Operation Shylock*

1993
E. Annie Proulx, *Postcards*

1992
Don DeLillo, *Mao II*

1991
John Edgar Wideman, *Philadelphia Fire*

1990
E. L. Doctorow, *Billy Bathgate*

1989
James Salter, *Dusk* (story collection)

1988
T. Coraghessan Boyle, *World's End*

1987
Richard Wiley, *Soldiers in Hiding*

1986
Peter Taylor, *The Old Forest and Other Stories*

1985
Tobias Wolff, *The Barracks Thief*

1984
John Edgar Wideman, *Sent for You Yesterday*

1983
Toby Olson, *Seaview*

1982
David Bradley, *The Chaneysville Incident*

1981
Walter Abish, *How German Is It?*

NOBEL PRIZE

Nobel Prizes in literature awarded to American novelists:

1993
Toni Morrison

1978
Isaac Bashevis Singer

1976
Saul Bellow

1962
John Steinbeck

1954
Ernest Hemingway

1949
William Faulkner

1938
Pearl Buck (Pearl Walsh Nie Sydenstricker)

1930
Sinclair Lewis

EDGAR AWARD

Established by the Mystery Writers of America to present annual awards for the best mystery novel published each year, the Edgar Awards are named after Edgar Allan Poe. Other categories include stories, criticism, and biographies of mystery writers.

2006
Jess Walter, *Citizen Vince*

2005
T. Jefferson Parker, *California Girl*

2004
Ian Rankin, *Resurrection Men*

2003
S. J. Rozan, *Winter and Night*

2002
T. Jefferson Parker, *Silent Joe*

2001
Joe R. Lansdale, *The Bottoms*

2000
Jan Burke, *Bones*

1999
Robert Clark, *Mr. White's Confession*

1998
James Lee Burke, *Cimarron Rose*

1997
Thomas H. Cook, *The Chatham School Affair*

1996
Dick Francis, *Come to Grief*

1995
Mary Willis Walker, *The Red Scream*

1994
Minette Walters, *The Sculptress*

1993
Margaret Maron, *Bootlegger's Daughter*

1992
Lawrence Block, *A Dance at the Slaughterhouse*

1991
Julie Smith, *New Orleans Mourning*

1990
James Lee Burke, *Black Cherry Blues*

1989
Stuart M. Kaminsky, *A Cold Red Sunrise*

1988
Aaron Elkins, *Old Bones*

1987
Barbara Vine, *A Dark-Adopted Eye*

1986
L. R. Wright, *The Suspect*

1985
Ross Thomas, *Briar Patch*

1984
Elmore Leonard, *La Brava*

1983
Rick Boyer, *Billingsgate Shoal*

1982
William Bayer, *Peregrine*

1981
Dick Francis, *Whip Hand*

1980
Arthur Maling, *The Rheingold Route*

1979
Ken Follett, *The Eye of the Needle*

1978
William Hallahan, *Catch Me: Kill Me*

1977
Robert B. Parker, *Promised Land*

1976
Brian Garfield, *Hopscotch*

1975
Jon Cleary, *Peter's Pence*

1974
Tony Hillerman, *Dance Hall of the Dead*

1973
Warren Kiefer, *The Lingala Code*

1972
Frederick Forsyth, *The Day of the Jackal*

1971
Maj Sjowall, Per Wahloo, *The Laughing Policeman*

1970
Dick Francis, *Forfeit*

1969
Jeffery Hudson, *A Case of Need*

1968
Donald E. Westlake, *God Save the Mark*

1967
Nicolas Freeling, *The King of the Rainy Country*

1966
Adam Hall, *The Quiller Memorandum*

1965
John le Carre, *The Spy Who Came in from the Cold*

1964
Eric Ambler, *The Light of Day*

1963
Ellis Peters, *Death and the Joyful Woman*

1962
J. J. Marric, *Gideon's Fire*

1961
Julian Symons, *The Progress of a Crime*

1960
Celia Fremlin, *The Hours before Dawn*

1959
Stanley Ellin, *The Eighth Circle*

1958
Ed Lacy, *Room to Swing*

1957
Charlotte Armstrong, *A Dram of Poison*

1956
Margaret Millar, *Beast in View*

1955
Raymond Chandler, *The Long Goodbye*

APPENDIX II

SELECTED BIBLIOGRAPHY

Adams, James Truslow. *The Founding of New England.* New York: Atlantic Monthly Press, 1921.

American Women Writers: A Critical Reference Guide from Colonial Times to the Present. 4 vols. New York: Ungar, 1983.

Ammons, Elizabeth. *Conflicting Stories: American Women Writers at the Turn into the Twentieth Century.* New York: Oxford University Press, 1992.

Banta, Martha. *Failure and Success in America: A Literary Debate.* Princeton, N.J.: Princeton University Press, 1978.

Barbour, J., and Tom Quirk, eds. *Writing the American Classics.* Chapel Hill: University of North Carolina Press, 1990.

Bardes, Barbara, and Suzanne Gossett. *Declarations of Independence: Women and Political Power in Nineteenth Century American Fiction.* New Brunswick, N.J.: Rutgers University Press, 1990.

Bateson, F. W., and H. T. Meserole. *A Guide to English and American Literature.* 3rd ed. London: Longman, 1976.

Baym, Nina. *Novels, Readers, and Reviewers: Responses to Fiction in Antebellum America.* Ithaca, N.Y.: Cornell University Press, 1984.

———. *Women's Fiction: A Guide to Novels by and about Women in America, 1820–70.* 2nd ed. Urbana: Illinois University Press, 1993.

Bercovitch, Sacvan, ed. *Cambridge History of American Literature.* 5 vols. New York: Cambridge University Press, 1994.

Bercovitch, Sacvan, and Myra Jehien, eds. *Ideology and Classic American Literature.* Cambridge: Cambridge University Press, 1986.

Bercovitch, Sacvan. *The Office of The Scarlet Letter.* Baltimore, Md.: Johns Hopkins University Press, 1991.

———. *The Puritan Origins of the American Self.* New Haven, Conn.: Yale University Press, 1975.

Bewley, Marius. *Complex Fate.* London: Chatto and Windus, 1952.

Bradbury, Malcolm, ed. *The Novel Today: Contemporary Writers on Modern Fiction.* Manchester, England: Manchester University Press, 1977.

Bradbury, Malcolm. *The Modern American Novel* (New Edition). Oxford and Boston: Oxford University Press, 1992.

Brodhead, Richard H. *Hawthorne, Melville and the Novel.* Chicago: University of Chicago Press, 1976.

Bruccoli, Matthew J., ed. *The Profession of Authorship in America, 1800–1870: The Papers of William Charvat.* Columbus: Ohio State University Press, 1968.

Bryer, Jackson R. *Sixteen Modern American Authors; A Survey of Research and Criticism.* Durham, N.C.: Duke University Press, 1974.

Buell, Lawrence. *Literary Transcendentalism: Style and Vision in the American Renaissance.* Ithaca, N.Y.: Cornell University Press, 1973.

Burgess, Anthony. *The Novel Now: A Guide to Contemporary Fiction.* New York: Norton, 1967.

Bynum, Victoria E. *Unruly Women: The Politics of Social & Sexual Control in the Old South.* Chapel Hill: University of North Carolina Press, 1992.

Cady, Edwin H. *The Light of Common Day: Realism in American Fiction.* Bloomington: Indiana University Press, 1971.

Cameron, Sharon, *The Corporeal Self: Allegories of the Body in Melville and Hawthorne.* New York: Columbia University Press, 1981.

Chase, Richard V. *The American Novel and Its Tradition.* Garden City, N.Y.: Doubleday, 1957.

Conn, Peter. *Literature in America: An Illustrated History.* New York: Cambridge University Press, 1989.

Contemporary Authors: A Bibliographical Guide to Current Writers in Fiction. Detroit: Gale Research, 1962.

Contemporary Poets, Dramatists, Essayists, and Novelists of the South: a Bio-Bibliographical Sourcebook. Edited by Robert Bain and Joseph M. Flora. Westport, Conn.: Greenwood Press, 1994.

Cowley, Malcolm. *The Flower and the Leaf: A Contemporary Record of American Writing since 1941.* New York: Viking, 1985.

Cunliffe, Marcus, ed. *American Literature to 1900.* New York: Penguin, 1993.

Dearborn, Mary. *Pocahontas's Daughters: Gender and Ethnicity in American Culture.* New York: Oxford University Press, 1986.

Donoghue, Denis. *Reading America: Essays on American Literature.* Berkeley: University of California Press, 1987.

Donohue, Agnes McNeill. *Hawthorne: Calvin's Ironic Stepchild.* Kent, Ohio: Kent State University Press, 1985.

Douglas, Ann. *The Feminization of American Culture.* New York: Knopf, 1977.

Duke, Maurice, ed. *American Women Writers: Bibliographical Essays.* Westport, Conn.: Greenwood Press, 1983.

Eagleton, Terry. *The Illusions of Postmodernism.* London: Blackwell Publishers, 1996.

Elliot, Emory, ed. *The Columbia History of the American Novel.* New York: Columbia University Press, 1988.

Feidelson, Charles. *Symbolism and American Literature.* Chicago: University of Chicago Press, 1953.

Fiedler, Leslie. *Love and Death in the American Novel.* 1960. Rev. ed. New York: Stein and Day, 1966.

Fifty Southern Writers before 1900: a Bio-Bibliographical Sourcebook. Edited by Robert Bain and Joseph M. Flora. Westport, Conn.: Greenwood Press, 1987

Fisher, Philip. *Hard Facts: Setting and Form in the American Novel.* New York: Oxford University Press, 1985.

Frye, Joanne S. *Living Stories Telling Lives: Women and the Novel in Contemporary Experience.* Ann Arbor: University of Michigan Press, 1986.

Gates, Henry Lewis, Jr., ed. *The Schomburg Library of 19th Century Black Women Writers.* 30 vols. New York: Oxford University Press, 1988.

Gates, Henry Louis, Jr. *The Signifying Monkey: A Theory of African-American Literary Criticism.* New York: Oxford University Press, 1988.

Gayle, Addison. *The Way of the New World: The Black Novel in America.* Garden City, N.Y.: Doubleday, 1975.

Gilbert, Sandra, and Susan Gubar. *The Madwoman in the Attic.* New Haven, Conn.: Yale University Press, 1979.

————. *No Man's Land: The Place of the Woman Writer in the 20th Century.* 3 vols. New Haven, Conn.: Yale University Press, 1987, 1988, 1994.

Gilmore, Michael. *American Romanticism and the Marketplace.* Chicago: University of Chicago Press, 1985.

Greenblatt, Stephen, and Giles Gunn, eds. *Redrawing the Boundaries: The Transformation of English and American Literary Studies.* New York: Modern Language Association, 1994.

Habegger, Alfred. *Gender, Fantasy and Realism in American Literature.* New York: Columbia University Press, 1982.

Harbert, Earl N., and Robert A. Rees. *Fifteen American Authors before 1900; Bibliographic Essays on Research and Criticism.* Rev. ed. Madison: University of Wisconsin Press, 1984.

Hart, James D. *The Popular Book: A History of America's Literary Taste.* Berkeley: University of California Press, 1961.

Hobson, Fred C. *Tell about the South.* Baton Rouge: Louisiana State University Press, 1983.

Hoffman, Daniel, ed. *Harvard Guide to Contemporary American Writing.* Cambridge, Mass.: Harvard University Press, 1979.

Holman, C. Hugh, comp. *The American Novel through Henry James.* 2nd ed. Arlington Heights, Ill.: AHM Publishing, 1979.

Horton, Rod, and Herbert Edwards. *Backgrounds of American Literary Thought.* 3rd ed. Englewood Cliffs, N.J.: Prentice Hall, 1974.

Horwitz, Howard. *By The Law of Nature: Form and Value in Nineteenth-Century America.* New York: Oxford University Press, 1991.

Howard, June. *Form and History in American Literary Naturalism.* Chapel Hill: University of North Carolina Press, 1985.

Howe, Irving. *The American Newness.* Cambridge, Mass.: Harvard University Press, 1986.

Huyssen, Andreas. *After the Great Divide: Modernism, Mass Culture, Postmodernism.* Bloomington: Indiana University Press, (1986).

James, Henry. *The Future of the Novel.* Edited by Leon Edel. New York: Vintage, 1956.

Jay, Paul. *Being In The Text: Self-Representation from Wordsworth to Roland Barthes.* Ithaca, N.Y.: Cornell University Press, 1984.

Jehlen, Myra. *American Incarnation.* Cambridge, Mass.: Harvard University Press, 1986.

Kaplan, Amy. *The Social Construction of American Realism.* Chicago: University of Chicago Press, 1988.

Karl, Frederic. *American Fictions 1940–1980: A Comprehensive History and Critical Evaluation.* New York: Harper and Row, 1983.

Kazin, Alfred. *On Native Grounds: An Interpretation of Modern American Prose Literature.* 1942. New York: Harcourt, 1995.

———. *A Writer's America.* Cambridge, Mass.: Harvard University Press, 1988.

Kenner, Hugh. *A Homemade World: The American Modernist Writers.* New York: William Morrow, 1975.

Knight, Brenda, ed. *Women of the Beat Generation.* Berkeley, Calif.: Conan Press, 1996.

Kostelanetz, Richard. *The Avant-Garde Tradition in Literature.* Buffalo, N.Y.: Prometheus Books, 1982.

Lang, Amy Schrager. *Prophetic Woman: Anne Hutchinson.* Berkeley: University of California Press, 1987.

Lawrence D. H. *Studies in Classic American Literature.* 1923. Reprint. Cambridge: Cambridge University Press, 2002.

Leary, Lewis G. *American Literature: A Study and Research Guide.* New York: St. Martin's Press, 1976.

Levin, Harry. *The Power of Blackness.* Athens: Ohio University Press, 1958.

Lewis, R. W. B. *American Adam.* Chicago: University of Chicago Press, 1955.

Litz, A. Walton. *Modern American Fiction: Essays in Criticism.* New York: Oxford University Press, 1963.

Lukács, George. *The Theory of the Novel.* Translated by Anna Bostock. London: Merlin Press, 1962.

Machor, James L., ed. *Readers in History: Nineteenth Century American Literature and the Contexts of Response.* Baltimore, Md.: Johns Hopkins University Press, 1993.

Manning, Carol S. *The Female Tradition in Southern Literature.* Urbana: University of Illinois Press, 1993.

Marx, Leo. *The Machine in the Garden: Technology and the Pastoral Ideal in America.* London: Oxford University Press, 1964.

Matthiessen, F. O. *American Renaissance.* New York: Oxford University Press, 1941.

Maxwell, D. E. *American Fiction.* New York: Columbia University Press, 1963.

McCormick, John. *American Literature 1919–1932: A Comparative History.* London: Routledge and Keegan Paul, 1971.

Messenger, Christian K. *Sport and the Spirit of Play in Contemporary American Fiction.* New York: Columbia University Press, 1990.

Miller, Perry. *The Raven and the Whale.* New York: Harcourt, 1956.

———. *Errand into the Wilderness.* Cambridge, Mass.: Harvard University Press, 1956.

———. *The New England Mind.* 1939. Cambridge, Mass.: Harvard University Press, 1953.

———. *The New England Mind: The Seventeenth Century.* New York: Macmillan, 1939.

Miller, Perry, and Thomas H. Johnson, eds. *The Puritans: A Sourcebook of Their Writings.* 2 vols. New York: American Book Company, 1938.

Muir, Edwin. *The Structure of the Novel.* London: Hogarth Press, 1928.

Myerson, Joel. *The American Renaissance in New England.* Detroit: Gale Research, 1978.

———, ed. *The Transcendentalists.* New York: Modern Language Association, 1984.

Newman, Charles. *The Post-Modern Aura: Fiction in an Age of Inflation.* Evanston, Ill.: Northwestern University Press, 1985.

Oelschlaeger, Max. *The Idea of Wilderness: From Prehistory to the Age of Ecoloqy.* New Haven, Conn.: Yale University Press, 1991.

Olster, Stacey Michele. *Reminiscence and Re-Creation in Contemporary American Fiction.* Cambridge: Cambridge University Press, 1989.

Parrington, Vernon L. *Main Currents in American Thought.* 3 vols. New York: Harcourt Brace, 1927.

Pease, Donald. *Visionary Compacts.* Madison: University of Wisconsin Press, 1987.

Pizer, Donald. *Realism and Naturalism in Nineteenth-Century American Literature*. Rev. ed. Carbondale: Southern Illinois University Press, 1984.

Poirier, Richard. *A World Elsewhere: The Place of Style in American Literature*. Madison: University of Wisconsin Press, 1966.

Poroush, David. *The Soft Machine: Cybernetic Fiction*. New York: Methuen, 1985.

Rees, Robert A., and Earl N. Harbert, eds. *Fifteen American Authors before 1900; Bibliographic Essays on Research and Criticism*. 1971. Rev. ed. Madison: University of Wisconsin Press, 1984.

Reynolds, David S. *Beneath the American Renaissance*. Cambridge, Mass.: Harvard University Press, 1988.

Reynolds, Larry. *The American Renaissance and the Revolutions of 1848*. New Haven, Conn.: Yale University Press, 1988.

Rideout, Walter. *The Radical Novel in the United States, 1900–1954*. Cambridge, Mass.: Harvard University Press, 1956.

Rogin, Michael. *Subversive Genealogy: The Politics and Art of Herman Melville*. Berkeley: University of California Press, 1985.

Rubin, Louis D., Jr. *A Bibliographical Guide to the Study of Southern Literature*. Baton Rouge: Louisiana State University Press, 1969.

———. *The Edge of the Swamp: A Study in the Literature and Society of the Old South*. Baton Rouge: Louisiana State University Press, 1989.

Ruoff, A. LaVonne Brown, and Jerry W. Ward, Jr., eds. *Redefining American Literary History*. New York: Modern Language Association, 1990.

Schirmeister, Pamela. *The Consolations of Space: The Place of Romance in Hawthorne, Melville and James*. Stanford, Calif.: Stanford University Press, 1990.

Showalter, Elaine, ed. *The New Feminist Criticism: Essays on Women, Literature & Theory*. New York: Pantheon, 1985.

Slotkin, Richard. *The Fatal Environment: The Myth of the Frontier in the Age of Industrialization, 1800–1890*. New York: Atheneum, 1985.

Smith, Henry Nash. *Virgin Land: The American West as Symbol and Myth*. Cambridge, Mass.: Harvard University Press, 1950.

Spiller, Robert E., et al. *Literary History of the United States: Bibliography*. 4th ed., rev. New York: Macmillan, 1974.

Spiller, Robert E. *The Cycle of American Literature: An Essay in Historical Criticism*. New York: New American Library, 1957.

Tichi, Cecilia. *Shifting Gears: Technology, Literature and Culture in Modernist America*. Chapel Hill: University of North Carolina Press, 1987.

Tompkins, Jane. *Sensational Designs: The Cultural Work of American Fiction, 1790–1860*. New York: Oxford University Press, 1985.

Turner, Darwin T. *Afro-American Writers*. New York: Appleton-Century-Crofts, 1970.

Van Doren, Carl. *The American Novel, 1789–1939*. New York: Macmillan, 1921. Revised and enlarged, 1940. Rev. ed., 1955.

Warren, Joyce W. *The American Narcissus: Individualism and Women in Nineteenth-Century American Fiction*. New Brunswick, N.J.: Rutgers University Press, 1984.

———. *The (Other) American Traditions: Nineteenth-Century Women Writers*. New Brunswick, N.J.: Rutgers University Press, 1993.

Wilde, Adam. *Middle Grounds: Studies in Contemporary American Fiction*. Philadelphia: University of Pennsylvania Press, 1987.

Wilson, Edmund. *The Shock of Recognition*. 1943. 2d ed. New York: Farrar, Straus, and Cudahy, 1955.

Woodress, James. *Eight American Authors; A Review of Research and Criticism*. Rev. ed. New York: Norton, 1971.

Yellin, Jean Fagan, and John C. Van Home, eds. *Women and Sisters: The Antislavery Feminists in American Culture*. Ithaca, N.Y.: Cornell University Press, 1994.

Young, Thomas D., and Ronald E. Fine, eds. *American Literature: A Critical Survey*. 2 vols. New York: American Book Company, 1968.

Ziff, Larzer. *Literary Democracy: The Declaration of Cultural Independence in America*. New York: Viking, 1981.

LIST OF CONTRIBUTORS

Adams, Jon   Western Michigan University

Adams, Morgan   Rancho Cucamonga, California

Ambrozic, Alex   Memorial University of Newfoundland, Canada

Anderson, Crystal   Ohio University

Antonaya, Marisa   Asian University, Thailand

Arnel, Jill   Oregon City, Oregon

Asya, Ferda   Bloomsburg University

Austenfeld, Thomas   North Georgia College and State University

Baena, Rosalia   Universidad de Navarra, Spain

Berger, Aimee   Texas Woman's University

Berkove, Lawrence J.   University of Michigan

Betz, Frederick   Southern Illinois University at Carbondale

Bezusko, Adriane   University of North Dakota

Blackwell, Brent M.   Ball State University

Bliven, Heather   De Paul University

Boal, David   University of Toulouse, France

Bowers, Maggie Ann   University of Antwerp/UIA, Belgium

Bradley, Patricia   Middle Tennessee State University

Brottman, David   University of Southern Indiana

Brownlie, Alan W.   Anne Arundel Community College

Buckman, Alyson   California State University at Sacramento

Califano, Sharon Kehl   University of New Hampshire

Camp, Mechel   Jackson State Community College

Campbell, Donna   Gonzaga University

Carey, Suzanne   Stanford University

Carlson, David J.   California State University at San Bernardino

Carson, Warren J.   University of South Carolina Upstate

Channing, Jill Ann   Wright State University

Clay, Alicia   Texas A & M University

Cohen, Sanda   The Elisabeth Morrow School, Englewood, N.J.

Cook, Chris O.   DePaul University

J. Randolph Cox   St. Olaf College

Craton, Lillie   Emory University

Crawford, Valerie Matthews   Georgia Perimeter College

Crowther, Kathryn E.   Emory University

Cummins, Amy E.   Fort Hays State University

D'Augustine, Allie M.   University of Pennsylvania

Dahm, Jacobia   Columbia University

Davis, Rocío G.   Universidad de Navarra, Spain

de Jesús, Melinda L.   Arizona State University

de Manuel, Dolores   Nassau Community College

De Ornellas, Kevin   Queen's University, Belfast, Ireland

DePietro, Thomas   Eastchester, New York

Delgado, Ana Beatriz   Universidad de Navarra, Spain

DeNuccio, Jerome   Graceland University

Despain, Max   University of Delaware

Diaz, Lisette Gibson   Capitol University

Dickison, Stephanie   Toronto, Ontario

Dittman, Michael   Franklin, Pa.

Dobbins, Zachary   University of Texas at Austin

Dorfman, John   New York, N.Y.

Dukess, Mona   Larchmont, N.Y.

Durnell, Laura   DePaul University

Edelstein, Sari   Brandeis University

Elkin, Lauren   City University of New York

Ellam, Julie L.   University of Hull

Elliott, Rosslyn   Emory University

Elliott, Winter   Glenville State College

Entzminger, Betina   Bloomsburg University

Ernst, Monty Kozbial   University of Wisconsin at Eau Claire

Evans, Amy   York Queen Mary, University of London, England

Fabiano, Mark   Wright State University

Fagan, Deirdre   University of Miami

Fahy, Thomas   University of North Carolina at Chapel Hill

Feerst, Alex   Duke University

Fenimore, David   University of Nevada at Reno

Flanagan, Kelly   Prior Lake High School

Flores, Nona C.   University of Illinois at Chicago

Fu, Bennett   National Taiwan University

García, Carmen Méndez   Universidad Complutense

Gentry, April   Savannah State University

Gold, Harriet   Université de Montréal, Canada

Grattan, William   University of Missouri

Grossberg, Blythe   New York, N.Y.

Gussman, Deborah   The Richard Stockton College of New Jersey

Haggard, Kendra   Northeastern State University of Oklahoma

Han, Jihee   Yonsei University, China

Haugen, Hayley Mitchell   Ohio University

Hausmann, Jessica   Drew University

Hayes, Sandra Chrystal   University of Southern California

Henderson, Katherine Usher   Point Park University

Hicks, Kathleen   Arizona State University

Hime, Laurie Howell   Miami Dade Community College

Hinkle, Lynda   Rutgers University

Ho, Jennifer   Mount Holyoke College

Hoeness-Krupsaw, Susanna   University of Southern Indiana

Hogan, Monika   University of Massachusetts

Horrine Kerri A.   Bellarmine University

Huey, Peggy J.   The University of Tampa

Hume, Beverly   Indiana University-Purdue University at Fort Wayne

Huskey, Paige   Wright State University

Jasmine, Randy   Dixie State College of Utah

Jesús, Melinda L. de   Arizona State University

Jin, Li   Beijing University of Technology

Johnsen, H. L.   Sam Houston State University

Jones, Dan   University of South Dakota

Josyph, Peter   New York, N.Y.

Keller, Jane   Eblen University of Baltimore

Kelley, James   Mississippi State University at Meridian

Kenemore, Scott   Logan Square, Chicago, Ill.

Kich, Martin   Wright State University—Lake Campus

Killoran, Helen   Ohio State University

Kiskis, Michael J.   Elmira College

Konkle, Lincoln   Trenton College of New Jersey

Kornreich, Leron   Los Angeles, Calif.

Kuhl, Nancy   Yale University

Lansky, Ellen   Inver Hills Community College

Leahy, Anna   North Central College

Lee, Patricia Becker   Fordham University

Leuschner, Eric   University of Missouri-Columbia

Lewis, Marilyn   Commerce, Texas

Lewis, Timothy Adrian   DePaul University

Li Jin [aka Jane Lee]   Beijing University of Technology, China

Li Wenxin   Suffolk County Community College of the State University of New York

Liukkonen, Petri   Kuusankoski Library, Finland

Lundquist, Susan   Everest

Lynn, Amy D.   Texas Tech University & Université de Limoges, France

Maas, Wendy   Drew University

Mahoney, Rita   De Paul University

Marovitz, Sanford E.   Kent State University

Martín-Junquera, Imelda   Universidad de León, Spain

Martin, Lowell   Meridian Community College, Meridian, Mississippi

Martin, Quentin   University of Colorado at Colorado Springs

Martucci, Elise A.   Fordham University

Massey, Christopher Lee   Wright University

Mathis, Andrew   Philadelphia, Pa.

Maxey, Ruth   University College London

Mayo, James   Jackson State Community College

McLoughlin, Kate   University of Oxford

Meyer, Kurtis L.   Edina, Minnesota

Meyer, Michael J.   DePaul University

Middlebrook, Geoffrey L.   California State University at San Bernardino

Miga, Michael   DePaul University

Miguela, Antonia Dom'nguez   University of Huelva, Spain

Miles, Kathryn   Unity College

Miller, Andy   University of Missouri–Columbia

Miller, Cynthia J.   Emerson College

Millichap, Joseph   Western Kentucky University

Mills, Fiona   University of North Carolina at Chapel Hill

Moore, Erika   New York, N.Y.

Moore, Erin   Flagler University

Moynihan, Susan Muchshima   University of Illinois at Urbana-Champaign

Murg, Stephanie   New York, N.Y.

Murphy, Bernice   Trinity College, Dublin, Ireland

Nanda, Ram Shankar   Sambalpur University, India

Neary, Gwen   Santa Monica College

Neary, Gwen   Sonoma State University/Santa Rosa Junior College

Nebrida, Patricia J.   DePaul University

Nimura, Tamiko   University of Puget Sound

Norris, Jan Schubert   San Antonio, Texas

O'Hagan, Christine   Long Island, N.Y.

Ostman, Heather   Iona College

Overall, Keri   DeVry University

Packwood, A. Nicholas   Wilfrid Laurier University, Waterloo, Ontario, Canada

Pamplin, Claire   Borough of Manhattan Community College

Panesar, Gurdip   Kaur University of Glasgow, Scotland

Parker, Eliot   Marshall University

Parry, Sally E.   Illinois State University

Pazos, José Gabriel Rodríguez   University of Navarra, Spain

Perel, Zivah   University of Delaware

Peterman, Terry   Texas A & M University at Commerce

Petrillo, Marion   Bloomsburg University

Pluck, Jay   Brooklyn, N.Y.

Pollock, Jeri   Rio de Janeiro, Brasil

Potter, Rebecca C.   University of Dayton

Quirk, Kevin

Rabin, Jessica   Anne Arundel Community College

Rakover, Jeff   Harvard University

Ramirez, Luz Elena   California State University at San Bernardino

Ramsden, Catherine   De Paul University

Redwine, Elizbeth Brewer   Emory University

Rich, Rachel   Utah State University

Royal, Derek P.   Texas A&M University at Commerce

Rozzell, Kristen

Rubin, Lance   Arapahoe Community College

Samuels, Wilfred D.   University of Utah

Sathyaraj, V.   Indian Institute of Technology (IIT), India

Scalia, Bill   Louisiana State University

Schrynemakers, Ilse   Brooklyn, N.Y.

Schwankle, David   California State University at San Bernardino

Sehulster, Patricia J.   Pace University

Senchyne, Jonathan William   Syracuse University

Shankar, Lavina Dhingra   Bates College

Shantz, Jeff   York University

Shearin, Gloria   Savannah State University

Sheffer, Jolie A.   University of Virginia

Shenk, Max   Montgomery County Community College, Bluebell, Pa.

Smith, Patrick A.   Bainbridge College

Snyder, Carey   Ohio University

Spencer, William C.   Delta State University

Suglia, Joseph   Northwestern University/De Paul University

Taylor, Corey M.   University of Delaware

Sweeney, Brian   Brown University

Thacker, Robert   St. Lawrence University, Canton, N.Y.

Thompson, Stella   Prairie View A&M University

Tomkins, David   University of Southern California

Trefzer, Annette   University of Mississippi

Trodd, Zoe   Harvard University

Twitchell-Waas, Jeffrey   OFS College, Singapore

Tynberg, Nan Claire   California State University, San Bernardino at Palm Desert

Unrue, Darlene   University of Nevada at Reno

Unrue, John   University of Nevada at Reno

Van Dover, J. K.   Lincoln University

Van Dyke, Annette   University of Illinois at Springfield

Verderame, Carla Lee   West Chester University

Vescio, Bryan   University of Wisconsin–Green Bay

Vials, Chris   University of Massachusetts

Vilmar, Christopher   Emory University

Walden, Daniel   Penn State University

Wall, Rachel G.   Georgia State University

Weaver, Carole   The College of New Rochelle

Weir, Zachary   Miami University of Ohio

Wendt, Kerry Higgins   Emory University

Yoder, Paul L.   Southern Illinois University

Westerman, Jennifer Hughes   University of Nevada, Reno

Whalen, Zach   University of Florida

Whitlark, Jim   Texas Tech University

Whitsun, Carolyn   Metrostate University

Wiehl, John   University of Kansas

Wilson, James M.   Flagler University

Woodard, Loretta G.   Marygrove College

Yoder, Paul   Southern Illinois University

Zuidema, Leah A.   Michigan State University

Zhou, Xiaojing   University of the Pacific

INDEX

H